# Contents

## Upfront

*Colour pages giving you information about this guide and how to get the best out of it.*

2 Welcome to the Guide
4 Sure Signs of Where to Stay
6 Wheelchair Accessible Scheme
7 A Look at Some of the Best

8 How to Use the Guide
10 Key to Symbols
11 Tourist Information Centres
12 England's Tourist Regions

## Places to Stay

*B&Bs, farmhouses and inns listed alphabetically by town within England's 11 tourist regions.*

17 London
35 Cumbria
61 Northumbria
83 North West
99 Yorkshire & Humberside
131 Heart of England

191 Middle England
215 East Anglia
251 West Country
313 South of England
349 South East England

## Plus...

379 Farm Holiday Groups

383 Group and Youth Section

## Information Pages

*Lots of useful information to help you choose the right place to stay.*

402 National Rating Scheme
404 National Accessible Scheme for Wheelchair Users
405 General Advice and Information

408 About the Guide Entries
411 What's On in England 1995
417 Enquiry Coupons
431 Index to Advertisers

## Town Index and Location Maps

*Use these to find places with accommodation and the relevant page numbers.*

425 Town Index
433 Location Maps
448 Finding a Place to Stay

## Key to Symbols

*The fold-out back cover gives a convenient key to all the symbols used in this guide.*

FRONT COVER: GEORGE HOTEL, CASTLE CARY, SOMERSET

# Welcome to the Guide

*This 'Where to Stay' guide is designed to give you all the information you need to help you find accommodation in England in the right place, at the right price and with the facilities and services that are right for you.*

Whatever your reason for staying away from home – holiday, shopping trip, on business or visiting friends or relatives – you're sure to find in this guide accommodation that suits you best.

### Sure Signs of Where to Stay
All the accommodation included in this guide has been inspected – or is awaiting inspection – under the English Tourist Board's national rating scheme. So where you see a rating in an accommodation entry you'll know that we've checked it out before you check in.

### Easy to Use
A unique and helpful feature of this 'Where to Stay' guide is that all the essential information you need about the accommodation is presented in a straightforward and easy-to-read style.

### Symbols
We use at-a-glance symbols to give you the detailed and necessary information about additional services and facilities. But there's no need to flick back and forth between pages to find out what all the symbols mean – just fold out the back cover and you can check them as you go.

### Town Index
Also at the back of the guide is a comprehensive town index to make it easy for you to check whether accommodation in a particular place is included in the guide.

### Where to Go
And there's more! Each of the 11 regional sections starts with lots of ideas on where to go and what to see in the region. Throughout the guide you'll also find thumbnail town descriptions to give you a quick picture of each place.

### Information
To complete the 'Where to Stay' package you'll find the Information Pages (starting on page 401) full of useful advice on such things as bookings, cancellations, complaints, etc.

### Location Maps
At the back of the guide you will find full-colour maps which not only pinpoint all those cities, towns and villages with accommodation listings, but also show major towns, motorways, main 'A' roads, airports, BR InterCity stations, main ferry routes, and much, much more.

'Where to Stay' is a series of official accommodation guides, all available from your local bookshop:

- Hotels & Guesthouses in England  £8.99
- Bed & Breakfast, Farmhouses, Inns & Hostels in England  £7.99
- Self-Catering Holiday Homes in England  £5.99
- Families Welcome £4.99
- Somewhere Special £6.99

# Sure Signs of Where to Stay

*When you see a Crown or Lodge rating at an establishment or in its advertising you can be sure that the accommodation has been inspected and found to meet Tourist Board standards for facilities and services.*

Since their introduction in 1987, the Tourist Board accommodation ratings have become recognised as the leading indicator of the standards you can expect to find at your selected establishment. In fact, over 30,000 places to stay throughout Britain now offer the reassurance of a national rating.

### Inspected
All accommodation included in this 'Where to Stay' guide has been inspected – or is awaiting inspection – under the national rating scheme.

The Crown or Lodge ratings which appear in entries are in two parts:

### Facilities
The number of Crown or Moon symbols indicates the range of facilities and services that you will find at the establishment – the more symbols, the wider the range.

### Standards
The quality standard of what is provided is indicated by the terms Approved, Commended, Highly Commended or De Luxe. The Tourist Board assessment for this quality grading takes into account such important aspects as warmth of welcome, atmosphere and efficiency of service as well as the quality of furnishings, fitments and equipment.
If no quality grade appears alongside the symbols it means the proprietor has yet to invite the Tourist Board to do a quality assessment. However, you can still be sure of a high standard of cleanliness and service appropriate to the type of establishment.

### Wheelchair Access
More and more establishments are making provision for those in wheelchairs or who have some difficulty in walking. Under a voluntary code, the Tourist Board inspects such establishments and awards symbols according to the category of accessibility.

## CROWN RATINGS

**Listed**
You can be sure that the accommodation will be clean and comfortable, but the range of facilities and services may be limited.

You will find additional facilities, including washbasin and chair in your bedroom, and you will have use of a telephone.

There will be a colour TV in your bedroom or in a lounge and you can enjoy morning tea/coffee in your bedroom. At least some of the bedrooms will have a private bath (or shower) and WC.

At least half of the bedrooms will have private bath (or shower) en-suite. You will also be able to order a hot evening meal.

Your bedroom will have a colour TV, radio and telephone, there will be lounge service until midnight and evening meals can be ordered up to 2030 hours. 90% of the bedrooms will have private bath and/or shower and WC en-suite.

Every bedroom will have private bath, fixed shower and WC en-suite. The restaurant will be open for breakfast, lunch and dinner (or you can take meals in your room from breakfast until midnight) and you will benefit from an all-night lounge service. A night porter will also be on duty.

More information on the national rating scheme is given on pages 402–403.

## LODGE RATINGS

'Lodge' ratings acknowledge the purpose-built bedroom accommodation that you will find along major roads and motorways. The range of facilities is indicated by Moon symbols.

In a One Moon 'Lodge', your bedroom will have at least a washbasin and radio or colour TV. Tea/coffee may be from a vending machine in a public area.

Your bedroom in a Two Moon 'Lodge' will have colour TV, tea/ coffee-making facilities and en-suite bath or shower with WC.

In a Three Moon 'Lodge', you will find colour TV and radio, tea/coffee-making facilities and comfortable seating in your bedroom and there will be a bath, shower and WC en-suite. The reception area will be manned throughout the night.

## QUALITY STANDARDS

The quality grades APPROVED, COMMENDED, HIGHLY COMMENDED and DE LUXE can apply to any of the Crown and Lodge ratings. A Listed or One Crown B&B with limited facilities can have a HIGHLY COMMENDED or even DE LUXE grade if what it provides is to a very high quality standard. A Four or Five Crown hotel with a wide range of facilities might have an APPROVED grade if what it provides is to a relatively modest quality standard.

## WHEELCHAIR ACCESS CATEGORIES

These symbols are sure signs of places to stay for wheelchair users and others who may have difficulty in walking. See page 404 for further information and a list of establishments in this guide which have received a wheelchair access category symbol following inspection by the Tourist Board.

# National Accessible Scheme for Wheelchair Users

Throughout England, the Tourist Boards are inspecting all types of places to stay, on holiday or business, that provide accessible accommodation for wheelchair users and others who may have difficulty walking. Those that meet the criteria can display their wheelchair access category and symbol at their premises and in their advertising – so look for the symbol when choosing where to stay.

The criteria the Tourist Boards have adopted do not, necessarily, conform to British Standards or to Building Regulations. They reflect what the boards understand to be acceptable to meet the practical needs of wheelchair users.

The Tourist Boards recognise three categories of accessibility:

🦽 **Category 1**
Accessible to all wheelchair users including those travelling independently

🦽 **Category 2**
Accessible to a wheelchair user with assistance

🦽 **Category 3**
Accessible to a wheelchair user able to walk short distances and up at least three steps

*If you have additional needs or special requirements of any kind, we strongly recommend that you make sure these can be met by your chosen establishment before you confirm your booking.*

*The National Accessible Scheme forms part of the Tourism for All Campaign that is being promoted by all three National Tourist Boards. Additional help and guidance on finding suitable holiday accommodation for those with special needs can be obtained from:*
**Holiday Care Service**
*2 Old Bank Chambers, Station Road, Horley, Surrey RH6 9HW.*
*Tel: (01293) 774535.*
*Fax: (01293) 784647.*
*Minicom: (01293) 776943.*

*Establishments included in this* **'Where to Stay'** *guide which have a wheelchair access category are listed on page 404.*

PHOTOGRAPHS COURTESY OF
THE COPTHORNE TARA, LONDON

# A Look at Some of the Best

The award of a national Crown or Lodge rating follows a visit to the establishment by a Tourist Board inspector to check the facilities and services available.

Where an establishment has also applied for a quality grade, the inspector, without revealing his or her identity, will stay overnight.

The inspector will judge the quality and presentation of the food – at both dinner and breakfast – the appearance of the building, the tidiness of the grounds and the standard of decor of all the public rooms and areas.

*BROADVIEW, CREWKERNE, SOMERSET*

*MIDDLE ORD MANOR HOUSE, BERWICK-UPON-TWEED, NORTHUMBERLAND*

The highest quality grade of DE LUXE is awarded only to those establishments found to offer facilities and services to an exceptionally high quality standard.

The following establishments included in this 'Where to Stay' guide have achieved a DE LUXE grade. You can use the Town Index at the back of the guide to find page numbers for their fully detailed entries.

From arrival to departure, the inspector will also assess such intangible aspects as warmth of welcome, efficiency of service, attitude and appearance of staff and the general atmosphere and ambience of the place.

At the end of the visit, the inspector is in a position to make an objective judgment of the facilities and services (for the Crown symbols) and a quality judgment of the standard of those items and the establishment generally (for the quality grade).

**Brereton House,** Holmes Chapel, Cheshire
**Broadview,** Crewkerne, Somerset
**Causa Grange,** Rosley, Cumbria
**Halfway House,** Crayke, N. Yorkshire
**Holmfield,** Kendal, Cumbria
**Hope House,** Tynemouth, Tyne & Wear
**Inwood Farm,** Church Stretton, Shropshire
**Middle Ord Manor House,** Berwick-upon-Tweed, Northumberland
**The Old Parsonage,** Royal Tunbridge Wells, Kent
**Shawswell Country House,** Rendcomb, Gloucestershire
**Tavern House,** Tetbury, Gloucestershire

# How to Use the Guide

*This 'Where to Stay' guide will help you to find accommodation in England which suits your mood and your pocket.*

*The content has been arranged so that you can quickly and easily find a place to stay in your chosen area.*

## Tourist Regions

The guide is divided into 11 sections corresponding to England's tourist regions (see pages 12–13).

Each regional section has an introduction, with a selection of ideas on interesting places to visit, followed by alphabetical listings of the region's cities, towns and villages and their accommodation establishments.

Colour maps locating all places with accommodation and a complete index to place names can be found at the back of this guide.

There are two main ways of using this guide to find suitable accommodation:

### ① Town Index

If you have a particular city, town or village in mind, check the name in the Town Index. If it is included, turn to the page number shown to find accommodation available there. You can then use the map reference alongside the place name to locate it on the colour maps. This will also enable you to identify other, nearby places with accommodation which might be equally suitable.

### ② Location Maps

If the place you want is not included in the Town Index (or you have only a general idea of the area in which you wish to stay), use the colour location maps to find places in the area which do have accommodation listings in this guide – the Town Index will give you page numbers for these places.

### The Place for You?

Each accommodation listing contains detailed information to enable you to make a judgment as to its suitability (see sample entry opposite). This information has been provided by the proprietors themselves and our aim has been to ensure that it is as objective and factual as possible.

## TAUNTON

Somerset
Map Ref 1D1

County town, well-known for its public schools, sheltered by gentle hill-ranges on the River Tone.

### Tower Hotel

COMMENDED

River Street, Taunton TA9 2PW
☎ (01823) 000111
Fax (01823) 000011
*Charming family-run hotel with walled garden and conservatory restaurant. Ideal base for exploring.*
Bedrooms: 10 single, 20 twin, 13 double
Bathrooms: 43 private
Bed & breakfast

| per night: | £min | £max |
|---|---|---|
| Double | 53.00 | 104.00 |

Lunch available
Evening meal 1930 (last orders 2130)
Parking for 40
Cards accepted: Access, Visa, Amex

10–70

— Town name
— Map reference
— Town description
— Establishment name
— National rating
— Address, telephone and fax numbers
— Establishment description
— Accommodation, prices and facilities

Information about additional services and facilities is represented by symbols – you will find a key to these symbols overleaf and inside the back cover flap (which can be kept open for easy reference).

## Check for Changes

*Please remember that changes may have occurred since the guide went to press or may occur during 1995. When you have found a suitable place to stay, therefore, we do advise you to contact the establishment to check not only its availability but also any other information about facilities which may be important to you.*

## Enquiry Coupons

*We have included enquiry coupons at the back of this guide to help you when contacting accommodation establishments or advertisers in this guide.*

*You may also find it useful to read the information pages at the back of this guide, particularly the section on cancellations.*

# Key to Symbols

Information about many of the services and facilities at accommodation listed in this guide is given in the form of symbols, which are explained below.

You will also find this key inside the back cover flap, which can be kept open for easy reference.

The national accommodation rating scheme – see pages 4 and 5 for further information.

The national accessible scheme for wheelchair users – see page 6 for further information.

| | |
|---|---|
| ♏♏ | Establishment is a member of a Regional Tourist Board |
| 🐴 | Children welcome (a number following gives minimum age) |
| ⚒ | Not all bedrooms have hot and cold water |
| 🛏ᴳ | Ground floor bedroom(s) |
| 🛏 | Traditional four poster bed(s) |
| ☎ | Telephone in all bedrooms |
| 📻 | Radio in all bedrooms |
| 📺 | Television in all bedrooms |
| 🫖 | Tea and coffee making facilities in all bedrooms |
| 💇 | Hairdryer in all bedrooms |
| UL | Unlicensed (alcoholic drinks not served) |
| 🔒 | Packed lunch provided |
| S | Special diets provided by arrangement |
| 🚭 | Facilities for non-smokers |
| R | Lounge for residents' use |
| TV | Colour television in lounge |
| ◗ | Night porter |
| ↕ | Passenger lift |
| ⃜ | Central heating throughout |
| ☰ | Full air conditioning |
| ⬛ | Ironing facilities available |

| | |
|---|---|
| 🛎 | Conference/meeting facilities (numbers following show capacity) |
| 🧖 | Sauna |
| 🏋 | Gym |
| ● | Games room |
| 🏊 | Indoor swimming pool |
| 🏊 | Outdoor swimming pool |
| 🏃 | Squash court(s) |
| 🎾 | Tennis court(s) |
| U | Riding and/or pony trekking nearby |
| 🎣 | Private fishing rights |
| ⚑ | Permanent or specific arrangements for golf |
| 🔫 | Private shooting rights |
| ✿ | Garden for guests' use |
| 🐕 | Dogs **not** accepted |
| 🚌 | Overnight coach parties **not** accepted |
| OAP | Reduced prices for senior citizens |
| ✦ | Special Christmas/New Year packages |
| SP | Reduced price packages (eg, special weekends/low season) |
| 🏛 | Building of historic, literary or architectural interest |
| T | Bookings can be made through most recognised travel agents and booking agencies |

# Use Your *i*'s

When it comes to your next England break, the first stage of your journey could be closer than you think. You've probably got a Tourist Information Centre nearby. But you might not have realised that it's there to serve the

local community – as well as visitors. So make us your first stop. We'll be happy to help you, wherever you're heading.

Many Information Centres can provide you with maps and guides, helping you plan well in advance. And sometimes it's even possible for us to book your accommodation, too.

A visit to your nearest Information Centre can pay off in other ways as well. We can point you in the right direction when it comes to finding out about all the special events which are happening in the local region.

In fact, we can give you details of places to visit within easy reach... and perhaps tempt you to plan a day trip or weekend away.

Across the country, there are more than 550 Tourist Information Centres so you're never far away. You'll find the address of your nearest Tourist Information Centre in your local Phone Book.

# England's Tourist Regions

England is divided into 11 tourist regions, each of which has its own section in this guide. The regions are shown on the map and also listed opposite together with an index which identifies the region in which each county is located.

Location maps showing all the places with accommodation listed in this guide and an index to the place names can be found at the back of the guide.

Northumbria

Cumbria

Yorkshire & Humberside

North West

Middle England

East Anglia

Heart of England

London

South East England

South of England

West Country

17  *London*
    *Greater London*

35  *Cumbria*
    *The County of Cumbria, including
    English Lakeland*

61  *Northumbria*
    *Cleveland, County Durham,
    Northumberland, Tyne & Wear*

83  *North West*
    *Cheshire, Greater Manchester,
    Lancashire, Merseyside*

99  *Yorkshire & Humberside*
    *North, South and West Yorkshire,
    Humberside*

131 *Heart of England*
    *Gloucestershire, Hereford &
    Worcester, Shropshire,
    Staffordshire, Warwickshire,
    West Midlands*

191 *Middle England*
    *Derbyshire, Leicestershire,
    Lincolnshire, Northamptonshire,
    Nottinghamshire*

215 *East Anglia*
    *Bedfordshire, Cambridgeshire,
    Essex, Hertfordshire, Norfolk,
    Suffolk*

251 *West Country*
    *Avon, Cornwall, Devon, Isles of
    Scilly, Somerset, Western Dorset,
    Wiltshire*

313 *South of England*
    *Berkshire, Buckinghamshire,
    Eastern Dorset, Hampshire,
    Isle of Wight, Oxfordshire*

349 *South East England*
    *East and West Sussex, Kent,
    Surrey*

## County Index

**Avon:** West Country
**Bedfordshire:** East Anglia
**Berkshire:** South of England
**Buckinghamshire:** South of England
**Cambridgeshire:** East Anglia
**Cheshire:** North West
**Cleveland:** Northumbria
**Cornwall:** West Country
**County Durham:** Northumbria
**Cumbria:** Cumbria
**Derbyshire:** Middle England
**Devon:** West Country
**Dorset (Eastern):** South of England
**Dorset (Western):** West Country
**East Sussex:** South East England
**Essex:** East Anglia
**Gloucestershire:** Heart of England
**Greater London:** London
**Greater Manchester:** North West
**Hampshire:** South of England
**Hereford & Worcester:** Heart of England
**Hertfordshire:** East Anglia
**Humberside:** Yorkshire & Humberside
**Isle of Wight:** South of England
**Isles of Scilly:** West Country
**Kent:** South East England
**Lancashire:** North West
**Leicestershire:** Middle England
**Lincolnshire:** Middle England
**Merseyside:** North West
**Norfolk:** East Anglia
**North Yorkshire:** Yorkshire & Humberside
**Northamptonshire:** Middle England
**Northumberland:** Northumbria
**Nottinghamshire:** Middle England
**Oxfordshire:** South of England
**Shropshire:** Heart of England
**Somerset:** West Country
**South Yorkshire:** Yorkshire & Humberside
**Staffordshire:** Heart of England
**Suffolk:** East Anglia
**Surrey:** South East England
**Tyne & Wear:** Northumbria
**Warwickshire:** Heart of England
**West Midlands:** Heart of England
**West Sussex:** South East England
**West Yorkshire:** Yorkshire & Humberside
**Wiltshire:** West Country

# THE ENGLAND FOR EXCELLENCE AWARDS 1993 WINNERS

The England for Excellence Awards were created by the English Tourist Board to recognise and reward the highest standards of excellence and quality in all major sectors of tourism in England. The coveted Leo statuette, presented each year to winners, has become firmly established as the ultimate accolade in the English tourism industry.

Over the past six years, the Leo has been won by all types and sizes of business with one common attribute – excellence in the facilities and services they offer.

Hotel of the Year sponsored by Yellow Pages
SWALLOW HOTEL, BIRMINGHAM

Holiday Destination of the Year sponsored by Marks & Spencer
NOTTINGHAM CITY & NOTTINGHAMSHIRE COUNTY COUNCILS – THE ENGLISH CIVIL WAR 350TH COMMEMORATION

Caravan Holiday Park of the Year sponsored by the National Caravan Council
NEW FOREST COUNTRY HOLIDAYS

Bed and Breakfast of the Year sponsored by Le Shuttle
HALFWAY HOUSE, CRAYKE

Tourism and the Environment Award sponsored by Center Parcs
'ECO-HULL' – BRITISH WATERWAYS & ALVECHURCH BOAT CENTRES

Tourist Information Centre of the Year sponsored by National Express
PICKERING TOURIST INFORMATION CENTRE

Visitor Attraction of the Year sponsored by Embassy Leisure Breaks by Jarvis
EUREKA! THE MUSEUM FOR CHILDREN, HALIFAX

Self-Catering Holiday of the Year sponsored by the Country Holidays Group
LONGLANDS AT CARTMEL

Tourism for All Award sponsored by Blackpool Pleasure Beach
PLYMOUTH DOME

Tourism Training Award sponsored by Poole Pottery
WHITE ROSE LINE, YORK

Travel and Tourism Industry Award sponsored by Sea Containers Ferries
HAVENWARNER

Outstanding Contribution to English Tourism Award sponsored by Hilton UK
SIR BOB SCOTT

Thames Tower
Black's Road
London W6 9EL

# Where to Stay in England '95

*All from your local bookshop*

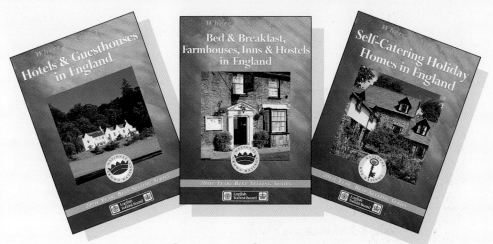

Hotels & Guesthouses £8.99

Bed & Breakfast, Farmhouses, Inns & Hostels £7.99

Self-Catering Holiday Homes £5.99

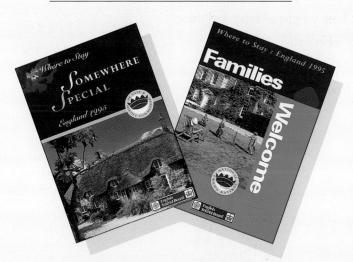

*New to the series*

Somewhere Special £6.99

Families Welcome £4.99

## FESTIVAL OF ARTS AND CULTURE

In 1995 the entire United Kingdom will be celebrating a year-long festival of Britain's arts, heritage, culture and entertainment – the biggest ever planned. Every month of the year, all over the country, you will find a wealth of events and attractions, from street festivals to grand opera, from open-air concerts to village fetes, from comedy to high drama. There is something for everyone to enjoy.

For further information please visit your local Tourist Information Centre.

# Where to Stay in England

*Published by:* English Tourist Board, Thames Tower, Black's Road, Hammersmith, London W6 9EL.
*Internal Reference Number:* ETB/213/95 CP/1386/36M/94
*Managing Editor:* Jane Collinson
*Compilation & Production:* Guide Associates, Croydon
*Design:* Celsius, Winchester
*Colour Photography:* Nigel Corrie (front cover); Celsius, Glyn Williams and Syndication International
*Illustrations:* Susie Louis
*Cartoons:* David Austin
*Cartography:* Colin Earl Cartography, Alton, and Line & Line, Thames Ditton
*Typesetting:* Computaprint, London, and Celsius
*Printing & Binding:* Bemrose Security Printing, Derby
*Advertisement Sales:* Madison Bell Ltd, 3 St. Peter's Street, Islington Green, London N1 8JD. Telephone: (0171) 359 7737.
© English Tourist Board (except where stated)

**IMPORTANT:**
The information contained in this guide has been published in good faith on the basis of information submitted to the English Tourist Board by the proprietors of the premises listed, who have paid for their entries to appear. The English Tourist Board cannot guarantee the accuracy of the information in this guide and accepts no responsibility for any error or misrepresentation. All liability for loss, disappointment, negligence or other damage caused by reliance on the information contained in this guide, or in the event of bankruptcy, or liquidation, or cessation of trade of any company, individual or firm mentioned, is hereby excluded. Please check carefully all prices and other details before confirming a reservation.

**The English Tourist Board**
The Board is a statutory body created by the Development of Tourism Act 1969 to develop and market England's tourism. Its main objectives are to provide a welcome for people visiting England; to encourage people living in England to take their holidays there; and to encourage the provision and improvement of tourist amenities and facilities in England. The Board has a statutory duty to advise the Government on tourism matters relating to England and, with Government approval and support, administers the national classification and grading schemes for tourist accommodation in England.

*There's little chance of running out of ideas on how to spend your time in London. There's sightseeing, of course – on foot or perhaps from the open top-deck of a bus. Browse around the museums and galleries, shop in world-renowned stores and ancient markets, experience new tastes in one of the thousands of restaurants. See a West End show or play (best to book in advance) or try new productions in the pubs and fringe theatres. London's waiting for you – come and be part of it!*

# LONDON

Greater London, comprising the 32 London boroughs

For more information on London, contact:
London Tourist Board and
Convention Bureau
26 Grosvenor Gardens
London SW1W ODU
Tel: (0171) 730 3450
Fax: (0171) 730 9367

Where to Go in London
– see pages 18–20

Where to Stay in London
– see pages 24–33

# WHERE TO GO

*You will find hundreds of interesting places to visit during your stay in London, just some of which are listed in these pages. Contact any Tourist Information Centre in the region for more ideas on days out in London.*

*An intriguing variety of arts and crafts can be admired at Camden Lock market.*

*Room, transatlantic telephone room, map room and Prime Minister's room, used by British Government during World War II.*

### Bankside Gallery
48 Hopton Street, London SE1 9JH
Tel: (0171) 928 7521
*Changing exhibitions of watercolours and prints. Home of The Royal Watercolour Society and The Royal Society of Painter-Etchers and Engravers.*

### British Museum
Great Russell Street, London WC1B 3DG
Tel: (0171) 636 1555
*One of the great museums of the world, showing the works of man from all over the world from prehistoric times to the present day. British Library Exhibition Galleries are in the museum.*

### Cabinet War Rooms
Clive Steps, King Charles Street, London SW1A 2AQ
Tel: (0171) 930 6961
*Underground headquarters, including Cabinet*

### Chessington World of Adventures
Leatherhead Road, Chessington, Surrey KT9 2NE
Tel: (01372) 729560
*A world of adventure, fun, exciting theme areas, rides, circus and the famous zoo. Rides include "Vampire" and "Professor Burp's Bubble Works".*

### Commonwealth Institute
Kensington High Street, London W8 6NQ
Tel: (0171) 603 4535
*Three floors of exhibition galleries depicting the history, landscape, wildlife and culture of 50 Commonwealth countries.*

### Design Museum
Shad Thames, London SE1 2YD
Tel: (0171) 403 6933
*Study collection showing the development of design in mass production. Review of new products, graphics gallery and changing programme of exhibitions.*

### Fenton House
Windmill Hill, London NW3 6RT
Tel: (0171) 435 3471
*William and Mary house containing Benton Fletcher collection of early keyboard instruments and Binning collection of porcelain and furniture.*

### Guards Museum
Wellington Barracks, Birdcage Walk, London SW1E 6HQ
Tel: (0171) 414 3271
*Collection of uniforms, colours and artefacts spanning over 300 years' history of the Foot Guards.*

## Guinness World of Records

The Trocadero, Coventry Street, Piccadilly Circus, London W1V 7FD
Tel: (0171) 439 7331
*Exhibition using models, videos, computers and electronic displays to bring to life the Guinness Book of Records.*

## Hampton Court Palace

Hampton Court, Surrey KT8 9AU
Tel: (0181) 781 9500
*Oldest Tudor palace in England. Tudor kitchens, tennis courts, maze, state apartments and King's apartments.*

## HMS Belfast

Morgan's Lane, Tooley Street, London SE1 2JH
Tel: (0171) 407 6434
*Naval museum in 11,500-tonne World War II cruiser moored on the Thames. Seven decks to explore.*

## Imperial War Museum

Lambeth Road, London SE1 6HZ
Tel: (0171) 416 5000
*The story of 20th C war from Flanders to the Gulf. Features include Blitz Experience, Trench Experience and Operation Jericho.*

## Kew Bridge Steam Museum

Green Dragon Lane, Brentford, Middlesex TW8 0EN
Tel: (0181) 568 4757
*Victorian waterworks housing massive steam-powered pumping engines. Steam railway, waterwheel, history of water. Tea room and shop.*

## London Zoo

Regent's Park, London NW1 4RY
Tel: (0171) 722 3333
*Over 8,000 animals including giant panda, venomous snakes, penguins and piranhas. Daily events, Lifewatch Conservation Centre and Moonlight World.*

## Madame Tussaud's

Marylebone Road, London NW1 5LR
Tel: (0171) 935 6861

*A welcome sight on a cold day: one of London's hot chestnut sellers.*

*Wax figures in themed settings, including The Garden Party, Superstars, The Chamber of Horrors and The Spirit of London.*

## Museum of London

150 London Wall, London EC2Y 5HN
Tel: (0171) 600 3699
*Galleries illustrate over 2,000 years of the capital's social history. Regular temporary exhibitions, lunchtime lecture programme.*

## Museum of the Moving Image

South Bank, Waterloo, London SE1 8XT
Tel: (0171) 928 3535
*A celebration of cinema and television. 44 exhibition areas, offering plenty of hands-on participation, and a cast of actors to tell visitors more.*

## National Army Museum

Royal Hospital Road, London SW3 4HT
Tel: (0171) 730 0717
*Histories of the British Army from 1485, the Indian Army up to independence in 1947 and colonial land forces. Battle of Waterloo exhibition.*

## National Gallery

Trafalgar Square, London WC2N 5DN
Tel: (0171) 839 3321
*Western painting from 1260 to 1920, including work by Van Gogh, Rembrandt, Cezanne, Turner, Gainsborough, Leonardo da Vinci, Renoir and Botticelli.*

## National Maritime Museum

Romney Road, Greenwich, London SE10 9NF
Tel: (0181) 858 4422
*Britain's maritime heritage illustrated through actual and model ships, paintings, uniforms, navigation and astronomy instruments, archives and photographs. Queen's House.*

## National Portrait Gallery

St Martin's Place, London WC2H 0HE
Tel: (0171) 306 0055

Collection of portraits of famous men and women from Middle Ages to the present day.

### National Postal Museum
King Edward Building, King Edward Street, London EC1A 1LP
Tel: (0171) 239 5420
One of the most important and extensive collections of postage stamps in the world, including Phillips and Berne collections. Temporary exhibitions.

### Natural History Museum
Cromwell Road, London SW7 5BD
Tel: (0171) 938 9123
Home of the wonders of the natural world, one of the most popular museums in the world and one of London's finest landmarks.

### Old Royal Observatory
Flamsteed House, Greenwich Park, Greenwich, London SE10 9NF
Tel: (0181) 858 4422
Museum of space and time. Greenwich Meridian, working telescopes and planetarium, timeball, intricate clocks, computer simulations, Wren's Octagon Room.

### Pollock's Toy Museum
1 Scala Street, London W1P 1LT
Tel: (0171) 636 3452

Toys of all kinds, including dolls, dolls' houses, teddy bears, tin toys, folk toys, toy theatres.

### Royal Air Force Museum
Grahame Park Way, Hendon, London NW9 5LL
Tel: (0181) 205 2266
Three halls displaying over 70 full-size aircraft. "Battle of Britain Experience", flight simulator, jet trainer, free film shows.

### Science Museum
Exhibition Road, South Kensington, London SW7 2DD
Tel: (0171) 938 8000
National Museum of Science and Industry. Full-size replica of Apollo II Lunar Lander, launch pad, Wellcome Museum of History of Medicine, flight lab, food for thought, optics.

### The Story of Telecommunications
145 Queen Victoria Street, London EC4V 4AT
Tel: (0171) 248 7444
Museum telling the story of telecommunications with set pieces and hands-on exhibits.

### The Theatre Museum
1E Tavistock Street, Covent Garden, London WC2E 7PA
Tel: (0171) 836 7891
Five galleries include permanent display of history of performance in the UK. Collection includes theatre, ballet, dance, rock and pop music, musical stage.

### Tower Hill Pageant
Tower Hill Terrace, London EC3N 4EE
Tel: (0171) 709 0081
Automatic vehicles transport visitors past tableaux depicting the history of the City and its port. Display of archaeological finds, shops, restaurant.

# FIND OUT MORE

A free information pack about holidays and attractions in London is available on written request from: London Tourist Board and Convention Bureau, 26 Grosvenor Gardens, London SW1W 0DU

**The "Wig & Pen", opposite the Law Courts, is a favourite watering-hole for the legal profession.**

LONDON

# TOURIST INFORMATION

Tourist and leisure information can be obtained from Tourist Information Centres throughout England. Details of centres and other information services in Greater London are given below. The symbol 🛏 means that an accommodation booking service is provided.

## TOURIST INFORMATION CENTRES

### Points of arrival

**Victoria Station, Forecourt, SW1** 🛏
Easter–October, daily 0800–1900.
November–Easter, reduced opening hours.
**Liverpool Street Underground Station, EC2** 🛏
Monday 0815–1900. Tuesday–Saturday
0815–1800. Sunday 0830–1645.
**Heathrow Terminals 1, 2, 3 Underground Station Concourse (Heathrow Airport)** 🛏
Daily 0830–1800.
**Heathrow Terminal 3 Arrivals Concourse** 🛏
**Waterloo International Arrivals Hall** 🛏
The above information centres provide a London and Britain tourist information service, offer a hotel accommodation booking service, stock free and saleable publications on Britain and London and sell theatre tickets, tourist tickets for bus and underground and tickets for sightseeing tours.

### Inner London

**British Travel Centre** 🛏
12 Regent Street, Piccadilly Circus, SW1Y 4PQ
Monday–Friday 0900–1830. Saturday–Sunday
1000–1600 (0900–1700 Saturdays
May–September).
**East End Visitor Centre**
107a Commercial Street, E1 6BG
Tel: (0181) 375 2549
Monday–Friday 0930–1630.
**Greenwich Tourist Information Centre** 🛏
46 Greenwich Church Street, SE10 9BL
Tel: (0181) 858 6376
April–September, daily 1000–1700.
October–March, reduced opening hours.
**Hackney Museum and Tourist Information Centre**
Central Hall, Mare Street, E8
Tel: (0181) 985 9055

Tuesday–Friday 1000–1700. Saturday 1330–1700.
**Islington Tourist Information Centre** 🛏
44 Duncan Street, E1 8BL
Tel: (0171) 278 8787
Monday–Saturday 1000–1700. Reduced winter opening hours.
**Lewisham Tourist Information Centre**
Lewisham Library, Lewisham High Street, SE13
Tel: (0181) 690 8325
Saturday, Monday 0930–1700. Tuesday,
Thursday 0930–2000. Friday 0930–1300.
**Selfridges** 🛏
Oxford Street, W1. Basement Services Arcade –
Duke Street entrance.
Open during normal store hours.
**Southwark Tourist Information Centre**
Hay's Galleria, Tooley Street, SE1
Monday–Friday 1100–1730. Saturday, Sunday
1200–1730.

### Outer London

**Bexley Tourist Information Centre** 🛏
Central Library, Townley Road, Bexleyheath
DA6 7HJ
Tel: (0181) 303 9052
Monday, Tuesday, Thursday 0930–2000. Friday
0930–1730. Saturday 0930–1700.
**Also at Hall Place Visitor Centre** 🛏
Bourne Road, Bexley
Tel: (01322) 558676
June–September, daily 1130–1630.
**Croydon Tourist Information Centre** 🛏
Katharine Street, Croydon CR9 1ET
Tel: (0181) 253 1009
Monday 0930–1900. Tuesday–Friday
0930–1800. Saturday 0900–1700.
**Harrow Tourist Information Centre**
Civic Centre, Station Road, Harrow HA1 2UJ
Tel: (0181) 424 1103
Monday–Friday 0900–1700.
**Hillingdon Tourist Information Centre**
Central Library, 14 High Street, Uxbridge UB8 1HD
Tel: Uxbridge (01895) 250706
Monday–Thursday 0930–2000. Friday
0930–1730. Saturday 0930–1600.
**Hounslow Tourist Information Centre**
24 The Treaty Centre, Hounslow High Street,
Hounslow TW3 1ES
Tel: (0181) 572 8279

Monday, Wednesday 0930–1730. Tuesday, Thursday–Saturday 0930–2000.

**Redbridge Tourist Information Centre**
Town Hall, High Road, Ilford, Essex IG1 1DD
Tel: (0181) 478 3020
Monday–Friday 0830–1700.

**Richmond Tourist Information Centre**
Old Town Hall, Whittaker Avenue, Richmond upon Thames TW9 1TP
Tel: (0181) 940 9125
Monday–Friday 0900–1800. Saturday 0900–1700. May–October, also Sunday 1015–1615.

**Twickenham Tourist Information Centre**
The Atrium, Civic Centre, York Street, Twickenham TW1 3BZ
Tel: (0181) 891 7272
Monday–Friday 0900–1700.

## Visitorcall

The London Tourist Board and Convention Bureau's 'phone guide to London operates 24 hours a day. To access a full range of information call 0839 123456. To access specific lines dial 0839 123 followed by:

What's on this week – 400
What's on next 3 months – 401
Sunday in London – 407
Rock and pop concerts – 422
Popular attractions – 480
Where to take children – 424
Museums – 429
Palaces (including Buckingham Palace) – 481
Current exhibitions – 403
Changing the Guard – 411
Popular West End shows – 416
Pubs and restaurants – 485
Calls cost 39p per minute cheap rate, 49p per minute at all other times.
To order a Visitorcall card please call (0171) 971 0026. Information for callers using push-button telephones: (0171) 971 0027.

## Artsline

London's information and advice service for disabled people on arts and entertainment. Call (0171) 388 2227.

## Hotel Accommodation Service

The London Tourist Board and Convention Bureau helps visitors to find and book accommodation at a wide range of prices in hotels and guesthouses, including budget accommodation, throughout the Greater London area. Reservations are made with hotels which are members of LTB, denoted in this guide with the symbol 🏨 by their name. Reservations can be made by credit card holders via the telephone accommodation reservations service on (0171) 824 8844 by simply giving the reservations clerk your card details (Access or Visa) and room requirements. LTB takes an administrative booking fee. The service operates Monday–Friday 0930–1730. Reservations on arrival are handled at the Tourist Information Centres operated by LTB at Victoria Station, Liverpool Street Station, Waterloo International, Selfridges and Heathrow. Go to any of them on the day when you need accommodation. A communication charge and a refundable deposit are payable when making a reservation.

## Which part of London?

The majority of tourist accommodation is situated in the central parts of London and is therefore very convenient for most of the city's attractions and night life.
However, there are many hotels in outer London which provide other advantages, such as easier parking. In the "Where to Stay" pages which follow, you will find accommodation listed under INNER LONDON (covering the E1 to W14 London Postal Area) and OUTER LONDON (covering the remainder of Greater London). Colour maps 6 and 7 at the back of the guide show place names and London Postal Area codes and will help you to locate accommodation in your chosen area of London.

# LONDON INDEX

*If you are looking for accommodation in a particular establishment in London and you know its name, this index will give you the page number of the full entry in the guide.*

### A — page no

| | |
|---|---|
| Aaron House Harrow | 32 |
| Abbey Court Hotel W2 | 29 |
| The Abbotts Hotel NW2 | 25 |
| Acorns Hotel WC1 | 32 |
| The Alice House West Drayton | 32 |

### B — page no

| | |
|---|---|
| Barry House Hotel W2 | 30 |
| Be My Guest SE26 | 27 |
| Bedknobs SE22 | 26 |
| 71 Berkshire Gardens N13 | 25 |
| Beverley House Hotel W2 | 30 |
| Brindle House Hotel SW1 | 27 |
| Byron Villa N11 | 24 |

### C — page no

| | |
|---|---|
| Camelot Hotel W2 | 30 |
| Caswell Hotel SW1 | 27 |
| "The Chimneys" Sidcup | 32 |
| Colliers Hotel SW1 | 27 |
| Compton Guest House SW19 | 29 |
| Corfton Guest House W5 | 31 |
| The Corner Lodge N20 | 25 |
| Creffield Lodge W5 | 31 |

### D — page no

| | |
|---|---|
| Demetriou Guest House W8 | 31 |
| Diana Hotel SE21 | 26 |

### E — page no

| | |
|---|---|
| 25 Eglington Road E4 | 24 |
| Elizabeth Hotel SW1 | 27 |
| Europa House Hotel W2 | 30 |

### F — page no

| | |
|---|---|
| Five Kings Guest House N7 | 24 |
| Five Sumner Place Hotel SW7 | 29 |

### G — page no

| | |
|---|---|
| Garth Hotel WC1 | 32 |
| Glynne Court Hotel W1 | 29 |
| Grange Lodge Hotel W5 | 31 |
| Green Court Hotel SW5 | 28 |

### H — page no

| | |
|---|---|
| Hyde Park Rooms Hotel W2 | 30 |

### I — page no

| | |
|---|---|
| Iverna Croydon | 32 |

### J — page no

| | |
|---|---|
| J and T Guest House NW10 | 25 |

### K — page no

| | |
|---|---|
| Kandara Guest House N1 | 24 |
| 152 Kensington Park Road W11 | 32 |

### L — page no

| | |
|---|---|
| Lancaster Court Hotel W2 | 30 |
| The Langorf Hotel NW3 | 25 |
| Lincoln House Hotel W1 | 29 |
| Luna-Simone Hotel SW1 | 27 |

### M — page no

| | |
|---|---|
| Meadow Croft Lodge SE9 | 26 |
| Merlyn Court Hotel SW5 | 28 |
| 41 Minard Road SE6 | 26 |

### N — page no

| | |
|---|---|
| Nayland Hotel W2 | 30 |

### P — page no

| | |
|---|---|
| Pane Residence N22 | 25 |
| Parkland Walk Guest House N19 | 25 |
| Parkwood Hotel W2 | 30 |
| The Plough Inn SW14 | 29 |
| Premier West Hotel W6 | 31 |

### R — page no

| | |
|---|---|
| Rhodes House Hotel W2 | 30 |
| Rilux House NW4 | 25 |
| Ruddimans Hotel W2 | 31 |

### S — page no

| | |
|---|---|
| St. Athan's Hotel WC1 | 32 |
| St. Georges Hotel SW1 | 27 |
| Sass House Hotel W2 | 31 |
| Sleeping Beauty Motel E10 | 24 |
| Stanley House Hotel SW1 | 27 |
| Hotel Strand Continental WC2 | 32 |
| Swiss House Hotel SW5 | 28 |

### W — page no

| | |
|---|---|
| Westpoint Hotel W2 | 31 |
| Wigmore Court Hotel W1 | 29 |
| Windermere Hotel SW1 | 27 |
| Windsor House SW5 | 28 |

### Y — page no

| | |
|---|---|
| York House Hotel SW5 | 29 |

THINK OF A NUMBER ... ADD ONE.

# PhONEday

All telephone numbers in the editorial and listings sections of this guide include the new PhONEday area codes. Please use the new codes when dialling.

# WHERE TO STAY

Accommodation entries in this section are listed under Inner London (covering the E1 to W14 London Postal Area) and Outer London (covering the remainder of Greater London). See colour location maps 6 and 7 at the back of this guide. If you want to look up a particular establishment, use the index to establishments (preceding page) to find the page number.

Symbols at the end of each accommodation entry give information about services and facilities. A 'key' to these symbols is inside the back cover flap, which can be kept open for easy reference.

## INNER LONDON

Colour maps 6 & 7 at the back of the guide show place names and London Postal Area codes and will help you to locate accommodation in your chosen area of London.

### LONDON E4

**25 Eglington Road**
**Listed**
North Chingford, London E4 7AN
☎ (0181) 529 1140
Fax (0181) 508 3837
*Comfortable Edwardian period family home with exclusive facilities in quiet suburb, easy access to City. Solar-heated swimming pool in landscaped garden. Gourmet meals on request.*
Bedrooms: 1 double, 1 twin
Bathrooms: 1 public

**Bed & breakfast**

| per night: | £min | £max |
|---|---|---|
| Single | 30.00 | |
| Double | 60.00 | |

**Half board**

| per person: | £min | £max |
|---|---|---|
| Daily | 45.00 | |

Lunch available
Evening meal 1700 (last orders 2300)
🍴🖳♿🏅🛏️📺🍽️♨️🚭🔌⚓💺⛵
♻✖️🅿️Ⓣ

### LONDON E10

**Sleeping Beauty Motel ♈**
Ⓒ **APPROVED**
543 Lea Bridge Road, Leyton, London E10 7EB
☎ (0181) 556 8080
Fax (0181) 556 8080
*All rooms en-suite with bath and showers, satellite TV. Lift, bar, car park.*

*Warm and friendly atmosphere. Prices are per room.*
Bedrooms: 15 double, 24 twin, 2 triple
Bathrooms: 41 private

**Bed & breakfast**

| per night: | £min | £max |
|---|---|---|
| Single | 30.00 | 35.00 |
| Double | 35.00 | 40.00 |

Parking for 34
Cards accepted: Access, Visa, Diners, Amex, Switch/Delta
🍴3🛏️♿🍷🖳☐🛏️📺♨️🔌🏛️⚓🚭
✖️Ⓣ

### LONDON N1

**Kandara Guest House ♈**
**Listed**
68 Ockendon Road, London N1 3NW
☎ (0171) 226 5721 & 226 3379
*Small family-run guesthouse near the Angel, Islington. Free street parking and good public transport to West End and City.*
Bedrooms: 4 single, 3 double, 2 twin, 1 triple
Bathrooms: 3 public

**Bed & breakfast**

| per night: | £min | £max |
|---|---|---|
| Single | 22.00 | 25.00 |
| Double | 32.00 | 35.00 |

Cards accepted: Access, Visa
🍴🛏️☐♿🖳⚓✖️🏛️ OAP SP Ⓣ

### LONDON N7

**Five Kings Guest House ♈**
🏠
59 Anson Road, Tufnell Park, London N7 0AR
☎ (0171) 607 3996 & 607 6466
*Privately-run guesthouse in a quiet residential area. 15 minutes to central London. Unrestricted parking in road.*

Bedrooms: 6 single, 3 double, 3 twin, 2 triple, 2 family rooms
Bathrooms: 9 private, 3 public, 2 private showers

**Bed & breakfast**

| per night: | £min | £max |
|---|---|---|
| Single | 16.00 | 17.00 |
| Double | 28.00 | 30.00 |

Cards accepted: Access, Visa
🍴🛏️♿🍷🖳📺📺♨️🏛️⚓🚭✖️🗝️⚓⛵
SP Ⓣ

### LONDON N11

**Byron Villa**
147 Bounds Green Road, New Southgate, London N11 2ED
☎ (0181) 888 1278
Fax (0181) 365 8625

*Victorian character guesthouse, convenient for central London, near underground, Alexandra Palace, M25. TV lounge, parking, English breakfast. Singles and groups welcome.*
Bedrooms: 1 double, 1 twin, 3 family rooms
Bathrooms: 2 public

**Bed & breakfast**

| per night: | £min | £max |
|---|---|---|
| Single | 20.00 | 24.00 |
| Double | 30.00 | 34.00 |

Parking for 4
🍴🛏️♿♿📺📺🏛️⚓🗝️✖️⚓ SP Ⓣ

## LONDON N13

### 71 Berkshire Gardens
**Listed**

Palmers Green, London N13 6AA
☎ (0181) 888 5573
*2-storey house with garden, 5 minutes'
bus ride from Wood Green Piccadilly
line underground station. Car parking
available.*
Bedrooms: 1 single, 1 double
Bathrooms: 1 public
**Bed & breakfast**

| per night: | £min | £max |
| --- | --- | --- |
| Single | 10.00 | 12.00 |
| Double | 20.00 | 24.00 |

| Half board per person: | £min | £max |
| --- | --- | --- |
| Daily | 13.00 | 15.00 |

Lunch available
Evening meal 1800 (last orders 2000)
Parking for 1

## LONDON N19

### Parkland Walk Guest House
**Listed COMMENDED**

12 Hornsey Rise Gardens, London
N19 3PR
☎ (0171) 263 3228
Fax (0171) 831 9489
Telex 262433
*Friendly Victorian family house in
residential area, Highgate/Crouch End.
Near many restaurants and convenient
for central London. Non-smokers only.
Recent British Tourist Authority award
winner - Best Small Hotel in London
competition.*
Bedrooms: 3 single, 2 double, 1 twin
Bathrooms: 2 private, 2 public
**Bed & breakfast**

| per night: | £min | £max |
| --- | --- | --- |
| Single | 23.00 | 32.00 |
| Double | 42.00 | 55.00 |

Cards accepted: Amex

## LONDON N20

### The Corner Lodge
**COMMENDED**

9 Athenaeum Road, Whetstone,
London N20 9AA
☎ (0181) 446 3720

*Charming, beautifully furnished
Edwardian house set in a tree-lined
avenue. Friendly family atmosphere.
Full English breakfast. 10 minutes
M1/M25, 5 minutes' walk to*

*underground, 20 minutes to central
London.*
Bedrooms: 1 double, 2 twin, 1 family
room
Bathrooms: 3 private, 1 public
**Bed & breakfast**

| per night: | £min | £max |
| --- | --- | --- |
| Single | 30.00 | 38.00 |
| Double | 42.00 | 50.00 |

Evening meal 1830 (last orders 1930)

## LONDON N22

### Pane Residence
**Listed**

154 Boundary Road, Wood Green,
London N22 6AE
☎ (0181) 889 3735
*In a pleasant location 6 minutes' walk
from Turnpike Lane underground
station and near Alexandra Palace.
Kitchen facilities available.*
Bedrooms: 1 single, 1 double, 1 twin
Bathrooms: 1 public
**Bed & breakfast**

| per night: | £min | £max |
| --- | --- | --- |
| Single | 16.00 | 16.00 |
| Double | 24.00 | 24.00 |

Parking for 2

## LONDON NW2

### The Abbotts Hotel
**Listed**

283-285 Willesden Lane, Willesden
Green, London NW2 5JA
☎ (0181) 459 5387
Fax (0181) 451 3034

*Homely and comfortable, a recently
refurbished all en-suite hotel.
Complimented for its friendly staff.
Within easy reach of motorways, central
London and Wembley complex.*
Bedrooms: 6 single, 4 double, 4 twin,
4 triple, 4 family rooms
Bathrooms: 22 private
**Bed & breakfast**

| per night: | £min | £max |
| --- | --- | --- |
| Single | 28.00 | 30.00 |
| Double | 38.00 | 41.00 |

| Half board per person: | £min | £max |
| --- | --- | --- |
| Daily | 35.00 | 38.00 |
| Weekly | 245.00 | 266.00 |

Evening meal 1800 (last orders 2030)
Parking for 15

Cards accepted: Access, Visa, Diners,
Amex

**Ad** Display advertisement appears on
page 28

## LONDON NW3

### The Langorf Hotel
**COMMENDED**

20 Frognal, Hampstead, London
NW3 6AG
☎ (0171) 794 4483
Fax (0171) 435 9055
*Three minutes' walk from Finchley
Road underground, this elegant
Edwardian residence in Hampstead
boasts attractive bedrooms with full
facilities. BTA Spencer Award runners-
up.*
Bedrooms: 1 single, 18 double, 8 twin,
4 triple
Bathrooms: 31 private
**Bed & breakfast**

| per night: | £min | £max |
| --- | --- | --- |
| Single | 45.00 | 61.00 |
| Double | 50.00 | 90.00 |

Lunch available
Evening meal 1800 (last orders 2300)
Cards accepted: Access, Visa, Diners,
Amex

## LONDON NW4

### Rilux House

1 Lodge Road, London NW4 4DD
☎ (0181) 203 0933
Fax (0181) 203 6446
*High standard, all private facilities,
kitchenette and garden. Quiet. Close to
underground, buses, M1, 20 minutes
West End. Convenient for Wembley,
easy route to Heathrow, direct trains to
Gatwick and Luton airports. Languages
spoken.*
Bedrooms: 1 single, 1 double
Bathrooms: 2 private
**Bed & breakfast**

| per night: | £min | £max |
| --- | --- | --- |
| Single | 27.00 | 35.00 |
| Double | 45.00 | 54.00 |

Parking for 1

## LONDON NW10

### J and T Guest House
**Listed**

98 Park Avenue North, Willesden
Green, London NW10 1JY
☎ (0181) 452 4085
Fax (0181) 450 2503
*Small guesthouse in north west London
close to underground. Easy access to
Wembley Stadium complex. 5 minutes
from M1.*

*Continued ▶*

## LONDON NW10

### Continued

Bedrooms: 1 single, 1 double, 3 twin,
1 triple
Bathrooms: 5 private, 1 public
**Bed & breakfast**

| per night: | £min | £max |
| --- | --- | --- |
| Single | 27.00 | 32.00 |
| Double | 39.00 | 45.00 |

Parking for 2
Cards accepted: Access, Visa
🛏🚪🛎📞🕾🖉♨🅿🍴🛁🚭Ⓣ

## LONDON SE6

### 41 Minard Road

**Listed**

Catford, London SE6 1NP
☎ (0181) 697 2596
*English home in quiet residential area
off A205 South Circular road. 10
minutes' walk to Hither Green station
for 20-minute journey to central
London.*
Bedrooms: 1 single, 2 twin
Bathrooms: 1 public
**Bed & breakfast**

| per night: | £min | £max |
| --- | --- | --- |
| Single | 17.00 | |
| Double | 34.00 | |

**Half board**

| per person: | £min | £max |
| --- | --- | --- |
| Daily | 23.50 | |
| Weekly | 164.50 | |

Evening meal 1700 (last orders 2000)
🛏🚪🛎🖉🕾📺🖥🅿♨✂🛄🚭SP

## LONDON SE9

### Meadow Croft Lodge ⚑

**☺ APPROVED**

96-98 Southwood Road, New Eltham,
London SE9 3QS
☎ (0181) 859 1488
Fax (0181) 850 8054
*Between A2 and A20, near New Eltham
station with easy access to London.
Warm and friendly atmosphere. TV in
rooms. British Tourist Authority London
B&B award 1990.*
Bedrooms: 4 single, 3 double, 9 twin,
1 family room
Bathrooms: 1 private, 4 public,
9 private showers
**Bed & breakfast**

| per night: | £min | £max |
| --- | --- | --- |
| Single | 21.00 | 27.00 |
| Double | 37.00 | 42.00 |

Parking for 9
Cards accepted: Access, Visa, Amex
🛏🚪🖉🕾✂♨📺🖥🅿♨🛄🚭Ⓣ

## LONDON SE21

### Diana Hotel

☺☺

88 Thurlow Park Road, London
SE21 8HY
☎ (0181) 670 3250
Fax (0181) 761 9152
*Comfortable and friendly family-run
hotel near Dulwich Village, a pleasant
suburb 10 minutes from central
London.*
Bedrooms: 2 single, 4 double, 3 twin,
3 triple
Bathrooms: 2 private, 2 public,
2 private showers
**Bed & breakfast**

| per night: | £min | £max |
| --- | --- | --- |
| Single | 28.00 | 38.00 |
| Double | 40.00 | 50.00 |

Evening meal 1800 (last orders 1930)
Parking for 3
🛏🚪🖉🕾📺🖥🅿♨🛄Ⓣ

## LONDON SE22

### Bedknobs

**Listed COMMENDED**

58 Glengarry Road, East Dulwich,
London SE22 8QD
☎ (0181) 299 2004
*Victorian family-run house, carefully
restored, providing modern-day comforts
and a friendly service. BTA London B
& B award 1992.*

Bedrooms: 1 double, 1 twin, 1 triple
Bathrooms: 2 public

**Bed & breakfast**

| per night: | £min | £max |
|---|---|---|
| Single | 19.50 | 25.00 |
| Double | 37.00 | 42.00 |

### LONDON SE26

## Be My Guest

COMMENDED

79 Venner Road, Sydenham, London
SE26 5HU
☎ (0181) 659 5413
Fax (0181) 776 8151
*Spacious Victorian residence, 15
minutes to central London from nearby
stations. Free travel in London with
reservations of 3 days or more. Car and
driver service by arrangement.*
Bedrooms: 1 twin, 2 family rooms
Bathrooms: 3 private

**Bed & breakfast**

| per night: | £min | £max |
|---|---|---|
| Single | 40.00 | 48.00 |
| Double | 48.00 | 57.00 |

**Half board**

| per person: | £min | £max |
|---|---|---|
| Daily | 33.00 | 63.00 |
| Weekly | 231.00 | 441.00 |

Lunch available
Evening meal 1900 (last orders 2000)
Parking for 2
Cards accepted: Access, Visa, Amex

### LONDON SW1

## Brindle House Hotel ⚄

Listed

1 Warwick Place North, London
SW1V 1QW
☎ (0171) 828 0057
Fax (0171) 931 8805
*Small and quiet (off main road) bed
and breakfast ideally located for
Victoria bus, train and underground
stations. Good atmosphere.*
Bedrooms: 4 single, 4 double, 2 twin,
2 triple
Bathrooms: 2 public, 5 private
showers

**Bed & breakfast**

| per night: | £min | £max |
|---|---|---|
| Single | 25.00 | 29.00 |
| Double | 36.00 | 44.00 |

Cards accepted: Access, Visa, Diners,
Amex

## Caswell Hotel

Listed

25 Gloucester Street, London
SW1V 2DB
☎ (0171) 834 6345
*Pleasant, family-run hotel, near Victoria
coach and rail stations, yet in a quiet
location.*
Bedrooms: 1 single, 6 double, 6 twin,
3 triple, 2 family rooms

---

Bathrooms: 7 private, 5 public

**Bed & breakfast**

| per night: | £min | £max |
|---|---|---|
| Single | 25.00 | 46.00 |
| Double | 33.00 | 59.00 |

## Colliers Hotel ⚄

97 Warwick Way, London SW1V 1QL
☎ (0171) 834 6931 & 828 0210
Fax (0171) 834 8439
*Modern-style family hotel with spacious
rooms. Very clean, budget priced,
centrally located. Ideal for easy
connections to London's major tourist
spots.*
Bedrooms: 4 single, 5 double, 5 twin,
3 triple, 2 family rooms
Bathrooms: 2 private, 3 public,
4 private showers

**Bed & breakfast**

| per night: | £min | £max |
|---|---|---|
| Single | 22.00 | 26.00 |
| Double | 32.00 | 36.00 |

Cards accepted: Access, Visa, Diners,
Amex

## Elizabeth Hotel ⚄

37 Eccleston Square, Victoria, London
SW1V 1PB
☎ (0171) 828 6812
Fax (0171) 828 6814

*Friendly, quiet hotel overlooking
magnificent gardens of stately
residential square (circa 1835), close to
Belgravia and within 5 minutes' walk of
Victoria*
Bedrooms: 12 single, 12 double,
6 twin, 4 triple, 9 family rooms
Bathrooms: 27 private, 6 public,
13 private showers

**Bed & breakfast**

| per night: | £min | £max |
|---|---|---|
| Single | 36.00 | 55.00 |
| Double | 55.00 | 80.00 |

Ad Display advertisement appears on
page 26

## Luna-Simone Hotel ⚄

Listed

47 Belgrave Road, London SW1V 2BB
☎ (0171) 834 5897
*Friendly, good value, bed and breakfast
hotel. Within easy walking distance of
Victoria rail, underground and coach
stations. Opposite bus stop.*
Bedrooms: 3 single, 11 double,
11 twin, 10 triple

---

Bathrooms: 25 private, 4 public

**Bed & breakfast**

| per night: | £min | £max |
|---|---|---|
| Single | 20.00 | 24.00 |
| Double | 28.00 | 48.00 |

Cards accepted: Access, Visa

## St. Georges Hotel

25 Belgrave Road, London SW1V 1RB
☎ (0171) 828 2061 & 828 2605
Fax (0171) 834 8439
Telex 24699 KISMET G
*Quiet, private family-run hotel.*
Bedrooms: 2 single, 4 double, 4 twin,
3 triple
Bathrooms: 3 private, 4 public,
4 private showers

**Bed & breakfast**

| per night: | £min | £max |
|---|---|---|
| Single | 18.00 | 25.00 |
| Double | 30.00 | 40.00 |

Cards accepted: Access, Visa, Diners,
Amex

## Stanley House Hotel ⚄

19-21 Belgrave Road, London
SW1V 1RB
☎ (0171) 834 5042 & 834 7292
Fax (0171) 834 8439
*Modern-style family hotel with spacious
rooms, all with intercom and radio.
Telex available.*
Bedrooms: 5 double, 12 twin, 1 triple,
13 family rooms
Bathrooms: 18 private, 5 public

**Bed & breakfast**

| per night: | £min | £max |
|---|---|---|
| Single | 20.00 | 32.00 |
| Double | 30.00 | 40.00 |

Cards accepted: Access, Visa, Diners,
Amex

## Windermere Hotel ⚄

COMMENDED

142-144 Warwick Way, Victoria,
London SW1V 4JE
☎ (0171) 834 5163 & 834 5480
Fax (0171) 630 8831
*Winner of the 1992 BTA Trophy, Small
Hotel Award. Winner of the Certificate
of Distinction in 1991. A friendly,
charming hotel with well-appointed
rooms and a licensed restaurant.*
Bedrooms: 3 single, 11 double, 5 twin,
1 triple, 3 family rooms
Bathrooms: 19 private, 2 public

**Bed & breakfast**

| per night: | £min | £max |
|---|---|---|
| Single | 34.00 | 55.00 |
| Double | 48.00 | 79.00 |

Lunch available
Evening meal 1800 (last orders 2100)
Cards accepted: Access, Visa, Amex

## LONDON SW5

### Green Court Hotel M
**Listed**

52 Hogarth Road, London SW5 0PU
☎ (0171) 370 0853
Fax (0171) 370 3998
*Nearest underground station Earl's
Court, 20 minutes to West End and
Heathrow Airport by train.
Knightsbridge and Kensington High
Street shops are also nearby.*
Bedrooms: 12 single, 8 double, 2 twin,
1 triple
Bathrooms: 18 private, 2 public,
1 private shower
**Bed & breakfast**

| per night: | £min | £max |
|---|---|---|
| Single | 18.00 | 22.00 |
| Double | 28.00 | 32.00 |

Cards accepted: Access, Visa, Amex
🕭 🕿 ▢ UL ⦿ ▥ 🖃 ✕ 🛥

### Merlyn Court Hotel M
2 Barkston Gardens, London
SW5 0EN
☎ (0171) 370 1640
Fax (0171) 370 4986

> Please check prices and
> other details at the time
> of booking.

*Well-established, family-run, good value
hotel in quiet Edwardian square, close
to Earl's Court and Olympia. Direct
underground link to Heathrow, the West
End and rail stations. Car park nearby.*
Bedrooms: 4 single, 4 double, 4 twin,
2 triple, 3 family rooms
Bathrooms: 10 private, 6 public,
3 private showers
**Bed & breakfast**

| per night: | £min | £max |
|---|---|---|
| Single | 28.00 | 45.00 |
| Double | 40.00 | 55.00 |

Cards accepted: Access, Visa
🕭 🕿 🕭 ▢ 🕭 🕿 UL 🖃 🎜 TV ▥ 🖃 OAP 🕭
SP T

### Swiss House Hotel M
**Listed** **COMMENDED**

171 Old Brompton Road, London
SW5 0AN
☎ (0171) 373 2769 & 373 9383
Fax (0171) 373 4983

*Very clean, comfortable and
conveniently situated hotel near London
museums, shopping/exhibition centres.
Gloucester Road underground station is
within easy walking distance. Recent
winner of BTA award for best value
B&B in London.*
Bedrooms: 2 single, 6 double, 2 twin,
6 triple
Bathrooms: 11 private, 1 public
**Bed & breakfast**

| per night: | £min | £max |
|---|---|---|
| Single | 35.00 | 49.00 |
| Double | 50.00 | 63.00 |

Cards accepted: Access, Visa, Diners,
Amex, Switch/Delta
🕭 🕿 🕭 ▢ UL 🎜 🕿 TV ⦿ ▥ 🖃
🌼 🛥 OAP 🕭 SP T

### Windsor House M
**Listed**

12 Penywern Road, London SW5 9ST
☎ (0171) 373 9087
Fax (0171) 385 2417

Budget-priced bed and breakfast establishment in Earl's Court. Easily reached from airports and motorway. The West End is minutes away by underground. NCP parking.
Bedrooms: 2 single, 5 double, 3 twin, 1 triple, 4 family rooms
Bathrooms: 1 private, 6 public, 11 private showers
**Bed & breakfast**

| per night: | £min | £max |
| --- | --- | --- |
| Single | 24.00 | 34.00 |
| Double | 28.00 | 44.00 |
| Parking for 10 | | |

🛇🕭📞🛏☐ψ⯑🅄🆂🌢🅃🅅◐⥮Ⅲ💼❄✕🅖
🆂🅿 🆃
**Ad** Display advertisement appears on page 28

### York House Hotel ⋀
🕭
28 Philbeach Gardens, London SW5 9EA
☎ (0171) 373 7519 & 373 7579
Fax (0171) 370 4641
Bed and breakfast hotel, conveniently located close to the Earl's Court and Olympia Exhibition Centres and the West End.
Bedrooms: 20 single, 3 twin, 11 triple, 4 family rooms
Bathrooms: 1 private, 9 public
**Bed & breakfast**

| per night: | £min | £max |
| --- | --- | --- |
| Single | 25.00 | 26.00 |
| Double | 40.00 | 42.00 |

Cards accepted: Access, Visa, Diners, Amex
🛇🕭📞🅄🌢❄✕🆂🅿🆃

---

## LONDON SW7

### Five Sumner Place Hotel ⋀
**Listed** **HIGHLY COMMENDED**
5 Sumner Place, South Kensington, London SW7 3EE
☎ (0171) 584 7586
Fax (0171) 823 9962
Recent winner of the Best Small Hotel in London Award. Situated in South Kensington, the most fashionable area. This family owned and run hotel offers first-class service and personal attention.
Bedrooms: 3 single, 10 double
Bathrooms: 13 private, 1 public
**Bed & breakfast**

| per night: | £min | £max |
| --- | --- | --- |
| Single | 60.00 | 79.00 |
| Double | 80.00 | 110.00 |

Cards accepted: Access, Visa, Diners, Amex
🛇🕭📞🛏☐ψ🅄◐⯑Ⅲ💼✕🐎
🄳🅰🄿🌢🆂🅿🕭

---

## LONDON SW14

### The Plough Inn
🕭🕭🕭 **APPROVED**
42 Christchurch Road, East Sheen, London SW14 7AF
☎ (0181) 876 7833 & 876 4533

Delightful old pub, part 16th C, next to Richmond Park. En-suite accommodation, traditional ales, home-cooked food.
Bedrooms: 4 double, 3 twin
Bathrooms: 7 private
**Bed & breakfast**

| per night: | £min | £max |
| --- | --- | --- |
| Single | 47.00 | 50.00 |
| Double | 60.00 | 65.00 |

**Half board**

| per person: | £min | £max |
| --- | --- | --- |
| Daily | 53.00 | 58.00 |

Lunch available
Evening meal 1930 (last orders 2130)
Parking for 4
Cards accepted: Access, Visa, Amex
🛇🕭📞☐ψ🛏Ⅲ💼🐎🆃

---

## LONDON SW19

### Compton Guest House
**Listed**
65 Compton Road, Wimbledon, London SW19 7QA
☎ (0181) 947 4488 & 879 3245
Family-run guesthouse in pleasant, peaceful area, 5 minutes from Wimbledon station (British Rail and District Line). Easy access to the West End, central London, M1, M2, M3, M4, and M25. Quality rooms, with excellent service. About 12 minutes' walk to Wimbledon tennis courts.
Bedrooms: 2 single, 1 double, 2 twin, 1 triple, 2 family rooms
Bathrooms: 2 public
**Bed & breakfast**

| per night: | £min | £max |
| --- | --- | --- |
| Single | 25.00 | 35.00 |
| Double | 35.00 | 55.00 |
| Parking for 2 | | |

🛇🕭📞☐ψ🅄🅄🗲Ⅲ💼✕🄳🅰🄿🌢🆂🅿🆃

---

## LONDON W1

### Glynne Court Hotel ⋀
**Listed**
41 Great Cumberland Place, Marble Arch, London W1H 7GH
☎ (0171) 262 4344
Fax (0171) 724 2071
Friendly hotel, convenient for shops and theatres. 3 minutes' walk from Marble Arch, Hyde Park and Oxford Street.

---

Bedrooms: 2 single, 4 double, 3 twin, 2 triple, 1 family room
Bathrooms: 6 public
**Bed & breakfast**

| per night: | £min | £max |
| --- | --- | --- |
| Single | 30.00 | 35.00 |
| Double | 40.00 | 45.00 |

Cards accepted: Access, Visa, Diners, Amex
🛇🕭📞☐ψ🅄◐Ⅲ💼✕🄳🅰🄿🌢
🆂🅿🆃

### Lincoln House Hotel ⋀
🕭 **COMMENDED**
33 Gloucester Place, London W1H 3PD
☎ (0171) 486 7630
Fax (0171) 486 0166
Fully refurbished Georgian hotel, in the heart of the West End, close to Oxford Street shops, theatres and nightlife.
Bedrooms: 4 single, 9 double, 5 twin, 4 triple
Bathrooms: 17 private, 1 public
**Bed & breakfast**

| per night: | £min | £max |
| --- | --- | --- |
| Single | 45.00 | 49.00 |
| Double | 59.00 | 65.00 |

Cards accepted: Access, Visa, Diners, Amex, Switch/Delta
🛇🕭📞☐ψ🅄🅄🅃🅅◐Ⅲ💼✕🐎
🆂🅿🏠🆃

### Wigmore Court Hotel ⋀
🕭🕭 **COMMENDED**
23 Gloucester Place, Portman Square, London W1H 3PB
☎ (0171) 935 0928
Fax (0171) 487 4254
Small, clean, fully refurbished family hotel. Large en-suite rooms - ideal for families. 3 minutes' walk to Oxford Street. Competitively priced.
Bedrooms: 5 single, 6 double, 4 twin, 3 triple, 2 family rooms
Bathrooms: 18 private, 1 public
**Bed & breakfast**

| per night: | £min | £max |
| --- | --- | --- |
| Single | 30.00 | 48.00 |
| Double | 40.00 | 60.00 |

Cards accepted: Access, Visa, Diners
🛇🕭📞☐🅄🅄🅃🅅◐Ⅲ💼✕🄳🅰🄿🌢
🆂🏠🆃

---

## LONDON W2

### Abbey Court Hotel ⋀
**Listed**
174 Sussex Gardens, London W2 1TP
☎ (0171) 402 0704
Fax (0171) 262 2055
Central London hotel, reasonable prices. Within walking distance of Lancaster Gate, Paddington station and Hyde Park. Car parking available at modest charge.
Bedrooms: 4 single, 7 double, 3 twin, 10 triple, 2 family rooms
Bathrooms: 10 public, 6 private showers

Continued ▶

## LONDON W2

*Continued*

**Bed & breakfast**

| per night: | £min | £max |
| --- | --- | --- |
| Single | 20.00 | |
| Double | 28.00 | |

Parking for 20
Cards accepted: Access, Visa, Amex

🛏🍴🛎📻🖥🕭📺📺📺▥💶🚗➤☘🅿 🛩 SP

[Ad] Display advertisement appears on page 33

## Barry House Hotel ▲▲

**APPROVED**

12 Sussex Place, London W2 2TP
☎ (0171) 723 7340 & 723 0994
Fax (0171) 723 9775
*We believe in family-like care.
Comfortable en-suite rooms with TV,
telephone and hospitality tray. Located
close to Hyde Park, the West End,
Paddington Station and many tourist
attractions.*
Bedrooms: 3 single, 2 double, 11 twin,
2 family rooms
Bathrooms: 14 private, 2 public

**Bed & breakfast**

| per night: | £min | £max |
| --- | --- | --- |
| Single | 28.00 | 36.00 |
| Double | 48.00 | 56.00 |

Cards accepted: Access, Visa, Diners,
Amex

🛏🍴🛎📻🖥🕭▥🇸🅜📺▥ 🚗🅄☘🅿 SP 🛩

## Beverley House Hotel ▲▲

👑👑

142 Sussex Gardens, London W2 1UB
☎ (0171) 723 3380
Fax (0171) 262 0324
*Recently refurbished bed and breakfast
hotel, serving traditional English
breakfast and offering high standards at
low prices. Close to Paddington station,
Hyde Park and museums.*
Bedrooms: 6 single, 5 double, 6 twin,
6 triple
Bathrooms: 23 private

**Bed & breakfast**

| per night: | £min | £max |
| --- | --- | --- |
| Single | 35.00 | 45.00 |
| Double | 38.00 | 60.00 |

Evening meal 1800 (last orders 2200)
Parking for 2
Cards accepted: Access, Visa, Diners,
Amex

🛏🍴🛎📻🖥🕭▥🅜◐▥ 🚗 SP 🛩

## Camelot Hotel ▲▲

👑👑 **COMMENDED**

45-47 Norfolk Square, Paddington,
London W2 1RX
☎ (0171) 262 1980 & 723 9118
Fax (0171) 402 3412
*Beautifully restored 19th C town house
"bed and breakfast" hotel offering
charming, stylish accommodation in
central London.*

Bedrooms: 14 single, 11 double,
12 twin, 4 triple, 6 family rooms
Bathrooms: 35 private, 1 public,
4 private showers

**Bed & breakfast**

| per night: | £min | £max |
| --- | --- | --- |
| Single | 36.50 | 50.00 |
| Double | 70.00 | 70.00 |

Cards accepted: Access, Visa, Diners,
Switch/Delta

🛏🍴🛎📻🖥🕭▥🇸🅜📺▥🔆🚗🅿
☘🅿 SP 🛩 T

## Europa House Hotel ▲▲

151 Sussex Gardens, London W2 2RY
☎ (0171) 723 7343 & 402 1923
Fax (0171) 224 9331
*Close to Hyde Park and convenient for
the Heathrow Airbus link. All rooms
with en-suite facilities, tea and coffee
making facilities, colour TV. English
breakfast included.*
Bedrooms: 2 single, 2 double, 7 twin,
5 triple, 2 family rooms
Bathrooms: 18 private, 1 public

**Bed & breakfast**

| per night: | £min | £max |
| --- | --- | --- |
| Single | 28.00 | 32.00 |
| Double | 42.00 | 45.00 |

Parking for 1
Cards accepted: Access, Visa, Diners

🛏🍴🛎🖥🕭▥🇸🅜📺◐▥ 🚗☘🅿 SP

## Hyde Park Rooms Hotel ▲▲

**Listed**

137 Sussex Gardens, Hyde Park,
London W2 2RX
☎ (0171) 723 0225 & 723 0965
*Small centrally located private hotel
with personal service. Clean,
comfortable and friendly. Within
walking distance of Hyde Park and
Kensington Gardens. Car parking
available.*
Bedrooms: 5 single, 6 double, 2 twin,
1 family room
Bathrooms: 5 private, 2 public

**Bed & breakfast**

| per night: | £min | £max |
| --- | --- | --- |
| Single | 20.00 | 35.00 |
| Double | 30.00 | 45.00 |

Parking for 3
Cards accepted: Access, Visa, Diners,
Amex, Switch/Delta

🛏🍴🛎🖥🕭▥◐▥ 🚗🅄☘🅿 SP
🛩 T

## Lancaster Court Hotel ▲▲

**Listed**

202-204 Sussex Gardens, Hyde Park,
London W2 3UA
☎ (0171) 402 8438
Fax (0171) 706 3794
*2 minutes from Lancaster Gate,
Paddington underground and Hyde
Park. 1 minute from Heathrow Airbus
stop. Oxford Street and theatres nearby.
Friendly, courteous service, meals can
be arranged for groups. Coach parties
welcome. Special group and low season
rates on request.*

Bedrooms: 13 single, 9 double, 4 twin,
6 triple, 10 family rooms
Bathrooms: 29 private, 2 public,
13 private showers

**Bed & breakfast**

| per night: | £min | £max |
| --- | --- | --- |
| Single | 20.00 | 35.00 |
| Double | 35.00 | 59.00 |

**Half board**

| per person: | £min | £max |
| --- | --- | --- |
| Daily | 30.00 | 45.00 |
| Weekly | 180.00 | 275.00 |

Evening meal 1900 (last orders 2230)
Parking for 10
Cards accepted: Access, Visa, Diners,
Amex

🛏🍴🛎📻🖥🕭✕◐▥ 🚗🍴2-30
🅄☘🅿 SP 🛩 T

## Nayland Hotel ▲▲

👑👑👑

132-134 Sussex Gardens, London
W2 1UB
☎ (0171) 723 4615
Fax (0171) 402 3292
*Centrally located, close to many
amenities and within walking distance
of Hyde Park and Oxford Street. Quality
you can afford.*
Bedrooms: 11 single, 8 double,
17 twin, 5 triple
Bathrooms: 41 private

**Bed & breakfast**

| per night: | £min | £max |
| --- | --- | --- |
| Single | 40.00 | 52.00 |
| Double | 46.00 | 64.00 |

Evening meal 1800 (last orders 2100)
Parking for 5
Cards accepted: Access, Visa, Diners,
Amex

🛏🍴🛎📻🖥🕭🍴📺◐▥▥ 🚗➤
🚗 🛩 T

## Parkwood Hotel ▲▲

👑👑 **APPROVED**

4 Stanhope Place, London W2 2HB
☎ (0171) 402 2241
Fax (0171) 402 1574
*Smart townhouse convenient for Hyde
Park and Oxford Street. Comfortable
bedrooms and friendly atmosphere.*
Bedrooms: 5 single, 2 double, 7 twin,
4 triple
Bathrooms: 12 private, 2 public

**Bed & breakfast**

| per night: | £min | £max |
| --- | --- | --- |
| Single | 39.50 | 55.00 |
| Double | 49.50 | 69.00 |

Evening meal 1830 (last orders 2130)
Cards accepted: Access, Visa

🛏🍴🛎📻🖥🕭🔆🅜✕🅜📺◐▥ 🚗
🚗🅿 SP

## Rhodes House Hotel ▲▲

👑👑 **APPROVED**

195 Sussex Gardens, London W2 2RJ
☎ (0171) 262 5617 & 262 0537
Fax (0171) 723 4054
*Rooms with private facilities and TV,
telephone, refrigerator and hairdryer.
Friendly atmosphere. Families*

*especially welcome. Near transport for sightseeing and shopping.*
Bedrooms: 3 single, 3 double, 4 twin, 4 triple, 4 family rooms
Bathrooms: 15 private, 1 public, 1 private shower
**Bed & breakfast**

| per night: | £min | £max |
|---|---|---|
| Single | 45.00 | 55.00 |
| Double | 55.00 | 65.00 |

Cards accepted: Access, Visa

### Ruddimans Hotel ▲
Listed · APPROVED
160-162 Sussex Gardens, London W2 1UD
☎ (0171) 723 1026 & 723 6715
Fax (0171) 262 2983
*Comfortable hotel close to West End and London's attractions, offering generous English breakfast and good service at reasonable prices. Car park.*
Bedrooms: 10 single, 12 double, 12 twin, 6 triple
Bathrooms: 26 private, 4 public
**Bed & breakfast**

| per night: | £min | £max |
|---|---|---|
| Single | 25.00 | 32.00 |
| Double | 38.00 | 45.00 |

Parking for 6

### Sass House Hotel ▲
Listed
10 & 11 Craven Terrace, London W2 3QD
☎ (0171) 262 2325
Fax (0171) 262 0889
*Budget accommodation, convenient for central London, Hyde Park and the West End. Paddington and Lancaster Gate underground stations nearby. Easy access to tourist attractions.*
Bedrooms: 4 single, 4 double, 4 twin, 6 triple
Bathrooms: 3 public
**Bed & breakfast**

| per night: | £min | £max |
|---|---|---|
| Single | 18.00 | |
| Double | 24.00 | |

Cards accepted: Access, Visa, Amex
Display advertisement appears on page 33

### Westpoint Hotel ▲
Listed
170-172 Sussex Gardens, London W2 1TP
☎ (0171) 402 0281
Fax (0171) 224 9114
*Inexpensive accommodation in central London. Close to Paddington and Lancaster Gate underground stations. Easy access to tourist attractions and Hyde Park.*
Bedrooms: 2 single, 17 double, 6 twin, 9 triple, 6 family rooms
Bathrooms: 23 private, 5 public, 1 private shower

**Bed & breakfast**

| per night: | £min | £max |
|---|---|---|
| Single | 20.00 | |
| Double | 28.00 | |

Parking for 15
Cards accepted: Access, Visa, Diners, Amex
Display advertisement appears on page 33

## LONDON W5

### Corfton Guest House
♛♛
42 Corfton Road, Ealing, London W5 2HT
☎ (0181) 998 1120
*Close to Ealing Broadway station, in a quiet residential area of considerable character.*
Bedrooms: 3 single, 4 double, 1 twin, 2 triple
Bathrooms: 5 private, 2 public
**Bed & breakfast**

| per night: | £min | £max |
|---|---|---|
| Single | 14.00 | 25.00 |
| Double | 23.00 | 30.00 |

Parking for 6

### Creffield Lodge ▲
Listed
2-4 Creffield Road, Ealing, London W5 3HN
☎ (0181) 993 2284
Fax (0181) 992 7082
Telex 935114

*Victorian-style property on ground and two upper floors, located in quiet residential road, adjacent to 150-bedroom Carnarvon Hotel.*
Bedrooms: 10 single, 4 double, 4 twin, 1 triple
Bathrooms: 5 private, 5 public
**Bed & breakfast**

| per night: | £min | £max |
|---|---|---|
| Single | 28.00 | 38.00 |
| Double | 38.00 | 48.00 |

Lunch available
Evening meal 1830 (last orders 2130)
Parking for 20
Cards accepted: Access, Visa, Diners, Amex

### Grange Lodge Hotel
♛♛
48-50 Grange Road, Ealing, London W5 5BX
☎ (0181) 567 1049
Fax (0181) 579 5350

*Quiet, comfortable hotel within a few hundred yards of the underground station. Midway between central London and Heathrow.*
Bedrooms: 7 single, 1 double, 4 twin, 2 triple
Bathrooms: 9 private, 2 public
**Bed & breakfast**

| per night: | £min | £max |
|---|---|---|
| Single | 24.00 | 35.00 |
| Double | 35.00 | 48.00 |

Parking for 10
Cards accepted: Access, Visa, Switch/ Delta

## LONDON W6

### Premier West Hotel ▲
♛♛
28-34 Glenthorne Road, Hammersmith, London W6 0LS
☎ (0181) 748 6181
Fax (0181) 748 2195
*Friendly hotel with affordable prices, conveniently situated for West End, Earl's Court and Olympia exhibition centres and Heathrow Airport.*
Bedrooms: 10 single, 4 double, 17 twin, 14 triple, 4 family rooms
Bathrooms: 41 private, 3 public
**Bed & breakfast**

| per night: | £min | £max |
|---|---|---|
| Single | 32.00 | 67.00 |
| Double | 42.00 | 77.00 |

Lunch available
Evening meal 1800 (last orders 2100)
Parking for 6
Cards accepted: Access, Visa, Diners, Amex

## LONDON W8

### Demetriou Guest House ▲
Listed · APPROVED
9 Strathmore Gardens, London W8 4RZ
☎ (0171) 229 6709
*Small, privately-owned B & B at reasonable prices. Very close to Kensington Gardens and Hyde Park and convenient for all amenities.*
Bedrooms: 1 single, 3 double, 3 twin, 2 triple
Bathrooms: 6 private, 3 public
**Bed & breakfast**

| per night: | £min | £max |
|---|---|---|
| Single | 28.00 | 30.00 |
| Double | 44.00 | 50.00 |

## LONDON W11

### 152 Kensington Park Road
Listed
London W11 2EP
☎ (0171) 727 7174
*Pleasantly situated Victorian terrace house, close to all amenities. Clients*
*Continued ▶*

## LONDON W11

### Continued

*receive individual attention in homely
and friendly surroundings.*
Bedrooms: 2 double, 1 triple
Bathrooms: 1 public
**Bed & breakfast**

| per night: | £min | £max |
|---|---|---|
| Double | 20.00 | 24.00 |

## LONDON WC1

### Acorns Hotel

42 Tavistock Place, London
WC1H 9RE
☎ (0171) 837 3077 & 837 2723
*Grade II listed Victorian house, well-
placed between West End and the City,
ideal for business or pleasure. Minutes'
walk to Russell Square, Euston and
King's Cross.*
Bedrooms: 2 single, 6 double, 4 twin,
2 triple
Bathrooms: 4 public
**Bed & breakfast**

| per night: | £min | £max |
|---|---|---|
| Single | 25.00 | 28.00 |
| Double | 30.00 | 39.00 |

Cards accepted: Access, Visa, Diners,
Amex

### Garth Hotel ♠

**Listed**

69 Gower Street, London WC1E 6HJ
☎ (0171) 636 5761
Fax (0171) 637 4854
*Centrally situated family-run bed and
breakfast accommodation, convenient
for shops, theatres and travel. TV in
rooms. Tea/coffee-making facilities.
Some rooms en-suite.*
Bedrooms: 3 single, 4 double, 5 twin,
3 triple, 2 family rooms
Bathrooms: 1 private, 3 public,
5 private showers
**Bed & breakfast**

| per night: | £min | £max |
|---|---|---|
| Single | 26.00 | 38.00 |
| Double | 36.00 | 50.00 |

Cards accepted: Access, Visa

### St. Athan's Hotel ♠

**Listed**

20 Tavistock Place, Russell Square,
London WC1H 9RE
☎ (0171) 837 9140 & 837 9627
Fax (0171) 833 8352
*Small family-run hotel offering bed and
breakfast.*

Bedrooms: 16 single, 15 double,
15 twin, 5 family rooms
Bathrooms: 6 private, 12 public
**Bed & breakfast**

| per night: | £min | £max |
|---|---|---|
| Single | 26.00 | 42.00 |
| Double | 36.00 | 52.00 |

Cards accepted: Access, Visa, Diners,
Amex

## LONDON WC2

### Hotel Strand Continental ♠

**Listed**

143 The Strand, London WC2R 1JA
☎ (0171) 836 4880
*Small hotel with friendly atmosphere,
near theatres and famous London
landmarks.*
Bedrooms: 10 single, 8 double, 2 twin,
2 triple
Bathrooms: 6 public
**Bed & breakfast**

| per night: | £min | £max |
|---|---|---|
| Single | 23.00 | 26.00 |
| Double | 29.00 | 34.00 |

## OUTER LONDON

Colour maps 6 & 7 at the back of
the guide show place names and
London Postal Area codes and will
help you to locate accommodation
in your chosen area of London.

## CROYDON

### Iverna

**Listed**

1 Annandale Road, Addiscombe,
Croydon CR0 7HP
☎ (0181) 654 8639
*Large house in a quiet road, close to
East Croydon station. London Victoria
15 minutes away. No smoking in public
areas.*
Bedrooms: 3 single, 1 twin
Bathrooms: 1 public
**Bed & breakfast**

| per night: | £min | £max |
|---|---|---|
| Single | 20.00 | 22.00 |
| Double | 36.00 | 40.00 |

Parking for 2

## HARROW

### Aaron House

48 Butler Road, Harrow, Middlesex
HA1 4DR
☎ (0181) 248 3831
*Family guesthouse near underground,
buses and BR station. 20 minutes from
central London, 30 minutes Heathrow.*

*In quiet residential area yet near all
amenities. Traditional breakfast.*
Bedrooms: 1 single, 2 double, 1 twin,
1 triple
Bathrooms: 2 public
**Bed & breakfast**

| per night: | £min | £max |
|---|---|---|
| Single | 22.00 | 28.00 |
| Double | 35.00 | 38.00 |

Lunch available
Evening meal 1800 (last orders 1930)

## HEATHROW AIRPORT

*See under West Drayton*

## SIDCUP

### "The Chimneys"

**Listed**

6 Clarence Road, Sidcup, Kent
DA14 4DL
☎ (0181) 309 1460
*Comfortable and friendly Victorian
home, within easy walking distance of
station and amenities. 30 minutes to
central London by train, 10 minutes
from M25.*
Bedrooms: 2 twin
Bathrooms: 1 public
**Bed & breakfast**

| per night: | £min | £max |
|---|---|---|
| Single | 18.00 | |
| Double | 30.00 | |

| **Half board** | | |
|---|---|---|
| per person: | £min | £max |
| Daily | 20.00 | 25.00 |
| Weekly | 140.00 | 150.00 |

## WEST DRAYTON

### The Alice House

**Listed** **APPROVED**

9 Hollycroft Close, Sipson, West
Drayton, Middlesex UB7 0JJ
☎ (0181) 897 9032
*Small, clean and comfortable
guesthouse. Convenient for the airport,
but with no noise from flight path. Car
service to airport available. Evening
meal by arrangement. Close M4, M25.
London 40 minutes. Parking.*
Bedrooms: 1 single, 1 double, 1 twin
Bathrooms: 1 public
**Bed & breakfast**

| per night: | £min | £max |
|---|---|---|
| Single | 28.00 | 32.00 |
| Double | 38.00 | 42.00 |

Evening meal 1800 (last orders 2000)
Parking for 6

# ACCOMMODATION

33

# SURE SIGNS
## OF WHERE TO STAY

**Throughout Britain, the tourist boards now inspect over 30,000 places to stay, every year, to help you find the ones that suit you best.**

Looking for somewhere convenient to stop overnight on a motorway or major road route? Look for the 'Lodge' **MOON**. The classifications: **ONE to THREE MOON** tell you the range of facilities you can expect. The more Moons, the wider the range.

Looking for a self-catering holiday home? Look for the **KEY**. The classifications: **ONE to FIVE KEY,** tell you the range of facilities and equipment you can expect. The more Keys, the wider the range.
THE GRADES: **APPROVED, COMMENDED, HIGHLY COMMENDED and DE LUXE,** whether alongside the **CROWNS**, **KEYS** or **MOONS** show the quality standard of what is provided. If no grade is shown, you can still expect a high standard of cleanliness.

Looking for a holiday caravan, chalet or camping park? Look for the **Q** symbol. The more ✓s in the Q (from one to five), the higher the quality standard of what is provided.

Looking for a hotel, guesthouse, inn, B&B or farmhouse? Look for the **CROWN**. The classifications: 'Listed', and then **ONE to FIVE CROWN**, tell you the range of facilities and services you can expect. The more Crowns, the wider the range.

**English Tourist Board**

**We've checked them out before you check in!**

More detailed information on the **CROWNS**, the **KEYS** and the **Q** is given in free *SURE SIGN* leaflets, available at any Tourist Information Centre.

*Unique in its richness and variety of landscape, climate, culture and history, Cumbria has as its core the Lake District's rugged fells, radiating valleys and, of course, the gleaming lakes. But there's a lesser-known Cumbria. Explore the long coastline of shingle beaches and sands, soaring*

# CUMBRIA

*cliffs, saltmarshes and flat coastal plains. Discover the Eden Valley – an area of lush farmland, meandering rivers and pretty villages. Or visit the North Pennines, truly England's last wilderness.*

The County of Cumbria, including English Lakeland

For more information on Cumbria, contact:
**Cumbria Tourist Board**
**Ashleigh**
**Holly Road**
**Windermere**
**Cumbria LA23 2AQ**
Tel: (015394) 44444
Fax: (015394) 44041

Where to Go in Cumbria
– see pages 36–39

Where to Stay in Cumbria
– see pages 40–59

# WHERE TO GO

*You will find hundreds of interesting places to visit during your stay in Cumbria, just some of which are listed in these pages. The number against each name will help you locate it on the map (page 38).*
*Contact any Tourist Information Centre in the region for more ideas on days out in Cumbria.*

**1** *Birdoswald Roman Fort*
Gilsland, Cumbria CA6 7DD
Tel: (016977) 47602
*Remains of Roman fort on Hadrian's Wall, with excellent views of Irthing Gorge. Visitor centre.*

**2** *Naworth Castle*
Brampton, Cumbria
Tel: (016977) 41156
*Historic border fortress, built in 1335 and renovated in 1602. Great hall, Gobelin tapestries, Pre-Raphaelite library, 14th C dungeons.*

**3** *Tullie House Museum and Art Gallery*
Castle Street, Carlisle, Cumbria CA3 8TP
Tel: (01228) 34781
*Major tourist complex housing museum, art gallery, education facility, lecture theatre, shops, garden restaurant, terrace bars.*

**4** *South Tynedale Railway*
Railway Station, Alston, Cumbria CA9 3JB
Tel: (01434) 381696
*2ft gauge railway following part of the route of the former Alston to Haltwhistle branch line through South Tynedale.*

**5** *Senhouse Roman Museum*
The Battery, Sea Brows, Maryport, Cumbria CA15 6JD
Tel: (01900) 816168
*Largest collection of Roman altars and inscriptions from a single site. Museum shows what Roman life was like in the North West.*

**6** *Hutton-in-the-Forest*
Skelton, Cumbria CA11 9TH
Tel: (017684) 84449
*14th C Pele Tower with later additions. Tapestries, furniture, paintings, china, armour. Formal gardens, dovecote, lake and woods with specimen trees.*

**7** *Mirehouse*
Underskiddaw, Cumbria CA12 4QE
Tel: (017687) 72287
*Manuscripts and portraits with many literary connections, Victorian schoolroom/nursery, antiques quiz, woodland and lakeside walk, 4 adventure playgrounds.*

**8** *Acorn Bank Garden*
Temple Sowerby, Cumbria CA10 1SP
Tel: (017683) 61893
*Spring bulbs, walled garden, outstanding herb garden, wild garden. 16th C house in garden is not normally open to the public.*

**Bridge House, Ambleside: one of Britain's smallest dwellings.**

**9** *Dalemain Historic House and Gardens*
Dacre, Penrith, Cumbria CA11 OHB
Tel: (017684) 86450
*Historic house with Georgian furniture.*
*Westmorland and Cumberland Yeomanry*
*Museum. Agricultural bygones, adventure*
*playground, licensed restaurant, gardens.*

**10** *Lakeland Bird of Prey Centre*
Old Walled Garden, Lowther, Cumbria
CA10 2HH
Tel: (01931) 712746
*Most types of hawk, falcon, buzzard, owl and*
*eagle are displayed either in aviaries or*
*"blocked out".*

**Grasmere's famous gingerbread is still**
**baked to a secret recipe dating from 1855.**

**11** *Whinlatter Forest Park Visitor Centre*
Braithwaite, Cumbria CA12 5TW
Tel: (017687) 78469
*Interpretative forestry exhibition with audio-*
*visual presentations. Working model of forest*
*operations, lecture theatre, shop, walks, trails,*
*orienteering.*

**12** *Dove Cottage and Wordsworth Museum*
Town End, Grasmere, Cumbria LA22 9SH
Tel: (015394) 35544
*Wordsworth's home 1799–1808. Poet's*
*possessions, museum with manuscripts,*
*farmhouse reconstruction, paintings and*
*drawings. Year-round programme of events.*

**13** *Rydal Mount*
Ambleside, Cumbria LA22 9LU
Tel: (015394) 33002
*Wordsworth's home for 37 years, with first*
*editions, portraits, memorabilia. Garden*
*landscaped by the poet.*

**14** *Eskdale Corn Mill*
Boot, Cumbria CA19 1TG
Tel: (019467) 23335
*Historic water-powered corn mill near Dalegarth*
*station, approached by a packhorse bridge.*
*Early wooden machinery, waterfalls, exhibition.*

**15** *Brockhole – Lake District National Park*
*Visitor Centre*
Windermere, Cumbria LA23 1LJ
Tel: (015394) 46601
*Exhibitions include the National Park Story, slide*
*shows and films. Shop, gardens, grounds,*
*adventure playground, dry stone walling area,*
*trails, events. Restaurant, tearoom.*

**16** *The World of Beatrix Potter Exhibition*
The Old Laundry, Crag Brow, Bowness-on-
Windermere, Cumbria LA23 3BT
Tel: (015394) 88444
*Exhibition interpreting the life and works of*
*Beatrix Potter, comprising 9-screen video wall*
*recreating scenes in three dimensions and film.*

**17** *Steam Yacht Gondola*
Pier Cottage, Coniston, Cumbria LA21 8AJ
Tel: (015394) 41288
*Steam-powered yacht, launched 1859 and now*
*completely renovated with opulent saloon,*
*carries 86 passengers. Piers at Coniston, Park-a-*
*Moor and Brantwood.*

**18** *Muncaster Castle, Gardens and Owl*
*Centre*
Ravenglass, Cumbria CA18 1RQ
Tel: (01229) 717614
*14th C pele tower with 15th and 19th C*
*additions. Gardens with exceptional collection*
*of rhododendrons and azaleas. Extensive*
*collection of owls.*

**19** *Ravenglass and Eskdale Railway and*
*Museum*
Ravenglass, Cumbria CA18 1SW
Tel: (01229) 717171

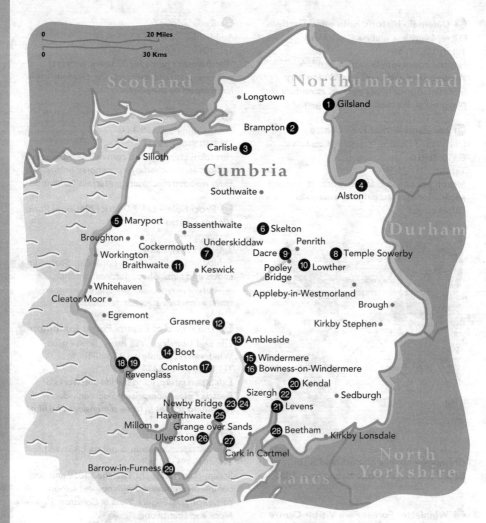

### Map Key

- 1 Gilsland
- 2 Brampton
- 3 Carlisle
- 4 Alston
- 5 Maryport
- 6 Skelton
- 7 Underskiddaw
- 8 Temple Sowerby
- 9 Dacre
- 10 Lowther
- 11 Braithwaite
- 12 Grasmere
- 13 Ambleside
- 14 Boot
- 15 Windermere
- 16 Bowness-on-Windermere
- 17 Coniston
- 18 Ravenglass
- 19 Ravenglass
- 20 Kendal
- 21 Levens
- 22 Sizergh
- 23 Newby Bridge
- 24 Newby Bridge
- 25 Haverthwaite
- 26 Ulverston
- 27 Cark in Cartmel
- 28 Beetham
- 29 Barrow-in-Furness

Map labels: Longtown, Silloth, Southwaite, Bassenthwaite, Cockermouth, Workington, Broughton, Keswick, Whitehaven, Cleator Moor, Egremont, Penrith, Pooley Bridge, Appleby-in-Westmorland, Brough, Kirkby Stephen, Sedbergh, Millom, Grange over Sands, Kirkby Lonsdale, Scotland, Northumberland, Durham, North Yorkshire, Lancs

0   20 Miles
0   30 Kms

---

England's oldest narrow gauge railway, running for 7 miles through glorious scenery to the foot of the country's highest hills. Most trains are steam-hauled.

### 20 *Kendal Museum*

Station Road, Kendal, Cumbria LA9 6BT
Tel: (01539) 721374
*Outstanding natural history gallery with reconstructions of Lake District habitats, world wildlife gallery, Westmorland gallery on local history, Alfred Wainwright display.*

### 21 *Levens Hall*

Kendal, Cumbria LA8 0PD
Tel: (015395) 60321
*Elizabethan mansion incorporating a pele tower. Topiary garden laid out in 1694, plant centre, steam collection, picnic and play areas, shop.*

### 22 *Sizergh Castle*

Kendal, Cumbria LA8 8AE
Tel: (015395) 60070
*Castle with 14th C pele tower, 15th C great hall and 16th C wings. Stuart connections. Rock garden, rose garden, daffodils.*

**㉓ Graythwaite Hall Gardens**
Newby Bridge, Cumbria LA12 8BA
Tel: (015395) 31248
*Rhododendrons, azaleas and flowering
shrubs. Laid out by T. Mawson 1888–1890.*

**㉔ Windermere Iron Steamboat
Company**
Lakeside Pier, Newby Bridge, Cumbria
LA12 8AS
Tel: (015395) 31188
*Three steamers sailing Windermere, also
motor launches and ferry service from
Lakeside to Fell Foot. Booking offices at
Lakeside, Bowness and Ambleside.*

**㉕ Lakeside and Haverthwaite Railway**
Haverthwaite Station, Ulverston, Cumbria
LA12 8AL
Tel: (015395) 31594
*Standard gauge steam railway operating a
daily service at Easter and from May to October.
Display of steam and diesel locomotives.*

**㉖ Heron Glass**
The Gill, Ulverston, Cumbria LA12 7BL
Tel: (01229) 581121
*New visitor centre with glass-makers
transforming molten glass into artistic shapes.*

**㉗ Holker Hall and Gardens**
Cark in Cartmel, Cumbria LA11 7PL
Tel: (015395) 58328
*Victorian wing, formal and woodland garden,
deer park, motor museum, adventure
playground, gift shop. Exhibitions, including
Timeless Toys and Teddies.*

**㉘ Heron Corn Mill and Museum of
Papermaking**
Waterhouse Mills, Beetham, Cumbria LA7 7AR
Tel: (015395) 63363
*Restored working corn mill with 14ft high
breastshot waterwheel. Museum of Papermaking.*

**㉙ The Dock Museum**
North Road, Barrow-in-Furness, Cumbria
LA14 2PW
Tel: (01229) 870871
*Based in the unique setting of a 19th C dry dock, the
museum presents the story of steel shipbuilding for
which Barrow-in-Furness is famous.*

*Cumbria is fine sheep country – great numbers
are reared on the hill farms and moorlands.*

# FIND OUT MORE

*Further information about holidays and
attractions in Cumbria is available from:*
**Cumbria Tourist Board**, *Ashleigh, Holly Road,
Windermere, Cumbria LA23 2AQ
Tel: (015394) 44444*

*These publications are available from the
Cumbria Tourist Board (post free):*
● **Cumbria The Lake District Touring Map**
*(including tourist information and touring
caravan and camping parks) £3.45*
● **Places to Visit and Things to Do in Cumbria
The Lake District** *(over 200 ideas for a great day
out) £1.25*
● **Short Walks – Good for Families** *(route
descriptions, maps and information for 14 walks
in the lesser-known areas of Cumbria) 95p*
● **Wordsworth's Lake District** *(folded map
showing major Wordsworthian sites plus
biographical details) 45p. Japanese language
version £1. Poster £1.*
● **Explore Cumbria by Car** *(route descriptions,
maps and information for 10 circular motor
tours) 95p*

# WHERE TO STAY

Accommodation entries in this regional section are listed in alphabetical order of place name, and then in alphabetical order of establishment.

Map references refer to the colour location maps at the back of this guide. The first figure is the map number; the letter and figure which follow indicate the grid reference on the map.

Symbols at the end of each accommodation entry give information about services and facilities. A 'key' to these symbols is inside the back cover flap, which can be kept open for easy reference.

## ALSTON

Cumbria
Map ref 5B2

Alston is the highest market town in England, set amongst the highest fells of the Pennines and close to the Pennine Way in an Area of Outstanding Natural Beauty. Mainly 17th C buildings with steep, cobbled streets.
*Tourist Information Centre*
☎ *(01434) 381696*

### Shield Hill House ⚲
♛♛

Garrigill, Alston CA9 3EX
☎ (01434) 381238
*Converted farmhouse with panoramic views. In the heart of the North Pennines, convenient for Borders, Lakes, Northumbria and dales. 3.5 miles from Alston on the B6277 Barnard Castle road. No smoking, please.*
Bedrooms: 2 double, 2 twin, 1 family room
Bathrooms: 5 private

**Bed & breakfast**

| per night: | £min | £max |
|---|---|---|
| Single | 16.50 | 17.50 |
| Double | 33.00 | 35.00 |

**Half board**

| per person: | £min | £max |
|---|---|---|
| Daily | 24.50 | 25.95 |
| Weekly | 145.00 | 165.00 |

Evening meal 1930 (last orders 1200)
Parking for 8
Cards accepted: Access, Visa
⌕♨⮹♿♿♿✆⟊⚘📺⛱⬛, ⬛✿✕
🚍 SP

## AMBLESIDE

Cumbria
Map ref 5A3

Market town situated at the head of Lake Windermere and surrounded by fells. The historic town centre is now a conservation area and the country around Ambleside is rich in historic and literary associations. Good centre for touring, walking and climbing.
*Tourist Information Centre*
☎ *(01539) 432582*

### The Anchorage
♛♛ COMMENDED

Rydal Road, Ambleside LA22 9AY
☎ (01539) 432046
*Modern detached guesthouse offering a good standard of accommodation and own private car park. 300 metres from town centre and amenities.*
Bedrooms: 4 double, 1 twin
Bathrooms: 2 private, 1 public

**Bed & breakfast**

| per night: | £min | £max |
|---|---|---|
| Double | 34.00 | 44.00 |

Parking for 7
Open February-November
⌕ 10 ⛁⛶⬛♨⚘ S ⛱⬛, ✕🚍

### Borrans Park Hotel ⚲
♛♛ ♛ HIGHLY COMMENDED

Borrans Road, Ambleside LA22 0EN
☎ (01539) 433454
*Peacefully situated between the village and lake. Enjoy candlelit dinners, 120 fine wines, and four-poster bedrooms with private spa baths.*
Wheelchair access category 3 ♿
Bedrooms: 9 double, 1 twin, 2 triple
Bathrooms: 12 private

**Bed & breakfast**

| per night: | £min | £max |
|---|---|---|
| Single | 27.50 | 47.50 |
| Double | 55.00 | 75.00 |

**Half board**

| per person: | £min | £max |
|---|---|---|
| Daily | 43.00 | 53.00 |
| Weekly | 229.00 | 299.00 |

Evening meal 1900 (last orders 1800)
Parking for 20
Cards accepted: Access, Visa
⌕♨♿⚭✆⛁⬛♨⟊♿ S ⛱✕⬛, ⬛
✿✕🚍♿ SP

### Brantfell House ⚲
♛♛ APPROVED

Rothay Road, Ambleside LA22 0EE
☎ (01539) 432239
*Warm friendly Victorian house, centrally located overlooking fells. Good cuisine, catering for all tastes - optional evening meal.*
Bedrooms: 1 single, 3 double, 1 twin, 1 triple
Bathrooms: 3 private, 2 public

**Bed & breakfast**

| per night: | £min | £max |
|---|---|---|
| Single | 13.50 | 17.00 |
| Double | 32.00 | 40.00 |

**Half board**

| per person: | £min | £max |
|---|---|---|
| Daily | 23.50 | 30.00 |
| Weekly | 156.00 | 210.00 |

Evening meal 1900 (last orders 2100)
Parking for 2
⌕⛶♨⚘S✕⛱📺⬛, ⬛✿♿ SP

### Foxghyll ⚲
♛♛ HIGHLY COMMENDED

Under Loughrigg, Rydal, Ambleside LA22 9LL
☎ (01539) 433292

*Large country house in secluded gardens with direct access to fells. All rooms en-suite, one with spa bath. Ample parking.*
Bedrooms: 2 double, 1 twin
Bathrooms: 3 private
**Bed & breakfast**

| per night: | £min | £max |
|---|---|---|
| Double | 42.00 | 52.00 |

Parking for 7
⊙ 10 ⌂ ▣ □ ↓ ⚲ ⓊⓁ ⏦ ⋈ ▥ ◪ ✈ ♪ ☼ ✗ ☕ ⌘

## The Gables Hotel ⋈
⚜ ⚜

Compston Road, Ambleside LA22 9DJ
☎ (01539) 433272
*In a quiet residential area overlooking the park, tennis courts, bowling green and Loughrigg Fell. Convenient for the shops, walking and water sports.*
Bedrooms: 3 single, 5 double, 1 twin, 4 triple
Bathrooms: 13 private
**Bed & breakfast**

| per night: | £min | £max |
|---|---|---|
| Single | 18.75 | 22.50 |
| Double | 37.50 | 45.00 |

**Half board**

| per person: | £min | £max |
|---|---|---|
| Daily | 31.25 | 35.00 |
| Weekly | 217.00 | |

Evening meal 1845 (last orders 1915)
Parking for 7
Open January-November
⊙ ⚶ □ ↓ ▣ Ⓢ ⏦ ⓉⓋ ▥ ⌘ ☕

## Glenside ⋈
⚜ COMMENDED

Old Lake Road, Ambleside LA22 0DP
☎ (01539) 432635
*17th C farm cottage, comfortable bedrooms with original oak beams, TV lounge. Between town and lake, ideal centre for walking. Private parking.*
Bedrooms: 2 double, 1 twin
Bathrooms: 1 public
**Bed & breakfast**

| per night: | £min | £max |
|---|---|---|
| Single | 14.00 | 16.00 |
| Double | 28.00 | 32.00 |

Parking for 3
⊙ 5 ↓ ⓊⓁ ⓘ ✗ ▥ ⓉⓋ ▥ ✗ ☕ OAP Ⓣ

## High Wray Farm
Listed

High Wray, Ambleside LA22 0JE
☎ (01539) 432280

*173-acre livestock farm. Charming 17th C farmhouse once owned by Beatrix Potter. In quiet location, ideal centre for touring or walking. Panoramic views and lake shore walks close by.*
Bedrooms: 2 double, 1 twin
Bathrooms: 1 private, 1 public
**Bed & breakfast**

| per night: | £min | £max |
|---|---|---|
| Single | 13.50 | 15.50 |
| Double | 27.00 | 31.00 |

Parking for 7
⊙ ⚶ ⓊⓁ ⓘ Ⓢ ✗ ▥ ⓉⓋ ☼ ☕ ⌘

## Laurel Villa ⋈
⚜ ⚜ ⚜ HIGHLY COMMENDED

Lake Road, Ambleside LA22 0DB
☎ (01539) 433240
*Detached Victorian house, visited by Beatrix Potter. En-suite bedrooms overlooking the fells. Within easy reach of Lake Windermere and the village. Private car park.*
Bedrooms: 7 double, 1 twin
Bathrooms: 8 private
**Bed & breakfast**

| per night: | £min | £max |
|---|---|---|
| Single | 50.00 | 50.00 |
| Double | 60.00 | 80.00 |

Evening meal 1900 (last orders 1700)
Parking for 10
Cards accepted: Access, Visa
▣ ▣ □ ↓ ⚲ Ⓢ ✗ ▥ ▥ ⌘ ☼ ✗ ☕ OAP Ⓢ Ⓣ

## Meadowbank
⚜

Rydal Road, Ambleside LA22 9BA
☎ (01539) 432710
*Country house in private garden with ample parking in grounds. Overlooking meadowland and fells, yet a level, easy walk to Ambleside. Good walking base.*
Bedrooms: 1 single, 2 double, 2 twin, 2 triple
Bathrooms: 3 private, 2 public
**Bed & breakfast**

| per night: | £min | £max |
|---|---|---|
| Single | 17.00 | 25.00 |
| Double | 34.00 | 42.00 |

Parking for 10
⊙ ⚶ □ ↓ ⓊⓁ Ⓢ ✗ ▥ ⓉⓋ ▥ ⌘ ☼ ✗ ☕ Ⓢ ⌘

## Mill Cottage Country Guesthouse and Restaurant
Listed APPROVED

Rydal Road, Ambleside LA22 9AN
☎ (01539) 434830
*Grade II listed restaurant and guesthouse in riverside location adjacent to the famous Bridge House.*
Bedrooms: 4 double, 1 family room

Bathrooms: 2 private, 1 public, 3 private showers
**Bed & breakfast**

| per night: | £min | £max |
|---|---|---|
| Single | 17.00 | 20.00 |
| Double | 30.00 | 34.00 |

**Half board**

| per person: | £min | £max |
|---|---|---|
| Daily | 25.00 | 27.00 |
| Weekly | 160.00 | 175.00 |

Lunch available
Evening meal 1800 (last orders 2130)
⊙ □ ↓ ⓘ Ⓢ ✗ ▥ ⌘ ☕ ☼ Ⓢ ⌘

## The Old Vicarage ⋈
⚜ ⚜ APPROVED

Vicarage Road, Ambleside LA22 9DH
☎ (01539) 433364
Fax (01539) 434734

*Quietly situated in own grounds in heart of village. Car park, quality en-suite accommodation, friendly service. Family-run. Pets welcome.*
Bedrooms: 7 double, 1 twin, 1 triple, 1 family room
Bathrooms: 10 private
**Bed & breakfast**

| per night: | £min | £max |
|---|---|---|
| Single | 23.00 | |
| Double | 46.00 | |

Parking for 12
⊙ ⚶ ▣ ▣ □ ↓ ⚲ ⓊⓁ ⓘ Ⓢ ✗ ▥ ▥ ⌘ Ⓣ ☼ ✗ Ⓢ ⌘

## Riverside Lodge Country House ⋈
⚜ ⚜ COMMENDED

Nr. Rothay Bridge, Ambleside LA22 0EH
☎ (01539) 434208

*Georgian country house of character with 2 acres of grounds through which the River Rothay flows. 500 yards from the centre of Ambleside.*
Bedrooms: 1 double, 1 twin, 1 triple
Bathrooms: 3 private
**Bed & breakfast**

| per night: | £min | £max |
|---|---|---|
| Double | 42.00 | 57.00 |

Parking for 20
Cards accepted: Access, Visa
⊙ 11 ⚶ ▣ ⓛ ▣ □ ↓ ⚲ ⓘ ✗ ▥ ▥ ⌘ ♪ ☼ ✗ ☕ ◌ Ⓢ ⌘

## AMBLESIDE
### Continued

### Rowanfield Country Guesthouse 🅜
**HIGHLY COMMENDED**
Kirkstone Road, Ambleside LA22 9ET
☎ (01539) 433686

*Idyllic setting, panoramic lake and mountain views. Laura Ashley style decor. Scrumptious food created by proprietor/chef. Special break prices.*
Wheelchair access category 3 ♿
Bedrooms: 5 double, 1 twin, 1 triple
Bathrooms: 7 private

**Bed & breakfast**

| per night: | £min | £max |
|---|---|---|
| Double | 48.00 | 56.00 |

**Half board**

| per person: | £min | £max |
|---|---|---|
| Daily | 39.00 | 43.00 |
| Weekly | 235.00 | 252.00 |

Evening meal 1900 (last orders 1930)
Parking for 8
Open March-December
Cards accepted: Access, Visa
🛏5♿🖳🖵♨🅂🖃🍴🅼🕮,🖂✿🚗🚭 SP 🏤

### Smallwood House Hotel 🅜
**APPROVED**
Compston Road, Ambleside LA22 9DJ
☎ (01539) 432330
*Family-run hotel in central position, offering warm and friendly service, good home cooking and value-for-money quality and standards.*
Bedrooms: 7 double, 3 twin, 3 triple, 2 family rooms
Bathrooms: 15 private, 2 public

**Bed & breakfast**

| per night: | £min | £max |
|---|---|---|
| Single | 18.00 | 25.00 |
| Double | 33.00 | 39.00 |

**Half board**

| per person: | £min | £max |
|---|---|---|
| Daily | 28.00 | 35.00 |
| Weekly | 185.00 | 200.00 |

Lunch available
Evening meal 1800 (last orders 2000)
Parking for 11
🛏♿🖳🖵♨🅂🖃🅼🕮,🖂 DAP 🚭 SP

### Wanslea Guest House 🅜
Lake Road, Ambleside LA22 0DB
☎ (01539) 433884

*Spacious, comfortable, family-run Victorian house offering good food, wines and fine views. Easy walk to lake and village. Honeymoons a speciality. Brochure available.*
Bedrooms: 1 single, 3 double, 3 triple, 1 family room
Bathrooms: 4 private, 3 public

**Bed & breakfast**

| per night: | £min | £max |
|---|---|---|
| Single | 18.00 | 27.50 |
| Double | 37.00 | 55.00 |

**Half board**

| per person: | £min | £max |
|---|---|---|
| Daily | 29.00 | 38.00 |
| Weekly | 170.00 | 248.00 |

Lunch available
Evening meal 1845 (last orders 1500)
🛏♨🅂🖃🅼🕮🖃,🖂🍴10-20✿ DAP 🚭 SP 🖵

### Windlehurst Guesthouse 🅜
Millans Park, Ambleside LA22 9AG
☎ (01539) 433137
*Victorian house in quiet location close to village. Commanding views of Loughrigg Fell. Comfortable rooms, friendly service. No-smoking. Dogs welcome.*
Bedrooms: 1 single, 2 double, 2 triple, 1 family room
Bathrooms: 2 private, 2 public

**Bed & breakfast**

| per night: | £min | £max |
|---|---|---|
| Single | 14.50 | 20.00 |
| Double | 28.00 | 44.00 |

Parking for 6
Open January-October
🛏🖵♨🖃🅂🍴🅼🕮🖃,🖂✿🚗

## APPLEBY-IN-WESTMORLAND
Cumbria
Map ref 5B3

Former county town of Westmorland, at the foot of the Pennines in the Eden Valley. The castle was rebuilt in the 17th C, except for its Norman keep, ditches and ramparts. It now houses a Rare Breeds Survival Trust Centre. Good centre for exploring the Eden Valley.
Tourist Information Centre
☎ (01768) 351177

### Bongate House 🅜
**COMMENDED**
Appleby-in-Westmorland CA16 6UE
☎ (01768) 351245

*Family-run Georgian guesthouse on the outskirts of a small market town. Large garden. Relaxed friendly atmosphere, good home cooking.*
Bedrooms: 1 single, 4 double, 2 twin, 1 triple
Bathrooms: 5 private, 1 public

**Bed & breakfast**

| per night: | £min | £max |
|---|---|---|
| Single | 16.00 | 16.00 |
| Double | 32.00 | 37.00 |

**Half board**

| per person: | £min | £max |
|---|---|---|
| Daily | 24.00 | 26.50 |
| Weekly | 150.00 | 170.00 |

Evening meal 1900 (last orders 1800)
Parking for 10
🛏7🖵♨♿🅂🅼🕮,🖂🚻🚹♪🕭✿🚭 SP 🏤🖵

### Bridge End Farm
Kirkby Thore, Penrith CA10 1UZ
☎ Kirkby Stephen (01768) 361362 & 352543
*450-acre arable & dairy farm. Relax in 18th C farmhouse in Eden Valley. Spacious rooms overlooking Pennine Hills, alongside River Eden. Delicious home-made breakfast and dinners.*
Bedrooms: 2 double, 1 twin
Bathrooms: 3 private, 1 public

**Bed & breakfast**

| per night: | £min | £max |
|---|---|---|
| Single | 16.00 | 18.00 |
| Double | 32.00 | 36.00 |

**Half board**

| per person: | £min | £max |
|---|---|---|
| Daily | 24.50 | 27.00 |
| Weekly | 165.00 | 175.00 |

Evening meal 1800 (last orders 1930)
Parking for 3
🛏🖳♿🖃🅂🍴🅼🕮🖃,🖂♪✿🚗

### Dufton Hall Farm
Dufton, Appleby-in-Westmorland CA16 6DD
☎ (01768) 351573
*60-acre mixed farm. Part of ancient hall, and working hill farm in village centre. 3.5 miles north-east of Appleby-in-Westmorland and close to Pennine Way.*
Bedrooms: 2 double, 1 twin
Bathrooms: 3 private

**Bed & breakfast**

| per night: | £min | £max |
|---|---|---|
| Single | 18.00 | |
| Double | 30.00 | |

**Half board**

| per person: | £min | £max |
|---|---|---|
| Daily | 25.00 | |
| Weekly | 175.00 | |

Evening meal 1800 (last orders 1900)
Parking for 3
Open April-October
🛏♿🖃🅂🅼🕮🖂✿✕🚗🏤

### Howgill House ⚑
COMMENDED

Appleby-in-Westmorland CA16 6UW
☎ (01768) 351574
*Private family-run house standing in a large garden. On B6542, half a mile from the town centre.*
Bedrooms: 1 single, 1 twin, 2 triple
Bathrooms: 2 public

**Bed & breakfast**

| per night: | £min | £max |
| --- | --- | --- |
| Single | 15.00 | |
| Double | 28.00 | |

Parking for 6
Open May-September

---

## ARNSIDE
Cumbria
Map ref 5A3

Small coastal village in an Area of Outstanding Natural Beauty, with spectacular views across the Kent Estuary of the Lakeland hills. Excellent base for bird-watching. The incoming tide creates an impressive tidal bore.

### Willowfield Hotel ⚑
COMMENDED

The Promenade, Arnside, Carnforth, Lancashire LA5 0AD
☎ (01524) 761354
*Non-smoking, relaxed, family-run hotel with panoramic outlook over estuary to Lakeland hills. Good home cooking and quiet situation.*
Bedrooms: 2 single, 3 double, 3 twin, 2 triple
Bathrooms: 3 private, 2 public

**Bed & breakfast**

| per night: | £min | £max |
| --- | --- | --- |
| Single | 17.00 | 20.00 |
| Double | 34.00 | 40.00 |

**Half board**

| per person: | £min | £max |
| --- | --- | --- |
| Daily | 26.50 | 29.50 |
| Weekly | 175.00 | 196.00 |

Evening meal from 1830
Parking for 10

---

## BORROWDALE
Cumbria
Map ref 5A3

Stretching south of Derwentwater to Seathwaite in the heart of the Lake District, the valley is walled by high fellsides. It can justly claim to be the most scenically impressive valley in the Lake District. Excellent centre for walking and climbing.

### Mary Mount ⚑

Borrowdale, Keswick CA12 5UU
☎ (01768) 777223

---

*Set in 4.5 acres of gardens and woodlands on the shores of Derwentwater, 2.5 miles from Keswick. Views across lake to Catbells and Maiden Moor. Families welcome.*
Bedrooms: 1 single, 5 double, 5 twin, 2 triple, 1 family room
Bathrooms: 14 private

**Bed & breakfast**

| per night: | £min | £max |
| --- | --- | --- |
| Single | 18.00 | 26.00 |
| Double | 36.00 | 52.00 |

Lunch available
Evening meal 1830 (last orders 2045)
Parking for 40
Open February-December
Cards accepted: Access, Visa

### Scawdel
Listed

Grange-in-Borrowdale, Keswick CA12 5UQ
☎ Keswick (01768) 777271
*Detached house with private parking in Grange village, 4 miles from Keswick. Excellent mountain views from most windows. Rooms have comfortable seating and orthopaedic beds.*
Bedrooms: 2 double, 1 twin
Bathrooms: 1 public

**Bed & breakfast**

| per night: | £min | £max |
| --- | --- | --- |
| Single | 17.50 | |
| Double | 31.00 | 35.00 |

Parking for 4

---

## BOWNESS-ON-SOLWAY
Cumbria
Map ref 5A2

Coastal village near the site of a Roman fort at the western end of Hadrian's Wall.

### Wallsend Guest House

Wallsend (The Old Rectory), Church Lane, Bowness-on-Solway, Carlisle CA5 5AF
☎ Kirkbride (01697) 351055
*Former rectory in an acre of grounds, on fringe of farming/fishing village near Solway Firth. Private parking. Start and finish of Hadrian's Wall walk and convenient for Cumbria coastal way and cycle way.*
Bedrooms: 2 double
Bathrooms: 1 public

**Bed & breakfast**

| per night: | £min | £max |
| --- | --- | --- |
| Single | 16.00 | 20.00 |
| Double | 24.00 | 34.00 |

Parking for 6

---

## BRAITHWAITE
Cumbria
Map ref 5A3

Braithwaite nestles at the foot of the Whinlatter Pass and has a magnificent backdrop of the mountains forming the Coledale Horseshoe.

### Coledale Inn ⚑

Braithwaite, Keswick CA12 5TN
☎ (01768) 778272
*Victorian country house hotel and Georgian inn, in a peaceful hillside position away from traffic, with superb mountain views.*
Bedrooms: 1 single, 5 double, 2 twin, 3 triple, 1 family room
Bathrooms: 12 private

**Bed & breakfast**

| per night: | £min | £max |
| --- | --- | --- |
| Single | 16.00 | 20.00 |
| Double | 36.00 | 52.00 |

Lunch available
Evening meal 1830 (last orders 2100)
Parking for 15
Cards accepted: Access, Visa

---

## BRAMPTON
Cumbria
Map ref 5B3

Pleasant market town whose character has changed very little over the past 150 years. The Moot Hall, in the market square, is a fine octagonal building which stands next to the stocks. A good centre for exploring Hadrian's Wall.

### Cracrop Farm ⚑
HIGHLY COMMENDED

Kirkcambeck, Brampton CA8 2BW
☎ Roadhead (01697) 748245
*425-acre mixed farm. Superior accommodation on farm which has won prizes in farming and wildlife competition. Farm trails in unspoilt, picturesque countryside. Relax in sauna and spa bath.*
Bedrooms: 1 single, 2 double, 1 twin
Bathrooms: 4 private, 1 public

**Bed & breakfast**

| per night: | £min | £max |
| --- | --- | --- |
| Single | 18.00 | 20.00 |
| Double | 36.00 | 40.00 |

Evening meal 1800 (last orders 1300)
Parking for 4
Cards accepted: Amex

### High Nook Farm
Listed

Low Row, Brampton CA8 2LU
☎ Hallbankgate (01697) 746273

*Continued* ▶

## BRAMPTON

### Continued

*100-acre livestock farm. Quiet location in the beautiful Irthing Valley, near the Roman Wall, convenient for Northumberland, Scottish borders and the Lake District. Good hourly bus service.*
Bedrooms: 1 double, 1 family room
Bathrooms: 1 public

**Bed & breakfast**

| per night: | £min | £max |
|---|---|---|
| Double | 22.00 | 24.00 |

**Half board**

| per person: | £min | £max |
|---|---|---|
| Daily | 16.50 | 17.50 |
| Weekly | 108.50 | 115.50 |

Evening meal 1800 (last orders 1500)
Parking for 3
Open May–September

### High Rigg Farm ⋀
APPROVED

Walton, Brampton CA8 2AZ
☎ (01697) 72117
*202-acre mixed farm. 18th C listed farmhouse on roadside, 1 mile from Walton and Roman Wall, 3.5 miles from Brampton. Family-run with pedigree cattle and sheep, farm trail to waterfall. Friendly atmosphere, delicious food. Good stopover or holiday base.*
Bedrooms: 1 family room
Bathrooms: 1 public

**Bed & breakfast**

| per night: | £min | £max |
|---|---|---|
| Single | 14.50 | 15.00 |
| Double | 27.00 | 28.00 |

**Half board**

| per person: | £min | £max |
|---|---|---|
| Daily | 21.50 | 22.50 |
| Weekly | 147.00 | 150.00 |

Evening meal 1800 (last orders 1400)
Parking for 4

### Howard House Farm ⋀
HIGHLY COMMENDED

Gilsland, Carlisle CA6 7AN
☎ Gilsland (01697) 747285
*250-acre livestock farm. Peaceful farm in comfortable and friendly surroundings, 7 miles north-east of Brampton and centre of Roman Wall. Birdoswald 2 miles, Housesteads 6 miles.*
Bedrooms: 1 double, 1 twin, 1 triple
Bathrooms: 1 private, 2 public

**Bed & breakfast**

| per night: | £min | £max |
|---|---|---|
| Single | 20.00 | 20.00 |
| Double | 32.00 | 38.00 |

Evening meal 1800 (last orders 1800)
Parking for 4

## BROUGHTON-IN-FURNESS

Cumbria
Map ref 5A3

Old market village whose historic charter to hold fairs is still proclaimed every year on the first day of August in the market square. Good centre for touring the pretty Duddon Valley.

### Black Cock Inn
Listed

Princes Street, Broughton-in-Furness LA20 6HQ
☎ (01229) 716529
Fax (01229) 716774
*16th C listed inn serving home-made fare and traditional ales. A haven within easy reach of Windermere, Coniston and the beautiful Duddon Valley.*
Bedrooms: 1 double, 2 twin, 1 family room
Bathrooms: 1 public

**Bed & breakfast**

| per night: | £min | £max |
|---|---|---|
| Single | 15.50 | 17.00 |
| Double | 31.00 | 31.00 |

Lunch available
Evening meal 1800 (last orders 2130)
Cards accepted: Access, Visa, Switch/Delta

### Cobblers Cottage ⋀
COMMENDED

Griffin Street, Broughton-in-Furness LA20 6HH
☎ (01229) 716413

*Quaint 17th C cottage offering delicious food in a cosy and relaxed atmosphere. Ideally situated for exploring South Lakes and beautiful Duddon Valley.*
Bedrooms: 2 double, 1 twin
Bathrooms: 1 private, 1 public

**Bed & breakfast**

| per night: | £min | £max |
|---|---|---|
| Single | 16.00 | 18.50 |
| Double | 32.00 | 37.00 |

**Half board**

| per person: | £min | £max |
|---|---|---|
| Daily | 25.00 | 30.50 |
| Weekly | 168.00 | 206.50 |

Evening meal 1900 (last orders 1700)

### Manor Arms
👑👑👑

The Square, Broughton-in-Furness LA20 6HY
☎ Barrow (01229) 716286

*18th C family-run freehouse with a welcoming atmosphere, in a picturesque market town. Awards for range of excellent traditional ales, well-appointed bedrooms.*
Bedrooms: 2 double, 1 twin
Bathrooms: 3 private

**Bed & breakfast**

| per night: | £min | £max |
|---|---|---|
| Single | 17.00 | 23.00 |
| Double | 28.00 | 38.00 |

Cards accepted: Access, Visa, Amex, Switch/Delta

## CALDBECK

Cumbria
Map ref 5A2

Quaint limestone village lying on the northern fringe of the Lake District National Park. John Peel, the famous huntsman who is immortalised in song, is buried in the churchyard. The fells surrounding Caldbeck were once heavily mined, being rich in lead, copper and barytes.

### Friar Hall ⋀
👑

Caldbeck, Wigton CA7 8DS
☎ (01697) 478633
*140-acre mixed farm. In the lovely village of Caldbeck overlooking the river. Ideal for touring the Lakes and Scottish Borders. On Cumbria Way route.*
Bedrooms: 2 double, 1 triple
Bathrooms: 2 public

**Bed & breakfast**

| per night: | £min | £max |
|---|---|---|
| Single | 17.50 | 18.50 |
| Double | 32.00 | 34.00 |

Parking for 3
Open March–October

### High Greenrigg House ⋀
👑👑👑

Caldbeck, Wigton CA7 8HD
☎ (01697) 478430
*Converted 17th C farmhouse in the remote northern fells of the Lake District National Park. Home cooking and a warm welcome. All rooms en-suite.*
Bedrooms: 4 double, 3 twin
Bathrooms: 7 private

**Bed & breakfast**

| per night: | £min | £max |
|---|---|---|
| Single | 19.50 | 19.50 |
| Double | 39.00 | 39.00 |

Evening meal 1900 (last orders 1600)
Parking for 8
Open March–December
Cards accepted: Access, Visa

## Oddfellows Arms Inn

**COMMENDED**

Caldbeck, Wigton CA7 8EA
☎ (01697) 478227
Fax (01697) 478227

*A 200-year-old inn, full of character.*
*Open fires, friendly locals, good ales*
*and food. Newly refurbished en-suite*
*bedrooms.*
Bedrooms: 2 double, 1 twin, 1 family
room
Bathrooms: 4 private

**Bed & breakfast**

| per night: | £min | £max |
|---|---|---|
| Single | 22.00 | 26.00 |
| Double | 40.00 | 50.00 |

**Half board**

| per person: | £min | £max |
|---|---|---|
| Daily | 30.00 | 40.00 |
| Weekly | 180.00 | 280.00 |

Lunch available
Evening meal 1830 (last orders 2100)
Parking for 6
Cards accepted: Access, Visa

⌂ 10 ⌸ ❒ ♥ ♦ ❘ ⑤ ✗ ▥ 🕮 🖚 ⚲ ⚔ ⚲
✿ ✗ 🚗 SP ⌘

## Swaledale Watch ⋀

Whelpo, Caldbeck, Wigton CA7 8HQ
☎ (01697) 478409
*300-acre mixed farm. Enjoy great*
*comfort, fine food, beautiful*
*surroundings and peaceful countryside*
*on our working farm, central for*
*touring or walking the rolling northern*
*fells.*
Bedrooms: 1 double, 1 twin, 1 triple
Bathrooms: 2 private, 1 public

**Bed & breakfast**

| per night: | £min | £max |
|---|---|---|
| Single | 15.00 | 18.00 |
| Double | 30.00 | 36.00 |

**Half board**

| per person: | £min | £max |
|---|---|---|
| Daily | 24.00 | 27.00 |
| Weekly | 168.00 | 189.00 |

Evening meal 1900 (last orders 1400)
Parking for 10

⌂ ⌶ ⌸ ❒ ♥ ▥ ⑤ ✗ ▥ 🕮 🖚 🖚
✗ 🚗

---

Colour maps at the
back of this guide
pinpoint all places which
have accommodation
listings in the guide.

---

Cumbria
Map ref 5A2

Near the Scottish border, this
cathedral city suffered years of
strife through the centuries, often
changing hands between England
and Scotland. The red sandstone
cathedral is the second smallest in
England. The castle, founded in
1092, now houses a museum.
*Tourist Information Centre*
☎ *(01228) 512444*

## Beech Croft

**COMMENDED**

Aglionby, Carlisle CA4 8AQ
☎ (01228) 513762
*Spacious, modern, detached house in a*
*delightful rural setting. 1 mile on the*
*A69 from M6 junction 43. High quality*
*accommodation in a friendly family*
*atmosphere.*
Bedrooms: 1 single, 2 double
Bathrooms: 1 private, 2 public

**Bed & breakfast**

| per night: | £min | £max |
|---|---|---|
| Single | 18.00 | 18.00 |
| Double | 34.00 | 38.00 |

Parking for 4

⌂ ⌶3 ⌸ ❒ ♥ ▥ ⑤ ✗ ▥ 🕮 🖚 ✿ 🚗

## Chatsworth Guesthouse

**COMMENDED**

22 Chatsworth Square, Carlisle
CA1 1HF
☎ (01228) 24023
*Ornate city centre listed Victorian town*
*house in quiet conservation area*
*overlooking Chatsworth Gardens. 5*
*minutes from bus and rail stations,*
*convenient for Sands Centre (sports and*
*leisure). Street parking.*
Bedrooms: 1 single, 3 twin, 2 family
rooms
Bathrooms: 2 private, 1 public

**Bed & breakfast**

| per night: | £min | £max |
|---|---|---|
| Single | 14.00 | 15.00 |
| Double | 25.00 | 34.00 |

**Half board**

| per person: | £min | £max |
|---|---|---|
| Daily | 20.00 | 23.00 |
| Weekly | 135.00 | 154.00 |

Evening meal 1700 (last orders 1830)
Parking for 2
Cards accepted: Access, Visa

⌂ ⌶2 ❒ ♥ ▥ ⑤ ▥ 🕮 🖚 🖚 ⏛ ✿ ✗ ⒹⒶⓅ
▧ SP ⌘ ⓣ

## Craighead

**APPROVED**

6 Hartington Place, Carlisle CA1 1HL
☎ (01228) 596767
*Grade II listed Victorian town house*
*with spacious rooms and original*
*features. Minutes' walk to city centre,*
*bus and rail stations. Friendly and*
*comfortable. Fresh farm food.*

---

Bedrooms: 2 single, 1 double, 1 twin,
1 family room
Bathrooms: 2 public

**Bed & breakfast**

| per night: | £min | £max |
|---|---|---|
| Single | 15.00 | 17.00 |
| Double | 28.00 | 32.00 |

⌂ ⌸ ❒ ♥ ▥ ⑤ ✗ ▥ 🕮 🖚 🖚 🚗 SP
⌘ ⓣ

## Croft End ⋀

**Listed**

Hurst, Ivegill, Carlisle CA4 0NL
☎ (01768) 484362
*Rural bungalow situated midway*
*junction 41 and 42 of M6, 4 miles west*
*of Southwaite service area.*
Bedrooms: 1 single, 2 double
Bathrooms: 1 public

**Bed & breakfast**

| per night: | £min | £max |
|---|---|---|
| Single | 13.00 | 15.00 |
| Double | 26.00 | 26.00 |

Parking for 4

⌂ ⌶1 ⌸ ⌸ ❒ ▥ ✗ ▥ 🕮 🖚 ✿ ✗ 🚗

## The Gill Farm ⋀

☎

Blackford, Carlisle CA6 4EL
☎ Kirklinton (01228) 75326
*124-acre arable & livestock farm. Ideal*
*halfway stopping place or a good base*
*for touring Cumbria's beauty spots. In*
*peaceful countryside, 3 miles from the*
*M6 junction 44. From Carlisle go north*
*to Blackford, fork right at sign for*
*Longpark, Cliff and Kirklinton, after*
*100 yards turn right, half a mile turn*
*left, Gill Farm on left up this road.*
Bedrooms: 1 double, 1 twin, 1 triple
Bathrooms: 2 public

**Bed & breakfast**

| per night: | £min | £max |
|---|---|---|
| Single | 16.00 | 18.00 |
| Double | 30.00 | 32.00 |

Evening meal 1800 (last orders 1600)
Parking for 6
Open January–November

⌂ ♥ ▥ ⑤ ▥ 🕮 🖚 🖚 ✿ ✗ 🚗 ⌘ ⓣ

## Metal Bridge House

☎

Rockcliffe, Carlisle CA6 4HG
☎ Rockcliffe (01228) 74695

*Just off A74 (Metal Bridge) 4 miles*
*north of junction 44 (Carlisle), large*
*detached house adjacent to*
*restaurant/bar. Country setting,*
*comfortable and spacious rooms,*
*friendly welcome.*
Bedrooms: 1 double, 2 twin
Bathrooms: 1 public

Continued ►

# CUMBRIA

## CARLISLE

*Continued*

**Bed & breakfast**

| per night: | £min | £max |
|---|---|---|
| Single | 18.00 | 20.00 |
| Double | 27.00 | 30.00 |

Parking for 5

### New Pallyards ▲▲

**COMMENDED**

Hethersgill, Carlisle CA6 6HZ
☎ Nicholforest (01228) 577 308
Fax (01228) 577 308
*65-acre mixed farm. Warmth and hospitality await you in this 18th C modernised farmhouse. Country setting, easily accessible from M6, A7, M74. All rooms en-suite. National award winner.*
Bedrooms: 1 single, 2 double, 1 twin, 1 triple
Bathrooms: 5 private, 1 public

**Bed & breakfast**

| per night: | £min | £max |
|---|---|---|
| Single | 18.80 | 23.80 |
| Double | 35.00 | 37.60 |

**Half board**

| per person: | £min | £max |
|---|---|---|
| Daily | 25.30 | 29.30 |
| Weekly | 145.00 | 165.00 |

Evening meal 1900 (last orders 1930)
Parking for 7
Cards accepted: Visa, Amex

### Park House Hotel

**Listed**

Park House Road, Kingstown, Carlisle CA6 4BY
☎ (01228) 26028
*Homely pub with good bar meals, a quarter of a mile from M6 junction 44.*
Bedrooms: 4 single, 1 twin
Bathrooms: 2 public

**Bed & breakfast**

| per night: | £min | £max |
|---|---|---|
| Single | 19.50 | 19.50 |
| Double | 36.00 | 36.00 |

Lunch available
Evening meal 1800 (last orders 2045)
Parking for 40
Cards accepted: Access, Visa

### Streethead Farm ▲▲

**Listed**

Ivegill, Carlisle CA4 0NG
☎ Southwaite (01697) 473327
*211-acre mixed & dairy farm. Distant hills, log fires, en-suite bedroom on working farm between Penrith and Carlisle (8 miles). 10 minutes from junctions 41 and 42 of M6. Ideal for Lakes or Scotland. Brochure available.*
Bedrooms: 1 double, 1 triple
Bathrooms: 1 public

**Bed & breakfast**

| per night: | £min | £max |
|---|---|---|
| Single | 16.00 | 18.00 |
| Double | 32.00 | 36.00 |

Evening meal 1830 (last orders 1000)
Parking for 2
Open March-October

## CARTMEL

Cumbria
Map ref 5A3

Picturesque conserved village based on a 12th C priory with a well-preserved church and gatehouse. Just half a mile outside the Lake District National Park, this is a peaceful base for walking and touring, with historic houses and beautiful scenery.

### Eeabank House ▲▲

123 Station Road, Cark in Cartmel, Grange-over-Sands LA11 7NY
☎ Flookburgh (01539) 558818
*Family-run guesthouse close to Holker Hall and gardens. Easy access to Lakes, good country walks. Ideal for touring.*
Bedrooms: 1 double, 1 twin, 1 triple
Bathrooms: 1 private, 1 public

**Bed & breakfast**

| per night: | £min | £max |
|---|---|---|
| Single | 16.50 | 18.50 |
| Double | 33.00 | 37.00 |

**Half board**

| per person: | £min | £max |
|---|---|---|
| Daily | 23.50 | 27.50 |
| Weekly | 160.00 | 190.00 |

Lunch available
Evening meal 1830 (last orders 2100)
Parking for 3
Cards accepted: Access, Visa

## CARTMEL FELL

Cumbria
Map ref 5A3

Small village set in tranquil countryside in an upland area of great beauty. Noted for its 16th C church with 3-tiered pulpit.

### Lightwood Farmhouse

**COMMENDED**

Cartmel Fell, Bowland Bridge, Grange-over-Sands LA11 6NP
☎ Newby Bridge (01539) 531454
*17th C farmhouse with original oak beams. Extensive views, large garden with streams. Home cooking. Just off the A592 near Bowland Bridge.*
Bedrooms: 5 double, 2 twin, 2 triple
Bathrooms: 5 private, 1 public

**Bed & breakfast**

| per night: | £min | £max |
|---|---|---|
| Double | 37.00 | 46.00 |

Evening meal from 1900
Parking for 10
Cards accepted: Access, Visa

## COCKERMOUTH

Cumbria
Map ref 5A2

Ancient market town at confluence of Rivers Cocker and Derwent. Birthplace of William Wordsworth in 1770. The house where he was born is at the end of the town's broad, tree-lined main street and is now owned by the National Trust. Good touring base for the Lakes.
*Tourist Information Centre*
☎ (01900) 822634

### Crag End Farm

**Listed**

Rogerscale, Lorton, Cockermouth CA13 0RG
☎ Lorton (01900) 85658
*250-acre mixed farm. In lovely surroundings and ideal for families, this peaceful working family farm is convenient for the Lakes, the shops and many walks. Home cooking using home-grown produce.*
Bedrooms: 1 single, 2 double, 1 twin
Bathrooms: 2 public

**Bed & breakfast**

| per night: | £min | £max |
|---|---|---|
| Single | 16.00 | |
| Double | 32.00 | |

**Half board**

| per person: | £min | £max |
|---|---|---|
| Daily | 24.00 | |
| Weekly | 168.00 | |

Evening meal from 1900
Parking for 10
Open February-November

## CONISTON

Cumbria
Map ref 5A3

Born from the mining industry, this village lies at the north end of Coniston Water. The scenery to the rear of the village is dominated by Coniston Old Man. Its most famous resident was John Ruskin, whose home, Brantwood, is open to the public. Good centre for walking.

### Arrowfield Country Guest House ▲▲

**HIGHLY COMMENDED**

Little Arrow, Coniston LA21 8AU
☎ (01539) 441741
*Elegant 19th C Lakeland house in beautiful rural setting. Adjacent to Coniston/Torver road (A593), 2 miles from Coniston village.*

46

Bedrooms: 1 single, 2 double, 2 twin
Bathrooms: 2 private, 1 public

**Bed & breakfast**

| per night: | £min | £max |
| --- | --- | --- |
| Single | 17.00 | 20.00 |
| Double | 30.00 | 44.00 |

**Half board**

| per person: | £min | £max |
| --- | --- | --- |
| Daily | 28.00 | 35.00 |
| Weekly | 196.00 | 221.00 |

Evening meal 1900 (last orders 0930)
Parking for 6
Open March-November
🛇 3 ⌂ ♦ ⛏ 🅰 🅂 ⚡ 🕅 📺 Ⅲ ❄ ✕ 🕭 🆂🅿

## Townson Ground ♠♠

⛉⛉ **COMMENDED**

East of Lake Road, Coniston
LA21 8AA
☎ (01539) 441272

*Fascinating 400-year-old farmhouse
providing first class accommodation
approximately 1 mile from Coniston.
Private parking and access to lake and
jetty.*
Bedrooms: 1 single, 1 double, 2 twin,
1 triple
Bathrooms: 4 private, 1 public

**Bed & breakfast**

| per night: | £min | £max |
| --- | --- | --- |
| Single | 17.00 | 19.00 |
| Double | 35.00 | 40.00 |

Parking for 10
Open February-November
🛇 3 ♦ 🅰 📺 Ⅲ ▪ ❄

## Yewdale Hotel ♠♠

⛉⛉ **COMMENDED**

Yewdale Road, Coniston LA21 8LU
☎ (01539) 441280
*Built of local materials in 1896 as a
bank, now a modern hotel skilfully
refurbished throughout. Reduced rate
breaks available.*
Bedrooms: 5 double, 2 twin, 3 triple
Bathrooms: 7 private, 2 public

**Bed & breakfast**

| per night: | £min | £max |
| --- | --- | --- |
| Double | 43.90 | 63.00 |

**Half board**

| per person: | £min | £max |
| --- | --- | --- |
| Daily | 32.90 | 42.45 |
| Weekly | 138.40 | 192.00 |

Lunch available
Evening meal (last orders 2100)
Parking for 6
Cards accepted: Access, Visa
🛇 ⛉ 🖵 ♦ ⛏ 🅰 🅂 ⚡ 🕅 Ⅲ ▪ 🛉 ☚ ∪
♪ ⊁ 🕭 🅳🅰🅿 🆂🅿 🕭 🆃

---

Cumbria
Map ref 5A2

Village in undulating countryside
on the banks of the River Caldew.
The churchyard is burial place to
two Bishops of Carlisle.

## Barn Close

**Listed**

Gaitsgill, Dalston, Carlisle CA5 7AH
☎ Raughton Head (01697) 476558
*Dated 1703, in tranquil countryside
with a secluded garden. Easy access M6
(junction 42), Carlisle and Borders.
Inns nearby.*
Bedrooms: 2 double, 1 twin
Bathrooms: 2 public

**Bed & breakfast**

| per night: | £min | £max |
| --- | --- | --- |
| Single | 16.50 | 16.50 |
| Double | 33.00 | 33.00 |

Parking for 4
Open May-October
⚳ 🅰 🅂 ⚡ 🕅 📺 Ⅲ ▪ 🕭 🏠 🆃

## Smithy Cottage

**Listed** **COMMENDED**

Bridge End, Dalston, Carlisle CA5 7BJ
☎ Carlisle (01228) 711659
*Jean and Peter Garnett offer a warm
welcome at their recently restored and
elegantly furnished authentic 18th C
smithy. Retaining much of its original
rustic charm, it will delight all who
appreciate the timeless qualities of a
traditional English home.*
Bedrooms: 1 double, 2 twin
Bathrooms: 1 private, 1 public

**Bed & breakfast**

| per night: | £min | £max |
| --- | --- | --- |
| Single | 18.50 | 22.00 |
| Double | 35.00 | 37.00 |

Parking for 5
Open January-November
🛏 5 🖵 ♦ ⛏ ✕ Ⅲ ⑧ ▪ ❄ ✕ 🕭 🏠

---

Cumbria
Map ref 5A3

Set on the beautiful Cartmel
Peninsula, this tranquil resort,
known as Lakeland's Riviera,
overlooks Morecambe Bay.
Pleasant seafront walks and
beautiful gardens. The bay attracts
many species of wading birds.

## High Bank

⛉

Methven Road, Grange-over-Sands
LA11 7DU
☎ (01539) 532902
*Spacious Victorian house in quiet
situation. Interesting garden, sea views,
and a good base for seeing Lake
Windermere and Coniston.*
Bedrooms: 1 single, 1 double, 1 twin
Bathrooms: 1 public

**Bed & breakfast**

| per night: | £min | £max |
| --- | --- | --- |
| Single | 15.00 | 15.00 |
| Double | 30.00 | 30.00 |

**Half board**

| per person: | £min | £max |
| --- | --- | --- |
| Daily | 22.00 | 22.00 |
| Weekly | 154.00 | 154.00 |

Evening meal 1830 (last orders 1600)
Parking for 2
☎ 5 ♦ 🕅 🅂 ⑧ ▪ ❄ ✕ 🕭

## Prospect House Hotel ♠♠

⛉⛉⛉

Kents Bank Road, Grange-over-Sands
LA11 7DJ
☎ (01539) 532116
*Our best advertisement is the many
return visits we receive every year.
Imaginative meals and a friendly
welcome are guaranteed.*
Bedrooms: 5 double, 2 twin
Bathrooms: 6 private, 1 public

**Bed & breakfast**

| per night: | £min | £max |
| --- | --- | --- |
| Single | 20.00 | 27.00 |
| Double | 39.00 | 44.00 |

**Half board**

| per person: | £min | £max |
| --- | --- | --- |
| Daily | 29.50 | 36.00 |
| Weekly | 180.00 | 215.00 |

Evening meal from 1900
Parking for 5
🛇 6 🖵 ♦ 🅰 🅂 ✕ 🕅 Ⅲ ▪ ❄ 🕭
🕅 🆂🅿

---

Cumbria
Map ref 5A3

Described by William Wordsworth
as "the loveliest spot that man
hath ever found", this village,
famous for its gingerbread, is in a
beautiful setting overlooked by
Helm Crag. Wordsworth lived at
Dove Cottage. The cottage and
museum are open to the public.

## Bramriggs

**Listed** **APPROVED**

Grasmere, Ambleside LA22 9RU
☎ (01539) 435360
*Small country house with garden
bordering footpath to Helvellyn.
Tranquil setting, spectacular views of
almost entire valley. 1 mile north of
Grasmere village. Lovely walking
country.*
Bedrooms: 1 single, 1 double, 1 twin
Bathrooms: 1 public

**Bed & breakfast**

| per night: | £min | £max |
| --- | --- | --- |
| Single | 15.00 | 18.00 |
| Double | 30.00 | 36.00 |

Parking for 7
🛇 🕅 ☏ 🖵 ♦ ⛏ 🅰 🅂 ⚡ 📺 ◑ 🔟 🔅 Ⅲ
⑧ ▪ ❄ 🕭 🆃

## GRASMERE

*Continued*

### Craigside House ⚑
**COMMENDED**

Grasmere, Ambleside LA22 9SG
☎ (01539) 435292
*Delightfully furnished Victorian house on the edge of the village near Dove Cottage. In a large, peaceful garden overlooking the lake and hills.*
Bedrooms: 2 double, 1 twin
Bathrooms: 3 private

**Bed & breakfast**

| per night: | £min | £max |
|---|---|---|
| Single | 27.00 | 50.00 |
| Double | 50.00 | 58.00 |

Parking for 6

### The Harwood ⚑
**Listed**

Red Lion Square, Grasmere, Ambleside LA22 9SP
☎ (01539) 435248
*Family-run hotel in the heart of Grasmere. Comfortable rooms all with private facilities and TV. Ideal for exploring the Lake District.*
Bedrooms: 1 single, 6 double
Bathrooms: 7 private

**Bed & breakfast**

| per night: | £min | £max |
|---|---|---|
| Single | 16.50 | 25.50 |
| Double | 33.00 | 51.00 |

Lunch available
Parking for 8
Cards accepted: Access, Visa

### Oak Bank Hotel ⚑
**COMMENDED**

Broadgate, Grasmere, Ambleside LA22 9TA
☎ (01539) 435217
*Built 100 years ago in Lakeland stone and now modernised throughout. Cordon bleu cuisine, good cellar - pamper yourself!*
Bedrooms: 1 single, 9 double, 4 twin, 1 family room
Bathrooms: 15 private

**Bed & breakfast**

| per night: | £min | £max |
|---|---|---|
| Single | 20.00 | 44.00 |
| Double | 40.00 | 88.00 |

**Half board**

| per person: | £min | £max |
|---|---|---|
| Daily | 30.00 | 55.00 |

Evening meal 1900 (last orders 2300)
Parking for 15
Open February-December
Cards accepted: Access, Visa, Switch/Delta

### Woodland Crag Guest House ⚑
**HIGHLY COMMENDED**

Howe Head Lane, Grasmere, Ambleside LA22 9SG
☎ (01539) 435351
*Charming Victorian Lakeland-stone house with lake and fell views. Beautiful walks radiate from here. Peacefully situated in landscaped grounds on edge of village. No smoking please.*
Bedrooms: 2 single, 2 double, 1 twin
Bathrooms: 3 private, 1 public

**Bed & breakfast**

| per night: | £min | £max |
|---|---|---|
| Single | 22.00 | 24.00 |
| Double | 48.00 | 50.00 |

Parking for 5
Open January-November

## GRAYRIGG

Cumbria
Map ref 5B3

### Punchbowl House ⚑
**COMMENDED**

Grayrigg, Kendal LA8 9BU
☎ (01539) 824345
*Spacious Victorian farmhouse with log fires, in peaceful surroundings between Lakes and Dales. Non-smoking.*
Bedrooms: 2 double, 1 twin
Bathrooms: 1 private, 1 public

**Bed & breakfast**

| per night: | £min | £max |
|---|---|---|
| Single | 15.50 | 26.00 |
| Double | 31.00 | 37.00 |

Parking for 6

## GREENODD

Cumbria
Map ref 5A3

### Machell Arms ⚑
**APPROVED**

Greenodd Village, Ulverston LA12 7QZ
☎ Ulverston (01229) 861 246
*Family-run pub in hillside village. 5 miles Windermere, 5 miles Coniston Water. Log fire, home-made food and real ale. Warm welcome.*
Bedrooms: 2 triple, 1 family room
Bathrooms: 1 public

**Bed & breakfast**

| per night: | £min | £max |
|---|---|---|
| Single | 15.00 | 17.00 |
| Double | 27.00 | 30.00 |

**Half board**

| per person: | £min | £max |
|---|---|---|
| Daily | 22.00 | 25.00 |
| Weekly | 140.00 | 160.00 |

Lunch available
Evening meal 1800 (last orders 2030)
Parking for 7

## HAVERTHWAITE

Cumbria
Map ref 5A3

Set in the Levens Valley south-west of Newby Bridge, on the north bank of River Leven. Headquarters of the Lakeside and Haverthwaite Railway Company.

### The Coach House ⚑
⚑

Hollow Oak, Haverthwaite, Ulverston LA12 8AD
☎ Ulverston (01539) 531622
*Friendly and comfortable coach house with original beams. Garden. Convenient for Holker Hall, Coniston and Windermere. Non-smokers only, please.*
Bedrooms: 2 double, 1 twin
Bathrooms: 2 public

**Bed & breakfast**

| per night: | £min | £max |
|---|---|---|
| Single | 13.00 | 15.00 |
| Double | 26.00 | 30.00 |

Parking for 3
Open March-October

## HAWKSHEAD

Cumbria
Map ref 5A3

Lying near Esthwaite Water, this village has great charm and character. Its small squares are linked by flagged or cobbled alleys and the main square is dominated by the market house, or Shambles, where the butchers had their stalls in days gone by.

### Balla Wray Cottage ⚑
**Listed**

High Wray, Ambleside LA22 0JQ
☎ Ambleside (01539) 432401
*Lakeland-stone cottage on west side of Windermere, in quiet secluded position with views over the lake. Balla Wray is shown on Ordnance Survey map (reference SD378999).*
Bedrooms: 1 double, 1 twin
Bathrooms: 2 private

**Bed & breakfast**

| per night: | £min | £max |
|---|---|---|
| Single | 19.50 | 21.00 |
| Double | 39.00 | 42.00 |

Parking for 2

### The Drunken Duck Inn ⚑
**COMMENDED**

Barngates, Ambleside LA22 0NG
☎ Ambleside (01539) 436347

*An old fashioned inn amidst
magnificent scenery. Oak-beamed bars,
cosy log fires and charming bedrooms.
Good food and beers.*
Bedrooms: 9 double, 1 twin
Bathrooms: 10 private
**Bed & breakfast**

| per night: | £min | £max |
| --- | --- | --- |
| Single | 44.00 | 50.00 |
| Double | 59.50 | 79.00 |

Lunch available
Evening meal 1830 (last orders 2100)
Parking for 60
Cards accepted: Access, Visa, Switch/
Delta

## Silverholme ⋀
COMMENDED
Graythwaite, Ulverston LA12 8AZ
☎ Newby Bridge (01539) 531332
*Set in its own grounds, overlooking
Lake Windermere, this small mansion
house provides a quiet, comfortable,
relaxed atmosphere. Home cooking.*
Bedrooms: 2 double, 1 twin
Bathrooms: 3 private
**Bed & breakfast**

| per night: | £min | £max |
| --- | --- | --- |
| Single | 19.50 | 21.50 |
| Double | 38.00 | 43.00 |

**Half board**

| per person: | £min | £max |
| --- | --- | --- |
| Daily | 29.00 | 31.00 |

Evening meal 1900 (last orders 1700)
Parking for 6

## KENDAL
Cumbria
Map ref 5B3

The "Auld Grey Town" lies in the
valley of the River Kent with a
backcloth of limestone fells.
Situated just outside the Lake
District National Park, it is a good
centre for touring the Lakes and
surrounding country. Ruined castle
was the birthplace of Catherine
Parr.
*Tourist Information Centre*
*☎ (01539) 725758*

## Fairways Guest House
COMMENDED
102 Windermere Road, Kendal
LA9 5EZ
☎ (01539) 725564
*On the main Kendal-Windermere road.
Victorian guesthouse with en-suite
facilities. TV, tea and coffee in all*

rooms. Four-poster bedrooms. Private
parking.
Bedrooms: 3 double
Bathrooms: 3 private, 1 public
**Bed & breakfast**

| per night: | £min | £max |
| --- | --- | --- |
| Double | 30.00 | 34.00 |

Parking for 4

## Gateside Farm
Listed COMMENDED
Windermere Road, Kendal LA9 5SE
☎ (01539) 722036
*300-acre dairy & livestock farm.
Traditional Lakeland farm easily
accessible from the motorway and on
the main tourist route through
Lakeland. One night and short stays are
welcome.*
Bedrooms: 3 double, 1 twin, 1 family
room
Bathrooms: 2 private, 2 public
**Bed & breakfast**

| per night: | £min | £max |
| --- | --- | --- |
| Single | 18.00 | 22.00 |
| Double | 32.00 | 35.00 |

**Half board**

| per person: | £min | £max |
| --- | --- | --- |
| Daily | 24.00 | |

Evening meal (last orders 1700)
Parking for 7

## Higher House Farm ⋀
COMMENDED
Oxenholme Lane, Natland, Kendal
LA9 7QH
☎ Sedgwick (01539) 561177

*17th C beamed farmhouse in tranquil
village south of Kendal, overlooking
Lakeland fells. Near M6 and Oxenholme
station. Delicious cuisine. Four-poster
bed.*
Bedrooms: 2 double, 1 family room
Bathrooms: 3 private
**Bed & breakfast**

| per night: | £min | £max |
| --- | --- | --- |
| Single | 15.00 | 24.50 |
| Double | 35.00 | 43.00 |

**Half board**

| per person: | £min | £max |
| --- | --- | --- |
| Daily | 29.50 | 33.50 |

Evening meal 1900 (last orders 2130)
Parking for 9

## Hill Fold Farm
APPROVED
Burneside, Kendal LA8 9AU
☎ (01539) 722574
*500-acre mixed farm. Log fires and
exposed beams. Overnight storage
heaters in bedrooms. Only 3 miles
north of Kendal and close to the rolling
hills of Potter Fell with its many quiet
walks.*
Bedrooms: 2 double, 1 twin
Bathrooms: 1 public
**Bed & breakfast**

| per night: | £min | £max |
| --- | --- | --- |
| Single | 14.00 | 15.00 |
| Double | 28.00 | 30.00 |

**Half board**

| per person: | £min | £max |
| --- | --- | --- |
| Daily | 19.00 | 20.00 |
| Weekly | 125.00 | 130.00 |

Evening meal 1930 (last orders 1600)
Parking for 6

## Holmfield ⋀
Listed DE LUXE
41 Kendal Green, Kendal LA9 5PP
☎ (01539) 720790
Fax (01539) 720790
*Elegant detached Edwardian house on
edge of town. Large gardens, panoramic
views, swimming pool, croquet. Lovely
bedrooms including four poster. No
smoking.*
Bedrooms: 2 double, 1 twin
Bathrooms: 2 public
**Bed & breakfast**

| per night: | £min | £max |
| --- | --- | --- |
| Single | 18.00 | 30.00 |
| Double | 32.00 | 42.00 |

Parking for 7

## Lyndhurst ⋀
8 South Road, Kendal LA9 5QH
☎ (01539) 727281
*Terraced house providing comfortable
accommodation, in a quiet area with
river view. 10 minutes' walk from the
town.*
Bedrooms: 2 single, 2 double, 1 twin,
1 triple
Bathrooms: 2 public
**Bed & breakfast**

| per night: | £min | £max |
| --- | --- | --- |
| Single | 14.00 | 15.50 |
| Double | 28.00 | 31.00 |

Parking for 4

## Park Lea
COMMENDED
15 Sunnyside, Kendal LA9 7DJ
☎ (01539) 740986
*Delightful Victorian house close to
castle and river, overlooking parkland.
Abbot Hall, Brewery Arts and town
centre 5 minutes' walk.*

*Continued* ▶

## KENDAL

### Continued

Bedrooms: 2 double, 1 twin
Bathrooms: 2 private, 1 public
**Bed & breakfast**

| per night: | £min | £max |
|---|---|---|
| Single | 15.00 | 18.00 |
| Double | 30.00 | 36.00 |

Parking for 2

## 7 Thorny Hills

**COMMENDED**

Kendal LA9 7AL
☎ (01539) 720207
*Beautiful, unspoilt Georgian town
house. Peaceful, pretty location close to
town centre. Good home cooking. Self-
catering available. Non-smokers only,
please.*
Bedrooms: 2 double, 1 twin
Bathrooms: 3 private
**Bed & breakfast**

| per night: | £min | £max |
|---|---|---|
| Single | 19.00 | 19.00 |
| Double | 34.00 | 34.00 |

| **Half board** | | |
|---|---|---|
| per person: | £min | £max |
| Daily | 26.00 | 26.00 |

Evening meal from 1800
Parking for 3
Open January-November

## KESWICK

Cumbria
Map ref 5A3

Beautifully positioned town beside
Derwentwater and below the
mountains of Skiddaw and
Blencathra. Excellent base for
walking, climbing, watersports and
touring. Motor-launches operate on
Derwentwater and motor boats,
rowing boats and canoes can be
hired.
*Tourist Information Centre*
☎ *(01768) 772645*

## Abacourt House ⋀

**HIGHLY COMMENDED**

26 Stanger Street, Keswick CA12 5JU
☎ (01768) 772967
*Victorian townhouse, lovingly restored
to a high standard in 1992. Beautifully
furnished, fully double glazed. Superior
en-suites in all bedrooms. Central, quiet,
cosy and friendly. Brochure available.*
Bedrooms: 4 double
Bathrooms: 4 private
**Bed & breakfast**

| per night: | £min | £max |
|---|---|---|
| Double | 40.00 | 40.00 |

Parking for 4
Open February-December

## Acorn House Hotel ⋀

**HIGHLY COMMENDED**

Ambleside Road, Keswick CA12 4DL
☎ (01768) 772553
*Delightful Georgian house in own
grounds. All bedrooms are of a high
standard. Close to town centre. Ideal
base for touring Lake District.*
Bedrooms: 6 double, 1 twin, 3 triple
Bathrooms: 10 private
**Bed & breakfast**

| per night: | £min | £max |
|---|---|---|
| Single | 22.50 | 35.00 |
| Double | 40.00 | 55.00 |

Parking for 10
Open February-November
Cards accepted: Access, Visa

## Bank Tavern

**Listed**

47 Main Street, Keswick CA12 5DS
☎ (01768) 772663
*A country pub in the town centre.*
Bedrooms: 2 double, 2 twin, 1 triple
Bathrooms: 1 public
**Bed & breakfast**

| per night: | £min | £max |
|---|---|---|
| Single | 14.00 | 15.00 |
| Double | 28.00 | 30.00 |

Lunch available
Evening meal 1800 (last orders 2100)
Parking for 5

## The Bay Tree ⋀

**Listed** **APPROVED**

1 Wordsworth Street, Keswick
CA12 4HU
☎ (01768) 773313
*Friendly guesthouse with lovely views
over river and Fitz Park to mountains.
3 minutes' walk from town centre.
Home-cooked food.*
Bedrooms: 4 double, 1 twin
Bathrooms: 1 private, 1 public
**Bed & breakfast**

| per night: | £min | £max |
|---|---|---|
| Double | 28.00 | 38.00 |

| **Half board** | | |
|---|---|---|
| per person: | £min | £max |
| Daily | 25.00 | 30.00 |
| Weekly | 168.00 | 203.00 |

Lunch available
Evening meal 1900 (last orders 1600)

## Beckstones Farm ⋀

**COMMENDED**

Thornthwaite, Keswick CA12 5SQ
☎ Braithwaite (01768) 778510
*4-acre smallholding. Converted Georgian
farmhouse in a typical Lakeland setting,
with extensive views of the mountains
and Thornthwaite Forest. 3 miles west
of Keswick.*
Bedrooms: 4 double, 1 twin
Bathrooms: 3 private, 1 public

| per night: | £min | £max |
|---|---|---|
| Single | 18.00 | 19.50 |
| Double | 36.00 | 39.00 |

Evening meal 1830 (last orders 1000)
Parking for 8
Open February-November

## Birkrigg Farm

**Listed**

Newlands, Keswick CA12 5TS
☎ Braithwaite (01768) 778278
*250-acre mixed farm. Pleasantly and
peacefully located in the Newlands
Valley. 5 miles from Keswick on the
Braithwaite to Buttermere road.*
Bedrooms: 1 single, 2 double, 1 twin,
1 triple, 1 family room
Bathrooms: 2 public
**Bed & breakfast**

| per night: | £min | £max |
|---|---|---|
| Single | 14.00 | 15.00 |
| Double | 28.00 | 30.00 |

Parking for 6
Open March-November

## Dancing Beck ⋀

Underskiddaw, Keswick CA12 4PZ
☎ (01768) 773800
*Lakeland house, with views of Derwent
Valley and Lakeland mountains, 2.5
miles from Keswick, just off A591
Keswick-Carlisle road.*
Bedrooms: 1 double, 2 twin
Bathrooms: 3 private, 2 public
**Bed & breakfast**

| per night: | £min | £max |
|---|---|---|
| Double | 36.00 | 39.00 |

Parking for 3
Open March-October

## Hazeldene Hotel ⋀

**APPROVED**

The Heads, Keswick CA12 5ER
☎ (01768) 772106
Fax (01768) 775435
*Beautiful and central with open views
of Skiddaw and Borrowdale and
Newlands Valleys. Midway between town
centre and Lake Derwentwater.*
Bedrooms: 5 single, 9 double, 4 twin,
4 triple
Bathrooms: 19 private, 2 public
**Bed & breakfast**

| per night: | £min | £max |
|---|---|---|
| Single | 19.00 | 25.00 |
| Double | 38.00 | 50.00 |

| **Half board** | | |
|---|---|---|
| per person: | £min | £max |
| Daily | 31.00 | 37.00 |
| Weekly | 209.00 | 248.00 |

Evening meal 1830 (last orders 1600)
Parking for 18
Open February-November

## Heatherlea

**Listed**

26 Blencathra Street, Keswick
CA12 4HP
☎ (01768) 772430
*Charming, friendly guesthouse, close to town centre, offering a warm welcome. Good home cooking, residential licence, own key. Lovely views. Non-smoking.*
Bedrooms: 2 double, 1 triple, 1 family room
Bathrooms: 4 private

**Bed & breakfast**

| per night: | £min | £max |
| --- | --- | --- |
| Single | 17.50 | 18.00 |
| Double | 26.50 | 27.00 |

Evening meal 1830 (last orders 1900)
☎🍷🖵♨️👤🐾✕🛏️🖩💆➔✕🚲🅂🄿🅃

## Keskadale Farm

**Listed**

Newlands Valley, Keswick CA12 5TS
☎ Braithwaite (01768) 778544
*300-acre livestock farm. Traditional Lakeland farm 6 miles from Keswick, 2.5 miles from Buttermere. Pleasantly situated in the Newland Valley with magnificent views from all bedrooms. A warm welcome awaits you.*
Bedrooms: 2 double, 1 twin
Bathrooms: 1 public

**Bed & breakfast**

| per night: | £min | £max |
| --- | --- | --- |
| Double | 28.00 | 32.00 |

Parking for 6
Open March-November
🕿🍷⬗♨️🆄🅐👤🅂✕🛏️📺🖩➔▶✿✕🚲🏠

## Ravensworth Hotel ♈

**HIGHLY COMMENDED**

Station Street, Keswick CA12 5HH
☎ (01768) 772476
*Small family-run licensed hotel, decorated to a high standard of comfort, situated close to Keswick's amenities. An ideal Lake District base.*
Bedrooms: 7 double, 1 twin
Bathrooms: 8 private

**Bed & breakfast**

| per night: | £min | £max |
| --- | --- | --- |
| Single | 15.00 | 34.00 |
| Double | 30.00 | 50.00 |

Parking for 5
Open March-November
Cards accepted: Access, Visa
🕿6⬗🖵♨️👤🅂✕🛏️📺🖩➔▶✕🚲🅂🄿

## Richmond House ♈

37-39 Eskin Street, Keswick
CA12 4DG
☎ (01768) 773965
*Family-run guesthouse, home-from-home, easy walking distance to town centre and lake. Vegetarians catered for. Non-smokers only please.*
Bedrooms: 2 single, 5 double, 1 twin, 1 triple
Bathrooms: 7 private, 2 public, 1 private shower

**Bed & breakfast**

| per night: | £min | £max |
| --- | --- | --- |
| Single | 14.00 | 20.00 |
| Double | 28.00 | 35.00 |

**Half board**

| per person: | £min | £max |
| --- | --- | --- |
| Daily | 31.00 | 37.00 |
| Weekly | 150.00 | 180.00 |

Evening meal 1900 (last orders 1700)
Cards accepted: Access, Visa
🕿8🏠🖵♨️🅂✕🛏️📺🖩➔🕿20✕🚲🅂🄿🅃

## Rickerby Grange ♈

**COMMENDED**

Portinscale, Keswick CA12 5RH
☎ (01768) 772344

*Detached country hotel in its own gardens, in a quiet village on the outskirts of Keswick. Provides imaginative cooking, a cosy bar and quiet lounge. Ground floor bedrooms available.*
Bedrooms: 2 single, 7 double, 1 twin, 3 triple
Bathrooms: 11 private, 1 public

**Bed & breakfast**

| per night: | £min | £max |
| --- | --- | --- |
| Single | 22.00 | 25.00 |
| Double | 44.00 | 50.00 |

**Half board**

| per person: | £min | £max |
| --- | --- | --- |
| Daily | 33.00 | 36.00 |
| Weekly | 215.00 | 235.00 |

Evening meal 1900 (last orders 1800)
Parking for 14
🕿5🏠🍷🖵♨️✕🛏️🖩➔✿✕🚲🅂

## Rowling End

**Listed COMMENDED**

31 Helvellyn Street, Keswick
CA12 4EP
☎ (01768) 774108
*Small, comfortable, family-run guesthouse. All rooms centrally-heated, with TV, tea and coffee facilities. Some en-suite available. Five minutes from town centre. Good home-cooked evening meals.*
Bedrooms: 2 double, 1 triple, 1 family room
Bathrooms: 2 private, 1 public

**Bed & breakfast**

| per night: | £min | £max |
| --- | --- | --- |
| Single | 15.00 | 18.00 |
| Double | 30.00 | 36.00 |

**Half board**

| per person: | £min | £max |
| --- | --- | --- |
| Daily | 25.00 | 28.00 |
| Weekly | 165.00 | 185.00 |

Open March-December
🕿🖵♨️🆄🅐👤✕🛏️🖩➔✕🚲🅂🄿

## Watendlath Guest House ♈

**Listed COMMENDED**

15 Acorn Street, Keswick CA12 4EA
☎ (01768) 774165
*Within easy walking distance of the lake, hills and town centre. We offer a warm and friendly welcome and traditional English breakfast.*
Bedrooms: 4 double, 1 twin
Bathrooms: 2 private, 1 public

**Bed & breakfast**

| per night: | £min | £max |
| --- | --- | --- |
| Double | 28.00 | 34.00 |

Open January-October
🕿⬗♨️🆄🅂🖩➔✕🚲🅂

## Whitehouse Guest House

**COMMENDED**

15 Ambleside Road, Keswick
CA12 4DL
☎ (01768) 773176
*Fully refurbished, small, friendly guesthouse 5 minutes' walk from the town centre. Colour TV, electric blankets, tea/coffee. Most rooms with en-suite facilities.*
Bedrooms: 4 double
Bathrooms: 3 private, 1 public, 1 private shower

**Bed & breakfast**

| per night: | £min | £max |
| --- | --- | --- |
| Double | 28.00 | 34.00 |

Parking for 3
Open March-October
🕿🖵♨️🆄📺🖩➔✕🚲

## KIRKBY STEPHEN

Cumbria
Map ref 5B3

Old market town close to the River Eden, with many fine Georgian buildings and an attractive market square. St Stephen's Church is known as the "Cathedral of the Dales". Good base for exploring the Eden Valley and the Dales.
*Tourist Information Centre*
☎ *(01768) 371199*

## Augill House Farm

**HIGHLY COMMENDED**

Brough, Kirkby Stephen CA17 4DX
☎ Brough (01768) 341305

Continued ▶

## KIRKBY STEPHEN

### Continued

*40-acre mixed farm. Spacious Georgian farmhouse, where the emphasis is on good food and hospitality. Enjoy super breakfasts and delicious 4-course dinners served in our lovely conservatory overlooking the garden.*
Bedrooms: 2 double, 1 twin
Bathrooms: 3 private

**Bed & breakfast**

| per night: | £min | £max |
|---|---|---|
| Double | 38.00 | 40.00 |

**Half board**

| per person: | £min | £max |
|---|---|---|
| Daily | 28.00 | 30.00 |
| Weekly | 175.00 | 175.00 |

Evening meal from 1900
Parking for 6

🐕 12 🏠 ♨ ✿ 🖲 ▮ ✠ 🅿 📺 🎚 🍽 ▶ ✽ ✈ 🚗 SP

### The Old Rectory
Crosby Garrett, Kirkby Stephen
CA17 4PW
☎ (01768) 372074

*A Grade II listed 17th C rectory, recently restored retaining oak beams and panelled rooms, in unique village setting. Ideal for walking or exploring Eden, Lakes or dales. Aga cooking.*
Bedrooms: 2 double, 1 twin
Bathrooms: 3 private

**Bed & breakfast**

| per night: | £min | £max |
|---|---|---|
| Single | 18.00 | 24.00 |
| Double | 30.00 | 36.00 |

**Half board**

| per person: | £min | £max |
|---|---|---|
| Daily | 23.00 | 28.00 |
| Weekly | 150.00 | 185.00 |

Evening meal 1800 (last orders 2100)
Parking for 3

🐕 🏠 ✿ ♨ 🖲 ▮ 🅿 ✠ 📺 🎚 🍽 ✽ 🚗 SP ♿

---

There are separate sections in this guide listing groups specialising in farm holidays and accommodation which is especially suitable for young people and organised groups.

---

## LAMPLUGH

Cumbria
Map ref 5A3

Near the A5086 between Cockermouth and Cleator Moor, Lamplugh is a scattered village famous for its "Lamplugh Pudding". Ideal touring base for the western Lake District.

### Briscoe Close Farm
**Listed** **COMMENDED**
Scalesmoor, Lamplugh, Workington
CA14 4TZ
☎ (01946) 861633
*Bungalow close to family-run farm. Near Loweswater and Ennerdale, half a mile from A5086. Home cooking using produce grown on farm.*
Bedrooms: 2 double
Bathrooms: 1 public

**Bed & breakfast**

| per night: | £min | £max |
|---|---|---|
| Single | 15.00 | |
| Double | 30.00 | |

**Half board**

| per person: | £min | £max |
|---|---|---|
| Daily | 21.00 | 22.00 |
| Weekly | 145.00 | |

Evening meal from 1900
Parking for 2

🐕 🏠 🖲 🎚 📺 🎚 ▮ 🍽 ✽ 🚗

---

## LANGDALE

Cumbria
Map ref 5A3

The two Langdale valleys (Great Langdale and Little Langdale) lie in the heart of beautiful mountain scenery. The craggy Langdale Pikes are almost 2500 ft high. An ideal walking and climbing area and base for touring.

### Britannia Inn 🏍
**COMMENDED**
Elterwater, Ambleside LA22 9HP
☎ Windermere (01539) 437210
Fax (01539) 437311

*A 400-year-old traditional Lake District inn on a village green in the beautiful Langdale Valley. A warm welcome to all. TV available in bedrooms.*
Bedrooms: 1 single, 9 double, 3 twin
Bathrooms: 7 private, 2 public

**Bed & breakfast**

| per night: | £min | £max |
|---|---|---|
| Single | 21.50 | 23.50 |
| Double | 43.00 | 65.00 |

---

Lunch available
Evening meal 1930 (last orders 1930)
Parking for 10
Cards accepted: Access, Visa, Switch/ Delta

🐕 📞 🖲 ♨ ✿ 🖲 S 📺 🎚 🍽 ✽ 🚗 SP ♿ T

### South View
**Listed**
Chapel Stile, Great Langdale, Ambleside LA22 9JJ
☎ (01539) 437248
*Comfortable Lakeland-stone house, tastefully modernised and furnished, in a quiet village with good views and easy access to the fells.*
Bedrooms: 2 double, 1 twin, 2 triple
Bathrooms: 2 private, 2 public

**Bed & breakfast**

| per night: | £min | £max |
|---|---|---|
| Single | 16.00 | 20.00 |
| Double | 31.00 | 38.00 |

🐕 ♨ 🖲 ▮ 📺 🎚 🍽 🚗 SP

---

## LAZONBY

Cumbria
Map ref 5B2

Busy, working village of stone cottages, set beside the River Eden amid sweeping pastoral landscape. Good fishing available.

### Bracken Bank Lodge Ltd
Lazonby, Penrith CA10 1AX
☎ (01768) 898241
Fax (01768) 898221
*Guesthouse and shooting/fishing lodge. 6 miles from Penrith, signposted to Lazonby on A6.*
Bedrooms: 5 single, 2 double, 3 twin
Bathrooms: 5 public, 1 private shower

**Bed & breakfast**

| per night: | £min | £max |
|---|---|---|
| Single | 17.63 | 21.15 |
| Double | 35.26 | 42.30 |

**Half board**

| per person: | £min | £max |
|---|---|---|
| Daily | 29.08 | 32.31 |

Lunch available
Evening meal 2000 (last orders 2000)
Parking for 10

🐕 ♨ 🖲 S ✠ 📺 🎚 🍽 ♟10-25 ↗ ✿ 🚗 ✖ SP

---

## LORTON

Cumbria
Map ref 5A3

High and Low Lorton are set in a beautiful vale north of Crummock Water and at the foot of the Whinlatter Pass. Church of St Cuthbert is well worth a visit.

### New House Farm 🏍
**HIGHLY COMMENDED**
Lorton, Cockermouth CA13 9UU
☎ (01900) 85404
*Spectacular valley and fell setting for this carefully restored 17th C Lakeland*

*stone house. Superb views from every room. Fine traditional cooking. Major tourism award winner 1994.*
Bedrooms: 3 double
Bathrooms: 3 private

**Bed & breakfast**

| per night: | £min | £max |
|---|---|---|
| Single | | 35.00 |
| Double | 60.00 | 70.00 |

**Half board**

| per person: | £min | £max |
|---|---|---|
| Daily | 50.00 | 55.00 |

Lunch available
Evening meal 1930 (last orders 1930)
Parking for 20
🛏 12 ♿ ☏ 🖥 🛆 S 🅿 🖨 📺 📖 ❄ 🐾 ⚘ SP 🏠 T

## LOWESWATER

Cumbria
Map ref 5A3

This scattered village lies between Loweswater, one of the smaller lakes of the Lake District, and Crummock Water. Several mountains lie beyond the village, giving lovely views.

### Brook Farm
**COMMENDED**
Thackthwaite, Loweswater, Cockermouth CA13 0RP
☎ Lorton (01900) 85606
*300-acre hill farm. In quiet surroundings and a good walking area, 5 miles from Cockermouth. Carrying sheep and suckler cows.*
Bedrooms: 1 double, 1 twin
Bathrooms: 1 public

**Bed & breakfast**

| per night: | £min | £max |
|---|---|---|
| Single | 15.50 | 17.00 |
| Double | 31.00 | 34.00 |

**Half board**

| per person: | £min | £max |
|---|---|---|
| Daily | 22.50 | 24.00 |
| Weekly | 154.00 | 161.00 |

Evening meal from 1900
Parking for 3
Open May-October
🛏 ♿ UL 🛆 🖥 📺 ❄ 🐾

### Kirkstile Inn 🅰
**COMMENDED**
Loweswater, Cockermouth CA13 0RU
☎ Lorton (01900) 85219
*A 16th C inn near an oak-fringed beck running between Loweswater and Crummock Water lakes, surrounded by fells.*
Bedrooms: 5 double, 2 twin, 3 triple
Bathrooms: 8 private, 2 public

**Bed & breakfast**

| per night: | £min | £max |
|---|---|---|
| Single | 32.00 | 42.00 |
| Double | 42.00 | 52.00 |

Lunch available
Evening meal 1830 (last orders 2100)
Parking for 40
Cards accepted: Access, Visa
🛏 🛆 S 🖥 📺 📖 🛆 🔍 ✦ ❄ ⚘ 🏠

## ORTON

Cumbria
Map ref 5B3

Small, attractive village with the background of Orton Scar, it has some old buildings and a spacious green. George Whitehead, the itinerant Quaker preacher, was born here in 1636.

### Vicarage 🅰
**Listed** **COMMENDED**
Orton, Penrith CA10 3RQ
☎ (01539) 624873
Fax (01539) 624873
*Warm, comfortable accommodation in a working vicarage overlooking rooftops and fells. Ideal for walkers visiting the Lakes and Yorkshire Dales.*
Bedrooms: 1 double, 2 twin
Bathrooms: 1 public

**Bed & breakfast**

| per night: | £min | £max |
|---|---|---|
| Single | 15.00 | |
| Double | 30.00 | |

**Half board**

| per person: | £min | £max |
|---|---|---|
| Daily | 23.00 | |

Evening meal 1900 (last orders 2100)
Parking for 2
🛏 🗟 📭 ♿ UL 🛆 S 🖥 📺 📖 🛆 ❄ ⚘ SP T

## OXEN PARK

Cumbria
Map ref 5A3

### The Manor House
**COMMENDED**
Oxen Park, Ulverston LA12 8HG
☎ Ulverston (01229) 861345

*18th C manor house between Lakes Windermere and Coniston, adjacent to Grizedale Forest. A haven of peace and comfort. In "Good Beer Guide".*
Bedrooms: 1 single, 3 double, 1 twin
Bathrooms: 5 private

**Bed & breakfast**

| per night: | £min | £max |
|---|---|---|
| Single | 22.50 | 25.00 |
| Double | 45.00 | 50.00 |

Lunch available
Evening meal 1830 (last orders 2130)
Parking for 25

Cards accepted: Access, Visa, Switch/Delta
🛏 🗟 ♿ 🛆 S 🖥 📺 📖 🛆 🔍 ⟳ ❄ ⚘ SP 🏠 T

## PATTERDALE

Cumbria
Map ref 5A3

Amongst the fells at the southern end of the Ullswater Valley, this village is dominated by Helvellyn and St Sunday Crag. Ideal centre for touring and outdoor activities.

### Fellside 🅰
**Listed** **APPROVED**
Hartsop, Patterdale, Penrith CA11 0NZ
☎ Glenridding (01768) 482532
*17th C Cumbrian farmhouse at the foot of Kirkstone Pass, perfect for fellwalkers; artists welcome. Magnificent scenery. Piano in the lounge.*
Bedrooms: 1 single, 1 double, 1 twin
Bathrooms: 2 public

**Bed & breakfast**

| per night: | £min | £max |
|---|---|---|
| Single | 14.00 | 16.00 |
| Double | 28.00 | 32.00 |

Parking for 3
🛏 ♿ UL 🛆 S 🖥 📺 📖 🛆 ❄ ⚘ SP 🏠 T

## PENRITH

Cumbria
Map ref 5B2

Ancient and historic market town, the northern gateway to the Lake District. Penrith Castle was built as a defence against the Scots. Its ruins, open to the public, stand in the public park. High above the town is the Penrith Beacon, made famous by William Wordsworth.
*Tourist Information Centre*
☎ *(01768) 67466*

### Glendale 🅰
**Listed** **APPROVED**
4 Portland Place, Penrith CA11 7QN
☎ (01768) 62579
*Victorian town house overlooking pleasant gardens. Spacious family rooms. Children and pets welcome. Special diets catered for on request.*
Bedrooms: 1 single, 1 double, 3 triple
Bathrooms: 1 public

**Bed & breakfast**

| per night: | £min | £max |
|---|---|---|
| Single | | 17.50 |
| Double | | 31.00 |

Parking for 1
🛏 📭 ♿ UL 🛆 S 🖥 📺 📖 🛆 🍽 SP

### Holmewood Guesthouse
**Listed** **COMMENDED**
5 Portland Place, Penrith CA11 7QN
☎ (01768) 63072 Changing to 863072
*Large Victorian terraced house run by proprietress and providing good*

Continued ▶

## PENRITH

*Continued*

facilities. Ideal for Lake District and stopover to or from Scotland.
Bedrooms: 1 double, 3 triple, 1 family room
Bathrooms: 1 private, 2 public

**Bed & breakfast**

| per night: | £min | £max |
|---|---|---|
| Single | 15.50 | 19.50 |
| Double | 29.00 | 45.00 |

Parking for 1

### Hornby Hall Country House

**Listed** **HIGHLY COMMENDED**

Hornby Hall Farm, Brougham, Penrith CA10 2AR
☎ Culgaith (01768) 891114

850-acre mixed farm. Farmhouse with interesting old hall. Fishing on Eamont available. Within easy reach of Lakes, Pennines and Yorkshire Dales. Home-cooked local produce.
Bedrooms: 2 single, 2 double, 3 twin
Bathrooms: 2 private, 3 public

**Bed & breakfast**

| per night: | £min | £max |
|---|---|---|
| Single | 18.00 | 29.00 |

**Half board**

| per person: | £min | £max |
|---|---|---|
| Daily | 32.00 | 46.00 |

Evening meal 1900 (last orders 2100)
Parking for 10
Cards accepted: Access, Visa, Amex

### Newton Rigg College ⋀

Penrith CA11 0AH
☎ (01768) 63791
Fax (01768) 67249
College in beautiful setting with standard and en-suite accommodation. Bar, dining room, shop, sporting facilities. Self-catering also available.
Bedrooms: 245 single, 12 twin
Bathrooms: 120 private, 28 public

**Bed & breakfast**

| per night: | £min | £max |
|---|---|---|
| Single | 15.00 | 20.00 |
| Double | 25.00 | 35.00 |

**Half board**

| per person: | £min | £max |
|---|---|---|
| Daily | 21.00 | 26.00 |
| Weekly | 135.00 | 170.00 |

Lunch available
Evening meal 1800 (last orders 1930)

Parking for 300
Open June-August and Christmas

### Old Victoria Hotel

**APPROVED**

46 Castlegate, Penrith CA11 7HY
☎ (01768) 62467
Family-run hotel with public bar. Bar lunches and evening meals. Home-cooked specialities. Your hosts are Roy and Christine Bacon.
Bedrooms: 4 double, 3 twin
Bathrooms: 2 private, 1 public, 5 private showers

**Bed & breakfast**

| per night: | £min | £max |
|---|---|---|
| Single | 20.00 | 25.00 |
| Double | 40.00 | 44.00 |

**Half board**

| per person: | £min | £max |
|---|---|---|
| Daily | 27.00 | 29.00 |
| Weekly | 170.00 | 180.00 |

Lunch available
Evening meal 1900 (last orders 2100)
Parking for 12

### Sockbridge Mill Trout Farm

**Listed** **COMMENDED**

Penrith CA10 2JT
☎ (01768) 65338
8-acre fish farm. Picturesque working trout farm on the River Eamont, off the B5320 between Pooley Bridge and Penrith.
Bedrooms: 2 double, 2 twin
Bathrooms: 2 public, 1 private shower

**Bed & breakfast**

| per night: | £min | £max |
|---|---|---|
| Single | 14.00 | 20.00 |
| Double | 24.00 | 36.00 |

**Half board**

| per person: | £min | £max |
|---|---|---|
| Daily | 22.00 | 28.00 |
| Weekly | 130.00 | 170.00 |

Parking for 6
Open April-October

### The White House ⋀

**COMMENDED**

Clifton, Penrith CA10 2EL
☎ (01768) 65115

Situated in rural area, an 18th C converted farmhouse where guests' comfort and enjoyment take priority. Ullswater, Hawswater, Eden Valley nearby. Fully licensed. For non-smokers only.

Bedrooms: 2 single, 1 double, 1 twin, 1 triple
Bathrooms: 2 private, 2 public

**Bed & breakfast**

| per night: | £min | £max |
|---|---|---|
| Single | 17.00 | 17.00 |
| Double | 36.00 | 40.00 |

**Half board**

| per person: | £min | £max |
|---|---|---|
| Daily | 28.50 | 31.50 |
| Weekly | 182.00 | 203.00 |

Evening meal 1900 (last orders 1200)
Parking for 8
Open January-October and Christmas

## PENRUDDOCK

Cumbria
Map ref 5A2

### Low Garth Guest House

**APPROVED**

Penruddock, Penrith CA11 0QU
☎ Greystoke (01768) 483492
Tastefully converted 18th C barn in peaceful surroundings with magnificent views, offering a warm welcome and Aga-cooked meals.
Bedrooms: 1 twin, 1 triple
Bathrooms: 2 private, 1 public

**Bed & breakfast**

| per night: | £min | £max |
|---|---|---|
| Single | 15.00 | 18.00 |
| Double | 30.00 | 36.00 |

**Half board**

| per person: | £min | £max |
|---|---|---|
| Daily | 25.00 | 29.00 |
| Weekly | 175.00 | 189.00 |

Evening meal 1800 (last orders 2000)
Parking for 8

## ROSLEY

Cumbria
Map ref 5A2

### Causa Grange ⋀

**DE LUXE**

Rosley, Wigton CA7 8DD
☎ Wigton (01697) 345358
Charming Victorian house set in the heart of the countryside yet only 8 miles from historic Carlisle. Overlooking Caldbeck Fells towards Lake District. Fine food and furnishings. Log fires. A warm welcome.
Bedrooms: 1 double, 1 twin
Bathrooms: 2 private, 1 public

**Bed & breakfast**

| per night: | £min | £max |
|---|---|---|
| Single | 20.00 | 25.00 |
| Double | 40.00 | 50.00 |

**Half board**

| per person: | £min | £max |
|---|---|---|
| Daily | 31.00 | 36.00 |
| Weekly | 190.00 | 210.00 |

Evening meal 1800 (last orders 2100)
Parking for 9

🔥 🖉 📺 📶 🅰 📡 ✂ ⚓ 📺 ⛟ 🈂 ☎ ✕ 🚐
🆂🅿 🏠

## ST BEES

Cumbria
Map ref 5A3

Small seaside village with a good beach, fine Norman church and a public school founded in the 16th C. Dramatic red sandstone cliffs make up impressive St Bees Head, parts of which are RSPB reserves and home to puffins and black guillemot.

### Stonehouse
Listed **APPROVED**

Main Street, Next to Railway Station, St Bees CA27 0DE
☎ Whitehaven (01946) 822 224
*Modernised Georgian listed farmhouse, conveniently and attractively situated next to station, shops and hotels. Start of coast-to-coast route. Golf-course, long-stay car park.*
Bedrooms: 1 single, 2 double, 2 twin, 1 family room
Bathrooms: 3 public, 1 private shower
**Bed & breakfast**

| per night: | £min | £max |
| --- | --- | --- |
| Single | 16.00 | 18.00 |
| Double | 30.00 | 36.00 |

Parking for 8

🐄 🎿 ⛺ ⛟ 🍴 ↯ 📶 🅰 📶 ⛉ 🅰 ↺ ⏰ ☼ ✕ 🚐
🅳🅰🅿 🏠

## SEDBERGH

Cumbria
Map ref 5B3

This busy market town set below the Howgill Fells is an excellent centre for walkers and touring the Dales and Howgills. The noted boys' school was founded in 1525.

### Dalesman Country Inn
👑 👑 👑 **COMMENDED**

Main Street, Sedbergh LA10 5BN
☎ (01539) 621183
*On entering Sedbergh from the M6 the Dalesman is the first inn on the left. 17th C but recently refurbished by local craftsmen. 10% discount on weekly bookings. Winter breaks available.*
Bedrooms: 4 double, 1 twin
Bathrooms: 4 private, 2 public
**Bed & breakfast**

| per night: | £min | £max |
| --- | --- | --- |
| Single | 33.00 | 36.00 |
| Double | 45.00 | 50.00 |

Lunch available
Evening meal 1800 (last orders 2130)
Parking for 12
Cards accepted: Access, Visa

🐄 ⛟ ↯ 🅭 🅰 📶 🅸 📺 📶 🅰 ↺ ⏰ ✕ 🚐 🆂🅿

## SHAP

Cumbria
Map ref 5B3

Village lying nearly 1000 ft above sea-level, amongst impressive moorland scenery. Shap Abbey, open to the public, is hidden in a valley nearby. Most of the ruins date from the early 13th C, but the tower is 16th C. The famous Shap granite and limestone quarries are nearby.

### Kings Arms Hotel 🏩
Listed

Main Street, Shap, Penrith CA10 3NU
☎ (01931) 716277
*Comfortable friendly accommodation on the fringe of the Lake District near M6 junction 39. Directly on the "Coast to Coast" walk.*
Bedrooms: 2 double, 2 twin, 2 triple
Bathrooms: 2 public
**Bed & breakfast**

| per night: | £min | £max |
| --- | --- | --- |
| Single | 20.00 | |
| Double | 36.00 | |

Lunch available
Evening meal 1830 (last orders 2000)
Parking for 15
Cards accepted: Access

🐄 🍴 ⛟ ↯ 🅸 🅰 ⏰ ☼ 🚐

## SILLOTH

Cumbria
Map ref 5A2

Small port and coastal resort on the Solway Firth with wide cobbled roads and an attractive green leading to the promenade and seashore known for its magnificent sunsets.
*Tourist Information Centre*
☎ *(01697) 331944*

### Nook Farm
Listed **APPROVED**

Beckfoot, Silloth, Carlisle CA5 4LG
☎ Allonby (01900) 881279
*90-acre livestock farm. Nook Farm welcomes guests to home cooking and free-range eggs. Within easy reach of lakes and on Cumbrian cycle way.*
Bedrooms: 1 double, 1 triple
Bathrooms: 1 public
**Bed & breakfast**

| per night: | £min | £max |
| --- | --- | --- |
| Single | 14.00 | 15.00 |
| Double | 27.50 | 30.00 |

Parking for 3
Open April-October

🐄 📶 ⏰ 📺 🅰 ☼ 🚐

---

We advise you to confirm your booking in writing.

## TROUTBECK

Cumbria
Map ref 5A3

On the Penrith to Keswick road, Troutbeck was the site of a series of Roman camps. The village now hosts a busy weekly sheep market.

### Troutbeck Inn 🏩
👑 👑

Troutbeck, Penrith CA11 0SJ
☎ Greystoke (01768) 483635
*Small, family-run country inn halfway between Keswick and Penrith. Approximately 10 minutes from the M6, Ullswater and Keswick, and ideal for all Lakeland activities. Good bar meals available.*
Bedrooms: 4 double, 1 triple
Bathrooms: 3 private, 1 public
**Bed & breakfast**

| per night: | £min | £max |
| --- | --- | --- |
| Single | 25.00 | |
| Double | 30.00 | 35.00 |

Evening meal 1830 (last orders 2100)
Parking for 50

🐄 🍴 ↯ 🅸 🅰 ⏰ 📺 📶 🅰 ⚓ 🚐

## ULLSWATER

Cumbria
Map ref 5A3

This beautiful lake, which is over 7 miles long, runs from Glenridding to Pooley Bridge. Lofty peaks ranging around the lake make an impressive background. A steamer service operates along the lake between Pooley Bridge, Howtown and Glenridding in the summer.

### Bridge End Farm 🏩
👑 👑 **COMMENDED**

Hutton, Hutton John, Penrith CA11 0LZ
☎ Greystoke (01768) 483273
*14-acre mixed farm Warmest hospitality in 17th C farmhouse, situated in own grounds with gardens to river. Lakeland fell views. 5 miles west of M6, half a mile A66, 3 miles Ullswater.*
Bedrooms: 2 double, 1 twin, 1 triple
Bathrooms: 4 private
**Bed & breakfast**

| per night: | £min | £max |
| --- | --- | --- |
| Double | 30.00 | 35.00 |

| Half board | | |
| --- | --- | --- |
| per person: | £min | £max |
| Daily | 23.00 | 25.00 |
| Weekly | 150.00 | 160.00 |

Evening meal 1830 (last orders 1700)
Parking for 6
Open March-October

🐄 📶 10 📶 🅰 ⏰ 📺 📶 🅰 ☼ ✕ 🚐 🏠

## ULLSWATER

*Continued*

### Cragside Cottage ⚫

Thackthwaite, Ullswater, Penrith
CA11 0ND
☎ Pooley Bridge (01768) 486385
*Mountainside location, 3 miles north of Ullswater. All rooms have toilet, shower and washbasin, tea-making facilities, TV. Reserved parking space. Breakfast served in room. Brochure available.*
Bedrooms: 4 double, 1 triple
Bathrooms: 5 private

**Bed & breakfast**

| per night: | £min | £max |
| --- | --- | --- |
| Double | 32.00 | 32.00 |

Parking for 5
Open March-October
Cards accepted: Access, Visa
➣🔥🍴☐♦ ⛫ 🛁 🚲

### Netherdene Guest House ⚫
**COMMENDED**

Troutbeck, Penrith CA11 0SJ
☎ Greystoke (01768) 483475
*Traditional country house in its own quiet grounds, with extensive mountain views, offering comfortable well-appointed rooms with personal attention. Ideal base for touring Lakeland.*
Bedrooms: 2 double, 1 twin, 1 triple
Bathrooms: 2 private, 2 public

**Bed & breakfast**

| per night: | £min | £max |
| --- | --- | --- |
| Single | 18.00 | 21.00 |
| Double | 29.00 | 37.00 |

**Half board**

| per person: | £min | £max |
| --- | --- | --- |
| Daily | 22.00 | 27.00 |
| Weekly | 145.00 | 170.00 |

Evening meal 1830 (last orders 1600)
Parking for 6
➣🕖☐♦⛫✕🛁📺⛭🚗✿✗🚲

### Swiss Chalet Inn ⚫
**APPROVED**

Pooley Bridge, Penrith CA10 2NN
☎ Pooley Bridge (01768) 486215
Fax (01768) 486215

*Set in charming village near shores of beautiful Ullswater, 5 miles from M6. All rooms en-suite, non-smoking. Swiss/Continental/English cuisine.*
Bedrooms: 1 single, 6 double, 2 twin, 1 triple, 1 family room
Bathrooms: 11 private

---

**Bed & breakfast**

| per night: | £min | £max |
| --- | --- | --- |
| Single | 27.00 | 32.00 |
| Double | 44.00 | 52.00 |

Lunch available
Evening meal 1800 (last orders 2145)
Parking for 40
Open February-December
Cards accepted: Access, Visa
➣🔥☐⛫♦⛏🇸✕🛁⛭🚗🍴🚲 SP ⊺

### Tymparon Hall
**COMMENDED**

Newbiggin, Stainton, Penrith
CA11 0HS
☎ Greystoke (01768) 483236
*150-acre livestock farm. Delightful 18th C manor house with peaceful surroundings, offering comfortable well appointed rooms. Lake Ullswater 10 minutes. Delicious home cooking.*
Bedrooms: 3 double
Bathrooms: 2 private, 1 public

**Bed & breakfast**

| per night: | £min | £max |
| --- | --- | --- |
| Single | 17.00 | 20.00 |
| Double | 35.00 | 40.00 |

**Half board**

| per person: | £min | £max |
| --- | --- | --- |
| Daily | 27.50 | 30.00 |
| Weekly | 180.00 | 200.00 |

Evening meal 1830 (last orders 1430)
Open April-October
➣☐♦⛫🇸✕🛁📺🚗✿🚲 OAP SP

### Ullswater House ⚫
**COMMENDED**

Pooley Bridge, Penrith CA10 2NN
☎ Pooley Bridge (01768) 486259
*Centrally situated in Pooley Bridge. The well appointed rooms are quiet, each having a fridge containing alcoholic and soft drinks.*
Bedrooms: 2 double, 1 twin
Bathrooms: 3 private

**Bed & breakfast**

| per night: | £min | £max |
| --- | --- | --- |
| Single | 18.50 | 28.50 |
| Double | 37.00 | 37.00 |

**Half board**

| per person: | £min | £max |
| --- | --- | --- |
| Daily | 28.50 | 28.50 |
| Weekly | 185.00 | 185.00 |

Evening meal 1900 (last orders 1900)
Parking for 4
➣🔥☐♦⛫🇸✕🛁⛭🚗✿🚲

### Waterside House ⚫
**COMMENDED**

Watermillock, Penrith CA11 0JH
☎ Pooley Bridge (01768) 486038
*A listed statesman's house, set in 10 acres of gardens and meadows on Ullswater's glorious shores. Peaceful and comfortable, an idyllic retreat from pressures. On A592 to Patterdale, 2 miles south of Pooley Bridge.*
Wheelchair access category 3 ♿
Bedrooms: 5 double, 1 twin, 1 triple
Bathrooms: 4 private, 3 public

---

**Bed & breakfast**

| per night: | £min | £max |
| --- | --- | --- |
| Double | 40.00 | 70.00 |

**Half board**

| per person: | £min | £max |
| --- | --- | --- |
| Daily | 35.00 | 50.00 |

Lunch available
Evening meal 1800 (last orders 2130)
Cards accepted: Access, Visa
➣🔥♦⛫🇸✕🛁📺🚗🍴10-20 ♪✿ 🚲✗ SP 🏠

## WINDERMERE

Cumbria
Map ref 5A3

Once a tiny hamlet before the introduction of the railway in 1847, now adjoins Bowness which is on the lakeside. Centre for sailing and boating. A good way to see the lake is a trip on a passenger steamer. Steamboat Museum has a fine collection of old boats.
*Tourist Information Centre*
*☎ (01539) 446499*

### Aaron Slack ⚫
**COMMENDED**

48 Ellerthwaite Road, Windermere
LA23 2BS
☎ (01539) 444649 & mobile 0374 638714
*Small, friendly guesthouse for non-smokers in a quiet part of Windermere, close to all amenities and concentrating on personal service.*
Bedrooms: 2 double, 1 twin
Bathrooms: 3 private

**Bed & breakfast**

| per night: | £min | £max |
| --- | --- | --- |
| Single | 15.00 | 20.00 |
| Double | 26.00 | 40.00 |

Cards accepted: Access, Visa, Amex
➣12☐♦⛫🇸✕🛁📺🚗✗ 🚲✗⊺

### The Beaumont Hotel ⚫
**HIGHLY COMMENDED**

Holly Road, Windermere LA23 2AF
☎ (01539) 447075

*Elegant Victorian house hotel with beautiful lounge. All rooms are en-suite, with colour TV, hairdryer, tea/coffee making facilities. Some four-posters. Warm, personal service.*
Bedrooms: 1 single, 6 double, 1 twin, 2 family rooms
Bathrooms: 10 private

| Bed & breakfast per night: | £min | £max |
|---|---|---|
| Single | 25.00 | 36.00 |
| Double | 40.00 | 56.00 |

Parking for 10
Open March-October
Cards accepted: Access, Visa, Amex, Switch/Delta

🛇6🔥🍽️📺🛜🟐🍴📶S✂️🐾📺🎬💻🖼️🚗❄️
✖️🚲OAP SP

## Beckmead House ⚭

🛏️ COMMENDED

5 Park Avenue, Windermere LA23 2AR
☎ (01539) 442757
*Delightful stone-built Victorian house with reputation for high standards, comfort and friendliness. Our a la carte breakfasts are famous. Convenient for lake, shops, restaurants and golf-course.*
Bedrooms: 1 single, 2 double, 1 twin, 1 family room
Bathrooms: 2 private, 1 public, 2 private showers

| Bed & breakfast per night: | £min | £max |
|---|---|---|
| Single | 15.50 | 17.50 |
| Double | 31.00 | 42.00 |

🛇🗝️📺🛜UL S📺💻🖼️🚗✖️🚲T

## Beckside Cottage ⚭

Listed

4 Park Road, Windermere LA23 2AW
☎ (01539) 442069 & 488105
*Small, comfortable cottage with en-suite bedrooms. Full central heating, colour TV and tea/coffee in all rooms. Full English breakfast served. Ideally situated, close to Windermere Villa.*
Bedrooms: 1 single, 3 double
Bathrooms: 4 private

| Bed & breakfast per night: | £min | £max |
|---|---|---|
| Single | 14.50 | 17.00 |
| Double | 29.00 | 36.00 |

Parking for 3

🛇9📺🛜UL💻🖼️🚗🚲EP

## Boston House ⚭

🛏️🛏️🛏️ COMMENDED

4 The Terrace, Windermere LA23 1AJ
☎ (01539) 443654
Fax (01539) 443654

*Charmingly peaceful Victorian listed building within 5 minutes' walk of trains and town centre. Delicious food, panoramic views, relaxed comfortable atmosphere, private parking.*
Bedrooms: 3 double, 1 twin, 1 triple, 1 family room
Bathrooms: 5 private, 2 public, 1 private shower

| Bed & breakfast per night: | £min | £max |
|---|---|---|
| Double | 31.00 | 42.00 |

| Half board per person: | £min | £max |
|---|---|---|
| Daily | 26.00 | 32.00 |
| Weekly | 160.00 | 200.00 |

Evening meal 1900 (last orders 1930)
Parking for 6
Open February-November
Cards accepted: Access, Visa

🛇🗝️📺🛜🟐🍴S✂️🐾📺💻🖼️🚗🚲
OAP 🚲SP🍴

## Cambridge House ⚭

Listed COMMENDED

9 Oak Street, Windermere LA23 1EN
☎ (01539) 443846
*Village centre location convenient for all amenities. Modern, comfortable rooms with en-suite facilities. Full English, Continental or vegetarian breakfast.*
Bedrooms: 5 double, 1 triple
Bathrooms: 6 private

| Bed & breakfast per night: | £min | £max |
|---|---|---|
| Single | 15.00 | 18.00 |
| Double | 29.00 | 36.00 |

🛇5🗝️📺🛜UL S💻🖼️🚗✖️🚲SP

## The Common Farm

Windermere LA23 1JQ
☎ (01539) 443433
*200-acre dairy farm. Picturesque and homely 17th C farmhouse in peaceful surroundings, less than 1 mile from Windermere village.*
Bedrooms: 1 double, 1 family room
Bathrooms: 1 public

| Bed & breakfast per night: | £min | £max |
|---|---|---|
| Single | 16.00 | 20.00 |
| Double | 28.00 | 32.00 |

Parking for 4
Open March-November

🛇5UL S📺📺💻🖼️U✖️🚲SP🍴

## Fairfield Country House Hotel ⚭

🛏️🛏️ COMMENDED

Brantfell Road, Bowness-on-Windermere, Windermere LA23 3AE
☎ (01539) 446565
Fax (01539) 446565
*Small, friendly 200-year-old country house with half an acre of peaceful secluded gardens. 2 minutes' walk from Lake Windermere and village. Private car park, leisure facilities.*
Bedrooms: 1 single, 4 double, 1 twin, 2 triple, 1 family room
Bathrooms: 9 private, 1 public

| Bed & breakfast per night: | £min | £max |
|---|---|---|
| Single | 24.00 | 28.00 |
| Double | 48.00 | 56.00 |

| Half board per person: | £min | £max |
|---|---|---|
| Daily | 39.00 | 43.00 |
| Weekly | 255.00 | 280.00 |

Evening meal 1900 (last orders 1900)
Parking for 14
Cards accepted: Access, Visa

🛇🔥📺🛜🟐🍴S✂️🐾📺💻🖼️🚗U⌀J
▶❄️✖️🚲🐾SP

## Fir Trees ⚭

🛏️🛏️ HIGHLY COMMENDED

Lake Road, Windermere LA23 2EQ
☎ (01539) 442272
Fax (01539) 442272
*Well-situated and handsome Victorian gentleman's residence offering elegant accommodation. Lovely bedrooms, scrumptious breakfasts and warm hospitality, all at exceptional value for money.*
Bedrooms: 5 double, 1 twin, 1 triple
Bathrooms: 7 private

| Bed & breakfast per night: | £min | £max |
|---|---|---|
| Single | 19.50 | 31.00 |
| Double | 39.00 | 51.00 |

Parking for 8
Cards accepted: Access, Visa, Amex

🛇🗝️📺🛜UL🟐✂️🐾📺💻🖼️🚗✖️🚲OAP
🚲SP

## Haisthorpe Guest House ⚭

🛏️🛏️ COMMENDED

Holly Road, Windermere LA23 2AF
☎ (01539) 443445
*Small, comfortable home-from-home in family-run guesthouse. Residents' lounge. Situated in a quiet location yet close to centre of village.*
Bedrooms: 4 double, 2 triple
Bathrooms: 4 private, 1 public

| Bed & breakfast per night: | £min | £max |
|---|---|---|
| Single | 13.00 | 18.00 |
| Double | 26.00 | 36.00 |

| Half board per person: | £min | £max |
|---|---|---|
| Daily | 20.00 | 25.50 |
| Weekly | 128.00 | 158.00 |

Evening meal 1900 (last orders 2000)
Parking for 3
Cards accepted: Access, Visa, Switch/Delta

🛇📺🛜🟐UL S📺💻🖼️🚗🚲OAP
🚲SP T

## Holly Lodge ⚭

🛏️🛏️ COMMENDED

6 College Road, Windermere LA23 1BX
☎ (01539) 443873
Fax (01539) 443873
*Traditional Lakeland stone guesthouse, built in 1854. In a quiet area off the main road, close to the village centre, buses, railway station and all amenities.*
Bedrooms: 1 single, 5 double, 2 twin, 3 triple
Bathrooms: 4 private, 2 public

Continued ▶

## WINDERMERE

### Continued

**Bed & breakfast**

| per night: | £min | £max |
|---|---|---|
| Single | 16.00 | 20.00 |
| Double | 32.00 | 40.00 |

**Half board**

| per person: | £min | £max |
|---|---|---|
| Daily | 26.00 | 30.00 |
| Weekly | 182.00 | 210.00 |

Evening meal from 1900
Parking for 7

### Laurel Cottage ⚑
COMMENDED

St. Martin's Square, Bowness-on-Windermere, Windermere LA23 3EF
☎ (01539) 445594
*Charming early 17th C cottage with front garden, situated in centre of Bowness. Superb selection of restaurants within one minute's stroll.*
Bedrooms: 2 single, 10 double, 1 twin, 2 triple
Bathrooms: 10 private, 2 public

**Bed & breakfast**

| per night: | £min | £max |
|---|---|---|
| Single | 21.00 | 23.00 |
| Double | 34.00 | 52.00 |

Parking for 8

### Oldfield House ⚑
COMMENDED

Oldfield Road, Windermere LA23 2BY
☎ (01539) 488445

*Friendly, informal atmosphere within a traditionally-built Lakeland residence. Quiet central location, free use of swimming and leisure club.*
Bedrooms: 2 single, 3 double, 1 triple, 1 family room
Bathrooms: 6 private, 1 public

**Bed & breakfast**

| per night: | £min | £max |
|---|---|---|
| Single | 19.00 | 27.00 |
| Double | 34.00 | 50.00 |

Parking for 7
Cards accepted: Access, Visa, Amex, Switch/Delta

### Park Beck Guest House ⚑
Listed

3 Park Road, Windermere LA23 2AW
☎ (01539) 444025

*Ideally situated Lakeland-stone guesthouse, close to all facilities. En-suite rooms with colour TV and tea/coffee making facilities.*
Bedrooms: 2 double, 1 twin, 1 triple
Bathrooms: 4 private

**Bed & breakfast**

| per night: | £min | £max |
|---|---|---|
| Single | 15.00 | 20.00 |
| Double | 29.00 | 40.00 |

Lunch available
Parking for 2

### The Poplars ⚑
COMMENDED

Lake Road, Windermere LA23 2EQ
☎ (01539) 442325 & 4446690
*Small family-run guesthouse on the main lake road, offering en-suite accommodation coupled with fine cuisine and homely atmosphere. Golf and fishing can be arranged.*
Bedrooms: 1 single, 3 double, 2 twin, 1 triple
Bathrooms: 6 private, 1 public

**Bed & breakfast**

| per night: | £min | £max |
|---|---|---|
| Single | 16.50 | 20.00 |
| Double | 33.00 | 40.00 |

**Half board**

| per person: | £min | £max |
|---|---|---|
| Daily | 27.00 | 30.50 |
| Weekly | 175.00 | 213.50 |

Evening meal 1830 (last orders 1900)
Parking for 7

### Rayrigg Villa
Listed

Ellerthwaite Square, Windermere LA23 1DP
☎ (01539) 488342

*Traditional detached family-run Lakeland guesthouse built in 1873. Totally refurbished and modernised in 1990.*
Bedrooms: 6 double, 1 triple, 1 family room
Bathrooms: 4 private, 2 public

**Bed & breakfast**

| per night: | £min | £max |
|---|---|---|
| Single | 15.00 | 24.00 |
| Double | 28.00 | 44.00 |

Parking for 9
Open May-October

### Sunny Bank House
Listed

Princes Road, Windermere LA23 2DD
☎ (01539) 442969

*Victorian house in quiet location. We share our home. A native proprietor with wide local knowledge.*
Bedrooms: 1 single, 1 double, 1 twin
Bathrooms: 1 public

**Bed & breakfast**

| per night: | £min | £max |
|---|---|---|
| Single | 13.00 | 15.00 |
| Double | 26.00 | 52.00 |

Parking for 1
Open April-October

### Villa Lodge ⚑⚑
COMMENDED

Cross Street, Windermere LA23 1AE
☎ (01539) 443318
Fax (01539) 443318

*Friendliness and cleanliness guaranteed. Peacefully situated in quiet cul-de-sac overlooking Windermere village. Splendid views from bedrooms.*
Bedrooms: 1 single, 3 double, 1 twin, 1 triple, 1 family room
Bathrooms: 4 private, 2 public

**Bed & breakfast**

| per night: | £min | £max |
|---|---|---|
| Single | 16.00 | 19.00 |
| Double | 36.00 | 50.00 |

Evening meal 1830 (last orders 1530)
Parking for 6

### Westbourne Hotel ⚑
⚑⚑ COMMENDED

Biskey Howe Road, Bowness-on-Windermere, Windermere LA23 2JR
☎ (01539) 443625
*In a peaceful area of Bowness within a short walk of the lake and shops. Highly recommended by our regular guests for comfort, decor and food.*
Bedrooms: 1 single, 4 double, 1 twin, 1 triple
Bathrooms: 7 private

**Bed & breakfast**

| per night: | £min | £max |
|---|---|---|
| Single | 20.00 | 30.00 |
| Double | 40.00 | 60.00 |

**Half board**

| per person: | £min | £max |
|---|---|---|
| Daily | 30.00 | 36.00 |
| Weekly | 200.00 | 240.00 |

Evening meal 1830 (last orders 1900)
Parking for 10
Cards accepted: Access, Visa

## Westwood

⚨⚨ COMMENDED

4 Ellerthwaite Road, Windermere
LA23 2AH
☎ (01539) 443514
*Traditional Lakeland stone semi-
detached house in a pleasant, central
position overlooking a small park.*
Bedrooms: 4 double
Bathrooms: 4 private
**Bed & breakfast**

| per night: | £min | £max |
| --- | --- | --- |
| Single | 16.00 | 20.00 |
| Double | 32.00 | 38.00 |

Parking for 4

🖵 ♨ ⅏ ﯼ 📺 ▥ ✕ 🚗 SP

## White Lodge Hotel ⋀

⚨⚨⚨ COMMENDED

Lake Road, Windermere LA23 2JS
☎ (01539) 443624
*Victorian family-owned hotel with good
home cooking, only a short walk from
Bowness Bay. All bedrooms have private
bathroom, colour TV and tea making
facilities, some with lake views and
four-posters.*
Bedrooms: 2 single, 7 double, 2 twin,
1 triple
Bathrooms: 12 private
**Bed & breakfast**

| per night: | £min | £max |
| --- | --- | --- |
| Single | 22.00 | 29.00 |
| Double | 42.00 | 52.00 |

**Half board**

| per person: | £min | £max |
| --- | --- | --- |
| Daily | 33.00 | 38.00 |
| Weekly | 150.00 | 180.00 |

Lunch available
Evening meal 1900 (last orders 2000)
Parking for 20
Open March-November
Cards accepted: Access, Visa

🖵 ♨ ⅏ 🖵 ♨ 🛅 S ﯼ 📺 ▥ 🖵 ▸ ❀ ✕ 🐾 SP
🏠 T

Cumbria
Map ref 5A2

A deep-water port on the west
Cumbrian coast. There are the
ruins of the 14th C Workington
Hall, where Mary Queen of Scots
stayed in 1568.
*Tourist Information Centre*
*☎ (01900) 602923*

## Morven Guest House ⋀

⚨⚨

Siddick Road, Siddick, Workington
CA14 1LE
☎ (01900) 602118
*Detached house north-west of
Workington. Ideal base for touring the
Lake District and west Cumbria. Large
car park.*
Bedrooms: 2 single, 1 double, 2 twin,
1 triple

Bathrooms: 4 private, 1 public
**Bed & breakfast**

| per night: | £min | £max |
| --- | --- | --- |
| Single | 20.00 | 30.00 |
| Double | 32.00 | 42.00 |

**Half board**

| per person: | £min | £max |
| --- | --- | --- |
| Daily | 28.00 | 38.00 |

Lunch available
Evening meal 1800 (last orders 1600)
Parking for 20

🖵 ♨ ⅏ 🖵 ♨ ﯼ ✁ ✕ 📺 ▥ 🖵 ❀ ✿
🖵 T

---

Please mention this guide
when making a booking.

---

There are separate
sections in this guide
listing groups
specialising in farm
holidays and
accommodation which
is especially suitable
for young people and
organised groups.

---

# KEY TO SYMBOLS

Information about many of the services and
facilities at accommodation listed in this guide
is given in the form of symbols. The key to
these symbols is inside the back cover flap.
You may find it helpful to keep the flap open
when referring to the accommodation listings.

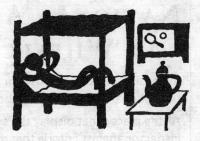

HOLIDAY
CANPAIGN.

# CHECK THE MAPS

The colour maps at the back of this guide show
all cities, towns and villages which have
accommodation listings in the guide. They will
enable you to check if there is suitable
accommodation in the vicinity of the place you
plan to visit.

# USE YOUR *i*'s

There are more than 550 Tourist Information Centres throughout England offering friendly help with accommodation and holiday ideas as well as suggestions of places to visit and things to do.

In your home town there may be a centre which can help you before you set out. You'll find the address of your nearest Tourist Information Centre in your local Phone Book.

# NATIONAL ACCESSIBLE SCHEME FOR WHEELCHAIR USERS

If you are a wheelchair user or someone who has difficulty walking, look for the national 'Accessible' symbol when choosing where to stay.

All the places that display the symbol have been checked by a Tourist Board inspector against criteria that reflect the practical needs of wheelchair users.

**There are three categories of accessibility, indicated by symbols:**

**Category 1:** Accessible to all wheelchair users including those travelling independently

**Category 2:** Accessible to a wheelchair user with assistance

**Category 3:** Accessible to a wheelchair user able to walk short distances and up at least three steps

Establishments in this 'Where to Stay' guide which have an access category are listed in the information pages at the back, together with further details of the scheme. Tourist Information Centre staff will also be pleased to help with finding suitable accommodation.

*Once an ancient kingdom, modern Northumbria combines four counties, each with its own unique identity and, together, making Northumbria the most diverse and interesting region in England. Away from the cities of Newcastle upon Tyne, Durham City and Sunderland (Britain's newest city) quiet roads lead you through unspoilt countryside. Relish the wild and beautiful national parks and enjoy the spectacular coastlines of high cliffs, castles and golden beaches. You'll experience a region proud of its past and confident of its future.*

# NORTHUMBRIA

The Counties of Cleveland, Durham, Northumberland and Tyne & Wear

For more information on Northumbria, contact:
**Northumbria Tourist Board**
**Aykley Heads**
**Durham DH1 5UX**
Tel: (0191) 384 6905
Fax: (0191) 386 0899

Where to Go in Northumbria
– see pages 62–65

Where to Stay in Northumbria
– see pages 66–82

# WHERE TO GO

*You will find hundreds of interesting places to visit during your stay in Northumbria, just some of which are listed in these pages. The number against each name will help you locate it on the map (page 65). Contact any Tourist Information Centre in the region for more ideas on days out in Northumbria.*

**❶ Lindisfarne Castle**
Holy Island, Berwick-upon-Tweed,
Northumberland TD15 2SH
Tel: (01289) 89244
*Tudor fort converted into a private home in 1903 for Edward Hudson by the architect Edwin Lutyens.*

**❷ Bamburgh Castle**
Bamburgh, Northumberland NE69 7DF
Tel: (01668) 214208
*Magnificent coastal castle completely restored in 1900. Collections of china, porcelain, furniture, paintings, arms and armour.*

**❸ Farne Islands**
Seahouses, off Northumberland coast
*Bird reserve holding around 55,000 pairs of breeding birds of 21 species. Also home to a large colony of grey seals.*

**❹ Alnwick Castle**
Alnwick, Northumberland NE66 1NQ
Tel: (01665) 510777
*Home of the Percys, Dukes of Northumberland, since 1309. Largest inhabited castle in England after Windsor.*

**❺ Cragside House, Gardens and Grounds**
Cragside, Rothbury, Northumberland NE65 7PX
Tel: (01669) 20333
*House built 1864–95 for the first Lord Armstrong,*

Tyneside industrialist. First house to be lit by electricity generated by water power.

**❻ Morpeth Chantry Bagpipe Museum**
The Chantry, Bridge Street, Morpeth,
Northumberland NE61 1PJ
Tel: (01670) 519466
*Set in a 13th C church building, museum showing the history and development of Northumbrian small pipes and the music.*

**❼ Chesters Roman Fort**
Chollerford, Humshaugh, Hadrian's Wall,
Northumberland NE46 4EP
Tel: (01434) 681379
*Fort built for 500 cavalrymen. Remains include 5 gateways, barrack blocks, commandant's house and headquarters. Finest military bathhouse in Britain.*

**❽ Sea Life Centre**
Grand Parade, Long Sands, Tynemouth,
Tyne & Wear NE30 4JF
Tel: (0191) 257 6100
*Over 30 hi-tech displays provide encounters with thousands of amazing sea creatures.*

**❾ The Fishing Experience**
Neville House, Fishquay, North Shields, Tyne & Wear NE30 1HE
Tel: (0191) 296 5449
*Exciting interactive visitor attraction bringing to life the story of the North Sea and the history of fishing in the north-east.*

*The technique used for smoking kippers at Craster hasn't changed for over 100 years.*

### 10 Housesteads Roman Fort
Hadrian's Wall, Northumberland NE47 6NN
Tel: (01434) 344363
*Best preserved and most impressive of the Roman forts. Vercovicium was 5-acre fort with extensive civil settlement.*

### 11 Souter Point Lighthouse
Coast Road, Whitburn, South Shields, Tyne & Wear SR6 7NH
Tel: (0191) 529 3061
*Lighthouse and associated buildings were constructed in 1871 and contained the most advanced lighthouse technology of the day.*

### 12 MetroCentre
Gateshead, Tyne & Wear NE11 9XX
Tel: (0191) 493 2046
*Over 350 shops with spacious malls, garden court, Mediterranean village, antique village, Roman forum, over 50 eating outlets, cinema, superbowl. Metroland indoor theme park with roller-coaster, dodgems, pirate ship, live entertainment.*

### 13 Gibside Chapel and Grounds
Gibside, Burnopfield, Newcastle upon Tyne, NE16 6BG
Tel: (01207) 542255
*Mausoleum of 5 members of the Bowes family, built to a design by James Paine between 1760 and 1812. Restored in 1965. Avenue of Turkey Oak trees.*

### 14 Wildfowl and Wetlands Trust
Washington, Tyne & Wear NE38 8LE
Tel: (0191) 416 5454
*Collection of 1,250 wildfowl of 108 varieties. Viewing gallery, picnic areas, hides and winter wild bird feeding station (bird food available). Flamingos.*

### 15 Beamish – The North of England Open Air Museum
Beamish, Co Durham DH9 0RG
Tel: (01207) 231811
*Open air museum of northern life around the turn of the century. Buildings re-erected to form a town with shops and houses. Colliery village, station and working farm.*

**The timber resource at Kielder, Europe's largest man-made forest, needs efficient management.**

### 16 Durham Castle
Palace Green, Durham DH1 3RW
Tel: (0191) 374 3863
*Castle with fine bailey founded in 1072, Norman chapel dating from 1080, kitchens and great hall dating from 1499 and 1284 respectively.*

### 17 Durham Cathedral
Durham, DH1 3EQ
Tel: (0191) 386 2367
*Widely considered to be the finest example of Norman church architecture in England. Tombs of St Cuthbert and the Venerable Bede.*

### 18 Killhope Leadmining Centre
Cowshill, St John's Chapel, Co Durham DL13 1AR
Tel: (01388) 537505
*Most complete lead mining site in Great Britain. Includes crushing mill with 34ft water wheel, reconstruction of Victorian machinery and miners' accommodation.*

### 19 High Force Waterfall
Forest-in-Teesdale, Middleton-in-Teesdale, Co Durham
Tel: (01833) 40209
*Most majestic of the waterfalls on the River Tees. The falls are only a short walk from a bus stop, car park and picnic area.*

*Longstone lighthouse on the Farne Islands: a long tradition of helping mariners.*

**20 Raby Castle**
Staindrop, Co Durham DL2 3AH
Tel: (01833) 660202
*Medieval castle in 200-acre park. 600-year-old kitchen and carriage collection. Walled gardens and deer park.*

**21 Saltburn Smugglers Heritage Centre**
Ship Inn, Saltburn-by-the-Sea, Cleveland
TS12 1HF
Tel: (01287) 625252
*Offers the sights, sounds and smells of Saltburn's smuggling heritage, with tales of John Andrew, "King of the Smugglers".*

**22 Butterfly World**
Preston Park, Yarm Road, Stockton-on-Tees,
Cleveland TS18 3RH
Tel: (01642) 791414
*Indoor tropical garden with exotic free-flying butterflies plus fascinating insects and reptiles.*

**23 Green Dragon Museum**
Theatre Yard, Stockton-on-Tees, Cleveland
TS18 1AT
Tel: (01642) 674308
*Local history museum recording development of Stockton. "1825, the Birth of Railways" is an exciting audio-visual show.*

**24 Preston Hall Museum**
Yarm Road, Stockton-on-Tees, Cleveland
TS18 3RH

Tel: (01642) 781184
*Social history museum with period street and rooms, working craftsmen, arms, armour, costume and toys. Set in 116 acres of beautiful parkland, with aviary, pitch and putt.*

**25 Captain Cook Birthplace Museum**
Stewart Park, Marton, Middlesbrough,
Cleveland TS7 6AS
Tel: (01642) 311211
*Early life and voyages of Captain Cook and the countries he visited. Exhibitions changing monthly.*

**26 Ormesby Hall**
Church Lane, Ormesby, Middlesbrough,
Cleveland TS7 9AS
Tel: (01642) 324188
*Mid-18th C house with fine decorative plasterwork, Jacobean doorway, stable block. Attributed to Carr of York.*

# FIND OUT MORE

*Further information about holidays and attractions in Northumbria is available from:*
**Northumbria Tourist Board**, *Aykley Heads, Durham DH1 5UX*
Tel: (0191) 384 6905

*These publications are available free from the Northumbria Tourist Board:*
● **Northumbria Breaks 1995**

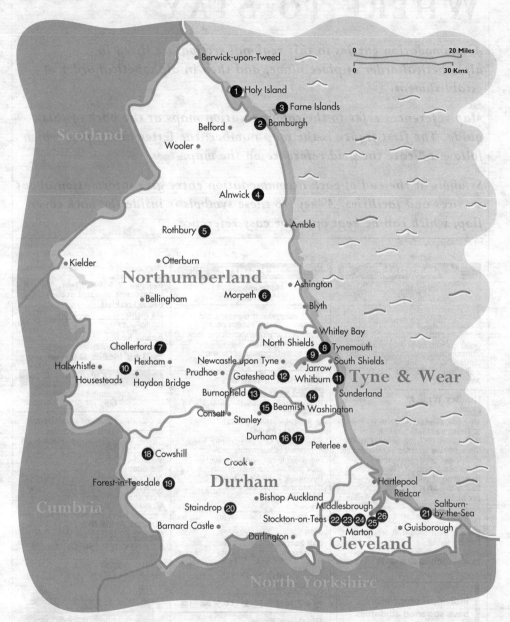

- **Bed & Breakfast map** – *Northumbria and Cumbria*
- **Great Days Out** *map/gazetteer*
- **Caravan and Camping Guide** – *Northumbria, Yorkshire & Humberside, Cumbria and North West*

- **Educational brochure**
*Also available are (prices include postage and packing):*
- **Northumbria touring map and guide** *£5*
- **Leisure Guide to Northumbria** *£11*
- **Walk Northumbria** *£6*

# WHERE TO STAY

*Accommodation entries in this regional section are listed in alphabetical order of place name, and then in alphabetical order of establishment.*

*Map references refer to the colour location maps at the back of this guide. The first figure is the map number; the letter and figure which follow indicate the grid reference on the map.*

*Symbols at the end of each accommodation entry give information about services and facilities. A 'key' to these symbols is inside the back cover flap, which can be kept open for easy reference.*

## ALLENDALE

Northumberland
Map ref 5B2

Attractive small town set amongst moors, 10 miles south-west of Hexham and claimed to be the geographical centre of Britain. Surrounded by unspoilt walking country, with many well-signposted walks along the East and West Allen Rivers.

### Hindley Wrae ⋀

Listed

Allendale, Hexham NE47 9ER
☎ Hexham (01434) 345237
*Dating from 1669, the house is listed Grade II. Very secluded, surrounded by wildlife and open countryside.*
Bedrooms: 2 twin
Bathrooms: 1 public
**Bed & breakfast**

| per night: | £min | £max |
|---|---|---|
| Single | 17.50 | 20.00 |
| Double | 35.00 | 40.00 |

Evening meal 1900 (last orders 2100)
Parking for 4
Open February-November
🛇🕭🎇🛢✗📺🛏️ 🛋️❄🛥️🅰️

---

Individual proprietors have supplied all details of accommodation. Although we do check for accuracy, we advise you to confirm the information at the time of booking.

## ALNMOUTH

Northumberland
Map ref 5C1

Quiet village with pleasant old buildings, at the mouth of the River Aln where extensive dunes and sands stretch along Alnmouth Bay. 18th C granaries, some converted to dwellings, still stand.

### High Buston Hall ⋀

♛♛♛ HIGHLY COMMENDED

High Buston, Alnmouth, Alnwick NE66 3QH
☎ Alnwick (01665) 830341
Fax (01665) 830341
*Elegant listed Georgian country house in tranquil village setting, with commanding sea views. Traditional good food and warm hospitality.*
Bedrooms: 2 double, 1 twin
Bathrooms: 3 private
**Bed & breakfast**

| per night: | £min | £max |
|---|---|---|
| Single | 35.00 | 40.00 |
| Double | 55.00 | 60.00 |

**Half board**

| per person: | £min | £max |
|---|---|---|
| Daily | 45.00 | 50.00 |

Evening meal from 1930
Parking for 9
Open February-November
🛇🛢⑤🎇🛏️📺🛏️ 🛋️🅾❄✗🛥️🆂🅿🅰️

### Hipsburn Farm

♛ HIGHLY COMMENDED

Lesbury, Alnwick NE66 3PY
☎ Alnwick (01665) 830206
*630-acre mixed farm. Comfortably furnished, spacious rooms, fully centrally heated. 1 mile from Alnmouth overlooking Aln*
estuary. Ideal centre for golfers - many courses nearby.
Bedrooms: 2 double, 1 twin
Bathrooms: 1 private, 1 public
**Bed & breakfast**

| per night: | £min | £max |
|---|---|---|
| Double | 36.00 | 38.00 |

Parking for 6
Open April-October
🛇🖵🛢✗🎇📺🛏️ 🛋️❄✗🅰️

## ALNWICK

Northumberland
Map ref 5C1

Ancient and historic market town, entered through the Hotspur Tower, an original gate in the town walls. The medieval castle, the second biggest in England and still the seat of the Dukes of Northumberland, was restored from ruin in the 18th C.
*Tourist Information Centre*
☎ (01665) 510665

### Masons Arms ⋀

♛♛ COMMENDED

Stamford Cott, Rennington, Alnwick NE66 3RX
☎ (01665) 577275
Fax (01665) 577894

*Country inn offering real ale and good food. En-suite bedrooms. 3.5 miles from A1 towards coast and beaches on B1340.*

Bedrooms: 2 single, 4 double, 1 twin, 3 triple
Bathrooms: 10 private

**Bed & breakfast**

| per night: | £min | £max |
|---|---|---|
| Single | 22.50 | |
| Double | 45.00 | |

Lunch available
Evening meal 1900 (last orders 2130)
Parking for 20
Cards accepted: Access, Visa, Switch/Delta

≿ 14 ⌂ ♨ ♦ ⋒ ⨼ ◳ ⴲ ꟿ2-20 ꟾ ✕ 

### Norfolk ♈

**HIGHLY COMMENDED**

41 Blakelaw Road, Alnwick NE66 1BA
☎ (01665) 602892
*Private detached house, quiet area. Tastefully furnished, comfort assured. Delicious 4-course evening meals using own garden produce. No smoking throughout.*
Bedrooms: 1 double, 1 twin
Bathrooms: 2 private

**Bed & breakfast**

| per night: | £min | £max |
|---|---|---|
| Single | 18.00 | |
| Double | 36.00 | |

**Half board**

| per person: | £min | £max |
|---|---|---|
| Daily | 25.00 | |
| Weekly | 169.00 | |

Evening meal 1830 (last orders 1700)
Parking for 2
Open May-October

≿ ⛱ ♒ ⋒ ⨼ ♈ ◳ ⴲ ⴼ ✕ ꟿ 

## AMBLE-BY-THE-SEA

Northumberland
Map ref 5C1

Small fishing town at the mouth of the River Coquet, with fine, quiet, sandy beaches to north and south. The harbour and estuary are popular for sailing and bird-watching. Coquet Island lies 1 mile offshore.

### The Hollies ♈

**COMMENDED**

3 Riverside Park, Amble-by-the-Sea, Morpeth NE65 0YR
☎ Alnwick (01665) 712323
*Detached bungalow quietly situated behind marina, offering bed and breakfast with optional evening meal. Tea/coffee facilities, colour TV. No smoking.*
Bedrooms: 1 double, 2 twin
Bathrooms: 1 private, 1 public

**Bed & breakfast**

| per night: | £min | £max |
|---|---|---|
| Single | 18.00 | 18.00 |
| Double | 27.00 | 29.00 |

**Half board**

| per person: | £min | £max |
|---|---|---|
| Daily | 18.50 | 23.00 |
| Weekly | 120.00 | 126.00 |

Evening meal from 1800
Parking for 3

≿ ⌂ ⛱ ♒ ⋒ ⓘ ◳ ⨼ ⴲ ◳ ⴼ ✿ ✕ ꟿ ⬚ SP

## BAMBURGH

Northumberland
Map ref 5C1

Village with a spectacular red sandstone castle standing 150 ft above the sea. On the village green the magnificent Norman church stands opposite a museum containing mementoes of the heroine Grace Darling.

### Burton Hall ♈

**Listed** **COMMENDED**

East Burton, Bamburgh NE69 7AR
☎ (01668) 214213 & 214458
Fax (01668) 214538
*Elegant, homely farmhouse with spacious rooms. 1.5 miles from Bamburgh, 3.5 miles from Seahouses. Head to Glororum crossroads, Burton signposted there.*
Bedrooms: 6 double, 2 twin
Bathrooms: 4 private, 3 public

**Bed & breakfast**

| per night: | £min | £max |
|---|---|---|
| Single | 18.00 | 25.00 |
| Double | 36.00 | 50.00 |

Parking for 10

≿ 4 ⛱ ⌂ ⛊ ♦ ⋒ ♈ ◳ ⴲ ⴼ ✿ ꟿ

### Glenander Guest House ♈

**HIGHLY COMMENDED**

27 Lucker Road, Bamburgh NE69 7BS
☎ (01668) 214 336
*Travellers from the south leave A1 by the B1341 at Adderstone garage. From the north, by the B1342 off the Belford bypass. Approximately 5 miles in either case.*
Bedrooms: 1 double, 2 twin
Bathrooms: 3 private

**Bed & breakfast**

| per night: | £min | £max |
|---|---|---|
| Single | 20.00 | |
| Double | 36.00 | |

≿ 6 ⛊ ⌂ ♒ ⋒ ⨼ ♈ ◳ ⴲ ⴼ ꟿ ⬚ SP

### Mizen Head Hotel ♈

**APPROVED**

Lucker Road, Bamburgh NE69 7BS
☎ (01668) 214254
*Privately-owned, fully licensed hotel in own grounds, with accent on good food and service. Convenient for beaches, castle and golf. 2 minutes' walk from village centre.*
Bedrooms: 3 single, 5 double, 4 twin, 4 family rooms
Bathrooms: 7 private, 3 public

**Bed & breakfast**

| per night: | £min | £max |
|---|---|---|
| Single | 20.00 | 32.00 |
| Double | 33.00 | 66.00 |

**Half board**

| per person: | £min | £max |
|---|---|---|
| Daily | 28.00 | 45.00 |
| Weekly | 179.00 | 275.00 |

Lunch available
Evening meal 1830 (last orders 2000)
Parking for 30
Cards accepted: Access, Visa

≿ ⌂ ♦ ⓘ ◳ ♈ ◳ ⴲ ꟿ8-30 ✿ ◳ SP ⬚

## BARDON MILL

Northumberland
Map ref 5B2

Small hamlet midway between Haydon Bridge and Haltwhistle, within easy walking distance of Vindolanda, an excavated Roman settlement, and near the best stretches of Hadrian's Wall.

### Winshields Farm

**COMMENDED**

Bardon Mill, Hexham NE47 7AN
☎ Haltwhistle (01434) 344243
*500-acre hill farm. 18th C farmhouse, situated just below highest point of Hadrian's Wall, with Pennine Way and Hadrian's Wall running through land.*
Bedrooms: 1 double, 1 twin, 1 triple
Bathrooms: 2 public

**Bed & breakfast**

| per night: | £min | £max |
|---|---|---|
| Single | 16.00 | 16.50 |
| Double | 32.00 | 33.00 |

Parking for 6
Open June-September

≿ ⛫ ♦ ⋒ ⓘ ♈ ◳ ⴲ ⴼ ✿ ꟿ

## BARNARD CASTLE

Durham
Map ref 5B3

High over the Tees, a thriving market town with a busy market square. Bernard Baliol's 12th C castle (now ruins) stands nearby. The Bowes Museum, housed in a grand 19th C French chateau, holds fine paintings and furniture. Nearby are some magnificent buildings.
*Tourist Information Centre*
☎ *(01833) 690909*

### East Mellwaters Farm ♈

**COMMENDED**

Bowes, Barnard Castle, County Durham DL12 9RH
☎ Teesdale (01833) 28269
*350-acre livestock farm. On A66, 2 miles west of Bowes. 17th C farmhouse in attractive setting with views. Sleep in modern comfort, dine by traditional open-fire range. Home-made bread.*
Bedrooms: 1 single, 2 double, 1 twin, 1 triple
Bathrooms: 5 private

*Continued* ▶

## BARNARD CASTLE

### Continued

**Bed & breakfast**

| per night: | £min | £max |
|---|---|---|
| Single | 15.00 | 18.00 |
| Double | 30.00 | 36.00 |

**Half board**

| per person: | £min | £max |
|---|---|---|
| Daily | 25.00 | 28.00 |
| Weekly | 150.00 | 170.00 |

Lunch available
Evening meal 1730 (last orders 1900)
Parking for 12
Cards accepted: Access

🛏🖵♿🛁✕🏰🖼⛏📷☎16-15🕛♪✔
❀🐾SP🏰

### George & Dragon Inn
**Listed**

Boldron, Barnard Castle, County
Durham DL12 9RF
☎ Teesdale (01833) 38215
*Attractive inn in beautiful Teesdale,*
*offering comfortable accommodation*
*and friendly hospitality.*
Bedrooms: 1 double, 1 twin
Bathrooms: 1 public

**Bed & breakfast**

| per night: | £min | £max |
|---|---|---|
| Single | 15.00 | 16.00 |
| Double | 30.00 | 32.00 |

**Half board**

| per person: | £min | £max |
|---|---|---|
| Daily | 20.00 | 21.00 |
| Weekly | 140.00 | 147.00 |

Lunch available
Evening meal 1900 (last orders 1730)
Parking for 20

🛏🖵♿🛁🖼📺🖼⛏🐾

### Old Well Inn
**COMMENDED**

21 The Bank, Barnard Castle, County
Durham DL12 8PH
☎ Teesdale (01833) 690130
*Historic inn and popular restaurant,*
*tastefully decorated, with spacious en-*
*suite bedrooms. Home-cooked food and*
*real ales. North Pennines Area of*
*Outstanding Natural Beauty.*
Bedrooms: 1 double, 1 twin, 1 triple
Bathrooms: 3 private, 1 public

**Bed & breakfast**

| per night: | £min | £max |
|---|---|---|
| Single | 25.00 | 30.00 |
| Double | 40.00 | 45.00 |

Lunch available
Evening meal 1900 (last orders 2130)
Cards accepted: Access, Visa, Switch/
Delta

🛏🖵♿🛁✕🖼⛏📷☎❀🐾OAP🏰

### West Roods Tourism M
**COMMENDED**

West Roods, West Rood Farm,
Boldron, Barnard Castle, County
Durham DL12 9SW
☎ Teesdale (01833) 690116

*58-acre mixed & dairy farm. In*
*Teesdale area, south of Barnard Castle,*
*2.5 miles east of Bowes on A66.*
*Activities from water divining to table*
*tennis. Home cooking using milk and*
*eggs from our own farm.*
Bedrooms: 1 single, 1 double, 1 twin
Bathrooms: 2 private, 1 public

**Bed & breakfast**

| per night: | £min | £max |
|---|---|---|
| Single | 16.00 | |
| Double | 32.00 | |

**Half board**

| per person: | £min | £max |
|---|---|---|
| Daily | 26.00 | 28.00 |

Evening meal 1700 (last orders 1800)
Parking for 6
Open March-October
Cards accepted: Visa, Diners, Amex

🛏🖵♿🖼📷🛁🖼⛏📷☎⛏♪❀🐾
🏰🎖

### Wilson House
**COMMENDED**

Barningham, Richmond, North
Yorkshire DL11 7EB
☎ Teesdale (01833) 21218
*Situated 1 mile from A66, 5 miles from*
*Barnard Castle. Period farmhouse with*
*spacious guest accommodation enjoying*
*magnificent views.*
Bedrooms: 2 single, 1 twin, 1 family
room
Bathrooms: 3 private, 1 public

**Bed & breakfast**

| per night: | £min | £max |
|---|---|---|
| Single | 12.00 | 18.00 |
| Double | 30.00 | 30.00 |

**Half board**

| per person: | £min | £max |
|---|---|---|
| Daily | 22.00 | 28.00 |
| Weekly | 154.00 | 165.00 |

Evening meal 1800 (last orders 2000)
Parking for 5
Open March-October

🛏🖧🖵♿🖼📷🛁🖼⛏📷🕛❀✕
🐾SP🏰

## BEADNELL

Northumberland
Map ref 5C1

Charming fishing village on
Beadnell Bay. Seashore lime kilns
(National Trust), dating from the
18th C, recall busier days as a
coal and lime port and a pub is
built on to a medieval pele tower
which survives from days of the
border wars.

### Beadnell House M
**COMMENDED**

Beadnell, Chathill NE67 5AT
☎ Seahouses (01665) 721380
Fax (01665) 720283
*Victorian mansion standing in its own*
*peaceful grounds. Offering B&B*
*accommodation with limited service.*
*Ideal base for touring coast.*

Bedrooms: 1 single, 3 double, 5 twin,
2 triple, 2 family rooms
Bathrooms: 6 private, 1 public

**Bed & breakfast**

| per night: | £min | £max |
|---|---|---|
| Single | 14.95 | 22.95 |
| Double | 27.90 | 43.90 |

**Half board**

| per person: | £min | £max |
|---|---|---|
| Daily | 19.00 | |
| Weekly | 130.00 | |

Evening meal 1900 (last orders 2100)
Parking for 20
Open April-October

🛏🖵♿🖼📷🛁🖼📺🖼⛏📷🕛❀✔OAP SP🏰🖼

### Shepherds Cottage
**Listed** **COMMENDED**

Beadnell, Chathill NE67 5AD
☎ Alnwick (01665) 720497

*Character cottage near Beadnell, with*
*spacious garden, tea and coffee*
*facilities, comfortable sitting room. Keys*
*for all-day access. Ample off-road*
*parking.*
Bedrooms: 2 double, 1 twin
Bathrooms: 1 private, 1 public

**Bed & breakfast**

| per night: | £min | £max |
|---|---|---|
| Single | 15.00 | 18.50 |
| Double | 30.00 | 37.00 |

Parking for 6

🖧♿🖼📷📺🖼⛏📷❀✕🐾🖼

## BELLINGHAM

Northumberland
Map ref 5B2

Set in the beautiful valley of the
North Tyne close to the Kielder
Forest, Kielder Water and lonely
moorland below the Cheviots. The
church has an ancient stone
wagon roof fortified in the 18th C
with buttresses.
*Tourist Information Centre*
☎ *(01434) 220616*

### Lyndale Guest House M
**HIGHLY COMMENDED**

Off the Square, (Kielder Water),
Bellingham, Hexham NE48 2AW
☎ Hexham (01434) 220361
*Attractive, comfortable bungalow with*
*pleasant walled garden and sun lounge*
*with panoramic views. Quality ground*
*floor en-suites. Good food, good walking*
*and quiet roads. Close to Hadrian's Wall*
*and Kielder Water. Amid moors and*
*national park area.*
Bedrooms: 1 double, 1 twin, 1 triple
Bathrooms: 3 private, 1 public

**Bed & breakfast**

| per night: | £min | £max |
|---|---|---|
| Single | 15.90 | 22.50 |
| Double | 31.00 | 44.00 |

**Half board**

| per person: | £min | £max |
|---|---|---|
| Daily | 25.90 | 32.50 |
| Weekly | 170.00 | 204.00 |

Evening meal 1800 (last orders 1600)
Parking for 6

🛏3♨🍴🖭☎♦♘Ⓤ🛡⬚✕🅜🅣�🛢↻♪⚡✿🖐⮐DAP SP T

## Mantle Hill

👑👑 COMMENDED

Hesleyside, Bellingham, Hexham
NE48 2LB
☎ (01434) 220428
Fax (01434) 220113
*Family home, built as dower house to historic Hesleyside Hall. 200 yards from North Tyne River with lovely views over unspoilt countryside. Licensed.*
Bedrooms: 1 double, 1 twin
Bathrooms: 2 private

**Bed & breakfast**

| per night: | £min | £max |
|---|---|---|
| Single | 20.00 | 23.00 |
| Double | 40.00 | 48.00 |

**Half board**

| per person: | £min | £max |
|---|---|---|
| Daily | 34.00 | 37.00 |

Evening meal 1900 (last orders 2100)
Parking for 8
Cards accepted: Visa

🛏3🍴🖭🛡🅜🅣🅜🛢🍴12☎↻♪✔✿⮐SP🖐

---

## BERWICK-UPON-TWEED

Northumberland
Map ref 5B1

Guarding the mouth of the Tweed, England's northernmost town with the best 16th C city walls in Europe. The handsome Guildhall and barracks date from the 18th C. Three bridges cross to Tweedmouth, the oldest built in 1634.
*Tourist Information Centre*
☎ *(01289) 330733*

## Ladythorne House

Listed

Cheswick, Berwick-upon-Tweed
TD15 2RW
☎ (01289) 387382
*Grade II listed building, dated 1721, set in farmland. Only 15 minutes' walk from the beaches.*
Bedrooms: 1 single, 1 double, 2 twin, 2 triple
Bathrooms: 3 public

**Bed & breakfast**

| per night: | £min | £max |
|---|---|---|
| Single | 11.00 | 15.00 |
| Double | 22.00 | 30.00 |

Parking for 8

🛏🐾Ⓤ🛡S🅜✕🅜🅣🛢✿🖐⚡SP🖐

## Middle Ord Manor House ▲▲

👑👑👑 DE LUXE

Middle Ord Farm, Berwick-upon-Tweed TD15 2XQ
☎ (01289) 306323

*550-acre mixed farm. Quality accommodation within Georgian farmhouse. Central for touring the Borders, coast and Holy Island. En-suites and four-poster bed available.*
Bedrooms: 2 double, 1 twin
Bathrooms: 3 private, 1 public

**Bed & breakfast**

| per night: | £min | £max |
|---|---|---|
| Single | 17.00 | 23.00 |
| Double | 34.00 | 46.00 |

Parking for 6
Open April-October

🖭🍴🖭🖭♦♘Ⓤ✕🅜🅣🛢↻✔✿✕🖐🖐

## The Old Vicarage Guest House ▲▲

👑👑👑 HIGHLY COMMENDED

24 Church Road, Tweedmouth,
Berwick-upon-Tweed TD15 2AN
☎ (01289) 306909

*Spacious, detached 19th C vicarage, recently refurbished to a high standard. 10 minutes' walk from town centre and beautiful beaches.*
Bedrooms: 1 single, 4 double, 1 twin, 1 triple
Bathrooms: 4 private, 1 public

**Bed & breakfast**

| per night: | £min | £max |
|---|---|---|
| Single | 14.00 | 17.00 |
| Double | 28.00 | 46.00 |

Parking for 4

🛏🐾🖭♦Ⓤ S🅜✕🅜🅣🛢DAP SP T

## Padua

👑👑👑 HIGHLY COMMENDED

Castle Terrace, Berwick-upon-Tweed
TD15 1NZ
☎ (01289) 306875
*Easy access from A1 bypass, on the outskirts of historic town. Classical 19th C architecture, large rooms. Peaceful and relaxed atmosphere, with high standard of comfort.*
Bedrooms: 2 double
Bathrooms: 2 private, 2 public

## Bed & breakfast

| per night: | £min | £max |
|---|---|---|
| Single | 20.00 | |
| Double | 40.00 | |

Parking for 6

🍴♦♘Ⓤ S✕🅜🅣🛢↻🛢↻🛢↻♪♪✿✕🖐🖐

## 8 Ravensdowne ▲▲

👑👑 COMMENDED

Berwick-upon-Tweed TD15 1HX
☎ (01289) 307883
*Sally Duke offers a year-round welcome in this listed Georgian townhouse, adjacent to the historic town walls. All-day access. Pets by arrangement.*
Bedrooms: 2 single, 1 double, 2 twin
Bathrooms: 2 private, 2 public

**Bed & breakfast**

| per night: | £min | £max |
|---|---|---|
| Single | 16.00 | 25.00 |
| Double | 32.00 | 40.00 |

Parking for 5

🛏🍴♦Ⓤ🛡♘✕🅜🅣🛢🛢🖐🖐

## 3 Scott's Place ▲▲

👑👑👑 HIGHLY COMMENDED

Berwick-upon-Tweed TD15 1LQ
☎ (01289) 305323
*Listed Grade II, Georgian terrace built in 1806. Close to the town walls, local tourist information office and town centre.*
Bedrooms: 2 double, 1 twin
Bathrooms: 3 private

**Bed & breakfast**

| per night: | £min | £max |
|---|---|---|
| Single | 15.00 | 25.00 |
| Double | 30.00 | 50.00 |

🍴🖭♦🖭S🅜🅣🛢🖐🖐

## Thornton Park Farm ▲▲

👑👑 COMMENDED

Berwick-upon-Tweed TD15 2LP
☎ (01289) 382231
*315-acre mixed farm. Large Georgian farmhouse in unspoilt countryside, just over 1 mile from the Scottish border, 4.5 miles to good beaches, and an ideal centre for touring. On A698. Secluded car park.*
Bedrooms: 1 double, 1 twin
Bathrooms: 2 private, 2 public

**Bed & breakfast**

| per night: | £min | £max |
|---|---|---|
| Single | 17.00 | 18.00 |
| Double | 34.00 | 36.00 |

Parking for 6
Open March-October

🛏5♦Ⓤ S🅣🅜🛢♪✿✕🖐✕🖐

All accommodation in this guide has been inspected, or is awaiting inspection, under the national Crown scheme.

## BISHOP AUCKLAND

Durham
Map ref 5C2

Busy market town on the bank of the River Wear. The Palace, a castellated Norman manor house altered in the 18th C, stands in beautiful gardens. Entered from the market square by a handsome 18th C gatehouse, the park is a peaceful retreat of trees and streams.
*Tourist Information Centre*
☎ *(01388) 604922*

### Five Gables

Binchester, Bishop Auckland, County Durham DL14 8AT
☎ Weardale (01388) 608204
*300 yards from A688 between Bishop Auckland and Spennymoor. Victorian house with views over countryside and Weardale. Within easy reach of popular tourist attractions in the North of England.*
Bedrooms: 1 double, 1 triple
Bathrooms: 1 private, 1 public
**Bed & breakfast**

| per night: | £min | £max |
| --- | --- | --- |
| Single | 20.00 | 30.00 |
| Double | 25.00 | 35.00 |

Open April-October
ⓣ5☐♦ⓊⓈ✕▥❈✕🐾SP

## BOWES

Durham
Map ref 5B3

Old stone village high up on a Roman road crossing the Pennines. Settled since Roman times, the town has a sturdy Norman castle keep and an ancient church with a Norman font and Roman inscribed stone.

### Ancient Unicorn Inn

Bowes, Barnard Castle, County Durham DL12 9HN
☎ Teesdale (01833) 628321
*16th C inn on the A66 with comfortable bedrooms, extensive bar menu. Ideal base for exploring the Lakes, Northumbria, Yorkshire Dales and Yorkshire Wolds.*
Bedrooms: 2 twin, 1 triple
Bathrooms: 3 private
**Bed & breakfast**

| per night: | £min | £max |
| --- | --- | --- |
| Single | | 19.00 |
| Double | | 30.00 |

Lunch available
Evening meal 1930 (last orders 2130)
Parking for 20
ⓣ💇☐♦🛏▥❖Ⓤ✕🐾🏧

## CARTERWAY HEADS

Northumberland
Map ref 5B2

Small hamlet on the A68, high on the moors at the head of the Derwent Valley overlooking Derwent reservoir.

### Greenhead House
👑👑👑 COMMENDED

A68, Carterway Heads, Consett DH8 9TP
☎ Edmundbyers (01207) 55676
*18th C stone, former coaching inn at A68 Carterway Heads crossroads to Edmundbyers and Shotley Bridge. Garden with uninterrupted views. Evening meals by arrangement. All rooms en-suite. Table licence.*
Bedrooms: 2 double, 1 twin
Bathrooms: 3 private
**Bed & breakfast**

| per night: | £min | £max |
| --- | --- | --- |
| Single | 20.00 | 20.00 |
| Double | 28.00 | 30.00 |

**Half board**

| per person: | £min | £max |
| --- | --- | --- |
| Daily | 19.00 | 25.00 |
| Weekly | 133.00 | 175.00 |

Lunch available
Evening meal 1800 (last orders 2000)
Parking for 10
ⓣ💇☎☐♦🍴✕▥ⓉⓋⓄ▥▤🏵🐾SP🏧

## CASTLESIDE

Durham
Map ref 5B2

Village on the edge of the North Pennines on the A68, one of the main routes from England to Scotland.

### Castlenook Guest House
👑👑

18-20 Front Street, Castleside, Consett, County Durham DH8 9AR
☎ Consett (01207) 506634
*On the A68 within easy reach of Durham City, Hadrian's Wall, Beamish Museum and MetroCentre. Excellent village amenities.*
Bedrooms: 1 double, 2 twin
Bathrooms: 3 private
**Bed & breakfast**

| per night: | £min | £max |
| --- | --- | --- |
| Single | 20.00 | 20.00 |
| Double | 30.00 | 30.00 |

**Half board**

| per person: | £min | £max |
| --- | --- | --- |
| Daily | 21.00 | 21.00 |
| Weekly | 140.00 | 140.00 |

Evening meal 1700 (last orders 1850)
Parking for 5
ⓣ☐♦ⓊⒾⓈ▥ⓉⓋ▥▤Ⓤ🏵🐾SP🏧

### Willerby Grange Farm
👑👑 COMMENDED

Allensford, Castleside, Consett, County Durham DH8 9BA
☎ Consett (01207) 508752
*Situated in beautiful Derwent Valley, self-contained apartments available also for bed and breakfast. Pony trekking nearby, livery on site. Easy travelling distance to Beamish museum, Gateshead MetroCentre, Hadrian's Wall. Moorland and woodland walks. Approximately 1 kilometre off A68 at Allensford.*
Bedrooms: 3 double, 2 twin
Bathrooms: 5 private
**Bed & breakfast**

| per night: | £min | £max |
| --- | --- | --- |
| Single | 25.00 | 35.00 |
| Double | 40.00 | 45.00 |

Parking for 100
Cards accepted: Access, Visa, Diners, Amex
ⓣ💇☎☐♦ⓊⒾ✕▥ⓉⓋ▥▤🐾Ⓤ▸🏵🐾

## CHESTER-LE-STREET

Durham
Map ref 5C2

Originally a Roman military site, town with modern commerce and light industry on the River Wear. The ancient church replaced a wooden sanctuary which sheltered the remains of St Cuthbert for 113 years. The Anker's house beside the church is now a museum.

### Low Urpeth Farm House
Listed HIGHLY COMMENDED

Ouston, Chester-le-Street, County Durham DH2 1BD
☎ (0191) 410 2901
Fax (0191) 410 0081
*500-acre arable & livestock farm. Leave A1(M) at Chester-le-Street. Take A693, signpost Beamish. At second roundabout turn right to Ouston. Pass garage, down hill, over roundabout and turn left into farm at "Trees Please" sign.*
Bedrooms: 1 double, 2 twin
Bathrooms: 2 private, 1 public
**Bed & breakfast**

| per night: | £min | £max |
| --- | --- | --- |
| Single | 18.00 | |
| Double | 32.00 | |

Parking for 6
ⓣ💇☐♦ⓊⓈ✕Ⓣ▥▤🏵✕🐾

### Waldridge Fell House
👑👑 HIGHLY COMMENDED

Waldridge Lane, Waldridge, Chester-Le-Street, County Durham DH2 3RY
☎ (0191) 389 1908
*Former village chapel, stone-built in 1868. Panoramic views and country walks. Children half price. Winter weekend breaks.*
Bedrooms: 3 triple, 2 family rooms

Bathrooms: 1 private, 1 public,
1 private shower

**Bed & breakfast**

| per night: | £min | £max |
|---|---|---|
| Single | 22.00 | 27.00 |
| Double | 36.00 | 41.00 |

Parking for 8

🛇🗻▭🗐ⓤⓛ🅰ⓢ✂️📺🖾,🛆❄🛒SP

## Waldridge Hall Farm ⋀

**Listed  HIGHLY COMMENDED**

Old Waldridge, Chester-Le-Street,
County Durham DH2 3SL
☎ (0191) 388 4210
*40-acre arable farm. Listed 18th C
farmhouse in pretty countryside,
between Durham City and the Beamish
Museum. A warm welcome with homely
accommodation. Vegetarians catered for.
No smoking in bedrooms.*
Bedrooms: 1 double, 1 twin, 1 triple
Bathrooms: 1 public

**Bed & breakfast**

| per night: | £min | £max |
|---|---|---|
| Single | 22.00 | 25.00 |
| Double | 30.00 | 35.00 |

Parking for 8
Open March-October

🛇❋🚲🗻▭🛆🚿ⓤⓛ🅰ⓢ✂️📺🖾,
🛆❄✗🛒🏠

## CONSETT

Durham
Map ref 5B2

Former steel town on the edge of
rolling moors. Modern
development includes the
shopping centre and a handsome
Roman Catholic church, designed
by a local architect. To the west,
the Derwent Reservoir provides
water sports and pleasant walks.

## Bee Cottage Farm ⋀

**HIGHLY COMMENDED**

Castleside, Consett, County Durham
DH8 9HW
☎ (01207) 508224

*46-acre livestock farm. 1.5 miles west of
the A68, between Castleside and Tow
Law. Unspoilt views. Ideally located for
Beamish Museum and Durham. No
smoking in main farmhouse.*
Bedrooms: 1 single, 3 double, 2 twin,
1 triple, 2 family rooms
Bathrooms: 3 private, 5 public

**Bed & breakfast**

| per night: | £min | £max |
|---|---|---|
| Single | 22.00 | |
| Double | 36.00 | |

---

**Half board**

| per person: | £min | £max |
|---|---|---|
| Daily | 30.00 | |
| Weekly | 210.00 | |

Lunch available
Evening meal 2015 (last orders 2130)
Parking for 20

🛇🗻🚲🅰ⓢ✂️🐾📺🕙🖾,🛆🅄❄🐾

## CORBRIDGE

Northumberland
Map ref 5B2

Small town on the River Tyne.
Close by are extensive remains of
the Roman military town
Corstopitum, with a museum
housing important discoveries from
excavations. The town itself is
attractive with shady trees, a 17th
C bridge and interesting old
buildings, notably a 14th C
vicarage.

## Fellcroft ⋀

**♛♛  HIGHLY COMMENDED**

Station Road, Corbridge NE45 5AY
☎ Hexham (01434) 632384
*Well-appointed stone-built Edwardian
house with full private facilities and
colour TV in all bedrooms. Quiet road
in country setting, half a mile south of
market square. Excellent choice of
eating places nearby. Non-smokers only
please.*
Bedrooms: 2 twin
Bathrooms: 2 private

**Bed & breakfast**

| per night: | £min | £max |
|---|---|---|
| Single | 18.50 | 20.50 |
| Double | 30.00 | 33.00 |

Evening meal 1900 (last orders 1945)
Parking for 2

🛇📞🖂▭🛆🐾ⓤⓛ🅰ⓢ📺🖾,🛆
✗🏠

## Fox & Hounds Hotel

**♛♛♛**

Stagshaw Bank, Corbridge NE45 5QW
☎ Hexham (01434) 633024
Fax (01434) 633024

*400-year-old coaching inn with a 70-seat
conservatory restaurant. On the A68,
just north of historic Corbridge and
next to Hadrian's Wall. Owners live on
premises.*
Bedrooms: 1 single, 4 double, 4 twin,
1 triple
Bathrooms: 10 private

**Bed & breakfast**

| per night: | £min | £max |
|---|---|---|
| Single | 26.50 | 26.50 |
| Double | 38.00 | 38.00 |

---

**Half board**

| per person: | £min | £max |
|---|---|---|
| Weekly | 175.00 | 175.00 |

Lunch available
Evening meal 1700 (last orders 2130)
Parking for 40
Cards accepted: Visa

🛇🗻🚲🛆🅰ⓢ🐾🕙🖾,🛆🔍🎵▸
❄SP🏠Ⓣ

## The Hayes Guest House ⋀

🚲

Newcastle Road, Corbridge NE45 5LP
☎ Hexham (01434) 632010
*Large house set amidst 7.5 acres of
woodland and gardens with delightful
views. Self-catering flat, caravan and
cottages also available. Ample car
parking.*
Bedrooms: 2 single, 1 double, 2 twin,
1 triple
Bathrooms: 2 public, 2 private
showers

**Bed & breakfast**

| per night: | £min | £max |
|---|---|---|
| Single | 15.50 | 15.50 |
| Double | 31.00 | 31.00 |

Parking for 14
Open January-November

🛇ⓤⓛ🅰ⓢ🐾📺⏸🖾,🛆🅄▸❄DAP SP
🏠Ⓣ

## COTHERSTONE

Durham
Map ref 5B3

## Glendale

**♛♛  HIGHLY COMMENDED**

Cotherstone, Barnard Castle, County
Durham DL12 9UH
☎ Teesdale (01833) 650384
*Dormer bungalow with beautiful
gardens and large pond, in quiet, rural
surroundings. Take Briscoe road from
Cotherstone for 200 yards.*
Bedrooms: 3 double
Bathrooms: 3 private, 1 public

**Bed & breakfast**

| per night: | £min | £max |
|---|---|---|
| Single | 16.00 | 22.00 |
| Double | 28.00 | 32.00 |

Parking for 4

🛇10🗻🖂▭🛆ⓤⓛ🅰✂️🐾🖾,🛆🅄▸
❄🛒SP

## Nether Hoyles ⋀

**Listed**

Marwood View, Cotherstone, Barnard
Castle, County Durham DL12 9PP
☎ Teesdale (01833) 650832
*Comfortable, friendly home in village, 4
miles from Barnard Castle on B6277.
Ideal base for walking or touring.
Packed lunches provided, diets catered
for.*
Bedrooms: 1 double, 1 triple
Bathrooms: 1 public

*Continued* ▶

## COTHERSTONE

*Continued*

**Bed & breakfast**

| per night: | £min | £max |
|---|---|---|
| Single | 14.00 | 14.00 |
| Double | 28.00 | 28.00 |

**Half board**

| per person: | £min | £max |
|---|---|---|
| Daily | 21.00 | 21.00 |

Evening meal 1800 (last orders 2100)
Open January-November

🛇🍴🖵♿ⓦ🅸ⓢ🍴▥✿🗙🐾🅂🅿🆃

## CRASTER

Northumberland
Map ref 5C1

Small fishing village with a fine
northward view of Dunstanburgh
Castle. Fishing cobles in the tiny
harbour, stone cottages at the
water's edge and a kippering shed
where Craster's famous delicacy is
produced give the village its
unspoilt charm.

### Cottage Inn ᴀ
🏆🏆🏆 COMMENDED

Dunstan Village, Craster, Alnwick
NE66 3ZS
☎ Embleton (01665) 576658
*Family-run inn half a mile from the sea.
All rooms are ground floor and have
garden view. Noted for food. Special
breaks available.*
Bedrooms: 2 double, 8 twin
Bathrooms: 10 private

**Bed & breakfast**

| per night: | £min | £max |
|---|---|---|
| Single | 29.50 | 35.00 |
| Double | 50.00 | 57.00 |

**Half board**

| per person: | £min | £max |
|---|---|---|
| Daily | 40.00 | 48.00 |
| Weekly | 245.00 | 320.00 |

Lunch available
Evening meal 1800 (last orders 2130)
Parking for 30
Cards accepted: Access, Visa

🛇🍴\☎🖵♿🅸ⓢ🍴▥🚗🅿🗙✿🛇🅂🅿

### Stonecroft
Listed COMMENDED

Dunstan, Craster, Alnwick NE66 3SZ
☎ Alnwick (01665) 576433
*Warm welcome awaits at large new
bungalow, tastefully decorated. In
peaceful rural setting, only minutes
from unspoilt coastline. Central for
touring, walking, historic attractions.
Craster half a mile.*
Bedrooms: 2 double
Bathrooms: 1 private, 1 public

**Bed & breakfast**

| per night: | £min | £max |
|---|---|---|
| Double | 27.00 | 33.00 |

Parking for 4
Open March-October

🛇🍴🖵♿ⓦ🅸ⓢ🍴▥✿🗙🐾

## CROOKHAM

Northumberland
Map ref 5B1

Pretty hamlet taking its name from
the winding course of the River Till
which flows in the shape of a
shepherd's crook. Three castles -
Etal, Duddo and Ford - can be
seen, and nearby the restored
Heatherslaw Mill is of great
interest.

### The Coach House ᴀ
🏆🏆🏆 HIGHLY COMMENDED

Crookham, Cornhill-on-Tweed
TD12 4TD
☎ (01890) 820293 & 820373
*Spacious rooms, arranged around a
courtyard, in rolling country near the
Scottish border. Home-cooked, quality
fresh food. Rooms specially equipped
for disabled guests.*
Wheelchair access category 1 ♿
Bedrooms: 2 single, 2 double, 5 twin
Bathrooms: 7 private, 2 public

**Bed & breakfast**

| per night: | £min | £max |
|---|---|---|
| Single | 17.00 | 31.00 |
| Double | 42.00 | 62.00 |

**Half board**

| per person: | £min | £max |
|---|---|---|
| Daily | 31.50 | 45.50 |
| Weekly | 220.50 | 318.50 |

Evening meal 1930 (last orders 1930)
Parking for 12
Open March-November
Cards accepted: Access, Visa

🛇🍴♿🅸ⓢ🅼📺▥🚗🗙✿🐾🛏

## DURHAM

Durham
Map ref 5C2

Ancient city with its Norman castle
and cathedral set on a bluff high
over the Wear. A market and
university town and regional
centre, spreading beyond the
market-place on both banks of the
river.
*Tourist Information Centre*
☎ *(0191) 384 3720*

### Bay Horse Inn ᴀ
🏆🏆🏆 COMMENDED

Brandon Village, Durham, County
Durham DH7 8ST
☎ (0191) 378 0498
*Ten stone-built chalets 3 miles from
Durham city centre. All have shower,
toilet, TV, tea and coffee facilities and
telephone. Ample car parking.*

Bedrooms: 3 double, 6 twin, 1 family
room
Bathrooms: 10 private

**Bed & breakfast**

| per night: | £min | £max |
|---|---|---|
| Single | 28.00 | 28.00 |
| Double | 37.00 | 37.00 |

Lunch available
Evening meal 1900 (last orders 2200)
Parking for 25
Cards accepted: Access, Visa

🛇🍴🖵\🖵♿🅸🗙🅼▥🚗▸✿🐾🆃

### Bees Cottage Guest House ᴀ
🏆🏆

Bridge Street, Durham, County
Durham DH1 4RT
☎ (0191) 384 5775
*Durham's oldest cottage. In city centre,
close to rail and bus stations. All rooms
en-suite with colour TV and hospitality
tray. Private parking.*
Bedrooms: 1 double, 2 twin, 1 triple
Bathrooms: 4 private

**Bed & breakfast**

| per night: | £min | £max |
|---|---|---|
| Single | 30.00 | 30.00 |
| Double | 42.00 | 42.00 |

Parking for 4

🛇🖵♿ⓦ🅸ⓢ🍴▥🚗🗙🐾🛏

### Castledene ᴀ
Listed COMMENDED

37 Nevilledale Terrace, Durham,
County Durham DH1 4QG
☎ (0191) 384 8386
*Edwardian end-of-terrace house half a
mile west of the market place. Within
walking distance of the riverside,
cathedral and castle.*
Bedrooms: 1 single, 2 twin
Bathrooms: 1 public

**Bed & breakfast**

| per night: | £min | £max |
|---|---|---|
| Single | 17.00 | |
| Double | | 34.00 |

Parking for 6

🛇7♿ⓦ🅸🅼📺▥🚗🐾

### Crakemarsh ᴀ
Listed HIGHLY COMMENDED

Mill Lane, Plawsworth Gate, Chester-
Le-Street, County Durham DH2 3LG
☎ (0191) 371 2464
*Comfortable residence with country
views. 10 minutes from Beamish
Museum, 2.5 miles Durham, 30 yards to
A167. Durham to Chester-le-Street,
Leamside/Finchale Priory turning at
Plawsworth Gate, first house on left.
Evening meals on request. Strictly no
smoking.*
Bedrooms: 1 double, 1 triple
Bathrooms: 1 public

**Bed & breakfast**

| per night: | £min | £max |
|---|---|---|
| Single | 23.00 | 25.00 |
| Double | 36.00 | |

Evening meal 1800 (last orders 1900)
Parking for 4

## Lothlorien

COMMENDED

Front Street, Witton Gilbert, Durham,
County Durham DH7 6SY
☎ (0191) 371 0067
*Period country cottage only 5 minutes
by car from Durham City centre and on
a direct route to Hadrian's Wall. A good
centre for touring.*
Bedrooms: 1 single, 1 double, 1 twin
Bathrooms: 2 public

| Bed & breakfast per night: | £min | £max |
| --- | --- | --- |
| Single | 17.00 | 17.00 |
| Double | 34.00 | 34.00 |

Parking for 3

## Trevelyan College ⋒

Elvet Hill Road, Durham, County
Durham DH1 3LN
☎ (0191) 374 3765 & 374 3768
Fax (0191) 374 3789
*Set in parkland within easy walking
distance of Durham City. Comfortable
Cloister Bar, TV lounges, ample
parking. Standard and en-suite rooms
available.*
Bedrooms: 253 single, 8 double,
27 twin
Bathrooms: 58 private, 47 public

| Bed & breakfast per night: | £min | £max |
| --- | --- | --- |
| Single | 17.50 | 26.90 |
| Double | 32.00 | 49.50 |

| Half board per person: | £min | £max |
| --- | --- | --- |
| Daily | 26.00 | 35.40 |

Lunch available
Evening meal 1830 (last orders 1930)
Parking for 100
Open March April, June September,
December

EMBLETON

Northumberland
Map ref 5C1

Coastal village beside a golf-
course spread along the edge of
Embleton Bay. The old church was
extensively restored in the 19th C.
The vicarage incorporates a
medieval pele tower.

## Doxford Farmhouse ⋒

COMMENDED

Chathill NE67 5DY
☎ Charlton Mires (01665) 579235

*400-acre mixed farm. Listed Georgian
farmhouse set in wooded grounds.
Pollution-free beaches and moorland are
within easy reach. Lake and woodland
nature trail. Home cooking and home-
made bread.*
Bedrooms: 1 double, 1 twin, 1 triple,
1 family room
Bathrooms: 1 private, 1 public

| Bed & breakfast per night: | £min | £max |
| --- | --- | --- |
| Single | 16.00 | 22.00 |
| Double | 32.00 | 36.00 |

| Half board per person: | £min | £max |
| --- | --- | --- |
| Daily | 24.00 | 28.00 |
| Weekly | 150.00 | 165.00 |

Evening meal 1830 (last orders 1400)
Parking for 8
Cards accepted: Visa

## FALSTONE

Northumberland
Map ref 5B2

Remote village on the edge of
Kielder Forest where it spreads
beneath the heathery slopes of the
south-west Cheviots along the
valley of the North Tyne. Just 1
mile west lies Kielder Water, a
vast man-made lake which adds
boating and fishing to forest
recreations.

## Blackcock Inn ⋒

COMMENDED

Falstone, Hexham NE48 1AA
☎ Hexham (01434) 240200
Fax (01434) 240036

*Traditional old country village inn close
to Kielder Water, offering cask ale, good
food and comfortable accommodation.
Non-smokers 10% discount.*
Bedrooms: 2 single, 2 double
Bathrooms: 3 private, 1 public

| Bed & breakfast per night: | £min | £max |
| --- | --- | --- |
| Single | 20.00 | 25.00 |
| Double | | 45.00 |

Lunch available
Evening meal 1900 (last orders 2100)
Parking for 12

## The Pheasant Inn (by Kielder Water) ⋒

COMMENDED

Stannersburn, Falstone, Hexham
NE48 1DD
☎ Hexham (01434) 240382

*Historic inn with beamed ceilings and
open fires. Home cooking. Fishing,
riding and all water sports nearby.
Close to Kielder Water, Hadrian's Wall
and the Scottish border.*
Bedrooms: 4 double, 3 twin, 1 family
room
Bathrooms: 8 private

| Bed & breakfast per night: | £min | £max |
| --- | --- | --- |
| Single | 25.00 | 35.00 |
| Double | 48.00 | 54.00 |

| Half board per person: | £min | £max |
| --- | --- | --- |
| Daily | 37.00 | 48.00 |

Lunch available
Evening meal 1900 (last orders 2100)
Parking for 30

## FOREST-IN-TEESDALE

Durham
Map ref 5B2

An area in Upper Teesdale of
widely dispersed farmsteads set in
wild but beautiful scenery with
High Force Waterfall and Cauldron
Snout. Once the hunting park of
the Earls of Darlington.

## Langdon Beck Hotel

Listed

Forest-in-Teesdale, Barnard Castle,
County Durham DL12 0XP
☎ Teesdale (01833) 22267
*A pleasant inn in the magnificent area
of Upper Teesdale where a friendly
welcome and home cooking are
assured. Ideal for walkers and nature
lovers.*
Bedrooms: 3 single, 1 double, 1 twin,
1 triple
Bathrooms: 2 private, 2 public

| Bed & breakfast per night: | £min | £max |
| --- | --- | --- |
| Single | 19.00 | 22.00 |
| Double | 38.00 | 44.00 |

Continued ▶

## FOREST-IN-TEESDALE

*Continued*

**Half board**

| per person: | £min | £max |
|---|---|---|
| Daily | 26.00 | 29.00 |
| Weekly | 176.00 | 197.00 |

Lunch available
Evening meal 1830 (last orders 1830)
Parking for 15
Open January-November
🛏 🖐 Ⓢ 💂 📺 🎮 ❄ 🚲

## HALLINGTON

Northumberland
Map ref 5B2

### Cuan Dor Cottage ⚇

**HIGHLY COMMENDED**

Hallington, Newcastle upon Tyne
NE19 2LW
☎ Hexham (01434) 672412
*Converted 19th C farm building. En-suite accommodation, log fires, traditional home cooking. 11 miles Hexham, 3.5 miles off A68.*
Bedrooms: 1 double, 1 twin
Bathrooms: 2 private

**Bed & breakfast**

| per night: | £min | £max |
|---|---|---|
| Double | 36.00 | 42.00 |

**Half board**

| per person: | £min | £max |
|---|---|---|
| Daily | 25.00 | 28.00 |
| Weekly | 150.00 | 170.00 |

Lunch available
Evening meal from 1950
Parking for 4
🛏 🖐 🖳 🖐 🔫 � 🛉 ✠ 💂 📺 🎮 ⏚
❄ ✗ 🚲 🎿 SP

## HALTWHISTLE

Northumberland
Map ref 5B2

Small market town with interesting
12th C church, old inns and
blacksmith's smithy. North of the
town are several important sites
and interpretation centres of
Hadrian's Wall. Ideal centre for
archaeology, outdoor activity or
touring holidays.
*Tourist Information Centre*
☎ *(01434) 322002*

### Broomshaw Hill Farm ⚇

**HIGHLY COMMENDED**

Willia Road, Haltwhistle NE49 9NP
☎ Hexham (01434) 320866
*5-acre livestock farm. Attractive modernised 18th C stone-built farmhouse. On conjunction of bridleway and footpath, both leading to Hadrian's Wall 1 mile away.*
Bedrooms: 1 twin, 1 triple
Bathrooms: 1 public

**Bed & breakfast**

| per night: | £min | £max |
|---|---|---|
| Double | 32.00 | 34.00 |

**Half board**

| per person: | £min | £max |
|---|---|---|
| Weekly | 160.00 | 175.00 |

Evening meal 1830 (last orders 0900)
Parking for 8
Open February-October
🛏 🖳 🖐 🔫 ⓤ 🛉 ⚓ 📺 🎮 ⏚ 🚪 U 🕯 ❄ 🚲 SP

### Hall Meadows ⚇

**COMMENDED**

Main Street, Haltwhistle NE49 0AZ
☎ (01434) 321021
*Built in 1888, a large family house with pleasant garden in the centre of Haltwhistle. Ideally placed for Hadrian's Wall.*
Bedrooms: 1 single, 1 double, 1 twin
Bathrooms: 1 public

**Bed & breakfast**

| per night: | £min | £max |
|---|---|---|
| Single | 16.00 | 16.00 |
| Double | 30.00 | 30.00 |

Parking for 3
🛏 🖳 🖐 🔫 💂 📺 🎮 ⏚ 🚪 ❄ 🚲

### Oaky Knowe Farm ⚇

**Listed** **COMMENDED**

Haltwhistle NE49 0NB
☎ Hexham (01434) 320648
*300-acre livestock farm. Overlooking the Tyne Valley, within walking distance of Haltwhistle and the Roman Wall, this comfortable farmhouse offers friendly family holidays.*
Bedrooms: 1 twin, 2 triple
Bathrooms: 1 public

**Bed & breakfast**

| per night: | £min | £max |
|---|---|---|
| Single | 16.00 | 16.00 |
| Double | 28.00 | 30.00 |

**Half board**

| per person: | £min | £max |
|---|---|---|
| Daily | 21.00 | 23.00 |
| Weekly | 140.00 | 155.00 |

Evening meal 1700 (last orders 1530)
Parking for 8
🛏 🖳 🖐 🖳 🔫 💂 📺 🎮 ⏚ 🚪 🖉 ❄ 🚲
OAP SP

## HAMSTERLEY

Durham
Map ref 5B2

Small village near Bedburn Beck,
at the edge of Durham's Pennines.
Just westward lies moorland
country of Hamsterley Common
and the beautiful Hamsterley
Forest with picnic areas and
nature trails.

### Dryderdale Hall ⚇

**⚇⚇⚇**

Hamsterley, County Durham
DL13 3NR
☎ Bishop Auckland (01388) 488494

*Large Victorian country house, set in 19 acres of parkland with stream and ponds, situated near Hamsterley Forest.*
Bedrooms: 1 double, 2 twin
Bathrooms: 3 private

**Bed & breakfast**

| per night: | £min | £max |
|---|---|---|
| Double | 40.00 | 45.00 |

Parking for 6
🛏 🖐 🖳 💂 📺 🎮 ❄ ✗ 🚲 🎏

## HAMSTERLEY FOREST

Durham

*See under Barnard Castle, Bishop Auckland, Tow Law*

## HAYDON BRIDGE

Northumberland
Map ref 5B2

Small town on the banks of the
South Tyne with an ancient
church, built of stone from sites
along the Roman Wall just north.
Ideally situated for exploring
Hadrian's Wall and the Border
country.

### Sewing Shields Farm ⚇

**Listed** **COMMENDED**

Hadrian's Wall, Haydon Bridge,
Hexham NE47 6NW
☎ Hexham (01434) 684418
*2000-acre hill farm. 17th C listed farmhouse, situated on top of Hadrian's Wall, 1 mile east of Housesteads, 5 miles north of Haydon Bridge. Breathtaking views.*
Bedrooms: 1 double, 1 twin, 1 family
room
Bathrooms: 2 public

**Bed & breakfast**

| per night: | £min | £max |
|---|---|---|
| Single | 15.00 | 15.00 |
| Double | 30.00 | 30.00 |

**Half board**

| per person: | £min | £max |
|---|---|---|
| Daily | 22.50 | 22.50 |
| Weekly | 150.00 | 150.00 |

Evening meal from 1800
Parking for 6
🛏 🖾 🖐 🔫 🖳 💂 Ⓢ ✂ 💂 📺 🎮 ⏚ 🚪 U ❄
🚲 OAP 🎿 SP 🎏

## HEIGHINGTON

Durham
Map ref 5C3

### Eldon House ⚇

**HIGHLY COMMENDED**

East Green, Heighington, Darlington,
County Durham DL5 6PP
☎ Aycliffe (01325) 312270
*17th C manor house with large garden overlooking the village green. Large, comfortable, well-appointed rooms. Ample parking. Tennis court. Coal/wood fire in sitting room.*
Bedrooms: 3 twin

Bathrooms: 3 private, 2 public

**Bed & breakfast**

| per night: | £min | £max |
|---|---|---|
| Single | 25.00 | 30.00 |
| Double | 35.00 | 40.00 |

Parking for 6

## HESLEDEN

Durham
Map ref 5C2

Small village south of the New Town of Peterlee near the County Durham coast.

## Golden Calf Hotel

Front Street, Hesleden, Hartlepool, Cleveland TS27 4PH
☎ Wellfield (01429) 836493
*Family-run inn with friendly service. Only 1 mile from A19 on Castle Eden road. 15 minutes to Teesside, 35 minutes to Newcastle, 12 miles to A1.*
Bedrooms: 2 double, 2 triple
Bathrooms: 1 public

**Bed & breakfast**

| per night: | £min | £max |
|---|---|---|
| Single | | 12.50 |
| Double | | 25.00 |

Lunch available
Evening meal 1900 (last orders 2200)
Parking for 20

## HEXHAM

Northumberland
Map ref 5B2

Old coaching and market town near Hadrian's Wall. Since pre-Norman times a weekly market has been held in the centre with its market-place and abbey park, and the richly-furnished 12th C abbey church has a superb Anglo-Saxon crypt.
*Tourist Information Centre*
☎ *(01434) 605225*

## Anick Grange

COMMENDED

Hexham NE46 4LP
☎ (01434) 603807
*363-acre mixed farm. 17th C farmhouse 1 mile from Hexham. Superb open views. Home cooking and warm welcome.*
Bedrooms: 1 single, 1 twin, 1 triple
Bathrooms: 1 private, 1 public

**Bed & breakfast**

| per night: | £min | £max |
|---|---|---|
| Single | 15.00 | 17.00 |
| Double | 30.00 | 34.00 |

Parking for 4
Open April-September

## "Aydon"

1 Osborne Avenue, Hexham NE46 3JP
☎ (01434) 602915
*Spacious, terraced Edwardian family home in quiet situation, offering a warm and friendly welcome. Tastefully renovated and furnished. 10 minutes' walk from town centre.*
Bedrooms: 1 double, 1 triple
Bathrooms: 1 public

**Bed & breakfast**

| per night: | £min | £max |
|---|---|---|
| Double | 30.00 | |

**Half board**

| per person: | £min | £max |
|---|---|---|
| Daily | 24.00 | |

Evening meal 1830 (last orders 1830)
Parking for 1

## Dene House ⋀

HIGHLY COMMENDED

Juniper, Hexham NE46 1SJ
☎ (01434) 673413

*Stone farmhouse with beamed ceilings, log fires and flowers everywhere. Very quietly situated in 9 acres of farmland, 4 miles south of Hexham.*
Bedrooms: 1 single, 1 double, 1 twin
Bathrooms: 1 private, 1 public

**Bed & breakfast**

| per night: | £min | £max |
|---|---|---|
| Single | 15.00 | 17.50 |
| Double | 30.00 | 35.00 |

**Half board**

| per person: | £min | £max |
|---|---|---|
| Daily | 25.00 | 27.50 |
| Weekly | 160.00 | 180.00 |

Evening meal 1800 (last orders 1900)
Parking for 3

## Laburnum House ⋀

HIGHLY COMMENDED

23 Leazes Crescent, Hexham NE46 3JZ
☎ (01434) 601828
*Very comfortable, spacious, Victorian family home 10-12 minutes' walk from town centre. Good home cooking. An ideal base for touring Northumbria.*
Bedrooms: 2 single, 1 double, 1 twin
Bathrooms: 1 public

**Bed & breakfast**

| per night: | £min | £max |
|---|---|---|
| Single | 16.00 | 18.00 |
| Double | 32.00 | 36.00 |

**Half board**

| per person: | £min | £max |
|---|---|---|
| Daily | 26.00 | 28.00 |
| Weekly | 170.00 | 183.00 |

Evening meal 1900 (last orders 1900)

## Rye Hill Farm ⋀

COMMENDED

Slaley, Hexham NE47 0AH
☎ (01434) 673259
Fax (01434) 673259

*30-acre livestock farm. Warm and comfortable barn conversion, 5 miles south of Hexham, where you can enjoy the peace of rural life. Noted for the food and the friendly atmosphere.*
Bedrooms: 2 double, 2 twin, 2 triple
Bathrooms: 6 private, 1 public

**Bed & breakfast**

| per night: | £min | £max |
|---|---|---|
| Single | 20.00 | 20.00 |
| Double | 36.00 | 36.00 |

**Half board**

| per person: | £min | £max |
|---|---|---|
| Daily | 28.00 | 30.00 |
| Weekly | 183.00 | 196.00 |

Evening meal 1930 (last orders 1700)
Parking for 6

## Stotsfold Hall ⋀

Steel, Hexham NE47 0HP
☎ (01434) 673270
*Beautiful house surrounded by 15 acres of gardens and woodland with streams and flowers. 6 miles south of Hexham.*
Bedrooms: 2 single, 1 double, 1 twin
Bathrooms: 3 public

**Bed & breakfast**

| per night: | £min | £max |
|---|---|---|
| Single | 17.50 | 17.50 |
| Double | 35.00 | 35.00 |

Parking for 6

Individual proprietors have supplied all details of accommodation. Although we do check for accuracy, we advise you to confirm the information at the time of booking.

## HOLY ISLAND

Northumberland
Map ref 5B1

Still an idyllic retreat, tiny island and fishing village and cradle of northern Christianity. It is approached from the mainland at low water by a causeway. The clifftop castle (National Trust) was restored by Sir Edwin Lutyens.

### Britannia
♛♛

Holy Island, Berwick-upon-Tweed TD15 2RX
☎ Berwick-upon-Tweed (01289) 89218
*Comfortable, friendly bed and breakfast in centre of Holy Island. Hot and cold water, tea-making facilities in all rooms. TV lounge. En-suite available.*
Bedrooms: 1 double, 1 twin, 1 triple
Bathrooms: 1 private, 1 public

**Bed & breakfast**

| per night: | £min | £max |
| --- | --- | --- |
| Double | 27.00 | 64.00 |

Parking for 4
Open March-November
🛇♨♿🍴♿📺🛏🔲🚗🏞🗙🚿

### Crown & Anchor Hotel ⚠
♛♛

Fenkle Street, Holy Island, Berwick-upon-Tweed TD15 2RX
☎ Berwick-upon-Tweed (01289) 89215
*Old-fashioned inn with public bar, no-smoking lounge bar and dining room. Bedrooms en-suite and centrally heated. Beautiful views and quietly situated.*
Bedrooms: 2 double, 1 twin
Bathrooms: 3 private, 1 public

**Bed & breakfast**

| per night: | £min | £max |
| --- | --- | --- |
| Single | 18.00 | 25.00 |
| Double | 30.00 | 40.00 |

Lunch available
Parking for 5
🔲♨♿📺🚗🗙🚿

### North View ⚠
♛♛♛ COMMENDED

Marygate, Holy Island, Berwick-upon-Tweed TD15 2SD
☎ Berwick-upon-Tweed (01289) 89222
*400-year-old listed building on historic and beautiful island. Ideally situated for visiting many of Northumberland's tourist attractions.*
Bedrooms: 2 double, 1 twin
Bathrooms: 3 private

**Bed & breakfast**

| per night: | £min | £max |
| --- | --- | --- |
| Single | 20.00 | 26.00 |
| Double | 40.00 | 42.00 |

**Half board**

| per person: | £min | £max |
| --- | --- | --- |
| Daily | 29.00 | 37.00 |

Lunch available
Evening meal 1900 (last orders 2100)
Parking for 6
🔲🖵♨♿🍴♿🅂🗙🛏🔲🚗🏵🗙🚗🚿 SP ⌂

## INGOE

Tyne and Wear
Map ref 5B2

### The Courtyard ⚠
Listed | HIGHLY COMMENDED

Wallridge Farm, Wallridge, Ingoe, Northumberland NE20 0SX
☎ Otterburn (01830) 30326
*Built around a courtyard garden, a conversion from old cow byres. Furnished with antiques. Private sitting-room for guests.*
Bedrooms: 1 double, 1 twin
Bathrooms: 1 public

**Bed & breakfast**

| per night: | £min | £max |
| --- | --- | --- |
| Single | 17.50 | 25.00 |
| Double | 35.00 | 50.00 |

**Half board**

| per person: | £min | £max |
| --- | --- | --- |
| Daily | 25.00 | 35.00 |
| Weekly | 150.00 | 225.00 |

Evening meal 1830 (last orders 2030)
Parking for 10
🛇5♨♿🍴♿📺🅂🗙🛏📺🔲🚗🎿♿⌖♨♿🗙🚗⌂

## KIELDER

Northumberland
Map ref 5B1

Wide area of forest established earlier this century on moors edging the North Tyne. Kielder village is overlooked by Kielder Castle, a former hunting lodge now a visitor centre. Forest and lake provide a wide variety of recreations which include boating, fishing and camping.

### Gowanburn
Listed

Kielder, Hexham NE48 1HL
☎ Hexham (01434) 250254
*Peacefully situated old farmhouse on the edge of Kielder Water within the forest, overlooking the beautiful reservoir.*
Bedrooms: 1 double, 1 twin, 1 triple
Bathrooms: 1 public

**Bed & breakfast**

| per night: | £min | £max |
| --- | --- | --- |
| Single | 15.00 | 15.00 |
| Double | 30.00 | 30.00 |

**Half board**

| per person: | £min | £max |
| --- | --- | --- |
| Daily | 23.00 | 23.00 |
| Weekly | 161.00 | |

Evening meal 1800 (last orders 1600)
Parking for 6
Open April-November
🛇⚡♿🍴♿📺🔲🚗🗙🚗🚿

## KIELDER FOREST

Northumberland

*See under Bellingham, Falstone*

## LESBURY

Northumberland
Map ref 5C1

### Dukes Ryde ⚠

Longhoughton Road, Lesbury, Alnwick NE66 3AT
☎ Alnwick (01665) 830855
*Delightful and imposing early 20th C house set in secluded gardens, on the outskirts of Lesbury village, near beaches and golf-courses.*
Bedrooms: 2 double, 1 twin
Bathrooms: 3 private

**Bed & breakfast**

| per night: | £min | £max |
| --- | --- | --- |
| Single | 20.00 | 25.00 |
| Double | 37.00 | 40.00 |

Parking for 6
🔲🖵♨♿🍴♿🅂🗙🛏🔲🚗🏵🗙🚗 SP

## MIDDLESBROUGH

Cleveland
Map ref 5C3

Boom-town of the mid 19th C, today's Teesside industrial and conference town has a modern shopping complex and predominantly modern buildings. An engineering miracle of the early 20th C is the Transporter Bridge which replaced an old ferry.
*Tourist Information Centre*
☎ (01642) 243425

### Maltby Farm ⚠
♛ APPROVED

Maltby, Middlesbrough TS8 0BP
☎ (01642) 590121
*187-acre mixed farm. Traditional Yorkshire farmhouse, over 200 years old, looking south on to the Cleveland Hills.*
Bedrooms: 1 single, 1 twin, 1 triple
Bathrooms: 1 public

**Bed & breakfast**

| per night: | £min | £max |
| --- | --- | --- |
| Single | 15.00 | 16.00 |
| Double | 30.00 | 32.00 |

**Half board**

| per person: | £min | £max |
| --- | --- | --- |
| Daily | 21.00 | 22.00 |
| Weekly | 132.00 | 135.00 |

Evening meal 1800 (last orders 2000)
Parking for 6
Open April-October
🛇♿🅂🅂🛏📺🔲🚗🗙🚗

---

**We advise you to confirm your booking in writing.**

## MIDDLETON-IN-TEESDALE

Durham
Map ref 5B3

Small stone town of hillside terraces overlooking the river, developed by the London Lead Company in the 18th C. Five miles up-river is the spectacular 70-ft waterfall, High Force.

### Bowbank House
⚜⚜ HIGHLY COMMENDED

Lunedale, Middleton-in-Teesdale, Barnard Castle, County Durham
DL12 0NJ
☎ (01833) 640637

*Bowbank was built at the turn of the 18th C. A typical Georgian property, with original stone roof, internal beams, coal fires and beautiful gardens.*
Bedrooms: 2 double, 1 twin
Bathrooms: 3 private, 3 public

**Bed & breakfast**

| per night: | £min | £max |
| --- | --- | --- |
| Single | 20.00 | 25.00 |
| Double | 30.00 | 35.00 |

Parking for 4
⛔🕿🍴❓⚘♿🔆🅿📺🖥️🖨️🅿✿
✕🐎🏠

### Brunswick House ♠
⚜⚜ COMMENDED

55 Market Place, Middleton-in-Teesdale, Barnard Castle, County Durham DL12 0QH
☎ Teesdale (01833) 640393

*18th C listed stone-built guesthouse retaining much character and many original features. Comfort, friendly service and home cooking are assured.*
Bedrooms: 2 double, 1 twin, 1 family room
Bathrooms: 4 private, 1 public

**Bed & breakfast**

| per night: | £min | £max |
| --- | --- | --- |
| Single | 20.00 | 28.00 |
| Double | | 40.00 |

**Half board**

| per person: | £min | £max |
| --- | --- | --- |
| Daily | 28.00 | 32.95 |
| Weekly | | 195.00 |

Lunch available
Evening meal 1930 (last orders 1900)
Parking for 5
⛔🕿🖵❓⚘♿🔆🅿🖥️🖨️🅿✿✕🐎❄
SP 🏠

### Wythes Hill Farm
📺

Lunedale, Middleton-in-Teesdale, Barnard Castle, County Durham
DL12 0NX
☎ Teesdale (01833) 640349
*550-acre mixed farm. Farmhouse with panoramic views, on the Pennine Way in lovely walking area. Farmhouse cooking. Peace and quiet, friendliness and comfort guaranteed.*
Bedrooms: 2 double, 1 twin
Bathrooms: 2 public

**Bed & breakfast**

| per night: | £min | £max |
| --- | --- | --- |
| Single | 15.00 | 16.00 |
| Double | 30.00 | 32.00 |

**Half board**

| per person: | £min | £max |
| --- | --- | --- |
| Daily | 23.00 | 24.00 |
| Weekly | 150.00 | 150.00 |

Evening meal 1800 (last orders 1830)
Parking for 3
Open April–October
🕿⚘♿UL ⚫🅂🅿📺🖥️🖨️🅿✿🐎 DAP

## NEWCASTLE UPON TYNE

Tyne and Wear
Map ref 5C2

Commercial and cultural centre of the North East, with a large indoor shopping centre, Quayside market, museums and theatres which offer an annual 6 week season by the Royal Shakespeare Company. Norman castle keep, medieval alleys, old Guildhall.
*Tourist Information Centre*
*☎ (0191) 261 0691 or 230 0030*

### Bywell
⚜⚜ COMMENDED

Sanderson House, 59 Sanderson Road, Jesmond, Newcastle upon Tyne
NE2 2DR
☎ (0191) 281 7615
*Large Victorian house with spacious bedrooms, located in quiet residential area close to city centre and all amenities. No smoking.*
Bedrooms: 1 double, 1 twin
Bathrooms: 1 private, 1 public

**Bed & breakfast**

| per night: | £min | £max |
| --- | --- | --- |
| Single | 18.00 | 20.00 |
| Double | 30.00 | 40.00 |

Parking for 1
⛔🖵⚘♿🅂🔆🖨️🅿✕🐎

---

**Please mention this guide when making a booking.**

---

### Grosvenor Hotel ♠
⚜⚜⚜ APPROVED

Grosvenor Road, Jesmond, Newcastle upon Tyne NE2 2RR
☎ (0191) 281 0543
Fax (0191) 281 9217
*Friendly hotel in quiet residential suburb, offering a wide range of facilities. Close to city centre.*
Bedrooms: 18 single, 9 double, 14 twin
Bathrooms: 33 private, 5 public

**Bed & breakfast**

| per night: | £min | £max |
| --- | --- | --- |
| Single | 25.00 | 40.00 |
| Double | 35.00 | 55.00 |

**Half board**

| per person: | £min | £max |
| --- | --- | --- |
| Daily | 30.00 | 60.00 |
| Weekly | 180.00 | 360.00 |

Lunch available
Evening meal 1830 (last orders 2100)
Parking for 30
Cards accepted: Access, Visa, Diners, Amex
⛔🏨📞🖵⚘♿🅂🅿📺⏰🖨️🅿
🕿2-120 DAP 🐎 SP T

### Whorlton Church Cottage
Stamfordham Road, Westerhope, Newcastle upon Tyne NE5 1NN
☎ (0191) 214 0473
*Secluded, 100-year-old stone cottage, set in beautiful landscaped gardens and surrounded by wonderful countryside and coast, yet only 3 miles from the city. Laura Ashley team designed the interior, retaining its charm.*
Bedrooms: 1 double, 1 twin
Bathrooms: 1 public

**Bed & breakfast**

| per night: | £min | £max |
| --- | --- | --- |
| Double | 33.00 | 35.00 |

Parking for 5
❄⚘♿UL 🅂🔆🖨️✿✕🐎

## NORHAM

Northumberland
Map ref 5B1

Border village on the salmon-rich Tweed, dominated by its dramatic castle ruin. Near Castle Street is the church, like the castle destroyed after the Battle of Flodden, but rebuilt. Norham Station Railway Museum is just outside the town.

### Dromore House ♠
Listed

12 Pedwell Way, Norham, Berwick-upon-Tweed TD15 2LD
☎ Berwick-upon-Tweed (01289) 382313
*Guesthouse in a small village on the River Tweed, between the Cheviot and Lammermuir Hills. Quiet beaches are within easy reach.*
Bedrooms: 1 double, 1 twin, 1 triple
Bathrooms: 2 private, 1 public
*Continued ►*

## NORHAM

*Continued*

**Bed & breakfast**

| per night: | £min | £max |
| --- | --- | --- |
| Single | 15.00 | 18.00 |
| Double | 30.00 | 36.00 |

**Half board**

| per person: | £min | £max |
| --- | --- | --- |
| Daily | 22.00 | 25.00 |
| Weekly | 134.00 | 189.00 |

Evening meal 1700 (last orders 1900)
Parking for 3

🛇♿🎿🖵♨️Ⓤ👤🖺🏍📺🖩💺🐾🏠

## OVINGTON

Northumberland
Map ref 5B2

Quiet village on the north bank of the River Tyne, linked to the adjacent village of Ovingham which has a 17th C packhorse bridge and was the birthplace of the famous artist and engraver Thomas Bewick.

### Southcroft

Listed **COMMENDED**

Ovington, Prudhoe NE42 6EE
☎ Prudhoe (01661) 832515
Fax (01661) 834312
*Comfortable, detached stone house in 4 acres, including three-quarters of an acre garden, enjoying open views across Tyne Valley. Just off A69 trunk road, midway between Newcastle upon Tyne and Hexham.*
Bedrooms: 1 single, 1 twin
Bathrooms: 1 public

**Bed & breakfast**

| per night: | £min | £max |
| --- | --- | --- |
| Single | 15.00 | 15.00 |
| Double | 30.00 | 30.00 |

Evening meal 1800 (last orders 1930)
Parking for 3

🛇10♿🖵♨️🏍Ⓤ👤📺🖩💺❄️✗🐾

## PLAWSWORTH

Durham
Map ref 5C2

### Lilac Cottage

Listed

Wheatley Well Lane, Plawsworth, Chester-Le-Street, County Durham DH2 3LD
☎ (0191) 371 2969
*Stone-built character Georgian cottage, located close to Durham and Chester-le-Street, to the east of the A167.*
Bedrooms: 1 twin
Bathrooms: 2 public

**Bed & breakfast**

| per night: | £min | £max |
| --- | --- | --- |
| Single | 15.00 | 15.00 |
| Double | 25.00 | 27.50 |

Parking for 4
Open March-November

🖵🖵♨️Ⓤ🎿🏍📺🖩💺❄️✗🐾🏠

## REDCAR

Cleveland
Map ref 5C3

Lively holiday resort near Teesside with broad sandy beaches, a fine racecourse, a large indoor funfair at Coatham and other seaside amusements. Britain's oldest existing lifeboat can be seen at the Zetland Museum.

### Waterside House ⋀

♛

35 Newcomen Terrace, Redcar TS10 1DB
☎ (01642) 481062
*Large terraced property overlooking the sea, close to town centre and leisure centre. Warm, friendly atmosphere with true Yorkshire hospitality.*
Bedrooms: 2 single, 3 triple, 1 family room
Bathrooms: 2 public

**Bed & breakfast**

| per night: | £min | £max |
| --- | --- | --- |
| Single | 14.00 | 16.00 |
| Double | 25.00 | 27.00 |

**Half board**

| per person: | £min | £max |
| --- | --- | --- |
| Daily | 19.50 | 22.50 |

Evening meal 1700 (last orders 1900)
🛇🖵♨️Ⓤ👤📺🖩💺🏠SP

## ROTHBURY

Northumberland
Map ref 5B1

Old market town on the River Coquet near the Simonside Hills. It makes an ideal centre for walking and fishing or for exploring this beautiful area from the coast to the Cheviots. Cragside House and Gardens (National Trust) are open to the public.

### Lorbottle West Steads

Listed

Thropton, Morpeth NE65 7JT
☎ Alnwick (01665) 574672
*310-acre mixed farm. Stone farmhouse with panoramic views of the Coquet Valley and Cheviot Hills. B6341 to Thropton, turn for Whittingham, turn at Lorbottle, first right.*
Bedrooms: 1 single, 1 double, 1 twin
Bathrooms: 1 public

**Bed & breakfast**

| per night: | £min | £max |
| --- | --- | --- |
| Single | 13.50 | 14.50 |
| Double | 28.00 | 31.00 |

Parking for 8
Open May-October

🛇🎿🖵♨️Ⓤ🅂🎿📺🖩💺🐾❄️🐾

### Thropton Demesne ⋀

👑👑 HIGHLY COMMENDED

Thropton, Morpeth NE65 7LT
☎ (01669) 20196
*24-acre mixed farm. Traditional farmhouse peacefully situated in the picturesque Coquet Valley. Spectacular views. Ideally placed for fishing, golf and walking.*
Bedrooms: 1 double, 1 twin, 1 triple
Bathrooms: 3 private

**Bed & breakfast**

| per night: | £min | £max |
| --- | --- | --- |
| Single | 18.00 | |
| Double | 36.00 | |

Parking for 6
🛇🖵♨️🏍Ⓤ👤🎿🖩💺🐾❄️🐾SP🏠

## ROWLANDS GILL

Tyne and Wear
Map ref 5C2

Adjacent to the Derwent Walk Country Park on the side of the River Derwent, opposite the National Trust Gibside Chapel.

### Chopwell Wood House ⋀

♛

Chopwell Woods, Rowlands Gill NE39 1LT
☎ (01207) 542765
*Large, attractive house in 600 acres of woodland in the Derwent Valley, within easy reach of Newcastle, Durham and Hexham. Near MetroCentre and Beamish Museum.*
Bedrooms: 1 double, 1 twin, 1 triple
Bathrooms: 1 public

**Bed & breakfast**

| per night: | £min | £max |
| --- | --- | --- |
| Single | 20.00 | |
| Double | 30.00 | 35.00 |

Parking for 6
🛇🖵🖵♨️🏍Ⓤ👤🎿📺🖩💺🐾Ⓤ❄️✗🐾

There are separate sections in this guide listing groups specialising in farm holidays and accommodation which is especially suitable for young people and organised groups.

## RYTON

Tyne and Wear
Map ref 5C2

On a wooded site above the Tyne,
Ryton has a 12th C church with a
Jacobean screen and good 19th C
oak carving. Small pit working,
notable for the spectacular 1826
Stargate Explosion, ceased in
1967. Easy access to the A1,
Hadrian's Wall and rural
Northumbria.

### Barmoor Old Manse ⋀

**Listed** **APPROVED**

The Old Manse, Barmoor, Ryton
NE40 3BD
☎ (0191) 413 2438
*Large stone Victorian house, built as
Manse for Congregational Church in
1862. Delightful garden. Near
MetroCentre, Roman Wall and Beamish
Museum.*
Bedrooms: 1 double, 2 twin
Bathrooms: 1 public

**Bed & breakfast**

| per night: | £min | £max |
| --- | --- | --- |
| Single | 16.00 | |
| Double | 32.00 | |

Parking for 2

## SALTBURN-BY-THE-SEA

Cleveland
Map ref 5C3

Set on fine cliffs just north of the
Cleveland Hills, a gracious
Victorian resort with later
developments and wide, firm
sands. A handsome Jacobean
mansion at Marske can be
reached along the sands.
*Tourist Information Centre
☎ (01287) 622422*

### Boulby Barns Farm

**Listed**

Easington, Loftus, Saltburn-by-the-Sea
TS13 4UT
☎ Guisborough (01287) 641306
*7-acre mixed farm. Traditional stone
farmhouse with accommodation on a
working smallholding in the national
park. Situated half a mile from A174,
close to Boulby Cliffs and the Cleveland
Way, with views of moors and sea.*
Bedrooms: 1 double, 2 twin
Bathrooms: 2 public

**Bed & breakfast**

| per night: | £min | £max |
| --- | --- | --- |
| Single | 16.50 | |
| Double | 33.00 | |

Parking for 8
Open April-November

## SEAHOUSES

Northumberland
Map ref 5C1

Small modern resort developed
around a 19th C herring port. Just
offshore, and reached by boat
from here, are the rocky Farne
Islands (National Trust) where
there is an important bird reserve.
The bird observatory occupies a
medieval pele tower.

### 'Leeholme' ⋀

**Listed** **COMMENDED**

93 Main Street, Seahouses NE68 7TS
☎ (01665) 720230
*A warm welcome awaits you at this
small homely bed and breakfast. 5
minutes' walk to Seahouses harbour
and shops. Hearty breakfast assured.*
Bedrooms: 1 double, 1 twin
Bathrooms: 1 public

**Bed & breakfast**

| per night: | £min | £max |
| --- | --- | --- |
| Single | 13.00 | |
| Double | 26.00 | |

Parking for 2
Open March-October

### Rowena

**Listed**

99 Main Street, Seahouses NE68 7TS
☎ (01665) 721309
*Comfortable bed and breakfast
accommodation, 5 minutes' walk from
the harbour where boats leave to visit
the Farne Islands.*
Bedrooms: 1 single, 1 double, 1 twin,
1 triple
Bathrooms: 1 private, 1 public

**Bed & breakfast**

| per night: | £min | £max |
| --- | --- | --- |
| Single | 14.50 | 14.50 |
| Double | 29.00 | 35.00 |

Parking for 3

### West Side Guest House

⚜

9 King Street, Seahouses NE68 7XN
☎ (01665) 720508
*Guesthouse in the village centre, within
walking distance of the harbour and
other facilities.*
Bedrooms: 1 single, 2 double, 1 twin
Bathrooms: 2 public

**Bed & breakfast**

| per night: | £min | £max |
| --- | --- | --- |
| Single | 15.00 | |
| Double | 28.00 | |

Parking for 8
Open April-October

## SLALEY

Northumberland
Map ref 5B2

Small hamlet, now a major golfing
venue, south of Corbridge near the
Derwent Reservoir.

### Rose and Crown Inn ⋀

⚜⚜⚜ **HIGHLY COMMENDED**

Main Street, Slaley, Hexham
NE47 0AA
☎ Hexham (01434) 673263
*Warm, friendly, family-run business
with good wholesome home cooking
and a la carte restaurant. All bedrooms
en-suite.*
Bedrooms: 1 single, 2 twin
Bathrooms: 3 private

**Bed & breakfast**

| per night: | £min | £max |
| --- | --- | --- |
| Single | 18.00 | 22.50 |
| Double | 36.00 | 45.00 |

**Half board**

| per person: | £min | £max |
| --- | --- | --- |
| Daily | 28.00 | 30.50 |

Lunch available
Evening meal 1830 (last orders 2200)
Parking for 32
Cards accepted: Access, Visa

## SPENNYMOOR

Durham
Map ref 5C2

Booming coal and iron town from
the 18th C until early in the
present century when traditional
industry gave way to lighter
manufacturing and trading estates
were built. On the moors south of
the town there are fine views of
the Wear Valley.

### Idsley House ⋀

⚜⚜ **COMMENDED**

4 Green Lane, Spennymoor, County
Durham DL16 6HD
☎ Bishop Auckland (01388) 814237
*Long-established Victorian guesthouse
on A167/A688 run by local family.
Ideal for Durham City. Suitable for
business or pleasure. Ample parking on
premises.*
Bedrooms: 1 single, 1 double, 2 twin,
1 triple
Bathrooms: 4 private, 1 public

**Bed & breakfast**

| per night: | £min | £max |
| --- | --- | --- |
| Single | 18.00 | 25.00 |
| Double | 33.00 | 35.00 |

Parking for 8

## STAINDROP

Durham
Map ref 5B3

### Gazebo House

ⓘⓘ HIGHLY COMMENDED

4 North Green, Staindrop, Darlington,
County Durham DL2 3JN
☎ Teesdale (01833) 660222
Fax (01833) 660222

*18th C house with listed gazebo
(illustrated) in garden. Adjacent Raby
Park and Castle. Ideal base for Lake
District and Yorkshire Dales.*
Bedrooms: 1 double, 1 twin
Bathrooms: 2 private

**Bed & breakfast**

| per night: | £min | £max |
|---|---|---|
| Single | 18.00 | |
| Double | 38.00 | |

**Half board**

| per person: | £min | £max |
|---|---|---|
| Daily | 30.00 | 31.00 |
| Weekly | 195.00 | 200.00 |

Evening meal 1900 (last orders 2200)
🛇📞🍴🖵☂🦮🛆🐾🚘⚹🎣🐾🏛

## STANLEY

Durham
Map ref 5C2

Small town on the site of a Roman
cattle camp. At the Beamish North
of England Open Air Museum
numerous set-pieces and displays
recreate industrial and social
conditions prevalent during the
area's past.

### Bushblades Farm

Listed

Harperley, Stanley, County Durham
DH9 9UA
☎ (01207) 232722
*60-acre livestock farm. Comfortable
Georgian farmhouse, in rural setting.
Within easy reach of Durham City,
Beamish Museum, A1M, MetroCentre
and Roman Wall.*
Bedrooms: 2 double, 1 twin
Bathrooms: 1 private, 1 public

**Bed & breakfast**

| per night: | £min | £max |
|---|---|---|
| Single | 20.00 | 25.00 |
| Double | 30.00 | 38.00 |

Parking for 6
🛇12🖵☂🦮⛛ℳ📺🛆✕🐾

## STEEL

Northumberland
Map ref 5B2

### Peth Head Cottage ⋀

ⓘⓘ HIGHLY COMMENDED

Juniper Village, Steel, Hexham
NE47 0LA
☎ Hexham (01434) 673286
Fax (01434) 673038

*Northumbrian stone cottage, situated in
quiet hamlet. Comfortable bedrooms and
attractive lounge for guests. Picturesque
rural location, ideal for walking
holidays.*
Bedrooms: 1 single, 1 double, 1 twin
Bathrooms: 3 private

**Bed & breakfast**

| per night: | £min | £max |
|---|---|---|
| Single | 17.50 | 20.00 |
| Double | 35.00 | 35.00 |

Parking for 5
🛇1🖵☂🦮⛛ℳ📺🛆🐾⚹🎣🐾📵

## STOCKTON-ON-TEES

Cleveland
Map ref 5C3

Teesside town first developed in
the 19th C around the ancient
market town with its broad main
street which has been the site of a
regular market since 1310. Green
Dragon Yard has a Georgian
theatre and there is a railway
heritage trail around the town.
*Tourist Information Centre*
☎ *(01642) 615080*

### Fulthorpe Farmhouse ⋀

ⓘⓘ COMMENDED

Wynyard Road, Thorpe Thewles,
Stockton-on-Tees TS21 3JQ
☎ Sedgefield (01740) 644627 &
644153
Fax (01740) 644627
*Traditional Georgian farmhouse set in
open farmland between picturesque
villages of Wolviston and Thorpe
Thewles, north of Stockton-on-Tees.
Panoramic views of Cleveland Hills.
Convenient for A19, A66 and A1.*
Bedrooms: 1 double, 1 twin, 1 triple
Bathrooms: 3 private

**Bed & breakfast**

| per night: | £min | £max |
|---|---|---|
| Single | 20.00 | 20.00 |
| Double | 40.00 | 40.00 |

**Half board**

| per person: | £min | £max |
|---|---|---|
| Daily | 30.00 | 30.00 |
| Weekly | 210.00 | 210.00 |

Evening meal 1900 (last orders 2030)
Parking for 10
🛇☂🦮ⓤⓛⓢ⛛ℳ📺🛆⚹✕🐾🏛

## SUNDERLAND

Tyne and Wear
Map ref 5C2

Ancient coal and shipbuilding port
on Wearside, with important
glassworks since the 17th C.
Today's industrial complex dates
from the 19th C. Modern building
includes the Civic Centre.
*Tourist Information Centre*
☎ *(0191) 565 0960 or (0191) 565
0990*

### Bed & Breakfast Stop ⋀

Listed COMMENDED

183 Newcastle Road, Fulwell,
Sunderland, Tyne & Wear SR5 1NR
☎ (0191) 548 2291
*Tudor-style semi-detached house on the
A1018 Newcastle to Sunderland road. 5
minutes to the railway station and 10
minutes to the seafront and city centre.*
Bedrooms: 1 single, 1 twin, 1 triple
Bathrooms: 1 public

**Bed & breakfast**

| per night: | £min | £max |
|---|---|---|
| Single | 15.00 | 17.00 |
| Double | 26.00 | 30.00 |

**Half board**

| per person: | £min | £max |
|---|---|---|
| Daily | 21.00 | 23.00 |
| Weekly | 123.00 | 140.00 |

Evening meal 1800 (last orders 1200)
Parking for 3
🛇3🖵☂🦮⛛ℳ📺🛆🐾ⓢⓟ

## TOW LAW

Durham
Map ref 5B2

### Butsfield Abbey Farm

ⓘ APPROVED

Satley, Tow Law, Bishop Auckland,
County Durham DL13 4JD
☎ Bishop Auckland (01388) 730509
*210-acre mixed farm. Farmhouse
cottage in a quiet rural setting. 1 mile
from A68 and 4 miles from Castleside.*
Bedrooms: 1 double
Bathrooms: 1 private, 1 public

**Bed & breakfast**

| per night: | £min | £max |
|---|---|---|
| Single | 15.00 | 15.00 |
| Double | 25.00 | 25.00 |

Parking for 4
🛇🦮🖵☂🦮⛛ⓤⓛℳ📺🛆🚶🐾🛇

## TYNEMOUTH

Tyne and Wear
Map ref 5C2

At the mouth of the Tyne, old Tyneside resort adjoining North Shields with its fish quay and market. The pier is overlooked by the gaunt ruins of a Benedictine priory and a castle. Splendid sands, amusement centre and park.

### Hope House ♨
**DE LUXE**

47 Percy Gardens, Tynemouth, North Shields NE30 4HH
☎ (0191) 257 1989
Fax (0191) 257 1989
*Double-fronted Victorian house with superb coastal views from most rooms. Tastefully furnished, with large bedrooms. Fine cuisine and quality wines.*
Bedrooms: 2 double, 1 twin
Bathrooms: 3 private, 1 public

**Bed & breakfast**

| per night: | £min | £max |
| --- | --- | --- |
| Single | 30.00 | 42.50 |
| Double | 37.50 | 50.00 |

**Half board**

| per person: | £min | £max |
| --- | --- | --- |
| Daily | 32.75 | 38.50 |

Lunch available
Evening meal 1800 (last orders 2100)
Parking for 5
Cards accepted: Access, Visa, Diners, Amex

## WARKWORTH

Northumberland
Map ref 5C1

A pretty village overlooked by its medieval castle. A 14th C fortified bridge across the wooded Coquet gives a superb view of 18th C terraces climbing to the castle. Upstream is a curious 14th C Hermitage and in the market square is the Norman church of St Lawrence.

### Beck 'N' Call ♨
**HIGHLY COMMENDED**

Birling West Cottage, Warkworth, Morpeth NE65 0XS
☎ Alnwick (01665) 711653
*Country cottage set in half an acre of terraced gardens with stream. First cottage on the right entering Warkworth from Alnwick.*
Bedrooms: 2 double, 1 triple
Bathrooms: 1 private, 1 public

**Bed & breakfast**

| per night: | £min | £max |
| --- | --- | --- |
| Single | 17.00 | |
| Double | 34.00 | |

Parking for 4

### Bide A While ♨
**Listed COMMENDED**

4 Beal Croft, Warkworth, Morpeth NE65 0XL
☎ Alnwick (01665) 711753
*Bungalow on small executive housing estate of 8 dwellings.*
Bedrooms: 1 double, 1 family room
Bathrooms: 1 private, 1 public

**Bed & breakfast**

| per night: | £min | £max |
| --- | --- | --- |
| Single | 14.00 | 16.50 |
| Double | 28.00 | 33.00 |

Parking for 3

### North Cottage ♨
**HIGHLY COMMENDED**

Birling, Warkworth, Morpeth NE65 0XS
☎ Alnwick (01665) 711263

*Attractive cottage, with ground floor, en-suite non-smoking rooms. Extensive gardens, with patio where visitors are welcome to relax.*
Bedrooms: 1 single, 2 double, 1 twin
Bathrooms: 3 private, 1 public

**Bed & breakfast**

| per night: | £min | £max |
| --- | --- | --- |
| Single | 17.00 | |
| Double | 34.00 | |

Parking for 8

## WESTGATE-IN-WEARDALE

Durham
Map ref 5B2

Small Weardale village with an old water-mill and a 19th C church. It is set at the entrance to the Bishops of Durham's former hunting ground, Old Park. Beautiful moorland, river and valley scenery to be explored.

### Wingate House Farm ♨
**HIGHLY COMMENDED**

Westgate-in-Weardale, Bishop Auckland, County Durham DL13 1LP
☎ Bishop Auckland (01388) 517281
*80-acre mixed farm. Victorian farmhouse in own grounds with*

terraced garden - 100 yards from A689 with level drive. Panoramic views, ideal touring centre.
Bedrooms: 1 twin, 1 triple
Bathrooms: 1 private, 1 public

**Bed & breakfast**

| per night: | £min | £max |
| --- | --- | --- |
| Double | 34.00 | 36.00 |

Parking for 4
Open April-October

## WHITLEY BAY

Tyne and Wear
Map ref 5C2

Traditional seaside resort with long beaches of sand and rock and many pools to explore. St Mary's lighthouse is open to the public.
*Tourist Information Centre*
☎ (0191) 252 4494

### Windsor Hotel ♨
**COMMENDED**

South Parade, Whitley Bay NE26 2RF
☎ (0191) 2518888 & 297 0272

*Private hotel close to the seafront and town centre. An excellent base in the north east for business or pleasure.*
Bedrooms: 5 single, 16 double, 43 twin
Bathrooms: 64 private

**Bed & breakfast**

| per night: | £min | £max |
| --- | --- | --- |
| Single | 35.00 | 54.00 |
| Double | 45.00 | 60.00 |

**Half board**

| per person: | £min | £max |
| --- | --- | --- |
| Daily | 30.00 | 50.00 |
| Weekly | 210.00 | 280.00 |

Lunch available
Evening meal 1800 (last orders 2130)
Parking for 26
Cards accepted: Access, Visa, Diners, Amex, Switch/Delta

---

There are separate sections in this guide listing groups specialising in farm holidays and accommodation which is especially suitable for young people and organised groups.

## WOOLER

Northumberland
Map ref 5B1

Old grey-stone town, market-place for foresters and hill farmers, set at the edge of the north-east Cheviots. This makes a good base for excursions to Northumberland's loveliest coastline, or for angling and walking in the Borderlands.

### Tilldale House ⋀

34-40 High Street, Wooler NE71 6BG
☎ (01668) 281 450
*Centrally situated stone-built property, 300 years old but now with all modern comforts. Evening meal available on request. Non-smokers only please.*
Bedrooms: 1 double, 1 twin, 1 family room
Bathrooms: 3 private, 1 public
**Bed & breakfast**

| per night: | £min | £max |
| --- | --- | --- |
| Single | 15.00 | 20.00 |
| Double | 30.00 | 38.00 |

**Half board**

| per person: | £min | £max |
| --- | --- | --- |
| Daily | 20.00 | 25.00 |
| Weekly | 120.00 | 170.00 |

Evening meal 1800 (last orders 2000)
Parking for 3

## WYLAM

Northumberland
Map ref 5B2

Well-kept village on the River Tyne, famous as the birthplace of the railway pioneer, George Stephenson. The cottage in which he was born is open to the public, and the Wylam Railway Museum also commemorates William Hedley and Timothy Hackworth.

### Wormald House ⋀

HIGHLY COMMENDED
Main Street, Wylam NE41 8DN
☎ (01661) 852529 & 852552

*Pleasant country home located near centre of Wylam, George Stephenson's birthplace. House stands on site of Timothy Hackworth's birthplace (Stephenson's contemporary).*
Bedrooms: 2 double, 1 twin
Bathrooms: 3 private
**Bed & breakfast**

| per night: | £min | £max |
| --- | --- | --- |
| Single | 16.50 | 17.50 |
| Double | 33.00 | 35.00 |

Parking for 4

There are separate sections in this guide listing groups specialising in farm holidays and accommodation which is especially suitable for young people and organised groups.

# pHONEday

All telephone numbers in the editorial and listings sections of this guide include the new PhONEday area codes. Please use the new codes when dialling.

# BOOKINGS

When enquiring about accommodation you may find it helpful to use the booking enquiry coupons which can be found towards the end of the guide.
These should be cut out and mailed direct to the establishments in which you are interested.
Do remember to include your name and address.

England's North West has welcomed visitors from all over the world, travellers and traders alike, for hundreds of years – and the welcome is just as warm today. A pleasant, cosmopolitan atmosphere pervades much of the region.

# NORTH WEST

You'll find echoes of Las Vegas in Blackpool's superb entertainments, Boston in Liverpool's Albert Dock complex and China when the Chinese New Year is celebrated in Manchester. Visit the beautiful Fylde coast and the windmills, parks and gardens will remind you of Holland. In fact, rather than a tour around the world, why not just take yourself off to the North West?

The Counties of Cheshire, Greater Manchester, Lancashire and Merseyside

For more information on the North West, contact:
North West Tourist Board
Swan House
Swan Meadow Road
Wigan Pier
Wigan
Lancashire WN3 5BB
Tel: (01942) 821222
Fax: (01942) 820002

Where to Go in the North West
– see pages 84–87

Where to Stay in the North West
– see pages 88–98

# WHERE TO GO

*You will find hundreds of interesting places to visit during your stay in the North West, just some of which are listed in these pages. The number against each name will help you locate it on the map (page 87). Contact any Tourist Information Centre in the region for more ideas on days out in the North West.*

**❶ Frontierland Western Theme Park**
Marine Road, Morecambe, Lancashire LA4 4DG
Tel: (01524) 410024
*Over 30 Wild West thrill rides and attractions, including Texas Tornado, Perculator, Stampede Roller Coaster. "Fun house" indoor complex.*

**❷ Lancaster Castle**
Shire Hall, Castle Parade, Lancaster LA1 1YJ
Tel: (01524) 64998
*Collection of coats of arms, dungeons, Crown Court, Grand Jury Room, Jane Scott's chair, external tour of castle walls.*

**❸ Sandcastle**
Promenade, Blackpool, Lancashire FY4 1BB
Tel: (01253) 343602
*Leisure pool, wave pool, giant slides, amusements, live entertainment, bars, cafés, showbar, shops, nightclub, children's playground, beer garden.*

**❹ Blackpool Pleasure Beach**
Ocean Boulevard, Blackpool, Lancashire FY4 1EZ
Tel: (01253) 341033
*Europe's greatest amusement park: Space Invader, Big Dipper, Revolution, etc. Funshineland for children. Summer season ice show, illusion show in Horseshoe Bar.*

**❺ Blackpool Sea Life Centre**
The Promenade, Blackpool, Lancashire FY1 5AA
Tel: (01253) 22445
*Tropical sharks up to 8ft in length housed in 100,000-gallon display with underwater walk-through tunnel.*

**❻ Blackpool Tower**
The Promenade, Blackpool, Lancashire FY1 4BJ
Tel: (01253) 22242

*Tower Ballroom, Bug World, Jungle Jim's playground, Out of this World, Undersea World, laser fantasy, lift ride. Tower Circus. Children's entertainment in Hornpipe Galley.*

**❼ Ribchester Museum of Childhood**
Church Street, Ribchester, Lancashire PR3 3YE
Tel: (01254) 878520
*Childhood toys, dolls, dolls' houses, 20-piece model fairground, Tom Thumb replica. Collectors' toy shop.*

**❽ Pleasureland Amusement Park**
Marine Drive, The Fun Coast, Southport, Merseyside PR8 1RX
Tel: (01704) 532717
*Traditional amusement park with wide variety of thrilling and family rides.*

**Britain's textile industry flourished in the North West during the 19th century.**

*Liverpool's impressive Metropolitan Cathedral of Christ the King is constructed of concrete and glass.*

**⑬ Granada Studios Tour**
Water Street, Manchester
M60 9EA
Tel: (0161) 832 9090
*The only major TV theme park in Europe, giving a unique insight into the fascinating world behind the TV screen. Visit three of the most famous streets on TV.*

**⑭ Museum of Science and Industry in Manchester**
Liverpool Road, Castlefield, Manchester
M3 4JP
Tel: (0161) 832 2244
*Based in the world's oldest passenger railway station, 15 galleries amaze, amuse and entertain.*

**⑨ Camelot Theme Park**
Park Hall Road, Charnock Richard, Lancashire
PR7 5LP
Tel: (01257) 453044
*Magical kingdom offering over 100 thrilling rides, fantastic medieval entertainment and lots of family fun.*

**⑩ Wildfowl and Wetland Centre**
Martin Mere, Burscough, Lancashire L40 0TA
Tel: (01704) 895181
*45 acres of gardens with over 1,600 ducks, geese and swans of 120 different kinds. Two flocks of flamingos. 300-acre wild area with 20-acre lake.*

**⑪ East Lancashire Railway**
Bolton Street Station, Bury, Lancashire BL9 0EY
Tel: (0161) 764 7790
*Eight-mile-long preserved railway operated principally by steam traction. Transport museum nearby.*

**⑫ Wigan Pier**
Wallgate, Wigan, Lancashire WN3 4EU
Tel: (01942) 323666
*"The Way We Were" – life in Wigan in 1900. Cotton machinery hall, world's largest steam-operated mill engine, waterbuses, shops, Victorian classroom, picnic gardens.*

**⑮ Knowsley Safari Park**
Prescot, Merseyside L34 4AN
Tel: (0151) 430 9009
*Five-mile drive through game reserves, set in 400 acres of parkland containing lions, tigers, elephants, rhinos, etc. Large picnic areas, children's amusement park.*

**⑯ Albert Dock**
The Colonnades, Albert Dock, Liverpool
L3 4AA
Tel: (0151) 708 7334
*Britain's largest Grade I listed historic building. Restored 4-sided dock, including shops, bars, restaurants, entertainment, marina and maritime museum.*

**⑰ Tate Gallery Liverpool**
Albert Dock, Liverpool L3 4BB
Tel: (0151) 709 3223
*North of England venue for the national collection of modern art.*

**⑱ Catalyst: The Museum of the Chemical Industry**
Gossage Building, Mersey Road, Widnes, Cheshire WA8 0DF
Tel: (0151) 420 1121
*Dramatic riverside observation gallery with*

interactive microcomputers, video and other displays telling the story of the chemical industry in Widnes and Runcorn.

### ⑲ Dunham Massey Hall and Park
Altrincham, Cheshire WA14 4SJ
Tel: (0161) 941 1025
*Historic house, garden and park with restaurant and shop.*

### ⑳ Bramall Hall
Bramall Park, Bramhall, Cheshire SK7 3NX
Tel: (0161) 485 3708
*Important Elizabethan manor house in 60 acres of landscaped grounds. Wall paintings, furniture, medieval stained glass, Victorian kitchen.*

### ㉑ Lyme Park
Disley, Cheshire SK12 2NX
Tel: (01663) 762023
*National Trust country estate with 1,377 acres of moorland, woodland and park. Magnificent house with 17 acres of historic gardens.*

### ㉒ Quarry Bank Mill
Styal, Cheshire SK9 4LA
Tel: (01625) 527468
*Georgian water-powered cotton spinning mill, with four floors of displays and demonstrations.*

### ㉓ Lady Lever Art Gallery
Port Sunlight Village, Bebington, Merseyside L62 5EQ
Tel: (0151) 645 3623

*The first Lord Leverhulme's magnificent collection of British paintings, 1750–1900, plus Wedgwood and oriental porcelain, British furniture.*

### ㉔ Port Sunlight Heritage Centre
95 Greendale Road, Port Sunlight, Merseyside L62 4XE
Tel: (0151) 644 6466
*In listed building, display showing creation of village, with photographs, drawings, models.*

### ㉕ Norton Priory Museum and Gardens
Tudor Road, Runcorn, Cheshire WA7 1SX
Tel: (01928) 569895
*Excavated Augustinian priory, remains of church, cloister and chapter house. Later site of Tudor mansion and Georgian house.*

### ㉖ Boat Museum
Dock Yard Road, Ellesmere Port, Cheshire L65 4EF
Tel: (0151) 355 5017
*Over 50 historic craft – largest floating collection in the world. Restored buildings, traditional cottages, workshops, steam engines, boat trips, shop, etc.*

### ㉗ Arley Hall and Gardens
Arley, Northwich, Cheshire CW9 6NA
Tel: (01565) 777353
*Early Victorian house and 15th C tythe barn in 12 acres of magnificent gardens. Collection of watercolours of the area. Woodland walk, craftsmen, shop.*

### ㉘ Macclesfield Silk Museum
The Heritage Centre, Roe Street, Macclesfield, Cheshire SK11 6UT
Tel: (01625) 613210
*Information centre, town history exhibition, silk museum, Sunday school, history exhibition, guided trails, tearoom, shop. Auditorium seats 450.*

### ㉙ Jodrell Bank Science Centre and Arboretum
Lower Withington, Cheshire SK11 9DL
Tel: (01477) 571339
*Exhibition and interactive exhibits on astronomy, space, satellites, energy, the environment. Planetarium, the Lovell telescope, 35-acre arboretum.*

*Lancashire Hot-Pot: a classic of British cooking.*

Cumbria
0 20 Miles
0 30 Kms
North Yorkshire
1 Morecambe
2 Lancaster
Fleetwood
Lancashire
Clitheroe
Blackpool 3 4 5 6
Ribchester 7
Nelson
Burnley
Preston
Lytham St Annes
Blackburn
Accrington
West Yorkshire
Darwen
Rawtenstall
Ramsbottom
Southport 8
9 Chorley
Charnock Richard
Rochdale
Burscough 10
Ormskirk
Bolton
11 Bury
Formby
Skelmersdale
12 Wigan
Greater Manchester
Oldham
Merseyside
Kirkby
St Helens
Salford
13 14 Manchester
New Brighton
15 Prescot
Stockport
Hoylake
Birkenhead
16 17 Huyton
Warrington
Altrincham
Cheadle
Port Sunlight 24
Liverpool
18 Widnes
19 Bramhall
21 Disley
Styal 22 20
Bebington 23
25 Runcorn
Derby
Arley 27
Knutsford
Wilmslow
Alderley Edge
26
Ellesmere Port
Northwich
28 Macclesfield
Chester
Cheshire
29 Lower Withington
Winsford
Congleton
Sandbach
Wales
Alsager
Crewe
Kidsgrove
Nantwich
Staffordshire

# Find Out More

*Further information about holidays and attractions in the North West is available from:* ***North West Tourist Board****, Swan House, Swan Meadow Road, Wigan Pier, Wigan, Lancashire WN3 5BB*
*Tel: (01942) 821222*

*These publications are available free from the North West Tourist Board:*

- ***North West Welcome Guide***
- ***Discover England's North West*** *(attractions map)*
- ***Overseas brochure***
- ***Group Visits***
- ***Bed & Breakfast map***
- ***Caravan and Camping Parks guide***

# WHERE TO STAY

*Accommodation entries in this regional section are listed in alphabetical order of place name, and then in alphabetical order of establishment.*

*Map references refer to the colour location maps at the back of this guide. The first figure is the map number; the letter and figure which follow indicate the grid reference on the map.*

*Symbols at the end of each accommodation entry give information about services and facilities. A 'key' to these symbols is inside the back cover flap, which can be kept open for easy reference.*

---

## ALDERLEY EDGE

Cheshire
Map ref 4B2

Picturesque town taking its name from the wooded escarpment towering above the Cheshire plain, with fine views and walks. A romantic local legend tells of the Wizard and sleeping warriors who will save the country in crisis. Excellent shops. Chorley Hall, nearby, boasts a moat.

### Dean Green Farm
HIGHLY COMMENDED

Nusery Lane, Nether Alderley, Macclesfield SK10 4TX
☎ Chelford (01625) 861401
*131-acre beef farm. Situated between A34 and A535 at Nether Alderley. Grade II oak-beamed farmhouse surrounded by pastureland looking towards Alderley Edge, convenient for Knutsford, Wilmslow and Macclesfield.*
Bedrooms: 1 double
Bathrooms: 1 private

**Bed & breakfast**

| per night: | £min | £max |
|---|---|---|
| Single | | 29.37 |
| Double | | 58.75 |

Evening meal 1800 (last orders 2100)
Parking for 10

---

The enquiry coupons at the back will help you when contacting proprietors.

---

## ALTRINCHAM

Greater Manchester
Map ref 4A2

Altrincham preserves the best of the old at its fascinating Old Market Place, with the best of the new on pedestrianised George Street. International fashion and high style interior design rub shoulders with unique boutiques and local speciality shops.
*Tourist Information Centre*
☎ (0161) 941 7337

### Ashley Mill ᴍ
HIGHLY COMMENDED

Ashley Mill Lane, Ashley, Altrincham, Cheshire WA14 3PU
☎ (0161) 928 5751
*17th C mill house set in 5 acres of delightful Cheshire countryside. A haven of peace and tranquillity, yet only 10 minutes from Manchester Airport. Car parking available.*
Bedrooms: 1 single, 2 double, 1 twin
Bathrooms: 1 public

**Bed & breakfast**

| per night: | £min | £max |
|---|---|---|
| Single | 20.00 | |
| Double | 40.00 | |

Evening meal from 1830
Parking for 32

### Belvedere Guest House
Listed APPROVED

58 Barrington Road, Altrincham, Cheshire WA14 1HY
☎ (0161) 941 5996 & Mobile 0850 237227
Fax (0161) 929 6450

10 minutes from Manchester Airport; free taxi service. Convenient for buses and trains. All rooms en-suite with satellite TV, tea/coffee-making facilities.
Bedrooms: 1 double, 2 twin, 1 triple
Bathrooms: 4 private

**Bed & breakfast**

| per night: | £min | £max |
|---|---|---|
| Single | 20.00 | 25.00 |
| Double | 34.00 | 38.00 |

Evening meal 1800 (last orders 1900)
Parking for 6
Cards accepted: Access, Visa, Amex

---

## BIRKENHEAD

Merseyside
Map ref 4A2

Founded in the 12th C by monks who operated the first Mersey ferry service, Birkenhead has some fine Victorian architecture, one of the best markets in the north west and several visitor attractions including, of course, the famous Mersey Ferry.
*Tourist Information Centre*
☎ (0151) 647 6780

### Ashgrove Guest House ᴍ
Listed

14 Ashville Road, Claughton, Birkenhead L43 8SA
☎ (0151) 653 3794
*Friendly, family-run establishment overlooking Birkenhead Park. 10 minutes' walk to train and 2 stops to Liverpool centre. Excellent shopping facilities nearby, numerous sports facilities. Owner is local guitar vocalist.*
Bedrooms: 2 single, 2 double, 1 twin
Bathrooms: 3 public

## Bed & breakfast

| per night: | £min | £max |
|---|---|---|
| Single | 14.00 | 19.00 |
| Double | 28.00 | 36.00 |

## Half board

| per person: | £min | £max |
|---|---|---|
| Daily | 17.50 | 25.00 |
| Weekly | 94.50 | 140.00 |

Lunch available
Evening meal 1800 (last orders 1600)
Parking for 10

🌃🐕☗🏠🖤⑁📶🛈💲⌁🏊📺🎞️🖥️🔌🔍🔥❄️
📶 OAP 🐾 🎏

---

Lancashire
Map ref 4A1

North east Lancashire market town. Waves Water Fun Centre; Lewis Textile Museum; Blackburn Museum; 19th C cathedral; Victorian landscaped Corporation Park.
*Tourist Information Centre*
☎ *(01254) 53277*

### Rose Cottage ⚹

👑👑👑

Longsight Road, Clayton Le Dale, Blackburn BB1 9EX
☎ Mellor (01254) 813223
Fax (01254) 813831
*100-year-old cottage, on A59, at the gateway to the Ribble Valley, 5 miles from M6 junction 31.*
Bedrooms: 1 double, 2 twin
Bathrooms: 2 private, 1 public

**Bed & breakfast**

| per night: | £min | £max |
|---|---|---|
| Single | 17.00 | 20.00 |
| Double | 28.00 | 32.00 |

Parking for 3

🌃🐕📞🖤☗♿🖥️⑁📶🛈💲⌁🖥️🔌🎏

---

Lancashire
Map ref 4A1

Britain's largest fun resort, with Blackpool Pleasure Beach, 3 piers and the famous Tower. Host to the spectacular autumn illuminations - "the greatest free show on earth".
*Tourist Information Centre*
☎ *(01253) 21623 or 25212*

### Sunray ⚹

👑👑👑 COMMENDED

42 Knowle Avenue, Blackpool FY2 9TQ
☎ (01253) 351937
*Modern semi in quiet residential part of north Blackpool. Friendly personal service and care. 1.75 miles north of tower along promenade. Turn right at Uncle Tom's Cabin. Sunray is about 300 yards on left.*
Bedrooms: 3 single, 2 double, 2 twin, 2 triple
Bathrooms: 9 private, 1 public

---

## Bed & breakfast

| per night: | £min | £max |
|---|---|---|
| Single | 24.00 | 28.00 |
| Double | 48.00 | 56.00 |

## Half board

| per person: | £min | £max |
|---|---|---|
| Daily | 34.00 | 38.00 |
| Weekly | 204.00 | 228.00 |

Evening meal 1750 (last orders 1500)
Parking for 6
Cards accepted: Access, Visa

🌃🐕📞🖤☗♿🖥️⑁📶🛈💲⌁🖥️🔌🖥️🎞️🖥️🔌🛢️❄️🎏
OAP SP T

---

Greater Manchester
Map ref 4A1

On the edge of the West Pennine Moors and renowned for its outstanding town centre architecture and fine shopping facilities. Attractions include the Water Place, Octagon Theatre, Bolton Market and the Last Drop Village.
*Tourist Information Centre*
☎ *(01204) 364333*

### Commercial Royal Hotel

👑👑👑 COMMENDED

13-15 Bolton Road, Moses Gate, Farnworth, Bolton BL4 7JN
☎ (01204) 73661
Fax (01204) 862488
*New, quality hotel offering a high standard of service and facilities rarely found in small hotels. Noted English/Italian restaurant. Two minutes from motorway network, 15 minutes from Manchester, 5 minutes from Bolton.*
Bedrooms: 6 single, 3 double, 1 triple
Bathrooms: 6 private, 2 public

**Bed & breakfast**

| per night: | £min | £max |
|---|---|---|
| Single | 24.00 | 39.00 |
| Double | 39.00 | 49.00 |

**Half board**

| per person: | £min | £max |
|---|---|---|
| Daily | 30.00 | 45.00 |
| Weekly | 200.00 | 280.00 |

Evening meal 1800 (last orders 2200)
Parking for 15
Cards accepted: Access, Visa, Diners, Amex

🌃🚿♿📞🖤☗♿⑁🛈💲⌁🖥️🎞️🖥️🔌
🛢️ OAP 🐾 SP

---

National Crown ratings were correct at the time of going to press but are subject to change. Please check at the time of booking.

---

Lancashire
Map ref 5A3

Village on the main A6 trunk road with the picturesque Lancaster Canal passing through it. An ideal touring base.

### Thwaite End Farm

👑👑

A6 Road, Bolton-le-sands, Carnforth LA5 9TN
☎ Carnforth (01524) 732551
*20-acre livestock farm. 17th C farmhouse in an ideal area for breaking your journey to and from Scotland. Well placed for touring the Lake District and Lancashire. Self-catering cottage also available.*
Bedrooms: 2 double, 1 twin
Bathrooms: 2 private, 2 public

**Bed & breakfast**

| per night: | £min | £max |
|---|---|---|
| Single | 17.00 | 18.00 |
| Double | 36.00 | 40.00 |

Parking for 4

📞🖤☗♿🖥️📺🎞️🖥️🔌🛢️❄️✗🎏

---

Lancashire
Map ref 4B1

"A town amidst the Pennines", set in the glorious Lancashire countryside. Towneley Hall has fine period rooms and is home to Burnley's art gallery and museum. The Kay-Shuttleworth collection of lace and embroidery can be seen at Gawthorpe Hall (National Trust).
*Tourist Information Centre*
☎ *(01282) 455485*

### Ormerod Hotel

👑👑👑 HIGHLY COMMENDED

121-123 Ormerod Road, Burnley BB11 3QW
☎ (01282) 423255
*Small bed and breakfast hotel in quiet, pleasant surroundings facing local parks. Recently refurbished, all en-suite facilities. 5 minutes from town centre.*
Bedrooms: 4 single, 2 double, 2 twin, 2 triple
Bathrooms: 10 private

**Bed & breakfast**

| per night: | £min | £max |
|---|---|---|
| Single | 19.00 | 24.00 |
| Double | 34.00 | 36.00 |

Parking for 7

🌃🚿☗♿🖥️⑁🛈📺🎞️🖥️🔌🛢️T

---

The town index at the back of this guide gives page numbers of all places with accommodation.

## BURWARDSLEY

Cheshire
Map ref 4A2

### The Pheasant Inn
😄😄😄 COMMENDED

Higher Burwardsley, Tattenhall,
Chester CH3 9PF
☎ Tattenhall (01829) 70434
Fax (01829) 71097

*300-year-old inn, half-timber and
sandstone construction, nestling on the
top of the Peckforton Hills.
Accommodation in delightfully
converted barn affording pleasant views
towards Chester.*
Bedrooms: 5 double, 2 twin, 1 triple
Bathrooms: 8 private

**Bed & breakfast
per night:**

|  | £min | £max |
| --- | --- | --- |
| Single | 40.00 | 40.00 |
| Double | 60.00 | 80.00 |

**Half board
per person:**

|  | £min | £max |
| --- | --- | --- |
| Daily | 42.50 | 45.00 |
| Weekly | 250.00 | 270.00 |

Lunch available
Evening meal 1930 (last orders 2200)
Parking for 60
Cards accepted: Access, Visa, Diners,
Amex
⏰🚿🍴📞🚪🧺🎣🅿🛏🎱📺🛗🚗🍽
✿🐾🔌 SP 🎏 T

## CHESTER

Cheshire
Map ref 4A2

Roman and medieval walled city
rich in architectural and
archaeological treasures. Fine
timber-framed and plaster
buildings. Shopping in the Rows
(galleried arcades reached by
steps from the street). 14th C
cathedral, castle and zoo.
*Tourist Information Centre
☎ (01244) 317962 or 351609 or
318916*

### Belgrave Hotel ⚠
😄😄 APPROVED

City Road, Chester CH1 3AE
☎ (01244) 312138
Fax (01244) 324951
*Near railway station, 5 minutes' walk to
city centre. Two bars, entertainment
some evenings. En-suite rooms with
colour TV, tea/coffee-making facilities.*
Bedrooms: 12 single, 4 double,
13 twin, 5 triple
Bathrooms: 34 private

**Bed & breakfast
per night:**

|  | £min | £max |
| --- | --- | --- |
| Single | 25.00 | 35.00 |
| Double | 35.00 | 49.00 |

**Half board
per person:**

|  | £min | £max |
| --- | --- | --- |
| Daily | 33.50 | 43.50 |
| Weekly | 134.00 | 174.00 |

Evening meal 1830 (last orders 2100)
Cards accepted: Access, Visa
⏰📞🚪🧺🛏🖀🎱📺🕐🚗🖐 DAP
🐾 SP

### Cheyney Lodge Hotel ⚠
😄😄 COMMENDED

77-79 Cheyney Road, Chester
CH1 4BS
☎ (01244) 381925
*Small, friendly hotel of unusual design,
featuring indoor garden and fish pond.
10 minutes' walk from city centre and
on main bus route. Personally
supervised with emphasis on good food.*
Bedrooms: 5 double, 2 twin, 1 triple
Bathrooms: 7 private, 1 public

**Bed & breakfast
per night:**

|  | £min | £max |
| --- | --- | --- |
| Single | 24.00 | 24.00 |
| Double | 38.00 | 42.00 |

**Half board
per person:**

|  | £min | £max |
| --- | --- | --- |
| Daily | 26.50 | 29.50 |

Lunch available
Evening meal 1800 (last orders 2100)
Parking for 12
Cards accepted: Access, Visa
⏰🖿🎏📞🚪🧺🎣🛏🖀🎱🚗🖐 SP T

### Eaton House
😄😄

36 Eaton Road, Handbridge, Chester
CH4 7EN
☎ (01244) 671346
*140-year-old Victorian house with all
modern facilities, in pleasant
conservation area, near river and town
centre.*
Bedrooms: 3 double
Bathrooms: 2 private, 1 public

**Bed & breakfast
per night:**

|  | £min | £max |
| --- | --- | --- |
| Double | 27.00 | 33.00 |

Parking for 5
⏰📞🚪🧺🎣 UL 🛏🖀🎱🚗🖐🎏
DAP 🐾 SP

### Golborne Manor ⚠
😄😄 COMMENDED

Platts Lane, Hatton Heath, Chester
CH3 9AN
☎ Tattenhall (01829) 70310 & Mobile
0850 267425
Fax (01244) 318084
*19th C manor house renovated to a
high standard, set in 3.5 acres. Lovely
rural setting with fine views. 5 miles
south of Chester, off A41 Whitchurch
road, turning right just after DP Motors.
Ample parking.*
Bedrooms: 1 twin, 1 family room
Bathrooms: 2 private, 1 public

**Bed & breakfast
per night:**

|  | £min | £max |
| --- | --- | --- |
| Single | 25.00 | 28.00 |
| Double | 38.00 | 40.00 |

Parking for 6
⏰🖿📞🚪🧺🛏🖀🎱🖐🚗🖐🛗🚗🛏🍽
🖐🎏🎏

### Grove House
😄😄

Holme Street, Tarvin, Chester
CH3 8EQ
☎ Tarvin (01829) 740893
*Warm welcome in relaxing
environment. Spacious, comfortable
rooms, attractive garden. Within easy
reach of Chester (4 miles) and major
tourist attractions. German, Italian,
French and Spanish spoken.*
Bedrooms: 1 double, 1 twin
Bathrooms: 2 private

**Bed & breakfast
per night:**

|  | £min | £max |
| --- | --- | --- |
| Single | 18.50 | 20.00 |
| Double | 40.00 | 50.00 |

Parking for 6
⏰ 12 🧺 UL S 🛏 📺 🎱 🚗🖐🐾🖐🎏

### Mitchells of Chester
😄😄 HIGHLY COMMENDED

Green Gables House, 28 Hough Green,
Chester CH4 8JQ
☎ (01244) 679004

*Tastefully restored, elegant Victorian
gentleman's residence, with steeply
pitched slated roofs, a sweeping
staircase, antique furniture in tall
rooms with moulded cornices. Compact
landscaped gardens. Close to city
centre.*
Bedrooms: 1 single, 1 double, 1 twin,
1 family room
Bathrooms: 4 private, 1 public

**Bed & breakfast
per night:**

|  | £min | £max |
| --- | --- | --- |
| Single | 23.00 | 25.00 |
| Double | 36.00 | 40.00 |

Parking for 5
⏰📞🧺🖐 UL S 🖐🛏 📺 🎱🚗✿🖐
DAP SP

### Moorings ⚠
😄😄 HIGHLY COMMENDED

14 Sandy Lane, Chester CH3 5UL
☎ (01244) 324485
*Award-winning B & B in elegant
riverside Victorian house with terraced
gardens to River Dee. Idyllic rural
aspect yet within easy walking distance
of city centre.*
Bedrooms: 1 double, 1 twin
Bathrooms: 1 private, 1 public

**Bed & breakfast**

| per night: | £min | £max |
|---|---|---|
| Single | 19.00 | 19.00 |
| Double | 30.00 | 38.00 |

Open February–December

⛺🏠♿🐾🅿️🎲📺🛏🚗🍴☼🚲

## Tickeridge House
♨♨

Whitchurch Road, Milton Green,
Chester CH3 9DS
☎ Tattenhall (01829) 70443
*Chester 5 miles on A41. Set in 3 acres
of gardens. All rooms on ground floor
with comfortable beds and prettily
decorated. A warm welcome awaits.
Come and meet the donkey.*
Bedrooms: 1 single, 1 double, 1 triple
Bathrooms: 1 private, 2 public

**Bed & breakfast**

| per night: | £min | £max |
|---|---|---|
| Single | 17.50 | 22.50 |
| Double | 30.00 | 35.00 |

Parking for 6
Cards accepted: Visa

⛺🏠♿🐾🍴🅿️📺🛏🚗☼🚲 DAP SP

Set between the Pennine moors
and the Lancashire Plain, Chorley
has been an important town since
medieval times, with its "Flat-Iron"
and covered markets. The rich
heritage includes Astley Hall and
Park, Hoghton Tower, Rivington
Country Park and the Leeds-
Liverpool Canal.

## Astley House Hotel ᴍ
Listed COMMENDED

3 Southport Road, Chorley PR7 1LB
☎ (01257) 272315
*A warm welcome awaits you at this
elegant Victorian house, lovingly
restored with quality furnishings and
fittings. Minutes' walk from town.*
Bedrooms: 4 single, 2 twin
Bathrooms: 3 private, 1 public

**Bed & breakfast**

| per night: | £min | £max |
|---|---|---|
| Single | 18.00 | 23.00 |
| Double | | 40.00 |

Evening meal from 1800
Parking for 6
Cards accepted: Access, Visa, Amex

⛺🏠♿🅿️📺🛏🚗🐾

National Crown ratings
were correct at the time
of going to press but
are subject to change.
Please check at the time
of booking.

Intriguing town with an 800-year-
old castle keep and a wide range
of award-winning shops. Good
base for touring Ribble Valley,
Trough of Bowland and Pennine
moorland. Country market on
Tuesdays and Saturdays.
*Tourist Information Centre*
☎ *(01200) 25566*

## Rakefoot Farm ᴍ
Listed COMMENDED

Chaigley, Clitheroe BB7 3LY
☎ Chipping (01995) 61332
*100-acre dairy farm. Traditional B & B
(with optional evening meal) in
farmhouse in beautiful Forest of
Bowland. 5 miles from Clitheroe, 12
miles M6 junctions 31/32. Panoramic
views, home cooking and a warm
welcome await. Self-catering also
available in new stone barn conversion.*
Bedrooms: 2 double, 1 twin
Bathrooms: 1 private, 1 public

**Bed & breakfast**

| per night: | £min | £max |
|---|---|---|
| Single | 15.00 | 18.00 |
| Double | 30.00 | 33.00 |

**Half board**

| per person: | £min | £max |
|---|---|---|
| Daily | 24.00 | 27.00 |
| Weekly | 157.50 | 178.50 |

Evening meal 1700 (last orders 1900)
Parking for 6

⛺🏠♿🍴🅿️📺🛏🚗🔌☼🐾 DAP 🚲 SP 🏠 T

Old market town with mixed
industries bordering the moorland
Bronte country. Nearby are the
ruins of Wycoller House, featured
in Charlotte Bronte's "Jane Eyre"
as Ferndean Manor.

## 148 Keighley Road
Listed HIGHLY COMMENDED

Colne BB8 0PJ
☎ (01282) 862002
*Edwardian town house with many
original features. Comfortable
accommodation with easy access to
Pendle, Bronte country and the
Yorkshire Dales. Non-smokers only
please.*
Bedrooms: 1 single, 2 double
Bathrooms: 2 public

**Bed & breakfast**

| per night: | £min | £max |
|---|---|---|
| Single | 15.00 | 15.00 |
| Double | 30.00 | 30.00 |

Parking for 1

⛺11🅿️♿🔌🛏🚗📺🛁🐾 SP

## Middle Beardshaw Head Farm
Listed APPROVED

Burnley Road, Trawden, Colne
BB8 8PP
☎ (01282) 865257
*15-acre dairy farm. 17th-18th C
Lancashire longhouse with oak beams,
panelling, log fires. Panoramic views
with pools, woods and stream. Half mile
from Trawden. Caravan and camping
site on farm, with bathroom, hot shower
and electricity.*
Bedrooms: 2 single, 1 family room
Bathrooms: 2 public, 1 private shower

**Bed & breakfast**

| per night: | £min | £max |
|---|---|---|
| Single | 17.50 | |
| Double | 35.00 | |

**Half board**

| per person: | £min | £max |
|---|---|---|
| Daily | 25.00 | |
| Weekly | 150.00 | |

Lunch available
Evening meal 1900 (last orders 2030)
Parking for 10

⛺🏠♿🅿️📺🛏🍴🚗☼🐾 SP 🏠

## Turnpike House
♨ COMMENDED

6 Keighley Road, Colne BB8 0JL
☎ (01282) 869596
*Large Victorian house with garden.
Ideal for exploring Bronte country,
Pendle, Forest of Bowland, Yorkshire
Dales. Close to coach and rail stations.
A warm welcome awaits you. Walkers
welcome, families a speciality.*
Bedrooms: 1 single, 1 double, 1 triple
Bathrooms: 1 public

**Bed & breakfast**

| per night: | £min | £max |
|---|---|---|
| Single | 14.00 | 15.00 |
| Double | 28.00 | 30.00 |

Evening meal 1800 (last orders 1930)
Parking for 1

⛺♿🅿️🛏📺🛁🚗☼🐾🏠

Important cattle market and silk
town on the River Dane, now
concerned with general textiles.
Nearby are Little Moreton Hall, a
Tudor house surrounded by a
moat, the Bridestones, a
chambered tomb, and Mow Cop,
topped by a folly.
*Tourist Information Centre*
☎ *(01260) 271095*

## Sandhole Farm ᴍ
♨♨ HIGHLY COMMENDED

Hulme Walfield, Congleton CW12 2JH
☎ Marton Heath (01260) 224419
Fax (01260) 224766
*200-acre arable and mixed farm.
Charming en-suite accommodation in*
*Continued ▶*

## CONGLETON

*Continued*

*tastefully converted stables adjacent to attractive traditional farmhouse. Two miles north of Congleton on A34.*
Wheelchair access category 3 ♿
Bedrooms: 3 single, 2 double, 7 twin, 1 triple
Bathrooms: 8 private, 2 public
**Bed & breakfast**

| per night: | £min | £max |
|---|---|---|
| Single | 25.00 | 30.00 |
| Double | 38.00 | 42.00 |

Parking for 40
Cards accepted: Access, Visa

### Yew Tree Farm
**Listed COMMENDED**
North Rode, Congleton CW12 2PF
☎ North Rode (01260) 223569
*77-acre mixed farm. Peaceful village setting. 20 minutes from M6. Guests are invited to look around the farm and get to know the animals.*
Bedrooms: 1 double, 2 twin
Bathrooms: 1 private, 1 public
**Bed & breakfast**

| per night: | £min | £max |
|---|---|---|
| Single | 15.00 | 18.00 |
| Double | 30.00 | 35.00 |

**Half board**

| per person: | £min | £max |
|---|---|---|
| Daily | 25.00 | 28.00 |

Evening meal 1800 (last orders 1900)
Parking for 3

## GARSTANG

Lancashire
Map ref 4A1

Picturesque country market town. Regarded as the gateway to the fells, it stands on the Lancaster Canal and is popular as a cruising centre. Close by are the remains of Greenhalgh Castle (no public access) and the Bleasdale Circle. Discovery Centre.
*Tourist Information Centre*
☎ *(01995) 602125*

### Guy's Thatched Hamlet ♙
**♛♛♛ COMMENDED**
Canalside, St. Michael's Road, Bilsborrow, Garstang, Preston PR3 0RS
☎ Brock (01995) 640849 & 640010
Fax (01995) 640141

> Symbols are explained
> on the flap inside the
> back cover.

*Friendly, family-run thatched canalside tavern, restaurant, pizzeria, lodgings, craft shops and cricket ground with thatched pavilion. Conference centre. Off junction 32 of M6, then 3 miles north on A6 to Garstang.*
Bedrooms: 2 single, 28 double, 20 twin, 4 triple
Bathrooms: 54 private
**Bed & breakfast**

| per night: | £min | £max |
|---|---|---|
| Single | 34.75 | 50.75 |
| Double | 37.50 | 58.00 |

**Half board**

| per person: | £min | £max |
|---|---|---|
| Daily | 28.75 | 39.00 |

Lunch available
Evening meal 1800 (last orders 2330)
Parking for 300
Cards accepted: Access, Visa, Amex, Switch/Delta

## GOOSNARGH

Lancashire
Map ref 4A1

### Isles Field Barn ♙
**Listed**
Skye House Lane, Goosnargh, Preston PR3 2EN
☎ Brock (01995) 640398
*10-acre livestock farm. Large spacious rooms, in tastefully converted stone barn, with exposed beams and stone fireplace. Approximately 5 miles from M6 (junction 32).*
Bedrooms: 1 double, 1 triple
Bathrooms: 2 private, 1 public
**Bed & breakfast**

| per night: | £min | £max |
|---|---|---|
| Single | 15.00 | 16.00 |
| Double | 30.00 | 32.00 |

Parking for 6

## GREAT ECCLESTON

Lancashire
Map ref 4A1

### Cartford Hotel ♙
**♛♛♛**
Cartford Lane, Little Eccleston, Preston PR3 0YP
☎ (01995) 670166
*A country riverside pub and coaching inn, with 1.5 miles of fishing rights. Within easy reach of Blackpool and the Lake District.*
Bedrooms: 5 double, 1 twin
Bathrooms: 6 private

| Bed & breakfast | | |
|---|---|---|
| per night: | £min | £max |
| Single | 29.50 | 31.50 |
| Double | 39.50 | 45.50 |

Lunch available
Evening meal 1900 (last orders 2130)
Parking for 100
Cards accepted: Access, Visa

## HALE

Cheshire
Map ref 4A2

### Rooftree
**Listed HIGHLY COMMENDED**
40 Arthog Road, Hale, Altrincham WA15 0LU
☎ (0161) 980 4906
Fax (0161) 980 4906
*Charming, characterful ivy-covered house offering peaceful seclusion and very comfortable accommodation within 10 miles of Manchester Airport.*
Bedrooms: 1 single, 1 twin
Bathrooms: 1 public
**Bed & breakfast**

| per night: | £min | £max |
|---|---|---|
| Single | 20.00 | 20.00 |
| Double | 40.00 | 40.00 |

Evening meal from 1900
Parking for 6
Open January-July, September-December

## HOLMES CHAPEL

Cheshire
Map ref 4A2

Large village with some interesting 18th C buildings and St Luke's Church encased in brick hiding the 15th C original.

### Tiree ♙
**Listed**
5 Middlewich Road, Cranage, Holmes Chapel, Crewe CW4 8HG
☎ (01477) 533716
*Modern house set in open country 3 miles from the M6 (junction 18) and close to the A50, 2 miles north of Holmes Chapel.*
Bedrooms: 1 single, 1 double, 1 twin
Bathrooms: 1 public
**Bed & breakfast**

| per night: | £min | £max |
|---|---|---|
| Single | 15.00 | 15.00 |
| Double | 28.00 | 28.00 |

Parking for 4

> Map references apply
> to the colour maps at the
> back of this guide.

## HYDE

Greater Manchester
Map ref 4B2

### Needhams Farm ♠
**Listed COMMENDED**

Uplands Road, Werneth Low, Gee
Cross, Hyde, Cheshire SK14 3AQ
☎ (0161) 368 4610
Fax (0161) 367 9106
*30-acre beef farm. 500-year-old
farmhouse with exposed beams in all
rooms and an open fire in bar/dining
room. Excellent views. Well placed for
Manchester city and the airport.*
Bedrooms: 1 single, 4 double, 1 twin,
1 triple
Bathrooms: 5 private, 1 public

| Bed & breakfast per night: | £min | £max |
|---|---|---|
| Single | 17.00 | 19.00 |
| Double | 30.00 | 32.00 |

| Half board per person: | £min | £max |
|---|---|---|
| Daily | 24.00 | 26.00 |

Lunch available
Evening meal 1900 (last orders 2130)
Parking for 12
Cards accepted: Access, Visa, Amex

### Wayside Cottage
**Listed HIGHLY COMMENDED**

106 Padfield Main Road, Padfield,
Hyde, Cheshire SK14 7ET
☎ Glossop (01457) 866495

*17th C farm buildings with oak beams
and antiques, 17th C four poster bed,
en-suite rooms, set in beautiful
countryside. Ideal for walking, fishing,
watersports, a relaxing and stress-free
break. Five minutes from motorway
network, 30 minutes from Manchester.*
Bedrooms: 2 double, 1 twin
Bathrooms: 2 private, 1 public

| Bed & breakfast per night: | £min | £max |
|---|---|---|
| Single | 18.00 | 20.00 |
| Double | 30.00 | 40.00 |

| Half board per person: | £min | £max |
|---|---|---|
| Daily | 25.50 | 27.50 |
| Weekly | 161.00 | 173.25 |

Evening meal 1800 (last orders 2000)
Parking for 1

## INGLEWHITE

Lancashire
Map ref 4A1

### Latus Hall Farm
**Listed COMMENDED**

Inglewhite, Preston PR3 2LN
☎ Brock (01995) 640368

*100-acre dairy farm. 300-year-old
farmhouse, 7 miles north of Preston,
2.5 miles from A6 at Bilsborrow. Oak
beams, log fires and a warm welcome.*
Bedrooms: 1 double, 1 twin, 1 triple
Bathrooms: 1 public

| Bed & breakfast per night: | £min | £max |
|---|---|---|
| Single | 13.50 | |
| Double | 27.00 | |

Parking for 6

## KNUTSFORD

Cheshire
Map ref 4A2

Delightful town with many buildings
of architectural and historic
interest. The setting of Elizabeth
Gaskell's "Cranford". Annual May
Day celebration and decorative
"sanding" of the pavements are
unique to the town. Popular
Heritage Centre.
*Tourist Information Centre*
☎ *(01565) 632611 or 632210*

### The Dog Inn
**COMMENDED**

Well Bank Lane, Over Peover,
Knutsford WA16 8UP
☎ Chelford (01625) 861421
Fax (01625) 861421
*Country pub renowned for its food and
homely atmosphere, approximately 3
miles from Knutsford in the heart of
Cheshire. Close to M6 and M56
motorways.*
Bedrooms: 1 double, 2 twin
Bathrooms: 3 private

| Bed & breakfast per night: | £min | £max |
|---|---|---|
| Single | 38.00 | 45.00 |
| Double | 58.00 | 70.00 |

| Half board per person: | £min | £max |
|---|---|---|
| Daily | 45.50 | 60.00 |
| Weekly | 316.00 | 420.00 |

Lunch available
Evening meal 1830 (last orders 2100)

---

Parking for 100
Cards accepted: Access, Visa, Switch/
Delta

### Laburnum Cottage Guest House ♠
**HIGHLY COMMENDED**

Knutsford Road, Mobberley, Knutsford
WA16 7PU
☎ Mobberley (01565) 872464
Fax (01565) 872464
*Small country house in Cheshire
countryside on B5085 close to Tatton
Park, 6 miles from Manchester Airport,
4 miles from M6 exit 19 and 4 miles
from M56. Taxi service to airport. Non-
smokers only please. Winner of NWTB
Place to Stay '93 Guesthouse Award.*
Bedrooms: 2 single, 1 double, 2 twin
Bathrooms: 3 private, 1 public

| Bed & breakfast per night: | £min | £max |
|---|---|---|
| Single | 28.00 | 38.00 |
| Double | 40.00 | 48.00 |

Parking for 8

## LANCASTER

Lancashire
Map ref 4A1

Interesting old county town on the
River Lune with history dating back
to Roman times. Norman castle,
St Mary's Church, Customs House,
City and Maritime Museums,
Ashton Memorial and Butterfly
House are among places of note.
Good centre for touring the Lake
District.
*Tourist Information Centre*
☎ *(01524) 32878*

### Lancaster Town House ♠
**COMMENDED**

11 Newton Terrace, Caton Road,
Lancaster LA1 3PB
☎ (01524) 65527
*Ideal for touring the area, close to M6
motorway. All rooms en-suite with
colour TV. Four-poster bedroom. Full
breakfast menu.*
Bedrooms: 1 single, 3 double, 1 twin
Bathrooms: 5 private

| Bed & breakfast per night: | £min | £max |
|---|---|---|
| Single | 22.00 | 25.00 |
| Double | 34.50 | 40.00 |

### Middle Holly Cottage ♠
**COMMENDED**

Middle Holly, Forton, Preston
PR3 1AH
☎ Forton (01524) 792399
*Former coaching inn, set in rural
surroundings. Adjacent A6 Lancaster
road, 7 miles south of city centre, 3
miles south of M6 junction 33.*

*Continued ►*

## LANCASTER

### Continued

*Convenient for all North Lancashire areas and only 30 minutes' drive to Lakes.*
Bedrooms: 1 single, 2 double, 1 twin, 1 triple
Bathrooms: 5 private
**Bed & breakfast**

| per night: | £min | £max |
|---|---|---|
| Single | 22.50 | 27.50 |
| Double | 34.50 | 39.50 |

Parking for 11
Cards accepted: Access, Visa

### The Old Mill House

Waggon Road, Lower Dolphinholme, Lancaster LA2 9AX
☎ Forton (01524) 791855
*17th C mill house with extensive landscaped gardens on River Wyre. Private woodland and ponds, adjacent to Forest of Bowland. 5 minutes from junction 33 of M6.*
Bedrooms: 2 double, 1 twin
Bathrooms: 1 private, 1 public
**Bed & breakfast**

| per night: | £min | £max |
|---|---|---|
| Single | 17.50 | 35.00 |
| Double | 35.00 | 46.00 |

| **Half board** | | |
|---|---|---|
| per person: | £min | £max |
| Daily | 28.50 | 46.00 |
| Weekly | 175.00 | 225.00 |

Evening meal 1900 (last orders 1200)
Parking for 5

## LIVERPOOL

### Merseyside
### Map ref 4A2

Exciting city, famous for the Beatles, football, the Grand National, theatres and nightlife. Liverpool has a magnificent waterfront, 2 cathedrals, 3 historic houses, museum, galleries and a host of attractions.
*Tourist Information Centre*
☎ *(0151) 709 3631*

### Anna's
COMMENDED

65 Dudlow Lane, Calderstones, Liverpool L18 2EY
☎ (0151) 722 3708
Fax (0151) 722 8699
*Large family house with friendly atmosphere, in select residential area close to all amenities. Direct transport routes to city centre. 1 mile from end of M62 motorway.*
Bedrooms: 1 double, 3 twin
Bathrooms: 1 public

**Bed & breakfast**

| per night: | £min | £max |
|---|---|---|
| Single | 17.00 | 18.00 |
| Double | 30.00 | 32.00 |

Parking for 6

### Somersby Guest House
COMMENDED

57 Green Lane, off Menlove Avenue, Liverpool L18 2EP
☎ (0151) 722 7549
*Attractive house with secure parking, delightfully situated in exclusive area with easy access to city centre, airport and M62.*
Bedrooms: 2 double, 1 twin
Bathrooms: 2 public

**Bed & breakfast**

| per night: | £min | £max |
|---|---|---|
| Single | 17.50 | 21.00 |
| Double | 35.00 | 35.00 |

Parking for 6

## MALPAS

### Cheshire
### Map ref 4A2

### Millhey Farm

Barton, Malpas SY14 7HY
☎ Broxton (01829) 782431
*140-acre mixed farm. Typical, lovely Cheshire black and white part-timbered farmhouse in conservation area, 9 miles from Chester, close to Welsh Border country. On A534, just off A41.*
Bedrooms: 1 triple, 1 family room
Bathrooms: 2 private, 1 public

**Bed & breakfast**

| per night: | £min | £max |
|---|---|---|
| Single | 15.00 | 15.00 |
| Double | 28.00 | 28.00 |

Parking for 2

## MANCHESTER

### Greater Manchester
### Map ref 4B1

The Gateway to the North, offering one of Britain's largest selections of arts venues and theatre productions, a wide range of chain stores and specialist shops, a legendary, lively nightlife, spectacular architecture and a plethora of eating and drinking places.
*Tourist Information Centre*
☎ *(0161) 234 3157/8*

### Baron Hotel

116 Palatine Road, West Didsbury, Manchester M20 9ZA
☎ (0161) 445 3877 & 434 3688
Fax (01203) 520680

*Comfortable, friendly, family-run hotel, all rooms with en-suite facilities. Ten minutes from Manchester Airport and city centre. Half a mile from the motorway network.*
Bedrooms: 10 single, 5 twin, 1 triple
Bathrooms: 16 private

**Bed & breakfast**

| per night: | £min | £max |
|---|---|---|
| Single | 25.00 | 28.50 |
| Double | 35.00 | 45.00 |

Evening meal 1900 (last orders 2030)
Parking for 25
Cards accepted: Access, Visa

### Ebor Hotel

402 Wilbraham Road, Chorlton-cum-Hardy, Manchester M21 0UH
☎ (0161) 881 1911 & 881 4855
*Hotel offering comfortable accommodation and friendly service, within easy reach of airport, Manchester city centre and motorway network.*
Bedrooms: 6 single, 2 double, 3 twin, 4 triple, 1 family room
Bathrooms: 7 private, 3 public

**Bed & breakfast**

| per night: | £min | £max |
|---|---|---|
| Single | 22.00 | 27.00 |
| Double | 32.00 | 37.00 |

| **Half board** | | |
|---|---|---|
| per person: | £min | £max |
| Daily | 28.00 | 33.00 |
| Weekly | 196.00 | 231.00 |

Evening meal 1830 (last orders 1700)
Parking for 20
Cards accepted: Access, Visa, Amex

### Parkside Guest House

58 Cromwell Road, Off Edge Lane, Stretford, Manchester M32 8QJ
☎ (0161) 865 2860
*Clean, comfortable, convenient. In a quiet pleasant area near Old Trafford football/cricket grounds. 15 minutes from airport and city centre by Metro. M63 exit 7. A warm and friendly welcome assured.*
Bedrooms: 1 double, 1 twin, 1 triple, 1 family room
Bathrooms: 4 private, 1 public

**Bed & breakfast**

| per night: | £min | £max |
|---|---|---|
| Single | 17.00 | 19.00 |
| Double | 31.00 | 33.00 |

Parking for 3

### Waterfall Farm Cottage
COMMENDED

7 Motcombe Grove, Gatley, Cheadle, Cheshire SK8 3TL
☎ (0161) 436 4732
*Small guesthouse, 2 miles from the airport, 5 miles from Stockport. Near 4 major motorways, ideal for touring the*

north west. Courtesy transport to/from airport. All rooms en-suite with tea/coffee facilities and TV.
Bedrooms: 1 double, 1 twin
Bathrooms: 2 private, 1 public

**Bed & breakfast**

| per night: | £min | £max |
|---|---|---|
| Single | 25.00 | |
| Double | 35.00 | |

Evening meal 1900 (last orders 2100)
Parking for 5
Cards accepted: Amex

📶🔥🚭📞💻🚿♿♨️Ⓜ️Ⓢ🅿️🍴📺▥🍷↕️❄️🚐Ⓣ

*See under Alderley Edge, Altrincham, Hyde, Knutsford, Manchester, Salford, Stockport*

## NANTWICH

Cheshire
Map ref 4A2

Old market town on the River Weaver made prosperous in Roman times by salt springs. Fire destroyed the town in 1583 and many buildings were rebuilt in Elizabethan style. Churche's Mansion (open to the public) survived the fire.
*Tourist Information Centre*
☎ *(01270) 610983 or 610880*

### Lea Farm
⚜️⚜️ COMMENDED

Wrinehill Road, Wybunbury, Nantwich CW5 7NS
☎ Crewe (01270) 841429

*160-acre dairy farm. Charming farmhouse in beautiful gardens where peacocks roam. Comfortable lounge, pool/snooker, fishing pool. Ideal surroundings.*
Bedrooms: 2 double, 1 triple
Bathrooms: 2 private, 1 public

**Bed & breakfast**

| per night: | £min | £max |
|---|---|---|
| Single | 14.00 | 18.00 |
| Double | 27.00 | 29.00 |

**Half board**

| per person: | £min | £max |
|---|---|---|
| Daily | 21.00 | 25.00 |
| Weekly | 140.00 | 165.00 |

Evening meal 1800 (last orders 1900)
Parking for 22

📶📺💻🚿♿Ⓢ🅿️✂️▥📺🍷↕️🚶🎣❄️🚐

### Oakland House ⚜️
⚜️⚜️ HIGHLY COMMENDED

252 Newcastle Road (A500), Blakelow, Shavington, Nantwich CW5 7ET
☎ Willaston (01270) 67134
*Friendly welcome, home comforts, rural views. Superior accommodation at reasonable rates. On A500 (A52) 5 miles from M6 junction 16. Within easy reach of historic Nantwich and Chester, Stapeley Water Gardens and Bridgemere Garden World.*
Bedrooms: 3 double, 2 twin
Bathrooms: 5 private

**Bed & breakfast**

| per night: | £min | £max |
|---|---|---|
| Single | 20.00 | 25.00 |
| Double | 30.00 | 32.00 |

Parking for 10

📶♿📺💻🚿♨️Ⓤ Ⓢ✂️▥📺🍷↕️❄️🚐

### Poole Bank Farm
⚜️⚜️ COMMENDED

Wettenhall Road, Poole, Nantwich CW5 6AL
☎ (01270) 625169
*200-acre dairy farm. 17th C timbered farmhouse in delightful Cheshire countryside, close to the historic town of Nantwich.*
Bedrooms: 2 double, 1 twin
Bathrooms: 1 private, 1 public

**Bed & breakfast**

| per night: | £min | £max |
|---|---|---|
| Single | 16.00 | 18.00 |
| Double | 27.00 | 31.00 |

Parking for 10

📶📺💻🚿♿Ⓢ▥❄️🎣🚐🏠

### Red Cow ⚜️
Listed

45 Beam Street, Nantwich CW5 7NF
☎ (01270) 628581
*Cottage with four letting bedrooms, adjoining 15th C timbered building. Real ale pub with inglenook fireplace, noted by CAMRA.*
Bedrooms: 2 single, 1 double, 1 twin
Bathrooms: 1 public

**Bed & breakfast**

| per night: | £min | £max |
|---|---|---|
| Single | 18.00 | 18.00 |
| Double | 36.00 | 36.00 |

Lunch available
Evening meal 1700 (last orders 2145)
Parking for 8

📶♿📺💻Ⓢ▥🍴🍷🔍❄️🚐🍷SP🏠

---

## NORTHWICH

Cheshire
Map ref 4A2

An important salt-producing town since Roman times, Northwich has been replanned with a modern shopping centre and a number of black and white buildings. Unique Anderton boat-lift on northern outskirts of town.

### Barratwich
Listed

Cuddington Lane, Cuddington, Northwich CW8 2SZ
☎ Sandiway (01606) 882412
*Attractive cottage set in lovely countryside, yet only 1 mile from A49 and A556. Close to Delamere Forest, 12 miles from Chester. Comfortable rooms.*
Bedrooms: 1 single, 2 twin
Bathrooms: 1 public

**Bed & breakfast**

| per night: | £min | £max |
|---|---|---|
| Single | 16.00 | |
| Double | 32.00 | |

**Half board**

| per person: | £min | £max |
|---|---|---|
| Daily | 24.50 | |
| Weekly | 170.00 | |

Evening meal 1900 (last orders 1400)
Parking for 4

📶3📺💻🚿♿🅰️Ⓢ▥🚐❄️🚐🏠

### Springfield Guest House ⚜️
⚜️⚜️ COMMENDED

Chester Road, Delamere, Oakmere, Northwich CW8 2HB
☎ Sandiway (01606) 882538
*Family guesthouse erected in 1863. On A556 close to Delamere Forest, midway between Chester and M6 motorway junction 19. Manchester Airport 25 minutes' drive.*
Bedrooms: 4 single, 1 double, 1 twin, 1 family room
Bathrooms: 2 private, 1 public

**Bed & breakfast**

| per night: | £min | £max |
|---|---|---|
| Single | 17.50 | 17.50 |
| Double | 30.00 | 30.00 |

Evening meal 1800 (last orders 2000)
Parking for 12

📶📺🚿♿Ⓤ🅰️Ⓢ▥📺🍷❄️🎣🚐🏠

---

There are separate sections in this guide listing groups specialising in farm holidays and accommodation which is especially suitable for young people and organised groups.

## OLDHAM

Greater Manchester
Map ref 4B1

The magnificent mill buildings which made Oldham one of the world's leading cotton-spinning towns still dominate the landscape. Ideally situated on the edge of the Peak District, it is now a centre of culture, sport and shopping.
*Tourist Information Centre*
☎ *(0161) 627 1024*

### Farrars Arms ᛗ

56 Oldham Road, Grasscroft, Oldham OL4 4HL
☎ Saddleworth (01457) 872124
*Old world public house with lots of character, in a lovely area of Saddleworth.*
Bedrooms: 1 single, 1 double, 1 twin
Bathrooms: 1 public

**Bed & breakfast**

| per night: | £min | £max |
|---|---|---|
| Single | | 20.00 |
| Double | | 38.00 |

Lunch available
Evening meal 1700 (last orders 1930)
Parking for 23
Cards accepted: Access, Visa

## PRESTON

Lancashire
Map ref 4A1

Scene of decisive Royalist defeat by Cromwell in the Civil War and later of riots in the Industrial Revolution. Local history exhibited in Harris Museum.
*Tourist Information Centre*
☎ *(01772) 253731*

### Brook House Guest House

ꛃ ꛃ ꛃ COMMENDED

544 Blackpool Road, Ashton, Preston PR2 1HY
☎ (01772) 728684
*Detached property 10 minutes from town centre and on bus route. TV lounge, car park, tea/coffee facilities, some en-suite rooms. Non-smoking establishment.*
Bedrooms: 2 single, 1 double, 1 twin
Bathrooms: 2 private, 1 public

**Bed & breakfast**

| per night: | £min | £max |
|---|---|---|
| Single | 20.00 | 30.00 |
| Double | 43.00 | 48.00 |

**Half board**

| per person: | £min | £max |
|---|---|---|
| Daily | 29.50 | 39.50 |
| Weekly | 196.50 | 276.50 |

Evening meal 1800 (last orders 1800)
Parking for 4
Cards accepted: Access, Visa

### Jenkinsons Farmhouse

Listed HIGHLY COMMENDED

Alston Lane, Longridge, Preston PR3 3BD
☎ (01772) 782624
*100-acre dairy & livestock farm. Old world farmhouse with panoramic views of the Ribble Valley. Traditional English cooking. Herbaceous gardens in a tranquil setting. M6 junction 31. Follow signs to Alston Hall, off the B6243 Preston to Longridge road.*
Bedrooms: 1 single, 2 double, 2 twin
Bathrooms: 3 public

**Bed & breakfast**

| per night: | £min | £max |
|---|---|---|
| Single | 20.00 | 20.00 |
| Double | 40.00 | 40.00 |

**Half board**

| per person: | £min | £max |
|---|---|---|
| Daily | 32.50 | 32.50 |

Evening meal from 1900
Parking for 10

### Olde Duncombe House ᛗ

ꛃ ꛃ ꛃ HIGHLY COMMENDED

Garstang Road, Bilsborrow, Preston PR3 0RE
☎ Brock (01995) 640336
*Traditional cottage-style bed and breakfast establishment set in rural surroundings alongside the picturesque Lancaster canal. 4 miles north of M6 junction 32.*
Bedrooms: 5 double, 2 twin, 2 triple
Bathrooms: 9 private

**Bed & breakfast**

| per night: | £min | £max |
|---|---|---|
| Single | 29.50 | 39.50 |
| Double | 39.50 | 49.50 |

Lunch available
Evening meal 1800 (last orders 2030)
Parking for 12
Cards accepted: Access, Visa

### Smithy Farm

Listed

Huntingdonhall Lane, Dutton, Longridge, Preston PR3 2ZT
☎ Ribchester (01254) 878250
*Set in the beautiful Ribble Valley, 20 minutes from the M6. Homely atmosphere, children half price.*
Bedrooms: 2 double, 1 twin
Bathrooms: 1 public

**Bed & breakfast**

| per night: | £min | £max |
|---|---|---|
| Single | 12.50 | 12.50 |
| Double | 25.00 | 25.00 |

**Half board**

| per person: | £min | £max |
|---|---|---|
| Daily | 17.50 | 17.50 |
| Weekly | 122.50 | 122.50 |

Evening meal 1900 (last orders 2130)
Parking for 4

## RIBBLE VALLEY

*See under Clitheroe*

## ROCHDALE

Greater Manchester
Map ref 4B1

Pennine mill town made prosperous by wool and later cotton- spinning, famous for the Co-operative Movement started in 1844 by a group of Rochdale working men. Birthplace of John Bright (Corn Law opponent) and more recently Gracie Fields. Fine neo-Gothic town hall.
*Tourist Information Centre*
☎ *(01706) 356592*

### Leaches Farm Bed and Breakfast

Listed

Leaches Farm, Ashworth Valley, Rochdale, Lancashire OL11 5UN
☎ (01706) 41116/7 & 228520
*140-acre livestock farm. 18th C Pennine hill farmhouse with panoramic views and moorland walks. 10 minutes from M62/M66.*
Bedrooms: 1 single, 1 double, 1 twin
Bathrooms: 1 public

**Bed & breakfast**

| per night: | £min | £max |
|---|---|---|
| Single | 18.00 | |
| Double | 34.00 | |

Parking for 6

## ST MICHAEL'S ON WYRE

Lancashire
Map ref 4A1

Village near Blackpool with interesting 13th C church of St Michael containing medieval stained glass window depicting sheep shearing, and clock tower bell made in 1548.

### Compton House ᛗ

ꛃ ꛃ COMMENDED

Garstang Road, St Michael's on Wyre, Preston PR3 0TE
☎ St. Michaels (01995) 679378
*Well-furnished country house in own grounds in a picturesque village, near M6 and 40 minutes from Lake District. Fishing in the Wyre. Antique restoration/reproduction of furniture undertaken on the premises.*
Bedrooms: 1 single, 1 double, 2 twin

Bathrooms: 4 private
**Bed & breakfast**

| per night: | £min | £max |
|---|---|---|
| Single | 17.50 | 17.50 |
| Double | 35.00 | 35.00 |

Parking for 6

🛏 🖛 🖵 ♦ ♖ 🗑 🛈 ⓢ 🛐 📺 🛋 🚗 ✿ 🚐

Greater Manchester
Map ref 4B1

Industrial city close to Manchester with Roman Catholic cathedral and university. Lowry often painted Salford's industrial architecture and much of his work is in the local art gallery.

## White Lodge Private Hotel
☻

87-89 Great Cheetham Street West, Broughton, Salford M7 9JA
☎ (0161) 792 3047
*Small, family-run hotel, close to city centre amenities and sporting facilities.*
Bedrooms: 3 single, 3 double, 3 twin
Bathrooms: 2 public
**Bed & breakfast**

| per night: | £min | £max |
|---|---|---|
| Single | 19.00 | |
| Double | 33.00 | |

Parking for 6

🛏 2 ⓢ 🛐 📺 🛋 🚗 🚐

Cheshire
Map ref 4A2

Small Cheshire town, originally important for salt production. Contains narrow, winding streets, timbered houses and a cobbled market-place. Town square has 2 Anglo-Saxon crosses to commemorate the conversion to Christianity of the king of Mercia's son.

## Canal Centre and Village Store ᴀ
Listed COMMENDED
Hassall Green, Sandbach CW11 OYB
☎ Crewe (01270) 762266

*The house and shop, built circa 1777 at the side of Lock 57 on the Trent and Mersey Canal, have served canal users for over 200 years. Off A533 near Sandbach and junction 17 on M6 - signposted. Gift shop, tearooms, store and licensed restaurant (Tues-Sat from 7pm).*

---

Bedrooms: 2 single, 1 double, 1 twin
Bathrooms: 1 public
**Bed & breakfast**

| per night: | £min | £max |
|---|---|---|
| Single | 15.00 | 16.00 |
| Double | 30.00 | 32.00 |

Lunch available
Evening meal 1900 (last orders 2130)
Parking for 5
Cards accepted: Access, Visa, Switch/Delta

🛏 🖵 ♦ 🛈 ⓢ ✂ 🛐 📺 🛋 🚗 ✿ 🚐

## Moss Cottage Farm
Listed COMMENDED
Hassall Road, Winterley, Sandbach CW11 0RU
☎ Crewe (01270) 583018
*Beamed farmhouse in quiet location just off A534, with lovely walks, fishing and golf. All rooms have tea-making facilities and hand basins.*
Bedrooms: 1 single, 1 double, 1 twin
Bathrooms: 2 public
**Bed & breakfast**

| per night: | £min | £max |
|---|---|---|
| Single | 13.50 | 15.00 |
| Double | 27.00 | 30.00 |

**Half board**

| per person: | £min | £max |
|---|---|---|
| Daily | 21.00 | 22.50 |
| Weekly | 147.00 | 157.50 |

Evening meal 1700 (last orders 2000)
Parking for 10

🛏 🖛 ♦ ♖ 🛈 ⓘ ✂ 🛐 📺 🛋 🚗 ✿ 🚐

Cheshire
Map ref 4B2

## Golden Cross Farm
♛♛
Siddington, Macclesfield SK11 9JP
☎ Marton Heath (01260) 224358
*45-acre dairy farm. Beautiful old farmhouse in the heart of Cheshire countryside. Lots of character. Adjacent Siddington Church. Closed over Christmas and New Year period. Non-smokers preferred.*
Bedrooms: 2 single, 2 double
Bathrooms: 1 private, 2 public
**Bed & breakfast**

| per night: | £min | £max |
|---|---|---|
| Single | 15.00 | 18.00 |
| Double | 30.00 | 36.00 |

Parking for 6

🛏 ♦ 🗑 ✂ 🛐 📺 🛋 🚗 ✿ ✗ 🚐

---

**National Crown ratings were correct at the time of going to press but are subject to change. Please check at the time of booking.**

---

Lancashire
Map ref 4A1

Ancient parish dating from 1175, mentioned in Domesday Book. Chapel and day school dating back to 1865. Mainly rural area to the north of St Anne's.

## Old Castle Farm ᴀ
Listed APPROVED
Garstang Road, Singleton, Blackpool FY6 8ND
☎ Poulton-le-Fylde (01253) 883839
*Take junction 3 off M55, follow Fleetwood sign to first traffic lights. Turn right, travel 200 yards on A586 to bungalow on the right.*
Bedrooms: 1 double, 1 twin, 1 triple
Bathrooms: 1 public
**Bed & breakfast**

| per night: | £min | £max |
|---|---|---|
| Single | 15.00 | |
| Double | 30.00 | |

Parking for 20
Open April-October

🛏 🖢 ♦ 🗑 ⓢ 🛐 📺 🛋 ✗ 🚐

Merseyside
Map ref 4A1

Delightful Victorian resort noted for its gardens, sandy beaches and six golf-courses, particularly Royal Birkdale. Attractions include the Atkinson Art Gallery, Southport Railway Centre, Pleasureland and the annual Southport Flower Show. Excellent shopping.
*Tourist Information Centre*
☎ *(01704) 533333*

## Sandy Brook Farm ᴀ
♛♛
52 Wyke Cop Road, Scarisbrick, Southport PR8 5LR
☎ Scarisbrick (01704) 880337
*27-acre arable farm. Small comfortable farmhouse in rural area of Scarisbrick, offering a friendly welcome. 3.5 miles from seaside town of Southport.*
Bedrooms: 1 single, 1 double, 2 twin, 1 triple, 1 family room
Bathrooms: 6 private
**Bed & breakfast**

| per night: | £min | £max |
|---|---|---|
| Single | 18.00 | 18.00 |
| Double | 30.00 | 30.00 |

Parking for 9

🛏 🖢 🖵 ♦ 🗑 ⓢ 📺 🛋 🚗 ✗ 🚐

---

**Establishments should be open throughout the year unless otherwise stated in the entry.**

## STOCKPORT

Greater Manchester
Map ref 4B2

Once an important cotton-spinning
and manufacturing centre,
Stockport has an impressive
railway viaduct, a shopping
precinct built over the River
Mersey and a new leisure
complex. Lyme Hall and Vernon
Park Museum nearby.
*Tourist Information Centre*
☎ *(0161) 474 3320/1*

### Northumbria House
👑

35 Corbar Road, Stockport, Cheshire
SK2 6EP
☎ (0161) 483 4000
*Edwardian house set in a large garden
in a quiet, residential area close to bus,
rail stations and airport. Lots of tourist
information. German and French
spoken. Non-smokers only, please.*
Bedrooms: 1 double, 1 twin
Bathrooms: 1 public
**Bed & breakfast**

| per night: | £min | £max |
|---|---|---|
| Single | 16.00 | 18.00 |
| Double | 30.00 | 35.00 |

Parking for 3
♿♒Ⓤ🅰Ⓢ🍴📺🛏🚗✻✗🏍

### Shire Cottage Farmhouse ⋔
👑👑 COMMENDED

Benches Lane, Chisworth, Hyde,
Cheshire SK14 6RY
☎ Glossop (01457) 866536
*180-acre mixed farm. Opposite
Woodheys Restaurant off the A626
Stockport to Glossop road, close to the
Peak District, Buxton, Derwent Dams
and Kinder Scout. 20 minutes from the
airport, 16 miles from Manchester city
centre. Swimming, horse riding, fishing
and boating nearby.*
Bedrooms: 1 single, 1 double, 1 twin,
1 triple
Bathrooms: 2 private, 2 public
**Bed & breakfast**

| per night: | £min | £max |
|---|---|---|
| Single | 17.00 | 24.00 |
| Double | 32.00 | 40.00 |

Parking for 7
🛥⛺🖵♒Ⓤ🅰Ⓢ🍴📺🛏🚗✻✗
🏍 DAP 🏳 SP

## STYAL

Cheshire
Map ref 4B2

### Willow Cottage ⋔
Listed

56 Hollin Lane, Styal, Wilmslow
SK9 4JH
☎ Wilmslow (01625) 523630
*A comfortable modern dormer bungalow
set in rural surroundings yet convenient
for motorways, airport, restaurants and
Styal Country Park and Mill.*
Bedrooms: 1 single, 1 twin
Bathrooms: 1 public
**Bed & breakfast**

| per night: | £min | £max |
|---|---|---|
| Single | 15.00 | 15.00 |
| Double | 30.00 | 35.00 |

Parking for 6
🛥3🖵♒Ⓤ🅰🍴📺🛏🚗✻✗🏍Ⓣ

## TARPORLEY

Cheshire
Map ref 4A2

Old town with gabled houses and
medieval church of St Helen
containing monuments to the Done
family, a historic name in this area.
Spectacular ruins of 13th C
Beeston Castle nearby.

### Swan Hotel at Tarporley ⋔
👑👑👑 COMMENDED

50 High Street, Tarporley CW6 0AG
☎ (01829) 733838
Fax (01829) 732932

*Historic Georgian coaching inn,
attractively and traditionally furnished.
High standard of food and warm
welcome. Well-appointed bedrooms.
Special breaks available, including
activities.*
Bedrooms: 2 single, 5 double, 7 twin
Bathrooms: 14 private

**Bed & breakfast**

| per night: | £min | £max |
|---|---|---|
| Single | 35.00 | 44.95 |
| Double | 45.00 | 59.00 |

| **Half board** per person: | £min | £max |
|---|---|---|
| Daily | 42.95 | 52.00 |

Lunch available
Evening meal 1800 (last orders 2200)
Parking for 49
Cards accepted: Access, Visa, Amex
🛥📺☎🖵♒🅰Ⓢ🛏🚗☎20-100✻♿
SP 🏧

## WADDINGTON

Lancashire
Map ref 4A1

One of the area's best-known
villages, with a stream and public
gardens gracing the main street.

### Peter Barn Country House
👑 HIGHLY COMMENDED

Cross Lane, Waddington, Clitheroe
BB7 3JH
☎ Clitheroe (01200) 28585

*Tastefully converted stone tythe barn
with beamed sitting room, antiques, log
fire, overlooking extensive gardens,
stream and ponds. Home-made muesli,
marmalade. Reduced rates for 3 or
more nights.*
Bedrooms: 2 double, 1 twin
Bathrooms: 3 private
**Bed & breakfast**

| per night: | £min | £max |
|---|---|---|
| Single | 25.00 | |
| Double | 35.00 | 39.00 |

Parking for 8
🛥♒Ⓤ🅰Ⓢ🍴📺📺🛏🚗✻✗🏍 SP 🏧

## WIRRAL

Merseyside

*See under Birkenhead*

*Whatever you're seeking from a holiday, you're sure to find it in Yorkshire & Humberside. It's a region with a unique mixture of history, beautiful countryside and coastline, lively cities and a host of activities and attractions to keep you entertained. Everything is on a grand scale. There are national parks, giving you plenty of space to breathe as you wander the moors and dales. There's the coastline, with a mix of towering cliffs, major seaside resorts and quaint fishing villages. There's the city centre heritage and attractions of places like York and Harrogate. You'll never be bored in Yorkshire & Humberside.*

# YORKSHIRE & HUMBERSIDE

The Counties of North Yorkshire, South Yorkshire, West Yorkshire and Humberside

For more information on Yorkshire & Humberside, contact:
**Yorkshire & Humberside Tourist Board**
312 Tadcaster Road
York YO2 2HF
Tel: (01904) 707961 or 707070
(24-hour brochure line)
Fax: (01904) 701414

Where to Go in Yorkshire & Humberside
 – see pages 100–103

Where to Stay in Yorkshire & Humberside
 – see pages 104–129

# WHERE TO GO

*You will find hundreds of interesting places to visit during your stay in Yorkshire & Humberside, just some of which are listed in these pages. The number against each name will help you locate it on the map (page 103). Contact any Tourist Information Centre in the region for more ideas on days out in Yorkshire & Humberside.*

**❶ Scarborough Millennium**
Harbourside, Scarborough, North Yorkshire YO11 1PG
Tel: (01723) 501000
*A time travel experience unlike any other. An epic adventure through 1,000 years from 966 to 1966.*

**❷ North Yorkshire Moors Railway**
Pickering Station, Pickering, North Yorkshire YO18 7AJ
Tel: (01751) 472508
*18-mile railway through the magnificent scenery of the North York Moors National Park.*

**❸ Flamingo Land Family Funpark, Zoo and Holiday Village**
Kirby Misperton, North Yorkshire YO17 0UX
Tel: (01653) 668287
*One-price family funpark with over 100 attractions, shows and Europe's largest privately-owned zoo.*

**❹ Fountains Abbey and Studley Royal Park**
Ripon, North Yorkshire HG4 3DZ
Tel: (01765) 608888
*Largest monastic ruin in Britain, founded by Cistercian monks in 1132. Landscaped garden laid out 1720–40 with lake, formal watergarden and temples, deer park.*

**❺ Dalby Forest Drive and Visitor Centre**
Low Dalby, North Yorkshire YO18 7LS
Tel: (01751) 460295
*9-mile scenic drive with picnic places, waymarked walks, wayfaring course. Visitor centre with forestry exhibition.*

*Toad-in-the-Hole, a variation on the famous Yorkshire Pudding and a firm favourite.*

**❻ Castle Howard**
Malton, North Yorkshire YO6 7BZ
Tel: (01653) 648333
*Set in 1,000 acres of parkland with nature walks, scenic lake and stunning rose gardens. Important furniture and works of art.*

**❼ Eden Camp Modern History Theme Museum**
Malton, North Yorkshire YO17 0SD
Tel: (01653) 697777
*Modern history theme museum depicting civilian way of life in Britain during World War II. Based in a genuine ex-Prisoner of War camp with original buildings.*

**❽ Sewerby Hall, Park and Zoo**
Sewerby, Bridlington, North Humberside YO15 1EA
Tel: (01262) 673769
*Zoo, aviary, old English walled garden, bowls, putting, golf, children's corner, museum, art gallery, Amy Johnson collection, novel train from park to North Beach.*

**❾ Yorkshire Dales Falconry and Conservation Centre**
Crows Nest, Giggleswick, North Yorkshire LA2 8AS
Tel: (01729) 825164

Falconry centre with many species of birds of prey from around the world including vultures, eagles, hawks, falcons and owls. Free-flying displays, lecture room and aviaries.

**⑩ Beningbrough Hall**
Shipton-by-Beningbrough, York, North Yorkshire YO6 1DD
Tel: (01904) 470666
*Handsome Baroque house built in 1716 with nearly 100 pictures from the National Portrait Gallery. Victorian laundry, potting shed, garden, adventure playground, National Trust shop.*

**⑪ Skipton Castle**
Skipton, North Yorkshire BD23 1AQ
Tel: (01756) 792442
*One of the most complete and well-preserved medieval castles in England. Beautiful Conduit Court with famous yew.*

**⑫ Bolton Abbey Estate**
Bolton Abbey, North Yorkshire BD23 6EX
Tel: (01756) 710533
*Ruins of 12th C priory in parkland setting by River Wharfe. Nature trails, fishing, fell walking in picturesque countryside.*

**⑬ Ripley Castle**
Ripley, North Yorkshire HG3 3AY
Tel: (01423) 770152
*Ingilby family home since 1345. Fine armour, furniture, chandeliers, panelling, priest's hiding hole.*

**⑭ Jorvik Viking Centre**
Coppergate, York YO1 1NT
Tel: (01904) 643211
*Visitors travel in electric cars down a time tunnel to a re-creation of Viking York. Excavated remains of Viking houses and display of objects found.*

**⑮ National Railway Museum**
Leeman Road, York YO2 4XJ
Tel: (01904) 621261
*Experience nearly 200 years of technical and social history of the railways and see how they shaped the world.*

**⑯ York Castle Museum**
The Eye of York, York YO1 1RY
Tel: (01904) 653611
*Popular museum of everyday life with reconstructed streets and period rooms, Edwardian park, costume and jewellery, arms and armour, craft workshops.*

**⑰ York Minster**
Deangate, York YO1 2JA
Tel: (01904) 624426
*The largest Gothic cathedral in England. Museum of Saxon and Norman remains, chapter house and crypt. Unrivalled views from Norman tower.*

**⑱ Harewood House**
Harewood, Leeds, West Yorkshire LS17 9LQ
Tel: (0113) 288 6225
*18th C Carr/Adam house, Capability Brown landscape. Fine Sevres and Chinese porcelain, English and Italian paintings, Chippendale furniture. Exotic bird garden.*

**⑲ Leeds City Art Gallery and Henry Moore Centre**
The Headrow, Leeds, West Yorkshire LS1 3AA
Tel: (0113) 247 8248
*19th and 20th C paintings, sculptures, prints and drawings. Permanent collection of 20th C sculpture in Henry Moore Centre.*

**Local iron ore gave Sheffield its prosperous steel and cutlery industries.**

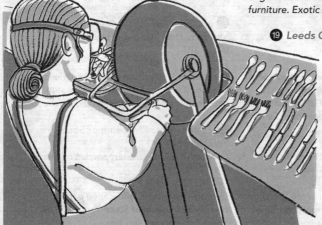

**20 Tropical World**
Canal Gardens, Roundhay Park,
Leeds LS8 1DF
Tel: (0113) 266 1850
*Greenhouses, butterfly house,
tropical house, jungle
experience, aquaria, insects
and fish.*

**21 Museum of Army
Transport**
Beverley, Humberside
HU17 ONG
Tel: (01482) 860445
*Army road, rail, sea and air
exhibits excitingly displayed in
two exhibition halls, plus the
huge, last remaining Blackburn
Beverley aircraft. D-Day
exhibition.*

*Cliffords Tower – the 13th century keep of York Castle, built by Henry III.*

**22 National Museum of Photography, Film
and Television**
Pictureville, Bradford, West Yorkshire BD1 1NQ
Tel: (01274) 307610
*The largest cinema screen (Imax) in Britain.
Kodak Museum. Fly on a magic carpet, operate
TV camera, become a newsreader for a day.*

**23 Eureka!**
Discovery Road, Halifax, West Yorkshire HX1 2NE
Tel: (01422) 330069
*Designed especially for children between 5 and
12 years of age. Visitors can touch, listen and
smell as well as look at exhibitions about the
body, work and communications.*

**24 Piece Hall**
Halifax, West Yorkshire HX1 1RE
Tel: (01422) 358087
*Historic colonnaded cloth hall, surrounding open-
air courtyard and comprising 40 speciality shops,
art gallery, weekly markets, new Calderdale
Kaleidoscope display, Tourist Information Centre.*

**25 Yorkshire Mining Museum**
Caphouse Colliery, New Road, Overton,
Wakefield, West Yorkshire WF4 4RH
Tel: (01924) 848806
*Exciting award-winning museum of the Yorkshire
coalfield, including guided underground tour of
authentic old workings.*

**26 Yorkshire Sculpture Park**
Bretton, West Yorkshire WF4 4LG
Tel: (01924) 830302
*Beautiful parkland containing regular exhibitions
of contemporary sculpture. Permanent
collections include work by Barbara Hepworth
and Henry Moore.*

**27 Normanby Hall**
Normanby, South Humberside DN15 9HU
Tel: (01724) 720588
*Regency mansion by Sir Robert Smirke, architect
of British Museum. Furnished and decorated in
period, with displays of costume.*

**28 National Fishing Heritage Centre**
Alexandra Dock, Grimsby, Humberside
DN31 1UF
Tel: (01472) 344867
*Spectacular 1950s steam trawler experience. See,
hear, smell and touch a series of re-created
environments. Museum displays, aquarium, shop.*

**29 Cusworth Hall Museum of South
Yorkshire Life**
Cusworth Lane, Doncaster, South Yorkshire
DN5 7TU
Tel: (01302) 782342
*Georgian mansion in landscaped park
containing Museum of South Yorkshire Life.
Special educational facilities.*

# FIND OUT MORE

Further information about holidays and attractions in Yorkshire & Humberside is available from:
*Yorkshire & Humberside Tourist Board,*
*312 Tadcaster Road, York YO2 2HF*
*Tel: (01904) 707961 or 707070 (24-hour brochure line)*

These publications are available free from the Yorkshire & Humberside Tourist Board:
● *Main holiday guide (information on the region, including hotels, self-catering and caravan and camping parks)*
● *Short Breaks*
● *Bed & Breakfast touring map*
● *Major events list*
● *What's On (3 issues per year)*
● *Attractions map*
● *Overseas brochure (French, Dutch, German, Italian, Spanish)*
● *Farm Holidays*
● *"Freedom" (caravan and camping guide)*
● *Getting Around Yorkshire & Humberside (guide to public transport)*
● *All Aboard (scenic railways)*

103

# WHERE TO STAY

*Accommodation entries in this regional section are listed in alphabetical order of place name, and then in alphabetical order of establishment.*

*Map references refer to the colour location maps at the back of this guide. The first figure is the map number; the letter and figure which follow indicate the grid reference on the map.*

*Symbols at the end of each accommodation entry give information about services and facilities. A 'key' to these symbols is inside the back cover flap, which can be kept open for easy reference.*

---

## AMPLEFORTH

North Yorkshire
Map ref 5C3

Stone-built village in Hambleton Hills. Famous for its abbey and college, a Benedictine public school, founded in 1802, of which Cardinal Hume was once abbot.

### Carr House Farm ⚏

Shallowdale, Ampleforth, York
YO6 4ED
☎ Coxwold (01347) 868526 & Mobile
0850 310188
*375-acre mixed farm. Good food, good welcome and good walking in peaceful "Herriot/Heartbeat" countryside. Romantic four-poster bedrooms. Just 30 minutes from York.*
Bedrooms: 3 double
Bathrooms: 3 private

**Bed & breakfast**

| per night: | £min | £max |
|---|---|---|
| Single | | 15.00 |
| Double | | 30.00 |

**Half board**

| per person: | £min | £max |
|---|---|---|
| Daily | | 23.00 |

Evening meal 1800 (last orders 1800)
Parking for 3

---

Please use the new PhONEday area telephone codes shown in establishment entries.

---

## ASKRIGG

North Yorkshire
Map ref 5B3

The name of this dales village means "ash tree ridge". It is centred on a steep main street of high, narrow 3-storey houses and thrived on cotton and later wool in 18th C. Once famous for its clock making.

### Home Farm

Listed HIGHLY COMMENDED

Stalling Busk, Askrigg, Leyburn
DL8 3DH
☎ Wensleydale (01969) 650360
*65-acre mixed farm. Licensed 17th C beamed, dales farmhouse with log fires, beautiful Victorian and antique furnishings, brass bedsteads and patchwork quilts. Traditional cooking and home-made bread.*
Bedrooms: 3 double
Bathrooms: 2 public

**Bed & breakfast**

| per night: | £min | £max |
|---|---|---|
| Double | 30.00 | 32.00 |

**Half board**

| per person: | £min | £max |
|---|---|---|
| Daily | 24.50 | 25.50 |

Evening meal 1900 (last orders 1900)
Parking for 4

### Milton House ⚏

Askrigg, Leyburn DL8 3HJ
☎ Wensleydale (01969) 650217
*Large, comfortable, family house in a beautiful dales village, central for touring or walking. Colour TV lounge and wholesome Yorkshire cooking.*

---

Bedrooms: 1 double, 1 triple, 1 family room
Bathrooms: 2 private, 1 public

**Bed & breakfast**

| per night: | £min | £max |
|---|---|---|
| Double | 30.00 | 36.00 |

**Half board**

| per person: | £min | £max |
|---|---|---|
| Daily | 25.00 | 28.00 |

Evening meal 1900 (last orders 1900)
Parking for 3

### Semergarth ⚏

Listed

Worton, Askrigg, Leyburn DL8 3EU
☎ Wensleydale (01969) 650244
*Stone-built house just off the A684. An ideal centre for walking and touring the dales. Enjoy the comfortable accommodation and warm welcome to our home.*
Bedrooms: 1 single, 1 double, 1 twin
Bathrooms: 1 public

**Bed & breakfast**

| per night: | £min | £max |
|---|---|---|
| Single | 14.50 | 15.50 |
| Double | 29.00 | 31.00 |

Parking for 2

### Thornsgill Guest House ⚏

COMMENDED

Moor Road, Askrigg, Leyburn
DL8 3HH
☎ Wensleydale (01969) 650617
*Spacious, early 20th C family house in the Yorkshire Dales National Park. En-suite bedrooms. Wholesome Yorkshire food. Relaxed friendly atmosphere.*
Bedrooms: 2 double, 1 twin
Bathrooms: 3 private

| **Bed & breakfast per night:** | £min | £max |
|---|---|---|
| Double | 37.00 | 39.00 |

Evening meal from 1830
Parking for 3

## AYSGARTH

North Yorkshire
Map ref 5B3

Famous for its beautiful Falls - a series of 3 cascades extending for half a mile on the River Ure in Wensleydale. There is a coach and carriage museum with a crafts centre at Old Yore Mill and a National Park Centre.

### Marlbeck

Listed

Aysgarth, Leyburn DL8 3AH
Wensleydale (01969) 663610
*Guests' recommendations: "Best B & B in Yorkshire - lovely room - comfy bed - great breakfast - charming hostess - great views - en-sweeter than ever - we'll be back".*
Bedrooms: 1 single, 1 double, 1 twin
Bathrooms: 1 private, 1 public

| **Bed & breakfast per night:** | £min | £max |
|---|---|---|
| Single | 16.00 | 30.00 |
| Double | 30.00 | 40.00 |

Open February-November

### Palmer Flatt Hotel

Aysgarth, Leyburn DL8 3SR
(01969) 663228
*Family-owned hotel offering guests a warm welcome, in the heart of Wensleydale near Aysgarth Falls.*
Bedrooms: 6 double, 2 twin, 1 family room
Bathrooms: 9 private

| **Bed & breakfast per night:** | £min | £max |
|---|---|---|
| Single | 22.50 | 30.00 |
| Double | 45.00 | 55.00 |

Lunch available
Evening meal 1900 (last orders 2130)
Parking for 30
Cards accepted: Access, Visa

## BAINBRIDGE

North Yorkshire
Map ref 5B3

This Wensleydale grey-stone village, with fine views of the River Bain, reputedly England's shortest river, was once a Roman settlement, some of it still visible. Boating and water-skiing on nearby Semerwater. Ancient foresters' custom of hornblowing still continues.

### Countersett Hall

HIGHLY COMMENDED

Countersett, Bainbridge, Leyburn DL8 3DD
Wensleydale (01969) 650373
Fax (01969) 650373
*Peaceful and welcoming 17th C yeoman's farmhouse close to Semerwater, the largest natural lake in Yorkshire. Ideal centre for exploring the Dales. Wonderful scenery. Walk out of our door straight on to the hills. Delicious traditional or vegetarian meals.*
Bedrooms: 1 single, 3 double
Bathrooms: 1 private, 2 public

| **Bed & breakfast per night:** | £min | £max |
|---|---|---|
| Single | 17.50 | 20.00 |
| Double | 35.00 | 40.00 |

| **Half board per person:** | £min | £max |
|---|---|---|
| Daily | 31.50 | 34.00 |

Evening meal 1930 (last orders 1700)
Parking for 6
Open March-October

### High Force Farm

Listed APPROVED

Bainbridge, Leyburn DL8 3DL
Wensleydale (01969) 650379
*470-acre hill farm. Used in the James Herriot TV series, close to Semerwater Lake. Friendly, relaxed atmosphere in non-smoking establishment.*
Bedrooms: 1 double, 1 triple
Bathrooms: 2 public

| **Bed & breakfast per night:** | £min | £max |
|---|---|---|
| Single | 13.00 | 15.00 |
| Double | 26.00 | 30.00 |

Parking for 3

## BEVERLEY

Humberside
Map ref 4C1

Beverley's most famous landmark is its beautiful medieval Minster with Percy family tomb. Many attractive squares and streets, notably Wednesday and Saturday Market, North Bar Gateway and the Museum of Army Transport, Flemingate. Famous racecourse.
*Tourist Information Centre*
*(01482) 867430*

### Eastgate Guest House

COMMENDED

7 Eastgate, Beverley, North Humberside HU17 0DR
Hull (01482) 868464
Fax (01482) 871899
*Family-run Victorian guesthouse, established and run by the same proprietor for 26 years. Close to the town centre, Beverley Minster, Museum of Army Transport and railway station.*
Bedrooms: 5 single, 5 double, 4 twin, 4 triple
Bathrooms: 7 private, 3 public

| **Bed & breakfast per night:** | £min | £max |
|---|---|---|
| Single | 15.00 | 30.00 |
| Double | 26.00 | 42.00 |

Check the introduction to this region for ideas on Where to Go.

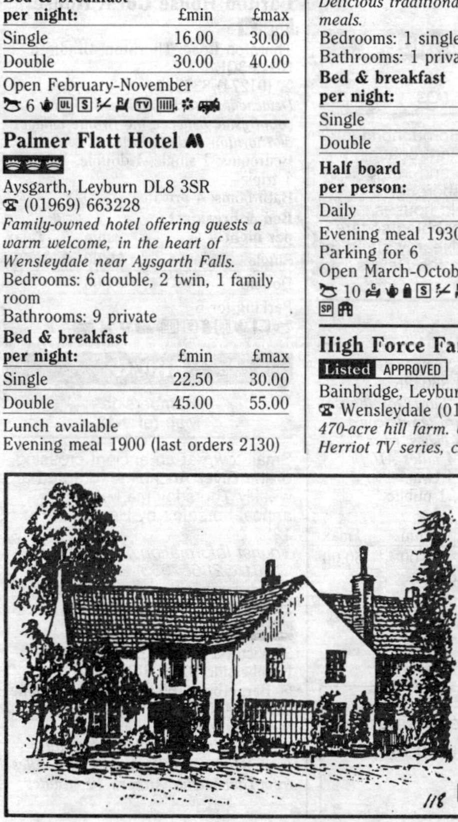

## BEVERLEY

*Continued*

### Rudstone Walk Farmhouse & Country Cottages ₥

🏆🏆 HIGHLY COMMENDED

South Cave, Brough, North
Humberside HU15 2AH
☎ North Cave (01430) 422230
Fax (01430) 424552
*303-acre arable farm. Architect-designed en-suite rooms with breakfast in historic farmhouse mentioned in the Domesday Book. Excellent location for Beverley, York, moors and coast.*
Wheelchair access category 3 ♿
Bedrooms: 7 double, 7 twin
Bathrooms: 14 private, 1 public

**Bed & breakfast**

| per night: | £min | £max |
|---|---|---|
| Single | 35.00 | 38.50 |
| Double | 44.00 | 65.00 |

Evening meal 1900 (last orders 1600)
Parking for 30
Cards accepted: Access, Visa, Amex, Switch/Delta
🛏🐾🖤📻📺🗝📱🖫📺⛏🖥🖨
🕻8-75🏌🚲🚜🏘📶🅿🏤
Ⓐ Display advertisement appears on page 105

## BINGLEY

West Yorkshire
Map ref 4B1

Bingley Five-Rise is an impressive group of locks on the Leeds and Liverpool Canal. Town claims to have first bred the Airedale terrier originally used for otter hunting. Among fine Georgian houses is Myrtle Grove where John Wesley stayed. East Riddlesden Hall is nearby.

### Ashley End

Listed

22 Ashley Road, Off Ashfield Crescent,
Bingley BD16 1DZ
☎ Bradford (01274) 569679
*Private house just off the main Bradford/Leeds road into Bingley. 5 minutes' walk to Bingley and 10 minutes' walk to the station. Twin room and single room have a wash basin.*
Bedrooms: 1 single, 2 twin
Bathrooms: 1 public

**Bed & breakfast**

| per night: | £min | £max |
|---|---|---|
| Single | 15.00 | 16.00 |
| Double | 30.00 | 32.00 |

🛏🖫🛁🖤📺🖥🚜

**Please check prices and other details at the time of booking.**

## BISHOP THORNTON

North Yorkshire
Map ref 5C3

Small village in Nidderdale, near Brimham Rocks.

### Hatton House Farm

🏆🏆 HIGHLY COMMENDED

Bishop Thornton, Harrogate HG3 3JA
☎ Harrogate (01423) 770315
*150-acre dairy & livestock farm. Farmhouse accommodation with special emphasis on well-presented, home-cooked food. Open all year round. No smoking indoors, please.*
Bedrooms: 2 double, 1 twin
Bathrooms: 1 public

**Bed & breakfast**

| per night: | £min | £max |
|---|---|---|
| Single | 18.00 | 21.00 |
| Double | 35.00 | 37.00 |

**Half board**

| per person: | £min | £max |
|---|---|---|
| Daily | 24.00 | 26.00 |
| Weekly | 155.00 | 170.00 |

Evening meal 1830 (last orders 1800)
Parking for 10
🛏🐾🖫🛁📺🖥📺🖨🚲◡🚜🌼
🏌🚜

## BOROUGHBRIDGE

North Yorkshire
Map ref 5C3

On the River Ure, Boroughbridge was once an important coaching centre with 22 inns and in the 18th C a port for Knaresborough's linens. It has fine old houses, many trees and a cobbled square with market cross. Nearby stand 3 megaliths known as the Devil's Arrows.

### Laurel Farm ₥

🏆🏆 COMMENDED

Brafferton, Helperby, York YO6 2NZ
☎ Harrogate (01423) 360436
*28-acre livestock farm. Large farmhouse with horses, sheep, hard tennis court, croquet lawn, glorious views, river walks. 12 miles York, 4 miles A1(M).*
Bedrooms: 2 double, 1 twin
Bathrooms: 1 private, 1 public

**Bed & breakfast**

| per night: | £min | £max |
|---|---|---|
| Double | 39.00 | 50.00 |

Evening meal from 1930
Parking for 6
🖤📻🛁🖤🖫🛁🖨🚲🔍🌼🚜🏘
🅿🏤

**Symbols are explained on the flap inside the back cover.**

## BRADFORD

West Yorkshire
Map ref 4B1

City founded on wool, with fine Victorian and modern buildings. Attractions include the cathedral, city hall, Cartwright Hall, Lister Park, Moorside Mills Industrial Museum and National Museum of Photography, Film and Television.
*Tourist Information Centre*
☎ *(01274) 753678*

### Brow Top Farm ₥

🏆🏆 HIGHLY COMMENDED

Baldwin Lane, Clayton, Bradford
BD14 6PS
☎ (01274) 882178
*300-acre mixed farm. Newly renovated farmhouse.*
Bedrooms: 2 double, 1 twin
Bathrooms: 3 private

**Bed & breakfast**

| per night: | £min | £max |
|---|---|---|
| Single | 20.00 | 20.00 |
| Double | 30.00 | 30.00 |

Parking for 4
🛏🖤🛁🖫🖤📺🖥🖨🌼🚜

### Carlton House Guest House

Listed

Thornton Road, Thornton, Bradford
BD13 3QE
☎ (01274) 833397
*Detached, Victorian house in open countryside between the Bronte villages of Thornton and Haworth.*
Bedrooms: 1 single, 1 double, 1 twin, 1 triple
Bathrooms: 4 private

**Bed & breakfast**

| per night: | £min | £max |
|---|---|---|
| Single | 19.00 | |
| Double | 31.00 | |

Parking for 6
🛏🖤🛁🖫🛁🖥🖨🌼🚜

## BRIGG

Humberside
Map ref 4C1

Small town at an ancient crossing of the River Ancholme, granted a weekly Thursday market and annual horsefair by Henry III in 1235.
*Tourist Information Centre*
☎ *(01652) 657053*

### Holcombe House ₥

🏆🏆🏆 COMMENDED

34 Victoria Road, Barnetby, South
Humberside DN38 6JR
☎ Barnetby (01652) 680655 & Mobile
0850 764002
*Pleasant, homely accommodation in centre of Barnetby village. 5 minutes from M180 and railway station, 3 miles from Humberside Airport, 10 minutes*

from Brigg, 15-30 minutes from Grimsby, Scunthorpe and Hull.
Bedrooms: 3 single, 3 twin
Bathrooms: 3 private, 2 public, 1 private shower

**Bed & breakfast**

| per night: | £min | £max |
|---|---|---|
| Single | 15.00 | 20.00 |
| Double | 25.00 | 30.00 |

**Half board**

| per person: | £min | £max |
|---|---|---|
| Daily | 20.00 | 25.00 |
| Weekly | 30.00 | 35.00 |

Evening meal 1900 (last orders 2000)
Parking for 4
Cards accepted: Access, Visa

## BURNT YATES

North Yorkshire
Map ref 4B1

On a hill, 1 mile north of the River Nidd, the village has a Free School founded in 1760.

### Bay Horse Inn ⋒

Burnt Yates, Harrogate HG3 3EJ
☎ Harrogate (01423) 770230
*Renowned 18th C inn with oak beams, open log fires and restaurant serving traditional English fare. In Nidderdale between Ripley and Pateley Bridge. Ideal base for racing in Yorkshire, golf courses and shooting parties.*
Bedrooms: 4 double, 8 twin, 2 triple
Bathrooms: 14 private

**Bed & breakfast**

| per night: | £min | £max |
|---|---|---|
| Single | 40.00 | 40.00 |
| Double | 55.00 | 55.00 |

**Half board**

| per person: | £min | £max |
|---|---|---|
| Daily | 42.45 | 42.45 |
| Weekly | 250.00 | 250.00 |

Lunch available
Evening meal 1900 (last orders 2200)
Parking for 80
Cards accepted: Access, Visa

## CLOUGHTON

North Yorkshire
Map ref 5D3

Village close to the east coast and North York Moors.

### Gowland Farm ⋒
Listed

Gowland Lane, Cloughton, Scarborough YO13 0DU
☎ Scarborough (01723) 870924
*In a quiet, peaceful location with superb views. 2 miles north of Cloughton on the A171 take a sharp left turn on to an unmarked road and house is half a mile*

down on the left. A warm welcome awaits you.
Bedrooms: 1 single, 1 double, 1 twin
Bathrooms: 1 public

**Bed & breakfast**

| per night: | £min | £max |
|---|---|---|
| Single | 13.50 | 13.50 |
| Double | 27.00 | 27.00 |

**Half board**

| per person: | £min | £max |
|---|---|---|
| Daily | 20.00 | 20.00 |
| Weekly | 130.00 | 130.00 |

Evening meal 1900 (last orders 2000)
Parking for 8
Open April-October

## COXWOLD

North Yorkshire
Map ref 5C3

This well-known beauty spot in Hambleton and Howardian Hills is famous as home of Laurence Sterne, the 18th C country parson and author of "Tristram Shandy" books who, in 1760, lived at Shandy Hall, now open to the public.

### Wakendale House
COMMENDED

Oldstead Grange, Coxwold, York YO6 4BJ
☎ (01347) 868351
*160-acre mixed farm. Comfortable accommodation with a friendly family in an attractive farmhouse set in lovely countryside. No smoking in the house.*
Bedrooms: 1 double, 1 twin, 1 triple
Bathrooms: 1 public

**Bed & breakfast**

| per night: | £min | £max |
|---|---|---|
| Double | 30.00 | |

Parking for 5
Open February-November

### Willows ⋒
Listed

12 Husthwaite Road, Coxwold, York YO6 4AE
☎ (01347) 868335
*Attractive village 20 miles north of York and 6 miles from Thirsk. Lounge for sole use of guests. Continental breakfast available when required at whatever time you wish.*
Bedrooms: 1 double
Bathrooms: 1 public

**Bed & breakfast**

| per night: | £min | £max |
|---|---|---|
| Single | 11.00 | 15.00 |
| Double | 22.00 | 30.00 |

Parking for 1

## CRAYKE

North Yorkshire
Map ref 5C3

Pretty hillside village once belonging to the Bishopric of Durham, hence the name of the village inn, the "Durham Ox".

### Halfway House ⋒
DE LUXE

Easingwold Road, Crayke, York YO6 4TJ
☎ Easingwold (01347) 822614
Fax (01347) 822942
*Elegant Victorian house and Georgian granary set in secluded gardens with 7-acre paddock, halfway between the market town of Easingwold and pretty village of Crayke. "Bed and Breakfast of the Year" winner in England for Excellence 1993.*
Bedrooms: 2 double, 1 twin
Bathrooms: 3 private, 2 public

**Bed & breakfast**

| per night: | £min | £max |
|---|---|---|
| Single | 40.00 | |
| Double | 60.00 | |

**Half board**

| per person: | £min | £max |
|---|---|---|
| Daily | 58.00 | |
| Weekly | 365.00 | |

Evening meal from 2000
Parking for 13
Cards accepted: Access, Visa

## CROPTON

North Yorkshire
Map ref 5C3

Moorland village at the top of a high ridge with stone houses, some of cruck construction, a Victorian church and the remains of a 12th C moated castle. Cropton Forest nearby.

### Burr Bank Cottage ⋒
HIGHLY COMMENDED

Cropton, Pickering YO18 8HL
☎ Lastingham (01751) 417777
Fax (01751) 417777
*Stone cottage in 10 acres with extensive views. Peaceful accommodation, a warm welcome and home cooking.*
Bedrooms: 1 double, 1 twin
Bathrooms: 2 private

**Bed & breakfast**

| per night: | £min | £max |
|---|---|---|
| Single | 21.00 | 21.00 |
| Double | 42.00 | 42.00 |

Continued ▶

We advise you to confirm your booking in writing.

## CROPTON

*Continued*

**Half board**

| per person: | £min | £max |
|---|---|---|
| Daily | 33.00 | 33.00 |
| Weekly | 231.00 | 231.00 |

Evening meal 1900 (last orders 1900)
Parking for 10

### High Farm ⚑

[COMMENDED]

Cropton, Pickering YO18 8HL
☎ Lastingham (01751) 417461
*Lovely Victorian house with large gardens. Easy access to the moors, coast and York. Open fires and a warm welcome.*
Bedrooms: 3 double
Bathrooms: 3 private

**Bed & breakfast**

| per night: | £min | £max |
|---|---|---|
| Single | 20.00 | 20.00 |
| Double | 34.00 | 36.00 |

Parking for 10
Open March-October and Christmas

## DANBY

North Yorkshire
Map ref 5C3

### Duke of Wellington ⚑

[COMMENDED]

Danby, Whitby YO21 2LY
☎ Guisborough (01287) 660351

*Traditional English inn in the centre of the village. On the North Yorkshire Moors, close to the Moors Centre and the east coast. Access by road and rail.*
Bedrooms: 1 single, 5 double, 1 twin, 2 triple
Bathrooms: 9 private, 1 public

**Bed & breakfast**

| per night: | £min | £max |
|---|---|---|
| Single | 19.00 | 22.00 |
| Double | 38.00 | 44.00 |

**Half board**

| per person: | £min | £max |
|---|---|---|
| Daily | 24.00 | |
| Weekly | 154.00 | |

Lunch available
Evening meal 1900 (last orders 2130)
Parking for 8
Cards accepted: Access, Visa, Amex

## DARLEY

North Yorkshire
Map ref 4B1

### Greenbanks ⚑

[Listed]

Nidd Side, Station Road, Darley,
Harrogate HG3 2PW
☎ Harrogate (01423) 780883
*In the village of Darley, on the banks of the River Nidd. Perfect for walkers and convenient for Harrogate.*
Bedrooms: 2 double, 1 twin
Bathrooms: 1 public

**Bed & breakfast**

| per night: | £min | £max |
|---|---|---|
| Single | 14.00 | 15.00 |
| Double | 25.00 | 27.00 |

## EASINGWOLD

North Yorkshire
Map ref 5C3

Market town of charm and character with a cobbled square and many fine Georgian buildings.

### The Old Vicarage ⚑

[COMMENDED]

Market Place, Easingwold, York
YO6 3AL
☎ (01347) 821015
*Delightful 18th C country house with extensive lawned gardens and croquet lawn. In centre of market town, 12 miles north of York, and ideal as a touring centre for North Yorkshire.*
Bedrooms: 1 single, 2 double, 2 twin
Bathrooms: 5 private

**Bed & breakfast**

| per night: | £min | £max |
|---|---|---|
| Single | 21.00 | 24.00 |
| Double | 39.00 | 42.00 |

Parking for 5
Open February-November

## EBBERSTON

North Yorkshire
Map ref 5D3

Picturesque village with a Norman church and hall, overlooking the Vale of Pickering.

### The Foxholm ⚑

Ebberston, Scarborough YO13 9NJ
☎ Scarborough (01723) 859550
*Small, family-run, fully licensed country hotel in rural setting. Ground-floor rooms. Overlooks peaceful gardens.*
Bedrooms: 4 double, 3 twin
Bathrooms: 7 private, 3 public

**Bed & breakfast**

| per night: | £min | £max |
|---|---|---|
| Single | 25.50 | 28.50 |
| Double | 47.00 | 53.00 |

Lunch available
Evening meal 1830 (last orders 2030)
Parking for 20

## ELLERBY

North Yorkshire
Map ref 5C3

### Ellerby Hotel ⚑

[COMMENDED]

Ellerby, Saltburn-by-the-Sea, Cleveland
TS13 5LP
☎ Whitby (01947) 840342
Fax (01947) 841221
*Residential country inn within the North York Moors National Park, 9 miles north of Whitby, 1 mile inland from Runswick Bay.*
Wheelchair access category 3 ♿
Bedrooms: 7 double, 2 triple
Bathrooms: 9 private

**Bed & breakfast**

| per night: | £min | £max |
|---|---|---|
| Single | 31.00 | 35.00 |
| Double | 46.00 | 55.00 |

Lunch available
Evening meal 1900 (last orders 2200)
Parking for 60
Cards accepted: Access, Visa, Switch/Delta

## ESCRICK

North Yorkshire
Map ref 4C1

Near York, Escrick has an impressive Victorian church, St Helen's, designed in 14th C style with colourful marble and stone features.

### Black Bull Inn ⚑

[COMMENDED]

Main Street, Escrick, York YO4 6JP
☎ York (01904) 728245

*Country inn set in the centre of a quiet village. 10 minutes' drive from the beautiful city of York.*
Bedrooms: 5 double, 2 twin, 1 family room
Bathrooms: 8 private

**Bed & breakfast**

| per night: | £min | £max |
|---|---|---|
| Single | 35.00 | 35.00 |
| Double | 48.00 | 58.00 |

Lunch available
Evening meal 1700 (last orders 2200)
Parking for 20
Cards accepted: Access, Visa

## FLAMBOROUGH

Humberside
Map ref 5D3

Village with strong seafaring tradition, high on chalk headland dominated by cliffs of Flamborough Head, a fortress for over 2000 years. St Oswald's Church is in the oldest part of Flamborough.

### The Grange ♙
Listed COMMENDED

Flamborough, Bridlington, North Humberside YO15 1AS
☎ Bridlington (01262) 850207
Fax (01262) 851359
*475-acre arable & livestock farm. Family-run Georgian farmhouse offering a warm welcome. Half a mile from the village, close to RSPB reserve at Bempton.*
Bedrooms: 1 double, 2 twin
Bathrooms: 2 public

**Bed & breakfast**

| per night: | £min | £max |
|---|---|---|
| Single | 13.00 | 14.50 |
| Double | 26.00 | 29.00 |

Parking for 6

## FLAXTON

North Yorkshire
Map ref 5C3

Attractive village with broad greens, just west of the A64 York to Malton highway.

### Grange Farm ♙

Oak Busk Lane, Flaxton, York YO6 7RL
☎ York (01904) 468219
*130-acre arable & livestock farm. South-facing, modernised farmhouse in its own gardens. 8 miles from York, off the A64 York to Scarborough road, through Flaxton village and right down Oak Busk Lane.*
Bedrooms: 2 double, 1 family room
Bathrooms: 1 private, 1 public

**Bed & breakfast**

| per night: | £min | £max |
|---|---|---|
| Single | 14.00 | 16.00 |
| Double | 28.00 | 32.00 |

Parking for 10

## GARFORTH

West Yorkshire
Map ref 4B1

### Myrtle House ♙
Listed

31 Wakefield Road, Garforth, Leeds LS25 1AN
☎ Leeds (0113) 286 6445
*Spacious Victorian terraced house between M62 and A1. All rooms have tea and coffee making facilities and TV.*
Bedrooms: 1 single, 1 double, 3 twin, 1 triple
Bathrooms: 3 public

**Bed & breakfast**

| per night: | £min | £max |
|---|---|---|
| Single | 15.00 | |
| Double | 30.00 | |

## GILLAMOOR

North Yorkshire
Map ref 5C3

Village much admired by photographers for its views of Farndale, including "Surprise View" from the churchyard.

### Royal Oak Inn ♙
COMMENDED

Gillamoor, York YO6 6HX
☎ Kirkbymoorside (01751) 431414
*Old country inn on the edge of the North York Moors. Tastefully renovated, with plenty of character and charm. Open log fires.*
Bedrooms: 5 double, 1 twin
Bathrooms: 6 private

**Bed & breakfast**

| per night: | £min | £max |
|---|---|---|
| Single | 25.00 | 34.00 |
| Double | 44.00 | 48.00 |

Lunch available
Evening meal 1900 (last orders 2100)
Parking for 9

## GOLCAR

West Yorkshire
Map ref 4B1

### 14 Grandstand ♙
Listed

Scapegoat Hill, Golcar, Huddersfield HD7 4NQ
☎ Huddersfield (01484) 658342
*Yorkshire stone-built cottage in quiet Pennine village. Panoramic views. Spacious, comfortable rooms with double glazing, central heating and colour TV. Warm welcome assured.*
Bedrooms: 1 double, 1 twin
Bathrooms: 2 public

**Bed & breakfast**

| per night: | £min | £max |
|---|---|---|
| Single | 16.00 | 18.00 |
| Double | 32.00 | 36.00 |

Evening meal from 1800
Parking for 2

## GRASSINGTON

North Yorkshire
Map ref 5B3

Tourists visit this former lead-mining village to see its "smiddy", antique and craft shops and Upper Wharfedale Museum of country trades. Popular with fishermen and walkers. Numerous prehistoric sites. Grassington Feast in October. National Park Centre.

### Clarendon Hotel ♙
COMMENDED

Hebden, Grassington, Skipton BD23 5DE
☎ Skipton (01756) 752446
*Yorkshire Dales village inn serving good food and ales. Personal supervision at all times. Steaks and fish dishes are specialities.*
Bedrooms: 2 double, 1 twin
Bathrooms: 3 private

**Bed & breakfast**

| per night: | £min | £max |
|---|---|---|
| Double | 40.00 | 50.00 |

Lunch available
Evening meal 1900 (last orders 2100)
Parking for 30

### Foresters Arms Hotel ♙
Listed

20 Main Street, Grassington, Skipton BD23 5AA
☎ (01756) 752349
*Formerly an old coaching inn, situated in picturesque village, serving lunch and evening meals and hand-pulled ales.*
Bedrooms: 1 single, 4 double, 2 triple
Bathrooms: 1 private, 2 public

**Bed & breakfast**

| per night: | £min | £max |
|---|---|---|
| Single | 16.00 | 20.00 |
| Double | 32.00 | 50.00 |

Lunch available
Evening meal 1800 (last orders 2030)
Parking for 2

### Franor House

3 Wharfeside Avenue, Threshfield, Skipton BD23 5BS
☎ (01756) 752115
*Large semi-detached house in quiet surroundings. Take B6265 from Skipton, turning right for Grassington. Wharfeside Avenue is half a mile - first turning on left.*
Bedrooms: 1 single, 1 twin, 1 triple

*Continued* ▶

## GRASSINGTON

*Continued*

Bathrooms: 3 private
**Bed & breakfast**

| per night: | £min | £max |
| --- | --- | --- |
| Single | 17.00 | 18.50 |
| Double | 30.00 | 35.00 |

Parking for 4
Open March-October and Christmas
♿ ♨ 🖵 ♦ Ⓤ 🅐 S 🅜 🎬 🏨 ♨ ❂ ♪ ▶ ✿ ✈ ⛳

### Grange Cottage ⋀

**HIGHLY COMMENDED**

Linton, Skipton BD23 5HH
☎ (01756) 752527
*Stone-built cottage with open fires and warm hospitality. In a quiet backwater of a picture postcard village, perfect for hiking and car touring in the dales.*
Bedrooms: 1 double, 1 twin
Bathrooms: 1 public, 1 private shower
**Bed & breakfast**

| per night: | £min | £max |
| --- | --- | --- |
| Single | 25.00 | 25.00 |
| Double | 35.00 | 37.00 |

Parking for 4
Open March-October
♿ ♨ ♦ Ⓤ 🅐 S ✂ 🅜 🎬 🏨 ♨ ❂ ✿ ⛳

## GREEN HAMMERTON

North Yorkshire
Map ref 4C1

### Bay Horse Inn & Motel ⋀

**COMMENDED**

York Road, Green Hammerton, York
YO5 8BN
☎ Boroughbridge (01423) 330338 & 331113
Fax (01423) 331279
*Village inn 10 miles from York and Harrogate on the A59 and 3 miles off the A1. Restaurant and bar meals. Weekly rates on request.*
Bedrooms: 2 single, 3 double, 4 twin, 1 triple
Bathrooms: 10 private
**Bed & breakfast**

| per night: | £min | £max |
| --- | --- | --- |
| Single | 30.00 | 30.00 |
| Double | 45.00 | 45.00 |

Lunch available
Evening meal 1900 (last orders 2130)
Parking for 40
Cards accepted: Access, Visa, Diners
♿ ♨ ♦ ☎ 🖵 ♦ 🅐 S 🏨 ❂ 🆈 SP T

National Crown ratings were correct at the time of going to press but are subject to change. Please check at the time of booking.

## GUNNERSIDE

North Yorkshire
Map ref 5B3

Taking its name from the Viking chieftain "Gunner", the village has a humpbacked bridge known as "Ivelet Bridge" spanning the river which is said to be haunted by a headless dog.

### Oxnop Hall

**COMMENDED**

Low Oxnop, Gunnerside, Richmond
DL11 6JJ
☎ Richmond (01748) 886253
*600-acre hill farm. Traditional farmhouse in the heart of Swaledale, featuring oak beams and mullion windows. All rooms have private facilities.*
Bedrooms: 1 single, 3 double, 1 twin, 1 family room
Bathrooms: 6 private
**Bed & breakfast**

| per night: | £min | £max |
| --- | --- | --- |
| Single | 20.00 | 21.00 |
| Double | 40.00 | 42.00 |

**Half board**

| per person: | £min | £max |
| --- | --- | --- |
| Daily | 31.50 | 33.00 |
| Weekly | 213.00 | 220.50 |

Evening meal 1630 (last orders 1630)
Parking for 5
Open March-November
♿ 7 ♨ ☎ ♦ ⓠ 🅐 S ✂ 🅜 🎬 🏨 ♨ ❂ ✈ ⛳ ♿

## HALIFAX

West Yorkshire
Map ref 4B1

Founded on the cloth trade, and famous for its building society, textiles, carpets and toffee. Most notable landmark is Piece Hall where wool merchants traded, now restored to house shops, museums and art gallery. Home also to Eureka! The Museum for Children.
*Tourist Information Centre*
☎ (01422) 368725

### The Elms

**♨**

Keighley Road, Illingworth, Halifax
HX2 8HT
☎ (01422) 244430
*Victorian residence with gardens and original ornate ceilings, within 3 miles of Halifax.*
Bedrooms: 2 single, 1 double, 1 triple
Bathrooms: 2 private, 1 public
**Bed & breakfast**

| per night: | £min | £max |
| --- | --- | --- |
| Single | 17.00 | 19.00 |
| Double | 34.00 | 38.00 |

**Half board**

| per person: | £min | £max |
| --- | --- | --- |
| Daily | 24.50 | 26.50 |

Evening meal 1800 (last orders 2000)
Parking for 14
♿ ♨ 🖵 ♦ Ⓤ 🅜 S 🅜 🎬 🏨 ♨ ❂ 🆈 8 ❂ ⛳ SP

## HARROGATE

North Yorkshire
Map ref 4B1

A major conference, exhibition and shopping centre, renowned for its spa heritage and award winning floral displays, spacious parks and gardens. Famous for antiques, toffee, fine shopping and excellent tea shops, also its Royal Pump Rooms and Baths.
*Tourist Information Centre*
☎ (01423) 525666

### Alamah ⋀

**COMMENDED**

88 Kings Road, Harrogate HG1 5JX
☎ (01423) 502187
*Comfortable rooms, personal attention, friendly atmosphere and full English breakfast. 300 metres from town centre. Garages/parking.*
Bedrooms: 2 single, 2 double, 2 twin, 1 family room
Bathrooms: 5 private, 2 private showers
**Bed & breakfast**

| per night: | £min | £max |
| --- | --- | --- |
| Single | 20.00 | 22.00 |
| Double | 42.00 | 45.00 |

**Half board**

| per person: | £min | £max |
| --- | --- | --- |
| Daily | 33.00 | |

Evening meal 1830 (last orders 1630)
Parking for 8
♿ 🖵 ♦ Ⓤ 🅐 🅜 🏨 ♨ 🆈 SP T

### The Belfry

**Listed**

27 Belmont Road, Harrogate
HG2 0LR
☎ (01423) 522783
*Friendly, family guesthouse within easy walking distance of the town centre and all tourist amenities. A wide choice of cooked breakfast is offered.*
Bedrooms: 2 single, 1 double, 1 twin
Bathrooms: 1 public
**Bed & breakfast**

| per night: | £min | £max |
| --- | --- | --- |
| Single | 15.50 | 16.50 |
| Double | 31.00 | 33.00 |

♿ ♨ 🖵 ♦ Ⓤ 🅐 S 🏨 ♨ ✈ ⛳

### Brooklands ⋀

**Listed COMMENDED**

5 Valley Drive, Harrogate HG2 0JJ
☎ (01423) 564609
*Overlooking Harrogate's beautiful valley gardens, a short walk to the town centre and an ideal base from which to*

*explore the magnificent sights and scenery of the Yorkshire Dales.*
Bedrooms: 1 single, 1 double, 2 twin, 1 family room
Bathrooms: 5 private

**Bed & breakfast**

| per night: | £min | £max |
|---|---|---|
| Single | 23.00 | 23.00 |
| Double | 39.00 | 39.00 |

Cards accepted: Access, Visa

### Knabbs Ash M

HIGHLY COMMENDED

Skipton Road, Felliscliffe, Harrogate HG3 2LT
☎ (01423) 771040
Fax (01423) 771515

*Set back off the A59 Harrogate to Skipton road, 6 miles west of Harrogate, in its own grounds. In a panoramic, tranquil setting. Ideal area for walking and exploring the Yorkshire Dales.*
Bedrooms: 2 double, 1 twin
Bathrooms: 3 private

**Bed & breakfast**

| per night: | £min | £max |
|---|---|---|
| Single | 25.00 | 25.00 |
| Double | 40.00 | 40.00 |

Parking for 6

### 17 Peckfield Close M

APPROVED

Hampsthwaite, Harrogate HG3 2ES
☎ (01423) 770765
*In picturesque village 4 miles from Harrogate off A59. Large, attractive garden. At start of Nidderdale Walk.*
Bedrooms: 1 single, 2 twin
Bathrooms: 1 public

**Bed & breakfast**

| per night: | £min | £max |
|---|---|---|
| Single | 14.00 | 16.00 |
| Double | 28.00 | 32.00 |

**Half board**

| per person: | £min | £max |
|---|---|---|
| Daily | 19.00 | 21.00 |
| Weekly | 133.00 | 147.00 |

Parking for 2

---

The symbol **M** after an establishment name indicates membership of a Regional Tourist Board.

---

North Yorkshire
Map ref 5B3

The capital of Upper Wensleydale on the famous Pennine Way, renowned for great cheeses. Popular with walkers. Dales National Park Information Centre and Folk Museum. Nearby is spectacular Hardraw Force waterfall.

### Ebor Guest House M

Burtersett Road, Hawes DL8 3NT
☎ Wensleydale (01969) 667337
*Small, family-run guesthouse, double-glazed and centrally-heated throughout. Walkers are particularly welcome. Centrally located for touring the dales.*
Bedrooms: 1 single, 2 double, 1 twin
Bathrooms: 2 private, 1 public

**Bed & breakfast**

| per night: | £min | £max |
|---|---|---|
| Single | 14.00 | 16.00 |
| Double | 28.00 | 32.00 |

Parking for 5

### Springbank House M

COMMENDED

Springbank, Townfoot, Hawes DL8 3NW
☎ Wensleydale (01969) 667376
*Delightful Victorian house near the centre of Hawes with superb views over the surrounding fells.*
Bedrooms: 2 triple
Bathrooms: 2 private

**Bed & breakfast**

| per night: | £min | £max |
|---|---|---|
| Double | 32.00 | |

Parking for 3
Open February-October

### White Hart Inn M

APPROVED

Main Street, Hawes DL8 3QL
☎ Wensleydale (01969) 667259
*Small country inn with a friendly welcome, offering home-cooked meals using local produce. An ideal centre for exploring the Yorkshire Dales.*
Bedrooms: 1 single, 4 double, 2 twin
Bathrooms: 2 public

**Bed & breakfast**

| per night: | £min | £max |
|---|---|---|
| Single | 17.50 | 17.50 |
| Double | 33.00 | 33.00 |

Lunch available
Evening meal 1900 (last orders 2100)
Parking for 7
Cards accepted: Access, Visa, Amex

---

North Yorkshire
Map ref 5C3

### Easterside Farm M

COMMENDED

Hawnby, York YO6 5QT
☎ Bilsdale (01439) 6277 Changing to 798277
*25-acre hill farm. Recently renovated large 18th C farmhouse with garden. Ideal base for touring North Yorkshire and all its splendours.*
Bedrooms: 1 double, 1 twin, 1 triple
Bathrooms: 3 private

**Bed & breakfast**

| per night: | £min | £max |
|---|---|---|
| Single | 15.00 | 17.00 |
| Double | 30.00 | 34.00 |

**Half board**

| per person: | £min | £max |
|---|---|---|
| Daily | 27.00 | 27.00 |
| Weekly | 175.00 | |

Evening meal 1830 (last orders 1930)

---

West Yorkshire
Map ref 4B1

This Pennine town is famous as home of the Bronte family. The parsonage is now a Bronte Museum where furniture and possessions of the family are displayed. Moors and Bronte waterfalls nearby and steam trains on the Keighley and Worth Valley Railway pass through.
*Tourist Information Centre*
☎ *(01535) 642329*

### Ebor House M

APPROVED

Lees Lane, Haworth, Keighley BD22 8RA
☎ Keighley (01535) 645869
*Yorkshire stone-built house of character, conveniently placed for the main tourist attractions of Haworth, including the Worth Valley Railway and Bronte Parsonage and Museum.*
Bedrooms: 3 twin
Bathrooms: 1 public

**Bed & breakfast**

| per night: | £min | £max |
|---|---|---|
| Single | 14.00 | |
| Double | 26.00 | |

Parking for 2

### Hole Farm M

COMMENDED

Dimples Lane, Haworth, Keighley BD22 8QS
☎ Keighley (01535) 644755
*8-acre smallholding. 17th C farmhouse, five minutes' walk from Bronte*

Continued ▶

## HAWORTH
### Continued

*Parsonage and two minutes' walk from the moors. Panoramic views of Haworth. Farm has peacocks, geese, cattle and horses.*
Bedrooms: 2 double
Bathrooms: 2 private

**Bed & breakfast**

| per night: | £min | £max |
|---|---|---|
| Double | 34.00 | |

Parking for 4

### The Lee
**Listed**

Lee Lane, Oxenhope, Keighley BD22 9RB
☎ (01535) 646311
*Detached 17th C house with 6 acres of land, 1.5 miles from the centre of Haworth. Close to the moors and waterfalls.*
Bedrooms: 1 double, 1 triple
Bathrooms: 2 private, 2 public

**Bed & breakfast**

| per night: | £min | £max |
|---|---|---|
| Single | 15.00 | 20.00 |
| Double | 30.00 | 30.00 |

Parking for 4

### Old White Lion Hotel
**COMMENDED**

Haworth, Keighley BD22 8DU
☎ Keighley (01535) 642313
Fax (01535) 646222
*Family-run, centuries old coaching inn. Candlelit restaurant using local fresh produce cooked to order and featured in food guides. Old world bars serving extensive range of bar snacks and real ales.*
Bedrooms: 3 single, 6 double, 2 twin, 4 triple
Bathrooms: 15 private

**Bed & breakfast**

| per night: | £min | £max |
|---|---|---|
| Single | 35.00 | 38.00 |
| Double | 46.00 | 50.00 |

**Half board**

| per person: | £min | £max |
|---|---|---|
| Daily | 34.00 | 49.00 |
| Weekly | 161.00 | 266.00 |

Lunch available
Evening meal 1900 (last orders 2200)
Parking for 10
Cards accepted: Access, Visa, Diners, Amex

The national Crown scheme is explained in full in the information pages at the back of this guide.

## HEBDEN BRIDGE
West Yorkshire
Map ref 4B1

Originally a small town on packhorse route, Hebden Bridge grew into a booming mill town in 18th C with rows of "up-and-down" houses of several storeys built against hillsides. Ancient "pace-egg play" custom held on Good Friday.
*Tourist Information Centre*
☎ *(01422) 843831*

### Cherry Tree Cottage
**COMMENDED**

Woodhouse Road, Todmorden, Lancashire OL14 5RJ
☎ Todmorden (01706) 817492
*Sympathetically restored, part 17th C country cottage with modern amenities and lovely views. Emphasis on fresh, home-cooked fare.*
Bedrooms: 2 twin
Bathrooms: 2 private

**Bed & breakfast**

| per night: | £min | £max |
|---|---|---|
| Single | 16.50 | 19.00 |
| Double | 33.00 | 38.00 |

**Half board**

| per person: | £min | £max |
|---|---|---|
| Daily | 23.50 | 26.00 |
| Weekly | 164.50 | 182.00 |

Evening meal 1800 (last orders 1900)
Parking for 2

### Robin Hood Inn
**Listed APPROVED**

Pecket Well, Hebden Bridge HX7 8QR
☎ (01422) 842593
*Traditional inn on the edge of Calderdale and Pennine Way, Bronte country, Hardcastle Crags. Near Hebden Bridge. Real ale and home-made food.*
Bedrooms: 1 single, 1 double, 1 twin, 1 triple
Bathrooms: 2 private, 2 public

**Bed & breakfast**

| per night: | £min | £max |
|---|---|---|
| Single | 16.50 | 20.00 |
| Double | 30.00 | 40.00 |

**Half board**

| per person: | £min | £max |
|---|---|---|
| Daily | 24.00 | 29.50 |
| Weekly | 90.00 | 135.00 |

Lunch available
Evening meal 1845 (last orders 2200)
Parking for 28
Cards accepted: Visa, Switch/Delta

Please mention this guide when making a booking.

## HELLIFIELD
North Yorkshire
Map ref 4B1

### Wenningber Farm
**HIGHLY COMMENDED**

Airton Road, Hellifield, Skipton BD23 4JR
☎ (01729) 850856
*80-acre mixed farm. Charming farmhouse, with log fire and oak beams, just 5 miles from Malham in the heart of the Yorkshire Dales.*
Bedrooms: 1 double, 1 twin
Bathrooms: 1 public

**Bed & breakfast**

| per night: | £min | £max |
|---|---|---|
| Single | 18.00 | 24.00 |
| Double | 32.00 | 36.00 |

Parking for 10

## HELMSLEY
North Yorkshire
Map ref 5C3

Pretty town on the River Rye at the entrance to Ryedale and the North York Moors, with large square and remains of 12th C castle, several inns and All Saints' Church.

### Sproxton Hall
**HIGHLY COMMENDED**

Sproxton, Helmsley, York YO6 5EQ
☎ (01439) 770225
Fax (01439) 771373
*300-acre mixed farm. 17th C Grade II listed stone farmhouse, beamed, beautifully decorated and comfortably furnished. In a peaceful setting with panoramic views, 1.5 miles from Helmsley. Excellent base for the North York Moors, York, the coast and dales. Non-smokers only please.*
Bedrooms: 2 double, 1 twin
Bathrooms: 1 private, 1 public

**Bed & breakfast**

| per night: | £min | £max |
|---|---|---|
| Single | 19.50 | |
| Double | 35.00 | 43.00 |

Parking for 10

### Stilworth House

1 Church Street, Helmsley, York YO6 5AD
☎ (01439) 771072 & 770507
*Elegant Georgian town house off the market square of Helmsley. All Saints Church to front and Helmsley Castle to the rear.*
Bedrooms: 3 double
Bathrooms: 3 private

**Bed & breakfast**

| per night: | £min | £max |
|---|---|---|
| Single | 25.00 | 35.00 |
| Double | 40.00 | 45.00 |

Evening meal from 1830
Parking for 4

🛏️♿🚭📞♨️📶Ⓢ🅿️📺🎬 ▦ 🚐❄️✕ 🚙 SP

## HOLMFIRTH

West Yorkshire
Map ref 4B1

This village has become famous as the location for the filming of the TV series "Last of the Summer Wine". It has a postcard museum and is on the edge of the Peak District National Park.
*Tourist Information Centre*
☎ *(01484) 687603*

### Aldermans Head Manor ♠

⚜️⚜️⚜️ HIGHLY COMMENDED

Hartcliffe Hill Road, Langsett,
Stocksbridge, Sheffield S30 5GY
☎ Barnsley (01226) 766209
Fax (01226) 766209
*Seven centuries ago Kirkstead Abbey monks owned the manor, which overlooks Langsett and Midhopestones reservoirs with the Peak District beyond. In village to the south east of Holmfirth.*
Bedrooms: 2 double, 2 twin
Bathrooms: 4 private

**Bed & breakfast**

| per night: | £min | £max |
|---|---|---|
| Single | 25.00 | 35.00 |
| Double | 40.00 | 50.00 |

**Half board**

| per person: | £min | £max |
|---|---|---|
| Daily | 40.00 | 50.00 |
| Weekly | 245.00 | 301.00 |

Evening meal from 1900
Parking for 12

🛏️12📞📶Ⓢ🅿️✕🎬📺▦🚐 ☎12❄️🚙

### Spring Head House ♠

Listed

15 Holmfirth Road, Shepley,
Huddersfield HD8 8BB
☎ Huddersfield (01484) 606300
Fax (01484) 608030
*Large Georgian house with a garden, close to Holmfirth and "Summer Wine" country and with easy access to the M1 and M62.*
Bedrooms: 1 single, 1 twin
Bathrooms: 1 private, 1 public

**Bed & breakfast**

| per night: | £min | £max |
|---|---|---|
| Single | 16.50 | 22.00 |
| Double | 33.00 | 33.00 |

Parking for 3
Cards accepted: Access, Visa

🛏️🅿️♨️📶Ⓢ✕📺▦🚐❄️✕🚙

### 29 Woodhead Road

⚜️ COMMENDED

Holmfirth, Huddersfield HD7 1JU
☎ (01484) 683962
*200-year-old family home, 5 minutes' walk from Holmfirth. Tea and coffee available at any time. Good walking area and pleasant countryside.*
Bedrooms: 1 twin
Bathrooms: 1 private

**Bed & breakfast**

| per night: | £min | £max |
|---|---|---|
| Single | 13.00 | 13.00 |
| Double | 26.00 | 26.00 |

Parking for 2

📞📺🅿️♨️📶▦🚐✕🚙🏇

## HUNTON

North Yorkshire
Map ref 5C3

### The Countryman's Inn

⚜️⚜️⚜️ COMMENDED

Hunton, Bedale DL8 1PY
☎ Bedale (01677) 450554
*Recently modernised village inn and restaurant, retaining its old world charm, with log fires and beamed ceilings. Four-poster room. Just off the A684 between Bedale and Leyburn, convenient for the Yorkshire Dales.*
Bedrooms: 6 double, 1 twin
Bathrooms: 7 private

**Bed & breakfast**

| per night: | £min | £max |
|---|---|---|
| Single | 27.00 | 30.00 |
| Double | 44.00 | 55.00 |

Evening meal 1900 (last orders 2130)
Parking for 20
Cards accepted: Access, Visa, Amex

▦🅿️♨️📞📶Ⓢ✕▦🚐🔍♨️⋃▶️✕🚙 SP

## HUSTHWAITE

North Yorkshire
Map ref 5C3

Attractive village beneath Hambleton Hills, of weathered brickwork houses and a green dominated by medieval church of St Nicholas with some Norman features.

### Flower of May

Listed

Husthwaite, York YO6 3SG
☎ Coxwold (01347) 868317
*153-acre mixed farm. Family-run farm with beautiful views of the Vale of York. Convenient for North York Moors, York and coast.*
Bedrooms: 1 single, 1 double, 1 twin
Bathrooms: 1 public

**Bed & breakfast**

| per night: | £min | £max |
|---|---|---|
| Single | 12.00 | 12.00 |
| Double | 24.00 | 24.00 |

Parking for 5
Open February-November

🛏️🚆♨️📶Ⓢ🅿️📺▦🚐❄️✕🚙

## ILKLEY

West Yorkshire
Map ref 4B1

This moorland town is famous for its ballad. The 16th C manor house, now a museum, displays local prehistoric and Roman relics. Popular walk leads up Heber's Ghyll to Ilkley Moor, with the mysterious Swastika Stone and White Wells, 18th C plunge baths.
*Tourist Information Centre*
☎ *(01943) 602319*

### Briarwood

⚜️ COMMENDED

Queens Drive, Ilkley LS29 9QW
☎ (01943) 600870
*Victorian ladies' residence with spacious rooms and excellent views. Visitors are entertained as house guests. 5 minutes' walk from Ilkley Moor and Ilkley College.*
Bedrooms: 2 twin
Bathrooms: 2 private, 1 public

**Bed & breakfast**

| per night: | £min | £max |
|---|---|---|
| Single | 15.00 | 17.00 |
| Double | 30.00 | 30.00 |

Parking for 5

🛏️📶Ⓢ🅿️📺▦🚐❄️✕🚙

### Moorview Hotel ♠

⚜️

104 Skipton Road, Ilkley LS29 9HE
☎ (01943) 600156 & 816572

*Imposing Victorian villa on bank of River Wharfe, at start of the Dales Way. Ideal touring centre for dales and Bronte country. Ample parking.*
Bedrooms: 1 single, 4 double, 2 twin, 2 triple, 4 family rooms
Bathrooms: 8 private, 3 public

**Bed & breakfast**

| per night: | £min | £max |
|---|---|---|
| Single | 28.00 | 38.00 |
| Double | 35.00 | 48.00 |

Evening meal 1900 (last orders 2100)
Parking for 15
Cards accepted: Access, Visa, Switch/Delta

🛏️🅿️♨️📶Ⓢ🅿️📺▦🚐❄️🚙

> Half board prices shown are per person but in some cases may be based on double/twin occupancy.

## INGLEBY GREENHOW

North Yorkshire
Map ref 5C3

Perched on the edge of Cleveland Hills, the village boasts the Norman church of St Andrew's with well-preserved carving and effigies of a priest and a knight. Ingleby Moor rises 1300 ft above village.

### Manor House Farm ⋀

ESS HIGHLY COMMENDED

Ingleby Greenhow, Middlesbrough, Cleveland TS9 6RB
☎ Great Ayton (01642) 722384

164-acre mixed farm. In a picture book setting surrounded by hills and forests, in the North York Moors National Park. Ideal for nature lovers, walking, touring, riding and relaxing. Fine food and wines.
Bedrooms: 1 double, 2 twin
Bathrooms: 2 private, 1 public

**Half board**

| per person: | £min | £max |
| --- | --- | --- |
| Daily | 35.00 | 38.00 |
| Weekly | 234.50 | 240.00 |

Evening meal 1900 (last orders 1600)
Parking for 66
Open January-November

⟡ 12 ⌷⌑♦🛆S⌀⋈🗚TV🛏.⛁∪♪↾ ✓❀🚗🏛

## INGLETON

North Yorkshire
Map ref 5B3

Thriving tourist centre for fell-walkers, climbers and pot-holers. Popular walks up beautiful Twiss Valley to Ingleborough Summit, Whernside, White Scar Caves and waterfalls.

### Ferncliffe Guest House ⋀

ESS ESS COMMENDED

55 Main Street, Ingleton, Carnforth, Lancashire LA6 3HJ
☎ (01524) 242405

Lovely detached stone-built house dated 1897. In the Three Peaks area of the dales and within easy reach of the

Lakes, 12 miles east of Lancaster and the M6.
Bedrooms: 1 double, 3 twin
Bathrooms: 4 private

**Bed & breakfast**

| per night: | £min | £max |
| --- | --- | --- |
| Single | 22.00 | 22.00 |
| Double | 38.00 | 38.00 |

**Half board**

| per person: | £min | £max |
| --- | --- | --- |
| Daily | 28.50 | 31.50 |
| Weekly | 189.00 | 210.00 |

Evening meal 1830 (last orders 1900)
Parking for 4
Open February-November

⟡⌷♦🛆⌐S🗚TV🛏.⛁🚗SP T

### Moorgarth Hall Country House Hotel

New Road, Ingleton, Carnforth, Lancashire LA6 3HL
☎ (01524) 241946
Fax (01524) 242252
Delightful Victorian family-run country house in wooded grounds with superb views. All rooms en-suite with colour TV and central heating. Log fires, relaxed atmosphere and home cooking. Children welcome, toys on hand!
Bedrooms: 1 single, 4 double, 3 twin
Bathrooms: 8 private

**Bed & breakfast**

| per night: | £min | £max |
| --- | --- | --- |
| Single | 25.00 | 30.00 |
| Double | 40.00 | 48.00 |

Evening meal 1930 (last orders 2030)
Parking for 12
Open February-December
Cards accepted: Access, Visa

⟡🖼⌑⌷♦🛆⌐S🗚🛏.⛁♦🚗 ✂SP

## KETTLEWELL

North Yorkshire
Map ref 5B3

Set in the spectacular scenery of the Yorkshire Dales National Park in Wharfedale, this former market town is a convenient stopping place for climbers and walkers. Dramatic rock formation of Kilnsey Crag is 3 miles south.

### Fold Farm ⋀

ESS HIGHLY COMMENDED

Kettlewell, Skipton BD23 5RJ
☎ Skipton (01756) 760886
Fax (01756) 760464

350-acre hill farm. 15th C farmhouse, with oak beams and spiral staircase, situated in quiet part of village close to

all amenities. Private parking away from road.
Bedrooms: 2 double, 1 twin
Bathrooms: 3 private

**Bed & breakfast**

| per night: | £min | £max |
| --- | --- | --- |
| Double | 35.00 | 40.00 |

Parking for 6
Open May-October

⟡ 10 ⌷⌑⌷♦🛆⌐S🗚⋈TV🛏.⛁ ∪↾✓❀✂🚗🏛

## KIRKBY

North Yorkshire
Map ref 5C3

### Dromonby Hall Farm ⋀

ESS COMMENDED

Busby Lane, Kirkby, Stokesley, Middlesbrough, Cleveland TS9 7AP
☎ Middlesbrough (01642) 712312
170-acre mixed farm. Modern farmhouse with superb views of hills and a short drive from coast. Beautiful walking and riding country and ideal for touring by car. Easy access from A19 and B1257. Enjoy quiet and peaceful surroundings.
Bedrooms: 1 double, 2 twin
Bathrooms: 1 public, 1 private shower

**Bed & breakfast**

| per night: | £min | £max |
| --- | --- | --- |
| Single | 15.00 | 17.50 |
| Double | 30.00 | 35.00 |

Parking for 6

⟡🖼⌷⌑♦🛆⌐💷⋈TV🛏.⛁∪❀ ✂🚗

## KIRKBYMOORSIDE

North Yorkshire
Map ref 5C3

Attractive market town with remains of Norman castle. Good centre for exploring moors. Nearby are wild daffodils of Farndale.

### Low Northolme Farm ⋀

ESS ESS HIGHLY COMMENDED

Salton, York YO6 6RP
☎ (01751) 432321
220-acre mixed farm. 18th C farmhouse set in peaceful area of Ryedale, 6 miles from Helmsley, just two miles south of A170.
Bedrooms: 1 twin, 1 triple
Bathrooms: 2 private

**Bed & breakfast**

| per night: | £min | £max |
| --- | --- | --- |
| Single | 17.00 | |
| Double | 34.00 | |

**Half board**

| per person: | £min | £max |
| --- | --- | --- |
| Daily | 26.50 | |

Evening meal 1830 (last orders 1930)
Parking for 6
Open March-October

⟡5⌷⌑♦🛆⌐⋈🗚TV🛏.⛁∪♪❀ 🚗

## LEEDS

West Yorkshire
Map ref 4B1

Large city with excellent modern shopping centre and splendid Victorian architecture. Museums and galleries including Temple Newsam House (the Hampton Court of the North) and Tetley's Brewery Wharf; also home of Opera North.
*Tourist Information Centre*
☎ *(0113) 247 8301*

### Eagle Tavern ♈

Listed

North Street, Leeds LS7 1AF
☎ (0113) 245 7146
*Traditional pub in a commercial district of Leeds, offering friendly service at reasonable prices. Close to the city centre. Colour TV in all rooms. Voted CAMRA pub of the year 1989, 1990 and 1992. Yorkshire pub of the year 1993.*
Bedrooms: 1 single, 6 twin, 2 triple
Bathrooms: 2 public

**Bed & breakfast**

| per night: | £min | £max |
| --- | --- | --- |
| Single | 20.00 | 20.00 |
| Double | 40.00 | 40.00 |

Evening meal 1730 (last orders 1900)
Parking for 12
❧ 🖃 ♨ S ▥ 🍴 ✕ ➾ 🏠

### The White House ♈

Listed  APPROVED

157 Middleton Park Road, Leeds
LS10 4LZ
☎ (0113) 271 1231
*Spacious, detached house. Excellent local transport from near the door. Convenient for M1, M62 and West Riding towns and ideal stopover for North/South travel. Non-smokers only, please.*
Bedrooms: 3 twin
Bathrooms: 1 public

**Bed & breakfast**

| per night: | £min | £max |
| --- | --- | --- |
| Single | 16.00 | |
| Double | 32.00 | |

Parking for 3
🕸 🖃 ➔ ♨ ▥ ✕ ▥ ➾ ✕ ➾

## LEEDS/BRADFORD AIRPORT

*See under Bingley, Bradford, Leeds, Otley*

National Crown ratings were correct at the time of going to press but are subject to change. Please check at the time of booking.

## LEEMING BAR

North Yorkshire
Map ref 5C3

Just off the A1 between dales and moors.

### Little Holtby

⚜⚜ HIGHLY COMMENDED

Leeming Bar, Northallerton DL7 9LH
☎ Northallerton (01609) 748762
*Recently restored old farmhouse retaining many features, including open fires, old beams, polished floors, and furnished with antiques. Beautiful views.*
Bedrooms: 1 double, 1 twin, 1 family room
Bathrooms: 1 private, 1 public

**Bed & breakfast**

| per night: | £min | £max |
| --- | --- | --- |
| Single | 20.00 | 20.00 |
| Double | 30.00 | 35.00 |

**Half board**

| per person: | £min | £max |
| --- | --- | --- |
| Daily | 27.50 | 27.50 |
| Weekly | 175.00 | 175.00 |

Evening meal 1930 (last orders 2100)
Parking for 10
❧ 🖃 ➔ ♨ ▥ ⓘ S ▥ 🍴 ▥ ➾ ❋ ➾ SP

## LEVISHAM

North Yorkshire
Map ref 5D3

Isolated moorland village overlooking Newton Dale with disused water-mill and church on Levisham Beck dating from Anglo-Saxon times.

### Horseshoe Inn ♈

⚜⚜ COMMENDED

Levisham, Pickering YO18 7NL
☎ Pickering (01751) 460240
*16th C inn at head of unspoilt village on edge of North York Moors, with moors railway passing through nearby Levisham station. 16 miles from coast.*
Bedrooms: 2 single, 2 double, 1 twin, 1 family room
Bathrooms: 3 private, 1 public

**Bed & breakfast**

| per night: | £min | £max |
| --- | --- | --- |
| Single | 21.00 | 23.00 |
| Double | 42.00 | 46.00 |

Lunch available
Evening meal 1900 (last orders 2100)
Parking for 100
❧ 🖃 ➔ ⓘ S ▥ ▥ U ➾ SP

The enquiry coupons at the back will help you when contacting proprietors.

## LONG MARSTON

North Yorkshire
Map ref 4C1

Close to the site of the Battle of Marston Moor, a decisive Civil War battle of 1644. A monument commemorates the event.

### Gill House Farm ♈

⚜⚜⚜ HIGHLY COMMENDED

Tockwith Road, Long Marston, York YO5 8PJ
☎ Rufforth (01904) 738379 & Mobile 0850 511140
*500-acre mixed farm. Peaceful period farmhouse set in glorious countryside overlooking the Vale of York. Warm welcome. Good bus route and lots of local eating places.*
Bedrooms: 2 double, 1 triple, 1 family room
Bathrooms: 4 private

**Bed & breakfast**

| per night: | £min | £max |
| --- | --- | --- |
| Double | 40.00 | |

Parking for 5
❧ ⛾ 🖃 ➔ ♨ ⛏ ⓘ S ✕ ▥ 🍴 ▥ ➾ ❋ ➾ 🏠

## LUND

Humberside
Map ref 4C1

### Clematis House, Farmhouse Bed & Breakfast ♈

⚜⚜

1 Eastgate, Lund, Driffield, North Humberside YO25 9TQ
☎ Driffield (01377) 217204
*389-acre arable & livestock farm. Family-run working farm in pretty rural village. Farmhouse with character, spacious yet cosy, with en-suite rooms and tea/coffee making facilities. Secluded walled garden, TV lounge.*
Bedrooms: 1 double, 1 twin
Bathrooms: 2 private

**Bed & breakfast**

| per night: | £min | £max |
| --- | --- | --- |
| Single | 18.50 | |
| Double | 34.00 | |

**Half board**

| per person: | £min | £max |
| --- | --- | --- |
| Daily | 26.00 | |
| Weekly | 163.80 | |

Evening meal 1800 (last orders 2000)
Parking for 4
❧ 🖃 ➔ ♨ ▥ S ✕ ▥ 🍴 ▥ ➾ U ❋ ✕ ➾ 🏠

The town index at the back of this guide gives page numbers of all places with accommodation.

## MALHAM

North Yorkshire
Map ref 5B3

Hamlet of stone cottages amid magnificent rugged limestone scenery in the Yorkshire Dales National Park. Malham Cove is a curving, sheer white cliff 240 ft high. Malham Tarn, one of Yorkshire's few natural lakes, belongs to the National Trust. National Park Centre.

### Beck Hall Guest House ⋀

Malham, Skipton BD23 4DJ
☎ Settle (01729) 830332
*Family-run guesthouse set in a spacious riverside garden. Homely atmosphere, four-poster beds, log fires and home cooking.*
Bedrooms: 11 double, 3 twin
Bathrooms: 11 private, 1 public
**Bed & breakfast**

| per night: | £min | £max |
|---|---|---|
| Single | 19.50 | 23.50 |
| Double | 29.00 | 37.00 |

**Half board**

| per person: | £min | £max |
|---|---|---|
| Daily | 21.00 | 25.00 |
| Weekly | 133.00 | 157.50 |

Lunch available
Evening meal 1900 (last orders 2000)
Parking for 30

### Miresfield Farm ⋀

Malham, Skipton BD23 4DA
☎ Airton (01729) 830414
*In national park. En-suite rooms, tea-making facilities, ground floor bedrooms, central heating. Two lounges. Home cooking. Private parking.*
Bedrooms: 6 double, 3 twin, 4 triple
Bathrooms: 11 private, 2 public
**Bed & breakfast**

| per night: | £min | £max |
|---|---|---|
| Single | 20.00 | 30.00 |
| Double | 38.00 | 42.00 |

**Half board**

| per person: | £min | £max |
|---|---|---|
| Daily | 30.00 | 34.00 |
| Weekly | 210.00 | 224.00 |

Evening meal 1830 (last orders 1200)
Parking for 16

Colour maps at the back of this guide pinpoint all places which have accommodation listings in the guide.

## MARKET WEIGHTON

Humberside
Map ref 4C1

Small town on the western side of the Yorkshire Wolds. A tablet in the parish church records the death of William Bradley in 1820 at which time he was 7 ft 9 in tall and weighed 27 stone!

### Arras Farmhouse ⋀

Listed
Arras Farm, Market Weighton, York YO4 3RN
☎ (01430) 872404
Fax (01430) 871500

*460-acre arable farm. Large farmhouse and grounds, peaceful and comfortable, on A1079 between Market Weighton and Beverley. 3 miles from Market Weighton at crossroads.*
Bedrooms: 2 double, 1 twin
Bathrooms: 2 private, 1 public
**Bed & breakfast**

| per night: | £min | £max |
|---|---|---|
| Single | 18.00 | 20.00 |
| Double | 30.00 | 34.00 |

Parking for 5

## MARTON

North Yorkshire
Map ref 5C3

### Orchard House ⋀

COMMENDED
Main Street, Marton, Sinnington, York YO6 6RD
☎ Kirkbymoorside (01751) 432904
*18th C former farmhouse in a peaceful village setting on the River Seven. Friendly relaxed atmosphere with log fires, low beams and high standards. Large gardens with river frontage.*
Bedrooms: 2 double, 1 twin
Bathrooms: 3 private
**Bed & breakfast**

| per night: | £min | £max |
|---|---|---|
| Single | 20.00 | 25.00 |
| Double | 30.00 | 38.00 |

Evening meal 1830 (last orders 1500)
Parking for 5
Open February-December

We advise you to confirm your booking in writing.

## MASHAM

North Yorkshire
Map ref 5C3

Famous market town on the River Ure, with a large market square. St Mary's Church has Norman tower and 13th C spire. Theakston's "Old Peculier" ale is brewed here.

### Lamb Hill Farm ⋀

COMMENDED
Masham, Ripon HG4 4DJ
☎ Ripon (01765) 689274
*390-acre mixed farm. Spacious and comfortable old farmhouse with views of the dales. Ideally situated for exploring Herriot country, yet only 45 minutes from York. 2 miles from Masham, A1 5 miles, Durham 1 hour.*
Bedrooms: 1 double, 1 twin, 1 triple
Bathrooms: 3 private
**Bed & breakfast**

| per night: | £min | £max |
|---|---|---|
| Single | 20.00 | 20.00 |
| Double | 32.00 | 32.00 |

Evening meal from 1900
Parking for 5
Open February-December

### Leighton Hall Farm

Listed APPROVED
Healey, Ripon HG4 4LS
☎ Ripon (01765) 689360
*540-acre mixed farm. Farmhouse is a former monastery with beautiful panoramic views. Between the dales and 5 minutes from a fishing reservoir. Also near a pony trekking centre.*
Bedrooms: 1 double, 1 family room
Bathrooms: 1 private, 1 public
**Bed & breakfast**

| per night: | £min | £max |
|---|---|---|
| Single | 13.00 | 15.00 |
| Double | 26.00 | 30.00 |

Evening meal from 1830
Parking for 3
Open April-October

### Pasture House ⋀

COMMENDED
Healey, Ripon HG4 4LJ
☎ Ripon (01765) 689149
Fax (01765) 689990
*100-year-old detached house in 3.5 acres at the foot of Colsterdale, a beautiful, small and quiet dale leading to grouse moors. Fishing and golf available by arrangement.*
Bedrooms: 1 double, 1 twin, 1 triple
Bathrooms: 2 public
**Bed & breakfast**

| per night: | £min | £max |
|---|---|---|
| Single | 12.00 | |
| Double | 24.00 | |

| Half board per person: | £min | £max |
|---|---|---|
| Daily | 20.00 | |
| Weekly | 135.00 | |

Lunch available
Evening meal from 1900
Parking for 6

## MYTON-ON-SWALE

North Yorkshire
Map ref 5C3

Small village on the mighty River Swale.

### Plump House Farm 🏵

Myton-on-Swale, York YO6 2RA
☎ Boroughbridge (01423) 360650
*160-acre mixed farm. A warm welcome with comfortable en-suite accommodation on a working family farm. Easy access to York and Harrogate and an ideal centre for the coast, dales and moors. Reductions for children.*
Bedrooms: 1 double, 1 family room
Bathrooms: 2 private

| Bed & breakfast per night: | £min | £max |
|---|---|---|
| Single | 13.00 | |
| Double | 26.00 | |

| Half board per person: | £min | £max |
|---|---|---|
| Daily | 19.00 | |

Evening meal 1800 (last orders 2000)
Parking for 4

## NORTHALLERTON

North Yorkshire
Map ref 5C3

Formerly a staging post on coaching route to the North and later a railway town. Today a lively market town and administrative capital of North Yorkshire. Parish church of All Saints dates from 1200.
*Tourist Information Centre*
☎ *(01609) 776864*

### Lovesome Hill Farm 🏵 COMMENDED

Lovesome Hill, Northallerton DL6 2PB
☎ (01609) 772311
*165-acre mixed farm. 19th C farmhouse. Tastefully converted granary adjoins with spacious, quality en-suite rooms. "You'll love it". North of Northallerton, twixt dales and moors.*
Bedrooms: 1 double, 1 triple, 1 family room
Bathrooms: 3 private

| Bed & breakfast per night: | £min | £max |
|---|---|---|
| Single | 20.00 | 24.00 |
| Double | 32.00 | 38.00 |

| Half board per person: | £min | £max |
|---|---|---|
| Daily | 24.50 | 27.50 |

Evening meal from 1900
Parking for 10
Open February-November

## NUNNINGTON

North Yorkshire
Map ref 5C3

On the River Rye, this picturesque village has a splendid Hall which houses some magnificent 17th C tapestries.

### Sunley Court 🏵 COMMENDED

Nunnington, York YO6 5XQ
☎ (01439) 748233
*200-acre arable and mixed farm. Modern farmhouse in open countryside. Home cooking, log fires and emphasis on comfort. Central to York, North York Moors and coast.*
Bedrooms: 2 single, 1 double, 1 twin
Bathrooms: 2 private, 1 public

| Bed & breakfast per night: | £min | £max |
|---|---|---|
| Single | 15.00 | |
| Double | 30.00 | |

| Half board per person: | £min | £max |
|---|---|---|
| Daily | 25.00 | |
| Weekly | 140.00 | |

Lunch available
Evening meal 1800 (last orders 2100)
Parking for 9
Open April-October

## OSMOTHERLEY

North Yorkshire
Map ref 5C3

The famous "Lyke Wake Walk", across the Cleveland Hills to Ravenscar 40 miles away, starts here in this ancient village. Attached to the village cross is a large stone table used as a "pulpit" by John Wesley.

### Quintana House 🏵 Listed COMMENDED

Back Lane, Osmotherley, Northallerton DL6 3BJ
☎ (01609) 883258
*Detached, stone cottage near national park village centre, within 90 metres of the Cleveland Way, affording panoramic views of Black Hambleton. Non-smokers only please.*
Bedrooms: 1 double, 1 twin
Bathrooms: 1 public

| Bed & breakfast per night: | £min | £max |
|---|---|---|
| Double | 29.00 | 30.00 |

| Half board per person: | £min | £max |
|---|---|---|
| Daily | 21.00 | 35.00 |
| Weekly | 142.00 | 245.00 |

Evening meal 1830 (last orders 2000)
Parking for 5

## OSWALDKIRK

North Yorkshire
Map ref 5C3

Village on the hillside overlooking the valley which separates the Howardian and Hambleton Hills. In the Domesday Book as "Oswaldeschurcha" meaning the church of Oswald.

### Thirklewood House 🏵 COMMENDED

Oswaldkirk, York YO6 5YB
☎ Ampleforth (01439) 3229
*Large country house in 2 acres of gardens on the B1257 between Helmsley and Malton. All rooms have central heating and tea/coffee making facilities. Friendly atmosphere.*
Bedrooms: 3 double
Bathrooms: 1 private, 1 public

| Bed & breakfast per night: | £min | £max |
|---|---|---|
| Double | 30.00 | 36.00 |

Parking for 6

## OTLEY

West Yorkshire
Map ref 4B1

Market and manufacturing town in Lower Wharfedale, the birthplace of Thomas Chippendale. Has a Maypole, several old inns, rebuilt medieval bridge and a local history museum. All Saints Church dates from Norman times.
*Tourist Information Centre*
☎ *(0113) 247 7707*

### Paddock Hill 🏵 APPROVED

Norwood, Otley LS21 2QU
☎ (01943) 465977
*Converted farmhouse on the B6451 with open fires and lovely views. Within easy reach of Herriot, Bronte and Emmerdale country, the dales, Skipton, Harrogate and Leeds. Reservoir fishing nearby.*
Bedrooms: 1 double, 2 twin
Bathrooms: 1 public, 1 private shower

*Continued ▶*

## OTLEY

*Continued*

### Bed & breakfast

| per night: | £min | £max |
|---|---|---|
| Single | 14.00 | 18.00 |
| Double | 28.00 | 32.00 |
| Parking for 3 | | |

### Wood Top Farm ▲▲

COMMENDED

Off Norwood Edge, Lindley, Otley
LS21 2QS
☎ (01943) 464010
*7-acre mixed farm. Quiet 18th C farmhouse in an Area of Outstanding Natural Beauty, half a mile off B6451. Ideal for nature lovers and central for Harrogate, Leeds, Skipton, York, Haworth and touring the Dales. Cosy bedrooms with adjoining private bathroom/dressing room, room service for tea and coffee, varied breakfast menu. Non-smoking.*
Bedrooms: 1 single, 1 twin
Bathrooms: 1 private

### Bed & breakfast

| per night: | £min | £max |
|---|---|---|
| Single | 18.00 | 20.00 |
| Double | 36.00 | 40.00 |
| Parking for 6 | | |

Open February-December

## PATELEY BRIDGE

North Yorkshire
Map ref 5C3

Small market town at centre of Upper Nidderdale. Flax and linen industries once flourished in this remote and beautiful setting.

### North Pasture Farm

Brimham Rocks, Summer Bridge, Harrogate HG3 4DW
☎ Harrogate (01423) 711470
*135-acre dairy farm. Parts of the house date back to 1400 and 1657. John Wesley preached in what is now the lounge.*
Bedrooms: 2 double, 1 twin
Bathrooms: 3 private

### Bed & breakfast

| per night: | £min | £max |
|---|---|---|
| Double | 37.00 | 39.00 |

### Half board

| per person: | £min | £max |
|---|---|---|
| Daily | 27.50 | 28.50 |
| Weekly | 185.00 | 192.50 |

Evening meal from 1830
Parking for 6
Open April-October

## PICKERING

North Yorkshire
Map ref 5D3

Market town and tourist centre on edge of North York Moors. Parish church has complete set of 15th C wall paintings depicting lives of saints. Part of 12th C castle still stands. Beck Isle Museum. The North York Moors Railway begins here.
*Tourist Information Centre*
☎ *(01751) 473791*

### Eden House ▲▲

COMMENDED

120 Eastgate, Pickering YO18 7DW
☎ (01751) 477297 & 472289
Fax (01751) 477297
*Listed cottage situated on the A170 road to the East Coast. On the outskirts of a small market town.*
Bedrooms: 2 double, 1 twin
Bathrooms: 1 private, 1 public

### Bed & breakfast

| per night: | £min | £max |
|---|---|---|
| Single | | 20.00 |
| Double | 32.00 | 35.00 |

### Half board

| per person: | £min | £max |
|---|---|---|
| Daily | 26.00 | 27.50 |
| Weekly | 156.00 | 165.00 |

Evening meal 1830 (last orders 2000)
Parking for 3

### Fox & Hounds Hotel ▲▲

COMMENDED

Main Street, Sinnington, York
YO6 6SQ
☎ (01751) 431577
*Old coaching inn, newly refurbished, with open fires and period furniture. In a rural setting west of Pickering. Fishing, riding and riverside walks close by. Private parking. Four ground floor bedrooms available.*
Bedrooms: 1 single, 5 double, 1 twin, 3 triple, 1 family room
Bathrooms: 10 private

### Bed & breakfast

| per night: | £min | £max |
|---|---|---|
| Single | 30.00 | 35.00 |
| Double | 47.00 | 57.00 |

### Half board

| per person: | £min | £max |
|---|---|---|
| Daily | 40.00 | 50.00 |
| Weekly | 234.50 | 304.50 |

Lunch available
Evening meal 1830 (last orders 2130)
Parking for 30
Cards accepted: Access, Visa

### Grindale House ▲▲

COMMENDED

123 Eastgate, Pickering YO18 7DW
☎ (01751) 476636
*Beautiful 18th C stone/pantile townhouse. Lovely rooms with antique furniture, private facilities, TVs. Car park. Friendly informal atmosphere. Non-smoking.*
Bedrooms: 2 double, 1 twin
Bathrooms: 3 private

### Bed & breakfast

| per night: | £min | £max |
|---|---|---|
| Single | 20.00 | 25.00 |
| Double | 34.00 | 44.00 |

Parking for 8

### Marton Hill ▲▲

Listed

Marton, Sinnington, York YO6 6RG
☎ Kirkbymoorside (01751) 431418
*55-acre livestock farm. 300-year-old country house with spectacular views. 3 miles from Kirkbymoorside on the Malton road, with good easy access.*
Bedrooms: 1 double, 1 twin
Bathrooms: 1 public

### Bed & breakfast

| per night: | £min | £max |
|---|---|---|
| Single | 11.00 | 12.50 |

Parking for 2
Open April-October

### The Old Vicarage ▲▲

COMMENDED

Yedingham, Malton YO17 8SL
☎ West Heslerton (01944) 728426
*Delightful, Georgian former vicarage set in large gardens with panoramic views of moors and wolds. Pretty village, with local inn, approximately 7 miles from Pickering, on River Derwent in the heart of Ryedale. Dinner by arrangement.*
Bedrooms: 2 double, 1 twin
Bathrooms: 3 private

### Bed & breakfast

| per night: | £min | £max |
|---|---|---|
| Single | 13.00 | 18.00 |
| Double | 26.00 | 36.00 |

### Half board

| per person: | £min | £max |
|---|---|---|
| Daily | 21.00 | 26.00 |

Parking for 4

### Rains Farm ▲▲

Allerston, Pickering YO18 7PQ
☎ Scarborough (01723) 859333
*120-acre arable farm. Renovated farmhouse, peaceful, picturesque location in the Vale of Pickering. Ideal touring base for moors and coast. Good food, warm welcome.*
Bedrooms: 2 double, 2 twin, 1 triple
Bathrooms: 5 private

| Bed & breakfast per night: | £min | £max |
|---|---|---|
| Single | 16.00 | 21.00 |
| Double | 32.00 | 34.00 |

| Half board per person: | £min | £max |
|---|---|---|
| Daily | 24.00 | 25.50 |
| Weekly | 165.00 | 172.50 |

Evening meal 1800 (last orders 1400)
Parking for 6
Open April-October

## Sunnyside ♠
HIGHLY COMMENDED

Carr Lane, Middleton, Pickering
YO18 8PD
☎ (01751) 476104
Fax (01751) 476104
*Large, south-facing chalet bungalow with private parking and a garden, in an open country aspect. Some ground floor rooms.*
Bedrooms: 1 double, 1 twin, 1 triple
Bathrooms: 3 private

| Bed & breakfast per night: | £min | £max |
|---|---|---|
| Single | 22.00 | 24.00 |
| Double | 32.00 | 36.00 |

Evening meal from 1930
Parking for 4
Open April-October
Cards accepted: Access, Visa

## RAVENSCAR
North Yorkshire
Map ref 5D3

Splendidly-positioned small coastal resort with magnificent views over Robin Hood's Bay. Its Old Peak is the end of the famous Lyke Wake Walk or "corpse way".

## Smugglers Rock Country Guest House ♠

Ravenscar, Scarborough YO13 0ER
☎ Scarborough (01723) 870044
*Georgian country house, reputedly a former smugglers' haunt, with panoramic views over the surrounding national park and sea. Half a mile from the village. Ideal centre for touring, walking and pony trekking.*
Bedrooms: 2 single, 2 double, 2 twin, 1 triple, 2 family rooms
Bathrooms: 9 private

| Bed & breakfast per night: | £min | £max |
|---|---|---|
| Single | 19.00 | 20.00 |
| Double | 38.00 | 40.00 |

| Half board per person: | £min | £max |
|---|---|---|
| Daily | 26.50 | 27.50 |
| Weekly | 169.00 | 175.00 |

Evening meal 1830 (last orders 1600)

Parking for 12
Open March-November

## REETH
North Yorkshire
Map ref 5B3

Once a market town and lead-mining centre, Reeth today serves holiday-makers in Swaledale with its folk museum and 18th C shops and inns lining the green at High Row.

## Springfield House ♠
Listed

Quaker Close, Reeth, Richmond
DL11 6UY
☎ Richmond (01748) 884634
*In the heart of Swaledale with wonderful walks and superb views. Excellent base for touring the dales. Comfortable rooms with TV. Warm welcome assured.*
Bedrooms: 1 single, 1 double, 1 twin
Bathrooms: 1 public

| Bed & breakfast per night: | £min | £max |
|---|---|---|
| Single | 15.00 | 16.00 |
| Double | 30.00 | 32.00 |

Parking for 3
Open March-November

## RICHMOND
North Yorkshire
Map ref 5C3

Market town on edge of Swaledale with 11th C castle, Georgian and Victorian buildings surrounding cobbled market-place. Green Howards' Museum is in the former Holy Trinity Church. Attractions include the Georgian Theatre, Richmondshire Museum and Easby Abbey.
*Tourist Information Centre*
☎ (01748) 850252

## Browson Bank ♠
COMMENDED

Dalton, Richmond DL11 7HE
☎ Darlington (01325) 718504 & 718246
*16th C converted barn, full of character, in beautiful farmland near Richmond and 6 miles west of Scotch Corner.*
Bedrooms: 3 triple
Bathrooms: 3 private, 1 public

| Bed & breakfast per night: | £min | £max |
|---|---|---|
| Single | 15.00 | 18.00 |
| Double | 30.00 | 32.00 |

Parking for 4

Ad Display advertisement appears on page 129

## Carlin House ♠
COMMENDED

6 Frenchgate, Richmond DL10 4JG
☎ (01748) 826771
*Grade II listed 18th C town house located at lower entrance to Richmond's market square. Geologists especially welcome.*
Bedrooms: 1 single, 1 double
Bathrooms: 2 private

| Bed & breakfast per night: | £min | £max |
|---|---|---|
| Single | 18.00 | 25.00 |
| Double | 36.00 | 40.00 |

Open January-November

## Holmedale ♠
COMMENDED

Dalton, Richmond DL11 7HX
☎ Teesdale (01833) 21236 Changing to 621236
*Georgian house in a quiet village, midway between Richmond and Barnard Castle. Ideal for the Yorkshire and Durham dales.*
Bedrooms: 1 double, 1 triple
Bathrooms: 1 public

| Bed & breakfast per night: | £min | £max |
|---|---|---|
| Single | 15.00 | 15.00 |
| Double | 25.00 | 25.00 |

| Half board per person: | £min | £max |
|---|---|---|
| Daily | 20.00 | 20.00 |
| Weekly | 125.00 | 125.00 |

Evening meal 1800 (last orders 1200)
Parking for 2

## Mount Pleasant Farm ♠
COMMENDED

Whashton, Richmond DL11 7JP
☎ (01748) 822784

*280-acre mixed farm. En-suite rooms in a converted stable, 1 suitable for disabled. Ideal for a family holiday and a pleasant place to stay. Noted for good food and warm welcome. Lots to see and do on the farm. Please ring for brochure and menus.*
Wheelchair access category 3 ♿
Bedrooms: 2 double, 1 twin, 1 triple, 2 family rooms
Bathrooms: 6 private

| Bed & breakfast per night: | £min | £max |
|---|---|---|
| Single | 18.50 | |
| Double | 34.00 | |

*Continued ▶*

## RICHMOND

*Continued*

**Half board**

| per person: | £min | £max |
|---|---|---|
| Daily | 26.00 | |
| Weekly | 182.00 | |

Evening meal 1830 (last orders 1200)
Parking for 6

🛇 👤 🗐 ♨ 🐾 🛎 S TV 🖫 🛢 🔍
♿ ✓ ✿ 🚲 DAP ⟲ SP

## RILLINGTON

North Yorkshire
Map ref 5D3

A stream runs through this large, attractive village which has a quaint old church and is on the main road to Scarborough.

### The Coach and Horses ⋒
**Listed**

1 Scarborough Road, Rillington,
Malton YO17 8LH
☎ (01944) 758373
*Grade II listed building dating back to the 18th C. Situated on the A64 midway between York and Scarborough.*
Bedrooms: 2 twin
Bathrooms: 1 public

**Bed & breakfast**

| per night: | £min | £max |
|---|---|---|
| Single | 16.00 | 20.00 |
| Double | 28.00 | 40.00 |

Lunch available
Evening meal 1800 (last orders 2130)
Parking for 20
Cards accepted: Access, Visa, Diners, Switch/Delta

🛇 🎇 🗐 👤 🛎 ✓ 🖫 🛢 🔍 ✿ 🚲 DAP 🏮

## RIPON

North Yorkshire
Map ref 5C3

Small, ancient city with impressive cathedral containing Saxon crypt which houses church treasures from all over Yorkshire. "Setting the Watch" tradition kept nightly by horn-blower in Market Square. Fountains Abbey nearby.

### The Coopers ⋒
👑👑

36 College Road, Ripon HG4 2HA
☎ (01765) 603708
*Spacious, comfortable Victorian house in quiet area. En-suite facilities available. Special rates for children. Cyclists welcome (storage for bicycles). Take-away meals acceptable in rooms.*
Bedrooms: 1 single, 1 twin, 1 triple
Bathrooms: 1 private, 1 public

**Bed & breakfast**

| per night: | £min | £max |
|---|---|---|
| Single | 15.00 | 16.00 |
| Double | 26.00 | 34.00 |

Parking for 3

🛇 🗐 👤 UL 🛎 S TV 🖫 🛢 🚲

### Lowgate Cottage ⋒
**Listed** **COMMENDED**

Lowgate Lane, Sawley, Ripon
HG4 3EL
☎ Sawley (01765) 620302
*Restored dwelling, peacefully located in one-third of an acre of beautiful gardens. 10 minutes' walking distance from Fountains Abbey and Studley Park.*
Bedrooms: 1 double, 1 twin
Bathrooms: 1 public

**Bed & breakfast**

| per night: | £min | £max |
|---|---|---|
| Single | 20.00 | |
| Double | 29.00 | |

**Half board**

| per person: | £min | £max |
|---|---|---|
| Daily | 22.00 | |
| Weekly | 150.00 | |

Parking for 4

🛇 🗐 👤 ♨ UL 👤 ✓ TV 🖫 🛢 ✿ 🚲 SP

### Mallard Grange ⋒
**Listed** **COMMENDED**

Aldfield, Ripon HG4 3BE
☎ Sawley (01765) 620242

*460-acre mixed farm. Set in the Yorkshire Dales, this peaceful 16th C farmhouse offers high quality traditionally furnished rooms. Historically linked to Fountains Abbey, just a few fields away.*
Bedrooms: 1 double, 1 twin
Bathrooms: 1 private

**Bed & breakfast**

| per night: | £min | £max |
|---|---|---|
| Double | 34.00 | 40.00 |

Parking for 4

🗐🗏 🗐 👤 UL 🛎 S ✓ 🛢 🔍 ✿ 🚲 SP

### Moor End Farm ⋒
👑👑

Knaresborough Road, Littlethorpe,
Ripon HG4 3LU
☎ (01765) 677419
*41-acre livestock farm. Between Bishop Monkton and Ripon on the Knaresborough road. Ideal centre for the dales and Herriot country. Home cooking and a warm Yorkshire welcome. Non-smokers only please.*
Bedrooms: 2 double, 1 twin
Bathrooms: 1 private, 1 public

**Bed & breakfast**

| per night: | £min | £max |
|---|---|---|
| Single | 18.00 | 20.00 |
| Double | 30.00 | 38.00 |

**Half board**

| per person: | £min | £max |
|---|---|---|
| Daily | 24.00 | 28.00 |
| Weekly | 161.00 | 189.00 |

Evening meal 1830 (last orders 1600)
Parking for 7
Open January-November

👤 UL 🛎 ✓ 🐾 TV 🖫 🛢 ✿ 🗡 🚲 DAP SP

### St George's Court ⋒
**Listed** **COMMENDED**

Old Home Farm, Grantley, Ripon
HG4 3EU
☎ Sawley (01765) 620618
*5 miles from Ripon, beautifully situated accommodation in renovated farm buildings. Comfortable rooms with colour TV. Breakfast served in the 17th C farmhouse.*
Bedrooms: 3 double, 1 twin, 1 family room
Bathrooms: 5 private

**Bed & breakfast**

| per night: | £min | £max |
|---|---|---|
| Single | 22.50 | |
| Double | 38.00 | |

**Half board**

| per person: | £min | £max |
|---|---|---|
| Daily | 29.00 | |

Evening meal 1900 (last orders 2000)
Parking for 12

🛇 🗐 👤 UL 🛎 S 🖫 ✿ 🚲 SP

## ROBIN HOOD'S BAY

North Yorkshire
Map ref 5D3

Picturesque village of red-roofed cottages with main street running from clifftop down ravine to seashore. Scene of much smuggling and shipwrecks in 18th C. Robin Hood reputed to have escaped to continent by boat from here.

### The Flask Inn
**Listed**

Fylingdales, Whitby YO22 4QH
☎ Whitby (01947) 880305

*Originally a 16th C monks' hostel, situated on the Whitby to Scarborough road (A171) in the glorious North York Moors National Park.*
Bedrooms: 3 double, 1 twin, 1 triple, 1 family room
Bathrooms: 6 private

**Bed & breakfast**

| per night: | £min | £max |
| --- | --- | --- |
| Single | 25.00 | 25.00 |
| Double | 40.00 | 40.00 |

Lunch available
Evening meal 1830 (last orders 2100)
Parking for 25

---

### RUFFORTH

North Yorkshire
Map ref 4C1

Village west of York. There is a small airfield, and it is also the home of the York Gliding Centre.

### Rosedale Guest House ⋒

COMMENDED

Wetherby Road, Rufforth, York
YO2 3QB
☎ York (01904) 738297
*Small, family-run guesthouse with a homely atmosphere and all facilities, in a delightful, unspoilt village 4 miles west of York on the B1224. Private parking available.*
Bedrooms: 1 single, 2 double, 1 twin, 1 triple
Bathrooms: 1 private, 2 public, 2 private showers

**Bed & breakfast**

| per night: | £min | £max |
| --- | --- | --- |
| Single | 13.00 | 17.00 |
| Double | 28.00 | 35.00 |

Parking for 5

---

### SCARBOROUGH

North Yorkshire
Map ref 5D3

Large, popular east coast seaside resort, formerly a spa town. Beautiful gardens and two splendid sandy beaches. Castle ruins date from 1100, fine Georgian and Victorian houses. Angling, cricket festivals. Scarborough Millenium depicts 1,000 years of town's history.
*Tourist Information Centre*
☎ (01723) 373333

### Ambassador Hotel ⋒

COMMENDED

Esplanade, Scarborough YO11 2AY
☎ (01723) 362841
Fax (01723) 362841
*Private Victorian hotel in centre of the Esplanade. Commanding South Cliff position with bay views. Full facilities, pleasant helpful staff, entertainment, lift, fine cuisine, public bar.*
Bedrooms: 12 single, 15 double, 12 twin, 7 triple, 3 family rooms
Bathrooms: 49 private

---

**Bed & breakfast**

| per night: | £min | £max |
| --- | --- | --- |
| Single | 23.00 | 38.00 |
| Double | 46.00 | 76.00 |

**Half board**

| per person: | £min | £max |
| --- | --- | --- |
| Daily | 28.50 | 48.00 |
| Weekly | 189.00 | 295.00 |

Evening meal 1800 (last orders 1930)
Cards accepted: Access, Visa, Amex, Switch/Delta

### East Ayton Lodge Country Hotel & Restaurant ⋒

Moor Lane, East Ayton, Scarborough
YO13 9EW
☎ (01723) 864227
Fax (01723) 862680

*Country hotel and restaurant in a beautiful 3-acre setting by the River Derwent, in the North York Moors National Park, only 3 miles from Scarborough.*
Bedrooms: 10 double, 4 twin, 2 triple, 1 family room
Bathrooms: 17 private

**Bed & breakfast**

| per night: | £min | £max |
| --- | --- | --- |
| Single | 30.00 | 50.00 |
| Double | 40.00 | 90.00 |

**Half board**

| per person: | £min | £max |
| --- | --- | --- |
| Daily | 30.00 | 62.50 |
| Weekly | 210.00 | 325.00 |

Lunch available
Evening meal 1800 (last orders 2100)
Parking for 50
Cards accepted: Access, Visa, Amex

---

### SELBY

North Yorkshire
Map ref 4C1

Small market town on the River Ouse, believed to have been birthplace of Henry I, with a magnificent abbey containing much fine Norman and Early English architecture.
*Tourist Information Centre*
☎ (01757) 703263

### Hazeldene Guest House ⋒

34 Brook Street, Doncaster Road,
Selby YO8 0AR
☎ (01757) 704809
Fax (01757) 709300
*Situated by the A19 in pleasant market town, only 12 miles from York. M62 and A1 are both 7 miles distant.*
Bedrooms: 2 single, 1 double, 2 twin, 2 triple, 1 family room
Bathrooms: 1 private, 2 public

**Bed & breakfast**

| per night: | £min | £max |
| --- | --- | --- |
| Single | 15.00 | 16.00 |
| Double | 28.00 | 36.00 |

Parking for 6

### Judith Parish ⋒

Listed

Villa Nuseries, 33 York Road, Riccall,
York YO4 6QG
☎ (01757) 248257
*Family-run house in a quiet village 9 miles south of York, offering comfortable, friendly accommodation. Kitchen and laundry facilities. Children and pets welcome.*
Bedrooms: 1 single, 1 double, 3 twin, 1 triple, 1 family room
Bathrooms: 3 private, 1 public

**Bed & breakfast**

| per night: | £min | £max |
| --- | --- | --- |
| Single | 14.00 | 19.00 |
| Double | 24.00 | 34.00 |

Parking for 10

---

Please mention this guide when making a booking.

There are separate sections in this guide listing groups specialising in farm holidays and accommodation which is especially suitable for young people and organised groups.

Individual proprietors have supplied all details of accommodation. Although we do check for accuracy, we advise you to confirm the information at the time of booking.

## SETTLE

North Yorkshire
Map ref 5B3

Town of narrow streets and
Georgian houses in an area of
great limestone hills and crags.
Panoramic view from Castleberg
Crag which stands 300 ft above
town.
*Tourist Information Centre*
☎ *(01729) 825192*

### Maypole Inn ⋏
⚜⚜⚜ COMMENDED

Maypole Green, Main Street, Long
Preston, Skipton BD23 4PH
☎ Long Preston (01729) 840219
*17th C inn, with open fires, on the
village green. Easy access to many
attractive walks in the surrounding
dales. 4 miles from Settle.*
Bedrooms: 1 single, 2 double, 1 twin,
1 triple, 1 family room
Bathrooms: 6 private

**Bed & breakfast**

| per night: | £min | £max |
|---|---|---|
| Single | 26.00 | |
| Double | 39.00 | |

Lunch available
Evening meal 1830 (last orders 2100)
Parking for 25
Cards accepted: Access, Visa, Diners,
Amex

🐾🖥♿🛎Ⓢ✂🅜📺🛏💺🍴10-60🔍
🚶 SP 🏠 Ⓣ

### The Riddings ⋏
⚜⚜⚜ HIGHLY COMMENDED

Long Preston, Skipton BD23 4QN
☎ Long Preston (01729) 840 231
*Grade II listed country house with
extensive formal and walled gardens,
private woodland and landscaped
waterfalls. Superb views over the Ribble
Valley.*
Bedrooms: 3 double, 1 twin
Bathrooms: 2 private, 1 public

**Bed & breakfast**

| per night: | £min | £max |
|---|---|---|
| Single | 25.00 | 35.00 |
| Double | 39.00 | 55.00 |

Evening meal 1830 (last orders 1000)
Parking for 14

🐾10🖥🖵♿🛎Ⓤ🅛Ⓢ✂🅜📺🛏💺
❀✈🚶 SP 🏠

### Scar Close Farm ⋏
⚜⚜⚜ COMMENDED

Feizor, Austwick, Lancaster LA2 8DF
☎ (01729) 823496
*250-acre dairy & livestock farm. High
standard en-suite farmhouse
accommodation and food in a
picturesque hamlet near Settle. A tourist
centre for the dales, Lakes and seaside.*
Bedrooms: 1 double, 1 twin, 1 triple,
1 family room
Bathrooms: 4 private

**Bed & breakfast**

| per night: | £min | £max |
|---|---|---|
| Double | 34.00 | 36.00 |

**Half board**

| per person: | £min | £max |
|---|---|---|
| Daily | 26.50 | 27.50 |
| Weekly | 175.00 | 180.00 |

Evening meal 1800 (last orders 1830)
Parking for 5

🐾♿🛎📞🅛🛎Ⓢ🅜📺🛏💺🚶Ⓤ❀✈
🚶 SP

## SHEFFIELD

South Yorkshire
Map ref 4B2

Local iron ore and coal gave
Sheffield its prosperous steel and
cutlery industries. The modern city
centre has many interesting
buildings - cathedral, Cutlers'
Hall, Crucible Theatre, Graves and
Mappin Art Galleries - and
Meadowhall shopping centre
nearby.
*Tourist Information Centre*
☎ *(0114) 273 4671 or 279 5901*

### Anna's Bed & Breakfast
Listed

981 Penistone Road, Hillsborough,
Sheffield S6 2DH
☎ (0114) 234 0108
*A clean, comfortable, welcoming bed
and breakfast establishment in cheaper
price range but offering good
wholesome food.*
Bedrooms: 2 single, 3 twin
Bathrooms: 2 public

**Bed & breakfast**

| per night: | £min | £max |
|---|---|---|
| Single | 15.00 | 17.50 |
| Double | 30.00 | 35.00 |

Parking for 5

🐾♿🖵♿🅛Ⓛ🛎Ⓢ🅜📺🛏💺🚶❀✈🚶

### Holme Lane Farm Private Hotel ⋏
⚜⚜⚜ COMMENDED

38 Halifax Road, Grenoside, Sheffield
S30 3PB
☎ (0114) 246 8858
*15-acre horses farm. Converted barn
and cottage on the A61, 3 miles from
the motorway and Sheffield, near
Meadowhall Shopping Centre and a
short run from the Peak District.*
Bedrooms: 4 single, 1 double, 2 twin
Bathrooms: 7 private

**Bed & breakfast**

| per night: | £min | £max |
|---|---|---|
| Single | 26.00 | 26.00 |
| Double | 45.00 | 45.00 |

Parking for 10
Cards accepted: Access, Visa

🐾♿🖵🖥♿🛎📞Ⓤ🅛Ⓢ✂🅜📺🛏💺🖵🔍
Ⓤ❀🚶🏠

We advise you to confirm
your booking in writing.

## STARBOTTON

North Yorkshire
Map ref 5B3

Quiet, picturesque village midway
between Kettlewell and Buckden in
Wharfedale. Many buildings belong
to the 17th C and several have
dated lintels.

### Bushey Lodge Farm
⚜⚜ COMMENDED

Starbotton, Skipton BD23 5HY
☎ Kettlewell (01756) 760424
*2000-acre mixed farm. Traditional dales
farmhouse in quiet position in Upper
Wharfedale village. Extensive views
along the valley. Both rooms are en-
suite with TV, tea/coffee facilities.*
Bedrooms: 1 double, 1 twin
Bathrooms: 2 private

**Bed & breakfast**

| per night: | £min | £max |
|---|---|---|
| Single | 17.00 | 19.00 |
| Double | 34.00 | 38.00 |

Parking for 6

🐾🖥🖵♿🛎Ⓤ🅛🛎Ⓢ📺🛏💺🖵❀✈🚶 OAP

## THIRSK

North Yorkshire
Map ref 5C3

Thriving market town with cobbled
square surrounded by old shops
and inns and also with a local
museum. St Mary's Church is
probably the best example of
Perpendicular work in Yorkshire.

### Doxford House ⋏
⚜⚜

Front Street, Sowerby, Thirsk YO7 1JP
☎ (01845) 523238
*Handsome, Georgian house with
attractive gardens and paddock with
animals, overlooking the greens of
Sowerby. Comfortable rooms - all en-
suite.*
Wheelchair access category 3 ♿
Bedrooms: 1 double, 1 twin, 2 triple
Bathrooms: 4 private

**Bed & breakfast**

| per night: | £min | £max |
|---|---|---|
| Single | 16.00 | 21.00 |
| Double | 32.00 | 32.00 |

**Half board**

| per person: | £min | £max |
|---|---|---|
| Daily | 24.00 | 29.00 |

Evening meal from 1830
Parking for 4

🐾♿♿🛎Ⓢ✂🅜📺🛏💺🖵❀🚶🏠

### Firtree Farmhouse
⚜⚜

Thormanby, York YO6 3NN
☎ (01845) 501201 & 501220
*650-acre arable farm. 18th C farmhouse
set in the Vale of York. 16 miles north
of York, 5 miles south of Thirsk.
Traditionally decorated rooms. Home*

cooked evening meals available. Dales and moors nearby.
Bedrooms: 3 triple
Bathrooms: 1 private, 1 public

**Bed & breakfast**

| per night: | £min | £max |
|---|---|---|
| Single | 15.00 | 20.00 |
| Double | 28.00 | 34.00 |

**Half board**

| per person: | £min | £max |
|---|---|---|
| Daily | 22.00 | 26.00 |
| Weekly | 140.00 | 170.00 |

Evening meal 1900 (last orders 2100)
Parking for 5

🛥️ 👶 ♿ 🔌 ⓘ 🆂 ✂ 🅜 📺 🛏️ , 🖨️ ⚲ ∪ ♪ ❄ 🚲 🐾 SP

## Garth House ⋀
**Listed**

Dalton, Thirsk YO7 3HY
☎ (01845) 577310
*50-acre livestock farm. Farmhouse set in a country village. Central for York, Harrogate and many historic, interesting places. Friendly welcome awaiting guests.*
Bedrooms: 1 double, 1 twin, 1 family room
Bathrooms: 2 public

**Bed & breakfast**

| per night: | £min | £max |
|---|---|---|
| Single | 12.00 | 14.00 |
| Double | 24.00 | 28.00 |

Parking for 6
Open March-November

🛥️ ⌸ ♿ ⓠ 🔌 📺 🛏️ , 🖨️ ❄ 🚲

## High House Farm ⋀
🛇

Sutton Bank, Thirsk YO7 2HA
☎ (01845) 597557
*113-acre mixed farm. Family-run, set in open countryside and offering some of the most magnificent views in North Yorkshire. Splendid walking country, ideal for quiet relaxing holiday. Good food and hospitality.*
Bedrooms: 1 double, 1 triple
Bathrooms: 1 public

**Bed & breakfast**

| per night: | £min | £max |
|---|---|---|
| Double | 30.00 | 35.00 |

Parking for 2
Open April-October

🛥️ ♿ 🔌 🅜 📺 🛏️ , 🖨️ ∪ ❄ ✗ 🚲 DAP

## Low Paradise ⋀
**Listed**

Boltby, Thirsk YO7 2HS
☎ (01845) 537253
*Ideal base for walking and pony trekking on the moors. Boltby is north east of Thirsk.*
Bedrooms: 1 double, 2 twin
Bathrooms: 1 public

**Bed & breakfast**

| per night: | £min | £max |
|---|---|---|
| Single | 16.00 | |
| Double | 30.00 | 30.00 |

**Half board**

| per person: | £min | £max |
|---|---|---|
| Daily | 25.00 | 25.00 |
| Weekly | 165.00 | 165.00 |

Lunch available
Evening meal 1800 (last orders 2000)
Parking for 4
Open April-October
Cards accepted: Access, Visa

🛥️ 3 🔌 ⓘ 🆂 ✂ 🅜 📺 🖨️ ∪ ♪ ❄ 🚲 SP 🐾

## Plump Bank ⋀
**COMMENDED**

Felixkirk Road, Thirsk YO7 2EW
☎ (01845) 522406
*From Thirsk take the A170 Scarborough road. After 1 mile turn left for Felixkirk and Boltby and house is on the left after 100 yards.*
Bedrooms: 2 double, 1 twin
Bathrooms: 3 private

**Bed & breakfast**

| per night: | £min | £max |
|---|---|---|
| Double | 32.00 | 36.00 |

Parking for 9
Open March-October

⬜ ♿ 📺 🛏️ , 🖨️ ∪ 🚲

## Station House
🛇

Station Road, Thirsk YO7 4LS
☎ (01845) 522063
*Old station-master's house with garden and private parking. Convenient for station. Ideal base for touring dales, moors. York 25 miles.*
Bedrooms: 1 single, 1 double, 1 triple
Bathrooms: 1 public

**Bed & breakfast**

| per night: | £min | £max |
|---|---|---|
| Single | 13.00 | 13.00 |
| Double | 26.00 | 26.00 |

Parking for 3
Open April-October

🛥️ ♿ 🔌 ⓘ 🆂 🅜 📺 🖨️ ❄ 🚲 🐾

## Thornborough House Farm
**COMMENDED**

South Kilvington, Thirsk YO7 2NP
☎ (01845) 522103
*206-acre mixed farm. 200-year-old farmhouse in an ideal position for walking and touring in the North York Moors and Yorkshire Dales.*
Bedrooms: 1 double, 1 twin, 1 family room
Bathrooms: 3 private, 1 public

**Bed & breakfast**

| per night: | £min | £max |
|---|---|---|
| Single | 13.00 | 17.00 |
| Double | 26.00 | 34.00 |

**Half board**

| per person: | £min | £max |
|---|---|---|
| Daily | 21.00 | 22.00 |
| Weekly | 130.00 | 160.00 |

Evening meal from 1830
Parking for 6
Cards accepted: Access, Visa

🛥️ ⌸ ⬜ ♿ ⓠ 🔌 🆂 ✂ 🅜 📺 🛏️ , 🖨️ ❄ 🚲 DAP 🐾 SP

Small village south of Aysgarth in Wensleydale.

## High Green House ⋀
**HIGHLY COMMENDED**

Thoralby, Leyburn DL8 3SU
☎ Wensleydale (01969) 663420
*Listed Georgian house with fine views, period furniture, beams, log fires. Walled garden to rear. Good traditional food. Excellent centre for touring and walking.*
Wheelchair access category 3 ♿
Bedrooms: 2 double, 1 twin
Bathrooms: 3 private

**Bed & breakfast**

| per night: | £min | £max |
|---|---|---|
| Double | 40.00 | 52.00 |

**Half board**

| per person: | £min | £max |
|---|---|---|
| Daily | 33.50 | 40.00 |
| Weekly | 221.00 | 266.00 |

Evening meal from 1900
Parking for 4
Open April-October
Cards accepted: Access, Visa

🛥️ 👶 ⌸ ⬜ ♿ ⓘ 🆂 ✂ 🅜 🛏️ , 🖨️ ❄ 🚲 SP 🐾

## The Buck Inn ⋀
**COMMENDED**

Thornton Watlass, Ripon HG4 4AH
☎ Bedale (01677) 422461
*Friendly village inn overlooking the delightful cricket green in a small village, 3 miles from Bedale on the Masham road, and close to the A1. In James Herriot country. Walking holidays with experienced leader.*
Bedrooms: 1 single, 2 double, 1 twin, 1 triple
Bathrooms: 5 private

**Bed & breakfast**

| per night: | £min | £max |
|---|---|---|
| Single | 28.00 | |
| Double | 48.00 | |

Lunch available
Evening meal 1830 (last orders 2130)
Parking for 40
Cards accepted: Access, Visa, Diners, Amex

🛥️ 👶 ⌸ ⬜ ⓘ 🆂 ✂ 🅜 📺 🛏️ , 🖨️ ▮ 2-70 ♦ ♪ ❄ 🚲 SP

> Establishments should be open throughout the year unless otherwise stated in the entry.

123

## THURLSTONE

South Yorkshire
Map ref 4B1

On the River Don and close to the Peak District National Park. Has some 19th C weavers' cottages with long upper windows.

### Weavers Cottages
♛♛

3-5 Tenter Hill, Thurlstone, Sheffield S30 6RG
☎ Barnsley (01226) 763350
*18th C weavers' cottages in conservation area and listed Grade II. Original workrooms converted into private suites with authentic furnishings.*
Bedrooms: 1 single, 1 double, 1 twin
Bathrooms: 2 private, 1 public
**Bed & breakfast**

| per night: | £min | £max |
|---|---|---|
| Single | 19.00 | 23.00 |
| Double | 38.00 | 46.00 |

Parking for 2
⌂ ✆ 🍴 ⌂ ♨ ♦ ℡ Ⓤ Ⓢ ✂ ⅓ ▣ ▥ ⎈ ✿ ✈ ⚒ ⌂

## WARTER

Humberside
Map ref 4C1

Picturesque Wolds village adjacent to the Wolds Way on the B1246 east coast road. Famous for its thatched cottages on the green and the priory, one of the "Lost great houses of East Yorkshire", destroyed in 1970.

### Rickman House Bed & Breakfast ♈
Listed COMMENDED

Huggate Road, Warter, York YO4 2SY
☎ Pocklington (01759) 304303
*Secluded 17th C wolds farmhouse in large garden, surrounded by parkland overlooking Warter village. Period furniture, log fires. Convenient for York, Beverley, Hull and east coast.*
Bedrooms: 2 double, 1 twin
Bathrooms: 1 private, 1 public
**Bed & breakfast**

| per night: | £min | £max |
|---|---|---|
| Single | 16.00 | 18.00 |
| Double | 32.00 | 34.00 |

Evening meal 1800 (last orders 2000)
Parking for 4
Cards accepted: Access, Visa
⌂ ⚘ 🍴 ♨ ♦ ℡ 🅿 Ⓢ ▣ ▥ ⎈ ✿ ⚒ Ⓣ

Please use the new PhONEday area telephone codes shown in establishment entries.

## WEST WITTON

North Yorkshire
Map ref 5B3

Popular Wensleydale village, where the burning of "Owd Bartle", effigy of an 18th C pig rustler, is held in August.

### Old Vicarage Guest House ♈
♛

Main Street, West Witton, Leyburn DL8 4LX
☎ Wensleydale (01969) 22108
*Substantially-built, tastefully-appointed, Grade II listed house of character converted to a guesthouse. Outstanding views of Wensleydale from the bedrooms.*
Bedrooms: 2 double, 1 twin
Bathrooms: 3 private
**Bed & breakfast**

| per night: | £min | £max |
|---|---|---|
| Single | 17.00 | 22.00 |
| Double | 30.00 | 34.00 |

Parking for 8
Open March-October
⌂ ⌂ ♦ ♨ ▥ ⎈ ⚒ ⌂

## WETHERBY

West Yorkshire
Map ref 4B1

Prosperous market town on the River Wharfe, noted for horse-racing.
*Tourist Information Centre*
☎ *(01937) 582706*

### 14 Woodhill View ♈
Listed COMMENDED

Wetherby LS22 6PP
☎ (01937) 581200
*Semi-detached house in a quiet residential area near the town centre.*
Bedrooms: 1 double, 1 twin
Bathrooms: 1 public
**Bed & breakfast**

| per night: | £min | £max |
|---|---|---|
| Single | 17.50 | |
| Double | 29.00 | |

Parking for 2
Cards accepted: Access, Visa
⌂ 🍴 ♦ Ⓤ Ⓢ ▥ ℡ 🅿 ⌂

There are separate sections in this guide listing groups specialising in farm holidays and accommodation which is especially suitable for young people and organised groups.

## WHITBY

North Yorkshire
Map ref 5D3

Quaint holiday town with narrow streets and steep alleys at the mouth of the River Esk. Captain James Cook, the famous navigator, lived in Grape Lane. 199 steps lead to St Mary's Church and St Hilda's Abbey overlooking harbour. Dracula connections. Sandy beach.
*Tourist Information Centre*
☎ *(01947) 602674*

### Ryedale House ♈
♛ APPROVED

154-158 Coach Road, Sleights, Whitby YO22 5EQ
☎ (01947) 810534
*Welcoming Yorkshire house (non-smoking) 3.5 miles from Whitby, with large garden, magnificent views and relaxing atmosphere. Delicious traditional and vegetarian menus, picnics, light meals. Minimum stay 2 nights. Sorry, no pets.*
Bedrooms: 2 double, 1 twin
Bathrooms: 2 private, 1 public
**Bed & breakfast**

| per night: | £min | £max |
|---|---|---|
| Double | 30.00 | 35.00 |

Parking for 3
Open March-November
♦ Ⓤ 🅰 Ⓢ ✂ ℡ ▥ ⎈ 🅿 ✿ ✈ ⚒

## YORK

North Yorkshire
Map ref 4C1

Ancient walled city nearly 2000 years old containing many well-preserved medieval buildings. Its Minster has over 100 stained glass windows. Attractions include Castle Museum, National Railway Museum, Jorvik Viking Centre and York Dungeon.
*Tourist Information Centre*
☎ *(01904) 620557 or 621756 or 643700*

### The Acer ♈
♛♛♛ APPROVED

52 Scarcroft Hill, The Mount, York YO2 1DE
☎ (01904) 653839 & 628046
Fax (01904) 640421

*Small Victorian hotel in a quiet residential area adjoining the Knavesmire and racecourse. Half a mile from the city centre.*
Bedrooms: 3 double, 2 twin, 1 triple

Bathrooms: 6 private

**Bed & breakfast**

| per night: | £min | £max |
|---|---|---|
| Single | 22.50 | 27.50 |
| Double | 45.00 | 55.00 |

**Half board**

| per person: | £min | £max |
|---|---|---|
| Daily | 35.00 | 40.00 |
| Weekly | 205.00 | 220.00 |

Lunch available
Evening meal 1800 (last orders 2000)
Parking for 4
Cards accepted: Access, Visa, Amex

🛏️🚻🛁📞🖂👄📺📻🍴🅂📶🖩 🖵 OAP 🚭 SP 🏮

### Arndale Hotel ⚄

👑👑 HIGHLY COMMENDED

290 Tadcaster Road, York YO2 2ET
☎ (01904) 702424

*Welcoming Victorian hotel directly overlooking racecourse, close to city centre. Period furnishings, antique half-tester/four-poster beds, whirlpool baths. Private car park.*
Bedrooms: 6 double, 2 twin, 1 triple
Bathrooms: 9 private

**Bed & breakfast**

| per night: | £min | £max |
|---|---|---|
| Single | 30.00 | 39.00 |
| Double | 39.00 | 56.00 |

Parking for 20

🛏️8🚻🛁🖂📞👄📺📻🍴🖩 🖵 ❄ 🍴 SP 🏮 T

### Arnot House ⚄

Listed

17 Grosvenor Terrace, Bootham, York YO3 7AG
☎ (01904) 641966
*Beautifully preserved Victorian town house with original cornices, fireplaces and staircase. Large rooms, tastefully decorated and well appointed. 5 minutes' walk from York Minster. Brochure available.*
Bedrooms: 1 single, 2 double, 2 twin, 1 triple
Bathrooms: 2 public

**Bed & breakfast**

| per night: | £min | £max |
|---|---|---|
| Single | 15.00 | 17.00 |
| Double | 30.00 | 34.00 |

**Half board**

| per person: | £min | £max |
|---|---|---|
| Daily | 24.75 | 26.75 |
| Weekly | 173.25 | 187.25 |

Evening meal from 1830
Parking for 2
Open February-November

🛏️5🚻🛁🖂👄📻🅂🖩 🖵 🍴 SP

### Avimore House Hotel ⚄

👑👑

78 Stockton Lane, York YO3 0BS
☎ (01904) 425556
*Edwardian house, now a family-run hotel with quiet rooms in a pleasant residential area on the east side of the city. Car park.*
Bedrooms: 2 single, 1 double, 2 twin, 1 triple
Bathrooms: 6 private

**Bed & breakfast**

| per night: | £min | £max |
|---|---|---|
| Single | 18.00 | 25.00 |
| Double | 32.00 | 46.00 |

Evening meal 1800 (last orders 1200)
Parking for 6

🛏️🚻🖵🖂📞👄📺🍴🅂🖩 🖵 🚗 OAP SP

### Beckfield House ⚄

Listed

Stockton Lane, York YO3 9UA
☎ (01904) 424475
*Country house on the outskirts of York with large private gardens. Close to the ring road. Non-smoking.*
Bedrooms: 2 double, 1 twin
Bathrooms: 1 private, 1 public

**Bed & breakfast**

| per night: | £min | £max |
|---|---|---|
| Single | 13.00 | 16.00 |
| Double | 26.00 | 40.00 |

**Half board**

| per person: | £min | £max |
|---|---|---|
| Daily | 19.00 | 26.00 |
| Weekly | 110.00 | 150.00 |

Lunch available
Evening meal 1900 (last orders 2000)
Parking for 6
Cards accepted: Access, Visa

🛏️🖵📻🅂👄📺🖩 🖵 🍴 SP T

### Beech House ⚄

👑👑👑

6-7 Longfield Terrace, Bootham, York YO3 7DJ
☎ (01904) 634581
*Small, family-run guesthouse with a warm welcome and a relaxing atmosphere only 5 minutes' walk from York Minster.*
Bedrooms: 1 single, 6 double, 1 twin
Bathrooms: 8 private

**Bed & breakfast**

| per night: | £min | £max |
|---|---|---|
| Single | 20.00 | 25.00 |
| Double | 34.00 | 44.00 |

Evening meal from 1800
Parking for 5

🛏️10📞🖵🖂👄📻🍴🖩 🖵 🍴 SP T

### The Bloomsbury Hotel ⚄

👑👑👑

127 Clifton, York YO3 6BL
☎ (01904) 634031
*Splendid Victorian family-run guesthouse with bedrooms on the*

*ground and first floors. Within walking distance of city centre.*
Bedrooms: 1 single, 3 double, 2 twin, 1 triple
Bathrooms: 4 private, 2 public

**Bed & breakfast**

| per night: | £min | £max |
|---|---|---|
| Single | 18.00 | |
| Double | 30.00 | |

Evening meal 1800 (last orders 0900)
Parking for 14

🛏️🚻🛁🖂👄📺📻🍴📶🖩 🖵 🍴 🏮 SP

### Bowen House ⚄

👑👑

4 Gladstone Street, Huntington Road, York YO3 7RF
☎ (01904) 636881

*Close to York Minster, this late Victorian town house combines high quality facilities with old-style charm. Private car park. Traditional/vegetarian breakfasts. Non-smoking throughout.*
Bedrooms: 1 single, 2 double, 1 twin, 1 family room
Bathrooms: 2 private, 1 public, 1 private shower

**Bed & breakfast**

| per night: | £min | £max |
|---|---|---|
| Single | 20.00 | 25.00 |
| Double | 32.00 | 44.00 |

Parking for 4
Cards accepted: Access, Visa

🛏️📻🖵🅂👄📺🖩 🖵 🍴 OAP SP T

### Burton Villa ⚄

Listed COMMENDED

22 Haxby Road, York YO3 7JX
☎ (01904) 626364

*Noted for friendly atmosphere, good breakfasts and high standards. 7 minutes' walk from York Minster. Private parking.*
Bedrooms: 1 single, 6 double, 1 twin, 1 triple, 2 family rooms
Bathrooms: 8 private, 1 public

**Bed & breakfast**

| per night: | £min | £max |
|---|---|---|
| Single | 15.00 | 30.00 |
| Double | 30.00 | 50.00 |

Parking for 7

🛏️🚻🖵👄📻🅂🍴📻🖩 🖵 🍴 SP T

## YORK

*Continued*

### Chilton Guest House ⋀
**Listed**

1 Claremont Terrace, Gillygate, York
YO3 7EJ
☎ (01904) 612465
*Small guesthouse in city centre, close to all historic attractions.*
Bedrooms: 2 double, 1 twin
Bathrooms: 3 private

**Bed & breakfast**

| per night: | £min | £max |
|---|---|---|
| Double | 34.00 | 40.00 |

Parking for 2

### City Centre Guest House ⋀
**Listed**

54 Walmgate, York YO1 2TJ
☎ (01904) 624048 & 652383
Fax (01904) 612494
*Quiet, city centre guesthouse offering a warm welcome. Lunches available on request.*
Bedrooms: 3 single, 2 double, 3 twin, 5 triple, 2 family rooms
Bathrooms: 5 private, 4 public

**Bed & breakfast**

| per night: | £min | £max |
|---|---|---|
| Single | 14.00 | 16.50 |
| Double | 28.00 | 33.00 |

**Half board**

| per person: | £min | £max |
|---|---|---|
| Daily | 20.50 | 23.00 |

Lunch available
Evening meal 1800 (last orders 1830)
Parking for 15
Cards accepted: Access, Visa, Switch/Delta

### City Guest House ⋀
👑

68 Monkgate, York YO3 7PF
☎ (01904) 622483
*Cosy guesthouse 3 minutes from York Minster. En-suite rooms and car parking. Non-smokers only, please.*
Bedrooms: 3 single, 2 double, 2 twin, 1 family room
Bathrooms: 6 private, 2 private showers

**Bed & breakfast**

| per night: | £min | £max |
|---|---|---|
| Single | 14.00 | 25.00 |
| Double | 30.00 | 45.00 |

Parking for 5
Cards accepted: Access, Visa

### Cumbria House ⋀
**Listed COMMENDED**

2 Vyner Street, Haxby Road, York
YO3 7HS
☎ (01904) 636817
*Family-run guesthouse, 10 minutes' walk from York Minster. En-suites*

*available. Easily located from ring road. Private car park. Brochure.*
Bedrooms: 1 single, 2 double, 2 triple
Bathrooms: 3 private, 1 public

**Bed & breakfast**

| per night: | £min | £max |
|---|---|---|
| Single | 18.00 | 25.00 |
| Double | 30.00 | 40.00 |

Parking for 5

### Curzon Lodge and Stable Cottages ⋀
👑👑 **COMMENDED**

23 Tadcaster Road, Dringhouses, York
YO2 2QG
☎ (01904) 703157

*Delightful 17th C listed house and former stables in pretty conservation area overlooking York racecourse, once a home of the Terry "chocolate" family. All en-suite, some four-posters. Many antiques. Large enclosed car park.*
Bedrooms: 1 single, 4 double, 3 twin, 2 triple
Bathrooms: 10 private

**Bed & breakfast**

| per night: | £min | £max |
|---|---|---|
| Single | 30.00 | 38.00 |
| Double | 46.00 | 56.00 |

Parking for 16
Cards accepted: Access, Visa

### Hotel Fairmount ⋀
👑

230 Tadcaster Road, Mount Vale, York
YO2 2ES
☎ (01904) 638298
Fax (01904) 639724
*Large, tastefully furnished, Victorian villa with open views over racecourse, 10 minutes from city centre. Ground floor rooms available for people with special needs.*
Bedrooms: 2 single, 6 double, 2 twin, 2 triple
Bathrooms: 12 private

**Bed & breakfast**

| per night: | £min | £max |
|---|---|---|
| Single | 30.00 | 30.00 |
| Double | 45.00 | 62.00 |

**Half board**

| per person: | £min | £max |
|---|---|---|
| Daily | 35.00 | 46.00 |

Lunch available
Evening meal 1900 (last orders 2100)
Parking for 12
Cards accepted: Access, Visa

### Foss Bank Guest House
👑

16 Huntington Road, York YO3 7RB
☎ (01904) 635548
*Small Victorian family-run guesthouse, comfortable and friendly, on the north-east side of the city. 5 minutes' walk from the city wall.*
Bedrooms: 2 single, 3 double, 1 twin
Bathrooms: 2 private, 4 private showers

**Bed & breakfast**

| per night: | £min | £max |
|---|---|---|
| Single | 16.00 | 18.00 |
| Double | 32.00 | 36.00 |

Parking for 5
Open February-December

### Four Seasons Hotel ⋀
👑👑 **COMMENDED**

7 St Peter's Grove, Bootham, York
YO3 6AQ
☎ (01904) 622621
Fax (01904) 430565
*Beautiful high-quality Victorian hotel, in a quiet location 5 minutes' walk from city centre. All rooms en-suite. Private car park.*
Bedrooms: 2 double, 1 twin, 1 triple, 1 family room
Bathrooms: 5 private, 1 public

**Bed & breakfast**

| per night: | £min | £max |
|---|---|---|
| Single | 32.00 | 32.00 |
| Double | 44.00 | 50.00 |

Parking for 6

### Hedley House ⋀
👑👑 **COMMENDED**

3-4 Bootham Terrace, York YO3 7DH
☎ (01904) 637404
*Family-run hotel close to the city centre. 1 ground floor bedroom. All rooms en-suite. Home cooking, special diets catered for.*
Bedrooms: 2 single, 5 double, 5 twin, 2 triple, 1 family room
Bathrooms: 15 private

**Bed & breakfast**

| per night: | £min | £max |
|---|---|---|
| Single | 20.00 | 32.00 |
| Double | 36.00 | 52.00 |

Lunch available
Evening meal 1830 (last orders 1900)
Parking for 12
Cards accepted: Access, Visa, Amex

### Hillcrest Guest House ⋀
👑👑

110 Bishopthorpe Road, York
YO2 1JX
☎ (01904) 653160
*Two elegantly converted Victorian town houses, close to the city centre, racecourse and station. It is our pleasure to offer individual attention, home cooking, comfort and good value.*

Bedrooms: 3 single, 5 double, 1 twin, 2 triple, 2 family rooms
Bathrooms: 7 private, 3 public

**Bed & breakfast**

| per night: | £min | £max |
| --- | --- | --- |
| Single | 15.00 | 19.00 |
| Double | 26.00 | 38.00 |

Evening meal 1800 (last orders 1500)
Parking for 8
Cards accepted: Access, Visa

## Holgate Hill Hotel M

APPROVED

124 Holgate Road, York YO2 4BB
☎ (01904) 653786
Fax (01904) 643223
*Family hotel where home cooking is a speciality. Close to the city centre, points of historic interest and the racecourse.*
Bedrooms: 6 single, 15 double, 7 twin, 4 triple, 1 family room
Bathrooms: 33 private, 2 public

**Bed & breakfast**

| per night: | £min | £max |
| --- | --- | --- |
| Single | 33.00 | |
| Double | 52.00 | |

**Half board**

| per person: | £min | £max |
| --- | --- | --- |
| Daily | 43.75 | |

Lunch available
Evening meal 1900 (last orders 2030)
Parking for 14
Cards accepted: Access, Visa, Diners, Amex, Switch/Delta

## Holly Lodge M

APPROVED

206 Fulford Road, York YO1 4DD
☎ (01904) 646005
*Listed Georgian building on the A19, convenient for both the north and south and within walking distance of the city centre. Quiet rooms and private car park.*
Bedrooms: 3 double, 1 twin, 1 family room
Bathrooms: 5 private

**Bed & breakfast**

| per night: | £min | £max |
| --- | --- | --- |
| Single | 25.00 | 30.00 |
| Double | 30.00 | 50.00 |

Parking for 5
Open January-November
Cards accepted: Access, Visa

## Jacobean Lodge Hotel M

COMMENDED

Plainville Lane, Wigginton, York YO3 8RG
☎ (01904) 762749
Fax (01904) 762749
*Converted 17th C farmhouse, 4 miles north of York. Set in picturesque gardens with ample parking. Open log*

fire, warm, friendly atmosphere and traditional cuisine.
Bedrooms: 2 single, 4 double, 1 triple, 1 family room
Bathrooms: 8 private, 1 public

**Bed & breakfast**

| per night: | £min | £max |
| --- | --- | --- |
| Single | 24.00 | 32.00 |
| Double | 39.00 | 56.00 |

Lunch available
Evening meal 1900 (last orders 2200)
Parking for 70
Cards accepted: Access, Visa

## The Lodge M

COMMENDED

Earswick Grange, Old Earswick, York YO3 9SW
☎ (01904) 761387
*Modern family house in its own grounds. Large comfortable rooms ideal for families. No smoking establishment. Easy access to York.*
Bedrooms: 1 double, 1 twin, 1 family room
Bathrooms: 2 public

**Bed & breakfast**

| per night: | £min | £max |
| --- | --- | --- |
| Single | 14.00 | 18.00 |
| Double | 28.00 | 30.00 |

Parking for 3

## Manor Cottage M

Listed

Middlethorpe, York YO2 1QB
☎ (01904) 634397
*Detached cottage in quiet cul-de-sac overlooking countryside. Three-quarters of a mile from Bishopthorpe village. Riverside walk to York nearby. Ideal for racecourse - walking distance.*
Bedrooms: 2 double
Bathrooms: 2 private, 1 public

**Bed & breakfast**

| per night: | £min | £max |
| --- | --- | --- |
| Single | 20.00 | 30.00 |
| Double | 30.00 | 50.00 |

Open January-November

## Manor Country Guest House M

COMMENDED

Acaster Malbis, York YO2 1UL
☎ (01904) 706723
Fax (01904) 706723

*Atmospheric manor in rural tranquillity, bordering river. Off the beaten track yet close for city, racecourse and A64.*

Private fishing in lake. En-suite rooms with full facilities.
Bedrooms: 5 double, 3 twin, 2 triple
Bathrooms: 10 private

**Bed & breakfast**

| per night: | £min | £max |
| --- | --- | --- |
| Single | 20.00 | 36.00 |
| Double | 36.00 | 52.00 |

**Half board**

| per person: | £min | £max |
| --- | --- | --- |
| Daily | 28.00 | 36.00 |
| Weekly | 196.00 | 252.00 |

Lunch available
Evening meal 1900 (last orders 2030)
Parking for 19

## Midway House Hotel M

COMMENDED

145 Fulford Road, York YO1 4HG
☎ (01904) 659272
*Family-run Victorian hotel with spacious en-suite bedrooms, near city centre, university and Fulford golf-course. Private parking. Non-smokers only, please.*
Bedrooms: 7 double, 3 twin, 2 triple
Bathrooms: 12 private, 1 public

**Bed & breakfast**

| per night: | £min | £max |
| --- | --- | --- |
| Single | 25.00 | 40.00 |
| Double | 36.00 | 50.00 |

**Half board**

| per person: | £min | £max |
| --- | --- | --- |
| Daily | 30.00 | 37.00 |
| Weekly | 210.00 | 250.00 |

Evening meal 1730 (last orders 1900)
Parking for 14
Cards accepted: Access, Visa, Diners, Amex

## Mulberry Guest House M

COMMENDED

124 East Parade, Heworth, York YO3 7YG
☎ (01904) 423468
*Beautifully appointed Victorian town house, a short walk from city centre. Lovingly furnished throughout. Warm welcome assured. No smoking. Easy parking.*
Bedrooms: 1 single, 1 double, 1 twin
Bathrooms: 1 private, 2 private showers

**Bed & breakfast**

| per night: | £min | £max |
| --- | --- | --- |
| Single | 14.00 | 18.50 |
| Double | 28.00 | 40.00 |

Parking for 2

## Orillia House M

89 The Village, Stockton-on-the-Forest, York YO3 9UP
☎ (01904) 400600
*A warm welcome awaits you in this 300-year-old house of charm and*

*Continued ▶*

## YORK

### Continued

*character, opposite church. Three miles north east of York.*
Bedrooms: 2 double, 1 twin, 2 triple
Bathrooms: 5 private

**Bed & breakfast**

| per night: | £min | £max |
|---|---|---|
| Double | 32.00 | 40.00 |

Parking for 10
Cards accepted: Access, Visa

symbols

### Primrose Lodge ᴍ
Listed

Hull Road, Dunnington, York
YO1 5LR
☎ (01904) 489140
*Spacious, modern rooms to which guests have their own private entrance. Colour TV, tea/coffee making facilities in every room. 5 minutes from York on A1079.*
Bedrooms: 2 double, 1 twin
Bathrooms: 3 private

**Bed & breakfast**

| per night: | £min | £max |
|---|---|---|
| Single | 20.00 | 22.00 |
| Double | 30.00 | 34.00 |

Parking for 6

symbols

### Ship Inn ᴍ
Listed COMMENDED

Acaster Malbis, York YO2 1UH
☎ (01904) 705609 & 703888
Fax (01904) 705971
*17th C coaching inn on the River Ouse, 3.5 miles from York city centre. Restaurant, bar meals, conservatory. Weddings catered for.*
Bedrooms: 5 double, 2 twin, 1 family room
Bathrooms: 8 private

**Bed & breakfast**

| per night: | £min | £max |
|---|---|---|
| Single | 37.50 | 37.50 |
| Double | 39.50 | 65.00 |

**Half board**

| per person: | £min | £max |
|---|---|---|
| Daily | 33.00 | 36.50 |

Lunch available
Evening meal 1900 (last orders 2130)
Parking for 60
Cards accepted: Access, Visa

symbols

### Stanley Guest House ᴍ
COMMENDED

Stanley Street, Haxby Road, York
YO3 7NW
☎ (01904) 637111
*Friendly, comfortable guesthouse, 10 minutes' walk to York Minster and city and close to many attractions. All rooms en-suite. Non-smokers only, please.*
Bedrooms: 2 single, 2 double, 1 twin, 1 triple
Bathrooms: 6 private

**Bed & breakfast**

| per night: | £min | £max |
|---|---|---|
| Single | 17.50 | 20.00 |
| Double | 32.00 | 35.00 |

Parking for 5
Cards accepted: Access, Visa

symbols

### Tower Guest House ᴍ
COMMENDED

2 Feversham Crescent, Wigginton
Road, York YO3 7HQ
☎ (01904) 655571 & 635924
*Comfortable and spacious 19th C guesthouse with friendly, informative hosts. Strolling distance from York Minster and city centre attractions.*
Bedrooms: 2 double, 1 twin, 2 triple
Bathrooms: 5 private

**Bed & breakfast**

| per night: | £min | £max |
|---|---|---|
| Single | 18.00 | 24.00 |
| Double | 34.00 | 40.00 |

Parking for 5
Cards accepted: Access, Visa

symbols

### Victoria Villa
Listed

72 Heslington Road, York YO1 5AU
☎ (01904) 631647
*Victorian town house, close to city centre. Offering clean and friendly accommodation and a full English breakfast.*
Bedrooms: 1 single, 2 double, 1 twin, 2 triple
Bathrooms: 2 public

**Bed & breakfast**

| per night: | £min | £max |
|---|---|---|
| Single | 17.00 | 20.00 |
| Double | 30.00 | 40.00 |

Parking for 4

symbols

### Warrens Guest House ᴍ
Listed

30 Scarcroft Road, York YO2 1NF
☎ (01904) 643139
*Small centrally heated guesthouse, all rooms en-suite with colour TV and tea/coffee making facilities. Full English breakfast served. Four-poster beds available. Car park.*
Bedrooms: 1 single, 1 double, 1 twin, 1 triple, 1 family room
Bathrooms: 5 private

**Bed & breakfast**

| per night: | £min | £max |
|---|---|---|
| Single | 24.00 | |
| Double | 35.00 | 42.00 |

symbols

### Wellgarth House ᴍ

Wetherby Road, Rufforth, York
YO2 3QB
☎ Rufforth (01904) 738592 & 738595
*Individual and attractive country guesthouse in the delightful village of Rufforth. Ideal touring base for York and the Yorkshire Dales.*
Bedrooms: 1 single, 3 double, 2 twin, 1 triple
Bathrooms: 7 private, 1 public

**Bed & breakfast**

| per night: | £min | £max |
|---|---|---|
| Single | 17.00 | |
| Double | 30.00 | 40.00 |

Parking for 10
Cards accepted: Access, Visa

symbols

### Winston House ᴍ

4 Nunthorpe Drive, Bishopthorpe
Road, York YO2 1DY
☎ (01904) 653171
*Close to racecourse and 10 minutes' walk to city centre, railway station. Character en-suite room with all facilities. Private car park.*
Bedrooms: 1 double
Bathrooms: 1 private

**Bed & breakfast**

| per night: | £min | £max |
|---|---|---|
| Double | 28.00 | 32.00 |

Parking for 6

symbols

> **Please mention this guide when making a booking.**

SUNNYSIDE FARM WELCOMES CAREFUL WALKERS.

# COUNTRY CODE

♣ Enjoy the countryside and respect its life and work ♣ Guard against all risk of fire ♣ Fasten all gates ♣ Keep your dogs under close control ♣ Keep to public paths across farmland ♣ Use gates and stiles to cross fences, hedges and walls ♣ Leave livestock, crops and machinery alone ♣ Take your litter home ♣ Help to keep all water clean ♣ Protect wildlife, plants and trees ♣ Take special care on country roads ♣ Make no unnecessary noise

# USE YOUR *i*'S

There are more than 550 Tourist Information Centres throughout England offering friendly help with accommodation and holiday ideas as well as suggestions of places to visit and things to do.

In your home town there may be a centre which can help you before you set out. You'll find the address of your nearest Tourist Information Centre in your local Phone Book.

# SURE SIGNS

## OF WHERE TO STAY

**Throughout Britain, the tourist boards now inspect over 30,000 places to stay, every year, to help you find the ones that suit you best.**

Looking for a hotel, guesthouse, inn, B&B or farmhouse? Look for the **CROWN**. The classifications: 'Listed', and then **ONE to FIVE CROWN,** tell you the range of facilities and services you can expect. The more Crowns, the wider the range.

Looking for somewhere convenient to stop overnight on a motorway or major road route? Look for the 'Lodge' **MOON.** The classifications: **ONE to THREE MOON** tell you the range of facilities you can expect. The more Moons, the wider the range.

Looking for a self-catering holiday home? Look for the **KEY**. The classifications: **ONE to FIVE KEY,** tell you the range of facilities and equipment you can expect. The more Keys, the wider the range.
THE GRADES: **APPROVED, COMMENDED, HIGHLY COMMENDED and DE LUXE,** whether alongside the **CROWNS, KEYS** or **MOONS** show the quality standard of what is provided. If no grade is shown, you can still expect a high standard of cleanliness.

Looking for a holiday caravan, chalet or camping park? Look for the **Q** symbol. The more ✓s in the Q (from one to five), the higher the quality standard of what is provided.

**We've checked them out before you check in!**

More detailed information on the **CROWNS**, the **KEYS** and the **Q** is given in free *SURE SIGN* leaflets, available at any Tourist Information Centre.

Think of the Cotswolds and the Malvern Hills. Think of the Wye Valley and the Forest of Dean. Think of the Potteries and the Black Country. Think of cities like Birmingham, Coventry, Worcester and Gloucester. Yes, this is the big Heart of England, a region of marked and splendid contrast. Exploration will reveal all. Take in the peaceful Marches which encompass the borderlands of England and Wales, tour Shakespeare country, follow the River Severn to the scene of the Industrial Revolution and....well, why not come and see for yourself?

# HEART OF ENGLAND

The Counties of Gloucestershire, Hereford & Worcester, Shropshire, Staffordshire, Warwickshire and West Midlands

For more information on the Heart of England, contact:
Heart of England Tourist Board
Lark Hill Road
Worcester WR5 2EF
Tel: (01905) 763436 or 763439
(24 hours)
Fax: (01905) 763450

Where to Go in the Heart of England
– see pages 132–135

Where to Stay in the Heart of England
– see pages 136–189

# WHERE TO GO

***You will find hundreds of interesting places to visit during your stay in the Heart of England, just some of which are listed in these pages. The number against each name will help you locate it on the map (page 135). Contact any Tourist Information Centre in the region for more ideas on days out in the Heart of England.***

---

**1 *Wedgwood Visitor Centre***
Barlaston, Stoke-on-Trent, Staffordshire ST12 9ES
Tel: (01782) 204141
*Located in the Wedgwood factory which lies within a 500-acre country estate. Potters and decorators can be seen at work. Museum and shop.*

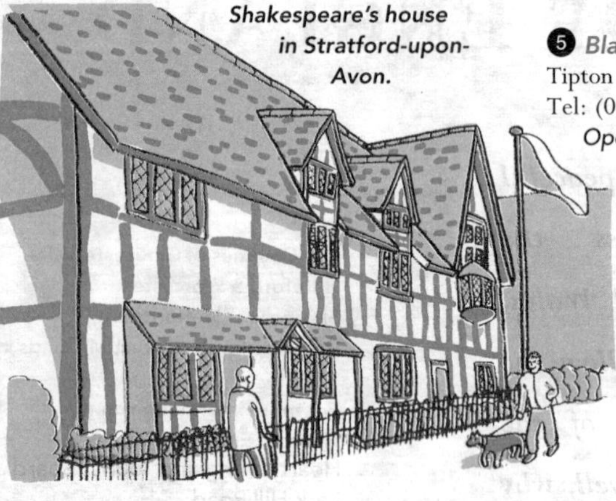

***Shakespeare's house in Stratford-upon-Avon.***

**2 *Alton Towers Theme Park***
Alton, Staffordshire ST10 4DB
Tel: (01538) 702200
*Over 125 rides and attractions including Haunted House, Runaway Mine Train, Congo River Rapids, Log Flume, The Beast, Corkscrew and Thunderlooper.*

**3 *Bass Museum, Visitor Centre and Shire Horse Stables***
Horninglow Street, Burton upon Trent, Staffordshire DE14 1JZ
Tel: (01283) 42031
*First major museum of brewing industry. Exhibition and story of different methods of transporting beer since the early 1800s. Shire horse stables.*

**4 *Ironbridge Gorge Museum***
Ironbridge, Shropshire TF8 7AW
Tel: (01952) 433522
*World's first cast iron bridge, Museum of the River visitor centre, tar tunnel, Jackfield Tile Museum, Coalport China Museum, Rosehill House, Blists Hill Museum, Museum of Iron.*

**5 *Black Country Museum***
Tipton Road, Dudley, West Midlands DY1 4SQ
Tel: (0121) 557 9643
*Open-air museum bringing Britain's industrial past to life. Shops, chapel, canal trip into limestone cavern houses, underground mining display and electric tramway.*

**6 *Sandwell Park Farm Visitors Centre***
Salters Lane, West Bromwich, West Midlands B71 4BG
Tel: (0121) 553 0220
*Restored 19th C working farm with livestock breeds of the period, traditional farming methods, displays and exhibitions. Tearooms and Victorian kitchen garden.*

**7 *Birmingham Museum of Science and Industry***
146 Newhall Street, Birmingham B3 1RZ
Tel: (0121) 235 1661
*Steam engines and locomotives, aircraft, veteran cars, motorcycles and other items of industrial or scientific interest.*

**8 *Cadbury World***
Linden Road, Bournville, Birmingham, West Midlands B30 2LD
Tel: (0121) 451 4180
*Story of chocolate from Aztec times to present day includes chocolate-making demonstration*

*Double Gloucester cheese and Worcestershire Sauce: a spicy combination.*

**13 Avoncroft Museum of Buildings**
Stoke Heath, Worcestershire B60 4JR
Tel: (01527) 831363
*Re-erected buildings saved from destruction, including a working windmill, a dovecote and a 1946 prefab.*

**14 Hatton Country World**
Dark Lane, Hatton, Warwickshire CV35 0XA
Tel: (01926) 842436
*100-acre haven of rural attractions including one of the finest collections of rare farm animals in the UK. Craft centre with 30 shops.*

**15 Warwick Castle**
Warwick, Warwickshire CV34 4QU
Tel: (01926) 408000
*Set in 60 acres of grounds. State rooms, armoury, dungeon, torture chamber, clock tower. Exhibits include "A Royal Weekend Party 1898", a preparation for battle scene and "Kingmaker Feasts".*

**16 Droitwich Spa Brine Baths Complex**
St Andrew's Road, Droitwich, Worcestershire WR9 8DN
Tel: (01905) 794894
*Unique experience of floating weightless in natural brine. Other fitness and health facilities available.*

**17 Ashorne Hall Nickelodeon**
Ashorne Hill, Nr Warwick, Warwickshire CV33 9QN
Tel: (01926) 651444
*Britain's only "nickelodeon" with unique presentation of automatic musical instruments. Vintage cinema showing silent films with Compton organ accompaniment.*

**18 Heritage Motor Centre**
Banbury Road, Gaydon, Warwickshire CV35 0BJ
Tel: (01926) 641188
*Purpose-built transport museum on 63-acre site. Collection of historic British cars, 4-wheel drive circuit, playground, picnic area, nature reserve.*

**19 Wellesbourne Watermill**
Kineton Road, Wellesbourne, Warwickshire CV35 9HG

and children's fantasy factory.
**9 National Motorcycle Museum**
Coventry Road, Bickenhill, West Midlands B92 0EJ
Tel: (01675) 443311
*Museum with a collection of 650 British machines from 1898–1993.*

**10 Museum of British Road Transport**
St Agnes Lane, Hales Street, Coventry, West Midlands CV1 1NN
Tel: (01203) 832425
*160 cars and commercial vehicles from 1896 on, 200 cycles from 1818 on and 50 motorcycles from 1920 on. Also Thrust 2, holder of land speed record.*

**11 Midland Air Museum**
Coventry Airport, Baginton, West Midlands CV8 3AZ
Tel: (01203) 301033
*Collection of over 28 historic aeroplanes. Sir Frank Whittle Jet Heritage Centre includes early jet aircraft and aero engines.*

**12 Severn Valley Railway**
The Railway Station, Bewdley, Worcestershire DY12 1BG
Tel: (01299) 401001
*Preserved standard gauge steam railway running 16 miles between Kidderminster, Bewdley and Bridgnorth. Collection of locomotives and passenger coaches.*

Tel: (01789) 470237
*Wooden waterwheel powers impressive machinery in working mill. Stoneground flour, conservation work including video of mill restoration, millpond, local crafts and exhibition.*

**20 Shakespeare's Birthplace**
Henley Street, Stratford-upon-Avon, Warwickshire CV37 6QW
Tel: (01789) 204016
*Half-timbered building furnished in period style, containing many fascinating books, manuscripts and objects. BBC TV Shakespeare costume exhibition.*

**21 The Commandery**
Sidbury, Worcester, Worcestershire WR1 2HU
Tel: (01905) 355071
*16th C timber-framed building with great hall and panelled rooms. Civil War audio-visual show and exhibition.*

**22 Worcester Cathedral**
10A College Green, Worcester WR1 2LH
Tel: (01905) 28854
*Norman crypt and Chapter House, King John's tomb, Prince Arthur's chantry, medieval cloisters and buildings. Facilities available for visually impaired.*

**Staffordshire has been the home of fine English pottery for over 300 years.**

**23 Elgar's Birthplace Museum**
Crown East Lane, Lower Broadheath, Worcestershire WR2 6RH
Tel: (01905) 333224
*Cottage in which Edward Elgar was born, now housing a museum of photographs, musical scores, letters and records associated with the composer.*

**24 The Lost Street Museum**
Palma Court, 27 Brookend Street, Ross-on-Wye, Herefordshire HR9 7EE
Tel: (01989) 62752
*Complete Edwardian street of shops including tobacconist, glassware, grocer, chemist, clothes store, pub and many others.*

**25 Jubilee Maze and Museum of Mazes**
Jubilee Park, Symonds Yat, Herefordshire HR9 6DA
Tel: (01600) 890360
*Traditional hedge maze with carved stone temple centrepiece, created to celebrate Queen Elizabeth's Jubilee in 1977. World's only "hands-on interactive" Museum of Mazes.*

**26 National Waterways Museum**
Llanthony Warehouse, Gloucester Docks, Gloucester GL1 2EH
Tel: (01452) 318054
*Three floors of dockside warehouse with lively displays telling the story of Britain's canals. Outside craft area with demonstrations, café and shop.*

**27 Robert Opie Collection – Museum of Advertising and Packaging**
Albert Warehouse, Gloucester Docks, Gloucester GL1 2EH
Tel: (01452) 302309
*Steeped in nostalgia, the Robert Opie Collection of packaging and advertising brings over 100 years of shopping basket history vividly to life.*

## FIND OUT MORE

*Further information about holidays and attractions in the Heart of England is available from:*
**Heart of England Tourist Board,** Lark Hill Road, Worcester WR5 2EF
Tel: (01905) 763436 or 763439 (24 hours)
*These publications are available free from the Heart of England Tourist Board:*

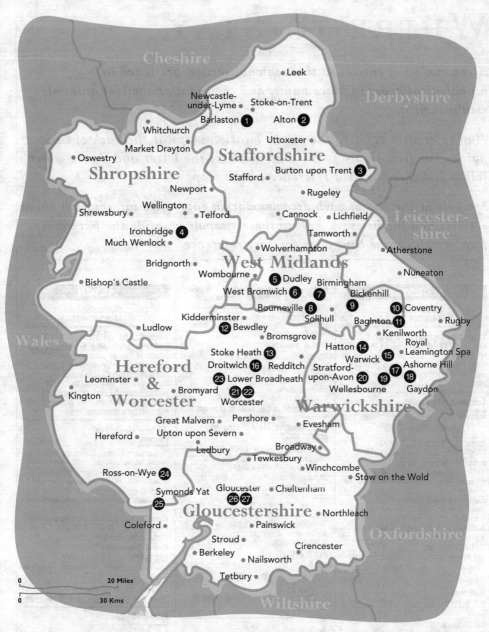

Cheshire

Derbyshire

• Leek

Newcastle-
under-Lyme
• Stoke-on-Trent
Barlaston ❶    Alton ❷

Whitchurch
• Uttoxeter
Market Drayton    **Staffordshire**
• Oswestry
Stafford •    Burton upon Trent ❸
**Shropshire**    Newport •
• Rugeley
Wellington    Leicester-
Shrewsbury •    • Telford    • Cannock    • Lichfield    shire
Ironbridge ❹    • Tamworth
Much Wenlock    • Atherstone
• Wolverhampton
Bridgnorth •    **West Midlands**    • Nuneaton
Wombourne •    Dudley
• Bishop's Castle    ❺    Birmingham
West Bromwich ❻    ❼    Bickenhill
Bourneville ❽    ❾    ❿ Coventry
Kidderminster •    Solihull    Baginton ⓫
• Ludlow    ⓬ Bewdley    • Rugby
Bromsgrove    • Kenilworth
**Wales**    Stoke Heath ⓭    Hatton ⓮    Royal
**Hereford**    Droitwich ⓰    Warwick ⓯ • Leamington Spa
Leominster •    Redditch    Stratford- ⓱ Ashorne Hill
**&**    ㉓ Lower Broadheath    upon-Avon ⓴ ⓲
Kington •    • Bromyard    ㉑㉒    Wellesbourne • Gaydon
**Worcester**    Worcester ⓳    **Warwickshire**
Great Malvern •    Pershore •
Hereford •    Upton upon Severn •    • Evesham
Ledbury •    Broadway •
• Tewkesbury
Ross-on-Wye ㉔    • Winchcombe
Symonds Yat    Gloucester • Cheltenham    • Stow on the Wold
㉕    ㉖㉗
**Gloucestershire**    • Northleach
Coleford •    • Painswick    **Oxfordshire**
Stroud •
• Berkeley    Cirencester •
• Nailsworth
Tetbury •    **Wiltshire**

0 ———— 20 Miles
0 ———— 30 Kms

• **Bed & Breakfast touring map**
• **A Guide to Great Escapes in the Heart of England** (short breaks)
• **Events list**
• **Fact sheets**
Also available are:
• **Places to Visit in the Heart of England** (over

700 attractions – with discounts, vouchers and places to visit in winter) £2.99
• **Cotswolds map** £2.95
• **Cotswold/Wyedean map** £2.60
• **Shropshire/Staffordshire map** £2.40
Please add 60p postage for up to 3 items, plus 25p for each additional 3 items.

# WHERE TO STAY

***Accommodation entries in this regional section are listed in alphabetical order of place name, and then in alphabetical order of establishment.***

***Map references refer to the colour location maps at the back of this guide. The first figure is the map number; the letter and figure which follow indicate the grid reference on the map.***

***Symbols at the end of each accommodation entry give information about services and facilities. A 'key' to these symbols is inside the back cover flap, which can be kept open for easy reference.***

## ALCESTER

Warwickshire
Map ref 2B1

Town has Roman origins and many old buildings around the High Street. It is close to Ragley Hall, the 18th C Palladian mansion with its magnificent baroque Great Hall.

### Icknield House 🅰

👑👑

54 Birmingham Road, Alcester
B49 5EG
☎ (01789) 763287 & 763681
*Comfortable, well-furnished Victorian house of character, on the Birmingham road, a few hundred yards off A435. Close to Warwick and the Cotswolds. 10 minutes from Stratford-upon-Avon. Excellent touring centre.*
Bedrooms: 2 single, 2 double, 1 twin, 1 triple
Bathrooms: 3 private, 1 public, 1 private shower

| **Bed & breakfast per night:** | £min | £max |
|---|---|---|
| Single | 20.00 | 25.00 |
| Double | 36.00 | 38.00 |

| **Half board per person:** | £min | £max |
|---|---|---|
| Daily | 27.00 | 32.00 |

Lunch available
Evening meal 1830 (last orders 1930)
Parking for 8
🎠 🛏 🖥 🫖 💨 [UL] 🔒 [S] 🪑 [TV] ◐ ♨ 👔 ✿ [OAP] [SP]

### Orchard Lawns 🅰

👑👑 HIGHLY COMMENDED

Wixford, Alcester B49 6DA
☎ Stratford-on-Avon (01789) 772668
*Bed and breakfast accommodation in a small village on B4085, 7 miles from Stratford-upon-Avon. TV lounge, garden. Ideal touring centre.*
Bedrooms: 1 single, 1 double, 1 twin
Bathrooms: 1 private, 1 public

| **Bed & breakfast per night:** | £min | £max |
|---|---|---|
| Single | 15.50 | 18.50 |
| Double | 31.00 | 37.00 |

Parking for 6
Cards accepted: Access, Visa
🎠 5 [UL] [S] 🚭 🪑 [TV] ♨ 👔 🏓 ✿ 🐕 🚜 🏠

### Sambourne Hall Farm 🅰

👑👑 COMMENDED

Wike Lane, Sambourne, Redditch, Worcestershire B96 6NZ
☎ Studley (01527) 852151
*315-acre arable & livestock farm. Mid-17th C farmhouse in a peaceful village, close to local pub. Just off the A435 between Alcester and Studley and 9 miles from Stratford-upon-Avon.*
Bedrooms: 1 double, 1 triple
Bathrooms: 2 private

| **Bed & breakfast per night:** | £min | £max |
|---|---|---|
| Single | 18.00 | 20.00 |
| Double | 35.00 | 35.00 |

Parking for 6
🎠 ☰ 💨 [UL] [S] 🚭 🪑 [TV] ♨ 👔 ✿ 🚜 🏠

National Crown ratings were correct at the time of going to press but are subject to change. Please check at the time of booking.

## ALTON

Staffordshire
Map ref 4B2

Alton Castle, an impressive 19th C building, dominates the village which is set in spectacular scenery. Nearby is Alton Towers, a romantic 19th C ruin with innumerable tourist attractions within one of England's largest theme parks in its 800 acres of magnificent gardens.

### Abbey Holidays

Listed

Tythe Barn House, Denstone Lane, Alton, Stoke-on-Trent ST10 4AX
☎ Oakamoor (01538) 702852
*Comfortable 17th C property. Car park. Garden. Reduced rates for children. 1 mile from Alton Towers. Self-catering also available.*
Bedrooms: 1 double, 3 triple, 2 family rooms
Bathrooms: 1 public

| **Bed & breakfast per night:** | £min | £max |
|---|---|---|
| Double | 30.00 | 35.00 |

Parking for 8
Open March-November
🎠 🍽 🫖 [UL] [S] 🪑 [TV] ♨ 👔 ✿ 🐕 🚜 [SP] 🏠

### Bank House

👑👑 APPROVED

Smithy Bank, Alton, Stoke-on-Trent ST10 4AA
☎ Oakamoor (01538) 702524
*Central in Alton village, 1 mile from Alton Towers and close to Dovedale and Manifold Valley. 3 good inns serving meals within 200 metres. Family-run.*
Bedrooms: 3 double, 3 triple
Bathrooms: 4 private, 1 public

**Bed & breakfast**

| per night: | £min | £max |
|---|---|---|
| Single | 17.50 | 17.50 |
| Double | 35.00 | 35.00 |

Parking for 6

## Bee Cottage ♠

Listed

Saltersford Lane, Alton, Stoke-on-Trent ST10 4AU
☎ Oakamoor (01538) 702802
*Traditional stone-built cottage, extended over a period of 200 years. In countryside, 1 mile from Alton Towers. Adjoining paddock and orchard extending to 2 acres.*
Bedrooms: 2 double, 1 twin
Bathrooms: 1 public

**Bed & breakfast**

| per night: | £min | £max |
|---|---|---|
| Single | 15.00 | 30.00 |
| Double | 30.00 | 35.00 |

Parking for 5
Open March-November

## Bradley Elms Farm ♠

COMMENDED

Threapwood, Cheadle, Stoke-on-Trent ST10 4RA
☎ Cheadle (01538) 753135
*Well-appointed farm accommodation providing a comfortable and relaxing atmosphere for that well-earned break. On the edge of the Staffordshire Moorlands. 3 miles from Alton Towers, close to the Potteries and the Peak District National Park.*
Bedrooms: 4 double, 3 twin, 1 triple, 1 family room
Bathrooms: 9 private, 1 public

**Bed & breakfast**

| per night: | £min | £max |
|---|---|---|
| Double | 33.00 | 36.00 |

**Half board**

| per person: | £min | £max |
|---|---|---|
| Daily | 28.00 | 34.00 |

Lunch available
Evening meal 1900 (last orders 2030)
Parking for 10

## Bulls Head Inn ♠

APPROVED

High Street, Alton ST10 4AQ
☎ Oakamoor (01538) 702307
Fax (01538) 702065
*In the village of Alton close to Alton Towers, an 18th C inn with real ale and home cooking.*
Bedrooms: 3 double, 1 twin, 2 family rooms
Bathrooms: 6 private, 1 public

**Bed & breakfast**

| per night: | £min | £max |
|---|---|---|
| Single | 25.00 | 40.00 |
| Double | 35.00 | 50.00 |

Lunch available
Evening meal 1900 (last orders 2200)
Parking for 10
Cards accepted: Access, Visa

## Talbot Inn ♠

Listed

Red Road, Alton, Stoke-on-Trent ST10 4BX
☎ Oakamoor (01538) 702767
*Charming country inn, delightful setting within view of Alton Towers, offering varied, interesting home-cooked food, real ale and comfortable accommodation.*
Bedrooms: 1 twin, 1 family room
Bathrooms: 1 public

**Bed & breakfast**

| per night: | £min | £max |
|---|---|---|
| Double | | 35.00 |

Lunch available
Evening meal 1830 (last orders 2100)
Parking for 20

## Wild Duck Inn

Listed

New Road, Alton, Stoke-on-Trent ST10 4AF
☎ Oakamoor (01538) 702218
*Large country inn, one mile from Alton Towers. Comfortable bedrooms, restaurant, bar and family lounge with games room.*
Bedrooms: 7 triple
Bathrooms: 2 private, 2 public

**Bed & breakfast**

| per night: | £min | £max |
|---|---|---|
| Double | 38.00 | 44.00 |

Evening meal 1900 (last orders 2030)
Parking for 50
Open March-November
Cards accepted: Access, Visa

## AMPNEY CRUCIS

Gloucestershire
Map ref 2B1

This is one of the 4 Ampney villages and is situated in pleasant countryside. Its church has Saxon features. The very attractive gardens at nearby Barnsley House are open Monday to Friday and offer plants for sale.

## Waterton Garden Cottage ♠

HIGHLY COMMENDED

Ampney Crucis, Cirencester GL7 5RX
☎ (01285) 851303
*Sympathetically converted part of Victorian stable block, retaining many original features. Walled garden, heated pool, croquet lawn. Tranquil situation, not too far from Cirencester.*
Bedrooms: 1 single, 2 double
Bathrooms: 3 private

**Bed & breakfast**

| per night: | £min | £max |
|---|---|---|
| Single | 25.00 | 35.00 |
| Double | | 45.00 |

**Half board**

| per person: | £min | £max |
|---|---|---|
| Daily | 45.00 | 55.00 |

Lunch available
Parking for 6

## AVON DASSETT

Warwickshire
Map ref 2C1

Village on the slopes of the Dasset Hills, with good views. The church, with its impressive tower and spire, dates from 1868 but incorporates a 14th C window with 15th C glass.

## Crandon House ♠

HIGHLY COMMENDED

Avon Dassett, Leamington Spa CV33 0AA
☎ Fenny Compton (01295) 770652

*20-acre mixed farm. Farmhouse offering a high standard of accommodation with superb views over unspoilt countryside. Quiet and peaceful. Easy access to Warwick, Stratford and Cotswolds. 4 miles from junctions 11 and 12 of M40.*
Bedrooms: 1 double, 2 twin
Bathrooms: 3 private

**Bed & breakfast**

| per night: | £min | £max |
|---|---|---|
| Single | 20.00 | 25.00 |
| Double | 34.00 | 39.00 |

**Half board**

| per person: | £min | £max |
|---|---|---|
| Daily | 29.00 | 36.00 |
| Weekly | 180.00 | 240.00 |

Evening meal from 1900
Parking for 22
Cards accepted: Access, Visa

All accommodation in this guide has been inspected, or is awaiting inspection, under the national Crown scheme.

## BALSALL COMMON

West Midlands
Map ref 4B3

Close to Kenilworth and within easy reach of Coventry.

### Avonlea
**Listed**

135 Kenilworth Road, Balsall Common, Coventry CV7 7EU
☎ Berkswell (01676) 532430 & Mobile 0850 915611
*A 19th C cottage extended to provide spacious and comfortable accommodation, set back from main A425 road. Ample off-road parking.*
Bedrooms: 1 double, 2 twin
Bathrooms: 1 public
**Bed & breakfast**

| per night: | £min | £max |
| --- | --- | --- |
| Single | 18.00 | 18.00 |
| Double | 36.00 | 36.00 |
| Parking for 5 | | |

### Blythe Paddocks

Barston Lane, Balsall Common, Coventry CV7 7BT
☎ Berkswell (01676) 533050
*Family home standing in 5 acres. Ten minutes from Birmingham Airport and the National Exhibition Centre. NAC Stoneleigh 8 miles. Countryside location.*
Bedrooms: 2 single, 1 double, 1 twin
Bathrooms: 1 public
**Bed & breakfast**

| per night: | £min | £max |
| --- | --- | --- |
| Single | 16.00 | 20.00 |
| Double | 32.00 | 40.00 |
| Parking for 10 | | |

### Edale
**Listed**

251 Station Road, Balsall Common, Coventry CV7 7EG
☎ Berkswell (01676) 533470
*Comfortable house with large garden and warm welcome. Ideally situated for NAC, NEC, Kenilworth, Warwick, Coventry. Easy access to airport, rail and motorway links. Near shops and eating establishments.*
Bedrooms: 1 double, 1 twin
Bathrooms: 2 public
**Bed & breakfast**

| per night: | £min | £max |
| --- | --- | --- |
| Single | 17.50 | 19.00 |
| Double | 35.00 | 38.00 |
| Parking for 7 | | |

> We advise you to confirm your booking in writing.

## BARLASTON

Staffordshire
Map ref 4B2

### Wedgwood Memorial College

Station Road, Barlaston, Stoke-on-Trent ST12 9DG
☎ Stoke-on-Trent (01782) 372105 & 373427
Fax (01782) 372393
*Pleasant, well-appointed adult residential college with relaxed, homely ambience. In a quiet village, yet close to National Trust downs and Potteries. Convenient for Peak District, Alton Towers. Good quality, home-cooked food with an imaginative repertoire of vegetarian dishes. Limited facilities for the disabled.*
Bedrooms: 9 single, 7 twin, 3 triple, 2 family rooms
Bathrooms: 7 public
**Bed & breakfast**

| per night: | £min | £max |
| --- | --- | --- |
| Single | 12.50 | 12.50 |
| Double | 25.00 | 25.00 |

**Half board**

| per person: | £min | £max |
| --- | --- | --- |
| Daily | 18.50 | 18.50 |
| Weekly | 129.50 | 129.50 |

Lunch available
Evening meal 1830 (last orders 1830)
Parking for 40

## BERKELEY

Gloucestershire
Map ref 2B1

Town dominated by the castle where Edward II was murdered. Dating from Norman times, it is still the home of the Berkeley family and is open to the public April to September and October Sundays. Slimbridge Wildfowl Trust is nearby.

### Pickwick Farm
**Listed** **COMMENDED**

Berkeley GL13 9EU
☎ Dursley (01453) 810241
*120-acre dairy farm. A warm welcome at this easily located family farm, formerly a coaching inn used by Charles Dickens. Close to Berkeley Castle, Slimbridge Wildfowl Trust and 3 golf courses. Non-smoking establishment.*
Bedrooms: 1 double, 2 twin
Bathrooms: 1 public
**Bed & breakfast**

| per night: | £min | £max |
| --- | --- | --- |
| Single | 16.00 | 16.00 |
| Double | 32.00 | 32.00 |
| Parking for 3 | | |

## BEWDLEY

Hereford and Worcester
Map ref 4A3

Attractive hillside town on the River Severn, approached by a bridge designed by Telford. The town has many elegant buildings and an interesting museum. It is the southern terminus of the Severn Valley Steam Railway.
*Tourist Information Centre*
☎ *(01299) 404740*

### Clay Farm
**HIGHLY COMMENDED**

Clows Top, Kidderminster, Worcestershire DY14 9NN
☎ Clows Top (01299) 832421
*98-acre mixed farm. Modern farmhouse with outstanding views. Bedrooms en-suite with tea-making facilities. TV lounge, central heating. Fly and coarse fishing pools. Brochures on request. On the B4202 Clows Top to Cleobury Mortimer road.*
Bedrooms: 2 double, 1 twin
Bathrooms: 2 private, 1 public
**Bed & breakfast**

| per night: | £min | £max |
| --- | --- | --- |
| Single | 16.00 | 18.00 |
| Double | 32.00 | 32.00 |
| Parking for 10 | | |

## BIBURY

Gloucestershire
Map ref 2B1

Village on the River Coln with stone houses and the famous 17th C Arlington Row, former weavers' cottages. Arlington Mill is now a folk museum. Trout farm and Bansley House Gardens nearby are open to the public.

### Cotteswold House
**HIGHLY COMMENDED**

Arlington, Bibury, Cirencester GL7 5ND
☎ Cirencester (01285) 740609
*Enjoy a relaxed friendly atmosphere in this family home. Ideally situated for touring the Cotswolds. All bedrooms en-suite with TV. Guest lounge/dining room. No smoking please. Parking.*
Bedrooms: 2 double, 1 twin
Bathrooms: 3 private
**Bed & breakfast**

| per night: | £min | £max |
| --- | --- | --- |
| Single | | 22.00 |
| Double | | 38.00 |
| Parking for 4 | | |

> Please mention this guide when making a booking.

## BIDFORD-ON-AVON

Warwickshire
Map ref 2B1

Attractive village with an ancient 8-arched bridge and a main street with some interesting 15th C houses.

### Broom Hall Inn ♨

♨♨ APPROVED

Bidford Road, Broom, Alcester B50 4HE
☎ Stratford-upon-Avon (01789) 773757

Family-owned country inn with carvery restaurant and extensive range of bar meals. Close to Stratford-upon-Avon and Cotswolds.
Bedrooms: 4 single, 4 double, 4 twin
Bathrooms: 12 private

**Bed & breakfast**

| per night: | £min | £max |
|---|---|---|
| Single | 37.50 | |
| Double | 60.00 | |

**Half board**

| per person: | £min | £max |
|---|---|---|
| Daily | 34.50 | |

Lunch available
Evening meal 1900 (last orders 2200)
Parking for 80
Cards accepted: Access, Visa, Diners, Amex

## BIRDLIP

Gloucestershire
Map ref 2B1

Hamlet at the top of a very steep descent down to the Gloucester Vale with excellent viewpoint over Crickley Hill Country Park.

### Beechmount

♨♨ COMMENDED

Birdlip, Gloucester GL4 8JH
☎ Gloucester (01452) 862262
Family-run guesthouse with personal attention. Ideal centre for the Cotswolds. Choice of menu for breakfast, unrestricted access.
Bedrooms: 1 single, 2 double, 2 twin, 2 triple
Bathrooms: 2 private, 1 public

**Bed & breakfast**

| per night: | £min | £max |
|---|---|---|
| Single | 14.00 | 30.00 |
| Double | 28.00 | 42.00 |

Evening meal (last orders 1900)
Parking for 7

## BIRMINGHAM

West Midlands
Map ref 4B3

Britain's second city, with many attractions including the City Art Gallery, Barber Institute of Fine Arts, 17th C Aston Hall, science and railway museums, Jewellery Quarter, Cadbury World, 2 cathedrals and Botanical Gardens. Good base for exploring Shakespeare country.
*Tourist Information Centre*
☎ *(0121) 643 2514*

### Awentsbury Hotel

♨♨

21 Serpentine Road, Selly Park, Birmingham B29 7HU
☎ (0121) 472 1258
Fax (0121) 472 1258
*Victorian country house set in its own large garden. Close to buses, trains, Birmingham University, BBC Pebble Mill, Queen Elizabeth Hospital, Selly Oak Hospital. Only 2 miles from the city centre and the convention centre.*
Bedrooms: 6 single, 2 double, 7 twin, 1 triple
Bathrooms: 6 private, 2 public, 5 private showers

**Bed & breakfast**

| per night: | £min | £max |
|---|---|---|
| Single | 26.00 | 36.00 |
| Double | 40.00 | 48.00 |

**Half board**

| per person: | £min | £max |
|---|---|---|
| Daily | 33.50 | 43.50 |
| Weekly | 210.00 | 275.00 |

Evening meal 1900 (last orders 1930)
Parking for 12
Cards accepted: Access, Visa, Diners, Amex

### Heath Lodge Hotel ♨

♨♨♨

Coleshill Road, Marston Green, Birmingham B37 7HT
☎ (0121) 779 2218
Fax (0121) 779 2218

*Licensed family-run hotel, quietly situated less than 2 miles from the*

National Exhibition Centre and Birmingham Airport. Courtesy car to airport.
Bedrooms: 8 single, 3 double, 7 twin
Bathrooms: 12 private, 1 public, 1 private shower

**Bed & breakfast**

| per night: | £min | £max |
|---|---|---|
| Single | 25.00 | 39.50 |
| Double | 32.00 | 50.00 |

Lunch available
Evening meal 1830 (last orders 2030)
Parking for 24
Cards accepted: Access, Visa, Diners, Amex

## BIRMINGHAM AIRPORT

West Midlands

*See under Balsall Common, Coleshill, Coventry, Hampton in Arden, Meriden, Solihull*

## BISHOP'S CASTLE

Shropshire
Map ref 4A3

A 12th C Planned Town with a castle site at the top of the hill and a church at the bottom of the main street. Many interesting buildings with original timber frames hidden behind present day houses. On the Welsh border close to the Clun Forest in quiet, unspoilt countryside.

### Castle Hotel

♨♨

The Square, Bishop's Castle SY9 5DG
☎ Bishops Castle (01588) 638403
*300-year-old unspoilt coaching inn. Large, well-kept garden with views over the town and valley.*
Bedrooms: 1 single, 4 double, 2 twin
Bathrooms: 2 private, 2 public

**Bed & breakfast**

| per night: | £min | £max |
|---|---|---|
| Single | 25.00 | 28.00 |
| Double | 40.00 | 45.00 |

Lunch available
Evening meal 1830 (last orders 2100)
Parking for 40
Cards accepted: Access, Visa

There are separate sections in this guide listing groups specialising in farm holidays and accommodation which is especially suitable for young people and organised groups.

## BLAKENEY

Gloucestershire
Map ref 2B1

Village in wooded hills near the Forest of Dean and the Severn Estuary. It is close to Lydney where the Dean Forest Railway has full size railway engines, a museum and steam days.

### Brook House Guest House

COMMENDED

Bridge Street, Blakeney GL15 4DY
☎ Dean (01594) 517101
*Attractive 17th C building in the Forest of Dean, set back from the main Gloucester/Chepstow road (A48). Ideal for walking, cycling, fishing and touring.*
Bedrooms: 2 single, 2 double
Bathrooms: 2 private, 1 public

**Bed & breakfast**

| per night: | £min | £max |
| --- | --- | --- |
| Single | 16.50 | 16.50 |
| Double | 30.00 | 36.00 |

Evening meal 1800 (last orders 1930)
Parking for 8

## BLEDINGTON

Gloucestershire
Map ref 2B1

Village close to the Oxfordshire border, with a pleasant green and a beautiful church.

### Kings Head Inn & Restaurant ♠

COMMENDED

The Green, Bledington, Oxford
OX7 6HD
☎ Kingham (01608) 658365
Fax (01608) 658365

*15th C inn located in the heart of the Cotswolds, facing the village green. Authentic lounge bars, full restaurant. Delightful en-suite rooms.*
Bedrooms: 11 double, 1 twin
Bathrooms: 12 private

**Bed & breakfast**

| per night: | £min | £max |
| --- | --- | --- |
| Single | 32.00 | 55.00 |
| Double | 52.00 | 60.00 |

Lunch available
Evening meal 1900 (last orders 2200)
Parking for 60
Cards accepted: Access, Visa

## BLOCKLEY

Gloucestershire
Map ref 2B1

This village's prosperity was founded in silk mills and other factories but now it is a quiet, unspoilt place. An excellent centre for exploring pretty Cotswold villages, especially Chipping Campden and Broadway.

### 21 Station Road ♠

COMMENDED

Blockley, Moreton-in-Marsh GL56 9ED
☎ (01386) 700402
*Beautifully presented Cotswold-stone house on edge of delightful village. Ideal base for touring Cotswolds and Shakespeare country. Tastefully decorated, comfortable, non-smoking accommodation with full en-suite facilities. A warm welcome awaits you.*
Bedrooms: 1 double, 2 twin
Bathrooms: 3 private

**Bed & breakfast**

| per night: | £min | £max |
| --- | --- | --- |
| Single | 20.00 | 20.00 |
| Double | 36.00 | 36.00 |

Parking for 9

## BODENHAM

Hereford and Worcester
Map ref 2A1

Attractive village with old timbered cottages and stone houses and an interesting church. Here the River Lugg makes a loop and flows under an ancient bridge at the end of the village.

### Maund Court

HIGHLY COMMENDED

Bodenham, Hereford HR1 3JA
☎ (01568) 84282
*150-acre mixed farm. Attractive 15th C farmhouse with a large garden, swimming pool and croquet. Riding, golf and pleasant walks nearby. Ideal centre for touring.*
Bedrooms: 1 single, 2 double, 1 twin
Bathrooms: 4 private

**Bed & breakfast**

| per night: | £min | £max |
| --- | --- | --- |
| Single | 17.00 | 18.00 |
| Double | 34.00 | 36.00 |

Evening meal from 1900
Parking for 8
Open March-November

Map references apply to the colour maps at the back of this guide.

## BOURTON-ON-THE-WATER

Gloucestershire
Map ref 2B1

The River Windrush flows through this famous Cotswold village which has a green, and cottages and houses of Cotswold stone. Its many attractions include a model village, Birdland, a Motor Museum and the Cotswold Perfumery.

### Berkeley Guesthouse ♠

COMMENDED

Moore Road, Bourton-on-the-Water, Cheltenham GL54 2AZ
☎ Cotswolds (01451) 810388
Fax (01451) 810388
*Detached house with a homely, relaxed atmosphere, furnished to a high standard. Personal attention. Attractive gardens, sun lounge, car park. No smoking.*
Bedrooms: 1 double, 1 twin, 1 triple
Bathrooms: 3 private

**Bed & breakfast**

| per night: | £min | £max |
| --- | --- | --- |
| Single | 16.00 | 20.00 |
| Double | 32.00 | 37.00 |

Parking for 4

### Coombe House ♠

HIGHLY COMMENDED

Rissington Road, Bourton-on-the-Water, Cheltenham GL54 2DT
☎ Cotswold (01451) 821966
Fax (01451) 810477
*Elegant, small "country house" style accommodation. Prettily appointed en-suite bedrooms. Delightful garden, ample parking. Non-smoking haven. Restaurants close by.*
Bedrooms: 3 double, 2 twin, 2 triple
Bathrooms: 7 private

**Bed & breakfast**

| per night: | £min | £max |
| --- | --- | --- |
| Single | 36.00 | 42.00 |
| Double | 50.00 | 65.00 |

Parking for 10
Cards accepted: Access, Visa, Amex

### Duke of Wellington Inn

Listed

Sherborne Street, Bourton-on-the-Water, Cheltenham GL54 2BY
☎ Cotswold (01451) 820539 & (Visitors) 821716
*16th C Cotswolds inn in the centre of the village, bordered by the River Windrush. Real ales and a beer garden.*
Bedrooms: 2 double, 1 twin
Bathrooms: 3 private

**Bed & breakfast**

| per night: | £min | £max |
| --- | --- | --- |
| Single | 25.00 | 26.00 |
| Double | 38.00 | 40.00 |

| Half board per person: | £min | £max |
| --- | --- | --- |
| Daily | 26.00 | 32.00 |
| Weekly | 180.00 | 220.00 |

Lunch available
Evening meal 1800 (last orders 2200)
Parking for 16

🛇 ☎ 🖳 □ ♥ 🛈 Ⓢ 🎹 ▥ ▣ ♨ Ʊ ✗ 🚲 SP 🏠

## Farncombe ⋀

♨♨

Clapton, Bourton-on-the-Water,
Cheltenham GL54 2LG
☎ Cotswold (01451) 820120
Fax (01451) 820120
*Quiet comfortable accommodation with
superb views of the Windrush Valley. In
the hamlet of Clapton, 2.5 miles from
Bourton-on-the-Water. No-smoking
house.*
Bedrooms: 2 double, 1 twin
Bathrooms: 1 private, 1 public,
2 private showers

| Bed & breakfast per night: | £min | £max |
| --- | --- | --- |
| Single | 18.00 | |
| Double | 32.00 | 40.00 |

Parking for 3

🖳 ▥ 🛈 Ⓢ ✗ 🎹 ▥ ▣ ♨ Ʊ ✗ 🚲

## Lamb Inn ⋀

♨♨♨ COMMENDED

Great Rissington, Bourton-on-the-
Water, Cheltenham GL54 2LP
☎ Cotswold (01451) 820388
Fax (01451) 820724
*Country inn in rural setting, with home-
cooked food, including steaks and local
trout, served in attractive restaurant.
Beer garden and real ale. Honeymoon
suite also available.*
Bedrooms: 8 double, 2 twin, 3 triple
Bathrooms: 8 private, 1 public

| Bed & breakfast per night: | £min | £max |
| --- | --- | --- |
| Single | 34.00 | 55.00 |
| Double | 44.00 | 72.00 |

| Half board per person: | £min | £max |
| --- | --- | --- |
| Daily | 45.00 | 62.00 |

Lunch available
Evening meal 1900 (last orders 2130)
Parking for 10
Cards accepted: Access, Visa, Amex

🛇 ☎ 🖱 ♥ 🛈 Ⓢ ✗ 🎹 ▥ ▣ �️ ♨ 🚲 SP 🏠

## Lansdowne House ⋀

♨ COMMENDED

Lansdowne, Bourton-on-the-Water,
Cheltenham GL54 2AT
☎ Cotswold (01451) 820812

*Large, period, stone family house, 2
minutes' level walk from the centre of
this much visited and delightful
Cotswold village.*
Bedrooms: 2 double, 1 triple
Bathrooms: 3 private

| Bed & breakfast per night: | £min | £max |
| --- | --- | --- |
| Single | 23.00 | 29.00 |
| Double | 29.00 | 35.00 |

Parking for 4

🛇 ☎ 🖳 □ ♥ ▥ 🛈 Ⓢ ✗ 🎹 ▥ ▣ ♨ ✗ 🚲 SP

## The Lawns ⋀

Listed

Station Road, Bourton-on-the-Water,
Cheltenham GL54 2ER
☎ Cotswold (01451) 821195
*Newly built traditional Cotswold stone
house, just 5 minutes' walk from the
centre of this picturesque village. Relax
in a comfortable lounge enjoying an
open log fire. Families and children
welcome. Discount winter breaks.*
Bedrooms: 1 double, 1 triple, 1 family
room
Bathrooms: 2 private, 1 public

| Bed & breakfast per night: | £min | £max |
| --- | --- | --- |
| Single | 16.00 | 25.00 |
| Double | 32.00 | 38.00 |

Parking for 9

🛇 □ ♥ ▥ Ⓢ ✗ 🎹 ▥ ▣ ♨ ✗ 🚲 SP

## Mousetrap Inn ⋀

♨♨ APPROVED

Lansdowne, Bourton-on-the-Water,
Cheltenham GL54 2AR
☎ Cotswold (01451) 820579
*Small homely inn with beer garden. TV
and tea/coffee makers in all rooms. Bar
meals, and open fires in winter.*
Bedrooms: 7 double, 2 twin
Bathrooms: 9 private

| Bed & breakfast per night: | £min | £max |
| --- | --- | --- |
| Single | 25.00 | |
| Double | 40.00 | 45.00 |

Lunch available
Evening meal 1830 (last orders 2100)
Parking for 12

🛇 ☎ □ ♥ 🛈 Ⓢ ✗ ▥ ▣ ⏎ ♨

## Rooftrees Guesthouse ⋀

♨♨

Rissington Road, Bourton-on-the-
Water, Cheltenham GL54 2DX
☎ Cotswold (01451) 821943
*Detached Cotswold-stone family house,
all rooms individually decorated, 8
minutes' level walk from village centre.
Home cooking with fresh local produce.
3 en-suite bedrooms: 2 rooms are on
ground floor, 2 rooms have four-posters.
No smoking.*
Bedrooms: 3 double
Bathrooms: 3 private, 1 public

| Bed & breakfast per night: | £min | £max |
| --- | --- | --- |
| Double | 37.00 | 40.00 |

Evening meal 1830 (last orders 1200)

Parking for 8
Cards accepted: Access, Visa, Switch/
Delta

🛇 ☎ 6 🖱 ▥ 🛈 🖳 □ ♥ ▥ 🛈 Ⓢ ✗ 🎹 ▥ ▣ ✗ 🚲

## Stepping Stone ⋀

♨♨

Rectory Lane, Great Rissington,
Cheltenham GL54 2LL
☎ Cotswold (01451) 821385
*Large detached house in country village
lane with private grounds and views
across the Windrush Valley.*
Bedrooms: 1 single, 2 double, 1 twin
Bathrooms: 2 private, 1 public

| Bed & breakfast per night: | £min | £max |
| --- | --- | --- |
| Single | 16.00 | 40.00 |
| Double | 30.00 | 42.00 |

Parking for 6

🛇 ☎ 10 🖱 □ ♥ ▥ 🎹 ▥ ▣ ♨ ✗ 🚲

## Strathspey ⋀

Listed APPROVED

Lansdown, Bourton-on-the-Water,
Cheltenham GL54 2AR
☎ Cotswold (01451) 820694
*Character, Cotswold-stone house 400
yards' walk from village centre. Quiet
location with pretty riverside walk.*
Bedrooms: 3 double
Bathrooms: 2 private, 1 public

| Bed & breakfast per night: | £min | £max |
| --- | --- | --- |
| Double | 32.00 | 38.00 |

Parking for 4
Open April-October

🛇 ☎ 12 🖱 🖳 □ ♥ ▥ 🛈 Ⓢ ✗ ▥ ▣ ✗ 🚲 DAP

## Upper Farm

♨♨

Clapton on the Hill, Bourton-on-the-
Water, Cheltenham GL54 2LG
☎ Cotswold (01451) 820453
*130-acre mixed farm. 17th C Cotswold
farmhouse in a quiet, unspoilt village
2.5 miles from Bourton-on-the-Water.
Magnificent views. Fresh farm produce.*
Bedrooms: 1 single, 2 double, 2 twin
Bathrooms: 2 private, 2 public

| Bed & breakfast per night: | £min | £max |
| --- | --- | --- |
| Single | 18.00 | 20.00 |
| Double | 30.00 | 38.00 |

Parking for 6
Open March-November

🛇 ☎ 5 🖱 🖳 □ ♥ ▥ 🛈 ✗ 🎹 ▥ ▣ Ʊ ✓ ♨ ✗ 🚲 🏠

National Crown ratings
were correct at the time
of going to press but
are subject to change.
Please check at the time
of booking.

## BRAILES

Warwickshire
Map ref 2C1

### Agdon Farm
**Listed**

Brailes, Banbury, Oxfordshire
OX15 5JJ
☎ (01608) 685226 & Mobile 0850
847786
*211-acre mixed farm. Old Cotswold-
stone house in an area of outstanding
beauty. We keep horses, cats aand dogs.
Well situated for touring the Cotswolds,
Oxford, Warwick and Stratford-upon-
Avon.*
Bedrooms: 2 double, 1 twin
Bathrooms: 1 public
**Bed & breakfast**

| per night: | £min | £max |
| --- | --- | --- |
| Single | 18.00 | |
| Double | 32.00 | |

**Half board**

| per person: | £min | £max |
| --- | --- | --- |
| Daily | 25.50 | |
| Weekly | 153.00 | |

Evening meal 1800 (last orders 2100)
Parking for 8

## BREDENBURY

Hereford and Worcester
Map ref 2A1

### Redhill Farm
**Listed**

Bredenbury, Bromyard, Herefordshire
HR7 4SY
☎ Bromyard (01885) 483255 &
483535
Fax (01885) 483535
*86-acre mixed & livestock farm. 17th C
farmhouse in peaceful, unspoilt
countryside with panoramic views.
Central for Malvern, Hereford,
Worcester, Ledbury and Ludlow.
Children and pets welcome. A home-
from-home on the A44 road.*
Bedrooms: 1 double, 1 twin, 1 triple
Bathrooms: 1 public
**Bed & breakfast**

| per night: | £min | £max |
| --- | --- | --- |
| Single | 14.00 | 15.00 |
| Double | 28.00 | 30.00 |

Evening meal 1900 (last orders 2100)
Parking for 23

Colour maps at the
back of this guide
pinpoint all places which
have accommodation
listings in the guide.

## BREDON'S NORTON

Hereford and Worcester
Map ref 2B1

Hamlet at the foot of Bredon Hill
with a substantial Victorian
mansion in Tudor style.

### Lampitt House ⚏
**COMMENDED**

Lampitt Lane, Bredon's Norton,
Tewkesbury, Gloucestershire
GL20 7HB
☎ Bredon (01684) 72295

*Large house set in 1.5 acre garden in
picturesque Cotswold village at the foot
of Bredon Hill. Extensive views.
Tewkesbury 4 miles. Beautiful hill and
riverside walks.*
Bedrooms: 2 double, 1 twin
Bathrooms: 3 private
**Bed & breakfast**

| per night: | £min | £max |
| --- | --- | --- |
| Single | 25.00 | |
| Double | 35.00 | |

**Half board**

| per person: | £min | £max |
| --- | --- | --- |
| Daily | 28.50 | |
| Weekly | 322.00 | |

Evening meal 1800 (last orders 2000)
Parking for 6

## BRETFORTON

Hereford and Worcester
Map ref 2B1

### The Pond House ⚏
**HIGHLY COMMENDED**

Lower Fields, Weston Road,
Bretforton, Evesham, Worcestershire
WR11 5QA
☎ Evesham (01386) 831687
*Superb country home in open farmland,
with panoramic views of Cotswold Hills.
Ideally placed for touring, 3 miles to
Broadway and Chipping Campden,
close to Stratford-upon-Avon.*
Bedrooms: 2 double, 1 twin
Bathrooms: 3 private
**Bed & breakfast**

| per night: | £min | £max |
| --- | --- | --- |
| Single | 20.50 | |
| Double | 31.00 | 38.00 |

Parking for 10

## BREWOOD

Staffordshire
Map ref 4B3

### The Blackladies
⚏⚏ **HIGHLY COMMENDED**

Brewood, Stafford ST19 9BH
☎ Wolverhampton (01902) 850210
*A fine 16th C manor house, formerly a
Benedictine priory, set in 5 acres of
grounds and surrounded by beautiful
countryside. Within easy reach of
motorway network.*
Bedrooms: 1 double, 1 twin, 1 family
room
Bathrooms: 3 private
**Bed & breakfast**

| per night: | £min | £max |
| --- | --- | --- |
| Single | 27.50 | 32.50 |
| Double | 50.00 | 60.00 |

Parking for 9

## BRIDGNORTH

Shropshire
Map ref 4A3

Red sandstone riverside town in 2
parts - High and Low - linked by a
cliff railway. Much of interest
including a ruined Norman keep,
half-timbered 16th C houses,
Midland Motor Museum and
Severn Valley Railway.
*Tourist Information Centre*
☎ *(01746) 763358*

### The Albynes
⚏

Nordley, Bridgnorth WV16 4SX
☎ (01746) 762261

*263-acre arable and mixed farm. Large
country house, peacefully set in
parkland with spectacular views of
Shropshire countryside. On B4373 -
Bridgnorth 3 miles, Ironbridge 4 miles.*
Bedrooms: 2 twin
Bathrooms: 2 private, 2 public
**Bed & breakfast**

| per night: | £min | £max |
| --- | --- | --- |
| Single | 17.50 | 19.00 |
| Double | 35.00 | 38.00 |

Parking for 8

### Aldenham Weir ⚏
**COMMENDED**

Muckley Cross, Bridgnorth WV16 4RR
☎ Morville (01746) 714352

*Superb country house, set in 11.5 acres, with working mill race, weir and trout stream for fishing. All rooms en-suite. Close to Ironbridge Gorge Museum. Quietly located off the A458, central between Much Wenlock and Bridgnorth.*
Bedrooms: 3 double, 2 twin, 1 triple
Bathrooms: 6 private
**Bed & breakfast**

| per night: | £min | £max |
|---|---|---|
| Single | | 25.00 |
| Double | | 38.00 |

Parking for 5

## Church House 🏠

Aston Eyre, Bridgnorth WV16 6XD
☎ Morville (01746) 714248

*You are invited to a peaceful holiday in this oak-beamed cottage on a 6-acre smallholding. Overlooking Shropshire's rolling hills, it nestles behind a Norman church. Evening meals by arrangement.*
Bedrooms: 1 double, 1 twin
Bathrooms: 2 private
**Bed & breakfast**

| per night: | £min | £max |
|---|---|---|
| Double | 30.00 | 34.00 |

**Half board**

| per person: | £min | £max |
|---|---|---|
| Daily | 50.00 | 54.00 |

Evening meal 1800 (last orders 2000)
Parking for 4
Open February-November

## Oldfield Cottage
**COMMENDED**
Oldfield, Bridgnorth WV16 6AQ
☎ Middleton Scriven (01746) 35257
Changing to 789257
*Traditional stone cottage in "Cadfael country". Exposed timbers and log fires. Large garden. Four miles from Bridgnorth. Extensive country views.*
Bedrooms: 1 double, 1 twin
Bathrooms: 1 private, 1 public
**Bed & breakfast**

| per night: | £min | £max |
|---|---|---|
| Single | 20.00 | 20.00 |
| Double | 35.00 | 35.00 |

---

**Half board**

| per person: | £min | £max |
|---|---|---|
| Daily | | 26.00 |

Parking for 2
Open February-October

## Park Grange Bed & Breakfast 🏠
Morville, Bridgnorth WV16 4RN
☎ Morville (01746) 31285 Changing to 714285
*12-acre livestock farm. Splendid beamed family house set in 12 acres, with goats, poultry, pony, wildlife and fishing pools. Children's play area. Look for Holiday Caravans sign. Quiet location midway between Bridgnorth and Much Wenlock just off A458.*
Bedrooms: 1 family room
Bathrooms: 1 private
**Bed & breakfast**

| per night: | £min | £max |
|---|---|---|
| Double | 34.00 | 36.00 |

Parking for 10
Open March-October

---

## BROADWAY
Hereford and Worcester
Map ref 2B1

Beautiful Cotswold village called the "Show village of England", with 16th C stone houses and cottages. Near the village is Broadway Tower with magnificent views over 12 counties and a country park with nature trails and adventure playground.

## Broadway Court 🏠
**Listed HIGHLY COMMENDED**
89 High Street, Broadway, Worcestershire WR12 7AL
☎ (01386) 852237
*Grade II listed barn conversion overlooking secluded, walled cottage garden with country views. Delightful and spacious en-suite bedrooms, beautiful panelled dining room. Two minutes' walk to village centre.*
Bedrooms: 2 double
Bathrooms: 2 private
**Bed & breakfast**

| per night: | £min | £max |
|---|---|---|
| Double | | 50.00 |

Parking for 10

## Cinnibar Cottage 🏠
**Listed HIGHLY COMMENDED**
45 Bury End, (Snowshill Rd.,), Broadway, Worcestershire WR12 7AF
☎ (01386) 858 623
*150-year-old Cotswold-stone cottage. Quiet situation with open country views, half a mile from Broadway village*

---

*green, along Snowshill road. Non-smoking establishment.*
Bedrooms: 1 double, 1 twin
Bathrooms: 1 public
**Bed & breakfast**

| per night: | £min | £max |
|---|---|---|
| Double | 31.00 | 35.00 |

Parking for 2

## Crown and Trumpet Inn 🏠
**APPROVED**
Church Street, Broadway, Worcestershire WR12 7AE
☎ (01386) 853202
*Traditional English inn with log fires and oak beams, quietly located just off the village green. Home-cooked local and seasonal English food.*
Bedrooms: 3 double, 1 twin
Bathrooms: 4 private
**Bed & breakfast**

| per night: | £min | £max |
|---|---|---|
| Double | 37.00 | 56.00 |

Lunch available
Evening meal 1830 (last orders 2130)
Parking for 6

## Eastbank 🏠
Station Drive, Broadway, Worcestershire WR12 7DF
☎ (01386) 852659
*Quiet location, half a mile from village. All rooms fully en-suite (bath/shower), with colour TV and beverage facilities. Homely atmosphere. Free brochure.*
Bedrooms: 2 double, 2 twin, 2 triple
Bathrooms: 6 private
**Bed & breakfast**

| per night: | £min | £max |
|---|---|---|
| Single | 15.00 | |
| Double | 30.60 | 50.00 |

Evening meal 1900 (last orders 1000)
Parking for 6

## Leasow House 🏠
**HIGHLY COMMENDED**
Laverton Meadow, Broadway, Worcestershire WR12 7NA
☎ Stanton (01386) 584526
Fax (01386) 584596

*17th C Cotswold-stone farmhouse tranquilly set in open countryside close to Broadway village.*
Bedrooms: 3 double, 2 twin, 2 triple
Bathrooms: 7 private

*Continued ►*

## BROADWAY

*Continued*

| Bed & breakfast per night: | £min | £max |
|---|---|---|
| Single | 30.00 | 45.00 |
| Double | 48.00 | 60.00 |

Parking for 14
Cards accepted: Access, Visa, Amex

### Manor Farm 🅜

COMMENDED

Wormington, Broadway,
Worcestershire WR12 7NL
☎ Stanton (01386) 73302
*400-acre arable & livestock farm.
Attractive Tudor farmhouse in quiet
village, 4 miles from Broadway. Access
to farm with animals and river fishing.*
Bedrooms: 2 double, 1 twin
Bathrooms: 3 private

| Bed & breakfast per night: | £min | £max |
|---|---|---|
| Single | 16.00 | 22.00 |
| Double | 30.00 | 42.00 |

Parking for 6

### Millhay Cottage

Listed

Bury End, Broadway, Worcestershire
WR12 7JS
☎ (01386) 858241
*House set in a superb garden off the
Snowshill road and adjacent to
Cotswold Way. The suite of two
bedrooms, bathroom and WC is let as a
family unit (1-4 persons).*
Bedrooms: 1 double, 1 twin
Bathrooms: 2 private, 1 public

| Bed & breakfast per night: | £min | £max |
|---|---|---|
| Single | 18.00 | 22.00 |
| Double | 36.00 | 44.00 |

Parking for 12

### Mount Pleasant Farm 🅜

HIGHLY COMMENDED

Childswickham, Broadway,
Worcestershire WR12 7HZ
☎ (01386) 853424
*250-acre mixed farm. Large Victorian
farmhouse with excellent views. Very
quiet accommodation with all modern
amenities. Approximately 3 miles from
Broadway.*
Bedrooms: 2 double, 1 twin
Bathrooms: 3 private

| Bed & breakfast per night: | £min | £max |
|---|---|---|
| Single | | 25.00 |
| Double | 35.00 | 40.00 |

Parking for 8

## Olive Branch Guest House 🅜

78 High Street, Broadway,
Worcestershire WR12 7AJ
☎ (01386) 853440
Fax (01386) 853440

*16th C house with modern amenities
close to centre of village. Traditional
English breakfast served. Reduced rates
for 3 nights or more.*
Bedrooms: 2 single, 2 double, 2 twin,
1 triple
Bathrooms: 5 private, 1 public

| Bed & breakfast per night: | £min | £max |
|---|---|---|
| Single | 17.00 | 19.50 |
| Double | 36.00 | 45.00 |

| Half board per person: | £min | £max |
|---|---|---|
| Daily | 25.00 | 31.00 |
| Weekly | 168.00 | 196.00 |

Evening meal 1900 (last orders 2000)
Parking for 8
Cards accepted: Amex

### Orchard Grove 🅜

HIGHLY COMMENDED

Station Road, Broadway,
Worcestershire WR12 7DE
☎ Evesham (01386) 853834
*Attractive detached Cotswold house, just
minutes from village centre, tastefully
appointed for guests' every comfort.
Warm welcome assured. Non-smokers
only, please.*
Bedrooms: 1 double, 1 triple
Bathrooms: 2 private

| Bed & breakfast per night: | £min | £max |
|---|---|---|
| Double | 40.00 | 45.00 |

Parking for 3

### Pine Tree Cottage 🅜

Listed COMMENDED

Laverton, Broadway, Worcestershire
WR12 7NA
☎ Stanton (01386) 584280
Fax (01386) 584280
*Small family bed and breakfast, 2 miles
from Broadway in peaceful village. Self-
catering also available.*
Bedrooms: 1 double, 1 twin
Bathrooms: 1 private

| Bed & breakfast per night: | £min | £max |
|---|---|---|
| Single | 18.00 | 21.00 |
| Double | 30.00 | 36.00 |

Parking for 3

## Shenberrow Hill

Listed

Stanton, Broadway, Worcestershire
WR12 7NE
☎ (01386) 584468
*9-acre horse farm. Attractive country
house, quietly situated in beautiful
unspoilt Cotswold village. Heated
swimming pool. Friendly, helpful
service. Inn nearby.*
Bedrooms: 2 twin, 2 family rooms
Bathrooms: 2 private, 1 public

| Bed & breakfast per night: | £min | £max |
|---|---|---|
| Single | 20.00 | |
| Double | 36.00 | 40.00 |

| Half board per night: | £min | £max |
|---|---|---|
| Daily | 27.00 | 29.00 |

Evening meal 1800 (last orders 2000)
Parking for 6

### Southwold House 🅜

COMMENDED

Station Road, Broadway,
Worcestershire WR12 7DE
☎ (01386) 853681
*Warm welcome, friendly service, good
cooking at this large Edwardian house,
only 4 minutes' walk from village
centre. Reductions for 2 or more nights;
bargain winter breaks.*
Bedrooms: 1 single, 5 double, 2 twin
Bathrooms: 5 private, 2 public

| Bed & breakfast per night: | £min | £max |
|---|---|---|
| Single | 17.00 | |
| Double | 34.00 | 42.00 |

Parking for 8
Cards accepted: Access, Visa, Amex

### White Acres Guesthouse 🅜

COMMENDED

Station Road, Broadway,
Worcestershire WR12 7DE
☎ (01386) 852320
*Spacious Victorian house with en-suite
bedrooms, 3 with four-poster beds. Off-
road parking. 4 minutes' walk from
village centre. Reductions for 2 or more
nights. Bargain winter breaks.*
Bedrooms: 5 double, 1 twin
Bathrooms: 6 private

| Bed & breakfast per night: | £min | £max |
|---|---|---|
| Double | 38.00 | 42.00 |

Parking for 8
Open March-November

### Windrush House 🅜

COMMENDED

Station Road, Broadway,
Worcestershire WR12 7DE
☎ (01386) 853577
*Edwardian guesthouse on the A44, half
a mile from the village centre, offering
personal service. Evening meals by*

*arrangement. 10 per cent reduction in tariff after 2 nights. A no smoking establishment.*
Bedrooms: 4 double, 1 twin
Bathrooms: 5 private

**Bed & breakfast**

| per night: | £min | £max |
|---|---|---|
| Single | 18.00 | 25.00 |
| Double | 36.00 | 44.00 |

**Half board**

| per person: | £min | £max |
|---|---|---|
| Daily | 30.00 | 34.00 |
| Weekly | 200.00 | 220.00 |

Parking for 5

🖵 ♿ 🅟 🕆 UL ♿ S ✂ ▥ 🖂 🐾 SP

## BROMSGROVE

Hereford and Worcester
Map ref 4B3

This market town near the Lickey Hills has an interesting museum and craft centre and 14th C church with fine tombs and a Carillon tower. The Avoncroft Museum of Buildings is nearby where many old buildings have been re-assembled, having been saved from destruction.
*Tourist Information Centre*
☎ *(01527) 831809*

### The Barn ⋒
♨♨ **COMMENDED**

Woodman Lane, Clent, Stourbridge, Worcestershire DY9 9PX
☎ Hagley (01562) 885879 & Kingswinford (01384) 401977
*Converted Georgian barn on smallholding. At foot of Clent Hills, access to hills from the property. Easy access to Birmingham and National Exhibition Centre.*
Bedrooms: 1 double, 1 family room
Bathrooms: 2 private

**Bed & breakfast**

| per night: | £min | £max |
|---|---|---|
| Single | 20.00 | |
| Double | 40.00 | |

Parking for 11

ኄ ♿ 🖭 📞 🕆 🖵 UL S ✂ ▥ 🖂 ✿ 🐾 🏮

### The Grahams
**Listed** **APPROVED**

95 Old Station Road, Bromsgrove, Worcestershire B60 2AF
☎ (01527) 874463
*Modern house in quiet pleasant location close to the A38, 3 miles from the M5 and 1.5 miles from the M42. Within easy reach of National Exhibition Centre, Worcester and Stratford. Car parking, TV lounge, tea/coffee facilities.*
Bedrooms: 2 single, 1 twin
Bathrooms: 1 public

**Bed & breakfast**

| per night: | £min | £max |
|---|---|---|
| Single | 15.00 | 15.00 |
| Double | 30.00 | 30.00 |

**Half board**

| per person: | £min | £max |
|---|---|---|
| Daily | 20.00 | 20.00 |
| Weekly | 120.00 | 120.00 |

Evening meal 1800 (last orders 0900)
Parking for 2

ኄ 2 ⌘ ♿ 🕆 UL ♿ ✂ ▥ 🖵 🖂 🐾 ⊕

### Hill Farm ⋒
♨♨ **COMMENDED**

Rocky Lane, Bournheath, Bromsgrove, Worcestershire B61 9HU
☎ (01527) 872403
*50-acre market garden farm. Georgian listed farmhouse, tastefully maintained throughout. Traditional farmhouse fare. Families welcome.*
Bedrooms: 2 single, 1 double, 2 twin
Bathrooms: 5 private

**Bed & breakfast**

| per night: | £min | £max |
|---|---|---|
| Single | 17.50 | 20.00 |
| Double | 35.00 | 40.00 |

**Half board**

| per person: | £min | £max |
|---|---|---|
| Daily | 29.00 | 31.50 |
| Weekly | 192.50 | 210.00 |

Evening meal 1800 (last orders 2000)
Parking for 6

ኄ 3 ♿ 🕆 UL 📞 S ▤ ▥ ▥ 🖂 ✿ 🐾 🏮

## BROMYARD

Hereford and Worcester
Map ref 2B1

Market town on the River Frome surrounded by orchards, with black and white houses and a Norman church. Nearby at Lower Brockhampton is a 14th C half-timbered moated manor house owned by the National Trust. Heritage Centre.
*Tourist Information Centre*
☎ *(01885) 482341 or 482038*

### Park House ⋒
♨♨

28 Sherford Street, Bromyard, Herefordshire HR7 4DL
☎ (01885) 482294
*Close to town centre, restaurant and shops, and a desirable location for touring. Ample parking.*
Bedrooms: 1 single, 1 double, 1 twin, 2 triple
Bathrooms: 3 private, 1 public

**Bed & breakfast**

| per night: | £min | £max |
|---|---|---|
| Single | 15.00 | 20.00 |
| Double | 28.00 | 30.00 |

Parking for 6

ኄ ♿ 🕆 ▤ 📞 S ✂ ▥ ▥ ▥ ✿ 🐾 🏮

---

**Check the introduction to this region for ideas on Where to Go.**

## BROSELEY

Shropshire
Map ref 4A3

### Lord Hill Guest House
**Listed**

Duke Street, Broseley TF12 5LU
☎ Telford (01952) 884270
*Former public house renovated to a high standard. Easy access to Ironbridge, Bridgnorth, Shrewsbury and Telford town centre.*
Bedrooms: 1 single, 1 double, 5 twin
Bathrooms: 2 private, 2 public, 1 private shower

**Bed & breakfast**

| per night: | £min | £max |
|---|---|---|
| Single | 16.00 | 18.00 |
| Double | 32.00 | 36.00 |

**Half board**

| per person: | £min | £max |
|---|---|---|
| Daily | 22.00 | 26.00 |
| Weekly | 154.00 | 182.00 |

Parking for 9

ኄ 8 ⌘ ♿ 🖵 ▤ ▥ ▥ ▥ ✿ 🐾 DAP SP

## BUCKNELL

Shropshire
Map ref 4A3

Village by the River Redlake with thatched black and white cottages, a Norman church and the remains of an Iron Age fort on a nearby hill. It is a designated Area of Outstanding Natural Beauty.

### The Hall ⋒
♨♨ **COMMENDED**

Bucknell SY7 0AA
☎ (01547) 4249
*200-acre mixed farm. Georgian farmhouse in the picturesque village of Bucknell, with a peaceful and relaxed atmosphere.*
Bedrooms: 2 double, 1 twin
Bathrooms: 1 private, 1 public

**Bed & breakfast**

| per night: | £min | £max |
|---|---|---|
| Single | 15.00 | 16.00 |
| Double | 30.00 | 32.00 |

**Half board**

| per person: | £min | £max |
|---|---|---|
| Daily | 23.00 | 24.00 |
| Weekly | 158.00 | |

Evening meal 1800 (last orders 1200)
Parking for 4
Open March-November

ኄ 7 🖵 🕆 UL ✂ ▥ ▥ ✿ 🐾 🏮

---

**The symbol ⋒ after an establishment name indicates membership of a Regional Tourist Board.**

## BURTON UPON TRENT

Staffordshire
Map ref 4B3

An important brewing town with the Bass Museum of Brewing, where the Bass shire horses are stabled. There are 3 bridges with views over the river and some interesting public buildings including the 18th C St Modwen's Church.
*Tourist Information Centre*
☎ *(01283) 516609*

### Hayfield House
Listed

13 Ashby Road, Woodville, Swadlincote, Derbyshire DE11 7BZ
☎ (01283) 225620
*Victorian villa on the A50 in South Derbyshire, close to the Leicestershire/Staffordshire/Derbyshire border.*
Bedrooms: 1 triple, 1 family room
Bathrooms: 1 private, 1 public

| Bed & breakfast per night: | £min | £max |
|---|---|---|
| Single | 15.00 | 15.00 |
| Double | 30.00 | 30.00 |

Evening meal 1800 (last orders 1900)
Parking for 3

### New Inn Farm
Listed

Needwood, Burton upon Trent DE13 9PB
☎ (01283) 75435
*122-acre mixed & dairy farm. In the heart of Needwood Forest on the main B5234 Newborough to Burton upon Trent road. B5017 goes right past the farmhouse gate. Central for Uttoxeter, Lichfield, Derby and Burton upon Trent.*
Bedrooms: 1 single, 1 double, 1 triple
Bathrooms: 1 public

| Bed & breakfast per night: | £min | £max |
|---|---|---|
| Single | 14.50 | 15.00 |
| Double | 29.00 | 30.00 |

Parking for 6

## CARDINGTON

Shropshire
Map ref 4A3

### Grove Farm
Listed

Cardington, Church Stretton SY6 7JZ
☎ Longville (01694) 771451
*7-acre mixed farm. Oak-beamed farmhouse built in 1667, in delightful village 5 miles from Church Stretton. Excellent walking country. Homely atmosphere.*
Bedrooms: 1 twin, 1 triple
Bathrooms: 1 public

| Bed & breakfast per night: | £min | £max |
|---|---|---|
| Single | 15.00 | 17.00 |
| Double | 28.00 | 30.00 |

Parking for 10

### Woodside Farm

Cardington, Church Stretton SY6 7LB
☎ Longville (01694) 771314
*36-acre livestock farm. Woodside is situated on a country lane, between Gretton and Chatwall. 6.5 miles from Church Stretton and 9 miles from Much Wenlock.*
Bedrooms: 1 double, 1 triple
Bathrooms: 1 public

| Bed & breakfast per night: | £min | £max |
|---|---|---|
| Single | 12.50 | 14.00 |
| Double | 25.00 | 28.00 |

| Half board per person: | £min | £max |
|---|---|---|
| Daily | 20.50 | 22.00 |

Evening meal 1800 (last orders 1900)
Parking for 4

## CHELTENHAM

Gloucestershire
Map ref 2B1

Cheltenham was developed as a spa town in the 18th C and has some beautiful Regency architecture, in particular the Pittville Pump Room. It holds international music and literature festivals and is also famous for its race meetings and cricket.
*Tourist Information Centre*
☎ *(01242) 522878*

### Elm Villa ⋒

49 London Road, Cheltenham GL52 6HE
☎ (01242) 231909
*Beautiful, detached, listed Victorian house, with its own special original architecture. Three minutes town centre, theatre, swimming pool, parks.*
Bedrooms: 1 double, 2 twin
Bathrooms: 1 public

| Bed & breakfast per night: | £min | £max |
|---|---|---|
| Single | 20.00 | 25.00 |
| Double | 36.00 | 38.00 |

Parking for 6

### Ham Hill Farm ⋒
Listed  COMMENDED

Whittington, Cheltenham GL54 4EZ
☎ (01242) 584415
*160-acre mixed farm. Farmhouse, built in 1983 to a high standard, with good views of the Cotswolds. 2 miles from Cheltenham, on the Cotswold Way.*
Bedrooms: 1 single, 4 double, 1 twin, 1 family room
Bathrooms: 6 private

| Bed & breakfast per night: | £min | £max |
|---|---|---|
| Single | 20.00 | 20.00 |
| Double | 34.00 | 35.00 |

Parking for 7

### Hamilton

46 All Saints Road, Cheltenham GL52 2HA
☎ (01242) 582845
*Early Victorian town house, with spacious accommodation, near town centre. Ideal for visitors to Stratford-upon-Avon, the Cotswolds and Forest of Dean.*
Bedrooms: 1 twin
Bathrooms: 1 private

| Bed & breakfast per night: | £min | £max |
|---|---|---|
| Single | 18.00 | 25.00 |
| Double | 32.00 | 50.00 |

Open January-November

### Hunting Butts ⋒
APPROVED

Swindon Lane, Cheltenham GL50 4NZ
☎ (01242) 524982
*200-acre arable & livestock farm. Farmhouse overlooking Cheltenham with views to the Malverns and Cleeve Hill, within walking distance of Cheltenham and all facilities. Also converted stable annexe, which includes 2 ground floor rooms adapted for disabled visitors.*
Wheelchair access category 3 ♿
Bedrooms: 2 double, 3 twin, 2 triple
Bathrooms: 5 private, 1 public

| Bed & breakfast per night: | £min | £max |
|---|---|---|
| Single | 18.50 | 21.00 |
| Double | 32.00 | 37.00 |

| Half board per person: | £min | £max |
|---|---|---|
| Daily | 27.50 | 30.00 |
| Weekly | 255.50 | 270.00 |

Parking for 20

### Kielder ⋒
COMMENDED

222 London Road, Charlton Kings, Cheltenham GL52 6HW
☎ (01242) 237138
*Comfortable family house on A40, near junction with A435. One and a quarter miles from town centre. Stair chairlift available. No smoking.*
Bedrooms: 1 double, 1 twin, 1 triple
Bathrooms: 1 private, 1 public

| Bed & breakfast per night: | £min | £max |
|---|---|---|
| Single | 17.00 | 25.00 |
| Double | 32.00 | 34.00 |

| Half board per person: | £min | £max |
|---|---|---|
| Daily | 27.00 | 34.00 |
| Weekly | 180.00 | 190.00 |

Evening meal from 1830
Parking for 5

🛏🍴☐🌙🕿 � ⛶✕🔺 🖾▦ 🖪❋✕🚐

## Lawn Hotel ⚠

☎ **COMMENDED**

5 Pittville Lawn, Cheltenham
GL52 2BE
☎ (01242) 526638

*Grade II listed Regency hotel within
Pittville Gardens. Friendly, relaxed
atmosphere, bright rooms and good
breakfast. Parking.*
Bedrooms: 6 single, 1 double, 2 triple
Bathrooms: 3 public

| Bed & breakfast per night: | £min | £max |
|---|---|---|
| Single | 15.00 | 19.00 |
| Double | 30.00 | 38.00 |

| Half board per person: | £min | £max |
|---|---|---|
| Daily | 25.00 | 29.00 |

Lunch available
Evening meal 1830 (last orders 1930)
Parking for 6

🛏🍴☐🝤🛡🔺⛶📺▦🖪❋ SP 🏮

## Lonsdale House ⚠

☎☎

Montpellier Drive, Cheltenham
GL50 1TX
☎ (01242) 232379
Fax (01242) 232379
*Regency house situated 5 minutes' walk
from the town hall, promenade,
shopping centre, parks and theatre.
Easy access to all main routes.*
Bedrooms: 5 single, 2 double, 1 twin,
2 triple, 1 family room
Bathrooms: 3 private, 4 public

| Bed & breakfast per night: | £min | £max |
|---|---|---|
| Single | 18.00 | 26.00 |
| Double | 36.00 | 48.00 |

Parking for 6
Cards accepted: Access, Visa

🛏3☐🕿🌙🛡🛡📺▦🖪❋🚐 SP 🏮 🅣

## Old Rectory ⚠

☎☎ **COMMENDED**

Woolstone, Cheltenham GL52 4RG
☎ Bishops Cleeve (01242) 673766

*Beautiful Victorian rectory in peaceful
hamlet, 4 miles north of the Regency
town of Cheltenham. Tranquil spot with
lovely views.*
Bedrooms: 1 double, 1 twin, 1 triple
Bathrooms: 3 private

| Bed & breakfast per night: | £min | £max |
|---|---|---|
| Single | | 25.00 |
| Double | | 39.00 |

Parking for 6

🛏🚲🍴☐🌙🕿 ⓘ⛶📺🖪⯈20↺
✕ 🚐🏮

## Old Stables ⚠

**Listed**

239A London Road, Charlton Kings,
Cheltenham GL52 6YE
☎ (01242) 583660
*Former coach house with separate B &
B accommodation, 2 miles east of
Cheltenham town centre on the A40.
Easy car access and parking.*
Bedrooms: 1 twin, 1 triple
Bathrooms: 1 public

| Bed & breakfast per night: | £min | £max |
|---|---|---|
| Single | 15.00 | 16.00 |
| Double | 28.00 | 30.00 |

Parking for 3

🛏1🗌ⓘ📺▦🖪❋🚐 SP

## St. Michaels ⚠

☎☎ **COMMENDED**

4 Montpellier Drive, Cheltenham
GL50 1TX
☎ (01242) 513587
*Elegant Edwardian guesthouse 5
minutes' stroll from town centre.
Delightful rooms with central heating,
refreshment tray, colour TV,
clock/radio, hairdryer. Quiet location.*
Bedrooms: 2 double, 1 twin, 2 triple
Bathrooms: 3 private, 1 public

| Bed & breakfast per night: | £min | £max |
|---|---|---|
| Single | 21.00 | 26.00 |
| Double | 36.00 | 41.00 |

Parking for 3
Cards accepted: Access, Visa

🛏☐🌙🕿 ⓘ Ⓢ⛶▦🖪🚐 OAP SP

## The Wynyards ⚠

☎☎ **COMMENDED**

Butts Lane, Woodmancote,
Cheltenham GL52 4QH
☎ (01242) 673876
*Secluded old Cotswold stone-house in
elevated position with panoramic views.
Set in open countryside on outskirts of
small village, 4 miles from Cheltenham.*
Bedrooms: 1 double, 2 twin
Bathrooms: 1 private, 2 public

| Bed & breakfast per night: | £min | £max |
|---|---|---|
| Single | 15.00 | 18.00 |
| Double | 26.00 | 32.00 |

Parking for 6

🛏📞🌙🕿 ⓘ⛶🔺📺◑▦🖪↺↻
❋✕🚐 SP

## CHIPPING CAMPDEN

Gloucestershire
Map ref 2B1

Outstanding Cotswold wool town
with many old stone gabled
houses, a splendid church, 17th C
almshouses and Woolstaplers Hall
Museum. Nearby are Kiftsgate
Court Gardens and Hidcote Manor
Gardens (National Trust).

## Brymbo ⚠

**Listed**

Honeybourne Lane, Mickleton,
Chipping Campden GL55 6PU
☎ Mickleton (01386) 438876
Fax (01386) 438113
*Comfortable, spacious farm building
conversion with large garden in
beautiful Cotswold countryside. 3 miles
Chipping Campden, close to Stratford
and Broadway. Free "4 wheel drive
tour" offer.*
Bedrooms: 2 double, 1 twin
Bathrooms: 2 private, 2 public

| Bed & breakfast per night: | £min | £max |
|---|---|---|
| Single | 14.00 | 21.00 |
| Double | 28.00 | 34.00 |

Parking for 4

🛏🚲🍴☐🌙🕿 ⓘ⛶🔺📺▦🖪❋
SP 🅣

## Haydon House

☎☎ **APPROVED**

Church Street, Chipping Campden
GL55 6JG
☎ Evesham (01386) 840275
*Comfortable historic house, converted
from a dairy and bakehouse,
surrounding a secluded vine-hung
courtyard. Centrally heated. No
smoking.*
Bedrooms: 1 single, 1 double, 1 twin
Bathrooms: 3 private

| Bed & breakfast per night: | £min | £max |
|---|---|---|
| Single | 20.00 | 22.00 |
| Double | 40.00 | 42.00 |

Open March-December

🛏10🍴🌙 ⓘ Ⓢ⛶▦🖪❋✕
🚐🏮

## Lower High Street

☎

Chipping Campden GL55 6DZ
☎ Evesham (01386) 840163
*Cotswold-stone house in Lower High
Street, conveniently situated for tours
and walks in the Cotswolds, shops and
restaurants.*
Bedrooms: 1 double, 1 twin
Bathrooms: 1 private, 1 public

| Bed & breakfast per night: | £min | £max |
|---|---|---|
| Double | 30.00 | 35.00 |

Open April-October

🛏🍴☐🌙 ⓘ Ⓢ▦🚐

## CHIPPING CAMPDEN

*Continued*

### Manor Farm **⋀**
👑👑 COMMENDED

Weston Subedge, Chipping Campden
GL55 6QH
☎ Evesham (01386) 840390
*500-acre mixed farm. Traditional 17th C
farmhouse, an excellent base for touring
the Cotswolds, Shakespeare country and
Hidcote Gardens. Warm, friendly
atmosphere. Walled garden. All rooms
en-suite with tea/coffee making
facilities, TV/radio. 1.5 miles from
Chipping Campden.*
Bedrooms: 2 double, 1 twin
Bathrooms: 3 private

**Bed & breakfast**

| per night: | £min | £max |
|---|---|---|
| Single | 25.00 | 25.00 |
| Double | 40.00 | 40.00 |

Parking for 8

### Orchard Hill House **⋀**
Listed HIGHLY COMMENDED

Broad Campden, Chipping Campden
GL55 6UU
☎ Evesham (01386) 841473

*17th C Cotswold-stone restored
farmhouse. Breakfast in our flagstoned
dining room with inglenook fireplace
around our 10 ft elm farmhouse table.*
Bedrooms: 2 double, 1 twin, 1 triple
Bathrooms: 4 private

**Bed & breakfast**

| per night: | £min | £max |
|---|---|---|
| Single | 35.00 | 40.00 |
| Double | 40.00 | 55.00 |

Parking for 6

### Sparlings
👑👑 COMMENDED

Leysbourne, High Street, Chipping
Campden GL55 6HL
☎ Evesham (01386) 840505

*Fully centrally heated, comfortable,
attractive 18th C Cotswold house in
Chipping Campden High Street. Walled
garden. Easy parking. Children over 6
welcome.*
Bedrooms: 1 double, 1 twin

Bathrooms: 2 private

**Bed & breakfast**

| per night: | £min | £max |
|---|---|---|
| Single | 25.00 | 25.00 |
| Double | 42.00 | 44.00 |

### Weston Park Farm **⋀**
👑👑

Dovers Hill, Chipping Campden
GL55 6UW
☎ Evesham (01386) 840835
*20-acre mixed farm. Self-contained wing
of secluded, magnificently situated
farmhouse, 1 mile from Chipping
Campden, adjacent to National Trust
land.*
Bedrooms: 1 triple
Bathrooms: 1 private

**Bed & breakfast**

| per night: | £min | £max |
|---|---|---|
| Single | 20.00 | |
| Double | 35.00 | 38.00 |

Parking for 10

### Wyldlands
Listed COMMENDED

Broad Campden, Chipping Campden
GL55 6UR
☎ Evesham (01386) 840478
*Welcoming, comfortable house in
picturesque village. Peaceful setting with
lovely views. Ideal for walking and
touring. Traditional inn nearby.
Reduced rates 3 nights or more.*
Bedrooms: 2 double, 1 twin
Bathrooms: 1 private, 2 public

**Bed & breakfast**

| per night: | £min | £max |
|---|---|---|
| Single | 18.00 | 20.00 |
| Double | 34.00 | 38.00 |

Parking for 4

## CHURCH STRETTON

Shropshire
Map ref 4A3

Church Stretton lies under the
eastern slope of the Longmynd
surrounded by hills. It is ideal for
walkers, with marvellous views,
golf and gliding. Wenlock Edge is
not far away.

### Acton Scott Farm **⋀**
👑👑 COMMENDED

Acton Scott, Church Stretton SY6 6QN
☎ Marshbrook (01694) 781260
*320-acre mixed farm. Conveniently
situated 17th C farmhouse of character
with comfortable, spacious rooms and
log fires. Beautiful countryside.*
Bedrooms: 1 double, 1 twin, 1 family
room
Bathrooms: 1 private, 1 public

**Bed & breakfast**

| per night: | £min | £max |
|---|---|---|
| Double | 26.00 | 40.00 |

Parking for 6
Open February-November

### Batchcott Hall
Listed COMMENDED

Picklescott, Church Stretton SY6 6NP
☎ Leebotwood (01694) 751234

*200-acre mixed farm. Friendly
atmosphere in a 16th C farmhouse.
Well-appointed, comfortable rooms,
colour TV. An idyllic spot on the edge
of the Longmynd with excellent views.*
Bedrooms: 1 double, 1 twin
Bathrooms: 2 private

**Bed & breakfast**

| per night: | £min | £max |
|---|---|---|
| Double | 40.00 | 44.00 |

Parking for 6

### Bottle and Glass
👑

Picklescott, Church Stretton SY6 6NR
☎ (01694) 751345
*Old world pub with letting rooms, on
the edge of the Long Mynd. Church
Stretton 4 miles away, Shrewsbury 9
miles.*
Bedrooms: 2 double, 1 triple
Bathrooms: 3 private

**Bed & breakfast**

| per night: | £min | £max |
|---|---|---|
| Single | 25.00 | 30.00 |
| Double | 35.00 | 45.00 |

Lunch available
Evening meal 1900 (last orders 2130)
Parking for 40

### Brook House Farm
Listed

Wall-under-Heywood, Church Stretton
SY6 7DS
☎ Longville (01694) 771308
*12-acre mixed farm. Attractive 18th C
stone farmhouse recently extended and
restored yet retaining its former
character, including a wealth of old oak.*
Bedrooms: 1 single, 1 double, 1 family
room
Bathrooms: 2 public

**Bed & breakfast**

| per night: | £min | £max |
|---|---|---|
| Single | 14.50 | 15.50 |
| Double | 29.00 | 31.00 |

Lunch available
Evening meal 1900 (last orders 1700)
Parking for 5

## The Elms ⋔
Listed

Little Stretton, Church Stretton
SY6 6RD
☎ (01694) 723084
*Victorian country house in spacious
grounds, decorated and furnished in
Victorian style.*
Bedrooms: 2 double, 1 twin
Bathrooms: 2 public

**Bed & breakfast**

| per night: | £min | £max |
| --- | --- | --- |
| Single | 18.00 | |
| Double | 31.00 | |

Parking for 3

## Gilberries Cottage ⋔
COMMENDED

Wall-under-Heywood, Church Stretton
SY6 7HZ
☎ Longville (01694) 771400
*Country cottage adjoining family farm,
in peaceful and beautiful countryside.
Ideal for walking. Numerous places of
interest nearby.*
Bedrooms: 1 twin, 1 triple
Bathrooms: 1 public

**Bed & breakfast**

| per night: | £min | £max |
| --- | --- | --- |
| Single | 20.00 | 20.00 |
| Double | 32.00 | 34.00 |

Parking for 8
Open February-November

## Inwood Farm ⋔
DE LUXE

All Stretton, Church Stretton SY6 6LA
☎ (01694) 724046
*Georgian farmhouse accommodation,
peaceful location, magnificent views.
Twelve acres of fields, trees and
gardens, furnished terrace, direct access
to Long Mynd hills.*
Bedrooms: 3 double
Bathrooms: 3 private

**Bed & breakfast**

| per night: | £min | £max |
| --- | --- | --- |
| Single | 30.00 | 30.00 |
| Double | 40.00 | 50.00 |

**Half board**

| per person: | £min | £max |
| --- | --- | --- |
| Daily | 34.00 | 44.00 |

Evening meal 1900 (last orders 2030)
Parking for 10

## Juniper Cottage

All Stretton, Church Stretton SY6 6HG
☎ (01694) 723427
*Quality cottage-style house, quiet village
in National Trust Shropshire Hills. One*

---

*mile north of Church Stretton on
B4370.*
Bedrooms: 1 double
Bathrooms: 1 private

**Bed & breakfast**

| per night: | £min | £max |
| --- | --- | --- |
| Double | 28.00 | 32.00 |

Parking for 5

## Sayang House
HIGHLY COMMENDED

Hope Bowdler, Church Stretton
SY6 7DD
☎ (01694) 723981
*Beautiful house in tranquil village in
the Stretton Hills. 1.75 miles from town
of Church Stretton. Residents' lounge
with oak beams and inglenook fireplace.
All accommodation en-suite and
furnished to highest possible standard.*
Bedrooms: 1 double, 2 twin
Bathrooms: 3 private

**Bed & breakfast**

| per night: | £min | £max |
| --- | --- | --- |
| Single | 21.00 | 23.00 |
| Double | 41.00 | 46.00 |

Parking for 10
Open January-November

## Wayside Inn
Listed

Marshbrook, Church Stretton
SY6 6QE
☎ (01694) 781208
*16th C inn, fully beamed and with log
fires. Excellent walking area. Meals
available 7 days a week.*
Bedrooms: 1 single, 1 double, 1 triple
Bathrooms: 1 public

**Bed & breakfast**

| per night: | £min | £max |
| --- | --- | --- |
| Single | 16.00 | 18.00 |
| Double | 32.00 | 36.00 |

Lunch available
Evening meal 1830 (last orders 2100)
Parking for 20

## Woodbank House
Listed

Watling Street South, Church Stretton
SY6 6PH
☎ (01694) 723454
*Victorian detached house in pleasant
rural setting, view of Stretton Hills.
Easy access to Church Stretton, A49
and footpaths. Private drive off A49.*
Bedrooms: 1 single, 1 double, 1 twin
Bathrooms: 2 public

**Bed & breakfast**

| per night: | £min | £max |
| --- | --- | --- |
| Single | 15.00 | 17.50 |
| Double | 30.00 | 35.00 |

Parking for 5

---

## Woolston Farm ⋔

Church Stretton SY6 6QD
☎ Marshbrook (01694) 781201
*350-acre mixed farm. Victorian
farmhouse in the small hamlet of
Woolston, off A49. Ideal position for
touring Shropshire. Outstanding views
and good farmhouse fare.*
Bedrooms: 2 double, 1 twin
Bathrooms: 1 public

**Bed & breakfast**

| per night: | £min | £max |
| --- | --- | --- |
| Single | 14.50 | |
| Double | 29.00 | |

**Half board**

| per person: | £min | £max |
| --- | --- | --- |
| Daily | 22.50 | |
| Weekly | 147.00 | |

Evening meal 1850 (last orders 2000)
Parking for 2
Open January-November

### CIRENCESTER

Gloucestershire
Map ref 2B1

"Capital of the Cotswolds",
Cirencester was Britain's second
most important Roman town with
many finds housed in the Corinium
Museum. It has a very fine
Perpendicular church and old
houses around the market place.
*Tourist Information Centre*
☎ *(01285) 654180*

## Chesil Rocks
Listed

Baunton Lane, Stratton, Cirencester
GL7 2LL
☎ (01285) 655031
*Pleasant and friendly home in a quiet
lane, with easy access to town and
country walks. Cheltenham, Gloucester
and Swindon within easy reach.*
Bedrooms: 2 single, 1 twin
Bathrooms: 1 public, 1 private shower

**Bed & breakfast**

| per night: | £min | £max |
| --- | --- | --- |
| Single | 15.00 | 15.00 |
| Double | 30.00 | 30.00 |

Parking for 3

## Eliot Arms Hotel Free House ⋔
COMMENDED

Clarks Hay, South Cerney, Cirencester
GL7 5UA
☎ (01285) 860215
Fax (01285) 860215
*Dating from the 16th C, a comfortable
Cotswold freehouse hotel, 2.5 miles
from Cirencester, just off the A419.
Reputation for fine food and hospitality.
Riverside gardens.*
Bedrooms: 1 single, 4 double, 6 twin

*Continued* ▶

## CIRENCESTER

### Continued

Bathrooms: 11 private
**Bed & breakfast**

| per night: | £min | £max |
|---|---|---|
| Single | 32.50 | |
| Double | 48.00 | 75.00 |

Lunch available
Evening meal 1830 (last orders 2200)
Parking for 30
Cards accepted: Access, Visa

[icons]

### The Masons Arms ⚑

High Street, Meysey Hampton,
Cirencester GL7 5JT
☎ (01285) 850164

*Seeking peace and tranquillity? Treat yourself to a break in this 17th C inn set beside the village green. Oak beams and log fire. A warm welcome awaits you.*
Bedrooms: 1 single, 6 double, 1 twin, 1 triple
Bathrooms: 9 private
**Bed & breakfast**

| per night: | £min | £max |
|---|---|---|
| Single | 28.00 | 35.00 |
| Double | 44.00 | 59.00 |

Lunch available
Evening meal 1900 (last orders 2130)
Parking for 8
Cards accepted: Access, Visa

[icons]

### Millstone

**HIGHLY COMMENDED**

Down Ampney, Cirencester GL7 5QR
☎ Down Ampney (01793) 750475
*Recently constructed Cotswold-style house, surrounded by open countryside. Spacious rooms, some en-suite, TV and tea-making facilities. Central for touring.*
Bedrooms: 2 double
Bathrooms: 2 private
**Bed & breakfast**

| per night: | £min | £max |
|---|---|---|
| Single | 23.00 | 25.00 |
| Double | 38.00 | 42.00 |

Parking for 4

[icons]

### The Old Rectory ⚑

**COMMENDED**

Rodmarton, Cirencester GL7 6PE
☎ (01285) 841246

*Old 17th C rectory set in three-quarters of an acre of gardens. Cirencester 6 miles, Tetbury 5 miles. Equidistant Swindon, Cheltenham and Gloucester.*
Bedrooms: 2 twin
Bathrooms: 2 private
**Bed & breakfast**

| per night: | £min | £max |
|---|---|---|
| Single | 20.00 | 25.00 |
| Double | 35.00 | 40.00 |

**Half board**

| per person: | £min | £max |
|---|---|---|
| Daily | 35.00 | 35.00 |

Evening meal 1900 (last orders 2100)
Parking for 6

[icons]

### Smerrill Barns ⚑

**COMMENDED**

Kemble, Cirencester GL7 6BW
☎ (01285) 770907
Fax (01285) 770907
*Accommodation in a listed barn, providing all modern facilities. Situated 3 miles from Cirencester on the A429.*
Bedrooms: 1 single, 4 double, 1 twin, 1 family room
Bathrooms: 7 private, 1 public
**Bed & breakfast**

| per night: | £min | £max |
|---|---|---|
| Single | 25.00 | 35.00 |
| Double | 40.00 | 55.00 |

Parking for 7
Cards accepted: Access, Visa

[icons]

### Tally Cottage ⚑

**Listed**

Woodmancote, Cirencester GL7 7EF
☎ North Cerney (01285) 831563
*A typical 16th C Cotswold stone village cottage with mullioned windows, beams and inglenook. Centrally heated and double glazed. Pretty, private small garden.*
Bedrooms: 1 twin
Bathrooms: 1 public
**Bed & breakfast**

| per night: | £min | £max |
|---|---|---|
| Single | 17.50 | 17.50 |
| Double | 35.00 | 35.00 |

Parking for 1

[icons]

### The Village Pub

**Listed** **APPROVED**

Barnsley, Cirencester GL7 5EF
☎ (01285) 740421
*The Village Pub has 5 rooms, all with private facilities, and is situated in a pretty Cotswold village.*
Bedrooms: 4 double, 1 twin
Bathrooms: 5 private
**Bed & breakfast**

| per night: | £min | £max |
|---|---|---|
| Single | | 30.00 |
| Double | | 45.00 |

Lunch available
Evening meal 1900 (last orders 2130)
Parking for 40
Cards accepted: Access, Visa, Amex

[icons]

### Warwick Cottage Guest House ⚑

**COMMENDED**

75 Victoria Road, Cirencester GL7 1ES
☎ (01285) 656279
*Attractive Victorian townhouse, 5 minutes from the town centre. Good base for touring the Cotswolds. Family rooms available as doubles or twins. Singles by arrangement. Bargain breaks available.*
Bedrooms: 2 double, 2 family rooms
Bathrooms: 4 private, 1 public
**Bed & breakfast**

| per night: | £min | £max |
|---|---|---|
| Double | 30.00 | 34.00 |

**Half board**

| per person: | £min | £max |
|---|---|---|
| Daily | 22.50 | 24.50 |
| Weekly | 138.00 | 159.00 |

Evening meal from 1830
Parking for 4

[icons]

### Windrush

**Listed**

The Whiteway, Baunton, Cirencester GL7 7BA
☎ (01285) 655942
*Large detached house in beautiful rural setting on the outskirts of Baunton village. One and a half miles north of Cirencester.*
Bedrooms: 1 single, 2 double
Bathrooms: 1 private, 1 public
**Bed & breakfast**

| per night: | £min | £max |
|---|---|---|
| Single | 20.00 | 20.00 |
| Double | 30.00 | 35.00 |

Parking for 3

[icons]

## CLEEVE HILL

Gloucestershire
Map ref 2B1

Settlement with wonderful all-round views, above Cheltenham on the road to Winchcombe and Broadway.

### Cleyne Hage ⚑

**APPROVED**

Southam Lane, Southam, Cheltenham GL52 3NY
☎ Cheltenham (01242) 518569
*Cotswold-stone house in secluded setting between B4632 and A435, on the Cotswold Way, 3 miles north of Cheltenham. Open view of hills and racecourse. Pets welcome. Off-road parking. Non-smokers only, please.*
Bedrooms: 2 single, 1 double, 1 twin
Bathrooms: 2 public

**Bed & breakfast**

| per night: | £min | £max |
|---|---|---|
| Single | 16.00 | 20.00 |
| Double | 25.00 | 35.00 |

Parking for 8
Cards accepted: Access, Visa

♿🐕➡️🛁🏸🖲️🔌✂️📻📺🕐🍴🛏️�'

---

## CLEOBURY MORTIMER

Shropshire
Map ref 4A3

Village with attractive timbered and Georgian houses and a church with a wooden spire. It is close to the Clee Hills with marvellous views.

### Cox's Barn

**Listed**

Bagginswood, Cleobury Mortimer, Kidderminster, Worcestershire DY14 8LS
☎ Stottesden (01746) 32415 & Mobile Phone 0860 135011
*124-acre mixed farm. Converted barn on working farm with spacious gardens overlooking beautiful countryside. Good home cooking, centrally heated. Evening meal optional.*
Bedrooms: 2 double, 1 twin
Bathrooms: 2 private, 1 public

**Bed & breakfast**

| per night: | £min | £max |
|---|---|---|
| Single | 14.00 | 16.00 |
| Double | 28.00 | 32.00 |

**Half board**

| per person: | £min | £max |
|---|---|---|
| Daily | 20.00 | 26.00 |

Lunch available
Evening meal 1800 (last orders 2000)
Parking for 6

### Kings Arms Hotel

Church Street, Cleobury Mortimer, Kidderminster, Worcestershire DY14 8BS
☎ (01299) 270252
*16th C coaching inn, famous for food, in centre of picturesque village. Close to golf, fishing, safari park and Severn Valley Railway.*
Bedrooms: 2 double, 1 twin
Bathrooms: 2 private, 1 public

**Bed & breakfast**

| per night: | £min | £max |
|---|---|---|
| Single | 18.00 | 25.00 |
| Double | 34.00 | 42.00 |

Lunch available
Evening meal 1900 (last orders 2100)
Parking for 6
Cards accepted: Access, Visa

---

### The Old Bake House

46/47 High Street, Cleobury Mortimer, Kidderminster, Worcestershire DY14 8DQ
☎ (01299) 270193
*Grade II listed townhouse, formerly both a public house and bakery, with 18th C frontage.*
Bedrooms: 3 twin
Bathrooms: 3 private

**Bed & breakfast**

| per night: | £min | £max |
|---|---|---|
| Single | 18.00 | 22.50 |
| Double | 36.00 | 40.00 |

**Half board**

| per person: | £min | £max |
|---|---|---|
| Daily | 28.00 | 32.50 |
| Weekly | 168.00 | 195.00 |

Evening meal 1900 (last orders 2000)
Parking for 2

---

## CLUN

Shropshire
Map ref 4A3

Small, ancient town on the Welsh border with flint and stone tools in its museum and Iron Age forts nearby. The impressive ruins of a Norman castle lie beside the River Clun and there are some interesting 17th C houses.

### Clun Farm

**Listed**

High Street, Clun, Craven Arms SY7 8JB
☎ (01588) 640432
*200-acre mixed farm. 16th C double cruck farmhouse situated in Clun High Street, within 200 metres of 3 public houses and restaurants.*
Bedrooms: 2 single, 1 double, 1 twin
Bathrooms: 1 private, 1 public

**Bed & breakfast**

| per night: | £min | £max |
|---|---|---|
| Single | 14.00 | 16.00 |
| Double | 28.00 | 32.00 |

Parking for 6

### Hurst Mill Farm ♠♠

Clun, Craven Arms SY7 0JA
☎ (01588) 640224
*100-acre mixed farm. Attractive farmhouse and old mill in the lovely Clun Valley. River and woodland trails, 2 riding ponies, pets welcome. Previous winner of "Great Shropshire Breakfast" challenge.*
Bedrooms: 1 double, 1 twin, 1 triple
Bathrooms: 2 public, 1 private shower

**Bed & breakfast**

| per night: | £min | £max |
|---|---|---|
| Single | 15.00 | 17.00 |
| Double | 30.00 | 32.00 |

---

**Half board**

| per person: | £min | £max |
|---|---|---|
| Daily | 23.00 | 24.00 |
| Weekly | 160.00 | 165.00 |

Evening meal 1800 (last orders 2000)
Parking for 8

### New House Farm

**COMMENDED**

Clun, Craven Arms SY7 8NJ
☎ Bishops Castle (01588) 638314
*325-acre mixed farm. Isolated 18th C stone farmhouse set high in the Clun hills, near Offa's Dyke. Scenic views, peaceful walking in unspoilt countryside.*
Bedrooms: 1 double, 1 twin, 1 triple
Bathrooms: 1 private, 2 public

**Bed & breakfast**

| per night: | £min | £max |
|---|---|---|
| Single | 16.50 | 18.50 |
| Double | 33.00 | 37.00 |

**Half board**

| per person: | £min | £max |
|---|---|---|
| Daily | 25.50 | 28.50 |
| Weekly | 110.00 | 120.00 |

Evening meal 1900 (last orders 2100)
Parking for 5
Open February-November

### Springhill Farm

**Listed**

Clun, Craven Arms SY7 8PE
☎ (01588) 640337
*275-acre mixed farm. Situated right on Offa's Dyke footpath with beautiful views of the Clun valley. 3 miles from Clun, 1 mile from the village of Newcastle.*
Bedrooms: 1 double, 1 triple, 1 family room
Bathrooms: 1 public

**Bed & breakfast**

| per night: | £min | £max |
|---|---|---|
| Double | 32.00 | 32.00 |

**Half board**

| per person: | £min | £max |
|---|---|---|
| Daily | 23.00 | 23.00 |

Parking for 4
Open March-October

---

## CLUNGUNFORD

Shropshire
Map ref 4A3

Village near the River Clun and Stokesay Castle, a 13th C fortified manor house with an Elizabethan gatehouse.

### Broadward Hall ♠♠

**Listed**

Clungunford, Craven Arms SY7 0QA
☎ Bucknell (01547) 4357

*Continued* ▶

## CLUNGUNFORD

### Continued

*176-acre mixed farm. Grade II listed, castellated building, 9 miles west of Ludlow in rural Clun Valley surroundings.*
Bedrooms: 2 twin, 1 triple
Bathrooms: 2 public

**Bed & breakfast**

| per night: | £min | £max |
|---|---|---|
| Single | 12.00 | 15.00 |
| Double | 24.00 | 30.00 |

**Half board**

| per person: | £min | £max |
|---|---|---|
| Daily | 21.00 | 24.00 |
| Weekly | 147.00 | |

Evening meal 1900 (last orders 0900)
Parking for 15
Open March-November

## CODSALL

Staffordshire
Map ref 4B3

Expanding residential village a few miles from Wolverhampton.

### Moors Farm and Country Restaurant

Chillington Lane, Codsall,
Wolverhampton WV8 1QF
☎ (01902) 842330
Fax (01902) 842330
*100-acre mixed farm. 200-year-old farmhouse, 1 mile from pretty village. All home produce used. Many local walks and places of interest.*
Bedrooms: 3 double, 1 twin, 1 family room
Bathrooms: 3 private, 2 public

**Bed & breakfast**

| per night: | £min | £max |
|---|---|---|
| Single | 23.00 | 29.00 |
| Double | 38.00 | 48.00 |

**Half board**

| per person: | £min | £max |
|---|---|---|
| Daily | 32.00 | 38.00 |
| Weekly | 180.00 | 250.00 |

Evening meal 1830 (last orders 1900)
Parking for 20

---

There are separate sections in this guide listing groups specialising in farm holidays and accommodation which is especially suitable for young people and organised groups.

---

## COLEFORD

Gloucestershire
Map ref 2A1

Small town in the Forest of Dean with the ancient iron mines at Clearwell Caves nearby, where mining equipment and geological samples are displayed. There are several forest trails in the area.
*Tourist Information Centre*
☎ *(01594) 836307*

### Millend House and Garden

Coleford GL16 8NF
☎ Dean (01594) 832128
*250-year-old traditional stone-built house, in 2 acres of lovely hillside gardens and woodlands. Situated at the end of a valley looking down towards Newland and the "Cathedral of the Forest".*
Bedrooms: 1 double, 2 twin
Bathrooms: 1 private, 1 public

**Bed & breakfast**

| per night: | £min | £max |
|---|---|---|
| Single | 16.00 | 32.00 |
| Double | 20.00 | 40.00 |

Parking for 4

## COLESHILL

Warwickshire
Map ref 4B3

Close to Birmingham's many attractions including the 17th C Aston Hall with its plasterwork and furnishings, the Railway Museum and Sarehole Mill, an 18th C water-powered mill restored to working order.

### Maxstoke Hall Farm

COMMENDED

Maxstoke, Coleshill, Birmingham
B46 2QT
☎ (01675) 463237
Fax (01675) 463237

*230-acre arable farm. Elegant farmhouse, 1634, with en-suite rooms. 10 minutes from M42 and M6, 15 minutes from National Exhibition Centre and Birmingham Airport.*
Bedrooms: 1 single, 1 twin
Bathrooms: 2 private

**Bed & breakfast**

| per night: | £min | £max |
|---|---|---|
| Single | 25.00 | 25.00 |
| Double | 44.00 | 44.00 |

**Half board**

| per person: | £min | £max |
|---|---|---|
| Daily | 35.00 | 35.00 |

Evening meal 1830 (last orders 2000)
Parking for 30

### Packington Lane Farm

Listed

Packington Lane, Coleshill,
Birmingham B46 3JJ
☎ (01675) 462228
Fax (01675) 462228
*250-acre mixed farm. Charming, traditional farmhouse. Beamed TV room. Radio, tea/coffee tray in rooms. 2.5 miles National Exhibition Centre, 3.5 miles airport and Birmingham International rail station, 5 minutes motorway network (M6/M42).*
Bedrooms: 1 single, 2 twin
Bathrooms: 1 private, 1 public

**Bed & breakfast**

| per night: | £min | £max |
|---|---|---|
| Single | | 18.00 |
| Double | 36.00 | 40.00 |

Parking for 8

## COLWALL

Hereford and Worcester
Map ref 2B1

Village on the slopes of the Malvern Hills close to the famous Herefordshire Beacon, site of a large Iron Age camp. The area offers excellent walks with the Worcestershire Beacon to the north.

### Hacketts

Listed APPROVED

Mathon Road, Colwall, Malvern,
Worcestershire WR13 6EW
☎ (01684) 40261
*3-acre arable farm. Well-built black and white house, completely remodernised and tastefully decorated. Situated on the roadside, with pleasant garden.*
Bedrooms: 1 single, 1 double, 1 twin
Bathrooms: 2 public

**Bed & breakfast**

| per night: | £min | £max |
|---|---|---|
| Single | 16.00 | 16.00 |
| Double | 32.00 | 32.00 |

Parking for 6
Open April-October

## CORSE

Gloucestershire
Map ref 2B1

### Kilmorie Guest House

Gloucester Road, Corse, Snigs End,
Staunton, Gloucester GL19 3RQ
☎ Gloucester (01452) 840224

*7-acre livestock & fruit farm. Built by Chartists in 1847, Grade II listed smallholding in conservation area. Modernised, comfortable and friendly. Ideally situated for touring Cotswolds, Forest of Dean and Malvern Hills. Pony riding.*
Bedrooms: 1 single, 3 double, 1 twin, 1 family room
Bathrooms: 2 private, 1 public

**Bed & breakfast**

| per night: | £min | £max |
| --- | --- | --- |
| Single | 12.50 | |
| Double | 25.00 | |

**Half board**

| per person: | £min | £max |
| --- | --- | --- |
| Daily | 19.00 | |
| Weekly | 129.50 | |

Lunch available
Evening meal from 1800
Parking for 8

## COTSWOLDS

*See under Ampney Crucis, Berkeley, Bibury, Birdlip, Bledington, Blockley, Bourton-on-the-Water, Bretforton, Broadway, Cheltenham, Chipping Campden, Cirencester, Cleeve Hill, Donnington, Fairford, Gloucester, Great Rissington, Guiting Power, Lechlade, Long Compton, Minchinhampton, Moreton-in-Marsh, Nailsworth, Naunton, Northleach, Nympsfield, Painswick, Rendcomb, Slimbridge, Stonehouse, Stow-on-the-Wold, Stroud, Teddington, Tetbury, Tewkesbury, Winchcombe*

## COVENTRY

West Midlands
Map ref 4B3

Modern city with a long history. It has many places of interest including the post-war and ruined medieval cathedrals, art gallery and museums, some 16th C almshouses, St Mary's Guildhall, Lunt Roman fort and the Belgrade Theatre.
*Tourist Information Centre*
☎ *(01203) 832303*

### Acorn Lodge Private Guest House M

Pond Farm, Upper Eastern Green Lane, Coventry CV5 7DP
☎ (01203) 465182

---

*300-year-old beamed farmhouse of character in secluded position. Ideally situated for touring Stratford and Warwick and 20 miles from National Exhibition Centre and Birmingham Airport. Friendly, informal atmosphere. Paddocks and ponies.*
Bedrooms: 2 single, 1 double, 1 twin
Bathrooms: 1 private, 2 public

**Bed & breakfast**

| per night: | £min | £max |
| --- | --- | --- |
| Single | 15.00 | |
| Double | 34.00 | |

Parking for 6

### Falcon Hotel M

13-19 Manor Road, Coventry CV1 2LH
☎ (01203) 258615
Fax (01203) 520680
*Situated close to Coventry railway station, ideal for the travelling businessman. Ten minutes from NEC, M6 motorway and Birmingham International Airport. Large free car park. Shops, social and cultural activities readily at hand.*
Bedrooms: 10 single, 11 double, 7 twin, 6 triple
Bathrooms: 34 private

**Bed & breakfast**

| per night: | £min | £max |
| --- | --- | --- |
| Single | 25.00 | 35.00 |
| Double | 40.00 | 48.00 |

**Half board**

| per person: | £min | £max |
| --- | --- | --- |
| Daily | 27.00 | 35.00 |

Lunch available
Evening meal 1900 (last orders 2145)
Parking for 50
Cards accepted: Access, Visa, Diners, Amex

### Mill Farmhouse M

Mill Lane, Fillongley, Coventry CV7 8EE
☎ Fillongley (01676) 41898
*Beautiful farmhouse set in picturesque countryside, offering peace and tranquillity. Detached bed and breakfast apartments with en-suite bathrooms and colour TV. Private car park and gardens. 15 minutes from Coventry, NEC, Birmingham Airport.*
Bedrooms: 1 single, 1 double, 1 twin
Bathrooms: 3 private

**Bed & breakfast**

| per night: | £min | £max |
| --- | --- | --- |
| Single | 17.00 | 30.00 |
| Double | 40.00 | |

Evening meal 1800 (last orders 0900)
Parking for 4

### Mount Guest House M

Listed
9 Coundon Road, Coventry CV1 4AR
☎ (01203) 225998

---

*Family guesthouse within walking distance of city and cathedral. Easy reach of the National Exhibition Centre and the Royal Showground. Snacks available.*
Bedrooms: 2 single, 6 twin, 2 triple
Bathrooms: 2 public

**Bed & breakfast**

| per night: | £min | £max |
| --- | --- | --- |
| Single | 13.00 | 15.00 |
| Double | 26.00 | 30.00 |

### Westwood Cottage

79 Westwood Heath Road, Westwood Heath, Coventry CV4 8GN
☎ (01203) 471084
*One of 4 sandstone farm cottages, circa 1834, in rural surroundings. Recently converted but with character maintained and offering comfortable accommodation for a small number of guests.*
Bedrooms: 2 single, 1 double, 1 twin
Bathrooms: 4 private

**Bed & breakfast**

| per night: | £min | £max |
| --- | --- | --- |
| Single | 18.00 | 18.00 |
| Double | 33.00 | 35.00 |

Parking for 5

### Woodlands M

Oak Lane, Allesley, Coventry CV5 9BX
☎ Meriden (01676) 22688 Changing to 522688
*Comfortable, detached and privately situated in a beautiful country lane only 150 yards from the A45. Ten minutes from NEC and Birmingham Airport, ideal for Coventry, Stratford-upon-Avon and Warwick.*
Bedrooms: 3 twin
Bathrooms: 1 public

**Bed & breakfast**

| per night: | £min | £max |
| --- | --- | --- |
| Single | 17.00 | 19.00 |
| Double | 34.00 | 36.00 |

Parking for 6

## CRAVEN ARMS

Shropshire
Map ref 4A3

Village close to Wenlock Edge and the Longmynd and an ideal centre for walking with many fine views. It is close to Stokesay Castle, a 13th C fortified manor house, the ruins of Hopton Castle and Ludlow.

### Castle View

Listed
148 Stokesay, Craven Arms SY7 9AL
☎ (01588) 673712

Continued ▶

## CRAVEN ARMS

### Continued

*Stone-built Victorian house. Within easy walking distance of Stokesay Castle.*
Bedrooms: 1 single, 1 double, 1 twin
Bathrooms: 2 public

**Bed & breakfast**

| per night: | £min | £max |
| --- | --- | --- |
| Single | 13.50 | 15.00 |
| Double | 27.00 | 30.00 |

Evening meal 1830 (last orders 1930)
Parking for 3

🐕 5 🍳 ❑ 🌸 ⓤ ⅏ ▥ ✿ 🛥

### Woodville ⋀

ⓦ HIGHLY COMMENDED

Clun Road, Craven Arms SY7 9AA
☎ (01588) 672476

*Large family house set in three-quarters of an acre in the heart of some of the most unspoilt countryside in Shropshire.*
Bedrooms: 2 double, 1 twin
Bathrooms: 3 private

**Bed & breakfast**

| per night: | £min | £max |
| --- | --- | --- |
| Double | 28.00 | 32.00 |

**Half board**

| per person: | £min | £max |
| --- | --- | --- |
| Daily | 22.50 | 24.50 |

Evening meal from 1900
Parking for 6

🐕 🐄 🌸 ⓤ ⅏ ▥ ✿ ▥ 🛥 ✿ ✕ 🛥

## DEERHURST

Gloucestershire
Map ref 2B1

### Deerhurst House ⋀

ⓦⓦ HIGHLY COMMENDED

Deerhurst, Gloucester GL19 4BX
☎ Tewkesbury (01684) 292135 &
Mobile 0850 520051
*Classical Georgian country house set in 3 acres on edge of ancient riverside village of Deerhurst, midway between Cheltenham, Tewkesbury and Gloucester.*
Bedrooms: 1 double, 1 twin
Bathrooms: 2 private

**Bed & breakfast**

| per night: | £min | £max |
| --- | --- | --- |
| Single | 20.00 | 25.00 |
| Double | 40.00 | 45.00 |

Parking for 10

🐕 ⅏ ❑ 🌸 🐄 ⓤ ▯ ⅏ ▥ ▥ 🛥 ✿ 🛥 ⓣ

## DIDMARTON

Gloucestershire
Map ref 2B2

Attractive village with stone houses and interesting architectural features. It has 2 churches, one of which has Georgian furnishings. Didmarton is close to Badminton House.

### The Old Rectory ⋀

ⓦⓦ

Didmarton, Badminton, Avon GL9 1DS
☎ Chipping Sodbury (01454) 238233
*Small former rectory in centre of village close to Westonbirt and Tetbury. Easy reach of Bath, M4 and Cirencester.*
Bedrooms: 2 double
Bathrooms: 2 private

**Bed & breakfast**

| per night: | £min | £max |
| --- | --- | --- |
| Single | 17.00 | 17.00 |
| Double | 30.00 | 35.00 |

Parking for 4
Open March-October

🐕 9 ❑ ⓤ ⅏ ▥ ⓣ ▥ 🛥 ✿ ✕ 🛥 🏠

## DILWYN

Hereford and Worcester
Map ref 2A1

Pretty black and white houses, a village green and a big medieval church form the focal point of this peaceful village which has now been by-passed by the Leominster to Brecon road.

### Bedford House

Dilwyn, Hereford HR4 8JJ
☎ Pembridge (01544) 388260
*20-acre mixed farm. Small, friendly farm offers peace and quiet, excellent accommodation, and good home cooking. Central for exploring Herefordshire, Worcestershire, Gloucestershire and Radnorshire. Welcome cup of tea.*
Bedrooms: 1 double, 1 twin, 1 triple
Bathrooms: 1 public

**Bed & breakfast**

| per night: | £min | £max |
| --- | --- | --- |
| Single | 16.00 | |
| Double | 30.00 | |

**Half board**

| per person: | £min | £max |
| --- | --- | --- |
| Daily | 23.00 | |
| Weekly | 160.00 | |

Evening meal from 1830
Parking for 3
Open March-November

🐕 🐄 🌸 ⓤ ▤ S ⅏ ▥ ⓣ ▥ 🛥 ❑ U ✦ ⥿
✦ ✿ 🛥

---

We advise you to confirm
your booking in writing.

---

## DONNINGTON

Gloucestershire
Map ref 2B1

### Holmleigh

Listed

Donnington, Moreton-in-Marsh
GL56 0XX
☎ Cotswold (01451) 830792
*15-acre dairy farm. Farmhouse accommodation with friendly welcome. In a peaceful setting with own private lane from the village of Donnington, 1 mile from Stow-on-the-Wold.*
Bedrooms: 2 twin
Bathrooms: 1 private, 1 public

**Bed & breakfast**

| per night: | £min | £max |
| --- | --- | --- |
| Single | 12.00 | 12.50 |
| Double | 24.00 | 25.00 |

Parking for 3
Open April-October

🐕 5 🐄 🛢 🌸 🐄 ⓤ ⅏ ⓤ ▯ ⅏ ▥ ⓣ ▥ 🛥 ✿ ✕ 🛥 🕸

## DROITWICH

Hereford and Worcester
Map ref 2B1

Old town with natural brine springs, now incorporated into the Brine Baths Health Centre, developed as a spa at the beginning of the 19th C. Of particular interest is the Church of the Sacred Heart with splendid mosaics. Fine parks and a Heritage Centre.
*Tourist Information Centre*
☎ *(01905) 774312*

### Church Farm ⋀

ⓦⓦ HIGHLY COMMENDED

Elmbridge, Droitwich, Worcestershire
WR9 0DA
☎ Cutnall Green (01299) 851627
*Beautiful listed Georgian farmhouse with panoramic views of Malvern Hills. Situated in peaceful village of Elmbridge yet only 2 miles from M5.*
Bedrooms: 2 twin
Bathrooms: 2 private

**Bed & breakfast**

| per night: | £min | £max |
| --- | --- | --- |
| Single | 25.00 | 25.00 |
| Double | 40.00 | 40.00 |

Parking for 7

❑ 🌸 ⓤ ⅏ ▥ 🛥 ❑ ▷ ✦ ✿ ✕ 🛥 🏠

### Richmond Guest House ⋀

Listed

3 Ombersley St. West, Droitwich,
Worcestershire WR9 8HZ
☎ Worcester (01905) 775722
Fax (01905) 794500
*Victorian-built guesthouse in the town centre, 5 minutes from railway station and bus route. English breakfast. 30 minutes from National Exhibition Centre via M5/M42.*
Bedrooms: 6 single, 1 double, 2 twin, 5 triple

Bathrooms: 3 public

**Bed & breakfast**

| per night: | £min | £max |
|---|---|---|
| Single | 15.00 | 16.00 |
| Double | 26.00 | 28.00 |

Parking for 12

## DUNTISBOURNE ABBOTS

Gloucestershire
Map ref 2B1

### Dixs Barn

Duntisbourne Abbots, Cirencester
GL7 7JN
☎ Cirencester (01285) 821249

*200-acre arable & livestock farm.
Converted barn with marvellous views
in an Area of Outstanding Natural
Beauty. Ideal centre for touring and
walking.*
Bedrooms: 1 double, 1 twin
Bathrooms: 2 private

**Bed & breakfast**

| per night: | £min | £max |
|---|---|---|
| Single | 16.00 | 17.00 |
| Double | 32.00 | 34.00 |

Parking for 6

## DYMOCK

Gloucestershire
Map ref 2B1

Village with one of the most
interesting churches in the area,
which has extensive Norman work
and a fragment of a manuscript
copy of St John's Gospel of the
8th C. On the village green is the
White House where John Kyrle,
the Man of Ross, was born in
1637. Also noted for the Dymock
poets.

### The Granary

**Listed**

Lower House Farm, Kempley, Dymock
GL18 2BS
☎ (01531) 890301
*130-acre dairy farm. Wing of farmhouse
offering good food, including large
breakfasts. Play area plus many
animals. Wonderful countryside with
many local attractions.*
Bedrooms: 2 double, 1 twin
Bathrooms: 3 private, 1 public

**Bed & breakfast**

| per night: | £min | £max |
|---|---|---|
| Single | 16.00 | 20.00 |
| Double | 32.00 | 40.00 |

**Half board**

| per person: | £min | £max |
|---|---|---|
| Daily | 25.00 | 30.00 |
| Weekly | 175.00 | 210.00 |

Evening meal 1800 (last orders 2100)
Parking for 6

## ECCLESHALL

Staffordshire
Map ref 4B3

Small market town has long
associations with the Bishops of
Lichfield, 6 of whom are buried in
the large 12th C parish church.
The ruined castle was formerly the
residence of these bishops.

### Cobblers Cottage

Kerry Lane, Eccleshall, Stafford
ST21 6EJ
☎ Stafford (01785) 850116
*Country cottage with en-suite bedrooms,
in a quiet lane on the edge of village,
with several pubs and restaurants
within walking distance.*
Bedrooms: 1 double, 1 twin
Bathrooms: 2 private

**Bed & breakfast**

| per night: | £min | £max |
|---|---|---|
| Single | 18.00 | 21.00 |
| Double | 30.00 | 36.00 |

Parking for 3

### Glenwood ⋔

**COMMENDED**

Croxton, Eccleshall, Stafford ST21 6PF
☎ Wetwood (01630) 620238

*16th C timber-framed cottage in an
ideal position for visiting the many
attractions of Staffordshire and
Shropshire.*
Bedrooms: 1 single, 1 double, 1 twin,
1 triple
Bathrooms: 1 private, 1 public

**Bed & breakfast**

| per night: | £min | £max |
|---|---|---|
| Single | 15.00 | 20.00 |
| Double | 28.00 | 36.00 |

Parking for 6

### The Round House ⋔

**HIGHLY COMMENDED**

Butters Bank, Croxton, Eccleshall,
Stafford ST21 6NN
☎ Wetwood (01630) 82631

*Quiet country house of character,
overlooking rolling countryside.
Tastefully furnished accommodation, all
rooms en-suite.*
Bedrooms: 2 double
Bathrooms: 1 private, 1 private shower

**Bed & breakfast**

| per night: | £min | £max |
|---|---|---|
| Single | 20.00 | |
| Double | 34.00 | |

Parking for 4

### Slindon House Farm

Slindon, Eccleshall, Stafford ST21 6LX
☎ Standon Rock (01782) 791237

*Farmhouse bed and breakfast situated
on the A519 in the village of Slindon, 2
miles from Eccleshall and 9 miles from
Newcastle-under-Lyme.*
Bedrooms: 1 double, 1 twin
Bathrooms: 1 private, 1 public

**Bed & breakfast**

| per night: | £min | £max |
|---|---|---|
| Single | 15.00 | 20.00 |
| Double | 30.00 | 40.00 |

Parking for 2

## ELMLEY CASTLE

Hereford and Worcester
Map ref 2B1

### The Cloisters

**HIGHLY COMMENDED**

Main Street, Elmley Castle, Pershore,
Worcestershire WR10 3HS
☎ Pershore (01386) 710241
*A stone and half-timbered Tudor house,
part of which dates back to the 14th C.
Located towards the end of the main
street, on the left-hand corner of
Ashton-under-Hill Lane. Elmley Castle,
at the foot of Bredon Hill, is one of the
most attractive villages in the Vale of
Evesham.*
Bedrooms: 1 double, 1 family room
Bathrooms: 2 private

**Bed & breakfast**

| per night: | £min | £max |
|---|---|---|
| Double | 39.00 | 41.00 |

Parking for 3

Please check prices and
other details at the time
of booking.

## EVESHAM

Hereford and Worcester
Map ref 2B1

Market town in the centre of a
fruit-growing area. There are
pleasant walks along the River
Avon and many old houses and
inns. A fine 16th C bell tower
stands between 2 churches near
the medieval Almonry Museum.
*Tourist Information Centre*
☎ *(01386) 446944*

### Chequers Inn ⋔
😃😃😃 COMMENDED

Fladbury, Pershore, Worcestershire
WR10 2PZ
☎ (01386) 860276 & 860527
Fax (01386) 861286
*14th C inn between Evesham and
Pershore, on the edge of the Cotswolds.
Off B4084 and A44, in a quiet village
location, 17 miles from Stratford-upon-
Avon.*
Bedrooms: 4 double, 3 twin, 1 triple
Bathrooms: 8 private

**Bed & breakfast**

| per night: | £min | £max |
|---|---|---|
| Single | 42.50 | 42.50 |
| Double | 55.00 | 65.00 |

Lunch available
Evening meal 1830 (last orders 2130)
Parking for 30
Cards accepted: Access, Visa, Amex

🛇🌂🍽️🖬🖻⬧🆂🎱🖺🖴🚲🏃🗡️💺🐎
🅿️🛏️ 🆂🅿️ 🏚️

### Far Horizon ⋔
😃😃 COMMENDED

Long Hyde Road, South Littleton,
Evesham, Worcestershire WR11 5TH
☎ (01386) 831691
*Elegant family home of character, with
fine views over surrounding Cotswolds
and Malvern Hills. Rural location 3
miles from Evesham.*
Bedrooms: 1 single, 1 double, 1 twin
Bathrooms: 3 private

**Bed & breakfast**

| per night: | £min | £max |
|---|---|---|
| Single | 16.00 | 17.50 |
| Double | 32.00 | 35.00 |

Parking for 3
Open March-November

🛇10🍽️🖬⬧🖽🗡️🖺🖴🏚️📺🗡️🐎

### Fircroft ⋔
😃😃 COMMENDED

84 Greenhill, Evesham, Worcestershire
WR11 4NH
☎ (01386) 45828
*Comfortable B & B offering a relaxed
and unobtrusive environment. Elegant
house in attractive gardens, situated
three quarters of a mile north of town
centre. No smoking.*
Bedrooms: 2 double, 1 twin
Bathrooms: 1 private, 2 public

**Bed & breakfast**

| per night: | £min | £max |
|---|---|---|
| Single | 20.00 | 25.00 |
| Double | 35.00 | 42.00 |

Parking for 6
Open March-October

🛇🖵⬧🖾🛈🆂⌫🖽🎱🗡️🐎📱🎱

### Glencoyne
Listed

Lenchwick, Evesham, Worcestershire
WR11 4TG
☎ (01386) 870901
*Ground floor accommodation in large
chalet bungalow with beautiful gardens
overlooking a lake. Two miles from
Evesham centre.*
Bedrooms: 1 twin
Bathrooms: 1 public

**Bed & breakfast**

| per night: | £min | £max |
|---|---|---|
| Single | 12.50 | 12.50 |
| Double | 25.00 | 25.00 |

Parking for 5

🛇5⬧🖽🆂🖺📺🖴📱🎱🗡️🐎

### Hill Barn Orchard ⋔
Listed

Church Lench, Evesham,
Worcestershire WR11 4UB
☎ (01386) 871035

*50-acre arable farm. North of Evesham
overlooking Church Lench and lakes in
orchard setting. Close to Cotswolds and
Stratford-upon-Avon. Flyfishing, good
pub food locally.*
Bedrooms: 1 double, 2 twin
Bathrooms: 1 private, 1 public

**Bed & breakfast**

| per night: | £min | £max |
|---|---|---|
| Single | 20.00 | 30.00 |
| Double | 30.00 | 40.00 |

**Half board**

| per person: | £min | £max |
|---|---|---|
| Daily | 30.00 | 35.00 |
| Weekly | 210.00 | 245.00 |

Parking for 12

🛇🎿⬧🖽🆂📺🖴📱🗡️🐎🏚️

### Park View Hotel ⋔
😃

Waterside, Evesham, Worcestershire
WR11 6BS
☎ (01386) 442639
*Family-run hotel offering comfortable
accommodation in a friendly
atmosphere. Riverside situation, close to
town centre. Ideal base for touring the
Cotswolds and Shakespeare country.*
Bedrooms: 10 single, 4 double,
10 twin, 1 triple, 1 family room
Bathrooms: 7 public

**Bed & breakfast**

| per night: | £min | £max |
|---|---|---|
| Single | 18.50 | 22.00 |
| Double | 33.50 | 39.00 |

Evening meal 1800 (last orders 1900)
Parking for 50
Cards accepted: Access, Visa, Diners,
Amex

🛇🛈🆂🖺📺📱🍴2-30 🆂🅿️ 🕂

## EWEN

Gloucestershire
Map ref 2B1

Village in the South Cotswolds of
attractive stone cottages and
houses.

### Wild Duck Inn ⋔
😃😃 COMMENDED

Drakes Island, Ewen, Cirencester
GL7 6BY
☎ Cirencester (01285) 770310 &
770364
Fax (01285) 770310

*15th C Cotswold-stone inn, set in a
rural position in the village. Two four-
poster rooms in the oldest part of the
building. All rooms with private
facilities. Delightful garden.*
Bedrooms: 5 double, 4 twin
Bathrooms: 9 private

**Bed & breakfast**

| per night: | £min | £max |
|---|---|---|
| Single | | 48.00 |
| Double | | 65.00 |

Lunch available
Evening meal 1900 (last orders 2145)
Parking for 50
Cards accepted: Access, Visa, Amex,
Switch/Delta

🛇🖾🖴🍽️🖵⬧🛈🆂🖺📺🖴📱🍴
🖰🏃🎱 🆂🅿️ 🏚️🕂

## FAIRFORD

Gloucestershire
Map ref 2B1

Small town with a 15th C wool
church famous for its complete
15th C stained glass windows,
interesting carvings and original
wall paintings. It is an excellent
touring centre and the Cotswolds
Wildlife Park is nearby.

### Waiten Hill Farm ⋔
😃😃

Fairford GL7 4JG
☎ Cirencester (01285) 712652
*350-acre mixed farm. Imposing 19th C
farmhouse, overlooking River Coln, old
mill and famous church. Short walk to*

*shops and restaurants. Ideal for touring the Cotswolds and water parks.*
Bedrooms: 2 double, 1 twin
Bathrooms: 1 private, 1 public

**Bed & breakfast**

| per night: | £min | £max |
|---|---|---|
| Single | 15.00 | 20.00 |
| Double | 30.00 | 35.00 |

Parking for 6

🐕 🖵 ♿ ⓌⓁ 🎿 📺 ▥ 🌣 🎯 SP Ⓣ

## FOREST OF DEAN

*See under Blakeney, Coleford, Corse, Newent, Newland*

## FOWNHOPE

Hereford and Worcester
Map ref 2A1

Attractive village close to the River Wye with black and white cottages and other interesting houses. It has a large church with a Norman tower and a 14th C spire.

### Green Man Inn ⋀⋀
👑👑👑 COMMENDED

Fownhope, Hereford HR1 4PE
☎ Hereford (01432) 860243
Fax (01432) 860207
*15th C black and white coaching inn, midway between Ross-on-Wye and Hereford, in the picturesque village of Fownhope. On B4224, close to the River Wye and set in the beautiful Wye Valley.*
Bedrooms: 1 single, 13 double, 1 twin, 4 triple
Bathrooms: 19 private

**Bed & breakfast**

| per night: | £min | £max |
|---|---|---|
| Single | 31.00 | 31.50 |
| Double | 49.00 | 50.00 |

**Half board**

| per person: | £min | £max |
|---|---|---|
| Daily | 35.25 | 37.75 |
| Weekly | 231.50 | 242.25 |

Lunch available
Evening meal 1900 (last orders 2100)
Parking for 80
Cards accepted: Access, Visa, Amex

🐕 ♿ 🖾 🖳 🗌 ♿ 🍴 🛈 S 🎿 📺 ▥
🖃 Ⓣ30-40 ♪ 🌣 🎿 SP 🎯

---

There are separate sections in this guide listing groups specialising in farm holidays and accommodation which is especially suitable for young people and organised groups.

---

## GLOUCESTER

Gloucestershire
Map ref 2B1

A Roman city and inland port, its cathedral is one of the most beautiful in Britain. Gloucester's many attractions include museums and the restored warehouses in the Victorian docks containing the National Waterways Museum, Robert Opie Collection and other attractions.
Tourist Information Centre
☎ (01452) 421188

### Hill Farm ⋀⋀
👑👑

Wainlodes Lane, Bishops Norton, Gloucester GL2 9LN
☎ (01452) 730351
*14th C thatched farmhouse in rural setting, close to River Severn, offering facilities for "get away from it all" breaks.*
Bedrooms: 3 double, 1 twin
Bathrooms: 2 private, 1 public

**Bed & breakfast**

| per night: | £min | £max |
|---|---|---|
| Single | 15.00 | 21.50 |
| Double | 30.00 | 43.00 |

**Half board**

| per person: | £min | £max |
|---|---|---|
| Daily | 25.00 | 31.50 |
| Weekly | 175.00 | 220.50 |

Evening meal 1845 (last orders 2030)
Parking for 12
Open January-November

🐕 ♿ 🖵 🍴 🛈 S 🎿 🖃 Ⓣ4-12 🌣 🎿
🎿 🎯

### Merrivale ⋀⋀
👑 COMMENDED

Tewkesbury Road, Norton, Gloucester GL2 9LQ
☎ (01452) 730412
*Large private house with a pleasant garden, 3 miles from Gloucester. TV and tea/coffee-making facilities in all bedrooms.*
Bedrooms: 2 double, 3 twin, 1 triple
Bathrooms: 1 public, 2 private showers

**Bed & breakfast**

| per night: | £min | £max |
|---|---|---|
| Single | 15.00 | 17.00 |
| Double | 30.00 | 34.00 |

Parking for 8

🐕 ♿ 🖵 ♿ ⓌⓁ 🛈 S 🎿 📺 ▥ 🌣 🎯

### Notley House and Coach House ⋀⋀
👑👑👑 COMMENDED

93 Hucclecote Road, Hucclecote, Gloucester GL3 3TR
☎ (01452) 611584
*Affordable quality accommodation. Ideal for historic Gloucester and the Cotswolds. Tastefully furnished en-suite rooms, suite with four-poster bed.*

---

Bedrooms: 1 single, 2 double, 2 twin, 2 triple
Bathrooms: 5 private, 2 private showers

**Bed & breakfast**

| per night: | £min | £max |
|---|---|---|
| Single | 23.00 | 35.00 |
| Double | 38.00 | 59.00 |

**Half board**

| per person: | £min | £max |
|---|---|---|
| Daily | 33.00 | 45.00 |
| Weekly | 208.00 | 284.00 |

Lunch available
Evening meal 1800 (last orders 1930)
Parking for 8
Cards accepted: Access, Visa

🐕 ♿ 🖾 🖳 🖵 ♿ 🍴 ⓌⓁ 🛈 S 🎿 🎿 📺 ▥ 🖃
🌣 🎿 🎯

## Severn Bank ⋀⋀
👑👑

Minsterworth, Gloucester GL2 8JH
☎ (01452) 750357
Fax (01452) 750357
*A fine riverside country house in 6 acres of grounds, 4 miles west of Gloucester. Viewpoint for Severn Bore Tidal Wave.*
Bedrooms: 1 single, 1 double, 1 triple
Bathrooms: 3 private, 1 public

**Bed & breakfast**

| per night: | £min | £max |
|---|---|---|
| Single | 17.50 | 19.50 |
| Double | 35.00 | 39.00 |

Parking for 6

🐕 🖵 ♿ ⓌⓁ 🎿 🎿 📺 ▥ 🖃 🌣 🎿 🎯 🎯

## GREAT RISSINGTON

Gloucestershire
Map ref 2B1

### The Malthouse
👑👑

Great Rissington, Cheltenham GL54 2LH
☎ Cotswolds (01451) 820582
*Cotswold-stone malthouse built in 1648, in sought after, quiet Cotswold village. Accommodation is a private suite with gallery bedroom. Non-smokers only please.*
Bedrooms: 1 double
Bathrooms: 1 private

**Bed & breakfast**

| per night: | £min | £max |
|---|---|---|
| Double | 40.00 | 42.50 |

Parking for 2

🖵 ♿ 🎿 ⓌⓁ S 🎿 🎿 📺 ▥ 🖃 Ⓤ 🌣 🎿
🎿 🎯

---

National Crown ratings were correct at the time of going to press but are subject to change. Please check at the time of booking.

## GUITING POWER

Gloucestershire
Map ref 2B1

Unspoilt village with stone cottages and a green. The Cotswold Farm Park, with a collection of rare breeds, an adventure playground and farm trail, is nearby.

### Farmers Arms

**APPROVED**

Guiting Power, Cheltenham GL54 5TZ
☎ (01451) 850358

*Country pub in lovely unspoilt Cotswold village, 13 miles from Cheltenham. Good access to local places of interest.*
Bedrooms: 1 twin, 1 triple
Bathrooms: 2 private

**Bed & breakfast**

| per night: | £min | £max |
|---|---|---|
| Single | 20.00 | 22.00 |
| Double | 35.00 | 38.00 |

**Half board**

| per person: | £min | £max |
|---|---|---|
| Daily | 26.00 | 35.00 |
| Weekly | 150.00 | 180.00 |

Lunch available
Evening meal 1900 (last orders 2115)
Parking for 24

## HAMPTON IN ARDEN

West Midlands
Map ref 4B3

### The Hollies ⋔

Kenilworth Road, Hampton in Arden, Solihull B92 0LW
☎ (01675) 442941 & 442681
Fax (01675) 442941
*Home from home comfort, 2.5 miles from NEC and Birmingham International Airport. Sky TV, ample parking.*
Bedrooms: 1 single, 3 double, 4 twin
Bathrooms: 5 private, 1 public

**Bed & breakfast**

| per night: | £min | £max |
|---|---|---|
| Single | 20.00 | 25.00 |
| Double | 34.00 | 40.00 |

Parking for 10

---

## HASELEY

Warwickshire
Map ref 4B3

Village which has an interesting church with many original features including box pews and candles.

### Shrewley Pools Farm ⋔

**Listed COMMENDED**

Haseley, Warwick CV35 7HB
☎ Warwick (01926) 484315
*260-acre mixed farm. Traditional mid-17th C beamed farmhouse set in 1 acre of gardens. 5 miles north of Warwick on the A4177.*
Bedrooms: 1 twin, 1 triple
Bathrooms: 1 private, 1 public

**Bed & breakfast**

| per night: | £min | £max |
|---|---|---|
| Single | 18.00 | 23.00 |
| Double | 36.00 | 40.00 |

**Half board**

| per person: | £min | £max |
|---|---|---|
| Daily | 23.00 | 30.50 |
| Weekly | 150.00 | 200.00 |

Lunch available
Evening meal 1800 (last orders 2100)
Parking for 10

## HENLEY-IN-ARDEN

Warwickshire
Map ref 2B1

Old market town which in Tudor times stood in the Forest of Arden. It has many ancient inns, a 15th C Guildhall and parish church. Coughton Court with its Gunpowder Plot connections is nearby.

### Irelands Farm ⋔

**HIGHLY COMMENDED**

Irelands Lane, Henley-in-Arden, Solihull, West Midlands B95 5SA
☎ (01564) 792476
*220-acre arable & livestock farm. Secluded farmhouse in peaceful countryside. Close to Stratford, Warwick, National Exhibition Centre and the Cotswolds. 1 mile off A3400 between Henley and M42.*
Bedrooms: 2 double, 1 twin
Bathrooms: 3 private

**Bed & breakfast**

| per night: | £min | £max |
|---|---|---|
| Single | 17.00 | 20.00 |
| Double | 30.00 | 40.00 |

Parking for 6

---

## HEREFORD

Hereford and Worcester
Map ref 2A1

Agricultural county town, its cathedral containing much Norman work and a large chained library. Among the city's varied attractions are several museums including the Cider Museum and the Old House.
*Tourist Information Centre*
☎ *(01432) 268430*

### Cwm Craig Farm

**COMMENDED**

Little Dewchurch, Hereford HR2 6PS
☎ Carey (01432) 840250
*190-acre arable & livestock farm. Spacious Georgian farmhouse on edge of Wye Valley, surrounded by superb, unspoilt countryside. 5 miles south of Hereford. Easy access from M50.*
Bedrooms: 1 double, 1 twin, 1 family room
Bathrooms: 1 private, 2 public

**Bed & breakfast**

| per night: | £min | £max |
|---|---|---|
| Single | 15.00 | 16.00 |
| Double | 28.00 | 34.00 |

Parking for 6

### Felton House

**HIGHLY COMMENDED**

Felton, Hereford HR1 3PH
☎ (01432) 820366
*Tranquil stone rectory offering Victorian/Edwardian charm with modern comforts. Four-poster and brass beds. Warm welcome assured. Wide breakfast choice. In tiny hamlet, 8 miles from Hereford, just off A417.*
Bedrooms: 1 single, 2 double, 1 twin
Bathrooms: 1 private, 1 public

**Bed & breakfast**

| per night: | £min | £max |
|---|---|---|
| Single | 16.00 | 18.00 |
| Double | 32.00 | 36.00 |

Parking for 6
Open January-November

### Grafton Villa Farm House

**HIGHLY COMMENDED**

Grafton, Hereford HR2 8ED
☎ (01432) 268689
*180-acre mixed farm. Character farmhouse beautifully furnished with antiques and lovely fabrics, surrounded by peaceful countryside. Ideal for touring Wye Valley. Set back off A49 Hereford/Ross-on-Wye road.*
Bedrooms: 1 double, 1 twin, 1 triple
Bathrooms: 3 private

**Bed & breakfast**

| per night: | £min | £max |
|---|---|---|
| Single | 18.50 | 20.00 |
| Double | 32.00 | 36.00 |

---

Please mention this guide when making a booking.

We advise you to confirm your booking in writing.

Evening meal 1900 (last orders 1600)
Parking for 10

🛇⛶⏍♿☎🛇🆑⑂🅿TV🎔▦⏏☕⟳✿ 🐾♻️

## Lower Bartestree Farm
⛌

Bartestree, Hereford HR1 4DT
☎ (01432) 851005
*Comfortable accommodation in a peaceful setting with splendid views. Home-made bread, preserves and crafts available. Off A438, 4 miles from city centre.*
Bedrooms: 1 twin, 1 triple
Bathrooms: 1 public

### Bed & breakfast
| per night: | £min | £max |
| --- | --- | --- |
| Single | | 16.00 |
| Double | | 30.00 |

Parking for 5

🛇⛶⏍♿🆑S🅿TV▦⏏☕⟳✿🐾

## Sink Green Farm
⛌⛌ COMMENDED

Rotherwas, Hereford HR2 6LE
☎ Holme Lacy (01432) 870223
*170-acre livestock farm. 16th C farmhouse on family-run farm. Overlooking River Wye and 3 miles from Hereford city centre. Establishment is non-smoking.*
Bedrooms: 2 double, 1 twin
Bathrooms: 3 private

### Bed & breakfast
| per night: | £min | £max |
| --- | --- | --- |
| Single | 19.00 | 23.00 |
| Double | 36.00 | 46.00 |

Parking for 10

🛇🚗🆑⛶⏍♿🅿S🅿TV▦⏏☕✎✿ 🐾SP

## IRONBRIDGE
Shropshire
Map ref 4A3

Small town on the Severn where the Industrial Revolution began. It has the world's first iron bridge built in 1774. The Ironbridge Gorge Museum, of exceptional interest, comprises a rebuilt turn-of-the-century town and sites spread over 2 miles.
*Tourist Information Centre*
☎ *(01952) 432166*

## The Old Church Guest House
⛌⛌

Park Avenue, Madeley, Telford TF7 5AB
☎ Telford (01952) 583745
*Church built c1874 in area of industrial revolution. Converted to guesthouse by present owners in 1994.*
Bedrooms: 2 double, 1 twin
Bathrooms: 3 private

### Bed & breakfast
| per night: | £min | £max |
| --- | --- | --- |
| Single | 20.00 | 30.00 |
| Double | 30.00 | 40.00 |

Parking for 3
Open February-November

♿🚗🆑⛶⏍♿🅿TV▦⏏☕✗ 🐾SP

## Paradise House ⋔
APPROVED

Coalbrookdale, Telford TF8 7NR
☎ Telford (01952) 433379
*Georgian family home with large, airy rooms, overlooking the valley. Central for museums and adjacent to the Shropshire Way footpath.*
Bedrooms: 1 double, 1 family room
Bathrooms: 2 private

### Bed & breakfast
| per night: | £min | £max |
| --- | --- | --- |
| Single | 19.00 | 25.00 |
| Double | 34.00 | 40.00 |

Parking for 2
Open February-November

🛇♿🆑⛶⏍♿🅿🆑S TV▦⏏☕✿✗ 🐾🏵

## 46 Wigmore
Listed APPROVED

Woodside, Telford TF7 5NB
☎ Telford (01952) 583748
*Privately-owned house with garden and garage at rear. TV in all rooms and hot and cold water at all times.*
Bedrooms: 1 single, 1 twin
Bathrooms: 1 public

### Bed & breakfast
| per night: | £min | £max |
| --- | --- | --- |
| Single | 8.00 | 12.00 |
| Double | 12.00 | 14.00 |

### Half board
| per person: | £min | £max |
| --- | --- | --- |
| Daily | 15.00 | 18.00 |
| Weekly | 90.00 | 100.00 |

Evening meal from 1700
Parking for 2

🆑⛶⏍♿🆑✗TV▦⏏☕🐾

## KENILWORTH
Warwickshire
Map ref 4B3

The main feature of the town is the ruined 12th C castle. It has many royal associations but was damaged by Cromwell. A good base for visiting Coventry, Leamington Spa and Warwick.
*Tourist Information Centre*
☎ *(01926) 52595*

## Banner Hill Farmhouse
⛌

Rouncil Lane, Kenilworth CV8 1NN
☎ (01926) 52850
*250-acre mixed farm. Farmhouse set in Warwickshire countryside. Local walks - bicycles available. Also a 30-foot residential van with 2 bedrooms, bathroom and kitchen.*
Bedrooms: 3 twin
Bathrooms: 1 private, 1 public

### Bed & breakfast
| per night: | £min | £max |
| --- | --- | --- |
| Single | 16.00 | 22.50 |
| Double | 34.00 | 38.00 |

### Half board
| per person: | £min | £max |
| --- | --- | --- |
| Daily | 20.00 | 25.00 |
| Weekly | 75.00 | 120.00 |

Lunch available
Parking for 8

🛇🆑⛶⏍♿🆑S🅿TV▦⏏☕🖉✿🐾

## Oldwych House Farm ⋔
⛌⛌ COMMENDED

Oldwych Lane, Fen End, Kenilworth CV8 1NR
☎ Berkswell (01676) 533552
*35-acre mixed farm. 14th C half-timbered farmhouse in open countryside. 2 pools, sheep, horses, abundant wildlife. Resident artist's gallery. 6 miles from NEC and NAC, 8 miles Warwick, 12 miles Stratford-upon-Avon, 4 miles junction 5 of M42.*
Bedrooms: 2 double
Bathrooms: 2 private

### Bed & breakfast
| per night: | £min | £max |
| --- | --- | --- |
| Single | 25.00 | 30.00 |
| Double | 40.00 | 40.00 |

Parking for 6

🛇7🚗🆑⛶⏍♿🅿⑂TV▦✿✗🐾 🏵T

## KIDDERMINSTER
Hereford and Worcester
Map ref 4B3

The town is the centre for carpet manufacturing. It has a medieval church with good monuments and a statue of Sir Rowland Hill, a native of the town and founder of the penny post. West Midlands Safari Park is nearby. Severn Valley railway station.

## Cedars Hotel ⋔
⛌⛌⛌ COMMENDED

Mason Road, Kidderminster, Worcestershire DY11 6AG
☎ (01562) 515595
Fax (01562) 751103
*Charming conversion of a Georgian building close to the River Severn, Severn Valley Railway and Worcestershire countryside. 15 minutes from the M5.*
Bedrooms: 1 single, 7 double, 7 twin, 1 triple, 4 family rooms
Bathrooms: 20 private

### Bed & breakfast
| per night: | £min | £max |
| --- | --- | --- |
| Single | 29.00 | 50.30 |
| Double | 38.70 | 61.00 |

Continued ▶

159

## KIDDERMINSTER

*Continued*

Evening meal 1900 (last orders 2030)
Parking for 23
Cards accepted: Access, Visa, Diners, Amex

🛏🐾♿🍴☕🖤🦮♦🛎🛁✂🅿🏧🖲 ❧
☎8-35 ✿ SP T

## KINETON

Warwickshire
Map ref 2C1

Attractive old village in rolling countryside. 1 mile from site of famous battle of Edgehill. Medieval church of St Peter.

### Willowbrook Farmhouse ⚲

🛏🛏

Lighthorne Road, Kineton, Warwick
CV35 0JL
☎ (01926) 640475
Fax (01926) 641747
*4-acre smallholding. Very comfortable house surrounded by lovely countryside, 3 miles to M40 (junction 12) and B4100, half a mile from Kineton village. Handy for Stratford-upon-Avon, Warwick and Cotswolds. Tea trays, antiques and friendly service.*
Bedrooms: 2 double, 1 twin
Bathrooms: 1 private, 2 public

**Bed & breakfast**

| per night: | £min | £max |
|---|---|---|
| Double | 30.00 | 37.00 |

Parking for 6

🛏🐾♦🛎🅖🖤🛁✂📺🖲.🛍⌱♿✿ SP

## KINGS CAPLE

Hereford and Worcester
Map ref 2A1

Quiet village set in a loop of the River Wye, one of the 3 Herefordshire parishes where pax cakes are given out after the service on Palm Sunday, together with the greeting "Peace and Good Neighbourhood".

### Ruxton Farm

🛏🛏 COMMENDED

Kings Caple, Hereford HR1 4TX
☎ Carey (01432) 840493
Fax (01432) 840592
*18-acre horse farm. 17th C farmhouse with original staircase and hound gate. Quiet tranquil location off the main road in beautiful Wye Valley. Ample parking. A non-smoking establishment.*
Bedrooms: 3 double
Bathrooms: 3 private

**Bed & breakfast**

| per night: | £min | £max |
|---|---|---|
| Single | 17.50 | 17.50 |
| Double | 35.00 | 35.00 |

Parking for 6

🛏☎10🅖🖤✂📺🖲.🛍⌱♿✿🚗🖲

## KINGSTONE

Hereford and Worcester
Map ref 2A1

Village near the Golden Valley, Abbey Dore Church and Kilpeck Church.

### Webton Court Farmhouse

🛏🛏

Kingstone, Hereford HR2 9NF
☎ Golden Valley (01981) 250220
*280-acre mixed farm. Large black and white Georgian farmhouse in a quiet and peaceful part of Herefordshire. Lunch provided upon request.*
Bedrooms: 1 single, 2 double, 2 twin, 1 triple, 2 family rooms
Bathrooms: 2 private, 3 public

**Bed & breakfast**

| per night: | £min | £max |
|---|---|---|
| Single | 15.00 | 20.00 |
| Double | 28.00 | 40.00 |

**Half board**

| per person: | £min | £max |
|---|---|---|
| Daily | 21.50 | 27.50 |
| Weekly | 143.50 | 192.50 |

Lunch available
Evening meal 1900 (last orders 2000)
Parking for 10

🛏🐾☐♦🛎🅖🖤📺🖲⌱♿✿🚗 OAP 🏛

## KINNERSLEY

Hereford and Worcester
Map ref 2A1

### The Old Rectory

🛏

Kinnersley, Hereford HR3 6QD
☎ Eardisley (01544) 327555 & 327541
Fax (01544) 327568
*Late 18th C listed Georgian house, set in small park. Large garden with croquet lawn. Situated on A4112 Leominster to Brecon road, opposite Kinnersley Church.*
Bedrooms: 2 twin
Bathrooms: 1 private, 1 public

**Bed & breakfast**

| per night: | £min | £max |
|---|---|---|
| Single | 25.00 | 25.00 |
| Double | 35.00 | 40.00 |

Parking for 9
Open February-November

🛏☎5♦🛎🅖🖤🛁✂🖲.🛍⌱♿⌱♿✿🚗

---

Individual proprietors have supplied all details of accommodation. Although we do check for accuracy, we advise you to confirm the information at the time of booking.

## LEAMINGTON SPA

Warwickshire
Map ref 4B3

18th C spa town with many fine Georgian and Regency houses. Tea can be taken in the 19th C Pump Room. The attractive Jephson Gardens are laid out alongside the river and there is a museum and art gallery.
*Tourist Information Centre*
☎ *(01926) 311470*

### Glendower Guesthouse ⚲

🛏🛏 APPROVED

8 Warwick Place, Leamington Spa
CV32 5BJ
☎ (01926) 422784
*Charming Victorian building with many original features in a central but quiet location, offering comfortable accommodation. Ideal for National Agricultural Centre, M40, NEC, Warwick Castle and for touring the Cotswolds.*
Bedrooms: 3 single, 2 double, 2 twin, 2 triple
Bathrooms: 2 private, 2 public

**Bed & breakfast**

| per night: | £min | £max |
|---|---|---|
| Single | 16.00 | |
| Double | 32.00 | |

Parking for 4

🛏☎1☐♦🛎🅖🖤📺🖲.🛍♿✿🖐 SP

### Hill Farm ⚲

🛏🛏

Lewis Road, Radford Semele,
Leamington Spa CV31 1UX
☎ (01926) 337571
*350-acre mixed farm. Farmhouse set in large attractive garden, 2 miles from Leamington town centre and close to Warwick Castle and Stratford-upon-Avon.*
Bedrooms: 3 double, 2 twin
Bathrooms: 3 private, 1 public

**Bed & breakfast**

| per night: | £min | £max |
|---|---|---|
| Single | 17.00 | 20.00 |
| Double | 30.00 | 36.00 |

Parking for 10

🛏🐾♦🛎🅖🖤✂📺🖲.🛍⌱♿✿🖐🚗

### Northton

🛏🛏 COMMENDED

77 Telford Avenue, Lillington,
Leamington Spa CV32 7HQ
☎ (01926) 425609
*Detached family home with large garden in quiet residential area off A445, 2.5 miles from National Agricultural Centre. No smoking and no pets please.*
Bedrooms: 1 single, 1 twin
Bathrooms: 2 private

**Bed & breakfast**

| per night: | £min | £max |
| --- | --- | --- |
| Single | 17.50 | 17.50 |
| Double | 35.00 | 35.00 |

Parking for 4
Open February-October
🛏🚪♿️ⓤⓛ✕🛁✗🐾

## The Orchard

Listed

3 Sherbourne Terrace, Clarendon
Street, Leamington Spa CV32 5SP
☎ (01926) 428198
*Victorian double-fronted terrace with
walled garden. 5 minutes' walk to town
centre. Overseas visitors and children
welcome.*
Bedrooms: 1 single, 1 twin, 1 triple
Bathrooms: 2 public

**Bed & breakfast**

| per night: | £min | £max |
| --- | --- | --- |
| Single | 15.00 | 18.00 |
| Double | 30.00 | 32.00 |

**Half board**

| per person: | £min | £max |
| --- | --- | --- |
| Daily | 19.00 | 22.00 |
| Weekly | 110.00 | 130.00 |

Lunch available
Evening meal from 1800
🛏🌂♿️ⓤⓛ🅸🆂✕📺🛁🍴✗🐾

## Snowford Hall 🏚

COMMENDED

Snowford Hall Farm, Hunningham,
Leamington Spa CV33 9ES
☎ Marton (01926) 632297
*250-acre arable and mixed farm. 18th C
farmhouse off the Fosse Way, on the
edge of Hunningham village. On
elevated ground overlooking quiet
surrounding countryside. Self-catering
also available.*
Bedrooms: 1 double, 2 twin
Bathrooms: 1 private, 1 public,
1 private shower

**Bed & breakfast**

| per night: | £min | £max |
| --- | --- | --- |
| Single | 16.00 | 25.00 |
| Double | 32.00 | 38.00 |

Parking for 4
🛏♿️🐕ⓤⓛ🅸📺🛁🍴✗🐾

### LECHLADE

Gloucestershire
Map ref 2B1

Attractive village on the River
Thames and a popular spot for
boating. It has a number of fine
Georgian houses and a 15th C
church. Nearby is Kelmscott
Manor, with its William Morris
furnishings, and 18th C Buscot
House (National Trust).

## Apple Tree House
♿️♿️

Buscot, Faringdon, Oxfordshire
SN7 8DA
☎ Faringdon (01367) 252592

*Listed property offering comfortable B
& B in National Trust village near
Lechlade. River Thames 5 minutes' walk
through village. Large garden.*
Bedrooms: 2 double, 1 twin
Bathrooms: 1 private, 1 public

**Bed & breakfast**

| per night: | £min | £max |
| --- | --- | --- |
| Single | 22.00 | |
| Double | 32.00 | 39.00 |

Parking for 8,
🛏♿️ⓤⓛ🅸🆂✕🅜📺🛁🍴✗🐾🏡

## Cambrai Lodge 🏚
♿️♿️

Oak Street, Lechlade GL7 3AY
☎ (01367) 253173 & (01793) 762527,
mobile 0860 150467
*Family-run guesthouse, recently
modernised, close to River Thames.
Ideal base for touring the Cotswolds.
Garden and ample parking.*
Bedrooms: 1 single, 2 double
Bathrooms: 2 private, 1 public

**Bed & breakfast**

| per night: | £min | £max |
| --- | --- | --- |
| Single | 15.00 | 24.00 |
| Double | 28.00 | 35.00 |

Parking for 13
🛏♿️🛋📪🚪♿️ⓤⓛ📺🛁🍴🍴✗🐾🐾 SP

### LEDBURY

Hereford and Worcester
Map ref 2B1

Town with cobbled streets and
many black and white timbered
houses, including the 17th C
market house and old inns. Nearby
is Eastnor Castle with an
interesting collection of tapestries
and armour.
*Tourist Information Centre*
☎ *(01531) 636147*

## Foley House Bed and
## Breakfast
♿️

39 Bye Street, Ledbury, Herefordshire
HR8 2AA
☎ (01531) 632471
*Attractive Victorian house tastefully
converted into a bed and breakfast in
the middle of Ledbury town. Parking at
rear.*
Bedrooms: 2 double
Bathrooms: 1 public

**Bed & breakfast**

| per night: | £min | £max |
| --- | --- | --- |
| Single | 15.00 | |
| Double | 30.00 | |

Parking for 6
Open January-November
🛏2♿️📪🚪♿️ⓤⓛ🛁🍴✗🐾 SP

Please mention this guide
when making a booking.

### LEEK

Staffordshire
Map ref 4B2

Old silk and textile town, with
some interesting buildings and a
number of inns dating from the
17th C. Its art gallery has displays
of embroidery. Brindley Mill,
designed by James Brindley, has
been restored as a museum.
*Tourist Information Centre*
☎ *(01538) 381000*

## Abbey Inn
♿️♿️ APPROVED

Abbey Green Road, Leek ST13 8SA
☎ (01538) 382865
*17th C inn with accommodation in a
separate annexe, set in beautiful
countryside, 1 mile from the town and
just off the main A523.*
Bedrooms: 2 single, 4 double, 1 twin
Bathrooms: 7 private

**Bed & breakfast**

| per night: | £min | £max |
| --- | --- | --- |
| Single | 27.00 | 27.00 |
| Double | 42.00 | 42.00 |

Lunch available
Evening meal 1830 (last orders 2100)
Parking for 60
Cards accepted: Access, Visa, Diners,
Amex
🛏♿️📞📪🚪♿️🅸🛁❄️✗ SP🏡

## Horton Hall 🏚
♿️♿️ HIGHLY COMMENDED

Horton, Leek ST13 8PH
☎ Rudyard (01538) 306270
*17th C stone manor house with
courtyard, walled garden and paddocks
overlooking the magnificent Horton
Valley. Within a mile of Rudyard Lake
and with easy access to the Peak
District, the Potteries and Alton Towers.*
Bedrooms: 1 double, 1 triple, 1 family
room
Bathrooms: 1 private, 1 public

**Bed & breakfast**

| per night: | £min | £max |
| --- | --- | --- |
| Single | 15.00 | 17.50 |
| Double | 30.00 | 35.00 |

Parking for 16
🛏🚪♿️🐕ⓤⓛ🅜📺🛁🍴♿️🍴☕️🐾🏡

## Three Horseshoes Inn &
## Restaurant 🏚
♿️♿️ COMMENDED

Buxton Road, Blackshaw Moor, Leek
ST13 8TW
☎ (01538) 300296
Fax (01538) 300320

*Continued ▶*

## LEEK

### Continued

*Log fire, slate floor, oak and pine beams, good food and wines. Cottage-style rooms. Convenient for Peak District National Park and Alton Towers.*
Bedrooms: 4 double, 2 twin
Bathrooms: 6 private

**Bed & breakfast**

| per night: | £min | £max |
|---|---|---|
| Single | 40.00 | 48.00 |
| Double | 46.00 | 55.00 |

**Half board**

| per person: | £min | £max |
|---|---|---|
| Daily | 38.00 | 48.00 |

Lunch available
Evening meal 1900 (last orders 2100)
Parking for 100
Cards accepted: Access, Visa, Switch/Delta

ॐ ८ ◻️ ◻️ ♨ 👃 ⓢ ⌘ 🔏 📺 🛍️ ◢ ∪ ✈ ✿ SP T

## LEINTWARDINE

Hereford and Worcester
Map ref 4A3

Attractive border village where the Rivers Teme and Clun meet. It has some black and white cottages, old inns and an impressive church. It is near Hopton Castle and the beautiful scenery around Clun.

### Lower House M
☵☵ HIGHLY COMMENDED

Adforton, Leintwardine, Craven Arms, Shropshire SY7 0NF
☎ Wigmore (01568) 86223
*House dates from early 17th C. Set in peaceful unspoilt countryside. Excellent walking in surrounding hills. Home cooking using local produce. A no-smoking establishment.*
Bedrooms: 2 double, 2 twin
Bathrooms: 4 private

**Bed & breakfast**

| per night: | £min | £max |
|---|---|---|
| Single | 21.00 | 23.00 |
| Double | 42.00 | 46.00 |

**Half board**

| per person: | £min | £max |
|---|---|---|
| Daily | 36.00 | 38.00 |
| Weekly | 245.00 | 245.00 |

Evening meal 1900 (last orders 1930)
Parking for 10
Open March-November

ॐ 10 ♨ 🔏 ⌘ 📺 🛍️ ◢ ∪ ✿ ✈ 🐴

The national Crown scheme is explained in full in the information pages at the back of this guide.

## LEOMINSTER

Hereford and Worcester
Map ref 2A1

The town owed its prosperity to wool and has many interesting buildings, notably the timber-framed Grange Court, a former town hall. The impressive Norman priory church has 3 naves and a ducking stool. Berrington Hall (National Trust) is nearby.
*Tourist Information Centre*
☎ *(01568) 616460*

### Heath House M
☵☵ HIGHLY COMMENDED

Humber, Stoke Prior, Leominster, Herefordshire HR6 0NF
☎ Steens Bridge (01568) 760385
*Attractive stone farmhouse full of beams and history, set in peaceful countryside. Room to move and relax in comfort.*
Bedrooms: 1 double, 1 twin, 1 triple
Bathrooms: 3 private

**Bed & breakfast**

| per night: | £min | £max |
|---|---|---|
| Single | 16.00 | 21.50 |
| Double | 37.00 | 40.00 |

**Half board**

| per person: | £min | £max |
|---|---|---|
| Daily | 27.00 | 37.50 |
| Weekly | 178.50 | 231.00 |

Evening meal 1900 (last orders 2000)
Parking for 6
Open March-November

ॐ 9 📶 🔏 👃 ⓢ ⌘ 🔏 📺 🛍️ ◢ ∪ ✈ ✿ 🐴 🐟 T

### Highfield M
☵☵ COMMENDED

Ivington Road, Newtown, Leominster, Herefordshire HR6 8QD
☎ (01568) 613216
*Elegant Edwardian house in large garden, outside town. Cosy fire in TV lounge. Comfortable and peaceful. Home cooking. Advanced booking advisable.*
Bedrooms: 1 double, 2 twin
Bathrooms: 1 private, 2 public

**Bed & breakfast**

| per night: | £min | £max |
|---|---|---|
| Double | 38.00 | 42.00 |

**Half board**

| per person: | £min | £max |
|---|---|---|
| Daily | 31.00 | 33.00 |
| Weekly | 210.00 | 224.00 |

Lunch available
Evening meal 1830 (last orders 1600)
Parking for 3

◻️ 👃 ⓢ ⌘ 🔏 📺 🛍️ ◢ ✿ ✈ 🐴 SP

### Home Farm
☵

Bircher, Leominster, Herefordshire HR6 0AX
☎ Yarpole (01568) 780525
*100-acre mixed farm. Traditional farmhouse accommodation with tea room on Welsh border, 4 miles north of Leominster and 7 miles south of*

Ludlow. On B4362. Paradise for walkers and country-lovers.
Bedrooms: 1 double, 1 twin, 1 triple
Bathrooms: 2 public, 1 private shower

**Bed & breakfast**

| per night: | £min | £max |
|---|---|---|
| Single | 16.00 | 20.00 |
| Double | 30.00 | 35.00 |

Parking for 6
Open February-November

ॐ ◻️ ♨ 🔏 🛍️ 👃 ✈ 🔏 📺 🛍️ ◢ ✿ 🐴

### Lower Bache M
☵☵☵ HIGHLY COMMENDED

Kimbolton, Leominster, Herefordshire HR6 0ER
☎ Leysters (01568) 750304

*17th C farmhouse in tranquil valley, with annexe comprising 3 suites, each with bedroom, bath/shower and sitting room. Period country furniture. Organic food. Wildlife, walking, ideal for touring base. Please ring for brochure.*
Bedrooms: 2 double, 1 twin
Bathrooms: 3 private

**Bed & breakfast**

| per night: | £min | £max |
|---|---|---|
| Single | 24.50 | |
| Double | 49.00 | |

**Half board**

| per person: | £min | £max |
|---|---|---|
| Daily | 35.50 | 42.00 |
| Weekly | 248.50 | 294.00 |

Lunch available
Evening meal 1950 (last orders 1230)
Parking for 10

ॐ 8 📶 ◻️ ♨ 👃 ⓢ ⌘ 🔏 📺 🛍️ ◢ T ∪ ✿ ✈ 🐴 🐟 SP 🐴

## LICHFIELD

Staffordshire
Map ref 4B3

Lichfield is Dr Samuel Johnson's birthplace and commemorates him with a museum and statue. The 13th C cathedral has 3 spires and the west front is full of statues. There is a regimental museum and Heritage Centre.
*Tourist Information Centre*
☎ *(01543) 252109*

### Coppers End M
☵☵ COMMENDED

Walsall Road, Muckley Corner, Lichfield WS14 0BG
☎ (01543) 372910
*Detached guesthouse of character and charm in its own grounds. Rural location with easy access to M6, Birmingham, Lichfield and M1. Residential licence.*

Bedrooms: 1 single, 2 double, 2 twin
Bathrooms: 1 private, 1 public

**Bed & breakfast**

| per night: | £min | £max |
| --- | --- | --- |
| Single | 21.00 | 28.00 |
| Double | 34.00 | 40.00 |

**Half board**

| per person: | £min | £max |
| --- | --- | --- |
| Daily | 24.00 | 35.00 |

Evening meal 1900 (last orders 2030)
Parking for 12
Cards accepted: Access, Visa, Diners, Amex

⛵♿️🛗❒☐♨🛏📠Ⓢ♨📺🎱,🚪▶☼🐎 ⒮🎏

## LONG COMPTON

Warwickshire
Map ref 2B1

Village with a restored church displaying Norman doorways and a thatched room above the lych gate. Several interesting old houses exist in the area.

### Butlers Road Farm ⚠

**Listed**

Long Compton, Shipston-on-Stour CV36 5JZ
☎ (01608) 684262
Fax (01608) 684262
*115-acre dairy farm. Listed old stone farmhouse situated adjacent to A3400 between Oxford and Stratford-upon-Avon.*
Bedrooms: 1 double, 1 twin
Bathrooms: 1 public

**Bed & breakfast**

| per night: | £min | £max |
| --- | --- | --- |
| Single | | 16.00 |
| Double | | 30.00 |

Parking for 4

⛵❒🛏🛏ⓈⒾ📺🎱,🚪🔦♿🐎

## LUDLOW

Shropshire
Map ref 4A3

Outstandingly interesting border town with a magnificent castle high above the River Teme, 2 half-timbered old inns and an impressive 15th C church. The Reader's House, with its 3-storey Jacobean porch, should also be seen.
*Tourist Information Centre*
☎ *(01584) 875053*

### Church Bank ⚠

**Listed**

Burrington, Ludlow SY8 2HT
☎ Wigmore (01568) 86426
*Stone cottage guesthouse in tiny village. Walking in hills and forests, and historic places to visit. Four-course dinner.*
Bedrooms: 1 double, 2 twin
Bathrooms: 2 public

**Bed & breakfast**

| per night: | £min | £max |
| --- | --- | --- |
| Single | 14.50 | 15.00 |
| Double | 27.00 | 28.00 |

**Half board**

| per person: | £min | £max |
| --- | --- | --- |
| Daily | 24.00 | 25.00 |
| Weekly | 160.00 | 160.00 |

Evening meal from 1900
Parking for 4
Open April-September

⛵🗝🛗Ⓘ♨ⓈⒾ📺🎱,🚪☼✕🐎

### The Church Inn ⚠

👑👑👑

Butter Cross, Ludlow SY8 1AW
☎ (01584) 872174
*Georgian inn, centrally located on one of the most ancient sites in Ludlow. Good food and CAMRA listed for ales.*
Bedrooms: 6 double, 2 twin, 1 triple
Bathrooms: 9 private

**Bed & breakfast**

| per night: | £min | £max |
| --- | --- | --- |
| Single | 28.00 | 28.00 |
| Double | 40.00 | 40.00 |

Lunch available
Evening meal 1800 (last orders 2100)
Cards accepted: Access, Visa

⛵☐♨ⓈⒾ✕🎱,🚪🐎🎏

### Corndene ⚠

👑👑

Coreley, Ludlow SY8 3AW
☎ (01584) 890324
*Country house of character in the heart of rural Shropshire. Beautiful and secluded situation only 5 minutes off A4117 (Ludlow 7 miles). Spacious en-suite rooms, tasty home cooking and relaxing atmosphere. No smoking indoors please.*
Bedrooms: 3 twin
Bathrooms: 3 private

**Bed & breakfast**

| per night: | £min | £max |
| --- | --- | --- |
| Single | 21.25 | 23.00 |
| Double | 37.00 | 41.00 |

**Half board**

| per person: | £min | £max |
| --- | --- | --- |
| Daily | 27.00 | 30.00 |
| Weekly | 170.00 | 182.00 |

Evening meal 1830 (last orders 2000)
Parking for 5

⛵🗝♨🛗ⓈⒾ✕📺🎱,🚪☼✕🐎

### Fairview ⚠

👑👑 **HIGHLY COMMENDED**

Green Lane, Onibury, Craven Arms SY7 9BL
☎ Bromfield (01584) 77505
*5-acre smallholding. 300-year-old cottage 6 miles north of Ludlow. Panoramic views of Wenlock Edge, Long Mynd and Clee Hills.*
Bedrooms: 2 double, 1 twin
Bathrooms: 1 private, 1 public

**Bed & breakfast**

| per night: | £min | £max |
| --- | --- | --- |
| Single | 15.50 | 17.00 |
| Double | 31.00 | 36.00 |

**Half board**

| per person: | £min | £max |
| --- | --- | --- |
| Daily | 26.00 | 27.00 |
| Weekly | 174.00 | 183.50 |

Evening meal 1930 (last orders 1930)
Parking for 8
Open April-October

⛵12♨🗝🛗Ⓘ♨ⓈⒾ✕📺🎱,🚪☼ ✕🐎

### Longlands ⚠

👑👑

Woodhouse Lane, Richards Castle, Ludlow SY8 4EU
☎ Richards Castle (01584) 74636
*35-acre livestock farm. Farmhouse set in lovely rural landscape. Home-grown produce. Convenient for Ludlow, Mortimer Forest and Croft Castle. Interesting 14th C church and remains of 11th C castle in village.*
Bedrooms: 1 double, 1 twin
Bathrooms: 2 private, 1 public

**Bed & breakfast**

| per night: | £min | £max |
| --- | --- | --- |
| Single | 17.50 | |
| Double | 34.00 | |

**Half board**

| per person: | £min | £max |
| --- | --- | --- |
| Daily | 25.00 | |

Evening meal 1830 (last orders 1930)
Parking for 2

⛵🗝♨🛗Ⓘ♨ⓈⒾ📺🎱,🚪♿☼🐎

### 28 Lower Broad Street ⚠

👑👑👑👑 **COMMENDED**

Ludlow SY8 1PQ
☎ (01584) 876996

*Listed town house of charm and character. Secluded walled garden. Emphasis on good food and wines, warm hospitality and quiet relaxed atmosphere.*
Bedrooms: 1 double, 1 twin
Bathrooms: 2 private, 1 public

**Bed & breakfast**

| per night: | £min | £max |
| --- | --- | --- |
| Single | 25.00 | 45.00 |
| Double | 40.00 | 55.00 |

Continued ▶

Symbols are explained on the flap inside the back cover.

## LUDLOW
### Continued

**Half board**

| per person: | £min | £max |
|---|---|---|
| Daily | 33.50 | 41.00 |
| Weekly | 250.00 | 275.00 |

Evening meal 1930 (last orders 2030)
Cards accepted: Access, Visa

### Seifton Court ⚑
COMMENDED

Culmington, Ludlow SY8 2DG
☎ Seifton (01584) 73214
*50-acre mixed farm. Period farmhouse, 5 miles from Ludlow on the B4365 road. Set in the beautiful Corve Dale valley. Near Longmynd, Ironbridge. Ideal for walking and visiting National Trust properties. Farmhouse fare using home-grown produce.*
Bedrooms: 1 single, 1 twin, 1 triple
Bathrooms: 3 private, 1 public

**Bed & breakfast**

| per night: | £min | £max |
|---|---|---|
| Single | 18.00 | 25.00 |
| Double | 36.00 | 40.00 |

**Half board**

| per person: | £min | £max |
|---|---|---|
| Daily | 29.00 | 35.00 |
| Weekly | 185.00 | 196.00 |

Lunch available
Evening meal 1800 (last orders 1900)
Parking for 7

### Spring Cottage
HIGHLY COMMENDED

Abdon, Craven Arms SY7 9HU
☎ Ditton Priors (01746) 34551
*10-acre livestock & horse farm. Superbly situated country cottage in peaceful position on Brown Clee Hill, midway between Ludlow, Bridgnorth and Much Wenlock. Panoramic views over unspoilt countryside, delightfully landscaped gardens, delicious home cooking. Ideal walking, rambling and riding country.*
Bedrooms: 1 single, 1 double, 1 twin
Bathrooms: 2 private

**Bed & breakfast**

| per night: | £min | £max |
|---|---|---|
| Single | 17.00 | 21.00 |
| Double | 30.00 | 35.00 |

**Half board**

| per person: | £min | £max |
|---|---|---|
| Daily | 25.00 | 30.00 |
| Weekly | 168.00 | 195.00 |

Parking for 8

### The Wheatsheaf Inn
APPROVED

Lower Broad Street, Ludlow SY8 1PH
☎ (01584) 872980

*Family-run mid 17th C beamed inn, 100 yards from the town centre, nestling under Ludlow's historic 13th C Broad Gate, the last remaining of 7 town gates.*
Bedrooms: 4 double, 1 twin
Bathrooms: 5 private, 1 public

**Bed & breakfast**

| per night: | £min | £max |
|---|---|---|
| Single | 20.00 | 25.00 |
| Double | 35.00 | 40.00 |

Lunch available
Evening meal 1830 (last orders 2100)

## MALVERN
### Hereford and Worcester
### Map ref 2B1

Spa town in Victorian times, its water is today bottled and sold worldwide. 6 resorts, set on the slopes of the Hills, form part of Malvern. Great Malvern Priory has splendid 15th C windows. It is an excellent walking centre.
*Tourist Information Centre*
☎ *(01684) 892289*

### Chestnut Hill ⚑

Green Lane, Malvern Wells, Malvern, Worcestershire WR14 4HU
☎ (01684) 564648
*House, garden and grounds just a mile from the Three Counties Showground, situated well away from the main road in a quiet but accessible position. Outdoor manege and bridle paths available for horse owners.*
Bedrooms: 2 double, 1 twin
Bathrooms: 1 private, 1 public

**Bed & breakfast**

| per night: | £min | £max |
|---|---|---|
| Single | 15.00 | 18.00 |
| Double | | 32.50 |

**Half board**

| per person: | £min | £max |
|---|---|---|
| Daily | 21.00 | 24.00 |

Parking for 4
Open March-November

### Cowleigh Park Farm
HIGHLY COMMENDED

Cowleigh Road, Malvern, Worcestershire WR13 5HJ
☎ (01684) 566750

*Beautifully restored, Grade II listed timbered farmhouse set in 2.5 acres of landscaped gardens. In a tranquil setting at the foot of the Malvern Hills. Ample secure parking.*

Bedrooms: 1 double, 2 twin
Bathrooms: 3 private

**Bed & breakfast**

| per night: | £min | £max |
|---|---|---|
| Single | 28.00 | |
| Double | 40.00 | |

Evening meal 1830 (last orders 1000)
Parking for 6

### Grove House Farm ⚑
COMMENDED

Guarlford, Malvern, Worcestershire WR14 3QZ
☎ (01684) 574256
Fax (01684) 574256
*370-acre mixed farm. Beautifully furnished large farmhouse at foot of the Malvern Hills, in peaceful surroundings. Close to Three Counties Showground.*
Bedrooms: 1 double, 1 twin, 1 triple
Bathrooms: 1 public

**Bed & breakfast**

| per night: | £min | £max |
|---|---|---|
| Single | 20.00 | |
| Double | 36.00 | 40.00 |

Parking for 8
Open January-November

### Nags Head

19-21 Bank Street, Malvern, Worcestershire WR14 2JG
☎ (01684) 574373
*Self-contained bedroom with sofa bed in lounge, sleeping capacity for four people, private kitchen, bathroom and lounge.*
Bedrooms: 1 double
Bathrooms: 1 private

**Bed & breakfast**

| per night: | £min | £max |
|---|---|---|
| Single | 17.50 | 20.00 |
| Double | 35.00 | 40.00 |

Lunch available
Parking for 2

### The Red Lion Inn
Listed COMMENDED

Stiffords Bridge, Malvern, Worcestershire WR13 5NN
☎ Ridgeway Cross (01886) 880318
*Traditional country inn offering traditional ales and home-cooked bar fare, also a la carte restaurant. Attractive patio and gardens. Ideally situated on A4103, 3 miles from Malvern and 9 miles west of Worcester.*
Bedrooms: 1 twin, 1 triple
Bathrooms: 1 public

**Bed & breakfast**

| per night: | £min | £max |
|---|---|---|
| Single | | 23.00 |
| Double | | 38.00 |

Lunch available
Evening meal 1900 (last orders 2130)
Parking for 60
Cards accepted: Access, Visa, Switch/Delta

## Robin's Orchard ⚑

**COMMENDED**

New Road, Castlemorton, Malvern,
Worcestershire WR13 6BT
☎ Birtsmorton (01684) 833251
*Set in beautiful countryside at southern
end of Malvern Hills, with superb
walking. Bordering Herefordshire,
Worcestershire and Gloucestershire,
within easy reach of Cotswolds and
Stratford. 5 minutes' drive from Three
Counties Showground.*
Bedrooms: 1 double, 1 twin, 1 triple
Bathrooms: 1 private, 1 public
**Bed & breakfast**

| per night: | £min | £max |
|---|---|---|
| Double | 30.00 | 40.00 |

Evening meal 1830 (last orders 1830)
Parking for 20
Open January-November

## The Wyche Inn ⚑

**APPROVED**

74 Wyche Road, Malvern,
Worcestershire WR14 4EQ
☎ (01684) 575396
*The highest inn in Worcestershire,
nestling on top of the Malvern Hills and
with spectacular views across the
Severn Valley.*
Bedrooms: 1 double, 2 twin, 3 triple
Bathrooms: 6 private
**Bed & breakfast**

| per night: | £min | £max |
|---|---|---|
| Single | 25.00 | 30.00 |
| Double | 40.00 | 45.00 |

Lunch available
Evening meal 1900 (last orders 2200)
Parking for 12
Cards accepted: Access, Visa

Shropshire
Map ref 4A2

Old market town with black and
white buildings and 17th C houses,
also acclaimed for its gingerbread.
Hodnet Hall is in the vicinity with
its beautiful landscaped gardens
covering 60 acres.
*Tourist Information Centre*
☎ *(01630) 652139*

## Heath Farm Bed and Breakfast

**Listed**

Heath Farm, Hodnet, Market Drayton
TF9 3JJ
☎ Hodnet (01630) 685570
*60-acre mixed farm. Traditional
farmhouse welcome. Situated 1.5 miles
south of Hodnet off the A442,
approached by private drive.*
Bedrooms: 1 single, 1 double, 1 twin
Bathrooms: 1 public

**Bed & breakfast**

| per night: | £min | £max |
|---|---|---|
| Single | 13.50 | 15.00 |
| Double | 25.00 | 30.00 |

Parking for 5

West Midlands
Map ref 4B3

Village halfway between Coventry
and Birmingham. Said to be the
centre of England, marked by a
cross on the green.

## Cooperage Farm Bed and Breakfast ⚑

Old Road, Meriden, Coventry CV7 7JP
☎ (01676) 23493
*6-acre mixed farm. 300-year-old red
brick, Grade II listed farmhouse, set in
beautiful countryside. Ideally situated
for the National Exhibition Centre,
airport and touring the centre of
England.*
Bedrooms: 1 double, 3 twin, 2 triple
Bathrooms: 4 private, 2 public
**Bed & breakfast**

| per night: | £min | £max |
|---|---|---|
| Single | 20.00 | 30.00 |
| Double | 40.00 | 45.00 |

| Half board per person: | £min | £max |
|---|---|---|
| Daily | 30.00 | 35.00 |
| Weekly | 260.00 | 260.00 |

Evening meal 1800 (last orders 1900)
Parking for 6

## Innellan House ⚑

**COMMENDED**

Eaves Green Lane, Meriden, Coventry
CV7 7JL
☎ (01676) 23005 & 22548
*Detached country house surrounded by
18 acres of meadowland. Approximately
one mile from Meriden village. Good
touring centre, convenient for the
railway, airport and the National
Exhibition Centre. Non-smokers only
please.*
Bedrooms: 3 twin
Bathrooms: 3 private
**Bed & breakfast**

| per night: | £min | £max |
|---|---|---|
| Single | 25.00 | 28.00 |
| Double | 40.00 | 45.00 |

Parking for 10

> Map references apply
> to the colour maps at the
> back of this guide.

Gloucestershire
Map ref 2B1

Stone-built town, with many 17th/
18th C buildings, owing its
existence to the wool and cloth
trades. A 17th C pillared market
house may be found in the town
square, near which is the Norman
and 14th C church.

## Hunters Lodge

**COMMENDED**

Dr Brown's Road, Minchinhampton,
Stroud GL6 9BT
☎ Brimscombe (01453) 883588
Fax (01453) 731449
*Cotswold stone house adjoining
Minchinhampton common and golf-
course. Ideal centre for Bath,
Gloucester, Cheltenham and Cotswolds.
Located 2 miles from A419 Stroud-
Cirencester road 1.5 miles from A46
(first house on right going into
Minchinhampton).*
Bedrooms: 1 double, 1 twin, 1 triple
Bathrooms: 3 private
**Bed & breakfast**

| per night: | £min | £max |
|---|---|---|
| Single | 20.00 | 25.00 |
| Double | 32.00 | 40.00 |

Parking for 8

## Sunnycroft ⚑

**Listed**

Chapel Lane, Minchinhampton, Stroud
GL6 9DL
☎ Stroud (01453) 883159
*Bungalow overlooking Gatcombe woods.
From Minchinhampton Post Office take
next turning left then half a mile down
country lane.*
Bedrooms: 1 double, 2 twin
Bathrooms: 1 public
**Bed & breakfast**

| per night: | £min | £max |
|---|---|---|
| Single | 14.00 | 16.00 |
| Double | 28.00 | 32.00 |

Parking for 3

Shropshire
Map ref 4A3

Village with a curious little church
of 1692 and a fine old black and
white hall. The lofty ridge known
as the Stiperstones is 4 miles to
the south.

## Cricklewood Cottage

**HIGHLY COMMENDED**

Plox Green, Minsterley, Shrewsbury
SY5 0HT
☎ Shrewsbury (01743) 791229
*Delightful 18th C cottage with
countryside views, at foot of*

Continued ▶

## MINSTERLEY
### Continued

*Stiperstones Hills. Exposed beams, inglenook fireplace, traditional furnishings. Lovely cottage garden. Excellent restaurants and inns nearby.*
Bedrooms: 1 double, 2 twin
Bathrooms: 3 private
**Bed & breakfast**

| per night: | £min | £max |
| --- | --- | --- |
| Single | 19.00 | 28.50 |
| Double | 34.00 | 38.00 |

**Half board**

| per person: | £min | £max |
| --- | --- | --- |
| Daily | 29.00 | 38.00 |
| Weekly | 189.00 | 248.50 |

Evening meal 1900 (last orders 1000)
Parking for 4

## MORETON-IN-MARSH
Gloucestershire
Map ref 2B1

Attractive town of Cotswold stone with 17th C houses, an ideal base for touring the Cotswolds. Some of the local attractions include Batsford Park Arboretum, the Jacobean Chastleton House and Sezincote Garden.

### Blue Cedar House ⋀
Stow Road, Moreton-in-Marsh GL56 0DW
☎ (01608) 650299
*Attractive detached residence set in half-acre garden in the Cotswolds, with pleasantly decorated, well-equipped accommodation and garden room. Close to village centre.*
Bedrooms: 1 single, 2 double, 1 family room
Bathrooms: 2 private, 2 public, 1 private shower
**Bed & breakfast**

| per night: | £min | £max |
| --- | --- | --- |
| Single | 18.00 | 20.00 |
| Double | 32.00 | 40.00 |

**Half board**

| per person: | £min | £max |
| --- | --- | --- |
| Daily | 24.00 | 27.50 |

Evening meal 1800 (last orders 1800)
Parking for 7
Open February-November

### The Cottage
Listed
Oxford Street, Moreton-in-Marsh GL56 0LA
☎ (01608) 651740

*Listed cottage in the town, built of Cotswold stone with beams and an inglenook fireplace. Within walking distance of railway station.*
Bedrooms: 2 double, 1 twin, 1 family room
Bathrooms: 2 private, 1 public
**Bed & breakfast**

| per night: | £min | £max |
| --- | --- | --- |
| Double | 35.00 | 40.00 |

Parking for 3
Open January, March-December

### Lower Farm Barn ⋀
Great Wolford, Shipston-on-Stour, Warwickshire CV36 5NQ
☎ Barton on the Heath (01608) 74435 & 674435
*900-acre arable farm. 18th C converted barn combines modern comforts with exposed beams and ancient stonework. Use of attractive drawing room. Quiet village between A34, A44 and A429.*
Bedrooms: 2 double
Bathrooms: 1 private, 1 public
**Bed & breakfast**

| per night: | £min | £max |
| --- | --- | --- |
| Single | 18.00 | 20.00 |
| Double | 28.00 | 32.00 |

Parking for 10

### Manor Farm ⋀
Listed
Great Wolford, Shipston-on-Stour, Warwickshire CV36 5NQ
☎ Barton-on-the-Heath (01608) 674247
Fax (01608) 674247

*270-acre mixed farm. Comfortable listed farmhouse in a small village with traditional pub, close to Moreton-in-Marsh. Open fire, TV lounge, lovely views. Ideal for Cotswolds and Stratford-upon-Avon.*
Bedrooms: 1 double, 1 twin
Bathrooms: 1 public
**Bed & breakfast**

| per night: | £min | £max |
| --- | --- | --- |
| Single | 16.00 | 20.00 |
| Double | 30.00 | 36.00 |

Parking for 12
Open March-November

### New Farm ⋀
COMMENDED
Dorn, Moreton-in-Marsh GL56 9NS
☎ (01608) 650782

*250-acre dairy farm. Old Cotswold farmhouse. All rooms spacious, en-suite and furnished with antiques and with colour TV, coffee and tea facilities. Dining room with large impressive fireplace. Full English breakfast served with hot crispy bread.*
Bedrooms: 1 double, 1 twin, 1 family room
Bathrooms: 3 private, 1 public
**Bed & breakfast**

| per night: | £min | £max |
| --- | --- | --- |
| Single | 16.00 | 16.50 |
| Double | 32.00 | 33.00 |

**Half board**

| per person: | £min | £max |
| --- | --- | --- |
| Daily | 26.00 | 26.50 |
| Weekly | 180.00 | 182.00 |

Parking for 10

### Old Farm ⋀
COMMENDED
Dorn, Moreton-in-Marsh GL56 9NS
☎ (01608) 650394
*250-acre mixed farm. Enjoy the delights of a 15th C farmhouse - a comfortable family home. Spacious bedrooms. Tennis and croquet. Children welcome. Surrounded by beautiful Cotswolds scenery.*
Bedrooms: 1 double, 1 twin, 1 triple
Bathrooms: 1 private, 1 public
**Bed & breakfast**

| per night: | £min | £max |
| --- | --- | --- |
| Single | 15.00 | |
| Double | 28.00 | |

Parking for 8
Open March-October

### Rest Harrow ⋀
COMMENDED
Evenlode Road, Moreton-in-Marsh GL56 0NJ
☎ (01608) 650653
*Large four-bedroomed house in rural location. Take Evenlode turning by Wellington public house on main A44 Oxford-London road, then half a mile on left.*
Bedrooms: 1 double, 1 triple
Bathrooms: 1 public

| Bed & breakfast per night: | £min | £max |
| --- | --- | --- |
| Single | 14.00 | 16.00 |
| Double | 26.00 | 28.00 |
| Parking for 3 | | |

🐕 🖵 🕯 ⓤⓛ 🛋 Ⓢ ⊁ 🎿 🔲 🞖 🗕 ✕ ⇛ DAP

## Twostones
⚜⚜

Evenlode, Moreton-in-Marsh
GL56 0NY
☎ (01608) 651104

*16th C priest cottage, on smallholding, in quiet village, 3 miles from Stow-on-the-Wold and 2.5 miles from Moreton-in-Marsh. Ideal for Stratford and Cotswolds.*
Bedrooms: 2 double, 1 twin
Bathrooms: 3 private

| Bed & breakfast per night: | £min | £max |
| --- | --- | --- |
| Double | 36.00 | 36.00 |
| Parking for 6 | | |

🐕 10 🕯 ⓤⓛ ⊁ 🎿 🔲 🞖 ✻ ✕ ⇛ 🏠

### MUCH WENLOCK

Shropshire
Map ref 4A3

Small town close to Wenlock Edge in beautiful scenery and full of interest. In particular there are the remains of an 11th C priory with fine carving and the black and white 16th C Guildhall.

## The Old Barn
⚜⚜ COMMENDED

45 Sheinton Street, Much Wenlock
TF13 6HR
☎ Telford (01952) 728191

*18th C barn, converted to cottage-style accommodation, in the beautiful town of Much Wenlock.*
Bedrooms: 2 double, 2 twin
Bathrooms: 4 private

| Bed & breakfast per night: | £min | £max |
| --- | --- | --- |
| Single | 25.00 | 28.00 |
| Double | 35.00 | 38.00 |
| Parking for 4 | | |
| Open January-November | | |

🐕 4 🖚 🖵 🕯 ⓤⓛ ⊁ 🔲 🗕 ✕ ⇛ 🏠

## Walton House 🏍
Listed COMMENDED

35 Barrow Street, Much Wenlock
TF13 6EP
☎ (01952) 727139

*Two minutes' walk from town centre. 5 miles from Ironbridge Gorge, 13 miles from Shrewsbury, 8 miles from Bridgnorth and 10 miles from Telford town centre. Lawns and patio.*
Bedrooms: 1 single, 2 twin
Bathrooms: 1 public

| Bed & breakfast per night: | £min | £max |
| --- | --- | --- |
| Single | | 15.00 |
| Double | | 28.00 |
| Parking for 2 | | |
| Open April-October | | |
| Cards accepted: Visa | | |

🐕 5 🖚 🕯 ⓤⓛ Ⓢ 🎿 🔲 🗕 ✻ ✕ ⇛

### NAILSWORTH

Gloucestershire
Map ref 2B1

Ancient wool town with several elegant Jacobean and Georgian houses, surrounded by wooded hillsides with fine views.

## Aaron Farm 🏍
⚜⚜ COMMENDED

Nympsfield Road, Nailsworth, Stroud
GL6 0ET
☎ Stroud (01453) 833598

*Former farmhouse, with large en-suite bedrooms and panoramic views of the Cotswolds. Ideal touring centre. Many walks and attractions within easy reach. Brochure on request.*
Bedrooms: 1 double, 2 twin
Bathrooms: 3 private

| Bed & breakfast per night: | £min | £max |
| --- | --- | --- |
| Single | 22.00 | 26.00 |
| Double | 32.00 | 36.00 |

| Half board per person: | £min | £max |
| --- | --- | --- |
| Daily | 32.00 | 36.00 |
| Weekly | 200.00 | 240.00 |
| Evening meal 1800 (last orders 2000) | | |
| Parking for 4 | | |

🐕 📞 🖃 🖵 🕯 ⓤⓛ 🛋 Ⓢ ⊁ 🎿 🔲 🞖 🗕 ✻ ⇛ ⚓ SP Ⓣ

## Apple Orchard House 🏍
⚜⚜⚜ COMMENDED

Orchard Close, Springhill, Nailsworth,
Stroud GL6 0LX
☎ (01453) 832503
Fax (01453) 836213

*Elegant and spacious house in pretty 1 acre garden. Panoramic views from bedrooms and sitting room of picturesque Cotswold hills. Excellent touring centre. In small, historic town, close to restaurants, M5, M4.*
Wheelchair access category 3 ♿
Bedrooms: 1 double, 2 twin
Bathrooms: 3 private

| Bed & breakfast per night: | £min | £max |
| --- | --- | --- |
| Single | 18.00 | 28.00 |
| Double | 29.00 | 36.00 |

| Half board per person: | £min | £max |
| --- | --- | --- |
| Daily | 26.50 | 28.50 |
| Weekly | 174.30 | 186.90 |
| Evening meal 1900 (last orders 1700) | | |
| Parking for 3 | | |
| Cards accepted: Access, Visa, Amex | | |

🐕 🖚 📞 🖵 🕯 ⓤⓛ 🛋 Ⓢ ⊁ 🎿 ⊞ 🔲 🗕 ∪ ⇟ ✻ SP Ⓣ

[Ad] Display advertisement appears on this page

## NAILSWORTH

*Continued*

### The Upper House

**COMMENDED**

Spring Hill, Nailsworth, Stroud
GL6 0LX
☎ Stroud (01453) 836606
*Large imposing 18th C Cotswold house
near the centre of a small market town.
All bedrooms en-suite. Antiques, exposed
beams, log fires in downstairs rooms.*
Bedrooms: 2 double, 1 twin
Bathrooms: 3 private

**Bed & breakfast**

| per night: | £min | £max |
|---|---|---|
| Single | 16.00 | 20.00 |
| Double | 32.00 | 40.00 |

Parking for 5

## NAUNTON

Gloucestershire
Map ref 2B1

A high place on the Windrush,
renowned for its wild flowers and
with an attractive dovecote.

### Eastern Hill Farm M

**Listed**

Naunton, Cheltenham GL54 3AF
☎ Guiting Power (01451) 850716
*77-acre arable and mixed farm. Recently
constructed traditional style Cotswolds
farmhouse. Within walking distance of
Bourton-on-the-Water and the
Slaughters.*
Bedrooms: 1 double, 1 twin, 1 triple
Bathrooms: 3 public

**Bed & breakfast**

| per night: | £min | £max |
|---|---|---|
| Single | 17.00 | 18.00 |
| Double | 34.00 | 36.00 |

Evening meal from 1900
Parking for 6

## NEWENT

Gloucestershire
Map ref 2B1

Small town with the largest
collection of birds of prey in
Europe at the Falconry Centre.
Flying demonstrations daily. Glass
workshop where visitors can watch
glass being blown. There is a
"seconds" shop. North of the
village are Three Choirs Vineyards.
*Tourist Information Centre*
☎ *(01531) 822145*

### Merton House

☎

7 Birches Lane, Newent GL18 1DN
☎ (01531) 820608
*Detached house in attractive gardens,
quiet rural setting, good view to the*

*Malverns and Cotswolds. 1.75 miles
from the market town of Newent.*
Bedrooms: 2 double
Bathrooms: 1 public

**Bed & breakfast**

| per night: | £min | £max |
|---|---|---|
| Single | 18.00 | 20.00 |
| Double | 28.00 | 30.00 |

Parking for 4

### 5 Onslow Road

**Listed**

Newent GL18 1TL
☎ (01531) 821677
*Modern 4 bedroomed house, on south
side of Newent. Last right turn out of
town off old Gloucester Road, third
house on left.*
Bedrooms: 1 single, 1 double, 1 twin
Bathrooms: 1 private, 1 public

**Bed & breakfast**

| per night: | £min | £max |
|---|---|---|
| Single | 13.50 | 18.00 |
| Double | 27.00 | 36.00 |

Parking for 2

## NEWLAND

Gloucestershire
Map ref 2A1

Probably the most attractive of the
villages of the Forest of Dean. The
church is often referred to as "the
Cathedral of the Forest"; it
contains a number of interesting
monuments and the Forest Miner's
Brass. Almshouses nearby were
endowed by William Jones,
founder of Monmouth School.

### Scatterford Farm

**COMMENDED**

Newland, Coleford GL16 8NG
☎ Dean (01594) 836562
Fax (01594) 836323
*Beautiful 15th C farmhouse with
spacious rooms set in the midst of
glorious walking country. Half-a-mile
from Newland village.*
Bedrooms: 2 double, 1 twin
Bathrooms: 3 private

**Bed & breakfast**

| per night: | £min | £max |
|---|---|---|
| Single | 19.50 | 19.50 |
| Double | 39.00 | 39.00 |

Parking for 8

All accommodation in this
guide has been inspected,
or is awaiting inspection,
under the national Crown
scheme.

## NEWPORT

Shropshire
Map ref 4A3

Small market town on the
Shropshire Union Canal has a
wide High Street and a church with
some interesting monuments.
Newport is close to Aqualate Mere
which is the largest lake in
Staffordshire.

### Lane End Farm

Chetwynd, Newport TF10 8BN
☎ Sambrook (01952) 550337
*Delightful period farmhouse set in
lovely countryside. Located on A41 near
Newport. Ideal touring base and
beautiful local walks.*
Bedrooms: 2 double
Bathrooms: 2 private

**Bed & breakfast**

| per night: | £min | £max |
|---|---|---|
| Single | 16.00 | 20.00 |
| Double | 35.00 | 40.00 |

**Half board**

| per person: | £min | £max |
|---|---|---|
| Daily | 23.50 | 27.50 |

Evening meal 1800 (last orders 2100)
Parking for 5

### Sambrook Manor

**Listed**

Sambrook, Newport TF10 8AL
☎ Sambrook (01952) 550256
*260-acre mixed farm. Old manor
farmhouse built in 1702. Close to Stoke
Potteries, Shrewsbury, Ironbridge,
Wolverhampton and many places of
historic interest.*
Bedrooms: 1 single, 1 double, 1 triple
Bathrooms: 2 public

**Bed & breakfast**

| per night: | £min | £max |
|---|---|---|
| Single | 15.00 | 15.00 |
| Double | 30.00 | 30.00 |

Parking for 10

There are separate
sections in this guide
listing groups
specialising in farm
holidays and
accommodation which
is especially suitable
for young people and
organised groups.

## NORTHLEACH

Gloucestershire
Map ref 2B1

Village famous for its beautiful 15th C wool church with its lovely porch and interesting interior. There are also some fine houses including a 17th C wool merchant's house containing Keith Harding's World of Mechanical Music, and the Cotswold Countryside Collection is in the former prison.

### Bank Villas Guesthouse ⚠️
😑😑

West-end, Northleach, Cheltenham GL54 3HG
☎ Cotswold (01451) 860464
*Attractive residence with leaded windows, situated off the historic Fosse Way. An excellent base for exploring the beautiful Cotswolds and local places of interest.*
Bedrooms: 2 single, 1 double, 1 twin, 1 triple
Bathrooms: 1 private, 2 public
**Bed & breakfast**

| per night: | £min | £max |
| --- | --- | --- |
| Single | 17.00 | 18.00 |
| Double | 30.00 | 32.00 |

### Northfield Bed & Breakfast ⚠️
😑😑😑 COMMENDED

Cirencester Road (A429), Northleach, Cheltenham GL54 3JL
☎ Cotswold (01451) 860427
*Detached family house in the country with large gardens and home-grown produce. Excellent centre for visiting the Cotswolds and close to local services.*
Bedrooms: 1 double, 1 twin, 1 triple
Bathrooms: 3 private
**Bed & breakfast**

| per night: | £min | £max |
| --- | --- | --- |
| Single | 20.00 | 20.00 |
| Double | 30.00 | 36.00 |

| **Half board** | | |
| per person: | £min | £max |
| Daily | 28.00 | 30.00 |

Evening meal 1800 (last orders 1900)
Parking for 10

---

**Individual proprietors have supplied all details of accommodation. Although we do check for accuracy, we advise you to confirm the information at the time of booking.**

## NUNEATON

Warwickshire
Map ref 4B3

Busy town with an art gallery and museum which has a permanent exhibition of the work of George Eliot. The library also has an interesting collection of material. Arbury Hall, a fine example of Gothic architecture, is nearby.
*Tourist Information Centre*
☎ *(01203) 384027*

### Triple 'A' Lodge Guest House
Listed

94-96 Coleshill Road, Chapel End, Nuneaton CV10 OPH
☎ Coventry (01203) 394515
Fax (01203) 394515
*Family-run guesthouse on the outskirts of Nuneaton, in the pleasant village of Chapel End. Tea/coffee facilities and colour TV in all rooms. Evening meals available.*
Bedrooms: 3 double, 3 twin
Bathrooms: 2 public
**Bed & breakfast**

| per night: | £min | £max |
| --- | --- | --- |
| Single | 15.00 | 20.00 |
| Double | 24.00 | 30.00 |

Evening meal 1800 (last orders 2130)
Parking for 12
Cards accepted: Diners, Amex

## NYMPSFIELD

Gloucestershire
Map ref 2B1

Pretty village high up in the Cotswolds, with a simple mid-Victorian church and a prehistoric long barrow nearby.

### Rose and Crown Inn ⚠️
😑😑😑 COMMENDED

Nympsfield, Stonehouse GL10 3TU
☎ Dursley (01453) 860240
Fax (01453) 860240
*300-year-old inn, in quiet Cotswold village, close to Cotswold Way. Easy access to M4/M5.*
Bedrooms: 1 double, 3 triple
Bathrooms: 4 private
**Bed & breakfast**

| per night: | £min | £max |
| --- | --- | --- |
| Single | 24.00 | 28.00 |
| Double | 39.00 | 48.00 |

Lunch available
Evening meal 1830 (last orders 2130)
Parking for 30
Cards accepted: Access, Visa, Amex

---

**We advise you to confirm your booking in writing.**

## OAKAMOOR

Staffordshire
Map ref 4B2

Small village below a steep hill amid the glorious scenery of the Churnet Valley. Its industrial links have now gone, as the site of the factory which made 20,000 miles of copper wire for the first Atlantic cable has been transformed into an attractive picnic site on the riverside.

### Bank House ⚠️
😑😑 HIGHLY COMMENDED

Farley Road, Oakamoor, Stoke-on-Trent ST10 3BD
☎ Leek (01538) 702810

*Peaceful, elegantly furnished home with log fires and beautiful views. Fine cuisine, home-made breads. Close to Alton Towers, the Peak Park and the Potteries.*
Bedrooms: 1 single, 1 double, 1 twin
Bathrooms: 3 private
**Bed & breakfast**

| per night: | £min | £max |
| --- | --- | --- |
| Single | 33.00 | |
| Double | 46.00 | 70.00 |

| **Half board** | | |
| per person: | £min | £max |
| Daily | 39.00 | 53.00 |
| Weekly | 218.00 | 297.00 |

Lunch available
Evening meal 1900 (last orders 2130)
Parking for 8
Cards accepted: Access, Visa

### Cotton Lane Farm
Cotton, Oakamoor, Stoke-on-Trent ST10 3DS
☎ (01538) 702033
*10-acre horse farm. Character farmhouse with log fires, oak beams, patchwork quilts, home-made bread. Ideal for walking, cycling and riding. Alton Towers 2 miles.*
Bedrooms: 1 single, 3 double, 1 twin
Bathrooms: 3 private, 3 public
**Bed & breakfast**

| per night: | £min | £max |
| --- | --- | --- |
| Single | 15.00 | 19.00 |
| Double | 30.00 | 35.00 |

*Continued ▶*

## OAKAMOOR

*Continued*

**Half board**

| per person: | £min | £max |
|---|---|---|
| Daily | 20.00 | 25.00 |
| Weekly | 105.00 | 140.00 |

Parking for 10

🛇🖵♿ⓌⒾⓈⒸⓉⓋ🏧﹏🚗∪❔✓✿ 🛶 SP

### Ribden Farm ♨
⚜⚜⚜ HIGHLY COMMENDED

Oakamoor, Stoke-on-Trent ST10 3BW
☎ (01538) 702830

*98-acre livestock farm. Grade II listed
18th C farmhouse in open countryside,
1.5 miles from Alton Towers. TV and
tea/coffee in all rooms.*
Bedrooms: 1 double, 1 twin, 1 family
room
Bathrooms: 3 private

**Bed & breakfast**

| per night: | £min | £max |
|---|---|---|
| Double | 30.00 | 36.00 |

Parking for 3

🛇♿ⓌⒾ✕Ⓜ️ⓉⓋ﹏🚗✿❌🛶🏮

## OMBERSLEY

Hereford and Worcester
Map ref 2B1

A particularly fine village full of
black and white houses including
the 17th C Dower House and
some old inns. The church
contains the original box pews.

### The Crown and Sandys
Arms ♨
⚜⚜ APPROVED

Ombersley, Droitwich, Worcestershire
WR9 0EW
☎ Worcester (01905) 620252
Fax (01905) 620769
*Freehouse with comfortable bedrooms,
draught beers and open fires. Home-
cooked meals available lunchtime and
evenings, 7 days a week.*
Bedrooms: 1 single, 5 double, 1 twin
Bathrooms: 6 private, 1 public

**Bed & breakfast**

| per night: | £min | £max |
|---|---|---|
| Single | 20.00 | 30.00 |
| Double | 35.00 | 40.00 |

Lunch available
Evening meal 1800 (last orders 2145)
Parking for 100
Cards accepted: Access, Visa, Switch/
Delta

🛇Ⓔ🖵♿🍴✕Ⓜ️ⓉⓋ﹏🚗▮10-30
∪✿❌🏮

## ONNELEY

Staffordshire
Map ref 4A2

### The Wheatsheaf Inn at
Onneley ♨
⚜⚜⚜⚜ COMMENDED

Bar Hill Road, Onneley, Madeley,
Crewe CW3 9QF
☎ Stoke-on-Trent (01782) 751581
Fax (01782) 751499
*18th C country inn with bars, Spanish
restaurant, conference and function
facilities. On A525, 3 miles from
Bridgemere and Keele University, 7
miles from Newcastle-under-Lyme.
Prices are per room.*
Bedrooms: 4 double, 1 twin
Bathrooms: 5 private

**Bed & breakfast**

| per night: | £min | £max |
|---|---|---|
| Single | 45.00 | 45.00 |
| Double | 45.00 | 60.00 |

Lunch available
Evening meal 1800 (last orders 2130)
Parking for 150
Cards accepted: Access, Visa, Diners,
Amex

🛇📞Ⓔ🖵♿🍴Ⓘ Ⓢ Ⓜ️﹏🚗▮2-100
◗∪❔✿ⓄⒶⓅ SP Ⓣ

## OSWESTRY

Shropshire
Map ref 4A3

Town close to the Welsh border,
the scene of many battles. To the
north are the remains of a large
Iron Age hill fort. An excellent
centre for exploring Shropshire
and Offa's Dyke.
*Tourist Information Centre*
☎ *(01691) 662488*

### April Spring Cottage
⚜

Nantmawr, Oswestry SY10 9HL
☎ Llansantffraid (01691) 828802
*Friendly guesthouse with cosy lounge,
comfortable bedrooms, traditional
cooking, sunny peaceful garden.
Spectacular unspoilt countryside, quiet
roads. Guided walking and painting.*
Bedrooms: 1 double, 1 twin
Bathrooms: 1 public

**Bed & breakfast**

| per night: | £min | £max |
|---|---|---|
| Single | 15.50 | |
| Double | 31.00 | |

**Half board**

| per person: | £min | £max |
|---|---|---|
| Daily | 23.00 | |
| Weekly | 161.00 | |

Evening meal 1830 (last orders 2000)
Parking for 6

🛇8🍴🖵♿🍴Ⓦ🍴ⒾⓈ✕ⓉⓋ﹏🚗∪❔
✿❌🏮

### Frankton House
⚜⚜

Welsh Frankton, Oswestry SY11 4PA
☎ (01691) 623422

*Large old farmhouse, completely
refurbished in 1993 as a guesthouse. In
rural Shropshire, close to A5. Canal
and hire boats nearby, also riding
stables.*
Bedrooms: 1 single, 1 double, 2 twin
Bathrooms: 2 private, 1 public

**Bed & breakfast**

| per night: | £min | £max |
|---|---|---|
| Single | 16.00 | 17.50 |
| Double | 32.00 | 35.00 |

Parking for 14
Open February-November

🖵♿🍴ⓌⒾ✕Ⓜ️ⓉⓋ﹏🚗✿❌🏮

### Pant-Hir
⚜⚜

Croesaubach, Oswestry SY10 9BH
☎ Llansilin (01691) 70457
*25-acre horse farm. Just outside
Oswestry in beautiful rural
surroundings lies this attractive
smallholding. The bedrooms are en-suite
with TV. Added attraction is the
miniature horse stud.*
Bedrooms: 1 double, 1 twin
Bathrooms: 2 private

**Bed & breakfast**

| per night: | £min | £max |
|---|---|---|
| Single | 25.00 | |
| Double | 32.00 | |

**Half board**

| per person: | £min | £max |
|---|---|---|
| Daily | 24.00 | |
| Weekly | 160.00 | |

Evening meal 1900 (last orders 2000)
Parking for 10
Open January-November

🛇10Ⓔ🖵♿🍴Ⓦ🍴Ⓜ️ⓉⓋ﹏🚗✿🏮

### Rhoswiel Lodge ♨
Listed

Weston Rhyn, Oswestry SY10 7TG
☎ Chirk (01691) 777609
*Victorian country house in pleasant
surroundings beside Llangollen Canal, 4
miles north of Oswestry. 300 yards from
the A5.*
Bedrooms: 1 double, 1 twin
Bathrooms: 2 private, 2 public

**Bed & breakfast**

| per night: | £min | £max |
|---|---|---|
| Single | 18.00 | 20.00 |
| Double | 32.00 | 35.00 |

Parking for 6

🛇🖵♿ⓌⒾⓈⓉⓋ﹏🚗✿❌🏮

## Three Firs

Listed

The High, Pant, Oswestry SY10 8LB
☎ (01691) 831375
*5-acre horse farm. Quiet, comfortable, homely countryside accommodation, adjoining golf-course, Offa's Dyke and bridleways. Open log fire, full English breakfast.*
Bedrooms: 2 family rooms
Bathrooms: 1 private, 1 public

**Bed & breakfast**

| per night: | £min | £max |
|---|---|---|
| Single | 15.00 | 19.00 |
| Double | 30.00 | 38.00 |

**Half board**

| per person: | £min | £max |
|---|---|---|
| Daily | 20.00 | 22.50 |
| Weekly | 120.00 | 135.00 |

Parking for 6

---

### PAINSWICK

Gloucestershire
Map ref 2B1

Picturesque wool town with inns and houses dating from the 14th C. Painswick House is a Palladian mansion with Chinese wallpaper. The churchyard is famous for its yew trees.

## Brookhouse Mill Cottage

Listed

Tibbiwell Lane, Painswick, Stroud
GL6 6YA
☎ (01452) 812854
Fax (01452) 812854

*17th C cottage with inglenook fireplaces and oak beams. Garden straddles trout stream, lake and waterfalls yet is within short distance of village centre. Patchwork quilts on beds and for sale. Use of swimming pool.*
Bedrooms: 1 double
Bathrooms: 1 private, 1 public

**Bed & breakfast**

| per night: | £min | £max |
|---|---|---|
| Single | 20.00 | 24.95 |
| Double | 36.00 | 38.00 |

Parking for 5

## The Dream Factory

APPROVED

Friday Street, Painswick, Stroud
GL6 6QJ
☎ (01452) 812379

*Grade II listed building, in the centre of the village known as the "Queen of the Cotswolds".*
Bedrooms: 1 double
Bathrooms: 1 private

**Bed & breakfast**

| per night: | £min | £max |
|---|---|---|
| Single | | 20.00 |
| Double | | 40.00 |

## Hambutts Mynd

Edge Road, Painswick, Stroud
GL6 6UP
☎ (01452) 812352
*Old corn windmill, c1700-50, with original beams. Panoramic views from all bedrooms. Close to village centre. Weekly rates available.*
Bedrooms: 1 single, 1 double, 1 twin
Bathrooms: 1 private, 1 public

**Bed & breakfast**

| per night: | £min | £max |
|---|---|---|
| Single | 19.00 | 22.00 |
| Double | 37.00 | 39.00 |

Parking for 3
Open February-December

## Upper Doreys Mill

Edge, Painswick, Stroud GL6 6NF
☎ (01452) 812459
*18th C cloth mill with log fires and old beams. By a stream and in a rural setting. Half a mile from Painswick, down Edge Lane.*
Bedrooms: 2 double, 1 twin
Bathrooms: 3 private

**Bed & breakfast**

| per night: | £min | £max |
|---|---|---|
| Single | 22.00 | |
| Double | 36.00 | |

Parking for 6

---

### RENDCOMB

Gloucestershire
Map ref 2B1

## Shawswell Country House

DE LUXE

Rendcomb, Cirencester GL7 7HD
☎ Cirencester (01285) 831779
*17th C country house with quality accommodation. Idyllic setting in 25 acres offering peace and tranquillity and wonderful views. From A435 take turning to Rendcomb and follow "no through road" to the end.*
Bedrooms: 1 single, 3 double, 1 twin
Bathrooms: 5 private

**Bed & breakfast**

| per night: | £min | £max |
|---|---|---|
| Single | 25.00 | 35.00 |
| Double | 45.00 | 55.00 |

**Half board**

| per person: | £min | £max |
|---|---|---|
| Daily | 41.00 | 51.00 |

Evening meal 1900 (last orders 2000)
Parking for 8
Open February-November

---

### ROCESTER

Staffordshire
Map ref 4B2

## The Leeze Guest House

63 High Street, Rocester, Uttoxeter
ST14 5JU
☎ (01889) 591146
Fax (01889) 591146
*Just off the B5030 Uttoxeter to Ashbourne road, handy for Peak District, Potteries, Alton Towers and Churnet Valley. Traditional country cooking.*
Bedrooms: 2 twin, 3 triple
Bathrooms: 1 private, 2 public

**Bed & breakfast**

| per night: | £min | £max |
|---|---|---|
| Single | 16.00 | 24.00 |
| Double | 28.00 | 34.00 |

**Half board**

| per person: | £min | £max |
|---|---|---|
| Daily | 22.00 | 32.00 |

Evening meal 1800 (last orders 1600)
Parking for 6

---

### ROCK

Hereford and Worcester
Map ref 4A3

## The Old Forge

Listed

Gorst Hill, Rock, Kidderminster,
Worcestershire DY14 9YG
☎ (01299) 266745
*Recently renovated country cottage, near the Wyre Forest. Ideal for country walks and visiting local places of interest. Short and midweek breaks.*
Bedrooms: 1 double, 1 twin
Bathrooms: 1 public

**Bed & breakfast**

| per night: | £min | £max |
|---|---|---|
| Single | 14.00 | 15.00 |
| Double | 26.00 | 28.00 |

Parking for 5

National Crown ratings were correct at the time of going to press but are subject to change. Please check at the time of booking.

## ROSS-ON-WYE

Hereford and Worcester
Map ref 2A1

Attractive market town with a 17th C market hall, set above the River Wye. There are lovely views over the surrounding countryside from the Prospect and the town is close to Goodrich Castle and the Welsh border.
*Tourist Information Centre*
☎ *(01989) 562768*

### The Arches Hotel
Walford Road, Ross-on-Wye, Herefordshire HR9 5TP
☎ (01989) 563348
*Small family-run hotel set in half an acre of lawned gardens, half a mile from town centre. Warm, friendly atmosphere. All rooms furnished to a high standard and with views of the garden. Victorian conservatory in which to relax.*
Bedrooms: 1 single, 4 double, 2 twin, 1 triple
Bathrooms: 6 private, 2 public, 2 private showers

**Bed & breakfast**

| per night: | £min | £max |
|---|---|---|
| Single | 18.00 | 24.00 |
| Double | 32.00 | 42.00 |

**Half board**

| per person: | £min | £max |
|---|---|---|
| Daily | 26.00 | 31.00 |
| Weekly | 178.00 | 213.00 |

Evening meal from 1900
Parking for 8
Cards accepted: Access, Visa
🛌🕹🖵🕯🅂🗝🗡🖩📠❄✕🚗 ᴼᴬᴾ 🆂🅿

### The Ashe ⋀
🛏
Bridstow, Ross-on-Wye, Herefordshire HR9 6QA
☎ (01989) 563336
*200-acre mixed farm. 15th C sandstone farmhouse with oak beams and panelling. In beautiful countryside. Ideal for walking and touring Wye Valley, Forest of Dean and Wales. 2 miles north of Ross-on-Wye. Golf, fishing and tennis on the farm.*
Bedrooms: 1 double, 1 twin
Bathrooms: 2 private

**Bed & breakfast**

| per night: | £min | £max |
|---|---|---|
| Single | 15.00 | 15.50 |
| Double | 30.00 | 31.00 |

Parking for 8
🛌🖵🆄🅂🗝🗡📺🖩📠❄🔑❄✕🚗 🆂🅿

### Brook House ⋀
🛏
Lea, Ross-on-Wye, Herefordshire HR9 7JZ
☎ (01989) 750710

*Fine Queen Anne Grade II listed house offering a warm welcome, comfortable rooms and open fires. Home-cooked and produced fare. Home-made muffins a speciality.*
Bedrooms: 2 double, 1 twin
Bathrooms: 1 private, 1 public, 2 private showers

**Bed & breakfast**

| per night: | £min | £max |
|---|---|---|
| Single | 17.00 | |
| Double | 31.00 | 36.00 |

Evening meal 1900 (last orders 1800)
Parking for 2
Cards accepted: Access, Visa, Amex
🛌8🖵🖵🖩🆄🗝🅂🗡🖩📺🖩📠❄🚗🆂🏵

### Edde Cross House ⋀
🏆 HIGHLY COMMENDED
Edde Cross Street, Ross-on-Wye, Herefordshire HR9 7BZ
☎ (01989) 565088
*Delightful Georgian town house overlooking river, with the atmosphere and character of a comfortable private home. Close to town centre. Bedrooms with colour TV and beverage tray. All rooms en-suite or with private bathroom. No smoking house.*
Bedrooms: 3 double, 1 twin
Bathrooms: 4 private

**Bed & breakfast**

| per night: | £min | £max |
|---|---|---|
| Single | 25.00 | 35.00 |
| Double | 40.00 | 46.00 |

Open February-November
🛌10🖵🕯🆄🅂🗡🖩❄🚗✕🚗🏵

### Lavender Cottage
Listed
Bridstow, Ross-on-Wye, Herefordshire HR9 6QB
☎ (01989) 62836
*Part 17th C character property, 1 mile from Ross-on-Wye. Take Hereford road, turn right to Foy and then first turning on left.*
Bedrooms: 1 double, 2 twin
Bathrooms: 1 public

**Bed & breakfast**

| per night: | £min | £max |
|---|---|---|
| Single | 18.00 | 20.00 |
| Double | 30.00 | 34.00 |

**Half board**

| per person: | £min | £max |
|---|---|---|
| Daily | 26.00 | 28.00 |
| Weekly | 160.00 | 170.00 |

Evening meal from 1830
Parking for 3
🛌5🖵🕯🆄🗝🗡📺🖩📠❄✕🚗🏵

### Linton Hall ⋀
🛏🛏🛏 HIGHLY COMMENDED
Gorsley, Ross-on-Wye, Herefordshire HR9 7SP
☎ Gorsley (01989) 720276
*Built c1888, set in 8.5 acres of gardens, woodlands and pasture. One mile from junction 3, M50 on B4215 to Newent.*
Bedrooms: 1 double, 2 twin
Bathrooms: 3 private

**Bed & breakfast**

| per night: | £min | £max |
|---|---|---|
| Single | 30.00 | 40.00 |
| Double | 50.00 | 60.00 |

**Half board**

| per person: | £min | £max |
|---|---|---|
| Daily | 45.00 | 57.50 |

Parking for 6
🖵🖩🕯🗝✕🖩📠❄🚗🔑🕯❄🚗🏵

### Merrivale Place ⋀
🛏 COMMENDED
The Avenue, Ross-on-Wye, Herefordshire HR9 5AW
☎ (01989) 564929
*Fine Victorian house in quiet tree-lined avenue. Large comfortable rooms and lovely views. Home cooking. Near town and river.*
Bedrooms: 1 double, 1 twin, 1 triple
Bathrooms: 2 public

**Bed & breakfast**

| per night: | £min | £max |
|---|---|---|
| Single | 18.00 | |
| Double | 32.00 | 35.00 |

**Half board**

| per person: | £min | £max |
|---|---|---|
| Daily | 25.00 | 26.50 |
| Weekly | 168.00 | 175.00 |

Evening meal 1830 (last orders 1600)
Parking for 6
Open March-October
🛌🕯🆄🅂🗡🖩📺🖩📠❄✕🚗🏵

### Norton House
🛏🛏 COMMENDED
Whitchurch, Ross-on-Wye, Herefordshire HR9 6DJ
☎ Monmouth (01600) 890046
*300-year-old former farmhouse, tastefully improved, with wealth of original features. Renowned home cooking, friendly atmosphere, quality and comfort paramount.*
Bedrooms: 3 double
Bathrooms: 3 private

**Bed & breakfast**

| per night: | £min | £max |
|---|---|---|
| Double | 37.00 | 40.00 |

**Half board**

| per person: | £min | £max |
|---|---|---|
| Daily | 31.45 | 32.95 |

Parking for 6
🖵🕯🆄🗝🅂🗡🖩📠❄✕🚗🆂🏵

### The Skakes ⋀
🛏🛏
Glewstone, Ross-on-Wye, Herefordshire HR9 6AZ
☎ (01989) 770456

*Country guesthouse combining 18th C character with 20th C comforts. Perfect for Symonds Yat, Wye Valley, Forest of Dean. Home cooking.*
Bedrooms: 2 single, 4 double, 2 twin
Bathrooms: 2 private, 3 public

**Bed & breakfast**

| per night: | £min | £max |
| --- | --- | --- |
| Single | 20.00 | 20.00 |
| Double | 30.00 | 40.00 |

**Half board**

| per person: | £min | £max |
| --- | --- | --- |
| Daily | 25.00 | 30.00 |
| Weekly | 157.50 | 189.00 |

Evening meal 1900 (last orders 1900)
Parking for 8
Cards accepted: Access, Visa

### Thatch Close

**COMMENDED**

Llangrove, Ross-on-Wye, Herefordshire
HR9 6EL
☎ Llangarron (01989) 770300
*13-acre mixed farm. Secluded Georgian country farmhouse midway between Ross-on-Wye and Monmouth. Home-produced vegetables and meat. Ideal for country lovers of any age. Guests welcome to help with animals. Map sent on request. Ordnance Survey: 51535196.*
Bedrooms: 1 double, 1 twin, 1 triple
Bathrooms: 3 private

**Bed & breakfast**

| per night: | £min | £max |
| --- | --- | --- |
| Double | 30.00 | 36.00 |

**Half board**

| per person: | £min | £max |
| --- | --- | --- |
| Daily | 25.00 | 46.00 |

Lunch available
Evening meal 1830 (last orders 1800)
Parking for 7

### Underhill Farm

Foy, Ross-on-Wye, Herefordshire
HR9 6RD
☎ (01989) 67950
*400-acre mixed farm. Old farmhouse within 300 yards of the River Wye, overlooking the Wye Valley, 4 miles from Ross-on-Wye. In an Area of Outstanding Natural Beauty.*
Bedrooms: 1 single, 1 double, 1 twin
Bathrooms: 1 public

Please mention this guide when making a booking.

**Bed & breakfast**

| per night: | £min | £max |
| --- | --- | --- |
| Single | 14.00 | 15.00 |
| Double | 28.00 | 30.00 |

Parking for 4
Open March-October

## RUGBY

Warwickshire
Map ref 4C3

Town famous for its public school which gave its name to Rugby Union football and which featured in "Tom Brown's Schooldays".
*Tourist Information Centre*
*☎ (01788) 535348*

### Lawford Hill Farm

Lawford Hill Lane, Rugby CV23 9HG
☎ (01788) 542001
*100-acre mixed farm. Bed and breakfast all the year round in this spacious Georgian farmhouse. Close to National Agricultural Centre, Stratford-upon-Avon and the Cotswolds.*
Bedrooms: 2 double, 1 twin
Bathrooms: 1 public

**Bed & breakfast**

| per night: | £min | £max |
| --- | --- | --- |
| Single | 15.00 | 18.00 |
| Double | 30.00 | 35.00 |

Parking for 6

### White Lion Inn

**Listed** **APPROVED**

Coventry Road, Pailton, Rugby
CV23 0QD
☎ (01788) 832359
*17th C coaching inn, recently refurbished but maintaining all old world features. Close to Rugby, Coventry and Stratford. Within 2 miles of motorways.*
Bedrooms: 6 twin
Bathrooms: 6 private, 2 public

**Bed & breakfast**

| per night: | £min | £max |
| --- | --- | --- |
| Single | 17.50 | 18.50 |
| Double | 35.00 | 37.00 |

Lunch available
Evening meal 1830 (last orders 2200)
Parking for 60
Cards accepted: Access, Visa

Individual proprietors have supplied all details of accommodation. Although we do check for accuracy, we advise you to confirm the information at the time of booking.

## RUSHTON SPENCER

Staffordshire
Map ref 4B2

Village with an interesting church built in the 14th C of wood, some of which still remains. It is close to the pleasant Rudyard Reservoir.

### Barnswood Farm

**Listed**

Rushton Spencer, Macclesfield,
Cheshire SK11 0RA
☎ (01260) 226261
*100-acre dairy farm. In a lovely setting overlooking Rudyard Lake 400 yards down the field. Alton Towers, Peak District and the Potteries all within a 15 mile radius. Homely welcome, English breakfast.*
Bedrooms: 1 double, 1 triple, 1 family room
Bathrooms: 1 public

**Bed & breakfast**

| per night: | £min | £max |
| --- | --- | --- |
| Single | 15.00 | |
| Double | 26.00 | |

Parking for 5

## RUYTON-XI-TOWNS

Shropshire
Map ref 4A3

Town got its name from the time when, at the beginning of the 14th C, it was one of 11 towns "joined" into 1 manor. It is situated above the River Perry and has the remains of a castle in the churchyard.

### Brownhill House

**COMMENDED**

Ruyton-XI-Towns, Shrewsbury
SY4 1LR
☎ Baschurch (01939) 260626
*Quality accommodation, all en-suite, with first-class service. Good food and conversation, bring your own wine, extensive breakfast menu, non-stop tea/coffee. Local pubs. Unique hillside garden. Phone/fax for details.*
Bedrooms: 1 twin, 1 triple
Bathrooms: 2 private, 1 public

**Bed & breakfast**

| per night: | £min | £max |
| --- | --- | --- |
| Single | 16.00 | |
| Double | 33.00 | |

**Half board**

| per person: | £min | £max |
| --- | --- | --- |
| Daily | 24.00 | |

Lunch available
Evening meal 1800 (last orders 1600)
Parking for 5

## SEVERN STOKE

Hereford and Worcester
Map ref 2B1

Village to the south of Worcester with a picturesque group of houses surrounding the church and magnificent views across the Severn to the Malvern Hills.

### Madge Hill House
≋≋

Severn Stoke, Worcester WR8 9JN
☎ (01905) 371362
*Georgian house in peaceful country setting, between Tewkesbury and Worcester on A38. En-suite bedrooms with TV.*
Bedrooms: 1 double, 1 twin
Bathrooms: 2 private
**Bed & breakfast**

| per night: | £min | £max |
|---|---|---|
| Single | 17.00 | |
| Double | 34.00 | |

Parking for 2

## SHIFNAL

Shropshire
Map ref 4A3

Small market town, once an important staging centre for coaches on the Holyhead road. Where industrialism has not prevailed, the predominating architectural impression is Georgian, though some timber-framed houses survived the Great Fire of 1591.

### Drayton Lodge ⋈
Listed

Opposite Shifnal Golf Club, Shifnal TF11 8QW
☎ Telford (01952) 460244
*Family farmhouse where our children have grown up and left the nest. We enjoy good company. Easy reach of Weston Park, Ironbridge and Cosford. Evening meal by arrangement.*
Bedrooms: 2 single, 1 double, 1 twin
Bathrooms: 1 private, 1 public
**Bed & breakfast**

| per night: | £min | £max |
|---|---|---|
| Single | 14.00 | 16.00 |
| Double | 25.00 | 30.00 |

Parking for 20

National Crown ratings were correct at the time of going to press but are subject to change. Please check at the time of booking.

## SHREWSBURY

Shropshire
Map ref 4A3

Beautiful historic town on the River Severn retaining many fine old timber-framed houses. Its attractions include Rowley's Museum with Roman finds, remains of a castle, Clive House Museum, St Chad's 18th C round church and rowing on the river.
*Tourist Information Centre*
*☎ (01743) 350761*

### Acton Burnell Farm
Listed

Acton Burnell, Shrewsbury SY5 7PQ
☎ Acton Burnell (01694) 731207
*300-acre arable farm. Comfortable farmhouse in village. Residents' lounge with TV. 8 miles from Shrewsbury and 6 miles from Church Stretton.*
Bedrooms: 1 twin
Bathrooms: 1 public
**Bed & breakfast**

| per night: | £min | £max |
|---|---|---|
| Single | 15.00 | |
| Double | 30.00 | |

Parking for 4
Open April-October

### Ashton Lees
≋≋ COMMENDED

Dorrington, Shrewsbury SY5 7JW
☎ Dorrington (01743) 718378
*Comfortable family home set in large secluded garden, 6 miles south of Shrewsbury on A49. Convenient for exploring the town and surrounding countryside.*
Bedrooms: 2 double, 1 twin
Bathrooms: 1 private, 1 public
**Bed & breakfast**

| per night: | £min | £max |
|---|---|---|
| Single | 17.00 | 34.00 |
| Double | 34.00 | |

Parking for 6

### The Bancroft ⋈
Listed

17 Coton Crescent, Shrewsbury SY1 2NY
☎ (01743) 231746
*This warm, friendly guesthouse, with central heating, welcome tray, and colour TV in rooms, is an easy walk to bus/railway and Brother Cadfael trail, alongside the river.*
Bedrooms: 1 single, 1 twin, 1 triple
Bathrooms: 1 public
**Bed & breakfast**

| per night: | £min | £max |
|---|---|---|
| Single | 16.00 | |
| Double | 30.00 | |

**Half board**

| per person: | £min | £max |
|---|---|---|
| Daily | 24.00 | |

Evening meal from 1830
Parking for 3
Cards accepted: Access, Visa

### Bull Inn
Listed

Butcher Row, Shrewsbury SY1 1UW
☎ (01743) 344728
*Town centre public house with beer garden serving drinks 11am-11pm Monday to Saturday, 12noon to 3pm Sunday. Food is served 9am-9.30pm (Sunday 12-2pm and 7pm-9.30pm)*
Bedrooms: 4 double, 3 twin
Bathrooms: 7 private, 2 public
**Bed & breakfast**

| per night: | £min | £max |
|---|---|---|
| Single | 35.00 | |
| Double | 50.00 | |

Lunch available
Evening meal 1800 (last orders 2130)

### Cardeston Park Farm
≋ COMMENDED

Ford, Shrewsbury SY5 9NH
☎ (01743) 884265
*150-acre mixed farm. Spacious farmhouse set in countryside on the English/Welsh border. On A458 Shrewsbury to Welshpool road, 7 miles from Shrewsbury, 13 miles from Welshpool.*
Bedrooms: 1 single, 1 double, 1 twin
Bathrooms: 2 private, 1 public
**Bed & breakfast**

| per night: | £min | £max |
|---|---|---|
| Single | 15.00 | 18.00 |
| Double | 30.00 | 32.00 |

Parking for 4

### Chatford House ⋈
≋

Bayston Hill, Shrewsbury SY3 0AY
☎ (01743) 718301
*5-acre mixed farm. Comfortable farmhouse built in 1776, 5.5 miles south of Shrewsbury off A49. Through Bayston Hill, take third right (Stapleton) then right to Chatford.*
Bedrooms: 3 twin
Bathrooms: 1 public
**Bed & breakfast**

| per night: | £min | £max |
|---|---|---|
| Single | 13.00 | 14.00 |
| Double | 26.00 | 28.00 |

Parking for 4
Open April-October

### Glynndene
Listed

Abbey Foregate, Shrewsbury SY2 6BL
☎ (01743) 352488
*Pleasant and friendly bed and breakfast, overlooking the Abbey church grounds. Ideal for touring "Brother Cadfael" country.*
Bedrooms: 2 double, 1 twin
Bathrooms: 1 public

**Bed & breakfast**

| per night: | £min | £max |
|---|---|---|
| Single | 14.00 | 16.00 |
| Double | 28.00 | 32.00 |

Parking for 3

♒3❑☆♆☜Ⓤ🄻🛈Ⓢ🏛,🚪🚋

## Hillsboro
Listed

1 Port Hill Gardens, Shrewsbury
SY3 8SH
☎ (01743) 231033
*Charming Edwardian private house in
quiet residential area, near park, river
and Shrewsbury School. 5 minutes from
town centre. Traditional breakfast a
speciality. Parking.*
Bedrooms: 1 double, 1 twin
Bathrooms: 1 public

**Bed & breakfast**

| per night: | £min | £max |
|---|---|---|
| Single | 15.00 | 15.00 |
| Double | 30.00 | 30.00 |

Parking for 2

♒8❑☆♆☜Ⓤ🄻🛈Ⓢ🗡🛏🏛,🚪✈🚋Ⓣ

## Merevale House
Listed COMMENDED

66 Ellesmere Road, Shrewsbury
SY1 2QP
☎ (01743) 243677
*Comfortable, attractive, detached
Victorian house, 10 minutes' walk from
town and railway station. On bus route.
Private parking. Many extra home
comforts. Brochure. Weekly reductions.*
Bedrooms: 3 double
Bathrooms: 1 public

**Bed & breakfast**

| per night: | £min | £max |
|---|---|---|
| Double | 30.00 | 30.00 |

Parking for 8

♒☐❑☆♆☜Ⓤ Ⓢ🏛,🚪✈🚋 SP

## Shorthill Lodge ♙
HIGHLY COMMENDED

Shorthill, Lea Cross, Shrewsbury
SY5 8JE
☎ (01743) 860864
*Attractive, comfortable house in open
country setting, inglenook log fire and
centrally heated in winter. Five miles
south of Shrewsbury, off A488. Nearby
pub, restaurant and golf course.
Brochure available.*
Bedrooms: 1 double, 1 twin
Bathrooms: 2 private, 1 public

**Bed & breakfast**

| per night: | £min | £max |
|---|---|---|
| Single | 20.00 | 20.00 |
| Double | 32.00 | 36.00 |

Parking for 3

♒☐❑☆♆🛈Ⓢ🗡🛏🆃🏛,🛲🚪◗
❄🚋

## The Stiperstones Guest House ♙
COMMENDED

18 Coton Crescent, Coton Hill,
Shrewsbury SY1 2NZ
☎ (01743) 246720 & 350303
Fax (01743) 350303
*Always a warm welcome. Tastefully
furnished accommodation, very
comfortable and clean with extensive
facilities. Off-road parking. Close to
town centre and river.*
Bedrooms: 1 single, 3 double, 1 twin,
1 triple
Bathrooms: 3 public

**Bed & breakfast**

| per night: | £min | £max |
|---|---|---|
| Single | 16.00 | 16.00 |
| Double | 30.00 | 32.00 |

**Half board**

| per person: | £min | £max |
|---|---|---|
| Daily | 24.00 | 24.00 |
| Weekly | 156.00 | 156.00 |

Evening meal 1930 (last orders 1200)
Parking for 8

♒☆❑☆♆Ⓤ🛈Ⓢ🗡🛏🆃🏛,🚪❄✈
🚋 DAP 🐾 SP

## Sydney House Hotel
♕♕♕

Coton Crescent, Coton Hill,
Shrewsbury SY1 2LJ
☎ (01743) 354681 & Freephone 0500
130243
Fax (01743) 354681
*Edwardian town house with period
features, 10 minutes' walk from town
centre and railway station. Most rooms
en-suite. All with direct dial telephone,
colour TV, hot drink facilities and
hairdryer.*
Bedrooms: 2 single, 2 double, 2 twin,
1 triple
Bathrooms: 4 private, 2 public

**Bed & breakfast**

| per night: | £min | £max |
|---|---|---|
| Single | 32.00 | 45.00 |
| Double | 42.00 | 55.00 |

**Half board**

| per person: | £min | £max |
|---|---|---|
| Daily | 30.00 | 52.50 |
| Weekly | 207.50 | 360.00 |

Lunch available
Evening meal 1930 (last orders 2100)
Parking for 7
Cards accepted: Access, Visa, Amex

♒☎☐❑☆♆🛈Ⓢ🗡🛏🏛,🚪
🆃10-15🔱✈🚋 DAP SP 🎣Ⓣ

## Upper Brompton Farm
♕♕ COMMENDED

Brompton, Cross Houses, Shrewsbury
SY5 6LE
☎ Cross Houses (01743) 761629

*316-acre arable & livestock farm.
Elegant Georgian farmhouse with
relaxed friendly atmosphere and
comfortable accommodation amid peace
and tranquillity. Home-cooked
farmhouse fare available.*
Bedrooms: 1 double, 1 twin, 1 family
room
Bathrooms: 3 private

**Bed & breakfast**

| per night: | £min | £max |
|---|---|---|
| Single | 28.00 | 30.00 |
| Double | 36.00 | 40.00 |

**Half board**

| per person: | £min | £max |
|---|---|---|
| Daily | 30.50 | 32.50 |

Evening meal from 1830
Parking for 10

♒🛏❑☆♆☜Ⓤ🛈Ⓢ🗡🛏🚪🔱✓
❄🚋

## The White House ♙
♕♕♕ COMMENDED

Hanwood, Shrewsbury SY5 8LP
☎ (01743) 860414

*Relaxing 16th C guesthouse with large,
peaceful gardens. Handy for
Shrewsbury, Ironbridge and mid-Wales.
Short breaks available all year.*
Bedrooms: 1 single, 4 double, 1 twin
Bathrooms: 2 private, 1 public

**Bed & breakfast**

| per night: | £min | £max |
|---|---|---|
| Single | 20.00 | 30.00 |
| Double | 40.00 | 50.00 |

**Half board**

| per person: | £min | £max |
|---|---|---|
| Daily | 32.50 | 46.00 |
| Weekly | 227.50 | 322.00 |

Evening meal 1930 (last orders 2030)
Parking for 15

♆🛈Ⓢ🗡🛏🆃🏛,🚪♪❄✈🚋 SP 🎣

## Woodstock
Listed COMMENDED

Stretton Lane, Halfway House,
Shrewsbury SY5 9EG
☎ (01743) 884373
*Old house with character in quiet
countryside setting, half a mile from the
main road and accessible to local
amenities. South-west of Shrewsbury.*
Bedrooms: 1 double, 1 twin, 1 triple
*Continued ▶*

## SHREWSBURY

*Continued*

Bathrooms: 2 private, 1 public
**Bed & breakfast**

| per night: | £min | £max |
|---|---|---|
| Single | 17.50 | 25.00 |
| Double | 30.00 | 40.00 |

Parking for 8

🛏🗝♨🕿♿👜✗🚭📺🎮💻🖨🌼🐕🏧

## SLIMBRIDGE

Gloucestershire
Map ref 2B1

The Wildfowl and Wetlands Trust Centre was founded by Sir Peter Scott and has the world's largest collection of wildfowl. Of special interest are the wild swans and the geese which wander around the grounds.

### Tudor Arms Lodge

👑👑 **COMMENDED**

Shepherds Patch, Slimbridge, Gloucester GL2 7BP
🕿 Dursley (01453) 890306
*Newly-built lodge adjoining an 18th C freehouse, alongside Gloucester and Sharpness Canal. Renowned Slimbridge Wildfowl and Wetlands Trust centre only 800 yards away.*
Bedrooms: 4 double, 5 twin, 2 triple, 1 family room
Bathrooms: 12 private
**Bed & breakfast**

| per night: | £min | £max |
|---|---|---|
| Single | 29.50 | 32.50 |
| Double | 39.50 | 42.50 |

**Half board**

| per person: | £min | £max |
|---|---|---|
| Daily | 28.60 | 38.40 |
| Weekly | 175.00 | 227.50 |

Lunch available
Evening meal 1900 (last orders 2200)
Parking for 70
Cards accepted: Access, Visa, Amex

🛏👤🕿🍴🗝♨🕿🛎📺💻🖨🛎15 🍷▶✗

There are separate sections in this guide listing groups specialising in farm holidays and accommodation which is especially suitable for young people and organised groups.

## SOLIHULL

West Midlands
Map ref 4B3

On the outskirts of Birmingham. Some Tudor houses and a 13th C church remain amongst the new public buildings and shopping centre. The 16th C Malvern Hall is now a school and the 15th C Chester House at Knowle is now a library.
*Tourist Information Centre*
🕿 (0121) 704 6130

### The Gate House

Listed

Barston Lane, Barston, Solihull B92 0JN
🕿 Barston (01675) 443274
*Early Victorian mansion house set in beautiful countryside. Close to the National Exhibition Centre, International Convention Centre, airport and motorway.*
Bedrooms: 1 single, 1 double, 2 twin
Bathrooms: 3 private, 1 public
**Bed & breakfast**

| per night: | £min | £max |
|---|---|---|
| Single | 20.00 | 25.00 |
| Double | 36.00 | 40.00 |

Parking for 20

🛏👤📭🗝♨🍷🕿🛎📺💻🖨🌼✗

## STIPERSTONES

Shropshire
Map ref 4A3

Below the spectacular ridge of the same name, from which superb views over moorland, forest and hills may be enjoyed.

### Sycamore Cottage

👑👑 **COMMENDED**

5 Perkins Beach, Stiperstones, Minsterley, Shrewsbury SY5 0PQ
🕿 Shrewsbury (01743) 790914
*Delightful accommodation in beamed cottage at foot of Stiperstones Hills. Log fires. Friendly welcome. Wonderful views. Ideal walking country.*
Bedrooms: 1 twin
Bathrooms: 1 private
**Bed & breakfast**

| per night: | £min | £max |
|---|---|---|
| Single | | 16.50 |
| Double | | 33.00 |

**Half board**

| per person: | £min | £max |
|---|---|---|
| Daily | | 24.50 |

Evening meal 1930 (last orders 2200)
Parking for 3

🗝🍷💻🖨🖐📖🚭

### Tankerville Lodge ⚠

👑 **COMMENDED**

Stiperstones, Minsterley, Shrewsbury SY5 0NB
🕿 Shrewsbury (01743) 791401

*Country house noted for warm hospitality, set in superb landscape which offers breathtaking views. Ideal touring base for Shropshire and Welsh borderland. Adjacent to Stiperstones Nature Reserve.*
Bedrooms: 1 double, 3 twin
Bathrooms: 2 public
**Bed & breakfast**

| per night: | £min | £max |
|---|---|---|
| Single | 15.75 | 18.25 |
| Double | 31.50 | 31.50 |

**Half board**

| per person: | £min | £max |
|---|---|---|
| Daily | 24.50 | 27.00 |
| Weekly | 160.48 | 177.98 |

Evening meal 1900 (last orders 0900)
Parking for 5

🛏5♨🕿🛎📺💻🖨🛎🌙🌼🐕SP

## STOKE-ON-TRENT

Staffordshire
Map ref 4B2

Famous for its pottery. Factories of several famous makers, including Josiah Wedgwood, can be visited. The City Museum has one of the finest pottery and porcelain collections in the world.
*Tourist Information Centre*
🕿 (01782) 284600

### The Hollies

👑👑

Clay Lake, Endon, Stoke-on-Trent ST9 9DD
🕿 (01782) 503252
*Delightful Victorian house in a quiet country setting off B5051. Convenient for M6, the Potteries and Alton Towers. Non-smokers only, please.*
Bedrooms: 2 double, 1 twin, 2 triple
Bathrooms: 3 private, 1 public
**Bed & breakfast**

| per night: | £min | £max |
|---|---|---|
| Single | 20.00 | 25.00 |
| Double | 30.00 | 36.00 |

Parking for 5

🛏🗝♨🕿🛎S🖐📺💻🖨🌼🐕SP

### The Limes ⚠

👑

Cheadle Road, Blythe Bridge, Stoke-on-Trent ST11 9PW
🕿 Blythe Bridge (01782) 393278
*Victorian residence of character in large, landscaped gardens, near Alton Towers, Wedgwood, the Potteries and Staffordshire moorlands.*
Bedrooms: 1 single, 1 double, 1 triple
Bathrooms: 1 public, 2 private showers
**Bed & breakfast**

| per night: | £min | £max |
|---|---|---|
| Single | 19.00 | 21.00 |
| Double | 35.00 | 37.00 |

Parking for 8

🛏7🍷🗝♨🖐🔌📺💻🖨🌼✗🐕🏧

## STONE

Staffordshire
Map ref 4B2

Town on the River Trent with the remains of a 12th C Augustinian priory. It is surrounded by pleasant countryside. Trentham Gardens with 500 acres of parklands and recreational facilities is within easy reach.

### Couldreys ⋀
COMMENDED

8 Airdale Road, Stone ST15 8DW
☎ (01785) 812500
Fax (01785) 811761
*Edwardian house quietly situated on town outskirts, providing every comfort plus home-made bread! Excellent restaurants within walking distance. Convenient for M6, Wedgwood and Potteries. Non-smokers only.*
Bedrooms: 1 twin
Bathrooms: 1 private

**Bed & breakfast**

| per night: | £min | £max |
|---|---|---|
| Single | | 20.00 |
| Double | | 32.00 |

Parking for 2

## STONEHOUSE

Gloucestershire
Map ref 2B1

Village in the Stroud Valley with an Elizabethan Court, later restored and altered by Lutyens.

### Merton Lodge

8 Ebley Road, Stonehouse GL10 2LQ
☎ (01453) 822018
*Former gentleman's residence offering a warm welcome. No smoking in the house. Three miles from junction 13 of M5. Take A419 to Stroud, over 3 roundabouts, under footbridge - located opposite garden centre. Short walk to carvery/pub.*
Bedrooms: 3 double
Bathrooms: 1 private, 2 public

**Bed & breakfast**

| per night: | £min | £max |
|---|---|---|
| Single | 14.00 | |
| Double | 28.00 | |

Parking for 6

National Crown ratings were correct at the time of going to press but are subject to change. Please check at the time of booking.

## STOURBRIDGE

West Midlands
Map ref 4B3

Town on the River Stour, famous for its glassworks. Several of the factories can be visited and glassware purchased at the factory shops.

### St. Elizabeth's Cottage
COMMENDED

Woodman Lane, Clent, Stourbridge DY9 9PX
☎ Hagley (01562) 883883
*Beautiful country cottage with lovely gardens and interior professionally decorated throughout. 20 minutes from Birmingham and close to motorway links.*
Bedrooms: 1 double, 1 twin
Bathrooms: 2 private

**Bed & breakfast**

| per night: | £min | £max |
|---|---|---|
| Single | 22.00 | 25.00 |
| Double | 44.00 | 50.00 |

Parking for 2

## STOW-ON-THE-WOLD

Gloucestershire
Map ref 2B1

Attractive Cotswold wool town with a large market-place and some fine houses, especially the old grammar school. There is an interesting church dating from Norman times. Stow-on-the-Wold is surrounded by lovely countryside and Cotswold villages.
*Tourist Information Centre
☎ (01451) 831082*

### Banks Farm ⋀
Listed COMMENDED

Upper Oddington, Moreton-in-Marsh GL56 0XG
☎ Cotswold (01451) 830475
*280-acre mixed farm. Cotswold stone farmhouse overlooking fields to 11th C church, 3 miles from Stow-on-the-Wold. Central for touring the Cotswolds. Pubs, good food within walking distance. 1994 prices held for advance bookings. Reduced rates for weekly B & B.*
Bedrooms: 1 double, 1 twin
Bathrooms: 1 public

**Bed & breakfast**

| per night: | £min | £max |
|---|---|---|
| Single | 16.50 | 18.00 |

Parking for 4
Open April-October

### Corsham Field Farmhouse ⋀

Bledington Road, Stow-on-the-Wold, Cheltenham GL54 1JH
☎ Cotswold (01451) 831750

*100-acre mixed farm. Homely farmhouse with breathtaking views. Ideally situated for exploring the Cotswolds. En-suite and standard rooms. Good pub food 5 minutes' walk away.*
Bedrooms: 1 double, 1 twin, 1 triple
Bathrooms: 1 private, 2 public

**Bed & breakfast**

| per night: | £min | £max |
|---|---|---|
| Single | 15.00 | 25.00 |
| Double | 25.00 | 35.00 |

Parking for 10

### Fairview Farmhouse

Bledington Road, Stow-on-the-Wold GL54 1AN
☎ Cotswold (01451) 830279
*3-acre smallholding. A warm welcome awaits at Fairview. Situated on "B" road only 1 mile from Stow. Outstanding panoramic views. Cosy bedrooms furnished to a high standard with colour TV, tea/coffee facilities. Full central heating and wood-burner in lounge.*
Bedrooms: 2 double, 1 twin
Bathrooms: 3 private

**Bed & breakfast**

| per night: | £min | £max |
|---|---|---|
| Double | 38.00 | 45.00 |

Evening meal 1830 (last orders 2000)
Parking for 7

### Honeybrook Cottage
COMMENDED

Main Street, Adlestrop, Moreton-in-Marsh GL56 0YN
☎ Moreton-in-Marsh (01608) 658884

*A warm welcome awaits you at this natural stone cottage in quiet village. Views over hills, good walking and touring area.*
Bedrooms: 1 double, 1 twin
Bathrooms: 2 private, 1 public

**Bed & breakfast**

| per night: | £min | £max |
|---|---|---|
| Single | 22.00 | 24.00 |
| Double | 37.00 | 40.00 |

Parking for 3

### Journeys End ⋀
COMMENDED

Evenlode, Moreton-in-Marsh GL56 0NN
☎ Moreton-in-Marsh (01608) 650786
*20-acre mixed farm. Peaceful, comfortable, modernised farmhouse in quiet village. Approximately 3 miles*

Continued ▶

## STOW-ON-THE-WOLD

### Continued

*from Moreton-in-Marsh and Stow-on-the-Wold. One bedroom is on ground floor.*
Bedrooms: 3 double, 1 twin, 1 family room
Bathrooms: 5 private

**Bed & breakfast**

| per night: | £min | £max |
|---|---|---|
| Single | 17.00 | 20.00 |
| Double | 34.00 | 40.00 |

Parking for 5

### Old Farmhouse Hotel ⋏

**APPROVED**

Lower Swell, Stow-on-the-Wold,
Cheltenham GL54 1LF
☎ Cotswold (01451) 830232
Fax (01451) 870962

*Sympathetically converted 16th C Cotswold-stone farmhouse in a quiet hamlet, 1 mile west of Stow-on-the-Wold. Offers warm and unpretentious hospitality.*
Bedrooms: 9 double, 4 twin, 1 family room
Bathrooms: 12 private, 1 public

**Bed & breakfast**

| per night: | £min | £max |
|---|---|---|
| Single | 18.50 | 55.00 |
| Double | 38.00 | 84.00 |

**Half board**

| per person: | £min | £max |
|---|---|---|
| Daily | 33.00 | 69.50 |
| Weekly | 133.50 | 284.00 |

Lunch available
Evening meal 1900 (last orders 2100)
Parking for 25
Cards accepted: Access, Visa

### Royalist Hotel ⋏

Digbeth Street, Stow-on-the-Wold,
Cheltenham GL54 1BN
☎ Cotswold (01451) 830670
*The oldest inn in England (947 AD) with all the inherent charm and character of the past, yet every modern-day facility as well.*
Bedrooms: 1 single, 7 double, 2 twin, 2 triple
Bathrooms: 12 private

**Bed & breakfast**

| per night: | £min | £max |
|---|---|---|
| Single | 35.00 | 45.00 |
| Double | 50.00 | 75.00 |

Lunch available

Parking for 10
Cards accepted: Access, Visa

### South Hill Farmhouse ⋏

Fosseway, Stow-on-the-Wold,
Cheltenham GL54 1JU
☎ Cotswold (01451) 831219
Fax (01451) 831219

*Base your touring holiday in this Victorian farmhouse. Individually furnished and spacious rooms, a hearty breakfast, lounge with open fires.*
Bedrooms: 2 double, 1 twin, 2 triple
Bathrooms: 4 private, 1 public

**Bed & breakfast**

| per night: | £min | £max |
|---|---|---|
| Double | 30.00 | 36.00 |

Parking for 6

## STRATFORD-UPON-AVON

Warwickshire
Map ref 2B1

Famous as Shakespeare's home town, Stratford's many attractions include his birthplace, New Place where he died, the Royal Shakespeare Theatre and Gallery, "The World of Shakespeare" audio-visual theatre and Hall's Croft (his daughter's house).
*Tourist Information Centre*
☎ *(01789) 293127*

### Abberley

**COMMENDED**

12 Albany Road, Stratford-upon-Avon CV37 6PG
☎ (01789) 295934
*Comfortable home set in a quiet residential area yet within easy walking distance of theatres and town centre. Non-smokers only please.*
Bedrooms: 1 twin
Bathrooms: 1 private

**Bed & breakfast**

| per night: | £min | £max |
|---|---|---|
| Double | 40.00 | 44.00 |

Parking for 2

### Allors

**Listed**

62 Evesham Road, Stratford-upon-Avon CV37 9BA
☎ (01789) 269982
*Comfortable en-suite accommodation in detached house with private sitting*

*facilities. Non-smoking. TV. Parking. Reductions for two or more nights.*
Bedrooms: 1 double, 1 twin
Bathrooms: 2 private

**Bed & breakfast**

| per night: | £min | £max |
|---|---|---|
| Double | 30.00 | 38.00 |

Parking for 3
Open February–November

### Braeside Guest House ⋏

129 Shipston Road, Stratford-upon-Avon CV37 7LW
☎ (01789) 261648
*Attractive detached family-run guesthouse, 10 minutes' walk from Royal Shakespeare Theatre and town centre along old tramway footpath. Ample parking.*
Bedrooms: 1 single, 1 twin, 1 triple
Bathrooms: 1 private, 1 public, 1 private shower

**Bed & breakfast**

| per night: | £min | £max |
|---|---|---|
| Single | 14.00 | 15.00 |
| Double | 30.00 | 34.00 |

Parking for 4

### Bronhill House ⋏

**Listed**

260 Alcester Road, Stratford-upon-Avon CV37 9JQ
☎ (01789) 299169
*Detached family house in elevated position, 1 mile from Stratford-upon-Avon. Family-run with relaxed friendly atmosphere. A non-smoking establishment.*
Bedrooms: 1 single, 2 double
Bathrooms: 2 public

**Bed & breakfast**

| per night: | £min | £max |
|---|---|---|
| Single | 15.00 | 18.00 |
| Double | 23.00 | 30.00 |

Parking for 5

### Carlton Guest House ⋏

**COMMENDED**

22 Evesham Place, Stratford-upon-Avon CV37 6HT
☎ (01789) 293548
*Tasteful decor, elegantly furnished, combining Victorian origins with modern facilities. A peaceful home, happily shared with guests.*
Bedrooms: 1 single, 2 double, 1 twin, 1 family room
Bathrooms: 3 private, 1 public

**Bed & breakfast**

| per night: | £min | £max |
|---|---|---|
| Single | 19.00 | 23.00 |
| Double | 42.00 | 46.00 |

Parking for 3

## Chadwyns Guest House ⚘

**Listed**

6 Broad Walk, Stratford-upon-Avon
CV37 6HS
☎ (01789) 269077
*Traditionally furnished Victorian house, family-run, close to town centre and theatre. Colour TV and tea/coffee making facilities in all rooms.*
Bedrooms: 1 single, 2 double, 1 twin, 2 family rooms
Bathrooms: 3 private, 2 public

**Bed & breakfast**

| per night: | £min | £max |
|---|---|---|
| Single | 16.00 | 16.00 |
| Double | 30.00 | 38.00 |

Parking for 2

🛏️⚘☐♨️🔥⛄☐🆂⛁🍽️🚗 OAP ♨️ SP

## Cherangani ⚘

👑 **COMMENDED**

61 Maidenhead Road, Stratford-upon-Avon CV37 6XU
☎ (01789) 292655
*Pleasant detached house in a quiet, residential area, offering warm, attractive accommodation. Within walking distance of the town and theatre.*
Bedrooms: 1 twin
Bathrooms: 1 public

**Bed & breakfast**

| per night: | £min | £max |
|---|---|---|
| Single | 15.00 | 17.00 |
| Double | 32.00 | 36.00 |

Parking for 3

🛏️5♨️⛄⛁♨️TV⛁☐🚗✈️🐎 OAP

## Church Farm ⚘

👑👑 **COMMENDED**

Dorsington, Stratford-upon-Avon CV37 8AX
☎ (01789) 720471 & Mobile 0831 504194
Fax (01789) 720830
*127-acre mixed farm. Situated in beautiful countryside, some rooms en-suite, TV, tea and coffee facilities. Close to Stratford-upon-Avon, Warwick, the Cotswolds and Evesham.*
Wheelchair access category 3 ♿
Bedrooms: 3 double, 2 twin, 2 family rooms
Bathrooms: 4 private, 2 public

**Bed & breakfast**

| per night: | £min | £max |
|---|---|---|
| Single | 18.00 | 23.00 |
| Double | 27.00 | 33.00 |

Parking for 12

🛏️⚘♨️⛄⛁🆂♨️TV⛁🚗☐🥃♪▶️☀️🔥

## Church Farm ⚘

👑👑 **COMMENDED**

Long Marston, Stratford-upon-Avon CV37 8RH
☎ (01789) 720275

*A very friendly welcome at this old family farmhouse in quiet village. Close to Stratford-upon-Avon, Warwick Castle and the Cotswolds.*
Bedrooms: 1 twin, 1 triple
Bathrooms: 2 private

**Bed & breakfast**

| per night: | £min | £max |
|---|---|---|
| Single | 17.00 | 26.00 |
| Double | 32.00 | 36.00 |

Parking for 4

🛏️☐♨️⛛⛁🆂♨️⛁🚗☀️🐎

## Clomendy Guest House ⚘

⛛

157 Evesham Road, Stratford-upon-Avon CV37 9BP
☎ (01789) 266957

*Small, detached, mock-Tudor family-run guesthouse, convenient for town centre, Anne Hathaway's cottage and theatres. Stratford-in-Bloom commendation winner. Rail/coach guests met and returned. No smoking, please.*
Bedrooms: 1 single, 1 double, 1 twin
Bathrooms: 1 public, 1 private shower
Continued ▶

---

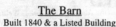

## STRATFORD-UPON-AVON
*Continued*

**Bed & breakfast**

| per night: | £min | £max |
|---|---|---|
| Single | 14.00 | 17.00 |
| Double | 26.00 | 34.00 |

Parking for 4

### Field View ⋒
*APPROVED*

35 Banbury Road, Stratford-upon-Avon CV37 7HW
☎ (01789) 292694
*10 minutes' walk from Stratford town centre, offering comfortable, family-type accommodation.*
Bedrooms: 1 double
Bathrooms: 1 public

**Bed & breakfast**

| per night: | £min | £max |
|---|---|---|
| Single | 14.00 | 16.00 |
| Double | 28.00 | 30.00 |

Parking for 3

### Green Gables ⋒
*COMMENDED*

47 Banbury Road, Stratford-upon-Avon CV37 7HW
☎ (01789) 205557
*Edwardian house in a residential area, within 10 minutes' walk of the town centre and theatre.*
Bedrooms: 1 double
Bathrooms: 1 private, 1 public

**Bed & breakfast**

| per night: | £min | £max |
|---|---|---|
| Double | 31.00 | 38.00 |

Parking for 3

### Highcroft ⋒
*COMMENDED*

Banbury Road, Stratford-upon-Avon CV37 7NF
☎ (01789) 296293

*Lovely country house in 2-acre garden, only 2 miles from Stratford-upon-Avon, on A422. Families welcome. Friendly, relaxed atmosphere.*
Bedrooms: 1 double, 1 family room
Bathrooms: 2 private

**Bed & breakfast**

| per night: | £min | £max |
|---|---|---|
| Single | 18.00 | 20.00 |
| Double | 33.00 | 35.00 |

Parking for 3

### Houndshill House ⋒

Banbury Road, Ettington, Stratford-upon-Avon CV37 7NS
☎ (01789) 740267
*Family-run pub with restaurant. 4 miles from Stratford-upon-Avon. Informal and friendly atmosphere.*
Bedrooms: 2 single, 3 double, 2 twin, 1 triple
Bathrooms: 8 private

**Bed & breakfast**

| per night: | £min | £max |
|---|---|---|
| Single | 28.00 | |
| Double | 45.00 | |

Lunch available
Evening meal 1900 (last orders 2200)
Parking for 50
Cards accepted: Access, Visa

### Hunters Moon Guest House ⋒

150 Alcester Road, Stratford-upon-Avon CV37 9DR
☎ (01789) 292888
*Detached guesthouse with en-suite rooms. On the A422 Stratford-Worcester road, 6 miles from M40 (junction 15). Close to Anne Hathaway's cottage and other Shakespearean properties.*
Bedrooms: 2 single, 2 double, 3 triple
Bathrooms: 7 private

**Bed & breakfast**

| per night: | £min | £max |
|---|---|---|
| Single | 17.00 | 30.00 |
| Double | 33.00 | 45.00 |

**Half board**

| per person: | £min | £max |
|---|---|---|
| Daily | 25.00 | 35.00 |
| Weekly | 150.00 | 210.00 |

Parking for 6
Cards accepted: Access, Visa, Diners, Amex

### Moonraker House ⋒
*COMMENDED*

40 Alcester Road, Stratford-upon-Avon CV37 9DB
☎ (01789) 299346 & 267115
Fax (01789) 295504
*Family-run, near town centre. Beautifully co-ordinated decor throughout. Some rooms with four-poster beds and garden terrace available for non-smokers.*
Bedrooms: 19 double, 3 twin, 2 triple
Bathrooms: 24 private

**Bed & breakfast**

| per night: | £min | £max |
|---|---|---|
| Single | 28.00 | 34.00 |
| Double | 39.00 | 60.00 |

Parking for 24
Cards accepted: Access, Visa

### Moss Cottage
*COMMENDED*

61 Evesham Road, Stratford-upon-Avon CV37 9BA
☎ (01789) 294770
*Pauline and Jim Rush welcome you to their charming detached cottage. Walking distance theatre/town. Spacious en-suite accommodation. Hospitality tray, TV. Parking.*
Bedrooms: 2 double
Bathrooms: 2 private

**Bed & breakfast**

| per night: | £min | £max |
|---|---|---|
| Single | 26.00 | 32.00 |
| Double | 34.00 | 40.00 |

Parking for 3
Open March-November

### Newlands ⋒
*COMMENDED*

7 Broad Walk, Stratford-upon-Avon CV37 6HS
☎ (01789) 298449
*Park your car at Sue Boston's home and take a short walk to the Royal Shakespeare Theatre, town centre and Shakespeare properties.*
Bedrooms: 1 single, 1 double, 1 twin, 1 triple
Bathrooms: 3 private, 1 public

**Bed & breakfast**

| per night: | £min | £max |
|---|---|---|
| Single | 19.00 | 22.00 |
| Double | 38.00 | 44.00 |

Parking for 2

### One Acre Guest House ⋒

One Acre, Barton Road, Welford-on-Avon, Stratford-upon-Avon CV37 8EZ
☎ (01789) 750477
*Family house in Shakespearean village with countryside views and a warm friendly atmosphere. 4 miles from Stratford-upon-Avon, off B439. Discount for weekly stays.*
Bedrooms: 1 double, 1 twin, 1 triple
Bathrooms: 3 private

**Bed & breakfast**

| per night: | £min | £max |
|---|---|---|
| Single | 18.00 | 20.00 |
| Double | 32.00 | 32.00 |

**Half board**

| per person: | £min | £max |
|---|---|---|
| Daily | 24.50 | 28.50 |

Lunch available
Evening meal 1800 (last orders 2100)
Parking for 6

### Oxstalls Farm
*COMMENDED*

Warwick Road, Stratford-upon-Avon CV37 0NS
☎ (01789) 205277

*Beautifully situated 60-acre stud farm overlooking the Welcome Hills and golf-course. 1 mile from Stratford-upon-Avon town centre and the Royal Shakespeare Theatre.*
Bedrooms: 1 single, 7 double, 4 twin, 7 triple
Bathrooms: 11 private, 2 public, 3 private showers

**Bed & breakfast**

| per night: | £min | £max |
|---|---|---|
| Single | 15.00 | 25.00 |
| Double | 32.00 | 50.00 |

Parking for 20

🛇🐾📭🖵♨🛆🗯🖳⅄🗚📺🛍🖵🗯⌗🏵✕⌂

Ad Display advertisement appears on page 179

## Parkfield ⋀
♨♨

3 Broad Walk, Stratford-upon-Avon CV37 6HS
☎ (01789) 293313
*Delightful Victorian house. Quiet location, 5 minutes' walk from theatre and town. Most rooms en-suite. Colour TV, tea and coffee facilities and parking. Choice of breakfast, including vegetarian. A non-smoking house.*
Bedrooms: 1 single, 1 double, 2 twin, 3 triple
Bathrooms: 5 private, 1 public

**Bed & breakfast**

| per night: | £min | £max |
|---|---|---|
| Single | 17.00 | 19.00 |
| Double | 34.00 | 44.00 |

Parking for 9
Cards accepted: Access, Visa, Diners, Amex

🛇📭🖵♨🗚ⓘ⅄🗚🛍🛆🗇

## The Poplars
**Listed**

Mansell Farm, Newbold-on-Stour, Stratford-upon-Avon CV37 8BZ
☎ (01789) 450540
*172-acre dairy farm. Modern farmhouse in picturesque surroundings offers friendly welcome. Two hostelries within walking distance serve good food. Six miles south of Stratford-upon-Avon on A3400.*
Bedrooms: 1 double, 1 twin, 1 triple
Bathrooms: 2 private, 1 public

**Bed & breakfast**

| per night: | £min | £max |
|---|---|---|
| Single | 15.00 | 16.50 |
| Double | 33.00 | 35.00 |

**Half board**

| per person: | £min | £max |
|---|---|---|
| Daily | 22.50 | 25.00 |
| Weekly | 157.50 | 168.00 |

Evening meal 1830 (last orders 2000)
Parking for 3
Open March-October

🛇♨🗚ⓘⓢ🗚🛍⌗🏵

## Ravenhurst ⋀
♨♨

2 Broad Walk, Stratford-upon-Avon CV37 6HS
☎ (01789) 292515

*Quietly situated, a few minutes' walk from the town centre and places of historic interest. Comfortable home, with substantial breakfast provided. Four-poster en-suite available.*
Bedrooms: 3 double, 2 twin
Bathrooms: 5 private

**Bed & breakfast**

| per night: | £min | £max |
|---|---|---|
| Double | 38.00 | 44.00 |

Parking for 4
Cards accepted: Access, Visa, Diners, Amex

🛇🏠🖵♨🗚🛍🛆✕🏵▥

## Sequoia House ⋀
♨♨

51-53 Shipston Road, Stratford-upon-Avon CV37 7LN
☎ (01789) 268852 & 294940
Fax (01789) 414559
*Beautifully-appointed private hotel with large car park and delightful garden walk to the theatre, riverside gardens and Shakespeare properties. Fully air-conditioned dining room.*
Bedrooms: 2 single, 10 double, 12 twin
Bathrooms: 20 private, 3 public, 1 private shower

**Bed & breakfast**

| per night: | £min | £max |
|---|---|---|
| Single | 29.00 | 49.00 |
| Double | 39.00 | 72.00 |

Lunch available
Parking for 33
Cards accepted: Access, Visa, Diners, Amex

🛇🏠📞🖵♨🗚ⓘⓢ⅄🗚🛍🛆
🍴10-60 ⊛🏵✕⌂ OAP SP ▥

## Uporchard
**Listed**

Kings Lane, Snitterfield, Stratford-upon-Avon CV37 0QB
☎ (01789) 731824
*Uporchard stands in 1 acre of gardens surrounded by orchards, 5 minutes from the centre of Stratford-upon-Avon with superb southerly views across the Avon Valley.*
Bedrooms: 1 double, 1 twin
Bathrooms: 1 public

---

**We advise you to confirm your booking in writing.**

---

**Bed & breakfast**

| per night: | £min | £max |
|---|---|---|
| Single | 20.00 | 25.00 |
| Double | 30.00 | 40.00 |

Parking for 5

🛇📭♨🗯🗚⅄🗚📺🛍🛆🏵✕🏵⌂ T

## Whitchurch Farm ⋀
♨♨

Wimpstone, Stratford-upon-Avon CV37 8NS
☎ Alderminster (01789) 450275
*260-acre mixed farm. Listed Georgian farmhouse set in park-like surroundings on the edge of the Cotswolds. Ideal for a touring holiday. Small village 4 miles south of Stratford-upon-Avon.*
Bedrooms: 2 double, 1 twin
Bathrooms: 3 private

**Bed & breakfast**

| per night: | £min | £max |
|---|---|---|
| Double | 32.00 | 34.00 |

**Half board**

| per person: | £min | £max |
|---|---|---|
| Daily | 24.00 | 26.00 |

Evening meal from 1830
Parking for 3

🛇♨ⓢ🗚📺🛍✕🏵▥

## Wood View ⋀
♨♨ HIGHLY COMMENDED

Pathlow, Stratford-upon-Avon CV37 0RQ
☎ (01789) 295778
*Beautifully situated comfortable home, with fine views over fields and woods. Ideal for touring Stratford-upon-Avon and the Cotswolds.*
Bedrooms: 2 twin
Bathrooms: 2 private

**Bed & breakfast**

| per night: | £min | £max |
|---|---|---|
| Single | 20.00 | 28.00 |

Parking for 6

🛇🏠🖵♨🗯🗚⅄🛍🛆⊛🔍🏵🏵

---

## STROUD
Gloucestershire
Map ref 2B1

This old town has been producing broadcloth for centuries and the local museum has an interesting display on the subject. It is surrounded by attractive hilly country.
*Tourist Information Centre*
☎ *(01453) 765768*

## Beechcroft
♨ COMMENDED

Brownshill, Stroud GL6 8AG
☎ (01453) 883422
*Edwardian house in quiet rural position, with open views. Evening meal by arrangement. Home-made bread and preserves. No smoking.*
Bedrooms: 1 double, 1 twin
Bathrooms: 1 public

*Continued ▶*

## STROUD

*Continued*

**Bed & breakfast**

| per night: | £min | £max |
|---|---|---|
| Single | | 16.00 |
| Double | | 28.00 |

**Half board**

| per person: | £min | £max |
|---|---|---|
| Daily | | 24.00 |
| Weekly | | 150.00 |

Evening meal from 1900
Parking for 4

### Cairngall Guest House

☞ APPROVED

65 Bisley Old Road, Stroud GL5 1NF
☎ (01453) 764595
*Unique, Bath-stone house in French style with porticoed west front, furnished to complement the architectural design.*
Bedrooms: 1 twin, 1 triple
Bathrooms: 1 public

**Bed & breakfast**

| per night: | £min | £max |
|---|---|---|
| Single | 15.00 | 18.00 |
| Double | 30.00 | 35.00 |

Parking for 3

### Downfield Hotel ⚑

☞☞☞

134 Cainscross Road, Stroud GL5 4HN
☎ (01453) 764496

*Imposing Georgian house in quiet location. Home cooking. 1 mile from town centre, 5 miles from M5 motorway, junction 13, on main A419 road.*
Bedrooms: 4 single, 9 double, 7 twin, 1 triple
Bathrooms: 11 private, 3 public

**Bed & breakfast**

| per night: | £min | £max |
|---|---|---|
| Single | 20.00 | 29.00 |
| Double | 29.00 | 35.00 |

**Half board**

| per person: | £min | £max |
|---|---|---|
| Daily | 25.00 | 50.00 |
| Weekly | 175.00 | 273.00 |

Evening meal 1830 (last orders 2000)
Parking for 23
Cards accepted: Access, Visa

### Hawthorns

☞☞

Lower Littleworth, Amberley, Stroud
GL5 5AW
☎ Stroudey (01453) 873535
*Grade II listed Queen Anne house in National Trust setting. Glorious 20-mile views. Wild badgers (floodlit) feed at nightfall within touching distance. Exceptional walking country, riding, hot-air ballooning. Warm welcome.*
Bedrooms: 2 double, 1 twin
Bathrooms: 3 private

**Bed & breakfast**

| per night: | £min | £max |
|---|---|---|
| Single | 20.00 | 25.00 |
| Double | 28.00 | 36.00 |

Parking for 3
Open March-October

### New Inn House ⚑

Listed  APPROVED

The Camp, Stroud GL6 7HL
☎ Cirencester (01285) 821336
*In a small hamlet amid unspoilt Cotswold countryside, convenient for Severn Wildfowl Trust and Prinknash Abbey. Guests have own door key. Separate tables. Non-smokers preferred.*
Bedrooms: 1 single, 1 twin
Bathrooms: 1 public

**Bed & breakfast**

| per night: | £min | £max |
|---|---|---|
| Single | 15.00 | 17.00 |
| Double | 30.00 | 34.00 |

Parking for 3
Open April-October

### Whitegates Farm

☞☞

Cowcombe Hill, Chalford, Stroud
GL6 8HP
☎ Cirencester (01285) 760758
*Peaceful hillside farmhouse with lovely views, gardens, orchards and 16 rambling acres. Good walking, central for touring. Non-smokers only, please. Spanish spoken.*
Bedrooms: 2 double
Bathrooms: 2 private

**Bed & breakfast**

| per night: | £min | £max |
|---|---|---|
| Single | 24.00 | 28.00 |
| Double | 36.00 | 40.00 |

**Half board**

| per person: | £min | £max |
|---|---|---|
| Daily | 30.50 | 34.50 |
| Weekly | 200.00 | 250.00 |

Evening meal 1900 (last orders 2000)
Parking for 6

### The Yew Tree Tea Rooms ⚑

☞☞

Walls Quarry, Brimscombe, Stroud
GL5 2PA
☎ (01453) 883428
Fax (01453) 883428

*Built c1669 of Cotswold stone. Once a fine brewhouse, entrance through ex-barley door. Picturesque views across valleys to Stroud and the surrounding hills. Amidst National Trust common land. Non-smokers only, please.*
Bedrooms: 1 twin
Bathrooms: 1 private

**Bed & breakfast**

| per night: | £min | £max |
|---|---|---|
| Single | 18.00 | 25.00 |
| Double | 36.00 | 40.00 |

Lunch available
Parking for 1
Open February-December

## TEDDINGTON

Gloucestershire
Map ref 2B1

Village a few miles east of Tewkesbury and north of Cheltenham, with just a few farms and houses, but an interesting church.

### Bengrove Farm

☞☞ COMMENDED

Bengrove, Teddington, Tewkesbury
GL20 8JB
☎ Cheltenham (01242) 620332
Fax (01242) 620851
*10-acre mixed farm. Large, interesting 14th C farmhouse with attractive rooms, timbered and beamed. 2 twin rooms, lounge and guests' bathroom. Comfortably furnished.*
Bedrooms: 2 twin
Bathrooms: 1 public

**Bed & breakfast**

| per night: | £min | £max |
|---|---|---|
| Single | 16.00 | 16.00 |
| Double | 28.00 | 28.00 |

Parking for 10

## TELFORD

Shropshire
Map ref 4A3

New Town named after Thomas Telford, the famous engineer who designed many of the country's canals, bridges and viaducts. It is close to Ironbridge with its monuments and museums to the Industrial Revolution, including restored 18th C buildings.
*Tourist Information Centre*
☎ *(01952) 291370*

### Allscott Inn

☞☞☞ APPROVED

Walcot, Wellington, Telford TF6 5EQ
☎ (01952) 248484
*Homely country inn offering delicious food and comfortable accommodation. Beer garden. Easy access Shrewsbury, Ironbridge and Telford.*
Bedrooms: 2 double, 2 twin

Bathrooms: 2 private, 1 public

**Bed & breakfast**

| per night: | £min | £max |
|---|---|---|
| Single | 20.00 | 28.00 |
| Double | 32.00 | 40.00 |

Lunch available
Evening meal 1900 (last orders 2200)
Parking for 50
Cards accepted: Amex

🛏🕯🖵🖨🌳✂🦮📺▥ 🚗🔍✿🚐

## Old Rectory

♨♨

Stirchley Village, Telford TF3 1DY
☎ (01952) 596308 & 596518
*Large, comfortable guesthouse dating
from 1734. Set in an acre of secluded
gardens, on edge of town park.
Convenient for town centre and
Ironbridge museums. Three miles from
M54 junction 4.*
Bedrooms: 2 single, 2 twin, 1 family
room
Bathrooms: 1 private, 2 public

**Bed & breakfast**

| per night: | £min | £max |
|---|---|---|
| Single | 18.00 | 23.00 |
| Double | 30.00 | 35.00 |

**Half board**

| per person: | £min | £max |
|---|---|---|
| Daily | 25.00 | 30.00 |
| Weekly | 157.00 | 187.00 |

Evening meal 1800 (last orders 2100)
Parking for 6

🛏🖵🖨💧🚻✂🦮📺▥ 🚗✿🚐 SP 🚒 T

---

### TETBURY

Gloucestershire
Map ref 2B2

Small market town with 18th C
houses and an attractive 17th C
Town Hall. It is a good touring
centre with many places of interest
nearby including Badminton House
and Westonbirt Arboretum.

## Tavern House ⋒

♨♨♨ DE LUXE

Willesley, Tetbury GL8 8QU
☎ (01666) 880444
Fax (01666) 880254

*A Grade II listed Cotswold stone house
(formerly a staging post) on the A433
Bath road, 1 mile from Westonbirt
Arboretum and 4 miles from Tetbury.*
Bedrooms: 3 double, 1 twin
Bathrooms: 4 private

---

**Bed & breakfast**

| per night: | £min | £max |
|---|---|---|
| Single | | 37.50 | 47.50 |
| Double | | 55.00 | 62.00 |

Parking for 4
Cards accepted: Access, Visa

🛏10🕯🖵🖨💧🦮▥🛁✂🦮▥ 🚗U
➤✿🦮🚐🌳 SP 🚒 T

---

### TEWKESBURY

Gloucestershire
Map ref 2B1

Tewkesbury's outstanding
possession is its magnificent
church, built as an abbey, with a
great Norman tower and beautiful
14th C interior. The town stands at
the confluence of the Severn and
Avon and has many old houses,
inns and several museums.
*Tourist Information Centre
☎ (01684) 295027*

## Abbots Court Farm ⋒

♨♨ APPROVED

Church End, Twyning, Tewkesbury
GL20 6DA
☎ (01684) 292515
Fax (01684) 292515
*450-acre arable & dairy farm. Large,
comfortable farmhouse in excellent
touring area. Most rooms en-suite. 3
games rooms, grass tennis court, fishing
available.*
Bedrooms: 1 single, 1 double, 2 twin,
2 triple, 2 family rooms
Bathrooms: 4 private, 1 public

**Bed & breakfast**

| per night: | £min | £max |
|---|---|---|
| Single | 17.00 | 19.00 |
| Double | 28.00 | 32.00 |

Parking for 20
Cards accepted: Visa

🛏🕯🖵💧🚻S⃝🦮📺▥ 🚗🔍🔍U♪
✿🚐 OAP SP 🚒

## Barn Hill Farmhouse ⋒

♨♨ COMMENDED

Bredons Norton, Tewkesbury
GL20 7HB
☎ Bredon (01684) 72704
Fax (01684) 72704

*10-acre livestock farm. Listed Cotswold-
stone farmhouse, c1611, in quiet
Bredon Hill village. Large comfortable
bedrooms, home cooking and a warm
welcome. Ideal touring centre, 30
minutes Cheltenham, Gloucester,
Worcester and Evesham.*
Bedrooms: 1 double, 1 triple
Bathrooms: 2 private

---

**Bed & breakfast**

| per night: | £min | £max |
|---|---|---|
| Single | 18.00 | 22.00 |
| Double | 32.00 | 38.00 |

**Half board**

| per person: | £min | £max |
|---|---|---|
| Daily | 24.00 | 29.00 |
| Weekly | 168.00 | 189.00 |

Evening meal 1830 (last orders 2000)
Parking for 12

🖵🖨💧🦮▥S⃝✂🦮📺▥ 🚗U✿
🚐🚒

## The Old Vicarage

♨♨ COMMENDED

Overbury, Tewkesbury GL20 7NT
☎ Overbury (01386) 725510
*Victorian vicarage in 1 acre of garden
in village of renowned beauty under
Bredon Hill. Comfortable centrally
heated rooms with own bathrooms.*
Bedrooms: 1 double, 1 twin
Bathrooms: 2 private

**Bed & breakfast**

| per night: | £min | £max |
|---|---|---|
| Single | 30.00 | |
| Double | 50.00 | |

Parking for 8

🖵🖨💧🦮▥🦮📺▥ 🚗✿🦮🚐

## Personal Touch ⋒

Listed

37 Tirle Bank Way, Tewkesbury
GL20 8ES
☎ (01684) 297692
*Semi-detached overlooking farmland.
Leave M5 at junction 9, Tewkesbury.
Second left past traffic lights, then left
and immediately right, follow road
round to right.*
Bedrooms: 2 twin
Bathrooms: 1 public

**Bed & breakfast**

| per night: | £min | £max |
|---|---|---|
| Single | 15.00 | 18.00 |
| Double | 30.00 | 30.00 |

**Half board**

| per person: | £min | £max |
|---|---|---|
| Daily | 22.00 | 22.00 |
| Weekly | 140.00 | 140.00 |

Lunch available
Evening meal from 1830
Parking for 2

🛏3🖵💧🦮🍴S⃝🦮📺▥ 🚗✂🚐 OAP

## Town Street Farm ⋒

♨♨ COMMENDED

Tirley, Gloucester GL19 4HG
☎ Gloucester (01452) 780442

*Continued* ▶

## TEWKESBURY

*Continued*

*500-acre mixed farm. 18th C farmhouse set in beautiful surroundings and within half a mile of the River Severn.*
Bedrooms: 1 twin, 1 triple
Bathrooms: 2 private, 1 public
**Bed & breakfast**

| per night: | £min | £max |
| --- | --- | --- |
| Single | 20.00 | 20.00 |
| Double | 30.00 | 30.00 |

Parking for 4

### Willow Cottages ⚈

Shuthonger Common, Tewkesbury
GL20 6ED
☎ (01684) 298599
*Peaceful former farmhouse with large garden. Comfortable rooms with TV, tea/coffee. Home cooking. Excellent walking/cycling. Fishing, golf, riding nearby.*
Bedrooms: 1 double, 1 twin, 1 family room
Bathrooms: 1 public
**Bed & breakfast**

| per night: | £min | £max |
| --- | --- | --- |
| Single | 15.00 | 16.00 |
| Double | 30.00 | 32.00 |

Evening meal 1930 (last orders 1200)
Parking for 5

## UPTON-UPON-SEVERN

Hereford and Worcester
Map ref 2B1

Attractive country town on the banks of the Severn and a good river cruising centre. It has many pleasant old houses and inns, and the pepperpot landmark is now the Heritage Centre.

### Pool House ⚈

**COMMENDED**

Hanley Road, Upton-upon-Severn,
Worcester WR8 0PA
☎ (01684) 592151
*Fine Queen Anne country house in large picturesque garden running down to the River Severn. Quiet, comfortable accommodation.*
Bedrooms: 3 double, 4 twin, 2 triple
Bathrooms: 6 private, 1 public
**Bed & breakfast**

| per night: | £min | £max |
| --- | --- | --- |
| Single | 22.00 | 31.50 |
| Double | 35.00 | 56.00 |

Parking for 20
Open February-November
Cards accepted: Access, Visa

### Tiltridge Farm and Vineyard ⚈

**HIGHLY COMMENDED**

Upper Hook Road, Upton-upon-Severn,
Worcester WR8 0SA
☎ (01684) 592906
Fax (01684) 594142

*9-acre vineyard & grazing farm. Fully renovated period farmhouse close to Upton and Malvern showground. Good food, warm welcome and wine from our own vineyard!*
Bedrooms: 1 double, 1 triple
Bathrooms: 2 private
**Bed & breakfast**

| per night: | £min | £max |
| --- | --- | --- |
| Single | 18.00 | 20.00 |
| Double | 34.00 | 40.00 |

**Half board**

| per person: | £min | £max |
| --- | --- | --- |
| Daily | 27.50 | 29.50 |
| Weekly | 178.50 | 192.50 |

Evening meal 1800 (last orders 2000)
Parking for 12

### Welland Court ⚈

Upton-upon-Severn, Worcester
WR8 0ST
☎ (01684) 594426 & 594413
Fax (01684) 594426
*Built c.1450 and enlarged in the 18th C. Recently rescued from a dilapidated state and modernised to a high standard. It lies at the foot of the Malvern Hills and is an ideal base for touring the Wye and Teme valleys.*
Bedrooms: 1 double, 1 twin
Bathrooms: 2 private, 1 public
**Bed & breakfast**

| per night: | £min | £max |
| --- | --- | --- |
| Single | 30.00 | 30.00 |
| Double | 60.00 | 60.00 |

**Half board**

| per person: | £min | £max |
| --- | --- | --- |
| Daily | 50.00 | 50.00 |
| Weekly | 240.00 | 240.00 |

Parking for 13

> Half board prices shown are per person but in some cases may be based on double/twin occupancy.

## UTTOXETER

Staffordshire
Map ref 4B2

Small market town, famous for its racecourse. There are half-timbered buildings around the Market Square.

### Stramshall Farm ⚈

**Listed** **COMMENDED**

Stramshall, Uttoxeter ST14 5AG
☎ (01889) 562363
*140-acre dairy & livestock farm. A large late-Victorian house of typical architecture. Set in attractive garden and in the centre of Stramshall village, 2 miles north of Uttoxeter.*
Bedrooms: 2 triple
Bathrooms: 1 public
**Bed & breakfast**

| per night: | £min | £max |
| --- | --- | --- |
| Single | 16.00 | 20.00 |
| Double | 26.00 | 32.00 |

Parking for 4
Open March-October

### West Lodge ⚈

**Listed** **HIGHLY COMMENDED**

Bramshall, Uttoxeter ST14 5BG
☎ (01889) 566000
*Detached residence in 1 acre of attractive garden, on the B5027, 2 miles from Uttoxeter. Easy access to the Derbyshire Dales and Alton Towers.*
Bedrooms: 1 double, 2 twin
Bathrooms: 2 public
**Bed & breakfast**

| per night: | £min | £max |
| --- | --- | --- |
| Single | 18.50 | 21.00 |
| Double | 28.00 | 32.00 |

Parking for 8

## VOWCHURCH

Hereford and Worcester
Map ref 2A1

Village in the Golden Valley by the River Dore and set in beautiful countryside. It has an interesting 14th C church and is close to Abbey Dore with its famous Cistercian church.

### Upper Gilvach Farm

**COMMENDED**

St. Margarets, Vowchurch, Hereford
HR2 0QY
☎ Michaelchurch (01981) 23618
*90-acre dairy farm. Between Golden Valley and Black Mountains. Very quiet with much historic interest. Family-run.*
Bedrooms: 2 double, 1 triple
Bathrooms: 3 private

| Bed & breakfast per night: | £min | £max |
|---|---|---|
| Double | 33.00 | 40.00 |
| Parking for 20 | | |

🐕♨UL🔓🛄📺⬛✿✕🚗

## WARWICK

Warwickshire
Map ref 2B1

Castle rising above the River Avon and 15th C Beauchamp Chapel attached to St Mary's Church, medieval Lord Leycester's Hospital almshouses and several museums. Nearby is Ashorne Hall Nickelodeon and the new National Heritage museum at Gaydon.
*Tourist Information Centre*
☎ *(01926) 492212*

### Avon Guest House ⋏
👑👑 APPROVED

7 Emscote Road, Warwick CV34 4PH
☎ (01926) 491367
*Family-run guesthouse, all rooms centrally heated with colour TV, tea/coffee facilities, some have own shower. Large locking car park. 5 miles from castle.*
Bedrooms: 3 single, 2 double, 2 twin, 3 triple
Bathrooms: 2 public, 4 private showers

| Bed & breakfast per night: | £min | £max |
|---|---|---|
| Single | 16.00 | 16.00 |
| Double | 30.00 | 32.00 |

| Half board per person: | £min | £max |
|---|---|---|
| Daily | 23.00 | 23.00 |
| Weekly | 161.00 | 161.00 |

Evening meal 1800 (last orders 1930)
Parking for 7

🐕♨🔓S✕📺🛄,🚗✿✕🚗

### The Croft ⋏
👑👑 COMMENDED

Haseley Knob, Warwick CV35 7NL
☎ Haseley Knob (01926) 484447
Fax (01926) 484447
*Friendly family atmosphere in picturesque rural setting. In Haseley Knob village off the A4177 between Balsall Common and Warwick, convenient for NEC, National Agricultural Centre, Stratford and Coventry. 15 minutes from Birmingham Airport.*
Bedrooms: 1 single, 2 double, 1 twin, 1 triple
Bathrooms: 5 private, 2 public

| Bed & breakfast per night: | £min | £max |
|---|---|---|
| Single | 18.50 | 29.00 |
| Double | 36.00 | 42.00 |

Evening meal 1800 (last orders 2000)
Parking for 10

🐕♨📞🛏🖵♨🔓UL🔓S✕📺🛄,🚗
✿🚗SP T

### 30 Eastley Crescent ⋏
👑👑 HIGHLY COMMENDED

Warwick CV34 5RX
☎ (01926) 496480
*Next to A46 and 5 minutes from the M40. Hairdryer, shoe cleaning, trouser press. Non-smoking establishment.*
Bedrooms: 1 single, 1 double
Bathrooms: 1 private, 1 public

| Bed & breakfast per night: | £min | £max |
|---|---|---|
| Single | 16.00 | 18.00 |
| Double | 32.00 | 34.00 |

Parking for 2

🐕♨8🖵♨🔓S✕📺🛄,🚗✿✕
🚗 OAP

### Forth House ⋏
👑👑 HIGHLY COMMENDED

44 High Street, Warwick CV34 4AX
☎ (01926) 401512
*Ground floor and first floor guest suites with private sitting rooms and bathrooms at the back of the house. Overlooking peaceful garden, in town centre.*
Bedrooms: 1 twin, 1 family room
Bathrooms: 2 private

| Bed & breakfast per night: | £min | £max |
|---|---|---|
| Single | 30.00 | 35.00 |
| Double | 40.00 | 50.00 |

Parking for 2

🐕♨📞🖵🖵♨🔓UL🔓✕📺🛄,🚗
▶✿🚗SP 🏠

### Fulbrook Edge ⋏
👑 COMMENDED

Sherbourne Hill, Warwick CV35 8AG
☎ (01926) 624242
*Old-fashioned hospitality in spectacular panoramic surroundings. All rooms at ground level. Croquet lawn. Midway Stratford/Warwick on the A46, a few minutes from the M40, junction 15. Wheelchair access category 3 ♿*
Bedrooms: 1 double, 2 twin
Bathrooms: 1 public

| Bed & breakfast per night: | £min | £max |
|---|---|---|
| Single | 25.00 | 27.00 |
| Double | 38.00 | 40.00 |

Parking for 6

♨🖵♨🔓✕📺🛄,🚗🔘↑✿✕
🚗 OAP 🏠

### Lower Watchbury Farm ⋏
👑👑 COMMENDED

Wasperton Lane, Barford, Warwick CV35 1DH
☎ (01926) 624772
*50-acre mixed farm. Well appointed accommodation on working farm, in rural surroundings outside Barford. M40 2 miles, Stratford-upon-Avon 7 miles, Warwick 3 miles.*
Bedrooms: 1 single, 1 double, 1 triple
Bathrooms: 3 private

| Bed & breakfast per night: | £min | £max |
|---|---|---|
| Single | 17.50 | 19.50 |
| Double | 35.00 | 39.00 |

Parking for 3

🐕🖵♨UL🔓📞♿✕📺🛄,🍴2-6✿
🚗SP

### Merrywood
Listed HIGHLY COMMENDED

Hampton on the Hill, Warwick CV35 8QR
☎ (01926) 492766
*Family house in small village 2 miles from Warwick, with open views from both of the rooms.*
Bedrooms: 1 single, 1 twin
Bathrooms: 2 public

| Bed & breakfast per night: | £min | £max |
|---|---|---|
| Single | 17.50 | 18.50 |
| Double | 27.50 | 30.00 |

Parking for 3

🐕1✕🖵♨UL🔓🛄,🚗✿✕🚗

### Northleigh House ⋏
👑👑 HIGHLY COMMENDED

Five Ways Road, Hatton, Warwick CV35 7HZ
☎ (01926) 484203 & Mobile 0374 101894

*Comfortable, peaceful country house where the elegant rooms are individually designed and have en-suite bathroom, fridge, kettle and remote-control TV.*
Bedrooms: 1 single, 5 double, 1 twin
Bathrooms: 7 private

| Bed & breakfast per night: | £min | £max |
|---|---|---|
| Single | 28.00 | 38.00 |
| Double | 38.00 | 55.00 |

Parking for 8
Open February-November
Cards accepted: Access, Visa

🐕🖵🖵♨UL🔓S✕📺🛄,🚗✿🚗

### Old Rectory ⋏
👑👑 COMMENDED

Vicarage Lane, Sherbourne, Warwick CV35 8AB
☎ Barford (01926) 624562
Fax (01926) 624562

*Continued* ▶

## WARWICK

*Continued*

*Georgian country house with beams and inglenook fireplaces, furnished with antiques. Well-appointed bedrooms, many with brass beds, some with direct-dial telephones, all with en-suite facilities and colour TV. Hearty breakfast, tray supper. Situated half a mile from M40 junction 15.*
Bedrooms: 4 single, 6 double, 2 twin, 1 triple, 1 family room
Bathrooms: 14 private

**Bed & breakfast**

| per night: | £min | £max |
|---|---|---|
| Single | 31.50 | 38.00 |
| Double | 40.00 | 48.00 |

Evening meal 1800 (last orders 2200)
Parking for 14
Cards accepted: Access, Visa

### Redlands Farm House

Banbury Road, Lighthorne, Warwick
CV35 0AH
☎ Leamington Spa (01926) 651241
*Built in local stone, mainly 17th C, tastefully restored and with a wealth of timber beams. Centrally located for Warwick and Stratford-upon-Avon, 2 miles from M40 junction 12.*
Bedrooms: 1 single, 1 double, 1 family room
Bathrooms: 1 private, 1 public

**Bed & breakfast**

| per night: | £min | £max |
|---|---|---|
| Single | 15.00 | 17.50 |
| Double | 32.00 | 35.00 |

Parking for 6
Open April-September

### The Seven Stars Public House

Listed

Friars Street, Warwick CV34 6HD
☎ (01926) 492658
*Black and white inn, built in 1610. Near town centre and racecourse and just a few minutes' walk from Warwick Castle.*
Bedrooms: 2 twin
Bathrooms: 1 public

**Bed & breakfast**

| per night: | £min | £max |
|---|---|---|
| Single | 12.50 | 15.00 |
| Double | 25.00 | 35.00 |

**Half board**

| per person: | £min | £max |
|---|---|---|
| Daily | 16.50 | 19.00 |
| Weekly | 100.00 | 130.00 |

Lunch available
Evening meal from 1800
Parking for 8
Cards accepted: Visa

### Shrewley House ⋒

HIGHLY COMMENDED

Hockley Road, Shrewley, Warwick
CV35 7AT
☎ Claverdon (01926) 842549
Fax (01926) 842216
*Listed 17th C farmhouse and home set amidst beautiful 1.5 acre gardens. King-sized four-poster bedrooms, all en-suite, with many thoughtful extras. Four miles from Warwick.*
Bedrooms: 2 double, 1 family room
Bathrooms: 3 private

**Bed & breakfast**

| per night: | £min | £max |
|---|---|---|
| Single | 37.00 | |
| Double | 55.00 | |

Evening meal from 1930
Parking for 22
Cards accepted: Access, Visa

### Tudor House Inn ⋒

90-92 West Street, Warwick
CV34 6AW
☎ (01926) 495447
Fax (01926) 492948
*Inn of character dating from 1472, with a wealth of beams. One of the few buildings to survive the great fire of Warwick in 1694. Opposite Warwick Castle and close to Warwick racecourse.*
Bedrooms: 3 single, 5 double, 2 twin, 1 family room
Bathrooms: 6 private, 1 public, 2 private showers

**Bed & breakfast**

| per night: | £min | £max |
|---|---|---|
| Single | 24.00 | |
| Double | 54.00 | |

**Half board**

| per person: | £min | £max |
|---|---|---|
| Daily | 34.00 | |

Lunch available
Evening meal 1800 (last orders 2300)
Parking for 6
Cards accepted: Access, Visa, Diners, Amex, Switch/Delta

## WATERHOUSES

Staffordshire
Map ref 4B2

Village in the valley of the River Hamps, once the terminus of the Leek and Manifold Light Railway, 8 miles of which is now a macadamised walkers' path.

### Ye Olde Crown ⋒

APPROVED

Leek Road, Waterhouses, Stoke-on-Trent ST10 3HL
☎ (01538) 308204
*On the edge of the Peak District National Park and at the start of the beautiful Manifold Valley. It is built of*

*natural stone and has a wealth of original oak beams.*
Bedrooms: 2 single, 3 double, 1 twin, 1 family room
Bathrooms: 5 private, 1 public

**Bed & breakfast**

| per night: | £min | £max |
|---|---|---|
| Single | 15.00 | 22.50 |
| Double | 35.00 | 35.00 |

**Half board**

| per person: | £min | £max |
|---|---|---|
| Daily | 22.00 | 35.00 |
| Weekly | 155.00 | 245.00 |

Lunch available
Evening meal 1900 (last orders 2200)
Parking for 50

## WEM

Shropshire
Map ref 4A3

Small town connected with Judge Jeffreys who lived in Lowe Hall. Well known for its ales.

### Chez Michael ⋒

Listed

23 Roden Grove, Wem, Shrewsbury
SY4 5HJ
☎ (01939) 232947
*Family-run, large bungalow, suitable for the elderly - children also very welcome. Large garden. Hawkstone Caves and Follies a short car ride away. Also convenient for medieval Shrewsbury.*
Bedrooms: 2 double
Bathrooms: 1 private, 1 public

**Bed & breakfast**

| per night: | £min | £max |
|---|---|---|
| Single | 14.00 | 16.00 |
| Double | 28.00 | 30.00 |

**Half board**

| per person: | £min | £max |
|---|---|---|
| Daily | 19.00 | 21.00 |

Evening meal 1700 (last orders 1830)
Parking for 2

### Forncet

Listed COMMENDED

Soulton Road, Wem, Shrewsbury
SY4 5HR
☎ (01939) 232996
*Spacious, centrally heated Victorian house on the edge of this small market town, 200 yards from British Rail station.*
Bedrooms: 1 single, 1 twin, 1 triple
Bathrooms: 2 public

**Bed & breakfast**

| per night: | £min | £max |
|---|---|---|
| Single | 13.00 | 15.00 |
| Double | 26.00 | 30.00 |

**Half board**

| per person: | £min | £max |
|---|---|---|
| Daily | 22.00 | 24.00 |

Evening meal 1830 (last orders 1930)
Parking for 4

🛇🕱⌨☺🖳🛈👗🅂🎗📺▦ 🚗🔌✿⊁🚜 SP

## Foxleigh House ♙
☀☀ COMMENDED

Foxleigh Drive, Wem, Shrewsbury
SY4 5BP
☎ (01939) 233528

Pretty bedrooms, private bathrooms in elegant country house on Shropshire Way. Ideal for touring. Comfort and warm welcome.
Bedrooms: 2 twin
Bathrooms: 2 private

**Bed & breakfast**

| per night: | £min | £max |
|---|---|---|
| Single | 18.00 | 20.00 |
| Double | 34.00 | 40.00 |

**Half board**

| per person: | £min | £max |
|---|---|---|
| Daily | 25.00 | 27.00 |
| Weekly | 175.00 | 185.00 |

Evening meal 1830 (last orders 2000)
Parking for 7

🛇10🖭⌨🖳👗🅂📺▦🖿✿🚜 SP🏠Ⓣ

## Lowe Hall Farm ♙
☀☀

Wem, Shrewsbury SY4 5UE
☎ (01939) 232236
150-acre dairy farm. Historically famous Grade II listed farmhouse, once the country residence of Judge Jeffreys, 1648-1689. High standard of food, decor and accommodation guaranteed.
Bedrooms: 1 double, 1 twin, 1 triple
Bathrooms: 1 private, 2 public

**Bed & breakfast**

| per night: | £min | £max |
|---|---|---|
| Single | 18.00 | 18.00 |
| Double | 32.00 | 32.00 |

**Half board**

| per person: | £min | £max |
|---|---|---|
| Daily | 24.00 | 24.00 |
| Weekly | 161.00 | 161.00 |

Evening meal 1830 (last orders 1930)
Parking for 8

🛇⌨🖳👗🅂📺▦🖿🔌🗡✿🚜

## Soulton Hall ♙
☀☀☀ COMMENDED

Wem, Shrewsbury SY4 5RS
☎ (01939) 232786
Fax (01939) 234097
Good home cooking and en-suite rooms at this Tudor manor house ensure a relaxing holiday. Moated Domesday site in grounds, private riverside and woodland walks.

---

Bedrooms: 1 single, 3 double, 1 twin, 1 triple
Bathrooms: 6 private

**Bed & breakfast**

| per night: | £min | £max |
|---|---|---|
| Single | 21.50 | 36.00 |
| Double | 43.00 | 58.00 |

**Half board**

| per person: | £min | £max |
|---|---|---|
| Daily | 36.50 | 45.00 |
| Weekly | 203.00 | 283.00 |

Evening meal 1900 (last orders 2030)
Parking for 23
Cards accepted: Access, Visa, Diners

🛇🖭⌨👗🅂🛈🅂✂▦🖿🖿 Ⓣ10🕊🗡⧉✿🚜 DAP ⊁SP🏠Ⓣ

### WENLOCK EDGE

Shropshire
Map ref 4A3

## The Wenlock Edge Inn ♙
☀☀ COMMENDED

Hilltop, Wenlock Edge, Much Wenlock TF13 6DJ
☎ Brockton (01746) 36403
Family run freehouse of Wenlock limestone, built about 1700. Peaceful location, fine views. Four miles from Much Wenlock on B4371.
Bedrooms: 2 double, 1 twin
Bathrooms: 3 private

**Bed & breakfast**

| per night: | £min | £max |
|---|---|---|
| Single | 40.00 | |
| Double | 55.00 | |

Lunch available
Evening meal 1900 (last orders 2100)
Parking for 40
Cards accepted: Access, Visa, Switch/Delta

🛇8🖭⌨🖳👗🅂✂▦📺▦🖿🕊⊁🚜🏠

### WEOBLEY

Hereford and Worcester
Map ref 2A1

One of the most beautiful Herefordshire villages and full of attractive black and white timber-framed houses. It is dominated by the church which has a fine spire.

## Ye Olde Salutation Inn ♙
☀☀☀ HIGHLY COMMENDED

Market Pitch, Weobley, Hereford HR4 8SJ
☎ (01544) 318443
Fax (01544) 318216

Traditional black and white country inn overlooking the main Broad Street.

---

Quality home-cooked bar meals and a la carte menu. Inglenook fireplace. Homely atmosphere.
Bedrooms: 3 double, 1 twin
Bathrooms: 4 private, 1 public

**Bed & breakfast**

| per night: | £min | £max |
|---|---|---|
| Single | 32.50 | 34.00 |
| Double | 55.00 | 60.00 |

Lunch available
Evening meal 1900 (last orders 2130)
Parking for 20
Cards accepted: Access, Visa, Diners, Amex, Switch/Delta

🛇12🖭🖭⌨👗🛈🅂✂▦📺▦🖿 Ⓣ6🕊🔌🕊⊁✿🚜SP🏠

### WILMCOTE

Warwickshire
Map ref 2B1

Village where Shakespeare's mother, Mary Arden, lived. Her home has an attractive cottage garden and now houses a museum of rural life.

## Dosthill Cottage
☀☀

The Green, Wilmcote, Stratford-upon-Avon CV37 9XJ
☎ Stratford-upon-Avon (01789) 266480
Old cottage on the village green, overlooking Mary Arden's house, with pleasant garden available to guests. Farmhouse museum and gardens.
Bedrooms: 2 double, 1 twin
Bathrooms: 3 private

**Bed & breakfast**

| per night: | £min | £max |
|---|---|---|
| Single | 20.00 | 28.00 |
| Double | 36.00 | 40.00 |

Parking for 6

🛇🖳⌨🖳👗🖳📺▦🖿✿🚜🏠

### WINCHCOMBE

Gloucestershire
Map ref 2B1

Ancient town with a folk museum and railway museum. To the south lies Sudeley Castle with its fine collection of paintings and toys and an Elizabethan garden.

## Mercia
☀☀ COMMENDED

Hailes Street, Winchcombe, Cheltenham GL54 5HU
☎ Cheltenham (01242) 602251
Black and white Cotswold-stone Tudor cottage with beamed walls and ceilings. Private parking at rear. Pleasant garden and views. 15 minutes from M5.
Bedrooms: 2 double, 1 twin
Bathrooms: 3 private

Continued ▶

## WINCHCOMBE

### Continued

**Bed & breakfast**

| per night: | £min | £max |
|---|---|---|
| Single | 17.00 | 20.00 |
| Double | 34.00 | 36.00 |

Parking for 3

🐕🛏️UL🛈S⚡🎔TV▥🖥🚗♻🔷🏠

### The Plaisterers Arms ⚔️
👑👑

Abbey Terrace, Winchcombe,
Cheltenham GL54 5LL
☎ Cheltenham (01242) 602358
Fax (01242) 602358

*Old Cotswold stone inn with en-suite
bed and breakfast accommodation, close
to Sudeley Castle and town centre.
Extensive menu, pub lunches, bar
snacks and evening meals available
every day. Large garden, patio and
children's area.*
Bedrooms: 2 double, 1 twin
Bathrooms: 3 private, 1 public

**Bed & breakfast**

| per night: | £min | £max |
|---|---|---|
| Single | 20.00 | 25.00 |
| Double | 35.00 | 40.00 |

Lunch available
Evening meal 1830 (last orders 2130)
Cards accepted: Access, Visa, Amex

🐕🗖🛏️S▥🎔🔍♻🏠🔷

### Postlip Hall Farm ⚔️
👑👑 HIGHLY COMMENDED

Winchcombe, Cheltenham GL54 5AQ
☎ Cheltenham (01242) 603351
*300-acre mixed farm. Family farm in
superb scenic location 1 mile from
Winchcombe, on side of Cleeve Hill.
Perfect centre for touring the Cotswolds,
Bath, Warwick. Great atmosphere.
Tranquillity guaranteed.*
Bedrooms: 1 double, 1 twin, 1 triple
Bathrooms: 3 private

**Bed & breakfast**

| per night: | £min | £max |
|---|---|---|
| Single | 16.50 | 25.00 |
| Double | 35.00 | 37.00 |

Parking for 6

🐕🛏️🎔UL🖊⚡TV▥🚗U✓♻🏠

### Sudeley Hill Farm ⚔️
👑👑 HIGHLY COMMENDED

Winchcombe, Cheltenham GL54 5JB
☎ Cheltenham (01242) 602344
*800-acre mixed farm. 15th C listed
farmhouse overlooking Sudeley Valley
and Castle. 1 mile out of Winchcombe.*
Bedrooms: 1 double, 1 twin, 1 triple

Bathrooms: 3 private

**Bed & breakfast**

| per night: | £min | £max |
|---|---|---|
| Single | 20.00 | 25.00 |
| Double | 40.00 | 40.00 |

Parking for 10

🐕🛏️🗖🎔⚡UL S⚡🎔TV▥🚗U⊨♻✗🏠🏠

### Wesley House Restaurant ⚔️
👑👑👑 COMMENDED

High Street, Winchcombe, Cheltenham
GL54 5LJ
☎ Cheltenham (01242) 602366

*Built in 1435, a former merchant's
house sympathetically restored to offer
quality accommodation and modern
British cooking. Warm and cosy in
winter with open log fires.*
Bedrooms: 1 single, 3 double, 2 twin
Bathrooms: 6 private

**Bed & breakfast**

| per night: | £min | £max |
|---|---|---|
| Single | 25.00 | 55.00 |
| Double | 45.00 | 65.00 |

**Half board**

| per person: | £min | £max |
|---|---|---|
| Daily | 40.00 | 55.00 |

Lunch available
Evening meal 1900 (last orders 2200)
Cards accepted: Access, Visa, Amex,
Switch/Delta

🐕📞🗖🛏️🎔🛈S⚡▥🚗U♻✗🏠🔷🏠

## WOOTTON WAWEN

### Warwickshire
### Map ref 2B1

Attractive village which has an
unspoilt church with an Anglo-
Saxon tower, the only chained
library in Warwickshire and some
good brasses and monuments.

### Wootton Park Farm ⚔️
👑👑 APPROVED

Alcester Road, Wootton Wawen,
Solihull, West Midlands B95 6HJ
☎ Henley-in-Arden (01564) 792673

*340-acre arable & dairy farm. Delightful
16th C half-timbered farmhouse with a
wealth of oak beams. 5 miles north of
Stratford-upon-Avon in quiet*

*countryside. Conveniently situated for
the National Agricultural Centre and the
National Exhibition Centre.*
Bedrooms: 1 double, 1 triple, 1 family
room
Bathrooms: 1 private, 1 public

**Bed & breakfast**

| per night: | £min | £max |
|---|---|---|
| Single | 22.00 | 25.00 |
| Double | 36.00 | 40.00 |

Parking for 6

🐕🛏️🎔UL S🎔TV▥🚗🔨✓♻🏠

### Yew Tree Farm ⚔️
👑👑 COMMENDED

Wootton Wawen, Solihull, West
Midlands B95 6BY
☎ Henley-in-Arden (01564) 792701
*800-acre arable & dairy farm. Fine
Georgian farmhouse conveniently
situated in village on the A3400, 6
miles from Stratford-upon-Avon. Large
en-suite bedrooms, with tea/coffee
facilities. Hearty English breakfast.
Farm walks.*
Bedrooms: 1 double, 1 twin
Bathrooms: 2 private

**Bed & breakfast**

| per night: | £min | £max |
|---|---|---|
| Single | | 22.50 |
| Double | | 35.00 |

Parking for 12

🐕5🗖🛏️🎔⚡UL🔨🎔TV▥🚗U♫♻✗🏠

## WORCESTER

### Hereford and Worcester
### Map ref 2B1

Lovely riverside city dominated by
its Norman and Early English
cathedral, King John's burial place.
Many old buildings including the
15th C Commandery and the 18th
C Guildhall. There are several
museums and the Royal Worcester
porcelain factory.
*Tourist Information Centre*
☎ *(01905) 726311*

### Burgage House ⚔️
Listed

4 College Precincts, Worcester
WR1 2LG
☎ (01905) 25396
*Comfortable accommodation in elegant
Georgian mews house in quiet cobbled
street next to cathedral. Close to River
Severn and cricket ground.*
Bedrooms: 1 single, 1 double, 1 twin,
1 triple
Bathrooms: 2 private, 2 public

**Bed & breakfast**

| per night: | £min | £max |
|---|---|---|
| Single | 22.00 | 24.00 |
| Double | 34.00 | 36.00 |

🐕❄🗖🛏️UL S⚡▥🚗✗🏠🔷🏠T

### Ivy Cottage ⋀
[CROWN CROWN] **COMMENDED**

Sinton Green, Hallow, Worcester
WR2 6NP
☎ (01905) 641123
*Charming cottage in quiet village, 4 miles north of Worcester, off A443 Worcester to Tenbury road. Good local restaurants.*
Bedrooms: 1 single, 1 double, 1 twin
Bathrooms: 3 private

**Bed & breakfast**

| per night: | £min | £max |
|---|---|---|
| Single | 16.00 | 20.00 |
| Double | 32.00 | 35.00 |

Parking for 4

### Little Lightwood Farm
[CROWN CROWN] **COMMENDED**

Lightwood Lane, Cotheridge, Worcester WR6 5LT
☎ Cotheridge (01905) 333236
*56-acre dairy farm. Farmhouse accommodation with en-suite rooms, tea-making facilities and heating in all bedrooms. Delightful views of the Malvern Hills. Just off the A44 from Worcester to Leominster, 3.5 miles from Worcester.*
Bedrooms: 2 double, 1 twin
Bathrooms: 3 private

**Bed & breakfast**

| per night: | £min | £max |
|---|---|---|
| Single | 18.00 | 22.00 |
| Double | 32.00 | 36.00 |

**Half board**

| per person: | £min | £max |
|---|---|---|
| Daily | 25.00 | 31.00 |
| Weekly | 168.00 | 182.00 |

Evening meal from 1800
Parking for 6
Open February-November

### Loch Ryan Hotel ⋀
[CROWN CROWN CROWN]

119 Sidbury, Worcester WR5 2DH
☎ (01905) 351143
Fax (01905) 764407
*Historic hotel, once home of Bishop Gore, close to cathedral, Royal Worcester Porcelain factory and Commandery. Attractive terraced garden. Imaginative food. Holders of Heartbeat and Worcester City clean food awards.*
Bedrooms: 1 single, 3 double, 5 twin, 1 family room
Bathrooms: 10 private

**Bed & breakfast**

| per night: | £min | £max |
|---|---|---|
| Single | 35.00 | 45.00 |
| Double | 45.00 | 55.00 |

Evening meal 1800 (last orders 1900)
Cards accepted: Access, Visa, Diners, Amex

### The Old Smithy ⋀
[Listed] **HIGHLY COMMENDED**

Pirton, Worcester WR8 9EJ
☎ (01905) 820482
*17th C half-timbered country house in peaceful countryside, only 4.5 miles from M5 motorway (junction 7) and Worcester city. Ideal central base for touring Cotswolds, Stratford-upon-Avon, Warwick and Potteries.*
Bedrooms: 1 double, 1 twin
Bathrooms: 1 public

**Bed & breakfast**

| per night: | £min | £max |
|---|---|---|
| Double | 30.00 | 40.00 |

**Half board**

| per person: | £min | £max |
|---|---|---|
| Daily | 23.00 | 28.00 |

Evening meal from 1830
Parking for 6

### Retreat Farm ⋀
[Listed] **HIGHLY COMMENDED**

Camp Lane, Grimley, Worcester WR2 6LU
☎ (01905) 640266
*60-acre arable farm. 17th C farmhouse, overlooking River Severn and Bevere Lock. Within walking distance of the Camp House Inn and Wagon Wheel Restaurant.*
Bedrooms: 2 double
Bathrooms: 2 private

**Bed & breakfast**

| per night: | £min | £max |
|---|---|---|
| Single | 20.00 | |
| Double | 38.00 | |

Parking for 14
Open April-October

## WORMSLEY
Hereford and Worcester
Map ref 2A1

### Hill Top Farm
[CROWN CROWN]

Wormsley, Hereford HR4 8LZ
☎ Bridge Sollars (01981) 22246
*200-acre arable & livestock farm. Comfortable stone-built farmhouse under brow of hill, deep in the Herefordshire countryside. Magnificent views over fields and woods to Black Mountains.*
Bedrooms: 1 twin, 1 triple
Bathrooms: 2 private, 1 public

**Bed & breakfast**

| per night: | £min | £max |
|---|---|---|
| Single | 14.00 | |
| Double | 34.00 | |

Parking for 6
Open February-November

## WYE VALLEY
*See under Fownhope, Hereford, Ross-on-Wye*

## YARKHILL
Hereford and Worcester
Map ref 2B1

### Garford Farm ⋀
[Listed]

Yarkhill, Hereford HR1 3ST
☎ Tarrington (01432) 890226
Fax (01432) 890707
*190-acre mixed farm. Picturesque black and white farmhouse on working farm. Very quiet but with easy access to the A4103 Hereford to Worcester road.*
Bedrooms: 1 double, 1 family room
Bathrooms: 1 public

**Bed & breakfast**

| per night: | £min | £max |
|---|---|---|
| Single | | 15.00 |
| Double | | 30.00 |

Parking for 6

## YOXALL
Staffordshire
Map ref 4B3

### The Moat ⋀
[CROWN CROWN] **HIGHLY COMMENDED**

Town Hill, Yoxall, Burton upon Trent DE13 8NN
☎ Burton upon Trent (01543) 472210
*Country house sited in 2.5 acres of garden, dry moated, of historic interest. Grounds listed Grade II.*
Wheelchair access category 3 ♿
Bedrooms: 3 twin
Bathrooms: 3 private, 1 public

**Bed & breakfast**

| per night: | £min | £max |
|---|---|---|
| Single | 25.00 | 30.00 |
| Double | 45.00 | 55.00 |

**Half board**

| per person: | £min | £max |
|---|---|---|
| Daily | 40.00 | 45.00 |

Parking for 6

# USE YOUR $i$'S

There are more than 550 Tourist Information Centres throughout England offering friendly help with accommodation and holiday ideas as well as suggestions of places to visit and things to do.

In your home town there may be a centre which can help you before you set out. You'll find the address of your nearest Tourist Information Centre in your local Phone Book.

# NATIONAL ACCESSIBLE SCHEME FOR WHEELCHAIR USERS

If you are a wheelchair user or someone who has difficulty walking, look for the national 'Accessible' symbol when choosing where to stay.

All the places that display the symbol have been checked by a Tourist Board inspector against criteria that reflect the practical needs of wheelchair users.

**There are three categories of accessibility, indicated by symbols:**

**Category 1:** Accessible to all wheelchair users including those travelling independently

**Category 2:** Accessible to a wheelchair user with assistance

**Category 3:** Accessible to a wheelchair user able to walk short distances and up at least three steps

Establishments in this 'Where to Stay' guide which have an access category are listed in the information pages at the back, together with further details of the scheme. Tourist Information Centre staff will also be pleased to help with finding suitable accommodation.

*Whether you're looking for peace and tranquillity or action and adventure, whether you want a traditional seaside holiday or an entertaining city break – whatever the season, the five counties of Middle England offer an unrivalled choice. Escape from the hustle and bustle of everyday life in the region's immensely varied countryside. You'll enjoy the hills and dales of Derbyshire and the gently rolling landscape of the Lincolnshire Wolds, the woods and waterways of Leicestershire and Northamptonshire – and the haunts of Robin Hood in Nottinghamshire.*

# MIDDLE ENGLAND

The Counties of Derbyshire, Leicestershire, Lincolnshire, Northamptonshire and Nottinghamshire

For more information on Middle England, contact:
**East Midlands Tourist Board**
**Exchequergate**
**Lincoln LN2 1PZ**
**Tel: (01522) 531521**
**Fax: (01522) 532501**

Where to Go in Middle England
– see pages 192–195

Where to Stay in Middle England
– see pages 196–213

# WHERE TO GO

*You will find hundreds of interesting places to visit during your stay in Middle England, just some of which are listed in these pages. The number against each name will help you locate it on the map (page 195). Contact any Tourist Information Centre in the region for more ideas on days out in Middle England.*

**❶ Gainsborough Old Hall**
Parnell Street, Gainsborough, Lincolnshire
DN21 2NB
Tel: (01427) 612669
*Late medieval timber-framed manor house built c1460, with fine medieval kitchen. Displays on the building and its restoration.*

**❷ Buxton Micrarium**
The Crescent, Buxton, Derbyshire SK17 6BQ
Tel: (01298) 78662
*Unique exhibition of the natural world under the microscope, using special push-button projection microscopes operated by visitors.*

**❸ Museum of Lincolnshire Life**
Burton Road, Lincoln LN1 3LY
Tel: (01522) 528448
*Agricultural, industrial and social history of Lincolnshire from 1800. Edwardian room setting. Display of craftwork in progress. World War I tank on display.*

**❹ Skegness Water Leisure Park**
Walls Lane, Ingoldmells, Lincolnshire PE25 1JF
Tel: (01754) 769019
*Water leisure park with cable tow water skiing, quad bikes, coarse fishing, narrow gauge railway.*

**❺ Chatsworth House and Garden, Farmyard and Adventure Playground**
Chatsworth, Bakewell, Derbyshire DE45 1PP
Tel: (01246) 582204
*Built 1687–1707. Collection of fine pictures, books, drawings, furniture. Garden laid out by Capability Brown with fountains, cascade. Farmyard with livestock, adventure playground.*

**Home of the Duke and Duchess of Devonshire, Chatsworth houses a collection of treasures.**

**❻ Rufford Country Park and Craft Centre**
Ollerton, Nottinghamshire NG22 9DF
Tel: (01623) 824153
*Parkland and 25-acre lake with ruins of Cistercian abbey. Woodland walks, formal gardens, sculpture garden. Craft centre with exhibitions of British craftsmanship.*

**❼ The National Tramway Museum**
Crich, Derbyshire DE4 5DP
Tel: (01773) 852565
*Collection of 50 trams from Britain and overseas built 1873–1953. Tram rides on one-mile route, period street scene, depots, power station, workshops.*

### 8 White Post Modern Farm Centre
Farnsfield, Nr Newark, Nottinghamshire
NG22 8HL
Tel: (01623) 882977
*Working farm with over 2,000 animals, including
llama. 8,000-egg incubator, free-range hens,
lakes, picnic areas, tea gardens, indoor
countryside night walk.*

### 9 Southwell Minster
Bishop's Drive, Southwell, Nottinghamshire
NG25 0JP
Tel: (01636) 812649
*Saxon tympanum, Norman nave and crossing,
Early English choir, outstanding foliage carving in
Chapter House. Ruins of archbishop's palace.*

### 10 Midland Railway Centre
Butterley Station, Ripley, Derbyshire DE5 3TL
Tel: (01773) 747674
*Over 25 locomotives and over 80 items of
historic rolling stock of Midland and LMS origin.
Steam-hauled passenger service, museum site,
country park.*

### 11 American Adventure
Pit Lane, Ilkeston, Derbyshire DE7 5SX
Tel: (01773) 531521
*American theme park with more than 100 rides
including Nightmare Niagara, Log Flume, Rocky
Mountain, Rapids Ride, The Missile. Motion Master
Simulator Cinema and many other attractions.*

### 12 Nottingham Industrial Museum
Courtyard Buildings, Wollaton Park,
Nottingham NG8 2AE
Tel: (0115) 928 4602
*18th C stables presenting history of Nottingham's
industries: printing, pharmacy, hosiery and lace.
Victorian beam engine, horse gin, transport.*

### 13 The Tales of Robin Hood
30–38 Maid Marian Way, Nottingham NG1 6GF
Tel: (0115) 941 4414
*Join the world's greatest medieval adventure and
hide out in the Sheriff's eerie cave. Ride through the
magical Greenwood and play the Silver Arrow game.*

### 14 Belton House, Park and Gardens
Belton, Lincolnshire NG32 2LS
Tel: (01476) 66116
*The crowning achievement of Restoration country*

*The Shires of Middle England are home to a
rich diversity of agricultural activity.*

*house architecture, built in 1685–88 for Sir John
Brownlow. Alterations by James Wyatt in 1777.*

### 15 Belvoir Castle
Belvoir, Lincolnshire NG32 1PD
Tel: (01476) 870262
*Present castle is fourth to be built on the site,
dating from 1816. Museum of Queens Royal
Lancers. Art treasures include works by Poussin,
Rubens, Holbein, Reynolds.*

### 16 Derby Industrial Museum
Silk Mill Lane, off Full Street, Derby DE1 3AR
Tel: (01332) 255308
*Displays on industries of Derbyshire, including
Rolls-Royce aero engines and railway engineering.
Museum is on site of former silk mill.*

### 17 Sudbury Hall
Sudbury, Derbyshire DE6 5HT
Tel: (01283) 585305
*Grand 17th C house. Plasterwork ceilings, ceiling
paintings, carved staircase and overmantel.
Museum of Childhood in former servants' wing.*

### 18 Great Central Railway
Great Central Station, Great Central Road,
Loughborough, Leicestershire LE11 1RW
Tel: (01509) 230726
*Preserved mainline steam railway operating
over 8.5 miles between Loughborough and
Leicester North.*

### 19 Ye Olde Pork Pie Shoppe
10 Nottingham Street, Melton Mowbray,
Leicestershire LE13 1NW
Tel: (01664) 62341

Pork pie shop and bakery in 17th C building. History of the town's pork pie industry, demonstrations of traditional craft of hand raising pork pies.

### ⑳ Springfields
Camelgate, Spalding, Lincolnshire PE12 6ET
Tel: (01775) 724843
25 acres of landscaped gardens with lake, woodland walk and palm house. New exhibition centre houses various events throughout the year.

### ㉑ Oakham Castle
Oakham, Leicestershire
Tel: (01572) 723654
Splendid 12th C great hall of fortified manor house. Unique horseshoe forfeits left by peers of the realm.

### ㉒ Newarke Houses Museum
The Newarke, Leicester LE2 7BY
Tel: (0116) 247 3222
Local history and crafts from 1485. Toys and games, clocks, mechanical instruments. 19th C street scene, early 20th C shop. Feature on Daniel Lambert, the 19th C giant.

### ㉓ Twycross Zoo
Twycross, Warwickshire CV9 3PX
Tel: (01827) 880250
Gorillas, orang-utans, chimpanzees, modern gibbon complex, elephants, lions, cheetahs, giraffes, reptile house, pets' corner, rides.

### ㉔ Rockingham Castle
Rockingham, Leicestershire LE16 8TH
Tel: (01536) 770240
Elizabethan house within walls of Norman castle. Fine pictures. Extensive views and gardens with roses and ancient yew hedge.

### ㉕ Foxton Locks Country Park
Gumley Road, Foxton, Leicestershire
Tel: (0116) 265 6914
Landscaped picnic site with woodland footpath to Grand Union Canal towpath, long flight of locks and remains of barge lift.

### ㉖ Stanford Hall and Motorcycle Museum
Lutterworth, Leicestershire LE17 6DH
Tel: (01788) 860250
William and Mary house on River Avon. Family

Bakewell puddings take pride of place among the region's culinary specialities.

costumes, furniture and pictures. Replica 1898 flying machine, motorcycle museum, rose garden, nature trail. Craft centre most Sundays.

### ㉗ Manor House Museum
Sheep Street, Kettering, Northamptonshire
Tel: (01536) 410333
Kettering's past, including shoe-making machinery, agricultural equipment and the Robinson car made in the town in 1907.

### ㉘ Holdenby House Gardens
Holdenby, Northampton NN6 8DJ
Tel: (01604) 770074
Remains of Elizabethan gardens with original entrance arches and terraces. King Charles Walk. Museum, craft shop, rare breeds of farm animals, falconry centre.

### ㉙ Church of the Holy Sepulchre
Sheep Street, Northampton NN1 3NL
Tel: (01604) 754782
England's largest Norman round church built c1100 with tower c1300. Restored by Gilbert Scott. Crusader window, Northamptonshire Regiment memorial chapel.

### ㉚ Sulgrave Manor
Sulgrave, Oxfordshire OX17 2SD
Tel: (01295) 760205
Small manor house of Shakespeare's time with furniture of period and fine kitchen. Early English home of ancestors of George Washington.

# FIND OUT MORE

Further information about holidays and attractions in Middle England is available from: **East Midlands Tourist Board**, Exchequergate, Lincoln LN2 1PZ Tel: (01522) 531521

These publications are available free from the

East Midlands Tourist Board:
- **Middle England '95** (general brochure)
- **The Peak District 1995**
- **Derbyshire – A Guide to Short Breaks**
- **Events list** (please send large stamped and addressed envelope)

Also available is (price includes postage and packing):
- **Shires of Middle England Leisure Map £3.50**

# WHERE TO STAY

*Accommodation entries in this regional section are listed in alphabetical order of place name, and then in alphabetical order of establishment.*

*Map references refer to the colour location maps at the back of this guide. The first figure is the map number; the letter and figure which follow indicate the grid reference on the map.*

*Symbols at the end of each accommodation entry give information about services and facilities. A 'key' to these symbols is inside the back cover flap, which can be kept open for easy reference.*

---

## ABTHORPE

Northamptonshire
Map ref 2C1

### Stone Cottage
Main Street, Abthorpe, Towcester
NN12 8QN
☎ Silverstone (01327) 857544
*Grade II listed cottage in delightful secluded position in conservation village. Convenient for Silverstone, Cotswolds, Oxford, M1 and M40 motorways.*
Bedrooms: 1 single, 2 twin
Bathrooms: 2 public

**Bed & breakfast**

| per night: | £min | £max |
| --- | --- | --- |
| Single | 18.00 | 18.00 |
| Double | 30.00 | 30.00 |

Parking for 8

🛏🖵🕭🔍🖳🛊Ⓢ🅿🕮🛒🎿🐾🚗🏧

## ALDWARK

Derbyshire
Map ref 4B2

### Tithe Farm ⋀
🏆 COMMENDED
Aldwark, Grange Mill, Matlock
DE4 4HX
☎ Carsington (01629) 540263
*Peacefully situated, within 10 miles of Matlock, Bakewell, Ashbourne, the dales and historic houses. Extensive breakfast menu with home-made bread and preserves.*
Bedrooms: 1 twin, 1 triple
Bathrooms: 2 private

---

**Bed & breakfast**

| per night: | £min | £max |
| --- | --- | --- |
| Single | 21.50 | 22.50 |
| Double | 34.00 | 36.00 |

Parking for 6
Open April-October

🛏🖵🕭🖳🛊Ⓢ🅿🕮📺🛒🏧🎿✗🚗Ⓣ

## ALFORD

Lincolnshire
Map ref 4D2

Busy market town with attractive Georgian houses and shops and a Folk Museum in the thatched manor house. A craft market is held on Fridays in the summer months and there is a restored and working 5-sailed tower mill.

### Halton House
🕭
50 East Street, Alford LN13 9EH
☎ Louth (01507) 462058
*Detached house in own gardens in the rural setting of a small market town on the edge of the Lincolnshire Wolds. A warm welcome awaits you. Non-smokers preferred.*
Bedrooms: 1 double, 1 twin
Bathrooms: 2 public

**Bed & breakfast**

| per night: | £min | £max |
| --- | --- | --- |
| Single | 15.00 | 15.00 |
| Double | 30.00 | 30.00 |

Parking for 3

🛏3🖵🕭🖳🗡🅿📺🛒✗🚗

---

Please mention this guide when making a booking.

---

## ALKMONTON

Derbyshire
Map ref 4B2

### Dairy House Farm ⋀
🏆🏆🏆 COMMENDED
Alkmonton, Longford, Ashbourne
DE6 3DG
☎ Ashbourne (01335) 330359
Fax (01335) 330359
*82-acre livestock farm. Old red brick farmhouse with oak beams, inglenook fireplace and a comfortable atmosphere. Guests have their own lounge and dining room. Non-smokers only and no pets please. Children over 12 only.*
Bedrooms: 3 single, 2 double, 1 twin
Bathrooms: 4 private, 1 public

**Bed & breakfast**

| per night: | £min | £max |
| --- | --- | --- |
| Single | 16.00 | 32.00 |
| Double | 32.00 | 38.00 |

**Half board**

| per person: | £min | £max |
| --- | --- | --- |
| Daily | 27.00 | 35.00 |
| Weekly | 189.00 | 210.00 |

Lunch available
Evening meal 1830 (last orders 1930)
Parking for 8

🕭🔍🛊Ⓢ🗡🅿📺🛒🚗🎿✗🚗

## AMBERGATE

Derbyshire
Map ref 4B2

### Lawn Farm
🕭
Whitewells Lane, Ambergate, Derby
DE5 2DN
☎ (01773) 852352

---

*240-acre livestock farm. Comfortable accommodation. Ideal for visiting stately homes, walking, fishing or touring.*
Bedrooms: 1 double, 1 family room
Bathrooms: 1 private, 1 public

**Bed & breakfast**

| per night: | £min | £max |
|---|---|---|
| Single | 12.50 | 25.00 |
| Double | 25.00 | 35.00 |

Parking for 3

---

## ANCASTER

Lincolnshire
Map ref 3A1

Large village on the Roman Ermine Street, within easy drive of Belton House, Grantham and the cathedral city of Lincoln.

## Woodlands ⋀

Listed

West Willoughby, Ancaster, Grantham NG32 3SH
☎ Loveden (01400) 230340

*12-acre mixed farm. Victorian stone farmhouse, in peaceful rural surroundings. A warm welcome, comfortable accommodation, and traditional farmhouse breakfast. Within easy reach of (A1) Grantham, Lincoln and many places of historic interest.*
Bedrooms: 1 triple, 1 family room
Bathrooms: 1 public

**Bed & breakfast**

| per night: | £min | £max |
|---|---|---|
| Single | 15.00 | 17.00 |
| Double | 28.00 | 30.00 |

Evening meal 1700 (last orders 2000)
Parking for 6
Open March-November

---

There are separate sections in this guide listing groups specialising in farm holidays and accommodation which is especially suitable for young people and organised groups.

---

## ASHBOURNE

Derbyshire
Map ref 4B2 .

Market town on the edge of the Peak District National Park and an excellent centre for walking. Its impressive church with 212-ft spire stands in an unspoilt old street. Ashbourne is well-known for gingerbread and its Shrovetide football match.
*Tourist Information Centre*
☎ *(01335) 343666*

## Bentley Brook Inn ⋀

🏵🏵🏵 COMMENDED

Fenny Bentley, Ashbourne DE6 1LF
☎ Thorpe Cloud (01335) 350278
Fax (01335) 350422

*Traditional family-run country inn with large garden in Peak District National Park. Close to Dovedale, Alton Towers and Chatsworth.*
Bedrooms: 1 single, 5 double, 2 twin, 1 triple
Bathrooms: 6 private, 2 public

**Bed & breakfast**

| per night: | £min | £max |
|---|---|---|
| Single | 17.50 | 37.00 |
| Double | 35.00 | 57.50 |

**Half board**

| per person: | £min | £max |
|---|---|---|
| Daily | 31.25 | 50.75 |
| Weekly | 165.00 | 199.00 |

Lunch available
Evening meal 1900 (last orders 2130)
Parking for 60
Cards accepted: Access, Visa, Diners, Amex & Switch/Delta

## Biggin Mill Farm ⋀

🏵🏵🏵 HIGHLY COMMENDED

Biggin-by-Hulland, Ashbourne DE6 3FN
☎ (01335) 370414

*18th C cosy rural "hideaway". Wooded grounds with stream, ducks and walks. Delicious meals and fine wines in relaxing quality surroundings. Optimally placed for sightseeing. Brochure. Telephone bookings only, please.*

---

Bedrooms: 2 double
Bathrooms: 2 private

**Bed & breakfast**

| per night: | £min | £max |
|---|---|---|
| Single | 47.50 | 47.50 |
| Double | 70.00 | 70.00 |

**Half board**

| per person: | £min | £max |
|---|---|---|
| Daily | 47.50 | 65.00 |

Evening meal 2000 (last orders 2000)
Parking for 2
Cards accepted: Access, Visa, Amex

## Collycroft Farm

Listed

Clifton, Ashbourne DE6 2GN
☎ (01335) 342187
*260-acre mixed farm. A warm welcome is assured in this pleasant farmhouse. Lovely garden and excellent views across the surrounding countryside. South of Ashbourne on the A515 Lichfield road.*
Bedrooms: 1 double, 1 twin, 1 triple
Bathrooms: 1 private, 1 public

**Bed & breakfast**

| per night: | £min | £max |
|---|---|---|
| Single | 17.00 | 17.00 |
| Double | 30.00 | 34.00 |

Parking for 8

## Little Park Farm

🏵 COMMENDED

Mappleton, Ashbourne DE6 2BR
☎ Thorpe Cloud (01335) 350341
*123-acre mixed farm. 300-year-old listed oak-beamed farmhouse, tastefully furnished. In the peaceful Dove Valley, 3 miles from Ashbourne. Superb views.*
Bedrooms: 2 double, 1 twin
Bathrooms: 1 public

**Bed & breakfast**

| per night: | £min | £max |
|---|---|---|
| Double | 26.00 | 32.00 |

**Half board**

| per person: | £min | £max |
|---|---|---|
| Daily | 21.00 | 24.00 |

Evening meal from 1830
Parking for 3
Open March-October

## Mercaston Hall ⋀

🏵🏵

Mercaston, Brailsford, Ashbourne DE6 3BL
☎ (01335) 360263
*55-acre mixed farm. Listed buildings in attractive, quiet countryside. Hard tennis court. Kedleston Hall (National Trust) 1 mile, Carsington Reservoir 5 minutes away.*
Bedrooms: 1 double, 1 twin
Bathrooms: 2 private, 1 public

*Continued* ▶

## ASHBOURNE

*Continued*

**Bed & breakfast**

| per night: | £min | £max |
|---|---|---|
| Single | 19.50 | 22.50 |
| Double | 29.00 | 35.00 |
| Parking for 16 | | |

⛳8🏠🖵♿🗲🛏︎ⓈⅢ☎🖵▥💼🅾
☂✿🚲🏤

### Shirley Hall Farm

😊😊 HIGHLY COMMENDED

Shirley, Ashbourne DE6 3AS
☎ (01335) 360346
*200-acre mixed farm. This peaceful
timbered manor house, complete with
part of its moat, is adjacent to superb
woodland walks and makes an excellent
centre for Sudbury and Kedleston Hall,
Chatsworth and Alton Towers.*
Bedrooms: 2 double, 1 twin
Bathrooms: 2 private, 1 public

**Bed & breakfast**

| per night: | £min | £max |
|---|---|---|
| Single | 17.00 | 20.00 |
| Double | 30.00 | 36.00 |
| Parking for 5 | | |

⛳3🏠🖵♿🗲🛏ⒾⓈⅢ☎▥💼🕭✿
🎦🚲🏤

## ASHFORD IN THE WATER

Derbyshire
Map ref 4B2

Limestone village in attractive
surroundings of the Peak District
approached by 3 bridges over the
River Wye. There is an annual
well-dressing ceremony and the
village was well-known in the 18th
C for its black marble quarries.

### Gritstone House 🗛

😊😊 HIGHLY COMMENDED

Greaves Lane, Ashford in the Water,
Bakewell DE45 1QH
☎ Bakewell (01629) 813563
*Charming 18th C Georgian house
offering friendly service and
accommodation designed with comfort
and style in mind. Ideal centre for
exploring the Peak District's scenery
and country houses, and close to an
extensive range of dining-out facilities.*
Bedrooms: 2 double, 1 twin
Bathrooms: 1 private, 1 public

**Bed & breakfast**

| per night: | £min | £max |
|---|---|---|
| Double | 34.00 | 42.00 |

🏠🖵♿🗲🛏ⓈⅢ☎▥💼🎦🚲🏤

The enquiry coupons
at the back will help
you when contacting
proprietors.

## ASHOVER

Derbyshire
Map ref 4B2

Unspoilt village with a 13th C
church.

### Old School Farm

😊

Uppertown, Ashover, Chesterfield
S45 0JF
☎ Chesterfield (01246) 590813
*25-acre mixed farm. A working farm
welcoming children but not pets,
suitable for visitors with their own
transport. In a small hamlet bordering
the Peak District, ideal for Chatsworth
House, Chesterfield and Matlock Bath.*
Bedrooms: 1 single, 1 double, 2 family
rooms
Bathrooms: 2 private, 1 public

**Bed & breakfast**

| per night: | £min | £max |
|---|---|---|
| Single | 16.00 | |
| Double | 32.00 | |

**Half board**

| per person: | £min | £max |
|---|---|---|
| Daily | 22.00 | |
| Weekly | 154.00 | |

Evening meal 1900 (last orders 0930)
Parking for 10
Open March-November

⛳🖧🏠🖵♿ⅢⓈ☎▥Ⅲ✿🎦🚲

## BAKEWELL

Derbyshire
Map ref 4B2

Pleasant market town, famous for
its pudding. It is set in beautiful
countryside on the River Wye and
is an excellent centre for exploring
the Derbyshire Dales, the Peak
District National Park, Chatsworth
and Haddon Hall.
*Tourist Information Centre*
*☎ (01629) 813227*

### Castle Cliffe Private Hotel 🗛

😊😊 COMMENDED

Monsal Head, Bakewell DE45 1NL
☎ Great Longstone (01629) 640258
*A Victorian stone house overlooking
beautiful Monsal Dale. Noted for its
friendly atmosphere, good food and
exceptional views.*
Bedrooms: 3 double, 4 twin, 2 family
rooms
Bathrooms: 2 private, 2 public,
6 private showers

**Bed & breakfast**

| per night: | £min | £max |
|---|---|---|
| Single | 25.00 | 35.00 |
| Double | 41.00 | 47.00 |

**Half board**

| per person: | £min | £max |
|---|---|---|
| Daily | 37.00 | 47.00 |
| Weekly | 190.00 | 250.00 |

Evening meal 1900 (last orders 1700)

Parking for 15
Cards accepted: Access, Visa

⛳♿🛡Ⓢ🛏☎▥Ⅲ💼🍴5-15✿🎦🚲
🍽🆂🅿

### Mandale House

😊😊

Haddon Grove, Bakewell DE4 1JF
☎ (01629) 812416

*200-acre beef farm. Farmhouse, quietly
positioned on the edge of Lathkill Dale,
3 miles from Bakewell. Varied breakfast
menu. All rooms en-suite.*
Bedrooms: 3 double
Bathrooms: 3 private

**Bed & breakfast**

| per night: | £min | £max |
|---|---|---|
| Single | 25.00 | 25.00 |
| Double | 36.00 | 40.00 |

Evening meal 1900 (last orders 1900)
Parking for 4
Open March-October

⛳♿🖵♿🛡ⒾⓈ🗲🛏☎▥Ⅲ💼✿🍽
🚲🆂

### Rowland Cottage 🗛

Listed

Rowland, Bakewell DE45 1NR
☎ Great Longstone (01629) 640365
*Nestling peacefully below Longstone
Edge since 1667. A warm welcome,
comfortable beds, delicious food and
relaxation await you. Come and share
our lovely home!*
Bedrooms: 1 double, 1 triple
Bathrooms: 1 private, 1 public

**Bed & breakfast**

| per night: | £min | £max |
|---|---|---|
| Double | 30.00 | 35.00 |

**Half board**

| per person: | £min | £max |
|---|---|---|
| Daily | 25.00 | 27.50 |
| Weekly | 175.00 | 192.50 |

Evening meal 1900 (last orders 2000)
Parking for 3

⛳♿🖧🏠🖵♿▥Ⓘ🛡Ⓢ🗲🛏☎▥Ⅲ💼
✿🚲🍽🆂🏤Ⓣ

## BAMFORD

Derbyshire
Map ref 4B2

Village in the Peak District near
the Upper Derwent Reservoirs of
Ladybower, Derwent and Howden.
An excellent centre for walking.

### Ye Derwent Hotel

😊😊

Main Road, Bamford, Sheffield
S30 2AY
☎ Hope Valley (01433) 651395

*Set amongst the rolling hills of the Peak National Park, the Derwent Hotel is a traditional 100-year-old inn, noted for its food, ale and country friendliness.*
Bedrooms: 4 single, 4 double, 1 twin, 1 triple
Bathrooms: 2 private, 2 public

**Bed & breakfast**

| per night: | £min | £max |
|---|---|---|
| Single | 25.00 | 30.00 |
| Double | 40.00 | 45.00 |

**Half board**

| per person: | £min | £max |
|---|---|---|
| Daily | 27.50 | 37.00 |
| Weekly | 190.00 | 250.00 |

Lunch available
Evening meal 1900 (last orders 2200)
Parking for 40
Cards accepted: Access, Visa

### Pioneer House ⚠

**COMMENDED**

Station Road, Bamford, Sheffield S30 2BN
☎ Hope Valley (01433) 650638
*Comfortable, spacious rooms, all with private facilities, in Edwardian family home. Friendly atmosphere, hearty breakfasts. Central location in Peak District.*
Bedrooms: 2 double, 1 twin
Bathrooms: 3 private

**Bed & breakfast**

| per night: | £min | £max |
|---|---|---|
| Double | 30.00 | 35.00 |

Evening meal 1800 (last orders 1930)
Parking for 8

### BELPER

Derbyshire
Map ref 4B2

### Chevin Green Farm ⚠

**COMMENDED**

Chevin Road, Belper, Derby DE56 2UN
☎ (01773) 822328
*38-acre mixed farm. Extended and improved 300-year-old beamed farmhouse accommodation with all bedrooms en-suite, an ideal base for exploring Derbyshire.*
Bedrooms: 2 single, 2 double, 1 twin, 1 triple
Bathrooms: 6 private

**Bed & breakfast**

| per night: | £min | £max |
|---|---|---|
| Single | 16.00 | 20.00 |
| Double | 28.00 | 36.00 |

Parking for 6

### BOSTON

Lincolnshire
Map ref 3A1

Historic town famous for its church tower, the Boston Stump, 272 ft high. Still a busy port, the town is full of interest and has links with Boston Massachusetts through the Pilgrim Fathers. The cells where they were imprisoned can be seen in the medieval Guildhall.
*Tourist Information Centre*
☎ *(01205) 356656*

### Bramley House

**Listed** **COMMENDED**

267 Sleaford Road, Boston PE21 7PQ
☎ (01205) 354538
*Small guesthouse, charmingly decorated, with warm and friendly personal service. Ample parking. Disabled welcome.*
Bedrooms: 4 single, 3 double, 2 twin
Bathrooms: 3 private, 2 public

**Bed & breakfast**

| per night: | £min | £max |
|---|---|---|
| Single | 17.50 | 29.50 |
| Double | 30.00 | 40.00 |

Evening meal 1800 (last orders 1930)
Parking for 20

### BRACKLEY

Northamptonshire
Map ref 2C1

Historic market town of mellow stone, with many fine buildings lining the wide High Street and Market Place. Sulgrave Manor (George Washington's ancestral home) and Silverstone Circuit are nearby.
*Tourist Information Centre*
☎ *(01280) 700111*

### Walltree House Farm ⚠

**COMMENDED**

Steane, Brackley NN13 5NS
☎ Banbury (01295) 811235
Fax (01295) 811147

*200-acre arable farm. Individual ground floor rooms in the courtyard adjacent to Victorian farmhouse, mostly en-suite. Gardens and woods to relax in. Near*

historic sites, shopping and sports. M40 junctions 10/11. County winners of Booker Silver Lapwing award for conservation.
Bedrooms: 2 double, 3 twin, 3 triple
Bathrooms: 7 private, 1 public

**Bed & breakfast**

| per night: | £min | £max |
|---|---|---|
| Single | 26.00 | 30.00 |
| Double | 40.00 | 50.00 |

**Half board**

| per person: | £min | £max |
|---|---|---|
| Daily | 32.00 | 42.00 |

Evening meal 1900 (last orders 1900)
Parking for 10
Cards accepted: Access, Visa

### Welbeck House ⚠

Pebble Lane, Brackley NN13 7DA
☎ (01280) 702364
*Large house in a quiet, attractive area of Brackley, close to the A43, M40 and many places of interest. We pride ourselves on full-scale breakfasts and a warm welcome to all.*
Bedrooms: 2 double, 1 twin
Bathrooms: 2 public

**Bed & breakfast**

| per night: | £min | £max |
|---|---|---|
| Single | 15.00 | |
| Double | 27.00 | |

Parking for 4

### BRADWELL

Derbyshire
Map ref 4B2

Small village in the beautiful Hope Valley. There is a well-dressing ceremony in August.

### Stoney Ridge ⚠

**HIGHLY COMMENDED**

Granby Road, Bradwell, Sheffield S30 2HU
☎ Hope Valley (01433) 620538
*Split-level bungalow, with good views, established gardens and an indoor heated pool. Near to Castleton.*
Bedrooms: 2 double, 1 twin
Bathrooms: 1 private, 1 public

**Bed & breakfast**

| per night: | £min | £max |
|---|---|---|
| Single | 22.00 | 22.00 |
| Double | 36.00 | 48.00 |

Parking for 8

The town index at the back of this guide gives page numbers of all places with accommodation.

## BROUGHTON ASTLEY

Leicestershire
Map ref 4C3

### The Old Farm House
**Listed**

Old Mill Road, Broughton Astley,
Leicester LE9 6PQ
☎ Sutton in the Elms (01455) 282254
*Recently converted Georgian farmhouse overlooking fields. Quietly situated behind the church, near village centre. Near junctions 20/21 of M1, junction 1 of M69. Well-behaved pets welcome. French spoken.*
Bedrooms: 3 twin
Bathrooms: 2 public

| Bed & breakfast per night: | £min | £max |
| --- | --- | --- |
| Single | 16.00 | 16.00 |
| Double | 32.00 | 32.00 |

| Half board per person: | £min | £max |
| --- | --- | --- |
| Daily | 22.00 | 27.00 |
| Weekly | 140.00 | 175.00 |

Parking for 4

## BUXTON

Derbyshire
Map ref 4B2

The highest market town in England and one of the oldest spas, with an elegant Crescent, Micrarium, Poole's Cavern, Opera House and attractive Pavilion Gardens. An excellent centre for exploring the Peak District.
*Tourist Information Centre*
☎ *(01298) 25106*

### Cotesfield Farm
Parsley Hay, Buxton SK17 0BD
☎ Longnor (01298) 83256
Fax (01298) 83256
*300-acre mixed farm. In the Peak District National Park on the Tissington Trail, this farmhouse offers peace and quiet. Access from the A515 Buxton to Ashbourne road.*
Bedrooms: 2 double, 1 twin
Bathrooms: 1 public

| Bed & breakfast per night: | £min | £max |
| --- | --- | --- |
| Single | 12.00 | 14.50 |
| Double | 24.00 | 29.00 |

Parking for 6

### Fairhaven
**Listed APPROVED**

1 Dale Terrace, Buxton SK17 6LU
☎ (01298) 24481
*Centrally placed with ample roadside parking, offering English home cooking in a warm and friendly atmosphere.*
Bedrooms: 1 single, 1 double, 1 twin, 2 triple, 1 family room
Bathrooms: 1 public

| Bed & breakfast per night: | £min | £max |
| --- | --- | --- |
| Single | 16.50 | 17.00 |
| Double | 28.50 | 29.00 |

| Half board per person: | £min | £max |
| --- | --- | --- |
| Daily | 21.00 | 23.00 |
| Weekly | 140.00 | 154.00 |

Evening meal 1800 (last orders 1600)
Cards accepted: Access, Visa, Amex

### Hawthorn Farm Guesthouse
**COMMENDED**

Fairfield Road, Buxton SK17 7ED
☎ (01298) 23230
*A 400-year-old former farmhouse which has been in the family for 10 generations. Full English breakfast.*
Bedrooms: 4 single, 2 double, 2 twin, 4 triple
Bathrooms: 5 private, 2 public

| Bed & breakfast per night: | £min | £max |
| --- | --- | --- |
| Single | 19.00 | 20.00 |
| Double | 38.00 | 46.00 |

Parking for 15
Open April-October

### Lynstone Guesthouse

3 Grange Road, Buxton SK17 6NH
☎ (01298) 77043
*A spacious homely house. Home cooking, traditional and vegetarian. Ideal base for touring and walking. Children welcome, cleanliness assured. Off-street parking. No smoking and no pets please.*
Bedrooms: 1 triple, 1 family room
Bathrooms: 1 private, 2 public

| Bed & breakfast per night: | £min | £max |
| --- | --- | --- |
| Double | 30.00 | 31.00 |

| Half board per person: | £min | £max |
| --- | --- | --- |
| Daily | 28.50 | 29.50 |
| Weekly | 166.00 | |

Evening meal 1800 (last orders 1800)
Parking for 3
Open March-December

### Oldfield House
**COMMENDED**

8 Macclesfield Road, Buxton SK17 9AH
☎ (01298) 24371
*Attractive detached Victorian guesthouse with gardens, close to the town centre and Pavilion Gardens. Spacious en-suite bedrooms. Non-smoking.*
Bedrooms: 2 double, 1 triple
Bathrooms: 3 private, 1 public

| Bed & breakfast per night: | £min | £max |
| --- | --- | --- |
| Single | 20.00 | 22.00 |
| Double | 34.00 | 35.00 |

### Pedlicote Farm
**Listed**

Peak Forest, Buxton SK17 8EG
☎ (01298) 22241
*1681 oak-beamed farmhouse conversion in the Peak Park, full of character, with a charming atmosphere and magnificent views.*
Bedrooms: 1 double, 2 twin
Bathrooms: 2 public

| Bed & breakfast per night: | £min | £max |
| --- | --- | --- |
| Single | 18.00 | 20.00 |
| Double | 28.00 | 30.00 |

| Half board per person: | £min | £max |
| --- | --- | --- |
| Daily | 25.00 | 27.00 |
| Weekly | 175.00 | 175.00 |

Lunch available
Evening meal 1830 (last orders 2030)
Parking for 9

### 8 Queens Road
**Listed**

Fairfield, Buxton SK17 7EX
☎ (01298) 78743
*Varied breakfast served anytime in your room. Guests' fridge. Walking distance from centre. Longer stay/off-peak discounts.*
Bedrooms: 1 double, 1 twin
Bathrooms: 1 public

| Bed & breakfast per night: | £min | £max |
| --- | --- | --- |
| Single | 14.00 | 15.50 |
| Double | 23.00 | 29.00 |

Parking for 3

### The Victorian Guesthouse
**COMMENDED**

5 Wye Grove, Off Macclesfield Road, Buxton SK17 9AJ
☎ (01298) 78759
*Attractive and comfortable surroundings, furnished in a tasteful Victorian manner, with a beautiful conservatory to relax in. En-suite rooms. Diets catered for. In a quiet cul-de-sac near town centre. Telephone for brochure.*
Bedrooms: 3 double
Bathrooms: 3 private, 1 public

| Bed & breakfast per night: | £min | £max |
| --- | --- | --- |
| Single | 20.00 | 30.00 |
| Double | 32.00 | 40.00 |

**Half board**

| per person: | £min | £max |
|---|---|---|
| Daily | 26.00 | 30.00 |
| Weekly | 170.00 | 200.00 |

Evening meal 1800 (last orders 1600)
Parking for 4

🦽🍴🖵🛈🖵🛈🆂🛏💻🧺

## Westlands

**Listed**

Bishops Lane, St. Johns Road, Buxton
SK17 6UN
☎ (01298) 23242
*Beautifully appointed small guesthouse
on country lane 1 mile from town
centre. Magnificent views overlooking
golf-course. Non smoking.*
Bedrooms: 2 double, 1 twin
Bathrooms: 1 public

**Bed & breakfast**

| per night: | £min | £max |
|---|---|---|
| Single | 20.00 | |
| Double | 28.00 | 30.00 |

Parking for 5

🦽🖵♿🖵🛈🆂🗲💻🛏⛽❅✕🧺 OAP
SP 🎏

Attractive village with castle
earthworks dating from Saxon
times and a parish church,
churchyard and several houses of
interest. It also has a duck pond
and stream.

## School Farm House

🏡🏡

4 High Street, Castle Bytham,
Grantham NG33 4RZ
☎ Stamford (01780) 410245
Fax (01780) 410245
*A family home in one of Lincolnshire's
attractive villages, 3 miles off A1.
Stamford is 8 miles south and
Grantham is 10 miles north. Non-
smokers only, please.*
Bedrooms: 1 single, 1 double, 1 twin
Bathrooms: 3 private, 1 public

**Bed & breakfast**

| per night: | £min | £max |
|---|---|---|
| Single | 20.00 | 25.00 |
| Double | 40.00 | 48.00 |

Parking for 4

🦽🍴🖵♿🖵🛈🆂🗲📺💻🛏⛽✕🧺🎏

A Norman castle once stood here.
The world's largest collection of
single-seater racing cars is
displayed at Donington Park
alongside the racing circuit, and an
Aeropark Visitor Centre can be
seen at nearby East Midlands
International Airport.

## High Barn Farm 🏍

**Listed**

Isley Walton, Castle Donington, Derby
DE74 2RL
☎ Derby (01332) 810360
*84-acre mixed farm. Accommodation in
delightfully converted barn, cottage and
farmhouse. Small and friendly,
peacefully rural, warm welcome
assured.*
Bedrooms: 2 single, 1 double, 5 twin,
1 family room
Bathrooms: 4 private, 3 public

**Bed & breakfast**

| per night: | £min | £max |
|---|---|---|
| Single | 16.00 | 21.00 |
| Double | 32.00 | 40.00 |

Parking for 16

🦽🖵♿🖵🆂🗲📺💻🛏⛽✕🧺

Large village in a spectacular Peak
District setting with ruined Peveril
Castle and 4 great show caverns,
where the Blue John stone and
lead were mined. One cavern
offers a mile-long underground
boat journey.

## Bargate Cottage

🏡🏡🏡 **COMMENDED**

Bargate, Pindale Road, Castleton,
Sheffield S30 2WG
☎ Hope Valley (01433) 620201
Fax (01433) 621739
*Unspoilt, renovated 17th C cottage
adjacent to Peveril Castle in the centre
of the village. An ideal base for
relaxing, walking or touring. Many
recreational facilities available locally.
Non-smokers only please.*
Bedrooms: 1 double, 2 triple
Bathrooms: 3 private

**Bed & breakfast**

| per night: | £min | £max |
|---|---|---|
| Single | 35.00 | |
| Double | 39.00 | 43.00 |

**Half board**

| per person: | £min | £max |
|---|---|---|
| Daily | 30.00 | |
| Weekly | 200.00 | |

Evening meal from 1830
Parking for 6

🦽3🖵♿🖵♿🖵🛈🆂🗲🛏💻🖵🚲🚶
♪🏌❅✕🦮🎏

## Hillside House

🏡🏡

Pindale Road, Castleton, Sheffield
S30 2WU
☎ Hope Valley (01433) 620312
*A homely guesthouse, with panoramic
views, in a quiet location on the
outskirts of the village. A good base for
touring and outdoor pursuits. Totally
non-smoking.*
Bedrooms: 1 double, 1 twin, 1 family
room
Bathrooms: 3 private, 1 public

**Bed & breakfast**

| per night: | £min | £max |
|---|---|---|
| Double | 33.00 | 38.00 |

Parking for 4
Open March-November

🦽5🍴🖵♿🖵🆂🗲💻🚶🏌❅✕🎏

## Ye Olde Cheshire Cheese Inn 🏍

**Listed**

How Lane, Castleton, Sheffield
S30 2WJ
☎ Hope Valley (01433) 620330 &
Mobile 0836 376439

*17th C inn in the heart of the Peak
District. En-suite rooms. Restaurant with
30 home-made dishes, including roast
wild boar, pheasant, game pie. Two
beamed lounge bars with real ale - no
pool tables or machines! Family-run.*
Bedrooms: 1 single, 4 double, 2 twin
Bathrooms: 6 private, 1 private shower

**Bed & breakfast**

| per night: | £min | £max |
|---|---|---|
| Single | 25.00 | 55.00 |
| Double | 45.00 | 55.00 |

**Half board**

| per person: | £min | £max |
|---|---|---|
| Daily | 31.11 | 41.80 |
| Weekly | 200.00 | 270.00 |

Lunch available
Evening meal 1800 (last orders 2100)
Parking for 65
Cards accepted: Access, Visa

🦽🖵♿🖵♿🖵🗲💻🍴⛴🚶♪🚲
🖂🎏

## CHESTERFIELD

Derbyshire
Map ref 4B2

Famous for the twisted spire of its parish church, Chesterfield has some fine modern buildings and excellent shopping facilities, including a large, traditional open-air market. Hardwick Hall and Bolsover Castle are nearby.
*Tourist Information Centre*
☎ *(01246) 207777/8*

### Abbeydale Hotel ⋀

♨♨♨ COMMENDED

Cross Street, Chesterfield S40 4TD
☎ (01246) 277849
Fax (01246) 558223
*Resident proprietors. Quiet location within walking distance of town centre, close to Peak District. Delicious food and wine. Short breaks available.*
Bedrooms: 5 single, 3 double, 3 twin
Bathrooms: 9 private, 1 public

**Bed & breakfast**

| per night: | £min | £max |
| --- | --- | --- |
| Single | 26.00 | 39.90 |
| Double | 45.00 | 52.00 |

**Half board**

| per person: | £min | £max |
| --- | --- | --- |
| Daily | 38.00 | 52.00 |
| Weekly | 250.00 | 340.00 |

Lunch available
Evening meal 1830 (last orders 2000)
Parking for 12
Cards accepted: Access, Visa, Diners, Amex
➤👪℡⌨🖵🍴☎🅿Ⓢ🅃

## CONINGSBY

Lincolnshire
Map ref 4D2

### White Bull Inn

♨♨♨ APPROVED

55 High Street, Coningsby, Lincoln LN4 4RB
☎ (01526) 342439
*A warm welcome awaits at this friendly pub with real ale, riverside beer garden and large children's playground. Traditional home-made meals are available every day, lunch time and evening. Half a mile from RAF Coningsby.*
Bedrooms: 2 single, 1 double, 1 twin
Bathrooms: 2 private, 2 public

**Bed & breakfast**

| per night: | £min | £max |
| --- | --- | --- |
| Single | 14.00 | 19.00 |
| Double | 23.00 | 35.00 |

**Half board**

| per person: | £min | £max |
| --- | --- | --- |
| Daily | 18.00 | 25.00 |
| Weekly | 120.00 | 160.00 |

Lunch available
Evening meal 1900 (last orders 2200)

---

Parking for 60
Cards accepted: Access, Visa
➤👪🏠⌨♿📵✂🖵📺🍴☎🅿🔍♪✿🎿Ⓢ🅿

## COTGRAVE

Nottinghamshire
Map ref 4C2

### Jerico Farm

♨♨ COMMENDED

Fosse Way, Cotgrave, Nottingham NG12 3HG
☎ Kinoulton (01949) 81733
*120-acre mixed farm. With lovely views over the Nottinghamshire Wolds, an excellent rural location for the business or holiday visitor yet only 8 miles from Nottingham with its universities, sports venues and tourist sites. Brochure available.*
Bedrooms: 1 double, 2 twin
Bathrooms: 1 private, 1 public

**Bed & breakfast**

| per night: | £min | £max |
| --- | --- | --- |
| Single | 17.00 | 22.00 |
| Double | 32.00 | 36.00 |

Parking for 4
➤5♿📵Ⓢ✂🖵🍴☎♪✿🎿🌾

## DERBY

Derbyshire
Map ref 4B2

Modern industrial city but with ancient origins. There is a wide range of attractions including several museums (notably Royal Crown Derby), a theatre, a concert hall, and the cathedral with fine ironwork and Bess of Hardwick's tomb.
*Tourist Information Centre*
☎ *(01332) 255802*

### Bonehill Farm

Listed

Etwall Road, Mickleover, Derby DE3 5DN
☎ (01332) 513553
*120-acre mixed farm. A traditional farmhouse in a rural setting, 3 miles from Derby. Alton Towers, the Peak District, historic houses and the Potteries are all within easy reach.*
Bedrooms: 1 double, 1 twin, 1 triple
Bathrooms: 1 private, 1 public

**Bed & breakfast**

| per night: | £min | £max |
| --- | --- | --- |
| Single | 15.00 | 18.00 |
| Double | 30.00 | 36.00 |

Parking for 6
➤♿📵🅰Ⓢ🖵📺🍴🅿🔍♪✿🌾🔦

---

> **We advise you to confirm your booking in writing.**

---

## DESBOROUGH

Northamptonshire
Map ref 4C3

### West Lodge Farm ⋀

♨♨ HIGHLY COMMENDED

Pipewell Road, Desborough, Kettering NN14 2SH
☎ Kettering (01536) 760552
*570-acre arable farm. Spacious Georgian farmhouse set in extensive gardens. Breakfast overlooking 600 acres of countryside. Close to A1/M1 link. Conservation prize winners, with woodlands.*
Bedrooms: 1 double, 1 twin
Bathrooms: 1 private, 1 public, 1 private shower

**Bed & breakfast**

| per night: | £min | £max |
| --- | --- | --- |
| Single | 20.00 | 24.00 |
| Double | 38.00 | 42.00 |

Parking for 5
➤℡⌨♿🖵📺🍴🅿
🕕6-30🔍♻✿🌾Ⓢ

## DOVERIDGE

Derbyshire
Map ref 4B2

### Cavendish Arms

Listed APPROVED

Derby Road, Doveridge, Derby DE6 5JR
☎ Uttoxeter (01889) 563820
*18th C village pub serving traditional food and ale, close to Alton Towers and the Peak District. On the A50 between Derby and Stoke-on-Trent.*
Bedrooms: 1 twin, 1 triple
Bathrooms: 1 public

**Bed & breakfast**

| per night: | £min | £max |
| --- | --- | --- |
| Single | 14.50 | |
| Double | 29.00 | |

Lunch available
Evening meal 1830 (last orders 2200)
Parking for 40
Cards accepted: Access, Visa, Switch/Delta
➤⌨♿🅰🍴🔍♻✿🌾

## EDALE

Derbyshire
Map ref 4B2

### Stonecroft ⋀

♨♨♨ COMMENDED

Grindsbrook, Edale, Sheffield S30 2ZA
☎ Hope Valley (01433) 670262

*Licensed country house accommodation with magnificent views at start of Pennine Way. Gourmet home-cooked meals - vegetarians and vegans welcomed. Drying facilities.*
Bedrooms: 1 double, 1 twin
Bathrooms: 1 private, 2 public

| **Bed & breakfast per night:** | £min | £max |
|---|---|---|
| Single | 26.00 | 28.00 |
| Double | 42.00 | 48.00 |

| **Half board per person:** | £min | £max |
|---|---|---|
| Daily | 33.00 | 40.00 |
| Weekly | 217.00 | 273.00 |

Evening meal from 1930
Parking for 5
[S] [TV] [SP]

## EDWINSTOWE

Nottinghamshire
Map ref 4C2

Village close to Sherwood Forest, famous for the legend of Robin Hood.
*Tourist Information Centre*
*☎ (01623) 824490*

### Duncan Wood Lodge

[Listed] COMMENDED
Carburton, Worksop S80 3BP
☎ Worksop (01909) 483614
*Countryside lodge in the heart of Sherwood Forest. One acre of gardens and orchard in woodland setting. Home-grown produce.*
Bedrooms: 1 single, 3 double, 3 twin, 1 family room
Bathrooms: 4 private, 2 public

| **Bed & breakfast per night:** | £min | £max |
|---|---|---|
| Single | 18.00 | 30.00 |
| Double | 35.00 | 40.00 |

Lunch available
Evening meal 1830 (last orders 2030)
Parking for 9
Cards accepted: Access, Visa
[S] [TV] 12 [SP]

## ELMESTHORPE

Leicestershire
Map ref 4C3

### Water Meadows Farm

[Listed] COMMENDED
22 Billington Road East, Elmesthorpe, Leicester LE9 7SB
☎ Earl Shilton (01455) 843417
*15-acre smallholding. Tudor-style, oak-beamed farmhouse with extensive gardens, including private conservation area, woodland and stream. Own produce, home cooking. On a private road. Central for visiting many places of scenic and historic interest.*
Bedrooms: 1 double, 1 family room
Bathrooms: 1 public

| **Bed & breakfast per night:** | £min | £max |
|---|---|---|
| Single | 17.50 | 17.50 |
| Double | 29.00 | 29.00 |

| **Half board per person:** | £min | £max |
|---|---|---|
| Daily | 21.50 | 24.50 |
| Weekly | 130.00 | 150.00 |

Evening meal from 1900
Parking for 10
2 [UL] [S] [TV] [SP]

## EYAM

Derbyshire
Map ref 4B2

Attractive village famous for the courage it showed during the plague of 1665. The church has several memorials to this time and there is a well-dressing ceremony in August. The fine 17th C manor house of Eyam Hall is open in summer, and Chatsworth is nearby.

### Royal Oak

APPROVED
Town Head, Eyam, Sheffield S30 1RE
☎ Hope Valley (01433) 631390
*A quaint pub in the historic and picturesque "plague village" of Eyam in the Peak Park, close to Bakewell and Buxton.*
Bedrooms: 1 double, 1 twin, 1 triple
Bathrooms: 3 private

| **Bed & breakfast per night:** | £min | £max |
|---|---|---|
| Single | 25.00 | 35.00 |
| Double | 35.00 | 45.00 |

| **Half board per person:** | £min | £max |
|---|---|---|
| Daily | 30.00 | 45.00 |
| Weekly | 190.00 | 280.00 |

Lunch available
Evening meal 1900 (last orders 2100)
Parking for 3
[S] [TV] [OAP] [SP] [T]

## FARNSFIELD

Nottinghamshire
Map ref 4C2

### Dower House

Lower Hexgreave Farm, Farnsfield, Newark NG22 8LT
☎ Mansfield (01623) 882020
Fax (01623) 882100
*1000-acre arable & horse farm. Attractive Victorian farmhouse on private estate in Sherwood Forest. All rooms overlook farmland and are en-suite. Open fires and central heating. Choice of menu. Out of season offers available.*
Bedrooms: 3 double, 1 twin
Bathrooms: 4 private

| **Bed & breakfast per night:** | £min | £max |
|---|---|---|
| Single | 20.00 | 20.00 |
| Double | 32.00 | 36.00 |

| **Half board per person:** | £min | £max |
|---|---|---|
| Daily | 24.00 | 26.00 |
| Weekly | 168.00 | 182.00 |

Evening meal 1800 (last orders 2000)
Parking for 11
Cards accepted: Access, Visa, Amex
[UL] [S] [TV] [OAP] [SP] [T]

## FOXTON

Leicestershire
Map ref 4C3

Attractive village established in the 8th C. The 13th C church contains part of a Saxon Cross and a "lepers window". The Grand Union Canal passes through the village. Within walking distance is historic Foxton Locks with its unique staircase flight of 10 locks, and Inclined Plane Museum.

### The Old Manse

Swingbridge Street, Foxton, Market Harborough LE16 7RH
☎ Market Harborough (01858) 545456
*Period house in large gardens with warm and friendly atmosphere, on edge of conservation village, 3 miles north of Market Harborough. Good food at both local inns.*
Bedrooms: 1 double, 2 twin
Bathrooms: 1 public

**Bed & breakfast**

| per night: | £min | £max |
|---|---|---|
| Single | 20.00 | 22.00 |
| Double | 35.00 | 38.00 |

Parking for 6

## GLOOSTON

Leicestershire
Map ref 4C3

### The Old Barn Inn ⚊ COMMENDED

Glooston, Market Harborough LE16 7ST
☎ East Langton (01858) 84215 & (01959) 54215 Changing to (01858) 545215
*A 16th C oak-beamed inn with log fires offering home-cooked food and a selection of traditional ales. In the village on a no-through-road.*
Bedrooms: 2 double, 1 twin
Bathrooms: 3 private

**Bed & breakfast**

| per night: | £min | £max |
|---|---|---|
| Single | | 37.50 |
| Double | | 49.50 |

**Half board**

| per person: | £min | £max |
|---|---|---|
| Daily | | 30.00 |

Lunch available
Evening meal 1900 (last orders 2130)
Parking for 13
Cards accepted: Access, Visa

---

Please mention this guide when making a booking.

## GUILSBOROUGH

Northamptonshire
Map ref 4C3

### Seven Piers
Listed

Coton, Northampton NN6 8RF
☎ Northampton (01604) 740322
*Detached, brick house with private garden, close to Ravensthorpe Reservoir and Althorpe House.*
Bedrooms: 2 single, 1 twin, 1 triple
Bathrooms: 1 public

**Bed & breakfast**

| per night: | £min | £max |
|---|---|---|
| Single | 15.00 | 15.00 |
| Double | 30.00 | 30.00 |

Parking for 3

## HATHERSAGE

Derbyshire
Map ref 4B2

Hillside village in the Peak District, dominated by the church with many good brasses and monuments to the Eyre family which provide a link with Charlotte Bronte. Little John, friend of Robin Hood, is said to be buried here.

### Hillfoot Farm ⚊
Listed COMMENDED

Castleton Road, Hathersage, Sheffield S30 1AH
☎ Hope Valley (01433) 651673
*Recently built accommodation on the existing farmhouse. All rooms are en-suite with colour TV, tea/coffee facilities. 2 rooms on ground floor, 3 on first floor. Large car park.*
Bedrooms: 2 double, 1 twin, 1 triple
Bathrooms: 4 private

**Bed & breakfast**

| per night: | £min | £max |
|---|---|---|
| Single | 18.50 | 36.00 |
| Double | 33.00 | |

**Half board**

| per person: | £min | £max |
|---|---|---|
| Daily | 26.00 | 45.50 |

Lunch available
Evening meal 1800 (last orders 1900)
Parking for 13

### The Old Vicarage
⚊⚊

Church Bank, Hathersage, Sheffield S30 1AB
☎ Hope Valley (01433) 651099
*In 1845 Charlotte Bronte stayed in this listed building which is beside Little John's grave overlooking the Hope Valley. Central for Chatsworth House, the caves, fishing and walking.*
Bedrooms: 2 double, 1 twin
Bathrooms: 1 private, 2 public, 1 private shower

---

**Bed & breakfast**

| per night: | £min | £max |
|---|---|---|
| Single | 20.00 | 20.00 |
| Double | 32.00 | 40.00 |

Parking for 3

### The Scotsmans Pack ⚊⚊

School Lane, Hathersage, Sheffield S30 1BZ
☎ Hope Valley (01433) 650253

*Traditional country inn in the heart of the Peak District National Park, combining the unique blend of old world charm with modern fittings.*
Bedrooms: 3 double, 1 twin
Bathrooms: 4 private

**Bed & breakfast**

| per night: | £min | £max |
|---|---|---|
| Single | 30.00 | 35.00 |
| Double | 55.00 | 65.00 |

**Half board**

| per person: | £min | £max |
|---|---|---|
| Daily | 42.00 | 47.00 |
| Weekly | 294.00 | 329.00 |

Lunch available
Evening meal 1800 (last orders 2030)
Parking for 13

## HAYFIELD

Derbyshire
Map ref 4B2

Village set in spectacular scenery at the highest point of the Peak District with the best approach to the Kinder Scout plateau via the Kinder Downfall. An excellent centre for walking. Three reservoirs close by.

### Bridge End Guesthouse and Restaurant ⚊
⚊

7 Church Street, Hayfield, Stockport, Cheshire SK12 5JE
☎ New Mills (01663) 747321
Fax (01663) 742121
*In the picturesque conservation area of Hayfield, adjoining Kinder Scout and extensive moorlands. Accessible to all parts of the Peak District National Park.*
Bedrooms: 3 double, 1 twin
Bathrooms: 4 private

**Bed & breakfast**

| per night: | £min | £max |
|---|---|---|
| Single | 30.00 | 35.00 |
| Double | 45.00 | 50.00 |

| Half board per person: | £min | £max |
|---|---|---|
| Daily | 48.00 | |
| Weekly | 300.00 | |

Lunch available
Evening meal 1900 (last orders 2200)
Parking for 6
Cards accepted: Access, Visa, Diners, Amex
🛇🖎⌨↺⚲🐾ⓈⓎ🛏TV◉▥.🖎
♉15🚭DAP🐾SP

## HOLBEACH
Lincolnshire
Map ref 3A1

Small town, mentioned in the Domesday Book, has a splendid 14th C church with a fine tower and spire. The surrounding villages also have interesting churches, and the area is well-known for its bulbfields.

### Cackle Hill House
Listed
Cackle Hill Lane, Holbeach, Spalding PE12 8BS
☎ (01406) 426721 & 424659
*70-acre mixed farm. An attractive farmhouse in a rural position, 1 mile from Holbeach and half a mile from the A17.*
Bedrooms: 1 double, 2 twin
Bathrooms: 1 private, 1 public

| Bed & breakfast per night: | £min | £max |
|---|---|---|
| Single | 17.00 | 19.00 |
| Double | 32.00 | 36.00 |

| Half board per person: | £min | £max |
|---|---|---|
| Daily | 26.00 | 29.00 |

Parking for 4
↻Ⓤ Ⓢ Ⓨ🛏TV▥.🖎✿✕🚜

## HOPE
Derbyshire
Map ref 4B2

Village in the Hope Valley which is an excellent base for walking in the Peak District and for fishing and shooting. There is a well-dressing ceremony each June and its August sheep dog trials are well-known. Castleton Caves are nearby.

### Underleigh House 🅰
HIGHLY COMMENDED
Off Edale Road, Hope, Sheffield S30 2RF
☎ (01433) 621372
*Secluded farmhouse-style home 1.5 miles from village. Magnificent countryside views from all rooms. En-suite facilities, colour TV and resident teddy bear. Gourmet houseparty dinners by owner chef.*
Bedrooms: 3 double, 2 twin
Bathrooms: 5 private

| Bed & breakfast per night: | £min | £max |
|---|---|---|
| Single | 16.00 | 35.00 |
| Double | 36.00 | 48.00 |

| Half board per person: | £min | £max |
|---|---|---|
| Daily | 31.00 | 50.00 |

Evening meal from 1930
Parking for 5
Cards accepted: Access, Visa
♿🖎⌨↺⚲🐾ⓈⓎ▥.🖎✿✕🚜🐾SP

## HUSBANDS BOSWORTH
Leicestershire
Map ref 4C3

### Mrs Armitage's B & B
APPROVED
31-33 High Street, Husbands Bosworth, Lutterworth LE17 6LJ
☎ Market Harborough (01858) 880066
*Village centre home of character on A427, with wholesome cooking and warm welcome. Good choice of reasonably-priced evening meals at nearby inn.*
Bedrooms: 3 twin
Bathrooms: 1 public

| Bed & breakfast per night: | £min | £max |
|---|---|---|
| Single | 14.00 | 15.00 |
| Double | 28.00 | 30.00 |

Parking for 6
↻⌨↺ⓊⓁ🐾ⓈⓂTV▥.✕🚜Ⓣ

## KERSALL
Nottinghamshire
Map ref 4C2

### Hill Farm Guesthouse
HIGHLY COMMENDED
Kersall, Newark NG22 0BJ
☎ Caunton (01636) 636274

*17th C farm cottage with splendid views over the countryside, a beamed dining room and a comfortable lounge with open log fire. Southwell Minster, Newark and the Sherwood Forest Visitor Centre are all nearby.*
Bedrooms: 1 double, 1 twin
Bathrooms: 1 private, 1 public

| Bed & breakfast per night: | £min | £max |
|---|---|---|
| Single | 16.00 | 17.50 |
| Double | 32.00 | 35.00 |

Parking for 6
🛇🖎⌨↺⚲ⓊⓁ🐾ⓈⓎ🛏TV◉▥.🖎✿✕🚜SP🐾

## KETTERING
Northamptonshire
Map ref 3A2

Ancient industrial town based on shoe-making. Wicksteed Park to the south has many children's amusements. The splendid 17th C ducal mansion of Boughton House is to the north.
*Tourist Information Centre*
☎ (01536) 410266 or 410333 ext 212

### Dairy Farm
COMMENDED
Cranford St Andrew, Kettering NN14 4AQ
☎ Cranford (01536) 330273
*350-acre mixed farm. 17th C thatched house with inglenook fireplaces and a garden with an ancient circular dovecote and mature trees. Good food.*
Bedrooms: 2 double, 1 twin
Bathrooms: 3 private, 1 public

| Bed & breakfast per night: | £min | £max |
|---|---|---|
| Single | 18.00 | 22.00 |
| Double | 36.00 | 44.00 |

| Half board per person: | £min | £max |
|---|---|---|
| Daily | 28.00 | 34.00 |

Evening meal 1900 (last orders 1200)
Parking for 5
🛇🖎🐾↺⚲ⓊⓁⓈⓂTV▥.🖎↺✿🚜🐾

## KIRBY MUXLOE
Leicestershire
Map ref 4C3

### Faith Cottage
Listed
400 Ratby Lane, Kirby Muxloe, Leicester LE9 9AQ
☎ Leicester (0116) 238 7435
*Old world cottage, convenient for Leicester and surrounding places of interest.*
Bedrooms: 1 single, 1 twin
Bathrooms: 1 private, 1 public

| Bed & breakfast per night: | £min | £max |
|---|---|---|
| Single | 17.50 | 17.50 |
| Double | 35.00 | 35.00 |

Parking for 3
🛇♉7⌨↺⚲ⓊⓁⓎⓂTV▥.✿✕🚜

Individual proprietors have supplied all details of accommodation. Although we do check for accuracy, we advise you to confirm the information at the time of booking.

## LANGHAM

Leicestershire
Map ref 4C3

Village with a fine church, whose tower and spire are a local landmark, and a 17th C hall and manor. Sailing and fishing facilities are available at Rutland Water, 2 miles away.

### The Old Hall ⚑

**Listed**

Langham, Oakham LE15 7JE
☎ Oakham (01572) 722923 & 770076
Fax (01572) 724386
*17th C country house, designed and enlarged by the famous architect, Hal Goodhart Rendel. Located in Langham village between Ruddles Brewery and the beautiful 16th C church with entrance under our clock tower in Church Street. Convenient for the A1 and near Rutland Water. Stables, billiard room, large garden.*
Bedrooms: 2 double, 1 twin
Bathrooms: 3 public

**Bed & breakfast**

| per night: | £min | £max |
|---|---|---|
| Single | 15.00 | 25.00 |
| Double | 25.00 | 35.00 |

Parking for 12
Cards accepted: Access, Visa
☎⬚💷♦♿⬚⬚⬚⬚⬚⬚⬚⬚⬚

## LEICESTER

Leicestershire
Map ref 4C3

Modern industrial city with a wide variety of attractions including Roman remains, ancient churches, Georgian houses and a Victorian clock tower. Excellent shopping precincts, arcades and market, museums, theatres, concert hall and sports and leisure centres.
*Tourist Information Centre*
☎(0116)265 0555 or 251 1301

### Glenfield Lodge Hotel

**APPROVED**

4 Glenfield Road, Leicester LE3 6AP
☎ (0116) 262 7554
*Small, friendly hotel with an interesting ornamental courtyard, home-cooked food and cosy, relaxed surroundings. Close to city centre.*
Bedrooms: 6 single, 3 double, 4 twin, 2 triple
Bathrooms: 3 public

**Bed & breakfast**

| per night: | £min | £max |
|---|---|---|
| Single | 15.50 | 15.50 |
| Double | 27.00 | 27.00 |

Evening meal 1730 (last orders 1830)
Parking for 3
☎⬚⬚⬚⬚⬚⬚⬚⬚⬚

## LINCOLN

Lincolnshire
Map ref 4C2

Ancient city dominated by the magnificent 11th C cathedral with its triple towers. A Roman gateway is still used and there are medieval houses lining narrow, cobbled streets. Other attractions include the Norman castle, several museums and the Usher Gallery.
*Tourist Information Centre*
☎ *(01522) 529828*

### Garden House ⚑

**COMMENDED**

Burton-By-Lincoln, Lincoln LN1 2RD
☎ (01522) 526120
Fax (01522) 523787
*Fully restored 300-year-old house with oak beams. A stairlift and wheelchair ramp are available. 1 mile north of Lincoln off the B1398.*
Wheelchair access category 3 ♿
Bedrooms: 1 double, 2 twin
Bathrooms: 2 private, 1 public

**Bed & breakfast**

| per night: | £min | £max |
|---|---|---|
| Single | 19.00 | 21.00 |
| Double | 38.00 | 42.00 |

Parking for 3
☎⬚⬚⬚♦♿⬚⬚⬚⬚⬚⬚⬚⬚⬚⬚⬚

### New Farm

Burton, Lincoln LN1 2RD
☎ (01522) 527326
*360-acre arable & dairy farm. Twin-bedded room with private bathroom. Use of lounge with colour TV. 2 miles north of Lincoln. Evening meal by prior arrangement. Coarse fishing in private lakes. Nature reserve close by.*
Bedrooms: 1 twin
Bathrooms: 1 private

**Bed & breakfast**

| per night: | £min | £max |
|---|---|---|
| Single | 20.00 | 20.00 |
| Double | 32.00 | 32.00 |

**Half board**

| per person: | £min | £max |
|---|---|---|
| Daily | 24.00 | 28.00 |
| Weekly | 165.00 | 190.00 |

Parking for 3
Open March-November
☎5⬚♦⬚⬚⬚⬚⬚⬚⬚⬚⬚⬚

## LONG BUCKBY

Northamptonshire
Map ref 4C3

### Murcott Mill

**COMMENDED**

Murcott, Long Buckby, Northampton
NN6 7QR
☎ (01327) 842236

*100-acre livestock farm. Imposing Georgian mill house overlooking open countryside. Recently renovated to a high standard, with open fires and en-suite bedrooms. Ideal stopover for M1 travellers.*
Bedrooms: 1 double, 2 twin
Bathrooms: 3 private, 1 public

**Bed & breakfast**

| per night: | £min | £max |
|---|---|---|
| Single | 18.00 | 20.00 |
| Double | 34.00 | 36.00 |

**Half board**

| per person: | £min | £max |
|---|---|---|
| Daily | 25.00 | |

Evening meal 1900 (last orders 2030)
Parking for 32
☎⬚⬚♦⬚⬚⬚⬚⬚⬚⬚⬚⬚

## LOUGHBOROUGH

Leicestershire
Map ref 4C3

Industrial town famous for its bell foundry and 47-bell Carillon Tower. The Great Central Railway operates steam railway rides of over 8 miles through the attractive scenery of Charnwood Forest.
*Tourist Information Centre*
☎ *(01509) 230131*

### De Montfort Hotel ⚑

**APPROVED**

88 Leicester Road, Loughborough
LE11 2AQ
☎ (01509) 216061
*Recently refurbished, friendly family-run hotel under new ownership. Close to town centre, Main Line Steam Trust, university and beautiful Leicestershire countryside.*
Bedrooms: 2 single, 1 double, 5 twin, 1 triple
Bathrooms: 6 private, 1 public

**Bed & breakfast**

| per night: | £min | £max |
|---|---|---|
| Single | 20.00 | 26.00 |
| Double | 30.00 | 38.00 |

Evening meal 1830 (last orders 1830)
Cards accepted: Access, Visa, Amex
☎⬚⬚⬚♦⬚⬚⬚⬚⬚⬚⬚⬚

There are separate sections in this guide listing groups specialising in farm holidays and accommodation which is especially suitable for young people and organised groups.

## LOUTH

Lincolnshire
Map ref 4D2

Attractive old market town set on the eastern edge of the Lincolnshire Wolds. St James's Church has an impressive tower and spire and there are the remains of a Cistercian abbey. The museum contains an interesting collection of local material.
*Tourist Information Centre*
☎ *(01507) 609289*

### Wickham House

**HIGHLY COMMENDED**

Church Lane, Conisholme, Louth LN11 7LX
☎ North Somercotes (01507) 358 465
*Attractive 18th C cottage in country lane. En-suite bedrooms. Beamed sitting and dining room, separate tables, library. No smoking in cottage please.*
Bedrooms: 1 single, 1 double, 1 twin
Bathrooms: 3 private

**Bed & breakfast**

| per night: | £min | £max |
| --- | --- | --- |
| Double | 36.00 | |

Parking for 4

## LUDFORD

Lincolnshire
Map ref 4D2

### Hainton Walk Farm

**Listed COMMENDED**

Ludford, Lincoln LN3 6AP
☎ Burgh on Bain (01507) 313242
*4-acre smallholding. Very peaceful and beautiful area on Lincolnshire Wolds. Outstanding views. Good food and homely atmosphere. Small pets welcome.*
Bedrooms: 1 single, 1 double, 1 triple
Bathrooms: 1 public

**Bed & breakfast**

| per night: | £min | £max |
| --- | --- | --- |
| Single | 14.00 | 14.00 |
| Double | 26.00 | 28.00 |

**Half board**

| per person: | £min | £max |
| --- | --- | --- |
| Daily | 20.50 | 21.50 |
| Weekly | 120.50 | 125.50 |

Evening meal 1900 (last orders 2130)
Parking for 7

Colour maps at the back of this guide pinpoint all places which have accommodation listings in the guide.

## MARKET DEEPING

Lincolnshire
Map ref 3A1

Attractive Fenland market town.

### Abbey House

**COMMENDED**

West End Road, Maxey, Peterborough PE6 9EJ
☎ (01778) 344642

*Listed former rectory, dating in part from 1190 AD, close to historic Stamford. Ideal for touring the eastern shires with their abundance of abbeys, cathedrals, stately homes and attractive stone villages.*
Bedrooms: 1 single, 4 double, 2 twin, 1 triple, 1 family room
Bathrooms: 7 private, 1 public

**Bed & breakfast**

| per night: | £min | £max |
| --- | --- | --- |
| Single | 19.00 | 30.00 |
| Double | 32.00 | 45.00 |

Parking for 12

## MARKET HARBOROUGH

Leicestershire
Map ref 4C3

There have been markets here since the early 13th C, and the town was also an important coaching centre, with several ancient hostelries. The early 17th C grammar school was once the butter market.
*Tourist Information Centre*
☎ *(01858) 468106*

### The Fox Inn ♈

**COMMENDED**

Church Street, Wilbarston, Market Harborough LE16 8QG
☎ Rockingham (01536) 771270
*An old ironstone village inn offering home-cooked food, real ales and traditional pub games. Near Rockingham Forest and Castle.*
Bedrooms: 2 double, 1 twin, 1 family room
Bathrooms: 4 private

**Bed & breakfast**

| per night: | £min | £max |
| --- | --- | --- |
| Single | 20.00 | 25.00 |
| Double | 30.00 | 40.00 |

**Half board**

| per person: | £min | £max |
| --- | --- | --- |
| Daily | 30.00 | 40.00 |
| Weekly | 175.00 | 210.00 |

Lunch available
Evening meal 1900 (last orders 2200)
Parking for 10
Cards accepted: Access, Visa

## MATLOCK

Derbyshire
Map ref 4B2

The town lies beside the narrow valley of the River Derwent surrounded by steep wooded hills. Good centre for exploring Derbyshire's best scenery.

### Farley Farm

Farley, Matlock DE4 5LR
☎ (01629) 582533
*250-acre mixed farm. Built in 1610 of natural stone, set in open countryside close to Peak District and many places of interest.*
Bedrooms: 1 double, 1 twin, 1 family room
Bathrooms: 2 public

**Bed & breakfast**

| per night: | £min | £max |
| --- | --- | --- |
| Single | 15.00 | 17.00 |
| Double | 30.00 | 30.00 |

**Half board**

| per person: | £min | £max |
| --- | --- | --- |
| Daily | 21.00 | 23.00 |
| Weekly | 147.00 | 147.00 |

Evening meal 1700 (last orders 1900)
Parking for 10

### Thornleigh ♈

11 Lime Grove Walk, Matlock DE4 3FD
☎ (01629) 57626
*Large Edwardian house with private parking, convenient for bus/rail stations and shops. Non-smokers only, please.*
Bedrooms: 1 single, 1 double, 1 triple
Bathrooms: 1 public

**Bed & breakfast**

| per night: | £min | £max |
| --- | --- | --- |
| Single | 14.00 | 14.00 |
| Double | 28.00 | 28.00 |

Parking for 3
Open March-November

Check the introduction to this region for ideas on Where to Go.

## MELTON MOWBRAY

Leicestershire
Map ref 4C3

Close to the attractive Vale of Belvoir and famous for its pork pies and Stilton cheese which are the subjects of special displays in the museum. It has a beautiful church with a tower 100 ft high.
*Tourist Information Centre*
☎ *(01664) 480992*

### Manor House M

COMMENDED

Church Lane, Saxelby, Melton Mowbray LE14 3PA
☎ (01664) 812269
*125-acre livestock farm. Home cooking and a warm welcome in this oak-beamed farmhouse. Parts date back several hundred years including a unique 400-year-old staircase.*
Bedrooms: 2 double, 1 twin, 1 family room
Bathrooms: 1 private, 1 public

**Bed & breakfast**

| per night: | £min | £max |
|---|---|---|
| Single | 25.00 | |
| Double | 37.00 | |

**Half board**

| per person: | £min | £max |
|---|---|---|
| Daily | 28.50 | |
| Weekly | 178.00 | |

Evening meal 1900 (last orders 1200)
Parking for 6
Open April-October
🛏🖵📞🍽🔌🅿🛆🔒📺🎬🖶, 🚗☼✕ 🐾🏕

## MIDDLETON

Northamptonshire
Map ref 4C3

### Valley View

🛏

3 Camsdale Walk, Middleton, Market Harborough, Leicestershire LE16 8YR
☎ Rockingham (01536) 770874
*An elevated, stone-built house with panoramic views of the Welland Valley. Within easy distance of Market Harborough and Corby.*
Bedrooms: 1 double, 1 twin
Bathrooms: 1 public

**Bed & breakfast**

| per night: | £min | £max |
|---|---|---|
| Single | 16.00 | 16.00 |
| Double | 32.00 | 32.00 |

Parking for 2
🛏🖵🔌🅿🎬📺🖶, 🛆☼🏕

### Please use the new PhONEday area telephone codes shown in establishment entries.

## MONYASH

Derbyshire
Map ref 4B2

### Sheldon House

HIGHLY COMMENDED

Chapel Street, Monyash, Bakewell DE45 1JJ
☎ Bakewell (01629) 813067
*Warm welcome in comfortable family home, ideal for walking. Good pub food locally, overseas visitors welcome. Non-smokers only please.*
Bedrooms: 3 double
Bathrooms: 3 private, 1 public

**Bed & breakfast**

| per night: | £min | £max |
|---|---|---|
| Single | 20.00 | 30.00 |
| Double | 35.00 | 38.00 |

Parking for 4
🛏7🖵🔌🅿🍴🆔🔒✕📺🖶,🛆🚶♂☼ ✕🏕

## MORETON PINKNEY

Northamptonshire
Map ref 2C1

### Barewell Fields

Listed  HIGHLY COMMENDED

Moreton Pinkney, Daventry NN11 3NJ
☎ Sulgrave (01295) 760754
*200-acre mixed farm. In a peaceful corner of the conservation village of Moreton Pinkney, convenient for many National Trust properties, Stratford and Silverstone, M1 and M40. Evening meals by arrangement only.*
Bedrooms: 1 single, 1 double, 1 twin
Bathrooms: 1 public

**Bed & breakfast**

| per night: | £min | £max |
|---|---|---|
| Single | 15.00 | 18.00 |
| Double | 30.00 | 36.00 |

**Half board**

| per person: | £min | £max |
|---|---|---|
| Daily | 25.00 | 30.00 |
| Weekly | 165.00 | 200.00 |

Evening meal 1800 (last orders 1900)
Parking for 4
Open January-November
🛏10🛁🖵🔌🅿🆔🔒📺📺🖶,🛆☼ ✕🏕

## MOUNTSORREL

Leicestershire
Map ref 4C3

### The Swan Inn

🛏

10 Loughborough Road, Mountsorrel, Loughborough LE12 7AT
☎ Leicester (0116) 230 2340
Fax (0116) 237 6115
*Traditional 17th C coaching inn in the heart of historic Mountsorrel, on the banks of the River Soar.*
Bedrooms: 1 single, 1 double, 1 twin
Bathrooms: 1 public

**Bed & breakfast**

| per night: | £min | £max |
|---|---|---|
| Single | 20.00 | 20.00 |
| Double | 32.00 | 32.00 |

**Half board**

| per person: | £min | £max |
|---|---|---|
| Daily | 22.00 | 26.00 |
| Weekly | 132.00 | 156.00 |

Lunch available
Evening meal 1900 (last orders 2130)
Parking for 12
Cards accepted: Access, Visa, Amex
🛏14🖵🔌🆔🔒📺🖶,🛆🚗✿🐾🏕

## NEWARK

Nottinghamshire
Map ref 4C2

The town has many fine old houses and ancient inns near the large, cobbled market-place. Substantial ruins of the 12th C castle, where King John died, dominate the riverside walk and there are several interesting museums. Sherwood Forest is nearby.
*Tourist Information Centre*
☎ *(01636) 78962*

### Willow Tree Inn M

Listed

Front Street, Barnby-in-the-Willows, Newark NG24 2SA
☎ Fenton Claypole (01636) 626613
Fax (01636) 626613
*17th C village inn, conveniently placed for historic Lincoln, Grantham, Newark and Sherwood. Known locally for good food and ales. Off the A17 and A1.*
Bedrooms: 1 single, 2 double, 2 triple
Bathrooms: 2 private, 1 public

**Bed & breakfast**

| per night: | £min | £max |
|---|---|---|
| Single | 18.00 | 38.00 |
| Double | 28.00 | 40.00 |

Lunch available
Evening meal 1900 (last orders 2230)
Parking for 50
Cards accepted: Access, Visa, Amex
🛏🛁🖵🔌🆔🖶,🛆🍴🔍☼✕ 🏕 OAP 🔗 SP 🏕

### There are separate sections in this guide listing groups specialising in farm holidays and accommodation which is especially suitable for young people and organised groups.

## NORTHAMPTON

Northamptonshire
Map ref 2C1

A bustling town and a shoe
manufacturing centre, with
excellent shopping facilities,
several museums and parks, a
theatre and a concert hall. Several
old churches include 1 of only 4
round churches in Britain.
*Tourist Information Centre*
☎ *(01604) 22677*

### Quinton Green Farm ⋀
⚬⚬

Quinton, Northampton NN7 2EG
☎ (01604) 863685
Fax (01604) 862230
*1200-acre arable & dairy farm.*
*Rambling 17th C farmhouse with lovely*
*views over own farmland. Convenient*
*for Northampton, M1 (junction 15) and*
*Milton Keynes.*
Bedrooms: 1 single, 1 double, 1 twin
Bathrooms: 2 private, 1 public
**Bed & breakfast**

| per night: | £min | £max |
|---|---|---|
| Single | 18.00 | 20.00 |
| Double | 35.00 | 40.00 |

Parking for 6
🛏🗄♿💷📺🖥📞♿🅿🛁🐾

## NOTTINGHAM

Nottinghamshire
Map ref 4C2

Attractive modern city with a rich
history. Outside its castle, now a
museum, is Robin Hood's statue.
Attractions include "The Tales of
Robin Hood"; the Lace Hall;
Wollaton Hall; museums and
excellent facilities for shopping,
sports and entertainment.
*Tourist Information Centre*
☎ *(0115) 947 0661 or 977 3558*

### Grantham Hotel ⋀
⚬⚬

24-26 Radcliffe Road, West Bridgford,
Nottingham NG2 5FW
☎ (0115) 981 1373
Fax (0115) 981 8567
*Family-run licensed hotel offering*
*modern accommodation in a*
*comfortable atmosphere. Convenient for*
*the centre of Nottingham, Trent Bridge*
*and the National Water Sports Centre.*
Bedrooms: 13 single, 2 double, 5 twin,
2 triple, 1 family room
Bathrooms: 13 private, 3 public
**Bed & breakfast**

| per night: | £min | £max |
|---|---|---|
| Single | 20.00 | 27.00 |
| Double | 35.00 | 39.00 |

**Half board**

| per person: | £min | £max |
|---|---|---|
| Daily | 23.00 | 34.00 |
| Weekly | 138.00 | 192.00 |

Evening meal 1800 (last orders 1930)
Parking for 20
Cards accepted: Access, Visa
🛏3🗄♿💷📺🖥📞

### Nelson & Railway Inn
**Listed** **APPROVED**

Station Road, Kimberley, Nottingham
NG16 2NR
☎ (0115) 938 2177
*A family-run village inn, 1 mile north of*
*junction 26 of the M1. Listed in "Good*
*Beer Guide".*
Bedrooms: 2 twin, 1 triple
Bathrooms: 1 public
**Bed & breakfast**

| per night: | £min | £max |
|---|---|---|
| Single | 19.00 | |
| Double | 33.00 | |

Lunch available
Evening meal 1700 (last orders 2200)
Parking for 50
🛏📭🗄♿💷📺🖥📞🍽♿✳✝🐾

## OAKHAM

Leicestershire
Map ref 4C3

Pleasant former county town of
Rutland. Fine 12th C Great Hall,
part of its castle, with a historic
collection of horseshoes. An
octagonal Butter Cross stands in
the market-place and Rutland
County Museum, Rutland Farm
Park and Rutland Water are of
interest.
*Tourist Information Centre*
☎ *(01572) 724329*

### Gnoll House
⚬⚬

9 Uppingham Road, Oakham
LE15 6JB
☎ (01572) 757531
*A modern house near the town centre,*
*overlooking open fields.*
Bedrooms: 1 double, 1 twin
Bathrooms: 2 private
**Bed & breakfast**

| per night: | £min | £max |
|---|---|---|
| Single | 15.00 | 20.00 |
| Double | | 35.00 |

Parking for 6
🛏🗄♿💷📺🖥📞♿🅿🛁🐾

### Milburn Motel ⋀
**Listed**

South Street, Oakham LE15 6BG
☎ (01572) 723330
*Modern residence with a bright,*
*comfortable atmosphere, in a central*
*part of Oakham.*
Bedrooms: 1 single, 1 double, 4 twin,
1 triple
Bathrooms: 3 private, 1 public

---

We advise you to confirm
your booking in writing.

---

**Bed & breakfast**

| per night: | £min | £max |
|---|---|---|
| Single | 17.50 | 27.50 |
| Double | 25.00 | 40.00 |

Parking for 7
🛏♿📞♿💷🖥🅿🐾

## OUNDLE

Northamptonshire
Map ref 3A1

Historic town situated on the River
Nene with narrow alleys and
courtyards and many stone
buildings, including a fine church
and historic inns.
*Tourist Information Centre*
☎ *(01832) 274333*

### Lilford Lodge Farm
⚬⚬ **COMMENDED**

Barnwell, Peterborough PE8 5SA
☎ (01832) 272230

*305-acre mixed farm. 19th C farmhouse,*
*recently converted, in the Nene Valley.*
*On the A605, 3 miles south of Oundle,*
*5 miles north of A14.*
Bedrooms: 1 single, 1 double, 1 twin
Bathrooms: 3 private
**Bed & breakfast**

| per night: | £min | £max |
|---|---|---|
| Single | 18.00 | 21.00 |
| Double | 36.00 | 36.00 |

Parking for 13
🛏📭♿💷📞📺🖥📞♿🅿🐾

## PEAK DISTRICT

*See under Aldwark, Ashbourne,*
*Ashford in the Water, Bakewell,*
*Bamford, Buxton, Castleton, Edale,*
*Eyam, Hathersage, Hayfield, Hope,*
*Monyash, Rowarth, Rowsley,*
*Tideswell, Winster*

## PEAK FOREST

Derbyshire
Map ref 4B2

### Devonshire Arms ⋀
⚬⚬

Peak Forest, Buxton SK17 8EJ
☎ Buxton (01298) 23875
*17th C former coaching inn located in*
*the heart of the Peak District, close to*
*all attractions. All rooms refurbished to*
*a high standard offering en-suite*
*facilities.*
Bedrooms: 2 double, 1 twin
Bathrooms: 3 private

*Continued* ▶

## PEAK FOREST

*Continued*

**Bed & breakfast**

| per night: | £min | £max |
| --- | --- | --- |
| Single | 20.00 | 20.00 |
| Double | 35.00 | 35.00 |

Lunch available
Evening meal 1830 (last orders 2145)
Parking for 40

🛇🗗📞🎣ⓈⓂ⏰️🌙U✿🎁

## RAGNALL

Nottinghamshire
Map ref 4C2

### Ragnall House

⬙⬙ COMMENDED

Ragnall, Newark NG22 0UR
☎ Dunham-on-Trent (01777) 228575
& Mobile 0374 455792
*Large listed Georgian family house in
over an acre of grounds in a small
village close to the River Trent. Good
local inns and restaurants nearby.*
Bedrooms: 1 single, 2 twin, 1 triple
Bathrooms: 1 private, 1 public,
1 private shower

**Bed & breakfast**

| per night: | £min | £max |
| --- | --- | --- |
| Single | 14.00 | 15.00 |
| Double | 28.00 | 30.00 |

Parking for 8

🛇🗗🌢️🍴ⓈⓂ️📺⏰️🌙✿SP🏮T

## ROWARTH

Derbyshire
Map ref 4B2

### Little Mill Inn ⋀

⬙⬙⬙

Rowarth, Stockport, Cheshire
SK12 5EB
☎ New Mills (01663) 743178 &
746305
*Delightful old country inn nestling in
the foothills of Derbyshire, with a
stream running through beautiful
gardens. Separate restaurant.*
Bedrooms: 3 double
Bathrooms: 3 private

**Bed & breakfast**

| per night: | £min | £max |
| --- | --- | --- |
| Single | 25.00 | |
| Double | 35.00 | |

**Half board**

| per person: | £min | £max |
| --- | --- | --- |
| Daily | | 35.00 |
| Weekly | | 45.00 |

Lunch available
Evening meal 1800 (last orders 2100)
Parking for 150
Cards accepted: Access, Visa, Diners,
Amex

🛇🛋️📞🗗🌢️🎣ⓈⓂ️🍽️🌙U🎣✿
OAP🔥SP🏮

## ROWSLEY

Derbyshire
Map ref 4B2

Village at the meeting point of the
Rivers Wye and Derwent, and on
the edge of the Haddon and
Chatsworth estates. 19th C water-
powered flour mill, working and
open to visitors, with craft
workshops.

### Vernon House

Listed COMMENDED

Bakewell Road, Rowsley, Matlock
DE4 2EB
☎ Matlock (01629) 734294

*Centred between Haddon Hall and
Chatsworth House, Vernon House offers
country house accommodation with
Georgian charm at an affordable price.
All rooms en-suite.*
Bedrooms: 2 double, 1 twin
Bathrooms: 3 private

**Bed & breakfast**

| per night: | £min | £max |
| --- | --- | --- |
| Single | 30.00 | 40.00 |
| Double | 50.00 | 60.00 |

Parking for 5

🛇🏰🖃🗗🌢️🎣ⓌⓁ🍽️⏰️🌙U✿🎣
🌾SP

## SAXILBY

Lincolnshire
Map ref 4C2

### Orchard Cottage

⬙⬙ COMMENDED

3 Orchard Lane, Saxilby, Lincoln
LN1 2HT
☎ Lincoln (01522) 703192

*Cottage-style house, with a guest annexe
in a pleasant garden, 6 miles from
Lincoln. Non-smokers only, please.*
Bedrooms: 1 single, 1 double, 1 triple
Bathrooms: 3 private

**Bed & breakfast**

| per night: | £min | £max |
| --- | --- | --- |
| Single | 17.00 | 21.00 |
| Double | 34.00 | 34.00 |

Parking for 2

🛇🖾🖃🗗🌢️ⓌⓁ🎣ⓈⓂ️🍽️🌾📺⏰️🌙U
✿🎣

## SHEARSBY

Leicestershire
Map ref 4C3

### Knaptoft House Farm

⬙⬙ HIGHLY COMMENDED

Bruntingthorpe Road, Shearsby,
Lutterworth LE17 6PR
☎ Leicester (0116) 247 8388
Fax (0116) 247 8388
*145-acre mixed farm. Beautifully-
appointed accommodation set in
peaceful rolling countryside close to
junction 1 of M6, junction 20 of M1.
Excellent pubs and restaurants nearby.*
Bedrooms: 2 double, 1 twin
Bathrooms: 1 private, 1 public,
2 private showers

**Bed & breakfast**

| per night: | £min | £max |
| --- | --- | --- |
| Single | 20.00 | |
| Double | 35.00 | 42.00 |

Parking for 5

🛇5🌢️ⓌⓁⓈ🍽️🌾📺⏰️🌙🎣✿🎣

## SHERWOOD FOREST

*See under Edwinstowe, Kersall,
Newark, Ragnall, Southwell, Upton*

## SKEGNESS

Lincolnshire
Map ref 4D2

Famous seaside resort with 6
miles of sandy beaches and
bracing air. Attractions include
swimming pools, bowling greens,
gardens, Natureland Marine Zoo,
golf-courses and a wide range of
entertainment at the Embassy
Centre. Nearby is Gibraltar Point
Nature Reserve.
*Tourist Information Centre
☎ (01754) 764821*

### Victoria Inn ⋀

⬙⬙

Wainfleet Road, Skegness PE25 3RG
☎ (01754) 767333
*Friendly, traditional inn with hotel
annexe providing home-cooked food.
Central for town and beach facilities.*
Bedrooms: 1 single, 3 double, 1 twin,
2 triple
Bathrooms: 4 private, 1 public

**Bed & breakfast**

| per night: | £min | £max |
| --- | --- | --- |
| Single | 14.00 | 15.00 |
| Double | 28.00 | 30.00 |

**Half board**

| per person: | £min | £max |
| --- | --- | --- |
| Daily | 17.00 | 25.00 |
| Weekly | 102.00 | 150.00 |

Lunch available
Evening meal 1800 (last orders 2200)
Parking for 20
Cards accepted: Access, Visa

🛇🖃🗗🌢️ⓈⓂ️🌾📺⏰️🌙🎣🔍✿🎣SP

## SKILLINGTON

Lincolnshire
Map ref 3A1

### Sproxton Lodge
Listed

Skillington, Grantham NG33 5HJ
☎ Grantham (01476) 860307
*213-acre arable farm. Quiet family farmhouse. Large lawns. Good breakfast. Large TV lounge with open fire. Located about 3 miles off the A1.*
Bedrooms: 1 single, 1 double, 1 triple
Bathrooms: 1 public

**Bed & breakfast**

| per night: | £min | £max |
|---|---|---|
| Single | 15.00 | 15.00 |
| Double | 30.00 | 30.00 |

Parking for 4

## SOUTHWELL

Nottinghamshire
Map ref 4C2

Town dominated by the Norman minster which has some beautiful 13th C stone carvings in the Chapter House. Charles I spent his last night of freedom in one of the inns. The original Bramley apple tree can still be seen.

### Barn Lodge
Listed COMMENDED

Duckers Cottage, Brinkley, Southwell NG25 0TP
☎ (01636) 813435
*Smallholding with panoramic views, 1 mile from the centre of Southwell and close to the racecourse, railway station and River Trent.*
Bedrooms: 1 double, 1 twin, 1 triple
Bathrooms: 3 private

**Bed & breakfast**

| per night: | £min | £max |
|---|---|---|
| Single | 20.00 | 20.00 |
| Double | 40.00 | 40.00 |

Parking for 3

## STAMFORD

Lincolnshire
Map ref 3A1

Exceptionally beautiful and historic town with many houses of architectural interest, several notable churches and other public buildings all in the local stone. Burghley House, built by William Cecil, is a magnificent Tudor mansion on the edge of the town.
*Tourist Information Centre*
☎ *(01780) 55611*

### Birch House
Listed

4 Lonsdale Road, Stamford PE9 2RW
☎ (01780) 54876 & Mbl 0850 185759
*Comfortable, family-run detached house on the outskirts of Stamford. All rooms have TV and tea/coffee-making facilities. Non-smokers only, please.*
Bedrooms: 2 single, 1 double, 1 twin
Bathrooms: 1 public

**Bed & breakfast**

| per night: | £min | £max |
|---|---|---|
| Single | 15.00 | 15.00 |
| Double | 30.00 | 30.00 |

Parking for 3

### 176 Casterton Road ⋒
Listed

Stamford PE9 2XX
☎ (01780) 63368
*Homely, modern detached house, a mile from the A1 on the B1081 and 1 mile from town centre.*
Bedrooms: 2 single, 1 double
Bathrooms: 1 public

**Bed & breakfast**

| per night: | £min | £max |
|---|---|---|
| Single | 14.00 | 14.00 |
| Double | 28.00 | 28.00 |

Parking for 3

### Dolphin Guesthouse
❅ ❅

12 East Street, Stamford PE9 1QD
☎ (01780) 55494
*En-suite accommodation next to the Dolphin Inn, renowned for its cask ales, friendliness and food. Off-road secure car parking and only 100 yards from the town centre.*
Bedrooms: 1 single, 1 double, 2 twin
Bathrooms: 2 private, 1 public

**Bed & breakfast**

| per night: | £min | £max |
|---|---|---|
| Single | 18.00 | 25.00 |
| Double | 36.00 | 50.00 |

**Half board**

| per person: | £min | £max |
|---|---|---|
| Daily | 22.00 | 33.00 |

Lunch available
Evening meal 1800 (last orders 2130)
Parking for 5
Cards accepted: Access, Visa, Amex, Switch/Delta

### The Manor Cottage
Listed HIGHLY COMMENDED

Stamford Road, Collyweston, Stamford PE9 3PN
☎ (01780) 83209
*Large stone-built Georgian house, set in 2 acres of grounds, with panoramic views, in the picturesque village of Collyweston, just 3 miles from historic Stamford.*
Bedrooms: 2 single, 1 double, 1 twin
Bathrooms: 1 private, 2 public

**Bed & breakfast**

| per night: | £min | £max |
|---|---|---|
| Single | 15.00 | 35.00 |
| Double | 30.00 | 60.00 |

Evening meal 1830 (last orders 2130)
Parking for 10
Cards accepted: Access, Visa

### Martins
Listed

20 High Street, Saint Martin's, Stamford PE9 2LF
☎ (01780) 52106
*Elegant, 17th C house near the town centre. Large rooms furnished with antiques. Walled garden and croquet. Street parking.*
Bedrooms: 3 twin
Bathrooms: 2 public

**Bed & breakfast**

| per night: | £min | £max |
|---|---|---|
| Single | 28.50 | 28.50 |
| Double | 45.00 | 50.00 |

**Half board**

| per person: | £min | £max |
|---|---|---|
| Daily | 37.50 | 43.50 |
| Weekly | 262.00 | 304.00 |

Evening meal 1930 (last orders 2030)
Parking for 3

### The Priory ⋒
❅ ❅ ❅ HIGHLY COMMENDED

Church Road, Ketton, Stamford PE9 3RD
☎ (01780) 720215
Fax (01780) 721881

*Grade II listed 16th C licensed country house near Stamford. En-suite rooms overlooking splendid gardens. Colour brochure available.*
Bedrooms: 2 double, 1 twin
Bathrooms: 2 private, 1 public

**Bed & breakfast**

| per night: | £min | £max |
|---|---|---|
| Single | 28.00 | 35.00 |
| Double | 38.00 | 55.00 |

**Half board**

| per person: | £min | £max |
|---|---|---|
| Daily | 31.50 | 40.00 |
| Weekly | 207.00 | 260.00 |

Lunch available
Evening meal 1900 (last orders 2100)
Parking for 10
Cards accepted: Access, Visa

---

Please check prices and other details at the time of booking.

## SUTTON-ON-TRENT

Nottinghamshire
Map ref 4C2

### Leylands
**Listed** **COMMENDED**

Great North Road, Sutton-on-Trent,
Newark NG23 6QN
☎ Newark (01636) 821710
Fax (01636) 822177
*Spacious accommodation with "old
world charm" in a rural setting,
designed and built by proprietors.
Convenient for Sherwood Forest,
Lincoln and Newark, and just 5 minutes
off the A1.*
Bedrooms: 1 single, 1 double, 1 twin
Bathrooms: 1 private, 1 public

**Bed & breakfast**

| per night: | £min | £max |
| --- | --- | --- |
| Single | 15.00 | |
| Double | 36.00 | 40.00 |

**Half board**

| per person: | £min | £max |
| --- | --- | --- |
| Daily | 23.00 | 28.00 |

Evening meal 1830 (last orders 2000)
Parking for 6

## TIDESWELL

Derbyshire
Map ref 4B2

Small town with a large 14th C
church known as the "Cathedral of
the Peak". There is a well-dressing
ceremony each June with Morris
dancing, and many choral events
throughout the year.

### Poppies
**Listed**

Bank Square, Tideswell, Buxton
SK17 8LA
☎ (01298) 871083
*Poppies offers a warm welcome,
comfortable accommodation and good
vegetarian and traditional home
cooking in a small restaurant, at the
centre of this picturesque mid Peak
District village.*
Bedrooms: 1 double, 1 twin, 1 triple
Bathrooms: 1 private, 1 public

**Bed & breakfast**

| per night: | £min | £max |
| --- | --- | --- |
| Single | 13.50 | 18.00 |
| Double | 27.00 | 36.00 |

**Half board**

| per person: | £min | £max |
| --- | --- | --- |
| Daily | 22.50 | 36.00 |
| Weekly | 140.50 | 220.00 |

Lunch available
Evening meal 1900 (last orders 2130)
Open February-December
Cards accepted: Access, Visa, Diners,
Amex

## UPPINGHAM

Leicestershire
Map ref 4C3

Quiet market town dominated by
its famous public school which
was founded in 1584. It has many
stone houses and is surrounded by
attractive countryside.

### Boundary Farm
☺☺

Glaston Road, Uppingham, Oakham
LE15 9PX
☎ (01572) 822354
*250-acre mixed farm. Family-run, within
walking distance of the historic market
town of Uppingham. Ideally placed to
explore Rutland Water and Stamford.*
Bedrooms: 1 double, 1 twin
Bathrooms: 2 private

**Bed & breakfast**

| per night: | £min | £max |
| --- | --- | --- |
| Single | 18.00 | |
| Double | 34.00 | |

Parking for 3
Open January-November

### Old Rectory ▲
☺☺

New Road, Belton in Rutland, Oakham
LE15 9LE
☎ Belton (01572) 86279 Changing to
717279
Fax (01572) 86343 Changing to
717343
*14-acre smallholding. Large Victorian
country house and annexe overlooking
Eye Brook valley and rolling Rutland
countryside. Cottage-style en-suite
rooms, quiet friendly atmosphere and
good food. Small farm environment.
Families welcome.*
Bedrooms: 1 single, 2 double, 1 twin,
1 triple
Bathrooms: 5 private, 1 public

**Bed & breakfast**

| per night: | £min | £max |
| --- | --- | --- |
| Single | 18.00 | |
| Double | 36.00 | |

Evening meal 1800 (last orders 1900)
Parking for 10
Cards accepted: Access, Visa

## UPTON

Nottinghamshire
Map ref 4C2

### Honey Cottage
☺☺☺ **HIGHLY COMMENDED**

The Green, Upton, Newark NG23 5SU
☎ Southwell (01636) 813318
*Attractive cottage in the heart of a
conservation village, ideal for touring
Robin Hood country. Bar and
restaurant meals available in village
pubs. Within easy reach of A1.*
Bedrooms: 2 twin
Bathrooms: 2 private

**Bed & breakfast**

| per night: | £min | £max |
| --- | --- | --- |
| Single | 25.00 | 25.00 |
| Double | 36.00 | 36.00 |

Parking for 4

## WEEDON

Northamptonshire
Map ref 2C1

### Globe Hotel ▲
☺☺☺ **COMMENDED**

High Street, Weedon, Northampton
NN7 4QD
☎ (01327) 340336
Fax (01327) 349058
*19th C countryside inn. Old world
atmosphere and freehouse hospitality
with good English cooking, available all
day. Meeting rooms. Close to M1,
Stratford and many tourist spots. Send
for information pack.*
Bedrooms: 4 single, 6 double, 5 twin,
3 triple
Bathrooms: 18 private

**Bed & breakfast**

| per night: | £min | £max |
| --- | --- | --- |
| Single | 28.50 | 42.00 |
| Double | 38.00 | 49.50 |

**Half board**

| per person: | £min | £max |
| --- | --- | --- |
| Daily | 38.50 | 48.50 |

Lunch available
Evening meal (last orders 2200)
Parking for 40
Cards accepted: Access, Visa, Diners,
Amex

## WESSINGTON

Derbyshire
Map ref 4B2

### Crich Lane Farm
**Listed**

Moorwood Moor Lane, Wessington,
Derby DE55 6DU
☎ Alfreton (01773) 835186
*44-acre dairy farm. Large garden in
peaceful surroundings, easy walking
distance of village and pubs. Pet
attractions and a warm and friendly
welcome to all. Easy access to M1 and
A38.*
Bedrooms: 1 single, 1 double, 1 twin
Bathrooms: 2 public

**Bed & breakfast**

| per night: | £min | £max |
| --- | --- | --- |
| Single | 14.00 | 15.00 |
| Double | 28.00 | 30.00 |

Parking for 10

## WEST HADDON

Northamptonshire
Map ref 4C3

### Pear Trees

[APPROVED]

31 Station Road, West Haddon, Northampton NN6 7AU
☎ (01788) 510389

*Attractive 18th C Northamptonshire-stone detached house in village, with good pubs/restaurants within walking distance. Four miles junction 18 M1/M6. Rugby 10 miles, Daventry 7 miles, Northampton 13 miles, nearest main line station 2 miles.*

Bedrooms: 1 double, 1 twin, 1 triple
Bathrooms: 2 private, 1 public

| **Bed & breakfast per night:** | £min | £max |
|---|---|---|
| Single | 18.00 | 18.00 |
| Double | 32.00 | 36.00 |

| **Half board per person:** | £min | £max |
|---|---|---|
| Daily | 25.00 | 25.00 |
| Weekly | 160.00 | 160.00 |

Evening meal 1900 (last orders 2030)
[UL] [S] [TV]

## WILLOUGHBY WATERLEYS

Leicestershire
Map ref 4C3

### The Old Rectory

[Listed]

Willoughby Waterleys, Leicester LE8 6UF
☎ Leicester (0116) 247 8474

*A listed Georgian rectory with many original features, in a conservation village 7 miles south of Leicester.*

Bedrooms: 1 double, 1 twin
Bathrooms: 1 private, 1 public

| **Bed & breakfast per night:** | £min | £max |
|---|---|---|
| Single | 18.00 | |
| Double | 36.00 | |

Parking for 4
[UL]

## WINSTER

Derbyshire
Map ref 4B2

Village with some interesting old gritstone houses and cottages, including the 17th C stone market hall now owned by the National Trust. It is a former lead mining centre.

### Brae Cottage

East Bank, Winster, Matlock DE4 2DT
☎ (01629) 650375

*Spacious, self contained cottage annexe ground level, with en-suite bathroom. Garage, patio and picturesque garden. Suitable for 2 to 4 people.*

Bedrooms: 1 family room
Bathrooms: 1 private

| **Bed & breakfast per night:** | £min | £max |
|---|---|---|
| Single | 14.00 | 14.00 |
| Double | 28.00 | 28.00 |

Parking for 2
[UL] [SP] [T]

### The Dower House

[HIGHLY COMMENDED]

Main Street, Winster, Matlock DE4 2DH
☎ Matlock (01629) 650213
Fax (01629) 650894

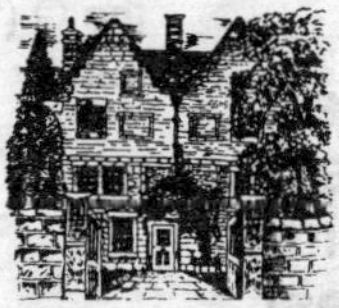

*Elizabethan country house offering peace and relaxation in a homely atmosphere. Home-made jams and marmalade. Close to Chatsworth and Haddon Hall. Resident Blue Badge Derbyshire tourist guide.*

Bedrooms: 1 double, 2 twin
Bathrooms: 3 private, 1 public

| **Bed & breakfast per night:** | £min | £max |
|---|---|---|
| Double | 36.00 | 55.00 |

Parking for 6
Open March-October
10 [S]

## WINWICK

Northamptonshire
Map ref 4C3

### Winwick Mill

Winwick, Northampton NN6 7PD
☎ West Haddon (01788) 510613
Fax (01788) 510613

*Converted watermill and millhouse, all rooms en-suite. Quiet secluded location with good access to main roads and motorways (M1, M6, M45).*

Bedrooms: 1 single, 1 double, 1 twin
Bathrooms: 3 private

| **Bed & breakfast per night:** | £min | £max |
|---|---|---|
| Single | 18.00 | |

| **Half board per person:** | £min | £max |
|---|---|---|
| Daily | 25.00 | |

Evening meal 1800 (last orders 2000)
Parking for 10
12 [UL] [S] [TV]

The symbol after an establishment name indicates membership of a Regional Tourist Board.

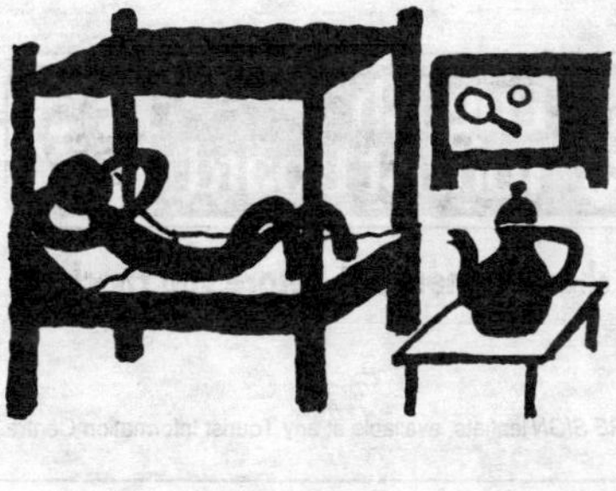

# KEY TO SYMBOLS

Information about many of the services and facilities at accommodation listed in this guide is given in the form of symbols. The key to these symbols is inside the back cover flap. You may find it helpful to keep the flap open when referring to the accommodation listings.

# SURE SIGNS
## OF WHERE TO STAY

**Throughout Britain, the tourist boards now inspect over 30,000 places to stay, every year, to help you find the ones that suit you best.**

Looking for a hotel, guesthouse, inn, B&B or farmhouse? Look for the **CROWN**. The classifications: 'Listed', and then **ONE to FIVE CROWN**, tell you the range of facilities and services you can expect. The more Crowns, the wider the range.

Looking for somewhere convenient to stop overnight on a motorway or major road route? Look for the 'Lodge' **MOON**. The classifications: **ONE to THREE MOON** tell you the range of facilities you can expect. The more Moons, the wider the range.

Looking for a self-catering holiday home? Look for the **KEY**. The classifications: **ONE to FIVE KEY**, tell you the range of facilities and equipment you can expect. The more Keys, the wider the range.
THE GRADES: **APPROVED, COMMENDED, HIGHLY COMMENDED and DE LUXE**, whether alongside the **CROWNS**, **KEYS** or **MOONS** show the quality standard of what is provided. If no grade is shown, you can still expect a high standard of cleanliness.

Looking for a holiday caravan, chalet or camping park? Look for the **Q** symbol. The more ✓s in the Q (from one to five), the higher the quality standard of what is provided.

English Tourist Board

**We've checked them out before you check in!**

More detailed information on the **CROWNS**, the **KEYS** and the **Q** is given in free *SURE SIGN* leaflets, available at any Tourist Information Centre.

214

*A rare place — that's East Anglia. Always a little apart, it has kept its character and its integrity. Its people have a sense of humour that's down to earth and accents that are a challenge to imitate. Experience the timeless quality of the sprawling Fens, the reedy Broads, the sandy heaths of Breckland and the Essex estuaries. Explore Bunyan's Bedford and the River Great Ouse, stroll the leafy lanes of Hertfordshire, visit historic cities such as Cambridge. You'll need more than a week in East Anglia!*

# EAST ANGLIA

The Counties of Bedfordshire, Cambridgeshire, Essex, Hertfordshire, Norfolk and Suffolk

For more information on East Anglia, contact:
**East Anglia Tourist Board**
**Toppesfield Hall**
**Hadleigh**
**Suffolk IP7 5DN**
Tel: (01473) 822922
Fax: (01473) 823063

Where to Go in East Anglia – see pages 216–219

Where to Stay in East Anglia – see pages 220–250

# WHERE TO GO

*You will find hundreds of interesting places to visit during your stay in East Anglia, just some of which are listed in these pages. The number against each name will help you locate it on the map (page 219). Contact any Tourist Information Centre in the region for more ideas on days out in East Anglia.*

Thatching, like many traditional country crafts, flourishes in East Anglia.

**1  Holkham Hall**
Wells-next-the-Sea, Norfolk NR23 1AB
Tel: (01328) 710733
*Classic 18th C Palladian-style mansion, part of a great agricultural estate, and a living treasure house of artistic and architectural history.*

**2  Sea Life Centre**
Southern Promenade, Hunstanton, Norfolk
PE36 5BH
Tel: (01485) 533576
*See a world only divers see, from the ocean tunnel. View and touch a variety of rock pool creatures. Also a seal rehabilitation centre.*

**3  Thursford Collection**
Thursford, Norfolk NR21 0AS
Tel: (01328) 878477
*Live musical shows, mechanical organs and Wurlitzer show.*

**4  Blickling Hall**
Blickling, Norfolk NR11 6NF
Tel: (01263) 733084
*Jacobean red brick mansion. Garden, orangery, parkland and lake. Fine tapestries and furniture.*

**5  Pensthorpe Waterfowl Park**
Pensthorpe, Fakenham, Norfolk NR21 0LN
Tel: (01328) 851465
*Large waterfowl and wildfowl collection. Information centre, conservation shop, adventure play area, walks and nature trails. Licensed restaurant.*

**6  Sainsbury Centre for Visual Arts**
University of East Anglia, Norwich, Norfolk
NR4 7TJ
Tel: (01603) 56060
*Robert and Lisa Sainsbury Collection is wide ranging and of international importance, housed in a remarkable building designed by N. Foster.*

**7  Sacrewell Farm and Country Centre**
Sacrewell, Thornhaugh, Peterborough,
Cambridgeshire PE8 6HJ
Tel: (01780) 782222
*500-acre farm, with working watermill, gardens, shrubberies, nature and general interest trails. 18th C buildings, displays of farm, rural and domestic bygones.*

**8  Oxburgh Hall**
Oxborough, King's Lynn, Norfolk PE33 9PS
Tel: (01366) 328258
*15th C moated red brick fortified manor house.*

Magnificent 80ft gatehouse, Mary Queen of Scots needlework, priest's hole, garden.

### 9 Pleasure Beach
South Beach Parade, Great Yarmouth, Norfolk NR30 3EH
Tel: (01493) 844585
*Roller coaster, terminator, log flume, flipper, monorail, breakdance, galloping horses, caterpillar, ghost train and fun house.*

### 10 Somerleyton Hall and Gardens
Somerleyton, Suffolk NR32 5QQ
Tel: (01502) 730224
*Anglo-Italian style building with state rooms, maze, garden. Miniature railway, shop and refreshment room.*

### 11 Pleasurewood Hills American Theme Park
Lowestoft, Suffolk NR32 5DZ
Tel: (01502)508200
*Tempest, chair lift, cine 180, railway, pirate ship, fort, Aladdin's cave, parrot shows, rollercoaster, waveswinger, Eye in the Sky, star ride Enterprise.*

### 12 Otter Trust
Earsham, Suffolk NR35 2AF
Tel: (01986) 893470
*A breeding and conservation headquarters with the largest collection of otters in the world. Also lakes with collection of waterfowl, deer, etc.*

### 13 Bressingham Steam Museum and Gardens
Bressingham, Norfolk IP22 2AB
Tel: (0137988) 386
*Steam rides through 5 miles of woodland, garden and nursery. Mainline locomotive and over 50 steam engines. Alan Bloom's "Dell" garden.*

### 14 Ancient House Museum
White Hart Street, Thetford, Norfolk IP24 1AA
Tel: (01842) 752599
*Museum of Thetford and Breckland life in a remarkable early Tudor house. Displays on local history, flint, archaeology and natural history.*

### 15 Ely Cathedral
Chapter House, The College, Ely, Cambridgeshire CB7 4DN
Tel: (01353) 667735
*One of England's finest cathedrals. Octagon is the crowning glory. Fine outbuildings. Guided tours and tower tours available. Brass rubbing and stained glass museum.*

### 16 Minsmere Nature Reserve (RSPB)
Westleton, Suffolk IP17 3BY
Tel: (0178873) 281
*Two 2-mile walks, 6 hides on coastal lagoon walk, 2 hides on reed bed. Birds include avocet, marsh harrier, bittern. Shop and reception area.*

### 17 Framlingham Castle
Framlingham, Suffolk IP8 9BT
Tel: (01728) 724189
*12th C curtain walls with 13 towers and Tudor brick chimneys. Built by Bigod family, Earls of Norfolk, home of Mary Tudor in 1553.*

### 18 Pakenham Watermill
Grimestone End, Pakenham, Suffolk
Tel: (01787) 247179
*Fine 18th C working watermill on Domesday site complete with oil engine and other subsidiary machinery. Restored by Suffolk Preservation Society.*

### 19 Ickworth House, Park and Gardens
Ickworth, Bury St Edmunds, Suffolk IP29 5QE
Tel: (01284) 735270
*Extraordinary oval house with flanking wings. Fine paintings and Georgian silver, Italian garden and park designed by Capability Brown.*

### 20 The National Horseracing Museum
99 High Street, Newmarket, Suffolk CB8 8JL
Tel: (01638) 667333
*5 permanent galleries telling the great story of the development of horseracing. British sporting art.*

*Colman's mustard: grown and processed in East Anglia.*

**21 Helmingham Hall Gardens**
Helmingham, Suffolk IP14 6EF
Tel: (01473) 890363
*Moated and walled garden with many rare roses and possibly the best kitchen garden in Britain. Highland cattle, safari rides in park to view red and fallow deer.*

**22 Imperial War Museum**
Duxford, Cambridgeshire CB2 4QR
Tel: (01223) 835000
*Over 120 aircraft plus tanks, vehicles and guns on display. Adventure playground, shops, restaurant.*

*Flatford Mill, captured in Constable's painting, epitomises the timeless charm of East Anglia.*

**23 Woburn Abbey**
Woburn, Bedfordshire MK43 0TP
Tel: (01525) 290666
*18th C Palladian mansion altered by Henry Holland, the Prince Regent's architect. Contains a collection of English silver, French and English furniture and an important art collection.*

**24 Mountfitchet Castle**
Stansted Mountfitchet, Essex CM24 8SP
Tel: (01279) 813237
*Reconstructed Norman motte and bailey castle and village of Domesday period. Grand hall, church, prison, siege tower and weapons.*

**25 Colchester Castle**
Colchester, Essex CO1 1TJ
Tel: (01206) 712931

*Norman keep on foundations of Roman temple. Archaeological material includes much on Roman Colchester.*

**26 Knebworth House, Gardens and Park**
Knebworth, Hertfordshire SG3 6PY
Tel: (01438) 812661
*Tudor mansion house refashioned in the 19th C by Bulwer-Lytton. Houses a collection of manuscripts, portraits, Jacobean banqueting hall, adventure playground and gift shop.*

**27 Whipsnade Wild Animal Park**
Zoological Society of London, Dunstable, Bedfordshire LU6 2LF
Tel: (01582) 872171
*Over 2,000 animals of 200 species in 600 acres of parkland. Children's playground, railway, Tiger Falls, sea-lions and birds of prey.*

**28 The Gardens of the Rose**
The Royal National Rose Society, Chiswell Green, St Albans, Hertfordshire AL2 3NR
Tel: (01727) 850461
*The Royal National Rose Society's garden, 20 acres of showground and trial ground for new varieties of rose. 30,000 roses of all types with 1,700 different varieties.*

**29 Hatfield House**
Hatfield Park, Hatfield, Hertfordshire AL9 5NQ
Tel: (01707) 262823
*Jacobean house built in 1611 and Old Palace built in 1497. Contains famous paintings, fine furniture and possessions of Queen Elizabeth I. Park and gardens.*

**30 Aldenham Country Park**
Dagger Lane, Elstree, Hertfordshire WD6 3AT
Tel: (0181) 953 9602
*65-acre reservoir, circular footpath and 175 acres of woods. Adventure playground, rare breed cattle, sheep, pigs and chickens. Angling, nature trail, horse-riding.*

Lincolnshire
Leicestershire
Northants
Cambridgeshire
Bedfordshire
Hertfordshire
Bucks
Greater London
Berkshire
Surrey
Kent

Norfolk
Suffolk
Essex

Wells-next-the-Sea **1**
Sheringham
Hunstanton **2**
Thursford
Cromer
Fakenham **3**
North Walsham
**4**
Pensthorpe **5**
Blickling
King's Lynn
East Dereham
Caister-on-Sea
Wisbech
Norwich **6**
Great Yarmouth **9**
Thornhaugh **7**
Peterborough
Swaffham
Wymondham
Oxborough **8**
Somerleyton **10**
March
Attleborough
Earsham
Bungay
Whittlesey
Thetford
**12**
Lowestoft
Yaxley
Chatteris
**14**
Diss
Halesworth
Southwold
Lakenheath
**13**
Bressingham
Ely **15**
Mildenhall
Westleton **16**
Pakenham
Huntingdon
St Ives
Bury St Edmunds **18**
Suffolk
Framlingham **17**
St Neots
**20**
**19**
Stowmarket
Aldeburgh
Cambridge
Newmarket
Ickworth
**21**
Great Shelford
Helmingham
Bedford
Duxford **22**
Haverhill
Ipswich
Sandy
Saffron Walden
Sudbury
Hadleigh
Leighton Buzzard
**23** Woburn
Letchworth
Stansted Mountfitchet
Colchester
Harwich
Hitchin
Knebworth
Essex
**25**
Dunstable **27**
Luton
**26**
**24**
Braintree
Clacton on Sea
Hemel Hempstead
Hertford
Bishop's Stortford
Coggeshall
Witham
West Mersea
**28** **29** Hatfield
Harlow
Chelmsford
Watford
St Albans
Chipping Ongar
Maldon
Burnham-on-Crouch
**30**
Elstree
Brentwood
Ingatestone
Basildon
Southend-on-Sea
Stanford-le-Hope
Grays
Tilbury

0        20 Miles
0        30 Kms

# FIND OUT MORE

Further information about holidays and attractions in East Anglia is available from:
**East Anglia Tourist Board**, Toppesfield Hall, Hadleigh, Suffolk IP7 5DN
Tel: (01473) 822922

These publications are available free from the East Anglia Tourist Board:
● *Bed & Breakfast Touring Map for the East of*

*England*
● *East Anglia, the Real England*
● *Places to Stay: Hotels, Guesthouses and Inns*
        *Self-Catering*
● *Camping and Caravanning Touring Map*
● *Freedom Holiday Parks in Eastern England*
Also available are (prices include postage and packing):
● *East Anglia Guide £4*
● *East Anglia Leisure Map £4*
● *A Day out of London Map £3.50*
● *Gardens to Visit in East Anglia £1.50*

# WHERE TO STAY

Accommodation entries in this regional section are listed in alphabetical order of place name, and then in alphabetical order of establishment.

Map references refer to the colour location maps at the back of this guide. The first figure is the map number; the letter and figure which follow indicate the grid reference on the map.

Symbols at the end of each accommodation entry give information about services and facilities. A 'key' to these symbols is inside the back cover flap, which can be kept open for easy reference.

## ALDEBURGH

Suffolk
Map ref 3C2

A prosperous port in the 16th C, now famous for the Aldeburgh Music Festival held annually in June. The 16th C Moot Hall, now a museum, is a timber-framed building once used as an open market.

### Faraway
Listed

28 Linden Close, Aldeburgh IP15 5JL
☎ (01728) 452571
Bungalow with garden and car parking. Very quiet, being off the main road.
Bedrooms: 1 single, 1 twin, 1 triple
Bathrooms: 1 public
**Bed & breakfast**

| per night: | £min | £max |
|---|---|---|
| Single | 14.00 | 15.00 |
| Double | 28.00 | 30.00 |

Parking for 3

### Tapp Cottage
35 Fawcett Road, Aldeburgh
IP15 5HQ
☎ (01728) 453672
Warm welcome at this family home, 3 minutes' walk to sea and town centre. Guests sitting room with TV, good home cooking.
Bedrooms: 1 double, 1 twin
Bathrooms: 1 public
**Bed & breakfast**

| per night: | £min | £max |
|---|---|---|
| Single | 16.00 | 23.00 |
| Double | 32.00 | 34.00 |

Evening meal 1800 (last orders 1800)

## ALDHAM

Essex
Map ref 3B2

### Old House ♙
Listed  COMMENDED

Ford Street, Aldham, Colchester CO6 3PH
☎ Colchester (01206) 240456
Bed and breakfast in 14th C family home with friendly atmosphere, oak beams, log fires, large garden and ample parking. Between Harwich and Cambridge, Felixstowe and London. On A604, 5 miles west of Colchester.
Bedrooms: 1 single, 1 twin, 1 triple
Bathrooms: 3 private, 1 public
**Bed & breakfast**

| per night: | £min | £max |
|---|---|---|
| Single | 20.00 | 25.00 |
| Double | 30.00 | 45.00 |

Parking for 8

There are separate sections in this guide listing groups specialising in farm holidays and accommodation which is especially suitable for young people and organised groups.

## AMPTHILL

Bedfordshire
Map ref 2D1

Busy market town with houses of distinctive Georgian character. Market established in 13th C, where traders sell their wares around the town pump, a Portland-stone obelisk presented to the town in 1785 by Lord Ossory.
Tourist Information Centre
☎ (01525) 402051

### House Beautiful
Listed

14 The Slade, Clophill, Bedford MK45 4BZ
☎ Silsoe (01525) 860517 & Silsoe (emergency ansaphone) 861703
Quiet country cottage in lovely summer gardens - log fire in winter. M1 junction 12 10 minutes, Luton Airport 20 minutes.
Bedrooms: 1 single, 1 double, 1 twin
Bathrooms: 1 public
**Bed & breakfast**

| per night: | £min | £max |
|---|---|---|
| Single | 15.00 | 20.00 |
| Double | 30.00 | 40.00 |

**Half board**

| per person: | £min | £max |
|---|---|---|
| Daily | 25.00 | 30.00 |
| Weekly | 175.00 | 210.00 |

Evening meal 1800 (last orders 2000)
Parking for 4

### Pond Farm
Listed

7 High Street, Pulloxhill, Bedford MK45 5HA
☎ Flitwick (01525) 712316

*70-acre arable & horse farm. Listed building, an ideal base for touring. Close to Woburn Abbey, Whipsnade Zoo, the Shuttleworth Collection of old aircraft and Luton Airport. Resident Great Dane.*
Bedrooms: 1 double, 1 twin, 1 triple
Bathrooms: 1 public

**Bed & breakfast**

| per night: | £min | £max |
|---|---|---|
| Single | 16.00 | 20.00 |
| Double | 28.00 | |

Parking for 6

## AYLSHAM

Norfolk
Map ref 3B1

Small town on the River Bure with an attractive market place and interesting church. Nearby is Blickling Hall (National Trust). Also the terminal of the Bure Valley narrow gauge steam railway which runs on 9 miles of the old Great Eastern trackbed, between Wroxham and Aylsham.

### Burgh House

Burgh Road, Aylsham, Norwich
NR11 6AR
☎ (01263) 733648 & 733567
*Secluded and peaceful country house in extensive wooded grounds, yet a minute's walk from town centre. Convenient for Broads, National Trust houses, Norwich and North Norfolk coast.*
Bedrooms: 1 double, 1 twin
Bathrooms: 2 private

**Bed & breakfast**

| per night: | £min | £max |
|---|---|---|
| Single | 17.50 | |
| Double | 35.00 | |

Parking for 10

### The Old Bank House

3 Norwich Road, Aylsham, Norwich
NR11 6BN
☎ (01263) 733843

*Relax in the comfort and traditional Victorian atmosphere of Aylsham's former private bank. We offer guests a friendly break, spacious welcoming bedrooms with TV and lovely countryside nearby.*
Bedrooms: 1 double, 1 twin, 1 triple
Bathrooms: 1 private, 2 public

**Bed & breakfast**

| per night: | £min | £max |
|---|---|---|
| Single | 16.00 | 16.00 |
| Double | 32.00 | 32.00 |

**Half board**

| per person: | £min | £max |
|---|---|---|
| Daily | 25.00 | 25.00 |
| Weekly | 150.00 | 150.00 |

Evening meal 1800 (last orders 2000)
Parking for 3
Cards accepted: Diners

### The Old Pump House 🏠
HIGHLY COMMENDED

Holman Road, Aylsham, Norwich
NR11 6BY
☎ (01263) 733789
*Comfortable, rambling 1750s family home, opposite thatched pump and 1 minute from church and historic marketplace. Pine-shuttered breakfast room overlooks peaceful garden. Non-smoking.*
Bedrooms: 3 double, 2 twin
Bathrooms: 3 private, 2 public

**Bed & breakfast**

| per night: | £min | £max |
|---|---|---|
| Single | 17.00 | 25.00 |
| Double | 34.00 | 40.00 |

**Half board**

| per person: | £min | £max |
|---|---|---|
| Daily | 27.00 | 35.00 |
| Weekly | 140.00 | 180.00 |

Evening meal from 1900
Parking for 7

## BABRAHAM

Cambridgeshire
Map ref 2D1

### Worsted Barrows

Babraham, Cambridge CB2 4AX
☎ Cambridge (01223) 833298
*Country house offering comfortable accommodation, 4 miles from M11. Convenient for Cambridge, Newmarket and for touring the pretty villages of Essex and Suffolk.*
Bedrooms: 3 double, 3 twin, 1 triple
Bathrooms: 6 private, 1 public

**Bed & breakfast**

| per night: | £min | £max |
|---|---|---|
| Single | 16.00 | 20.00 |
| Double | 30.00 | 32.00 |

**Half board**

| per person: | £min | £max |
|---|---|---|
| Daily | 26.00 | 36.00 |

Evening meal 1700 (last orders 1930)
Parking for 9

## BACTON

Suffolk
Map ref 3B2

### Brickwall Farm
HIGHLY COMMENDED

Broad Road, Bacton, Stowmarket
IP14 4HP
☎ (01449) 780197
*17th C listed farmhouse which has been sympathetically restored. Centrally situated for exploring Mid-Suffolk and the Heritage Coast.*
Bedrooms: 3 double
Bathrooms: 3 private

**Bed & breakfast**

| per night: | £min | £max |
|---|---|---|
| Single | 24.00 | |
| Double | 35.00 | |

**Half board**

| per person: | £min | £max |
|---|---|---|
| Daily | 34.00 | |
| Weekly | 150.00 | |

Evening meal 1900 (last orders 2100)
Parking for 5
Open January-October, December

## BARNHAM

Suffolk
Map ref 3B2

### Rymer Farm
COMMENDED

Barnham, Thetford, Norfolk IP24 2PP
☎ Elveden (01842) 890233
Fax (01842) 890653
*550-acre arable farm. 17th C farmhouse. Lovely walks, flower arranger's garden, carp fishing. 400 yards off A134 signposted to RAF Honington.*
Bedrooms: 1 single, 1 double, 1 twin
Bathrooms: 2 private, 1 public

**Bed & breakfast**

| per night: | £min | £max |
|---|---|---|
| Single | 16.00 | 20.00 |
| Double | 32.00 | 36.00 |

Parking for 10

Please mention this guide when making a booking.

Individual proprietors have supplied all details of accommodation. Although we do check for accuracy, we advise you to confirm the information at the time of booking.

## BECCLES

Suffolk
Map ref 3C1

Fire destroyed the town in the 16th C and it was rebuilt in Georgian red brick. The River Waveney, on which the town stands, is popular with boating enthusiasts and has an annual regatta. Home of Beccles and District Museum and the William Clowes Printing Museum.

### Rose Cottage
Listed  COMMENDED

21 Kells Way, Geldeston, Beccles NR34 0LU
☎ Kirby Cane (01508) 518451

*Parts of the cottage date back to 1600, with inglenook fireplaces, beams and studwork. Quiet Waveney Valley position in south Norfolk.*
Bedrooms: 2 single, 2 double
Bathrooms: 1 public

**Bed & breakfast**

| per night: | £min | £max |
|---|---|---|
| Single | 15.00 | 15.00 |
| Double | 27.00 | 27.00 |

Parking for 3

🛇 🖵 🛈 🎜 🖭 ⟊ 🖴 ✿ ✕ 🐎

## BEDFORD

Bedfordshire
Map ref 2D1

Busy county town with interesting buildings and churches near the River Ouse which has pleasant riverside walks. Many associations with John Bunyan including Bunyan Meeting House, museum and statue. The Bedford Museum and Cecil Higgins Art Gallery are of interest.
*Tourist Information Centre*
☎ (01234) 215226

### Firs Farm
👑👑 COMMENDED

Stagsden, Bedford MK43 8TB
☎ (01234) 822344
*504-acre arable farm. Family-run, set in quiet surroundings quarter-of-a-mile south of A422, midway between Bedford and Milton Keynes (M1 junction 14).*
Bedrooms: 2 double, 1 twin
Bathrooms: 1 private, 1 public

**Bed & breakfast**

| per night: | £min | £max |
|---|---|---|
| Single | 15.00 | 20.00 |
| Double | 30.00 | 35.00 |

Parking for 4

🛇 5 🛆 🖭 🛈 🎜 🗠 🖭 🎛 🖴 ⟊ ✿ 🐎

## BEETLEY

Norfolk
Map ref 3B1

### Peacock House
Listed  HIGHLY COMMENDED

Peacock Lane, Old Beetley, Dereham NR20 4DG
☎ Dereham (01362) 860371
*Beautiful period farmhouse in rural setting, 3.5 miles from Dereham. Ideal for Norwich, Sandringham and coast. Full English breakfast and a warm welcome.*
Bedrooms: 1 single, 2 double
Bathrooms: 2 private

**Bed & breakfast**

| per night: | £min | £max |
|---|---|---|
| Single | 16.00 | 16.00 |
| Double | 32.00 | 32.00 |

Parking for 4

🛇 🖵 🛆 🖭 🛈 🖫 🗠 🎜 🖭 🎛 🖴 ✿ 🐎 🏵

## BEYTON

Suffolk
Map ref 3B2

### Manorhouse
👑👑 HIGHLY COMMENDED

The Green, Beyton, Bury St Edmunds IP30 9AF
☎ (01359) 270960
Fax (01284) 752561

*Listed 16th C former farmhouse with 20th C comforts, overlooking delightful village green. Good local hostelries. 4 miles east of Bury St Edmunds, off A45. Well placed for touring Suffolk and Norfolk.*
Bedrooms: 1 double, 1 twin
Bathrooms: 2 private

**Bed & breakfast**

| per night: | £min | £max |
|---|---|---|
| Double | 36.00 | 40.00 |

Parking for 5

🛇 8 🖵 🖵 🛆 🎔 🖭 🛈 🖫 🗠 🎜 🖭 🖴 ✿ ✕ 🐎 🏵

---

We advise you to confirm your booking in writing.

---

## BISHOP'S STORTFORD

Hertfordshire
Map ref 2D1

Fine old town on the River Stort with many interesting buildings, particularly Victorian, and an imposing parish church. The vicarage where Cecil Rhodes was born is now a museum.
*Tourist Information Centre*
☎ (01279) 652274

### The Thatch
Listed  COMMENDED

Cambridge Road, Ugley, Bishop's Stortford CM22 6HZ
☎ Rickling (01799) 543440
*Situated in hamlet just north of Bishop's Stortford. Thatched property set in lovely countryside, with warm and friendly atmosphere. Convenient for Stansted airport and M11. Airport parking available.*
Bedrooms: 2 double, 1 twin
Bathrooms: 2 private, 1 public

**Bed & breakfast**

| per night: | £min | £max |
|---|---|---|
| Single | 18.00 | 20.00 |
| Double | 30.00 | 40.00 |

Parking for 7

🛇 🖵 🖵 🎔 🖭 🛈 🖫 🗠 🎜 🖭 🎛 🖴 ✿ 🐎 🅃

## BLAKENEY

Norfolk
Map ref 3B1

Picturesque village on the north coast of Norfolk and a former port and fishing village. 15th C Guildhall. Marshy creeks extend towards Blakeney Point (National Trust) and are a paradise for naturalists, with trips to the reserve and to see the seals from Blakeney Quay.

### Flintstones Guest House ⋈
Listed  COMMENDED

Wiveton, Holt NR25 7TL
☎ Cley (01263) 740337
*Attractive licensed guesthouse in picturesque rural surroundings near village green. 1 mile from Cley and Blakeney with good sailing and bird-watching. All rooms with private facilities. Non-smokers only, please.*
Bedrooms: 1 double, 1 twin, 3 triple
Bathrooms: 5 private

**Bed & breakfast**

| per night: | £min | £max |
|---|---|---|
| Single | 21.50 | 24.50 |
| Double | 32.00 | 37.00 |

---

Please mention this guide when making a booking.

---

| Half board per person: | £min | £max |
|---|---|---|
| Daily | 26.00 | 28.50 |
| Weekly | 182.00 | |

Evening meal 1900 (last orders 1700)
Parking for 5

🛏️⚿🖵♦🛎️Ⓢ⤢🗄️TV🛏️⟍🞿🚲SP

### BLYTHBURGH

Suffolk
Map ref 3C2

### Little Thorbyns

Listed COMMENDED

The Street, Blythburgh, Halesworth
IP19 9LS
☎ (01502) 478664
*Good, comfortable accommodation and
a warm welcome. Close to Minsmere
RSPB sanctuary and Southwold,
Walberswick and Dunwich beaches.
Three-day mini-break £70 per person.*
Bedrooms: 1 single, 1 double, 1 twin
Bathrooms: 2 public

| Bed & breakfast per night: | £min | £max |
|---|---|---|
| Single | 16.00 | 17.00 |
| Double | 32.00 | 34.00 |

| Half board per person: | £min | £max |
|---|---|---|
| Daily | 23.00 | 24.00 |
| Weekly | 150.00 | 157.50 |

Parking for 4

🛏️⤢♦🖳🛎️Ⓢ⤢🗄️TV🛏️⟍🞿🚲SP

### BRAINTREE

Essex
Map ref 3B2

The Heritage Centre in the Town
Hall describes Braintree's former
international importance in wool,
silk and engineering. St Michael's
parish church includes some
Roman bricks and Braintree
market was first chartered in 1199.
*Tourist Information Centre*
☎ (01376) 550066

### Corkers

🖥️

Shalford Green, Braintree CM7 5AZ
☎ Great Dunmow (01371) 850376
*Two 16th C original farm cottages,
tastefully converted. Lathe and plaster
with oak beams. Half a mile from
Shalford.*
Bedrooms: 2 single, 1 double
Bathrooms: 1 public

| Bed & breakfast per night: | £min | £max |
|---|---|---|
| Single | 15.00 | 15.00 |
| Double | 30.00 | 30.00 |

Parking for 3

🛏️5⤢🖵♦🖳⟍🞿⤢🗄️TV🛏️⟍🞿🗙
🚲🏠


### Spicers Farm

🏆 COMMENDED

Rotten End, Wethersfield, Braintree
CM7 4AL
☎ Great Dunmow (01371) 851021
*70-acre mixed & arable farm.
Farmhouse with large garden in area
designated of special landscape value.
Lovely views of quiet rural countryside
yet convenient for Harwich, Stansted,
Cambridge and Constable country. 6
miles north west of Braintree.*
Bedrooms: 1 double, 2 twin
Bathrooms: 3 private, 1 public

| Bed & breakfast per night: | £min | £max |
|---|---|---|
| Single | 15.00 | 18.00 |
| Double | 30.00 | 36.00 |

Parking for 10

🛏️4⤢🖵♦🖳Ⓢ🗄️TV🛏️⟍🞿🗙
🚲SP

### BRAMERTON

Norfolk
Map ref 3C1

### Rolling Acre

Wood's End, Bramerton, Norwich
NR14 7ED
☎ Surlingham (01508) 8529
*Norwich 12 minutes. This delightful
home in idyllic countryside enjoys
beautiful views across the Yare Valley.
Nearby riverside inn serves excellent
meals.*
Bedrooms: 1 twin, 1 triple
Bathrooms: 1 private

| Bed & breakfast per night: | £min | £max |
|---|---|---|
| Single | 17.50 | 20.00 |
| Double | 32.00 | 35.00 |

Parking for 2
Cards accepted: Diners

🛏️3⤢🖵♦🖳⟍🖳TV🛏️⟍🞿🚲

### BROCKDISH

Norfolk
Map ref 3C2

### Grove Thorpe

🏆🏆 HIGHLY COMMENDED

Grove Road, Brockdish, Diss IP21 4JE
☎ Hoxne (01379) 75305
*Built in 1650, this Grade II listed
property is three-quarters of a mile
from the villages of Brockdish and
Thorpe Abbotts on a quiet country lane.
Set in secluded gardens and grounds of
5 acres. Livery facilities for horses. Diss
5 miles.*
Bedrooms: 1 double, 1 twin
Bathrooms: 1 private, 1 public

| Bed & breakfast per night: | £min | £max |
|---|---|---|
| Single | 28.00 | 28.00 |
| Double | 36.00 | 50.00 |

| Half board per person: | £min | £max |
|---|---|---|
| Daily | 28.00 | 37.00 |
| Weekly | 175.00 | 224.00 |


Lunch available
Evening meal 1800 (last orders 1930)
Parking for 14

🛏️12♦🖳🖳🛎️Ⓢ⤢🗄️TV🛏️⟍🞿🗙
🗙🚲🗙SP

### BROOKE

Norfolk
Map ref 3C1

### Welbeck House

Listed

Brooke, Norwich NR15 1AT
☎ (01508) 550292
*Attractive, quiet Georgian farmhouse
near buses and local pubs. Good local
knowledge of nature reserves and
specialist plant nurseries. Dogs and
children over 12 welcome.*
Bedrooms: 1 single, 1 double, 1 twin
Bathrooms: 1 public

| Bed & breakfast per night: | £min | £max |
|---|---|---|
| Single | 16.00 | |
| Double | 32.00 | 40.00 |

Parking for 10

🛏️⤢♦🖳Ⓢ⤢TV🛏️⟍🞿🚲🏠

### BROXTED

Essex
Map ref 2D1

### Old Post Office

🏆 COMMENDED

Church End, Broxted, Dunmow
CM6 2BU
☎ Bishops Stortford (01279) 850050
*Warm welcome assured at our
comfortable family home in a quiet
village. Convenient for Stansted Airport,
M11 and many attractive local villages.
Non-smokers only, please.*
Bedrooms: 1 single, 1 twin, 1 triple
Bathrooms: 3 private, 1 public

| Bed & breakfast per night: | £min | £max |
|---|---|---|
| Single | 18.50 | 18.50 |
| Double | 32.00 | 34.00 |

Parking for 6

🛏️5♦🖳⟍🖳⤢🗄️TV🛏️⟍🞿🗙🚲T

### BRUISYARD

Suffolk
Map ref 3C2

### High House Farm

Listed

Badingham Road, Bruisyard,
Saxmundham IP17 2EQ
☎ Badingham (01728) 638429
*Comfortable accommodation in a quiet
setting close to A12 and the market
towns of Framlingham and
Saxmundham, convenient for touring
heritage coast and rural Suffolk.*
Bedrooms: 1 single, 2 twin
Bathrooms: 1 public

*Continued* ▶

## BRUISYARD

*Continued*

**Bed & breakfast**

| per night: | £min | £max |
| --- | --- | --- |
| Single | 12.50 | 12.50 |
| Double | 30.00 | 30.00 |

🛏5 ♨ ⒰ TV ▥ ◗ ✿ 🚲

## BRUNDALL

Norfolk
Map ref 3C1

### Hawthorn Lodge

**Listed**

34 The Street, Brundall, Norwich
NR13 5LJ
☎ Norwich (01603) 716618 & 0850
382929
Fax (01603) 716618
*Comfortable accommodation in family
atmosphere. Situated in Broadland
village, close to River Yare, 6 miles
from Norwich.*
Bedrooms: 1 twin
Bathrooms: 1 private

**Bed & breakfast**

| per night: | £min | £max |
| --- | --- | --- |
| Single | 17.00 | 19.00 |
| Double | 32.00 | 35.00 |

**Half board**

| per person: | £min | £max |
| --- | --- | --- |
| Daily | 24.00 | 26.00 |
| Weekly | 150.00 | 160.00 |

Evening meal 1900 (last orders 2100)
Parking for 2

🛏 ⒠ ⌷ ♨ ⒰ ▤ ▥ ◗ ✕ 🚲 SP

## BULPHAN

Essex
Map ref 3B3

### Bonny Downs Farm

**Listed** **APPROVED**

Doesgate Lane, Bulphan, Upminster
RM14 3TB
☎ Basildon (01268) 542129
*60-acre mixed farm. Large comfortable
farmhouse offering home-cooked food.
Conveniently placed for all road links:
M25, A13 and A127 to London and
south-east England.*
Bedrooms: 2 twin, 1 triple
Bathrooms: 1 private, 1 public

**Bed & breakfast**

| per night: | £min | £max |
| --- | --- | --- |
| Single | 20.00 | 20.00 |
| Double | 30.00 | 30.00 |

**Half board**

| per person: | £min | £max |
| --- | --- | --- |
| Daily | 28.00 | 28.00 |
| Weekly | 180.00 | 180.00 |

Evening meal 1800 (last orders 2000)
Parking for 4

🛏 ♿ ⒠ ♨ ⒰ ▤ ▥ ✕ ⒨ TV ◗ ▥ ◗ ✓ ✿ ✕ 🚲

## BUNGAY

Suffolk
Map ref 3C1

Market town and yachting centre
on the River Waveney with the
remains of a great 12th C castle.
In the market-place stands the
Butter Cross, rebuilt in 1689 after
being largely destroyed by fire.
Nearby at Earsham is the Otter
Trust.

### Dove Restaurant

**APPROVED**

Wortwell, Harleston, Norfolk
IP20 0EN
☎ Homersfield (01986) 788 315
*A former railway hotel, now an
established international restaurant
offering accommodation. On the
Norfolk/Suffolk border. Good centre for
the Waveney Valley.*
Bedrooms: 2 double, 1 twin
Bathrooms: 2 private

**Bed & breakfast**

| per night: | £min | £max |
| --- | --- | --- |
| Single | 15.00 | 16.50 |
| Double | 28.00 | 30.00 |

**Half board**

| per person: | £min | £max |
| --- | --- | --- |
| Daily | 22.50 | 28.50 |

Lunch available
Evening meal 1900 (last orders 2130)
Parking for 16
Cards accepted: Access, Visa

🛏 ⒠ ♨ ⒮ S ✕ ⒨ TV ▥ ◗ 🍴 ∪ ↾ ✿ 🚲

## BUNTINGFORD

Hertfordshire
Map ref 2D1

### Southfields Farm

**Listed**

Throcking, Buntingford SG9 9RD
☎ Royston (01763) 281224
*Warm, comfortable farmhouse 1.5 miles
off A10 midway between London and
Cambridge. TV, tea and coffee facilities.
Closed at Christmas. No smoking in
bedrooms.*
Bedrooms: 1 single, 1 twin
Bathrooms: 1 public

**Bed & breakfast**

| per night: | £min | £max |
| --- | --- | --- |
| Single | 15.00 | 20.00 |
| Double | 30.00 | 40.00 |

Parking for 5

⌷ ♨ ⒰ ✕ ▥ ◗ ✿ ✕ 🚲

---

All accommodation in this
guide has been inspected,
or is awaiting inspection,
under the national Crown
scheme.

## BURNHAM OVERY STAITHE

Norfolk
Map ref 3B1

### Domville Guest House ⋀

**COMMENDED**

Glebe Lane, Burnham Overy Staithe,
King's Lynn PE31 8JQ
☎ Fakenham (01328) 738298
*Standing in own grounds in a quiet
lane, close to the sea. Closed for
Christmas.*
Bedrooms: 3 single, 2 double, 2 twin
Bathrooms: 2 private, 2 public

**Bed & breakfast**

| per night: | £min | £max |
| --- | --- | --- |
| Single | 16.00 | 17.00 |
| Double | 32.00 | 34.00 |

**Half board**

| per person: | £min | £max |
| --- | --- | --- |
| Daily | 23.00 | 29.00 |
| Weekly | 161.00 | 203.00 |

Evening meal 1900 (last orders 1200)
Parking for 10

🛏6 ♿ ⒰ ⒮ S 🛉 ✕ ⒨ TV ✿ ✕ 🚲

## BURWELL

Cambridgeshire
Map ref 3B2

One of the largest villages in the
county with a wide main street
running for about 2 miles. The
soaring 100-ft tower of the church
of St Mary is an unmistakable
landmark above the fenland
fringes, its octagonal upper section
is influenced by the tower of Ely
Cathedral.

### The Meadow House

**Listed**

2A High Street, Burwell, Cambridge
CB5 0HB
☎ Newmarket (01638) 741926 &
741354
Fax (01638) 743424

*Large well equipped modern house set
in grounds of 2 acres, close to
Newmarket Racecourse, Cambridge and
Ely. King size double beds.*
Bedrooms: 2 double, 1 twin
Bathrooms: 1 private, 2 public

**Bed & breakfast**

| per night: | £min | £max |
| --- | --- | --- |
| Single | 18.00 | 20.00 |
| Double | 36.00 | 38.00 |

Evening meal 1800 (last orders 1900)
Parking for 14

🛏1 ⒠ ⌷ ♨ ⒰ ⒮ S ✕ ▥ ◗ ✿ ✕ 🚲

## BURY ST EDMUNDS

Suffolk
Map ref 3B2

Ancient market and cathedral town which takes its name from the martyred Saxon King, St Edmund. Bury St Edmunds has many fine buildings including the Athenaeum and Moyses Hall, reputed to be the oldest Norman house in the county.
*Tourist Information Centre*
☎ *(01284) 764667*

### Elms Farm

Depden, Bury St Edmunds IP29 4BS
☎ Chevington (01284) 850289
*470-acre mixed farm. 17th C farmhouse in a quiet rural position at the highest point in Suffolk. 7 miles south-west of Bury St Edmunds.*
Bedrooms: 1 double, 1 twin
Bathrooms: 1 public
**Bed & breakfast**

| per night: | £min | £max |
|---|---|---|
| Single | 16.00 | 20.00 |
| Double | 32.00 | 35.00 |

Parking for 10

### The Leys
COMMENDED

113 Fornham Road, Bury St Edmunds IP32 6AT
☎ (01284) 760225
*Lovely, spacious Victorian house in own grounds, close to the A45 and railway station. Pay-phone, home-made bread and preserves.*
Bedrooms: 1 double, 1 twin, 1 triple
Bathrooms: 1 private, 1 public
**Bed & breakfast**

| per night: | £min | £max |
|---|---|---|
| Single | 20.00 | 30.00 |
| Double | 34.00 | 40.00 |

Parking for 6

### Malthouse
Listed

20 Eastern Way, Bury St Edmunds IP32 7AB
☎ (01284) 753185
*Peacefully located away from main road but only 15 minutes' walk from town centre. Dining room overlooks the garden.*
Bedrooms: 1 single, 2 twin
Bathrooms: 1 public
**Bed & breakfast**

| per night: | £min | £max |
|---|---|---|
| Single | 15.00 | 16.00 |
| Double | 30.00 | 32.00 |

Parking for 4

### Maundrell House
Listed COMMENDED

109 Fornham Road, Bury St Edmunds IP32 6AS
☎ (01284) 705884
*Large Edwardian semi-detached town house. Twin rooms overlook garden. Close to town centre, station and A45. Guests are assured of a warm welcome and good food. Meeting from coach or train by arrangement.*
Bedrooms: 1 single, 2 twin
Bathrooms: 1 public
**Bed & breakfast**

| per night: | £min | £max |
|---|---|---|
| Single | 15.00 | |
| Double | 30.00 | |

**Half board**

| per person: | £min | £max |
|---|---|---|
| Daily | 23.00 | |

Parking for 2

### South Hill House
Listed COMMENDED

43 Southgate Street, Bury St Edmunds IP33 2AZ
☎ (01284) 755650
Fax (01284) 755650
*Grade II* listed townhouse, reputed to be the school mentioned in Charles Dickens' Pickwick Papers. 10 minutes' walk from town centre, 2 minutes' drive from A45.*
Bedrooms: 1 twin, 1 family room
Bathrooms: 2 private
**Bed & breakfast**

| per night: | £min | £max |
|---|---|---|
| Single | 20.00 | 25.00 |
| Double | 35.00 | 40.00 |

Parking for 4

## CAMBRIDGE

Cambridgeshire
Map ref 2D1

A most important and beautiful city on the River Cam with 31 colleges forming one of the oldest universities in the world. Numerous museums, good shopping centre, restaurants, theatres, cinema and fine bookshops.
*Tourist Information Centre*
☎ *(01223) 322640*

### Antwerp Guest House M

36 Brookfields, Mill Road, Cambridge CB1 3NW
☎ (01223) 247690
*On A1134 ring road between Addenbrookes Hospital and Cambridge Airport. Near the city's amenities, and bus and railway stations. Pleasant gardens.*
Bedrooms: 4 double, 4 twin
Bathrooms: 2 private, 2 public

**Bed & breakfast**

| per night: | £min | £max |
|---|---|---|
| Single | 20.00 | 25.00 |
| Double | 30.00 | 35.00 |

Lunch available
Evening meal 1830 (last orders 1600)
Parking for 8

### Bridge Hotel (Motel) M

Clayhythe, Waterbeach, Cambridge CB5 9HZ
☎ (01223) 860252
Fax (01223) 440448

*Picturesque riverside 17th C hotel with motel rooms, between A45 and A10 (B1047). 4 miles from Cambridge. Fishing, walking, boating.*
Bedrooms: 7 single, 16 double, 5 twin
Bathrooms: 28 private
**Bed & breakfast**

| per night: | £min | £max |
|---|---|---|
| Single | 30.00 | 35.00 |
| Double | 45.00 | 55.00 |

Lunch available
Evening meal 1830 (last orders 2130)
Parking for 50
Cards accepted: Access, Visa, Amex, Switch/Delta

### Carlton Lodge
Listed

245 Chesterton Road, Cambridge CB4 1AS
☎ (01223) 67792 & 566877
*Small family-run business within 1 mile of the city centre, and with easy access from M11 and A45.*
Bedrooms: 1 double, 1 twin, 1 triple
Bathrooms: 3 private, 1 public
**Bed & breakfast**

| per night: | £min | £max |
|---|---|---|
| Single | 17.00 | 30.00 |
| Double | 38.00 | 40.00 |

Parking for 6

### Cristinas

47 St. Andrews Road, Cambridge CB4 1DL
☎ (01223) 65855 & 327700
*Small family-run business in quiet location, a short walk from city centre and colleges.*
Bedrooms: 3 double, 2 twin, 1 triple
Bathrooms: 5 private, 2 public

Continued ▶

## CAMBRIDGE

### Continued

**Bed & breakfast**

| per night: | £min | £max |
| --- | --- | --- |
| Single | 24.00 | 25.00 |
| Double | 35.00 | 43.00 |
| Parking for 8 | | |

🛏🚲☐♨🔌♿📺🛍🍴✈

## Dykelands Guest House ♨
👑

157 Mowbray Road, Cambridge
CB1 4SP
☎ (01223) 244300
*Detached guesthouse offering modern accommodation. On south side of city. Ideally located for city centre and for touring the secrets of the Cambridgeshire countryside. Children and vegetarians especially welcome.*
Bedrooms: 1 single, 2 double, 2 twin, 2 triple, 1 family room
Bathrooms: 3 private, 1 public, 2 private showers

**Bed & breakfast**

| per night: | £min | £max |
| --- | --- | --- |
| Single | 19.50 | 24.50 |
| Double | 33.00 | 39.00 |
| Parking for 7 | | |

Cards accepted: Access, Visa, Amex, Switch/Delta

🛏🚲🚾☐♨🔌ⓘⓢ🍴📺🛍🍴🏧SP T

## Foxhounds
**Listed**

71 Cambridge Road, Wimpole, Royston, Hertfordshire SG8 5QD
☎ (01223) 207344
*Former pub, part 17th C, now a family home. On A603, 9 miles from Cambridge and within easy reach of Wimpole Hall (National Trust). Sitting room for guests, large garden.*
Bedrooms: 1 single, 2 twin
Bathrooms: 2 public

**Bed & breakfast**

| per night: | £min | £max |
| --- | --- | --- |
| Single | 16.00 | 18.00 |
| Double | 30.00 | 32.00 |
| Parking for 3 | | |

🛏🏊♿🔌ⓢ🍴📺🛍🍴🏧

## King's Tithe
**HIGHLY COMMENDED**

13a Comberton Road, Barton, Cambridge CB3 7BA
☎ (01223) 263610
*Very quiet private house, 2 twin bedrooms with adjacent bathroom and separate toilet. Good bar food available at local village pubs. On B1046 off A603 (exit junction 12 of M11).*
Bedrooms: 2 twin
Bathrooms: 1 public

---

**We advise you to confirm your booking in writing.**

---

**Bed & breakfast**

| per night: | £min | £max |
| --- | --- | --- |
| Single | 23.00 | 26.00 |
| Double | 34.00 | 40.00 |

Parking for 3
Open February-December

🛏8🚾☐♨🔌ⓤ🍴🛍🍴🏧

## Leys Cottage ♨
**Listed** **APPROVED**

56 Wimpole Road, Barton, Cambridge CB3 7AB
☎ (01223) 262482
Fax (01223) 264166
*Part 17th C house with modern extension in a quiet and secluded spot but within easy reach of Cambridge, M11 and A45. On A603 Cambridge-Sandy road.*
Bedrooms: 1 single, 1 double, 1 twin
Bathrooms: 2 private, 1 public

**Bed & breakfast**

| per night: | £min | £max |
| --- | --- | --- |
| Single | 20.00 | 25.00 |
| Double | 30.00 | 38.00 |

Evening meal 1900 (last orders 2030)
Parking for 4
Cards accepted: Diners

🛏🚾🚲☐♨🔌ⓘⓢ🍴📺🛍🍴♨

## The Manor House
**Listed** **APPROVED**

High Street, Oakington, Cambridge CB4 5AG
☎ (01223) 232450
*Enjoy a quiet, relaxing stay at this 16th C manor house with antique furniture throughout, spacious country garden, heated covered swimming pool, drawing room and children's playroom. 4 miles north west of Cambridge.*
Bedrooms: 3 double, 1 twin
Bathrooms: 2 public

**Bed & breakfast**

| per night: | £min | £max |
| --- | --- | --- |
| Single | 19.00 | 25.00 |
| Double | 29.00 | 40.00 |

**Half board**

| per person: | £min | £max |
| --- | --- | --- |
| Daily | 26.50 | 32.50 |
| Weekly | 159.00 | 195.00 |

Evening meal 1830 (last orders 2000)
Parking for 8
Cards accepted: Access, Visa

🛏🏊♿🔌♨ⓘ🍴📺🛍🍴🏧✕⚓
♨⌂▶🍴♨🏛 T

## The Old Rectory
**Listed**

Green End, Landbeach, Cambridge CB4 4ED
☎ (01223) 861507
Fax (01223) 441276
*Only 10 minutes from Cambridge centre, historic spacious former rectory in secluded grounds. Donkeys and rare breed sheep. Antique furniture throughout. All rooms en-suite. Aga home cooking. Families welcome.*
Bedrooms: 1 triple, 1 family room
Bathrooms: 2 private, 1 public

---

**Bed & breakfast**

| per night: | £min | £max |
| --- | --- | --- |
| Single | 20.00 | 22.00 |
| Double | 35.00 | 37.00 |
| Parking for 11 | | |

🛏🚾☐♨🔌ⓘⓢ🍴📺🛍🍴🏧✈⚓
♨ SP 🏛

## The Old Rectory
**Listed** **COMMENDED**

High Street, Swaffham Bulbeck, Cambridge CB5 0LX
☎ (01223) 811986 & 812009
*Georgian former vicarage set in own grounds. Located 6 miles from Cambridge and 4 miles from Newmarket.*
Bedrooms: 1 double, 1 twin, 1 triple
Bathrooms: 1 private, 1 public

**Bed & breakfast**

| per night: | £min | £max |
| --- | --- | --- |
| Single | 17.00 | 22.00 |
| Double | 34.00 | 44.00 |
| Parking for 10 | | |

🛏☐♨🔌ⓘⓢ🍴🛍🍴🏧🔧♨🏛

## Segovia Lodge
👑👑

2 Barton Road, Newnham, Cambridge CB3 9JZ
☎ (01223) 354105 & 323011
*Within walking distance of the city centre and colleges. Next to cricket and tennis fields. Warm welcome, personal service and both rooms with private facilities. Non-smokers only please.*
Bedrooms: 1 double, 1 twin
Bathrooms: 2 private, 1 public

**Bed & breakfast**

| per night: | £min | £max |
| --- | --- | --- |
| Double | 40.00 | 44.00 |
| Parking for 4 | | |

🛏10🚾♨🔌ⓤⓘⓢ🍴📺🛍🍴🏧
♨✕♨

## Tenison Towers Guest House
**Listed**

148 Tenison Road, Cambridge CB1 2DP
☎ (01223) 566511
*Near the railway station and city centre. Parking facilities. Evening meals available on request.*
Bedrooms: 1 single, 1 double, 1 twin, 1 triple, 1 family room
Bathrooms: 3 public

**Bed & breakfast**

| per night: | £min | £max |
| --- | --- | --- |
| Single | 16.00 | 18.00 |
| Double | 24.00 | 28.00 |

Evening meal 1700 (last orders 2100)
Parking for 2

🛏🚾☐♨🔌ⓤⓘ🍴🛍🍴🏧✕ DAP ♨ SP

## Woodfield House
👑👑

Madingley Hill, Coton, Cambridge CB3 7PH
☎ Madingley (01954) 210265
*New farmhouse set on a hill with beautiful views. 1.5 miles from*

*Cambridge, half a mile from M11. Sorry, no smoking.*
Bedrooms: 1 twin, 1 triple
Bathrooms: 1 private, 1 public

| **Bed & breakfast per night:** | £min | £max |
|---|---|---|
| Single | 18.00 | 25.00 |
| Double | 32.00 | 36.00 |

Parking for 4

## CASTLE HEDINGHAM

Essex
Map ref 3B2

### Little Chelmshoe House

Gestingthorpe Road, Great Maplestead CO9 3AB
☎ Sudbury (01787) 462385 & 460532
Fax (01787) 462312
Telex Mobile 0836 329560

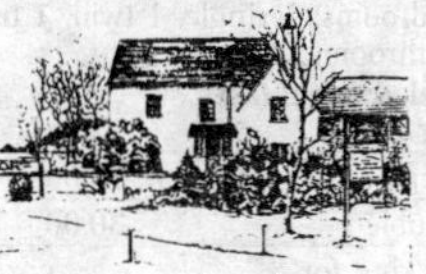

*Secluded 17th C farmhouse, offering quality accommodation surrounded by lovely countryside. Croquet lawn, swimming pool, whirlpool bath. Free transport to local restaurants.*
Bedrooms: 2 double
Bathrooms: 2 private

| **Bed & breakfast per night:** | £min | £max |
|---|---|---|
| Single | 45.00 | |
| Double | | 65.00 |

Parking for 9
Cards accepted: Visa, Amex

## CAWSTON

Norfolk
Map ref 3B1

Village with one of the finest churches in the country. St Agnes, built in the Perpendicular style, was much patronised by Michael de la Pole, Earl of Suffolk (1414), and has a magnificent hammer-beam roof and numerous carved angels.

### Grey Gables Country House Hotel & Restaurant

Norwich Road, Cawston, Norwich NR10 4EY
☎ Norwich (01603) 871259

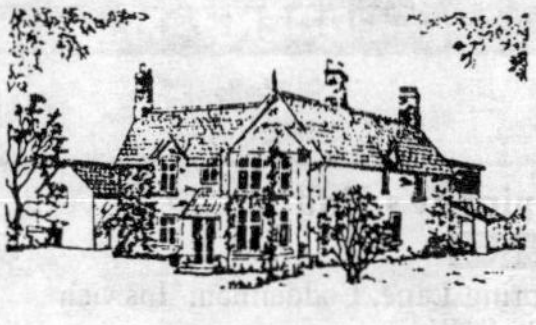

*Former rectory in pleasant, rural setting, 10 miles from Norwich, coast and Broads. Wine cellar, emphasis on food. Comfortably furnished with many antiques.*
Bedrooms: 2 single, 5 double, 1 twin
Bathrooms: 6 private, 1 public

| **Bed & breakfast per night:** | £min | £max |
|---|---|---|
| Single | 19.00 | 40.00 |
| Double | 38.00 | 60.00 |
| **Half board per person:** | **£min** | **£max** |
| Daily | 34.50 | 46.00 |
| Weekly | 219.00 | 238.00 |

Lunch available
Evening meal 1900 (last orders 2100)
Parking for 15
Cards accepted: Access, Visa
3-12

## CHATTERIS

Cambridgeshire
Map ref 3A2

### Cross Keys Inn Hotel

APPROVED
16 Market Hill, Chatteris PE16 6BA
☎ March (01354) 693036 & 692644
Fax (01354) 693036

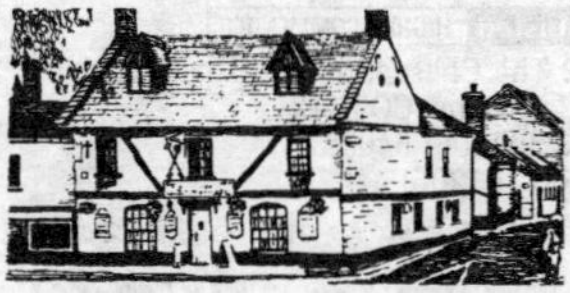

*Elizabethan coaching inn built around 1540, Grade II listed. A la carte menu and bar meals. Friendly atmosphere, oak-beamed lounge with log fires. Ideally placed in the heart of the Fens.*
Bedrooms: 1 double, 5 twin, 1 triple
Bathrooms: 5 private, 1 public

| **Bed & breakfast per night:** | £min | £max |
|---|---|---|
| Single | 21.50 | 32.50 |
| Double | 32.50 | 45.00 |

Lunch available
Evening meal 1900 (last orders 2200)
Parking for 10
Cards accepted: Access, Visa, Diners, Amex
10-40

## CHEDISTON

Suffolk
Map ref 3C2

### Saskiavill

Chediston, Halesworth IP19 OAR
☎ Halesworth (01986) 873067
*Travelling west from Halesworth on the B1123, turn right after 2 miles at the signpost for Chediston Green. After crossing the hump-backed bridge over the stream, Saskiavill is the fourth property on the left.*
Bedrooms: 1 double, 1 twin, 1 triple
Bathrooms: 3 private, 2 public

| **Bed & breakfast per night:** | £min | £max |
|---|---|---|
| Single | 17.00 | 18.00 |
| Double | 34.00 | 36.00 |
| **Half board per person:** | **£min** | **£max** |
| Daily | 20.00 | 22.00 |
| Weekly | 130.00 | 144.00 |

Evening meal from 1830
Parking for 8
Open January-October
3

## CHELMSFORD

Essex
Map ref 3B3

The county town of Essex, originally a Roman settlement, Caesaromagus, thought to have been destroyed by Boudicca. Growth of the town's industry can be traced in the excellent museum in Oaklands Park. 15th C parish church has been Chelmsford Cathedral since 1914.
*Tourist Information Centre*
*☎ (01245) 283400*

### Neptune Cafe Motel

Listed
Burnham Road, Latchingdon, Chelmsford CM3 6EX
☎ Maldon (01621) 740770
*Cafe with adjoining chalet block, which includes 2 units suitable for physically disabled. Village location between Malden and Burnham-on-Crouch.*
Bedrooms: 4 double, 2 twin, 4 triple
Bathrooms: 10 private

| **Bed & breakfast per night:** | £min | £max |
|---|---|---|
| Single | 20.00 | 20.00 |
| Double | 28.00 | 30.00 |
| **Half board per person:** | **£min** | **£max** |
| Daily | 25.00 | 25.00 |

Lunch available
Parking for 40

Please mention this guide when making a booking.

## CHELMSFORD

*Continued*

### Springford
**Listed** | **APPROVED**

8 Well Lane, Galleywood, Chelmsford
CM2 8QY
☎ (01245) 257821
*Family home at Galleywood, south of
Chelmsford. Take B1007 out of the town
or Galleywood turn-off from A12. Well
Lane is near White Bear pub.*
Bedrooms: 1 single, 2 twin
Bathrooms: 1 public

**Bed & breakfast**

| per night: | £min | £max |
|---|---|---|
| Single | 14.00 | 15.00 |
| Double | 28.00 | 30.00 |

**Half board**

| per person: | £min | £max |
|---|---|---|
| Daily | 21.00 | 22.00 |
| Weekly | 147.00 | 154.00 |

Evening meal 1700 (last orders 2030)
Parking for 3

### 25 West Avenue
**Listed**

Maylandsea, Chelmsford CM3 6AE
☎ Maldon (01621) 740972
Fax (01621) 740945
*Detached four-bedroomed private
residence. From Maldon on B1018 or
from South Woodham Ferrers on B1012
to Latchingdon, then on to Steeple
Road to Maylandsea (about 2 miles).*
Bedrooms: 1 double, 1 twin
Bathrooms: 1 public

**Bed & breakfast**

| per night: | £min | £max |
|---|---|---|
| Single | 14.00 | 16.00 |
| Double | 28.00 | 30.00 |

Parking for 5

## CHOSELEY

Norfolk
Map ref 3B1

### Choseley Farmhouse
**Listed**

Choseley, Docking, King's Lynn
PE31 8PQ
☎ Thornham (01485) 512331
*17th C Norfolk farmhouse with Tudor
chimneys. Foundations are thought to
date back to original abbey of 1250.*
Bedrooms: 1 double, 2 twin
Bathrooms: 1 public

**Bed & breakfast**

| per night: | £min | £max |
|---|---|---|
| Single | 15.00 | 15.00 |
| Double | 30.00 | 30.00 |

Parking for 10
Open July-September

## CODDENHAM

Suffolk
Map ref 3B2

### Spinney's End
**Listed**

Spring Lane, Coddenham, Ipswich
IP6 9TW
☎ (01449) 79451
*100-acre mixed farm. Large spacious
bungalow set in attractive landscaped
gardens with farmland views, in a
peaceful location. Full English breakfast
is served and evening meals are
available at public houses and inns
within 1-2 mile radius.*
Bedrooms: 2 double, 1 twin
Bathrooms: 1 public

**Bed & breakfast**

| per night: | £min | £max |
|---|---|---|
| Single | 18.00 | 18.00 |
| Double | 30.00 | 30.00 |

Parking for 12

## COLCHESTER

Essex
Map ref 3B2

Britain's oldest recorded town
standing on the River Colne and
famous for its oysters. Numerous
historic buildings, ancient remains
and museums. Plenty of parks and
gardens, extensive shopping
centre, theatre and zoo.
*Tourist Information Centre*
☎ (01206) 712920

### The Chase
**Listed** | **HIGHLY COMMENDED**

2 The Chase, Straight Road, Lexden,
Colchester CO3 5BU
☎ (01206) 540587
Fax (01206) 44471

*60-year-old house of real character.
Quiet yet convenient for town and other
facilities. In large, beautiful secluded
gardens.*
Bedrooms: 3 twin
Bathrooms: 2 private, 1 public

**Bed & breakfast**

| per night: | £min | £max |
|---|---|---|
| Single | 25.00 | |
| Double | 35.00 | |

Parking for 6

### 11 Harvest End
**Listed**

Stanway, Colchester CO3 5YX
☎ (01206) 43202

---

*Family home in quiet residential area,
convenient for A12. Easy access to
coast, ferries and Constable country.
Spacious bedrooms, parking. No
smoking, please.*
Bedrooms: 1 single, 1 double, 1 twin
Bathrooms: 1 public

**Bed & breakfast**

| per night: | £min | £max |
|---|---|---|
| Single | 16.50 | 17.00 |
| Double | 32.00 | 33.00 |

Parking for 2

### The Maltings
**Listed**

Mersea Road, Abberton, Colchester
CO5 7NR
☎ (01206) 735780
*Attractive period house with a wealth of
beams and an open log fire, in walled
garden with swimming pool.*
Bedrooms: 1 single, 1 twin, 1 triple
Bathrooms: 2 public

**Bed & breakfast**

| per night: | £min | £max |
|---|---|---|
| Single | 15.00 | 18.00 |
| Double | 30.00 | 36.00 |

Parking for 8

### Scheregate Hotel **M**
**Listed** | **APPROVED**

36 Osborne Street, via St John's
Street, Colchester CO2 7DB
☎ (01206) 573034
*Interesting 15th C building, centrally
situated, providing accommodation at
moderate prices.*
Bedrooms: 12 single, 9 twin, 1 triple,
1 family room
Bathrooms: 1 private, 6 public

**Bed & breakfast**

| per night: | £min | £max |
|---|---|---|
| Single | 17.50 | 25.00 |
| Double | 30.00 | 45.00 |

Parking for 30
Cards accepted: Access, Visa

## COLTISHALL

Norfolk
Map ref 3C1

On the River Bure, with an RAF
station nearby. The village is
attractive with many pleasant 18th
C brick houses and a thatched
church.

### Risings
**Listed**

Church Street, Coltishall, Norwich
NR12 7DW
☎ Norwich (01603) 737549
Fax (01603) 737549
*Delightful 17th C Dutch gabled country
home with enclosed garden, 200 yards
from Coltishall Staithe, central for all*

*Broadland touring. All diets catered for,
vegetarian a speciality.*
Bedrooms: 1 double, 2 twin
Bathrooms: 1 public
**Bed & breakfast**

| per night: | £min | £max |
|---|---|---|
| Single | 18.00 | 24.00 |
| Double | 32.00 | 40.00 |

Parking for 3
Cards accepted: Access, Visa

## CROMER
Norfolk
Map ref 3C1

Once a small fishing village and
now famous for its fishing boats
that still work off the beach and
offer freshly caught crabs.
Excellent bathing on sandy
beaches fringed by cliffs. The town
boasts a fine pier, theatre,
museum and a lifeboat station.
*Tourist Information Centre*
☎ *(01263) 512497*

### The Crowmere
Listed

4 Vicarage Road, Cromer NR27 9DQ
☎ (01263) 513056
*Charming Victorian residence in quiet
road close to beach/town centre and all
amenities. Tea/coffee making facilities
and TV in all rooms. Most rooms are
en-suite. Family suites available.*
Bedrooms: 4 double, 2 twin, 3 family
rooms
Bathrooms: 7 private, 1 public
**Bed & breakfast**

| per night: | £min | £max |
|---|---|---|
| Single | 16.00 | 19.00 |
| Double | 32.00 | 38.00 |

Parking for 6

## DANBURY
Essex
Map ref 3B3

### Southways
Listed

Copt Hill, Danbury, Chelmsford
CM3 4NN
☎ Chelmsford (01245) 223428
*Pleasant country house with large
garden adjoining an area of National
Trust common land.*
Bedrooms: 2 twin
Bathrooms: 1 public
**Bed & breakfast**

| per night: | £min | £max |
|---|---|---|
| Single | 16.00 | 16.00 |
| Double | 30.00 | 30.00 |

Parking for 2

## DARSHAM
Suffolk
Map ref 3C2

### Priory Farm ⋔
Listed COMMENDED

Darsham, Saxmundham IP17 3QD
☎ Yoxford (01728) 668459
*135-acre mixed farm. Comfortable 17th
C farmhouse, ideally situated for
exploring Suffolk and heritage coast.
Cycle hire available from own hire fleet.*
Bedrooms: 1 single, 1 double, 1 twin
Bathrooms: 1 public
**Bed & breakfast**

| per night: | £min | £max |
|---|---|---|
| Single | 15.00 | 20.00 |
| Double | 30.00 | 40.00 |

Parking for 10
Open March-October

## DEBDEN GREEN
Essex
Map ref 2D1

### Wigmores Farm
Listed COMMENDED

Debden Green, Saffron Walden
CB11 3LX
☎ Thaxted (01371) 830050
*16th C thatched farmhouse in open
countryside, 1.5 miles from Thaxted just
off the Thaxted to Debden road.*
Bedrooms: 2 double, 1 twin
Bathrooms: 2 public
**Bed & breakfast**

| per night: | £min | £max |
|---|---|---|
| Single | 19.00 | 20.00 |
| Double | 34.00 | 34.00 |

**Half board**

| per person: | £min | £max |
|---|---|---|
| Daily | 29.00 | 31.00 |
| Weekly | 203.00 | 217.00 |

Lunch available
Evening meal 1900 (last orders 2100)
Parking for 12

## DEDHAM
Essex
Map ref 3B2

A former wool town. Dedham Vale
is an area of outstanding natural
beauty and there is a countryside
centre in the village. This is John
Constable country and Sir Alfred
Munnings lived at Castle House
which is open to the public.

### May's Barn Farm ⋔
HIGHLY COMMENDED

May's Lane, Off Long Road West,
Dedham, Colchester CO7 6EW
☎ Colchester (01206) 323191
*300-acre arable farm. Tranquil old
farmhouse with outstanding views over*

*Dedham Vale in Constable country.
Quarter mile down unmade lane.
Comfortable, spacious rooms. With
private facilities.*
Bedrooms: 1 double, 1 twin
Bathrooms: 2 private
**Bed & breakfast**

| per night: | £min | £max |
|---|---|---|
| Single | 20.00 | 25.00 |
| Double | 34.00 | 38.00 |

Parking for 7

## DEREHAM
Norfolk
Map ref 3B1

East Dereham is famous for its
associations with the poet William
Cowper and also Bishop Bonner,
chaplain to Cardinal Wolsey. His
home is now a museum. Around
the charming market-place are
many notable buildings.

### Chapel Farm
♕♕

Dereham Road, Whinburgh, Dereham
NR19 1AA
☎ (01362) 698433
*Farmhouse B & B with full facilities,
including CH, outdoor heated swimming
pool, international standard snooker
table. En-suite rooms. Pub close by.*
Bedrooms: 3 double
Bathrooms: 2 private, 1 public
**Bed & breakfast**

| per night: | £min | £max |
|---|---|---|
| Single | 17.00 | 20.00 |
| Double | 34.00 | 40.00 |

Parking for 10
Cards accepted: Diners

### Clinton House
Listed HIGHLY COMMENDED

Well Hill, Clint Green, Yaxham,
Dereham NR19 1RX
☎ (01362) 692079
*Charming 18th C country house, full of
character, in peaceful location.
Tennis/croquet. Good touring centre.
Breakfast served in beautiful
conservatory.*
Bedrooms: 1 single, 2 double, 1 twin
Bathrooms: 1 private, 2 public
**Bed & breakfast**

| per night: | £min | £max |
|---|---|---|
| Single | 18.00 | 22.00 |
| Double | 30.00 | 34.00 |

Evening meal 1700 (last orders 1730)
Parking for 10

## DERSINGHAM

Norfolk
Map ref 3B1

Large parish church, mostly of Perpendicular period, with 14th C font and Elizabethan barn dated 1672.

### Jersey House
**Listed**
1 Senters Road, Dersingham, King's Lynn PE31 6JL
☎ (01485) 540035
*Bright, airy, modernised house with four bedrooms and pleasant garden. Within walking distance of Sandringham estate, near junction of Heath and Manor roads. Catholic household.*
Bedrooms: 2 twin
Bathrooms: 2 private
**Bed & breakfast**

| per night: | £min | £max |
|---|---|---|
| Single | 15.00 | 17.50 |
| Double | 25.00 | 30.00 |

Parking for 3

## DISS

Norfolk
Map ref 3B2

Old market town built around 3 sides of the Mere, a placid water of 6 acres. Although modernised, some interesting Tudor, Georgian and Victorian buildings around the market-place remain. St Mary's church has a fine knapped flint chancel.
*Tourist Information Centre*
☎ *(01379) 650523*

### South View
**Listed**
High Road, Roydon, Diss IP22 3RU
☎ (01379) 651620
*Comfortable bungalow set in half-acre secluded garden. Close to Bressingham Gardens/Steam Museum and Diss. Central for colleges, castles, cathedrals and churches of East Anglia and wildlife reserves.*
Bedrooms: 2 twin
Bathrooms: 2 private, 1 public
**Bed & breakfast**

| per night: | £min | £max |
|---|---|---|
| Single | 20.00 | 20.00 |
| Double | 32.00 | 34.00 |

Parking for 4

### Strenneth ♨
**COMMENDED**
Airfield Road, Fersfield, Diss IP22 2BP
☎ Bressingham (01379) 688182
Fax (01379) 688260
*Renovated period farmhouse, family-run. All en-suite. Ground floor rooms,*

four-poster and executive rooms. Licensed, pets welcome.
Bedrooms: 1 single, 4 double, 2 twin
Bathrooms: 7 private
**Bed & breakfast**

| per night: | £min | £max |
|---|---|---|
| Single | 22.00 | |
| Double | 44.00 | |

**Half board**

| per person: | £min | £max |
|---|---|---|
| Daily | 35.00 | |

Evening meal 1900 (last orders 1200)
Parking for 10
Cards accepted: Access, Visa

## DOWNHAM MARKET

Norfolk
Map ref 3B1

Market town above the surrounding Fens on the River Ouse. Oxburgh Hall (National Trust) is 8 miles east, a magnificent 15th C moated dwelling owned by one family, the Bedingfields, for almost 500 years.

### The Dial House ♨
**COMMENDED**
Railway Road, Downham Market PE38 9EB
☎ (01366) 388358
Fax (01366) 382198

*Family-run, comfortable Georgian house with en-suite rooms. Good home cooking. Ideal centre for touring quiet East Anglian countryside, historic houses, bird and wildlife sanctuaries.*
Bedrooms: 1 double, 2 twin
Bathrooms: 2 private, 1 public
**Bed & breakfast**

| per night: | £min | £max |
|---|---|---|
| Single | 19.00 | 25.00 |
| Double | 29.00 | 35.00 |

**Half board**

| per person: | £min | £max |
|---|---|---|
| Daily | 28.00 | 34.00 |
| Weekly | 176.00 | 220.00 |

Evening meal 1800 (last orders 2130)
Parking for 6

**Symbols are explained on the flap inside the back cover.**

## EAST BERGHOLT

Suffolk
Map ref 3B2

John Constable, the famous East Anglian artist, was born here in 1776 and at the church of St Mary are reminders of his family's associations with the area. 1 mile south of the village are Flatford Mill and Willy Lott's cottage, both made famous by Constable in his paintings.

### Rosemary
**Listed**
Rectory Hill, East Bergholt, Colchester CO7 6TH
☎ Colchester (01206) 298241
*Pleasant family house set in lovely garden of 1 acre in the centre of Constable country. Wide variety of plants and collection of old fashioned roses. A non-smoking establishment.*
Bedrooms: 1 single, 2 twin
Bathrooms: 1 public
**Bed & breakfast**

| per night: | £min | £max |
|---|---|---|
| Single | 17.00 | |
| Double | 34.00 | |

Parking for 2

## ELMSWELL

Suffolk
Map ref 3B2

### Kiln Farm Guest House
**COMMENDED**
Kiln Lane, Elmswell, Bury St Edmunds IP30 9QR
☎ (01359) 240442
*Victorian farmhouse and converted barns set in 3 acres. In quiet lane half a mile from A1088 roundabout off A45. Self-catering accommodation available.*
Bedrooms: 1 single, 1 double, 1 twin, 1 family room
Bathrooms: 4 private
**Bed & breakfast**

| per night: | £min | £max |
|---|---|---|
| Single | 18.00 | 20.00 |
| Double | 32.00 | 36.00 |

**Half board**

| per person: | £min | £max |
|---|---|---|
| Daily | 26.00 | 30.00 |

Evening meal 1830 (last orders 1900)
Parking for 7

## ELSING

Norfolk
Map ref 3B1

### Bartles Lodge
**COMMENDED**
Elsing, East Dereham NR20 3EA
☎ Dereham (01362) 637177

*Rural setting in 5 acres, own private fishing lake. Perfect peace and tranquillity yet central for Broads, coast and city of Norwich.*
Bedrooms: 3 double, 3 twin, 1 triple
Bathrooms: 7 private

**Bed & breakfast**

| per night: | £min | £max |
| --- | --- | --- |
| Single | 22.00 | 28.00 |
| Double | 44.00 | 50.00 |

**Half board**

| per person: | £min | £max |
| --- | --- | --- |
| Daily | 29.50 | 35.50 |
| Weekly | 165.00 | 220.00 |

Evening meal 1830 (last orders 2000)
Parking for 30
Cards accepted: Access, Visa

ॐ 12 ⬛ ⊞ ⚓ ⬇ ⚲ ⋈ TV ⊞ ◢ ♈ 10 ✦ ❋ ⊶ ⟡ SP

---

## ELY

Cambridgeshire
Map ref 3A2

Until the 17th C when the Fens were drained, Ely was an island. The cathedral, completed in 1189, dominates the surrounding area. One particular feature is the central octagonal tower with a fan-vaulted timber roof and wooden lantern.
*Tourist Information Centre*
☎ *(01353) 662062*

### Hill House Farm
⬛⬛ COMMENDED

9 Main Street, Coveney, Ely CB6 2DJ
☎ (01353) 778369
*240-acre arable farm. High quality en-suite accommodation and food, in fine Victorian farmhouse. Situated in unspoilt Fenland village 3 miles west of Ely, with open views of the surrounding countryside, and easy access to Cambridge. No smoking and no pets, please.*
Bedrooms: 1 double, 1 twin, 1 triple
Bathrooms: 2 private

**Bed & breakfast**

| per night: | £min | £max |
| --- | --- | --- |
| Single | 25.00 | 32.00 |
| Double | 36.00 | 40.00 |

Parking for 4

ॐ 4 ⬛ ⊞ ⬇ ⚲ ⋈ ▦ ◢ ∪ ❋ ✦ ⊶

### 38 Lynn Road
⬛ APPROVED

Ely CB6 1DA
☎ (01353) 664706
*Family home built in 1927, offering bed and breakfast with evening meal on request. Five minutes' walk from Cathedral. Situated on A10.*
Bedrooms: 2 twin, 1 triple
Bathrooms: 1 public

**Bed & breakfast**

| per night: | £min | £max |
| --- | --- | --- |
| Single | 18.00 | 22.50 |
| Double | 30.00 | 39.00 |

---

**Half board**

| per person: | £min | £max |
| --- | --- | --- |
| Daily | 19.50 | 22.50 |
| Weekly | 136.50 | 157.50 |

Evening meal 1800 (last orders 1900)
Parking for 3

ॐ ⊞ ⬇ ⊎ ⋈ ⓘ S ⊁ ⋈ TV ❋ ⊶ OAP

### Spinney Abbey
⬛⬛

Stretham Road, Wicken, Ely CB7 5XQ
☎ (01353) 720971
*150-acre dairy farm. Spacious Georgian farmhouse set in 1 acre of garden. All rooms with private facilities. Farm borders Wicken Fen Nature Reserve.*
Bedrooms: 1 double, 1 twin, 1 triple
Bathrooms: 3 private

**Bed & breakfast**

| per night: | £min | £max |
| --- | --- | --- |
| Double | 36.00 | 38.00 |

Parking for 4

ॐ 5 ⊡ ⬇ ⋈ TV ▦ ◢ ९ ❋ ✗ ⊶ 🔔

---

## EPPING

Essex
Map ref 2D1

Epping retains its identity as a small market town despite its nearness to London. Epping Forest covers 2000 acres and at Chingford Queen Elizabeth I's Hunting Lodge houses a display on the forest's history and wildlife.

### Uplands
Listed APPROVED

181a Lindsey Street, Epping CM16 6RF
☎ Waltham Cross (01992) 573733
*Private house with rural views. Close to M25, M11 for Stansted Airport and Central Line underground for London. Pay phone available.*
Bedrooms: 2 single, 2 triple
Bathrooms: 2 public

**Bed & breakfast**

| per night: | £min | £max |
| --- | --- | --- |
| Single | 16.00 | |
| Double | 32.00 | |

Parking for 6

ॐ ⬛ ⊡ ⬇ ⋈ ⊁ ▦ ◢ ❋ ✗ ⊶

---

## EYKE

Suffolk
Map ref 3C2

### The Old House ⋏
⬛⬛ COMMENDED

Eyke, Woodbridge IP12 2QW
☎ (01394) 460213
*Lovely Grade II listed house, 1620. Comfortable and friendly, with beams, open fires, large, interesting garden and views over Deben Valley. Centre of village and edge of heritage coast. Good choice of food.*
Bedrooms: 1 double, 2 triple
Bathrooms: 3 private

---

**Bed & breakfast**

| per night: | £min | £max |
| --- | --- | --- |
| Single | 22.00 | |
| Double | 35.00 | |

**Half board**

| per person: | £min | £max |
| --- | --- | --- |
| Daily | 27.50 | 32.00 |

Evening meal 1800 (last orders 1000)
Parking for 8

ॐ ⊞ ⬇ ⋈ ⓘ S ⊁ ⋈ ▦ ◢ ❋ ⊶ 🔔

---

## FAKENHAM

Norfolk
Map ref 3B1

Attractive, small market town dates from Saxon times and was a Royal Manor until the 17th C. Its market place has 2 old coaching inns, both showing traces of earlier work behind Georgian facades, and the parish church has a commanding 15th C tower.

### Highfield Farm
Listed COMMENDED

Great Ryburgh, Fakenham NR21 7AL
☎ Great Ryburgh (01328) 78249
Changing to 829249
*500-acre mixed farm. Large country house style farmhouse in 2-acre garden, set amongst 500 acres of rolling countryside. 10 miles from coast and 3 miles from Fakenham.*
Bedrooms: 1 double, 2 twin
Bathrooms: 1 private, 2 public

**Bed & breakfast**

| per night: | £min | £max |
| --- | --- | --- |
| Double | 34.00 | 40.00 |

Evening meal 1900 (last orders 1400)
Parking for 8
Cards accepted: Diners

ॐ 12 ⊞ ⬇ ▦ S ⋈ TV ◢ ९ ∪ ❋ ✗ ⊶

### The Old Brick Kilns ⋏
⬛⬛⬛ COMMENDED

Little Barney, Fakenham NR21 ONL
☎ Thursford (01328) 878305
Fax (01328) 878948
*Character house with landscaped gardens in a rural setting. Take the A148 Fakenham/Cromer road, after 5 miles take B1354 to Aylsham, for 200 yards. Turn right into Barney, first left to Little Barney House at end of lane.*
Bedrooms: 1 single, 1 double, 1 twin
Bathrooms: 3 private

**Bed & breakfast**

| per night: | £min | £max |
| --- | --- | --- |
| Single | 18.50 | 21.00 |
| Double | 37.00 | 42.00 |

**Half board**

| per person: | £min | £max |
| --- | --- | --- |
| Daily | 31.50 | 34.00 |
| Weekly | 127.75 | 218.75 |

*Continued ▶*

## FAKENHAM

### Continued

Evening meal 1800 (last orders 1000)
Parking for 8
Cards accepted: Access, Visa, Diners, Amex, Switch/Delta

🛏🍴🖥♨🍷🈸💺📺🖲🛉♿💷🌸🚗 SP

### Sculthorpe Mill ₥
♔♔♔

Lynn Road, Sculthorpe, Fakenham
NR21 9QG
☎ (01328) 856161 & 862675
Fax (01328) 856651

Grade II listed watermill in 6 acres of watermeadows straddling the River Wensum. A la carte and set menus served in oak-beamed restaurant overlooking river. Extensive range of bar food. En-suite rooms, including four-poster.
Bedrooms: 2 single, 2 double, 1 twin, 1 triple
Bathrooms: 6 private

**Bed & breakfast**

| per night: | £min | £max |
|---|---|---|
| Single | 25.00 | 35.00 |
| Double | 40.00 | 65.00 |

**Half board**

| per person: | £min | £max |
|---|---|---|
| Daily | 35.00 | 50.00 |
| Weekly | 210.00 | 300.00 |

Lunch available
Evening meal 1830 (last orders 2130)
Parking for 50
Cards accepted: Access, Visa, Amex

🛏🍴☎🖥♨🍷🈸💷🛉 🚗🔧6-60 ♨🍷🛡🌸🚗🈺 SP 🏠

## FELIXSTOWE

Suffolk
Map ref 3C2

Seaside resort that developed at the end of the 19th C. Lying in a gently curving bay with a 2-mile-long beach and backed by a wide promenade of lawns and floral gardens. Ferry links to the continent.
*Tourist Information Centre*
☎ *(01394) 276770*

### Fludyer Arms Hotel ₥
♔♔♔ APPROVED

Undercliff Rd. East, Felixstowe
IP11 7LU
☎ (01394) 283279
Fax (01394) 670754

Closest hotel to the sea in Felixstowe. Two fully licensed bars and family room overlooking the sea. All rooms have superb sea views. Colour TV. Specialises in home-cooked food, with children's and vegetarian menus available.
Bedrooms: 3 single, 5 double, 1 twin
Bathrooms: 6 private, 1 public

**Bed & breakfast**

| per night: | £min | £max |
|---|---|---|
| Single | 24.00 | 32.00 |
| Double | 38.00 | 46.00 |

Lunch available
Evening meal 1900 (last orders 2100)
Parking for 14
Cards accepted: Access, Visa, Amex

🛏🖥♨🍷💷🈸📺🖲🛉♿🍴🌸🚗

## FELSTED

Essex
Map ref 3B2

### Potash Farm
♔ COMMENDED

Cobblers Green, Causeway End Road, Felsted, Dunmow CM6 3LX
☎ Great Dunmow (01371) 820510

160-acre arable farm. Lovely old 15th C listed farmhouse set in a large half moated garden, within walking distance of Felsted centre. Convenient for Stansted and London.
Bedrooms: 1 double, 2 twin
Bathrooms: 1 public

**Bed & breakfast**

| per night: | £min | £max |
|---|---|---|
| Single | 15.00 | 16.00 |
| Double | 30.00 | 32.00 |

**Half board**

| per person: | £min | £max |
|---|---|---|
| Daily | 23.00 | 24.00 |

Evening meal 1800 (last orders 1930)
Parking for 6

🛏🖥🖤♨🍷🈸🖤💺📺🖲🛉♿🌸
🍴🚗🏠

---

The national Crown scheme is explained in full in the information pages at the back of this guide.

## FRAMLINGHAM

Suffolk
Map ref 3C2

Pleasant old market town with an interesting church, impressive castle and some attractive houses round Market Hill. The town's history can be traced at the Lanman Museum.

### The Falcon Inn
♔♔ APPROVED

Earl Soham, Framlingham, Woodbridge IP13 7SA
☎ Earl Soham (01728) 685263
15th C inn with exposed beams opposite bowls green and overlooking open fields. 3 miles from Framlingham. Ideal for touring East Anglia.
Bedrooms: 1 double, 2 twin
Bathrooms: 2 private, 1 public

**Bed & breakfast**

| per night: | £min | £max |
|---|---|---|
| Single | 19.00 | 25.00 |
| Double | 38.00 | 45.00 |

**Half board**

| per person: | £min | £max |
|---|---|---|
| Daily | 25.00 | 35.00 |
| Weekly | 165.00 | 225.00 |

Lunch available
Evening meal 1800 (last orders 2130)
Parking for 24

🛏♨🍷🈸🖤📺🖲🛉♿🍴8-30♿🍷🌸🚗
DAP SP 🏠 T

### High House Farm ₥
♔♔ COMMENDED

Cransford, Framlingham, Woodbridge IP13 9PD
☎ Rendham (01728) 663461
240-acre arable farm. Beautifully restored 15th C farmhouse featuring exposed beams, inglenooks and attractive gardens. Large family room. Situated between Framlingham and Saxmundham.
Bedrooms: 1 double, 1 family room
Bathrooms: 2 private

**Bed & breakfast**

| per night: | £min | £max |
|---|---|---|
| Single | 24.00 | |
| Double | 34.00 | 36.00 |

Parking for 4

🛏🍴♨🈸🍷💺📺🖲🛉♿🍴🚗🌸🚗🏠

### Shimmens Pightle ₥
Listed COMMENDED

Dennington Road, Framlingham, Woodbridge IP13 9JT
☎ Framlimgham (01728) 724036
Brian and Phyllis Collett's home is set in an acre of landscaped garden overlooking fields, on outskirts of Framlingham. Ground floor rooms with washbasins. Locally-cured bacon and home-made marmalade.
Bedrooms: 1 double, 2 twin
Bathrooms: 1 public

**Bed & breakfast per night:**

| | £min | £max |
|---|---|---|
| Double | 33.00 | 38.00 |

Parking for 4
Cards accepted: Diners
🐴 7 🛏 🫖 💇 [UL] [S] 🚭 [TV] ♨ ◢ ✿ 🐕 🚐

## FRESSINGFIELD

Suffolk
Map ref 3C2

### Chippenhall Hall ⚑

♛♛♛ HIGHLY COMMENDED

Fressingfield, Eye IP21 5TD
☎ (01379) 868180
Fax (01379) 86272
*Listed Tudor manor, heavily beamed and with inglenook fireplaces, in 7 secluded acres. Fine food and wines. 1 mile south of Fressingfield on B1116.*
Bedrooms: 3 double
Bathrooms: 3 private

**Bed & breakfast per night:**

| | £min | £max |
|---|---|---|
| Single | 48.00 | 54.00 |
| Double | 54.00 | 60.00 |

**Half board per person:**

| | £min | £max |
|---|---|---|
| Daily | 50.00 | 53.00 |
| Weekly | 341.00 | 361.00 |

Lunch available
Evening meal 1930 (last orders 1800)
Parking for 12
Cards accepted: Access, Visa
🐴 12 🗓 🫖 💇 🔒 [S] 🚭 🛋 [TV] ♨ ◢ 🏊 🐎
⚑ ✿ 🐕 🚐 🍃 🏛 [T]

## FRINTON-ON-SEA

Essex
Map ref 3C2

Sedate town that developed as a resort at the end of the 19th C and still retains an air of Victorian gentility. Fine sandy beaches, good fishing and golf.

### Hodgenolls Farmhouse

♛ COMMENDED

Pork Lane, Great Holland, Frinton-on-Sea CO13 0ES
☎ Clacton (01255) 672054
*Early 17th C timber-framed farmhouse in rural setting close to sandy beaches, Constable country, historic Colchester and Harwich. Non-smoking establishment.*
Bedrooms: 2 double, 1 twin
Bathrooms: 1 private, 1 public

**Bed & breakfast per night:**

| | £min | £max |
|---|---|---|
| Single | 18.00 | 19.00 |
| Double | 36.00 | 38.00 |

Parking for 5
Open April-October
🐴 🖥 🫖 [UL] [S] 🚭 🛋 [TV] ♨ ◢ ✿ 🐕 🚐

## GARBOLDISHAM

Norfolk
Map ref 3B2

### Ingleneuk Lodge ⚑

♛♛♛ COMMENDED

Hopton Road, Garboldisham, Diss IP22 2RQ
☎ (01953) 81541 Changing to 681541

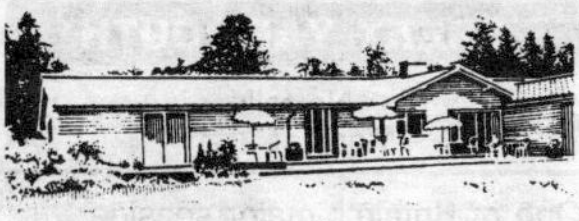

*Modern single-level home in 10 acres of wooded countryside. South-facing patio, riverside walk. Very friendly atmosphere. On B1111, 1 mile south of village.*
Wheelchair access category 2 ♿
Bedrooms: 3 single, 3 double, 2 twin, 2 triple
Bathrooms: 10 private, 1 public

**Bed & breakfast per night:**

| | £min | £max |
|---|---|---|
| Single | 22.00 | 31.50 |
| Double | 36.00 | 49.00 |

**Half board per person:**

| | £min | £max |
|---|---|---|
| Daily | 32.00 | 45.50 |
| Weekly | 210.00 | 294.00 |

Evening meal 1830 (last orders 1300)
Parking for 20
Cards accepted: Access, Visa, Amex
🐴 🛏 📞 🖥 🫖 [S] 🚭 🛋 ♨ ◢ ⊤2 ✿ 🚐
[SP] [T]

## GISSING

Norfolk
Map ref 3B2

### Old Rectory ⚑

♛♛ HIGHLY COMMENDED

Gissing, Diss IP22 3XB
☎ Tivetshall (01379) 77575
Fax (01379) 774427
*Elegant Victorian house in 3 acres. Peaceful, comfortable, tastefully decorated and furnished. Four-course, candlelit dinner available by arrangement. Tea/coffee-making facilities, colour TV and extensive range of toiletries available in all rooms. Indoor pool.*
Bedrooms: 1 double, 2 twin
Bathrooms: 3 private

**Bed & breakfast per night:**

| | £min | £max |
|---|---|---|
| Single | 36.00 | 40.00 |
| Double | 48.00 | 58.00 |

Evening meal 1945 (last orders 1945)
Parking for 6
Cards accepted: Access, Visa
🐴 8 🖥 🫖 💇 [UL] 🔒 [S] 🚭 🛋 [TV] ♨ ◢ 🏊 ✿
🐕 🚐 🍃 [SP] 🏛

## GRAYS

Essex
Map ref 3B3

### Stifford Clays Farmhouse

Stifford Clays Road, North Stifford, Grays RM16 3NL
☎ (01375) 375918
*200-year-old farmhouse with 3 acres of gardens and spacious, en-suite bedrooms. Close to Thurrock Lakeside, M25 Dartford crossing.*
Bedrooms: 6 single, 4 double, 5 twin, 2 family rooms
Bathrooms: 17 private

**Bed & breakfast per night:**

| | £min | £max |
|---|---|---|
| Single | 22.00 | 24.00 |
| Double | 28.00 | 31.00 |

Parking for 18
Cards accepted: Access, Visa
🐴 🛏 🖥 🫖 [UL] 🔒 🛋 [TV] ◐ ♨ ◢ ✿ 🚐 [SP]

## GREAT BARDFIELD

Essex
Map ref 3B2

### Bell Cottage

[Listed]

Bell Lane, Great Bardfield, Braintree CM7 4TH
☎ (01371) 810149
*Delightful 16th C thatched cottage, close to village centre, with grounds overlooking Pant Valley. Four miles from Thaxted, 2 miles from Finchingfield.*
Bedrooms: 1 single, 1 double, 1 family room
Bathrooms: 1 public

**Bed & breakfast per night:**

| | £min | £max |
|---|---|---|
| Single | 15.00 | 15.00 |
| Double | 30.00 | 30.00 |

Parking for 4
🐴 [UL] [S] 🛋 [TV] ♨ 🚐 🏛

## GREAT BIRCHAM

Norfolk
Map ref 3B1

### King's Head Hotel ⚑

♛♛♛

Great Bircham, King's Lynn PE31 6RJ
☎ Syderstone (01485) 23265
*Country inn with 3 bars, Italian restaurant and beer gardens, near Sandringham, King's Lynn and the coast. English and Italian cuisine, fresh Norfolk seafood and produce, traditional Sunday lunch. Two-night breaks available.*
Bedrooms: 2 double, 3 twin
Bathrooms: 5 private

**Bed & breakfast per night:**

| | £min | £max |
|---|---|---|
| Single | 30.00 | 33.00 |
| Double | 50.00 | 55.00 |

Continued ►

## GREAT BIRCHAM

### Continued

**Half board**

| per person: | £min | £max |
|---|---|---|
| Daily | 55.00 | 60.00 |
| Weekly | 335.00 | 355.00 |

Lunch available
Evening meal 1900 (last orders 2200)
Parking for 80
Cards accepted: Access, Visa

🛥🗂♿👶🏃📺🛏 ▪🔒▪▪🚭🅿 🅟🅰🅟 🆂🅿
🏠 🅣

## GREAT DUNMOW

Essex
Map ref 3B2

On the main Roman road from Bishop's Stortford to Braintree. Doctor's Pond near the square, was where the first lifeboat was tested in 1785. Home of the Dunmow Flitch trials held every 4 years on Whit Monday.

### Cowels Cottage
♨♨

Cowels Farm Lane, Lindsell, Dunmow CM6 3QG
☎ Gt Dunmow (01371) 870454
*Pink cottage, overlooking farmland in tranquil, secluded garden. Centrally heated, private sitting room and bathrooms, TV.*
Bedrooms: 1 single, 1 family room
Bathrooms: 2 private, 1 public
**Bed & breakfast**

| per night: | £min | £max |
|---|---|---|
| Single | 18.00 | |
| Double | 36.00 | |

Parking for 4

🛥🚲🗂♿🔒▪📺🛏▪🅿🚭🚗

### Homelye Farm
Listed

Homelye Chase, Braintree Road, Dunmow CM6 3AW
☎ (01371) 872127
*Bed and breakfast accommodation on quiet farm situated off the A120 1 mile east of Dunmow. Convenient for Stansted Airport and M11 to London.*
Bedrooms: 1 single, 1 double, 1 twin
Bathrooms: 3 private
**Bed & breakfast**

| per night: | £min | £max |
|---|---|---|
| Single | 18.50 | 20.00 |
| Double | 37.00 | 40.00 |

Parking for 6

🚲🗂♿🔒▪🏃📺🛏▪🅿🚭🚗

### Yarrow
♨♨ COMMENDED

27 Station Road, Felsted, Great Dunmow CM6 3HD
☎ (01371) 820878
*Edwardian house. South-facing bedrooms with garden and countryside*

---

*views. Ample parking. Quarter-of-a-mile to restaurants and pub in lovely village.*
Bedrooms: 2 double, 1 twin
Bathrooms: 1 private, 2 public
**Bed & breakfast**

| per night: | £min | £max |
|---|---|---|
| Single | 15.00 | 18.00 |
| Double | 28.00 | 34.00 |

Parking for 6

🛥🗂♿🔒▪🏃▪🛏▪🅿🚭🚗🚗

## GREAT YARMOUTH

Norfolk
Map ref 3C1

One of Britain's major seaside resorts with 5 miles of seafront and every possible amenity including an award winning leisure complex offering a huge variety of all-weather facilities. Busy harbour and fishing centre.
*Tourist Information Centre*
☎ *(01493) 842195 or (accommodation) 846344*

### Manor Farm Cottage
♨♨

Browston, Great Yarmouth NR31 9DP
☎ (01493) 604557
*144-acre arable farm. Peaceful, rural setting. Opposite country club with dining and sports facilities. One mile from A143, signposted Browston.*
Bedrooms: 1 double
Bathrooms: 1 private
**Bed & breakfast**

| per night: | £min | £max |
|---|---|---|
| Single | 18.00 | 20.00 |
| Double | 32.00 | 35.00 |

Parking for 4

🛥🚲♿🔒▪🏃📺🛏▪🅿🚭🚗 🅟🅰🅟 🆂🅿

### Spindrift Private Hotel 🅼
♨♨ APPROVED

36 Wellesley Road, Great Yarmouth NR30 1EU
☎ (01493) 858674
*Attractively situated small private hotel, close to all amenities and with Beach Coach Station and car park at rear. Front bedrooms have sea views.*
Bedrooms: 2 single, 2 double, 1 twin, 1 triple, 1 family room
Bathrooms: 5 private, 1 public
**Bed & breakfast**

| per night: | £min | £max |
|---|---|---|
| Single | 16.00 | 25.00 |
| Double | 28.00 | 40.00 |

Cards accepted: Access, Visa, Amex

🛥3🗂♿👶🆂🏃📺🛏▪🅿🚗🚗 🆂🅿

---

Colour maps at the back of this guide pinpoint all places which have accommodation listings in the guide.

---

## HACHESTON

Suffolk
Map ref 3C2

### Cherry Tree House
Listed

Hacheston, Woodbridge IP13 0DR
☎ Wickham Market (01728) 746371
Fax (01728) 746371
*Large farmhouse built in 1641, with mature garden for guests' use. Ample parking. Imaginative English and continental cooking using fresh garden produce. Evening meal by arrangement.*
Bedrooms: 1 single, 1 twin, 1 triple
Bathrooms: 2 public
**Bed & breakfast**

| per night: | £min | £max |
|---|---|---|
| Single | 16.00 | 20.00 |
| Double | 30.00 | 36.00 |

**Half board**

| per person: | £min | £max |
|---|---|---|
| Daily | 22.50 | 28.00 |

Evening meal 1830 (last orders 2000)
Parking for 3

🛥🗂🛏▪🏃▪🅿🚭🚗🚗🏠

## HADLEIGH

Suffolk
Map ref 3B2

Former wool town, lying on a tributary of the River Stour. The church of St Mary stands among a remarkable cluster of medieval buildings.
*Tourist Information Centre*
☎ *(01473) 823824*

### French's Farm
Listed

Hadleigh, Ipswich IP7 5PQ
☎ Ipswich (01473) 824215
*Large period country house set in magnificent grounds, offering well-appointed, peaceful accommodation and friendly service. Horse riding facilities available.*
Bedrooms: 2 double, 1 twin
Bathrooms: 2 private, 1 public
**Bed & breakfast**

| per night: | £min | £max |
|---|---|---|
| Single | 20.00 | 25.00 |
| Double | 35.00 | 38.00 |

**Half board**

| per person: | £min | £max |
|---|---|---|
| Daily | 22.00 | 27.00 |
| Weekly | 130.00 | 160.00 |

Evening meal 1800 (last orders 2000)
Parking for 15

🛥🗂♿🔒🛏▪🅿🔍🕐🚭🚗

### Howells
♨♨ COMMENDED

93 Angel Street, Hadleigh IP7 5EY
☎ Ipswich - After 4pm/Weekends (01473) 828117
*Retired hotelier offering guests every comfort to ensure an enjoyable stay.*

*Secluded location near town centre.
Large en-suite double bedroom, own
sitting room with TV.*
Bedrooms: 1 double
Bathrooms: 1 private

**Bed & breakfast**

| per night: | £min | £max |
|---|---|---|
| Single | 20.00 | 20.00 |
| Double | 35.00 | 35.00 |

Parking for 1

## Mount Pleasant Farm 🅰

APPROVED

Offton, Ipswich IP8 4RP
☎ Ipswich (01473) 658896
Fax (01473) 658896

*8-acre mixed farm. Genuinely secluded,
typical Suffolk farmhouse. 30 minutes
from the sea and 5 minutes from water
park. Many local beauty spots. Evening
meals a speciality.*
Bedrooms: 2 double, 1 twin
Bathrooms: 3 private

**Bed & breakfast**

| per night: | £min | £max |
|---|---|---|
| Single | 18.00 | 18.00 |
| Double | 27.50 | 30.00 |

**Half board**

| per person: | £min | £max |
|---|---|---|
| Daily | 21.75 | 26.00 |
| Weekly | 152.25 | 182.00 |

Lunch available
Evening meal 1900 (last orders 1000)
Parking for 10

## Odds and Ends House 🅰

131 High Street, Hadleigh, Ipswich
IP7 5EG
☎ Ipswich (01473) 822032
*Comfortable house within walking
distance of shops, pubs and restaurants
and swimming pool. Ground floor
rooms with wheelchair facilities
available in recently converted garden
annexe.*
Wheelchair access category 3 ♿
Bedrooms: 3 single, 2 double, 4 twin
Bathrooms: 5 private, 2 public

**Bed & breakfast**

| per night: | £min | £max |
|---|---|---|
| Single | 19.00 | 30.00 |
| Double | 38.00 | 45.00 |

Lunch available
Evening meal 1900 (last orders 1700)
Parking for 3

## Town House Fruit Farm

Listed

Hook Lane, Hadleigh, Ipswich
IP7 5PH
☎ (01473) 823260
Fax (01473) 827161
*85-acre fruit farm. Converted barn close
to Constable country and East Anglian
wool villages. Near Harwich and
Felixstowe.*
Bedrooms: 2 double, 1 twin
Bathrooms: 2 public

**Bed & breakfast**

| per night: | £min | £max |
|---|---|---|
| Single | 15.00 | |
| Double | 30.00 | |

Parking for 6

**HARTEST**

Suffolk
Map ref 3B2

## Giffords Hall

COMMENDED

Hartest, Bury St Edmunds IP29 4EX
☎ Bury St Edmunds (01284) 830464

*Georgian farmhouse just outside Hartest
village, operating a vineyard and small
country living with flowers and animals
on 33 acres.*
Bedrooms: 1 double, 2 twin
Bathrooms: 3 private

**Bed & breakfast**

| per night: | £min | £max |
|---|---|---|
| Single | 22.00 | 24.00 |
| Double | 34.00 | 38.00 |

Parking for 20
Cards accepted: Access, Visa

**HEMINGFORD GREY**

Cambridgeshire
Map ref 3A2

## 38 High Street

COMMENDED

Hemingford Grey, Huntingdon
PE18 9BJ
☎ Saint Ives (01480) 301203
*Private detached house in centre of
village, with large garden and quiet
surroundings. All home cooking. 1 mile
from the A604. Sorry, no smoking or
pets.*
Bedrooms: 2 single, 2 double
Bathrooms: 1 public

**Bed & breakfast**

| per night: | £min | £max |
|---|---|---|
| Single | 18.00 | 18.00 |
| Double | 36.00 | 36.00 |

**Half board**

| per person: | £min | £max |
|---|---|---|
| Daily | 28.00 | 28.00 |
| Weekly | 126.00 | 126.00 |

Evening meal 1930 (last orders 1600)
Parking for 4
Open January-November

**HETHERSETT**

Norfolk
Map ref 3B1

## Magnolia House

Listed

Cromwell Close, Hethersett NR9 3HD
☎ Norwich (01603) 810749
Fax (01603) 810749
*Family-run B & B. All rooms centrally
heated, colour TV, hot and cold water,
tea/coffee making facilities, own key.
Laundry available. Private car park.*
Bedrooms: 2 single, 3 double, 1 twin
Bathrooms: 3 public

**Bed & breakfast**

| per night: | £min | £max |
|---|---|---|
| Single | 16.00 | 18.00 |
| Double | 28.00 | 32.00 |

Parking for 7
Cards accepted: Diners

**HEVINGHAM**

Norfolk
Map ref 3B1

## Marsham Arms Inn 🅰

COMMENDED

Holt Road, Hevingham, Norwich
NR10 5NP
☎ Norwich (01603) 754268
Fax (01603) 754839
*Set in peaceful Norfolk countryside
within reach of Norwich, the Broads
and the coast. Comfortable and spacious
accommodation, good food and a fine
selection of ales.*
Bedrooms: 3 double, 5 twin
Bathrooms: 8 private

**Bed & breakfast**

| per night: | £min | £max |
|---|---|---|
| Single | 35.00 | 40.00 |
| Double | 45.00 | 60.00 |

**Half board**

| per person: | £min | £max |
|---|---|---|
| Daily | 30.00 | 40.00 |

Lunch available
Evening meal 1800 (last orders 2200)
Parking for 100
Cards accepted: Access, Visa, Amex,
Switch/Delta

## HIGHAM

Suffolk
Map ref 3B2

### The Bauble ♨

👑👑 HIGHLY COMMENDED

Higham, Colchester CO7 6LA
☎ (01206) 37254
Fax (01206) 37263
*Modernised country house in mature gardens adjacent to the Rivers Brett and Stour. Ideal for touring Constable country and wool industry villages. Will accept children over 12 years old.*
Bedrooms: 1 single, 2 twin
Bathrooms: 1 private, 2 public,
2 private showers

**Bed & breakfast**

| per night: | £min | £max |
|---|---|---|
| Single | 20.00 | 25.00 |
| Double | 38.00 | 45.00 |

Parking for 5

## HINTLESHAM

Suffolk
Map ref 3B2

### Birch Farm

Silver Hill, Hintlesham, Ipswich
IP8 3NJ
☎ (01473) 652249

*80-acre mixed farm. Traditional farm cottage set in picturesque valley and farmland. En-suite bedrooms, lounge and dining area are located in a beautifully converted annexe with own courtyard. Twin bedroom can be used as single. Evening meals by arrangement.*
Bedrooms: 1 double, 1 twin
Bathrooms: 2 private

**Bed & breakfast**

| per night: | £min | £max |
|---|---|---|
| Single | 18.00 | 20.00 |
| Double | 35.00 | 40.00 |

Parking for 2

### College Farm

👑👑 HIGHLY COMMENDED

Hintlesham, Ipswich IP8 3NT
☎ (01473) 652253
Fax (01473) 652253
*600-acre arable & livestock farm. Beamed 15th C farmhouse in rural setting 6 miles west of Ipswich, offering a warm welcome and comfortable*

*accommodation. Close to Constable country and Lavenham.*
Bedrooms: 1 single, 1 double, 1 triple
Bathrooms: 1 private, 1 public

**Bed & breakfast**

| per night: | £min | £max |
|---|---|---|
| Single | 16.00 | 20.00 |
| Double | 32.00 | 36.00 |

Parking for 10
Cards accepted: Diners

## HINXTON

Cambridgeshire
Map ref 2D1

### Lordship Farm

👑 COMMENDED

Mill Lane, Hinxton, Saffron Walden,
Essex CB10 1RD
☎ Saffron Walden (01799) 530242

*400-acre arable farm. 16th C house, extensively remodelled, originally moated. In small village near the river, midway between Cambridge and Saffron Walden.*
Bedrooms: 1 double, 2 twin
Bathrooms: 1 public, 3 private showers

**Bed & breakfast**

| per night: | £min | £max |
|---|---|---|
| Single | 15.00 | |
| Double | 30.00 | |

Parking for 6

## HITCHAM

Suffolk
Map ref 3B2

### Wetherden Hall

Listed APPROVED

Hitcham, Ipswich IP7 7PZ
☎ Bildeston (01449) 740412
*270-acre arable and mixed farm. A warm welcome awaits you at this attractive farmhouse on the edge of a very pretty village. Private fishing. Good centre for visiting medieval Lavenham, Bury St Edmunds, Ipswich, Cambridge and Constable country.*
Bedrooms: 1 double, 1 triple
Bathrooms: 1 public

**Bed & breakfast**

| per night: | £min | £max |
|---|---|---|
| Single | 15.00 | 16.00 |
| Double | 28.00 | 30.00 |

Parking for 6
Open March-October

## HUNTINGDON

Cambridgeshire
Map ref 3A2

Attractive, interesting town which abounds in associations with the Cromwell family. The town is connected to Godmanchester by a beautiful 14th C bridge over the great River Ouse.
*Tourist Information Centre*
☎ *(01480) 425831*

### The Elms

👑👑 COMMENDED

Banks End, Wyton, Huntingdon
PE17 2AA
☎ (01480) 453523
*Rambling Edwardian house in open countryside on outskirts of picturesque riverside village, 2 miles from Huntingdon and St Ives. Friendly and welcoming. No smoking please.*
Bedrooms: 2 single, 1 double, 1 twin
Bathrooms: 2 private, 1 public

**Bed & breakfast**

| per night: | £min | £max |
|---|---|---|
| Single | 17.50 | |
| Double | 35.00 | |

Parking for 4

### Prince of Wales ♨

👑👑 COMMENDED

Potton Road, Hilton, Huntingdon
PE18 9NG
☎ (01480) 830257
Fax (01480) 830257
*Traditional village inn with comfortable and well-equipped en-suite bedrooms. Convenient for St Ives, Huntingdon, St Neots and Cambridge. On B1040, south east of Huntingdon.*
Bedrooms: 2 single, 1 double, 1 twin
Bathrooms: 4 private

**Bed & breakfast**

| per night: | £min | £max |
|---|---|---|
| Single | 20.00 | 35.00 |
| Double | 40.00 | 45.00 |

Lunch available
Evening meal 1900 (last orders 2115)
Parking for 9
Cards accepted: Access, Visa, Amex,
Switch/Delta

## INGATESTONE

Essex
Map ref 3B3

### Eibiswald

Listed HIGHLY COMMENDED

85 Mill Road, Stock, Ingatestone
CM4 9LR
☎ Stock (01277) 840631
Fax (01277) 840631
*Anglo-Austrian hospitality. Comfortable, modern house in quiet, pleasant rural surroundings. Close to village centre. Railway 4 miles. Convenient for Chelmsford, Brentwood, Basildon. 5*

*minutes from A12 on B1007, signposted Billericay.*
Bedrooms: 3 double
Bathrooms: 1 private, 1 public
**Bed & breakfast**

| per night: | £min | £max |
| --- | --- | --- |
| Single | 24.80 | 30.00 |
| Double | 35.00 | 42.00 |

Parking for 7

🛇 12 ▭◻⬚🛈§✕📺▥ 🖉⚲❋ 🐎🏠ⓉⓉ

## KERSEY

Suffolk
Map ref 3B2

A most picturesque village, which was famous for cloth-making, set in a valley with a water-splash. The church of St Mary is an impressive building at the top of the hill.

### Red House Farm
**Listed  COMMENDED**
Kersey, Ipswich IP7 6EY
☎ Boxford (01787) 210245
*Listed farmhouse between Kersey and Boxford, central for Constable country. Rooms with wash basins, TV and tea-making facilities. Twin bedroom and ground floor annexe single en-suite. Swimming pool.*
Bedrooms: 1 single, 2 double, 1 twin
Bathrooms: 3 private, 1 public
**Bed & breakfast**

| per night: | £min | £max |
| --- | --- | --- |
| Single | 18.00 | 20.00 |
| Double | 32.00 | 34.00 |

**Half board**

| per person: | £min | £max |
| --- | --- | --- |
| Daily | 26.00 | 28.00 |
| Weekly | 182.00 | 196.00 |

Evening meal 1900 (last orders 1000)
Parking for 5

⬚◻♦️🖳⬚🛈§📺▥ 🖉⚲∪⌇❋ 🐎🏠

## KESSINGLAND

Suffolk
Map ref 3C1

Seaside village whose church tower has served as a landmark to sailors for generations. Nearby is the Suffolk Wildlife and Country Park.

### The Old Rectory
**☸☸ HIGHLY COMMENDED**
157 Church Road, Kessingland, Lowestoft NR33 7SQ
☎ Lowestoft (01502) 740020
*Beautiful late Georgian house in 2 acres of garden, well back from road ensuring peace and quiet. A warm welcome awaits. Spacious, comfortable, delightfully furnished rooms, most with antiques.*
Bedrooms: 1 double, 1 family room
Bathrooms: 2 private, 2 public

---

**Bed & breakfast**

| per night: | £min | £max |
| --- | --- | --- |
| Single | 22.00 | 24.00 |
| Double | 40.00 | 44.00 |

Parking for 6
Open May–September

🛇6♨◻🖳🛈🚳§✕📺▥🖉❋🐎🏠🏠

## KING'S LYNN

Norfolk
Map ref 3B1

A busy town with many outstanding buildings. The Guildhall and Town Hall are both built of flint in a striking chequer design. Behind the Guildhall in the Old Gaol House the sounds and smells of prison life 2 centuries ago are recreated.
*Tourist Information Centre*
☎ *(01553) 763044*

### Maranatha Guest House 🅼
**☸ APPROVED**
115 Gaywood Road, Gaywood, King's Lynn PE30 2PU
☎ (01553) 774596
*Large carrstone and brick residence with gardens front and rear. 10 minutes' walk from the town centre. Direct road to Sandringham and the coast.*
Bedrooms: 2 single, 2 double, 2 twin
Bathrooms: 1 private, 2 public
**Bed & breakfast**

| per night: | £min | £max |
| --- | --- | --- |
| Single | 15.00 | 17.00 |
| Double | 26.00 | 30.00 |

**Half board**

| per person: | £min | £max |
| --- | --- | --- |
| Daily | 18.00 | 21.00 |

Lunch available
Evening meal 1800 (last orders 1800)
Parking for 9

🛇◻♦️🛈§📺▥🖉🐎🖎

## KINGS LANGLEY

Hertfordshire
Map ref 2D1

### Woodcote House
**☸☸ COMMENDED**
7 The Grove, Chipperfield Road, Kings Langley WD4 9JF
☎ (01923) 262077

*Timber-framed house, sitting in 1 acre of landscaped gardens with quiet rural aspect. Convenient for M1 and M25 and close to Watford and Hemel Hempstead.*
Bedrooms: 2 single, 1 double, 1 twin

---

Bathrooms: 4 private
**Bed & breakfast**

| per night: | £min | £max |
| --- | --- | --- |
| Single | 20.00 | 24.00 |
| Double | 38.00 | 40.00 |

Evening meal 1800 (last orders 2100)
Parking for 8

🛇▭🖳§✕🙍📺▥ 🖉∪❋🐎🏠

## LAVENHAM

Suffolk
Map ref 3B2

A former prosperous wool town of timber-framed buildings with the cathedral-like church and its tall tower. The market-place is 13th C and the Guildhall now houses a museum.

### The Great House Restaurant and Hotel 🅼
**☸☸☸☸**
Market Place, Lavenham, Sudbury CO10 9QZ
☎ Sudbury (01787) 247431
*Famous and historic 15th C house with covered outside courtyard, quietly and ideally located, full of warmth and oak furniture for a relaxing stay. French cuisine. Menu changing daily.*
Bedrooms: 1 double, 1 twin, 1 triple, 1 family room
Bathrooms: 4 private
**Bed & breakfast**

| per night: | £min | £max |
| --- | --- | --- |
| Single | 49.50 | 60.00 |
| Double | 66.00 | 78.00 |

**Half board**

| per person: | £min | £max |
| --- | --- | --- |
| Daily | 48.95 | |

Lunch available
Evening meal 1900 (last orders 2230)
Parking for 10
Open February–December
Cards accepted: Access, Visa

🛇✆▭🖳♦️🙍📺▥ 🖉🍴❋🐎🏠SP 🏠Ⓣ

### The Red House
**Listed**
29 Bolton Street, Lavenham, Sudbury CO10 9RG
☎ (01787) 248074

*In the best of the medieval East Anglian villages, a large Victorian house which was the village bakehouse. Full central heating, large garden. Only a step from pubs.*
Bedrooms: 2 double, 1 twin
Bathrooms: 3 private

Continued ▶

## LAVENHAM

*Continued*

**Bed & breakfast**

| per night: | £min | £max |
|---|---|---|
| Double | 40.00 | 45.00 |

**Half board**

| per person: | £min | £max |
|---|---|---|
| Daily | 32.50 | 35.00 |

Evening meal 1930 (last orders 2000)
Parking for 6
Open March-November and Christmas

🛇🦽 UL 🛇 S ⚲ ⋈ TV ▥ 🖃 ✿ 🖦 🚲

## LAWSHALL

Suffolk
Map ref 3B2

### Brighthouse Farm

👑👑 **COMMENDED**

Melford Road, Lawshall, Bury St
Edmunds IP29 4PX
☎ Bury St Edmunds (01284) 830385
*300-acre arable & livestock farm. A
warm welcome awaits you at this 200-
year-old farmhouse set in 3 acres of
gardens. Close to many places of
historic interest. Good pubs and
restaurants nearby.*
Bedrooms: 2 double, 1 twin
Bathrooms: 3 private, 1 public

**Bed & breakfast**

| per night: | £min | £max |
|---|---|---|
| Single | 16.00 | 25.00 |
| Double | 32.00 | 40.00 |

Parking for 10

🛇🦽⚲ UL 🛇 S ⚲ TV ▥ 🖃 ⚲✿ 🖦 🏮

## LITTLE TEY

Essex
Map ref 3B2

### Knaves Farm House

**Listed**

Great Tey Road, Little Tey, Colchester
CO6 1JA
☎ Colchester (01206) 211039
*Charming early Victorian farmhouse in
1 acre of well-kept garden with
traditional Essex barns. 400 yards from
A120 towards Great Tey.*
Bedrooms: 1 single, 1 double
Bathrooms: 1 private

**Bed & breakfast**

| per night: | £min | £max |
|---|---|---|
| Single | 20.00 | 25.00 |
| Double | 30.00 | 35.00 |

Parking for 1

🛇🦽🖭⚲❦ UL 🏮 ▥ 🖃✿ 🖦 🏮

---

Half board prices shown
are per person but in some
cases may be based on
double/twin occupancy.

---

## LITTLE WALSINGHAM

Norfolk
Map ref 3B1

Little Walsingham is larger than its
neighbour Great Walsingham and
more important because of its long
history as a religious shrine to
which many pilgrimages were
made. The village has many
picturesque buildings of the 16th C
and later.

### St David's House

Friday Market, Little Walsingham,
Walsingham NR22 6BY
☎ Fakenham (01328) 820633
*16th C brick house in a delightful
medieval village. From Fakenham
(A148) take the B1105 - the village is
fully signposted.*
Bedrooms: 1 twin, 2 triple
Bathrooms: 3 private, 2 public

**Bed & breakfast**

| per night: | £min | £max |
|---|---|---|
| Single | 16.00 | |
| Double | 32.00 | |

**Half board**

| per person: | £min | £max |
|---|---|---|
| Daily | 23.50 | |

Lunch available
Evening meal from 1800

🛇🦽⚲ UL ⚲⋈ 🖦

## LONG MELFORD

Suffolk
Map ref 3B2

One of Suffolk's loveliest villages,
remarkable for the length of its
main street. Holy Trinity Church is
considered to be the finest village
church in England. The National
Trust own the Elizabethan Melford
Hall and nearby Kentwell Hall is
also open to the public.

### The George & Dragon

Long Melford, Sudbury CO10 9JB
☎ Sudbury (01787) 371285
Fax (01787) 312428
*English country inn offering traditional
service and hospitality. The best in both
beer and beef.*
Bedrooms: 1 single, 1 twin, 1 triple,
1 family room
Bathrooms: 1 private, 2 public,
1 private shower

**Bed & breakfast**

| per night: | £min | £max |
|---|---|---|
| Single | | 20.00 |
| Double | | 40.00 |

**Half board**

| per person: | £min | £max |
|---|---|---|
| Daily | | 30.00 |
| Weekly | | 55.00 |

Lunch available
Evening meal 1800 (last orders 2200)

---

Parking for 20
Cards accepted: Access, Visa

🛇🖭🗖🖃 S ⚲⋈ TV ▥ 🖃♦❦ U✿
DAP 🦯 SP 🏮

## LOWESTOFT

Suffolk
Map ref 3C1

Seaside town with wide sandy
beaches. Important fishing port
with picturesque fishing quarter.
Home of the famous Lowestoft
porcelain and birthplace of
Benjamin Britten. East Point
Pavilion's exhibition describes the
Lowestoft story.
*Tourist Information Centre*
☎ *(01502) 523000*

### Church Farm

**Listed** **HIGHLY COMMENDED**

Corton, Lowestoft NR32 5HX
☎ (01502) 730359
Fax (01502) 730359

*220-acre arable farm. Victorian
farmhouse with a warm, welcoming
atmosphere. Quietly situated on the
Suffolk coast between Lowestoft and
Great Yarmouth. Clean, comfortable, en-
suite rooms, generous English breakfast.
Non-smoking establishment.*
Bedrooms: 3 double
Bathrooms: 3 private

**Bed & breakfast**

| per night: | £min | £max |
|---|---|---|
| Double | 34.00 | 35.00 |

Parking for 4
Open March-October

🛇🖭 12🦽🖭🗖❦ UL S ⚲ ▥ 🖃 ♦✿
⋈ 🖦

### Hall Farm

**Listed** **COMMENDED**

Jay Lane, Church Lane, Lound,
Lowestoft NR32 5LJ
☎ (01502) 730415
*101-acre arable farm. Traditional 16th C
Suffolk farmhouse within 2 miles of the
sea. Clean, comfortable accommodation
with generous English breakfast. Farm
down a quiet, private lane half-a-mile
from A12.*
Bedrooms: 1 single, 1 double, 1 twin,
1 triple
Bathrooms: 2 private, 1 public

**Bed & breakfast**

| per night: | £min | £max |
|---|---|---|
| Single | 15.00 | 15.00 |
| Double | 32.00 | 32.00 |

Parking for 6
Open March-October

🛇🦯⚲ UL S ⚲⋈ TV ▥ 🖃 ♦ 🖦 DAP

## Oak Farm

`Listed` `COMMENDED`

Market Lane, Blundeston, Lowestoft
NR32 5AP
☎ (01502) 731622

*125-acre mixed & livestock farm.
Working farm in peaceful countryside
location, 10 minutes from coast. House
was originally Victorian cottages. Guest
stairs lead to rooms. Generous
farmhouse breakfast. Reductions for
children. No smoking, please.*
Bedrooms: 1 double, 1 twin
Bathrooms: 1 public
**Bed & breakfast**

| per night: | £min | £max |
|---|---|---|
| Single | 15.00 | |
| Double | 28.00 | |

Parking for 2
Open February–November
🛏 2 🎿 ❏ ⬗ ⓤ ⌇ ⌷ ▥ 🖪 ❀ ✕ 🚜

### LUDHAM

Norfolk
Map ref 3C1

Pleasant Broadland village with
Womack Broad close by. The
centre of the village has some
very attractive Georgian houses
and the church is outstanding.

## Bra-Lo End

`Listed`

Johnson Street, Ludham, Great
Yarmouth NR29 5NY
☎ Horning (01692) 631285 & Mobile
0831 766712
*Large 3-bedroom family house, 500
yards from River Ant at Ludham
Bridge, where you can fish, hire day
boats and bird-watch.*
Bedrooms: 2 double
Bathrooms: 1 public
**Bed & breakfast**

| per night: | £min | £max |
|---|---|---|
| Single | 15.00 | |
| Double | 30.00 | |

Parking for 4
🛏 🎿 ❏ ⬗ ⓤ ⌷ ▥ 🖪 ❀ 🚜

### MARGARET RODING

Essex
Map ref 2D1

## Greys

`Listed`

Ongar Road, Margaret Roding,
Dunmow CM6 1QR
☎ Good Easter (01245) 231509
*340-acre arable and mixed farm.
Formerly 2 cottages pleasantly situated*

---

*on family farm just off A1060 at
telephone kiosk. Beamed throughout,
large garden. Tea/coffee available.
Singles by arrangement.*
Bedrooms: 2 double, 1 twin
Bathrooms: 1 public
**Bed & breakfast**

| per night: | £min | £max |
|---|---|---|
| Double | 32.00 | |

Parking for 6
🛏 10 ⬗ ⓤ ⌇ ⌷ ⌷ ▥ ❀ ✕ 🚜 🏧

### MELTON CONSTABLE

Norfolk
Map ref 3B1

## Lowes Farm

👑👑

Edgefield, Melton Constable
NR24 2EX
☎ Holt (01263) 712317
*Grade II listed farmhouse built in 1637
occupying a superb position in the
Glaven Valley. Quality accommodation,
oak beams, antique furniture, log fires
in winter.*
Bedrooms: 2 double
Bathrooms: 2 private, 1 public
**Bed & breakfast**

| per night: | £min | £max |
|---|---|---|
| Double | 40.00 | 40.00 |

Parking for 15
📭 ⬗ ⓤ Ⓢ ⌇ ⌷ ⌷ ⓣⓥ ◐ ▥ 🖪 ❀ ✕ 🚜
🏧 Ⓣ

### MIDDLETON

Suffolk
Map ref 3C2

## Rose Farm

👑👑

Middleton, Saxmundham IP17 3NG
☎ Westleton (01728) 648456
*Quality bed and breakfast in a
delightful, rurally situated 17th C
farmhouse. Ideal for Aldeburgh,
Minsmere, Southwold and the beautiful
Suffolk heritage coastline.*
Bedrooms: 2 double, 1 twin
Bathrooms: 3 private
**Bed & breakfast**

| per night: | £min | £max |
|---|---|---|
| Single | 18.00 | 20.00 |
| Double | 36.00 | 40.00 |

Parking for 6
🛏 🍴 ❏ ⬗ ⓤ 🛍 Ⓢ ⌇ ⌷ ⓣⓥ ▥ ❀ ✕ 🚜

### MUCH HADHAM

Hertfordshire
Map ref 2D1

## Daneswood ⋀

`HIGHLY COMMENDED`

Much Hadham SG10 6DT
☎ (01279) 842519
*A small, listed country house, built in
the style of Edwin Lutyens, in 25 acres
of gardens and bluebell woods. 15
minutes from Stansted Airport.*
Bedrooms: 1 twin

---

Bathrooms: 1 private
**Bed & breakfast**

| per night: | £min | £max |
|---|---|---|
| Single | 25.00 | 25.00 |
| Double | 40.00 | 40.00 |

Parking for 4
🛏 12 📭 ❏ ⬗ ⓠ ⓤ ⌇ ▥ ▸ ✕ 🚜 🏧

### MUNDESLEY

Norfolk
Map ref 3C1

Small seaside resort with a superb
sandy beach and excellent
bathing. Nearby is a smock-mill
still with cap and sails.

## The Grange

`COMMENDED`

High Street, Mundesley-on-Sea,
Norwich NR11 8JL
☎ (01263) 721556
*Beautiful, well-furnished house with
friendly atmosphere, in attractive
garden. Ideal for the Broads and
Norwich, bird-watching, fishing and the
beach.*
Bedrooms: 2 double, 1 twin, 1 triple
Bathrooms: 2 public
**Bed & breakfast**

| per night: | £min | £max |
|---|---|---|
| Single | 16.00 | 18.00 |
| Double | 32.00 | 36.00 |

Parking for 10
🛏 2 ⬗ ⓤ ⌇ ⌷ ⓣⓥ ▥ 🖪 ❀ ✕ 🚜 SP

### NAYLAND

Suffolk
Map ref 3B2

Charmingly located village on the
River Stour owing its former
prosperity to the cloth trade. The
hub of the village is the 15th C
Alston Court. The altar-piece of St
James Church was painted by
John Constable.

## Leavenheath Farm

`Listed` `HIGHLY COMMENDED`

Locks Lane, Leavenheath, Colchester
CO6 4PF
☎ Colchester (01206) 262322
*30-acre mixed farm. Small fruit farm
with pedigree sheep, free-range
chickens, geese and ancient bluebell
wood in Stour Valley. Lovely
refurbished oak-beamed Suffolk
farmhouse offering peace and
tranquillity with home cooking. Winter
log fires and a warm welcome.*
Bedrooms: 3 double, 1 twin
Bathrooms: 4 private, 1 public
**Bed & breakfast**

| per night: | £min | £max |
|---|---|---|
| Single | 15.00 | 20.00 |
| Double | 32.00 | 40.00 |

Continued ▶

## NAYLAND

*Continued*

**Half board**

| per person: | £min | £max |
|---|---|---|
| Daily | 25.00 | 30.00 |
| Weekly | 150.00 | 180.00 |

Lunch available
Evening meal 1900 (last orders 2100)
Parking for 26

🛏🍴🗝🎍📞🛇⚡🕅📺🛏️🔌📞☾
✓❄🚐

## NEWMARKET

Suffolk
Map ref 3B2

Centre of the English horse-racing
world and the headquarters of the
Jockey Club and National Stud.
Racecourse and horse sales. The
National Horse Racing Museum
traces the history and
development of the Sport of Kings.
*Tourist Information Centre*
☎ *(01638) 667200*

### Westley House

**Listed**

Westley Waterless, Newmarket
CB8 0RQ
☎ (01638) 508112
Fax (01638) 508113
*Spacious Georgian-style former rectory
in quiet rural area 5 miles south of
Newmarket and convenient for
Cambridge. Large comfortable bedrooms
and drawing room opening on to 5
acres of garden, trees and paddocks.
Visitors are our guests. Advance
bookings only please.*
Bedrooms: 1 single, 2 twin
Bathrooms: 2 public

**Bed & breakfast**

| per night: | £min | £max |
|---|---|---|
| Single | 18.50 | 20.00 |
| Double | 37.00 | 40.00 |

**Half board**

| per person: | £min | £max |
|---|---|---|
| Daily | 28.50 | 30.00 |

Evening meal 1930 (last orders 2100)
Parking for 6

🛏⚡🛇🗝✕🕅📺🛏️🔌📞❄🚐⌧

## NORFOLK BROADS

*See under Aylsham, Beccles,
Brundall, Bungay, Cawston,
Coltishall, Great Yarmouth,
Hevingham, Lowestoft, Ludham,
North Walsham, Norwich,
Rackheath, Rollesby, Salhouse,
South Walsham, Stalham,
Wroxham*

We advise you to confirm
your booking in writing.

## NORTH WALSHAM

Norfolk
Map ref 3C1

Weekly market has been held here
for 700 years. 1 mile south of town
is a cross commemorating the
Peasants' Revolt of 1381. Nelson
attended the local Paston
Grammar School, founded in 1606
and still flourishing.

### Geoffrey the Dyer House

👑👑

Church Plain, Worstead, North
Walsham NR28 9AL
☎ Smallburgh (01692) 536562
*Carefully restored 17th C weaver's
residence, full of character and comfort,
close to beach, Broads and Norwich. In
centre of conservation village.*
Bedrooms: 2 double, 1 twin
Bathrooms: 3 private

**Bed & breakfast**

| per night: | £min | £max |
|---|---|---|
| Single | 17.50 | 24.00 |
| Double | 32.00 | 38.00 |

**Half board**

| per person: | £min | £max |
|---|---|---|
| Daily | 26.00 | 32.50 |

Lunch available
Evening meal 1830 (last orders 2200)
Parking for 4
Cards accepted: Diners

🛏🍴🗝⚡🕅📞🛇⚡✕🕅📺🛏️🚐🏠

### The Old Hall

**Listed**

Edingthorpe, North Walsham
NR28 9TJ
☎ Walcot (01692) 650189

*Grade II listed Elizabethan hall set in
countryside near coast. Beautiful
gardens. Take B1150 from North
Walsham to Bacton for approximately 2
miles, turn left at crossroads to
Edingthorpe/Mundesley. Non-smokers
only, please.*
Bedrooms: 2 double, 1 twin
Bathrooms: 2 private, 2 public

**Bed & breakfast**

| per night: | £min | £max |
|---|---|---|
| Single | 18.00 | 18.00 |
| Double | 36.00 | 50.00 |

**Half board**

| per person: | £min | £max |
|---|---|---|
| Daily | 27.50 | 34.50 |
| Weekly | 174.50 | 216.50 |

Evening meal 1800 (last orders 2000)
Parking for 6

🛏🍴🗝⚡🕅📞🛇📺🛏️🔌📞❄▶️❄
✕🚐⌧ SP 🏠

## NORWICH

Norfolk
Map ref 3C1

Beautiful cathedral city and county
town on the River Wensum with
many fine museums and medieval
churches. Norman castle, Guildhall
and interesting medieval streets.
Good shopping centre and market.
*Tourist Information Centre*
☎ *(01603) 666071*

### Arodet House

👑👑

132 Earlham Road, Norwich NR2 3HF
☎ (01603) 503522
*Convenient for university. Walking
distance to city centre. Separate guest
lounge. Tea/coffee facilities. Personal
keys.*
Bedrooms: 2 single, 2 double
Bathrooms: 1 private, 1 public

**Bed & breakfast**

| per night: | £min | £max |
|---|---|---|
| Single | 16.00 | 17.00 |
| Double | 32.00 | 37.00 |

🛏⚡🛇🗝🕅📺🛏️🚐🏠

### Cavell House

**Listed**

Swardeston, Norwich NR14 8D2
☎ Mulbarton (01508) 578195
*Birthplace of nurse Edith Cavell.
Georgian farmhouse on edge of
Swardeston village. Off B1113 south of
Norwich, 7 miles from centre. Rural
setting. Close to university.*
Bedrooms: 1 single, 1 double, 1 twin
Bathrooms: 2 public

**Bed & breakfast**

| per night: | £min | £max |
|---|---|---|
| Single | 10.00 | 18.50 |
| Double | 30.00 | 35.00 |

Parking for 10

🛏5🐾🗝🍴⚡🛇⚡🛇✕🛏️🚐📞
📞❄🚐 DAP 🏠

### Church Farm Guest House

👑👑 **COMMENDED**

Church Street, Horsford, Norwich
NR10 3DB
☎ (01603) 898020 & 898582
Fax (01603) 891649
*Quiet, modernised 17th C farmhouse.
Separate entrance, lounge and dining
room for guests. Approximately 4 miles
north of Norwich.*
Bedrooms: 3 double, 2 family rooms
Bathrooms: 5 private

**Bed & breakfast**

| per night: | £min | £max |
|---|---|---|
| Single | 14.00 | 20.00 |
| Double | 32.00 | 36.00 |

Parking for 20

🛏🐾🍴⚡🛇⚡🕅📺🛏️🚐❄✕🚐

## Gables Farm ᐱ
🅦 HIGHLY COMMENDED
Hemblington Hall Road, Hemblington,
Norwich NR13 4PT
☎ South Walsham (01603) 270239 &
Mobile 0860 786263
Fax (01603) 270548

*Delightful, secluded listed 17th C
thatched farmhouse in large garden
surrounded by farmland. Within easy
reach of Norwich, Norfolk Broads, the
coast and many nature reserves.*
Bedrooms: 1 twin, 1 family room
Bathrooms: 2 private
**Bed & breakfast**

| per night: | £min | £max |
|---|---|---|
| Single | 22.00 | |
| Double | 37.00 | |

Parking for 6
➤8🖭🗌♨🖵⬧🖃🔆📺🗔✿✕🛲🏠

## Kingsley Lodge
🅦🅦 COMMENDED
3 Kingsley Road, Norwich NR1 3RB
☎ (01603) 615819
*Quiet, friendly Edwardian house near
bus station, under 10 minutes' walk to
city centre. Spacious bedrooms with en-
suite bathrooms, TV, tea/coffee making
facilities. No smoking.*
Bedrooms: 2 single, 1 double, 1 twin
Bathrooms: 4 private
**Bed & breakfast**

| per night: | £min | £max |
|---|---|---|
| Single | 22.00 | 25.00 |
| Double | 36.00 | 38.00 |

Open February-December
➤🗌♨🖵S🔆🖃🗔⬧✕🛲

## Oakfield
🅦🅦 HIGHLY COMMENDED
Yelverton Road, Framingham Earl,
Norwich NR14 7SD
☎ Framingham Earl (01508) 492605
*Superior accommodation in beautiful,
quiet setting on edge of village 4 miles
south-east of Norwich. Splendid
breakfasts. Local pubs serve good
evening meals.*
Bedrooms: 1 single, 1 double, 1 twin
Bathrooms: 1 private, 1 public
**Bed & breakfast**

| per night: | £min | £max |
|---|---|---|
| Single | 16.00 | 18.00 |
| Double | 32.00 | 36.00 |

Parking for 6
➤12🖭🗌♨🖵⬧🔆🖃📺🗔⬧✿
✕🛲

## Rosedale ᐱ
Listed
145 Earlham Road, Norwich NR2 3RG
☎ (01603) 53743

*Friendly, family-run Victorian
guesthouse and restaurant on main
B1108, 1 mile from city centre.
Shopping centre, restaurants and
university nearby.*
Bedrooms: 3 single, 1 double, 3 twin,
1 triple
Bathrooms: 2 public
**Bed & breakfast**

| per night: | £min | £max |
|---|---|---|
| Single | 14.00 | 17.00 |
| Double | 28.00 | 32.00 |

Parking for 2
➤4🗌♨🖵⬧S🔆🖃🗔⬧✕🛲🏠

## Witton Hall Farm
🅦🅦
Witton, Norwich NR13 5DN
☎ (01603) 714580
*500-acre dairy farm. Elegant Georgian
farmhouse in the heart of Norfolk.
Peaceful, mature grounds. Swimming
pool in walled garden.*
Bedrooms: 1 double, 1 twin, 1 family
room
Bathrooms: 3 private
**Bed & breakfast**

| per night: | £min | £max |
|---|---|---|
| Single | 15.00 | 20.00 |
| Double | 30.00 | 33.00 |

Parking for 4
Cards accepted: Diners
➤🗌♨🖵🗋✿🖃📺🗔⬧⟲✿🛲

## PETERBOROUGH
Cambridgeshire
Map ref 3A1

Prosperous and rapidly expanding
cathedral city on the edge of the
Fens on the River Nene. Catherine
of Aragon is buried in the
cathedral. City Museum and Art
Gallery. Ferry Meadows Country
Park has numerous leisure
facilities.
*Tourist Information Centre
☎ (01733) 317336*

## Stoneacre ᐱ
🅦🅦
Elton Road, Wansford, Peterborough
PE8 6JT
☎ Stamford (01780) 783283
*Modern country house in rural and
secluded position with delightful views
across the River Nene Valley. Half a
mile from A1, 10 minutes from
Peterborough and Stamford. Large
grounds with mini golf-course.*
Bedrooms: 3 double, 1 twin
Bathrooms: 3 private, 2 public
**Bed & breakfast**

| per night: | £min | £max |
|---|---|---|
| Single | 21.00 | 34.00 |
| Double | 27.00 | 45.00 |

Parking for 24
➤5🖭🖭🗌♨🖵⬧🖃S🔆🖃📺🗔⬧
↕4-25🔍⟲🍴✿🛲🏠🏳

## QUIDENHAM
Norfolk
Map ref 3B1

## Manor Farm
Listed
Quidenham, Norwich NR16 2NY
☎ (01953) 887540
*950-acre arable farm. Large secluded
farmhouse set in beautiful surroundings.
Home cooking, fresh vegetables, own
eggs.*
Bedrooms: 2 single, 1 double, 1 twin
Bathrooms: 1 public
**Bed & breakfast**

| per night: | £min | £max |
|---|---|---|
| Single | 15.00 | |
| Double | 30.00 | |

**Half board**

| per person: | £min | £max |
|---|---|---|
| Daily | 25.00 | |

Evening meal 1900 (last orders 2000)
Parking for 10
➤6⬧♨🖵⬧S🖃📺🗔⬧✿✕🛲

## RACKHEATH
Norfolk
Map ref 3C1

## Barn Court
Listed APPROVED
6 Back Lane, Rackheath, Norwich
NR13 6NN
☎ Norwich (01603) 782536
Fax (01603) 782536
*Spacious accommodation in a
traditional Norfolk barn conversion,
built around a courtyard. Ideal base for
exploring Norfolk - 3 miles Norwich.
Friendly atmosphere with good home
cooking.*
Bedrooms: 2 double, 1 twin
Bathrooms: 2 public
**Bed & breakfast**

| per night: | £min | £max |
|---|---|---|
| Single | 16.00 | 20.00 |
| Double | 32.00 | 38.00 |

Parking for 4
Open February-December
➤⬧🖭🗌♨🖵⬧🖃S🔆🖃📺🗔⬧✿
🛲🏠

## RADWINTER
Essex
Map ref 3B2

## The Plough Inn
🅦 APPROVED
Sampford Road, Radwinter, Saffron
Walden CB10 2TL
☎ Saffron Walden (01799) 599222
*16th C inn with lovely garden views of
countryside. Self-contained
accommodation in garden. Lunch and
evening meal available in the pub. 5
miles from Saffron Walden and 6 miles
from Finchingfield.*
Bedrooms: 1 double, 1 twin

Continued ▶

## RADWINTER

*Continued*

Bathrooms: 2 private
**Bed & breakfast**

| per night: | £min | £max |
|---|---|---|
| Single | 22.00 | |
| Double | 36.00 | |

Lunch available
Evening meal 1900 (last orders 2200)
Parking for 20

⛴🚪🖵⬛🆂🛏🚿✕🚗🏠

## RAMSEY

Cambridgeshire
Map ref 3A2

### The Leys 🅼
Listed

25 Bury Road, Ramsey, Huntingdon
PE17 1NE
☎ (01487) 813221 & 710053
*Large family house with a friendly
atmosphere. On B1040 on the southern
outskirts of Ramsey, between
Huntingdon and Peterborough.*
Bedrooms: 1 single, 1 twin, 2 triple
Bathrooms: 2 public
**Bed & breakfast**

| per night: | £min | £max |
|---|---|---|
| Single | 12.00 | 15.00 |
| Double | 24.00 | 30.00 |

Parking for 10

🐕🛇⛴🚪➡🖵⬛🅸🆂🛏📺🖵🚘🍴10
✿🚗

## RICKMANSWORTH

Hertfordshire
Map ref 2D2

Old town, where 3 rivers meet,
now mainly residential. The High
Street is full of interesting
buildings, including the home of
William Penn. Moor Park Mansion,
a fine 18th C house, is now a golf
clubhouse.

### 6 Swallow Close
Listed

Nightingale Road, Rickmansworth
WD3 2DZ
☎ (01923) 720069
*In a quiet cul-de-sac, 5 minutes' walk
from underground station, 30 minutes
to London. Convenient for M25 and
Watford. All food home-made. Non-
smokers only, please.*
Bedrooms: 1 single, 1 double, 1 triple
Bathrooms: 1 private, 1 public
**Bed & breakfast**

| per night: | £min | £max |
|---|---|---|
| Single | 18.00 | 19.00 |
| Double | 36.00 | 38.00 |

Parking for 3

🐕5⛴➡🖵⬛✕🖵🚘✿✕🚗

## ROLLESBY

Norfolk
Map ref 3C1

Rollesby Broad forms part of the
Ormesby Broad complex and fine
views can be seen from the road
which runs through the middle.

### The Old Court House 🅼
👑 COMMENDED

Court Road, Rollesby, Great Yarmouth
NR29 5HG
☎ Great Yarmouth (01493) 369665

*18th C workhouse set in 4 acres in a
peaceful, rural location near the
Broads. Family-run with private bar and
home cooking. Large games area.
Bicycles for hire. Tennis, fishing and
riding nearby.*
Bedrooms: 2 double, 1 twin, 1 triple,
4 family rooms
Bathrooms: 5 private, 2 public
**Bed & breakfast**

| per night: | £min | £max |
|---|---|---|
| Double | 38.00 | 45.00 |

**Half board**

| per person: | £min | £max |
|---|---|---|
| Daily | 29.00 | 32.50 |
| Weekly | 184.00 | 205.00 |

Evening meal 1830 (last orders 1830)
Parking for 20
Open February-November

🐕⛴🚪➡🍴⬛🆂🛏📺🖵🚘🍴15♠↺
🔍∪🏸✿✕🚗🏠

## SAFFRON WALDEN

Essex
Map ref 2D1

Takes its name from the saffron
crocus once grown around the
town. The church of St Mary has
superb carvings, magnificent roofs
and brasses. A town maze can be
seen on the common. Two miles
south-west is Audley End, a
magnificent Jacobean mansion
owned by English Heritage.
*Tourist Information Centre*
☎ *(01799) 510444*

### Bridge End Orchard
👑👑 HIGHLY COMMENDED

Bridge Street, Saffron Walden
CB10 1BT
☎ (01799) 522001
*Comfortable accommodation in secluded
location, 5 minutes from town centre.
Convenient for amenities and
restaurants. Friendly atmosphere.
Private parking.*
Bedrooms: 2 double, 1 twin

Bathrooms: 3 private
**Bed & breakfast**

| per night: | £min | £max |
|---|---|---|
| Single | 19.50 | 21.00 |
| Double | 38.00 | 39.00 |

Parking for 3
Open January-November

⛴🚪🖵🛏📺🖵✿✕🚗

### The Delles
Listed HIGHLY COMMENDED

Carmen Street, Great Chesterford,
Saffron Walden CB10 1NR
☎ (01799) 530256 & Cellnet 0860
246740

*Tudor/Georgian house dating from
1520, with 2.5 acre gardens offering
peace and comfort. Situated in centre of
conservation area, yet close to
Cambridge, Imperial War Museum and
M11.*
Bedrooms: 2 double, 1 twin
Bathrooms: 2 public
**Bed & breakfast**

| per night: | £min | £max |
|---|---|---|
| Single | 17.50 | 22.00 |
| Double | 35.00 | 35.00 |

**Half board**

| per person: | £min | £max |
|---|---|---|
| Daily | 27.50 | 32.00 |

Evening meal 1830 (last orders 2100)
Parking for 6

🐕2⛴🚪➡🖵⬛🆂🛏📺🖵🚘✿✿
🚗🏠T

### Elmdon Bury
👑👑 HIGHLY COMMENDED

Elmdon, Saffron Walden CB11 4NF
☎ Royston (01763) 838220
*350-acre arable farm. Recently restored
red brick Essex farmhouse with
outstanding thatched barns. Set in
beautiful grounds behind church, in
centre of Elmdon village, to the West of
Saffron Walden. Large spacious rooms.*
Bedrooms: 1 double, 1 twin
Bathrooms: 2 private
**Bed & breakfast**

| per night: | £min | £max |
|---|---|---|
| Single | 20.00 | 25.00 |
| Double | 40.00 | 50.00 |

Evening meal 1930 (last orders 2030)
Parking for 10

⛴➡🖵✕🖵🚘↺🔍✿🚗🏠

### 1 Gunters Cottages
👑👑

Thaxted Road, Saffron Walden
CB10 2UT
☎ (01799) 522091
*Rebuilt 19th C cottages with views over
open farmland. Indoor heated
swimming pool. On Thaxted/Saffron*

*Walden road, 2 miles from Saffron
Walden.*
Bedrooms: 1 double
Bathrooms: 1 private
**Bed & breakfast**

| per night: | £min | £max |
|---|---|---|
| Single | 20.00 | 22.00 |
| Double | 30.00 | 35.00 |

Parking for 4

## Pond Mead

Widdington, Saffron Walden
CB11 3SB
☎ (01799) 540201
*Comfortable old house on the edge of
Widdington village, with its ancient
tithe barn and wildlife park. Easy access
to Stansted Airport, Cambridge and
M11.*
Bedrooms: 1 single, 1 double, 1 triple
Bathrooms: 2 private, 1 public
**Bed & breakfast**

| per night: | £min | £max |
|---|---|---|
| Single | 12.00 | 17.00 |
| Double | 30.00 | 30.00 |

Parking for 5

## Rockells Farm

Duddenhoe End, Saffron Walden
CB11 4UY
☎ Royston (01763) 838053
*420-acre arable farm. Georgian house in
rolling countryside with plenty of
opportunities for walking and
sightseeing. The 3-acre lake provides
excellent fishing. Stansted Airport 20
minutes by car, Cambridge 30 minutes
and London 1 hour.*
Bedrooms: 1 single, 1 twin, 1 triple
Bathrooms: 3 private, 1 public
**Bed & breakfast**

| per night: | £min | £max |
|---|---|---|
| Single | 16.00 | 18.00 |
| Double | 32.00 | 36.00 |

**Half board**

| per person: | £min | £max |
|---|---|---|
| Daily | 23.50 | 25.50 |

Evening meal from 1800
Parking for 4

## Rowley Hill Lodge

COMMENDED

Little Walden, Saffron Walden
CB10 1UZ
☎ (01799) 525975
Fax (01799) 516622
*Quiet farm lodge with large garden, 1
mile from centre of Saffron Walden.
Stansted Airport, Cambridge and
Duxford 20 minutes.*
Bedrooms: 1 single, 1 twin
Bathrooms: 1 private, 1 public

**Bed & breakfast**

| per night: | £min | £max |
|---|---|---|
| Single | 17.50 | 19.50 |
| Double | 35.00 | 35.00 |

Parking for 4

## Yardley's

COMMENDED

Orchard Pightle, Hadstock, Cambridge
CB1 6PQ
☎ Cambridge (01223) 891822
*Comfortable modern house with
conservatory and gardens, in quiet
village location. Hadstock is off A604
Colchester/Cambridge road at Linton,
20 minutes from Cambridge. Non-
smoking establishment.*
Bedrooms: 1 single, 1 double, 1 twin
Bathrooms: 2 private, 2 public
**Bed & breakfast**

| per night: | £min | £max |
|---|---|---|
| Single | 17.00 | 18.00 |
| Double | 34.00 | 38.00 |

Parking for 6

## Yeoman Cottage

Listed  APPROVED

Hempstead, Saffron Walden
CB10 2PH
☎ Radwinter (01799) 599345
*Comfortable timbered 14th C house with
antique furniture and charming
gardens, in village famous for William
Harvey and Dick Turpin. Convenient for
Cambridge, Thaxted and Stansted. Good
local restaurants.*
Bedrooms: 1 single, 1 twin
Bathrooms: 1 public
**Bed & breakfast**

| per night: | £min | £max |
|---|---|---|
| Single | 17.50 | |
| Double | 35.00 | |

Parking for 3

## ST ALBANS

Hertfordshire
Map ref 2D1

As Verulamium this was one of the
largest towns in Roman Britain and
its remains can be seen in the
museum. The Norman cathedral
was built from Roman materials to
commemorate Alban, the first
British Christian martyr.
*Tourist Information Centre*
☎ (01727) 864511

## Amaryllis

Listed

25 Ridgmont Road, St Albans
AL1 3AG
☎ (01727) 862755 & Mobile 0850
662371
*Friendly, informal family home close to
city centre. Convenient for M1 and*

*M25. Central London 20 minutes by
train. Non-smokers only please.*
Bedrooms: 1 single, 1 twin, 1 triple
Bathrooms: 1 public
**Bed & breakfast**

| per night: | £min | £max |
|---|---|---|
| Single | 13.00 | 20.00 |
| Double | 30.00 | 32.00 |

Parking for 1

## 2 The Limes

Listed

Spencer Gate, St Albans AL1 4AT
☎ (01727) 831080
*Modern, detached house in a quiet cul-
de-sac, within 10 minutes' walk of the
city centre. Home-baked bread.*
Bedrooms: 1 single, 1 twin
Bathrooms: 1 public
**Bed & breakfast**

| per night: | £min | £max |
|---|---|---|
| Single | 15.00 | 17.00 |
| Double | 30.00 | 34.00 |

Parking for 1

## The Squirrels

Listed  APPROVED

74 Sandridge Road, St Albans
AL1 4AR
☎ (01727) 840497
*Edwardian terraced house, 10 minutes'
walk from town centre.*
Bedrooms: 1 twin
Bathrooms: 1 private
**Bed & breakfast**

| per night: | £min | £max |
|---|---|---|
| Single | 15.00 | 17.50 |
| Double | 25.00 | 27.50 |

## SALHOUSE

Norfolk
Map ref 3C1

Village above the tree-fringed
Salhouse Broad. The church of All
Saints has a thatched roof and a
14th C arcade.

## Brooks Bank

COMMENDED

Lower Street, Salhouse, Norwich
NR13 6RW
☎ Norwich (01603) 720420
*18th C house situated in the centre of
Broadland. Guests' own private
accommodation. Illustrated brochure.
Our pleasure is your comfort.*
Bedrooms: 2 double, 1 twin
Bathrooms: 3 private
**Bed & breakfast**

| per night: | £min | £max |
|---|---|---|
| Single | 18.00 | 22.00 |
| Double | 30.00 | 35.00 |

Parking for 4

## SANDY

Bedfordshire
Map ref 2D1

Small town on the River Ivel on
the site of a Roman settlement.
Sandy is mentioned in Domesday.

### Highfield Farm
**HIGHLY COMMENDED**

Great North Road, Sandy SG19 2AQ
☎ (01767) 682332

*300-acre arable farm. Beautifully
peaceful, comfortable farmhouse. Most
rooms en-suite. Cambridge, the
Shuttleworth Collection, RSPB and
London in easy reach. Most guests
return.*
Bedrooms: 2 double, 3 twin, 1 triple
Bathrooms: 4 private, 1 public
**Bed & breakfast**

| per night: | £min | £max |
| --- | --- | --- |
| Single | 19.00 | 25.00 |
| Double | 32.00 | 36.00 |

Parking for 8

## SAXLINGHAM THORPE

Norfolk
Map ref 3B1

### The Lodge
**HIGHLY COMMENDED**

Cargate Lane, Saxlingham Thorpe,
Norwich NR15 1TU
☎ Swainsthorpe (01508) 471422

*Listed Regency country house with
spacious, elegantly furnished rooms.
Situated in secluded grounds close to
Norwich and A140. Candlelit dinners
available.*
Bedrooms: 1 single, 1 double, 1 twin
Bathrooms: 3 private
**Bed & breakfast**

| per night: | £min | £max |
| --- | --- | --- |
| Single | 28.00 | |
| Double | 48.00 | |

---

**Half board**

| per person: | £min | £max |
| --- | --- | --- |
| Daily | 41.00 | 45.00 |
| Weekly | 258.30 | 283.50 |

Evening meal 1930 (last orders 2000)
Parking for 12

## SAXMUNDHAM

Suffolk
Map ref 3C2

The church of St John the Baptist
has a hammer-beam roof and
contains a number of good
monuments.

### Little Orchard
**Listed**  **HIGHLY COMMENDED**

Middleton, Saxmundham IP17 3NT
☎ Westleton (01728) 648385
*Charming early 18th C house with open
views all around. Ideally situated for
sea and countryside, Snape Maltings
and Concert Hall and Minsmere nature
reserve. First house on left on B1125
coming from Theberton off the B1122.*
Bedrooms: 2 double
Bathrooms: 2 private
**Bed & breakfast**

| per night: | £min | £max |
| --- | --- | --- |
| Single | 16.00 | |
| Double | 32.00 | |

**Half board**

| per person: | £min | £max |
| --- | --- | --- |
| Daily | 26.00 | |

Evening meal 1900 (last orders 2000)
Parking for 3

## SHELLEY

Suffolk
Map ref 3B2

### Sparrows

Shelley, Ipswich IP7 5RQ
☎ Colchester (01206) 337381
*Peaceful 15th C house in unspoilt
Suffolk countryside. Central base for
touring. Excellent pubs close by.
Bicycles available. Grass tennis court.*
Bedrooms: 1 single, 1 double
Bathrooms: 1 public
**Bed & breakfast**

| per night: | £min | £max |
| --- | --- | --- |
| Single | 18.00 | 20.00 |
| Double | 34.00 | 40.00 |

**Half board**

| per person: | £min | £max |
| --- | --- | --- |
| Daily | 30.00 | 35.00 |
| Weekly | 200.00 | 235.00 |

Evening meal 1900 (last orders 2030)
Parking for 6

---

## SHERINGHAM

Norfolk
Map ref 3B1

Holiday resort with Victorian and
Edwardian hotels and a sand and
shingle beach where the fishing
boats are hauled up. The North
Norfolk Railway operates from
Sheringham station during the
summer. Other attractions include
museums, theatre and Splash Fun
Pool.

### The Bay Leaf Guest House
**Listed**

10 St. Peters Road, Sheringham
NR26 8QY
☎ (01263) 823779
*Charming Victorian licensed
guesthouse, open all year. Conveniently
situated in the town. Near golf-course
and woodlands, adjacent to steam
railway and 5 minutes from sea.*
Bedrooms: 1 double, 3 twin, 2 triple
Bathrooms: 6 private
**Bed & breakfast**

| per night: | £min | £max |
| --- | --- | --- |
| Single | 17.00 | 23.00 |
| Double | 34.00 | 46.00 |

**Half board**

| per person: | £min | £max |
| --- | --- | --- |
| Daily | 26.00 | 35.00 |
| Weekly | 167.00 | 192.00 |

Evening meal 1800 (last orders 1930)
Parking for 4
Cards accepted: Access, Visa

## SLOLEY

Norfolk
Map ref 3C1

### Sloley Farm
**COMMENDED**

Sloley, Norwich NR12 8HJ
☎ Smallburgh (01692) 536281
Fax (01692) 535162
*400-acre mixed farm. Comfortable
farmhouse set in peaceful countryside,
4 miles from Norfolk Broads and within
easy reach of the coast. Off B1150
Norwich to North Walsham road.*
Bedrooms: 2 double, 1 twin
Bathrooms: 1 public
**Bed & breakfast**

| per night: | £min | £max |
| --- | --- | --- |
| Single | 16.00 | 17.50 |
| Double | 30.00 | 32.00 |

**Half board**

| per person: | £min | £max |
| --- | --- | --- |
| Daily | 24.00 | 25.50 |
| Weekly | 168.00 | 178.50 |

Evening meal from 1800
Parking for 5
Cards accepted: Diners

## SOUTH CREAKE

Norfolk
Map ref 3B1

The interesting church of St Mary
is a good example of how a large
church would have looked in the
15th C. Nearby is the site of an
ancient Iron Age encampment.

### Avondale Farm
Listed

Avondale Road, South Creake,
Fakenham NR21 9PH
☎ Fakenham (01328) 823254
*Large detached farmhouse with large
garden overlooking village green.
Situated between Fakenham and
Burnham Market.*
Bedrooms: 2 double
Bathrooms: 1 public
**Bed & breakfast**

| per night: | £min | £max |
|---|---|---|
| Single | 15.00 | |
| Double | 30.00 | |

Parking for 3
Open April-September

## SOUTH LOPHAM

Norfolk
Map ref 3B2

### Malting Farm

Blo Norton Road, South Lopham, Diss
IP22 2HT
☎ Bressingham (01379) 88201
Changing to 687201
*70-acre dairy farm. Recently renovated,
timber-framed farmhouse with inglenook
fireplaces and four-poster beds. Crafts,
including embroidery, patchwork,
spinning. See the cows being milked.*
Bedrooms: 2 double, 1 twin
Bathrooms: 1 private, 1 public
**Bed & breakfast**

| per night: | £min | £max |
|---|---|---|
| Single | 20.00 | |

**Half board**

| per person: | £min | £max |
|---|---|---|
| Daily | 34.00 | |

Parking for 10
Cards accepted: Diners

There are separate
sections in this guide
listing groups
specialising in farm
holidays and
accommodation which
is especially suitable
for young people and
organised groups.

## SOUTH MIMMS

Hertfordshire
Map ref 2D1

Best known today for its location
at the junction of the M25 and the
A1M.
*Tourist Information Centre*
☎ *(01707) 643233*

### The Black Swan
Listed

62-64 Blanche Lane, South Mimms,
Potters Bar EN6 3PD
☎ Potters Bar (01707) 644180
*Comfortable accommodation in oak-
beamed bedrooms or self-contained flats
in quietly located listed building.
Breakfast provided.*
Bedrooms: 2 double
Bathrooms: 2 private, 1 public
**Bed & breakfast**

| per night: | £min | £max |
|---|---|---|
| Single | 25.00 | 25.00 |
| Double | 35.00 | 35.00 |

Parking for 7

## SOUTH WALSHAM

Norfolk
Map ref 3C1

Village famous for having 2
churches in adjoining churchyards.
South Walsham Broad consists of
an inner and outer section, the
former being private. Alongside,
the Fairhaven Garden Trust has
woodland and water-gardens open
to the public.

### Old Hall Farm ⋀

South Walsham, Norwich NR13 6DT
☎ Norwich (01603) 270271
*82-acre arable farm. Thatched
farmhouse dating from 17th C on the
edge of Broadland village. Good centre
for Norwich, Broads and coast.*
Bedrooms: 1 single, 3 double, 1 twin
Bathrooms: 1 private, 1 public
**Bed & breakfast**

| per night: | £min | £max |
|---|---|---|
| Single | 13.50 | |
| Double | 27.00 | 37.00 |

Parking for 5
Open April-October

National Crown ratings
were correct at the time
of going to press but
are subject to change.
Please check at the time
of booking.

## SOUTHEND-ON-SEA

Essex
Map ref 3B3

On the Thames Estuary and the
nearest seaside resort to London.
Famous for its pier and unique pier
trains. Other attractions include
Peter Pan's Playground, indoor
swimming pools, indoor
rollerskating and ten pin bowling.
*Tourist Information Centre*
☎ *(01702) 215120*

### Aldridge Guest House
Listed APPROVED

17 Hartington Road, Southend-on-Sea
SS1 2HR
☎ (01702) 614555
*Friendly accommodation, close to
seafront, pier and shops. Choice of
breakfast served in your room. All
rooms en-suite with colour TV and tea-
making facilities.*
Bedrooms: 1 double, 2 twin, 1 triple
Bathrooms: 4 private
**Bed & breakfast**

| per night: | £min | £max |
|---|---|---|
| Single | 15.00 | 16.00 |
| Double | 25.00 | 27.00 |

## SOUTHWOLD

Suffolk
Map ref 3C2

Pleasant and attractive seaside
town with a triangular market
square and spacious greens
around which stand flint, brick and
colour-washed cottages. The
parish church of St Edmund is one
of the greatest churches in Suffolk.

### Albert House
Listed

16 Dunwich Road, Southwold
IP18 6LJ
☎ (01502) 722218
*Victorian terrace with yesterday's charm
and today's standard, peacefully situated
just off the seafront in the heart of
Southwold.*
Bedrooms: 2 double, 1 twin
Bathrooms: 1 public
**Bed & breakfast**

| per night: | £min | £max |
|---|---|---|
| Single | 22.00 | 30.00 |
| Double | 35.00 | 40.00 |

All accommodation in this
guide has been inspected,
or is awaiting inspection,
under the national Crown
scheme.

## STALHAM

Norfolk
Map ref 3C1

Lies on the edge of the Broads.

### Bramble House
COMMENDED

Cat's Common, Norwich Road,
Smallburgh, Norwich NR12 9NS
☎ Smallburgh (01692) 535069
*Friendliness and comfort guaranteed in
this large country house, set in 1.5
acres in the heart of Broadland. All
rooms en-suite. Brochure available.*
Bedrooms: 1 single, 2 double
Bathrooms: 3 private

**Bed & breakfast**
| per night: | £min | £max |
| --- | --- | --- |
| Single | 17.00 | 20.00 |
| Double | 34.00 | 35.00 |

Parking for 8
Cards accepted: Diners

## STOKE HOLY CROSS

Norfolk
Map ref 3C1

### Salamanca Farm ⋀

Stoke Holy Cross, Norwich NR14 8QJ
☎ Framingham Earl (01508) 492322
*175-acre mixed farm. Picturesque village
near Norwich. Comfortable Victorian
farmhouse in a flower arranger's
garden. Guests have been welcomed for
20 years.*
Bedrooms: 3 double, 1 twin
Bathrooms: 4 private, 1 public

**Bed & breakfast**
| per night: | £min | £max |
| --- | --- | --- |
| Single | 17.00 | |
| Double | 34.00 | |

Parking for 8
Cards accepted: Diners

## STOKE-BY-NAYLAND

Suffolk
Map ref 3B2

Picturesque village with a fine
group of half-timbered cottages
near the church of St Mary, the
tower of which was one of
Constable's favourite subjects. In
School Street are the Guildhall
and the Maltings, both 16th C
timber-framed buildings.

### The Angel Inn ⋀
COMMENDED

Polstead Street, Stoke-by-Nayland,
Colchester CO6 4SA
☎ Colchester (01206) 263245
Fax (01206) 37386
*Beautifully restored freehouse and
restaurant in the historic village of*

*Stoke-by-Nayland, in the heart of
Constable country.*
Bedrooms: 1 single, 4 double, 1 twin
Bathrooms: 6 private

**Bed & breakfast**
| per night: | £min | £max |
| --- | --- | --- |
| Single | 44.00 | 44.00 |
| Double | 57.50 | 57.50 |

Lunch available
Evening meal 1830 (last orders 2100)
Parking for 25
Cards accepted: Access, Visa, Diners,
Amex, Switch/Delta

### Nether Hall
Listed

Thorington Street, Stoke-by-Nayland,
Colchester CO6 4ST
☎ Higham (01206) 37373

*A charming 15th C country house with
grounds adjoining the River Box and in
the heart of Constable country. On the
B1068, 3 miles from the A12.*
Bedrooms: 1 single, 2 double
Bathrooms: 3 private

**Bed & breakfast**
| per night: | £min | £max |
| --- | --- | --- |
| Single | 21.00 | 21.00 |
| Double | 42.00 | 42.00 |

Parking for 6

### Thorington Hall
Listed  APPROVED

Stoke-by-Nayland, Colchester CO6 4SS
☎ Higham (01206) 337329
*Beautiful farmhouse belonging to the
National Trust, with friendly
atmosphere. In rural setting, in the
heart of Constable country.*
Bedrooms: 2 single, 2 double
Bathrooms: 2 private, 1 public

**Bed & breakfast**
| per night: | £min | £max |
| --- | --- | --- |
| Single | 15.00 | 17.50 |
| Double | 30.00 | 35.00 |

Parking for 4
Open April-October

National Crown ratings
were correct at the time
of going to press but
are subject to change.
Please check at the time
of booking.

## STRATFORD ST MARY

Suffolk
Map ref 3B2

Set in countryside known as
Constable country.

### Teazles
Listed  APPROVED

Stratford St Mary, Colchester
CO7 6LU
☎ Colchester (01206) 323148
*Attractive 16th C country house in heart
of Constable country. Just off A12 on
B1029 to Dedham, leaving church on
right. Refurbished in 1971, now our
family home to which we welcome
guests.*
Bedrooms: 1 single, 1 double, 1 twin
Bathrooms: 2 public

**Bed & breakfast**
| per night: | £min | £max |
| --- | --- | --- |
| Single | 16.00 | 17.50 |
| Double | 32.00 | 37.00 |

Parking for 7

## SUDBURY

Suffolk
Map ref 3B2

Former important cloth and market
town on the River Stour. Birthplace
of Thomas Gainsborough whose
home is now an art gallery and
museum. The Corn Exchange is
an excellent example of early
Victorian civic building.

### St. Mary Hall
COMMENDED

Belchamp Walter, Sudbury CO10 7BB
☎ Great Yeldham (01787) 237202
*Lovely medieval manor house, with
beautiful garden, surrounded by quiet
countryside. Tennis court, croquet lawn,
swimming pool. In small village to the
west of Sudbury.*
Bedrooms: 2 single, 1 double, 1 twin
Bathrooms: 4 private, 3 public

**Bed & breakfast**
| per night: | £min | £max |
| --- | --- | --- |
| Single | 26.00 | |
| Double | 48.00 | 56.00 |

**Half board**
| per person: | £min | £max |
| --- | --- | --- |
| Daily | 40.00 | 44.00 |

Parking for 4
Cards accepted: Access, Visa

The enquiry coupons
at the back will help
you when contacting
proprietors.

## THAXTED

Essex
Map ref 3B2

Small town rich in outstanding buildings and dominated by its hilltop medieval church. The magnificent Guildhall was built by the Cutlers' Guild in the late 14th C. A windmill built in 1804 has been restored and houses a rural museum.

### Folly House

🏛🏛 COMMENDED

Watling Lane, Thaxted, Dunmow CM6 2QY
☎ (01371) 830618
*Sunny, light, spacious house, with sweeping views over hills, in the historic and picturesque village of Thaxted. Attentive friendly service. Sky TV in all rooms. Transport to Stansted Airport.*
Bedrooms: 1 double, 2 twin
Bathrooms: 1 private, 1 public

**Bed & breakfast**

| per night: | £min | £max |
| --- | --- | --- |
| Single | 18.00 | 25.00 |
| Double | 36.00 | 45.00 |

**Half board**

| per person: | £min | £max |
| --- | --- | --- |
| Daily | 28.00 | 38.00 |
| Weekly | 150.00 | 175.00 |

Evening meal 1800 (last orders 2030)
Parking for 6
🛇🍴🖥🖵🕯♿🗠⚿🛏📺🖩.🖨🅿♨
🗙🚲

### Piggots Mill

🏛🏛 HIGHLY COMMENDED

Watling Lane, Thaxted, Dunmow CM6 2QY
☎ (01371) 830379
*850-acre arable farm. Traditional Essex barn, now a secluded farmhouse offering excellent accommodation in the centre of Thaxted. Garden leads into meadow giving access to attractive walks.*
Bedrooms: 1 double, 1 twin
Bathrooms: 2 private

**Bed & breakfast**

| per night: | £min | £max |
| --- | --- | --- |
| Single | 28.00 | 30.00 |
| Double | 42.00 | 45.00 |

Parking for 10
🛇🛇12🖥🍴🖵♿🗠🕯🖩S⚿🛏🖩.🖨U♨
🗙🚲🅿🏢🅃

Colour maps at the back of this guide pinpoint all places which have accommodation listings in the guide.

## THETFORD

Norfolk
Map ref 3B2

Small, medieval market town with numerous reminders of its long history: the ruins of the 12th C priory, Iron Age earthworks at Castle Hill and a Norman castle mound. Timber-framed Ancient House is now a museum.

### Church Cottage

🏛 COMMENDED

Breckles, Attleborough NR17 1EW
☎ Great Hockham (01953) 498286
Fax (01953) 498320
*Charming 18th C home in beautiful Breckland. Ideal for touring East Anglia. Own coarse fishing. Heated outdoor swimming pool. Home-made bread. On B1111, 9 miles north-east of Thetford.*
Bedrooms: 2 double, 1 twin
Bathrooms: 2 public

**Bed & breakfast**

| per night: | £min | £max |
| --- | --- | --- |
| Single | 16.00 | 17.00 |
| Double | 32.00 | 34.00 |

Parking for 10
🛇10🖥🕯🖵ⓊⓁS🕭🖩📺🖩.🖨🅿🗠⚘
🚲🏢

### East Farm

🏛

Barnham, Thetford IP24 2PB
☎ Elveden (01842) 890231
*995-acre arable and mixed farm. Large rooms with superb views in farmhouse on working farm on outskirts of village. Central in East Anglia for many attractions.*
Bedrooms: 1 double, 1 twin
Bathrooms: 2 private

**Bed & breakfast**

| per night: | £min | £max |
| --- | --- | --- |
| Single | 21.00 | 22.00 |
| Double | 36.00 | 36.00 |

Parking for 4
🛇🖥🕯🖵ⓊⓁ🕭🖪🖩📺🖩.🖨⚘🗙🚲

## THOMPSON

Norfolk
Map ref 3B1

### College Farm 🏔

Listed

Thompson, Thetford IP24 1QG
☎ Caston (01953) 483318
*14th C farmhouse, formerly a college of priests. In quiet village away from main road. Meals provided at nearby inns.*
Bedrooms: 1 double, 2 twin
Bathrooms: 3 private, 1 public

**Bed & breakfast**

| per night: | £min | £max |
| --- | --- | --- |
| Single | 17.00 | 18.00 |
| Double | 34.00 | 36.00 |

Parking for 10
🛇7🖵ⓊⓁS🖩.🖨🗠⚘🗙🚲🏢

## THORNHAM

Norfolk
Map ref 3B1

### The Chequers Inn

Listed APPROVED

Thornham, Hunstanton PE36 6LY
☎ (01485) 512229
*Picturesque Grade II listed freehouse with beams and low ceilings, open fires and real ales. On main A149 road, close to RSPB sanctuary and sea. Food always available.*
Bedrooms: 1 single, 2 double
Bathrooms: 3 private

**Bed & breakfast**

| per night: | £min | £max |
| --- | --- | --- |
| Single | 20.00 | 25.00 |
| Double | 40.00 | 50.00 |

Lunch available
Evening meal 1800 (last orders 2200)
Parking for 31
Cards accepted: Access, Visa
🖵🕯S✂🖩.🖨🗠☏🖩🚲🖢🅿🏢

## THORPE MORIEUX

Suffolk
Map ref 3B2

### Mount Farm House

🏛🏛

Thorpe Morieux, Bury St Edmunds IP30 0NQ
☎ Lavenham (01787) 248428

*19th C farmhouse in quiet location, close to historic Lavenham. Free use of sauna, swimming pool and tennis court. Non-smokers please.*
Bedrooms: 3 double
Bathrooms: 3 private

**Bed & breakfast**

| per night: | £min | £max |
| --- | --- | --- |
| Double | 33.00 | 38.00 |

Evening meal 1930 (last orders 2130)
Parking for 12
🖵🕯🖩ⓊⓁ✂🗠☏🖢🗙🚲🏢

## TIPTREE

Essex
Map ref 3B3

### Linden

Listed

8 Clarkesmead, Maldon Road, Tiptree, Colchester CO5 0BX
☎ (01621) 819737
Fax (01621) 818033
*Modern architect-designed house in quiet cul-de-sac, off Maldon Road on edge of Tiptree.*

Continued ►

## TIPTREE

*Continued*

Bedrooms: 1 single, 1 double, 1 twin,
1 family room
Bathrooms: 1 private, 2 public,
1 private shower

**Bed & breakfast**

| per night: | £min | £max |
|---|---|---|
| Single | 20.00 | 22.00 |
| Double | 40.00 | 44.00 |

Parking for 6
Cards accepted: Access, Visa

## TIVETSHALL ST MARY

Norfolk
Map ref 3B2

### The Old Ram Coaching Inn

HIGHLY COMMENDED

Ipswich Road, Tivetshall St Mary,
Norwich NR15 2DE
☎ Pulham Market (01379) 676794
Fax (01379) 608399
*Situated off A140 Norwich/Ipswich road
15 miles south of Norwich. This 17th C
coaching inn has recently opened 5 en-
suite guest rooms, offering telephone,
satellite TV, hairdryer, trouser press and
tea/coffee making facilities.*
Bedrooms: 4 double, 1 triple
Bathrooms: 5 private

**Bed & breakfast**

| per night: | £min | £max |
|---|---|---|
| Single | 35.00 | 40.00 |
| Double | 50.00 | 55.00 |

Lunch available
Evening meal 1800 (last orders 2200)
Parking for 150
Cards accepted: Access, Visa, Switch/
Delta

## TOFT

Cambridgeshire
Map ref 2D1

### West View

Listed COMMENDED

6 Hardwick Road, Toft, Cambridge
CB3 7RQ
☎ Cambridge (01223) 263287 &
264202
*Self-contained accommodation joined to
main house. Easily reached through
Barton and Comberton. 6 miles from
Cambridge with bus service.*
Bedrooms: 2 single, 2 double
Bathrooms: 2 public

**Bed & breakfast**

| per night: | £min | £max |
|---|---|---|
| Single | 18.00 | 20.00 |
| Double | 30.00 | 35.00 |

Parking for 3

## WARE

Hertfordshire
Map ref 2D1

Interesting riverside town with
picturesque summer-houses lining
the tow-path of the River Lea. The
town has many timber-framed and
Georgian houses and the famous
Great Bed of Ware is now in the
Victoria and Albert Museum.

### Ashridge

COMMENDED

3 Belle Vue Road, Ware SG12 7BD
☎ (01920) 463895
*Comfortable, Edwardian residence in
quiet cul-de-sac. 10 minutes' walk from
Ware and station. Non-smokers only
please.*
Bedrooms: 2 single, 1 double, 1 twin
Bathrooms: 2 public

**Bed & breakfast**

| per night: | £min | £max |
|---|---|---|
| Single | 16.50 | 20.00 |
| Double | 33.00 | 40.00 |

**Half board**

| per person: | £min | £max |
|---|---|---|
| Daily | 22.50 | 27.00 |

Evening meal 1830 (last orders 1200)
Parking for 4

## WATFORD

Hertfordshire
Map ref 2D1

Large town with many industries
but with some old buildings,
particularly around St Mary's
Church which contains some fine
monuments. The grounds of
Cassiobury Park, once the home of
the Earls of Essex, form a
public park and golf-course.

### The Millwards

Listed

30 Hazelwood Road, Croxley Green,
Rickmansworth WD3 3EB
☎ (01923) 233751 & 226666
*Quiet, homely canalside residence.
Pleasant location. Convenient London
(Metropolitan line), Moor Park,
Wembley, Heathrow, Rickmansworth,
M1 and M25, Watford and Croxley
Business Centre.*
Bedrooms: 1 single, 2 twin
Bathrooms: 2 public

**Bed & breakfast**

| per night: | £min | £max |
|---|---|---|
| Single | 17.00 | 17.00 |
| Double | 30.00 | 32.00 |

Parking for 2

## WELLS-NEXT-THE-SEA

Norfolk
Map ref 3B1

Seaside resort and small port on
the north coast. The Buttlands is a
large tree-lined green surrounded
by Georgian houses and from here
narrow streets lead to the quay.

### Scarborough House Hotel

COMMENDED

Clubbs Lane, Wells-next-the-Sea
NR23 1DP
☎ Fakenham (01328) 710309 &
711661
*Licensed hotel with restaurant, log fires,
four-poster beds, private parking.
Perfect for bird-watchers and ramblers.
Dogs welcome.*
Bedrooms: 9 double, 4 twin, 1 family
room
Bathrooms: 14 private

**Bed & breakfast**

| per night: | £min | £max |
|---|---|---|
| Single | 29.00 | 34.00 |
| Double | 48.00 | 58.00 |

**Half board**

| per person: | £min | £max |
|---|---|---|
| Daily | 37.00 | 50.00 |
| Weekly | 240.00 | 300.00 |

Evening meal 1930 (last orders 2100)
Parking for 14
Cards accepted: Access, Visa, Diners,
Amex, Switch/Delta

## WEST BERGHOLT

Essex
Map ref 3B2

### Hill House

Listed

Gravel Hill, Nayland, Colchester
CO6 4JB
☎ Colchester (01206) 262782
*Delightful Tudor house set in pretty
village amidst Constable country. Good
base for touring and walking. Excellent
pubs locally. Easy access Harwich.*
Bedrooms: 1 single, 1 twin
Bathrooms: 1 private, 1 public

**Bed & breakfast**

| per night: | £min | £max |
|---|---|---|
| Single | 18.00 | 20.00 |
| Double | 36.00 | 38.00 |

Parking for 2

## WEYBREAD

Suffolk
Map ref 3C2

### Pear Tree Farm

Listed

The Street, Weybread, Diss, Norfolk
IP21 5TH
☎ Fressingfield (01379) 86753

15th C farmhouse with most beams exposed. Surrounded by fields. Large garden and lawns. Five minutes from large fishing area and also central for the coast and Norwich.
Bedrooms: 1 single, 1 twin, 1 triple
Bathrooms: 1 public

**Bed & breakfast**

| per night: | £min | £max |
|---|---|---|
| Single | 13.00 | 15.00 |
| Double | 26.00 | 30.00 |

**Half board**

| per person: | £min | £max |
|---|---|---|
| Daily | 19.00 | 21.00 |
| Weekly | 133.00 | 147.00 |

Evening meal 1800 (last orders 2000)
Parking for 5
Open January-October
Cards accepted: Diners
⌂ 🛗 📲 ⚡ 🅿 📺 🛏 ❄ ✕ 🐎

## WISBECH

Cambridgeshire
Map ref 3A1

The town is the centre of the agricultural and flower-growing industries of Fenland. Peckover House (National Trust) is an important example of domestic architecture.
*Tourist Information Centre*
☎ (01945) 583263

### Stratton Farm
**COMMENDED**

West Drove North, Walton Highway,
Wisbech PE14 7DP
☎ (01945) 880162
*22-acre livestock farm. All ground floor en-suite accommodation in peaceful setting, with heated swimming pool and private fishing. Wheelchair facilities. Non-smokers only please. Home-produced sausages, bacon and eggs. Wheelchair access category 3* 🦽
Bedrooms: 2 double, 1 twin
Bathrooms: 3 private

**Bed & breakfast**

| per night: | £min | £max |
|---|---|---|
| Single | 21.00 | 22.00 |
| Double | 42.00 | 44.00 |

Parking for 6
Cards accepted: Diners
⌂ 6 🛗 📲 ⚡ 🅿 📺 🛏 ❄ SP

## WIX

Essex
Map ref 3B2

### New Farm House Ⓜ
♛♛♛

Spinnell's Lane, Wix, Manningtree
CO11 2UJ
☎ Clacton (01255) 870365
Fax (01255) 870837

50-acre arable farm. Modern comfortable farmhouse in large garden, 10 minutes' drive to Harwich and convenient for Constable country. From Wix village crossroads, take Bradfield Road, turn right at top of hill; first house on left.
Bedrooms: 3 single, 1 double, 3 twin, 5 family rooms
Bathrooms: 7 private, 2 public

**Bed & breakfast**

| per night: | £min | £max |
|---|---|---|
| Single | 19.00 | 23.00 |
| Double | 37.00 | 42.00 |

**Half board**

| per person: | £min | £max |
|---|---|---|
| Daily | 29.00 | 31.50 |
| Weekly | 183.00 | 198.50 |

Evening meal 1830 (last orders 1730)
Parking for 18
Cards accepted: Access, Visa
⌂ 🛗 📲 ⚡ 🅿 📺 🛏 ❄ ✕

## WOODBRIDGE

Suffolk
Map ref 3C2

Once a busy seaport, the town is now a sailing centre on the River Deben. There are many buildings of architectural merit including the Bell and Angel Inns. The 18th C Tide Mill is now restored and open to the public.

### Moat Barn
♛♛♛ **HIGHLY COMMENDED**

Bredfield, Woodbridge IP13 6BD
☎ Charsfield (01473) 37520 Changing
to 737520
Fax (01473) 37520
*Renovated Suffolk barn with exposed beams and original features, standing in grounds of over 1 acre. In Bredfield village, with pub and church, just 3 miles from the market town of Woodbridge.*
Bedrooms: 2 double, 1 twin
Bathrooms: 1 private, 2 public

**Bed & breakfast**

| per night: | £min | £max |
|---|---|---|
| Single | 20.00 | 30.00 |
| Double | 40.00 | 50.00 |

Parking for 10
⌂ 🛗 📲 ⚡ 🅿 📺 🛏 ❄

### Otley House
♛♛♛ **HIGHLY COMMENDED**

Helmingham Road, Otley, Ipswich
IP6 9NR
☎ Helmingham (01473) 890 253
Fax (01473) 890 009

17th C country house set in mature peaceful grounds with lakes and large lawn, 5 miles north-west of Woodbridge. Billiard room, drawing room, Regency dining room. Open fires. English and continental cooking. Smoking in billiard room only.
Bedrooms: 2 double, 2 twin
Bathrooms: 4 private

**Bed & breakfast**

| per night: | £min | £max |
|---|---|---|
| Single | 36.00 | 40.00 |
| Double | 48.00 | 52.00 |

**Half board**

| per person: | £min | £max |
|---|---|---|
| Daily | 40.50 | 42.50 |
| Weekly | 283.50 | 297.50 |

Evening meal 1930 (last orders 1600)
Parking for 8
Open March-October
⌂ 12 🛗 📲 ⚡ 🅿 📺 🛏 ❄ ✕

## WOODHAM FERRERS

Essex
Map ref 3B3

### Woolfe's Cottage
**Listed**

The Street, Woodham Ferrers,
Chelmsford CM3 5RG
☎ Chelmsford (01245) 320037
*Large converted Victorian cottage in historic village, 12 miles from Chelmsford on the B1418. Many excellent walking trails for ramblers.*
Bedrooms: 1 double, 1 twin
Bathrooms: 1 public

**Bed & breakfast**

| per night: | £min | £max |
|---|---|---|
| Single | 15.50 | 16.50 |
| Double | 29.50 | 31.00 |

Parking for 2
⌂ 🛗 📲 ⚡ 🅿 📺 🛏 ❄ ✕

There are separate sections in this guide listing groups specialising in farm holidays and accommodation which is especially suitable for young people and organised groups.

## WROXHAM

Norfolk
Map ref 3C1

Yachting centre on the River Bure which houses the headquarters of the Norfolk Broads Yacht Club. The church of St Mary has a famous doorway and the manor house nearby dates back to 1623.

### Holly Cottage

👑 COMMENDED

Church Lane, Wroxham, Norwich NR12 8SH
☎ Norwich (01603) 783401
*Detached, modernised 200-year-old riverside cottage with artist's studio, near church in oldest part of Broadland village of Wroxham. Ample parking and beautiful gardens. Terraced down to River Bure.*
Bedrooms: 2 double, 2 twin
Bathrooms: 4 private

**Bed & breakfast**

| per night: | £min | £max |
|---|---|---|
| Single | 16.00 | 22.00 |
| Double | 36.00 | 40.00 |

Parking for 5

🛏10🕹♨🌢ⓊⒾⓈ✂🔥📺📺Ⅲ🗂☀🚗

### Manor Barn House

👑 COMMENDED

Back Lane, Rackheath, Wroxham, Norwich NR13 6NN
☎ Norwich (01603) 783543
*Traditional Norfolk barn conversion with exposed beams, in quiet setting with pleasant gardens. Just off the A1151, 2 miles from Wroxham.*
Bedrooms: 3 double, 2 twin
Bathrooms: 5 private

**Bed & breakfast**

| per night: | £min | £max |
|---|---|---|
| Single | 18.00 | 25.00 |
| Double | 30.00 | 36.00 |

Parking for 8

🛏3🕹♨🌢Ⓤ🔥✂🔥📺Ⅲ🗂🅿∪▶☀ 🚗 SP 🏵

### Wroxham Park Lodge 🏔

👑 COMMENDED

142 Norwich Road, Wroxham, Norwich NR12 8SA
☎ (01603) 782991
*Comfortable Victorian house in lovely gardens, 1 mile from Wroxham Broads and town centre. Central for all Broads amenities. Open all year round.*
Bedrooms: 2 double, 1 twin
Bathrooms: 3 private, 1 public

**Bed & breakfast**

| per night: | £min | £max |
|---|---|---|
| Single | 22.50 | 25.00 |
| Double | 36.00 | 38.00 |

Parking for 6

🛏👑🌢Ⓤ♨Ⓘ📺Ⅲ🗂☀🐾 SP

## WYMONDHAM

Norfolk
Map ref 3B1

Busy market town with a charming octagonal market cross. In 1615 a great fire destroyed most of its buildings but the Green Dragon Inn, now one of the oldest in the country, survived.

### Rose Farm

Listed

School Lane, Suton, Wymondham NR18 9JN
☎ (01953) 603512
*2-acre poultry farm. Homely farmhouse accommodation within easy reach of Norwich, Broads and Breckland. Bus and train services close by.*
Bedrooms: 2 single, 1 double, 1 triple
Bathrooms: 2 public

**Bed & breakfast**

| per night: | £min | £max |
|---|---|---|
| Single | 18.00 | 22.00 |
| Double | 36.00 | 44.00 |

Parking for 4
Cards accepted: Diners

🛏👑♨🌢Ⓤ♨ⒾⓈ✂📺📺Ⅲ🅿∪ 🗂☀🚗

### Turret House

Listed

27 Middleton Street, Wymondham NR18 0AB
☎ (01953) 603462
Fax (01953) 603462
*Large Victorian house in centre of Wymondham within walking distance of shops, restaurants and historic abbey. Convenient for Norwich.*
Bedrooms: 1 double, 1 twin
Bathrooms: 1 public

**Bed & breakfast**

| per night: | £min | £max |
|---|---|---|
| Single | 13.50 | 13.50 |
| Double | 27.00 | 27.00 |

Parking for 2
Cards accepted: Visa

🛏👑🍴🔥♨Ⓤ✂Ⅲ✕🚗

### Willow Farm

Listed COMMENDED

Wattlefield, Wymondham NR18 9PA
☎ (01953) 604679

*Comfortable farmhouse offering high standard of hospitality in relaxed atmosphere. Two miles south down B1135 from Wymondham fork right. Willow Farm three quarters of a mile on the left.*
Bedrooms: 1 single, 1 double, 1 twin
Bathrooms: 2 public

**Bed & breakfast**

| per night: | £min | £max |
|---|---|---|
| Single | 16.00 | 16.00 |
| Double | 32.00 | 32.00 |

Parking for 3

🛏👑♨🔥Ⓤ🅹📺Ⅲ🖨☀🚗

Without doubt, the West Country can claim to be England's most popular holiday playground, especially for those in search of the sea. The vast coastline offers some of the best scenery in the country. Golden sands, rugged cliffs, sheltered coves, friendly resorts, picturesque fishing villages and fascinating off-shore islands all combine to form a magnetic attraction. Add the Exmoor and Dartmoor national parks, the historic cities and towns you'll find inland, the literary connections of Thomas Hardy and Sir Arthur Conan Doyle and so much more – the West Country has something for everyone.

# WEST COUNTRY

The Counties of Avon, Cornwall, Devon, Dorset (western), Somerset, Wiltshire and the Isles of Scilly

For more information on the West Country, contact:
West Country Tourist Board
60 St David's Hill
Exeter EX4 4SY
Tel: (01392) 76351
Fax: (01392) 420891

Where to Go in the West Country
– see pages 252–256

Where to Stay in the West Country
– see pages 257–311

# WHERE TO GO

*You will find hundreds of interesting places to visit during your stay in the West Country, just some of which are listed in these pages. The number against each name will help you locate it on the map (pages 254–255). Contact any Tourist Information Centre in the region for more ideas on days out in the West Country.*

**❶ Oldown**
Tockington, Avon BS12 4PG
Tel: (01454) 413605
*Victorian estate with walled kitchen garden, gardens, farm, woodland, park and Iron Age fort. Forest adventure area with scramble nets, climbing frames and Burma bridges.*

**❷ Great Western Railway Museum**
Faringdon Road, Swindon, Wiltshire SN1 5BJ
Tel: (01793) 493189
*Historic Great Western Railway locomotives and wide range of models, nameplates, tickets, posters and illustrations.*

**❸ The Exploratory Hands-on Science Centre**
Bristol Old Station, Temple Gate, Bristol BS1 6QU
Tel: (0117) 925 2008

**A wide variety of fine fish is brought home by the Cornish fishermen...**

*Exhibition of lights, lenses, lasers, bubbles, bridges, illusions, gyroscopes and much more, all housed in Brunel's original engine shed and drawing office.*

**❹ Bowood House and Gardens**
Bowood Estate, Calne, Wiltshire SN11 0LZ
Tel: (01249) 812102
*18th C house by Robert Adam. Collections of paintings, watercolours, Victoriana, Indiana and porcelain. Landscaped park with lake, terraces, waterfall, grottos.*

**❺ Avebury Museum**
Avebury, Nr Marlborough, Wiltshire SN8 1RF
Tel: (016723) 250
*Founded by Alexander Keiller in 1930s and containing one of the most important prehistoric archaeological collections in Britain. Remains from Avebury area.*

**❻ Fox Talbot Museum of Photography**
Lacock, Wiltshire SN15 2LG
Tel: (01249) 730459
*Displays of apparatus and photographs related to Fox Talbot. Gallery with seasonal exhibitions.*

**❼ Roman Baths Museum**
Pump Room, Abbey Church Yard, Bath BA1 1LZ
Tel: (01225) 461111
*Roman baths and temple precinct, hot springs and Roman monuments. Jewellery, coins, curses and votive offerings from the sacred spring.*

**❽ Court Farm Country Park**
Wolverhill Road, Banwell, Avon BS24 6DL
Tel: (01934) 822383
*Working dairy farm with farming museum, cider house, traditional livestock and rare breeds, race and shire horse stud, conservation lakes and play area.*

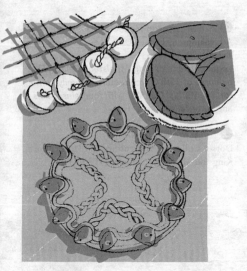

*...and some fish end up in the quaintly-named Stargazy Pie.*

**⑨ Cheddar Showcaves**
Cheddar Gorge, Somerset BS27 3QF
Tel: (01934) 742343
*Beautiful caves located in Cheddar Gorge. Gough's Cave with cathedral-like caverns and Cox's Cave with stalagmites and stalactites. Also "The Crystal Quest" fantasy adventure.*

**⑩ Rode Bird Gardens**
Rode, Somerset BA3 6QW
Tel: (01373) 830326
*Hundreds of exotic birds in lovely natural surroundings. 17 acres of woodland, gardens and lakes with children's play areas, pets' corner, miniature steam railway, clematis collection.*

**⑪ Wookey Hole Caves and Papermill**
Wookey Hole, Wells, Somerset BA5 1BB
Tel: (01749) 672243
*Spectacular caves and legendary home of the Witch of Wookey. Working Victorian papermill, with fairground memories, old penny arcade, magical mirror maze and cave diving museum.*

**⑫ Longleat House**
Warminster, Wiltshire BA12 7NN
Tel: (01985) 844400
*Great Elizabethan house with "lived-in" atmosphere – members of the family about daily. Important libraries and Italian ceilings. Safari park.*

**⑬ Stourhead House and Gardens**
Stourton, Wiltshire BA12 6QH
Tel: (01747) 840348
*Landscaped garden laid out 1741–80, with lakes and temples, rare trees and plants. House begun in 1721 contains fine paintings and Chippendale furniture.*

**⑭ Wilton House**
Wilton, Wiltshire SP2 0BJ
Tel: (01722) 743115
*Home of the Earls of Pembroke for almost 450 years. Famous Double and Single Cube rooms, renowned art collection. Adventure playground, woodland walk.*

**⑮ Salisbury and South Wiltshire Museum**
The King's House, 65 The Close, Salisbury, Wiltshire SP1 2EN
Tel: (01722) 332151
*Grade I listed building. Stonehenge collection, the Salisbury Giant and early man. History of Old Sarum, Salisbury, Romans to Saxons, ceramics, Wedgwood, picture and costume exhibitions.*

**⑯ Fleet Air Arm Museum**
Royal Naval Air Station, Yeovilton, Somerset BA22 8HT
Tel: (01935) 840565
*46 historic naval aircraft, displays, models, uniforms and other artefacts. Exhibitions on Concorde, Kamikaze, The Wrens, Harrier Jump Jet, Korea and World Wars I and II.*

**⑰ The Big Sheep**
Abbotsham, Devon EX39 5AP
Tel: (01237) 472366
*Award-winning all-weather attraction combining sheep racing, sheepdog trials, sheep milking, baby lambs and duck trialling. Adventure playground, lake and nature trail.*

**⑱ Rosemoor Garden – Royal Horticultural Society**
Rosemoor, Torrington, Devon EX38 8PH
Tel: (01805) 24067
*Garden of rare horticultural interest. Trees, shrubs, roses, alpines and arboretum. Nursery of rare plants. Garden is being expanded from 8 to 40 acres.*

**⑲ Killerton House**
Broadclyst, Nr Exeter, Devon EX5 3LE

Tel: (01392) 881345
18th C house built for the Acland family, now
housing collection of costumes shown in various
room settings. 15 acres of hillside garden with
rare trees and shrubs.

**20 *Parnham***
Beaminster, Dorset DT8 3NA
Tel: (01308) 862204
Tudor manor house with additions and
embellishments by John Nash in 1810. Home of
John Makepeace and his famous furniture-
making workshops. 14 acres of gardens.

**21 *Athelhampton House and Gardens***
Athelhampton, Dorset DT2 7LG
Tel: (01305) 848363
Legendary site of King Athelstan's Palace. Fine
example of 15th C architecture, a family home
for 5 centuries. Gardens with fountains, pools
and waterfalls.

**22 *Kingston Maurward Park***
Dorset College of Agriculture and Horticulture,
Kingston Maurward, Dorset DT2 9PY

0 ─── 20 Miles
0 ─── 30 Kms

Isles of Scilly
St Mary's

Combe Martin
Lynton
Minehead
Woolacombe
Ilfracombe
Williton
Braunton
Barnstaple
Abbotsham **17**
Bideford
South Molton
Torrington **18**
Sampford Peverell
Bude
Holsworthy
Tiverton
Crediton
Broadclyst
**Devon**
Exeter **19**
Tintagel
Launceston
Budleigh Salterton
Camelford
Bovey Tracey
Exmouth
Padstow
**Cornwall**
Teignmouth Dawlish
Wadebridge
Dobwalls
Tavistock
Newton Abbot
Babbacombe
Ashburton
Newquay
Lostwithiel
Liskeard **28**
Buckfastleigh **27**
Torquay **26**
Saltash
Totnes
Paignton
Carthew **29**
St Blazey
Plymouth
Brixham
St Austell
Fowey
Dartmouth
Redruth
Truro
Kingsbridge
St Ives **30**
Camborne
Salcombe
Hayle
Penzance **31** Marazion
Falmouth
Land's End

Tel: (01305) 264738
*Farm animal park, formal gardens, nature trail, walled garden, lake and walks.*

### 23 The Dinosaur Museum
Icen Way, Dorchester, Dorset DT1 1EW
Tel: (01305) 269880
*Only museum in Britain devoted exclusively to dinosaurs. Fossils, full-size dinosaur reconstructions plus audio-visual, "hands-on" and computerised displays and video gallery.*

### 24 Abbotsbury Sub-Tropical Gardens
Abbotsbury, Dorset
Tel: (01305) 871387
*Exotic trees, shrubs and herbaceous plants in 20 acres – an English Heritage Grade I garden.*

### 25 Weymouth Sea Life Park
Lodmoor Country Park, Weymouth, Dorset DT4 7SX
Tel: (01305) 761070
*Spectacular displays of British marine life where*

visitors come face to face with a wide variety of creatures. Also tropical jungle full of birds.

**26** *Model Village*
Hampton Avenue, Babbacombe, Devon TQ1 3LA
Tel: (01803) 328669
*Hundreds of models and figures to 1/12th scale, laid out in 4 acres of beautiful gardens to represent a model English countryside with modern town, villages and rural areas.*

**27** *Buckfast Abbey*
Buckfastleigh, Devon TQ11 0EE
Tel: (01364) 642519
*Large Benedictine monastery rebuilt on medieval foundations. Many art treasures in the abbey church, exhibition and audio-visual show. Attractive gardens.*

**28** *Dobwalls Family Adventure Park*
Dobwalls, Nr Liskeard, Cornwall PL14 6HD
Tel: (01579) 20325
*Two miles of scenically dramatic miniature railway based on the American railroad scene. Edwardian countryside exhibition. Children's Adventureland.*

**29** *Wheal Martyn China Clay Heritage Centre*
Carthew, St Austell, Cornwall PL26 8XG
Tel: (01726) 850362
*Restored 19th C clay works with working water wheels, static steam locomotives and fully restored 1916 Peerless lorry. Nature trail, children's adventure trail.*

**30** *Tate Gallery St Ives*
Porthmeor Beach, St Ives, Cornwall TR26 1TG
Tel: (01736) 796226
*A major new gallery showing changing groups of work from the Tate Gallery's pre-eminent collection of St Ives painting and sculpture. Extensive education programme.*

**The splendid new Tate Gallery, overlooking the bay at St Ives.**

**31** *St Michael's Mount*
Marazion, Cornwall TR17 0HT
Tel: (01736) 710507
*Originally the site of a Benedictine chapel, the castle on its rock dates from the 14th C. Fine views towards Land's End and the Lizard.*

# FIND OUT MORE

*Further information about holidays and attractions in the West Country is available from:*
**West Country Tourist Board**, 60 St David's Hill, Exeter EX4 4SY
Tel: (01392) 76351

*These publications are available free from the West Country Tourist Board:*
- **England's West Country – Holidays '95**
- **Bed and Breakfast Touring Map for the West Country '95**
- **West Country Inspected Holiday Homes '95**
- **Activity and Leisure Holidays '95**
- **West Country Short Breaks '94/'95**
- **Commended Hotels and Guesthouses '95**
*Also available is:*
- **Places to Visit £1.95**

WEST COUNTRY

# WHERE TO STAY

*Accommodation entries in this regional section are listed in alphabetical order of place name, and then in alphabetical order of establishment.*

*Map references refer to the colour location maps at the back of this guide. The first figure is the map number; the letter and figure which follow indicate the grid reference on the map.*

*Symbols at the end of each accommodation entry give information about services and facilities. A 'key' to these symbols is inside the back cover flap, which can be kept open for easy reference.*

---

## ABBOTSBURY

Dorset
Map ref 2A3

Beautiful village near Chesil Beach, with a long main street of mellow stone and thatched cottages and the ruins of a Benedictine monastery. High above the village on a hill is a prominent 15th C chapel. Abbotsbury's famous swannery and sub-tropical gardens lie just outside the village.

### Linton Cottage
`Listed` `COMMENDED`
Abbotsbury, Weymouth DT3 4JL
☎ (01305) 871339
*Victorian cottage in picturesque setting. Our own honey on the breakfast table, and dinners just that extra bit special.*
Bedrooms: 2 double, 1 twin
Bathrooms: 1 private, 1 public

**Bed & breakfast**

| per night: | £min | £max |
|---|---|---|
| Single | 27.50 | 32.00 |
| Double | 35.00 | 38.00 |

**Half board**

| per person: | £min | £max |
|---|---|---|
| Daily | 27.50 | 29.00 |
| Weekly | 170.00 | 185.00 |

Evening meal from 1830
Parking for 4
🛇🍴♨ⓤⓢ⅊⊁ⓉⅤ🖩🛏❀✕🚗

### Swan Lodge ♠♠
♛♛
Rodden Row, Abbotsbury, Weymouth DT3 4JL
☎ (01305) 871249
*Situated on the B3157 coastal road between Weymouth and Bridport. Swan*

---

*Inn public house opposite, where food is served all day, is under the same ownership.*
Bedrooms: 2 double, 2 twin, 1 triple
Bathrooms: 2 private, 1 public

**Bed & breakfast**

| per night: | £min | £max |
|---|---|---|
| Single | 28.00 | 35.00 |
| Double | 40.00 | 50.00 |

Lunch available
Evening meal 1800 (last orders 2200)
Parking for 10
Cards accepted: Access, Visa
🛇🍴♨ⓤⓢ⅊⊁ⓉⅤ🖩🛏📶20-80🍷 Ͻ❀🚗OAP✣SP

---

## ALLERFORD

Somerset
Map ref 1D1

Village with picturesque stone and thatch cottages and a packhorse bridge, set in the beautiful Vale of Porlock.

### Fern Cottage ♠♠
♛♛♛ `COMMENDED`
Allerford, Minehead TA24 8HN
☎ Porlock (01643) 862215

*Large 16th C traditional Exmoor cottage in National Trust wooded vale. Dramatic scenery and wildlife. Fine classic cooking and comprehensive wine list.*
Bedrooms: 3 double, 1 twin

---

Bathrooms: 4 private

**Bed & breakfast**

| per night: | £min | £max |
|---|---|---|
| Single | 27.50 | 28.50 |
| Double | 48.00 | 50.00 |

**Half board**

| per person: | £min | £max |
|---|---|---|
| Daily | 34.75 | 36.25 |
| Weekly | 218.90 | 228.40 |

Evening meal 1900 (last orders 1800)
Parking for 7
Cards accepted: Access, Visa, Switch/ Delta
🛇🍴♨ⓢ⅊⊁ⓉⅤ🖩🛏⊙♇🚗✣SP Ⓣ

---

## AMESBURY

Wiltshire
Map ref 2B2

Standing on the banks of the River Avon, this is the nearest town to Stonehenge on Salisbury Plain. The area is rich in prehistoric sites.
*Tourist Information Centre*
☎ (01980) 622833

### Church Cottage
`Listed` `HIGHLY COMMENDED`
Church Street, Amesbury, Salisbury SP4 7EY
☎ (01980) 624650
*Period 18th C property with beams and antiques, only 2 miles from Stonehenge. Attractive patio and gardens, lovely bedrooms, delicious English breakfast. Evening meal available.*
Bedrooms: 3 double
Bathrooms: 3 private

Continued ▶

## AMESBURY

*Continued*

**Bed & breakfast**

| per night: | £min | £max |
| --- | --- | --- |
| Single | 22.00 | 27.00 |
| Double | 30.00 | 38.00 |

Evening meal 1900 (last orders 2030)

🛳10 🖭▢ ♦ ♉ ⓤ 🅸 Ⓢ ⽊ 🏛 🖧 🌣 ✕ 🚗 SP 🏠 Ⓣ

### Ratfyn Barrow House

`Listed`

Ratfyn Road, Amesbury, Salisbury
SP4 7DZ
☎ Shrewton (01980) 623422

*Comfortable accommodation in pleasant
surroundings off main road. Site of an
ancient barrow, a listed monument.*
Bedrooms: 1 double, 2 twin
Bathrooms: 1 private, 1 public

**Bed & breakfast**

| per night: | £min | £max |
| --- | --- | --- |
| Single | 18.00 | 18.00 |
| Double | 28.00 | 30.00 |

Parking for 4
Open April-October

🛳5▢♦♉ⓤ⽊🏛🖧🌣🚗

## ASHBRITTLE

Somerset
Map ref 1D1

### Lower Westcott Farm

👑👑

Ashbrittle, Wellington TA21 0HZ
☎ Clayhanger (01398) 6296
*220-acre mixed farm. On
Devon/Somerset borders in peaceful,
scenic countryside. Ideal for touring
Exmoor, Quantocks, coast. Noted for
comfort, homeliness and farmhouse
cooking. All rooms have spectacular
views across valley.*
Bedrooms: 2 triple
Bathrooms: 1 private, 1 public

**Bed & breakfast**

| per night: | £min | £max |
| --- | --- | --- |
| Single | 14.00 | 17.00 |
| Double | 28.00 | 34.00 |

**Half board**

| per person: | £min | £max |
| --- | --- | --- |
| Daily | 20.00 | 24.00 |
| Weekly | 130.00 | 150.00 |

Evening meal 1830 (last orders 1700)
Parking for 4

🛳♦♉ⓤ🅸Ⓢ🎿📺🖧🌣U✓✿
✕🚗

## ASHBURTON

Devon
Map ref 1C2

Formerly a thriving wool centre
and important as one of
Dartmoor's four stannary towns.
Today's busy market town has
many period buildings. Ancient
tradition is maintained in the
annual ale-tasting and bread-
weighing ceremony. Good centre
for exploring Dartmoor or the
south Devon coast.

### New Cott Farm

👑👑 `COMMENDED`

Poundsgate, Newton Abbot TQ13 7PD
☎ Poundsgate (01364) 3421
Fax (01364) 3421
*130-acre mixed farm. Friendly welcome,
pleasing accommodation, beautiful
views. Ideal area for walking or just
enjoying Dartmoor. Lots of lovely home-
made food.*
Bedrooms: 2 double, 1 twin, 1 triple
Bathrooms: 4 private

**Bed & breakfast**

| per night: | £min | £max |
| --- | --- | --- |
| Double | 33.00 | 34.00 |

**Half board**

| per person: | £min | £max |
| --- | --- | --- |
| Daily | 26.00 | 27.00 |
| Weekly | 160.00 | |

Evening meal 1830 (last orders 1600)
Parking for 4

🛳♦🖭▢♦♉ⓤ🅸Ⓢ🎿📺🖧🖧🖧🚗U
🖊✓✿✕🚗↺

### Wellpritton Farm

👑👑 `HIGHLY COMMENDED`

Holne, Newton Abbot TQ13 7RX
☎ Poundsgate (01364) 3273
*15-acre mixed farm. Plenty of
mouthwatering farm-produced food in a
tastefully modernised farmhouse on the
edge of Dartmoor. Special diets catered
for by arrangement. A warm welcome
and caring personal attention.*
Bedrooms: 2 double, 2 twin
Bathrooms: 3 private, 1 public

**Bed & breakfast**

| per night: | £min | £max |
| --- | --- | --- |
| Single | 17.00 | 18.00 |
| Double | 34.00 | 36.00 |

**Half board**

| per person: | £min | £max |
| --- | --- | --- |
| Daily | 25.00 | 26.00 |
| Weekly | 154.00 | 154.00 |

Evening meal from 1900
Parking for 4

🛳♦🖭▢♦♉ⓤ🅸Ⓢ🎿📺🖧🖧🖧🚗
✕🚗

---

Map references apply
to the colour maps at the
back of this guide.

## ASHTON KEYNES

Wiltshire
Map ref 2B2

Village beside the River Thames,
with houses standing along the
edge of the stream reached by
bridges from the road on the
opposite bank. Nearby stands the
manor, Ashton House.

### Corner Cottage

👑👑 `APPROVED`

Fore Street, Ashton Keynes, Swindon
SN6 6NP
☎ Cirencester (01285) 861454
*Homely 17th C Cotswold stone cottage
in centre of best kept village within the
Cotswold Water Park. Ideal for water
sports and touring Cotswolds.*
Bedrooms: 1 double, 1 family room
Bathrooms: 2 private

**Bed & breakfast**

| per night: | £min | £max |
| --- | --- | --- |
| Single | 20.00 | 22.00 |
| Double | 35.00 | 38.00 |

Parking for 4

🛳♦♉ⓤ🅸Ⓢ🎿📺🖧🌣✕🚗

## AVEBURY

Wiltshire
Map ref 2B2

Set in a landscape of earthworks
and megalithic standing stones,
Avebury has a fine church and an
Elizabethan manor. Remains from
excavations may be seen in the
museum. The area abounds in
important prehistoric sites, among
them Silbury Hill. Stonehenge
stands about 20 miles due south.

### New Inn

`Listed` `APPROVED`

Winterbourne Monkton, Swindon
SN4 9NW
☎ (01672) 539240
*Small and friendly country pub only 1
mile from Avebury. Good, central
touring position.*
Bedrooms: 2 double, 3 twin
Bathrooms: 5 private

**Bed & breakfast**

| per night: | £min | £max |
| --- | --- | --- |
| Double | 33.00 | 37.00 |

Lunch available
Evening meal 1830 (last orders 2130)
Parking for 20

🛳♦▢♦🅸Ⓢ🖧🖧🚗🔔✕🚗

---

All accommodation in this
guide has been inspected,
or is awaiting inspection,
under the national Crown
scheme.

## BANTHAM

Devon
Map ref 1C3

Village at the mouth of the River Avon, with a fine sandy beach.

### Sloop Inn ⚔

🏆🏆 **COMMENDED**

Bantham, Kingsbridge TQ7 3AJ
☎ Kingsbridge (01548) 560489 &
5560215
Fax (01548) 560489
*Part 16th C inn in old world fishing
village. Some rooms overlook sea and
estuary. Menu majors on local seafood.
Featured in pub guides.*
Bedrooms: 3 double, 2 triple
Bathrooms: 5 private

| Bed & breakfast per night: | £min | £max |
|---|---|---|
| Double | 52.00 | 54.00 |

| Half board per person: | £min | £max |
|---|---|---|
| Daily | 40.00 | 44.00 |
| Weekly | 280.00 | 290.00 |

Lunch available
Evening meal 1900 (last orders 2200)
Parking for 35

🛏🍽🛜🕮📶🛢🚪🏧 OAP SP

## BARNSTAPLE

Devon
Map ref 1C1

At the head of the Taw Estuary, once a ship-building and textile town, now an agricultural centre with attractive period buildings, a modern civic centre and leisure centre. Attractions include Queen Anne's Walk, a charming colonnaded arcade and Pannier Market.
*Tourist Information Centre
☎ (01271) 388583*

### The Cedars Lodge Inn

🏆🏆🏆 **COMMENDED**

Bickington Road, Barnstaple
EX31 2HP
☎ (01271) 71784
Fax (01271) 25733
*Country house with lodges in 3 acres.
All en-suite, satellite TV. Pub and
restaurant. Just off North Devon link
road.*
Bedrooms: 9 double, 8 twin, 6 family rooms
Bathrooms: 23 private

| Bed & breakfast per night: | £min | £max |
|---|---|---|
| Single | 32.00 | 37.00 |
| Double | 43.00 | 53.00 |

| Half board per person: | £min | £max |
|---|---|---|
| Daily | 42.00 | |
| Weekly | 290.00 | |

Lunch available
Evening meal 1830 (last orders 2200)

Parking for 100
Cards accepted: Access, Visa, Amex

🛏🍽🕮🛒🏧🛜🛢🍴📶🛜
🍴2-150 🎯❄🚲 SP

### Home Park Farm Accommodation

🏆🏆 **COMMENDED**

Lower Blakewell, Muddiford,
Barnstaple EX31 4ET
☎ (01271) 42955

*70-acre livestock farm. Come and share
our beautiful corner of north Devon and
sample our Devonshire hospitality.
Paradise for the garden lover. Take A39
Lynton road from Barnstaple, fork left
B3230, second left and continue to end
of road. SAE for brochure.*
Bedrooms: 1 double, 1 triple, 1 family room
Bathrooms: 3 private

| Bed & breakfast per night: | £min | £max |
|---|---|---|
| Single | 15.00 | 18.50 |
| Double | 30.00 | 35.00 |

| Half board per person: | £min | £max |
|---|---|---|
| Daily | 22.50 | 25.00 |
| Weekly | 135.00 | 150.00 |

Lunch available
Evening meal 1800 (last orders 1800)
Parking for 4

🛏5🍽🛒🕮🛜🛢🍴📶🛜🛢
❄🚲 OAP SP 🍴

### The Red House

🏆 **HIGHLY COMMENDED**

Brynsworthy, Roundswell, Barnstaple
EX31 3NP
☎ (01271) 45966
*Country house, panoramic views. All
rooms colour TV, shower, hairdryer,
tea/coffee facilities, central heating.
Good pub food near.*
Bedrooms: 1 double, 1 twin
Bathrooms: 1 public, 2 private showers

| Bed & breakfast per night: | £min | £max |
|---|---|---|
| Single | 17.00 | 18.00 |
| Double | 30.00 | 34.00 |

Parking for 7

🛏12🍽🛒🛜📶🍴📶❄🍴🚲

### The Spinney

🏆 **COMMENDED**

Shirwell, Barnstaple EX31 4JR
☎ Shirwell (01271) 850282
*Regency former rectory with spacious
accommodation, set in over an acre of
grounds with views of Exmoor. Meals
made from local market-day produce.*

Bedrooms: 1 single, 1 double, 1 twin, 2 triple
Bathrooms: 1 private, 2 public

| Bed & breakfast per night | £min | £max |
|---|---|---|
| Single | 16.00 | 19.00 |
| Double | 32.00 | 38.00 |

| Half board per person | £min | £max |
|---|---|---|
| Daily | 23.00 | 26.00 |
| Weekly | 132.00 | 150.00 |

Evening meal 1900 (last orders 1700)
Parking for 7

🛏🛢🕮🛜📺📶🛢❄🚲 SP 🍴

### Waytown Farm

🏆🏆 **COMMENDED**

Shirwell, Barnstaple EX31 4JN
☎ Shirwell (01271) 850396
*240-acre mixed farm. Pleasantly situated
17th C farmhouse, 3 miles from
Barnstaple. Exmoor and beaches within
easy reach. Home cooking, comfortable
accommodation. Access at all times.*
Bedrooms: 1 double, 1 twin, 1 triple
Bathrooms: 2 private, 1 public

| Bed & breakfast per night: | £min | £max |
|---|---|---|
| Single | 20.00 | 21.00 |
| Double | 36.00 | 38.00 |

| Half board per person: | £min | £max |
|---|---|---|
| Daily | 24.00 | 26.00 |
| Weekly | 150.00 | 160.00 |

Evening meal 1830 (last orders 1600)
Parking for 6
Open January-November

🛏🍽🛢🕮📺📶🛢🚲🍴❄✈
🚲🍴

## BATH

Avon
Map ref 2B2

Georgian spa city beside the River Avon. Important Roman site with impressive reconstructed baths, uncovered in 19th C. Bath Abbey built on site of monastery where first king of England was crowned (AD 973). Fine architecture in mellow local stone. Pump Room and museums.
*Tourist Information Centre
☎ (01225) 462831*

### Ashley Villa Hotel ⚔

🏆🏆🏆

26 Newbridge Road, Bath BA1 3JZ
☎ (01225) 421683 & 428887
Fax (01225) 313604
*Comfortably furnished licensed hotel
with relaxing informal atmosphere,
close to city centre. All rooms en-suite.
Swimming pool. Car park.*
Bedrooms: 2 single, 7 double, 2 twin, 3 triple
Bathrooms: 14 private

*Continued* ▶

## BATH

*Continued*

**Bed & breakfast**

| per night: | £min | £max |
|---|---|---|
| Single | 39.00 | 45.00 |
| Double | 49.00 | 59.00 |

Evening meal 1800 (last orders 2100)
Parking for 10
Cards accepted: Access, Visa, Amex, Switch/Delta

### Astor House
👑 COMMENDED

14 Oldfield Road, Bath BA2 3ND
☎ (01225) 429134
*Lovely Victorian house with comfortable, spacious rooms and large secluded garden. Peaceful, elegant atmosphere.*
Bedrooms: 1 double, 1 twin, 1 triple
Bathrooms: 3 private, 2 public

**Bed & breakfast**

| per night: | £min | £max |
|---|---|---|
| Single | 18.00 | 24.00 |
| Double | 36.00 | 46.00 |

Parking for 4
Open February–December

### Bloomfield House M
👑👑 HIGHLY COMMENDED

146 Bloomfield Road, Bath BA2 2AS
☎ (01225) 420105
Fax (01225) 481958
*Fine Regency country house with superb views over the city, offering antique furniture, silk curtains and a warm welcome.*
Bedrooms: 1 single, 5 double
Bathrooms: 6 private

**Bed & breakfast**

| per night: | £min | £max |
|---|---|---|
| Single | 35.00 | 45.00 |
| Double | 45.00 | 105.00 |

Parking for 9
Cards accepted: Access, Visa

### Cherry Tree Villa
👑

7 Newbridge Hill, Bath BA1 3PW
☎ (01225) 331671
*Modernised, tastefully decorated Victorian house with friendly atmosphere, within easy walking distance of city centre through pleasant park.*
Bedrooms: 1 single, 1 double, 1 triple
Bathrooms: 1 public

**Bed & breakfast**

| per night: | £min | £max |
|---|---|---|
| Single | 15.00 | 18.00 |
| Double | 30.00 | 36.00 |

Parking for 4

### Church Farm
👑👑

Monkton Farleigh, Bradford-on-Avon,
Wiltshire BA15 2QJ
☎ (01225) 858583 & Mobile 0374 277665
*52-acre mixed farm. Converted barn in Wiltshire countryside. Traditional facilities with guest lounge. Livery stables. 5 minutes to new 18-hole golf-course, 10 minutes to Bath.*
Bedrooms: 3 double
Bathrooms: 1 private, 1 public

**Bed & breakfast**

| per night: | £min | £max |
|---|---|---|
| Single | 20.00 | 22.50 |
| Double | 32.00 | 38.00 |

Parking for 5

### Dorset Villa
👑👑 APPROVED

14 Newbridge Road, Bath BA1 3JX
☎ (01225) 425975

*Victorian house half a mile from Royal Crescent. En-suite rooms available. TV and coffee/tea facilities in all rooms.*
Bedrooms: 5 double, 1 twin
Bathrooms: 5 private, 1 public, 1 private shower

**Bed & breakfast**

| per night: | £min | £max |
|---|---|---|
| Double | 42.00 | 52.00 |

Evening meal 1900 (last orders 2100)
Parking for 6
Cards accepted: Access, Visa

### Fern Cottage
👑👑 COMMENDED

74 Monkton Farleigh, Bradford-on-Avon, Wiltshire BA15 2QJ
☎ (01225) 859412
Fax (01225) 859412
*Delightful stone-built 17th C cottage, set in fine gardens in peaceful conservation village between Bath and Bradford-on-Avon. Well-appointed rooms.*
Bedrooms: 1 double, 1 twin, 1 triple
Bathrooms: 1 private, 1 public

**Bed & breakfast**

| per night: | £min | £max |
|---|---|---|
| Single | 25.00 | |
| Double | 40.00 | 45.00 |

Parking for 5

### Forres Guest House
👑

172 Newbridge Road, Lower Weston,
Bath BA1 3LE
☎ (01225) 427698

*Edwardian family guesthouse with helpful hosts, who are ex-teachers and love Bath. River Avon and Cotswold Way close by. Traditional and vegetarian breakfasts. Colour TV and beverages in all rooms.*
Bedrooms: 2 double, 2 twin, 1 triple
Bathrooms: 5 private

**Bed & breakfast**

| per night: | £min | £max |
|---|---|---|
| Single | 20.00 | 22.00 |
| Double | 30.00 | 40.00 |

Parking for 5
Open April–October

### Gainsborough Hotel M
👑👑👑

Weston Lane, Bath BA1 4AB
☎ (01225) 311380
Fax (01225) 447411

*Spacious and comfortable country house hotel in own lovely grounds near the botanical gardens, and within easy walking distance of the city centre. High ground, nice views, own large car park. 5-course breakfast, friendly staff, warm welcome.*
Bedrooms: 2 single, 8 double, 4 twin, 1 triple, 1 family room
Bathrooms: 16 private

**Bed & breakfast**

| per night: | £min | £max |
|---|---|---|
| Single | 31.00 | 41.00 |
| Double | 49.00 | 62.00 |

Evening meal 1900 (last orders 2000)
Parking for 18
Cards accepted: Access, Visa, Amex

### Georgian Guest House
Listed

34 Henrietta Street, Bath BA2 6LR
☎ (01225) 424103
Fax (01225) 859267
*Central Bath. Grade I listed Georgian town house, next to Henrietta Park and only 2 minutes' walk to town centre.*
Bedrooms: 3 double, 2 twin, 3 triple, 1 family room
Bathrooms: 2 private, 1 public, 7 private showers

**Bed & breakfast**

| per night: | £min | £max |
|---|---|---|
| Single | 18.00 | 25.00 |
| Double | 36.00 | 45.00 |

Cards accepted: Access, Visa, Amex

## Haute Combe House

👑👑👑

176 Newbridge Road, Bath BA1 3LE
☎ (01225) 420061
Fax (01225) 420061
*Fully-equipped en-suite rooms in comfortable, period surroundings. Easy access to city attractions. Special off-season rates. Telephone for brochure.*
Bedrooms: 2 single, 3 double, 3 twin, 3 triple
Bathrooms: 11 private

**Bed & breakfast**

| **per night:** | £min | £max |
|---|---|---|
| Single | 28.00 | 39.00 |
| Double | 38.00 | 50.00 |

Evening meal 1900 (last orders 1800)
Parking for 11
Cards accepted: Access, Visa, Amex
🐴 ♿ ☎ 📻 🖵 ☕ 🔌 🔒 [S] 🚭 🛋 [TV] [IIII] 🚗 🍸 🌞 🚌 [SP] [T]

## The Hollies

👑👑 [COMMENDED]

Hatfield Road, Wellsway, Bath BA2 2BD
☎ (01225) 313366

*Grade II early Victorian family house, 15 minutes walk to city centre, overlooking parish church and gardens. Pretty guestrooms, comfortably furnished. Sunny secluded garden.*
Bedrooms: 2 double, 1 twin
Bathrooms: 3 private

**Bed & breakfast**

| **per night:** | £min | £max |
|---|---|---|
| Single | 18.00 | 25.00 |
| Double | 36.00 | 50.00 |

Parking for 6
🐴 1 📻 🖵 ☕ [UL] 🔒 [S] 🚭 🛋 [IIII] 🚗 🌞 ✈ 🚌 [SP] 🏠

## Kennard Hotel 🅰

👑👑 [COMMENDED]

11 Henrietta Street, Bath BA2 6LL
☎ (01225) 310472
Fax (01225) 460054
*Converted Georgian house in quiet street. A few minutes' level walk to city centre, abbey, Roman Baths, Pump Room and Henrietta Park.*
Bedrooms: 2 single, 9 double, 1 twin, 1 family room
Bathrooms: 11 private, 1 public

**Bed & breakfast**

| **per night:** | £min | £max |
|---|---|---|
| Single | 30.00 | 34.00 |
| Double | 48.00 | 58.00 |

Cards accepted: Access, Visa, Diners, Amex, Switch/Delta
♿ ☎ 📻 🖵 ☕ [UL] 🛋 [IIII] 🚗 🌞 ✈ 🚌 [SP] 🏠 [T]

## Kinlet Villa Guest House

👑 [COMMENDED]

99 Wellsway, Bath BA2 4RX
☎ (01225) 420268
*Edwardian villa retaining original features and furnishings. Walking distance from city centre, good bus service, unrestricted parking. Non-smokers only, please.*
Bedrooms: 1 double, 1 triple
Bathrooms: 1 public

**Bed & breakfast**

| **per night:** | £min | £max |
|---|---|---|
| Double | 30.00 | 34.00 |

🐴 🖵 ☕ [UL] [S] 🚭 🛋 [TV] [IIII] 🚗 ✈ 🚌 [SP]

## Lamp Post Villa

👑👑 [APPROVED]

3 Crescent Gardens, Upper Bristol Road, Bath BA1 2NB
☎ (01225) 331221
Fax (01225) 426783
*Semi-detached bay windowed property of Edwardian period, still maintaining many original features.*
Bedrooms: 3 single, 2 double, 1 twin, 1 family room
Bathrooms: 4 private, 1 public

**Bed & breakfast**

| **per night:** | £min | £max |
|---|---|---|
| Double | 45.00 | 55.00 |

Parking for 5
Cards accepted: Access, Visa, Diners, Amex
🐴 ♿ ☎ 📻 🖵 ☕ 🔌 [UL] 🚭 🛋 [TV] [IIII] 🚗 🚌

## Marlborough House

👑👑

1 Marlborough Lane, Bath BA1 2NQ
☎ (01225) 318175 & 466127
*Recently renovated Victorian house 5 minutes' level walk from city centre and 2 minutes from Royal Crescent. Light and airy rooms, four-poster. Non-smoking, private parking. 10% discount for 3 nights or more.*
Bedrooms: 2 single, 3 double
Bathrooms: 1 private, 1 public, 2 private showers

**Bed & breakfast**

| **per night:** | £min | £max |
|---|---|---|
| Single | 20.00 | 25.00 |
| Double | 38.00 | 50.00 |

Parking for 3
Cards accepted: Access, Visa, Amex
🐴 🛏 📻 🖵 ☕ 🔌 [UL] [S] 🚭 🛋 [TV] [IIII] 🚗 ✈ 🚌 🎺 [SP]

## Meadowland

👑👑 [HIGHLY COMMENDED]

36 Bloomfield Park, Bath BA2 2BX
☎ (01225) 311079
*Set in its own quiet secluded grounds and offering the highest standards in beautifully appointed en-suite accommodation. Private parking, lovely gardens. Non-smokers only, please. A peaceful retreat for the discerning traveller.*
Bedrooms: 2 double, 1 twin
Bathrooms: 3 private

**Bed & breakfast**

| **per night:** | £min | £max |
|---|---|---|
| Single | 35.00 | 40.00 |
| Double | 48.00 | 58.00 |

Parking for 6
Cards accepted: Access, Visa
🐴 3 📻 🖵 ☕ 🔌 [UL] [S] 🚭 🛋 [TV] [IIII] 🚗 U ⛳ 🌞 ✈ 🚌 [SP]

## Membland Guest House

[Listed]

7 Pulteney Terrace, Pulteney Road, Bath BA2 4HJ
☎ (01225) 336712
*5 minutes' walk to Roman baths, abbey, train/coach stations, city shops, tranquil canalside. Private parking, comfortable rooms and generous breakfast.*
Bedrooms: 1 twin, 1 triple
Bathrooms: 1 public, 1 private shower

**Bed & breakfast**

| **per night:** | £min | £max |
|---|---|---|
| Single | 22.00 | 33.00 |
| Double | 27.00 | 37.00 |

Parking for 2
Open February-December
🐴 🖵 ☕ [UL] 🔒 [S] [IIII] 🚗 🚌 [OAP] [SP] [T]

## Oakleigh House 🅰

👑👑 [COMMENDED]

19 Upper Oldfield Park, Bath BA2 3JX
☎ (01225) 315698
Fax (01225) 448223
*Quietly situated Victorian home only 10 minutes from city centre. All rooms en-suite with colour TV, tea/coffee making facilities, etc. Private car park.*
Bedrooms: 3 double, 1 twin
Bathrooms: 4 private

**Bed & breakfast**

| **per night:** | £min | £max |
|---|---|---|
| Single | 35.00 | 45.00 |
| Double | 45.00 | 60.00 |

Parking for 4
Cards accepted: Access, Visa
📻 🖵 ☕ 🔌 [UL] [S] 🚭 🛋 [IIII] 🚗 ✈ 🚌 [OAP] [SP]

## The Old School House 🅰

👑👑👑 [HIGHLY COMMENDED]

Church Street, Bathford, Bath BA1 7RR
☎ (01225) 859593
Fax (01225) 859590

*Pretty Victorian schoolhouse of Bath stone in peaceful conservation area overlooking Avon Valley. 3 miles to Bath centre. Country house ambience with candlelit dinners and winter log fires. Ground floor en-suite rooms. Licensed, non-smoking.*
Bedrooms: 3 double, 1 twin
Bathrooms: 4 private

*Continued* ►

## BATH
*Continued*

**Bed & breakfast**

| per night: | £min | £max |
|---|---|---|
| Single | 45.00 | 45.00 |
| Double | 60.00 | 75.00 |

**Half board**

| per person: | £min | £max |
|---|---|---|
| Daily | 49.50 | 64.50 |
| Weekly | 335.00 | 435.00 |

Evening meal 1900 (last orders 2000)
Parking for 6
Cards accepted: Access, Visa

### Orchard House
COMMENDED
24 Box Road, Bathford, Bath BA1 7QD
☎ (01225) 859072
*Small family-run guesthouse on A4 Chippenham road. Quiet, rural location, on bus route 3 miles from city centre. Ideal for walking the Avon Canal and Cotswold Way. Non-smoking.*
Bedrooms: 1 double, 1 twin, 1 triple
Bathrooms: 2 private, 1 public

**Bed & breakfast**

| per night: | £min | £max |
|---|---|---|
| Single | 20.00 | 22.00 |
| Double | 32.00 | 40.00 |

Parking for 4

### Poplar Farm ᴁ
Listed COMMENDED
Stanton Prior, Bath BA2 9HX
☎ Mendip (01761) 470382

*350-acre mixed farm. 17th C farmhouse, 5 miles west of Bath and within easy reach of park-and-ride for Bristol and Bath. Idyllic village beneath Iron Age fort. Good walks, peace and quiet. What more?*
Bedrooms: 1 double, 1 twin, 1 family room
Bathrooms: 3 private, 2 public

**Bed & breakfast**

| per night: | £min | £max |
|---|---|---|
| Single | 15.00 | 20.00 |
| Double | 30.00 | 40.00 |

Parking for 8

### The Priory Wing
54 Lyncombe Hill, Bath BA2 4PJ
☎ (01225) 336395

*Peaceful Georgian listed building bordering meadowland yet only 10 minutes' walk from city centre and railway/bus stations. Original fireplaces. One bedroom adjoins flagstone, panelled, entrance hall. Non-smokers only please.*
Bedrooms: 1 double, 1 twin
Bathrooms: 2 private

**Bed & breakfast**

| per night: | £min | £max |
|---|---|---|
| Single | 20.00 | 20.00 |
| Double | 40.00 | 40.00 |

Parking for 2

### Hotel Saint Clair
COMMENDED
1 Crescent Gardens, Upper Bristol Road, Bath BA1 2NA
☎ (01225) 425543
Fax (01225) 425543
*Small family hotel 5 minutes' walk from city, 2 minutes from Royal Crescent. Large public car park 1 minute away. One night stays welcome.*
Bedrooms: 5 double, 2 twin, 2 triple, 1 family room
Bathrooms: 7 private, 1 public

**Bed & breakfast**

| per night: | £min | £max |
|---|---|---|
| Single | 22.00 | 28.00 |
| Double | 34.00 | 44.00 |

Cards accepted: Access, Visa, Amex

### Sampford
11 Oldfield Road, Bath BA2 3ND
☎ (01225) 310053
*In a quiet residential area half a mile south of city centre off the A367 Exeter road.*
Bedrooms: 1 double, 1 twin, 1 triple
Bathrooms: 1 public, 3 private showers

**Bed & breakfast**

| per night: | £min | £max |
|---|---|---|
| Single | 15.00 | 15.00 |
| Double | 30.00 | 30.00 |

Parking for 2

### Seven Springs
Listed APPROVED
4 High Street, Woolley, Bath BA1 8AR
☎ (01225) 858001
*In small country hamlet of Woolley, 3 miles from Bath city centre and 4 miles from M4. Lovely walks on public footpaths. Ideal for touring West Country. Bedrooms can be let as twins, doubles or family rooms. Payphone available.*
Bedrooms: 2 family rooms
Bathrooms: 2 private

**Bed & breakfast**

| per night: | £min | £max |
|---|---|---|
| Double | 32.00 | 40.00 |

Parking for 8

### Sheridan
95 Wellsway, Bearflat, Bath BA2 4RU
☎ (01225) 429562
*Quiet, comfortable family guesthouse. A few minutes' drive from city centre and on main bus route to city and railway station. A non-smoking house.*
Bedrooms: 1 single, 1 twin, 1 triple
Bathrooms: 2 public

**Bed & breakfast**

| per night: | £min | £max |
|---|---|---|
| Single | 16.00 | 18.00 |
| Double | 32.00 | 34.00 |

### Wansdyke Cottage
Listed COMMENDED
Marksbury Gate, Bath BA2 9HE
☎ (01225) 873674

*Cottage-style accommodation including self-contained suite of bedroom, bathroom, kitchen and lounge. 5 miles west of Bath on A39.*
Bedrooms: 1 single, 2 double, 1 twin
Bathrooms: 1 private, 2 public

**Bed & breakfast**

| per night: | £min | £max |
|---|---|---|
| Single | 14.00 | 18.00 |
| Double | 28.00 | 35.00 |

**Half board**

| per person: | £min | £max |
|---|---|---|
| Daily | 21.00 | 25.00 |
| Weekly | 147.00 | 175.00 |

Evening meal 1900 (last orders 1700)
Parking for 4

### Wellsway Guest House
51 Wellsway, Bath BA2 4RS
☎ (01225) 423434
*Comfortable, clean, warm, small guesthouse on bus route. Colour TV in bedrooms. Close to local shops, only a few minutes' walk to city centre.*
Bedrooms: 1 single, 1 double, 1 twin, 1 triple
Bathrooms: 1 public

**Bed & breakfast**

| per night: | £min | £max |
|---|---|---|
| Single | 16.00 | 18.00 |
| Double | 24.00 | 34.00 |

Parking for 3

### Wheelwrights Arms ᴁ
Listed
Monkton Combe, Bath BA2 7HD
☎ Limpley Stoke (01225) 722287

*Ideal centre for sightseeing, a short distance from Bath. Guest rooms are in converted 17th C stables and barn.*
Bedrooms: 6 double, 2 twin
Bathrooms: 8 private

**Bed & breakfast**

| per night: | £min | £max |
|---|---|---|
| Single | 30.00 | 35.00 |
| Double | 40.00 | 45.00 |

**Half board**

| per person: | £min | £max |
|---|---|---|
| Daily | 35.00 | 35.00 |
| Weekly | 220.00 | 250.00 |

Lunch available
Evening meal 1930 (last orders 2100)
Parking for 30
Cards accepted: Access, Visa
⛷ 14 🖴 ❧ ⌨ ♨ 🅟 ▥ 🖳 ◪ ❋ ✕ 🚲 SP ⌘ T

## BEAMINSTER

Dorset
Map ref 2A3

Old country town of mellow local stone set amid hills and rural vales. Mainly Georgian buildings; attractive almshouses date from 1603. The 17th C church with its ornate, pinnacled tower was restored inside by the Victorians. Parnham, a Tudor manor house, lies 1 mile south.

### The Old Vicarage
Listed
Clay Lane, Beaminster DT8 3BU
☎ (01308) 863200
*Large, spacious mid-Victorian vicarage close to town centre, set in its own grounds of three-quarters of an acre. Hardy's Emminster Vicarage (as in "Tess of the D'Urbervilles").*
Bedrooms: 2 double, 1 twin
Bathrooms: 2 private, 1 public

**Bed & breakfast**

| per night: | £min | £max |
|---|---|---|
| Single | 14.00 | 16.50 |
| Double | 28.00 | 33.00 |

Parking for 6
Open May-October
⛷ ♨ ▥ S ✕ 🖳 ❋ 🚲 ⌘

## BECKINGTON

Somerset
Map ref 2B2

### Eden Vale Farm
Listed
Mill Lane, Beckington, Bath BA3 6SN
☎ Frome (01373) 830371 & 0374 760505
*80-acre dairy farm. Working farm, originally a cornmill, dating back to Domesday. Secluded riverside setting, three-quarters of a mile from Beckington village. Bath, Longleat and Cheddar within easy reach.*
Bedrooms: 2 double, 1 twin
Bathrooms: 3 private

**Bed & breakfast**

| per night: | £min | £max |
|---|---|---|
| Single | 16.00 | 18.00 |
| Double | 30.00 | 34.00 |

Parking for 21
⛷ 🖴 ⌨ ♨ ▥ 🅟 S ✕ 🖳 🖳 ◪ ∪ ⌨ ❋ 🚲 ⌘

## BERRYNARBOR

Devon
Map ref 1C1

Small village set in a wooded valley, close to Exmoor and to the wild North Devon coast.

### Langleigh House
👑 👑
The Village, Berrynarbor, Ilfracombe EX34 9SG
☎ Combe Martin (01271) 883410
*Friendly family-run guesthouse providing all home-cooked food, in the beautiful North Devon village of Berrynarbor.*
Bedrooms: 1 single, 3 double, 1 triple, 1 family room
Bathrooms: 4 private, 1 public

**Bed & breakfast**

| per night: | £min | £max |
|---|---|---|
| Single | 14.50 | 15.50 |
| Double | 29.00 | 31.00 |

**Half board**

| per person: | £min | £max |
|---|---|---|
| Daily | 21.00 | 22.00 |
| Weekly | 140.00 | 146.00 |

Evening meal 1830 (last orders 1200)
Parking for 6
⛷ ♨ ▥ 🅟 S 🖳 🖳 ◪ ❋ 🚲

## BIDEFORD

Devon
Map ref 1C1

The home port of Sir Richard Grenville, the town with its 17th C merchants' houses flourished as a shipbuilding and cloth town. The bridge of 24 arches was built about 1460. Charles Kingsley stayed here while writing Westward Ho!
*Tourist Information Centre*
☎ *(01237) 477676*

### Sunset Hotel 🅼
👑 👑 👑
Landcross, Bideford EX39 5JA
☎ (01237) 472962
*Small, elegant country hotel in peaceful, picturesque location, specialising in home cooking. Delightful en-suite bedrooms with beverages and colour TV. Book with confidence. A non-smoking establishment.*
Bedrooms: 1 double, 1 twin, 1 triple, 1 family room
Bathrooms: 4 private

**Bed & breakfast**

| per night: | £min | £max |
|---|---|---|
| Double | 46.00 | 48.00 |

**Half board**

| per person: | £min | £max |
|---|---|---|
| Daily | 33.00 | 35.00 |
| Weekly | 220.00 | 225.00 |

Evening meal 1900 (last orders 1900)
Parking for 6
Open February-November
Cards accepted: Access, Visa
⛷ ▱ ♨ 🅟 S ✕ 🖳 🖳 ◑ 🖳 ◪ ❋ 🚲 DAP SP T

## BISHOP'S LYDEARD

Somerset
Map ref 1D1

### Slimbridge Station Farm
👑 COMMENDED
Bishop's Lydeard, Taunton TA4 3BX
☎ Bishops Lydeard (01823) 432223
*120-acre dairy farm. Victorian house next to the privately-owned West Somerset Steam Railway, which has a limited number of trains running in the summer.*
Bedrooms: 1 single, 1 double, 1 twin
Bathrooms: 1 public

**Bed & breakfast**

| per night: | £min | £max |
|---|---|---|
| Single | 15.00 | 17.00 |
| Double | 30.00 | 34.00 |

Parking for 4
⛷ ▱ ▱ ♨ ▥ S ✕ 🖳 🖳 🖳 ❋ 🚲

## BLAGDON

Avon
Map ref 2A2

Village beneath the north-facing slopes of the Mendips, in a countryside of woods and lanes. Just below the Yeo Valley is Blagdon Lake, a large reservoir.

### Butcombe Farm
👑 👑 COMMENDED
Aldwick Lane, Blagdon, Bristol BS18 6UW
☎ (01761) 462380
Fax (01761) 462300
*Domesday Book manor house with 15th C Assize court and many historic features in an Area of Outstanding Natural Beauty in Mendip Hills.*
Bedrooms: 4 double, 2 twin
Bathrooms: 6 private

**Bed & breakfast**

| per night: | £min | £max |
|---|---|---|
| Single | | 39.00 |
| Double | | 49.00 |

Evening meal 1800 (last orders 2130)
Parking for 28
⛷ 🖴 ❧ ▱ 🖴 ♨ ▥ 🅟 S ✕ 🖳 🖳 ◪ 🍴 ✵ ❀ ⟲ ∪ ⌨ ✕ 🚲 ◿ SP ⌘

## BODMIN

Cornwall
Map ref 1B2

County town south-west of Bodmin Moor with a ruined priory and church, containing the casket said to have held relics of St Petroc, to whom the church is dedicated. Nearby are Lanhydrock House and Pencarrow House.
*Tourist Information Centre*
☎ *(01208) 76616*

### Treffry Farm ⚏

HIGHLY COMMENDED

Lanhydrock, Bodmin PL30 5AF
☎ (01208) 74405
Fax (01208) 74405

*200-acre dairy farm. Lovely Georgian farmhouse in beautiful countryside adjoining National Trust Lanhydrock. Central for coast, moors and walks.*
Bedrooms: 1 double, 2 twin
Bathrooms: 2 private, 1 public, 1 private shower

**Bed & breakfast**

| per night: | £min | £max |
|---|---|---|
| Single | 18.00 | 19.00 |
| Double | 36.00 | 38.00 |

Evening meal 1830 (last orders 1200)
Parking for 3
Open March-October

## BOSCASTLE

Cornwall
Map ref 1B2

Small, unspoilt village in Valency Valley. Active as a port until onset of railway era, its natural harbour affords rare shelter on this wild coast. Attractions include spectacular blow-hole, Celtic field strips, part-Norman church. St Juliot Church nearby, was restored by Thomas Hardy.

### The Old Coach House ⚏

*Relax and enjoy this beautiful 300-year-old former coach house. All rooms en-suite with colour TV, teamaker, hairdryer, etc. Friendly and helpful owners.*
Wheelchair access category 3 ♿
Bedrooms: 1 single, 3 double, 1 twin, 1 triple
Bathrooms: 6 private

Tintagel Road, Boscastle PL35 0AS
☎ (01840) 250398

**Bed & breakfast**

| per night: | £min | £max |
|---|---|---|
| Single | 15.00 | 22.00 |
| Double | 30.00 | 44.00 |

Parking for 9
Open March-October
Cards accepted: Access, Visa, Amex

### Tolcarne House Hotel and Restaurant ⚏

COMMENDED

Tintagel Road, Boscastle PL35 0AS
☎ (01840) 250654
*Delightful house of character in own grounds with lovely views to the dramatic Cornish coastline. All rooms en-suite. Restaurant and bar. Warm welcome.*
Bedrooms: 1 single, 6 double, 1 twin
Bathrooms: 8 private

**Bed & breakfast**

| per night: | £min | £max |
|---|---|---|
| Single | 20.00 | 25.00 |
| Double | 36.00 | 50.00 |

**Half board**

| per person: | £min | £max |
|---|---|---|
| Daily | 28.00 | 35.00 |
| Weekly | 196.00 | 231.00 |

Evening meal 1900 (last orders 2130)
Parking for 15
Open January-October
Cards accepted: Access, Visa, Switch/Delta

## BOVEY TRACEY

Devon
Map ref 1D2

Standing by the river just east of Dartmoor National Park, this old town has good moorland views. Its church, with a 14th C tower, holds one of Devon's finest medieval rood screens.

### Frost Farmhouse

COMMENDED

Frost Farm, Hennock Road, Bovey Tracey, Newton Abbot TQ13 9PP
☎ (01626) 833266
*220-acre mixed farm. Pretty pink-washed thatched farmhouse. Country furnishings, log fires, good country food. Quiet location, back to nature experience.*
Bedrooms: 2 double, 1 twin
Bathrooms: 3 private

**Bed & breakfast**

| per night: | £min | £max |
|---|---|---|
| Single | 18.00 | 18.00 |
| Double | 36.00 | 36.00 |

**Half board**

| per person: | £min | £max |
|---|---|---|
| Daily | 27.50 | 27.50 |
| Weekly | 180.00 | 180.00 |

Evening meal from 1900
Parking for 6

### Lower Elsford Cottage

Listed HIGHLY COMMENDED

Bovey Tracey, Newton Abbot TQ13 9NY
☎ Lustleigh (01647) 7408
*17th C stone cottage near the reservoirs at Hennock, overlooking village of Lustleigh with outstanding scenic views. Complete peace and quiet. Full English breakfast.*
Bedrooms: 1 single, 1 double
Bathrooms: 1 private, 1 public

**Bed & breakfast**

| per night: | £min | £max |
|---|---|---|
| Single | 17.00 | 20.00 |
| Double | 34.00 | 36.00 |

Parking for 4

### Sandy Meadow

Listed

Manaton, Newton Abbot TQ13 9UN
☎ Manaton (01647) 221263
*Bungalow set in tranquil countryside with moorland views. At crossroads in Manaton by Kestor Inn take lane signposted Southcott. Bungalow is approximately one-third of a mile.*
Bedrooms: 1 single, 1 double
Bathrooms: 2 public

**Bed & breakfast**

| per night: | £min | £max |
|---|---|---|
| Single | 12.50 | 12.50 |
| Double | 25.00 | 30.00 |

Parking for 2

## BOX

Wiltshire
Map ref 2B2

### Lorne House

London Road, Box, Corsham SN14 9NA
☎ Bath (01225) 742597
*Victorian property, recently refurbished, on main A4 road opposite Brunel's famous Box tunnel between Bath and Chippenham. Warm and welcoming.*
Bedrooms: 1 double, 3 triple
Bathrooms: 4 private

**Bed & breakfast**

| per night: | £min | £max |
|---|---|---|
| Single | 20.00 | 25.00 |
| Double | 35.00 | 40.00 |

Parking for 6
Cards accepted: Access, Visa

## BRADFORD-ON-AVON

Wiltshire
Map ref 2B2

Huddled beside the river, the buildings of this former cloth-weaving town reflect continuing prosperity from the Middle Ages. There is a tiny Anglo-Saxon church, part of a monastery. The part-14th C bridge carries a medieval chapel, later used as a gaol.
*Tourist Information Centre*
☎ *(01225) 865797*

### Brookfield House
👑👑 HIGHLY COMMENDED
Vaggs Hill, Southwick, Trowbridge BA14 9NA
☎ Frome (01373) 830615
*150-acre dairy farm. Delightful converted country barn in quiet rural setting. Relaxed, warm and friendly atmosphere. Dairy farm 100 yards away.*
Bedrooms: 2 double, 1 twin
Bathrooms: 1 private, 2 public
**Bed & breakfast**

| per night: | £min | £max |
| --- | --- | --- |
| Single | 20.00 | 30.00 |
| Double | 34.00 | 40.00 |

Parking for 10

### Irondale House
👑👑 HIGHLY COMMENDED
67 High Street, Rode, Bath BA3 6PB
☎ Frome (01373) 830730
*Late 18th C family house in quiet village. Lovely walled garden, wonderful views and a warm, friendly welcome. 10 miles from Bath.*
Bedrooms: 2 twin
Bathrooms: 2 private
**Bed & breakfast**

| per night: | £min | £max |
| --- | --- | --- |
| Single | 35.00 | |
| Double | 40.00 | |

**Half board**

| per person: | £min | £max |
| --- | --- | --- |
| Daily | 62.00 | |

Parking for 1

### Midway Cottage
👑👑 COMMENDED
10 Farleigh Wick, Bradford-on-Avon BA15 2PU
☎ (01225) 863932
Fax (01225) 868152
*Restored Victorian country cottage on the A363 between Bath and Bradford-on-Avon offering comfortable accommodation and a friendly welcome.*
Bedrooms: 2 double, 1 twin
Bathrooms: 3 private

**Bed & breakfast**

| per night: | £min | £max |
| --- | --- | --- |
| Single | 20.00 | 25.00 |
| Double | 35.00 | 40.00 |

Parking for 8

## BRENDON

Devon
Map ref 1C1

Small village on the East Lyn River, in beautiful Lorna Doone country between Exmoor and the dramatic North Devon coast. Watersmeet (National Trust) is nearby.

### Brendon House Hotel
👑👑👑
Brendon, Lynton EX35 6PS
☎ (01598) 7206
*Comfortable 18th C house set in beautiful gardens overlooking the East Lyn river, with an informal and friendly atmosphere. Home-produced food and interesting wine list. Dogs welcome.*
Bedrooms: 2 double, 1 twin, 1 triple, 1 family room
Bathrooms: 4 private, 1 public
**Bed & breakfast**

| per night: | £min | £max |
| --- | --- | --- |
| Single | 17.50 | 19.50 |
| Double | 35.00 | 39.00 |

**Half board**

| per person: | £min | £max |
| --- | --- | --- |
| Daily | 28.00 | 30.00 |
| Weekly | 186.00 | 200.00 |

Evening meal 1930 (last orders 2000)
Parking for 5
Open March-November

## BRIDESTOWE

Devon
Map ref 1C2

Small Dartmoor village with a much restored 15th C church, and Great Links Tor rising to the south-east.

### White Hart Inn
👑👑
Fore Street, Bridestowe, Okehampton EX20 4EL
☎ (01837) 86318
*17th C inn, family-run for 30 years, primarily noted for good food. En-suite accommodation. Close to Dartmoor National Park, Lydford Gorge and fishing at Roadford Lake.*
Bedrooms: 2 double
Bathrooms: 2 private
**Bed & breakfast**

| per night: | £min | £max |
| --- | --- | --- |
| Single | 25.00 | |
| Double | 42.50 | |

Lunch available
Evening meal 1900 (last orders 2130)
Parking for 20
Cards accepted: Access, Visa, Diners, Amex

## BRIDGWATER

Somerset
Map ref 1D1

Former medieval port on the River Parrett, now small industrial town with mostly 19th C or modern architecture. Georgian Castle Street leads to West Quay and site of 13th C castle razed to the ground by Cromwell. Birthplace of Cromwellian admiral Robert Blake is now museum. Arts centre.

### Chinar
👑👑
17 Oakfield Road, Bridgwater TA6 7LX
☎ (01278) 458639

*Detached modern house in a quiet locality and with attractive small garden. Very comfortable beds and imaginative breakfasts. Off-road parking.*
Bedrooms: 1 single, 1 double
Bathrooms: 2 private, 1 public
**Bed & breakfast**

| per night: | £min | £max |
| --- | --- | --- |
| Single | 16.00 | 20.00 |
| Double | 30.00 | 35.00 |

Evening meal 1830 (last orders 1600)
Parking for 2

### Cokerhurst Farm
👑👑 COMMENDED
87 Wembdon Hill, Bridgwater TA6 7QA
☎ (01278) 422330 & Mobile 0850 692065

*105-acre arable farm. West of Bridgwater, off A39. Old farmhouse set in quiet countryside with peaceful garden overlooking the lake and farm.*
Bedrooms: 1 double, 1 twin, 1 triple
Bathrooms: 1 private, 1 public

Continued ▶

## BRIDGWATER

### Continued

**Bed & breakfast**

| per night: | £min | £max |
| --- | --- | --- |
| Single | 17.00 | 22.50 |
| Double | 34.00 | 45.00 |

Parking for 143
Open March-November

🛇⌨▢♨⬔🅤🅛🎇📺🛌🛇⤳✿🏮

### Walnut Tree Inn ⚮

👑👑👑👑 COMMENDED

North Petherton, Bridgwater TA6 6QA
☎ North Petherton (01278) 662255
Fax (01278) 663946
*Set in the heart of Somerset. 18th C
coaching inn on A38, 1 mile from M5
exit 24. A welcome stopover for
businessmen and tourists.*
Bedrooms: 2 single, 21 double, 5 twin
Bathrooms: 28 private

**Bed & breakfast**

| per night: | £min | £max |
| --- | --- | --- |
| Single | 32.00 | 56.00 |
| Double | 54.00 | 86.00 |

**Half board**

| per person: | £min | £max |
| --- | --- | --- |
| Daily | 43.00 | |

Lunch available
Evening meal 1900 (last orders 2200)
Parking for 74
Cards accepted: Access, Visa, Diners,
Amex, Switch/Delta

🛇🖪⌨▢📞🅤🛆🅢🎇🅞🅸🎬⬛🛇
🕓4-80 ❁❋ 🆂🅿 🆃

### Wembdon Farm

👑👑 HIGHLY COMMENDED

Hollow Lane, Wembdon, Bridgwater
TA5 2BD
☎ (01278) 453097

*380-acre arable & dairy farm. Enjoy bed
and breakfast at this homely farmhouse.
En-suite rooms with tea/coffee making
facilities, lounge, dining room and
lovely gardens. Convenient for
Quantock, Mendip and Polden Hills,
Somerset Levels and coast. Golf and
fishing nearby. Non-smokers only
please.*
Bedrooms: 2 double
Bathrooms: 2 private

**Bed & breakfast**

| per night: | £min | £max |
| --- | --- | --- |
| Double | 39.00 | 39.00 |

Parking for 4
Open April-October

🛇▢♨🅤🎇🎬⬛🛇✿🛠⤳

### West Bower Manor

Listed COMMENDED

West Bower Lane, Durleigh,
Bridgwater TA5 2AT
☎ (01278) 422895
*Peaceful medieval manor house beside
a lake. Home-made bread, free-range
breakfasts.*
Bedrooms: 2 double, 1 twin
Bathrooms: 3 private

**Bed & breakfast**

| per night: | £min | £max |
| --- | --- | --- |
| Single | 20.00 | 35.00 |
| Double | 30.00 | 45.00 |

Parking for 6

🛇12🖻⌨▢♨🛆🛈🅢🎇🎬📺⬛🛇
❋✿🛠⤳🏮

### Woodlands

👑 COMMENDED

35 Durleigh Road, Bridgwater
TA6 7HY
☎ (01278) 423442
*Listed building in 2 acres landscaped
gardens. Antique furniture, log fires,
total tranquillity and seclusion yet close
to town centre.*
Bedrooms: 1 single, 2 double, 1 twin
Bathrooms: 3 private, 1 public

**Bed & breakfast**

| per night: | £min | £max |
| --- | --- | --- |
| Single | 18.00 | 20.00 |
| Double | 37.00 | 40.00 |

**Half board**

| per person: | £min | £max |
| --- | --- | --- |
| Daily | 27.00 | 34.00 |
| Weekly | 160.00 | 200.00 |

Evening meal 1830 (last orders 2000)
Parking for 4
Cards accepted: Access, Visa

🛇10⌨▢♨🅤🅛🅢🎇📺⬛🛇✿🛠
⤳🆂🏮

## BRIDPORT

### Dorset
### Map ref 2A3

Market town and chief producer of
nets and ropes just inland of
dramatic Dorset coast. Old, broad
streets built for drying and twisting,
long gardens for rope-walks.
Grand arcaded Town Hall and
Georgian buildings. Local history
museum has Roman relics.
*Tourist Information Centre*
☎ *(01308) 424901*

### Britmead House ⚮

👑👑👑 COMMENDED

West Bay Road, Bridport DT6 4EG
☎ (01308) 422941

*Elegant, spacious, tastefully decorated
house. Lounge and dining room
overlooking garden. West Bay
Harbour/Coastal Path, 10 minutes' walk
away. Renowned for hospitality,
delicious meals and comfort.*
Bedrooms: 4 double, 3 twin
Bathrooms: 6 private, 1 private shower

**Bed & breakfast**

| per night: | £min | £max |
| --- | --- | --- |
| Single | 24.00 | 33.00 |
| Double | 38.00 | 52.00 |

**Half board**

| per person: | £min | £max |
| --- | --- | --- |
| Daily | 31.00 | 38.00 |
| Weekly | 189.00 | 224.00 |

Evening meal 1900 (last orders 1700)
Parking for 8
Cards accepted: Access, Visa, Diners,
Amex

🛇🖪⌨▢♨🖐🍴🛈🅢🎇🎬⬛🛇❁✿
🛠🆂🆃

### Little Wych ⚮

👑👑 APPROVED

Burton Road, Bridport DT6 4GJ
☎ (01308) 420899
Fax (01308) 420899

*Spacious country house in beautiful
gardens with panoramic views of west
bay and surrounding countryside.
Peaceful location.*
Bedrooms: 2 double, 2 twin, 2 family
rooms
Bathrooms: 6 private

**Bed & breakfast**

| per night: | £min | £max |
| --- | --- | --- |
| Single | 20.00 | 24.00 |
| Double | 32.00 | 40.00 |

Parking for 16

🛇🖪🅤🎇📺⬛✿🛠⤳🆂🏮

### The Marquis of Lorne

👑👑 COMMENDED

Nettlecombe, Bridport DT6 3SY
☎ Powerstock (01308) 485236
Fax (01308) 485666
*Picturesque 16th C village inn only 4
miles from coast and Bridport. Large
garden and children's play area. Quality
bar meals.*
Bedrooms: 1 single, 3 double, 2 twin,
1 family room
Bathrooms: 4 private, 1 public

**Bed & breakfast**

| per night: | £min | £max |
| --- | --- | --- |
| Single | 22.00 | 22.00 |
| Double | 44.00 | 50.00 |

Lunch available
Evening meal 1830 (last orders 2130)

Parking for 50
Cards accepted: Access, Visa

## New House Farm

Mangerton Lane, Bradpole, Bridport
DT6 3SF
☎ (01308) 422884
*Modern, comfortable farmhouse set in rural Dorset hills.*
Bedrooms: 1 family room
Bathrooms: 1 private

**Bed & breakfast**

| per night: | £min | £max |
| --- | --- | --- |
| Single | 15.00 | 18.00 |
| Double | 30.00 | 36.00 |

**Half board**

| per person: | £min | £max |
| --- | --- | --- |
| Daily | 23.00 | 26.00 |
| Weekly | 140.00 | 160.00 |

Lunch available
Evening meal 1800 (last orders 2000)
Parking for 10
Open March-November

## BRISTOL

Avon
Map ref 2A2

Famous for maritime links, historic harbour, Georgian terraces and Brunel's Clifton suspension bridge. Many attractions including SS Great Britain, Bristol Zoo, museums and art galleries and top name entertainments. Events include Balloon Fiesta and Regatta.
*Tourist Information Centre*
☎ (0117) 926 0767

## Albany Guest House

500 Bath Road, Brislington, Bristol
BS4 3JY
☎ (0117) 977 8710
*Comfortable, tastefully-furnished Victorian semi, on main A4 2 miles from city centre and 1 mile from station. Off-road parking.*
Bedrooms: 1 single, 2 double, 1 twin
Bathrooms: 2 private, 1 public

**Bed & breakfast**

| per night: | £min | £max |
| --- | --- | --- |
| Single | 18.00 | 21.00 |
| Double | 27.00 | 31.00 |

Parking for 3

## The Bowl Inn and Restaurant M

COMMENDED

16 Church Road, Lower Almondsbury,
Bristol BS12 4DT
☎ Almondsbury (01454) 612757 & 613717
Fax (01454) 619910

*12th C building, once a priory, nestling on the edge of the Severn Vale. 3 minutes from M4/M5 interchange.*
Bedrooms: 3 double, 5 twin
Bathrooms: 8 private

**Bed & breakfast**

| per night: | £min | £max |
| --- | --- | --- |
| Single | 20.00 | 44.50 |
| Double | 39.00 | 86.80 |

**Half board**

| per person: | £min | £max |
| --- | --- | --- |
| Daily | 36.50 | 54.00 |
| Weekly | 255.50 | 378.00 |

Lunch available
Evening meal 1830 (last orders 2200)
Parking for 40
Cards accepted: Access, Visa, Diners, Amex, Switch/Delta

## Crown and Anchor

6 Hotwell Road, Clifton Wood, Bristol
BS8 4UD
☎ (0117) 929 0304
*Family-run, welcoming public house in 150-year-old building. View of "SS Great Britain" on River Avon in Bristol Harbour.*
Bedrooms: 1 single, 6 twin, 1 triple
Bathrooms: 4 private, 4 private showers

**Bed & breakfast**

| per night: | £min | £max |
| --- | --- | --- |
| Single | 17.50 | 25.00 |
| Double | 27.00 | 35.00 |

**Half board**

| per person: | £min | £max |
| --- | --- | --- |
| Daily | 20.00 | 30.00 |
| Weekly | 120.00 | 200.00 |

Evening meal 1700 (last orders 2100)

## 8 Southover Close

Listed

Westbury-on-Trym, Bristol BS9 3NG
☎ (0117) 950 0754
*Semi-detached house in quiet cul-de-sac 3 miles from centre of Bristol - off main Falcondale Road, just outside Westbury village.*
Bedrooms: 1 single, 1 double
Bathrooms: 1 public

**Bed & breakfast**

| per night: | £min | £max |
| --- | --- | --- |
| Single | 15.00 | |
| Double | 30.00 | |

Parking for 4
Open January-November

## Westbury Park Hotel

HIGHLY COMMENDED

37 Westbury Road, Bristol BS9 3AU
☎ (0117) 962 0465
Fax (0117) 962 8607
*Friendly family-run hotel on Durdham Downs, close to centre and M5 junction 17.*
Bedrooms: 1 single, 5 double, 2 twin
Bathrooms: 5 private, 1 public

**Bed & breakfast**

| per night: | £min | £max |
| --- | --- | --- |
| Single | 25.00 | 37.00 |
| Double | 38.00 | 48.00 |

Parking for 5
Cards accepted: Access, Visa

## BRIXHAM

Devon
Map ref 1D2

Famous for its trawling fleet in the 19th C, a steeply-built fishing port overlooking the harbour and fish market. A statue of William of Orange recalls his landing here before deposing James II. There is an aquarium and museum. Good cliff views and walks.
*Tourist Information Centre*
☎ (01803) 852861

## Richmond House Private Hotel M

COMMENDED

Higher Manor Road, Brixham
TQ5 8HA
☎ (01803) 882391
*Detached Victorian house with "Laura Ashley" interior, sun trap garden and adjacent car park. En-suite available. Convenient for shops and harbour, yet quiet location. First left after Golden Lion.*
Bedrooms: 1 single, 1 double, 1 twin, 3 triple, 1 family room
Bathrooms: 2 private, 2 public

**Bed & breakfast**

| per night: | £min | £max |
| --- | --- | --- |
| Single | 18.00 | |
| Double | 32.00 | |

Parking for 5
Cards accepted: Access, Visa

## BROAD CHALKE

Wiltshire
Map ref 2B3

Delightful River Ebble Valley village with a 13th C church displaying a notable porch and central tower.

## The Queens Head Inn

Broad Chalke, Salisbury SP5 5EN
☎ Salisbury (01722) 780344

*Continued* ▶

## BROAD CHALKE

*Continued*

*15th C building with stone walls and old beams. Set in the beautiful Chalke Valley, 8 miles from Salisbury.*
Bedrooms: 3 double, 1 twin
Bathrooms: 4 private

**Bed & breakfast**

| per night: | £min | £max |
| --- | --- | --- |
| Single | 25.00 | 25.00 |
| Double | 45.00 | 45.00 |

Lunch available
Evening meal 1900 (last orders 2115)
Parking for 40
Cards accepted: Access, Visa

## BROAD HINTON

Wiltshire
Map ref 2B2

Village 4 miles north of Avebury with its stone circle, museum and manor house. Good centre for walking and cycling, with easy access to the Ridgeway National Trail 2 miles north west.

### Weir Farm

Listed COMMENDED
Broad Hinton, Swindon SN4 9NE
☎ Swindon (01793) 731207
Fax (01793) 731207
*800-acre mixed farm. Attractive, comfortable period farmhouse on working farm with lovely views. On A4361, 6 miles from Swindon and near the Ridgeway, Avebury and Marlborough.*
Bedrooms: 1 single, 1 double, 1 twin
Bathrooms: 1 public

**Bed & breakfast**

| per night: | £min | £max |
| --- | --- | --- |
| Single | 18.00 | 22.00 |
| Double | 30.00 | 36.00 |

Parking for 4
Open January, March-December

## BUCKFASTLEIGH

Devon
Map ref 1C2

Small manufacturing and market town just south of Buckfast Abbey on the fringe of Dartmoor. Return trips can be taken by steam train on a reopened line along the beautiful Dart Valley.

### Wellpark Farm

Listed COMMENDED
Dean Prior, Buckfastleigh TQ11 0LY
☎ (01364) 643775
*500-acre arable & dairy farm. Enjoy a farm holiday on this working farm overlooking Dartmoor. Delicious food, well-appointed accommodation,*

*comfortable relaxing atmosphere. Large enclosed garden with children's play area.*
Bedrooms: 1 double, 1 family room
Bathrooms: 1 public

**Bed & breakfast**

| per night: | £min | £max |
| --- | --- | --- |
| Single | 10.00 | 15.00 |
| Double | 20.00 | 30.00 |

**Half board**

| per person: | £min | £max |
| --- | --- | --- |
| Daily | 19.00 | 24.00 |
| Weekly | 130.00 | 155.00 |

Evening meal 1800 (last orders 0800)
Parking for 3
Open March-October

## BUCKLAND MONACHORUM

Devon
Map ref 1C2

Village just north of Buckland Abbey, home of Sir Francis Drake. Founded by Cistercians, the building is of unique interest through its conversion into a country home by Sir Richard Grenville. Now a museum of Drake and Grenville mementoes, including Drake's drum. Beautiful gardens.

### Store Cottage

19 The Village, Buckland Monachorum, Yelverton PL20 7NA
☎ Yelverton (01822) 853117 & Mobile 0850 193495

*South-facing listed stone house in centre of village. Excellent meals at village pub. Unspoilt countryside at western edge of Dartmoor National Park.*
Bedrooms: 1 double, 1 twin
Bathrooms: 2 private

**Bed & breakfast**

| per night: | £min | £max |
| --- | --- | --- |
| Single | 18.00 | 18.00 |
| Double | 36.00 | 36.00 |

Open April-October

## BUDE

Cornwall
Map ref 1C2

Resort on dramatic Atlantic coast. High cliffs give spectacular sea and inland views. Golf-course, cricket pitch, folly, surfing, coarse-fishing and boating. Mother-town Stratton was base of Royalist Sir Bevil Grenville.
*Tourist Information Centre*
☎ *(01288) 354240*

### Clovelly House

COMMENDED
4 Burn View, Bude EX23 8BY
☎ (01288) 352761
*In a level location, opposite golf club and close to all amenities. All rooms with tea/coffee facilities, satellite TV, some en-suite.*
Bedrooms: 2 single, 2 double, 1 twin, 1 triple
Bathrooms: 3 private, 1 public

**Bed & breakfast**

| per night: | £min | £max |
| --- | --- | --- |
| Single | 13.50 | 18.00 |
| Double | 28.00 | 37.00 |

Parking for 2

### Lower Northcott Farm

COMMENDED
Poughill, Bude EX23 9EL
☎ (01288) 352350
*400-acre mixed farm. Georgian farmhouse in secluded grounds with children's safe play area. Visitors welcome to wander around and meet the animals.*
Bedrooms: 1 single, 1 twin, 3 family rooms
Bathrooms: 3 private, 1 public, 1 private shower

**Bed & breakfast**

| per night: | £min | £max |
| --- | --- | --- |
| Single | 15.00 | |
| Double | 30.00 | |

**Half board**

| per person: | £min | £max |
| --- | --- | --- |
| Daily | 21.00 | |
| Weekly | 140.00 | |

Evening meal 1830 (last orders 1830)
Parking for 4

Individual proprietors have supplied all details of accommodation. Although we do check for accuracy, we advise you to confirm the information at the time of booking.

Check the introduction to this region for ideas on Where to Go.

## BURBAGE

Wiltshire
Map ref 2B2

Village close to Savernake Forest, famous as a habitat for deer. Close by are the remains of Wolf Hall mansion, where a great banquet in honour of Jane Seymour took place in 1536.

### The Old Vicarage **

HIGHLY COMMENDED

Burbage, Marlborough SN8 3AG
☎ Marlborough (01672) 810495
Fax (01672) 810663
*Victorian country house in 2-acre garden, offering peace, comfort and delicious food. Within easy reach of Avebury, Bath, Oxford and Salisbury.*
Bedrooms: 1 single, 1 double, 1 twin
Bathrooms: 3 private
**Bed & breakfast**

| per night: | £min | £max |
|---|---|---|
| Single | 35.00 | |
| Double | 60.00 | |

Parking for 10
Cards accepted: Access, Visa, Amex

## BURNHAM-ON-SEA

Somerset
Map ref 1D1

Small Victorian resort with sandy beaches, a few minutes from junction 22 of the M5. Ideal base for touring Somerset. Good sporting facilities, championship golf-course.
*Tourist Information Centre*
*☎ (01278) 787852*

### Priors Mead

23 Rectory Road, Burnham-on-Sea TA8 2BZ
☎ (01278) 782116 & Mobile 0860 573018
Fax (01934) 822392
*Friendly, quiet Edwardian house with beautiful grounds and swimming pool. Large rooms either en-suite or with private facilities. Near championship golf course and sea. Ideal touring centre.*
Bedrooms: 2 double, 1 twin
Bathrooms: 3 private
**Bed & breakfast**

| per night: | £min | £max |
|---|---|---|
| Single | 17.00 | 19.00 |
| Double | 30.00 | 32.00 |

Parking for 3

## BURTON BRADSTOCK

Dorset
Map ref 2A3

Lying amid fields beside the River Bride, a village of old stone houses, a 14th C church and a village green. The beautiful coast road from Abbotsbury to Bridport passes by and Iron Age forts top the surrounding hills. The sheltered river valley makes a staging post for migrating birds.

### The Bramleys **

COMMENDED

Annings Lane, Burton Bradstock, Bridport DT6 4QN
☎ (01308) 897954
*New, spacious family home with large garden and conservatory. Sunday lunch/evening meals optional. Close to golf and beach.*
Bedrooms: 2 double, 1 twin
Bathrooms: 2 public
**Bed & breakfast**

| per night: | £min | £max |
|---|---|---|
| Single | | 12.50 |
| Double | 15.00 | 25.00 |

**Half board**

| per person: | £min | £max |
|---|---|---|
| Daily | | 30.00 |

Evening meal 1830 (last orders 2000)
Parking for 3

### Bridge Cottage Stores

Listed COMMENDED

87 High Street, Burton Bradstock, Bridport DT6 4RA
☎ Bridport (01308) 897222
*Self-contained en-suite accommodation in rooms above village shop and tea room. Close to beach, on Bridport to Weymouth road.*
Bedrooms: 2 double, 1 twin
Bathrooms: 3 private
**Bed & breakfast**

| per night: | £min | £max |
|---|---|---|
| Single | 14.15 | 24.50 |
| Double | 28.30 | 39.00 |

Lunch available
Parking for 8

### Three Horseshoes

APPROVED

Mill Street, Burton Bradstock, Bridport DT6 4QZ
☎ (01308) 897259
*Thatched inn with car park and garden on the B3157 Bridport to Weymouth road.*
Bedrooms: 2 double, 1 twin
Bathrooms: 1 public
**Bed & breakfast**

| per night: | £min | £max |
|---|---|---|
| Single | 15.50 | 17.50 |
| Double | 31.00 | 33.00 |

Lunch available
Evening meal 1830 (last orders 2115)
Parking for 14

## CALLINGTON

Cornwall
Map ref 1C2

A quiet market town standing on high ground above the River Lynher. The 15th C church of St Mary's has an alabaster monument to Lord Willoughby de Broke, Henry VII's marshal. A 15th C chapel, 1 mile east, houses Dupath Well, one of the Cornish Holy Wells.

### Dozmary **

Listed COMMENDED

Tors View Close, Tavistock Road, Callington PL17 7DY
☎ Liskeard (01579) 83677
*A deceptively spacious dormer bungalow providing comfortable accommodation with good facilities, just a few minutes from Callington town centre.*
Bedrooms: 1 double, 1 twin, 1 family room
Bathrooms: 2 private, 1 public
**Bed & breakfast**

| per night: | £min | £max |
|---|---|---|
| Single | 13.00 | 16.00 |
| Double | 26.00 | 28.00 |

Parking for 4
Open January-November

## CASTLE CARY

Somerset
Map ref 2B2

One of south Somerset's most attractive market towns, with a picturesque winding high street of golden stone and thatch, markethouse and famous round 18th C lock-up.

### George Hotel **

COMMENDED

Market Place, Castle Cary BA7 7AH
☎ (01963) 350761

*15th C thatched coaching inn with en-suite rooms, 2 bars and noted restaurant. Centrally located for many National Trust houses and gardens, Cheddar, Wells, Glastonbury and Bath.*
Bedrooms: 4 single, 5 double, 5 twin, 1 family room
Bathrooms: 15 private

*Continued ▶*

## CASTLE CARY

*Continued*

**Bed & breakfast**

| per night: | £min | £max |
|---|---|---|
| Single | 40.00 | 45.00 |
| Double | 50.00 | 65.00 |

**Half board**

| per person: | £min | £max |
|---|---|---|
| Daily | 45.00 | 60.00 |

Lunch available
Evening meal 1900 (last orders 2130)
Parking for 10
Cards accepted: Access, Visa, Switch/Delta

ち亡と咲口◆🏠⌕🌂📺▥. ☎♣20
⊍🅿🚗🐾 SP 🏧 T

## CHAGFORD

Devon
Map ref 1C2

Handsome stone houses, some from the Middle Ages, grace this former stannary town on northern Dartmoor. It is a popular centre for walking expeditions and for tours of the antiquities on the rugged moor. There is a splendid 15th C granite church, said to be haunted by the poet Godolphin.

### St. Johns West

👑👑

Murchington, Chagford, Newton Abbot TQ13 8HJ
☎ (01647) 432468
*Splendid country house within Dartmoor National Park, 1.5 miles north-west of Chagford. Walkers welcome. Sorry - non-smoking throughout. Brochure with pleasure.*
Bedrooms: 1 double, 1 twin, 1 family room
Bathrooms: 2 private, 1 public

**Bed & breakfast**

| per night: | £min | £max |
|---|---|---|
| Single | 15.00 | 15.00 |
| Double | 30.00 | 40.00 |

**Half board**

| per person: | £min | £max |
|---|---|---|
| Daily | 24.50 | 29.50 |
| Weekly | 154.35 | 185.85 |

Evening meal 1800 (last orders 2000)
Parking for 6

ち咲口◆🅄l◆S⌕🌂📺▥. ☎⊍✿
🚗🏧

National Crown ratings were correct at the time of going to press but are subject to change. Please check at the time of booking.

## CHARD

Somerset
Map ref 1D2

Market town in hilly countryside. The wide main street has some handsome buildings, among them the Guildhall, court house and almshouses. Modern light industry and dairy produce have replaced 19th C lace making which came at decline of cloth trade.
*Tourist Information Centre*
☎ *(01460) 67463*

### Wambrook Farm

Listed

Wambrook, Chard TA20 3DF
☎ (01460) 62371
*300-acre mixed farm. Attractive listed farmhouse 2 miles from Chard in beautiful rural hills. Children welcome. From Chard take A30 towards Honiton, follow signs.*
Bedrooms: 1 double, 1 twin, 1 triple
Bathrooms: 1 private, 1 public

**Bed & breakfast**

| per night: | £min | £max |
|---|---|---|
| Single | 16.00 | 22.00 |
| Double | 28.00 | 32.00 |

Parking for 8
Open April-November
Cards accepted: Visa

ち◆🅄lS🌂▥. ☎✿🛏🐾🚗

## CHEDDAR

Somerset
Map ref 1D1

Large village at foot of Mendips just south of the spectacular Cheddar Gorge. Close by are Roman and Saxon sites and famous show caves. Traditional Cheddar cheese is still made here.

### Constantine

Listed

Lower New Road, Cheddar BS27 3DY
☎ (01934) 742732
*Very friendly family home, close to village and Gorge with beautiful views. Large garden available to guests. Children welcome.*
Bedrooms: 1 single, 1 double, 1 triple
Bathrooms: 1 public, 1 private shower

**Bed & breakfast**

| per night: | £min | £max |
|---|---|---|
| Single | | 14.00 |
| Double | | 28.00 |

Parking for 6

ち亡咲▣◆🅄lS⌕🌂📺▥. ☎✿🛏🚗

### Tor Farm ♨

👑 HIGHLY COMMENDED

Nyland, Cheddar BS27 3UD
☎ (01934) 743710
*33-acre mixed farm. On A371 between Cheddar and Draycott (take the road signposted Nyland). Quiet and peaceful*

on Somerset Levels. Ideally situated for visiting Cheddar, Bath, Wookey Hole, Glastonbury, Wells and coast.
Bedrooms: 2 single, 4 double, 1 twin, 1 family room
Bathrooms: 6 private, 2 public

**Bed & breakfast**

| per night: | £min | £max |
|---|---|---|
| Single | 17.50 | |
| Double | 30.00 | 43.00 |

Evening meal 1900 (last orders 1800)
Parking for 10
Cards accepted: Access, Visa

ち亡咲◆🅄⌕🌂📺▥. ☎20⊍♣✿🛏✖
SP T

## CHEW MAGNA

Avon
Map ref 2A2

Prosperous redstone village in the Mendip Hills with fine houses, cottages and inns of varying periods. High Street rises between railed, raised pavements with lofty 15th C tower.

### Woodbarn Farm

👑👑

Denny Lane, Chew Magna, Bristol BS18 8SZ
☎ (01275) 332599
*70-acre mixed farm. Central for touring Bath, Bristol, Wells and Cheddar. 3 minutes from Chew Valley Lake. En-suite bedrooms. Large farmhouse breakfasts. Warm welcome.*
Bedrooms: 1 double, 1 family room
Bathrooms: 2 private

**Bed & breakfast**

| per night: | £min | £max |
|---|---|---|
| Single | 18.00 | 20.00 |
| Double | 34.00 | 38.00 |

Parking for 2
Open March-December

ち3◆🅄l◆⌕🌂📺▥. ☎✿✖🚗

## CHICKERELL

Dorset
Map ref 2B3

### Stonebank

👑👑

14 West Street, Chickerell, Weymouth DT3 4DY
☎ Weymouth (01305) 760120
*Charming 17th C former farmhouse, close to coastal path and Chesil Beach. Ideal for exploring the Dorset coast and countryside.*
Bedrooms: 2 double
Bathrooms: 2 private

**Bed & breakfast**

| per night: | £min | £max |
|---|---|---|
| Double | 30.00 | 35.00 |

Parking for 2
Open April-September

咲口◆🅄lS⌕🌂📺▥. ☎✿✖🛏🚗

## CHIDEOCK

Dorset
Map ref 1D2

Village of sandstone thatched cottages in a valley near the dramatic Dorset coast. The church holds an interesting processional cross in mother-of-pearl and the manor house close by is associated with the Victorian Roman Catholic church. Seatown has a pebble beach and limestone cliffs.

### Park Farmhouse Bed and Breakfast

Park Farmhouse, Main Street, Chideock, Bridport DT6 6JD
☎ Bridport (01297) 89157

*Built around 1750 in attractive West Dorset village of Chideock. Grade II listed, partly thatched, former farmhouse in a conservation area. Resident cordon bleu cook!*
Bedrooms: 1 single, 3 double, 1 twin
Bathrooms: 3 private, 1 public

**Bed & breakfast**

| per night: | £min | £max |
|---|---|---|
| Single | 15.00 | 28.50 |
| Double | 33.00 | 44.00 |

**Half board**

| per person: | £min | £max |
|---|---|---|
| Daily | 25.00 | 37.00 |
| Weekly | 160.00 | 245.00 |

Evening meal 1930 (last orders 2030)
Parking for 6
Cards accepted: Visa

---

Please mention this guide when making a booking.

---

There are separate sections in this guide listing groups specialising in farm holidays and accommodation which is especially suitable for young people and organised groups.

## CHIPPENHAM

Wiltshire
Map ref 2B2

Ancient market town with modern industry. Notable early buildings include the medieval Town Hall and the gabled 15th C Yelde Hall, now a local history museum. On the outskirts Hardenhuish has a charming hilltop church by the Georgian architect John Wood of Bath.
*Tourist Information Centre*
☎ *(01249) 657733*

### Frogwell House

132 Hungerdown Lane, Chippenham SN14 0BD
☎ (01249) 650328
Fax (01249) 650328
*An imposing late 19th C house built of local stone, modernised to provide comfortable and appealing accommodation.*
Bedrooms: 1 single, 1 double, 2 twin
Bathrooms: 2 private, 1 public

**Bed & breakfast**

| per night: | £min | £max |
|---|---|---|
| Single | 15.00 | 22.00 |
| Double | 30.00 | 40.00 |

**Half board**

| per person: | £min | £max |
|---|---|---|
| Daily | 21.00 | 27.00 |

Evening meal from 1800
Parking for 6

### Goulters Mill Farm

Listed
Goulters Mill, Nettleton, Chippenham SN14 7LL
☎ Castle Combe (01249) 782555

*Secluded 17th C mill cottage in garden and woodland open to public. On B4039 2 miles west of Castle Combe down track opposite turning to Littleton Drew.*
Bedrooms: 1 single, 1 double, 1 twin, 1 triple
Bathrooms: 2 private, 1 public

**Bed & breakfast**

| per night: | £min | £max |
|---|---|---|
| Single | 15.00 | 20.00 |
| Double | 30.00 | 60.00 |

Evening meal 1830 (last orders 2000)
Parking for 4

### 75 Rowden Hill

Chippenham SN15 2AL
☎ (01249) 652981
*Near National Trust village of Lacock and attractive Castle Combe. Corsham Court also nearby. Friendly welcome assured.*
Bedrooms: 2 double, 1 twin
Bathrooms: 1 public

**Bed & breakfast**

| per night: | £min | £max |
|---|---|---|
| Single | | 14.50 |
| Double | | 25.00 |

Parking for 5
Open April-October

## CHITTOE HEATH

Wiltshire
Map ref 2B2

### Wayside

COMMENDED
Chittoe Heath SN15 2EH
☎ Devizes (01380) 850458
Fax (01380) 850458
*Family-run establishment with informal atmosphere, in the heart of Wiltshire, with downs, historic houses and ancient sites. Bath, Salisbury and Marlborough all within 20 mile radius.*
Bedrooms: 1 single, 1 triple
Bathrooms: 2 private

**Bed & breakfast**

| per night: | £min | £max |
|---|---|---|
| Single | | 20.00 |
| Double | | 38.00 |

**Half board**

| per person: | £min | £max |
|---|---|---|
| Daily | | 27.50 |
| Weekly | | 170.00 |

Lunch available
Evening meal 1900 (last orders 2100)
Parking for 14

## CHULMLEIGH

Devon
Map ref 1C2

Small, hilly town above the Little Dart River, long since by-passed by the main road. The large 15th C church is noted for its splendid rood screen and 38 carved wooden angels on the roof.

### The Old Bakehouse

HIGHLY COMMENDED
South Molton Street, Chulmleigh EX18 7BW
☎ (01769) 580074

Continued ▶

## CHULMLEIGH

### Continued

*16th C merchant's house with licensed restaurant and en-suite bedrooms in converted bakehouse. Situated in beautiful Taw Valley between Dartmoor and Exmoor. Cosy wood burning stoves, unique atmosphere.*
Bedrooms: 1 double, 2 twin
Bathrooms: 3 private

**Bed & breakfast**

| per night: | £min | £max |
| --- | --- | --- |
| Single | 24.00 | 24.00 |
| Double | 36.00 | 36.00 |

**Half board**

| per person: | £min | £max |
| --- | --- | --- |
| Daily | 28.00 | 34.00 |
| Weekly | 175.00 | 215.00 |

Lunch available
Evening meal 1930 (last orders 2100)

## CLOVELLY

Devon
Map ref 1C1

Clinging to wooded cliffs, fishing village with steep cobbled street zigzagging, or cut in steps, to harbour. Carrying sleds stand beside whitewashed flower-decked cottages. Charles Kingsley's father was rector of the church set high up near the Hamlyn family's Clovelly Court.

### Fuchsia Cottage

Listed  APPROVED
Burscott, Clovelly, Bideford EX39 5RR
☎ (01237) 431398
*Private house with comfortable ground and first floor en-suite accommodation. Surrounded by beautiful views of sea and country. Evening meal by arrangement.*
Bedrooms: 1 single, 1 double, 1 triple
Bathrooms: 2 private, 1 public

**Bed & breakfast**

| per night: | £min | £max |
| --- | --- | --- |
| Single | | 12.00 |
| Double | | 30.00 |

**Half board**

| per person: | £min | £max |
| --- | --- | --- |
| Daily | | 21.00 |
| Weekly | | 147.00 |

Evening meal from 1830
Parking for 3
Open April-October

## COLYTON

Devon
Map ref 1D2

Surrounded by fertile farmland, this small riverside town was an early Saxon settlement. Medieval prosperity from the wool trade built the grand church tower with its octagonal lantern and the church's fine west window.

### Smallicombe Farm

COMMENDED
Northleigh, Colyton EX13 6BU
☎ Wilmington (01404) 831310
*17-acre mixed farm. Small farm with friendly cows, pigs, sheep and goats. In Area of Outstanding Natural Beauty. Glorious rural views from the farmhouse. All rooms en-suite. Reduced rates for children and weekly stays.*
Bedrooms: 1 double, 1 family room
Bathrooms: 2 private

**Bed & breakfast**

| per night: | £min | £max |
| --- | --- | --- |
| Single | 17.00 | 19.00 |
| Double | 34.00 | 38.00 |

**Half board**

| per person: | £min | £max |
| --- | --- | --- |
| Daily | 26.50 | 28.50 |

Evening meal (last orders 1600)
Parking for 10

## CORSHAM

Wiltshire
Map ref 2B2

Growing town with old centre showing Flemish influence, legacy of former prosperity from weaving. The church, restored last century, retains Norman features. The Elizabethan Corsham Court, with additions by Capability Brown, has fine furniture.

### Boyds Farm

COMMENDED
Gastard, Corsham SN13 9PT
☎ (01249) 713146
*211-acre arable farm. Attractive 16th C listed farmhouse in the peaceful village of Gastard. Bath, Lacock, Castle Combe and numerous attractions are close by.*
Bedrooms: 1 double, 1 triple
Bathrooms: 1 private, 2 public

**Bed & breakfast**

| per night: | £min | £max |
| --- | --- | --- |
| Single | 16.00 | 18.00 |
| Double | 30.00 | 32.00 |

Parking for 6

### Halfway Firs

Listed
5 Halfway Firs, Corsham SN13 0PJ
☎ Bath (01225) 810552
*Situated 7 miles from Bath on A4, 5 miles from Chippenham and 1 mile from Corsham, overlooking open farmland.*
Bedrooms: 1 single, 1 double, 1 triple
Bathrooms: 1 public

**Bed & breakfast**

| per night: | £min | £max |
| --- | --- | --- |
| Single | 15.00 | 16.00 |
| Double | 26.00 | 30.00 |

Parking for 4

### Spiders Barn

COMMENDED
Cross Keys, Corsham SN13 0DT
☎ (01249) 712012
*Converted period barn. Guest accommodation is self-contained with own kitchen for tea and coffee. Peaceful and secluded with lovely views.*
Bedrooms: 2 double, 1 twin
Bathrooms: 3 private

**Bed & breakfast**

| per night: | £min | £max |
| --- | --- | --- |
| Single | 25.00 | 28.00 |
| Double | 35.00 | 40.00 |

Parking for 8

## COSSINGTON

Somerset
Map ref 1D1

### Brookhayes Farm

Listed
Cossington, Bridgwater TA7 8LW
☎ Bridgwater (01278) 722559
*On edge of lovely village of Cossington, with its leafy lanes, 15th C church and fantastic views over moors and hills. Only 5 minutes from M5, between Bridgwater and Glastonbury.*
Bedrooms: 1 double, 2 twin
Bathrooms: 2 private, 1 public

**Bed & breakfast**

| per night: | £min | £max |
| --- | --- | --- |
| Single | 16.00 | |
| Double | 36.00 | |

Open April-September

## CRACKINGTON HAVEN

Cornwall
Map ref 1C2

Tiny village on the North Cornwall coast, with a small sandy beach and surf bathing. The highest cliffs in Cornwall lie to the south.

### Coombe Barton Inn

Crackington Haven, Bude EX23 0JG
☎ St. Gennys (01840) 230345
Fax (01840) 230788

*Warm and friendly inn beside the beach, serving good food, local ales and fine wines and offering comfortable accommodation.*
Bedrooms: 1 single, 2 double, 1 twin, 1 family room
Bathrooms: 3 private, 2 public

**Bed & breakfast**

| per night: | £min | £max |
| --- | --- | --- |
| Single | 15.50 | 19.50 |
| Double | 35.00 | 55.00 |

Lunch available
Evening meal 1800 (last orders 2200)
Parking for 40
Open March-October
Cards accepted: Access, Visa, Diners, Amex, Switch/Delta

## Treworgie Barton ⋀⋀
HIGHLY COMMENDED

Crackington Haven, Bude EX23 0NL
☎ St Gennys (01840) 230233
*106-acre mixed farm. In secluded setting 2 miles from unspoilt cove. Good farmhouse cooking. Turn right at Wainhouse corner 10 miles south of Bude on A39, then follow farm signs.*
Bedrooms: 3 double, 1 twin, 1 family room
Bathrooms: 5 private

**Bed & breakfast**

| per night: | £min | £max |
| --- | --- | --- |
| Single | 17.00 | 23.00 |
| Double | 34.00 | 46.00 |

**Half board**

| per person: | £min | £max |
| --- | --- | --- |
| Daily | 30.00 | 36.00 |
| Weekly | 200.00 | 242.00 |

Evening meal 1830 (last orders 1800)
Parking for 5
Open February-September, November

## CREDITON
Devon
Map ref 1D2

Ancient town in fertile valley, once prosperous from wool, now active in cider-making. Said to be the birthplace of St Boniface. The 13th C Chapter House, the church governors' meeting place, holds a collection of armour from the Civil War.

## Birchmans Farm
COMMENDED

Colebrooke, Crediton EX17 5AD
☎ Bow (01363) 82393
*200-acre mixed farm. In the centre of Devon within easy reach of Exeter and Dartmoor. Home produce. All rooms en-suite with tea and coffee-making facilities.*
Bedrooms: 2 double, 1 twin
Bathrooms: 3 private

**Bed & breakfast**

| per night: | £min | £max |
| --- | --- | --- |
| Single | 14.00 | 16.00 |
| Double | 28.00 | 32.00 |

Evening meal (last orders 1830)
Parking for 6

## CREWKERNE
Somerset
Map ref 1D2

This charming little market town on the Dorset border nestles in undulating farmland and orchards in a conservation area. Built of local sandstone with Roman and Saxon origins. The magnificent St Bartholomew's Church dates from 15th C; St Bartholomew's Fair is held in September.

## Broadview ⋀⋀
DE LUXE

43 East Street, Crewkerne TA18 7AG
☎ (01460) 73424
*Unusual colonial bungalow residence c1926. Set in an acre of secluded feature gardens with many unusual plants. Friendly, relaxing atmosphere and carefully furnished en-suite rooms. Quality, traditional home cooking.*
Bedrooms: 1 double, 2 twin
Bathrooms: 3 private

**Bed & breakfast**

| per night: | £min | £max |
| --- | --- | --- |
| Single | 30.00 | 35.00 |
| Double | | 46.00 |

**Half board**

| per person: | £min | £max |
| --- | --- | --- |
| Daily | | 35.00 |
| Weekly | | 245.00 |

Evening meal 1830 (last orders 1200)
Parking for 6

## The Manor Arms
COMMENDED

North Perrott, Crewkerne TA18 7SG
☎ (01460) 72901
*16th C Grade II listed coaching inn set in the centre of a conservation area. Bar and restaurant menus with home-made meals.*
Bedrooms: 3 double, 2 twin
Bathrooms: 5 private

**Bed & breakfast**

| per night: | £min | £max |
| --- | --- | --- |
| Single | 28.00 | 31.00 |
| Double | 39.00 | 45.00 |

**Half board**

| per person: | £min | £max |
| --- | --- | --- |
| Daily | 32.00 | 43.00 |
| Weekly | 160.00 | 200.00 |

Lunch available
Evening meal 1900 (last orders 2130)

Parking for 24
Cards accepted: Access, Visa

## CRICKLADE
Wiltshire
Map ref 2B2

Standing on the upper Thames, an old town and former Anglo-Saxon settlement. The Roman road from Cirencester passes through and canals pass to north and south. The church, its lofty Tudor tower dominating the town, has work of varying periods from the 12th C to 1930.

## Waterhay Farm
COMMENDED

Leigh, Cricklade, Swindon SN6 6QY
☎ Cirencester (01285) 861253
*160-acre dairy farm. Cotswold-stone beamed farmhouse, dining room/TV lounge with splendid inglenook fireplace. Peaceful surroundings on edge of water park.*
Bedrooms: 1 twin, 1 triple
Bathrooms: 2 private

**Bed & breakfast**

| per night: | £min | £max |
| --- | --- | --- |
| Single | 17.00 | 20.00 |
| Double | 34.00 | 38.00 |

Parking for 4

## CROYDE
Devon
Map ref 1C1

Pretty village with thatched cottages near Croyde Bay. To the south stretch Saunton Sands and their dunelands Braunton Burrows with interesting flowers and plants, nature reserve and golf-course. Cliff walks and bird-watching at Baggy Point, west of the village.

## Combas Farm
Listed COMMENDED

Croyde, Braunton EX33 1PH
☎ (01271) 890398

*140-acre mixed farm. Old world 16th C farmhouse, in secluded situation only three-quarters of a mile from Woolacombe Bay "Blue Flag" beach. Home cooking using own produce.*
Bedrooms: 1 single, 2 double, 1 twin, 1 triple, 1 family room
Bathrooms: 2 public

*Continued ►*

## CROYDE

*Continued*

**Bed & breakfast**

| per night: | £min | £max |
|---|---|---|
| Single | 15.50 | 18.00 |
| Double | 31.00 | 36.00 |

**Half board**

| per person: | £min | £max |
|---|---|---|
| Daily | 23.50 | 26.00 |
| Weekly | 148.00 | 163.00 |

Evening meal 1830 (last orders 1630)
Parking for 10
Open March-November

ॐ♨♠☎ऀ⑤◆☆☑☉◻◷↾✓❀
◫ ⑳ SP ◰ T

### Denham Farm and Country House ♙

⚜⚜⚜ **COMMENDED**

North Buckland, Braunton EX33 1HY
☎ (01271) 890297
Fax (01271) 890297

*160-acre mixed farm. Sample home cooking in this delightful country house, a "little gem" off the beaten track. Enjoy peace and tranquillity amid beautiful unspoilt countryside, near miles of golden sands.*
Bedrooms: 6 double, 1 twin, 1 triple, 2 family rooms
Bathrooms: 10 private

**Bed & breakfast**

| per night: | £min | £max |
|---|---|---|
| Double | 40.00 | 50.00 |

**Half board**

| per person: | £min | £max |
|---|---|---|
| Daily | 32.00 | 37.00 |
| Weekly | 198.00 | 217.00 |

Evening meal 1900 (last orders 1900)
Parking for 8
Cards accepted: Access, Visa

ॐ◻◻♨☉◷↾✂☑☉◻◻, ◻◖❀✕
◫ ⑳ ◹ SP

## CUCKLINGTON

Somerset
Map ref 2B3

### Hale Farm

⚜⚜

Cucklington, Wincanton BA9 9PN
☎ Wincanton (01963) 33342
*28-acre mixed farm. 17th C farmhouse with beams, in peaceful situation near A303. Central for touring. Bedrooms en-suite, home cooking.*
Bedrooms: 2 double, 1 twin
Bathrooms: 3 private

**Bed & breakfast**

| per night: | £min | £max |
|---|---|---|
| Single | 16.00 | 16.00 |
| Double | 32.00 | 32.00 |

Parking for 3
Open April-October

ॐ6♨☑⑤↾◻☑☉◻✿◻◻

## CULLOMPTON

Devon
Map ref 1D2

Market town on former coaching routes, with pleasant tree-shaded cobbled pavements and some handsome 17th C houses. Earlier prosperity from the wool industry is reflected in the grandness of the church with its fan-vaulted aisle built by a wool-stapler in 1526.

### The Manor House Hotel ♙

⚜⚜

2/4 Fore Street, Cullompton
EX15 1JL
☎ (01884) 32281
Fax (01884) 38344
*Built in 1603 and formerly the grand town house of a local wool merchant. Recently restored. Situated deep in Devon country town of Cullompton. Proprietor-run.*
Bedrooms: 1 single, 5 double, 3 twin, 1 triple
Bathrooms: 10 private

**Bed & breakfast**

| per night: | £min | £max |
|---|---|---|
| Single | 39.50 | 42.50 |
| Double | 49.50 | 54.50 |

**Half board**

| per person: | £min | £max |
|---|---|---|
| Daily | 32.50 | 36.50 |
| Weekly | 210.00 | 235.00 |

Lunch available
Evening meal 1900 (last orders 2100)
Parking for 46
Cards accepted: Access, Visa

ॐ5◻◖◻◻♨☜☑⑤↾◻▥, ◻
◻4-50 ◖❀✕◫ ⑳ ◹ SP ◻

## DARTMOOR

*See under Ashburton, Bovey Tracey, Bridestowe, Buckfastleigh, Buckland Monachorum, Chagford, Drewsteignton, Dunsford, Holne, Ilsington, Lustleigh, Lydford, Moretonhampstead, Okehampton, Peter Tavy, Tavistock, Widecombe-in-the-Moor, Yelverton*

---

National Crown ratings were correct at the time of going to press but are subject to change. Please check at the time of booking.

---

## DARTMOUTH

Devon
Map ref 1D3

Ancient port at mouth of Dart. Has fine period buildings, notably town houses near Quay and Butterwalk of 1635. Harbour castle ruin. In 12th C Crusader fleets assembled here. Royal Naval College dominates from Hill. Carnival, June; Regatta, August.
*Tourist Information Centre*
☎ *(01803) 834224*

### Boringdon House

⚜⚜⚜ **HIGHLY COMMENDED**

1 Church Road, Dartmouth TQ6 9HQ
☎ (01803) 832235
*Welcoming Georgian house in large secluded garden overlooking Dartmouth town and harbour. Spacious attractive rooms. Courtyard parking. Short walk to town centre. No smoking please.*
Bedrooms: 1 double, 2 twin
Bathrooms: 3 private

**Bed & breakfast**

| per night: | £min | £max |
|---|---|---|
| Single | 36.00 | 43.00 |
| Double | 42.00 | 49.00 |

Parking for 3
Open March-December

◻◻♨☑⑤↾▥, ◻❀✕◫ ⑳ T

## DAWLISH

Devon
Map ref 1D2

Small resort, developed in Regency and Victorian periods beside Dawlish Water. Town centre has ornamental riverside gardens with black swans. One of British Rail's most scenic stretches was built by Brunel alongside jagged red cliffs between the sands and the town.
*Tourist Information Centre*
☎ *(01626) 863589*

### Smallacombe Farm

⚜⚜

Dawlish EX7 0PS
☎ (01626) 862536
*140-acre livestock farm. Secluded farm, 10 minutes from Dawlish and within easy reach of Dartmoor, Exeter and Torquay. En-suite available, children welcome. Ring for a brochure.*
Bedrooms: 2 double, 1 twin
Bathrooms: 1 private, 1 public

**Bed & breakfast**

| per night: | £min | £max |
|---|---|---|
| Single | 15.00 | 16.50 |
| Double | 30.00 | 33.00 |

**Half board**

| per person: | £min | £max |
|---|---|---|
| Daily | 25.00 | 28.00 |
| Weekly | 164.50 | |

Evening meal 1830 (last orders 1830)
Parking for 10

## DEVIZES

Wiltshire
Map ref 2B2

Old market town standing on the Kennet and Avon Canal. Rebuilt Norman castle, good 18th C buildings. St John's church has 12th C work and Norman tower. Museum of Wiltshire's archaeology and natural history reflects wealth of prehistoric sites in the county.
*Tourist Information Centre*
☎ *(01380) 729408*

### Aspiro

46 The Green, Poulshot, Devizes SN10 1RT
☎ (01380) 828465
*On green in exceptionally quiet village. Large secluded garden with much birdlife. Delightful old pub with restaurant nearby. German spoken.*
Bedrooms: 1 double, 1 twin, 1 triple
Bathrooms: 1 public

**Bed & breakfast**

| per night: | £min | £max |
| --- | --- | --- |
| Single | 18.00 | 18.00 |
| Double | 30.00 | 30.00 |

**Half board**

| per person: | £min | £max |
| --- | --- | --- |
| Daily | 26.00 | |

Evening meal 1900 (last orders 2000)
Parking for 11

### Pinecroft

Potterne Road (A360), Devizes SN10 5DA
☎ (01380) 721433
Fax (01380) 728368
*Comfortable Georgian family house with spacious rooms, exquisite garden and private parking. Only 3 minutes' walk from town centre.*
Bedrooms: 2 double, 1 twin, 1 family room
Bathrooms: 4 private

**Bed & breakfast**

| per night: | £min | £max |
| --- | --- | --- |
| Single | 18.00 | 24.00 |
| Double | 30.00 | 38.00 |

Parking for 7
Cards accepted: Access, Visa, Amex

### Spout Cottage

HIGHLY COMMENDED
Stert, Devizes SN10 3JD
☎ (01380) 724336
*Delightfully situated thatched cottage in secluded valley. Idyllic peaceful retreat. Well appointed centrally heated rooms,*

*inglenook fireplace, beamed ceilings. Delicious, imaginative food.*
Bedrooms: 1 single, 1 double, 1 twin
Bathrooms: 2 public

**Bed & breakfast**

| per night: | £min | £max |
| --- | --- | --- |
| Single | 18.50 | 20.00 |
| Double | 33.00 | 35.00 |

**Half board**

| per person: | £min | £max |
| --- | --- | --- |
| Daily | 31.50 | 33.00 |

Lunch available
Evening meal from 2000
Parking for 4

## DODDISCOMBSLEIGH

Devon
Map ref 1D2

Riverside village amid hilly countryside just east of Dartmoor. Former manor house stands beside granite church. Spared from the Roundheads by its remoteness, the church's chief interest lies in glowing 15th C windows said to contain Devon's finest collection of medieval glass.

### Great Leigh Farm & Guesthouse

Doddiscombsleigh, Exeter EX6 7RF
☎ Christow (01647) 52058
Fax (01647) 52058

*180-acre livestock farm. Secluded farmhouse and converted barns, traditionally furnished. Beams in bedrooms, inglenook fireplace and beams in dining room. Snooker room. Fishing on River Teign.*
Bedrooms: 3 double, 1 twin
Bathrooms: 4 private

**Bed & breakfast**

| per night: | £min | £max |
| --- | --- | --- |
| Single | 24.00 | 34.50 |
| Double | 45.00 | 60.00 |

**Half board**

| per person: | £min | £max |
| --- | --- | --- |
| Daily | 42.50 | 54.50 |
| Weekly | 270.00 | 381.50 |

Lunch available
Evening meal 1930 (last orders 2100)
Parking for 10
Cards accepted: Access, Visa, Switch/Delta

### Whitemoor Farm

Doddiscombsleigh, Exeter EX6 7PU
☎ Christow (01647) 52423
*284-acre mixed farm. Homely 16th C thatched farmhouse, surrounded by garden and own farmland. Within easy reach of Dartmoor, the coast, Exeter, forest walks, birdwatching and Haldon Racecourse. Evening meal on request with good local inn nearby. Swimming pool available.*
Bedrooms: 2 single, 1 double, 1 twin
Bathrooms: 1 public

**Bed & breakfast**

| per night: | £min | £max |
| --- | --- | --- |
| Single | 16.50 | 17.50 |
| Double | 32.00 | 35.00 |

Evening meal 1900 (last orders 2000)
Parking for 5
Cards accepted: Visa

## DORCHESTER

Dorset
Map ref 2B3

Busy medieval county town destroyed by fires in 17th and 18th C. Cromwellian stronghold and scene of Judge Jeffrey's Bloody Assize after Monmouth Rebellion of 1685. Tolpuddle Martyrs were tried in Shire Hall. Museum has Roman and earlier exhibits and Hardy relics.
*Tourist Information Centre*
☎ *(01305) 267992*

### Castleview

APPROVED
8 Edward Road, Dorchester DT1 2HJ
☎ (01305) 263507
*Excellent base for touring beautiful Dorset, offering TV, washbasin with softened water and tea/coffee-making facilities in all rooms.*
Bedrooms: 2 single, 1 double, 1 twin
Bathrooms: 2 private, 1 public

**Bed & breakfast**

| per night: | £min | £max |
| --- | --- | --- |
| Single | 14.00 | |
| Double | 18.00 | |

Parking for 4

### Churchview Guest House

Winterbourne Abbas, Dorchester DT2 9LS
☎ Martinstown (01305) 889296

Continued ▶

Please check prices and other details at the time of booking.

## DORCHESTER

*Continued*

*Beautiful 17th C guesthouse set in a small village 5 miles west of Dorchester. Noted for its warm welcome, comfort and delicious home cooking.*
Bedrooms: 6 double, 4 twin
Bathrooms: 4 private, 2 public

**Bed & breakfast**

| per night: | £min | £max |
| --- | --- | --- |
| Single | 17.50 | 23.00 |
| Double | 35.00 | 46.00 |

**Half board**

| per person: | £min | £max |
| --- | --- | --- |
| Daily | 27.50 | 33.00 |
| Weekly | 180.00 | 220.00 |

Evening meal 1900 (last orders 1900)
Parking for 10
Cards accepted: Access, Visa, Switch/ Delta

### The Dower House

COMMENDED

Bradford Peverell, Dorchester
DT2 9SF
☎ (01305) 266125

*Grade II listed village house set in 4.5 acres of partially walled garden. Warm welcome and home baking. Three miles north-west of Dorchester.*
Bedrooms: 1 double, 1 twin
Bathrooms: 2 private

**Bed & breakfast**

| per night: | £min | £max |
| --- | --- | --- |
| Single | 16.00 | 17.50 |
| Double | 32.00 | 35.00 |

Parking for 3
Open March-October

### Mountain Ash

APPROVED

30 Mountain Ash Road, Dorchester
DT1 2PB
☎ (01305) 264811
*Comfortable accommodation close to transport, Records Office and museums. Washbasins, TV, beverage facilities in bedrooms. Owner knowledgeable about Dorset.*
Bedrooms: 1 single, 1 double, 1 twin
Bathrooms: 1 public

**Bed & breakfast**

| per night: | £min | £max |
| --- | --- | --- |
| Single | 15.00 | 18.00 |
| Double | 30.00 | 36.00 |

Parking for 5

### Riverhill House

COMMENDED

7 East Hill, Charminster, Dorchester
DT2 9QL
☎ (01305) 265614
*Pretty 18th C house in Hardy country, set in attractive grounds of 2 acres. Accommodation with every comfort.*
Bedrooms: 1 double, 2 twin
Bathrooms: 1 private, 2 public

**Bed & breakfast**

| per night: | £min | £max |
| --- | --- | --- |
| Single | 15.00 | |
| Double | 30.00 | 36.00 |

**Half board**

| per person: | £min | £max |
| --- | --- | --- |
| Daily | 23.00 | 26.00 |
| Weekly | 155.00 | 175.00 |

Evening meal 1800 (last orders 2030)
Parking for 6

## DREWSTEIGNTON

Devon
Map ref 1C2

Pretty village of thatched cottages overlooking the steep, wooded Teign valley at the northern edge of Dartmoor. The tree-shaded square shelters a fine 15th C church. To the west is Sir Edwin Lutyens' dramatic Castle Drogo in a romantic setting high over the Teign Gorge.

### The Old Rectory

Drewsteignton, Exeter EX6 6QT
☎ (01647) 281269
Fax (01647) 281269
*Georgian family house in two acres on edge of unspoilt Dartmoor village. Good walking and touring centre. Private guest wing. Home produce.*
Bedrooms: 2 double, 1 twin
Bathrooms: 1 private, 1 public

**Bed & breakfast**

| per night: | £min | £max |
| --- | --- | --- |
| Single | 18.00 | 21.00 |
| Double | 30.00 | 36.00 |

**Half board**

| per person: | £min | £max |
| --- | --- | --- |
| Daily | 24.00 | |

Evening meal 1800 (last orders 2100)
Parking for 3

We advise you to confirm your booking in writing.

## DULVERTON

Somerset
Map ref 1D1

Set among woods and hills of south-west Exmoor, a busy riverside town with a 13th C church. The Rivers Barle and Exe are rich in salmon and trout. The information centre at the Exmoor National Park Headquarters at Dulverton is open throughout the year.

### Highercombe

COMMENDED

Dulverton TA22 9PT
☎ (01398) 23451
*Relaxing, peacefully situated farmhouse, 14th C origins. Set in 8 acres of grounds and gardens. Close to open moorland. Beautiful views.*
Bedrooms: 2 double, 1 twin
Bathrooms: 3 private

**Bed & breakfast**

| per night: | £min | £max |
| --- | --- | --- |
| Single | 21.00 | 24.00 |
| Double | 32.00 | 38.00 |

Parking for 10

### Highercombe Farm

Listed

Dulverton TA22 9PT
☎ (01398) 23616
*450-acre livestock farm. In the heart of Exmoor next to open moorland with red deer and wild ponies. Superb 60 mile views. Antiques, friendly welcome, quality cooking.*
Bedrooms: 3 double
Bathrooms: 2 public

**Bed & breakfast**

| per night: | £min | £max |
| --- | --- | --- |
| Single | 14.00 | 16.00 |
| Double | 27.00 | 30.00 |

**Half board**

| per person: | £min | £max |
| --- | --- | --- |
| Daily | 23.50 | 30.00 |
| Weekly | 164.00 | 182.00 |

Evening meal 1800 (last orders 2000)
Parking for 4
Open March-November

### Newhouse Farm

COMMENDED

Oakford, Tiverton, Devon EX16 9JE
☎ Oakford (01398) 5347

*42-acre livestock farm. Charming 16th C farmhouse featuring oak beams and inglenook fireplace. Pretty en-suite*

*bedrooms with colour TV. Home-baked bread, delicious country cooking, warm hospitality.*
Bedrooms: 3 double
Bathrooms: 3 private

**Bed & breakfast**

| per night: | £min | £max |
| --- | --- | --- |
| Single | 18.00 | 19.00 |
| Double | 34.00 | 36.00 |

**Half board**

| per person: | £min | £max |
| --- | --- | --- |
| Daily | 27.00 | 28.00 |
| Weekly | 170.00 | 175.00 |

Evening meal 1930 (last orders 1700)
Parking for 3

### Springfield Farm

🏵🏵 COMMENDED

Dulverton TA22 9QD
☎ (01398) 23722
*270-acre livestock farm. Peacefully situated in Exmoor, 1.25 miles walk from Tarr Steps, with magnificent moorland and woodland views. Comfortable accommodation with friendly service and good food.*
Bedrooms: 1 single, 1 double, 1 twin
Bathrooms: 1 private, 1 public

**Bed & breakfast**

| per night: | £min | £max |
| --- | --- | --- |
| Single | 16.00 | 20.00 |
| Double | 30.00 | 36.00 |

**Half board**

| per person: | £min | £max |
| --- | --- | --- |
| Daily | 26.00 | |
| Weekly | 175.00 | |

Evening meal 1800 (last orders 2000)
Parking for 11
Open April-October

## DUNSFORD

Devon
Map ref 1D2

### Royal Oak Inn 🏍

Listed APPROVED

Dunsford, Exeter EX6 7DA
☎ Christow (01647) 52256
*Beautiful en-suite rooms in Victorian country inn, in the heart of a charming thatched village in the Teign Valley. Always 6 real ales and unusual home-made meals served 7 days a week.*
Bedrooms: 4 double, 2 twin, 2 triple
Bathrooms: 5 private, 1 public

**Bed & breakfast**

| per night: | £min | £max |
| --- | --- | --- |
| Single | 18.00 | 25.00 |
| Double | 31.50 | 40.00 |

Lunch available
Evening meal 1830 (last orders 2100)
Parking for 40
Cards accepted: Access, Visa

## DUNSTER

Somerset
Map ref 1D1

Ancient town with views of Exmoor. The hilltop castle has been continuously occupied since 1070. Medieval prosperity from cloth built 16th C octagonal Yarn Market and the church. A riverside mill, packhorse bridge and 18th C hilltop folly occupy other interesting corners in the town.

### Yarn Market Hotel (Exmoor) 🏍

🏵🏵🏵 APPROVED

25 High Street, Dunster, Minehead TA24 6SF
☎ (01643) 821425
Fax (01643) 821199
*Central and accessible hotel in quaint English village, an ideal location from which to explore the Exmoor National Park.*
Bedrooms: 1 double, 1 twin, 1 triple, 1 family room
Bathrooms: 4 private

**Bed & breakfast**

| per night: | £min | £max |
| --- | --- | --- |
| Single | 17.50 | 30.00 |
| Double | 35.00 | 60.00 |

**Half board**

| per person: | £min | £max |
| --- | --- | --- |
| Daily | 26.00 | 38.50 |
| Weekly | 168.00 | 255.50 |

Evening meal 1800 (last orders 2000)
Parking for 5
Cards accepted: Access, Visa, Amex

## EAST ALLINGTON

Devon
Map ref 1C3

### Lower Grimpstonleigh 🏍

🏵🏵 HIGHLY COMMENDED

East Allington, Totnes TQ9 7QH
☎ (01548) 521258
Fax (01548) 521258

*A tranquil retreat which combines the charm of an old world farmstead with spacious modern living. Beautifully furnished. Exceptionally high standards of comfort and service. Log fires.*
Bedrooms: 2 double
Bathrooms: 2 private

**Bed & breakfast**

| per night: | £min | £max |
| --- | --- | --- |
| Single | 25.00 | 30.00 |
| Double | 50.00 | 50.00 |

**Half board**

| per person: | £min | £max |
| --- | --- | --- |
| Daily | 40.00 | 45.00 |

Evening meal 1900 (last orders 2100)
Parking for 6

## EAST BUDLEIGH

Devon
Map ref 1D2

### Thorn Mill Farm

🏵🏵 HIGHLY COMMENDED

Frogmore Road, East Budleigh, Budleigh Salterton EX9 7BB
☎ Exmouth (01395) 444088

*Country hosts, David and Jennie Capel-Jones, welcome you to share their picturesque 16th C family home, with beamed lounge, inglenook fireplace, period features. Overlooking River Otter valley and footpaths to coastal paths.*
Bedrooms: 1 single, 1 double, 1 twin
Bathrooms: 1 private, 1 public

**Bed & breakfast**

| per night: | £min | £max |
| --- | --- | --- |
| Single | 18.00 | 22.00 |
| Double | 36.00 | 50.00 |

Parking for 3

## ENFORD

Wiltshire
Map ref 2B2

### Enford House

Enford, Pewsey SN9 6DJ
☎ Stonehenge (01980) 670414
*Listed country house with pretty garden. In attractive village 7 miles from Stonehenge. Ideal centre for walking and cycling. Good food at local village pub.*
Bedrooms: 1 double, 1 twin, 1 triple
Bathrooms: 3 private

**Bed & breakfast**

| per night: | £min | £max |
| --- | --- | --- |
| Single | 17.00 | |
| Double | 30.00 | |

Evening meal 1830 (last orders 1300)
Parking for 8

## EXETER

Devon
Map ref 1D2

University city rebuilt after the 1940s around its cathedral. Attractions include 13th C cathedral with fine west front; notable waterfront buildings; Maritime Museum; Guildhall; Royal Albert Memorial Museum; underground passages; Northcott Theatre.
*Tourist Information Centre*
☎ *(01392) 265700*

### Clock Tower Hotel ᴍ
⌂
16 New North Road, Exeter EX4 4HF
☎ (01392) 424545
Fax (01392) 218445
*Homely accommodation in the city centre. Coach and railway stations within 10 minutes' walk. All modern facilities. En-suite rooms.*
Bedrooms: 3 single, 6 double, 3 twin, 1 triple, 1 family room
Bathrooms: 8 private, 2 public

**Bed & breakfast**

| per night: | £min | £max |
| --- | --- | --- |
| Single | 15.00 | 19.00 |
| Double | 25.00 | 33.00 |

**Half board**

| per person: | £min | £max |
| --- | --- | --- |
| Daily | 24.00 | 32.00 |
| Weekly | 140.00 | 160.00 |

Evening meal 1800 (last orders 1600)
Cards accepted: Access, Visa, Diners, Amex

⌂☎⌕♨♿§⌗🅿🅿💻📺🅱🚗🚼🅿ᴛ

### Culm Vale Country House
⌂⌂
Stoke Canon, Exeter EX5 4EG
☎ (01392) 841615
*Comfortable accommodation in beautiful old country house 4 miles north east of Exeter. Friendly relaxed atmosphere, lovely gardens, ample free parking. Ideal touring centre.*
Bedrooms: 2 double, 1 twin
Bathrooms: 1 private, 1 public

**Bed & breakfast**

| per night: | £min | £max |
| --- | --- | --- |
| Single | 16.00 | 20.00 |
| Double | 30.00 | 32.00 |

Evening meal from 1830
Parking for 6

⌂♨♿🅱📺💻🅿⌕🚶♿✕🚗🅿

### The Grange
⌂
Stoke Hill, Exeter EX4 7JH
☎ (01392) 59723
*Country house set in 3 acres of woodlands, 1.5 miles from the city centre. Ideal for holidays and off-season breaks. En-suite rooms available.*
Bedrooms: 2 double, 2 twin
Bathrooms: 4 private

**Bed & breakfast**

| per night: | £min | £max |
| --- | --- | --- |
| Single | 18.00 | 20.00 |
| Double | 28.00 | 30.00 |

Parking for 11

⌂⌂♨♿🅱💻🅿⌕🚶♿✕🚗🅿🅿

### Hayne Barton
ᴹᴹᴹ **COMMENDED**
Whitestone, Exeter EX4 2JN
☎ Longdown (01392) 811268
*16-acre mixed farm. Listed farmhouse dating from 1086 (Domesday Book) set in gardens, woodland and fields overlooking Alphinbrook Valley. 4 miles from Exeter Cathedral and convenient for Dartmoor and Torquay.*
Bedrooms: 2 double, 1 twin
Bathrooms: 3 private

**Bed & breakfast**

| per night: | £min | £max |
| --- | --- | --- |
| Single | 22.00 | 24.00 |
| Double | 38.00 | 40.00 |

**Half board**

| per person: | £min | £max |
| --- | --- | --- |
| Daily | 30.00 | 32.00 |
| Weekly | 170.00 | 180.00 |

Evening meal 1930 (last orders 2030)
Parking for 10

⌂⌂⌂♨♿🅱§⌂🅿✕🅱📺💻🅿⌕🚶♿✕🚗🅿🅿

### Marianne Pool Farm
**Listed**
Clyst St George, Exeter EX3 0NZ
☎ Topsham (01392) 874939

*200-acre mixed farm. Peacefully situated thatched Devon longhouse, overlooking countryside in quiet rural area near Exeter. Comfortably furnished, spacious rooms. 5 minutes from junction 30 of M5.*
Bedrooms: 1 twin, 1 family room
Bathrooms: 1 public

**Bed & breakfast**

| per night: | £min | £max |
| --- | --- | --- |
| Single | 15.00 | 16.00 |
| Double | 30.00 | 32.00 |

Parking for 2
Open April-October

⌂♨♿🅱✕🅱📺🚗⌕♿✕🚗🅿

### Rydon Farm
⌂⌂
Woodbury, Exeter EX5 1LB
☎ Woodbury (01395) 232341

---

Please mention this guide when making a booking.

---

*280-acre dairy farm. 16th C Devon longhouse with exposed beams and inglenook fireplace. Spacious individually furnished and decorated rooms, one with romantic four-poster. En-suite facilities.*
Bedrooms: 1 double, 1 twin, 1 triple
Bathrooms: 3 private

**Bed & breakfast**

| per night: | £min | £max |
| --- | --- | --- |
| Single | 17.00 | 23.00 |
| Double | 34.00 | 46.00 |

Parking for 5

⌂🅱♨♿🅱§🅱📺💻🚗♿🚗🅿
🅿🅿

## EXMOOR

*See under Allerford, Brendon, Dulverton, Dunster, Lynton, Parracombe, Timberscombe, West Anstey, Wheddon Cross, Winsford*

## EXMOUTH

Devon
Map ref 1D2

Developed as a seaside resort in George III's reign, set against the woods of the Exe Estuary and red cliffs of Orcombe Point. Extensive sands, small harbour, chapel and almshouses, a model railway and A la Ronde, a 16-sided house.
*Tourist Information Centre*
☎ *(01395) 263744*

### The Mews
⌂
Knappe Cross, Brixington Lane, Exmouth EX8 5DL
☎ (01395) 272198
*Large part of a delightfully secluded mews building in a country setting. Midway between Exmouth and Woodbury Common. We ask that guests refrain from smoking.*
Bedrooms: 1 single, 1 double, 1 twin
Bathrooms: 1 public

**Bed & breakfast**

| per night: | £min | £max |
| --- | --- | --- |
| Single | 13.50 | 15.00 |
| Double | 27.00 | 30.00 |

Parking for 10

⌂4♿§🅱✕🅱📺💻♿✕🚗

### The Swallows
⌂⌂⌂ **COMMENDED**
11 Carlton Hill, Exmouth EX8 2AJ
☎ (01395) 263937
*Attractive Georgian house only 300 yards from seafront, pleasantly converted to modern standards and*

*providing comfortable guest accommodation.*
Bedrooms: 1 single, 2 double, 2 twin, 1 family room
Bathrooms: 6 private

**Bed & breakfast**

| per night: | £min | £max |
| --- | --- | --- |
| Single | 17.00 | 25.00 |
| Double | 32.00 | 40.00 |

**Half board**

| per person: | £min | £max |
| --- | --- | --- |
| Daily | 26.00 | 34.00 |
| Weekly | 173.00 | 220.00 |

Evening meal from 1800
Parking for 3

## FENNY BRIDGES

Devon
Map ref 1D2

### Skinners Ash Farm

Listed COMMENDED

Fenny Bridges, Honiton EX14 0BH
☎ Honiton (01404) 850231
*127-acre mixed farm. Traditional farmhouse offering cream teas to order and with rare animals and birds. Situated on A30, 3 miles from Honiton and close to local beaches.*
Bedrooms: 1 double, 1 family room
Bathrooms: 2 private

**Bed & breakfast**

| per night: | £min | £max |
| --- | --- | --- |
| Single | 15.50 | 15.50 |
| Double | 31.00 | 31.00 |

**Half board**

| per person: | £min | £max |
| --- | --- | --- |
| Daily | 22.50 | 22.50 |
| Weekly | 145.50 | 145.50 |

Lunch available
Evening meal 1900 (last orders 2100)
Parking for 7

## FIGHELDEAN

Wiltshire
Map ref 2B2

### Vale House

Listed

Figheldean, Salisbury SP4 8JJ
☎ Stonehenge (01980) 670713
*Secluded house in centre of picturesque village, 4 miles north of Amesbury on A345. Pub food nearby. Stonehenge 2 miles.*
Bedrooms: 1 single, 2 twin
Bathrooms: 2 public

**Bed & breakfast**

| per night: | £min | £max |
| --- | --- | --- |
| Single | 12.00 | 14.00 |
| Double | 24.00 | 28.00 |

Parking for 3

## FONTHILL GIFFORD

Wiltshire
Map ref 2B3

### Beckford Arms ♈

♛♛♛ HIGHLY COMMENDED

Fonthill Gifford, Tisbury, Salisbury SP3 6PX
☎ Tisbury (01747) 870385
Fax (01747) 851496

*Tastefully refurbished, stylish and comfortable 18th C inn, between Tisbury and Hindon in area of outstanding beauty. 2 miles A303. Convenient for Salisbury and Shaftesbury.*
Bedrooms: 2 single, 4 double, 1 twin
Bathrooms: 5 private, 2 private showers

**Bed & breakfast**

| per night: | £min | £max |
| --- | --- | --- |
| Single | 19.50 | 29.50 |
| Double | 39.00 | 54.50 |

**Half board**

| per person: | £min | £max |
| --- | --- | --- |
| Weekly | 192.50 | 192.50 |

Lunch available
Evening meal 1900 (last orders 2200)
Parking for 42
Cards accepted: Access, Visa, Amex

## FOWEY

Cornwall
Map ref 1B3

Set on steep slopes at the mouth of the Fowey River, important clayport and fishing town. Ruined forts guarding the shore recall days of "Fowey Gallants" who ruled local seas. The lofty church rises above the town. Ferries to Polruan and Bodinnick; August Regatta.
*Tourist Information Centre*
☎ *(01726) 833616*

### King of Prussia ♈

♛ APPROVED

Town Quay, Fowey PL23 1AT
☎ (01726) 832450
*Small, friendly inn, very comfortable, with all rooms overlooking town, quay and River Fowey. Easy reach of shops and restaurants.*
Bedrooms: 2 double, 4 triple
Bathrooms: 6 private

**Bed & breakfast**

| per night: | £min | £max |
| --- | --- | --- |
| Double | 48.50 | 50.00 |

**Half board**

| per person: | £min | £max |
| --- | --- | --- |
| Daily | 34.50 | |
| Weekly | 227.00 | |

Lunch available
Cards accepted: Access, Visa

## FROME

Somerset
Map ref 2B2

Old market town with modern light industry, its medieval centre watered by the River Frome. Above Cheap Street with its flagstones and watercourse is the church showing work of varying periods. Interesting buildings include 18th C wool merchants' houses.
*Tourist Information Centre*
☎ *(01383) 467271*

### Fourwinds Guest House

♛♛♛ COMMENDED

19 Bath Road, Frome BA11 2HJ
☎ (01373) 462618
*Chalet bungalow with some bedrooms on ground floor. TV and tea-making facilities. Licensed, good food.*
Bedrooms: 1 single, 2 double, 1 twin, 1 triple, 1 family room
Bathrooms: 6 private

**Bed & breakfast**

| per night: | £min | £max |
| --- | --- | --- |
| Single | 20.00 | 30.00 |
| Double | 40.00 | 45.00 |

Lunch available
Evening meal 1800 (last orders 1900)
Parking for 12

## GEORGE NYMPTON

Devon
Map ref 1C1

### West Trayne

♛♛

George Nympton, South Molton EX36 4JE
☎ South Molton (01769) 572534
*Grade II listed 16th C country house with large garden. Beamed dining room with genuine inglenook. Very comfortable accommodation. Good food.*
Bedrooms: 2 double, 1 twin
Bathrooms: 1 private, 1 public

**Bed & breakfast**

| per night: | £min | £max |
| --- | --- | --- |
| Single | 14.00 | 15.00 |
| Double | 28.00 | 30.00 |

Continued ▶

We advise you to confirm your booking in writing.

## GEORGE NYMPTON

*Continued*

**Half board**

| per person: | £min | £max |
| --- | --- | --- |
| Daily | 21.00 | 22.00 |
| Weekly | 147.00 | 154.00 |

Evening meal 1900 (last orders 1700)
Parking for 5

🏇 8 ⓤ Ⓢ 🅼 📺 🛏 ❅ 🐾 🏠

## GLASTONBURY

Somerset
Map ref 2A2

Market town associated with Joseph of Arimathea and the birth of English Christianity. Built around its 7th C abbey said to be the site of King Arthur's burial. Glastonbury Tor with its ancient tower gives panoramic views over flat country and the Mendip Hills.
*Tourist Information Centre*
☎ *(01458) 832954*

### Laverley House

⚜⚜

West Pennard, Glastonbury BA6 8NE
☎ Pilton (01749) 890696
*Grade II listed Georgian farmhouse in rural position with views towards Mendips. On the A361, 4 miles east of Glastonbury.*
Bedrooms: 2 double, 1 family room
Bathrooms: 3 private

**Bed & breakfast**

| per night: | £min | £max |
| --- | --- | --- |
| Single | 18.50 | 25.00 |
| Double | 37.00 | 37.00 |

Parking for 6
Open March-November

🏇🕯️🖵👄🔥ⓤⓈ⤢🅼📺🛏🚌∪↑ ❅🐾🏠

### Middlewick Farm

⚜⚜

Wick, Glastonbury BA6 8JW
☎ (01458) 832351
*20-acre beef farm. Tasteful barn conversion with ground floor accommodation and indoor heated swimming pool, set in 20 acres of gardens and apple orchards. From Glastonbury take A361 Shepton Mallet road for 1.5 miles, take left turn signposted Wick, continue for 1.5 miles.*
Bedrooms: 2 double, 1 twin
Bathrooms: 3 private

**Bed & breakfast**

| per night: | £min | £max |
| --- | --- | --- |
| Single | 21.00 | 24.00 |
| Double | 32.00 | 34.00 |

**Half board**

| per person: | £min | £max |
| --- | --- | --- |
| Daily | 25.00 | 33.00 |
| Weekly | 175.00 | 241.00 |

Evening meal 1900 (last orders 2030)
Parking for 20

🏇🖵👄🔥ⓤ🛡️Ⓢ⤢🅼📺🛏🚌🔌 ❅🗡️🐾🏠

### Pippin

**Listed** **APPROVED**

4 Ridgeway Gardens, Glastonbury BA6 8ER
☎ (01458) 834262
*Peaceful location with short walk to town centre or the Tor. Superb views over Chalice Hill. Every comfort.*
Bedrooms: 1 single, 1 double, 1 twin
Bathrooms: 1 private, 1 public

**Bed & breakfast**

| per night: | £min | £max |
| --- | --- | --- |
| Single | 12.50 | 14.00 |
| Double | 27.00 | 32.00 |

Parking for 2

🏇🌂🖵👄🔥ⓤ⤢🅼📺🛏🚌🐾

### Wick Hollow House

⚜⚜

8 Wick Hollow, Glastonbury BA6 8JJ
☎ (01458) 833595
*Peaceful, self-contained accommodation with private sitting room, on ground floor of lovely house overlooking Chalice Hill. Special rates for stays of more than 3 nights. Children half price.*
Bedrooms: 1 family room
Bathrooms: 1 private

**Bed & breakfast**

| per night: | £min | £max |
| --- | --- | --- |
| Single | 25.00 | 30.00 |
| Double | 35.00 | 40.00 |

Parking for 2

🏇🌂🖳👄🔥ⓤ🛡️Ⓢ⤢🅼📺🛏🚌🐾 ❅🗡️🅞🆂🅿

## GRAMPOUND

Cornwall
Map ref 1B3

### Perran House Ⓜ

⚜⚜

Fore Street, Grampound, Truro TR2 4RS
☎ St. Austell (01726) 882066
*Delightful listed cottage in the pretty village of Grampound, between St Austell and Truro. Central for touring.*
Bedrooms: 1 single, 3 double, 1 twin
Bathrooms: 3 private, 1 public

**Bed & breakfast**

| per night: | £min | £max |
| --- | --- | --- |
| Single | 13.00 | 14.50 |
| Double | 26.00 | 33.00 |

Parking for 6
Cards accepted: Access, Visa

🏇🖳🖵👄🔥ⓤ🛡️Ⓢ🅼📺🛏🚌❅🗡️🐾 🏠🅣

---

Please mention this guide
when making a booking.

---

## GREINTON

Somerset
Map ref 1D1

### West Town Farm

⚜⚜ **COMMENDED**

Greinton, Bridgwater TA7 9BW
☎ Ashcott (01458) 210277
*Original part of house is over 200 years old, with large inglenook fire and bread oven, flagstone floors and Georgian front. Listed building. Non-smoking establishment.*
Bedrooms: 1 double, 1 twin
Bathrooms: 2 private

**Bed & breakfast**

| per night: | £min | £max |
| --- | --- | --- |
| Single | 18.00 | 20.00 |
| Double | 36.00 | 40.00 |

Parking for 2
Open March-September

🏇 03 🖵👄🔥ⓤⓈ⤢🅼🛏❅🐾🗡️

## HARTLAND

Devon
Map ref 1C1

Hamlet on high, wild country near Hartland Point. Just west, the parish church tower makes a magnificent landmark; the light, unrestored interior holds one of Devon's finest rood screens. There are spectacular cliffs around Hartland Point and the lighthouse.

### Elmscott Farm

⚜⚜

Hartland, Bideford EX39 6ES
☎ (01237) 441276
*650-acre mixed farm. In a coastal setting, quietly situated near the Devon/Cornwall border. Signposted from the main A39, about 4 miles away.*
Bedrooms: 2 double, 1 twin
Bathrooms: 1 private, 1 public

**Bed & breakfast**

| per night: | £min | £max |
| --- | --- | --- |
| Single | 15.00 | 16.00 |
| Double | 30.00 | 32.00 |

**Half board**

| per person: | £min | £max |
| --- | --- | --- |
| Daily | 23.50 | 24.50 |

Evening meal 1800 (last orders 2000)
Parking for 8
Open April-October

🏇👄ⓤⓈ🅼📺🅠∪↑❅🗡️🐾

---

Individual proprietors
have supplied all details
of accommodation.
Although we do check for
accuracy, we advise you
to confirm the information
at the time of booking.

---

## HELSTON

Cornwall
Map ref 1B3

Handsome town with steep, main street and narrow alleys. In medieval times it was a major port and stannary town. Most buildings date from Regency and Victorian periods. The famous May dance, the Furry, is thought to have pre-Christian origins. A museum occupies the old Butter Market.

### Longstone Farm ⚇
COMMENDED
Trenear, Helston TR13 0HG
☎ (01326) 572483
*62-acre dairy farm. In peaceful countryside in west Cornwall. Ideal for touring and beaches. Flambards, horse riding and swimming pool nearby. B3297 to Redruth, left for Coverack Bridges. Right at bottom of hill, continue left for about 1.5 miles to Longstone Farm.*
Bedrooms: 3 single, 3 double, 1 twin, 1 triple
Bathrooms: 3 private, 2 public

**Bed & breakfast**
| per night: | £min | £max |
|---|---|---|
| Single | 14.00 | 17.00 |
| Double | 28.00 | 34.00 |

**Half board**
| per person: | £min | £max |
|---|---|---|
| Daily | 21.50 | 25.50 |
| Weekly | 135.00 | 150.00 |

Evening meal 1800 (last orders 0900)
Parking for 6
Open March-October

### Riverside ⚇
COMMENDED
Nantithet, Cury, Helston TR12 7RB
☎ Mullion (01326) 241027

*Small guesthouse, friendly and relaxing, in rural situation midway between Helston and Mullion. Enjoy home cooking including vegetarian dishes. Ideal for touring and walking. Within 2 miles of beaches, Mullion Golf Club and Flambards Theme Park.*
Bedrooms: 2 double, 1 twin, 1 family room
Bathrooms: 1 private, 2 public

**Bed & breakfast**
| per night: | £min | £max |
|---|---|---|
| Single | 13.50 | 18.50 |
| Double | 27.00 | 37.00 |

**Half board**
| per person: | £min | £max |
|---|---|---|
| Daily | 23.50 | 28.50 |
| Weekly | 164.50 | 182.00 |

Evening meal 1900 (last orders 2030)
Parking for 6

## HENSTRIDGE

Somerset
Map ref 2B3

Village with a rebuilt church containing the Tudor Carent tomb.

### Quiet Corner Farm ⚇
COMMENDED
Henstridge, Templecombe BA8 0RA
☎ Stalbridge (01963) 363045
Fax (01963) 363045
*5-acre livestock & fruit farm. Comfortable, welcoming 18th C farmhouse and lovely old barns, some converted to holiday cottages. In conservation village with excellent eating places and shops. Beautiful gardens and orchards. Miniature Shetland pony stud.*
Bedrooms: 2 double, 1 twin
Bathrooms: 1 private, 1 public, 1 private shower

**Bed & breakfast**
| per night: | £min | £max |
|---|---|---|
| Single | 20.00 | 25.00 |
| Double | 35.00 | 39.00 |

Parking for 8

## HIGHWORTH

Wiltshire
Map ref 2B2

### Roves Farm
COMMENDED
Sevenhampton, Highworth, Swindon SN6 7QG
☎ Swindon (01793) 763939
Fax (01793) 763939
*450-acre arable & livestock farm. Spacious, comfortable, quiet accommodation surrounded by beautiful countryside. Panoramic views, farm trail to woods, ponds and river. Signposted in Sevenhampton village.*
Bedrooms: 1 twin, 1 triple
Bathrooms: 2 private

**Bed & breakfast**
| per night: | £min | £max |
|---|---|---|
| Single | 19.50 | 20.00 |
| Double | 32.00 | 33.00 |

Parking for 5

---

We advise you to confirm your booking in writing.

---

## HOLNE

Devon
Map ref 1C2

Woodland village on south-east edge of Dartmoor. Its 15th C church has a painted medieval screen. Charles Kingsley was born at the vicarage. Holne Woods slope to the River Dart.

### Dodbrooke Farm
Listed
Michelcombe, Holne, Newton Abbot TQ13 7SP
☎ Poundsgate (01364) 3461
*23-acre livestock farm. Listed 17th C longhouse in idyllic setting at foot of Dartmoor, on farm with animals and large gardens. From Ashburton on A38 take road to Two Bridges, fork left for Holne then follow signs to Michelcombe.*
Bedrooms: 2 single, 2 twin
Bathrooms: 1 public

**Bed & breakfast**
| per night: | £min | £max |
|---|---|---|
| Single | 14.00 | 15.00 |
| Double | 30.00 | 31.00 |

**Half board**
| per person: | £min | £max |
|---|---|---|
| Daily | 22.00 | 23.50 |
| Weekly | 144.20 | 150.50 |

Evening meal from 1930
Parking for 3
Open January-November

### Hazelwood
Listed APPROVED
Holne, Newton Abbot TQ13 7SJ
☎ Poundsgate (01364) 631235
*Near Ashburton, family-run bed and breakfast in village with panoramic views. Village amenities include shop, post office and period pub.*
Bedrooms: 1 single, 1 double
Bathrooms: 1 public

**Bed & breakfast**
| per night: | £min | £max |
|---|---|---|
| Single | 14.00 | 15.00 |
| Double | 28.00 | 30.00 |

Parking for 3

## HOLNEST

Dorset
Map ref 2B3

### Bookham Stud and Ryewater Farm
Listed COMMENDED
Holnest, Sherborne DT9 5PL
☎ (01963) 210248
*80-acre horse farm. Old stone farmhouse in peaceful situation, surrounded by beautiful garden. Take A352 from Sherborne, 5 miles on turn*
Continued ▶

## HOLNEST

### Continued

left at signpost to Boyshill, half-a-mile
on turn left.
Bedrooms: 1 single, 2 twin
Bathrooms: 1 private, 1 public

**Bed & breakfast**

| per night: | £min | £max |
|---|---|---|
| Single | 14.00 | 18.00 |
| Double | 40.00 | 50.00 |
| Parking for 22 | | |

## ILSINGTON

Devon
Map ref 1D2

### Narracombe Farm

**COMMENDED**

Ilsington, Newton Abbot TQ13 9RD
☎ Haytor (01364) 661243 & 661506
Fax (01364) 661516
*220-acre mixed farm. A lovely old
Devon longhouse full of character and
charm. Spacious, peaceful, attractive
and welcoming. Set in beautiful
surroundings.*
Bedrooms: 1 twin, 1 triple
Bathrooms: 1 public

**Bed & breakfast**

| per night: | £min | £max |
|---|---|---|
| Single | 15.00 | 16.00 |
| Double | 30.00 | 32.00 |

**Half board**

| per person: | £min | £max |
|---|---|---|
| Daily | | 25.00 |
| Weekly | | 168.00 |

Evening meal from 1830
Parking for 4

## IVYBRIDGE

Devon
Map ref 1C2

Town set in delightful woodlands
on the River Erme. Brunel
designed the local railway viaduct.
South Dartmoor Leisure Centre.
*Tourist Information Centre*
☎ (01752) 897035

### Hillhead Farm

**Listed**

Ugborough, Ivybridge PL21 0HQ
☎ Plymouth (01752) 892674
*77-acre mixed farm. Spacious family
farmhouse, surrounded by fields. All
home-cooked and largely home-grown
food. From A38 turn off at Wrangton
Cross, turn left, take third right over
crossroads, after half a mile go straight
over next crossroads, after three-
quarters of a mile turn left, farm is 75
yards on left.*
Bedrooms: 2 double, 2 twin
Bathrooms: 1 public

**Bed & breakfast**

| per night: | £min | £max |
|---|---|---|
| Single | 14.00 | |
| Double | 28.00 | |

**Half board**

| per person: | £min | £max |
|---|---|---|
| Daily | 21.00 | |
| Weekly | 133.00 | |

Evening meal 1900 (last orders 2100)
Parking for 5

## KENTISBEARE

Devon
Map ref 1D2

Pretty village at the foot of the
Blackdown Hills. The church has a
magnificent carved 15th C screen,
and nearby is a medieval priest's
house with a minstrels' gallery and
oak screens.

### Knowles House

**Listed**

Broad Road, Kentisbeare, Cullompton
EX15 2EU
☎ (01884) 266209
*Country house with beautiful gardens
and woodland on edge of the
Blackdown Hills. 5 minutes M5,
junction 28, left on A373, left to
Sheldon, 1.5 miles on left.*
Bedrooms: 1 double, 1 twin
Bathrooms: 2 private

**Bed & breakfast**

| per night: | £min | £max |
|---|---|---|
| Single | 16.00 | 16.00 |
| Double | 32.00 | 32.00 |
| Parking for 4 | | |

### Millhayes

**Listed** **HIGHLY COMMENDED**

Kentisbeare, Cullompton EX15 2AF
☎ (01884) 6412 Changing to 266412
Fax (01884) 6412
*Situated in the picturesque village of
Kentisbeare, only 3 miles from the M5
junction 28. It is approximately halfway
between Taunton and Exeter and within
easy reach of both north and south
coasts.*
Bedrooms: 2 single, 1 double, 1 twin
Bathrooms: 2 private, 1 public

**Bed & breakfast**

| per night: | £min | £max |
|---|---|---|
| Single | 17.50 | 17.50 |
| Double | 39.00 | 39.00 |
| Parking for 8 | | |

Symbols are explained
on the flap inside the
back cover.

## KINGSBRIDGE

Devon
Map ref 1C3

Formerly important as a port, now
a market town overlooking head of
beautiful, wooded estuary winding
deep into rural countryside.
Summer art exhibitions;
Cookworthy Museum.
*Tourist Information Centre*
☎ (01548) 853195

### The Ashburton Arms

**Listed** **COMMENDED**

West Charleton, Kingsbridge TQ7 2AH
☎ (01548) 531242
*Friendly village freehouse serving real
ale and home-cooked food. Comfortable
accommodation. Sorry, no pets. No
smoking on first floor.*
Bedrooms: 2 single, 1 double, 1 twin
Bathrooms: 1 public

**Bed & breakfast**

| per night: | £min | £max |
|---|---|---|
| Single | 15.50 | 16.60 |
| Double | 33.00 | 36.00 |

**Half board**

| per person: | £min | £max |
|---|---|---|
| Daily | 19.95 | 22.75 |
| Weekly | 210.00 | |

Lunch available
Evening meal 1900 (last orders 2100)
Parking for 15
Cards accepted: Access, Visa

### Court Barton Farmhouse ⋀

**COMMENDED**

Aveton Gifford, Kingsbridge TQ7 4LE
☎ (01548) 550312

*40-acre mixed farm. Beautiful 16th C
manor farmhouse, below the church 100
yards from A379. Splendid hospitality
guaranteed.*
Bedrooms: 1 single, 2 double, 2 twin,
2 family rooms
Bathrooms: 6 private, 1 private shower

**Bed & breakfast**

| per night: | £min | £max |
|---|---|---|
| Single | 16.00 | 24.00 |
| Double | 32.00 | 48.00 |
| Parking for 10 | | |

### Crannacombe Farm

Hazelwood, Loddiswell, Kingsbridge
TQ7 4DX
☎ (01548) 550256

*80-acre mixed farm. Period farmhouse in the Avon Valley - an Area of Outstanding Natural Beauty. Private bathrooms, TV and CH in bedrooms. Lovely river walks and views. 10 minutes from Kingsbridge.*
Bedrooms: 1 double, 1 family room
Bathrooms: 2 private

**Bed & breakfast**

| per night: | £min | £max |
|---|---|---|
| Single | 16.00 | 16.50 |
| Double | 32.00 | 33.00 |

**Half board**

| per person: | £min | £max |
|---|---|---|
| Daily | 25.00 | 26.00 |
| Weekly | 175.00 | 182.00 |

Evening meal 1830 (last orders 1900)
Parking for 8

## Globe Inn

Frogmore, Kingsbridge TQ7 2NR
☎ Frogmore (01548) 531351
*Friendly village freehouse at the head of Frogmore Creek. Atmospheric restaurant and bars. Real ales, good food, open fires, beer garden and parking.*
Bedrooms: 3 double, 2 twin, 1 family room
Bathrooms: 3 private, 2 public

**Bed & breakfast**

| per night: | £min | £max |
|---|---|---|
| Single | 15.00 | 25.00 |
| Double | 30.00 | 45.00 |

Lunch available
Evening meal 1800 (last orders 2200)
Parking for 20
Cards accepted: Access, Visa, Switch/Delta

## Tor Cottage

**COMMENDED**

The Mounts, East Allington, Totnes TQ9 7QJ
☎ East Allington (01548) 521316 & Mobile 0836 359320
*Small friendly guesthouse in rural setting. Guests' lounge and garden with pleasant relaxing views. Close to Dartmouth and Salcombe. Ideal for touring and long stay.*
Bedrooms: 2 double, 1 twin
Bathrooms: 3 private

**Bed & breakfast**

| per night: | £min | £max |
|---|---|---|
| Single | 24.00 | 30.00 |
| Double | 32.00 | 38.00 |

**Half board**

| per person: | £min | £max |
|---|---|---|
| Daily | 24.00 | 27.00 |
| Weekly | 168.00 | 189.00 |

Evening meal from 1800
Parking for 3
Open February-November

## LANGTON HERRING

Dorset
Map ref 2A3

## Fox Barrow

**COMMENDED**

Langton Herring, Weymouth DT3 4NT
☎ Abbotsbury (01305) 871463
*Renovated Victorian farmhouse in centre of conservation village on heritage coast. Homely, comfortable, personal attention. Adjacent church and village inn.*
Bedrooms: 2 double, 1 twin, 3 family rooms
Bathrooms: 3 private, 1 public

**Bed & breakfast**

| per night: | £min | £max |
|---|---|---|
| Double | 36.00 | 40.00 |

Parking for 3

## LANIVET

Cornwall
Map ref 1B2

Small village with a large church displaying a lofty tower, a 14th C font and a churchyard with interesting features. A ruined tower from a former priory can also be seen.

## Bokiddick Farm

**COMMENDED**

Lanivet, Bodmin PL30 5HP
☎ Bodmin (01208) 831481
*185-acre dairy farm. Farmhouse accommodation in central Cornwall. Warm welcome, friendly atmosphere, good home cooking, en-suite bedrooms with tea/coffee facilities and colour TV. Peaceful location, wonderful views.*
Bedrooms: 1 double, 1 triple
Bathrooms: 2 private

**Bed & breakfast**

| per night: | £min | £max |
|---|---|---|
| Single | 18.00 | |
| Double | 34.00 | |

**Half board**

| per person: | £min | £max |
|---|---|---|
| Daily | 27.00 | |
| Weekly | 182.00 | |

Parking for 4
Open April-October

---

**Individual proprietors have supplied all details of accommodation. Although we do check for accuracy, we advise you to confirm the information at the time of booking.**

## LAUNCESTON

Cornwall
Map ref 1C2

Medieval "Gateway to Cornwall", county town until 1838, founded by the Normans under their hilltop castle near the original monastic settlement. This market town, overlooked by its castle ruin, has a square with Georgian houses and an elaborately-carved granite church.
*Tourist Information Centre*
☎ *(01566) 772321*

## Eagle House Hotel

Castle Street, Launceston PL15 8BA
☎ (01566) 772036
*Town house hotel within the wall of Launceston Castle, 2 minutes' walk from town centre and overlooking Cornish countryside. Golf and fishing nearby.*
Bedrooms: 1 single, 8 double, 6 twin
Bathrooms: 15 private

**Bed & breakfast**

| per night: | £min | £max |
|---|---|---|
| Single | 20.00 | 24.00 |
| Double | 40.00 | 48.00 |

**Half board**

| per person: | £min | £max |
|---|---|---|
| Daily | 27.50 | 31.50 |
| Weekly | 140.00 | 168.00 |

Lunch available
Evening meal 1830 (last orders 2130)
Parking for 50
Cards accepted: Access, Visa

## Falcondale

**Listed**

St Giles on the Heath, Launceston PL15 9RT
☎ (01566) 773036
*Relaxing atmosphere in rural home. Beautiful views. Private entrance for those seeking that peaceful getaway. Centrally positioned for major tourist attractions of both Devon and Cornwall.*
Bedrooms: 1 double, 1 twin
Bathrooms: 1 public

**Bed & breakfast**

| per night: | £min | £max |
|---|---|---|
| Double | 24.00 | 32.00 |

Parking for 3

## The Old Vicarage

**HIGHLY COMMENDED**

Treneglos, Launceston PL15 8UQ
☎ Canworthy Water (01566) 781351
*Elegant Georgian vicarage set in peaceful seclusion near spectacular north Cornwall coast. Renowned for hospitality and good food. High standard of furnishings and personal attention. Non-smoking.*
Bedrooms: 2 double

*Continued* ▶

## LAUNCESTON

*Continued*

Bathrooms: 2 private

**Bed & breakfast**

| per night: | £min | £max |
|---|---|---|
| Single | 16.00 | 19.00 |
| Double | 32.00 | 38.00 |

**Half board**

| per person: | £min | £max |
|---|---|---|
| Daily | 26.00 | 29.00 |
| Weekly | 182.00 | 192.50 |

Evening meal 1800 (last orders 2130)
Parking for 10
Open April-October

ॐ 2 ⌸⌷ ♠ ⚑ ⓌⒾ Ⓢ ⌿ ⋈ Ⓣ🅥 ⇘ ∪
▶ ❈ ✕ 🏘 🜚

### Wheatley Farm ⚠

Maxworthy, Launceston PL15 8LY
☎ Canworthy Water (01566) 781232
Fax (01566) 781232
*232-acre mixed farm. The warmest of welcomes awaits you. Ten minutes' drive to spectacular north coast. En-suite rooms, one with romantic four-poster. Colour TV. Delicious cooking our speciality.*
Bedrooms: 2 double, 2 family rooms
Bathrooms: 4 private

**Bed & breakfast**

| per night: | £min | £max |
|---|---|---|
| Double | 38.00 | 42.00 |

**Half board**

| per person: | £min | £max |
|---|---|---|
| Daily | 30.00 | 33.00 |

Evening meal 1830 (last orders 1400)
Parking for 4
Open April-September

ॐ 🛏 📞 ⌸⌷ ♠ ⚑ ⓌⒾ Ⓢ ⌿ ⋈ Ⓣ🅥 ▥ ⇘
🍷 ∪ ❈ ✕ 🏘

## LEWDOWN

Devon
Map ref 1C2

Small village on the very edge of Dartmoor. Lydford Castle is 4 miles to the east.

### Stowford Grange Farm

Stowford, Lewdown, Okehampton
EX20 4BZ
☎ (01566) 83298
*240-acre mixed farm. Listed building, quiet village. Home-cooked food, fresh vegetables and poultry. 10 miles from Okehampton and 7 miles from Launceston. Half a mile from old A30, turn right at Royal Exchange.*
Bedrooms: 3 double
Bathrooms: 2 public

**Bed & breakfast**

| per night: | £min | £max |
|---|---|---|
| Single | 14.00 | 15.50 |
| Double | 29.00 | 31.00 |

**Half board**

| per person: | £min | £max |
|---|---|---|
| Daily | 19.00 | 20.00 |
| Weekly | 115.50 | 119.00 |

Evening meal from 1900
Parking for 5
Open February-November

🛏 ♠ ⌷ ⓌⒾ Ⓢ ⌿ Ⓣ🅥 ▥ ♪ ▶ ⚆ ❈ ✕ 🏘

## LISKEARD

Cornwall
Map ref 1C2

Former stannary town with a livestock market and light industry, at the head of a valley running to the coast. Handsome Georgian and Victorian residences and a Victorian Guildhall reflect the prosperity of the mining boom. The large church has an early 20th C tower and a Norman font.

### Tregondale Farm

Menheniot, Liskeard PL14 3RG
☎ (01579) 342407
*180-acre mixed farm. Characteristic farmhouse in beautiful countryside. En-suite bedrooms with TV and tea/coffee. Home-produced food our speciality. Log fires, tennis court. North east of Menheniot, between A38 and A390.*
Bedrooms: 1 double, 1 twin, 1 triple
Bathrooms: 3 private

**Bed & breakfast**

| per night: | £min | £max |
|---|---|---|
| Single | 18.00 | 20.00 |
| Double | 32.00 | 36.00 |

**Half board**

| per person: | £min | £max |
|---|---|---|
| Daily | 25.00 | 27.00 |
| Weekly | 171.50 | 175.00 |

Evening meal 1900 (last orders 1800)
Parking for 3

ॐ ⌸⌷ ♠ ⓌⒾ Ⓢ ⌿ ⋈ Ⓣ🅥 ⇘ ∪ ⚋ ❈ ✕ 🏘

### Tresulgan Farm

Menheniot, Liskeard PL14 3PU
☎ Widegates (01503) 240268
Fax (01503) 240268

*145-acre dairy farm. Picturesque views from modernised 17th C farmhouse which has retained its character. Lots to do in this beautiful area and a warm and friendly welcome awaits you.*
Bedrooms: 1 double, 1 triple, 1 family room
Bathrooms: 3 private

**Bed & breakfast**

| per night: | £min | £max |
|---|---|---|
| Single | 19.00 | 20.00 |
| Double | 35.00 | 37.00 |

**Half board**

| per person: | £min | £max |
|---|---|---|
| Daily | 25.00 | 27.00 |
| Weekly | 175.00 | 180.00 |

Evening meal 1830 (last orders 1930)
Parking for 4
Open March-November

ॐ ♠ ⚑ ⓌⒾ 🍴 Ⓢ ⋈ Ⓣ🅥 ▥ ⇘ ∪ ❈ 🏘
DAP SP

## LITTLE BEDWYN

Wiltshire
Map ref 2C2

### Harrow Inn

Little Bedwyn, Marlborough SN8 3JP
☎ Marlborough (01672) 870871
Fax (01672) 870401
*Country inn on south-east side of quiet, unspoilt village close to Kennet and Avon Canal. Excellent restaurant, attractive garden.*
Bedrooms: 1 single, 2 twin
Bathrooms: 3 private

**Bed & breakfast**

| per night: | £min | £max |
|---|---|---|
| Single | 25.00 | 25.00 |
| Double | 40.00 | 45.00 |

Lunch available
Evening meal 1930 (last orders 2100)
Parking for 1
Cards accepted: Access, Visa

ॐ ⌸⌷ ♠ ⚑ Ⓢ ▥ ⚋ ❈ 🏘 Ⓣ

## LODDISWELL

Devon
Map ref 1C3

### Tunley Farm

Loddiswell, Kingsbridge TQ7 4ED
☎ Kingsbridge (01548) 550279
*180-acre dairy farm. Enjoy our comfortable, spacious accommodation in relaxed family atmosphere. Splendid breakfasts. Peaceful countryside near coast and Dartmoor.*
Bedrooms: 1 family room
Bathrooms: 1 private

**Bed & breakfast**

| per night: | £min | £max |
|---|---|---|
| Double | 32.00 | |

Parking for 3
Open March-October

ॐ ⌸⌷ ♠ ⚑ ⓌⒾ Ⓢ ⌿ ⋈ Ⓣ🅥 ▥ ⇘ ✓ ❈
✕ 🏘 🜚

Map references apply to the colour maps at the back of this guide.

## LONG SUTTON

Somerset
Map ref 2A3

### The Old Mill
☺☺ COMMENDED
Knole, Long Sutton, Langport
TA10 9HY
☎ (01458) 241599
Fax (01458) 241710
*Old watermill comfortably furnished with antiques. Modern facilities, farmhouse-style breakfast, mill stream gardens. Idyllically yet centrally located for business or pleasure. Half a mile off A372. 4 miles Podimore/Langport.*
Bedrooms: 2 double, 1 twin
Bathrooms: 3 private

**Bed & breakfast**

| per night: | £min | £max |
|---|---|---|
| Single | 18.50 | 25.00 |
| Double | 37.00 | 45.00 |

**Half board**

| per person: | £min | £max |
|---|---|---|
| Daily | 31.00 | 37.00 |
| Weekly | 200.00 | 250.00 |

Evening meal 1830 (last orders 2000)
Parking for 6
☎ 10 ▣ ❏ ♨ ➍ ⑩ Ⓢ 斌 TV ➋ U ➤
❋ ✕ 🐎 SP 🏛 T

## LOOE

Cornwall
Map ref 1C2

Small resort developed around former fishing and smuggling ports occupying the deep estuary of the East and West Looe Rivers. Narrow winding streets, with old inns; museum and art gallery are housed in interesting old buildings. Shark fishing centre, boat trips; busy harbour.

### Bucklawren Farm ⋔
☺☺☺ HIGHLY COMMENDED
St. Martin-by-Looe, Looe PL13 1NZ
☎ Widegates (01503) 240738
Fax (01503) 240481

*534-acre arable & dairy farm. Set in glorious countryside with beautiful sea views. Only 1.5 miles from beach. Family and en-suite accommodation with colour TV. Delicious farmhouse cooking.*
Bedrooms: 1 double, 1 twin, 1 triple, 2 family rooms
Bathrooms: 5 private

---

**Bed & breakfast**

| per night: | £min | £max |
|---|---|---|
| Single | 16.00 | 23.00 |
| Double | 32.00 | 38.00 |

**Half board**

| per person: | £min | £max |
|---|---|---|
| Daily | 25.00 | 28.00 |
| Weekly | 164.50 | 175.00 |

Evening meal 1800 (last orders 1800)
Parking for 10
Open March-October
Cards accepted: Access, Visa
☎ ▣ ❏ ♨ ➍ ⑩ Ⓐ Ⓢ 斌 TV ◑ 🛏 ➋
➋ ➤ ❋ ✕ 🐎 DAP SP 🏛

### Coombe Farm ⋔
☺☺ HIGHLY COMMENDED
Widegates, Looe PL13 1QN
☎ Widegates (01503) 240223

*Country house in lovely grounds with superb views to sea. All rooms en-suite. Candlelit dining. Home cooking. Glorious walks and beaches nearby. Ideally situated for touring Cornwall and Devon.*
Bedrooms: 1 single, 2 double, 2 twin, 2 triple, 3 family rooms
Bathrooms: 10 private

**Bed & breakfast**

| per night: | £min | £max |
|---|---|---|
| Single | 18.00 | 24.00 |
| Double | 36.00 | 48.00 |

**Half board**

| per person: | £min | £max |
|---|---|---|
| Daily | 30.00 | 36.00 |
| Weekly | 200.00 | 240.00 |

Evening meal 1900 (last orders 1900)
Parking for 12
Open March-October
☎ 10 ♨ ❄ ▣ ❏ ♨ ➍ 🛏 Ⓢ 斌 TV 🛏
➋ ◉ ⟲ U ➤ 🐎 ❋ SP

### Hall Barton Farm
☺☺ COMMENDED
Pelynt, Looe PL13 2LG
☎ Lanreath (01503) 220203
*275-acre arable & livestock farm. Grade II listed farmhouse overlooking fields in village of of Pelynt on B3359. 3 miles from Looe and Polperro. Close to coarse fishing. Pony trekking, woodland walks.*
Bedrooms: 2 double, 1 twin
Bathrooms: 2 private, 1 public,
1 private shower

**Bed & breakfast**

| per night: | £min | £max |
|---|---|---|
| Single | 14.00 | 18.00 |
| Double | 28.00 | 32.00 |

Parking for 10
Open March-December
☎ ❏ ♨ ⑩ TV ➋ ❋ 🐎 🏛

---

### Stonerock Cottage
☺☺ COMMENDED
Portuan Road, Hannafore, Looe
PL13 2DN
☎ (01503) 263651
*Modernised, old world cottage facing south to the Channel. Ample free parking. 2 minutes from the beach, shops, tennis and other amenities.*
Bedrooms: 1 single, 2 double, 1 twin
Bathrooms: 1 private, 2 public

**Bed & breakfast**

| per night: | £min | £max |
|---|---|---|
| Single | 15.00 | 16.00 |
| Double | 30.00 | 38.00 |

Parking for 4
Open February-October
☎ ⌂ ❏ ♨ ⑩ Ⓐ TV ⑩ 🛏 ➋ ❋ ✕ 🐎
SP 🏛

## LUSTLEIGH

Devon
Map ref 1D2

Riverside village of pretty thatched cottages gathered around its 15th C church. The traditional Mayday festival has dancing round the maypole. Just west is Lustleigh Cleave, where Dartmoor is breached by the River Bovey which flows through a deep valley of boulders and trees.

### Eastwrey Barton Hotel ⋔
☺☺☺ HIGHLY COMMENDED
Lustleigh, Newton Abbot TQ13 9SN
☎ (01647) 7338
*Well-appointed 17th C country house hotel. Peaceful, relaxing and renowned for good food and personal service.*
Bedrooms: 3 double, 3 twin
Bathrooms: 6 private

**Bed & breakfast**

| per night: | £min | £max |
|---|---|---|
| Single | 29.00 | 58.00 |
| Double | 58.00 | 58.00 |

**Half board**

| per person: | £min | £max |
|---|---|---|
| Daily | 42.00 | 42.00 |
| Weekly | 264.00 | 264.00 |

Evening meal 1930 (last orders 1930)
Parking for 20
Open March-October
Cards accepted: Access, Visa
☎ 12 ❏ ♨ ⑩ Ⓢ 斌 ▥ ➋ ❋ 🐎 SP T

### The Mill
Listed
Lustleigh, Newton Abbot TQ13 9SS
☎ (01647) 7357
*12-acre smallholding. Historic riverside millhouse on edge of beautiful Dartmoor village. Exposed beams, antique furniture, home-grown produce.*
Bedrooms: 1 single, 1 double, 1 twin
Bathrooms: 2 public

*Continued* ▶

## LUSTLEIGH

*Continued*

**Bed & breakfast**

| per night: | £min | £max |
|---|---|---|
| Single | 16.00 | 17.50 |
| Double | 32.00 | 35.00 |

**Half board**

| per person: | £min | £max |
|---|---|---|
| Daily | | 24.50 |
| Weekly | | 154.00 |

Evening meal from 1830
Parking for 3

🐾 5 🎷 ♨ ꮗ 🛈 Ⓢ ≯ ⅏ 📺 🖾 ▪ 🖙 🎵 ✿ 🐴 🏵

## LYDFORD

Devon
Map ref 1C2

Former important tin mining town, a small village on edge of West Dartmoor. Remains of Norman castle where all falling foul of tinners' notorious "Lydford Law" were incarcerated. Bridge crosses River Lyd where it rushes through a mile-long gorge of boulders and trees.

### Castle Inn and Hotel ⋔

**Listed** COMMENDED

Lydford, Okehampton EX20 4BH
☎ (01822) 82242 & 82252
Fax (01822) 82454

*Enchanting, romantic 16th C inn, 150 yards from Lydford Gorge and next to castle. Noted for food and wines. Woodland walks.*
Bedrooms: 1 single, 5 double, 2 twin
Bathrooms: 6 private, 1 public

**Bed & breakfast**

| per night: | £min | £max |
|---|---|---|
| Single | 27.50 | 37.50 |
| Double | 40.00 | 55.00 |

**Half board**

| per person: | £min | £max |
|---|---|---|
| Daily | 42.00 | 62.00 |
| Weekly | 225.00 | 260.00 |

Lunch available
Evening meal 1830 (last orders 2130)
Parking for 50
Cards accepted: Access, Visa, Diners, Amex, Switch/Delta

🐾 🍽 ⮸ ♨ 🛈 Ⓢ ≯ ⅏ 🛂 📻 🖾 ▪ 🖙 ✿ ⚲ 🏵 Ⓣ

## LYME REGIS

Dorset
Map ref 1D2

Pretty, historic fishing town and resort set against the fossil-rich cliffs of Lyme Bay. In medieval times it was an important port and cloth centre. The Cobb, a massive stone breakwater, shelters the ancient harbour which is still lively with boats.
*Tourist Information Centre*
☎ *(01297) 442138*

### Coverdale Guest House

♛

Woodmead Road, Lyme Regis
DT7 3AB
☎ (01297) 442882
*Homely family guesthouse situated in a quiet residential area with fine sea and country views. Short walk to town and beach. No smoking.*
Bedrooms: 2 single, 5 double, 1 twin
Bathrooms: 5 private, 1 public

**Bed & breakfast**

| per night: | £min | £max |
|---|---|---|
| Single | 12.00 | 16.00 |
| Double | 24.00 | 38.00 |

**Half board**

| per person: | £min | £max |
|---|---|---|
| Daily | 20.50 | 27.00 |
| Weekly | 118.65 | 160.00 |

Evening meal 1830 (last orders 1630)
Parking for 12
Open March-October

🐾 3 ⮸ ♨ 🛈 Ⓢ ≯ ⅏ 📺 🖾 ▪ 🖙 ᴰᴬᴾ ⱾⱣ

### Lydwell House ⋔

♛ COMMENDED

Lyme Road, Uplyme, Lyme Regis
DT7 3TJ
☎ (01297) 443522
Fax (01297) 445897
*Delightful Edwardian house ideally located for coast and country walking. Short distance to Lyme Regis town centre and beaches.*
Bedrooms: 1 single, 1 double, 1 twin, 2 family rooms
Bathrooms: 2 private, 1 public

**Bed & breakfast**

| per night: | £min | £max |
|---|---|---|
| Single | 15.00 | 19.00 |
| Double | 28.00 | 36.00 |

Evening meal 1800 (last orders 2000)
Parking for 7

🐾 ⮸ 🛈 Ⓢ ≯ ⅏ 📺 🖾 ▪ 🖙 ✿ ∪ ⚲ 🐴 ⱾⱣ

### Southernhaye

♛ COMMENDED

Pound Road, Lyme Regis DT7 3HX
☎ (01297) 443077
*Distinctive Edwardian house in quiet location with panoramic views over Lyme Bay, about 10 minutes' walk from town and beach.*
Bedrooms: 1 double, 1 twin
Bathrooms: 1 public

**Bed & breakfast**

| per night: | £min | £max |
|---|---|---|
| Single | 18.00 | 18.00 |
| Double | 30.00 | 34.00 |

Parking for 2

⮸ ꮗ Ⓢ ⅏ 📺 🖾 ▪ 🖙 ✿ ≯ 🐴 🏵

### Springfield

♛♛ COMMENDED

Woodmead Road, Lyme Regis DT7 3LJ
☎ (01297) 443409
*Elegant Georgian house in partly walled garden, with well-proportioned, tastefully decorated rooms, many enjoying views over the sea.*
Bedrooms: 1 single, 2 double, 2 twin, 1 triple, 1 family room
Bathrooms: 3 private, 2 public

**Bed & breakfast**

| per night: | £min | £max |
|---|---|---|
| Single | 15.00 | 18.00 |
| Double | 26.00 | 38.00 |

Parking for 9
Open February-November

🐾 ⮸ ꮗ 📺 🖾 ▪ 🖙 ✿ 🐴 🏵

### White House

♛♛ COMMENDED

47 Silver Street, Lyme Regis DT7 3HR
☎ (01297) 443420
*Fine views of Dorset coastline from rear of this 18th C guesthouse. A short walk from beach, gardens and shops.*
Bedrooms: 5 double, 2 twin
Bathrooms: 7 private

**Bed & breakfast**

| per night: | £min | £max |
|---|---|---|
| Double | 36.00 | 40.00 |

Parking for 6
Open April-October

🖵 ☐ ⮸ ꮗ 🛈 ≯ ⅏ 🖾 ▪ 🖙 ⱾⱣ 🏵

## LYNTON

Devon
Map ref 1C1

Hilltop resort on Exmoor coast linked to its seaside twin, Lynmouth, by a water-operated cliff railway which descends from the town hall. Spectacular surroundings of moorland cliffs with steep chasms of conifer and rocks through which rivers cascade.
*Tourist Information Centre*
☎ *(01598) 52225 Changing to 752225*

### Ingleside Hotel ⋔

♛♛♛

Lynton EX35 6HW
☎ (01598) 52223 Changing to 752223
*Family-run hotel with high standards in elevated position overlooking village. Ideal centre for exploring Exmoor.*
Bedrooms: 4 double, 1 twin, 2 triple
Bathrooms: 7 private

## Bed & breakfast

| per night: | £min | £max |
| --- | --- | --- |
| Single | 24.00 | 26.00 |
| Double | 42.00 | 46.00 |

## Half board

| per person: | £min | £max |
| --- | --- | --- |
| Daily | 33.00 | 35.00 |
| Weekly | 217.00 | 231.00 |

Evening meal 1900 (last orders 1800)
Parking for 10
Open March-October
Cards accepted: Access, Visa

⛒ 5 ♿ ⬜ 🖥 ♻ 🐾 Ⓢ 🍴 📺 🛏 🔌 🪑 ✖
🐾 DAP SP T

### Sandrock Hotel ⋀

Longmead, Lynton EX35 6DH
☎ (01598) 53307 Changing to 753307

Comfortable family-run hotel, quietly
situated near local beauty spots, bowls
green and tennis courts.
Bedrooms: 2 single, 4 double, 3 twin
Bathrooms: 7 private, 1 public

## Bed & breakfast

| per night: | £min | £max |
| --- | --- | --- |
| Single | 19.50 | 25.00 |
| Double | 39.00 | 52.00 |

## Half board

| per person: | £min | £max |
| --- | --- | --- |
| Daily | 30.00 | 37.00 |
| Weekly | 195.50 | 229.00 |

Evening meal 1900 (last orders 2000)
Parking for 9
Open February-November
Cards accepted: Access, Visa, Amex

⛒ ☎ 🖥 ⬜ ♻ 🐾 Ⓢ 🍴 🛏 🔌 🔍 🐾 DAP
SP T

### MALMESBURY

Wiltshire
Map ref 2B2

Overlooking the River Avon, an old
town dominated by its great
church, once a Benedictine abbey.
The surviving Norman nave and
porch are noted for fine
sculptures, 12th C arches and
musicians' gallery.
*Tourist Information Centre*
☎ *(01666) 823748*

### Flisteridge Cottage

Flisteridge Road, Upper Minety,
Malmesbury SN16 9PS
☎ (01666) 860343
*Quiet secluded country cottage in rural
surroundings. Take A429
Cirencester/Malmesbury road, turn off
at Crudwell, signpost Oaksey and*

---

*Minety, on to C class road, through
Eastcourt and Flisteridge woods.
Cottage is down gravel drive signposted
on right.*
Bedrooms: 1 single, 1 double, 1 twin
Bathrooms: 1 private, 1 public

## Bed & breakfast

| per night: | £min | £max |
| --- | --- | --- |
| Single | 14.00 | 16.50 |
| Double | 28.00 | 33.00 |

Parking for 6

⛒ 11 ♿ 🖥 ⬜ ♻ 🐾 Ⓢ 🍴 📺 🔌 🪑 🐾
🐾 SP

### Lovett Farm

Little Somerford, Malmesbury
SN15 5BP
☎ (01666) 823268
*65-acre livestock farm. Comfortable
spacious accommodation in modern
well appointed farmhouse. Ideally
situated for visiting Bath, the Cotswolds
and Stonehenge.*
Bedrooms: 1 double, 1 twin
Bathrooms: 2 private

## Bed & breakfast

| per night: | £min | £max |
| --- | --- | --- |
| Single | 15.00 | 17.00 |
| Double | 28.00 | 32.00 |

Parking for 5

⛒ 🖥 ⬜ ♻ 🐾 🍴 📺 🛏 🔌 🐾 ✖ 🐾

### Manor Farm

Corston, Malmesbury SN16 0HF
☎ (01666) 822148 & 0374 675783

*436-acre mixed farm. Relax and unwind
in charming 17th C Cotswolds
farmhouse. Excellent meals available in
village pub. Ideally situated for visiting
Cotswolds, Bath and Stonehenge.*
Bedrooms: 2 double, 1 twin, 2 triple,
1 family room
Bathrooms: 4 private, 1 public,
1 private shower

## Bed & breakfast

| per night: | £min | £max |
| --- | --- | --- |
| Single | 16.00 | 20.00 |
| Double | 32.00 | 40.00 |

Parking for 12
Cards accepted: Access, Visa

⛒ 🖥 ⬜ ♻ 🐾 🪑 📺 🛏 🔌 ✖ 🐾 🐾

### Marsh Farmhouse

Crudwell Road, Malmesbury SN16 9JL
☎ (01666) 822208
*A pleasant farmhouse with en-suite
rooms. Situated outside England's oldest
borough and within reach of M4 and
M5 motorways.*
Bedrooms: 1 single, 2 double, 2 twin

---

Bathrooms: 5 private

## Bed & breakfast

| per night: | £min | £max |
| --- | --- | --- |
| Single | 25.00 | 27.50 |
| Double | 38.00 | 41.00 |

## Half board

| per person: | £min | £max |
| --- | --- | --- |
| Daily | 27.50 | 38.00 |

Parking for 6
Cards accepted: Visa

⛒ ♿ ⬜ ♻ 🐾 🍴 🛏 🔌 ✖ 🐾 SP

### Stonehill Farm

Charlton, Malmesbury SN16 9DY
☎ (01666) 823310

*180-acre dairy farm. Delightful 15th C
farmhouse offering a warm welcome in
a relaxed atmosphere. 3 pretty rooms,
en-suite. Dogs welcome.*
Bedrooms: 2 double, 1 twin
Bathrooms: 1 private, 1 public

## Bed & breakfast

| per night: | £min | £max |
| --- | --- | --- |
| Single | 14.00 | 20.00 |
| Double | 28.00 | 40.00 |

Parking for 6

⛒ ♿ ♻ ⬜ 🪑 📺 🛏 🔌 🐾

### MARLBOROUGH

Wiltshire
Map ref 2B2

Important market town, in a river
valley cutting through chalk
downlands. The broad main street,
with colonnaded shops on one
side, shows a medley of building
styles, mainly from the Georgian
period. Lanes wind away on either
side and a church stands at each
end.
*Tourist Information Centre*
☎ *(01672) 513989*

### Cadley House

Savernake Forest, Marlborough
SN8 4NE
☎ (01672) 513407
Fax (01672) 511654
*Comfortable Victorian country house;
own secluded grounds, in historic
forest. Gracious reception rooms and
large well-furnished en-suite bedrooms.
Touring centre for Avebury,
Stonehenge, Salisbury, Bath, Cotswolds.
Excellent pubs and restaurants nearby.*
Bedrooms: 1 double, 2 twin
Bathrooms: 3 private

Continued ▶

## MARLBOROUGH

### Continued

**Bed & breakfast**

| per night: | £min | £max |
| --- | --- | --- |
| Single | 22.50 | 30.00 |
| Double | 32.50 | 50.00 |

Parking for 12

🐕🖵♿👤🖂 UL ⚡🏷 IIII. 🚗 ♨6-14 ✿ 🚲
SP 🏫

### Laurel Cottage Guest House

👑👑 HIGHLY COMMENDED

Southend, Ogbourne St George,
Marlborough SN8 1SG
☎ Ogbourne St George (01672)
841288

*16th C thatched cottage, in a delightful
rural setting. Low beamed ceilings and
inglenook fireplace. Non-smokers only,
please.*
Bedrooms: 2 double, 2 twin
Bathrooms: 2 private, 1 public

**Bed & breakfast**

| per night: | £min | £max |
| --- | --- | --- |
| Single | 26.00 | 34.00 |
| Double | 33.00 | 50.00 |

Parking for 5
Open April-October

🐕🖵🎇♿👤 UL 🔒 S 🏷 TV IIII. 🚗 ►✿✗
🚲🏫

## MARTINSTOWN

Dorset
Map ref 2B3

### Old Post Office

Listed

Martinstown, Dorchester DT2 9LF
☎ (01305) 889254
*Grade II listed Georgian cottage
tastefully modernised throughout. Large
garden with many small animals. Good
rural base, children and pets welcome.*
Bedrooms: 1 double, 2 twin
Bathrooms: 2 public

**Bed & breakfast**

| per night: | £min | £max |
| --- | --- | --- |
| Single | 15.00 | 20.00 |
| Double | 25.00 | 35.00 |

**Half board**

| per person: | £min | £max |
| --- | --- | --- |
| Daily | 25.00 | 30.00 |

Evening meal 2000 (last orders 1630)
Parking for 3

🐕🖵♿👤 UL 🔒 S TV IIII. 🚗►✿🚲🏫

## MARTOCK

Somerset
Map ref 2A3

Small town with many handsome
buildings of Ham stone and a
beautiful old church with tie-beam
roof. Medieval treasurer's house,
Georgian market house, 17th C
manor.

### Wychwood ⚜

👑👑 COMMENDED

7 Bearley Road, Martock TA12 6PG
☎ (01935) 825601
*Quality B & B in quiet position just off
A303 between Montacute and Tintinhull.
Ideal for visiting the eight classic
gardens of South Somerset. Near
Glastonbury and Wells. Brochure.*
Bedrooms: 1 single, 1 double, 1 twin
Bathrooms: 3 private

**Bed & breakfast**

| per night: | £min | £max |
| --- | --- | --- |
| Single | 17.00 | 19.00 |
| Double | 32.00 | 36.00 |

**Half board**

| per person: | £min | £max |
| --- | --- | --- |
| Daily | 26.00 | 29.00 |

Evening meal 1830 (last orders 2000)
Parking for 3

🐕 8 🖵🖂♿🎇 UL 🔒 S ✁🏷 IIII. 🚗
✿✗🚲

## MEVAGISSEY

Cornwall
Map ref 1B3

Small fishing town, a favourite with
holidaymakers. Earlier prosperity
came from pilchard fisheries, boat-
building and smuggling. By the
harbour are fish cellars, some
converted, and a local history
museum is housed in an old boat-
building shed. Handsome
Methodist chapel; shark fishing,
sailing.

### Auraville

👑

The Drive, Trevarth, Mevagissey, St
Austell PL26 6RX
☎ (01726) 843293
*Private residence in quiet and peaceful
surroundings, a short walk from the
harbour. Central for touring Cornwall.*
Bedrooms: 1 single, 2 double, 1 twin
Bathrooms: 2 public

**Bed & breakfast**

| per night: | £min | £max |
| --- | --- | --- |
| Single | 14.50 | |
| Double | | 29.00 |

Parking for 4

🐕🖵♿ UL 🔒 S ✁🏷 TV IIII. 🚗✿✗🚲
SP T

### Honeycomb House

👑

Polkirt Hill, Mevagissey, St Austell
PL26 6UR
☎ St Austell (01726) 842200
*Victorian house with sweeping
unsurpassed views of harbour and
coastline. Some rooms have a balcony,
all have TV and tea/coffee facilities.
Evening meal available.*
Bedrooms: 2 double, 1 twin
Bathrooms: 1 public

**Bed & breakfast**

| per night: | £min | £max |
| --- | --- | --- |
| Single | 17.00 | 20.00 |
| Double | 28.00 | 35.00 |

**Half board**

| per person: | £min | £max |
| --- | --- | --- |
| Daily | 22.00 | 25.00 |

Evening meal from 1900

🐕🖵♿ UL 🔒 S 🏷 ◐ IIII. ✗🚲 SP

### Rising Sun Inn

👑

Portmellon Cove, Mevagissey, St
Austell PL26 6PL
☎ (01726) 843235
*17th C inn right next to the beach at
Portmellon Cove, and overlooking
Chapel Point and surrounding
countryside.*
Bedrooms: 3 double, 1 twin, 1 triple
Bathrooms: 5 private

**Bed & breakfast**

| per night: | £min | £max |
| --- | --- | --- |
| Double | 35.00 | 45.00 |

Lunch available
Evening meal 1830 (last orders 2130)
Parking for 60
Open March-September
Cards accepted: Access, Visa

🐕🖵♿🎇 S ✁ IIII. 🚗♟ ❤✗ SP 🏫

### Steep House ⚜

👑👑

Portmellon Cove, Mevagissey, St
Austell PL26 2PH
☎ (01726) 843732

*Refreshingly clean and comfortable with
large garden and covered (summertime)
heated pool. Superb seaside views,
private parking, licensed, Christmas
celebrations.*
Bedrooms: 4 double, 1 twin, 2 triple
Bathrooms: 2 private, 2 public,
1 private shower

**Bed & breakfast**

| per night: | £min | £max |
| --- | --- | --- |
| Single | 16.00 | |
| Double | 32.00 | |

| Half board per person: | £min | £max |
|---|---|---|
| Daily | 27.00 | |
| Weekly | 185.00 | |

Lunch available
Evening meal 1900 (last orders 1700)
Parking for 12
Cards accepted: Access, Visa, Amex

☎10 ⌂ ⟐ ⓢ ⤢ ⋈ TV ◐ ▥ 🛏 ⌕ ❋ ✕ DAP ⍨ SP 🏠 T

## MINEHEAD

Somerset
Map ref 1D1

Victorian resort with spreading sands developed around old fishing port on the coast below Exmoor. Former fishermen's cottages stand beside the 17th C harbour; cobbled streets climb the hill in steps to the church. Boat trips, steam railway. Hobby Horse festival 1 May.
*Tourist Information Centre*
*☎ (01643) 702624*

### Higher Rodhuish Farm

⍣⍣ COMMENDED

Rodhuish, Minehead TA24 6QL
☎ Washford (01984) 640253
*700-acre mixed farm. Comfortable accommodation on working farm, 6 miles east of Minehead on edge of Exmoor National Park. Ideal centre for walking, riding, touring coast and moors.*
Bedrooms: 1 double, 1 twin
Bathrooms: 2 private

| Bed & breakfast per night: | £min | £max |
|---|---|---|
| Single | 16.00 | 18.00 |
| Double | 32.00 | 36.00 |

| Half board per person: | £min | £max |
|---|---|---|
| Daily | 24.50 | 26.00 |
| Weekly | 163.00 | 174.50 |

Evening meal 1930 (last orders 2030)
Parking for 4

⍨⍩ ⌂ ⟐ ⓤ🗠 ⓐ ⋈ TV ▥ 🛏 ✦ ❋ 🚗 🏠 T

### Hillside

⍣ HIGHLY COMMENDED

Higher Allerford, Minehead TA24 8HS
☎ Porlock (01643) 862831
Fax (01643) 862447

*Thatched cottage owned by the National Trust. Wonderful views overlooking the picturesque village of Allerford, 100 yards above the Packhorse Bridge.*
Bedrooms: 1 double, 1 twin
Bathrooms: 1 public

| Bed & breakfast per night: | £min | £max |
|---|---|---|
| Single | 15.50 | 16.50 |
| Double | 31.00 | 33.00 |

Parking for 4

⍨2 ⌂ ⟐ ⓠ ▥ ⓐ ⓢ ⤢ ⋈ TV ◐ ▥ 🛏
U ❋ 🚗 ⍨

### Kildare Lodge ♠

⍣⍣ COMMENDED

Townsend Road, Minehead TA24 5RQ
☎ (01643) 702009
Fax (01643) 706516

*Family-run, Edwin Lutyens designed, Grade II listed building. Elegant a la carte restaurant; character filled licensed bar; bar meals; well appointed en-suite accommodation, including family rooms.*
Bedrooms: 1 single, 4 double, 2 twin, 2 family rooms
Bathrooms: 9 private

| Bed & breakfast per night: | £min | £max |
|---|---|---|
| Single | 27.50 | 37.50 |
| Double | 47.50 | 57.50 |

| Half board per person: | £min | £max |
|---|---|---|
| Daily | 31.00 | 37.50 |
| Weekly | 199.00 | 225.00 |

Lunch available
Evening meal 1830 (last orders 2030)
Parking for 28
Cards accepted: Access, Visa, Diners

⍨⍩ ⓛ ⌂ ⟐ ⓠ ⓢ ⋈ TV ▥ 🛏
↑5-75 U ▶ ❋ DAP ⍨ SP 🏠 T

## MORETONHAMPSTEAD

Devon
Map ref 1C2

Small market town with a row of 17th C almshouses standing on the Exeter road. Surrounding moorland is scattered with ancient farmhouses, prehistoric sites.

### Cookshayes Country Guest House ♠

⍣⍣⍣ COMMENDED

33 Court Street, Moretonhampstead, Newton Abbot TQ13 8LG
☎ (01647) 40374
*Licensed guesthouse on edge of Dartmoor. Ornamental gardens with ample parking. Traditionally furnished. Accent on food and comfort.*
Bedrooms: 1 single, 4 double, 2 twin, 1 triple
Bathrooms: 6 private, 2 public

| Bed & breakfast per night: | £min | £max |
|---|---|---|
| Single | 21.50 | 21.50 |
| Double | 35.00 | 42.00 |

| Half board per person: | £min | £max |
|---|---|---|
| Daily | 32.00 | 35.50 |
| Weekly | 217.00 | 241.50 |

Evening meal 1900 (last orders 1700)
Parking for 15
Open March-October
Cards accepted: Access, Visa, Amex

⍨7 ⍩ ⌂ ⟐ ⓠ ⓐ ⓢ ⤢ ⋈ ▥ 🛏 ❋ 🚗
DAP SP T

### Great Doccombe Farm

⍥

Doccombe, Moretonhampstead, Newton Abbot TQ13 8SS
☎ (01647) 40694
*8-acre mixed farm. 300-year-old farmhouse in Dartmoor National Park. Comfortable rooms, ideal for walking the Teign Valley and Dartmoor.*
Bedrooms: 2 double, 1 twin
Bathrooms: 3 private, 2 public

| Bed & breakfast per night: | £min | £max |
|---|---|---|
| Double | 32.00 | 36.00 |

Parking for 6

⍨⍩ ⌂ ⟐ ⓠ ⓤ ⓐ ⓢ ⤢ ▥ 🛏 ❋ 🚗
SP 🏠

### Great Sloncombe Farm

⍣⍣⍣ HIGHLY COMMENDED

Moretonhampstead, Newton Abbot TQ13 8QF
☎ (01647) 40595 Changing to 440595
*170-acre dairy farm. 13th C Dartmoor farmhouse. Comfortable rooms, central heating, en-suite. Large wholesome farmhouse breakfasts and delicious dinners. Friendly Devonshire welcome.*
Bedrooms: 2 double, 1 twin
Bathrooms: 3 private

| Bed & breakfast per night: | £min | £max |
|---|---|---|
| Single | 18.00 | 20.00 |
| Double | 36.00 | 40.00 |

| Half board per person: | £min | £max |
|---|---|---|
| Daily | 28.00 | 30.00 |

Evening meal 1830 (last orders 1000)
Parking for 3

⍨8 ⌂ ⟐ ⓠ ⓤ ⓐ ⓢ ⤢ ⋈ TV ▥ 🛏
U ❋ 🚗 SP 🏠

### Wooston Farm

⍣⍣ HIGHLY COMMENDED

Moretonhampstead, Newton Abbot TQ13 8QA
☎ (01647) 40367
*280-acre mixed farm. Situated within Dartmoor National Park above the Teign Valley, with scenic views and walks. Two rooms are en-suite, one with 4-poster bed.*
Bedrooms: 2 double, 1 twin
Bathrooms: 3 private

*Continued* ▶

## MORETONHAMPSTEAD

*Continued*

**Bed & breakfast**

| per night: | £min | £max |
| --- | --- | --- |
| Double | 34.00 | 40.00 |

**Half board**

| per person: | £min | £max |
| --- | --- | --- |
| Daily | 27.00 | 30.00 |

Evening meal 1800 (last orders 1830)
Parking for 5

🛇🏠⏰🖵👆🏸Ⓤ️🅂📶🛏📺🚗Ⓤ
❄🚜

## MORWENSTOW

Cornwall
Map ref 1C2

Scattered parish on the wild north Cornish coast. The church, beautifully situated in a deep combe by the sea, has a fine Norman doorway and 15th C bench-ends. Its unique vicarage was built by the 19th C poet-priest Robert Hawker. Nearby are Cornwall's highest cliffs.

### Cornakey Farm

👑

Morwenstow, Bude EX23 9SS
☎ (01288) 331260
*220-acre mixed farm. Convenient coastal walking area with extensive views of sea and cliffs from bedrooms. Home cooking, games room. Reduced rates for children. Good touring centre.*
Bedrooms: 2 triple
Bathrooms: 2 private

**Bed & breakfast**

| per night: | £min | £max |
| --- | --- | --- |
| Single | 14.00 | 16.00 |
| Double | 28.00 | 32.00 |

**Half board**

| per person: | £min | £max |
| --- | --- | --- |
| Daily | 20.00 | 23.00 |
| Weekly | 133.00 | |

Evening meal 1830 (last orders 1730)
Parking for 2

🛇👆🅄🛏📺🅀Ⓤ❄✕🚜 SP 🏠

### Lopthorne Farm

👑👑

Morwenstow, Bude EX23 9PJ
☎ (01288) 331226
*100-acre mixed farm. Traditional old farmhouse in peaceful rural area, overlooking fields and wooded valleys. Home cooking our speciality. 7 miles north of Bude.*
Bedrooms: 1 double, 1 twin, 2 triple
Bathrooms: 2 private, 1 public, 2 private showers

**Bed & breakfast**

| per night: | £min | £max |
| --- | --- | --- |
| Single | 13.50 | 15.00 |
| Double | 27.00 | 30.00 |

**Half board**

| per person: | £min | £max |
| --- | --- | --- |
| Daily | 20.50 | 22.00 |
| Weekly | 135.00 | 140.00 |

Evening meal 1830 (last orders 1030)
Parking for 4
Open April-October

🛇👆🐾🅀🅄🅂🏸🛏📺🛏🚗❄✕🚜 OAP

## MULLION

Cornwall
Map ref 1B3

Small holiday village with a golf-course, set back from the coast. The church has a serpentine tower of 1500, carved roof and beautiful medieval bench-ends. Beyond Mullion Cove, with its tiny harbour, wild untouched cliffs stretch south-eastward toward Lizard Point.

### Alma House Hotel & Restaurant

`Listed`

Churchtown, Mullion, Helston TR12 7BZ
☎ Helston (01326) 240509 & 241039
*Close to beaches, shops and golf course, with sea views across Mount's Bay. Well-appointed accommodation, candlelit restaurant and bar.*
Bedrooms: 2 double, 1 twin
Bathrooms: 1 private, 1 public

**Bed & breakfast**

| per night: | £min | £max |
| --- | --- | --- |
| Single | 17.85 | 19.35 |
| Double | 31.00 | 35.70 |

**Half board**

| per person: | £min | £max |
| --- | --- | --- |
| Daily | 24.35 | 26.70 |
| Weekly | 166.45 | 183.40 |

Lunch available
Evening meal 1830 (last orders 2200)
Parking for 18
Open March-October
Cards accepted: Access, Visa, Diners, Amex

🛇🏠🖵👆🅂🏸🛁🚗✕🚜

## MYLOR BRIDGE

Cornwall
Map ref 1B3

### Penmere Guest House

👑👑 COMMENDED

10 Rosehill, Mylor Bridge, Falmouth TR11 5LZ
☎ Falmouth (01326) 374470
*Beautifully restored Victorian property enjoying splendid creek views, close to yachting centres. Lovely garden, perfect for a relaxing stay.*
Bedrooms: 2 double, 2 twin, 2 triple
Bathrooms: 4 private, 1 public

**Bed & breakfast**

| per night: | £min | £max |
| --- | --- | --- |
| Single | 22.00 | 25.00 |
| Double | 40.00 | 47.00 |

Parking for 6

🛇🖵👆🅄🏸👆✕🛏🛏🚗❄🚜

## NEWQUAY

Cornwall
Map ref 1B2

Popular resort spread over dramatic cliffs around its old fishing port. Many beaches with abundant sands, caves and rock pools; excellent surf. Pilots' gigs are still raced from the harbour and on the headland stands the stone Huer's House from the pilchard-fishing days.
*Tourist Information Centre*
☎ (01637) 871345

### Degembris Farmhouse ⋀

👑👑 HIGHLY COMMENDED

St Newlyn East, Newquay TR8 5HY
☎ Mitchell (01872) 510555
Fax (01872) 510230
*165-acre arable farm. 18th C listed Cornish farmhouse overlooking beautiful wooded valley. Our country trail will take you through natural woodland and fields visiting the pond and exploring the valley of the bluebells.*
Bedrooms: 1 single, 1 double, 1 twin, 1 triple, 1 family room
Bathrooms: 2 private, 2 public

**Bed & breakfast**

| per night: | £min | £max |
| --- | --- | --- |
| Single | 16.00 | |
| Double | 32.00 | |

**Half board**

| per person: | £min | £max |
| --- | --- | --- |
| Daily | 24.50 | |
| Weekly | 171.50 | |

Evening meal from 1800
Parking for 8
Open April-October

🛇🖵👆🅄👆🛏📺🛏🚗🅀✓❄✕ 🚜🏠

### Manuels Farm

👑👑 HIGHLY COMMENDED

Quintrell Downs, Newquay TR8 4NY
☎ (01637) 873577
*44-acre mixed farm. In a sheltered valley 2 miles inland from Newquay, offering the peace of the countryside with the charm of a traditional 17th C farmhouse. Beautifully furnished, log fires and delicious country cooking.*
Bedrooms: 1 double, 1 triple, 1 family room
Bathrooms: 1 private, 2 public

**Bed & breakfast**

| per night: | £min | £max |
| --- | --- | --- |
| Single | 18.00 | 20.00 |
| Double | 36.00 | 40.00 |

**Half board**

| per person: | £min | £max |
| --- | --- | --- |
| Daily | 27.00 | 29.00 |
| Weekly | 185.00 | 200.00 |

Evening meal 1830 (last orders 1630)
Parking for 6

🛥🕯♨🖳 ⓊⓁ 🛅 Ⓢ ✂ 🐾 📺 🎽 ➡ ✓ 🖊 🚲
SP 🎏

## Pendeen Hotel
♛♛ COMMENDED

Alexandra Road, Porth, Newquay
TR7 3ND
☎ (01637) 873521
Fax (01637) 873521
*Well established family-run hotel, in its
own grounds. 2 miles from Newquay
and close to beach. Good food served
with friendly and efficient service.*
Bedrooms: 1 single, 8 double, 2 twin,
2 triple, 2 family rooms
Bathrooms: 15 private

**Bed & breakfast**

| per night: | £min | £max |
| --- | --- | --- |
| Single | 17.00 | 25.00 |
| Double | 33.00 | 50.00 |

**Half board**

| per person: | £min | £max |
| --- | --- | --- |
| Daily | 23.00 | 32.00 |
| Weekly | 130.00 | 192.00 |

Evening meal 1830 (last orders 1700)
Parking for 15
Open January-October, December
Cards accepted: Access, Visa, Amex

🛥🕯🖳♨ 🛅 Ⓢ ✂ 🐾 📺 🎽 ➡ 🖊 ✈ 🚲
SP T

## Rose Cottage
♛♛

Shepherds Farm, St Newlyn East,
Newquay TR8 5NW
☎ Zelah (01872) 540502
*600-acre mixed farm. Decorated to a
high standard, all rooms en-suite with
colour TV and tea-making facilities.
Ideal for touring and beaches, 1 mile
from A30. A warm welcome awaits.*
Bedrooms: 2 double, 1 twin
Bathrooms: 3 private

**Bed & breakfast**

| per night: | £min | £max |
| --- | --- | --- |
| Single | 15.00 | 17.00 |
| Double | 30.00 | 34.00 |

**Half board**

| per person: | £min | £max |
| --- | --- | --- |
| Daily | 23.00 | |
| Weekly | 145.00 | 160.00 |

Evening meal 1800 (last orders 1000)
Parking for 3

🛥🖳♨🕯 🛅 Ⓢ 🐾 📺 🎽 ➡ 🕛 ❋ 🚲
OAP SP

The town index at the
back of this guide gives
page numbers of all places
with accommodation.

Devon
Map ref 1C3

Hillside village overlooking wooded
estuary of the River Yealm, with
attractive waterside cottages and
yacht anchorage.

## Maywood Cottage
♛♛ COMMENDED

Bridgend, Newton Ferrers, Plymouth
PL8 1AW
☎ Plymouth (01752) 872372
*Cottage on 3 levels, close to River
Yealm estuary. Part old, all modernised.
Take Bridgend - Noss Mayo road off
B3186 (leading to Newton Ferrers).
Maywood is at bottom of hill on right
just before estuary.*
Bedrooms: 3 twin
Bathrooms: 3 private

**Bed & breakfast**

| per night: | £min | £max |
| --- | --- | --- |
| Single | 15.00 | 25.00 |
| Double | 25.00 | 45.00 |

**Half board**

| per person: | £min | £max |
| --- | --- | --- |
| Daily | 23.50 | 33.50 |
| Weekly | 150.00 | 200.00 |

Evening meal 1800 (last orders 2030)
Parking for 3

🛥🕯♨ ⓊⓁ 🛅 Ⓢ 📺 🎽 ➡ 🐾 ❋ 🚲 OAP ⅍
SP 🎏

Devon
Map ref 1C3

## Slade Barn
Listed COMMENDED

Netton Farm, Noss Mayo, Plymouth
PL8 1HA
☎ Plymouth (01752) 872235
Fax (01752) 872235
*50-acre arable farm. Attractive coastal
barn conversion. Indoor pool, games
room, tennis court, gardens. Fabulous
National Trust walks. Up-market B & B
and self-catering. SAE for colour
brochure. Children over 10 welcome.*
Bedrooms: 2 double, 1 twin
Bathrooms: 2 public, 1 private shower

**Bed & breakfast**

| per night: | £min | £max |
| --- | --- | --- |
| Single | 15.00 | 18.50 |
| Double | 30.00 | 36.00 |

Parking for 6

🎿🖳🕯 ⓊⓁ ✓ 📺 🎽 ➡ 🐾 🕛 ⅍ ❋ 🖊
🚲

Establishments should be
open throughout the year
unless otherwise stated
in the entry.

Devon
Map ref 1C2

Busy market town near the high
tors of northern Dartmoor. The
Victorian church, with William
Morris windows and a 15th C
tower, stands on the site of a
Saxon church. A Norman castle
ruin overlooks the river to the west
of the town. Museum of Dartmoor
Life in a restored mill.

## Higher Cadham Farm
♛ COMMENDED

Jacobstowe, Okehampton EX20 3RB
☎ Exbourne (01837) 85647

*139-acre mixed farm. 16th C farmhouse
on a traditional Devon farm, 5 miles
from Dartmoor and within easy reach
of coast. On the Tarka trail.*
Bedrooms: 1 single, 1 double, 1 twin,
1 family room
Bathrooms: 1 public

**Bed & breakfast**

| per night: | £min | £max |
| --- | --- | --- |
| Single | 14.00 | 15.00 |
| Double | 28.00 | 30.00 |

**Half board**

| per person: | £min | £max |
| --- | --- | --- |
| Daily | 21.00 | 22.00 |
| Weekly | 125.00 | 125.00 |

Lunch available
Evening meal 1900 (last orders 2000)
Parking for 6

🛥3🖳🕯♨ 🛅 Ⓢ 📺 🎽 ➡ 🐾 ❋ 🖊
🚲 T

## Oxenham Arms 🏰
♛♛♛ COMMENDED

South Zeal, Okehampton EX20 2JT
☎ (01837) 840244
Fax (01837) 840791
*In the centre of Dartmoor village,
originally built in the 12th C. Wealth of
granite fireplaces, oak beams, mullion
windows. Various diets available on
request.*
Bedrooms: 3 double, 3 twin, 2 triple
Bathrooms: 8 private

**Bed & breakfast**

| per night: | £min | £max |
| --- | --- | --- |
| Single | 40.00 | 45.00 |
| Double | 45.00 | 50.00 |

**Half board**

| per person: | £min | £max |
| --- | --- | --- |
| Daily | 37.50 | 40.00 |
| Weekly | 210.00 | 227.50 |

*Continued ▶*

## OKEHAMPTON

### Continued

Lunch available
Evening meal 1930 (last orders 2100)
Parking for 8
Cards accepted: Access, Visa, Diners,
Amex

### Week Farm

**COMMENDED**

Bridestowe, Okehampton EX20 4HZ
☎ Bridestowe (01837) 86221
Changing to 861221

*180-acre dairy & livestock farm. A
warm welcome awaits you at this
homely 17th C farmhouse three-quarters
of a mile from the old A30 and 6 miles
from Okehampton. Home cooking and
every comfort. Come and spoil
yourselves.*
Bedrooms: 3 double, 1 triple, 1 family
room
Bathrooms: 5 private

| Bed & breakfast per night: | £min | £max |
| --- | --- | --- |
| Single | 19.00 | 20.00 |
| Double | 38.00 | 40.00 |

| Half board per person: | £min | £max |
| --- | --- | --- |
| Daily | 29.00 | 30.00 |
| Weekly | 200.00 | 210.00 |

Evening meal 1900 (last orders 1700)
Parking for 10

## OSMINGTON

Dorset
Map ref 2B3

Attractive village near the coast on
the road to Weymouth. Close by
on a hillside is an equestrian figure
of George III, Weymouth's patron,
cut into the chalk.

### Dingle Dell

**Listed HIGHLY COMMENDED**

Church Lane, Osmington, Weymouth
DT3 6EW
☎ Preston (01305) 832378
*Attractive rose-covered house with
charming garden in quiet location on
edge of village. Large, sunny, well-
furnished rooms with views over
countryside. Warm and friendly
atmosphere.*
Bedrooms: 1 double, 1 twin
Bathrooms: 1 private, 1 public

| Bed & breakfast per night: | £min | £max |
| --- | --- | --- |
| Double | 35.00 | 39.00 |

Parking for 3
Open March-October

## OTTERTON

Devon
Map ref 1D2

Village on the banks of the River
Otter, close to the sea. Beautiful
thatched cottages of cob or
pinkish stone and a church with a
15th C tower, overlooking the river.
A craft centre is housed in an
ancient mill nearby. Spectacular
red sandstone cliffs rise to 500 ft
toward Sidmouth.

### Ropers Cottage

Ropers Lane, Otterton, Budleigh
Salterton EX9 7JF
☎ Colaton Raleigh (01395) 568826
Fax (01395) 568206
*16th C modernised cottage with beams
and inglenook fireplace, in picturesque
village 2 miles from sea. Pleasant
country and river walks.*
Bedrooms: 1 double, 2 twin
Bathrooms: 1 private, 1 public

| Bed & breakfast per night: | £min | £max |
| --- | --- | --- |
| Single | 15.00 | 18.00 |
| Double | 30.00 | 36.00 |

Parking for 4
Open April-October

## OTTERY ST MARY

Devon
Map ref 1D2

Former wool town with modern
light industry set in countryside on
the River Otter. The Cromwellian
commander, Fairfax, made his
headquarters here briefly during
the Civil War. The interesting
church, dating from the 14th C, is
built to cathedral plan.

### Fluxton Farm Hotel

Ottery St Mary EX11 1RJ
☎ (01404) 812818
*Former farmhouse in beautiful country
setting. Comfortable en-suite bedrooms,
2 sitting rooms, large gardens. Home-
cooked food served in candlelit dining
room. Log fires in season. Cat lovers'
paradise.*
Bedrooms: 3 single, 3 double, 4 twin,
2 triple
Bathrooms: 10 private, 1 public

| Bed & breakfast per night: | £min | £max |
| --- | --- | --- |
| Single | 23.00 | 25.00 |
| Double | 46.00 | 50.00 |

| Half board per person: | £min | £max |
| --- | --- | --- |
| Daily | 29.50 | 32.50 |
| Weekly | 195.00 | 210.00 |

Evening meal 1850 (last orders 1800)
Parking for 20

### Pitt Farm

**Listed**

Ottery St Mary EX11 1NL
☎ (01404) 812439
*190-acre mixed farm. Thatched 16th C
farmhouse offering country fare. On
B3176, half a mile off A30 and within
easy reach of all east Devon coastal
resorts.*
Bedrooms: 1 single, 1 double, 2 twin,
2 family rooms
Bathrooms: 3 public

| Bed & breakfast per night: | £min | £max |
| --- | --- | --- |
| Single | 16.00 | 20.00 |
| Double | 32.00 | 40.00 |

| Half board per person: | £min | £max |
| --- | --- | --- |
| Daily | 23.00 | 26.00 |
| Weekly | 161.00 | 182.00 |

Evening meal 1900 (last orders 1700)
Parking for 6
Cards accepted: Amex

## PADSTOW

Cornwall
Map ref 1B2

Old town encircling its harbour on
the Camel Estuary. The 15th C
church has notable bench-ends.
There are fine houses on North
Quay and Raleigh's Court House
on South Quay. Tall cliffs and
golden sands along the coast and
ferry to Rock. Famous 'Obby 'Oss
Festival on 1 May.

### Old Mill Country House

**COMMENDED**

Little Petherick, Padstow PL27 7QT
☎ Rumford (01841) 540388
*16th C listed corn mill with waterwheel.
Set in own gardens by stream in
country village. Retains original
character, period furnishings.*
Bedrooms: 4 double, 2 twin
Bathrooms: 6 private, 1 public

| Bed & breakfast per night: | £min | £max |
| --- | --- | --- |
| Double | 45.00 | 52.00 |

Evening meal 1900 (last orders 1800)
Parking for 15
Open March-October

## PARRACOMBE

Devon
Map ref 1C1

Pretty village spreading over the slopes of a river valley on the western edge of Exmoor.

### Fox and Goose Inn M

Parracombe, Barnstaple EX31 4PE
☎ (01598) 3239
*19th C country coaching inn next to Heddon River, set in Exmoor National Park in the quiet village of Parracombe. Good home-cooked food.*
Bedrooms: 3 double, 1 twin
Bathrooms: 1 public, 4 private showers
**Bed & breakfast**

| per night: | £min | £max |
| --- | --- | --- |
| Single | 15.00 | 16.50 |
| Double | 30.00 | 33.00 |

Lunch available
Evening meal 1900 (last orders 2100)
Parking for 20
Cards accepted: Access, Visa

## PELYNT

Cornwall
Map ref 1C2

### Trenake Farm

COMMENDED

Pelynt, Looe PL13 2LT
☎ Lanreath (01503) 220216
*286-acre mixed farm. 14th C farmhouse, 5 miles from Looe and 3 miles from Talland Bay beach.*
Bedrooms: 1 single, 1 double, 1 triple
Bathrooms: 1 public
**Bed & breakfast**

| per night: | £min | £max |
| --- | --- | --- |
| Single | 14.50 | 15.00 |
| Double | 29.00 | 30.00 |

Parking for 6
Open April-October

## PENDEEN

Cornwall
Map ref 1A3

Small village on the beautiful coast road from Land's End to St Ives. A romantic landscape of craggy inland cliffs covered with bracken shelving to a rocky shore. There are numerous prehistoric sites, disused tin mines, a mine museum at Geevor and a lighthouse at Pendeen.

### Bosigran Farm

Listed APPROVED

Pendeen, Penzance TR20 8YX
☎ Penzance (01736) 796940
*280-acre livestock farm. 18th C farmhouse on cliffs overlooking sea.*

*Wonderful walking country and good beaches nearby. A real farmhouse welcome.*
Bedrooms: 2 double, 1 twin
Bathrooms: 1 public
**Bed & breakfast**

| per night: | £min | £max |
| --- | --- | --- |
| Single | 15.00 | 20.00 |
| Double | 30.00 | 40.00 |

Parking for 6

### Trewellard Manor Farm

COMMENDED

Pendeen, Penzance TR19 7SU
☎ Penzance (01736) 788526
*300-acre dairy farm. Friendly and comfortable atmosphere, home cooking and seasonal open fires.*
Bedrooms: 2 double, 1 twin
Bathrooms: 1 private, 1 public, 1 private shower
**Bed & breakfast**

| per night: | £min | £max |
| --- | --- | --- |
| Single | 15.00 | 18.00 |
| Double | 30.00 | 38.00 |

Parking for 2

## PENSFORD

Avon
Map ref 2A2

### Green Acres

Listed

Stanton Wick, Pensford BS18 4BX
☎ Mendip (01761) 490397
*A friendly welcome awaits you in peaceful setting, off A37/A368. Relax and enjoy panoramic views across Chew Valley to Dundry Hills.*
Bedrooms: 1 double, 2 twin
Bathrooms: 4 public
**Bed & breakfast**

| per night: | £min | £max |
| --- | --- | --- |
| Single | 15.00 | 20.00 |
| Double | 30.00 | |

Parking for 21

## PENTEWAN

Cornwall
Map ref 1B3

Tiny 19th C port with a pretty square, hidden from the main road, overlooked by a Regency terrace with luxuriant flower gardens and a Methodist chapel. Separated by the River Winnick from a broad, sandy beach.

### Polrudden Farm M

Listed

Pentewan, St Austell PL26 6BJ
☎ St Austell (01726) 843213
*75-acre mixed farm. Modern farmhouse with fantastic views and walks, 3 miles*

*from St Austell and 2 miles from Mevagissey. Peace and tranquillity.*
Bedrooms: 1 double, 2 twin
Bathrooms: 2 public
**Bed & breakfast**

| per night: | £min | £max |
| --- | --- | --- |
| Single | 15.00 | 17.50 |
| Double | 30.00 | 35.00 |

Parking for 13

## PENZANCE

Cornwall
Map ref 1A3

Resort and fishing port on Mount's Bay with mainly Victorian promenade and some fine Regency terraces. Former prosperity came from tin trade and pilchard fishing. Grand Georgian style church by harbour. Georgian Egyptian building at head of Chapel Street and Morrab Gardens.
*Tourist Information Centre*
☎ *(01736) 62207*

### Halcyon Guest House

6 Chyandour Square, Penzance
TR18 3LW
☎ (01736) 66302
*Granite Tudor-style house overlooking Mount's Bay and St Michael's Mount in a private road between town and beach. Private parking.*
Bedrooms: 1 double, 1 twin, 1 triple, 1 family room
Bathrooms: 4 private
**Bed & breakfast**

| per night: | £min | £max |
| --- | --- | --- |
| Single | 20.00 | 24.00 |
| Double | 36.00 | 40.00 |

Evening meal 1830 (last orders 1830)
Parking for 4
Open March-October

### Menwidden Farm

Listed APPROVED

Ludgvan, Penzance TR20 8BN
☎ (01736) 740415
*40-acre mixed farm. Centrally situated in west Cornwall. Warm family atmosphere and home cooking. Turn right at Crowlas crossroads on the A30 from Hayle, signpost Vellanoweth on right turn. Last farm on left.*
Bedrooms: 1 single, 2 double, 1 triple, 1 family room
Bathrooms: 2 public
**Bed & breakfast**

| per night: | £min | £max |
| --- | --- | --- |
| Single | 14.00 | |
| Double | 28.00 | |

Continued ▶

## PENZANCE

*Continued*

**Half board**

| per person: | £min | £max |
|---|---|---|
| Daily | 22.00 | |
| Weekly | 150.00 | |

Evening meal 1800 (last orders 1800)
Parking for 8
Open February-November
Cards accepted: Amex

### Penalva

⚜⚜⚜ APPROVED

Alexandra Road, Penzance TR18 4LZ
☎ (01736) 69060
*Well positioned imposing Victorian hotel, near all amenities, offering full central heating, good food and service. Non-smokers only please.*
Bedrooms: 1 single, 3 double, 1 twin
Bathrooms: 4 private

**Bed & breakfast**

| per night: | £min | £max |
|---|---|---|
| Single | 10.00 | 16.00 |
| Double | 24.00 | 32.00 |

**Half board**

| per person: | £min | £max |
|---|---|---|
| Daily | 20.00 | 26.00 |
| Weekly | 140.00 | 182.00 |

Evening meal 1830 (last orders 1900)

### Rose Farm

⚜⚜ COMMENDED

Chyanhal, Buryas Bridge, Penzance TR19 6AN
☎ (01736) 731808
*25-acre livestock & horse farm. Small farm with many animals. Near beaches and shops. Land's End 7 miles, Mousehole 2 miles. Lovely walks. Four-poster bed available. Cosy and relaxing.*
Bedrooms: 2 double, 1 family room
Bathrooms: 3 private

**Bed & breakfast**

| per night: | £min | £max |
|---|---|---|
| Double | 35.00 | 38.00 |

Parking for 10

### Tregoddick House

Listed

Madron, Penzance TR20 8SS
☎ (01736) 62643
*Detached period house with walled gardens. Interior has some original fittings, granite fireplaces, etc. Located in attractive village close to West Penwith moors.*
Bedrooms: 2 twin
Bathrooms: 2 private

---

**Bed & breakfast**

| per night: | £min | £max |
|---|---|---|
| Single | 16.00 | 17.50 |
| Double | 32.00 | 35.00 |

Parking for 2
Open January-November

### Woodstock Guest House

⚜⚜

29 Morrab Road, Penzance TR18 4AZ
☎ (01736) 69049
*Well-appointed, centrally situated guesthouse. Helpful, friendly service. Tea-making facilities, radio, TV and hairdryer all inclusive.*
Bedrooms: 1 single, 1 double, 1 twin, 2 triple
Bathrooms: 1 private, 2 public

**Bed & breakfast**

| per night: | £min | £max |
|---|---|---|
| Single | 10.00 | 16.00 |
| Double | 20.00 | 38.00 |

Cards accepted: Access, Visa, Diners, Amex

## PERRANUTHNOE

Cornwall
Map ref 1B3

Small village on Mount's Bay, with lovely cliff walks.

### Ednovean House

⚜⚜⚜

Perranuthnoe, Penzance TR20 9LZ
☎ Penzance (01736) 711071

*Stands in 1 acre of gardens, with superb views of St Michael's Mount and Mount's Bay. Ideal centre for touring and walking.*
Bedrooms: 2 single, 4 double, 2 twin, 1 triple
Bathrooms: 6 private, 1 public

**Bed & breakfast**

| per night: | £min | £max |
|---|---|---|
| Single | 18.00 | 22.00 |
| Double | 34.00 | 44.00 |

**Half board**

| per person: | £min | £max |
|---|---|---|
| Daily | 30.50 | 35.50 |
| Weekly | 192.00 | 223.00 |

Lunch available
Evening meal 1900 (last orders 2000)
Parking for 12
Cards accepted: Access, Visa, Amex

---

## PETER TAVY

Devon
Map ref 1C2

### Churchtown

Listed

Peter Tavy, Tavistock PL19 9NN
☎ Mary Tavy (01822) 810477
*Peaceful Victorian house in own grounds on edge of village. Beautiful moorland views. 5 minutes' walk to excellent pub food.*
Bedrooms: 2 single, 2 double
Bathrooms: 4 public, 2 private showers

**Bed & breakfast**

| per night: | £min | £max |
|---|---|---|
| Single | 14.00 | 15.00 |
| Double | 28.00 | 30.00 |

Parking for 6

## PIDDLETRENTHIDE

Dorset
Map ref 2B3

### The Poachers Inn ⚐

⚜⚜⚜ COMMENDED

Piddletrenthide, Dorchester DT2 7QX
☎ (01300) 348358
*Country inn with riverside garden, in beautiful Piddle Valley. Swimming pool. All rooms en-suite, colour TV, tea-making facilities, telephone. Residents' lounge. Brochure available.*
Bedrooms: 8 double, 1 twin, 2 family rooms
Bathrooms: 11 private

**Bed & breakfast**

| per night: | £min | £max |
|---|---|---|
| Double | 42.00 | 50.00 |

**Half board**

| per person: | £min | £max |
|---|---|---|
| Daily | 31.00 | 35.00 |
| Weekly | 196.00 | 208.00 |

Lunch available
Evening meal 1700 (last orders 2130)
Parking for 30
Cards accepted: Access, Visa

## PILLATON

Cornwall
Map ref 1C2

Peaceful village on the slopes of the River Lynher in steeply-wooded country near the Devon border. Within easy reach of the coast and rugged walking country on Bodmin Moor.

### The Weary Friar Inn ⚐

⚜⚜⚜ COMMENDED

Pillaton, Saltash PL12 6QS
☎ Liskeard (01579) 50238

*Charming country inn noted for its quality food and interesting combination of modern comforts with 12th C character. Ideally placed for exploring inland and coastal areas.*
Bedrooms: 9 double, 2 twin, 1 triple
Bathrooms: 12 private

**Bed & breakfast**

| per night: | £min | £max |
|---|---|---|
| Single | 30.00 | 35.00 |
| Double | 45.00 | 50.00 |

**Half board**

| per person: | £min | £max |
|---|---|---|
| Daily | 32.50 | 45.00 |
| Weekly | 200.00 | 245.00 |

Lunch available
Evening meal 1900 (last orders 2130)
Parking for 30
Cards accepted: Access, Visa

☎□♨🗄⑤✕🏃📺📺🖾▣🍴🛎🏋10-20♨
❋✕🏮

## PLYMOUTH
Devon
Map ref 1C2

Devon's largest city, major port and naval base. Old houses on the Barbican and ambitious architecture in modern centre, with aquarium, museum and art gallery, the Dome - a heritage centre on the Hoe. Superb coastal views over Plymouth Sound from the Hoe.
*Tourist Information Centre*
☎ *(01752) 264849*

### Bowling Green Hotel ♨
HIGHLY COMMENDED
9-10 Osborne Place, Lockyer Street, Plymouth PL1 2PU
☎ (01752) 667485
Fax (01752) 255150
*Rebuilt Victorian property with views of Dartmoor. Overlooking Sir Francis Drake's bowling green on beautiful Plymouth Hoe. Centrally situated for the Barbican, Theatre Royal and leisure/conference centre.*
Bedrooms: 1 single, 6 double, 2 twin, 3 triple
Bathrooms: 8 private, 4 private showers

**Bed & breakfast**

| per night: | £min | £max |
|---|---|---|
| Single | 27.00 | 34.00 |
| Double | 36.00 | 44.00 |

Parking for 4
Cards accepted: Access, Visa, Diners, Amex, Switch/Delta

☎♨📞🖵🗄♨🍴🗄⑤✕📺📺📀🖾▣
🅾🆂🅿

### Gabber Farm
COMMENDED
Down Thomas, Plymouth PL9 0AW
☎ (01752) 862269
*120-acre mixed & dairy farm. On the south Devon coast, near Bovisand and Wembury. Lovely walks in the area. Near diving centre. Directions are provided. Friendly welcome assured. Special rates for OAPs.*
Bedrooms: 1 double, 2 twin, 1 triple, 1 family room
Bathrooms: 2 private, 1 public

**Bed & breakfast**

| per night: | £min | £max |
|---|---|---|
| Single | 15.00 | 17.00 |
| Double | 30.00 | 34.00 |

**Half board**

| per person: | £min | £max |
|---|---|---|
| Daily | 23.00 | 25.00 |
| Weekly | 145.00 | 155.00 |

Evening meal 1900 (last orders 1800)
Parking for 4

☎□♨🖄🖵⑤✕🏃📺🖾▣🌸🏮
🅾🆃

### Lamplighter Hotel
103 Citadel Road, The Hoe, Plymouth PL1 2RN
☎ (01752) 663855
*Small friendly hotel on Plymouth Hoe, 5 minutes' walk from the city centre and seafront.*
Bedrooms: 5 double, 2 twin, 1 triple, 1 family room
Bathrooms: 7 private, 1 public, 2 private showers

**Bed & breakfast**

| per night: | £min | £max |
|---|---|---|
| Single | 20.00 | 22.00 |
| Double | 30.00 | 34.00 |

Parking for 4
Cards accepted: Access, Visa

☎□♨🖄🖵⑤✕🏃📺🖾▣🍴✕🏮

### Osmond Guest House
42 Pier Street, Plymouth PL1 3BT
☎ (01752) 229705
*Elegant Edwardian house, converted to modern standards, 20 yards from seafront. Resident proprietors offer courtesy "pick-up" from stations.*
Bedrooms: 1 single, 3 double, 1 twin, 2 triple
Bathrooms: 2 private, 2 public, 1 private shower

**Bed & breakfast**

| per night: | £min | £max |
|---|---|---|
| Single | 14.00 | 20.00 |
| Double | 26.00 | 34.00 |

Parking for 4

☎♨🖄🖵♨🍴⑤✕🖾▣🍴🛎🅾
🆂🏮

### Phantele Guest House
COMMENDED
176 Devonport Road, Stoke, Plymouth PL1 5RD
☎ (01752) 561506

*Small family-run guesthouse about 2 miles from city centre. Convenient base for touring. Close to continental and Torpoint ferries.*
Bedrooms: 2 single, 1 double, 1 twin, 2 triple
Bathrooms: 2 private, 2 public

**Bed & breakfast**

| per night: | £min | £max |
|---|---|---|
| Single | 14.50 | 20.50 |
| Double | 27.00 | 34.00 |

**Half board**

| per person: | £min | £max |
|---|---|---|
| Daily | 20.50 | 26.50 |
| Weekly | 123.00 | 153.00 |

Evening meal 1830 (last orders 1700)
☎♨🖄♨🍴⑤✕🏃📺🖾▣🍴✕🏮

## PORTHLEVEN
Cornwall
Map ref 1B3

Old fishing port with handsome Victorian buildings overlooking Mount's Bay. An extensive, shingly beach reaches south-east towards the Loe Bar, where the pebbles make a lake on the landward side.

### Harbour Inn ♨
COMMENDED
Commercial Road, Porthleven, Helston TR13 9JD
☎ Helston (01326) 573876
*150-year-old inn on harbour edge. Restaurant open 7 days a week. Most bedrooms en-suite, many with harbour views.*
Bedrooms: 1 single, 6 double, 2 twin, 1 family room
Bathrooms: 8 private, 1 public, 2 private showers

**Bed & breakfast**

| per night: | £min | £max |
|---|---|---|
| Single | 32.00 | |
| Double | 60.00 | |

**Half board**

| per person: | £min | £max |
|---|---|---|
| Daily | 43.00 | |

Lunch available
Evening meal 1830 (last orders 2130)
Parking for 10
Cards accepted: Access, Visa, Diners, Amex

☎♨📞🖵♨🖄⑤✕🏃📺🖾▣🍴✕🏮
🆂🅿🆃

There are separate sections in this guide listing groups specialising in farm holidays and accommodation which is especially suitable for young people and organised groups.

## PORTLAND

Dorset
Map ref 2B3

Joined by a narrow isthmus to the coast, a stony promontory sloping from the lofty landward side to a lighthouse on Portland Bill at its southern tip. Villages are built of the white limestone for which the "isle" is famous.

### Alessandria Hotel and Italian Restaurant M

APPROVED

71 Wakeham Easton, Portland, Weymouth DT5 1HW
☎ (01305) 822270 & 820108
Fax (01305) 820561
*Italy on Portland. Warm and friendly Italian hospitality from chef/proprietor Giovanni. Spacious en-suite bedrooms with all facilities. Food prepared and cooked to order. Three bedrooms on ground floor.*
Bedrooms: 4 single, 6 double, 4 twin, 2 family rooms
Bathrooms: 12 private, 3 public, 4 private showers

**Bed & breakfast**

| per night: | £min | £max |
|---|---|---|
| Single | 25.00 | 45.00 |
| Double | 40.00 | 55.00 |

**Half board**

| per person: | £min | £max |
|---|---|---|
| Daily | 37.00 | 55.00 |
| Weekly | 195.00 | 245.00 |

Evening meal 1900 (last orders 2100)
Parking for 19
Cards accepted: Access, Visa, Diners, Amex, Switch/Delta

## PORTREATH

Cornwall
Map ref 1B3

Formerly developed as a mining port, small resort with some handsome 19th C buildings. Cliffs, sands and good surf.

### Bensons

Listed COMMENDED

1 The Hillside, Portreath, Redruth TR16 4LL
☎ Redruth (01209) 842534
*Situated in a valley overlooking the sea. Close to beach and harbour. Ideally suited for touring Cornwall. Lovely clifftop walks in surrounding National Trust land.*
Bedrooms: 2 double, 2 twin
Bathrooms: 4 private

**Bed & breakfast**

| per night: | £min | £max |
|---|---|---|
| Single | 25.00 | 25.00 |
| Double | 35.00 | 40.00 |

Parking for 5

### Cliff House

Listed

The Square, Portreath, Redruth TR16 4LB
☎ Truro (01209) 842008
*Seaside cottage, a stone's throw from the harbour and 2 minutes from beach. On the North Atlantic coast.*
Bedrooms: 2 single, 1 double, 1 twin
Bathrooms: 4 private, 2 public

**Bed & breakfast**

| per night: | £min | £max |
|---|---|---|
| Single | 15.00 | 17.50 |
| Double | 30.00 | 35.00 |

Parking for 6

## POWERSTOCK

Dorset
Map ref 2A3

Hilly village of mellow stone houses, overlooked by its church. Partly rebuilt in the 19th C, the church retains a fine Norman chancel arch, gargoyles and 15th C carvings in the south porch.

### Oakleigh House

HIGHLY COMMENDED

Townsend, Powerstock, Bridport DT6 3TE
☎ (01308) 485526
*Large country house with outstanding views and indoor heated swimming pool, in the heart of a beautiful Dorset village, full of charm and character. Five minutes from coast and Bridport. Lovely walking country.*
Bedrooms: 1 double, 1 twin
Bathrooms: 2 private

**Bed & breakfast**

| per night: | £min | £max |
|---|---|---|
| Single | | 26.00 |
| Double | 38.00 | 38.00 |

Parking for 4
Open February-November

### Powerstock Mill

COMMENDED

Powerstock, Bridport DT6 3SL
☎ (01308) 485213
*50-acre dairy farm. Comfortable old farmhouse nestling in a valley, in an Area of Outstanding Natural Beauty. Only 4 miles away from beautiful coastline. High tea and babysitting provided on request.*
Bedrooms: 1 double, 1 twin
Bathrooms: 1 public

**Bed & breakfast**

| per night: | £min | £max |
|---|---|---|
| Single | 18.00 | 20.00 |
| Double | 36.00 | 40.00 |

**Half board**

| per person: | £min | £max |
|---|---|---|
| Daily | 27.50 | 30.00 |
| Weekly | 192.50 | 210.00 |

Evening meal 1800 (last orders 2000)
Parking for 7

## PRIDDY

Somerset
Map ref 2A2

Village in the Mendips, formerly a lead-mining centre, with old inns dating from the mining era. The area is rich in Bronze Age remains, among them the Priddy nine barrows. There is a sheep fair in the village every August.

### Highcroft

COMMENDED

Wells Road, Priddy, Wells BA5 3AU
☎ Wells (01749) 673446
*A natural stone country house with large lawns. From Wells take A39 to Bristol for 3 miles, turn left to Priddy and Highcroft is on right after about 2 miles.*
Bedrooms: 1 single, 1 double, 1 twin, 1 triple
Bathrooms: 2 private, 1 public

**Bed & breakfast**

| per night: | £min | £max |
|---|---|---|
| Single | 16.00 | 16.00 |
| Double | 32.00 | 34.00 |

Parking for 5

## REDLYNCH

Wiltshire
Map ref 2B3

### Lower Pensworth Farm

Redlynch, Salisbury SP5 2JU
☎ Downton (01725) 510322 & (Mobile) 0374 475352
*350-acre dairy farm. Attractive farmhouse in secluded, lovely rural setting surrounded by wooded countryside. Excellent walks, good for touring New Forest and Salisbury.*
Bedrooms: 1 double, 1 twin
Bathrooms: 1 public

**Bed & breakfast**

| per night: | £min | £max |
|---|---|---|
| Single | 17.00 | 20.00 |
| Double | 30.00 | 34.00 |

Parking for 4
Open February-November

## ST AGNES

Cornwall
Map ref 1B3

Small town in a once-rich mining area on the north coast. Terraced cottages and granite houses slope to the church. Some old mine workings remain, but the attraction must be the magnificent coastal scenery and superb walks. St Agnes Beacon offers one of Cornwall's most extensive views.

### Penkerris

Penwinnick Road, St Agnes TR5 0PA
☎ (01872) 552262
*Enchanting Edwardian residence with own grounds in unspoilt Cornish village. Beautiful rooms, log fires in winter, home cooking. Dramatic cliff walks and beaches nearby.*
Bedrooms: 1 single, 2 double, 2 twin, 2 triple
Bathrooms: 2 private, 3 public

**Bed & breakfast**

| per night: | £min | £max |
| --- | --- | --- |
| Single | 15.00 | 20.00 |
| Double | 27.00 | 35.00 |

**Half board**

| per person: | £min | £max |
| --- | --- | --- |
| Daily | 22.50 | 27.50 |
| Weekly | 125.00 | 145.00 |

Lunch available
Evening meal from 1830
Parking for 8
Cards accepted: Access, Visa, Switch/Delta

## ST IVES

Cornwall
Map ref 1B3

Old fishing port, artists' colony and holiday town with good surfing beach. Fishermen's cottages, granite fish cellars, a sandy harbour and magnificent headlands typify a charm that has survived since the 19th C pilchard boom. Tate Gallery opened in 1993.
*Tourist Information Centre*
☎ *(01736) 796297*

### The Anchorage Guest House

COMMENDED

5 Bunkers Hill, St Ives TR26 1LJ
☎ Penzance (01736) 797135
*18th C fisherman's cottage guesthouse with exceptional decor. Short walk to beach. Full of old world charm, centrally heated.*
Bedrooms: 1 single, 4 double, 1 twin, 1 family room
Bathrooms: 5 private, 1 public

**Bed & breakfast**

| per night: | £min | £max |
| --- | --- | --- |
| Single | 16.00 | 19.00 |
| Double | 32.00 | 38.00 |

Cards accepted: Access, Visa, Amex

### The Grey Mullet

2 Bunkers Hill, St Ives TR26 1LJ
☎ (01736) 796635
*18th C listed house in old St Ives. 20 yards from harbour, beaches, cliff walks and 2 minutes from the Tate Gallery.*
Bedrooms: 1 single, 5 double, 1 twin
Bathrooms: 3 private, 2 public

**Bed & breakfast**

| per night: | £min | £max |
| --- | --- | --- |
| Single | 16.00 | 18.00 |
| Double | 32.00 | 40.00 |

### Seagulls Guest House

4 Godrevy Terrace, St Ives TR26 1JA
☎ Penzance (01736) 797273
*Panoramic sea views, 2 minutes to beaches, town centre and Tate Gallery. Superior rooms with private facilities. Free parking.*
Bedrooms: 1 single, 4 double
Bathrooms: 4 private, 1 public

**Bed & breakfast**

| per night: | £min | £max |
| --- | --- | --- |
| Single | 14.00 | 22.00 |
| Double | 28.00 | 44.00 |

Parking for 10

### Tregony Guest House

1 Clodgy View, St Ives TR26 1JG
☎ Penzance (01736) 795884
*Comfortable, licensed guesthouse, overlooking the island and Porthmeor beach. Ideally situated for St Ives Tate Gallery. Cuisine prepared by chef/proprietor.*
Bedrooms: 3 double, 2 family rooms
Bathrooms: 2 private, 2 public

**Bed & breakfast**

| per night: | £min | £max |
| --- | --- | --- |
| Double | 32.00 | 40.00 |

Evening meal 1800 (last orders 1830)

Individual proprietors have supplied all details of accommodation. Although we do check for accuracy, we advise you to confirm the information at the time of booking.

## ST KEW

Cornwall
Map ref 1B2

Old village sheltered by trees standing beside a stream. The church is noted for its medieval glass showing the Passion and the remains of a scene of the Tree of Jesse.

### Tregellist Farm

COMMENDED

Tregellist, St Kew, Bodmin PL30 3HG
☎ Bodmin (01208) 880537
*125-acre mixed farm. Farmhouse, built in 1989, offering old-fashioned hospitality. Set in tiny hamlet with lovely views and pleasant walks. Central for coast and moors. Children welcome. 1.5 miles from A39.*
Bedrooms: 1 double, 1 twin, 1 family room
Bathrooms: 3 private

**Bed & breakfast**

| per night: | £min | £max |
| --- | --- | --- |
| Single | 16.00 | 18.00 |

**Half board**

| per person: | £min | £max |
| --- | --- | --- |
| Daily | 25.00 | 27.00 |

Evening meal from 1800
Parking for 6
Open February-October

## ST NEOT

Cornwall
Map ref 1C2

### Colliford Tavern

Colliford Lake, St Neot, Liskeard PL14 6PZ
☎ Cardinham (01208) 821335
Fax (01208) 821335
*Family-run freehouse near Colliford Lake. Cosy bar and dining room. Real ale, home-cooked specialities. Ideal base for exploring Cornwall.*
Bedrooms: 3 double, 2 twin
Bathrooms: 5 private

**Bed & breakfast**

| per night: | £min | £max |
| --- | --- | --- |
| Single | 24.00 | 29.50 |
| Double | 32.00 | 43.00 |

Lunch available
Evening meal 1900 (last orders 2130)
Parking for 50
Open April-September and Christmas
Cards accepted: Access, Visa, Amex

Please use the new PhONEday area telephone codes shown in establishment entries.

## SALCOMBE

Devon
Map ref 1C3

Sheltered yachting resort of whitewashed houses and narrow streets in a balmy setting on the Salcombe Estuary. Palm, myrtle and other Mediterranean plants flourish. There are sandy bays and creeks for boating.

### Torre View Hotel

**COMMENDED**

Devon Road, Salcombe TQ8 8HJ
☎ (01548) 842633
*Large detached residence with every modern comfort, commanding extensive views of the estuary and surrounding countryside. Congenial atmosphere.*
Bedrooms: 4 double, 2 twin, 2 triple
Bathrooms: 8 private

**Bed & breakfast**
| per night: | £min | £max |
|---|---|---|
| Single | 22.00 | 28.00 |
| Double | 43.00 | 52.00 |

**Half board**
| per person: | £min | £max |
|---|---|---|
| Daily | 32.00 | 36.50 |
| Weekly | 218.00 | 242.00 |

Evening meal 1900 (last orders 1800)
Parking for 5
Open February-October
Cards accepted: Access, Visa

## SALISBURY

Wiltshire
Map ref 2B3

Beautiful city and ancient regional capital set amid water meadows. Buildings of all periods are dominated by the cathedral whose spire is the tallest in England. Built between 1220 and 1258, it is one of the purest examples of Early English architecture.
*Tourist Information Centre*
*☎ (01722) 334956*

### The Bell Inn

Warminster Road, South Newton, Salisbury SP2 0QD
☎ (01722) 743336
*300-year-old roadside inn offering full en-suite facilities. Extensive range of bar meals. 6 miles north west of Salisbury.*
Bedrooms: 1 single, 1 double, 1 twin
Bathrooms: 3 private

**Bed & breakfast**
| per night: | £min | £max |
|---|---|---|
| Single | 18.00 | |
| Double | 32.00 | 34.00 |

Lunch available
Evening meal 1900 (last orders 2100)
Parking for 60

### Beulah

**Listed**

144 Britford Lane, Salisbury SP2 8AL
☎ (01722) 333517
*Bungalow in quiet road 1.25 miles from city centre, overlooking meadows. No-smoking establishment.*
Bedrooms: 1 single, 1 family room
Bathrooms: 1 public

**Bed & breakfast**
| per night: | £min | £max |
|---|---|---|
| Single | 14.00 | 16.00 |
| Double | 28.00 | 32.00 |

Parking for 4

### Byways House

31 Fowlers Road, Salisbury SP1 2QP
☎ (01722) 328364
Fax (01722) 322146
*Attractive family-run Victorian house close to cathedral in quiet area of city centre. Car park. Bedrooms en-suite with colour TV. Traditional English and vegetarian breakfasts.*
Bedrooms: 4 single, 8 double, 8 twin, 2 triple, 1 family room
Bathrooms: 19 private, 1 public

**Bed & breakfast**
| per night: | £min | £max |
|---|---|---|
| Single | 22.00 | 30.50 |
| Double | 39.00 | 56.00 |

Parking for 15
Cards accepted: Access, Visa

### Castlewood

45 Castle Road, Salisbury SP1 3RH
☎ (01722) 421494 & 324809
*Large Edwardian house, tastefully restored throughout. Pleasant 10 minutes' riverside walk to city centre and cathedral.*
Bedrooms: 2 single, 1 double, 1 twin, 1 family room
Bathrooms: 2 private, 1 public

**Bed & breakfast**
| per night: | £min | £max |
|---|---|---|
| Single | 18.00 | 25.00 |
| Double | 28.00 | 35.00 |

Parking for 4

### Cranston Guest House

**APPROVED**

5 Wain-a-Long Road, Salisbury SP1 1LJ
☎ (01722) 336776
*Large detached town house covered in Virginia creeper. 10 minutes' walk from town centre and cathedral.*
Bedrooms: 2 single, 3 double, 2 twin, 2 family rooms
Bathrooms: 7 private, 1 public

**Bed & breakfast**
| per night: | £min | £max |
|---|---|---|
| Single | 14.00 | 16.00 |
| Double | 30.00 | 32.00 |

Evening meal 1800 (last orders 1900)
Parking for 4

### The Gallery

**Listed COMMENDED**

36 Wyndham Road, Salisbury SP1 3AB
☎ (01722) 324586
*A warm welcome awaits you at The Gallery, situated within easy walking distance of cathedral, museum and shopping centre. A non-smoking establishment.*
Bedrooms: 1 double, 2 twin
Bathrooms: 3 private

**Bed & breakfast**
| per night: | £min | £max |
|---|---|---|
| Double | 28.00 | 34.00 |

### Hayburn Wyke Guest House

72 Castle Road, Salisbury SP1 3RL
☎ (01722) 412627
*Family-run spacious guesthouse adjacent to Victoria Park. Short walk from the cathedral and city centre and Old Sarum. Stonehenge 9 miles.*
Bedrooms: 2 double, 2 twin, 2 triple
Bathrooms: 2 private, 1 public

**Bed & breakfast**
| per night: | £min | £max |
|---|---|---|
| Single | 20.00 | |
| Double | 32.00 | 39.00 |

Parking for 6

### Kelebrae

101 Castle Road, Salisbury SP1 3RP
☎ (01722) 333628
*Family home, opposite Victoria Park within walking distance of city centre. Convenient for Stonehenge. Parking.*
Bedrooms: 2 double, 1 twin
Bathrooms: 1 private, 1 public

**Bed & breakfast**
| per night: | £min | £max |
|---|---|---|
| Double | 30.00 | 32.00 |

Parking for 4

### Leena's Guest House

50 Castle Road, Salisbury SP1 3RL
☎ (01722) 335419
*Attractive Edwardian house with friendly atmosphere, close to riverside walks and park. Modern facilities include en-suite and ground-floor rooms.*
Bedrooms: 1 single, 2 double, 2 twin, 1 family room
Bathrooms: 4 private, 1 public, 1 private shower

| Bed & breakfast per night: | £min | £max |
|---|---|---|
| Single | 16.00 | |
| Double | 30.00 | 36.00 |

Parking for 7

🛏🅿🖵♿ⓊⓁ⒮✂🎿📺◐🛒🅰❄✕🚗🅂🄿

## The Old Bakery
👑

35 Bedwin Street, Salisbury SP1 3UT
☎ (01722) 320100
*15th C city centre house of charm and character. High standard of comfort and service. Cosy oak-beamed bedrooms.*
Bedrooms: 1 single, 1 double, 1 twin
Bathrooms: 2 private, 1 public

| Bed & breakfast per night: | £min | £max |
|---|---|---|
| Single | 16.00 | 20.00 |
| Double | 32.00 | 42.00 |

🖵♿ⓊⓁ⒮📺🛒🅰✕🚗🄿

## Richburn Guest House
👑👑 APPROVED

23 & 25 Estcourt Road, Salisbury
SP1 3AP
☎ (01722) 325189
*Large, tastefully renovated Victorian house with homely family atmosphere. All modern amenities and large car park. Close to city centre and parks.*
Bedrooms: 2 single, 4 double, 2 twin, 1 triple, 1 family room
Bathrooms: 2 private, 2 public

| Bed & breakfast per night: | £min | £max |
|---|---|---|
| Single | 16.50 | 17.00 |
| Double | 28.00 | 36.00 |

Parking for 10

🛏🅿♿ⓊⓁ⒮✂🎿📺🛒🅰🍴

## Swaynes Firs Farm
👑 APPROVED

Grimsdyke, Coombe Bissett, Salisbury
SP5 5RF
☎ Martin Cross (01725) 519240
*15-acre mixed farm. Country farmhouse in pleasant position with good views. Ancient Roman ditch on farm. Peacocks, ducks, chickens and horses are reared on the farm.*
Bedrooms: 2 twin, 1 family room
Bathrooms: 3 private

| Bed & breakfast per night: | £min | £max |
|---|---|---|
| Single | 16.00 | 18.00 |
| Double | 32.00 | 36.00 |

Parking for 9

🛏🅿🖵♿🎣ⓊⓁ🔌📺🛒🅰♻❄🚗

## SALISBURY PLAIN

*See under Amesbury, Figheldean, Salisbury, Shrewton, Warminster, Winterbourne Stoke*

## SHALDON

Devon
Map ref 1D2

Pretty resort facing Teignmouth from the south bank of the Teign Estuary. Regency houses harmonise with others of later periods; there are old cottages and narrow lanes. On the Ness, a sandstone promontory nearby, a tunnel built in the 19th C leads to a beach revealed at low tide.

## Fonthill
👑👑 HIGHLY COMMENDED

Torquay Road, Shaldon, Teignmouth
TQ14 0AX
☎ (01626) 872344
Fax (01626) 872344

*Lovely Georgian family home in superb grounds overlooking River Teign. Very comfortable rooms in a peaceful setting. Restaurants nearby.*
Bedrooms: 3 twin
Bathrooms: 3 private

| Bed & breakfast per night: | £min | £max |
|---|---|---|
| Single | 28.00 | 32.00 |
| Double | 44.00 | 50.00 |

Parking for 5

🛏♿ⓊⓁ⒮✂🎿📺🛒🅰🔍▶❄✕🚗

## SHEPTON MALLET

Somerset
Map ref 2A2

Important, stone-built market town beneath the south-west slopes of the Mendips. Thriving rural industries include glove and shoe making, dairying and cider making; the remains of a medieval "shambles" in the square date from the town's prosperity as a wool centre.

## Hurlingpot Farm
👑👑 COMMENDED

Chelynch, Doulting, Shepton Mallet
BA4 4PY
☎ (01749) 880256
*Lovely 300-year-old farmhouse in a peaceful country setting, 2 miles east of Shepton Mallet. A361 to Doulting, then take Chelynch road. Turn left past Poachers Pocket pub and left again into farm entrance.*
Bedrooms: 2 single, 1 double, 1 twin
Bathrooms: 4 private

| Bed & breakfast per night: | £min | £max |
|---|---|---|
| Single | 20.00 | 25.00 |
| Double | | 35.00 |

Parking for 6

🛏🖵♿ⓊⓁ🛒🅰🍴❄✕🚗🅂🄿🏠

## Pecking Mill Inn and Hotel
👑👑👑

A371, Evercreech, Shepton Mallet
BA4 6PG
☎ (01749) 830336 & 830006
*16th C inn with oak-beamed restaurant and open log fire. Old world atmosphere with all modern amenities.*
Bedrooms: 1 single, 5 double
Bathrooms: 6 private

| Bed & breakfast per night: | £min | £max |
|---|---|---|
| Single | 28.00 | 33.00 |
| Double | 38.00 | 44.00 |

| Half board per person: | £min | £max |
|---|---|---|
| Daily | 29.50 | |

Lunch available
Evening meal 1900 (last orders 2200)
Parking for 23
Cards accepted: Access, Visa, Diners, Amex

🛏☎🍺🖵♿🐾🔓🅰⒮📺🛒🅰🍴🥄🅂🏠🅃

## Temple House Farm
👑👑 COMMENDED

Doulting, Shepton Mallet BA4 4RQ
☎ (01749) 880294
Fax (01749) 880688
*200-acre dairy farm. 400-year old listed farmhouse with all facilities. In rural area within easy reach of Wells, Bath, Shepton Mallet, the walking delights of the Mendips and plenty of tourist attractions.*
Bedrooms: 2 double
Bathrooms: 1 private, 1 public

| Bed & breakfast per night: | £min | £max |
|---|---|---|
| Single | 15.00 | |
| Double | 30.00 | |

| Half board per person: | £min | £max |
|---|---|---|
| Daily | 22.00 | |

🛏☎🖵♿🐾🔓ⓊⓁ🅰Ⓢ📺🛒🅰♻❄✕🚗🏠

There are separate sections in this guide listing groups specialising in farm holidays and accommodation which is especially suitable for young people and organised groups.

## SHERBORNE

Dorset
Map ref 2B3

Historic town of Ham stone, a business and market centre for a wide area and a developing cultural centre with a range of activities. The home of Dorset Opera. In Anglo-Saxon times it was a cathedral city and until the Dissolution there was a monastery here.
*Tourist Information Centre*
☎ *(01935) 815341*

### The Alders

🏠🏠 COMMENDED

Sandford Orcas, Sherborne DT9 4SB
☎ (01963) 220666
*Secluded stone house set in old walled garden, in picturesque conservation village near Sherborne. Excellent food available in friendly village pub.*
Bedrooms: 1 double, 1 twin
Bathrooms: 2 private

**Bed & breakfast**
| per night: | £min | £max |
| --- | --- | --- |
| Single | 18.50 | 21.00 |
| Double | 37.00 | 42.00 |

Parking for 6

### Quinns

🏠🏠 HIGHLY COMMENDED

Marston Road, Sherborne DT9 4BL
☎ (01935) 815008
*Delightful accommodation in modern house. All rooms en-suite, TV, tea/coffee making facilities. Spacious lounge. Dinners by arrangement. Car park.*
Bedrooms: 1 single, 1 double, 1 twin
Bathrooms: 3 private

**Bed & breakfast**
| per night: | £min | £max |
| --- | --- | --- |
| Single | 21.00 | 25.00 |
| Double | 42.00 | 50.00 |

**Half board**
| per person: | £min | £max |
| --- | --- | --- |
| Daily | 35.00 | 39.00 |

Evening meal from 1900
Parking for 4

## SHREWTON

Wiltshire
Map ref 2B2

### Ashwick House

🏠🏠

Upper Backway, Shrewton, Salisbury SP3 4DE
☎ (01980) 621138
*Large village house in quiet position. Ideal touring centre for Salisbury, Bath, New Forest, Stonehenge (2 miles). Walking distance of 2 pubs. Parking in driveway.*
Bedrooms: 2 twin
Bathrooms: 1 private, 1 public

**Bed & breakfast**
| per night: | £min | £max |
| --- | --- | --- |
| Single | 13.50 | 15.00 |
| Double | 27.00 | 30.00 |

**Half board**
| per person: | £min | £max |
| --- | --- | --- |
| Daily | 19.50 | 25.00 |
| Weekly | 120.00 | 160.00 |

Evening meal 1900 (last orders 2030)
Parking for 5

## SIDMOUTH

Devon
Map ref 1D2

Charming resort set amid lofty red cliffs where the River Sid meets the sea. The wealth of ornate Regency and Victorian villas recalls the time when this was one of the south coast's most exclusive resorts. Museum; August International Festival of Folk Arts.
*Tourist Information Centre*
☎ *(01395) 516441*

### Broad Oak

🏠🏠 HIGHLY COMMENDED

Sid Road, Sidmouth EX10 8QP
☎ (01395) 513713

*Listed Victorian villa in delightful gardens overlooking "The Byes". A peaceful location, only a short stroll from the town centre and Esplanade.*
Bedrooms: 1 single, 1 double, 1 twin
Bathrooms: 2 private, 1 public

**Bed & breakfast**
| per night: | £min | £max |
| --- | --- | --- |
| Single | 20.00 | 20.00 |
| Double | 46.00 | 50.00 |

Parking for 4
Open February-November

### Lower Pinn Farm

🏠🏠

Pinn, Sidmouth EX10 0NN
☎ (01395) 513733
*220-acre mixed farm. Situated in an Area of Outstanding Natural Beauty, 2 miles west of unspoilt coastal resort of Sidmouth. Comfortable, spacious rooms.*
Bedrooms: 2 double, 1 twin
Bathrooms: 2 private, 1 public

**Bed & breakfast**
| per night: | £min | £max |
| --- | --- | --- |
| Double | 34.00 | 38.00 |

Parking for 3

### Wiscombe Linhaye Farm

🏠

Southleigh, Colyton EX13 6JF
☎ Farway (01404) 87342
*30-acre beef farm. In quiet countyside within easy reach of Sidmouth and Lyme Regis. Ground floor bedrooms. Hot drink facilities and hair-dryer in all rooms.*
Wheelchair access category 3 ♿
Bedrooms: 2 double, 1 twin
Bathrooms: 3 private, 1 public

**Bed & breakfast**
| per night: | £min | £max |
| --- | --- | --- |
| Single | 17.00 | 18.00 |
| Double | 32.00 | 35.00 |

**Half board**
| per person: | £min | £max |
| --- | --- | --- |
| Daily | 22.00 | 25.00 |
| Weekly | 154.00 | 160.00 |

Evening meal from 1830
Parking for 5
Open April-October

## SLAPTON

Devon
Map ref 1D3

### Start House

🏠🏠 COMMENDED

Start, Slapton, Kingsbridge TQ7 2QD
☎ Kingsbridge (01548) 580254
*Situated in quiet hamlet, 1 mile from Slapton. Comfortable house overlooking beautiful valley. Large garden. Ideal for wildlife and walking.*
Bedrooms: 1 single, 2 double, 1 twin
Bathrooms: 2 private, 1 public

**Bed & breakfast**
| per night: | £min | £max |
| --- | --- | --- |
| Single | 17.00 | 18.50 |
| Double | 34.00 | 37.00 |

**Half board**
| per person: | £min | £max |
| --- | --- | --- |
| Daily | 28.00 | 29.50 |
| Weekly | 180.00 | 190.00 |

Evening meal 1830 (last orders 1000)
Parking for 4
Open January-November

There are separate sections in this guide listing groups specialising in farm holidays and accommodation which is especially suitable for young people and organised groups.

## SOUTH MOLTON

Devon
Map ref 1C1

Busy market town at the mouth of the Yeo Valley near southern Exmoor. Wool, mining and coaching brought prosperity between the Middle Ages and the 19th C and the fine square with Georgian buildings, a Guildhall and Assembly Rooms reflect this former affluence.

### Kerscott Farm

HIGHLY COMMENDED

Bishop's Nympton, South Molton EX36 4QG
☎ Bishop's Nympton (01769) 550262
*70-acre mixed farm. Peaceful old world 16th C Exmoor farmhouse mentioned in Domesday Book. Superb views. Fascinating interior/antiques. Scrumptious, hearty country cooking from Aga. Ideal friendly rural retreat. Non-smokers only.*
Bedrooms: 2 double, 1 twin
Bathrooms: 3 private, 1 public
**Bed & breakfast**

| per night: | £min | £max |
| --- | --- | --- |
| Double | 28.00 | 33.00 |

**Half board**

| per person: | £min | £max |
| --- | --- | --- |
| Daily | 21.00 | 23.00 |

Evening meal 1830 (last orders 1400)
Parking for 8

### Meadow Farm

HIGHLY COMMENDED

East Buckland, Barnstaple EX32 0TB
☎ (01598) 760375
*9-acre mixed farm. Idyllic rural setting. Spacious bungalow, surrounded by lovely gardens. Extensive views to Exmoor. Plenty of good food, friendly atmosphere. Easy drive coast and sandy beaches. 3 miles from A361.*
Bedrooms: 2 double
Bathrooms: 2 private
**Bed & breakfast**

| per night: | £min | £max |
| --- | --- | --- |
| Double | 32.00 | |

**Half board**

| per person: | £min | £max |
| --- | --- | --- |
| Daily | 26.00 | |
| Weekly | 165.00 | |

Evening meal from 1900
Parking for 3

The symbol **M** after an establishment name indicates membership of a Regional Tourist Board.

## STANTON DREW

Avon
Map ref 2A2

### Valley Farm **M**

HIGHLY COMMENDED

Sandy Lane, Stanton Drew, Bristol BS18 4EL
☎ Pill (01275) 332723
*64-acre beef farm. New farmhouse in old village with Druid stones. Quiet location, central for Bath, Wells, Cheddar. Tea/coffee facilities in bedrooms, TV lounge.*
Bedrooms: 3 double
Bathrooms: 3 private, 1 public
**Bed & breakfast**

| per night: | £min | £max |
| --- | --- | --- |
| Single | 18.00 | 20.00 |
| Double | 30.00 | 36.00 |

Parking for 4

## STARCROSS

Devon
Map ref 1D2

Small village on the western shore of the Exe Estuary, with a harbour and 19th C seaside villas. Powderham Castle and Park, just north, make a pleasant excursion and a pedestrian ferry crosses the water to Exmouth.

### The Old Vicarage **M**

COMMENDED

Starcross, Exeter EX6 8PX
☎ (01626) 890206

*Enjoy the relaxed, friendly atmosphere of this interesting old house set in 3 acres on Exe Estuary village edge. River views from some bedrooms. Easy access to Exeter, beaches and Dartmoor. Good local inns nearby.*
Bedrooms: 2 double, 2 twin, 1 family room
Bathrooms: 3 private, 1 public
**Bed & breakfast**

| per night: | £min | £max |
| --- | --- | --- |
| Single | 15.00 | 22.00 |
| Double | 30.00 | 40.00 |

Parking for 6

Please mention this guide when making a booking.

## STOKE ST GREGORY

Somerset
Map ref 1D1

### Parsonage Farm

Listed

Stoke St Gregory, Taunton TA3 6ET
☎ Burrowbridge (01823) 698205
*120-acre dairy farm. Large Georgian farmhouse and garden on ridge overlooking the Somerset Levels. Lovely views, good base for touring. Well-stocked coarse fishing half a mile away.*
Bedrooms: 2 twin, 1 family room
Bathrooms: 1 public
**Bed & breakfast**

| per night: | £min | £max |
| --- | --- | --- |
| Single | 15.00 | 17.00 |
| Double | 30.00 | 34.00 |

Parking for 8
Open March-October

## STOKE-IN-TEIGNHEAD

Devon
Map ref 1D2

### Deane Thatch Accommodation **M**

COMMENDED

Deane Road, Stoke-in-Teignhead, Newton Abbot TQ12 4QU
☎ Shaldon (01626) 873724

*Thatched Devonshire cob cottage and linhay. Quiet rural position near sea. Private facilities, large garden, home produce. Open all year.*
Bedrooms: 1 double, 1 family room
Bathrooms: 2 private
**Bed & breakfast**

| per night: | £min | £max |
| --- | --- | --- |
| Single | 20.00 | 25.00 |
| Double | 30.00 | 40.00 |

Parking for 3

Individual proprietors have supplied all details of accommodation. Although we do check for accuracy, we advise you to confirm the information at the time of booking.

## SWINDON

Wiltshire
Map ref 2B2

Wiltshire's industrial and commercial centre, an important railway town in the 19th C, situated just north of the Marlborough Downs. The railway village created in the mid-19th C has been preserved. Railway museum, art gallery, theatre and leisure centre.
*Tourist Information Centre*
☎ *(01793) 530328*

### Internos

3 Turnpike Road, Blunsdon, Swindon, Wiltshire SN2 4EA
☎ (01793) 721496
*Detached red brick house off A419, 4 miles north of Swindon and 6 miles from M4 junction 15.*
Bedrooms: 1 single, 1 twin, 1 triple
Bathrooms: 2 public

**Bed & breakfast**

| per night: | £min | £max |
|---|---|---|
| Single | 19.00 | 23.00 |
| Double | 32.00 | 32.00 |

Parking for 6

### Relian Guest House

151-153 County Road, Swindon SN1 2EB
☎ (01793) 521416
*Quiet house adjacent to Swindon Town Football Club and short distance from town centre. Close to bus and rail stations, and A345. Free car park at rear.*
Bedrooms: 4 single, 2 double, 2 twin
Bathrooms: 3 private, 3 private showers

**Bed & breakfast**

| per night: | £min | £max |
|---|---|---|
| Single | 17.00 | 25.00 |
| Double | 32.00 | 40.00 |

## SYDLING ST NICHOLAS

Dorset
Map ref 2B3

### Magiston Farm
**Listed**

Sydling St Nicholas DT2 9NR
☎ Maiden Newton (01300) 320295
*400-acre arable farm. 350-year-old farmhouse, set beside the Sydling River in the heart of Dorset's peaceful countryside. 5 miles north of Dorchester.*
Bedrooms: 2 single, 1 double, 2 twin
Bathrooms: 1 private, 1 public

---

**Bed & breakfast**

| per night: | £min | £max |
|---|---|---|
| Single | 15.50 | |
| Double | 31.00 | |

**Half board**

| per person: | £min | £max |
|---|---|---|
| Daily | 25.00 | |
| Weekly | 175.00 | |

Evening meal from 1900
Parking for 10

## TAUNTON

Somerset
Map ref 1D1

County town, well-known for its public schools, sheltered by gentle hill-ranges on the River Tone. Medieval prosperity from wool has continued in marketing and manufacturing and the town retains many fine period buildings.
*Tourist Information Centre*
☎ *(01823) 274785*

### Prockters Farm

West Monkton, Taunton TA2 8QN
☎ West Monkton (01823) 412269
*300-acre mixed farm. 300-year-old farmhouse, 3 miles from M5. Inglenook fireplaces, brass beds, collection of farm antiques. Large garden. Ground floor en-suite bedrooms. Tea and cake on arrival.*
Bedrooms: 3 double, 2 twin
Bathrooms: 2 private, 3 public

**Bed & breakfast**

| per night: | £min | £max |
|---|---|---|
| Single | 21.00 | 25.00 |
| Double | 34.00 | 42.00 |

Parking for 6
Cards accepted: Amex

## TAVISTOCK

Devon
Map ref 1C2

Old market town beside the River Tavy on the western edge of Dartmoor. Developed around its 10th C abbey, of which some fragments remain, it became a stannary town in 1305 when tin-streaming thrived on the moors. Tavistock Goose Fair, October.

### April Cottage
**HIGHLY COMMENDED**

Mount Tavy Road, Tavistock PL19 9JB
☎ (01822) 613280
*Victorian riverside character cottage in pretty garden. Dining-room overlooks river. 150 metres from town centre and excellent pub food. Modern comforts include en-suite. Homely and welcoming.*

---

Bedrooms: 2 double, 1 twin
Bathrooms: 1 private, 1 public

**Bed & breakfast**

| per night: | £min | £max |
|---|---|---|
| Single | 16.00 | 18.00 |
| Double | 26.00 | 32.00 |

Parking for 4

### Mallards Guesthouse

48 Plymouth Road, Tavistock PL19 8BU
☎ (01822) 615171
*Tastefully restored Victorian guesthouse. Centre of Tavistock overlooking the park. Quiet, family-run with home cooking. Close to Dartmoor. Ideally situated for touring Devon and Cornwall.*
Bedrooms: 3 double, 3 twin
Bathrooms: 6 private

**Bed & breakfast**

| per night: | £min | £max |
|---|---|---|
| Single | 25.00 | 30.00 |
| Double | 32.00 | 36.00 |

**Half board**

| per person: | £min | £max |
|---|---|---|
| Daily | 25.00 | 27.00 |
| Weekly | 154.00 | 168.00 |

Evening meal 1830 (last orders 1530)
Parking for 6

### The Old Coach House Hotel
**APPROVED**

Ottery, Tavistock PL19 8NS
☎ (01822) 617515
*Lovely country hotel set on the edge of Dartmoor. Good English food in an old world setting with traditional West Country hospitality. Ideal for walking, touring or relaxing. Three-night bargain breaks available.*
Bedrooms: 4 double, 1 twin, 1 triple
Bathrooms: 6 private

**Bed & breakfast**

| per night: | £min | £max |
|---|---|---|
| Single | 22.00 | 30.00 |
| Double | 40.00 | 56.00 |

**Half board**

| per person: | £min | £max |
|---|---|---|
| Daily | 30.00 | 40.00 |
| Weekly | 139.50 | 198.00 |

Lunch available
Evening meal 1930 (last orders 2230)
Parking for 8
Cards accepted: Access, Visa

### Wringworthy Farm
**Listed**

Mary Tavy, Tavistock PL19 9LT
☎ Mary Tavy (01822) 810434
*120-acre livestock farm. Elizabethan farmhouse with modern comforts, in quiet valley near the moors. Within easy reach of sea and well placed for touring.*

Bedrooms: 2 double, 1 twin
Bathrooms: 2 public

**Bed & breakfast**

| per night: | £min | £max |
| --- | --- | --- |
| Single | 15.00 | 16.00 |
| Double | 30.00 | 32.00 |

Parking for 3
Open March-November

 ⌂ ▯ ⚲ ⛁ Ⓢ ⌨ TV ▥ ▣ ❄ ✕ 🛥 🏠

## TIMBERSCOMBE

Somerset
Map ref 1D1

## Wellum
♔

Brook Street, Timberscombe,
Minehead TA24 7TG
☎ (01643) 841234
*Spacious stone-built 18th C house in
Exmoor National Park. Commanding
views towards Dunkery Beacon and
surrounding rural landscape.*
Bedrooms: 1 single, 1 double, 1 twin
Bathrooms: 1 public

**Bed & breakfast**

| per night: | £min | £max |
| --- | --- | --- |
| Single | 12.00 | 15.00 |
| Double | 24.00 | 30.00 |

**Half board**

| per person: | £min | £max |
| --- | --- | --- |
| Daily | 20.00 | 23.00 |
| Weekly | 140.00 | 140.00 |

Evening meal 1930 (last orders 2000)
Open February-November

⌂ ⚲ ⛁ ▯ Ⓢ ⌨ ▥ ▣ ❄ 🛥 🏠 SP

## TINTAGEL

Cornwall
Map ref 1B2

Coastal village near the legendary
home of King Arthur. There is a
lofty headland with the ruin of a
Norman castle and traces of a
Celtic monastery are still visible in
the turf.

## Castle Villa
♔♔ COMMENDED

Molesworth Street, Tintagel PL34 0BZ
☎ Camelford (01840) 770373 &
770203
*Over 150 years old, Castle Villa is
within easy walking distance of the 11th
C church, post office and King Arthur's
castle.*
Bedrooms: 1 single, 3 double, 1 twin
Bathrooms: 1 private, 2 public

**Bed & breakfast**

| per night: | £min | £max |
| --- | --- | --- |
| Single | 14.50 | 16.50 |
| Double | 29.00 | 38.00 |

Evening meal 1900 (last orders 2100)
Parking for 6
Cards accepted: Access, Visa

⌂ ⌱ ▯ ⚲ ⛁ Ⓢ ⌨ TV ▥ ▣ 🛥 OAP ⚑ SP

## Tintagel Arms
♔♔♔ COMMENDED

Fore Street, Tintagel PL34 ODB
☎ Camelford (01840) 770780
*Centre of village, within walking
distance of King Arthur's Castle and
cliffs. Family-run inn with home
cooking.*
Bedrooms: 1 single, 4 double, 2 triple
Bathrooms: 7 private

**Bed & breakfast**

| per night: | £min | £max |
| --- | --- | --- |
| Single | 17.50 | 25.00 |
| Double | 35.00 | 45.00 |

Lunch available
Evening meal 1800 (last orders 2200)
Parking for 10
Cards accepted: Access, Visa, Amex

⌂ ▯ ⚲ 🐾 ⛁ Ⓢ ▥ ▣ ✕ 🛥 SP

## TIVERTON

Devon
Map ref 1D2

Busy market and textile town,
settled since the 9th C, at the
meeting of 2 rivers. Town houses,
Tudor almshouses and parts of the
fine church were built by wealthy
cloth merchants; a medieval castle
is incorporated into a private
house; Blundells School.
*Tourist Information Centre
☎ (01884) 255827*

## Hornhill
♔♔ HIGHLY COMMENDED

Exeter Hill, Tiverton EX16 4PL
☎ (01884) 253352

*75-acre mixed farm. Country house with
superb views. Home cooking using local
produce. Comfortable bedrooms, one
with Victorian four poster. Peaceful
relaxed atmosphere. Ten minutes from
M5.*
Bedrooms: 2 double, 1 twin
Bathrooms: 3 private

**Bed & breakfast**

| per night: | £min | £max |
| --- | --- | --- |
| Single | 17.50 | 19.00 |
| Double | 32.00 | 38.00 |

**Half board**

| per person: | £min | £max |
| --- | --- | --- |
| Daily | 27.50 | 29.00 |
| Weekly | 180.00 | 185.00 |

Evening meal 1830 (last orders 1930)
Parking for 4

⌂ 12 ⚲ ⛁ 🔲 ▯ ⚲ 🐾 ▥ ✕ 🛥 🏠

## Lodge Hill Farm
## Guesthouse ♨
♔♔ APPROVED

Ashley, Tiverton EX16 5PA
☎ (01884) 252907
Fax (01884) 242090
*Ideally situated in a peaceful rural
setting in the beautiful Exe Valley.
Perfect base for exploring Devon. Easily
accessible on A396, 1 mile south of
Tiverton.*
Bedrooms: 3 single, 2 double, 1 twin,
2 family rooms
Bathrooms: 6 private, 2 public

**Bed & breakfast**

| per night: | £min | £max |
| --- | --- | --- |
| Single | 18.00 | 18.00 |
| Double | 34.00 | 34.00 |

**Half board**

| per person: | £min | £max |
| --- | --- | --- |
| Daily | 28.00 | 28.00 |
| Weekly | 180.00 | 180.00 |

Evening meal 1730 (last orders 2000)
Parking for 12
Cards accepted: Access, Visa

⌂ ⚲ ⌱ ▯ ⚲ 🐾 Ⓢ ⌨ TV ▥ ▣ 🛥 6
❄ 🛥 ⚑ SP T

## Lower Collipriest Farm
♔♔♔ HIGHLY COMMENDED

Tiverton EX16 4PT
☎ (01884) 252321

*221-acre dairy & livestock farm. Lovely
thatched farmhouse in beautiful Exe
Valley. Of particular interest to
naturalists. Traditional and speciality
cooking. Coasts and moors within easy
reach. Brochure available.*
Bedrooms: 3 single, 2 twin
Bathrooms: 5 private

**Bed & breakfast**

| per night: | £min | £max |
| --- | --- | --- |
| Single | 20.00 | 22.50 |
| Double | 40.00 | 45.00 |

**Half board**

| per person: | £min | £max |
| --- | --- | --- |
| Daily | 27.00 | 29.00 |
| Weekly | 186.00 | 190.00 |

Evening meal 1900 (last orders 1200)
Parking for 4
Open February-November

🔲 ⚲ 🐾 ⛁ ▯ ⚲ 🐾 Ⓢ ✕ ⌨ TV ▥ 🛥 ∪ ✓
❄ ✕ 🛥 🏠

## Marchweeke Farm
♔♔ COMMENDED

Witheridge, Tiverton EX16 8NY
☎ (01884) 860418

Continued ▶

## TIVERTON

### Continued

*107-acre mixed farm. Lovely Devon longhouse with peaceful atmosphere and panoramic views. Good home cooking, access at all times, central heating. Children welcome. Brochure available.*
Bedrooms: 1 double, 1 twin
Bathrooms: 2 private

**Bed & breakfast**

| per night: | £min | £max |
| --- | --- | --- |
| Single | 15.00 | 16.00 |
| Double | 30.00 | 32.00 |

**Half board**

| per person: | £min | £max |
| --- | --- | --- |
| Daily | 23.00 | 23.00 |
| Weekly | 140.00 | 140.00 |

Evening meal 1800 (last orders 2100)
Parking for 2
Open February-November

## TOLPUDDLE

### Dorset
### Map ref 2B3

### Park Pale
Listed

Southover, Tolpuddle, Dorchester
DT2 7HG
☎ Puddletown (01305) 848524
*17th C cottage surrounded by Hardy countryside. In Tolpuddle take the Southover road, then first right and follow Park Pale sign for half a mile.*
Bedrooms: 2 single, 1 twin
Bathrooms: 1 public

**Bed & breakfast**

| per night: | £min | £max |
| --- | --- | --- |
| Single | 15.00 | 17.50 |
| Double | 32.00 | 32.00 |

Parking for 5
Open April-October

### Wessex Fly Fishing ♠
⌒⌒ APPROVED

Lawrences Farm, Southover,
Tolpuddle, Dorchester DT2 7HF
☎ Puddletown (01305) 848460
Fax (01305) 848516
*Peaceful rural estate, comfortable rooms, first class lake and river trout fishing. Central Dorset location with sandy beaches and tourist attractions within easy reach. Friendly family atmosphere.*
Bedrooms: 1 double, 1 twin

Bathrooms: 2 private

**Bed & breakfast**

| per night: | £min | £max |
| --- | --- | --- |
| Single | 19.00 | 19.00 |
| Double | 22.00 | 22.00 |

Parking for 6

## TORQUAY

### Devon
### Map ref 1D2

Devon's grandest resort, developed from a fishing village. Smart apartments and terraces rise from the seafront and Marine Drive along the headland gives views of beaches and colourful cliffs.
*Tourist Information Centre*
☎ *(01803) 297428*

### Barn Hayes Country Hotel ♠
⌒⌒⌒ HIGHLY COMMENDED

Brim Hill, Maidencombe, Torquay
TQ1 4TR
☎ (01803) 327980

*Warm, friendly and comfortable country house hotel in an Area of Outstanding Natural Beauty overlooking countryside and sea. Relaxation is guaranteed in these lovely surroundings by personal service, good food and fine wines.*
Bedrooms: 2 single, 4 double, 2 twin, 2 triple, 2 family rooms
Bathrooms: 10 private, 1 public

**Bed & breakfast**

| per night: | £min | £max |
| --- | --- | --- |
| Single | 24.00 | 27.00 |
| Double | 48.00 | 54.00 |

**Half board**

| per person: | £min | £max |
| --- | --- | --- |
| Daily | 36.00 | 39.00 |
| Weekly | 231.00 | 252.00 |

Lunch available
Evening meal 1830 (last orders 1900)
Parking for 16
Open February-December
Cards accepted: Access, Visa

### Chelston Manor Hotel
⌒⌒⌒

Old Mill Road, Torquay TQ2 6HW
☎ (01803) 605142

*Old world bed and breakfast inn. Reputation for pub food. Sun-trap gardens with heated swimming pool.*
Bedrooms: 1 single, 7 double, 4 twin, 1 triple
Bathrooms: 9 private, 1 public

**Bed & breakfast**

| per night: | £min | £max |
| --- | --- | --- |
| Single | 15.00 | 20.00 |
| Double | 30.00 | 40.00 |

Lunch available
Evening meal 1800 (last orders 2130)
Parking for 40
Open April-October

### Claver Guest House ♠
Listed

119 Abbey Road, Torquay TQ2 5NP
☎ (01803) 297118
*A warm welcome awaits you. Close to beach, harbour and all entertainments. Home-cooked food, you'll never leave the table hungry!*
Bedrooms: 1 single, 2 double, 1 twin, 2 triple, 2 family rooms
Bathrooms: 1 private, 2 public

**Bed & breakfast**

| per night: | £min | £max |
| --- | --- | --- |
| Single | 12.00 | |
| Double | 24.00 | |

**Half board**

| per person: | £min | £max |
| --- | --- | --- |
| Daily | 18.50 | |
| Weekly | 110.00 | |

Evening meal 1800 (last orders 1800)
Parking for 4
Open January-November

### Craig Court Hotel
⌒⌒ APPROVED

10 Ash Hill Road, Torquay TQ1 3HZ
☎ (01803) 294400
*Small hotel situated a short distance from the town centre and the harbour. Quiet location with a lovely garden and choice of menus.*
Bedrooms: 2 single, 4 double, 2 twin, 2 family rooms
Bathrooms: 5 private, 3 public

**Bed & breakfast**

| per night: | £min | £max |
| --- | --- | --- |
| Single | 16.50 | 22.50 |
| Double | 33.00 | 45.00 |

**Half board**

| per person: | £min | £max |
| --- | --- | --- |
| Daily | 22.00 | 30.00 |
| Weekly | 154.00 | 196.00 |

Evening meal 1800 (last orders 0900)
Parking for 10
Open April-October
🛏🚴♿💺📶Ⓢ🅿️📺➿❊🚗 SP 🏤 T

## Gainsboro Hotel

🏆 COMMENDED

22 Rathmore Road, Torquay TQ2 6NY
☎ (01803) 292032
*Family-run hotel providing friendly
atmosphere. Close to station, seafront
and amenities.*
Bedrooms: 1 single, 3 double, 2 twin,
1 triple
Bathrooms: 3 private, 1 public

**Bed & breakfast**

| per night: | £min | £max |
|---|---|---|
| Single | 11.00 | 16.00 |
| Double | 22.00 | 32.00 |

Parking for 5
Open March-October
Cards accepted: Access, Visa
🛏6♿💺📶Ⓤ🅿️📺➿❊🚗 DAP

## Kingston House ⚠

🏆

75 Avenue Road, Torquay TQ2 5LL
☎ (01803) 212760

*Elegant Victorian building, tastefully
modernised. Conveniently situated for
the town and seafront. Family-run,
offering traditional home cooking, with
a choice of daily menu.*
Bedrooms: 1 single, 3 double, 1 triple,
1 family room
Bathrooms: 6 private

**Bed & breakfast**

| per night: | £min | £max |
|---|---|---|
| Single | 15.50 | 22.50 |
| Double | 27.00 | 35.00 |

**Half board**

| per person: | £min | £max |
|---|---|---|
| Daily | 22.00 | 24.50 |
| Weekly | 135.00 | 159.00 |

Evening meal 1800 (last orders 1630)
Parking for 6
Open April-October
Cards accepted: Access, Visa
🛏8♿💺📶🔑Ⓢ🅿️➿❊🚗
DAP SP

## Maple Lodge

🏆 COMMENDED

36 Ash Hill Road, Torquay TQ1 3JD
☎ (01803) 297391
*Detached guesthouse with beautiful
views. Relaxed atmosphere, home
cooking, en-suite and shower rooms.
Centrally situated for town and beaches.*
Bedrooms: 1 single, 2 double, 1 twin,
2 triple, 1 family room
Bathrooms: 5 private, 1 public,
1 private shower

---

**Bed & breakfast**

| per night: | £min | £max |
|---|---|---|
| Single | 12.50 | 16.50 |
| Double | 25.00 | 33.00 |

**Half board**

| per person: | £min | £max |
|---|---|---|
| Daily | 18.00 | 22.00 |
| Weekly | 120.00 | 149.00 |

Evening meal from 1800
Parking for 5
Open March-October
🛏🚴♿💺🔑Ⓤ🔑Ⓢ🅿️📺➿❊🚗 DAP SP

Devon
Map ref 1C1

Perched high above the River
Torridge, with a charming market
square, Georgian Town Hall and a
museum. The famous Dartington
Crystal Factory, Rosemoor
Gardens and Plough Arts Centre
are all located in the town.

## Flavills Farm

Listed

Kingscott, St Giles in the Wood,
Torrington EX38 7JW
☎ (01805) 623530 & 623250
*125-acre mixed farm. 15th C farmhouse
in conservation area of picturesque
hamlet. Peaceful atmosphere.*
Bedrooms: 1 single, 1 double, 1 triple
Bathrooms: 1 public

**Bed & breakfast**

| per night: | £min | £max |
|---|---|---|
| Single | 12.00 | 12.00 |
| Double | 24.00 | 24.00 |

Parking for 6
Open April-September
🛏🚳Ⓤ🔑📺➿❊🚗🏤

Devon
Map ref 1D2

Old market town steeply built near
the head of the Dart Estuary.
Remains of medieval gateways, a
noble church, 16th C Guildhall and
medley of period houses recall
former wealth from cloth and
shipping, continued in rural and
water industries.
*Tourist Information Centre*
☎ *(01803) 863168*

## Old Church House Inn ⚠

🏆 COMMENDED

Torbryan, Newton Abbot TQ12 5UR
☎ Ipplepen (01803) 812372
*13th C coaching house of immense
character and old world charm with
inglenook fireplaces, stone walls and
oak beamed ceilings. Situated in a
beautiful valley between Dartmoor and
Torquay.*
Bedrooms: 5 double, 1 twin, 1 triple
Bathrooms: 7 private

---

**Bed & breakfast**

| per night: | £min | £max |
|---|---|---|
| Single | 27.50 | 35.00 |
| Double | 55.00 | 60.00 |

**Half board**

| per person: | £min | £max |
|---|---|---|
| Daily | 40.00 | 45.00 |
| Weekly | 240.00 | 270.00 |

Lunch available
Evening meal 1800 (last orders 2130)
Parking for 30
Cards accepted: Access, Visa
🛏🚴📶🔑💺♿📶Ⓢ🅿️📺➿
🍴40-60 ♿ 🔑➿❊ DAP 🚗 SP 🏤 T

## The Old Forge at Totnes ⚠

🏆 HIGHLY COMMENDED

Seymour Place, Totnes TQ9 5AY
☎ (01803) 862174
*Delightful 600-year-old stone building,
with walled garden, cobbled driveway
and working smithy. Cottage suite
suitable for family or disabled guests.
No smoking indoors. Extensive breakfast
menu including traditional, vegetarian,
fish, continental and special diet.*
Bedrooms: 1 single, 5 double, 2 twin,
2 family rooms
Bathrooms: 8 private, 1 public

**Bed & breakfast**

| per night: | £min | £max |
|---|---|---|
| Single | 30.00 | 44.00 |
| Double | 40.00 | 60.00 |

Parking for 10
Cards accepted: Access, Visa
🛏🚴📶🔑💺♿🔑📺➿🅿️
❊🚗🏤 SP 🏤 T

## Sea Trout Inn

🏆 COMMENDED

Staverton, Totnes TQ9 6PA
☎ (01803) 762274
Fax (01803) 762506
*Delightful beamed country inn, in
attractive village by the River Dart,
offering food and friendly atmosphere.
Good base for walking and touring
Dartmoor and south Devon.*
Bedrooms: 6 double, 3 twin, 1 triple
Bathrooms: 10 private

**Bed & breakfast**

| per night: | £min | £max |
|---|---|---|
| Single | 37.50 | 39.50 |
| Double | 44.00 | 54.00 |

**Half board**

| per person: | £min | £max |
|---|---|---|
| Daily | 36.00 | 40.00 |
| Weekly | 235.00 | 265.00 |

Lunch available
Evening meal 1900 (last orders 2145)
Parking for 50
Cards accepted: Access, Visa, Amex
🛏🚴📶🔑💺📶Ⓢ➿🅿️🍴❊🚗 DAP
SP 🏤 T

---

We advise you to confirm
your booking in writing.

## TROWBRIDGE

Wiltshire
Map ref 2B2

Wiltshire's administrative centre, a handsome market and manufacturing town with a wealth of merchants' houses and other Georgian buildings.
*Tourist Information Centre*
☎ (01225) 777054

### Welam House

COMMENDED

Bratton Road, West Ashton, Trowbridge BA14 6AZ
☎ (01225) 755908
*Located in quiet village, garden with trees and lawn with a view of Westbury White Horse. Ideally situated for touring. Bowls and mini-golf for guests.*
Bedrooms: 1 double, 1 twin, 1 triple
Bathrooms: 3 private

**Bed & breakfast**

| per night: | £min | £max |
| --- | --- | --- |
| Double | 32.00 | 32.00 |

Parking for 6
Open March-November
🐎🗢🖦ⓢ🕪📺🛏️🖧💷☼✕🐾🏠

## TRURO

Cornwall
Map ref 1B3

Cornwall's administrative centre and cathedral city, set at the head of Truro River on the Fal Estuary. A medieval stannary town, it handled mineral ore from west Cornwall; fine Georgian buildings recall its heyday as a society haunt in the second mining boom.
*Tourist Information Centre*
☎ (01872) 74555

### Arrallas ₩

HIGHLY COMMENDED

Ladock, Truro TR2 4NP
☎ Mitchell (01872) 510379
Fax (01872) 510200
*320-acre arable & dairy farm. Signed from opposite the Clock Garage, Summercourt. Farmhouse accommodation set in truly rural situation. Good food, warm welcome, attention to detail. Closed December/ January. Listed building.*
Bedrooms: 2 double, 1 twin
Bathrooms: 3 private

**Bed & breakfast**

| per night: | £min | £max |
| --- | --- | --- |
| Double | 32.00 | 39.00 |

**Half board**

| per person: | £min | £max |
| --- | --- | --- |
| Daily | 24.50 | 31.00 |
| Weekly | 166.50 | 198.50 |

Evening meal from 1900
Parking for 8
Open February-November
🐎🖦🖳🕪🖦ⓤⓛⓢ🕪📺🛏️🖧💷☼✕
🐾ˢᴾ🏠

### Bissick Old Mill ₩

HIGHLY COMMENDED

Ladock, Truro TR2 4PG
☎ St Austell (01726) 882557
*Listed 300-year-old watermill, providing comfortable accommodation with all the facilities expected from a larger establishment. Reputation for cuisine. Truro is only 10 minutes' drive.*
Bedrooms: 1 single, 2 double, 1 twin
Bathrooms: 3 private, 1 public

**Bed & breakfast**

| per night: | £min | £max |
| --- | --- | --- |
| Single | 25.00 | 30.00 |
| Double | 50.00 | 54.00 |

**Half board**

| per person: | £min | £max |
| --- | --- | --- |
| Daily | 35.50 | 43.00 |
| Weekly | 223.50 | 271.00 |

Lunch available
Evening meal 1900 (last orders 1700)
Parking for 9
Cards accepted: Access, Visa
🐎10🖦🖳🕪💷ⓢ🕪🛏️🖧💷☼🐾
ˢᴾ🏠

### Marcorrie Hotel ₩

20 Falmouth Road, Truro TR1 2HX
☎ (01872) 77374
Fax (01872) 41666
*Family-run hotel 5 minutes' walk from city centre and cathedral. Ideal for business or holiday, central for visiting the country houses and gardens of Cornwall.*
Bedrooms: 3 single, 3 double, 2 twin, 1 triple, 3 family rooms
Bathrooms: 10 private, 1 public, 1 private shower

**Bed & breakfast**

| per night: | £min | £max |
| --- | --- | --- |
| Single | 19.50 | |
| Double | 39.00 | |

**Half board**

| per person: | £min | £max |
| --- | --- | --- |
| Daily | 27.50 | |
| Weekly | 190.00 | |

Evening meal 1900 (last orders 1700)
Parking for 16
Cards accepted: Access, Visa, Amex
🐎🖦🕽🖳🕪💷ⓢ🕪🛏️📺🖦🖧💷
🍴10-20🕽☼🐾ˢᴾ🏠Ⓣ

### Rock Cottage

HIGHLY COMMENDED

Blackwater, Truro TR4 8EU
☎ (01872) 560252

*18th C beamed cottage, old world charm. Formerly village schoolmaster's home. Haven for non-smokers. Comfort,*

*hospitality, friendly service, a la carte menu.*
Bedrooms: 2 double, 1 twin
Bathrooms: 3 private

**Bed & breakfast**

| per night: | £min | £max |
| --- | --- | --- |
| Single | 18.50 | |
| Double | 37.00 | |

Evening meal 1900 (last orders 1500)
Parking for 4
🐎🖦🖳🕪ⓤⓛ🕪🛏️📺🖦🖧💷☼✕🐾

## UGBOROUGH

Devon
Map ref 1C2

### Venn Farm

COMMENDED

Ugborough, Ivybridge PL21 0PE
☎ South Brent (01364) 73240
*70-acre mixed farm. Set amid peaceful surroundings of South Hams. Children encouraged to help on farm. "Carve your own roast" a speciality.*
Bedrooms: 2 twin, 2 family rooms
Bathrooms: 3 private

**Bed & breakfast**

| per night: | £min | £max |
| --- | --- | --- |
| Single | 17.00 | |
| Double | 34.00 | |

**Half board**

| per person: | £min | £max |
| --- | --- | --- |
| Daily | 26.00 | |

Evening meal 1830 (last orders 1830)
Parking for 6
Open February-November
🐎🖦🖳🕪ⓤⓛ📺🖦🖧🔍✓🐾

## WARMINSTER

Wiltshire
Map ref 2B2

Attractive stone-built town high up to the west of Salisbury Plain. A market town, it originally thrived on cloth and wheat. Many prehistoric camps and barrows nearby, along with Longleat House and Safari Park.
*Tourist Information Centre*
☎ (01985) 218548

### Belmont Bed & Breakfast

Listed

9 Boreham Road, Warminster BA12 9JP
☎ (01985) 212799
*Spacious, friendly and comfortable accommodation with many facilities. Situated 10 minutes' drive from Longleat, en-route to Bath/Salisbury.*
Bedrooms: 2 double, 1 twin
Bathrooms: 1 public

**Bed & breakfast**

| per night: | £min | £max |
| --- | --- | --- |
| Double | 30.00 | 34.00 |

Parking for 4
🐎🕽🖳🖦ⓤⓛⓢ🕪🛏️🖦🖧🔍☼✕🐾
ⒹⒶⓅ🐾ˢᴾ

## WATCHET

Somerset
Map ref 1D1

Small port on Bridgwater Bay, sheltered by the Quantocks and the Brendon Hills. A thriving paper industry keeps the harbour busy; in the 19th C it handled iron from the Brendon Hills. Cleeve Abbey, a ruined Cistercian monastery, is 3 miles to the south-west.

### Wood Advent Farm

ⓦⓦⓦ COMMENDED

Roadwater, Watchet TA23 ORR
☎ Washford (01984) 640920

*350-acre mixed farm. Situated in Exmoor National Park, ideal for touring the many beauty spots. Country cooking, using mostly home-produced food.*
Bedrooms: 3 double, 2 twin
Bathrooms: 5 private

**Bed & breakfast**

| per night: | £min | £max |
| --- | --- | --- |
| Single | 17.50 | 23.50 |
| Double | 35.00 | 47.00 |

**Half board**

| per person: | £min | £max |
| --- | --- | --- |
| Daily | 29.50 | 35.50 |
| Weekly | 170.00 | 220.00 |

Lunch available
Evening meal 1900 (last orders 2100)
Parking for 13

## WELLS

Somerset
Map ref 2A2

Small city set beneath the southern slopes of the Mendips. Built between 1180 and 1424, the magnificent cathedral is preserved in much of its original glory and with its ancient precincts forms one of our loveliest and most unified groups of medieval buildings.
*Tourist Information Centre*
☎ *(01749) 672552*

### Beaconsfield Farm ⋔

ⓦⓦ HIGHLY COMMENDED

Easton, Wells BA5 1DU
☎ (01749) 870308
*Period character farmhouse in 4 acres of gardens and grounds with magnificent views. Beautifully decorated*

en-suite available. Village pub/restaurant 100 yards.
Bedrooms: 3 double
Bathrooms: 1 private, 1 public

**Bed & breakfast**

| per night: | £min | £max |
| --- | --- | --- |
| Double | 30.00 | 35.00 |

Parking for 10
Open April-October

### Bekynton House

ⓦⓦ COMMENDED

7 St Thomas Street, Wells BA5 2UU
☎ (01749) 672222
*Comfortable well-appointed house with cathedral views makes this an ideal place to park your car and walk to the cathedral, Bishop's Palace and market place in a couple of minutes.*
Bedrooms: 1 single, 3 double, 2 twin, 2 triple
Bathrooms: 6 private, 2 public

**Bed & breakfast**

| per night: | £min | £max |
| --- | --- | --- |
| Single | 22.00 | 25.00 |
| Double | 38.00 | 46.00 |

Parking for 6
Cards accepted: Access, Visa

### Fenny Castle House ⋔

ⓦⓦⓦ COMMENDED

Fenny Castle, Wookey, Wells BA5 1NN
☎ (01749) 672265
*Riverside setting overlooking motte and bailey castle. Country house in 60 acres on boundary of Levels. Restaurant, lounge bar, delightful accommodation.*
Bedrooms: 1 single, 3 double, 2 twin
Bathrooms: 6 private

**Bed & breakfast**

| per night: | £min | £max |
| --- | --- | --- |
| Single | 25.00 | 28.00 |

**Half board**

| per person: | £min | £max |
| --- | --- | --- |
| Daily | 35.00 | 40.00 |

Lunch available
Evening meal 1800 (last orders 2100)
Parking for 60
Cards accepted: Access, Visa, Amex

### Franklyns Farm

ⓦⓦ COMMENDED

Chewton Mendip, Bath BA3 4NB
☎ Chewton Mendip (01761) 241372
*350-acre arable & dairy farm. Comfortable and cosy modern farmhouse in heart of Mendips, in a peaceful setting with superb views. Situated on Emborough B3114 road. Ideal for touring Wells, Cheddar and Bath.*
Bedrooms: 1 double, 2 twin
Bathrooms: 2 private, 1 public

| per night: | £min | £max |
| --- | --- | --- |
| Single | 18.00 | |
| Double | 32.00 | 34.00 |

Parking for 5

### Home Farm

Stoppers Lane, Coxley, Wells BA5 1QS
☎ (01749) 672434
*15-acre pig farm. 1.5 miles from Wells, in a quiet spot just off A39. Extensive views of Mendip Hills. Pleasant rooms.*
Bedrooms: 1 single, 3 double, 2 twin, 1 triple
Bathrooms: 3 private, 2 public

**Bed & breakfast**

| per night: | £min | £max |
| --- | --- | --- |
| Single | 16.00 | 18.50 |
| Double | 33.00 | 38.00 |

Parking for 12

### Littlewell Farm Guest House

ⓦⓦ HIGHLY COMMENDED

Coxley, Wells BA5 1QP
☎ (01749) 677914
*Converted 200-year-old farmhouse enjoying extensive rural views of beautiful countryside. All bedrooms have shower or bathroom en-suite. Located 1 mile south-west of Wells.*
Bedrooms: 1 single, 2 double, 2 twin
Bathrooms: 5 private

**Bed & breakfast**

| per night: | £min | £max |
| --- | --- | --- |
| Single | 19.50 | 23.00 |
| Double | 35.00 | 40.00 |

**Half board**

| per person: | £min | £max |
| --- | --- | --- |
| Daily | 30.00 | 35.00 |

Evening meal 1900 (last orders 2000)
Parking for 11

### Manor Farm

Old Bristol Road, Upper Milton, Wells BA5 3AH
☎ (01749) 673394
*130-acre beef farm. Elizabethan manor house, Grade II* listed, on the southern slopes of the Mendips, 1 mile north of Wells. Superb view.*
Bedrooms: 2 double, 1 twin
Bathrooms: 1 public

**Bed & breakfast**

| per night: | £min | £max |
| --- | --- | --- |
| Single | 16.00 | 17.00 |
| Double | 28.00 | 30.00 |

Parking for 6

### Tor Guest House

ⓦⓦ COMMENDED

20 Tor Street, Wells BA5 2US
☎ (01749) 672322 & 672084

Continued ▶

## WELLS

### Continued

Historic, sympathetically restored 17th
C building in delightful grounds
overlooking the cathedral and Bishop's
Palace. Attractive, comfortable, and
tastefully furnished throughout. 3
minutes' walk to town centre. Ample
parking.
Bedrooms: 1 single, 2 double, 2 twin,
3 family rooms
Bathrooms: 5 private, 2 public

**Bed & breakfast**

| per night: | £min | £max |
|---|---|---|
| Single | 22.00 | 35.00 |
| Double | 35.00 | 50.00 |

Evening meal 1830 (last orders 1000)
Parking for 10
Cards accepted: Access, Visa

## WEST ANSTEY

Devon
Map ref 1D1

### Partridge Arms Farm ᴹ
**COMMENDED**

Yeo Mill, West Anstey, South Molton
EX36 3NU
☎ Anstey Mills (01398) 4217
200-acre mixed farm. Old established
family farm. Well placed for touring,
walking, riding, fishing, Exmoor
National Park, north Devon, west
Somerset and coastal resorts.
Bedrooms: 3 double, 2 twin, 2 family
rooms
Bathrooms: 4 private, 1 public

**Bed & breakfast**

| per night: | £min | £max |
|---|---|---|
| Single | 17.50 | 22.00 |
| Double | 35.00 | 44.00 |

**Half board**

| per person: | £min | £max |
|---|---|---|
| Daily | 25.50 | 30.00 |
| Weekly | 175.00 | 203.00 |

Evening meal 1845 (last orders 1600)
Parking for 10

## WEST BAGBOROUGH

Somerset
Map ref 1D1

### Bashfords Farmhouse ᴹ
**HIGHLY COMMENDED**

West Bagborough, Taunton TA4 3EF
☎ Bishops Lydeard (01823) 432015
Delightful old farmhouse, built of local
stone, set in the centre of a quiet village
in the Quantock Hills. One mile off the
A358 Taunton-Minehead road.
Bedrooms: 2 double, 1 twin
Bathrooms: 1 private, 1 public

**Bed & breakfast**

| per night: | £min | £max |
|---|---|---|
| Single | 17.00 | 22.50 |
| Double | 32.50 | 37.50 |

Parking for 5

## WEST BAY

Dorset
Map ref 2A3

### Egdon
**Listed**

Third Cliff Walk, West Bay, Bridport
DT6 4HX
☎ Bridport (01308) 422542
Quiet house with panoramic views of
Lyme Bay and countryside. 2 minutes
from beaches, harbour and coastal
walks, golf-course nearby.
Bedrooms: 1 double, 1 twin, 1 triple
Bathrooms: 1 public

**Bed & breakfast**

| per night: | £min | £max |
|---|---|---|
| Single | 12.50 | 16.00 |
| Double | 25.00 | 32.00 |

Parking for 3

## WESTON-SUPER-MARE

Avon
Map ref 1D1

Large, friendly resort developed in
the 19th C. Traditional seaside
attractions include theatres and a
dance hall. The museum shows a
Victorian seaside gallery and has
Iron Age finds from a hill fort on
Worlebury Hill in Weston Woods.
Tourist Information Centre
☎ (01934) 626838

### Conifers

63 Milton Road, Weston-super-Mare
BS23 2SP
☎ (01934) 624404
Semi-detached corner guesthouse
standing back in a large garden.
Completely refurbished for bed and
breakfast use. 24 years' experience.
Bedrooms: 1 single, 1 double, 1 twin
Bathrooms: 1 private, 1 public

**Bed & breakfast**

| per night: | £min | £max |
|---|---|---|
| Single | 16.00 | 20.00 |
| Double | 28.00 | 36.00 |

Parking for 4
Open January-November

### Purn House Farm ᴹ
**APPROVED**

Bleadon, Weston-super-Mare
BS24 0QE
☎ (01934) 812324
700-acre mixed farm. Comfortable 17th
C farmhouse only 3 miles from Weston-
super-Mare. En-suite available with TV.

1 ground floor room. Peaceful yet not
isolated, on bus route to town centre
and station.
Bedrooms: 1 double, 1 triple, 4 family
rooms
Bathrooms: 6 private, 1 public

**Bed & breakfast**

| per night: | £min | £max |
|---|---|---|
| Single | 16.00 | 20.00 |
| Double | 32.00 | 40.00 |

**Half board**

| per person: | £min | £max |
|---|---|---|
| Daily | 23.00 | 27.00 |
| Weekly | 135.00 | 155.00 |

Evening meal 1830 (last orders 1000)
Parking for 10
Open February-November

## WEYMOUTH

Dorset
Map ref 2B3

Ancient port and one of the
south's earliest resorts. Curving
beside a long, sandy beach, the
elegant Georgian esplanade is
graced with a statue of George III
and a cheerful Victorian Jubilee
clock tower.
Tourist Information Centre
☎ (01305) 765221

### Fairlight
**Listed**

50 Littlemoor Road, Preston,
Weymouth DT3 6AA
☎ (01305) 832293
Homely atmosphere in family bungalow.
Children and one-nighters welcome.
Freshly cooked food. Half a mile
Boleaze Cove, 3 miles Weymouth.
Bedrooms: 1 double, 1 family room
Bathrooms: 1 public

**Bed & breakfast**

| per night: | £min | £max |
|---|---|---|
| Single | 15.00 | 17.00 |
| Double | 29.00 | 34.00 |

**Half board**

| per person: | £min | £max |
|---|---|---|
| Daily | 21.50 | 24.50 |
| Weekly | 129.00 | 147.00 |

Evening meal from 1900
Parking for 2

### New Salsudas Hotel

22 Lennox Street, Weymouth
DT4 7HE
☎ (01305) 771903
Private hotel close to town centre in
quiet position 300 yards from beach,
station and gardens. Convenient for
nature reserve and many attractions.
Warm and friendly, winter or summer.
Bedrooms: 1 double, 2 twin, 1 triple,
2 family rooms
Bathrooms: 6 private, 1 public

| Bed & breakfast per night: | £min | £max |
|---|---|---|
| Single | 15.00 | 21.00 |
| Double | 28.00 | 36.00 |

| Half board per person: | £min | £max |
|---|---|---|
| Weekly | 135.00 | 160.00 |

Evening meal 1800 (last orders 1830)
Parking for 3
Cards accepted: Access, Visa

## WHEDDON CROSS

Somerset
Map ref 1D1

Crossroads hamlet in the heart of Exmoor National Park.

### Triscombe Farm ✦

Wheddon Cross, Minehead TA24 7HA
☎ Winsford (01643) 85227
*50-acre livestock farm. Old hunting lodge set in quiet valley 1 mile south of Wheddon Cross on A396. Home cooking using local and home produce. Warm friendly atmosphere.*
Bedrooms: 2 single, 1 double, 2 twin
Bathrooms: 2 public

| Bed & breakfast per night: | £min | £max |
|---|---|---|
| Single | 17.00 | 17.00 |
| Double | 34.00 | 34.00 |

| Half board per person: | £min | £max |
|---|---|---|
| Daily | 24.50 | 24.50 |
| Weekly | 170.00 | 170.00 |

Evening meal 1900 (last orders 2000)
Parking for 22
Open March-October

## WHITEPARISH

Wiltshire
Map ref 2B3

### Brickworth Farmhouse
Listed COMMENDED

Brickworth Lane, Whiteparish, Salisbury, Wilts SP5 2QE
☎ (01794) 884663
Fax (01794) 884581

*Charming 18th C listed farmhouse, featured in "Ideal Home": perfect location off A36 for visiting Wiltshire, Hampshire and Dorset.*
Bedrooms: 1 single, 1 double, 1 family room
Bathrooms: 1 private, 1 public

| Bed & breakfast per night: | £min | £max |
|---|---|---|
| Single | 18.00 | 20.00 |
| Double | 32.50 | 38.00 |

Parking for 20

## WIDECOMBE-IN-THE-MOOR

Devon
Map ref 1C2

Old village in pastoral country under the high tors of East Dartmoor. The "Cathedral of the Moor" stands near a tiny square, once used for archery practice, which has a 16th C Church House among other old buildings.

### Buzzards Reach ✦
Listed COMMENDED

Widecombe Hill, Widecombe-in-the-Moor, Newton Abbot TQ13 7TE
☎ (01364) 2205
*Extensive views from comfortable en-suite accommodation with own access, adjoining moorland house overlooking the Widecombe Valley. Private parking and access to open moorland. Ideal for touring Dartmoor, Devon and Cornwall.*
Bedrooms: 3 double
Bathrooms: 3 private

| Bed & breakfast per night: | £min | £max |
|---|---|---|
| Double | 32.00 | |

Parking for 20

### Higher Venton Farm
Listed

Widecombe-in-the-Moor, Newton Abbot TQ13 7TF
☎ (01364) 2235
*40-acre beef farm. 17th C thatched farmhouse with a homely atmosphere and farmhouse cooking. Ideal for touring Dartmoor. 16 miles from the coast.*
Bedrooms: 1 double, 1 twin, 1 triple
Bathrooms: 1 private, 1 public

| Bed & breakfast per night: | £min | £max |
|---|---|---|
| Single | 18.00 | 19.00 |
| Double | 30.00 | 32.00 |

Parking for 5

### Sheena Tower ✦

Widecombe-in-the-Moor, Newton Abbot TQ13 7TE
☎ (01364) 2308
*Comfortable moorland guesthouse overlooking Widecombe village, offering a relaxed holiday in picturesque surroundings. Well placed for discovering Dartmoor.*
Bedrooms: 1 single, 2 double, 1 twin, 1 triple, 1 family home
Bathrooms: 2 private, 2 public

| Bed & breakfast per night: | £min | £max |
|---|---|---|
| Single | 14.00 | 16.00 |
| Double | 28.00 | 32.00 |

| Half board per person: | £min | £max |
|---|---|---|
| Daily | 21.50 | 23.50 |
| Weekly | 147.50 | 161.50 |

Evening meal 1900 (last orders 1200)
Parking for 10
Open February-October

## WINCANTON

Somerset
Map ref 2B3

Thriving market town, rising from the rich pastures of Blackmoor Vale near the Dorset border, with many attractive 18th C stone buildings. Steeplechase racecourse.

### Lower Church Farm

Rectory Lane, Charlton Musgrove, Wincanton BA9 8ES
☎ (01963) 32307
*60-acre livestock farm. 18th C brick farmhouse with beams and inglenooks, in a quiet area surrounded by lovely countryside. Ideal for touring.*
Bedrooms: 2 double, 1 twin
Bathrooms: 3 private

| Bed & breakfast per night: | £min | £max |
|---|---|---|
| Double | | 30.00 |

Parking for 4

## WINSFORD

Somerset
Map ref 1D1

Small village on the River Exe in splendid walking country under Winsford Hill. On the other side of the hill is a Celtic standing stone, the Caratacus Stone, and nearby across the River Barle stretches an ancient packhorse bridge, Tarr Steps, built of great stone slabs.

### Larcombe Foot
COMMENDED

Winsford, Minehead TA24 7HS
☎ (01643) 85306
*Comfortable country house in tranquil, beautiful setting, overlooking River Exe. Lovely walks on doorstep. Ideal for touring Exmoor and north Devon coast.*
Bedrooms: 1 single, 1 double, 1 twin
Bathrooms: 3 private

*Continued ▶*

## WINSFORD

### Continued

**Bed & breakfast**

| per night: | £min | £max |
|---|---|---|
| Single | | 17.50 |
| Double | | 35.00 |

Parking for 3
Open April-October

🐎 6 ♨ ⓤ 🅿 📺 �🏠 ⚓ U ♨ ✿ 🚗

## WINTERBOURNE STOKE

Wiltshire
Map ref 2B2

### Scotland Lodge 🏍

☖☖☖ COMMENDED

Winterbourne Stoke, Salisbury
SP3 4TF
☎ Shrewton (01980) 620943 & Mobile
0860 272599
Fax (01980) 620943
*Historic, comfortable country house with private bathrooms. Helpful service, delicious breakfasts. Ideal touring base. French and some German spoken. Self-contained unit also available for self-catering.*
Bedrooms: 1 double, 2 twin
Bathrooms: 3 private

**Bed & breakfast**

| per night: | £min | £max |
|---|---|---|
| Single | 25.00 | 30.00 |
| Double | 35.00 | 45.00 |

Parking for 5

🐎 ⌖ ⬜ ♨ ⓤ 🅂 ✂ 🖾 ⬛ ⚓ ⓣ12 ✿ ✗ 🚗 OAP SP 🏮

## WOODBURY

Devon
Map ref 1D2

Attractive village, with Woodbury Common to the east, affording a panoramic coastal view from Berry Head to Portland Bill. Woodbury Castle Iron Age fort lies at a height of some 600 ft.

### Higher Bagmores Farm

☖

Woodbury, Exeter EX5 1LA
☎ (01395) 232261
*200-acre mixed farm. Set in delightful Devon countryside. Exmouth 5 miles, Exeter 7 miles, M5 junction 30, 2 miles.*
Bedrooms: 1 single, 1 double, 1 triple
Bathrooms: 2 public

**Bed & breakfast**

| per night: | £min | £max |
|---|---|---|
| Single | 14.00 | |
| Double | 28.00 | |

Parking for 4
Open January-November

🐎 ♨ 🅿 📺 🖾 ⬛ ✿ ✗ 🚗

## WOOTTON BASSETT

Wiltshire
Map ref 2B2

Small hillside town with attractive old buildings and a 13th C church. The church and the half-timbered town hall were both restored in the 19th C and the stocks and ducking pool are preserved.

### Little Cotmarsh Farm
### Cotmarsh

Listed COMMENDED

Broad Town, Wootton Bassett,
Swindon SN4 7RA
☎ Swindon (01793) 731322
*108-acre mixed farm. Comfortable 300-year-old farmhouse with inglenooks and beams, situated 4 miles south of M4 junction 16, in peaceful hamlet. Equal distances from Bath, Cotswolds and Oxford. Excellent amenities for wet days in and around Swindon.*
Bedrooms: 1 double, 1 twin, 1 triple
Bathrooms: 1 private, 1 public

**Bed & breakfast**

| per night: | £min | £max |
|---|---|---|
| Single | 16.00 | 17.00 |
| Double | 30.00 | 34.00 |

Parking for 6

🐎 ⌖ ♨ ⓤ ✂ 🖾 ⬛ ✿ ✗ 🚗 🏮

## YELVERTON

Devon
Map ref 1C2

Village on the edge of Dartmoor, where ponies wander over the flat common. Buckland Abbey is 2 miles south-west, while Burrator Reservoir is 2 miles to the east.

### Blowiscombe Barton 🏍

☖☖☖ COMMENDED

Milton Combe, Yelverton PL20 6HR
☎ (01822) 854853
Fax (01822) 854853

*Modernised farmhouse surrounded by rolling farmland. Beautiful garden and heated swimming pool. Close village pub and Dartmoor National Park. Plymouth/Tavistock 8 miles.*
Bedrooms: 2 double, 1 twin
Bathrooms: 3 private

**Bed & breakfast**

| per night: | £min | £max |
|---|---|---|
| Single | 20.00 | 23.00 |
| Double | 35.00 | 39.00 |

**Half board**

| per person: | £min | £max |
|---|---|---|
| Daily | 27.00 | 32.00 |

Evening meal 1830 (last orders 1200)
Parking for 6
Cards accepted: Access, Visa

🐎 ⌖ ⬜ ♨ ⓤ 🅂 🅿 📺 🖾 ⬛ ⚓ U ⯈ ✿ ✗ 🚗 ⓣ

### Greenwell Farm

☖☖☖ COMMENDED

Meavy, Yelverton PL20 6PY
☎ (01822) 853563
Fax (01822) 853563
*220-acre livestock farm. Fresh country air, breathtaking views and scrumptious farmhouse cuisine. This busy family farm welcomes you to share our countryside and wildlife.*
Bedrooms: 1 double, 1 twin, 1 triple
Bathrooms: 3 private

**Bed & breakfast**

| per night: | £min | £max |
|---|---|---|
| Single | 19.00 | 22.00 |
| Double | 38.00 | 44.00 |

**Half board**

| per person: | £min | £max |
|---|---|---|
| Daily | 30.00 | 33.00 |
| Weekly | 195.00 | 205.00 |

Evening meal 1900 (last orders 1200)
Parking for 8

🐎 ⌖ 🅴 ⬜ ♨ ♨ ⒤ 🅂 🅿 📺 🖾 ⬛ ⚓ ⓣ14 U ✿ ✗ 🚗 SP 🏮

## YEOVIL

Somerset
Map ref 2A3

Lively market town, famous for glove making, set in dairying country beside the River Yeo. Interesting parish church. Museum of South Somerset at Hendford Manor.
*Tourist Information Centre*
☎ *(01935) 71279*

### Holywell House

☖☖☖ HIGHLY COMMENDED

Holywell, East Coker, Yeovil
BA22 9NQ
☎ West Coker (01935) 862612
Fax (01935) 863035

*Beautifully renovated country home with fine amenities. Three acres of lovely grounds, tennis court, idyllic rural setting. Quiet location off A30 2 miles west of Yeovil. Suites available.*
Bedrooms: 2 double, 1 family room
Bathrooms: 3 private

**Bed & breakfast**

| per night: | £min | £max |
|---|---|---|
| Single | 30.00 | 35.00 |
| Double | 50.00 | 60.00 |

**Half board**

| per person: | £min | £max |
|---|---|---|
| Daily | 45.00 | 50.00 |

Evening meal 1900 (last orders 2030)
Parking for 15

🛏🚫🖵♿🖵💷Ⓢ🅿🖵🛁♨🕿12 ♦
🔍↺⑁※✕🖩 SP 🏧 T

## Southwoods

🛏 APPROVED

3 Southwoods, Yeovil BA20 2QQ
🕿 (01935) 22178
*Charming Edwardian house, close to town centre, ski-slope, leisure centre/swimming pool and wooded beauty spot. Relaxed, friendly atmosphere.*
Bedrooms: 1 single, 1 double, 1 twin
Bathrooms: 1 public

**Bed & breakfast**

| per night: | £min | £max |
|---|---|---|
| Single | 15.00 | 20.00 |
| Double | 30.00 | 36.00 |

Parking for 3

🛏🚫♿🖵Ⓢ🅿TV🖩♨🏧

Somerset
Map ref 2A3

## Cary Fitzpaine

🛏 APPROVED

Yeovilton, Yeovil BA22 8JB
🕿 Charlton Mackerell (01458) 223250
Fax (01458) 223250

---

*600-acre mixed farm. Elegant Georgian manor farmhouse in idyllic setting. 2 acres of gardens. High standard of accommodation.*
Bedrooms: 1 single, 1 double, 1 twin, 1 triple
Bathrooms: 4 private, 2 public

**Bed & breakfast**

| per night: | £min | £max |
|---|---|---|
| Single | 15.00 | 18.00 |
| Double | 30.00 | 36.00 |

Parking for 11
Open April-November

🛏🚫♿🖵💷🛅Ⓢ🅿TV🖩♨↺✿
🏧 SP

## Courtry Farm

Listed

Bridgehampton, Yeovil BA22 8HF
🕿 Ilchester (01935) 840327
*590-acre mixed farm. Farmhouse with ground floor rooms, en-suite, TV, tea-making facilities. Tennis court. Fleet Air Arm Museum half a mile.*
Bedrooms: 1 twin, 1 triple
Bathrooms: 2 private

**Bed & breakfast**

| per night: | £min | £max |
|---|---|---|
| Single | 18.00 | |
| Double | 30.00 | |

Parking for 20

🛏🚲🚫♿🖵✕🖩♨🔍✿🏧🏧

---

The national Crown scheme is explained in full in the information pages at the back of this guide.

---

Wiltshire
Map ref 2B2

Pretty village of thatched cottages set high over the Dorset border. Zeals House dates from the medieval period and has some 19th C work. The Palladian Stourhead House (National Trust), in its magnificent gardens, lies further north.

## Cornerways Cottage 🅰

🛏

Longcross, Zeals, Warminster BA12 6LL
🕿 Bourton (01747) 840477
*18th C cottage with original beams. Ideal position for touring Stourhead, Stonehenge, Shaftesbury and other local attractions. Riding, fishing, golf and walking locally. Close to A303, midway for London or Devon and Cornwall. Two miles from Stourhead House and Gardens, 4 miles from Longleat.*
Bedrooms: 3 double
Bathrooms: 3 private

**Bed & breakfast**

| per night: | £min | £max |
|---|---|---|
| Single | 16.00 | 18.00 |
| Double | 30.00 | 32.00 |

**Half board**

| per person: | £min | £max |
|---|---|---|
| Daily | 21.00 | 22.00 |

Parking for 6

🛏🚫♿🖵💷🛅✕🅿TV🖩♨↺♩✿
🏧 OAP

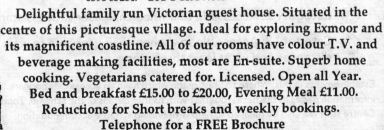

# Use your *i*'s

There are more than 550 Tourist Information Centres throughout England offering friendly help with accommodation and holiday ideas as well as suggestions of places to visit and things to do.

In your home town there may be a centre which can help you before you set out. You'll find the address of your nearest Tourist Information Centre in your local Phone Book.

# National Accessible Scheme for Wheelchair Users

If you are a wheelchair user or someone who has difficulty walking, look for the national 'Accessible' symbol when choosing where to stay.

All the places that display the symbol have been checked by a Tourist Board inspector against criteria that reflect the practical needs of wheelchair users.

**There are three categories of accessibility, indicated by symbols:**

**Category 1:** Accessible to all wheelchair users including those travelling independently

**Category 2:** Accessible to a wheelchair user with assistance

**Category 3:** Accessible to a wheelchair user able to walk short distances and up at least three steps

Establishments in this 'Where to Stay' guide which have an access category are listed in the information pages at the back, together with further details of the scheme. Tourist Information Centre staff will also be pleased to help with finding suitable accommodation.

The Royal County of Berkshire, home of England's best known symbols — the River Thames and Windsor Castle — lies neatly at the centre of this region. To the south you'll find rural Dorset, the bright lights of Bournemouth, the holiday kingdom of the Isle of Wight and the heaths and woodlands of Hampshire. To the north are Buckinghamshire — with its dramatic Chiltern Hills and modern Milton Keynes — and Oxfordshire, gateway to the Cotswolds and home of the world-famous university.

# SOUTH OF ENGLAND

The Counties of Berkshire, Buckinghamshire, Dorset (eastern), Hampshire, Isle of Wight and Oxfordshire

For more information on the South of England, contact:
Southern Tourist Board
40 Chamberlayne Road
Eastleigh
Hampshire SO50 5JH
Tel: (01703) 620006
Fax: (01703) 620010

Where to Go in the South of England
– see pages 314–317

Where to Stay in the South of England
– see pages 318–348

# WHERE TO GO

*You will find hundreds of interesting places to visit during your stay in the South of England, just some of which are listed in these pages. The number against each name will help you locate it on the map (page 317). Contact any Tourist Information Centre in the region for more ideas on days out in the South of England.*

---

**❶ Broughton Castle**
Banbury, Oxfordshire OX15 5EB
Tel: (01295) 262624
*Medieval moated house built in 1300 and enlarged between 1550 and 1600. The home of Lord and Lady Saye and Sele. Civil War connections.*

**❷ Blenheim Palace**
Woodstock, Oxfordshire OX20 1PX
Tel: (01993) 811091
*Birthplace of Sir Winston Churchill, designed by Vanbrugh with park designed by Capability Brown. Adventure play area, maze, butterfly house and Churchill exhibition.*

**❸ Cotswold Wildlife Park**
Bradwell Grove, Burford, Oxfordshire OX18 4JW
Tel: (01993) 823006
*Wildlife park in 200 acres of gardens and woodland, with a variety of animals from all over the world.*

**❹ Waterperry Gardens**
Waterperry, Oxfordshire OX33 1JZ
Tel: (01844) 339254
*Ornamental gardens covering 6 acres of 83-acre 18th C Waterperry House estate. Saxon village church, garden shop, tea shop.*

**❺ The Oxford Story**
6 Broad Street, Oxford, Oxfordshire OX1 3AJ
Tel: (01865) 728822
*Heritage centre depicting 800 years of university history in sights, sounds, personalities and smells. Visitors are transported in moving desks with commentary of their choice.*

**❻ Didcot Railway Centre**
Great Western Railway, Didcot, Oxfordshire OX11 7NJ

*Aromatic (and vampire-vanquishing) garlic is grown on the Isle of Wight.*

Tel: (01235) 817200
*Living museum recreating the golden age of the Great Western Railway. Steam locomotives and trains, engine shed and small relics museum. Steam days and gala events.*

**❼ Bekonscot Model Village**
Warwick Road, Beaconsfield, Buckinghamshire HP9 2PL
Tel: (01494) 672919
*A complete model village of the 1930s, with zoo, cinema, minster, cricket match and 1,400 inhabitants.*

**❽ Beale Park**
The Child-Beale Wildlife Trust, Church Farm, Lower Basildon, Berkshire RG8 9NH
Tel: (01734) 845172
*Established 36 years ago, the park features wildfowl, pheasants, Highland cattle, rare sheep, llamas. Narrow gauge railway and pets' corner.*

SOUTH OF ENGLAND

**9 Stratfield Saye House**
The Wellington Office, Stratfield Saye,
Hampshire RG7 2BT
Tel: (01256) 882882
*Built in 1630, the house displays many personal
possessions of the Iron Duke, including funeral
hearse (part of Wellington Exhibition).*

**10 The Vyne**
Sherborne St John, Hampshire RG26 5DX
Tel: (01256) 881337
*Original house dating back to Henry VII's time,
extensively altered in mid 17th C. Tudor chapel,
beautiful gardens and lake.*

**11 Andover Museum**
6 Church Close, Andover, Hampshire SP10 1DP
Tel: (01264) 366283
*The "Story of Andover" galleries. The Museum
of the Iron Age – life as revealed by excavations
at Iron Age hill fort, Danebury Ring.*

**12 Museum of Army Flying**
Middle Wallop, Hampshire SO20 8DY
Tel: (01264) 384421
*Award-winning and unique collection of flying
machines and displays depicting the role of
army flying since the late 19th C.*

**13 Jane Austen's House**
Chawton, Hampshire GU34 1SD
Tel: (01420) 83262
*17th C house where Jane Austen lived from
1809–1817, and wrote or revised her 6 great
novels. Letters, pictures, memorabilia, garden.*

**14 Romany Folklore Museum and
Workshop**
Limesend Yard, High Street, Selborne,
Hampshire GU34 3JW
Tel: (01420) 511486
*Museum depicting all aspects of gypsy life in
Great Britain. Van builder's workshops.*

**15 Gilbert White's House and Garden and
the Oates Museum**
The Wakes, Selborne, Hampshire GU34 3JH
Tel: (01420) 511275
*Historic house and garden, home of Gilbert*

*Windsor Castle: a principal residence of
English monarchs since William the Conqueror.*

*White, author of "The Natural History of
Selborne". Exhibition on Frank Oates, explorer,
and Captain Oates of Antarctic fame.*

**16 Marwell Zoological Park**
Colden Common, Winchester, Hampshire
SO21 1JH
Tel: (01962) 777407
*Large zoo breeding endangered species. Over
800 animals including big cats, giraffes, deer,
zebras, monkeys, hippos and birds.*

**17 The Sir Harold Hillier Gardens and
Arboretum**
Jermyns Lane, Ampfield, Hampshire SO51 0QA
Tel: (01794) 368787
*The largest collection of trees and shrubs of its
kind in the British Isles.*

**18 Broadlands**
Romsey, Hampshire SO51 9ZD
Tel: (01794) 516878
*Home of the late Lord Mountbatten.
Magnificent 18th C house and contents. Superb*

*Students and the Oxford Don – familiar sights in the university city.*

views across River Test. Mountbatten exhibition and audio-visual presentation.

**19 Tudor House Museum**
St Michael's Square, Bugle Street, Southampton SO1 0AD
Tel: (01703) 332513
*Large half-timbered Tudor house with exhibitions on Tudor, Georgian and Victorian domestic and local history. Unique Tudor garden.*

**20 Staunton Country Park**
Middle Park Way, Havant, Hampshire PO9 5HB
Tel: (01705) 453405
*Reconstructed Victorian glasshouses with displays of exotic plants in the charming setting of the historic walled gardens. Ornamental farm with wide range of farm animals.*

**21 Royal Signals Museum**
Blandford Camp, Blandford Forum, Dorset DT11 8RH
Tel: (01258) 482248
*History of Army communication from Crimea to the Gulf. Vehicles, uniforms, medals and badges on display.*

**22 The New Forest Owl Sanctuary**
Crow Lane, Crow, Ringwood, Hampshire BH24 3EA
Tel: (01425) 476487
*Sanctuary for barn owls destined to be released into the wild. Incubation room, hospital unit and 100 aviaries.*

**23 Kingston Lacy**
Wimborne Minster, Dorset BH21 4EA
Tel: (01202) 883402
*17th C house designed for Sir Ralph Bankes by Sir Roger Pratt, altered by Sir Charles Barry in the 19th C. Collection of paintings, 250 acres of wooded park and herd of Devon cattle.*

**24 Beaulieu Palace House**
Beaulieu, Hampshire SO42 7ZN
Tel: (01590) 612345
*Home of Lord and Lady Montagu. National Motor Museum, monastic life exhibition.*

**25 The D Day Museum and Overlord Embroidery**
Clarence Esplanade, Portsmouth, Hampshire PO5 3PA
Tel: (01705) 827261
*Incorporates Overlord embroidery depicting Allied invasion of Normandy.*

**26 Compton Acres**
Canford Cliffs, Poole, Dorset BH13 7ES
Tel: (01202) 700778
*Gardens include Italian, Japanese, sub-tropical glen, rock, water and heather. Collection of statues.*

**27 The Tank Museum**
Bovington Camp, Wareham, Dorset BH20 6JG
Tel: (01929) 463953
*Largest and most comprehensive museum collection of armoured fighting vehicles in the world.*

**28 Butterfly World and Fountain World**
Staplers Road, Wootton, Ryde, Isle of Wight PO33 4RW
Tel: (01983) 883430
*Tropical indoor garden with butterflies from around the world. Fountain World has water features and huge fish. Italian and Japanese garden.*

# FIND OUT MORE

*Further information about holidays and attractions in the South of England is available from:*
**Southern Tourist Board, 40 Chamberlayne Road, Eastleigh, Hampshire SO50 5JH Tel: (01703) 620006**

Hereford & Worcester

Warwickshire

Northants

Beds

Gloucestershire

Avon

Wiltshire

Cropredy

Newport Pagnell

Wolverton
Milton Keynes

Banbury ①

Buckingham
Bletchley

Chipping Norton

Bucks

Bicester

Aylesbury

Woodstock ②

Waterperry

Wendover

Burford ③
Witney

Oxford ⑤

④

Thame

Chesham

Princes Risborough

Oxfordshire

Faringdon

Abingdon

High Wycombe

Wantage

Didcot ⑥

Wallingford

Beaconsfield ⑦

Marlow

Maidenhead
Slough

Henley-on-Thames

Lower Basildon ⑧

Twyford

Windsor

Berkshire

Reading

Hungerford

Newbury

Wokingham

Bracknell

Stratfield Saye ⑨

Farnborough
Fleet

Sherborne St John ⑩

Basingstoke

Aldershot

Surrey

Andover ⑪

Hampshire

Alton

⑫

Chawton ⑬

Middle Wallop

⑭ ⑮ Selborne

Winchester

Liss

Gillingham

Ampfield

Colden Common

Petersfield

Shaftesbury

Romsey ⑱ ⑰

⑯

West Sussex

Dorset (eastern)

Fordingbridge

Eastleigh

Totton

⑲ Southampton

Lyndhurst

Ringwood ㉒

Fawley

Waterlooville
Locks Heath

㉕ Havant

Blandford Forum ㉑

Brockenhurst

Beaulieu

Lee-on-the-Solent

Wimborne Minster ㉓

West Moors

Lymington

Gosport

㉕ Portsmouth

Poole ㉖

Christchurch

Cowes

Ryde

Wareham ㉗

Bournemouth

Newport

㉘ Wootton

Yarmouth
Freshwater

Swanage

Isle of Wight

Sandown
Shanklin
Ventnor

0                    20 Miles

0                    30 Kms

317

# WHERE TO STAY

*Accommodation entries in this regional section are listed in alphabetical order of place name, and then in alphabetical order of establishment.*

*Map references refer to the colour location maps at the back of this guide. The first figure is the map number; the letter and figure which follow indicate the grid reference on the map.*

*Symbols at the end of each accommodation entry give information about services and facilities. A 'key' to these symbols is inside the back cover flap, which can be kept open for easy reference.*

---

## ABINGDON

Oxfordshire
Map ref 2C1

Attractive former county town on River Thames with many interesting buildings, including 17th C County Hall, now a museum, in the market-place and the remains of an abbey.
*Tourist Information Centre*
☎ *(01235) 522711*

### 1 Long Barn
Listed

Sutton Courtenay, Abingdon OX14 4BQ
☎ (01235) 848251
*17th C village house 8 miles from Oxford, 2 miles from Abingdon. Easy access to Henley and the Cotswolds.*
Bedrooms: 1 twin
Bathrooms: 1 private
**Bed & breakfast**

| per night: | £min | £max |
|---|---|---|
| Single | 15.00 | 15.00 |
| Double | 30.00 | 30.00 |

Parking for 3
🛇 8 ⓊⒷ ⓉⓋ ▥ 🖨 ✿ 🐎 🛖

There are separate sections in this guide listing groups specialising in farm holidays and accommodation which is especially suitable for young people and organised groups.

---

## ALTON

Hampshire
Map ref 2C2

Pleasant old market town standing on the Pilgrim's Way, with some attractive Georgian buildings. The parish church still bears the scars of bullet marks, evidence of a bitter struggle between the Roundheads and the Royalists.
*Tourist Information Centre*
☎ *(01420) 88448*

### Glen Derry
Listed COMMENDED

52 Wellhouse Road, Beech, Alton GU34 4AG
☎ (01420) 83235
*Peaceful, secluded family home set in 3.5 acres of garden. Warm welcome assured. Ideal base for Watercress Steam Railway, Winchester and Portsmouth.*
Bedrooms: 1 twin, 1 family room
Bathrooms: 1 private, 1 public
**Bed & breakfast**

| per night: | £min | £max |
|---|---|---|
| Single | 18.00 | 26.00 |
| Double | 28.00 | 36.00 |

Parking for 14
🛇 🕭 ⬛ ♨ ⓊⒷ ✭ ½ ⅍ ⓉⓋ ▥ 🖨 ✿ 🐎

National Crown ratings were correct at the time of going to press but are subject to change. Please check at the time of booking.

---

## AMERSHAM

Buckinghamshire
Map ref 2D1

Old town with many fine buildings, particularly in the High Street. There are several interesting old inns.

### The Barn
Listed HIGHLY COMMENDED

Rectory Hill, Old Amersham, Amersham HP7 0BT
☎ (01494) 722701
*17th C tithe barn with a wealth of beams. 6 minutes' walk from Amersham station. Easy access to M25 and M40.*
Bedrooms: 2 single, 1 double, 1 twin
Bathrooms: 1 public
**Bed & breakfast**

| per night: | £min | £max |
|---|---|---|
| Single | 27.50 | 30.00 |
| Double | 48.00 | 48.00 |

Parking for 7
🛇 8 ⚿ ⓊⒷ ☐ ♨ ⍾ ⓊⒷ ½ ⅍ ⓉⓋ ▥ 🖨 ✿ ✠ 🐎 🛖

---

## AMPORT

Hampshire
Map ref 2C2

### Broadwater ⋀
♿♿ COMMENDED

Amport, Andover SP11 8AY
☎ Andover (01264) 772240
Fax (01264) 772240

Please mention this guide when making a booking.

Grade II listed thatched cottage. From A303 (from Andover) take turn off to Hawk Conservancy/Amport. At T-junction, turn right, take first road right (East Cholderton). Broadwater is first cottage on the right.
Bedrooms: 2 twin
Bathrooms: 2 private, 1 public

**Bed & breakfast**

| per night: | £min | £max |
|---|---|---|
| Single | 18.00 | 22.00 |
| Double | 36.00 | 40.00 |

| Half board per person: | £min | £max |
|---|---|---|
| Daily | 28.00 | 32.00 |
| Weekly | 190.00 | 225.00 |

Evening meal 1830 (last orders 2030)
Parking for 3

---

## ANDOVER

Hampshire
Map ref 2C2

Town that achieved importance from the wool trade and now has much modern development. A good centre for visiting places of interest.
*Tourist Information Centre*
☎ *(01264) 324320*

### Malt Cottage ♠
HIGHLY COMMENDED

Upper Clatford, Andover SP11 7QL
☎ (01264) 323469
Fax (01264) 334100
*Country house with idyllic 6-acre garden, lake and stream. Set in charming Hampshire village within easy reach of Salisbury, Romsey, Stonehenge and London/Exeter road.*
Bedrooms: 1 double, 1 twin
Bathrooms: 2 private

**Bed & breakfast**

| per night: | £min | £max |
|---|---|---|
| Single | 25.00 | 37.00 |
| Double | 36.00 | 43.00 |

| Half board per person: | £min | £max |
|---|---|---|
| Daily | 30.50 | 34.00 |

Evening meal from 1800
Parking for 5

### The Old Barn ♠
Listed HIGHLY COMMENDED

Amport, Andover SP11 8AE
☎ (01264) 710410 & Mobile 0860 844772
Fax (01264) 710410

---

Converted old barn, in small village approximately 3 miles south west of Andover. Secluded, but only three-quarters of a mile from A303.
Bedrooms: 2 double
Bathrooms: 2 private

**Bed & breakfast**

| per night: | £min | £max |
|---|---|---|
| Single | 20.00 | 23.00 |
| Double | 30.00 | 34.00 |

Parking for 4

---

## ASCOT

Berkshire
Map ref 2C2

Small country town famous for its racecourse which was founded by Queen Anne. The race meeting each June is attended by the Royal Family.

### Birchcroft House ♠
HIGHLY COMMENDED

Birchcroft, Brockenhurst Road, South Ascot, Ascot SL5 9HA
☎ (01344) 20574
*Charming Edwardian country house in beautiful wooded gardens. Quality en-suite rooms. Ideal base for touring and golf at Wentworth, Sunningdale or Berkshire courses. Easy access M25, M4, M3. Heathrow only 25 minutes.*
Bedrooms: 1 double, 2 twin
Bathrooms: 3 private

**Bed & breakfast**

| per night: | £min | £max |
|---|---|---|
| Single | 28.00 | 35.00 |
| Double | 38.00 | 46.00 |

Parking for 6

### Tanglewood ♠

Birch Lane, off Longhill Road, Chavey Down, Ascot SL5 8RF
☎ Winkfield Row (01344) 882528
*En-suite bedrooms in spacious, modern bungalow. Quiet secluded location, large wooded garden. Four miles from Windsor and 15 miles from Heathrow (pick up possible). Convenient for Wentworth, Sunningdale, Ascot, Bracknell, Thames Valley and London.*
Bedrooms: 1 single, 2 twin
Bathrooms: 2 private, 1 public

**Bed & breakfast**

| per night: | £min | £max |
|---|---|---|
| Single | 15.00 | 25.00 |
| Double | 25.00 | 50.00 |

Evening meal 1900 (last orders 2000)
Parking for 6

---

## AYLESBURY

Buckinghamshire
Map ref 2C1

Historic county town in the Vale of Aylesbury. The cobbled market square has a Victorian clock tower and the 15th C King's Head Inn (National Trust). Interesting county museum and 13th C parish church. Twice-weekly livestock market.

### 9 Ballard Close ♠

Aylesbury HP21 9UY
☎ (01296) 84465

Comfortable, attractive house and garden. Parking. Convenient for London, Oxford, Cotswolds, Chiltern Hills and many National Trust properties including Waddesdon Manor.
Bedrooms: 1 single, 1 double, 1 twin
Bathrooms: 1 public

**Bed & breakfast**

| per night: | £min | £max |
|---|---|---|
| Single | 17.50 | 22.50 |
| Double | 33.00 | 35.00 |

Parking for 8

### The Old Wheatsheaf Inn
Listed COMMENDED

Weedon, Aylesbury HP22 4NS
☎ (01296) 641581

Old Elizabethan coaching inn, furnished with antiques. Courtyard surrounded by self-catering cottage and stable-cots. Home-from-home treatment and atmosphere. Garden with National Gardens Scheme.
Bedrooms: 1 single, 2 double, 2 twin
Bathrooms: 3 private, 2 public

**Bed & breakfast**

| per night: | £min | £max |
|---|---|---|
| Single | 30.00 | 35.00 |
| Double | 60.00 | 60.00 |

Lunch available
Evening meal 1830 (last orders 2200)
Parking for 14

## BAMPTON

Oxfordshire
Map ref 2C1

Small market town, well known for its Spring Bank Holiday Monday Fete with Morris Dance Festival.

### Romany Inn

**Listed**

Bridge Street, Bampton, Oxford
OX18 2HA
☎ (01993) 850237
*17th C listed Georgian building, just refurbished. Lounge bar, separate restaurant, chef/proprietor. Noted in pub and beer guides.*
Bedrooms: 4 double, 2 twin, 2 triple
Bathrooms: 8 private

**Bed & breakfast**

| per night: | £min | £max |
|---|---|---|
| Single | 21.00 | 21.00 |
| Double | 30.00 | 30.00 |

**Half board**

| per person: | £min | £max |
|---|---|---|
| Daily | 26.00 | |
| Weekly | 160.00 | |

Lunch available
Evening meal 1830 (last orders 2200)
Parking for 6
Cards accepted: Access, Visa
☺ ♨ ⌂ ♦ ⓘ ⅓ Å TV ▥ 🖩 ♨ ✕ 📶 🏠

## BANBURY

Oxfordshire
Map ref 2C1

Famous for its cattle market, cakes and nursery rhyme Cross. Founded in Saxon times, it has some fine houses and interesting old inns. A good centre for touring Warwickshire and the Cotswolds.
*Tourist Information Centre*
☎ *(01295) 259855*

### The Lodge

**HIGHLY COMMENDED**

Main Road, Middleton Cheney,
Banbury OX17 2PP
☎ (01295) 710355
*200-year-old lodge in lovely countryside, on outskirts of historic village, 3 miles east of Banbury on A422 and 1 mile from M40.*
Bedrooms: 1 double, 1 twin
Bathrooms: 2 private

**Bed & breakfast**

| per night: | £min | £max |
|---|---|---|
| Double | 42.00 | 45.00 |

Parking for 5
☺ 3 ♨ ⓤ Å TV ◑ ▥ 🖩 ♨ ✕ 📶 🏠

### "Roxtones"

**Listed**

Malthouse Lane, Shutford, Banbury
OX15 6PB
☎ (01295) 788240
*Stone-fronted semi-bungalow with garden surrounds, orchard and lawns. 6*

miles from Banbury, 16 miles from Stratford-upon-Avon and 2 miles from Broughton Castle.
Bedrooms: 2 single, 1 double
Bathrooms: 1 public

**Bed & breakfast**

| per night: | £min | £max |
|---|---|---|
| Single | | 15.00 |
| Double | | 25.00 |

**Half board**

| per person: | £min | £max |
|---|---|---|
| Daily | | 21.50 |
| Weekly | | 140.00 |

Evening meal 1900 (last orders 2100)
Parking for 3
Open April-September
☺ ♨ ⓤ ⓢ Å TV ▥ ✕ 📶

### Studleigh Farm

**Listed**

Wales Street, King's Sutton, Banbury
OX17 3RR
☎ (01295) 811979
*Renovated and modernised farmhouse, built circa 1700, on 8 acres of pastureland in a picturesque village. On direct Oxford-London rail line. Non-smokers only, please.*
Bedrooms: 1 double, 1 twin
Bathrooms: 2 private

**Bed & breakfast**

| per night: | £min | £max |
|---|---|---|
| Single | 27.00 | 30.00 |
| Double | 40.00 | 44.00 |

Parking for 3
♦ ⓤ ⓢ ✕ TV ▥ ♪ ♨ ✕ 📶 🏠

### Treetops Guest House

♛

28 Dashwood Road, Banbury
OX16 8HD
☎ (01295) 254444
*Comfortable accommodation. En-suite facilities available. Pets welcome. In an elegant Victorian town house on the A361, 5 minutes' walk from town centre.*
Bedrooms: 1 double, 1 twin, 2 triple, 1 family room
Bathrooms: 2 private, 2 public

**Bed & breakfast**

| per night: | £min | £max |
|---|---|---|
| Single | 16.00 | 20.00 |
| Double | 32.00 | 40.00 |

Lunch available
Parking for 2
☺ ♨ ⓤ ⓘ Å TV ▥ 📶

## BARTON ON SEA

Hampshire
Map ref 2B3

Seaside village with views of the Isle of Wight. Within easy driving distance of the New Forest.

### Bank Cottage

♛♛

Grove Road, Barton on Sea, New Milton BH25 7DN
☎ New Milton (01425) 613677

*Spacious en-suite rooms with every comfort and facility. Very warm welcome. Secure parking. Delicious home-made food. Close to pub and beach.*
Bedrooms: 2 double, 1 twin
Bathrooms: 3 private, 1 public

**Bed & breakfast**

| per night: | £min | £max |
|---|---|---|
| Single | 18.00 | 20.00 |
| Double | 28.00 | 37.00 |

**Half board**

| per person: | £min | £max |
|---|---|---|
| Daily | 21.50 | 45.00 |
| Weekly | 130.00 | 280.00 |

Evening meal from 1900
Parking for 4
☺ ⌂ ♦ ⓤ ⓘ ⓢ Å 🖩 ▥ ♨ ♣ ✕ 📶 ▨ SP

## BEAULIEU

Hampshire
Map ref 2C3

Beautifully situated among woods and hills on the Beaulieu river, the village is both charming and unspoilt. The 13th C ruined Cistercian abbey and 14th C Palace House stand close to the National Motor Museum. There is a maritime museum at Bucklers Hard.

### Coolderry Cottage ⚠

**Listed**

Masseys Lane, East Boldre, Beaulieu
SO42 7WE
☎ (01590) 612428
*Charming, peacefully located forest cottage, with friendly family atmosphere. Ideal base for forest and coastal activities. Pub meals walking distance. Admission to Exbury/Beaulieu reduced or inclusive with 3/5 nights (except July/August). Non-smoking.*
Bedrooms: 1 double, 1 twin
Bathrooms: 1 public

**Bed & breakfast**

| per night: | £min | £max |
|---|---|---|
| Single | 13.00 | 16.50 |

Parking for 4
☺ ⌂ ♦ ⓤ ⓢ ✕ TV ▥ 🖩 📶 OAP SP

### Leygreen Farm House ⚠

♛♛

Lyndhurst Road, Beaulieu,
Brockenhurst SO42 7YP
☎ Lymington (01590) 612355
*Comfortable Victorian farmhouse with large garden. Convenient for Beaulieu, Bucklers Hard museums and Exbury*

Gardens. Reductions for 3 days or more.

Bedrooms: 2 double, 1 twin
Bathrooms: 3 private, 1 public

**Bed & breakfast**

| per night: | £min | £max |
|---|---|---|
| Single | 16.00 | 20.00 |
| Double | 28.00 | 36.00 |

Parking for 6

⌂ 🖵 ♨ ⬚ S 📺 ▥ ▦ 🚗 ❀ 🚜 ◻ SP

## BICESTER

Oxfordshire
Map ref 2C1

Market town with large army depot and well-known hunting centre with hunt established in the late 18th C. The ancient parish church displays work of many periods. Nearby is the Jacobean mansion of Rousham House with gardens landscaped by William Kent.

### Manor Farm

Listed

Poundon, Bicester OX6 0BB
☎ (01869) 277212
*300-acre arable and mixed farm. 400-year-old farmhouse, tranquil, spacious and comfortable, a warm welcome to all. Take A421 Bicester to Buckingham road. Poundon turn is 3 miles along on right.*
Bedrooms: 1 single, 1 double, 1 triple
Bathrooms: 2 public

**Bed & breakfast**

| per night: | £min | £max |
|---|---|---|
| Single | 16.00 | 18.00 |
| Double | 32.00 | 36.00 |

Parking for 12

⌂ 🗴 🖵 ♨ ⬚ � ▥ 📺 ▥ 🚗 U ❀ 🚜 ◻

## BLANDFORD FORUM

Dorset
Map ref 2B3

Almost completely destroyed by fire in 1731, the town was rebuilt in a handsome Georgian style. The church is large and grand and the town is the hub of a rich farming area.
*Tourist Information Centre*
☎ *(01258) 454770*

### Church House

🏛🏛 COMMENDED

Church Road, Shillingstone, Blandford Forum DT11 0SL
☎ Child Okeford (01258) 860646
Fax (01258) 860646

Charming, 18th C thatched farmhouse, near Blandford. Pretty gardens, en-suite bathrooms, four-poster, log fires, home cooking. Ideal for touring, walking, exploring.
Bedrooms: 1 double, 1 twin, 1 triple
Bathrooms: 3 private, 2 public

**Bed & breakfast**

| per night: | £min | £max |
|---|---|---|
| Single | 22.00 | 25.00 |
| Double | 34.00 | 40.00 |

**Half board**

| per person: | £min | £max |
|---|---|---|
| Daily | 30.00 | 36.00 |
| Weekly | 200.00 | 250.00 |

Lunch available
Evening meal 1800 (last orders 1930)
Parking for 3

⌂ 🖵 10 ▦ ♨ ⬚ 🛇 S ⫝̸ X ▥ 📺 ▥ 🚗 U ▸ ❀ X 🚜 SP ▦ T

### Farnham Farm House ⋔

Listed APPROVED

Farnham, Blandford Forum DT11 8DG
☎ Tollard Royal (01725) 516254
Fax (01725) 516254
*350-acre arable farm. 19th C farmhouse in the Cranborne Chase with extensive views to the south. Within easy reach of the coast.*
Bedrooms: 1 double, 1 twin, 1 triple
Bathrooms: 1 private, 1 public

**Bed & breakfast**

| per night: | £min | £max |
|---|---|---|
| Single | 17.50 | 20.00 |
| Double | 35.00 | 40.00 |

Parking for 7

⌂ ♨ ⬚ S ▥ 📺 ▥ 🚗 ₹ ❀ 🚜

### Meadow House

▦

Tarrant Hinton, Blandford Forum DT11 8JG
☎ Tarrant Hinton (01258) 830498
*17th-18th C brick and flint farmhouse set in 4.5 acres. Warm welcome in peaceful, comfortable family home. Noted for delicious home-produced English breakfast. Excellent base for touring.*
Bedrooms: 1 single, 1 double, 1 triple
Bathrooms: 3 public

**Bed & breakfast**

| per night: | £min | £max |
|---|---|---|
| Single | 15.00 | 20.00 |
| Double | 30.00 | 40.00 |

Parking for 6

⌂ 🖵🗲 ♨ ⬚ S ⫝̸ ▥ 📺 ▥ 🚗 ₹ ❀ X 🚜

---

Individual proprietors have supplied all details of accommodation. Although we do check for accuracy, we advise you to confirm the information at the time of booking.

## BLETCHINGDON

Oxfordshire
Map ref 2C1

Thatched and stone-roofed cottages surround the village green with magnificent views of Ot Moor and the hills beyond.

### Stonehouse Farm

Listed

Weston Road, Bletchingdon, Oxford OX5 3EA
☎ (01869) 350585
*560-acre arable farm. 17th C Cotswold farmhouse. Ideal touring centre. 15 minutes north of Oxford, 20 minutes south of Banbury and 10 minutes from Blenheim Palace. Between the A4260 and A34, junction 9 of M40. 1 hour from Heathrow.*
Bedrooms: 1 double, 1 twin, 1 triple
Bathrooms: 2 public

**Bed & breakfast**

| per night: | £min | £max |
|---|---|---|
| Single | 15.00 | 20.00 |
| Double | 30.00 | 40.00 |

Parking for 11

⌂ 🖵 ♨ 🗲 ⬚ S 🚗 U ❀ X 🚜 ▦ T

## BOURNEMOUTH

Dorset
Map ref 2B3

Seaside town set among the pines with a mild climate, sandy beaches and fine coastal views. The town has wide streets with excellent shops, a pier, a pavilion, museums and conference centre.
*Tourist Information Centre*
☎ *(01202) 789789*

### Bay View Hotel

🏛🏛🏛 COMMENDED

Southbourne Overcliff Drive, Bournemouth BH6 3QB
☎ (01202) 429315
*Clifftop location on more relaxing side of Bournemouth. Scrumptious home-cooked food. Panoramic sea views from most rooms. Special Christmas programme.*
Bedrooms: 2 single, 9 double, 3 twin
Bathrooms: 12 private, 1 public

**Bed & breakfast**

| per night: | £min | £max |
|---|---|---|
| Single | 17.00 | 25.00 |
| Double | 34.00 | 52.00 |

**Half board**

| per person: | £min | £max |
|---|---|---|
| Daily | 24.50 | 33.50 |
| Weekly | 154.50 | 208.50 |

Evening meal 1830 (last orders 1930)
Parking for 12
Cards accepted: Access, Visa

⌂ 6 ▦ 🖵 📞 ♨ 🗲 ⬚ S ⫝̸ ▥ 📺 ▥ 🚗 🔌 ❀ X ◻ ◪ SP

## BOURNEMOUTH

*Continued*

### The Cottage 𝗔
😊😊😊 COMMENDED
12 Southern Road, Southbourne,
Bournemouth BH6 3SR
☎ (01202) 422764

*Charming character family-run hotel.
Restful location. Noted for home-
prepared fresh cooking, cleanliness and
tastefully furnished accommodation.
Ample parking. Non-smoking.*
Bedrooms: 1 single, 1 double, 2 twin,
1 triple, 2 family rooms
Bathrooms: 4 private, 2 public,
1 private shower

**Bed & breakfast**

| per night: | £min | £max |
| --- | --- | --- |
| Single | 16.50 | 20.50 |
| Double | 33.00 | 45.00 |

**Half board**

| per person: | £min | £max |
| --- | --- | --- |
| Daily | 24.00 | 30.00 |
| Weekly | 156.00 | 178.00 |

Evening meal 1800 (last orders 1800)
Parking for 8
Open February-November
🛇🖰4🏧🕯⏦🛅S⊁🛏📺🛋🖂🛪🛍 DAP SP

### Downside Private Hotel
😊
52 Westbourne Park Road,
Bournemouth BH4 8HQ
☎ (01202) 763109
*Small friendly hotel in quiet position
near chines, close to sea, shops,
entertainments. Personal service, long
or short stays welcome.*
Bedrooms: 2 single, 2 double, 1 twin,
4 family rooms
Bathrooms: 2 private, 2 public,
2 private showers

**Bed & breakfast**

| per night: | £min | £max |
| --- | --- | --- |
| Single | 12.50 | 15.50 |
| Double | 25.00 | 31.00 |

**Half board**

| per person: | £min | £max |
| --- | --- | --- |
| Daily | 18.50 | |
| Weekly | 122.50 | 145.50 |

Evening meal from 1800
Parking for 5
Open April-September and Christmas
Cards accepted: Access, Visa
🛇🖰🖰💤⏦🛅S🛏📺🛋🖂🛪🛍 DAP
🕯 SP T

### The Garthlyn Hotel 𝗔
😊😊😊 COMMENDED
6 Sandbourne Road, Alum Chine,
Westbourne, Bournemouth BH4 8JH
☎ (01202) 761016
*Hotel of character with lovely gardens.
Good quality beds. 4 minutes' walk to
beaches (hut available). Car park in
grounds.*
Bedrooms: 1 single, 5 double, 1 twin,
1 triple, 2 family rooms
Bathrooms: 9 private, 1 public

**Bed & breakfast**

| per night: | £min | £max |
| --- | --- | --- |
| Single | 20.25 | 28.50 |
| Double | 40.50 | 52.00 |

**Half board**

| per person: | £min | £max |
| --- | --- | --- |
| Daily | 27.00 | 36.00 |
| Weekly | 169.00 | 215.00 |

Evening meal 1800 (last orders 1900)
Parking for 9
Cards accepted: Access, Visa, Switch/
Delta
🛇🖰4🏧💤⏦🛅S⊁🛏📺🛋🖂🏧🛪
🛍 DAP 🕯 SP

### The Golden Sovereigns
### Hotel 𝗔
😊😊😊
97 Alumhurst Road, Alum Chine,
Bournemouth BH4 8HR
☎ (01202) 762088

*Attractively decorated Victorian hotel of
character, in a quiet yet convenient
location 4 minutes' walk from beach.
Comfortable rooms, traditional and Old
English home-cooked food.*
Bedrooms: 1 single, 2 double, 2 twin,
1 triple, 2 family rooms
Bathrooms: 5 private, 2 public

**Bed & breakfast**

| per night: | £min | £max |
| --- | --- | --- |
| Single | 14.50 | 22.00 |
| Double | 29.00 | 44.00 |

**Half board**

| per person: | £min | £max |
| --- | --- | --- |
| Daily | 20.00 | 29.50 |
| Weekly | 130.00 | 180.00 |

Lunch available
Evening meal 1800 (last orders 1600)
Parking for 9
Cards accepted: Access, Visa
🛇🖰💤⏦🛅S⊁🛏📺🛋🖂🅿 DAP 🕯 SP

### Mayfield Private Hotel
😊😊
46 Frances Road, Bournemouth
BH1 3SA
☎ (01202) 551839
*Overlooking public gardens with tennis,
bowling, putting greens. Central for sea,*
shops and main rail/coach stations.
*Some rooms with shower or
toilet/shower. Licensed.*
Bedrooms: 1 single, 4 double, 2 twin,
1 family room
Bathrooms: 4 private, 2 public,
3 private showers

**Bed & breakfast**

| per night: | £min | £max |
| --- | --- | --- |
| Single | 13.50 | 16.00 |
| Double | 27.00 | 32.00 |

**Half board**

| per person: | £min | £max |
| --- | --- | --- |
| Daily | 19.00 | 21.00 |
| Weekly | 110.00 | 126.00 |

Evening meal from 1800
Parking for 5
Open January-November
🛇🖰6🖰💤⏦🛅S🛏📺🛋❄🏧 DAP SP

### Pinewood 𝗔
Listed COMMENDED
197 Holdenhurst Road, Bournemouth
BH8 8DG
☎ (01202) 292684
*Friendly guesthouse, close to rail, coach
stations and all amenities. Tea, coffee
and satellite TV in all rooms.*
Bedrooms: 1 single, 3 double, 1 twin,
3 triple
Bathrooms: 2 public

**Bed & breakfast**

| per night: | £min | £max |
| --- | --- | --- |
| Single | 14.00 | 15.00 |
| Double | 28.00 | 30.00 |

Parking for 8
🛇🖰5🖰💤📵⏦🛅S🛋🖂🛪🏧

### Sun Haven
😊
39 Southern Road, Southbourne,
Bournemouth BH6 3SS
☎ (01202) 427560
*Quality establishment. Colour TV in
bedrooms, central heating, snacks and
tea/coffee facilities. Parking. Ideal for
Bournemouth, Christchurch, New Forest
and local beauty spots. Beach 150
yards.*
Bedrooms: 2 single, 3 double, 1 twin,
2 triple
Bathrooms: 3 public

**Bed & breakfast**

| per night: | £min | £max |
| --- | --- | --- |
| Single | 16.00 | 18.00 |
| Double | 32.00 | 36.00 |

Parking for 6
Open April-September
🛇🖰💤📵⏦🛅S🛏📺🛋🖂🏧 DAP SP

### Willowdene Hotel
😊😊 HIGHLY COMMENDED
43 Grand Avenue, Southbourne,
Bournemouth BH6 3SY
☎ (01202) 425370
*Detached Edwardian house, for those
who require quality accommodation
with a happy relaxed atmosphere. 200
yards from sandy beach, with views
over Poole Bay, Isle of Wight Needles
and Purbeck Hills. Non smoking.*
Bedrooms: 3 double, 1 twin, 1 triple

Bathrooms: 4 private, 1 public
**Bed & breakfast**

| per night: | £min | £max |
|---|---|---|
| Single | 16.00 | 18.00 |
| Double | 32.00 | 36.00 |

Parking for 8
Open April-October

🛇 👶 💧 🔌 🛇 🛇 ✦ ✕ 📺 �📱 🛒 🐾 ✕ 🐎
OAP SP

## BRACKNELL

Berkshire
Map ref 2C2

Designated a New Town in 1949, the town has ancient origins. Set in heathlands, it is an excellent centre for golf and walking. South Hill Park, an 18th C mansion, houses an art centre.
*Tourist Information Centre*
☎ *(01344) 868196*

### Bear Farm

Binfield, Bracknell RG12 5QE
☎ Twyford (01734) 343286
*65-acre mixed farm. 17th C oak-beamed farmhouse surrounded by 2 acres of well- kept gardens, with en-suite guest bedrooms in an adjoining converted farm building.*
Bedrooms: 1 double, 1 twin
Bathrooms: 2 private
**Bed & breakfast**

| per night: | £min | £max |
|---|---|---|
| Single | 23.00 | 24.00 |
| Double | 40.00 | 42.00 |

Parking for 6
Cards accepted: Access, Visa

🛇 4 👶 💧 📱 🛇 👶 🔌 📺 🛒 🐾 ✕ ✦ 🐎 🏠

## BRAMDEAN

Hampshire
Map ref 2C3

Village astride the A272, 1 mile west of the site of a Roman villa.

### Dean Farm
Listed

Kilmeston, Alresford SO24 0NL
☎ (01962) 771286
*200-acre mixed farm. Comfortable, 18th C farmhouse in Kilmeston, a small and peaceful village 1.5 miles off the A272 between Petersfield and Winchester.*
Bedrooms: 2 double, 1 triple
Bathrooms: 1 public
**Bed & breakfast**

| per night: | £min | £max |
|---|---|---|
| Single | 16.50 | 16.50 |
| Double | 33.00 | 33.00 |

Parking for 3

🛇 10 ⛏ 🔌 🛇 📱 S ✕ 📺 ⏶ 🛒 ✦ ✕ 🐎

## BRANSGORE

Hampshire
Map ref 2B3

Situated in extensive woodlands. In the church of St Mary is a lovely Perpendicular font which is said to have come from Christchurch.

### Wiltshire House M
🛑🛑 HIGHLY COMMENDED

West Road, Bransgore, Christchurch, Dorset BH23 8BD
☎ (01425) 672450
*Friendly, informal accommodation in an early Victorian gentleman's residence, set in a large secluded garden.*
Bedrooms: 1 single, 1 twin, 1 family room
Bathrooms: 1 private, 2 public
**Bed & breakfast**

| per night: | £min | £max |
|---|---|---|
| Single | 14.00 | 16.00 |
| Double | 28.00 | 32.00 |

Parking for 4

🛇 ⛏ 🔲 👶 💧 🔌 ✕ 📺 ⏶ ∪ ✦ ✕ 🐎
OAP SP T

## BRIMPTON

Berkshire
Map ref 2C2

### Manor Farm M
Listed

Brimpton, Reading RG7 4SQ
☎ Woolhampton (01734) 713166
*600-acre mixed farm. Family farm in Brimpton village. Interesting house and chapel, once of the Knights Hospitallers. Close to A4, M4 and M3.*
Bedrooms: 1 double, 1 twin
Bathrooms: 1 public
**Bed & breakfast**

| per night: | £min | £max |
|---|---|---|
| Single | 18.50 | 20.00 |
| Double | 35.00 | 40.00 |

Parking for 4

🛇 ⛏ 🔲 👶 💧 🔌 📺 🛒 ✦ ✕ 🐎 🏠

## BRIZE NORTON

Oxfordshire
Map ref 2C1

Village closely associated with the American Air Force. The medieval church is the only church in England dedicated to St Brice, from whom the village takes its name.

### Stonelands Barn
Brize Norton, Oxford OX18 3YH
☎ Carterton (01993) 844840
Fax (01993) 844840
*Large, private, converted Cotswold barn, full of historical interest. Horses welcome.*
Bedrooms: 2 twin

Bathrooms: 2 public
**Bed & breakfast**

| per night: | £min | £max |
|---|---|---|
| Single | 17.50 | 18.00 |
| Double | 35.00 | 38.00 |

Evening meal 2000 (last orders 2030)
Parking for 8
Open January-November

🛇 8 🛆 🔌 🛇 👶 💧 📺 ⏶ 🛒 ✦ 🐾 🐎 🏠

## BUCKINGHAM

Buckinghamshire
Map ref 2C1

Interesting old market town surrounded by rich farmland. It has many Georgian buildings, including the Town Hall and Old Jail and many old almshouses and inns. Stowe School nearby has magnificent 18th C landscaped gardens.

### Folly Farm M
🛑🛑 COMMENDED

Padbury, Buckingham MK18 2HS
☎ Winslow (01296) 712413
*500-acre arable farm. On A413 between Winslow and Padbury, 2 miles south of Buckingham. Substantial farmhouse opposite Folly Inn. Convenient for Stowe Landscape Gardens, Silverstone circuit and Addington Equestrian Centre. Evening meals by arrangement.*
Bedrooms: 3 double
Bathrooms: 3 private
**Bed & breakfast**

| per night: | £min | £max |
|---|---|---|
| Single | 17.50 | 18.00 |
| Double | 30.00 | 34.00 |

Parking for 10

🛇 🔲 👶 💧 🔌 S ✕ 📺 ⏶ ✦ ✕ 🐎

## BURFORD

Oxfordshire
Map ref 2B1

One of the most beautiful Cotswold wool towns with Georgian and Tudor houses, many antique shops and a picturesque High Street sloping to the River Windrush.
*Tourist Information Centre*
☎ *(01993) 823558*

### The Dower House
🛑

Westhall Hill, Fulbrook, Oxford OX18 4BJ
☎ (01993) 822596
*Elegant, restored period accommodation in an imposing Cotswold dower house. Superb and tranquil setting, with commanding views over Burford and beautiful surrounding countryside. South-facing bedrooms and picturesque gardens.*
Bedrooms: 2 double
Bathrooms: 1 private, 1 public
*Continued* ▶

## BURFORD

*Continued*

### Bed & breakfast

| per night: | £min | £max |
| --- | --- | --- |
| Single | 15.00 | 32.00 |
| Double | 32.00 | 36.00 |
| Parking for 3 | | |

🏠 ⛔ Ⓢ ⅍ 🅿 📺 🛏 🚗 ✕ 🐾 🎭

### Hillborough Hotel
♛♛♛

The Green, Milton-under-Wychwood,
Oxford OX7 6JH
☎ Shipton-under-Wychwood (01993)
830501

*Victorian country house facing village
green. Open fires. Friendly bar.
Restaurant open to non-residents. Leafy
conservatory coffee lounge. Pretty
gardens.*
Bedrooms: 4 double, 3 twin, 3 triple
Bathrooms: 10 private

### Bed & breakfast

| per night: | £min | £max |
| --- | --- | --- |
| Single | 35.00 | 40.00 |
| Double | 48.00 | 58.00 |

### Half board

| per person: | £min | £max |
| --- | --- | --- |
| Daily | 45.00 | 50.00 |
| Weekly | 234.00 | 270.00 |

Lunch available
Evening meal 1900 (last orders 2130)
Parking for 15
Open February-December
Cards accepted: Access, Visa, Amex

🏠 ⛔ 📞 🖥 📺 ⓘ Ⓢ ⅍ 🅿 📺 🛏 🚗
🍴10-20 ✿ ✕ SP

### Rookery Farm
Listed COMMENDED

Burford Road, Brize Norton, Oxford
OX18 3NL
☎ Carterton (01993) 842957

*2-acre smallholding. 18th C Cotswold
farmhouse, pleasantly situated in small
Oxfordshire village with lovely views of
surrounding countryside. Generous
farmhouse breakfast.*
Bedrooms: 2 double, 1 twin
Bathrooms: 1 public

### Bed & breakfast

| per night: | £min | £max |
| --- | --- | --- |
| Single | 20.00 | 20.00 |
| Double | 35.00 | 35.00 |
| Parking for 4 | | |

🏠 ⛔ ⅍ ⛔ 🅿 📺 🛏 🚗 ✕ 🐾 🎭

### St Winnow
Listed

160 The Hill, Burford, Oxford
OX18 4QY
☎ (01993) 823843
*Listed Cotswold property in
conservation area, on the hill above the
High Street. Terraced house with
garden and garage, plus limited parking
at rear.*
Bedrooms: 1 single, 1 double, 1 twin
Bathrooms: 1 public

### Bed & breakfast

| per night: | £min | £max |
| --- | --- | --- |
| Single | 20.00 | 25.00 |
| Double | 32.00 | 40.00 |
| Parking for 2 | | |

🏠 ⅍ ⛔ ⓘ Ⓢ ⅍ 🅿 📺 🛏 🚗 ✕ 🐾 🎭

## BURLEY

Hampshire
Map ref 2B3

Attractive centre from which to
explore the south-west part of the
New Forest. There is an ancient
earthwork on Castle Hill nearby,
which also offers good views.

### Brandon Thatch ♔
♛ HIGHLY COMMENDED

Charles' Lane, Bagnum, Ringwood
BH24 3DA
☎ Ringwood (01425) 474256
Fax (01425) 478452

*A warm, friendly welcome awaits you at
this delightful 17th C thatched country
house set in 3.5 acres of garden and
woodlands. Guest sitting room with TV,
video and sky TV. Horses and dogs by
arrangement. A non-smoking house.*
Bedrooms: 2 double, 1 twin
Bathrooms: 3 private, 1 public

### Bed & breakfast

| per night: | £min | £max |
| --- | --- | --- |
| Double | 48.00 | 60.00 |
| Parking for 13 | | |

🏠 ⅍ ⛔ ⓘ Ⓢ ⅍ 🅿 📺 🛏 🚗 ∪ ʏ ✿
🐾 SP 🎭

### Rosebay Cottage
♛ COMMENDED

Chapel Lane, Burley, Ringwood
BH24 4DJ
☎ (01425) 402471
Fax (01425) 403174

*Delightful, 100-year-old forest cottage,
with a duck pond and paddock with
foal. Friendly atmosphere. 8 minutes'
walk to village centre, direct access to
forest.*
Bedrooms: 2 double, 1 twin
Bathrooms: 3 private

### Bed & breakfast

| per night: | £min | £max |
| --- | --- | --- |
| Double | 30.00 | 34.00 |
| Parking for 5 | | |

🏠 5 ⛔ ⅍ ⛔ ⓘ Ⓢ ⅍ 🅿 📺 ▶ ✿ 🎭

## BURSLEDON

Hampshire
Map ref 2C3

### Dodwell Cottage ♔
♛♛ COMMENDED

Dodwell Lane, Bursledon,
Southampton SO31 1AD
☎ Southampton (01703) 406074
Fax (01489) 578659
*Comfortable, beamed 18th C country
cottage, close to River Hamble and
country park. Ample parking.
Restaurants nearby. Easy access
Portsmouth/Southampton ferries.*
Bedrooms: 1 double, 1 twin, 1 family
room
Bathrooms: 1 private, 1 public

### Bed & breakfast

| per night: | £min | £max |
| --- | --- | --- |
| Single | 23.00 | 27.50 |
| Double | 36.00 | 45.00 |

### Half board

| per person: | £min | £max |
| --- | --- | --- |
| Daily | 32.00 | 36.50 |

Evening meal 1800 (last orders 1900)
Parking for 10
Open February-December

🏠 5 ⛔ ⓘ Ⓢ ⅍ 🅿 📺 🛏 🚗 🍴6-12 ∪
✿ ✕ DAP 🎭

## CADNAM

Hampshire
Map ref 2C3

Village with numerous attractive
cottages and an inn close to the
entrance of the M27.

### Walnut Cottage ♔
♛♛ HIGHLY COMMENDED

Old Romsey Road, Cadnam,
Southampton SO4 2NP
☎ Southampton (01703) 812275
*150-year-old cottage, with attractive
garden and all rooms en-suite. Close to
forest and local hostelries.*
Bedrooms: 1 double, 2 twin
Bathrooms: 3 private

### Bed & breakfast

| per night: | £min | £max |
| --- | --- | --- |
| Single | 28.00 | 30.00 |
| Double | 40.00 | 42.00 |
| Parking for 3 | | |

🏠 14 ⛔ 🖥 ⛔ ⅍ ⛔ ⓘ ⅍ 📺 🛏 🚗
✿ ✕ 🐾 SP

## CHALFONT ST GILES

Buckinghamshire
Map ref 2D2

Pretty, old village in wooded Chiltern Hills only 20 miles from London. Good walking and touring centre for Cotswolds, Oxford and Thames Valley.

### Pickwicks ⋒
COMMENDED

Nightingales Lane, Chalfont St Giles HP8 4SH
☎ (01494) 874123
Fax (01494) 874123

*Large, old Tudor-style house in 1.25 acres of beautiful, peaceful gardens. Convenient for London, Heathrow, M40, M25, underground station and Bekonscot Model Village. Newlands College close by.*
Bedrooms: 1 single, 1 double, 1 twin
Bathrooms: 1 public
**Bed & breakfast**

| per night: | £min | £max |
|---|---|---|
| Single | 30.00 | 35.00 |
| Double | 40.00 | 45.00 |

Parking for 20

## CHANDLERS FORD

Hampshire
Map ref 2C3

### St Lucia
Listed

68 Shaftesbury Avenue, Chandlers Ford, Eastleigh SO5 3BP
☎ (01703) 262995
Fax (01703) 262995
*Homely accommodation well placed for touring, near Winchester, the south coast and the New Forest. Evening meals, home-grown produce in season. Non-smokers only please.*
Bedrooms: 2 single, 1 double, 1 twin
Bathrooms: 1 public
**Bed & breakfast**

| per night: | £min | £max |
|---|---|---|
| Single | 13.50 | 17.00 |
| Double | 29.00 | 31.00 |

**Half board**

| per person: | £min | £max |
|---|---|---|
| Daily | 17.00 | 27.50 |
| Weekly | 105.00 | 175.00 |

Evening meal 1830 (last orders 1830)
Parking for 5

## CHARLBURY

Oxfordshire
Map ref 2C1

Large Cotswold village with beautiful views of the Evenlode Valley just outside the village and close to the ancient Forest of Wychwood.

### Banbury Hill Farm
COMMENDED

Enstone Road, Charlbury, Oxford OX7 3JH
☎ (01608) 810314
*54-acre mixed farm. Cotswold-stone farmhouse with extensive views across Evenlode Valley. Ideal touring centre for Blenheim Palace, Oxford and the Cotswolds.*
Bedrooms: 1 single, 2 double, 1 twin, 1 triple
Bathrooms: 3 private, 1 public
**Bed & breakfast**

| per night: | £min | £max |
|---|---|---|
| Single | 16.00 | 20.00 |
| Double | 32.00 | 40.00 |

**Half board**

| per person: | £min | £max |
|---|---|---|
| Daily | 25.00 | |

Evening meal 1830 (last orders 2100)
Parking for 6

## COMPTON

Berkshire
Map ref 2C2

Village lies above a hollow on the eastern slope of the Berkshire Downs, a little south of the Ridgeway and the ancient British stronghold of Perborough Castle.

### The Compton Swan Hotel ⋒
◆◆◆

High Street, Compton, Newbury RG16 0NH
☎ Newbury (01635) 578269
Fax (01635) 578269
*Recently refurbished country hotel with games room, lounge, restaurant, extensive a la carte menu, large garden and a bar with a range of real ales. Close to the Ridgeway.*
Bedrooms: 1 double, 3 twin, 1 family room
Bathrooms: 3 private, 1 public, 2 private showers
**Bed & breakfast**

| per night: | £min | £max |
|---|---|---|
| Single | 32.00 | 32.00 |
| Double | 40.00 | 44.00 |

**Half board**

| per person: | £min | £max |
|---|---|---|
| Daily | 35.00 | 45.00 |
| Weekly | 200.00 | 240.00 |

Lunch available
Evening meal 1800 (last orders 2200)

Parking for 30
Cards accepted: Access, Visa

## COMPTON

Hampshire
Map ref 2C3

### Manor House
Listed

Place Lane, Compton, Winchester SO21 2BA
☎ Twyford (01962) 712162
*Comfortable country house, 8 minutes from Shawford railway station and 2 miles from city of Winchester. Non-smokers preferred.*
Bedrooms: 1 double
Bathrooms: 1 public
**Bed & breakfast**

| per night: | £min | £max |
|---|---|---|
| Single | 11.00 | 11.00 |
| Double | 22.00 | 22.00 |

Parking for 1

## CORFE CASTLE

Dorset
Map ref 2B3

One of the most spectacular ruined castles in Britain. Norman in origin, the castle was a Royalist stronghold during the Civil War and held out until 1645. The village had a considerable marble-carving industry in the Middle Ages.

### Bradle Farmhouse
COMMENDED

Bradle Farm, Church Knowle, Wareham BH20 5NU
☎ (01929) 480712

*550-acre mixed farm. Picturesque farmhouse in the heart of Purbeck. Superb views of castle and surrounding countryside, beach 2 miles. Warm family atmosphere with evening meals arranged at local inn.*
Bedrooms: 1 double, 1 twin, 1 triple
Bathrooms: 2 private, 1 public
**Bed & breakfast**

| per night: | £min | £max |
|---|---|---|
| Single | 18.00 | 23.00 |
| Double | 32.00 | 36.00 |

Continued ►

## CORFE CASTLE

*Continued*

**Half board**

| per person: | £min | £max |
|---|---|---|
| Weekly | 173.00 | 185.00 |

Evening meal 1830 (last orders 2000)
Parking for 3

⌂ ♨ ⟐ ▢ ♥ ⬙ 🅸 🆂 ⵌ 📺 ⛁ 🖃 🐾 ✕ 🚗
🅾🅰🅿 🆂🅿 🏠

## CRANBORNE

Dorset
Map ref 2B3

Village with an interesting
Jacobean manor house. Lies
south-east of Cranborne Chase,
formerly a forest and hunting
preserve.

## Clematis

♛♛

Edmondsham, Cranborne BH21 5RJ
☎ Verwood (01202) 822954
*Friendly country home on edge of
village in peaceful rural location. Easy
access to M27, ideally situated for New
Forest/coast. Well appointed bedrooms
with private facilities. Lounge. Golf,
riding, fishing nearby.*
Bedrooms: 1 double, 1 twin
Bathrooms: 2 private

**Bed & breakfast**

| per night: | £min | £max |
|---|---|---|
| Single | 16.00 | 18.00 |
| Double | 32.00 | 36.00 |

Parking for 4

⌂ ♨ ⟐ ▢ ♥ ⵌ 🅸 ✂ ⬙ 📺 ⛁ 🖃 🐾 🅿 ⛽ ✽
✕ 🚗 ✍ 🆂🅿

## The Fleur de Lys ♨

♛♛♛ COMMENDED

5 Wimborne Street, Cranborne,
Wimborne Minster BH21 5PP
☎ (01725) 517282
Fax (01725) 517631
*Charming old-world coaching inn, close
to the New Forest, with a cosy
atmosphere and friendly hospitality.
Restaurant and bar. En-suite
accommodation.*
Bedrooms: 1 single, 4 double, 3 twin
Bathrooms: 7 private, 1 private shower

**Bed & breakfast**

| per night: | £min | £max |
|---|---|---|
| Single | 27.00 | 35.00 |
| Double | 36.00 | 50.00 |

**Half board**

| per person: | £min | £max |
|---|---|---|
| Daily | 32.00 | 48.00 |
| Weekly | 200.00 | 300.00 |

Lunch available
Evening meal 1900 (last orders 2145)
Parking for 35
Cards accepted: Access, Visa, Amex,
Switch/Delta

⌂ ⛺ ⟐ ▢ ♥ ⵌ 🅸 ⛁ 🖃 🐾 🍴12 🚗 🆂🅿 🏠 🆃

## CUDDESDON

Oxfordshire
Map ref 2C1

## The Bat & Ball Inn ♨

♛ COMMENDED

28 High Street, Cuddesdon, Oxford
OX44 9HJ
☎ Oxford (01865) 874379
*Old coaching inn with scenic views and
interesting collection of cricket
memorabilia. Cuddesdon is an attractive
small village, well placed for Oxford and
the M40.*
Bedrooms: 5 double, 1 twin
Bathrooms: 6 private

**Bed & breakfast**

| per night: | £min | £max |
|---|---|---|
| Single | 35.00 | |
| Double | 40.00 | |

Lunch available
Evening meal 1830 (last orders 2100)
Parking for 15
Cards accepted: Access, Visa

♨ ⟐ ▢ ♥ 🅸 🆂 ⛁ 🖃 🐾 🍴15 ⛽ ✽ 🚗
✍ 🆂🅿 🏠

## CURDRIDGE

Hampshire
Map ref 2C3

## Bay Tree House

Listed HIGHLY COMMENDED

Blind Lane, Curdridge, Southampton
SO3 2BL
☎ Botley (01489) 784656
*Set in rural Meon Valley, a spacious
country house with idyllic gardens.
Swimming pool and tennis court.
Convenient for New Forest, Winchester,
Southampton and Portsmouth.*
Bedrooms: 1 single, 2 double, 1 twin
Bathrooms: 1 private, 1 public

**Bed & breakfast**

| per night: | £min | £max |
|---|---|---|
| Single | 20.00 | |
| Double | 40.00 | |

Parking for 9

⌂ ⛺6 ☒ ⟐ ▢ ♥ ⵌ 🅸 ✂ ✂ 📺 ⛁ 🖃 🐾 ✍ ⛽
✽ ✕ 🚗 🆃

## DEDDINGTON

Oxfordshire
Map ref 2C1

Attractive former market town with
a large market square and many
fine old buildings.

## Hill Barn

Listed

Milton Gated Road, Deddington,
Banbury OX5 4TS
☎ (01869) 38631
*Converted barn set in open countryside
with views overlooking valley and hills.
Banbury-Oxford road, half a mile before
Deddington, turn right to Milton Gated
Road. Hill Barn is 100 yards on the
right.*

Bedrooms: 1 double, 2 twin
Bathrooms: 1 public

**Bed & breakfast**

| per night: | £min | £max |
|---|---|---|
| Single | 15.00 | 20.00 |
| Double | 30.00 | 36.00 |

Parking for 6

⌂ ♨ ⬙ ⵌ 📺 ⛁ 🖃 🚗 ⛽ ✽ ✕ 🚗 🏠

## Unicorn Hotel

♛♛♛ APPROVED

Market Place, Deddington, Banbury
OX15 0SE
☎ (01869) 338838
Fax (01869) 338036
*17th C Cotswold border coaching inn,
10 minutes from M40 junctions 10 and
11, on A4260 Banbury to Oxford road.*
Bedrooms: 4 single, 3 double, 1 twin,
1 triple
Bathrooms: 9 private

**Bed & breakfast**

| per night: | £min | £max |
|---|---|---|
| Single | 35.00 | 39.50 |
| Double | 45.00 | 49.50 |

**Half board**

| per person: | £min | £max |
|---|---|---|
| Daily | 30.00 | 35.00 |
| Weekly | 180.00 | 210.00 |

Lunch available
Evening meal 1900 (last orders 2100)
Parking for 33
Cards accepted: Access, Visa, Diners,
Amex

⌂ ⛺ ⟐ ▢ ♥ 🅸 🆂 ⵌ 📺 ⛁ 🖃 🐾 🍴 ♨ ⛽
✽ 🅾🅰🅿 ✍ 🆂🅿 🏠 🆃

## DENMEAD

Hampshire
Map ref 2C3

Comparatively modern town,
south-west of the original
settlement.

## Forest Gate

Listed

Hambledon Road, Denmead,
Waterlooville PO7 6EX
☎ Waterlooville (01705) 255901
*Listed Georgian house on outskirts of
village in large garden. Within easy
reach of maritime Portsmouth and
continental ferries. Dinner by
arrangement.*
Bedrooms: 2 twin
Bathrooms: 2 private

**Bed & breakfast**

| per night: | £min | £max |
|---|---|---|
| Single | 20.00 | 22.00 |
| Double | 32.00 | 36.00 |

**Half board**

| per person: | £min | £max |
|---|---|---|
| Daily | 31.50 | 33.50 |
| Weekly | 200.00 | 215.00 |

Evening meal from 1930
Parking for 4

⌂ ♨ ⟐ ▢ ♥ ⵌ ✂ 📺 ⛁ 🖃 🐾 ⛽ ✽ ✕ 🚗 🏠

## DIBDEN

Hampshire
Map ref 2C3

Small village on the edge of the New Forest with a full recreation centre. Picturesque 13th C church overlooks Southampton Water.

### Dale Farm Guest House ₳

Manor Road, Applemore Hill, Dibden, Southampton SO4 5TJ
☎ Southampton (01703) 849632
*Friendly, family-run 18th C converted farmhouse, in wooded setting with large garden. 250 yards from A326, adjacent to riding stables and 15 minutes from beach.*
Bedrooms: 1 single, 2 double, 2 twin, 1 triple
Bathrooms: 1 public, 1 private shower

**Bed & breakfast**

| per night: | £min | £max |
|---|---|---|
| Single | 15.00 | |
| Double | 29.00 | |

**Half board**

| per person: | £min | £max |
|---|---|---|
| Daily | 23.00 | |
| Weekly | 160.00 | |

Evening meal 1800 (last orders 1100)
Parking for 10

---

## EAST HENDRED

Oxfordshire
Map ref 2C2

### Monks Court
Listed

Newbury Road, East Hendred, Wantage OX12 8LG
☎ Abingdon (01235) 833797 & Abingdon (Work) 815907
*Comfortable family house on outskirts of beautiful village. Only 1.5 miles from the Ridgeway and 3 miles from A34. Convenient for Oxford and Newbury.*
Bedrooms: 1 single, 2 double, 1 twin
Bathrooms: 1 private, 2 public

**Bed & breakfast**

| per night: | £min | £max |
|---|---|---|
| Single | 16.00 | 19.00 |
| Double | 32.00 | 34.00 |

Parking for 3

---

National Crown ratings were correct at the time of going to press but are subject to change. Please check at the time of booking.

---

## FAREHAM

Hampshire
Map ref 2C3

Lies on a quiet backwater of Portsmouth Harbour. The High Street is lined with fine Georgian buildings.
*Tourist Information Centre*
☎ *(01329) 221342*

### Giblet Ore Cottage
Listed

82 Hill Head Road, Hill Head, Fareham PO14 3JP
☎ Stubbington (01329) 663050
*Private house on seafront overlooking Solent and Isle of Wight. Beach, bird-watching and surfboarding facilities nearby.*
Bedrooms: 1 single, 1 double
Bathrooms: 1 private, 1 public

**Bed & breakfast**

| per night: | £min | £max |
|---|---|---|
| Single | 16.00 | 18.00 |
| Double | 32.00 | 34.00 |

Parking for 2

### Seven Sevens Private Hotel

56 Hill Head Road, Hill Head, Fareham PO14 3JL
☎ Stubbington (01329) 662408
*In the village of Hill Head, overlooking the Solent towards the Isle of Wight. 1 minute's walk from beach. Close to the various tourist attractions of Portsmouth and Winchester.*
Bedrooms: 2 single, 2 double, 1 triple
Bathrooms: 3 private, 3 public

**Bed & breakfast**

| per night: | £min | £max |
|---|---|---|
| Single | 16.50 | 19.50 |
| Double | 28.00 | 30.00 |

Parking for 6

---

## FARINGDON

Oxfordshire
Map ref 2C2

Ancient stone-built market town in the Vale of the White Horse. The 17th C market hall stands on pillars and the 13th C church has some fine monuments. A great monastic tithe barn is nearby at Great Coxwell.

### White Horse Inn ₳
Listed  COMMENDED

Woolstone, Faringdon SN7 7QL
☎ Uffington (01367) 820566 & 820726
Fax (01367) 820566

---

16th C inn 10 miles from M4 and close to White Horse Hill. Log fires, oak beams. Real ales, a la carte restaurant and bar snacks.
Bedrooms: 2 double, 3 twin, 1 triple
Bathrooms: 6 private

**Bed & breakfast**

| per night: | £min | £max |
|---|---|---|
| Single | 35.00 | 40.00 |
| Double | 45.00 | 55.00 |

**Half board**

| per person: | £min | £max |
|---|---|---|
| Daily | 50.00 | 60.00 |
| Weekly | 350.00 | 420.00 |

Lunch available
Evening meal 1900 (last orders 2200)
Parking for 80
Cards accepted: Access, Visa, Diners, Amex, Switch/Delta

---

## FLEET

Hampshire
Map ref 2C2

*Tourist Information Centre*
☎ *(01252) 811151*

### The Webbs ₳
Listed

12 Warren Close, Fleet, Aldershot GU13 9LT
☎ Aldershot (01252) 615063
Fax (01252) 629873
*Homely, friendly atmosphere. Families welcome (no age limit). Close to Fleet station, A30 and M3, exit 4A.*
Bedrooms: 2 single, 1 twin
Bathrooms: 2 public

**Bed & breakfast**

| per night: | £min | £max |
|---|---|---|
| Single | 17.00 | 17.00 |
| Double | 34.00 | 34.00 |

**Half board**

| per person: | £min | £max |
|---|---|---|
| Daily | 25.00 | 25.00 |

Evening meal 1830 (last orders 1700)
Parking for 2

---

Colour maps at the back of this guide pinpoint all places which have accommodation listings in the guide.

## FORDINGBRIDGE

Hampshire
Map ref 2B3

On the north-west edge of the New Forest. A medieval bridge crosses the Avon at this point and gave the town its name. A good centre for walking, exploring and fishing.

### Hillbury

Listed

2 Fir Tree Hill, Camel Green Road, Alderholt, Fordingbridge SP6 3AY
☎ (01425) 652582
Fax (01425) 652582
*Bungalow in quiet situation with easy access to M27. Ideal touring base for New Forest and South Coast. Riding, swimming, golf and fishing nearby. Sorry, no pets or smokers.*
Bedrooms: 1 single, 1 twin, 1 triple
Bathrooms: 1 private, 1 public

| **Bed & breakfast per night:** | £min | £max |
|---|---|---|
| Single | 15.00 | 17.00 |
| Double | 30.00 | 34.00 |

Parking for 5
[UL] [S] [T]

## GERRARDS CROSS

Buckinghamshire
Map ref 2D2

On the London Road, Gerrards Cross is distinguished by its wide gorse and beech tree common.

### Dovetails

Listed

Upway, Chalfont Heights, Chalfont St Peter, Gerrards Cross SL9 0AS
☎ (01753) 882639
*60-year-old detached house in large garden, on a quiet, private estate.*
Bedrooms: 2 twin
Bathrooms: 1 public

| **Bed & breakfast per night:** | £min | £max |
|---|---|---|
| Single | 20.00 | 25.00 |
| Double | 35.00 | 40.00 |

| **Half board per person:** | £min | £max |
|---|---|---|
| Daily | 27.50 | 32.50 |
| Weekly | 185.00 | 200.00 |

Evening meal 1800 (last orders 2000)
Parking for 2
[UL] [S] [T]

Half board prices shown are per person but in some cases may be based on double/twin occupancy.

## GORING

Oxfordshire
Map ref 2C2

Riverside town on the Oxfordshire/Berkshire border, linked by an attractive bridge to Streatley with views to the Goring Gap.

### The John Barleycorn

👑

Manor Road, Goring, Reading, Berkshire RG8 9DP
☎ (01491) 872509
*16th C inn with exposed beams. Real ale, home-cooked food. Close to the river, lovely walks.*
Bedrooms: 1 single, 1 double, 1 triple
Bathrooms: 2 public

| **Bed & breakfast per night:** | £min | £max |
|---|---|---|
| Single | 25.00 | |
| Double | 40.00 | |

Lunch available
Evening meal 1900 (last orders 2200)
Parking for 2
Cards accepted: Access, Visa, Switch/Delta
[S]

## GREAT HORWOOD

Buckinghamshire
Map ref 2C1

### Mill Farm

Listed

Winslow Road, Great Horwood, Milton Keynes MK17 0NY
☎ Winslow (01296) 712527
*52-acre livestock farm. House in a quiet location, with views across open country. On B4033 between Winslow and Great Horwood. Access to North Bucks Way. Non-smokers only, please.*
Bedrooms: 1 double, 1 triple
Bathrooms: 1 public

| **Bed & breakfast per night:** | £min | £max |
|---|---|---|
| Single | 15.50 | 15.50 |
| Double | 30.00 | 30.00 |

Parking for 25
[UL] [S] [TV]

## HAMBLEDON

Hampshire
Map ref 2C3

In a valley, surrounded by wooded downland and marked by an air of Georgian prosperity. It was here that cricket was given its first proper rules. The Bat and Ball Inn at Broadhalfpenny Down is the cradle of cricket.

### Cams

👑👑

Hambledon, Waterlooville PO7 4SP
☎ Portsmouth (01705) 632865
Fax (01705) 632691
*Comfortable, listed family house in beautiful setting with large garden on the edge of Hambledon village. Two pubs within walking distance. Evening meal by arrangement.*
Bedrooms: 1 double, 2 twin
Bathrooms: 1 private, 1 public, 1 private shower

| **Bed & breakfast per night:** | £min | £max |
|---|---|---|
| Single | 15.00 | 16.00 |
| Double | 30.00 | 36.00 |

| **Half board per person:** | £min | £max |
|---|---|---|
| Daily | 25.00 | 30.00 |
| Weekly | 160.00 | 195.00 |

Evening meal from 1900
Parking for 6
[UL] [TV]

### Mornington House

Listed

Speltham Hill, Hambledon, Waterlooville PO7 4RU
☎ Portsmouth (01705) 632704
*18th C private house with 2 acres of garden and paddock, in the centre of Hambledon behind the George Inn, 2 miles from famous Bat and Ball Inn.*
Bedrooms: 2 twin
Bathrooms: 1 public

| **Bed & breakfast per night:** | £min | £max |
|---|---|---|
| Single | 16.00 | 16.00 |
| Double | 30.00 | 30.00 |

Parking for 6
[UL] [S] [TV]

### Nightingale Cottage

👑👑 HIGHLY COMMENDED

Hoegate, Hambledon, Waterlooville PO7 4RD
☎ Portsmouth (01705) 632447
Fax (01705) 632027
*Country house with picturesque garden on outskirts of Hambledon, adjacent to Hoegate Common but only half a mile from B2150. In an Area of Outstanding Natural Beauty.*
Bedrooms: 2 double, 1 twin
Bathrooms: 3 private, 1 public

| **Bed & breakfast per night:** | £min | £max |
|---|---|---|
| Single | 20.00 | 25.00 |
| Double | 38.00 | |

Parking for 8
Cards accepted: Access, Visa
11 [UL] [S] [TV] [SP]

National Crown ratings were correct at the time of going to press but are subject to change. Please check at the time of booking.

## HAVANT

Hampshire
Map ref 2C3

Once a market town famous for making parchment. Nearby at Leigh Park extensive early 19th C landscape gardens and parklands are open to the public. Right in the centre of the town stands the interesting 13th C church of St Faith.
*Tourist Information Centre*
☎ *(01705) 480024*

### The Old Mill Guest House M

Mill Lane, Bedhampton, Havant
PO9 3JH
☎ Portsmouth (01705) 454948
Fax (01705) 499677
*Georgian house in large grounds by a lake abundant in wildlife. Modernised, comfortable retreat. John Keats rested here.*
Bedrooms: 1 twin, 4 triple
Bathrooms: 5 private

| Bed & breakfast per night: | £min | £max |
|---|---|---|
| Single | 23.00 | 25.00 |
| Double | 36.00 | 39.00 |
| Parking for 10 | | |

## HAYLING ISLAND

Hampshire
Map ref 2C3

Small, flat island of historic interest, surrounded by natural harbours and with fine sandy beaches, linked to the mainland by a road.

### Newtown House Hotel M

Manor Road, Hayling Island
PO11 0QR
☎ Portsmouth (01705) 466131
Fax (01705) 461366
*18th C converted farmhouse, set in own grounds a quarter of a mile from seafront. Indoor leisure complex with heated pool, gym, steamroom, jacuzzi and sauna. Tennis.*
Bedrooms: 10 single, 11 double, 4 twin, 3 triple
Bathrooms: 28 private, 2 public

| Bed & breakfast per night: | £min | £max |
|---|---|---|
| Single | 35.00 | |
| Double | 55.00 | |

| Half board per person: | £min | £max |
|---|---|---|
| Daily | 48.00 | |
| Weekly | 290.00 | |

Lunch available
Evening meal 1900 (last orders 2130)
Parking for 45

Cards accepted: Access, Visa, Diners, Amex

## HENLEY-ON-THAMES

Oxfordshire
Map ref 2C2

The famous Thames Regatta is held in this prosperous and attractive town at the beginning of July each year. The town has many Georgian buildings and old coaching inns and the parish church has some fine monuments.

### Alftrudis

HIGHLY COMMENDED
8 Norman Avenue, Henley-on-Thames
RG9 1SG
☎ (01491) 573099
*Friendly detached Victorian house in quiet, private road, centrally situated two minutes' walk from the station, town centre and the river. Easy parking.*
Bedrooms: 1 double, 1 twin, 1 triple
Bathrooms: 1 private, 1 public

| Bed & breakfast per night: | £min | £max |
|---|---|---|
| Single | 20.00 | 25.00 |
| Double | 30.00 | 36.00 |
| Parking for 2 | | |

### Crowsley House

Listed
Crowsley Road, Shiplake, Henley-on-Thames RG9 3JT
☎ Wargrave (01734) 403197
*Attractive house in quiet riverside village, close to Henley-on-Thames. Convenient for Oxford, London, Windsor and Heathrow.*
Bedrooms: 1 double, 2 twin
Bathrooms: 2 public

| Bed & breakfast per night: | £min | £max |
|---|---|---|
| Single | 18.00 | |
| Double | 36.00 | |
| Parking for 4 | | |

### Lenwade M

COMMENDED
3 Western Road, Henley-on-Thames
RG9 1JL
☎ (01491) 573468
*Victorian house in quiet surroundings, within walking distance of the River Thames and town centre. Children welcome. Parking available.*
Bedrooms: 2 double, 2 twin
Bathrooms: 2 private, 2 public

| Bed & breakfast per night: | £min | £max |
|---|---|---|
| Single | 20.00 | 25.00 |
| Double | 30.00 | 40.00 |
| Parking for 2 | | |

### Loreparmoor M

Listed   HIGHLY COMMENDED
Little Parmoor Farm, Frieth, Henley-on-Thames RG9 6NL
☎ High Wycombe (01494) 881600
*220-acre mixed farm. Retreat to the Hambleden Valley. 16th C farmhouse with oak beams and log fires. Peaceful walks in magnificent beechwoods. Ten minutes from Henley and Marlow.*
Bedrooms: 1 double, 2 twin
Bathrooms: 1 private, 1 public

| Bed & breakfast per night: | £min | £max |
|---|---|---|
| Single | 20.00 | 30.00 |
| Double | 36.00 | 45.00 |

Parking for 4
Cards accepted: Access, Visa

### Mervyn House M

COMMENDED
4 St Marks Road, Henley-on-Thames
RG9 1LJ
☎ (01491) 575331 & 411747
*Victorian house, situated in a residential road, very close to Henley town centre, station, restaurant, pubs and river. Convenient for Windsor, Oxford and London, M4 and M40.*
Bedrooms: 2 double, 1 twin
Bathrooms: 1 public

| Bed & breakfast per night: | £min | £max |
|---|---|---|
| Single | 15.99 | 21.00 |
| Double | 28.00 | 35.00 |

### New Lodge M

COMMENDED
Henley Park, Henley-on-Thames
RG9 6HU
☎ (01491) 576340
*Victorian lodge in parkland in Area of Outstanding Natural Beauty. Lovely walks and views. Only 1 mile from Henley, 45 minutes from Heathrow.*
Bedrooms: 2 double
Bathrooms: 2 private

| Bed & breakfast per night: | £min | £max |
|---|---|---|
| Single | 22.00 | 26.00 |
| Double | 29.00 | 39.00 |

Parking for 7

### Pennyford House M

APPROVED
Peppard Common, Henley-on-Thames
RG9 5JE
☎ Rotherfield Greys (01491) 628272
*Family home offering evening meals and packed lunches, by prior arrangement.*
Bedrooms: 3 double
Bathrooms: 3 private, 1 public

Continued ▶

329

## HENLEY-ON-THAMES

*Continued*

**Bed & breakfast**

| per night: | £min | £max |
|---|---|---|
| Single | 17.00 | 27.50 |
| Double | 33.00 | 50.00 |

**Half board**

| per person: | £min | £max |
|---|---|---|
| Daily | 28.00 | 35.00 |

Parking for 7

♿ ⌂ ❒ ♦ ⓤⓛ 🅸 ⓢ ⌿ 📺 ⛁ 🗟 ▸ ✿ ⇝ SP

### Windy Brow

**Listed**

204 Victoria Road, Wargrave, Reading,
Berkshire RG10 8AJ
☎ Reading (01734) 403336
*Friendly accommodation in a spacious
Victorian house with garden
overlooking farmland. 3 miles from
Henley-on-Thames, 12 miles from
Windsor. Heathrow Airport half an hour
away. Colour TV and tea/coffee
facilities in rooms. Excellent pub food
locally.*
Bedrooms: 1 single, 1 double, 1 twin,
1 triple
Bathrooms: 3 private, 2 public

**Bed & breakfast**

| per night: | £min | £max |
|---|---|---|
| Single | 17.50 | 35.00 |
| Double | 36.00 | 45.00 |

Parking for 7

♿ ⌖ ⌂ ♦ ⓤⓛ ⓢ ⌿ ⛁ 🗟 ✿ ⇝ SP 🏠

## HOOK NORTON

Oxfordshire
Map ref 2C1

Quiet town with a history dating
back 1000 years when the
Normans built and buttressed its
chancel walls against attack from
the invading Danes.

### Pear Tree Inn

**COMMENDED**

Scotland End, Hook Norton, Banbury
OX15 5NU
☎ (01608) 737482
*Old beamed pub, near famous Hook
Norton brewery. 5 miles from Chipping
Norton, close to Banbury and the
Cotswolds.*
Bedrooms: 1 double
Bathrooms: 1 private

**Bed & breakfast**

| per night: | £min | £max |
|---|---|---|
| Single | 20.00 | |
| Double | 35.00 | |

Lunch available
Evening meal 1800 (last orders 2000)
Parking for 11

♿ ⌂ ♦ 🅸 ⓢ ⛁ 🗟 ▸ ∪ ▸ ✿ ⇝ SP

## HORTON

Dorset
Map ref 2B3

### The Horton Inn ⚠

**COMMENDED**

Cranborne Road, Horton, Wimborne
Minster BH21 5AD
☎ Witchampton (01258) 840252
Fax (01258) 841400
*18th C coaching inn set in the beautiful
Dorset downlands, with scenic views.
High standard of cuisine using fresh
local produce. Warm welcome.*
Bedrooms: 1 single, 1 double, 3 twin,
1 triple
Bathrooms: 2 private, 1 public

**Bed & breakfast**

| per night: | £min | £max |
|---|---|---|
| Single | 17.50 | 40.00 |
| Double | 40.00 | 50.00 |

Lunch available
Evening meal 1900 (last orders 2130)
Parking for 100
Cards accepted: Access, Visa, Switch/
Delta

♿ ⌂ ❒ ♦ 🅸 ⓢ ⛁ 🗟 📷 6-30 ∪ ▸ ▸
✎ ✿ ⇝ ⚲ SP 🏠

## HYTHE

Hampshire
Map ref 2C3

### Changri-La

**HIGHLY COMMENDED**

12 Ashleigh Close, Hythe,
Southampton SO4 6QP
☎ Southampton (01703) 846664
*Spacious comfortable home, in unique
position on edge of New Forest, a few
minutes' drive from Beaulieu and other
places of interest. Golf-course, pony
trekking and sports complex nearby.*
Bedrooms: 1 single, 1 double, 1 twin
Bathrooms: 2 public

**Bed & breakfast**

| per night: | £min | £max |
|---|---|---|
| Single | 14.50 | 15.00 |
| Double | 28.00 | 30.00 |

Parking for 3

⌖ ♦ ⓤⓛ ⓢ 🅿 📺 ⛁ 🗟 ✕ ⇝

## ISLE OF WIGHT

*See under Ryde, Ryde-Wootton,
Shalfleet*

## KIMMERIDGE

Dorset
Map ref 2B3

### Kimmeridge Farmhouse

**Listed**

Kimmeridge, Wareham BH20 5PE
☎ Corfe Castle (01929) 480990
*750-acre mixed farm. Farmhouse built
in the 16th C, with lovely views of
surrounding countryside and sea. Warm
family atmosphere and spacious*

*facilities. Evening meals by
arrangement with local inn.*
Bedrooms: 2 double, 1 twin
Bathrooms: 1 private, 1 public

**Bed & breakfast**

| per night: | £min | £max |
|---|---|---|
| Single | 20.00 | 25.00 |
| Double | 32.00 | 35.00 |

Parking for 3

♿ ⌖ ⌂ ❒ ♦ ⓤⓛ ⓢ ⛁ 🗟 ▸ ✿ ✕ ⇝ 🏠

## KINGSTON LISLE

Oxfordshire
Map ref 2C2

### The Blowing Stone Inn ⚠

**COMMENDED**

Kingston Lisle, Wantage OX12 9QL
☎ Faringdon (01367) 820288
*Village inn with conservatory
restaurant. Open 7 days a week.
Situated 5 miles from Wantage on the
B4507.*
Bedrooms: 2 double, 1 twin
Bathrooms: 3 private, 1 public

**Bed & breakfast**

| per night: | £min | £max |
|---|---|---|
| Single | 25.00 | |
| Double | 42.00 | 45.00 |

Lunch available
Evening meal 1900 (last orders 2130)
Parking for 30
Cards accepted: Access, Visa, Amex

♿ ⌂ ❒ ♦ 🅸 ⓢ ⌿ ⛁ ® ◕ ▸ ▸ ✎ ✿ ✕
⚲ SP

## LAMBOURN

Berkshire
Map ref 2C2

Attractive village among the
Downs on the River Lambourn.
Famous for its racing stables.

### Lodge Down ⚠

**COMMENDED**

Lambourn, Newbury RG16 7BJ
☎ Marlborough (01672) 40304
Fax (01672) 40304

*70-acre arable farm. Country house with
quality accommodation and en-suite
bathrooms, set in lovely grounds. Exit
junction 14 of M4, take B4000 and
follow signs to Baydon. Lodge Down is
1 mile before Baydon (300 metres down
drive).*
Bedrooms: 1 single, 1 twin, 1 triple
Bathrooms: 2 private, 1 public

**Bed & breakfast**

| per night: | £min | £max |
|---|---|---|
| Single | 20.00 | 20.00 |
| Double | 40.00 | 40.00 |

Evening meal 1830 (last orders 2030)
Parking for 5

🐾🛴♿🗢🖾UL🗇⚡📺📖,🖾🗢🔍↻♪❄
🚗🗦SP

## LITTLE LONDON

Hampshire
Map ref 2C2

### Bangla 🅜
Listed

Silchester Road, Little London,
Basingstoke RG26 5EP
☎ Basingstoke (01256) 850735
*Modern, chalet bungalow in village of
Little London, 6 miles from
Basingstoke. Adjacent to Pamber Forest
Nature Reserve.*
Bedrooms: 1 single, 1 double, 1 twin
Bathrooms: 2 public
**Bed & breakfast**

| per night: | £min | £max |
|---|---|---|
| Single | 12.50 | 15.00 |
| Double | 27.00 | |

Parking for 4

🐾🛴🗢🖳🍴♿UL🗇S📺📖,🖾❄
🚗DAPSP

## LITTLE WITTENHAM

Oxfordshire
Map ref 2C2

### Rooks Orchard
👑👑 HIGHLY COMMENDED

Little Wittenham, Abingdon OX14 4QY
☎ Clifton Hampden (01865) 407765
*Attractive, peaceful and welcoming
listed 17th C house and garden, in
pretty Thameside village next to nature
reserve and Wiltenham Clumps.
"Wonderful breakfasts". Abingdon,
Didcot and Wallingford approximately 4
miles, Oxford 9 miles.*
Bedrooms: 1 double, 1 family room
Bathrooms: 2 private, 1 public
**Bed & breakfast**

| per night: | £min | £max |
|---|---|---|
| Single | 20.00 | 25.00 |
| Double | 38.00 | 44.00 |

Parking for 6

🐾🛴🗢🖳♿UL🗇S🍴♿📺📖,🖾❄
🚗DAP🗦🏠

## LYMINGTON

Hampshire
Map ref 2C3

Small, pleasant town with bright
cottages and attractive Georgian
houses, lying on the edge of the
New Forest with a ferry service to
the Isle of Wight. A sheltered
harbour makes it a busy yachting
centre.

### Admiral House
Listed

5 Stanley Road, Lymington SO41 3SJ
☎ (01590) 674339
*House exclusively for guests, with the
owner next door. 200 yards from
countryside conservation area and
marinas. Many pubs and restaurants
nearby.*
Bedrooms: 1 single, 1 twin, 1 triple
Bathrooms: 1 public
**Bed & breakfast**

| per night: | £min | £max |
|---|---|---|
| Single | 11.00 | 12.50 |
| Double | 22.00 | 25.00 |

🐾🛴♿UL🗗📺📖,🖾↻❄🚗

### Altworth 🅜
Listed APPROVED

12 North Close, Lymington SO41 9BT
☎ (01590) 674082
*Near centre of town in quiet residential
street, 5 minutes from bus/railway
stations and Isle of Wight ferry. Within
30 minutes of Southampton and
Bournemouth, with Brockenhurst and
New Forest area only 10 minutes away.*
Bedrooms: 1 single, 1 double, 1 triple
Bathrooms: 1 public
**Bed & breakfast**

| per night: | £min | £max |
|---|---|---|
| Single | 13.50 | 14.00 |
| Double | 24.00 | 25.00 |

Open April-October

🐾🛴♿S📖✕

### Our Bench 🅜
👑👑 COMMENDED

9 Lodge Road, Pennington, Lymington
SO41 8HH
☎ (01590) 673141
Fax (01590) 673141

*Some en-suite ground floor bedrooms,
separate TV lounge, indoor heated pool,
jacuzzi and sauna. Non-smokers only
please and, sorry, no children.*
Bedrooms: 1 single, 1 double, 1 twin
Bathrooms: 3 private
**Bed & breakfast**

| per night: | £min | £max |
|---|---|---|
| Single | 17.00 | 23.00 |
| Double | 35.00 | 39.00 |

**Half board**

| per person: | £min | £max |
|---|---|---|
| Daily | 22.00 | 30.00 |
| Weekly | 154.00 | 210.00 |

Evening meal 1900 (last orders 2100)
Parking for 5

🛴♿🗢🖾♿S✕📺📖,🖾🗢🔍↻
❄✕🚗DAPSP T

## LYNDHURST

Hampshire
Map ref 2C3

The "capital" of the New Forest,
surrounded by attractive woodland
scenery and delightful villages. The
town is dominated by the Victorian
Gothic-style church where the
original Alice in Wonderland is
buried.
*Tourist Information Centre
☎ (01703) 282269*

### Burton House 🅜
👑👑

Romsey Road, Lyndhurst SO43 7AA
☎ Southampton (01703) 282445
*Continued ▶*

## LYNDHURST

### Continued

*Lovely house in half-acre garden, near the village centre. All rooms with en-suite shower, WC and washbasin. Parking in grounds.*
Bedrooms: 1 single, 2 double, 1 twin, 1 triple, 1 family room
Bathrooms: 6 private

**Bed & breakfast**

| per night: | £min | £max |
| --- | --- | --- |
| Single | 20.00 | |
| Double | 32.00 | 38.00 |

Parking for 8

☎ ⛔ Ⓢ ♨ 📺 🛏 ■ ⚓ ❀ ✕ ♣

### Forest Cottage

Listed

High Street, Lyndhurst SO43 7BH
☎ Southampton (01703) 283461
*Charming 300-year-old cottage with welcoming atmosphere in the village, yet open forest only yards away. Guest lounge with open fire.*
Bedrooms: 1 single, 1 double, 1 twin
Bathrooms: 2 public

**Bed & breakfast**

| per night: | £min | £max |
| --- | --- | --- |
| Single | 16.00 | 17.00 |
| Double | 30.00 | 32.00 |

Parking for 3

⛔ ⓘ Ⓢ ♨ 📺 🛏 ■ ⚓ ❀ ✕ ♣ SP

### Little Hayes ⋀

👑 HIGHLY COMMENDED

43 Romsey Road, Lyndhurst
SO43 7AR
☎ Southampton (01703) 283000

*Lovely Victorian home, beautifully restored and furnished. Spacious rooms, friendly atmosphere and wonderful breakfast. Close to village centre and forest walks.*
Bedrooms: 2 double, 1 twin
Bathrooms: 1 private, 1 public

**Bed & breakfast**

| per night: | £min | £max |
| --- | --- | --- |
| Single | 20.00 | 25.00 |
| Double | 32.00 | 38.00 |

Parking for 4
Open February-October
Cards accepted: Access, Visa, Switch/
Delta

☎ 5 □ ♨ ⛔ ⓘ Ⓢ ♨ 📺 🛏 ■ ⚓ ✕ ♣ OAP SP

### The Penny Farthing Hotel ⋀

👑 COMMENDED

Romsey Road, Lyndhurst SO43 7AA
☎ Southampton (01703) 284422
Fax (01703) 284488

*Perfectly situated small hotel, 1 minute's walk from village centre, shops, restaurants, 2 minutes from open forest. Tastefully furnished rooms ensure a comfortable stay.*
Bedrooms: 3 single, 5 double, 1 twin, 1 triple, 1 family room
Bathrooms: 11 private

**Bed & breakfast**

| per night: | £min | £max |
| --- | --- | --- |
| Single | 25.00 | 35.00 |
| Double | 45.00 | 70.00 |

Parking for 15
Cards accepted: Access, Visa

☎ ⛁ 📞 ◫ □ ♨ ⓘ Ⓢ ♨ 📺 🛏 ■ ∪ ♣ SP
[Ad] Display advertisement appears on page 331

## MAIDENHEAD

### Berkshire
### Map ref 2C2

Attractive town on the River Thames which is crossed by an elegant 18th C bridge and by Brunel's well-known railway bridge. It is a popular place for boating with delightful riverside walks. The Courage Shire Horse Centre is nearby.
*Tourist Information Centre*
☎ *(01628) 781110*

### Cartlands Cottage

👑 APPROVED

Kings Lane, Cookham Dean, Cookham, Maidenhead SL6 9AY
☎ Marlow (01628) 482196
*Family room in self-contained garden studio. Meals in delightful timbered character cottage with exposed beams. Traditional cottage garden. National Trust common land. Very quiet.*
Bedrooms: 1 triple
Bathrooms: 1 private, 1 public

**Bed & breakfast**

| per night: | £min | £max |
| --- | --- | --- |
| Single | 18.00 | 20.00 |
| Double | 34.00 | 37.00 |

Parking for 4

☎ ⛁ ㈅ ◫ □ ♨ ♦ ⛏ ⛔ ⓘ ✕ 📺 🛏 ■
❀ ♣

### Moor Farm ⋀

👑 HIGHLY COMMENDED

Ascot Road, Holyport, Maidenhead
SL6 2HY
☎ (01628) 33761
Fax (01628) 33761
*100-acre mixed farm. 700-year-old medieval manor in picturesque Holyport village. 4 miles from Windsor, 12 miles from Heathrow.*
Bedrooms: 2 twin

Bathrooms: 2 private
**Bed & breakfast**

| per night: | £min | £max |
| --- | --- | --- |
| Double | 38.00 | 45.00 |

Parking for 4

☎ ⛔ Ⓢ ✕ ♨ 📺 🛏 ■ ⚓ ∪ ♦ ❀ ✕ ♣ ⊞

### "Sheephouse Manor" ⋀

👑 COMMENDED

Sheephouse Road, Maidenhead
SL6 8HJ
☎ (01628) 776902
Fax (01628) 25138
*Charming 16th C farmhouse in tranquil setting, close to River Thames. All rooms en-suite. Sauna, jacuzzi and gym available. Easy access to M4/M40.*
Bedrooms: 2 single, 2 double, 1 twin
Bathrooms: 5 private

**Bed & breakfast**

| per night: | £min | £max |
| --- | --- | --- |
| Single | 28.00 | 32.00 |
| Double | 38.00 | 44.00 |

Parking for 12
Cards accepted: Access, Visa, Switch/
Delta

☎ 1 ㈅ ⛏ □ ♦ ⛔ Ⓢ ♨ 📺 🛏 ■ ⚓ ⟲
✕ ● ❀ ♣ ⊞

## MARLOW

### Buckinghamshire
### Map ref 2C2

Attractive Georgian town on the River Thames, famous for its 19th C suspension bridge. The High Street contains many old houses and there are connections with writers including Shelley and the poet T S Eliot.

### Acha Pani ⋀

Listed COMMENDED

Bovingdon Green, Marlow SL7 2JL
☎ (01628) 483435
*Modern house with large garden, in quiet location 1 mile north of Marlow. No children or dogs please.*
Bedrooms: 1 single, 1 double, 1 twin
Bathrooms: 1 private, 1 public

**Bed & breakfast**

| per night: | £min | £max |
| --- | --- | --- |
| Single | 15.00 | 17.00 |
| Double | 30.00 | 35.00 |

Parking for 3

◫ ♦ ⛔ ⓘ Ⓢ ♨ 📺 🛏 ■ ⚓ ❀ ✕ ♣

### Holly Tree House ⋀

👑 HIGHLY COMMENDED

Burford Close, Marlow Bottom,
Marlow SL7 3NF
☎ (01628) 891110 & Mobile 0860 459880
Fax (01628) 481278
*Detached house set in large gardens with fine views over the valley. Quiet yet convenient location. Large car park. All rooms fully en-suite. Outdoor heated swimming pool.*
Bedrooms: 1 single, 4 double
Bathrooms: 5 private

| **Bed & breakfast per night:** | £min | £max |
|---|---|---|
| Single | 54.50 | |
| Double | 67.50 | 72.50 |

Parking for 10
Cards accepted: Access, Visa, Amex
🐴 🚿 ☎ 🛏 🖵 ☕ 🔑 [UL] [S] 📖 [TV] 📺 🧺
🏌8 🎣 ✿ 🚐

## 2 Hyde Green

[Listed]
Marlow SL7 1QL
☎ (01628) 483526
*Comfortable family home. Quietly situated yet only a few minutes' level walk from town centre, River Thames and station (Paddington 1 hour).*
Bedrooms: 1 double, 2 twin
Bathrooms: 2 private, 1 public

| **Bed & breakfast per night:** | £min | £max |
|---|---|---|
| Single | 22.00 | 25.00 |
| Double | 32.00 | 35.00 |

Parking for 2
🐴 🛏 🖵 ☕ [UL] 🚭 📺 🧺 ✈ 🚐

## Little Parmoor

[Listed]
Frieth, Henley-on-Thames, Oxfordshire RG9 6NL
☎ High Wycombe (01494) 881447
Fax (01494) 883012
*Period country house in Area of Outstanding Natural Beauty in the Chiltern Hills. Close to Marlow and Henley and easy access to Heathrow.*
Bedrooms: 1 single, 1 twin
Bathrooms: 1 private, 1 public

| **Bed & breakfast per night:** | £min | £max |
|---|---|---|
| Single | 18.00 | |
| Double | 44.00 | |

| **Half board per person:** | £min | £max |
|---|---|---|
| Daily | 31.00 | 35.00 |

Evening meal from 1930
Parking for 5
🐴 5 🖵 ☕ [UL] 🔒 [S] 🚭 📖 📺 🧺 U ✿ 🚐 🏠

## Monkton Farmhouse

[Listed] [COMMENDED]
Monkton Farm, Little Marlow, Marlow SL7 3RF
☎ High Wycombe (01494) 521082
Fax (01494) 443905
*150-acre dairy farm. 14th C cruckhouse set in beautiful countryside, easily reached by motorway, and close to shopping and sporting facilities.*
Bedrooms: 1 single, 1 twin, 1 triple
Bathrooms: 1 public

| **Bed & breakfast per night:** | £min | £max |
|---|---|---|
| Single | 18.00 | 20.00 |
| Double | 36.00 | 40.00 |

Parking for 6
🐴 5 🍴 🛏 🖵 ☕ 🔑 [UL] [S] 🚭 📖 📺 🧺
🏌10-30 ⛳ 🏏 ✿ ✈ 🚐 🏠

## 5 Pound Lane

[Listed]
Marlow SL7 2AE
☎ (01628) 482649
*Older style house, just off town centre, 2 minutes from River Thames and leisure complex. Double room has own balcony with delightful view.*
Bedrooms: 1 double, 1 twin
Bathrooms: 1 public

| **Bed & breakfast per night:** | £min | £max |
|---|---|---|
| Single | 22.00 | 25.00 |
| Double | 35.00 | 38.00 |

Parking for 2
🐴 🛏 🖵 ☕ 🔑 [UL] 🔒 [S] 🚭 📺 🧺 ✈ 🚐

## MILTON ABBAS

Dorset
Map ref 2B3

Sloping village street of thatched houses. A boys' school lies in Capability Brown's landscaped gardens amid hills and woods where the town once stood. The school chapel, former abbey church, can be visited.

## Dunbury Heights

[Listed] [HIGHLY COMMENDED]
Winterborne Stickland, Blandford Forum DT11 0DH
☎ (01258) 880445
*Always a friendly welcome at this brick and flint cottage. Outstanding views to Poole and Isle of Wight. 6 miles from Blandford Forum and 1 mile from the picturesque village of Milton Abbas.*
Bedrooms: 1 double, 1 twin
Bathrooms: 1 private, 1 public

| **Bed & breakfast per night:** | £min | £max |
|---|---|---|
| Single | 15.00 | 20.00 |
| Double | 30.00 | 35.00 |

Parking for 10
🐴 ☕ [UL] [S] 📖 [TV] 📺 🧺 ✿ 🚐

## MILTON KEYNES

Buckinghamshire
Map ref 2C1

Designated a New Town in 1967, Milton Keynes offers a wide range of housing and is abundantly planted with trees. It has excellent shopping facilities and 3 centres for leisure and sporting activities. The Open University is based here.
*Tourist Information Centre*
*☎ (01908) 232525*

## Chantry Farm

👑👑 [COMMENDED]
Pindon End, Hanslope, Milton Keynes MK19 7HL
☎ (01908) 510269
*600-acre mixed farm. Stone farmhouse built in 1650 with inglenook fireplaces, surrounded by open countryside. 15 minutes to city centre. Swimming pool, trout lake, table tennis, clay pigeon shooting.*
Bedrooms: 1 double, 2 twin
Bathrooms: 1 public, 1 private shower

| **Bed & breakfast per night:** | £min | £max |
|---|---|---|
| Single | 16.00 | 20.00 |
| Double | 35.00 | 36.00 |

Parking for 7
🐴 🖵 ☕ [UL] 🔒 [S] 📖 [TV] 📺 🧺 🏌 🎾 🎣 U
🏊 ⛳ 🏏 ✿ 🚐 [SP] 🏠

## Conifers Bed & Breakfast ♿

[Listed]
29 William Smith Close, Woolstone, Milton Keynes MK15 0AN
☎ (01908) 674506
*Every bedroom has a door leading to guests' garden patio. Only 1 mile from junction 14 of M1. Close to city centre, BR station and "National Bowl".*
Bedrooms: 1 single, 1 double, 1 twin
Bathrooms: 1 public

| **Bed & breakfast per night:** | £min | £max |
|---|---|---|
| Single | 17.50 | 20.00 |
| Double | 35.00 | 35.00 |

🐴 🍴 🚿 🖵 ☕ [UL] 🚭 [TV] 📺 ✿ ✈ 🚐

## The Croft ♿

👑👑
Little Crawley, Newport Pagnell MK16 9LT
☎ North Crawley (01234) 391296
*Spacious bungalow in open countryside, 15 minutes' drive from city centre. Nearby inns serve evening meals. Convenient for Bedford or Northampton.*
Bedrooms: 1 single, 2 double, 1 twin
Bathrooms: 2 private, 1 public

| **Bed & breakfast per night:** | £min | £max |
|---|---|---|
| Single | 14.50 | 15.50 |
| Double | 28.00 | 30.00 |

Parking for 6
🐴 4 🚿 🖵 ☕ [UL] 📺 🧺 ✿ ✈ 🚐

## The Grange Stables ♿

👑
Winslow Road, Great Horwood, Milton Keynes MK17 0QN
☎ Aylesbury (01296) 712051
Fax (01296) 714991
*A recently converted stable block offering comfortable and spacious accommodation. Conveniently situated opposite the Swan pub.*
Bedrooms: 3 twin
Bathrooms: 1 public, 1 private shower

| **Bed & breakfast per night:** | £min | £max |
|---|---|---|
| Single | 25.00 | 28.20 |
| Double | 35.00 | 41.12 |

Parking for 5
Cards accepted: Access, Visa
🐴 🚿 ☎ 🖵 ☕ 🔑 [UL] 🚭 📺 🧺 ✈ 🚐 🚫
[SP] 🏠

## MILTON KEYNES

### Continued

### Haversham Grange
Haversham, Milton Keynes MK19 7DX
☎ (01908) 312389
Fax (01908) 221554
*Large 14th C stone house with many interesting features. Set in own gardens backing on to lakes.*
Bedrooms: 3 twin
Bathrooms: 2 private, 1 public

**Bed & breakfast**

| per night: | £min | £max |
|---|---|---|
| Single | 20.00 | 23.00 |
| Double | 40.00 | 40.00 |

Parking for 6

🕙 8 🛏 ♿ 🏴 S ⅍ ⌶ ▦ ◨ 🔌 ☎ 10-12 🔍 ✝ 🌸 ✈ 🐾 🏠

### Michelville House
👑
Newton Road, Bletchley, Milton Keynes MK3 5BN
☎ (01908) 371578
*Clean compact establishment within easy reach of railway station, M1, shopping and sporting facilities. 10 minutes from Milton Keynes shopping centre.*
Bedrooms: 10 single, 6 twin
Bathrooms: 4 public

**Bed & breakfast**

| per night: | £min | £max |
|---|---|---|
| Single | 17.00 | 22.00 |
| Double | 32.00 | 40.00 |

Parking for 16

🕙 ♿ 🏴 ▦ ⌶ ▦ ✈

### Mill Farm
👑👑 COMMENDED
Gayhurst, Newport Pagnell MK16 8LT
☎ Newport Pagnell (01908) 611489
*505-acre mixed farm. 17th C farmhouse. Tennis, riding and fishing available on the farm. Good touring centre for Woburn, Oxford, Cambridge and Whipsnade.*
Bedrooms: 1 single, 1 twin, 1 triple
Bathrooms: 1 private, 2 public

**Bed & breakfast**

| per night: | £min | £max |
|---|---|---|
| Single | 15.00 | 20.00 |
| Double | 30.00 | 40.00 |

**Half board**

| per person: | £min | £max |
|---|---|---|
| Daily | 22.50 | 27.50 |

Evening meal 1900 (last orders 1600)
Parking for 12

🕙 ♿ 🛏 ♿ 🏴 S ⅍ ⌶ TV ▦ 🔌 🔍 ♿ U ♿ 🌸 🐾 SP 🏠

### Spinney Lodge Farm
👑
Forest Road, Hanslope, Milton Keynes MK19 7DE
☎ (01908) 510267
*350-acre arable and mixed farm. Victorian farmhouse in secluded situation. Superb walking facilities in*

---

*Salcey Forest. 15 minutes Milton Keynes and M1 junction 14, 8 minutes M1 junction 15.*
Bedrooms: 1 double, 1 twin
Bathrooms: 2 private

**Bed & breakfast**

| per night: | £min | £max |
|---|---|---|
| Single | 17.00 | 20.00 |
| Double | 32.00 | 40.00 |

Evening meal 1830 (last orders 1630)
Parking for 6

🕙 12 🛏 ♿ 🏴 S ⅍ ⌶ ▦ 🔌 ✝ ✈ 🐾 🏠

### Swan Revived Hotel ♠
👑👑👑 HIGHLY COMMENDED
High Street, Newport Pagnell, Milton Keynes MK16 8AR
☎ (01908) 610565
Fax (01908) 210995
*Independently owned and family-run, town house hotel, renowned former coaching inn, where guests can enjoy every modern comfort. Convenient for thriving new city of Milton Keynes.*
Bedrooms: 17 single, 20 double, 3 twin, 2 triple
Bathrooms: 42 private

**Bed & breakfast**

| per night: | £min | £max |
|---|---|---|
| Single | 30.00 | 58.00 |
| Double | 55.00 | 70.00 |

**Half board**

| per person: | £min | £max |
|---|---|---|
| Daily | 40.00 | 70.00 |

Lunch available
Evening meal 1915 (last orders 2200)
Parking for 18
Cards accepted: Access, Visa, Diners, Amex, Switch/Delta

🕙 ♿ 🛏 🕭 ♿ 🖂 🛏 ♿ 🖤 S ⅍ ▦ ◉ 🖃 ▦ 🔌 ☎ 2-75 DAP SP 🏠 T

## MINSTEAD

### Hampshire
### Map ref 2C3

Cluster of thatched cottages and detached period houses. The church, listed in the Domesday Book, has private boxes - one with its own fireplace.

### Acres Down Farm ♠
Listed
Minstead, Lyndhurst SO43 7GE
☎ Southampton (01703) 813693

*50-acre mixed farm. Homely New Forest working commoners' farm, in quiet surroundings opening directly on to open forest. Also self-catering cottage.*
Bedrooms: 2 double, 1 twin
Bathrooms: 1 public

---

**Bed & breakfast**

| per night: | £min | £max |
|---|---|---|
| Single | 15.00 | |
| Double | 30.00 | |

Parking for 6

🕙 ✂ ♿ 🏴 S ⅍ ⌶ TV ▦ 🔌 ☎ ✝ 🌸 ✈ 🐾 🏠

### Grove House
Listed
Newtown, Minstead, Lyndhurst SO43 7GG
☎ Southampton (01703) 813211
*9-acre smallholding. Attractive family home, set in quiet, rural position 3 miles from Lyndhurst, with superb walking, birdwatching and riding (stabling available).*
Bedrooms: 1 family room
Bathrooms: 1 private

**Bed & breakfast**

| per night: | £min | £max |
|---|---|---|
| Double | 30.00 | 35.00 |

Parking for 1

🕙 🖃 🛏 ♿ 🏴 S ⅍ ▦ 🌸 🏠

## MINSTER LOVELL

### Oxfordshire
### Map ref 2C1

Picturesque village on the River Windrush with thatched cottages and 19th C houses. Minster Lovell Hall, built in the 15th C by the Lovell family, is the subject of several legends and now stands in ruins in a beautiful riverside setting.

### Hill Grove Farm ♠
👑 HIGHLY COMMENDED
Crawley Road, Minster Lovell, Oxford OX8 5NA
☎ Witney (01993) 703120
Fax (01993) 700528
*300-acre mixed farm. Cotswold farmhouse run on a family basis, in an attractive rural setting overlooking the Windrush Valley. Pleasant rural walks.*
Bedrooms: 1 double, 1 twin
Bathrooms: 2 private

**Bed & breakfast**

| per night: | £min | £max |
|---|---|---|
| Double | 36.00 | 42.00 |

Parking for 4

🕙 🛏 ♿ 🏴 S ⅍ ⌶ TV ▦ 🔌 ✝ 🌸 ✈ 🐾

## MOCKBEGGAR

### Hampshire
### Map ref 2B3

### Plantation Cottage
👑👑 HIGHLY COMMENDED
Mockbeggar, Ringwood BH24 3NL
☎ Ringwood (01425) 477443
*Charming 200-year-old, Grade II listed cottage, set in lovely one-acre gardens and two-acre paddocks within New Forest.*
Bedrooms: 2 double, 1 twin

Bathrooms: 3 private
**Bed & breakfast**

| per night: | £min | £max |
|---|---|---|
| Single | 25.00 | 30.00 |
| Double | 40.00 | 45.00 |

Parking for 6

## NETHER WALLOP

Hampshire
Map ref 2C2

Winding lane leads to thatched cottages, cob walls of clay and straw and colourful gardens with the Wallop Brook running by St Andrew's Church. This has 11th C origins and a fine mural urging Sunday observance.

### The Great Barn

Five Bells Lane, Nether Wallop, Stockbridge SO20 8EN
☎ Andover (01264) 782142
*16th C barn, self-contained unit with private bathrooms. In beautiful village of Nether Wallop, setting for Agatha Christie's "Miss Marple" stories.*
Bedrooms: 1 double, 1 twin
Bathrooms: 2 private
**Bed & breakfast**

| per night: | £min | £max |
|---|---|---|
| Single | 25.00 | 25.00 |
| Double | 35.00 | 35.00 |

Parking for 2

## NEW FOREST

*See under Barton on Sea, Beaulieu, Bransgore, Burley, Cadnam, Dibden, Fordingbridge, Hythe, Lymington, Lyndhurst, Minstead, Mockbeggar, Ringwood, Sway, Tiptoe, Totton*

## NEWBURY

Berkshire
Map ref 2C2

Ancient town surrounded by the Downs and on the Kennet and Avon Canal. It has many buildings of interest, including the 17th C Cloth Hall, which is now a museum. The famous racecourse is nearby.
*Tourist Information Centre*
☎ *(01635) 30267*

### Mousefield Farm

**Listed**
Long Lane, Shaw, Newbury RG16 9LG
☎ (01635) 40333
*500-acre dairy farm. Farmhouse overlooking our own farmland, set in an Area of Outstanding Natural Beauty. Well-kept gardens and plenty of nature trails.*
Bedrooms: 1 twin, 2 triple

---

Bathrooms: 3 public
**Bed & breakfast**

| per night: | £min | £max |
|---|---|---|
| Single | 18.00 | 20.00 |
| Double | 36.00 | 40.00 |

**Half board**

| per person: | £min | £max |
|---|---|---|
| Daily | 25.00 | 27.00 |
| Weekly | 170.00 | 180.00 |

Evening meal 1830 (last orders 2030)
Parking for 12

### The Old Farmhouse

Downend Lane, Chieveley, Newbury RG16 8TN
☎ Chieveley (01635) 248361
*Small country farmhouse on edge of village. Within 1 mile of M4/A34 (junction 13) and close to Newbury. Accommodation in self-contained annexe.*
Bedrooms: 1 double, 1 family room
Bathrooms: 2 private, 1 public
**Bed & breakfast**

| per night: | £min | £max |
|---|---|---|
| Single | 18.50 | 20.00 |
| Double | 35.00 | 36.00 |

Parking for 5

## NEWTON LONGVILLE

Buckinghamshire
Map ref 2C1

### The Old Rectory

Drayton Road, Newton Longville, Milton Keynes MK17 0BH
☎ Milton Keynes (01908) 375794

*Brick built, listed Georgian house (1769), 6 miles south of Milton Keynes in village setting.*
Bedrooms: 2 double, 1 twin
Bathrooms: 1 private, 2 public, 1 private shower
**Bed & breakfast**

| per night: | £min | £max |
|---|---|---|
| Single | 15.00 | 18.00 |
| Double | 30.00 | 40.00 |

**Half board**

| per person: | £min | £max |
|---|---|---|
| Daily | 22.00 | 27.00 |
| Weekly | 140.00 | 165.00 |

Evening meal 1800 (last orders 2000)
Parking for 6

---

## OWSLEBURY

Hampshire
Map ref 2C3

Small farming village with Marwell Conservation Zoo close by.

### Tayinloan

**Listed** **HIGHLY COMMENDED**
Owslebury, Winchester SO21 1LP
☎ Winchester (01962) 777359
*Private house with extensive rural views. 4 miles from M3, 11 miles from M27. Easy access to Eastleigh Airport, 9 miles away, and Portsmouth ferries. Non-smokers only please.*
Bedrooms: 3 twin
Bathrooms: 3 private, 1 public
**Bed & breakfast**

| per night: | £min | £max |
|---|---|---|
| Single | 18.00 | 19.50 |
| Double | 36.00 | 39.00 |

Parking for 3

## OXFORD

Oxfordshire
Map ref 2C1

Beautiful university town with many ancient colleges, some dating from the 13th C, and numerous buildings of historic and architectural interest. The Ashmolean Museum has outstanding collections. Lovely gardens and meadows with punting on the Cherwell.
*Tourist Information Centre*
☎ *(01865) 726871*

### Acorn Guest House

**Listed**
260 Iffley Road, Oxford OX4 1SE
☎ (01865) 247998
*Situated midway between the centre of town and the ring-road and therefore convenient for local amenities and more distant attractions.*
Bedrooms: 2 single, 1 twin, 3 triple
Bathrooms: 2 public
**Bed & breakfast**

| per night: | £min | £max |
|---|---|---|
| Single | 20.00 | 26.00 |
| Double | 34.00 | 40.00 |

Parking for 5
Cards accepted: Access, Visa

### All Views

**COMMENDED**
67 Old Witney Road, On main A40, Eynsham, Oxford OX8 1PU
☎ (01865) 880891
*7-acre livestock farm. 1991-built Cotswold-stone chalet bungalow, adjacent A40 between Oxford and Witney. Designed with guests' comfort in mind. All rooms have full facilities.*
Bedrooms: 1 single, 2 double, 1 twin

*Continued* ▶

## OXFORD

*Continued*

Bathrooms: 4 private
**Bed & breakfast**

| per night: | £min | £max |
|---|---|---|
| Single | 30.00 | 36.00 |
| Double | 40.00 | 46.00 |

Parking for 30

🛇 8 👥 🛏 📞 🖭 🗗 ♨ 🖤 UL 🕅 TV 🞕 🗮 ⚓ ✿
✕ 🛋 SP

### Becket House
**Listed**

5 Becket Street, Oxford OX1 7PP
☎ (01865) 724675
*Friendly guesthouse convenient for rail
and bus station, within walking distance
of city centre and colleges. Good, clean
accommodation, en-suite rooms.*
Bedrooms: 4 single, 1 double, 3 twin,
1 triple
Bathrooms: 2 private, 3 public
**Bed & breakfast**

| per night: | £min | £max |
|---|---|---|
| Single | 20.00 | 40.00 |
| Double | 32.00 | 50.00 |

Cards accepted: Access, Visa

🛇 👥 🗗 ♨ UL 🕅 S TV 🞕 🗮 ⚓ 🛋

### The Bungalow
**Listed**

Cherwell Farm, Mill Lane, Old
Marston, Oxford OX3 0QF
☎ (01865) 57171
*Modern bungalow set in 5 acres, in
quiet location with views over open
countryside, but within 3 miles of city
centre. No smoking.*
Bedrooms: 2 double, 1 twin
Bathrooms: 1 private, 1 public
**Bed & breakfast**

| per night: | £min | £max |
|---|---|---|
| Single | 18.00 | 20.00 |
| Double | 34.00 | 45.00 |

Parking for 4
Open April-October

🛇 6 ⚁ 👥 🗗 ♨ 🖤 UL 🕅 ✕ TV 🞕 🗮 ⚓ ✿
✕ 🛋

### Cherwell Croft
**COMMENDED**

72 Church Street, Kidlington
OX5 2BB
☎ Kidlington (01865) 373371
*Georgian stone-built house in its own
grounds. Quiet and attractive part of
Kidlington by St Mary's Church. 4 miles
from Oxford and 2 miles from
Blenheim.*
Bedrooms: 1 single, 1 double, 1 twin
Bathrooms: 1 public
**Bed & breakfast**

| per night: | £min | £max |
|---|---|---|
| Single | 16.00 | 18.00 |
| Double | 30.00 | 32.00 |

Parking for 3

🛇 ⚁ ♨ UL 🕅 S TV 🞕 🗮 ⚓ ✿ 🛋 🞖

### Gables 🏨
**COMMENDED**

6 Cumnor Hill, Oxford OX2 9HA
☎ (01865) 862153
*Gables offers warm hospitality combined
with a high standard of comfort and
service. Easy access to Cotswolds and
city centre.*
Bedrooms: 2 single, 2 double, 1 twin,
1 triple
Bathrooms: 5 private, 2 public
**Bed & breakfast**

| per night: | £min | £max |
|---|---|---|
| Single | 18.00 | 24.00 |
| Double | 36.00 | 44.00 |

Parking for 8
Cards accepted: Access, Visa

🛇 ⚁ 🗗 ♨ UL 🕅 ✕ 🞕 TV 🞕 🗮 ⚓ 🛋

### High Hedges
**COMMENDED**

8 Cumnor Hill, Oxford OX2 9HA
☎ (01865) 863395
*Close to city centre, offering a high
standard of accommodation for a
comfortable and happy stay in Oxford.*
Bedrooms: 2 double, 1 twin
Bathrooms: 1 private, 1 public
**Bed & breakfast**

| per night: | £min | £max |
|---|---|---|
| Double | 34.00 | 40.00 |

Parking for 3

🛇 ⚁ 🗗 ♨ UL 🕅 S 🞕 🕅 TV 🞕 🗮 ⚓ ✿
🛋 OAP

### Isis Guest House 🏨
**Listed  APPROVED**

45-53 Iffley Road, Oxford OX4 1ED
☎ (01865) 248894 & 242466
*Modernised, Victorian, city centre
guesthouse within walking distance of
colleges and shops. Easy access to ring
road.*
Bedrooms: 12 single, 6 double,
17 twin, 2 triple
Bathrooms: 14 private, 10 public
**Bed & breakfast**

| per night: | £min | £max |
|---|---|---|
| Single | 19.00 | 25.00 |
| Double | 38.00 | 42.00 |

Parking for 18
Open June-September
Cards accepted: Access, Visa

🛇 ⚁ 📞 ♨ UL 🕅 ✕ 🞕 🗮 ⚓ OAP T

### 21 Lincoln Road
🏨

Oxford OX1 4TB
☎ (01865) 246944
*Cosy semi-detached home offering
ground floor room with separate access
to street. Convenient for north and
south ring roads and within walking
distance of city centre.*
Bedrooms: 1 single
Bathrooms: 1 private
**Bed & breakfast**

| per night: | £min | £max |
|---|---|---|
| Single | 20.00 | 23.00 |

Parking for 2

⚁ 🗗 ♨ 🞕 UL S ✕ 🞕 ✿ ✕ 🛋

### Mount Pleasant 🏨
**APPROVED**

76 London Road, Headington, Oxford
OX3 9AJ
☎ (01865) 62749
Fax (01865) 62749
*Small, family-run hotel offering full
facilities. On the A40 and convenient
for Oxford shopping, hospitals, colleges,
visiting the Chilterns and the Cotswolds.*
Bedrooms: 2 double, 5 twin, 1 triple
Bathrooms: 8 private
**Bed & breakfast**

| per night: | £min | £max |
|---|---|---|
| Single | 35.00 | 45.00 |
| Double | 45.00 | 75.00 |

**Half board**

| per person: | £min | £max |
|---|---|---|
| Daily | 35.00 | 47.50 |

Lunch available
Evening meal 1800 (last orders 2130)
Parking for 6
Cards accepted: Access, Visa, Diners,
Amex

🛇 📞 🗗 ♨ 🞖 🞕 S ✕ 🕅 🞕 🗮 ⚓ ✕ 🛋
SP T

### Newton House 🏨
🞖

82-84 Abingdon Road, Oxford
OX1 4PL
☎ (01865) 240561
*Centrally located, Victorian townhouse
with comfortable homely
accommodation, warm welcome and
friendly atmosphere. Special diets
catered for on request.*
Bedrooms: 7 double, 4 twin, 1 triple,
1 family room
Bathrooms: 5 private, 3 public
**Bed & breakfast**

| per night: | £min | £max |
|---|---|---|
| Single | 20.00 | 37.00 |
| Double | 30.00 | 47.00 |

Parking for 8
Cards accepted: Access, Visa, Amex

🛇 ⚁ 🗗 ♨ 🞕 S 🞕 🞖 🞕 🞕 🗮 ⚓ ✕ OAP SP

### 7 Princes Street
**Listed**

Oxford OX4 1DD
☎ (01865) 726755
*Restored Victorian artisan's cottage,
furnished with many antiques. Short
walk from Magdalen Bridge and central
Oxford.*
Bedrooms: 1 single, 1 double
Bathrooms: 1 public
**Bed & breakfast**

| per night: | £min | £max |
|---|---|---|
| Single | 16.00 | 20.00 |
| Double | 30.00 | 32.00 |

Parking for 2

🛇 ⚁ ♨ UL 🕅 TV 🞕 🗮 ⚓ ✿ ✕ 🛋

### West Farm
**Listed**

Eaton, Abingdon OX13 5PR
☎ (01865) 862908

*1100-acre arable & livestock farm.
Comfortable, centrally heated farmhouse
on working farm, 5 miles west of
Oxford. Children welcome (equipment,
toys etc.). Tennis court. Excellent centre
for touring, also frequent cheap coaches
from Oxford to London.*
Bedrooms: 1 single, 1 double, 1 triple
Bathrooms: 2 public
**Bed & breakfast**

| per night: | £min | £max |
| --- | --- | --- |
| Single | 18.50 | 22.00 |
| Double | 37.00 | 44.00 |

Parking for 6

## PETERSFIELD
Hampshire
Map ref 2C3

Grew prosperous from the wool
trade and was famous as a
coaching centre. Its attractive
market square is dominated by a
statue of William III. Close by are
Petersfield Heath with numerous
ancient barrows and Butser Hill
with magnificent views.
*Tourist Information Centre*
☎ *(01730) 268829*

### Westmark House
Listed
Sheet, Petersfield GU31 5AT
☎ (01730) 263863
*Pleasant Georgian country house, with
hard tennis court and heated pool. Take
the A3 north from Petersfield. Turn
right on to A272 towards Rogate and
Midhurst. Westmark House is first
house on the left.*
Bedrooms: 1 single, 1 double, 1 twin
Bathrooms: 1 public
**Bed & breakfast**

| per night: | £min | £max |
| --- | --- | --- |
| Single | 22.00 | 24.00 |
| Double | 44.00 | 48.00 |

**Half board**

| per person: | £min | £max |
| --- | --- | --- |
| Daily | 37.00 | 39.00 |

Evening meal 1900 (last orders 2030)
Parking for 3

---

Check the introduction
to this region for ideas
on Where to Go.

---

## POOLE
Dorset
Map ref 2B3

Tremendous natural harbour
makes Poole a superb boating
centre. The harbour area is
crowded with historic buildings
including the 15th C Town Cellars
housing a maritime museum.
*Tourist Information Centre*
☎ *(01202) 673322*

### Ashdell ♏
Listed
85 Dunyeats Road, Broadstone
BH18 8AF
☎ Bournemouth (01202) 692032
*Comfortable, secluded accommodation
in wood land setting and pleasant
garden. Breakfast choice. Coast/historic
countryside, golf course and ferry
terminal 4 miles. Driveway parking. On
bus route Wimborne/Poole.*
Bedrooms: 1 double, 2 twin
Bathrooms: 1 public
**Bed & breakfast**

| per night: | £min | £max |
| --- | --- | --- |
| Single | 14.00 | 17.00 |
| Double | 23.50 | 27.50 |

Evening meal from 1830
Parking for 3

### Homeleigh
Listed  HIGHLY COMMENDED
105 Wimborne Road, Poole BH15 2BP
☎ Bournemouth (01202) 673697
*Small, friendly, non-smoking
establishment, near town centre,
harbour, beaches and bus/rail stations.
Within easy reach of coast and New
Forest.*
Bedrooms: 2 twin
Bathrooms: 1 public
**Bed & breakfast**

| per night: | £min | £max |
| --- | --- | --- |
| Single | 13.00 | 15.00 |
| Double | 26.00 | 30.00 |

Parking for 2

### The Inn in the Park
26 Pinewood Road, Branksome Park,
Poole BH13 6JS
☎ Bournemouth (01202) 761318
*Small, friendly, family-owned pub with
sun terrace, log fire and easy access to
the beach.*
Bedrooms: 3 double, 1 twin, 1 triple
Bathrooms: 5 private
**Bed & breakfast**

| per night: | £min | £max |
| --- | --- | --- |
| Single | 25.00 | 30.00 |
| Double | 35.00 | 50.00 |

Lunch available
Evening meal 1900 (last orders 2130)
Parking for 15
Cards accepted: Access, Visa

---

## PORTSMOUTH & SOUTHSEA
Hampshire
Map ref 2C3

The first dock was built in 1194.
HMS Victory, Nelson's flagship, is
here and Charles Dickens' former
home is open to the public.
Neighbouring Southsea has a
promenade with magnificent views
of Spithead.
*Tourist Information Centre*
☎ *(01705) 826722*

### Britannia Guest House
8 Outram Road, Southsea, Hampshire
PO5 1QU
☎ (01705) 814234
*Large bedrooms are capable of
accommodating families of up to six
persons per room. You are sure of a
warm welcome in this family-run house.*
Bedrooms: 1 double, 2 triple, 2 family
rooms
Bathrooms: 2 public
**Bed & breakfast**

| per night: | £min | £max |
| --- | --- | --- |
| Single | 15.00 | 15.00 |
| Double | 30.00 | 30.00 |

**Half board**

| per night: | £min | £max |
| --- | --- | --- |
| Daily | 21.00 | 21.00 |
| Weekly | 135.00 | 135.00 |

Evening meal 1800 (last orders 1830)
Open June–September

### Hamilton House ♏
COMMENDED
95 Victoria Road North, Southsea,
Portsmouth, Hampshire PO5 1PS
☎ (01705) 823502
Fax (01705) 823502
*Delightful family-run guesthouse, 5
minutes by car to ferry terminals and
tourist attractions. Some en-suite rooms
also available. Breakfast served from
6am.*
Bedrooms: 1 single, 2 double, 2 twin,
1 triple, 2 family rooms
Bathrooms: 3 private, 2 public
**Bed & breakfast**

| per night: | £min | £max |
| --- | --- | --- |
| Single | 16.00 | 18.00 |
| Double | 32.00 | 36.00 |

**Half board**

| per person: | £min | £max |
| --- | --- | --- |
| Daily | 21.00 | 23.00 |
| Weekly | 144.00 | 158.00 |

Evening meal from 1800

## PORTSMOUTH & SOUTHSEA

*Continued*

### Hillside Lodge

**Listed**

1 Blake Road, Farlington, Portsmouth, Hampshire PO6 1ET
☎ Cosham (01705) 372687
*Comfortable house, situated on hill slope with fine views to Isle of Wight. No restrictions. Off-road parking.*
Bedrooms: 1 single, 1 double, 1 twin
Bathrooms: 1 private, 1 public

| Bed & breakfast per night: | £min | £max |
|---|---|---|
| Single | 14.00 | 14.00 |
| Double | 28.00 | 36.00 |

| Half board per person: | £min | £max |
|---|---|---|
| Daily | 20.00 | 24.00 |
| Weekly | 126.00 | |

Evening meal 1830 (last orders 1930)
Parking for 3

### The Saltings ▲

**HIGHLY COMMENDED**

19 Bath Square, Portsmouth, Hampshire PO1 2JL
☎ (01705) 821031
*Elegant town house on waterfront, overlooking Portsmouth Harbour entrance. Located on Spice Island, in the heart of Old Portsmouth. Attractively furnished rooms with spectacular views. Within strolling distance of Maritime Heritage and museums. Non-smokers only, please.*
Bedrooms: 1 double, 1 twin
Bathrooms: 1 public

| Bed & breakfast per night: | £min | £max |
|---|---|---|
| Single | 30.00 | 30.00 |
| Double | 40.00 | 44.00 |

Open February-December

### Victoria Court Hotel ▲

**♛♛♛**

29 Victoria Road North, Southsea, Hampshire PO5 1PL
☎ (01705) 820305
*Comfortable Victorian house in the heart of Southsea. Portsmouth's naval heritage is reflected in the dining room where home cooking is served. Ideal centre for touring the New Forest and West Sussex.*
Bedrooms: 2 double, 2 twin, 4 triple
Bathrooms: 8 private, 1 public

| Bed & breakfast per night: | £min | £max |
|---|---|---|
| Single | 28.00 | 35.00 |
| Double | 30.00 | 43.00 |

| Half board per person: | £min | £max |
|---|---|---|
| Daily | 38.00 | 53.00 |
| Weekly | 266.00 | 371.00 |

Evening meal from 1830
Cards accepted: Access, Visa, Diners

## READING

Berkshire
Map ref 2C2

Busy, modern county town with large shopping centre and many leisure and recreation facilities. There are several interesting museums and the Duke of Wellington's Stratfield Saye is nearby.
*Tourist Information Centre*
☎ *(01734) 566226*

### Belstone ▲

**Listed   HIGHLY COMMENDED**

36 Upper Warren Avenue, Caversham, Reading RG4 7EB
☎ (01734) 477435
*Friendly welcome in elegant Victorian family house. Quiet tree-lined avenue near river and farmland. Convenient for town centre by car. Non-smokers only please.*
Bedrooms: 1 double, 1 twin
Bathrooms: 1 public

| Bed & breakfast per night: | £min | £max |
|---|---|---|
| Single | 25.00 | 27.50 |
| Double | 35.00 | 40.00 |

Parking for 2

### Dittisham Guest House

**Listed   COMMENDED**

63 Tilehurst Road, Reading RG3 2JL
☎ (01734) 569483 & Mobile 0850 767029
*Renovated Edwardian property with garden, in a quiet but central location.*
Bedrooms: 4 single, 1 twin
Bathrooms: 3 private, 1 public

| Bed & breakfast per night: | £min | £max |
|---|---|---|
| Single | 19.00 | 27.50 |
| Double | 27.50 | 45.00 |

Parking for 7
Cards accepted: Access, Visa

### The Elms

**♛♛ COMMENDED**

Gallowstree Road, Rotherfield Peppard, Henley-on-Thames, Oxfordshire RG9 5HT
☎ (01734) 723164
*Bed and breakfast near Henley. Heated swimming pool. All normal services, large garden, good parking. Excellent pub close by.*
Bedrooms: 1 double, 1 twin
Bathrooms: 2 private

| Bed & breakfast per night: | £min | £max |
|---|---|---|
| Single | 15.00 | 20.00 |
| Double | 30.00 | 40.00 |

| Half board per person: | £min | £max |
|---|---|---|
| Daily | 24.50 | 29.50 |

Evening meal 1930 (last orders 2000)
Parking for 13

### 10 Greystoke Road

**Listed   COMMENDED**

Caversham, Reading RG4 0EL
☎ (01734) 475784
*Private home in quiet, residential area. TV lounge, tea and coffee-making facilities. Non-smokers only, please.*
Bedrooms: 1 single, 1 double
Bathrooms: 2 public

| Bed & breakfast per night: | £min | £max |
|---|---|---|
| Single | 16.00 | 19.00 |
| Double | 26.00 | 29.00 |

Parking for 2

### The Six Bells

**♛♛♛ COMMENDED**

Beenham Village, Beenham, Reading RG7 5NX
☎ Woolhampton (01734) 713368
*Village pub, overlooking farmland. Four miles from Theale M4 junction 12, 1 mile off A4. Newly-built bedrooms. Home cooking always available - varied menu.*
Bedrooms: 1 single, 2 double, 1 twin
Bathrooms: 4 private

| Bed & breakfast per night: | £min | £max |
|---|---|---|
| Single | 36.00 | |
| Double | 49.00 | |

Lunch available
Evening meal 1830 (last orders 2130)
Parking for 35
Cards accepted: Access, Visa

### Warren Dene Hotel

**♛♛♛ COMMENDED**

1017 Oxford Road, Tilehurst, Reading RG3 6TL
☎ (01734) 422556
Fax (01734) 422556
*Small, elegant Victorian hotel on the outskirts of Reading. Period bar lounge and decor throughout. Most rooms en-suite, family rooms available. Conveniently situated for Heathrow Airport and motorway access to Gatwick.*
Bedrooms: 1 single, 2 double, 2 twin, 1 triple, 2 family rooms
Bathrooms: 5 private, 2 public

| Bed & breakfast per night: | £min | £max |
|---|---|---|
| Single | 24.00 | 35.00 |
| Double | 35.00 | 42.00 |

**Half board**

| per person: | £min | £max |
| --- | --- | --- |
| Daily | 29.00 | 45.00 |

Lunch available
Evening meal 1800 (last orders 2100)
Parking for 9

[symbols]

## RINGWOOD

Hampshire
Map ref 2B3

Market town by the River Avon comprising old cottages, many of them thatched. Although just outside the New Forest, there is heath and woodland nearby and it is a good centre for horse-riding and walking.

### Homeacres ♨

COMMENDED

Homelands Farm, Three Legged Cross, Wimborne Minster, Dorset BH21 6QZ
☎ Verwood (01202) 822422
Fax (01202) 822422

*270-acre mixed farm. Large chalet bungalow of traditional design, with inglenook fireplace in drawing room. Extensive garden, with access to large patio from drawing room. Wheelchair access category 3* ♿
Bedrooms: 1 single, 1 twin, 1 triple, 2 family rooms
Bathrooms: 5 private, 1 public

**Bed & breakfast**

| per night: | £min | £max |
| --- | --- | --- |
| Single | 17.00 | 19.00 |
| Double | 28.00 | 38.00 |

Parking for 8

[symbols]

## ROMSEY

Hampshire
Map ref 2C3

Town grew up around the important abbey and lies on the banks of the River Test, famous for trout and salmon. Broadlands House, home of the late Lord Mountbatten, is open to the public.
*Tourist Information Centre*
☎ *(01794) 512987*

### Country Accommodation ♨

COMMENDED

The Old Post Office, New Road, Michelmersh, Romsey SO51 0NL
☎ (01794) 368739

*In pretty village location, interesting conversion from old forge, bakery and post office. All ground floor rooms, some beamed. On-site parking.*
Bedrooms: 1 double, 2 twin, 1 triple
Bathrooms: 4 private

**Bed & breakfast**

| per night: | £min | £max |
| --- | --- | --- |
| Single | 25.00 | 25.00 |
| Double | 40.00 | 40.00 |

Parking for 10
Cards accepted: Access, Visa

[symbols]

### 8 The Meads ♨

Listed

Romsey SO51 8HB
☎ (01794) 512049
*Small town house in pleasant, quiet location in town centre, with view of the abbey. Parking.*
Bedrooms: 1 double, 1 twin
Bathrooms: 1 public

**Bed & breakfast**

| per night: | £min | £max |
| --- | --- | --- |
| Single | 18.00 | 20.00 |
| Double | 30.00 | 32.00 |

Parking for 1
Open April-October

[symbols]

### Pyesmead Farm

Listed

Plaitford, Romsey SO51 6EE
☎ West Wellow (01794) 323386
*70-acre livestock farm. Small, family-run stock farm, situated on edge of the New Forest, west of Romsey. Easy access from A36, Southampton to Salisbury road.*
Bedrooms: 2 double, 1 twin
Bathrooms: 1 public

**Bed & breakfast**

| per night: | £min | £max |
| --- | --- | --- |
| Single | 17.00 | 17.00 |
| Double | 27.00 | 27.00 |

**Half board**

| per person: | £min | £max |
| --- | --- | --- |
| Daily | 21.00 | 24.50 |

Evening meal from 1900
Parking for 10

[symbols]

> All accommodation in this guide has been inspected, or is awaiting inspection, under the national Crown scheme.

## RYDE

Isle of Wight
Map ref 2C3

The island's chief entry port, connected to Portsmouth by ferries and hovercraft. 7 miles of sandy beaches with a half-mile pier, esplanade and gardens.
*Tourist Information Centre*
☎ *(01983) 562905*

### Sillwood Acre

HIGHLY COMMENDED

Church Road, Binstead, Ryde PO33 3TB
☎ Isle of Wight (01983) 563553
*Large Victorian house near Ryde, convenient for the ferry and hovercraft terminals. Two spacious en-suite rooms. Non-smoking.*
Bedrooms: 1 double, 1 triple
Bathrooms: 2 private

**Bed & breakfast**

| per night: | £min | £max |
| --- | --- | --- |
| Single | 16.00 | 18.00 |
| Double | 32.00 | 36.00 |

Parking for 3

[symbols]

## RYDE-WOOTTON

Isle of Wight
Map ref 2C3

Village runs uphill from Wootton Creek, popular with yachtsmen for its sailing school and boatyards.

### Bridge House ♨

HIGHLY COMMENDED

Kite Hill, Wootton Bridge, Ryde PO33 4LA
☎ Isle of Wight (01983) 884163
*Georgian listed building with gardens down to water's edge. Traditional English breakfast with home-made preserves. A no-smoking haven!*
Bedrooms: 2 double, 1 twin
Bathrooms: 1 public, 1 private shower

**Half board**

| per person: | £min | £max |
| --- | --- | --- |
| Daily | 30.00 | 38.00 |

Parking for 4

[symbols]

## SAUNDERTON

Buckinghamshire
Map ref 2C1

Small village close to the Ridgeway long distance footpath. The site of a Roman villa is near the church.

### Hunter's Gate

Listed  APPROVED

Deanfield, Saunderton, High Wycombe HP14 4JR
☎ High Wycombe (01494) 481446
*Continued ▶*

## SAUNDERTON

*Continued*

*6-acre smallholding. 4-bedroomed house with a 1 bedroom flat above garage, in a valley overlooked by Bledlow Ridge, half-a-mile from Wycombe/Princes Risborough road. Set in 5 acres in a quiet area but only half-a-mile to BR station for London.*
Bedrooms: 1 double, 1 twin
Bathrooms: 1 private, 1 public

**Bed & breakfast**

| per night: | £min | £max |
|---|---|---|
| Single | 15.00 | 15.00 |
| Double | 30.00 | 30.00 |

Parking for 4

## SELBORNE

Hampshire
Map ref 2C2

Village made famous by Gilbert White, who was a curate here and is remembered for his classic book "The Natural History of Selborne", published in 1788. His house is now a museum.

### 8 Goslings Croft

**Listed** HIGHLY COMMENDED

Selborne, Alton GU34 3HZ
☎ (01420) 511285
Fax (01420) 577451
*Family home, set on edge of historic village, adjacent to National Trust land. Ideal base for walking and touring. Non-smokers only please.*
Bedrooms: 1 twin
Bathrooms: 1 private

**Bed & breakfast**

| per night: | £min | £max |
|---|---|---|
| Single | 19.50 | 19.50 |
| Double | 29.50 | 29.50 |

Parking for 1
Cards accepted: Access, Visa

## SHALFLEET

Isle of Wight
Map ref 2C3

### The Old Malthouse ₩

1 Mill Road, Shalfleet, Newport PO30 4NE
☎ Isle of Wight (01983) 531329
*Family-run B & B in 250-year-old character house, in conservation village, opposite the New Inn. Cyclists and walkers welcome.*
Bedrooms: 1 single, 1 double, 1 triple
Bathrooms: 3 private

**Bed & breakfast**

| per night: | £min | £max |
|---|---|---|
| Single | 15.00 | 17.00 |
| Double | 30.00 | 34.00 |

Parking for 2

## SHIPTON BELLINGER

Hampshire
Map ref 2B2

### Parsonage Farm

COMMENDED

Shipton Bellinger, Tidworth SP9 7UF
☎ Stonehenge (01980) 842404
*Former farmhouse of 16th/17th C origins in quiet village. Walled garden, stables, paddocks. Situated off A338 opposite parish church and Boot Inn.*
Bedrooms: 1 single, 1 twin, 1 triple
Bathrooms: 1 private, 2 public

**Bed & breakfast**

| per night: | £min | £max |
|---|---|---|
| Single | 15.00 | 18.00 |
| Double | 30.00 | 35.00 |

Parking for 6

## SHIPTON-UNDER-WYCHWOOD

Oxfordshire
Map ref 2B1

Situated in the ancient Forest of Wychwood with many fine old houses and an interesting parish church. Nearby is Shipton Court, a gabled Elizabethan house set in beautiful grounds that include an ornamental lake and a tree-lined avenue approach.

### Garden Cottage

**Listed**

Fiddlers Hill, Shipton-under-Wychwood, Chipping Norton OX7 6DR
☎ (01993) 830640
*Modern, stone cottage on edge of village, quiet with nice views. 5 minutes' walk from popular local pub. Off main A361 Shipton to Burford road.*
Bedrooms: 2 double, 1 twin
Bathrooms: 1 private, 1 public

**Bed & breakfast**

| per night: | £min | £max |
|---|---|---|
| Single | 15.00 | 25.00 |
| Double | 30.00 | 40.00 |

Parking for 4

## SIXPENNY HANDLEY

Dorset
Map ref 2B3

### The Barleycorn House

Deanland, Sixpenny Handley, Salisbury, Wiltshire SP5 5PD
☎ Handley (01725) 552583
Fax (01725) 552090
*Converted 17th C inn retaining original period features, in peaceful surroundings with many nearby walks. Relaxed atmosphere and home cooking.*
Bedrooms: 1 single, 1 double, 1 twin
Bathrooms: 2 private, 1 public

**Bed & breakfast**

| per night: | £min | £max |
|---|---|---|
| Single | 18.00 | 18.00 |
| Double | 36.00 | 36.00 |

**Half board**

| per person: | £min | £max |
|---|---|---|
| Daily | 26.50 | 26.50 |
| Weekly | 172.90 | 172.90 |

Evening meal from 1830
Parking for 5

## SOULDERN

Oxfordshire
Map ref 2C1

### Tower Fields

Tusmore Road, Souldern, Bicester OX6 9HY
☎ Bicester (01869) 346554
Fax (01869) 345157
*14-acre rarebreeds farm. Converted 18th C cottages and smallholding with rare breeds of poultry, sheep and cattle. Small collection of vintage cars.*
Bedrooms: 1 double, 1 twin
Bathrooms: 2 private

**Bed & breakfast**

| per night: | £min | £max |
|---|---|---|
| Single | 22.00 | 22.00 |
| Double | 40.00 | 44.00 |

Parking for 2

## SOUTHAMPTON

Hampshire
Map ref 2C3

One of Britain's leading seaports with a long history, now a major container port. In the 18th C it became a fashionable resort with the assembly rooms and theatre. The old Guildhall and the Wool House are now museums. Sections of the medieval wall can still be seen.
*Tourist Information Centre*
☎ (01703) 221106

### Ashelee Lodge ₩

**Listed** COMMENDED

36 Atherley Road, Shirley, Southampton SO1 5DQ
☎ (01703) 222095
*Homely guesthouse, garden with pool. Half a mile from city centre, near station, M27 and Sealink ferryport. Good touring base for New Forest, Salisbury and Winchester.*
Bedrooms: 1 single, 1 double, 1 twin, 1 triple
Bathrooms: 1 public

**Bed & breakfast**

| per night: | £min | £max |
|---|---|---|
| Single | 14.00 | 15.00 |
| Double | 28.00 | 30.00 |

Evening meal from 1800

Parking for 2
Cards accepted: Access, Visa

[icons]

### Beacon Guest House

Listed

49 Archers Road, Southampton
SO1 2NF
☎ (01703) 225910 & Mobile 0860
224625
*Friendly, comfortable accommodation,
commercial and private. Close to city
centre, restaurants, docks and county
cricket ground, with easy access to the
New Forest and Winchester.*
Bedrooms: 1 single, 1 twin, 2 triple,
2 family rooms
Bathrooms: 2 public

**Bed & breakfast**

| per night: | £min | £max |
|---|---|---|
| Single | 12.50 | 16.00 |
| Double | 25.00 | 28.00 |

Parking for 4

[icons]

## SOUTHSEA

Hampshire

*See under Portsmouth & Southsea*

## STANDLAKE

Oxfordshire
Map ref 2C1

13th C church with an octagonal
tower and spire standing beside
the Windrush. The interior of the
church is rich in woodwork.

### Blenheim Cottage

Listed

47 Abingdon Road, Standlake, Witney
OX8 7QH
☎ Oxford (01865) 300718
*Recently extended and modernised
cottage in a rural setting on the A415.
Situated at the Witney end of Standlake.*
Bedrooms: 1 twin
Bathrooms: 1 private

**Bed & breakfast**

| per night: | £min | £max |
|---|---|---|
| Single | 20.00 | |
| Double | 32.00 | |

Parking for 1
Open May-September

[icons]

> **Individual proprietors
> have supplied all details
> of accommodation.
> Although we do check for
> accuracy, we advise you
> to confirm the information
> at the time of booking.**

## STOCKBRIDGE

Hampshire
Map ref 2C2

Set in the Test Valley which has
some of the best fishing in
England. The wide main street has
houses of all styles, mainly Tudor
and Georgian.

### Carbery Guest House ♠

COMMENDED

Salisbury Hill, Stockbridge SO20 6EZ
☎ Andover (01264) 810771
Fax (01264) 811022
*Fine old Georgian house in an acre of
landscaped gardens and lawns,
overlooking the River Test. Games and
swimming facilities, riding and fishing
can be arranged. Ideal for touring the
south coast and the New Forest.*
Bedrooms: 4 single, 4 double, 2 twin,
1 triple
Bathrooms: 8 private, 1 public

**Bed & breakfast**

| per night: | £min | £max |
|---|---|---|
| Single | 22.00 | 29.50 |
| Double | 44.00 | 48.00 |

**Half board**

| per person: | £min | £max |
|---|---|---|
| Daily | 32.50 | 40.00 |
| Weekly | 223.00 | 275.00 |

Evening meal 1900 (last orders 1800)
Parking for 12

[icons]

## STUDLAND

Dorset
Map ref 2B3

On a beautiful stretch of coast and
good for walking, with a National
Nature Reserve to the north. The
Norman church is the finest in the
country, with superb rounded
arches and vaulting. Brownsea
Island, where the first scout camp
was held, lies in Poole Harbour.

### Bankes Arms Hotel ♠

Manor Road, Studland, Swanage
BH19 3AU
☎ (01929) 450225

*Lovely old inn with large gardens,
overlooking the sea. En-suite rooms
with colour TV and and tea-making.
Home-cooked lunches and evening bar-
meals. Sandy beaches, water sports,
residents' moorings in bay, golf, riding.*
Bedrooms: 1 single, 3 double, 2 twin,
3 triple

Bathrooms: 5 private, 1 public

**Bed & breakfast**

| per night: | £min | £max |
|---|---|---|
| Single | 20.00 | 25.00 |
| Double | 40.00 | 55.00 |

Lunch available
Evening meal 1900 (last orders 2130)
Parking for 12
Cards accepted: Access, Visa

[icons]

## SUTTON SCOTNEY

Hampshire
Map ref 2C2

### Knoll House

COMMENDED

Wonston, Sutton Scotney, Winchester
SO21 3LR
☎ Winchester (01962) 760273 &
883550
*Take Andover road from Winchester to
Sutton Scotney. Turn right at village
hall to Wonston. Situated on right hand
side almost opposite Wonston Arms.*
Bedrooms: 1 double, 1 twin
Bathrooms: 2 private

**Bed & breakfast**

| per night: | £min | £max |
|---|---|---|
| Single | 16.00 | 16.00 |
| Double | 32.00 | 32.00 |

**Half board**

| per person: | £min | £max |
|---|---|---|
| Daily | 23.00 | 23.00 |
| Weekly | 161.00 | 161.00 |

Evening meal 1830 (last orders 2030)
Parking for 2

[icons]

## SWAY

Hampshire
Map ref 2C3

Small village on the south-western
edge of the New Forest. It is
noted for its 220-ft tower,
Peterson's Folly, built in the 1870s
by a retired Indian judge to
demonstrate the value of concrete
as a building material.

### Redwing Farm

Listed

Pitmore Lane, Sway, Lymington
SO41 6BW
☎ Lymington (01590) 683319
*24-acre pedigree farm. Beamed cottage
rooms, en-suite, overlooking fields and
gardens. Small TV lounge. Beautifully
situated walking/ touring New Forest
base.*
Bedrooms: 2 single, 2 double
Bathrooms: 3 private, 1 public

Continued ▶

## SWAY
### Continued

**Bed & breakfast**

| per night: | £min | £max |
|---|---|---|
| Single | 17.50 | 18.00 |
| Double | 36.00 | 36.00 |

Parking for 10

## TIPTOE
Hampshire
Map ref 2C3

### Candleford House
Listed

Middle Road, Tiptoe, Lymington SO41 0FX
☎ Lymington (01590) 682069
*Modern, Georgian-style house, not overlooked, on edge of New Forest. Central for Lymington, Milford-on-Sea, Bournemouth and Southampton.*
Bedrooms: 1 single, 1 double, 1 twin
Bathrooms: 1 public

**Bed & breakfast**

| per night: | £min | £max |
|---|---|---|
| Single | 15.50 | |
| Double | 29.00 | |

Parking for 3
Open March-October

## TOTTON
Hampshire
Map ref 2C3

### Jubilee Cottage

303 Salisbury Road, Totton, Southampton SO4 3LZ
☎ Southampton (01703) 862397
*Victorian house convenient for Romsey, M27, New Forest, continental and Isle of Wight ferries. Bed and breakfast accommodation with private facilities. French spoken.*
Bedrooms: 1 twin, 1 triple
Bathrooms: 2 private

**Bed & breakfast**

| per night: | £min | £max |
|---|---|---|
| Single | 15.00 | 15.00 |
| Double | 30.00 | 30.00 |

Parking for 2

Individual proprietors have supplied all details of accommodation. Although we do check for accuracy, we advise you to confirm the information at the time of booking.

## UFFINGTON
Oxfordshire
Map ref 2C2

Village famous for the great White Horse cut in the chalk, possibly dating from the Iron Age. Above it is Uffington Castle, a prehistoric hill fort.

### Shotover House
HIGHLY COMMENDED

Uffington, Faringdon SN7 7RH
☎ Faringdon (01367) 820351

*Traditional 19th C chalkstone cottage in pretty rose-filled garden, on edge of peaceful village and with views of the White Horse.*
Bedrooms: 1 single, 1 double, 1 twin
Bathrooms: 3 private

**Bed & breakfast**

| per night: | £min | £max |
|---|---|---|
| Single | | 25.00 |
| Double | | 50.00 |

**Half board**

| per person: | £min | £max |
|---|---|---|
| Daily | 35.00 | 40.00 |
| Weekly | 210.00 | 240.00 |

Evening meal from 1900
Parking for 3
Open March-October

## WALLINGFORD
Oxfordshire
Map ref 2C2

Site of an ancient ford over the River Thames, now crossed by a 900-ft-long bridge. The town has many timber-framed and Georgian buildings, Gainsborough portraits in the 17th C Town Hall and a few remains of a Norman Castle.
*Tourist Information Centre*
☎ *(01491) 826972*

### North Farm
HIGHLY COMMENDED

Shillingford Hill, Wallingford OX10 8NB
☎ Warborough (01865) 858406
*500-acre mixed farm. Comfortable farmhouse close to River Thames, in a quiet position with lovely views and walks. Pygmy goats, chickens and sheep.*
Bedrooms: 1 double, 1 twin
Bathrooms: 2 private

**Bed & breakfast**

| per night: | £min | £max |
|---|---|---|
| Single | 28.00 | 35.00 |
| Double | 38.00 | 43.00 |

Parking for 9

## WARBOROUGH
Oxfordshire
Map ref 2C2

### Blenheim House
HIGHLY COMMENDED

11-13 The Green North, Warborough, Wallingford OX10 7DW
☎ (01865) 858445
Fax (01865) 858445
*Old village house set in 2.5 acres of garden. Swimming pool.*
Bedrooms: 1 double, 1 twin
Bathrooms: 2 private

**Bed & breakfast**

| per night: | £min | £max |
|---|---|---|
| Single | 20.00 | 22.00 |
| Double | 40.00 | 45.00 |

Parking for 4

## WARNFORD
Hampshire
Map ref 2C3

### Paper Mill
Listed COMMENDED

Peake Lane, Warnford, Southampton SO3 1LA
☎ West Meon (01730) 829387

*Self-contained mill house in unique setting on River Meon. Take A272 from Petersfield or Winchester to West Meon Hut traffic lights, turn south on A32, follow road to Warnford, past George and Falcon and turn left into Peake Lane.*
Bedrooms: 1 double
Bathrooms: 1 private

**Bed & breakfast**

| per night: | £min | £max |
|---|---|---|
| Single | 25.00 | |
| Double | 45.00 | |

Parking for 1
Open April-September

We advise you to confirm your booking in writing.

## WENDOVER

Buckinghamshire
Map ref 2C1

Historic town on the Icknield Way set amid beautiful scenery and spectacular views of the Chilterns. There are many old timbered cottages and inns, one visited by Oliver Cromwell. The church has some interesting carving.
*Tourist Information Centre*
☎ *(01296) 696759*

### The Red Lion Hotel ⋀
😊😊😊

9 High Street, Wendover, Aylesbury HP22 6DU
☎ (01296) 622266
Fax (01296) 625077

*17th C coaching inn. Great location for walking in Chilterns. Excellent reputation for food and drink. Popular with locals.*
Bedrooms: 4 single, 14 double, 4 twin, 4 triple
Bathrooms: 26 private

**Bed & breakfast**

| per night: | £min | £max |
| --- | --- | --- |
| Single | 39.95 | 44.95 |
| Double | 49.95 | 54.95 |

**Half board**

| per person: | £min | £max |
| --- | --- | --- |
| Daily | 36.97 | 51.95 |

Lunch available
Evening meal 1800 (last orders 2200)
Parking for 60
Cards accepted: Access, Visa, Diners, Amex, Switch/Delta
🛇🛆🗚🖳📞☐🖐🛈⑤✂🖂🏧🖥📖🕭⇃👫
SP 🏠

## WEST LULWORTH

Dorset
Map ref 2B3

Well-known for Lulworth Cove, the almost landlocked circular bay of chalk and limestone cliffs.

### Graybank Guest House
Listed

Main Road, West Lulworth, Wareham BH20 5RL
☎ (01929) 400256
*Victorian guesthouse in beautiful countryside, 5 minutes' walk from Lulworth Cove. TV in most bedrooms. Ideal walking and touring base.*
Bedrooms: 1 single, 2 double, 1 twin, 1 triple, 2 family rooms
Bathrooms: 3 public

**Bed & breakfast**

| per night: | £min | £max |
| --- | --- | --- |
| Single | 17.00 | 19.00 |
| Double | 34.00 | 38.00 |

Parking for 7
Open January-November
🛇4☐🖐🖳⑤✂🏧🖥✿🐾SP🏠

### Newlands Farm
Listed   COMMENDED

West Lulworth, Wareham BH20 5PU
☎ (01929) 400376
Fax (01929) 400536
*750-acre arable & livestock farm. 19th C farmhouse, with outstanding views to sea and distant Purbeck Hills. At Durdle Door, 1 mile west of Lulworth Cove.*
Bedrooms: 1 double, 1 triple
Bathrooms: 1 public, 2 private showers

**Bed & breakfast**

| per night: | £min | £max |
| --- | --- | --- |
| Double | 36.00 | 40.00 |

Parking for 10
Open January-November
🛇☐🖐🖳🛈⑤✂🖂🕭⇃✿✂🐾

### The Old Barn ⋀
Listed

Lulworth Cove, West Lulworth, Wareham BH20 5RL
☎ (01929) 41305

*Converted old barn in peaceful, picturesque coastal village. Choice of rooms with continental breakfast or please-yourself-rooms with eight self-catering facilities. Large gardens. Ideal base for touring Dorset.*
Bedrooms: 2 single, 2 double, 1 twin, 1 triple, 1 family room
Bathrooms: 3 public

**Bed & breakfast**

| per night: | £min | £max |
| --- | --- | --- |
| Single | 16.00 | 18.50 |
| Double | 32.00 | 40.00 |

Parking for 9
Cards accepted: Access, Visa
🛇🛆🗚🖳🖐⑤✂🕭🖂⇃✿🐾DAPSP

## WEST STOUR

Dorset
Map ref 2B3

### The Ship Inn
😊😊😊 COMMENDED

West Stour, Gillingham SP8 5RP
☎ East Stour (01747) 838640
*18th C mail coach inn with fine views over the Dorset countryside. Log fires during winter and traditional hand-pumped ales throughout the year. Central for touring the West Country.*

*Good home-cooked food served 7 days a week.*
Bedrooms: 1 single, 3 double, 1 twin, 1 triple, 1 family room
Bathrooms: 7 private, 1 public

**Bed & breakfast**

| per night: | £min | £max |
| --- | --- | --- |
| Single | 28.00 | |
| Double | 38.00 | 42.00 |

Lunch available
Evening meal 1900 (last orders 2130)
Parking for 50
Cards accepted: Access, Visa
🛇☐🖐🛈⑤✂🖂🖳📺🖂⇃🕭⇃✿🐾SP🏠

## WESTBURY

Buckinghamshire
Map ref 2C1

### Mill Farm House
Listed

Westbury, Brackley, Northamptonshire NN13 5JS
☎ Brackley (01280) 704843
*1000-acre mixed farm. Grade II listed farmhouse, overlooking a colourful garden including a covered heated swimming pool. Situated in the centre of Westbury village.*
Bedrooms: 1 double, 1 triple
Bathrooms: 1 public

**Bed & breakfast**

| per night: | £min | £max |
| --- | --- | --- |
| Single | 16.00 | 20.00 |
| Double | 32.00 | 45.00 |

**Half board**

| per person: | £min | £max |
| --- | --- | --- |
| Daily | 28.00 | 40.00 |
| Weekly | 180.00 | 240.00 |

Evening meal 1930 (last orders 2130)
Parking for 6
🛇🖳⑤🖂📺🖥🖂🕭⇃✿🐾DAPSP🏠

## WICKHAM

Hampshire
Map ref 2C3

Lying in the Meon Valley, this market town is built around the Square and in Bridge Street can be seen some timber-framed cottages. Still the site of an annual horse fair.

### Montrose ⋀
😊😊 HIGHLY COMMENDED

Solomons Lane, Shirrell Heath, Southampton SO32 2HU
☎ (01329) 833345
*Attractive, comfortable accommodation in lovely Meon Valley, offering comfort and personal attention. Equidistant from main towns and convenient for continental ferries and motorway links.*
Bedrooms: 2 double, 1 twin
Bathrooms: 1 private, 1 public
*Continued ▶*

## WICKHAM

*Continued*

**Bed & breakfast**

| per night: | £min | £max |
| --- | --- | --- |
| Single | 22.00 | 26.00 |
| Double | 40.00 | 45.00 |

Parking for 6

♿🅿🚭🟥Ⓤ🟥✂🟥📺🎦🕳🖥❄✈🚐

## WIMBORNE MINSTER

Dorset
Map ref 2B3

Market town centred on the twin-towered Minster Church of St Cuthberga which gave the town the second part of its name. Good touring base for the surrounding countryside, depicted in the writings of Thomas Hardy.
*Tourist Information Centre*
☎ *(01202) 886116*

### Acacia House

👑👑 HIGHLY COMMENDED

2 Oakley Road, Wimborne Minster BH21 1QJ
☎ Bournemouth (01202) 883958
Fax (01202) 881943

*Beautifully decorated rooms are what the discerning traveller expects. What comes as a surprise is Eveline Stimpson's tea and cake welcome.*
Bedrooms: 1 single, 1 double, 1 twin, 1 triple
Bathrooms: 3 private, 1 public

**Bed & breakfast**

| per night: | £min | £max |
| --- | --- | --- |
| Single | 16.00 | 25.00 |
| Double | 34.00 | 40.00 |

Parking for 3

♿🅿🚭🟥🟥Ⓤ🅂🟥📺🕳🖥❄✈🚐

### Ashton Lodge ♨

👑👑 COMMENDED

10 Oakley Hill, Wimborne Minster BH21 1QH
☎ Bournemouth (01202) 883423
*Large, detached, family house, with attractive gardens and relaxed, friendly atmosphere. Off-street parking available. Pay phone. Children welcome.*
Bedrooms: 1 single, 1 double, 1 twin, 1 triple
Bathrooms: 3 private, 3 public

**Bed & breakfast**

| per night: | £min | £max |
| --- | --- | --- |
| Single | 17.00 | 17.00 |
| Double | 35.00 | 37.00 |

Parking for 4

♿🅿🚭🟥Ⓤ🟥🅂✂🟥📺🕳🖥❄✈🚐

### Granville

👑👑

54 Wimborne Road West, Wimborne Minster BH21 2DP
☎ Bournemouth (01202) 886735 & 695428
*Detached, double-fronted house in country setting, with sweeping drive, in three quarters of an acre garden. Ample parking space.*
Bedrooms: 3 twin, 1 triple, 2 family rooms
Bathrooms: 4 private, 1 public

**Bed & breakfast**

| per night: | £min | £max |
| --- | --- | --- |
| Single | 17.00 | 25.00 |
| Double | 32.00 | 40.00 |

**Half board**

| per person: | £min | £max |
| --- | --- | --- |
| Daily | 23.00 | 31.00 |
| Weekly | 150.00 | 200.00 |

Evening meal 1800 (last orders 2100)
Parking for 11
Cards accepted: Access, Visa

♿🅿🅿🟥🟥Ⓤ🅂🟥📺🕳🖥

### Hopewell ♨

👑👑 COMMENDED

Little Lonnen, Colehill, Wimborne Minster BH21 7BB
☎ (01202) 880311
*Modern, owner-designed family house, standing in 6 acres, featuring free-range rare breed domestic ducks. About 2 miles from Wimborne.*
Bedrooms: 1 single, 1 double, 1 twin
Bathrooms: 2 private, 1 public

**Bed & breakfast**

| per night: | £min | £max |
| --- | --- | --- |
| Single | 19.00 | 21.00 |
| Double | 38.00 | 42.00 |

Parking for 6
Cards accepted: Access

♿🟥🟥🚭🟥Ⓤ✂🟥🖥❄✈🚐

### Northill House ♨

👑👑👑 COMMENDED

Horton, Wimborne Minster BH21 7HL
☎ Witchampton (01258) 840407

*Mid-Victorian former farmhouse, modernised to provide comfortable bedrooms, all en-suite. Log fires and cooking using fresh produce. Ideal touring centre.*
Wheelchair access category 1 ♿

Bedrooms: 5 double, 3 twin, 1 triple
Bathrooms: 9 private

**Bed & breakfast**

| per night: | £min | £max |
| --- | --- | --- |
| Single | 37.00 | 37.00 |
| Double | 65.00 | 65.00 |

**Half board**

| per person: | £min | £max |
| --- | --- | --- |
| Daily | 45.50 | 50.00 |
| Weekly | 286.65 | 315.00 |

Evening meal 1930 (last orders 1830)
Parking for 12
Open February-December
Cards accepted: Access, Visa, Amex

♿8♿📞🟥🟥🟥🅂🟥🖥❄✒✈🚐 SP

### Twynham

Listed

67 Poole Road, Wimborne Minster BH21 1QB
☎ (01202) 887310
*A friendly, family home, recently refurbished with vanity unit, TV and beverages in rooms. Within walking distance of town centre.*
Bedrooms: 2 double
Bathrooms: 2 public

**Bed & breakfast**

| per night: | £min | £max |
| --- | --- | --- |
| Single | 15.00 | 18.00 |
| Double | 25.00 | 30.00 |

Parking for 2

♿🟥🟥🚭🟥Ⓤ✂🖥❄✈🚐

### Vines Close Farm

👑👑

Henbury, Wimborne Minster BH21 3RW
☎ Sturminster Marshall (01258) 857278 & 857086
Fax (01258) 857278
*60-acre mixed farm. Modern house close to A31 trunk road. Easy access, ample parking. Within easy reach of Bournemouth, Poole (ferry) and Isle of Purbeck.*
Bedrooms: 2 double, 1 twin
Bathrooms: 1 private, 1 public

**Bed & breakfast**

| per night: | £min | £max |
| --- | --- | --- |
| Single | | 14.00 |
| Double | 28.00 | 30.00 |

Parking for 6
Open January-November

♿🅿🟥🟥🟥Ⓤ🟥✂🟥📺🖥❄✈🚐

There are separate sections in this guide listing groups specialising in farm holidays and accommodation which is especially suitable for young people and organised groups.

## WINCHESTER

Hampshire
Map ref 2C3

King Alfred the Great made Winchester the capital of Saxon England. A magnificent Norman cathedral, with one of the longest naves in Europe, dominates the city. Home of Winchester College founded in 1382.
*Tourist Information Centre*
☎ *(01962) 840500*

### Cathedral View ⚑
🏠🏠🏠 COMMENDED

9A Magdalen Hill, Winchester
SO23 0HJ
☎ (01962) 863802
*Edwardian guesthouse with views across historic city and cathedral. 5 minutes' walk from city centre. En-suite facilities, TV, parking.*
Bedrooms: 3 double, 1 twin, 1 triple
Bathrooms: 5 private, 1 public

**Bed & breakfast**

| per night: | £min | £max |
|---|---|---|
| Single | 30.00 | 30.00 |
| Double | 38.00 | 44.00 |

Evening meal 1900 (last orders 0900)
Parking for 4

### 85 Christchurch Road ⚑
🏠🏠 COMMENDED

Winchester SO23 9QY
☎ (01962) 868661
*Comfortable, friendly Victorian family house in St Cross, Winchester. Ideal for exploring city and Hampshire. Off-street parking. Non-smokers only please.*
Bedrooms: 1 single, 1 double, 1 twin
Bathrooms: 1 private, 2 public

**Bed & breakfast**

| per night: | £min | £max |
|---|---|---|
| Single | 16.00 | 19.00 |
| Double | 32.00 | 38.00 |

Parking for 3

### Dellbrook ⚑
🏠🏠 COMMENDED

Hubert Road, St Cross, Winchester
SO23 9RG
☎ (01962) 865093 & 841472
Fax (01962) 865093
*Comfortable, spacious, welcoming Edwardian house in quiet area of Winchester close to water meadows and 12th C St Cross Hospital.*
Bedrooms: 1 twin, 2 triple
Bathrooms: 2 private, 1 public

**Bed & breakfast**

| per night: | £min | £max |
|---|---|---|
| Single | 23.00 | 28.00 |
| Double | 36.00 | 40.00 |

**Half board**

| per person: | £min | £max |
|---|---|---|
| Daily | 30.00 | 32.00 |
| Weekly | 200.00 | 214.00 |

Evening meal 1800 (last orders 1400)
Parking for 4
Cards accepted: Access, Visa

### The Farrells ⚑
🏠🏠 COMMENDED

5 Ranelagh Road, St Cross,
Winchester SO23 9TA
☎ (01962) 869555
*A warm welcome awaits you at this comfortable Victorian house close to city centre, St Cross Hospital and water meadows.*
Bedrooms: 2 double, 1 twin
Bathrooms: 2 private, 2 public

**Bed & breakfast**

| per night: | £min | £max |
|---|---|---|
| Single | 16.00 | 16.00 |
| Double | | 30.00 |

**Half board**

| per person: | £min | £max |
|---|---|---|
| Daily | | 38.00 |

Parking for 2

### 32 Hyde Street
🏠

Winchester SO23 7DX
☎ (01962) 851621
*Attractive 18th C town house close to city centre and recreational amenities.*
Bedrooms: 1 double, 1 triple
Bathrooms: 1 public

**Bed & breakfast**

| per night: | £min | £max |
|---|---|---|
| Single | 17.00 | 18.00 |
| Double | 28.00 | 30.00 |

### Ivy House
Listed HIGHLY COMMENDED

45 Vernham Road, Greenacres,
Winchester SO22 6BS
☎ (01962) 855512
*Situated in quiet residential road, 5 minutes' drive from city centre. Family-run house, decorated and furnished to a high standard.*
Bedrooms: 1 single, 1 double, 1 twin
Bathrooms: 1 public

**Bed & breakfast**

| per night: | £min | £max |
|---|---|---|
| Single | 16.00 | |
| Double | 35.00 | |

**Half board**

| per person: | £min | £max |
|---|---|---|
| Daily | 24.50 | 26.00 |

Evening meal from 1930
Parking for 3
Open January-November

### Markland House

44 St Cross Road, Winchester
SO23 9PS
☎ (01962) 854901
*Delightful Victorian house, close to cathedral, college, St Cross Hospital,*

water meadows and town centre. A warm welcome awaits you.
Bedrooms: 2 double, 2 twin
Bathrooms: 4 private

**Bed & breakfast**

| per night: | £min | £max |
|---|---|---|
| Single | 32.00 | 35.00 |
| Double | 42.00 | 45.00 |

Parking for 3
Cards accepted: Access, Visa

### Shawlands ⚑
🏠🏠 COMMENDED

46 Kilham Lane, Winchester
SO22 5QD
☎ (01962) 861166

*Attractive, modern house, situated in a quiet, elevated position overlooking open countryside. Delightful garden. 1.5 miles from city centre.*
Wheelchair access category 3 ♿
Bedrooms: 2 double, 1 twin
Bathrooms: 1 private, 2 public

**Bed & breakfast**

| per night: | £min | £max |
|---|---|---|
| Single | 18.00 | 20.00 |
| Double | 32.00 | 36.00 |

Parking for 4

### Stratton House ⚑
🏠🏠

Stratton Road, St Giles Hill,
Winchester SO23 0JQ
☎ (01962) 863919 & 864529
Fax (01962) 842095
*A lovely old Victorian house with an acre of grounds, in an elevated position on St Giles Hill.*
Bedrooms: 2 single, 2 double, 2 twin, 1 triple
Bathrooms: 7 private, 3 public

**Bed & breakfast**

| per night: | £min | £max |
|---|---|---|
| Single | 25.00 | 35.00 |
| Double | 40.00 | 50.00 |

**Half board**

| per person: | £min | £max |
|---|---|---|
| Daily | 30.00 | 40.00 |
| Weekly | 210.00 | 280.00 |

Evening meal 1800 (last orders 1600)
Parking for 8

### "Sycamores" ⚑
Listed COMMENDED

4 Bereweeke Close, Winchester
SO22 6AR
☎ (01962) 867242

*Continued* ▶

## WINCHESTER

### Continued

Detached house with open garden, in a quiet area 10 minutes' walk from the railway station. Family home.
Bedrooms: 2 double, 1 twin
Bathrooms: 1 public, 2 private showers

**Bed & breakfast**

| per night: | £min | £max |
|---|---|---|
| Single | 16.00 | 16.00 |
| Double | 32.00 | 32.00 |

Parking for 3

☎7 ⌨ ☐ ♨ ⒰ ⒮ ✂ 🗕 ▥ ■ ❄ ✗ 🚐

## The Wessex Centre Sparsholt College ♨

Sparsholt, Winchester SO21 2NF
☎ (01962) 776647 & 797259
Fax (01962) 776636
Agricultural college offering modern hostel accommodation during vacation periods (March/April, June-September). Comfortable bedrooms, picturesque surroundings, good food, sports facilities.
Bedrooms: 180 single, 12 twin
Bathrooms: 192 private

**Bed & breakfast**

| per night: | £min | £max |
|---|---|---|
| Single | 19.76 | |
| Double | 34.84 | |

**Half board**

| per person: | £min | £max |
|---|---|---|
| Daily | 24.91 | |
| Weekly | 144.56 | |

Lunch available
Evening meal 1800 (last orders 1930)
Parking for 200
Open March-April, June-September
Cards accepted: Access, Visa

☎ ♨ ♨ ⒮ ✂ 🗕 ▥ ■ ▯10-200 ✗ ● ✗ ♨ ∪ ↑ ✓ ❄ 🅿

## WINDSOR

Berkshire
Map ref 2D2

Town dominated by the spectacular castle and home of the Royal Family for over 900 years. Parts are open to the public. There are many attractions including the Great Park, Eton and trips on the river.
*Tourist Information Centre*
*☎ (01753) 852010*

## Barbara Clemens
☒

49 Longmead, Windsor SL4 5PZ
☎ (01753) 866019
Fax (01753) 830964
A home-from-home with private facilities in quiet residential area. 1.25 miles from town centre and Windsor Castle.
Bedrooms: 1 double, 1 triple
Bathrooms: 2 private

**Bed & breakfast**

| per night: | £min | £max |
|---|---|---|
| Single | 21.00 | 21.00 |
| Double | 38.00 | 38.00 |

Parking for 2

⌨ ☐ ♨ ⒰ ⒮ ✂ 🗕 ▥ ■ ✗ 🚐

## Chasela
Listed

30 Convent Road, Windsor SL4 3RB
☎ (01753) 860410
Warm, modern house a mile from the castle. Easy access M4, M40, M25, M3, Heathrow. TV, tea/coffee facilities in rooms. Breakfast room overlooks lovely garden. Payphone.
Bedrooms: 1 single, 1 twin
Bathrooms: 1 public

**Bed & breakfast**

| per night: | £min | £max |
|---|---|---|
| Single | 16.00 | 20.00 |
| Double | 32.00 | 40.00 |

Parking for 5

☎3 ☐ ♨ ⒰ ▥ ■ ■ ❄ ✗ 🚐

## The Crown & Cushion Inn
Listed

84 High Street, Eton, Windsor
SL4 6AF
☎ (01753) 861531
Family-run establishment, 15th C in part, close to Eton College. Windsor Castle and River Thames. Traditional lunchtime/evening meals.
Bedrooms: 5 single, 1 double, 2 twin
Bathrooms: 1 public, 1 private shower

**Bed & breakfast**

| per night: | £min | £max |
|---|---|---|
| Single | 25.00 | |
| Double | 50.00 | |

**Half board**

| per person: | £min | £max |
|---|---|---|
| Daily | 28.00 | |
| Weekly | 195.00 | |

Lunch available
Evening meal 1730 (last orders 2030)
Parking for 10
Cards accepted: Access, Visa, Amex

☎10 ☐ ♨ ♨ ⒮ ▥ ⒯ ■ ■ ▯30 ❄ ✗ 🚐 ⌂

## Halcyon House
👑 COMMENDED

131 Clarence Road, Windsor SL4 5AR
☎ (01753) 863262
A warm welcome at a family-run guesthouse, 10 minutes' walk from the town centre and river. Ideal base for London. Off-street parking.
Bedrooms: 2 double, 2 twin
Bathrooms: 3 private, 1 public

**Bed & breakfast**

| per night: | £min | £max |
|---|---|---|
| Single | 26.00 | 36.00 |
| Double | 35.00 | 42.00 |

Parking for 6

⌨ ☐ ♨ ⒰ ⒮ ✂ 🗕 ▥ ■ ❄ ✗ 🚐

## 1 Stovell Road
Listed

Windsor SL4 5JB
☎ (01753) 852055
A separate, self-contained garden flat with its own lounge. Only 100 yards to the river and the leisure centre and 7 minutes' walk to the town centre.
Bedrooms: 1 double, 1 twin
Bathrooms: 2 private

**Bed & breakfast**

| per night: | £min | £max |
|---|---|---|
| Single | 30.00 | 30.00 |
| Double | 40.00 | 40.00 |

Parking for 2

♨ ☎ ⒰ ⒮ ✂ 🗕 ⒯ ▥ ■ ⊚ ■ ❄ ✗ 🚐 ⒯

## Tanglewood
Listed HIGHLY COMMENDED

Oakley Green, Windsor SL4 4PZ
☎ (01753) 860034
Picturesque chalet-style guesthouse in beautiful garden. Rural area overlooking open fields on B3024. Windsor 10 minutes' drive, Heathrow 15 miles. Excellent meals at nearby pub.
Bedrooms: 2 twin
Bathrooms: 1 public

**Bed & breakfast**

| per night: | £min | £max |
|---|---|---|
| Single | 20.00 | 20.00 |
| Double | 34.00 | 34.00 |

Parking for 2
Open May-September

☎ ☐ ♨ ⒰ ▥ ■ ❄ ✗ 🚐

## WINSLOW

Buckinghamshire
Map ref 2C1

Small town with Georgian houses, a little market square and a fine church with 15th C wall-paintings. Winslow Hall, built to the design of Sir Christopher Wren in 1700, is open to the public.

## Manor Farm Stables
Listed

High Street, North Marston, Buckingham MK18 3PS
☎ North Marston (01296) 670252 & 670708
Comfortable converted stables within easy reach of National Trust properties, Milton Keynes and Aylesbury. Breakfast served in farmhouse.
Bedrooms: 1 single, 2 double, 2 twin, 1 triple
Bathrooms: 6 private

**Bed & breakfast**

| per night: | £min | £max |
|---|---|---|
| Single | 20.00 | 25.00 |
| Double | 39.00 | 45.00 |

Parking for 8

☎ ♨ ⌨ ☐ ♨ ⒰ ▥ ■ ✗ 🚐 🚐

## WINTERBORNE STICKLAND

Dorset
Map ref 2B3

### Restharrow

😊😊 HIGHLY COMMENDED

North Street, Winterborne Stickland,
Blandford Forum DT11 0NH
☎ Milton Abbas (01258) 880936 &
Mobile 0850 285645
*Comfortable accommodation in pretty
village at head of Winterborne Valley,
in the "Heart of Dorset". Friendly base
for exploring the county.*
Bedrooms: 2 double
Bathrooms: 2 private
**Bed & breakfast**

| per night: | £min | £max |
|---|---|---|
| Single | 22.00 | 28.00 |
| Double | 32.00 | 38.00 |

Parking for 3

☎🛏️🖐️🔌🛜📶💲🗝️📺🛋️🖨️✈️ 🐕 SP

## WITNEY

Oxfordshire
Map ref 2C1

Town famous for its blanket-
making and mentioned in the
Domesday Book. The market-place
contains the Butter Cross, a
medieval meeting place, and there
is a green with merchants' houses.
*Tourist Information Centre*
☎ *(01993) 775802*

### Field View

😊😊 HIGHLY COMMENDED

Wood Green, Witney OX8 6DE
☎ (01993) 705485
*Situated in two acres on edge of the
bustling market town of Witney. Ideal
for Oxford University and the Cotswolds.*
Bedrooms: 1 double, 2 twin
Bathrooms: 2 private, 1 private shower
**Bed & breakfast**

| per night: | £min | £max |
|---|---|---|
| Single | 22.00 | 24.00 |
| Double | 36.00 | 44.00 |

Parking for 10

☎🛏️🖐️🔌💲🗝️📺🛋️📶✈️🐕

## WOKINGHAM

Berkshire
Map ref 2C2

Pleasant town which grew up
around the silk trade and has
some half-timbered and Georgian
houses.

### Tudor Place

92 Arbor Lane, Winnersh, Wokingham
RG11 5JD
☎ (01734) 785007
Fax (01734) 785018
*Tudor-style house with en-suite facilities.
Within 10 minutes' drive of*

*Wokingham, Bracknell and Reading.
Ideal choice for computer training
courses.*
Bedrooms: 3 double
Bathrooms: 3 private
**Bed & breakfast**

| per night: | £min | £max |
|---|---|---|
| Single | 35.00 | 50.00 |
| Double | 50.00 | 60.00 |

Parking for 10
Cards accepted: Access, Visa

🛜🖐️🔌🗝️🛋️🖨️🍽️10 🐾✈️🐕

## WOODSTOCK

Oxfordshire
Map ref 2C1

Small country town clustered
around the park gates of Blenheim
Palace, the superb 18th C home of
the Duke of Marlborough. The
town has well-known inns and an
interesting museum. Sir Winston
Churchill was born and buried
nearby.

### Gorselands Farmhouse Auberge ⋀

😊😊

Boddington Lane, Long Hanborough,
Witney OX8 6PU
☎ Freeland (01993) 881895
Fax (01993) 882799
*Stone country farmhouse with exposed
beams, snooker room, conservatory.
Convenient for Blenheim Palace, Oxford
and Cotswold villages. Evening meals
available. Licensed for wine and beer.
Grass tennis court.*
Bedrooms: 1 single, 2 double, 1 twin,
2 family rooms
Bathrooms: 6 private, 1 public
**Bed & breakfast**

| per night: | £min | £max |
|---|---|---|
| Single | 17.50 | 25.00 |
| Double | 28.00 | 35.00 |

| Half board per person: | £min | £max |
|---|---|---|
| Daily | 24.45 | 27.95 |
| Weekly | 150.00 | 180.00 |

Evening meal 1900 (last orders 2100)
Parking for 7
Cards accepted: Access, Visa, Amex

🛜🖐️🔌💲🗝️📺🛋️🖨️🅿️🍷🔍 🐾🐕 SP 🎱🌐

### The Laurels

😊😊 HIGHLY COMMENDED

Hensington Road, Woodstock
OX20 1JL
☎ (01993) 812583

*Fine Victorian house, charmingly
furnished with an emphasis on comfort
and quality. Just off town centre and a
short walk from Blenheim Palace.*
Bedrooms: 1 double, 1 twin, 1 triple
Bathrooms: 3 private
**Bed & breakfast**

| per night: | £min | £max |
|---|---|---|
| Single | 28.00 | 38.00 |
| Double | 35.00 | 45.00 |

Parking for 3
Cards accepted: Access, Visa

🛜7🛏️🖐️🔌💲🗝️🛋️🖨️✈️🐕 DAP T

### Plane Tree House

😊

15 High Street, Woodstock, Oxford
OX20 1TE
☎ (01993) 813075
*Located in Woodstock town centre, 2
minutes' from Blenheim Palace. Ideal
base for touring the Cotswolds.*
Bedrooms: 1 double, 1 twin, 1 triple
Bathrooms: 1 public
**Bed & breakfast**

| per night: | £min | £max |
|---|---|---|
| Single | 20.00 | 25.00 |
| Double | 30.00 | 35.00 |

🛜🛏️🖐️🔌💲🗝️📺🛋️✈️🐕

### Punch Bowl Inn ⋀

Listed APPROVED

12 Oxford Street, Woodstock, Oxford
OX20 1TR
☎ (01993) 811218
Fax (01993) 811393
*Family-run pub in the centre of
Woodstock, close to Blenheim Palace. A
good touring centre for Oxford and the
Cotswolds.*
Bedrooms: 2 single, 4 double, 2 twin,
1 triple, 1 family room
Bathrooms: 3 private, 3 public
**Bed & breakfast**

| per night: | £min | £max |
|---|---|---|
| Single | 28.00 | 31.00 |
| Double | 38.00 | 41.00 |

Lunch available
Evening meal 1800 (last orders 2130)
Parking for 20
Cards accepted: Access, Visa, Amex

🛜🛏️🖐️💲🗝️🛋️🖨️🐾🎱🐕 T

### The Ridings

😊😊

32 Banbury Road, Woodstock, Oxford
OX20 1LQ
☎ (01993) 811269
*Detached house in a quiet, rural setting.
10 minutes' walk to town centre and
Blenheim Palace. Go past the Tourist
Information Centre for 300 yards then
take left fork along Banbury Road.*
Bedrooms: 2 twin, 1 triple
Bathrooms: 1 private, 1 public

*Continued* ▶

---

Please mention this guide
when making a booking.

---

## WOODSTOCK

*Continued*

**Bed & breakfast**

| per night: | £min | £max |
| --- | --- | --- |
| Single | 25.00 | 30.00 |
| Double | 36.00 | 40.00 |

Parking for 4
Open March-November
🛌🍴🚪🛗♿🚭🅿️📺🛏️❄️🐾

### Shepherds Hall Inn

♛♛

Witney Road, Freeland, Witney
OX8 8HQ
☎ Freeland (01993) 881256
*Well-appointed inn offering good*
*accommodation. All rooms en-suite.*
*Ideally situated for Oxford, Woodstock*
*and the Cotswolds, on the A4095*
*Woodstock to Witney road.*
Bedrooms: 1 single, 1 double, 2 twin,
1 triple
Bathrooms: 5 private

**Bed & breakfast**

| per night: | £min | £max |
| --- | --- | --- |
| Single | 20.00 | 25.00 |
| Double | 35.00 | 40.00 |

Lunch available
Evening meal 1900 (last orders 2200)
Parking for 50
Cards accepted: Access, Visa
🛌🍴🚪🛗♿🛏️❄️🐾

## YARNTON

Oxfordshire
Map ref 2C1

### Eltham Villa Guest House

♛♛♛ COMMENDED

148 Woodstock Road, Yarnton,
Kidlington OX5 1PW
☎ Kidlington (01865) 376037
Fax (01865) 376037
*Situated on the main A44 between the*
*historic town of Woodstock and the*
*University City of Oxford. A few*
*minutes' drive from Blenheim Palace.*
Bedrooms: 2 single, 1 double, 2 twin,
2 family rooms
Bathrooms: 7 private

**Bed & breakfast**

| per night: | £min | £max |
| --- | --- | --- |
| Single | 20.00 | 30.00 |
| Double | 30.00 | 40.00 |

**Half board**

| per person: | £min | £max |
| --- | --- | --- |
| Daily | 30.00 | 40.00 |
| Weekly | 200.00 | 250.00 |

Evening meal 1900 (last orders 2000)
Parking for 7
Cards accepted: Amex
🛌🍴🚪🛗♿🚭🛗🅂🛏️📺🛏️📠❄️
🍴🐾🚭🆂🆃

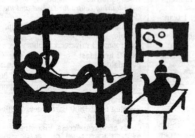

# KEY TO SYMBOLS

Information about many of the services and
facilities at accommodation listed in this guide
is given in the form of symbols. The key to
these symbols is inside the back cover flap. You
may find it helpful to keep the flap open when
referring to the accommodation listings.

# CHECK THE MAPS

The colour maps at the back of this guide show
all cities, towns and villages which have
accommodation listings in the guide. They will
enable you to check if there is suitable
accommodation in the vicinity of the place you
plan to visit.

*This is England's 'garden' region of orchards, vineyards and oasthouses, of unspoilt and well-kept villages in distinctive local styles. Walk the beaches and explore the old towns of Sussex and Kent where, long ago, smuggling was a way of life. If you can't spare a week, try a short break in one of the famous resorts — from Herne Bay in the east to Bognor Regis in the west. Full of historic houses, cathedrals and castles, there's not a dull mile from Surrey to the sea.*

# SOUTH EAST ENGLAND

**The Counties of East Sussex, Kent, Surrey and West Sussex**

For more information on South East England, contact:
South East England Tourist Board
The Old Brew House
Warwick Park
Tunbridge Wells
Kent TN2 5TU
Tel: (01892) 540766
Fax: (01892) 511008

Where to Go in South East England
– see pages 350–353

Where to Stay in South East England
– see pages 354–377

# WHERE TO GO

You will find hundreds of interesting places to visit during your stay in South East England, just some of which are listed in these pages. The number against each name will help you locate it on the map (page 353). Contact any Tourist Information Centre in the region for more ideas on days out in South East England.

**1 Powell Cotton Museum, Quex House and Gardens**
Quex Park, Birchington, Kent CT7 0BH
Tel: (01843) 842168
Regency house with period furniture. Museum with ethnograhic collections, diorama of African and Asian animals, weapons, archaeology, Chinese porcelain.

Epsom is the home of the Derby – the most famous horse race in the world.

**2 Royal Engineers Museum**
Prince Arthur Road, Gillingham, Kent
Tel: (01634) 406397
The characters, lives and work of Britain's soldier-engineers, 1066–1945. Medals, uniforms, scientific and technical equipment. Collection of ethnography and decorative arts.

**3 The Historic Dockyard**
Chatham, Kent ME4 4TE
Tel: (01634) 812551
Historic 18th C 80-acre dockyard, now a museum. Eight galleries including the award-winning "Wooden Walls". Sail and colour loft, ordnance mews, ropery, wagon rides.

**4 Brogdale Horticultural Trust**
Brogdale Farm, Brogdale Road, Faversham, Kent ME13 8XZ
Tel: (01795) 535286
National Fruit Collection with 4,000 varieties of fruit in 30 acres of orchard: apples, pears, cherries, plums, currants, quinces, medlars, etc.

**5 The Royal Horticultural Society's Garden**
Wisley, Surrey GU23 6QB
Tel: (01483) 224234
RHS establishment with 250 acres of vegetable, fruit and ornamental gardens. Trial grounds, glasshouses, rock garden, ponds, rose gardens, model and specialist gardens.

**6 Belmont**
Belmont Park, Throwley, Kent ME13 OHH
Tel: (01795) 890202

Late 18th C country mansion designed by Samuel Wyatt, seat of the Harris family since 1801. Harris clock collection, mementoes of connections with India. Gardens and pinetum.

**7 Guildford Cathedral**
Stag Hill, Guildford, Surrey GU2 5UP
Tel: (01483) 65287
Anglican cathedral, foundation stone laid in 1936 and consecrated in 1961. Notable glass engravings, embroidered kneelers, modern furnishings. Brass rubbing centre.

**8 Birdworld and Underwaterworld**
Holt Pound, Farnham, Surrey GU10 4LD
Tel: (01420) 22140
20 acres of garden and parkland with ostriches, flamingoes, hornbills, parrots, emus, pelicans, etc. Penguin island, tropical and marine fish, plant area, seashore walk.

**9 Whitbread Hop Farm**
Beltring, Paddock Wood, Kent TN12 6PY
Tel: (01622) 872068
Largest collection of Victorian oasts in the world. Hop story exhibition. Shire horses, birds of prey, animal village, nature trail, working pottery.

**10 Iden Croft Herbs**
Frittenden Road, Staplehurst, Kent TN12 0DH
Tel: (01580) 891432
Large fresh herb farm with walled garden and variety of aromatic gardens, demonstrating the beauty and use of herbs. Thyme rockery of special interest.

**11 Dover Castle and Hellfire Corner**
Dover, Kent CT16 1HU
Tel: (01304) 201628
One of most powerful medieval fortresses in Western Europe. St Mary in Castro Saxon church, Roman lighthouse, Hellfire Corner. All the Queen's Men exhibition and Battle of Waterloo model.

**12 Bedgebury National Pinetum**
Goudhurst, Kent TN17 2SL
Tel: (01580) 211044
Forestry Commission's superb collection of specimen conifers in 150 acres, with lake and stream. Also many rhododendrons and azaleas. Visitor centre.

**13 Leonardslee Gardens**
Lower Beeding, West Sussex RH13 6PP
Tel: (01403) 891212
Renowned spring-flowering shrub garden in a valley: rhododendrons, camellias, azaleas, lakes, paths. Good views, autumn tints, rock garden, bonsai exhibition, alpine house.

**14 The Bluebell Railway – Living Museum**
Sheffield Park Station, Sheffield Park, East Sussex TN22 3QL
Tel: (01825) 722370
7.5-mile standard gauge track from Sheffield Park to Horsted Keynes with extension to New Coombe Bridge. Largest collection of engines in the south. Victorian stations and museum.

The clock at Abinger Hammer, struck on the hour by "Jack the Smith".

**15 Brickwall House and Gardens**
Northiam, East Sussex TN31 6NL
Tel: (01797) 223329
Formal garden with terracotta entrance gates. 18th C bowling alley, sunken topiary garden, yew hedges, chess garden, arboretum. Jacobean house with 17th C plaster ceilings.

**16 Great Dixter House and Gardens**
Northiam, East Sussex TN31 6PH
Tel: (01797) 253160
Fine example of 15th C manor house with antique furniture and needlework. Unique great

351

hall restored by Lutyens, who also designed the garden – topiary, meadow garden, flower beds.

**⑰ Rye Town Model Sound and Light Show**
The Heritage Centre, Strand Quay, Rye, East Sussex TN31 7AY
Tel: (01797) 226696
Fascinating combination of detailed model of the ancient town with dramatic sound and light effects, telling the story of Rye through the ages.

**⑱ Buckleys Yesterday's World**
89–90 High Street, Battle, East Sussex TN33 0AQ
Tel: (01424) 775378
Over 50,000 exhibits in a Wealden hall house recall shopping and domestic life from 1850 to 1950 with smells and commentaries. Railway station, play village, garden.

**⑲ Bignor Roman Villa**
Bignor, West Sussex RH20 1PH
Tel: (017987) 259
Remains of large villa containing probably the finest mosaic pavements outside Italy. Hypocaust under-floor heating system, Roman artefacts.

**⑳ Weald and Downland Open Air Museum**
Singleton, West Sussex PO18 OEU
Tel: (01243) 811348
Open-air museum of 35 rescued historic buildings from South East England reconstructed on downland country park site, including medieval farmstead and watermill.

**㉑ A Smuggler's Adventure at St Clement's Caves**
West Hill, Hastings, East Sussex TN34 3HY
Tel: (01424) 422964
One acre of caves, housing the largest smuggling exhibition in the country. Museum, audio-visual show and 50 life-size figures with dramatic sound and lighting effects.

**㉒ The Wildfowl and Wetlands Centre**
Mill Road, Arundel, West Sussex BN18 9PB
Tel: (01903) 883355
Reserve in 60 acres of watermeadows. Tame swans, ducks, geese and many wild birds. Film theatre and visitor centre with gallery.

**㉓ Denmans Garden**
Denmans, Fontwell, West Sussex BN18 0SU

Tel: (01243) 542808
Walled, gravel and water gardens, natural layout of trees, climbers and wall shrubs for all-year interest. Glass areas. School of Garden Design.

**㉔ Pallant House**
9 North Pallant, Chichester, West Sussex PO19 1TJ
Tel: (01243) 774557
Queen Anne residence containing Bow Porcelain collection, Hussey and Kearley painting collections, Rembrandt to Picasso, sculptures by Moore. Temporary exhibitions. Old kitchen.

**㉕ Charleston Farmhouse**
Firle, Lewes, East Sussex BN8 6LL
Tel: (01323) 811265
17th–18th C farmhouse, home of Vanessa and Clive Bell and Duncan Grant. House and contents decorated by the artists. Newly restored garden room. Traditional flint-walled garden.

**㉖ Brighton Sea Life Centre**
Marine Parade, Brighton BN2 1TB
Tel: (01273) 604234
Ocean life on a grand scale featuring over 35 displays of fascinating marine creatures with underwater tunnel.

**㉗ Foredown Tower Countryside Centre**
Foredown Road, Portslade, East Sussex BN41 2EW
Tel: (01273) 422540
Converted water tower 1909, housing exhibitions on the Downs and water. Camera obscura gives views of South Downs and coast. Touch screen computer, weather station with satellite, slide shows.

**㉘ Smarts Amusement Park**
Seafront, Littlehampton, West Sussex BN17 5LL
Tel: (01903) 721200
Large indoor and outdoor amusement park for all ages. Many rides including dodgems, Waltzer, Cyclone Roller Coaster, waterslides.

**㉙ Eastbourne Pier**
Grand Parade, Eastbourne, East Sussex BN21 3EL
Tel: (01323) 410466
Well-preserved Victorian seaside pier with coastal views, family amusement arcade, disco, family entertainment room, shops, fishing and boats.

**30** *Earnley Butterflies and Gardens*
133 Almodington Lane, Earnley, West Sussex
PO20 7JR
Tel: (01243) 512637
*Ornamental butterfly house, covered theme gardens, exotic bird garden, children's play area, small animal farm, pottery.*

# FIND OUT MORE

*Further information about holidays and attractions in South East England is available from:*
**South East England Tourist Board,** *The Old Brew House, Warwick Park, Tunbridge Wells, Kent TN2 5TU*
Tel: (01892) 540766

*These publications are available free from the South East England Tourist Board:*
- **Holiday Selector**
- **Accommodation Guide**
- **Short Breaks South East**
- **Diary of Events**

*Summer pudding, made with fruit from the "Garden of England".*

- **Favourite Gardens and Garden Hotels**
- **Bed and Breakfast Touring Map**
- **Holidays for Walkers**
- **Holidays for Cyclists**
*Also available is (price includes postage and packing):*
- **South East England Leisure Map £4**

# WHERE TO STAY

Accommodation entries in this regional section are listed in alphabetical order of place name, and then in alphabetical order of establishment.

Map references refer to the colour location maps at the back of this guide. The first figure is the map number; the letter and figure which follow indicate the grid reference on the map.

Symbols at the end of each accommodation entry give information about services and facilities. A 'key' to these symbols is inside the back cover flap, which can be kept open for easy reference.

## ALDINGTON

Kent
Map ref 3B4

Once the home of Elizabeth Barton, the "Holy Maid" or "Nun of Kent".

### Hogben Farm
Listed

Church Lane, Aldington, Ashford
TN25 7EH
☎ (01233) 720219
*Small 16th C country house, surrounded by pretty garden and 17 acres of farmland. Convenient for Channel ports, Channel Tunnel, Canterbury, Rye, Tenterden and Romney Marsh. Evening meals by prior arrangement.*
Bedrooms: 1 double, 2 twin
Bathrooms: 1 public

**Bed & breakfast**

| per night: | £min | £max |
| --- | --- | --- |
| Single | 15.00 | 17.00 |
| Double | 30.00 | 34.00 |

**Half board**

| per person: | £min | £max |
| --- | --- | --- |
| Daily | 25.00 | 27.00 |
| Weekly | 150.00 | 162.00 |

Evening meal 1800 (last orders 2000)
Parking for 6

The enquiry coupons at the back will help you when contacting proprietors.

## ALKHAM

Kent
Map ref 3C4

### Owler Lodge ⋒
❦❦❦ HIGHLY COMMENDED

Alkham Valley Road, Alkham, Dover
CT15 7BX
☎ Dover (01304) 826375
*Small family run guesthouse with inglenook and beams. In the middle of the village of Alkham on B2060 between Dover and Folkestone. 3 miles from Channel Tunnel, 4 miles from Dover Docks.*
Bedrooms: 2 double, 1 twin
Bathrooms: 3 private

**Bed & breakfast**

| per night: | £min | £max |
| --- | --- | --- |
| Single | 18.00 | 20.00 |
| Double | 36.00 | 40.00 |

**Half board**

| per person: | £min | £max |
| --- | --- | --- |
| Daily | 24.00 | 26.00 |

Evening meal 1800 (last orders 2100)
Parking for 6

## APPLEDORE

Kent
Map ref 3B4

A centre for shipping in the Middle Ages, this village now lies on the edge of Romney Marsh and the sea is 7 miles away.

### Court Lodge ⋒
❦❦ HIGHLY COMMENDED

Appledore, Ashford TN26 2DD
☎ (01233) 83403

*1100-acre arable farm. Victorian farmhouse set in 4 acres of mature garden and farmland, in the picturesque village of Appledore overlooking Romney Marsh. Close to Rye, Tenterden and Channel ports.*
Bedrooms: 1 double, 1 twin
Bathrooms: 2 private

**Bed & breakfast**

| per night: | £min | £max |
| --- | --- | --- |
| Single | 25.00 | |
| Double | 37.00 | |

Parking for 2

## ARDINGLY

West Sussex
Map ref 2D3

Famous for the South of England Agricultural Showground and public school. Nearby is Wakehurst Place (National Trust), the gardens of which are administered by the Royal Botanic Gardens, Kew.

### Coneybury ⋒
❦❦ COMMENDED

Hook Lane, West Hoathly, East Grinstead RH19 4PX
☎ Sharpthorne (01342) 810200
Fax (01342) 810887
*Secluded country estate with spectacular views, ideal for exploring Sussex, Surrey, Kent. B2028 to north end*

*Ardingly village high street, right down Cob Lane (steep hill) for 1 mile, third entrance on right.*
Bedrooms: 1 double, 1 twin
Bathrooms: 1 private, 1 public

**Bed & breakfast**

| per night: | £min | £max |
|---|---|---|
| Single | 20.00 | 25.00 |
| Double | 38.00 | 45.00 |

Parking for 3

## Old Knowles

**Listed   HIGHLY COMMENDED**

Church Lane, Ardingly, Haywards Heath RH17 6UR
☎ Haywards Heath (01444) 892259
Fax (01444) 892259
*14th C country house situated in rural surroundings. Good access to Gatwick Airport, London and National Trust locations.*
Bedrooms: 2 double, 1 twin
Bathrooms: 3 private

**Bed & breakfast**

| per night: | £min | £max |
|---|---|---|
| Single | 20.00 | 25.00 |
| Double | 38.00 | 45.00 |

Parking for 6

## ARUNDEL

West Sussex
Map ref 2D3

Picturesque, historic town on the River Arun, dominated by Arundel Castle, home of the Dukes of Norfolk. There are many 18th C houses, the Toy and Military Museum, Wildfowl and Wetlands Centre and Museum and Heritage Centre.
*Tourist Information Centre*
☎ (01903) 882268

## Arundel Park Inn & Travel Lodge ⚑

Station Approach, Arundel BN18 9JL
☎ (01903) 882588
Fax (01903) 883808
*Refurbished to high standard, 3 bedrooms on ground floor. Pleasant lounge bar, informal restaurant serving high quality food. Central to many places of interest. Two minutes from station, 5 minutes to centre of Arundel.*
Bedrooms: 1 single, 8 double, 2 twin, 1 family room
Bathrooms: 12 private

**Bed & breakfast**

| per night: | £min | £max |
|---|---|---|
| Single | 32.00 | 38.00 |
| Double | 42.00 | 48.00 |

Lunch available
Evening meal 1830 (last orders 2100)

Parking for 60
Cards accepted: Access, Visa, Switch/Delta

## Arundel Vineyards ⚑

**COMMENDED**

The Vineyard, Church Lane, Lyminster, Arundel BN17 7QF
☎ (01903) 883393
*3-acre fruit farm. Modern farmhouse in English vineyard in beautiful countryside. From Arundel, turn south on to A284 Littlehampton/Lyminster road (new split junction). Signposted 1 mile on right.*
Bedrooms: 1 double, 1 twin
Bathrooms: 2 private

**Bed & breakfast**

| per night: | £min | £max |
|---|---|---|
| Single | 24.00 | |
| Double | 36.00 | |

Parking for 15

## Mill Lane House ⚑

Slindon, Arundel BN18 0RP
☎ Slindon (01243) 814440
*18th C house in beautiful National Trust village. Magnificent views to coast. Pubs within easy walking distance. One mile from A29/A27 junction.*
Bedrooms: 1 single, 3 double, 2 twin, 1 triple
Bathrooms: 7 private, 1 public

**Bed & breakfast**

| per night: | £min | £max |
|---|---|---|
| Single | 23.50 | 23.50 |
| Double | 36.00 | 36.00 |

**Half board**

| per person: | £min | £max |
|---|---|---|
| Daily | 27.25 | 32.75 |
| Weekly | 177.50 | 214.25 |

Evening meal 1900 (last orders 1000)
Parking for 7

## Pindars ⚑

**HIGHLY COMMENDED**

Lyminster, Arundel BN17 7QF
☎ (01903) 882628
*Charming country house in small village offers comfortable bedrooms, good food and warm hospitality. Beautiful garden. Non-smoking. Convenient for A27.*
Bedrooms: 2 double, 1 twin
Bathrooms: 1 private, 1 public

**Bed & breakfast**

| per night: | £min | £max |
|---|---|---|
| Double | 30.00 | 42.00 |

**Half board**

| per person: | £min | £max |
|---|---|---|
| Daily | 40.00 | 54.00 |

Evening meal from 1700

Parking for 7
Cards accepted: Access, Visa

## ASHFORD

Kent
Map ref 3B4

Once a market centre for the farmers of the Weald of Kent and Romney Marsh. The town centre has a number of Tudor and Georgian houses.
*Tourist Information Centre*
☎ (01233) 629165

## Fishponds Farm ⚑

Pilgrims Way, Brook, Ashford TN25 5PP
☎ (01233) 812398
*Rural farmhouse with lake in Wye Downs Nature Reserve, 3 miles south-east of Wye on lane to Brabourne.*
Bedrooms: 1 double, 1 twin
Bathrooms: 2 private

**Bed & breakfast**

| per night: | £min | £max |
|---|---|---|
| Single | 20.00 | |
| Double | 32.00 | |

Parking for 10

## Meadowside ⚑

**HIGHLY COMMENDED**

Church Road, Mersham, Ashford TN25 6NT
☎ (01233) 502458
*Two miles from junction 10 M20, convenient for Channel Tunnel and ports, Leeds and Sissinghurst Castles, Canterbury and Tenterden. Large comfortable rooms en-suite (shower), tea-making, colour TV. Non-smokers only, please.*
Bedrooms: 1 double, 1 twin
Bathrooms: 2 private

**Bed & breakfast**

| per night: | £min | £max |
|---|---|---|
| Single | 20.00 | 20.00 |
| Double | 36.00 | 40.00 |

Parking for 2

## Warren Cottage ⚑

**APPROVED**

136 The Street, Willesborough, Ashford TN25 0NB
☎ (01233) 621905 & 632929
Fax (01233) 623400
*300-year-old guesthouse with oak beams, open fireplaces and a cosy atmosphere. On old coaching route with easy access to M20 and a short drive from many places of interest.*
Bedrooms: 2 single, 2 double, 1 twin
Bathrooms: 5 private, 1 public

Continued ▶

## ASHFORD

*Continued*

| **Bed & breakfast per night:** | £min | £max |
|---|---|---|
| Single | 25.00 | 50.00 |
| Double | 50.00 | 100.00 |

| **Half board per person:** | £min | £max |
|---|---|---|
| Daily | 34.00 | 59.00 |
| Weekly | 170.00 | 295.00 |

Lunch available
Evening meal 1830 (last orders 2130)
Parking for 8
Cards accepted: Access, Visa, Switch/Delta

## AYLESFORD

Kent
Map ref 3B3

### Wickham Lodge

[COMMENDED]

73 High Street, Aylesford ME20 7AY
☎ Maidstone (01622) 717267
Fax (01622) 718791

*Period house fronting river by Aylesford Bridge. Lawns to river bank in front, walled garden to rear. Quiet position close to M2/M20 motorways. French spoken.*

Bedrooms: 1 single, 1 double, 1 triple
Bathrooms: 3 private

| **Bed & breakfast per night:** | £min | £max |
|---|---|---|
| Single | 25.00 | 25.00 |
| Double | 45.00 | 50.00 |

| **Half board per person:** | £min | £max |
|---|---|---|
| Daily | 33.50 | 33.50 |
| Weekly | 234.50 | 234.50 |

Evening meal from 2000
Parking for 4
Cards accepted: Access, Visa

**National Crown ratings were correct at the time of going to press but are subject to change. Please check at the time of booking.**

## BATTLE

East Sussex
Map ref 3B4

The Abbey at Battle was built on the site of the Battle of Hastings, when William defeated Harold II and so became the Conqueror in 1066. The museum has a fine collection relating to the Sussex iron industry.
*Tourist Information Centre*
*☎ (01424) 773721*

### Kitchenham Farm

[Listed]

Ashburnham, Battle TN33 9NP
☎ Ninfield (01424) 892221

*700-acre arable and mixed farm. Friendly family atmosphere in beautiful 18th C farmhouse. Traditional buildings offer perfect backdrop for stunning views. Large comfortable rooms.*

Bedrooms: 1 double, 2 twin
Bathrooms: 1 public

| **Bed & breakfast per night:** | £min | £max |
|---|---|---|
| Single | 20.00 | 20.00 |
| Double | 32.00 | 34.00 |

| **Half board per person:** | £min | £max |
|---|---|---|
| Daily | 25.00 | 27.00 |
| Weekly | 170.00 | 170.00 |

Evening meal 1900 (last orders 2000)
Parking for 7

### Moons Hill Farm

Moons Hill Farm, The Green, Ninfield, Battle TN33 9LH
☎ Ninfield (01424) 892645

*10-acre mixed farm. Modernised farmhouse in Ninfield village centre, in the heart of "1066" country. A warm welcome and Sussex home cooking. Pub opposite.*

Bedrooms: 2 double, 1 twin
Bathrooms: 2 private, 1 public

| **Bed & breakfast per night:** | £min | £max |
|---|---|---|
| Single | 15.00 | 17.50 |
| Double | 30.00 | 35.00 |

Parking for 12
Open January-November

## BIDDENDEN

Kent
Map ref 3B4

Perfect village with black and white houses, a tithe barn and a pond. Part of the village is grouped around a green with a village sign depicting the famous Biddenden Maids. It was an important centre of the Flemish weaving industry, hence the beautiful Old Cloth Hall.

### Bettmans Oast

[HIGHLY COMMENDED]

Hareplain Road, Biddenden, Ashford TN27 8LJ
☎ (01580) 291463

*Grade II listed oast house and converted barn set in 10 acres near Sissinghurst Castle, quarter mile from Three Chimneys pub. Lovely gardens and log fires in winter.*

Bedrooms: 1 family room
Bathrooms: 1 private

| **Bed & breakfast per night:** | £min | £max |
|---|---|---|
| Single | 20.00 | 20.00 |
| Double | 40.00 | 40.00 |

| **Half board per person:** | £min | £max |
|---|---|---|
| Daily | 30.00 | 35.00 |
| Weekly | 200.00 | 230.00 |

Evening meal 1900 (last orders 2100)
Parking for 4

### Bishopsdale Oast

[HIGHLY COMMENDED]

Biddenden, Ashford TN27 8DR
☎ (01580) 291027 & 292065
Fax (01580) 292321

*18th C double kiln oast. Outstanding views, business facilities, professional cooks. Tenterden 2 miles, Cranbrook 5 miles. Signpost on bend.*

Bedrooms: 2 double
Bathrooms: 2 private

| **Bed & breakfast per night:** | £min | £max |
|---|---|---|
| Single | 30.00 | 40.00 |
| Double | 40.00 | 50.00 |

| **Half board per person:** | £min | £max |
|---|---|---|
| Daily | 32.50 | 40.00 |
| Weekly | 227.50 | 280.00 |

Lunch available
Evening meal 1830 (last orders 2000)
Parking for 6

## BIRCHINGTON

Kent
Map ref 3C3

Town on the north coast of Kent with sandy beaches and rock pools. Powell Cotton Museum is in nearby Quex Park.

### Woodchurch Farmhouse

**Listed**

Woodchurch, Birchington CT7 0HE
☎ Thanet (01843) 832468
*6-acre arable farm. This Elizabethan farmhouse provides a warm welcome and ensures a comfortable stay. An excellent base for exploring south-east Kent.*
Bedrooms: 1 double, 2 twin
Bathrooms: 1 public

**Bed & breakfast**

| per night: | £min | £max |
|---|---|---|
| Single | 14.50 | 14.50 |
| Double | 29.00 | 29.00 |

Parking for 6

⌖☆♿♨🖊️UL🖊️TV①🖥️🅿️🚲U❄✱🚐🏠

## BREDE

East Sussex
Map ref 3B4

J M Barrie reputedly invented Peter Pan's Captain Hook whilst staying at Brede Place.

### Layces The Tea House

**COMMENDED**

Chitcombe Road, Broad Oak, Brede, Rye TN31 6EU
☎ (01424) 882836
*Situated six miles west of Rye. Very comfortable residence in 2 acres of gardens with wonderful views from all rooms. Ideal base for visiting many historic towns. Non-smokers only, please.*
Bedrooms: 1 double, 1 twin
Bathrooms: 2 private

**Bed & breakfast**

| per night: | £min | £max |
|---|---|---|
| Single | 15.00 | 20.00 |
| Double | 30.00 | 33.00 |

**Half board**

| per person: | £min | £max |
|---|---|---|
| Daily | 22.00 | 27.00 |
| Weekly | 154.00 | 189.00 |

Evening meal 1800 (last orders 2000)
Parking for 4
Open March-October

🖊️🖥️□🖊️UL🔒🖊️✂🖥️🅿️❄✱🚐

---

The town index at the back of this guide gives page numbers of all places with accommodation.

---

## BRIGHTON & HOVE

East Sussex
Map ref 2D3

Brighton's attractions include the Royal Pavilion, Volks Railway, Sea Life Centre and Marina, Conference Centre and "The Lanes" and several theatres. Neighbouring Hove is a resort in its own right.
*Tourist Information Centre*
*☎ (01273) 323755; for Hove*
*(01273) 746100 or 778087*

### 'Brighton' Marina House Hotel ⋒

♨♨♨

8 Charlotte Street, Marine Parade, Brighton BN2 1AG
☎ (01273) 605349 & 679484
Fax (01273) 605349

*Cosy, elegantly furnished, well-equipped, clean, comfortable, caring, family-run. Near sea, central for Palace Pier, Royal Pavilion, conference and exhibition halls, the famous Lanes, tourist attractions. Flexible breakfast, check-in/out times. Offering all facilities. Free street parking. Best in price range.*
Bedrooms: 3 single, 4 double, 3 triple
Bathrooms: 7 private, 1 public

**Bed & breakfast**

| per night: | £min | £max |
|---|---|---|
| Single | 13.50 | 23.00 |
| Double | 25.00 | 45.00 |

**Half board**

| per person: | £min | £max |
|---|---|---|
| Daily | 25.00 | 35.00 |
| Weekly | 165.00 | 222.00 |

Lunch available
Evening meal 1830 (last orders 1700)
Cards accepted: Access, Visa, Diners, Amex

⌖♨♿📞🖊️□♨🖊️🔒S🖊️🖥️🅿️✱
✂ OAP SP T

### Cavalaire House ⋒

♨♨ **COMMENDED**

34 Upper Rock Gardens, Brighton BN2 1QF
☎ (01273) 696899
Fax (01273) 600504
*Victorian townhouse, close to sea and town centre. Resident proprietors offer comfortably furnished rooms with or without private facilities. Book 7 nights and get 1 night free.*
Bedrooms: 1 single, 3 double, 3 twin, 2 triple
Bathrooms: 4 private, 1 public, 4 private showers

**Bed & breakfast**

| per night: | £min | £max |
|---|---|---|
| Single | 18.00 | 19.00 |
| Double | 28.00 | 45.00 |

Cards accepted: Access, Visa, Diners, Amex

⌖5🖊️□♨🖊️🖊️UL🖥️✂🖥️🖥️🅿️🚲🏠

### Diana House ⋒

**Listed**

25 St. Georges Terrace, Brighton BN2 1JJ
☎ (01273) 605797
*Warm and friendly, conveniently situated for town, conference centre and marina. Tea/coffee facilities, colour TV and central heating. Own key for access.*
Bedrooms: 4 double, 2 twin, 2 triple, 1 family room
Bathrooms: 1 private, 6 private showers

**Bed & breakfast**

| per night: | £min | £max |
|---|---|---|
| Single | 14.00 | 18.00 |
| Double | 28.00 | 36.00 |

Cards accepted: Access, Visa

⌖□♨🖊️UL S①🖥️🅿️🚲 OAP SP

## BURWASH

East Sussex
Map ref 3B4

Village of old houses, many from the Tudor and Stuart periods. One of the old ironmasters' houses is Bateman's (National Trust) which was the home of Rudyard Kipling.

### Woodlands Farm

**Listed**

Heathfield Road, Burwash, Etchingham TN19 7LA
☎ (01435) 882794

*55-acre mixed farm. Modernised 16th C farmhouse set away from road, amidst fields and woods. Friendly welcome and fresh food. Near Batemans.*
Bedrooms: 2 double, 1 twin
Bathrooms: 1 private, 2 public

**Bed & breakfast**

| per night: | £min | £max |
|---|---|---|
| Single | 15.50 | 18.00 |
| Double | 31.00 | 36.00 |

**Half board**

| per person: | £min | £max |
|---|---|---|
| Daily | 23.50 | 26.00 |

Parking for 4
Open April-December

⌖♿🖊️UL🔒🖊️TV🖥️🖥️✱🚐🏠

## CANTERBURY

Kent
Map ref 3B3

Place of pilgrimage since the martyrdom of Becket in 1170 and the site of Canterbury Cathedral. Visit St Augustine's Abbey, St Martin's (the oldest church in England), Royal Museum and Art Gallery and the Canterbury Tales. Nearby is Howletts Wild Animal Park.
*Tourist Information Centre*
☎ *(01227) 766567*

### Alicante Guest House ⚠

**Listed** **COMMENDED**

4 Roper Road, Canterbury CT2 7EH
☎ (01227) 766277
*Family-run for 11 years, offering friendly, helpful service in comfortable surroundings. Competitive prices for long and short stays.*
Bedrooms: 1 single, 2 double, 1 twin, 1 triple, 1 family room
Bathrooms: 2 public, 1 private shower
**Bed & breakfast**

| per night: | £min | £max |
|---|---|---|
| Single | 18.00 | 20.00 |
| Double | 32.00 | 36.00 |

Cards accepted: Access, Visa, Diners

### Bower Farm House

**Listed** **COMMENDED**

Stelling Minnis, Canterbury CT4 6BB
☎ Stelling Minnis (01227) 709430
*Delightful heavily beamed 17th C farmhouse between the villages of Stelling Minnis and Bossingham. Canterbury and Hythe are approximately 7 miles away.*
Bedrooms: 1 single, 1 double, 1 twin
Bathrooms: 2 private, 1 public
**Bed & breakfast**

| per night: | £min | £max |
|---|---|---|
| Single | 17.50 | 17.50 |
| Double | 35.00 | 35.00 |

Parking for 8

### Bridge House

**Listed**

The Green, Chartham, Canterbury CT4 7JW
☎ (01227) 738354
*Well-equipped house on banks of River Stour, next to village green. Tea/coffee upon request. Colour TV. Canterbury 3 miles on A28.*
Bedrooms: 2 twin
Bathrooms: 2 public
**Bed & breakfast**

| per night: | £min | £max |
|---|---|---|
| Single | 18.00 | 20.00 |
| Double | 30.00 | 34.00 |

Parking for 5

### Cathedral Gate Hotel ⚠

36 Burgate, Canterbury CT1 2HA
☎ (01227) 464381
Fax (01227) 462800
*Central position at main entrance to the cathedral. Car parking nearby. Baby listening service. Old world charm at reasonable prices. English breakfast extra.*
Bedrooms: 5 single, 7 double, 8 twin, 2 triple, 2 family rooms
Bathrooms: 12 private, 3 public, 2 private showers
**Bed & breakfast**

| per night: | £min | £max |
|---|---|---|
| Single | 21.00 | 45.00 |
| Double | 40.00 | 68.00 |

Evening meal 1900 (last orders 2100)
Parking for 12
Cards accepted: Access, Visa, Diners, Amex

### Clare-Ellen Guest House ⚠

**HIGHLY COMMENDED**

9 Victoria Road, Wincheap, Canterbury CT1 3SG
☎ (01227) 760205
Fax (01227) 784482

*Victorian house with large, elegant en-suite rooms, 8 minutes' walk from city centre. 5 minutes to BR Canterbury East station. Car park and garage available.*
Bedrooms: 1 single, 2 double, 1 twin, 1 family room
Bathrooms: 4 private, 2 public
**Bed & breakfast**

| per night: | £min | £max |
|---|---|---|
| Single | 20.00 | 24.00 |
| Double | 40.00 | 46.00 |

Parking for 9
Cards accepted: Access, Visa, Diners

### The Corner House ⚠

**Listed**

113 Whitstable Road, Canterbury CT2 8EF
☎ (01227) 761352
*Just a few minutes' walking distance from city, university, shops and restaurants. Spacious family house and friendly hospitality.*
Bedrooms: 1 double, 2 twin
Bathrooms: 2 public
**Bed & breakfast**

| per night: | £min | £max |
|---|---|---|
| Double | 28.00 | 36.00 |

Parking for 4

### Crossways

☒

Field Way, Sturry, Canterbury CT2 0BH
☎ (01227) 711059
*Small, family-run early Victorian home, 3 miles from Canterbury on A28 Margate road. On main bus and rail routes.*
Bedrooms: 1 single, 1 double, 1 twin
Bathrooms: 2 private, 1 public, 1 private shower
**Bed & breakfast**

| per night: | £min | £max |
|---|---|---|
| Single | 16.00 | 17.00 |
| Double | 32.00 | 34.00 |

Parking for 6

### The Farmhouse, Upper Mystole Park Farm

**HIGHLY COMMENDED**

Pennypot Lane, Mystole, Canterbury CT4 7BT
☎ (01227) 730589
*90-acre fruit farm. Modern farmhouse in the heart of Kent and with magnificent views. Set between historic Canterbury and beautiful Chilham (A28). Dover 25 minutes. Good home cooking.*
Bedrooms: 2 double, 1 twin
Bathrooms: 2 private, 1 public
**Bed & breakfast**

| per night: | £min | £max |
|---|---|---|
| Single | 18.00 | 20.00 |
| Double | 32.00 | 35.00 |

**Half board**

| per person: | £min | £max |
|---|---|---|
| Daily | 24.00 | 26.00 |
| Weekly | 165.00 | 175.00 |

Evening meal 1830 (last orders 2000)
Parking for 6

### Magnolia House ⚠

**HIGHLY COMMENDED**

36 St Dunstans Terrace, Canterbury CT2 8AX
☎ (01227) 765121
Fax (01227) 765121

*Georgian house in attractive city street. Close to university, gardens, river and city centre. Very quiet house within a walled garden, ideal for guests to relax in. Four-poster suite available.*
Bedrooms: 1 single, 4 double, 2 twin
Bathrooms: 7 private
**Bed & breakfast**

| per night: | £min | £max |
|---|---|---|
| Single | 36.00 | 38.00 |
| Double | 50.00 | 80.00 |

| Half board per person: | £min | £max |
|---|---|---|
| Daily | 36.00 | 50.00 |

Parking for 4
Cards accepted: Access, Visa, Amex

🛇🖚🖭🖳◔⬥Ⓤ🛄🚲Ⓢ✂🏵📺🅿❀
✕🚐 OAP SP 🏠 T

## Old House

**Listed**

Garlinge Green, Canterbury CT4 5RT
☎ (01227) 700284

*Charming Grade II listed 16th C cottage
in tranquil 1.5 acre garden, on the
downs in Area of Outstanding Natural
Beauty. Antiques, log fire, beams,
croquet. Convenient for Canterbury and
Channel ports.*
Bedrooms: 2 double
Bathrooms: 1 private, 1 public

| Bed & breakfast per night: | £min | £max |
|---|---|---|
| Single | 20.00 | 25.00 |
| Double | 35.00 | 40.00 |

Parking for 2

🛇🖚🖭◔Ⓤ🅂✂🏵📺🛄🚲🅿❀🚐🏠

## Old Stone House ⚠

**Listed**

The Green, Wickhambreaux,
Canterbury CT3 1RQ
☎ (01227) 728591

*One of the oldest houses in Kent, parts
dating from 12th C. Once the home of
Joan Plantagenet, wife of the Black
Prince. Ten minutes west of Canterbury,
30 minutes from Folkestone and Dover.*
Bedrooms: 1 single, 2 double, 1 twin
Bathrooms: 2 private, 1 public

| Bed & breakfast per night: | £min | £max |
|---|---|---|
| Single | 15.00 | 20.00 |
| Double | 34.00 | 40.00 |

Parking for 4

🛇🖚🛆◔⬥Ⓤ🛄🚲❀✕🚐🏠

## Oriel Lodge ⚠

⬥⬥ **HIGHLY COMMENDED**

3 Queens Avenue, Canterbury
CT2 8AY
☎ (01227) 462845

*In a residential road near city centre,
Edwardian family house of warm period
character. Clean, comfortable bedrooms,
lounge area with log fire. Smoking in
lounge area only.*
Bedrooms: 1 single, 3 double, 1 twin,
1 triple
Bathrooms: 2 private, 2 public

| Bed & breakfast per night: | £min | £max |
|---|---|---|
| Single | 19.00 | 24.00 |
| Double | 33.00 | 54.00 |

Parking for 6

🛇6🖚🖭◔⬥Ⓤ🅂✂🚲🛄🚲❀✕🚐
SP 🏠 T

## Pointers Hotel ⚠

⬥⬥⬥ **COMMENDED**

1 London Road, Canterbury CT2 8LR
☎ (01227) 456846
Fax (01227) 831131

*Family-run Georgian hotel close to city
centre, cathedral and university.*
Bedrooms: 2 single, 8 double, 2 twin,
2 triple
Bathrooms: 8 private, 2 public,
2 private showers

| Bed & breakfast per night: | £min | £max |
|---|---|---|
| Single | 30.00 | 38.00 |
| Double | 42.00 | 58.00 |

| Half board per person: | £min | £max |
|---|---|---|
| Daily | 35.00 | 51.00 |
| Weekly | 217.00 | 280.00 |

Evening meal 1930 (last orders 2030)
Parking for 10
Cards accepted: Access, Visa, Diners,
Amex

🛇🕻🖚🖭◔⬥👫🍽◑🛄🚲🅿 SP 🏠 T

## St Stephens Guest House ⚠

**Listed** **COMMENDED**

100 St Stephens Road, Canterbury
CT2 7JL
☎ (01227) 767644
*Mock-Tudor house set in attractive
garden within easy walking distance of
the city centre and cathedral. Colour TV
in rooms. Car park.*
Bedrooms: 3 single, 8 double, 1 twin
Bathrooms: 4 private, 3 public

| Bed & breakfast per night: | £min | £max |
|---|---|---|
| Single | 19.00 | 23.00 |
| Double | 35.00 | 44.00 |

Parking for 10
Cards accepted: Access, Visa

🛇🛆◔⬥Ⓤ🛄🚲Ⓢ⬥🛄🚲🅿❀✕T

## Thanington Hotel ⚠

⬥⬥ **HIGHLY COMMENDED**

140 Wincheap, Canterbury CT1 3RY
☎ (01227) 453227
Fax (01227) 453225

*Beautiful bed and breakfast hotel with
indoor heated swimming pool and
games room. 5 minutes' walk city
centre, 30 minutes' drive from Dover.
Colour brochure available.*
Bedrooms: 5 double, 3 twin, 2 family
rooms
Bathrooms: 10 private

| Bed & breakfast per night: | £min | £max |
|---|---|---|
| Single | 40.00 | 47.00 |
| Double | 58.00 | 63.00 |

Parking for 12
Cards accepted: Access, Visa, Diners,
Amex

🛇🛆🕻🖚🖭◔⬥👫✂🏵📺🛄🚲🚲◉
❀🚐 SP 🏠 T

## Well House

⬥⬥

The Green, Chartham, Canterbury
CT4 7JW
☎ (01227) 738762
*In a very quiet position, on village
green next to 15th C church. Just off
A28, 2 miles from Canterbury.*
Bedrooms: 1 double, 1 twin
Bathrooms: 2 private

| Bed & breakfast per night: | £min | £max |
|---|---|---|
| Single | 20.00 | |
| Double | 30.00 | |

Parking for 2

🛇🖭◔⬥👫Ⓤ🅂🛄🚲❀🚐

## Wingham Well Farmhouse ⚠

**Listed** **COMMENDED**

Wingham, Canterbury CT3 1NW
☎ (01227) 720253
*15th C half-timbered farmhouse, listed
Grade II, on 160-acre arable farm. Off
A257 between Canterbury and
Sandwich. Channel ports and tunnel 30
minutes' drive.*
Bedrooms: 1 double, 1 twin
Bathrooms: 2 private

*Continued* ▶

## CANTERBURY

### Continued

**Bed & breakfast**

| per night: | £min | £max |
|---|---|---|
| Double | 35.00 | 45.00 |

Parking for 4

### Yorke Lodge ⚑

**COMMENDED**

50 London Road, Canterbury CT2 8LF
☎ (01227) 451243
Fax (01227) 462006
*Spacious, elegant Victorian town house close to city centre. Relax and enjoy a special bed and breakfast.*
Bedrooms: 1 single, 4 double
Bathrooms: 5 private

**Bed & breakfast**

| per night: | £min | £max |
|---|---|---|
| Single | 22.00 | 30.00 |
| Double | 40.00 | 45.00 |

Parking for 4
Cards accepted: Access, Visa, Amex

### Zan Stel Lodge ⚑

**Listed   COMMENDED**

140 Old Dover Road, Canterbury
CT1 3NX
☎ (01227) 453654
*Elegant Edwardian guesthouse offering a high standard of cleanliness and service. Enjoy breakfast in the spacious dining room overlooking delightful walled garden. 10 minutes' walk to city. Non smoking.*
Bedrooms: 2 double, 2 triple
Bathrooms: 2 private, 1 public

**Bed & breakfast**

| per night: | £min | £max |
|---|---|---|
| Double | 34.00 | 45.00 |

Parking for 4

## CHELWOOD GATE

East Sussex
Map ref 2D2

Small village on the edge of the Ashdown Forest.

### Holly House ⚑

Beaconsfield Road, Chelwood Gate,
Haywards Heath, West Sussex
RH17 7LF
☎ (01825) 740484

*Early Victorian forest farmhouse converted to comfortable family home.*

---

*Warm welcome, long views, acre garden. Situated in Ashdown Forest village.*
Bedrooms: 1 double, 2 twin
Bathrooms: 3 private

**Bed & breakfast**

| per night: | £min | £max |
|---|---|---|
| Single | 16.00 | 25.00 |
| Double | 34.00 | 38.00 |

**Half board**

| per person: | £min | £max |
|---|---|---|
| Daily | 26.00 | 35.00 |
| Weekly | 156.00 | 210.00 |

Parking for 4

## CHICHESTER

West Sussex
Map ref 2C3

The county town of West Sussex with a beautiful Norman cathedral. Noted for its Georgian architecture but also has modern buildings like the Festival Theatre. Surrounded by places of interest, including Fishbourne Roman Palace and Weald and Downland Open-Air Museum.
*Tourist Information Centre*
☎ *(01243) 775888*

### Barford

Bosham Lane, Bosham, Chichester
PO18 8HL
☎ (01243) 573393
*Comfortable cottage-style bungalow in the centre of a picturesque village and within a few minutes' walk of the harbour. Cycle hire available.*
Bedrooms: 2 double, 1 twin
Bathrooms: 1 public

**Bed & breakfast**

| per night: | £min | £max |
|---|---|---|
| Single | 15.00 | 17.00 |
| Double | 30.00 | 34.00 |

Lunch available
Evening meal 1800 (last orders 2100)
Parking for 1

### Hedgehogs

**Listed**

45 Whyke Lane, Chichester PO19 2JT
☎ (01243) 780022
*About half-a-mile from city centre, bus/railway stations and theatre. Secluded garden. Guests' own bathroom, TV lounge. Weekly terms available. Cyclists and hikers welcome. No smoking.*
Bedrooms: 2 double, 1 twin
Bathrooms: 2 public

**Bed & breakfast**

| per night: | £min | £max |
|---|---|---|
| Single | 15.00 | 18.00 |
| Double | 30.00 | 36.00 |

Parking for 4

---

### Stanes Farm

Hares Lane, Funtington, Chichester
PO18 9DW
☎ Bosham (01243) 575558
Fax (01243) 575701
*Comfortable accommodation in peaceful secluded family home with large garden, situated at foot of the South Downs, three quarters of a mile north of Funtington.*
Bedrooms: 1 double, 1 twin
Bathrooms: 1 public

**Bed & breakfast**

| per night: | £min | £max |
|---|---|---|
| Single | 18.00 | 20.00 |
| Double | 36.00 | 36.00 |

Parking for 6

## CHIDDINGSTONE

Kent
Map ref 2D2

Pleasant village of 16th and 17th C, preserved by the National Trust, with an 18th C "castle" and attractive Tudor inn.

### Hoath Holidays ⚑

**Listed   APPROVED**

Hoath House, Chiddingstone Hoath,
Edenbridge TN8 7DB
☎ Cowden (01342) 850362
*Tudor family house with beamed and panelled rooms and extensive gardens. Convenient for Chartwell, Hever, Penshurst, Gatwick and London.*
Bedrooms: 2 twin
Bathrooms: 1 public, 1 private shower

**Bed & breakfast**

| per night: | £min | £max |
|---|---|---|
| Single | 15.00 | 22.00 |
| Double | 30.00 | 44.00 |

Parking for 8

## CHILHAM

Kent
Map ref 3B3

Extremely pretty village of mostly Tudor and Jacobean houses. The village rises to the spacious square with the castle and the 15th C church. The grounds of the Jacobean House, laid out by Capability Brown, are open to the public.

### Jullieberrie House ⚑

**Listed   COMMENDED**

Canterbury Road, Chilham, Canterbury
CT4 8DX
☎ Canterbury (01227) 730488
*Modern house with lovely views over lake and woodland. On the A28 Ashford to Canterbury road, close to Chilham village.*
Bedrooms: 2 double, 2 twin

Bathrooms: 2 private, 1 public

**Bed & breakfast**

| per night: | £min | £max |
|---|---|---|
| Single | 20.00 | 25.00 |
| Double | 30.00 | 36.00 |

Parking for 5

🛇🖵⌕♿Ⓤ🕴💷▬❀🚗

## The Woolpack Inn ⋀

👑👑👑 COMMENDED

High Street, Chilham, Canterbury
CT4 8DL
☎ Canterbury (01227) 730208 &
730351
Fax (01227) 731053
*A fine bed and victuals have been
offered here for 200 years. Dine on
Kentish fare and enjoy the friendly bar.*
Bedrooms: 6 double, 3 twin, 1 triple,
1 family room
Bathrooms: 11 private

**Bed & breakfast**

| per night: | £min | £max |
|---|---|---|
| Single | 37.50 | |
| Double | 47.50 | |

Lunch available
Evening meal 1900 (last orders 2130)
Parking for 30
Cards accepted: Access, Visa, Switch/
Delta

🛇♿♨📞🖾🖵♿💷🍴❀🚗SP🏠

### CLIFTONVILLE

Kent

*See under Margate*

### CRANBROOK

Kent
Map ref 3B4

Old town, a centre for the weaving
industry in the 15th C. The 72-ft
high Union Mill is a 3-storeyed
windmill, still in working order.

## Hallwood Farm House ⋀

Listed

Hallwood Farm, Cranbrook TN17 2SP
☎ (01580) 713204
*10-acre arable farm. 15th C hall house
with beams and open inglenook.*
Bedrooms: 1 double, 2 twin
Bathrooms: 1 public

**Bed & breakfast**

| per night: | £min | £max |
|---|---|---|
| Single | 20.00 | 20.00 |
| Double | 40.00 | 40.00 |

**Half board**

| per person: | £min | £max |
|---|---|---|
| Daily | 35.00 | 35.00 |
| Weekly | 220.00 | 220.00 |

Evening meal 1930 (last orders 2030)
Parking for 3
Open April-October

🛇♿Ⓤ✂🕅❀🚗🏠

## Tolehurst Barn ⋀

👑👑 COMMENDED

Cranbrook Road, Frittenden,
Cranbrook TN17 2BP
☎ (01580) 714385

*Converted 17th C beamed barn in
farmland - quiet and rural, all modern
conveniences. On A229, convenient for
the heart of Kent and places of historic
interest. Only 5 minutes from
Sissinghurst. Languages spoken.*
Bedrooms: 2 double, 1 triple
Bathrooms: 2 private

**Bed & breakfast**

| per night: | £min | £max |
|---|---|---|
| Single | 15.00 | 17.00 |
| Double | 30.00 | 34.00 |

**Half board**

| per person: | £min | £max |
|---|---|---|
| Daily | 23.00 | 25.00 |

Evening meal 1900 (last orders 2100)
Parking for 6

🛇🖾🖵♿Ⓤ🕴S🕅TV💷▬❀🚗
🏠Ⓣ

## The White Horse Inn ⋀

👑

High Street, Cranbrook TN17 3EX
☎ (01580) 712615
*Victorian public house and restaurant
in the centre of the smallest town in
Kent, once the capital of the Weald.*
Bedrooms: 1 single, 1 twin, 1 triple
Bathrooms: 1 public

**Bed & breakfast**

| per night: | £min | £max |
|---|---|---|
| Single | 22.00 | |
| Double | 32.00 | |

Lunch available
Evening meal 1830 (last orders 2130)
Parking for 12
Cards accepted: Access, Visa

🛇🖵♨♿💷🍴£50∪🅿❀✂🚗Ⓣ

### CRAWLEY

West Sussex
Map ref 2D2

One of the first New Towns built
after World War II, but it also has
some old buildings. Set in
magnificent wooded countryside.

## Caprice Guest House ⋀

Listed COMMENDED

Bonnetts Lane, Ifield, Crawley
RH11 0NY
☎ (01293) 528620
*Small, friendly, family-run guesthouse
surrounded by farmland and close to all
amenities. 10 minutes south of Gatwick
Airport.*

Bedrooms: 1 double, 2 twin
Bathrooms: 1 private, 1 public

**Bed & breakfast**

| per night: | £min | £max |
|---|---|---|
| Single | 25.00 | 35.00 |
| Double | 35.00 | 45.00 |

Parking for 6
Cards accepted: Access, Visa, Amex

🛇♨♿🖵♿Ⓤ💷S✂🕅TV💷▬❀✂
🚗Ⓣ

## The Manor House ⋀

👑👑 COMMENDED

Bonnets Lane, Ifield, Crawley
RH11 0NY
☎ (01293) 510000 & 512298
*100-year-old manor house in pleasant
rural surroundings on Gatwick's
doorstep. Family-run establishment
offering comfortable and spacious
accommodation.*
Bedrooms: 1 single, 2 double, 2 twin,
1 family room
Bathrooms: 4 private, 1 public

**Bed & breakfast**

| per night: | £min | £max |
|---|---|---|
| Single | 25.00 | 35.00 |
| Double | 35.00 | 45.00 |

Parking for 25
Cards accepted: Access, Visa

🛇🖾🖵♿Ⓤ✂💷▬❀✂🚗SPⓉ

### DEAL

Kent
Map ref 3C4

Coastal town and popular holiday
resort. Deal Castle was built by
Henry VIII as a fort and the
museum is devoted to finds
excavated in the area. Also the
Time-Ball Tower museum. Angling
available from both beach and
pier.
*Tourist Information Centre*
☎ (01304) 369576

## Beggars Leap

Listed

Lower Mill Lane, Deal CT14 9AG
☎ (01304) 373263
*Large Spanish-style house. From Dover
take A258 to Deal Castle, turn left,
Gilford Road, past Tides Leisure Pool,
turn right then 1st left, 1st house on
right. No smoking.*
Bedrooms: 1 double, 1 twin
Bathrooms: 1 public

**Bed & breakfast**

| per night: | £min | £max |
|---|---|---|
| Single | 19.00 | 20.00 |
| Double | 40.00 | 42.00 |

Parking for 4

🖾🖵🖵♿Ⓤ✂🕅TV💷🍴❀✂🚗

We advise you to confirm
your booking in writing.

## DORKING

Surrey
Map ref 2D2

Ancient market town and a good centre for walking, delightfully set between Box Hill and the Downs.

### Bulmer Farm

Holmbury St Mary, Dorking RH5 6LG
☎ (01306) 730210
*30-acre beef farm. 17th C character farmhouse with beams and inglenook fireplace, in the Surrey hills. Choice of twin rooms in the house or double/twin en-suite rooms in tastefully converted barn adjoining the house. Village is 5 miles from Dorking.*
Bedrooms: 3 double, 5 twin
Bathrooms: 5 private, 2 public

**Bed & breakfast**

| per night: | £min | £max |
| --- | --- | --- |
| Single | 18.00 | 30.00 |
| Double | 34.00 | 38.00 |

Parking for 12

### Crossways Farm

Raikes Lane, Abinger Hammer, Dorking RH5 6PZ
☎ (01306) 730173
*200-acre arable & livestock farm. 17th C listed farmhouse in a small village south-west of Dorking. Good centre for London, the South East and airports. Large comfortable rooms.*
Bedrooms: 1 twin, 1 triple
Bathrooms: 2 private, 1 public

**Bed & breakfast**

| per night: | £min | £max |
| --- | --- | --- |
| Single | 18.00 | 25.00 |
| Double | 30.00 | 36.00 |

Evening meal 1900 (last orders 1900)
Parking for 3

### Mark Ash

Listed COMMENDED

Abinger Common, Dorking RH5 6JA
☎ (01306) 731326
*Victorian house in lovely garden opposite village green. Area of Outstanding Natural Beauty. One mile off A25. Dorking 4 miles, Guildford 8 miles. Convenient for Gatwick Airport.*
Bedrooms: 1 double, 1 twin
Bathrooms: 2 private, 1 public

**Bed & breakfast**

| per night: | £min | £max |
| --- | --- | --- |
| Single | 20.00 | 25.00 |
| Double | 40.00 | 40.00 |

Parking for 4
Open March-November

### Steyning Cottage

Listed

Horsham Road, South Holmwood, Dorking RH5 4NE
☎ (01306) 888481
*Detached tile-hung house adjacent to A24 and within walking distance of Leith Hill. Gatwick Airport approximately 20 minutes away, Heathrow 45 minutes. French spoken.*
Bedrooms: 1 single, 2 twin
Bathrooms: 1 public

**Bed & breakfast**

| per night: | £min | £max |
| --- | --- | --- |
| Single | 15.00 | 20.00 |
| Double | 28.00 | 32.00 |

**Half board**

| per person: | £min | £max |
| --- | --- | --- |
| Daily | 23.00 | 28.00 |
| Weekly | 105.00 | 196.00 |

Evening meal 1900 (last orders 2000)
Parking for 4

### The Waltons

Listed

5 Rose Hill, Dorking RH14 2EG
☎ (01306) 883127
*House retains all its period features. Central location with beautiful views. Surrounded by National Trust land. Friendly atmosphere.*
Bedrooms: 1 double, 1 twin
Bathrooms: 2 public

**Bed & breakfast**

| per night: | £min | £max |
| --- | --- | --- |
| Single | 15.00 | 20.00 |
| Double | 30.00 | 35.00 |

**Half board**

| per person: | £min | £max |
| --- | --- | --- |
| Daily | 23.50 | 26.00 |
| Weekly | 94.00 | 104.00 |

Evening meal 1800 (last orders 2100)
Parking for 3

## DOVER

Kent
Map ref 3C4

A Cinque Port and busiest passenger port in the world. Still a historic town and seaside resort beside the famous White Cliffs. The White Cliffs Experience attraction traces the town's history through the Roman, Saxon, Norman and Victorian periods.
*Tourist Information Centre*
☎ *(01304) 205108*

### Coldred Court Farm ⋀

HIGHLY COMMENDED

Church Road, Coldred, Dover CT15 5AQ
☎ (01304) 830816
*7-acre mixed farm. 1620 farmhouse full of old world charm, with modern*

*facilities. Situated 1 mile from the A2, 10 minutes from Dover.*
Bedrooms: 2 double, 1 twin
Bathrooms: 3 private

**Bed & breakfast**

| per night: | £min | £max |
| --- | --- | --- |
| Single | 25.00 | 32.00 |
| Double | 38.00 | 45.00 |

**Half board**

| per person: | £min | £max |
| --- | --- | --- |
| Daily | 31.00 | 44.00 |
| Weekly | 200.00 | 270.00 |

Evening meal 1800 (last orders 2030)
Parking for 13

### Elmo Guest House ⋀

120 Folkestone Road, Dover CT17 9SP
☎ (01304) 206236
*Conveniently situated for ferries and Hoverport terminals and 10 minutes' drive to Channel Tunnel. Within easy reach of the town centre and railway station. Overnight stops our speciality.*
Bedrooms: 1 single, 2 double, 1 triple, 1 family room
Bathrooms: 2 public

**Bed & breakfast**

| per night: | £min | £max |
| --- | --- | --- |
| Single | 14.00 | 16.00 |
| Double | 24.00 | 30.00 |

Parking for 7

### Esther House

Listed COMMENDED

55 Barton Road, Dover CT16 2NF
☎ (01304) 241332
*Non-smoking B and B with warm Christian atmosphere. Close to ferries and town centre. Ideal for short breaks and overnight stops to Continent. Early breakfasts. Evening meals by arrangement.*
Bedrooms: 1 single, 1 twin, 1 triple
Bathrooms: 1 public

**Bed & breakfast**

| per night: | £min | £max |
| --- | --- | --- |
| Single | 12.00 | 18.00 |
| Double | 24.00 | 34.00 |

### The Norman Guest House

Listed

75 Folkestone Road, Dover CT17 9RZ
☎ (01304) 207803
*Opposite Dover Priory railway station and close to shops, ferries, hovercraft ports and all amenities. Only 15 minutes' drive to Eurotunnel.*
Bedrooms: 1 single, 2 double, 2 twin, 1 triple, 2 family rooms
Bathrooms: 2 public

| Bed & breakfast per night: | £min | £max |
|---|---|---|
| Single | 12.00 | 16.00 |
| Double | 24.00 | 32.00 |

Parking for 6

## St Albans Bed & Breakfast

71 Folkestone Road, Dover CT17 9RZ
☎ (01304) 206308
*Family-run guesthouse, directly opposite Dover Priory railway station, 3 minutes from docks, 10 minutes from Channel Tunnel. Perfect for overnight stays. Early breakfasts available.*
Bedrooms: 1 single, 3 double, 1 twin
Bathrooms: 1 public

| Bed & breakfast per night: | £min | £max |
|---|---|---|
| Single | 14.00 | 18.00 |
| Double | 20.00 | 32.00 |

## Woodpeckers

Chapel Lane, St-Margarets-at-Cliffe, Dover CT15 6BQ
☎ (01304) 852761

*10 minutes from Dover docks, in the quiet village of St Margarets, behind the village pond. En-suite facilities.*
Bedrooms: 1 twin, 1 triple
Bathrooms: 2 private

| Bed & breakfast per night: | £min | £max |
|---|---|---|
| Single | 20.00 | 20.00 |
| Double | 32.00 | 34.00 |

Parking for 4

## EAST DEAN

East Sussex
Map ref 2D3

Pretty village on a green near Friston Forest and Birling Gap.

## Birling Gap Hotel ♠♠♠ APPROVED

East Dean, Eastbourne BN20 0AB
☎ Eastbourne (01323) 423197
Fax (01323) 423030

*Magnificent Seven Sisters clifftop position, with views of country, sea, beach. Superb downland walks. Old world "Thatched Bar" and "Oak Room Restaurant". Coffee shop and games room, function and conference suite.*
Bedrooms: 1 single, 5 double, 2 twin, 2 triple
Bathrooms: 10 private, 1 public

| Bed & breakfast per night: | £min | £max |
|---|---|---|
| Single | 20.00 | 50.00 |
| Double | 30.00 | 55.00 |

| Half board per person: | £min | £max |
|---|---|---|
| Weekly | 172.50 | 287.00 |

Lunch available
Parking for 100
Cards accepted: Access, Visa, Diners, Amex, Switch/Delta

## EAST GRINSTEAD

West Sussex
Map ref 2D2

A number of fine old houses stand in the High Street, one of which is Sackville College, founded in 1609.

## Middle House Cookhams
### COMMENDED

Sharpthorne, East Grinstead RH19 4HU
☎ (01342) 810566
*Central portion of large 100-year-old country house, with open southerly aspect. In village south of East Grinstead.*
Bedrooms: 1 single, 1 double, 1 twin
Bathrooms: 2 private, 1 public

| Bed & breakfast per night: | £min | £max |
|---|---|---|
| Single | 20.00 | 22.50 |
| Double | 40.00 | 50.00 |

Parking for 4

## White Horse Inn
### ♠♠ APPROVED

Holtye, Cowden, Edenbridge, Kent TN8 7ED
☎ Cowden (01342) 850640
Fax (01342) 850032

*Built in the 13th C. Refurbished with every modern facility yet retaining its old world charm. New restaurant, beamed and with oak furniture. Bar with underwater fish tank with koi carp. Every assistance for the disabled.*
Bedrooms: 9 double, 1 twin
Bathrooms: 10 private

| Bed & breakfast per night: | £min | £max |
|---|---|---|
| Single | 35.00 | 40.00 |
| Double | 40.00 | 50.00 |

Lunch available
Evening meal 1800 (last orders 2200)
Parking for 40
Cards accepted: Access, Visa, Amex, Switch/Delta

## EASTBOURNE

East Sussex
Map ref 3B4

One of the finest, most elegant resorts on the south-east coast situated beside Beachy Head. Long promenade, plenty of gardens, theatres, Towner Art Gallery, "How We Lived Then" museum of shops and social history.
*Tourist Information Centre*
☎ (01323) 411400

## Bay Lodge Hotel ♠
### ♠♠♠ COMMENDED

61-62 Royal Parade, Eastbourne BN22 7AQ
☎ (01323) 732515
Fax (01323) 735009
*Small seafront hotel opposite Redoubt Gardens, close to bowling greens and entertainments. Large sun-lounge. All double/twin bedrooms are en-suite. Non-smokers' lounge.*
Bedrooms: 3 single, 5 double, 4 twin
Bathrooms: 9 private, 2 public

| Bed & breakfast per night: | £min | £max |
|---|---|---|
| Single | 18.00 | 22.00 |
| Double | 36.00 | 44.00 |

| Half board per person: | £min | £max |
|---|---|---|
| Daily | 28.00 | 33.00 |
| Weekly | 164.00 | 199.00 |

Evening meal 1800 (last orders 1800)
Open March-October and Christmas
Cards accepted: Access, Visa

## Edelweiss Private Hotel ♠

10-12 Elms Avenue, Eastbourne BN21 3DN
☎ (01323) 732071
Fax (01323) 732071
*Family-run hotel 50 yards from the pier. Comfortable bedrooms with TV, tea-making and hairdryer. En-suite rooms available. Licensed bar, guests' lounge.*
Bedrooms: 2 single, 6 double, 5 twin, 1 family room
Bathrooms: 3 private, 4 public

Continued ▶

## EASTBOURNE

*Continued*

**Bed & breakfast**

| per night: | £min | £max |
|---|---|---|
| Single | 13.50 | 18.00 |
| Double | 27.00 | 36.00 |

**Half board**

| per person: | £min | £max |
|---|---|---|
| Daily | 17.50 | 22.00 |
| Weekly | 105.00 | 143.00 |

Evening meal 1800 (last orders 1500)
Cards accepted: Access, Visa

## ELHAM

Kent
Map ref 3B4

In the Nailbourne Valley on the chalk downlands, this large village has an outstanding collection of old houses. Abbot's Fireside, built in 1614, has a timbered upper storey resting on brackets carved into figures.

### Tye
Listed

Collards Lane, Elham, Canterbury
CT4 6UF
☎ (01303) 840271
Fax (01303) 840271
*Country house, less than a mile from the village, beautifully situated on top of a hill with lovely views and walks. Very quiet.*
Bedrooms: 1 single, 2 twin
Bathrooms: 1 public

**Bed & breakfast**

| per night: | £min | £max |
|---|---|---|
| Single | 17.00 | 17.00 |
| Double | 34.00 | 34.00 |

Parking for 6

## ENGLEFIELD GREEN

Surrey
Map ref 2D2

### 4 Fircroft M
Listed

Bagshot Road, Englefield Green,
Egham TW20 0RS
☎ Egham (01784) 432893
*Detached house, 10 minutes from Windsor, 15 minutes from M25, near Wentworth Golf Club. Convenient for trains to Waterloo.*
Bedrooms: 1 single, 1 twin
Bathrooms: 1 public

**Bed & breakfast**

| per night: | £min | £max |
|---|---|---|
| Single | 16.50 | 16.50 |
| Double | 32.00 | 32.00 |

Parking for 3

## FAIRLIGHT

East Sussex
Map ref 3B4

Village conveniently situated between Hastings Country Park and the sea.

### The Harbour

Channel Way, Fairlight, Hastings
TN35 4BP
☎ Hastings (01424) 814633
*Cliff top bungalow between Rye and Hastings. Access country park from garden. Map sent on request. Pets by arrangement. Sea views from both bedrooms.*
Bedrooms: 1 double, 1 twin
Bathrooms: 2 private

**Bed & breakfast**

| per night: | £min | £max |
|---|---|---|
| Single | 20.00 | 20.00 |
| Double | 25.00 | 25.00 |

Parking for 6
Open April-September

## FARNHAM

Surrey
Map ref 2C2

Town noted for its Georgian houses. Willmer House (now a museum) has a facade of cut and moulded brick with fine carving and panelling in the interior. The 12th C castle has been occupied by Bishops of both Winchester and Guildford.
*Tourist Information Centre*
☎ (01252) 715109

### Borderfield Farm
Listed

Boundary Road, Rowledge, Farnham
GU10 4EP
☎ (01252) 793985
*20-acre mixed farm. Working smallholding full of friendly animals, set in attractive countryside. Two good pubs in the village. Easy reach of London, coast and New Forest.*
Bedrooms: 2 single, 1 twin
Bathrooms: 1 private, 1 public

**Bed & breakfast**

| per night: | £min | £max |
|---|---|---|
| Single | 16.00 | 17.00 |
| Double | | 32.00 |

Parking for 10
Open March-November

---

Please check prices and other details at the time of booking.

---

## FAVERSHAM

Kent
Map ref 3B3

Historic town, once a port, dating back to prehistoric times. Abbey Street has more than 50 listed buildings. Roman and Anglo-Saxon finds and other exhibits can be seen in a museum in the Maison Dieu at Ospringe. Fleur de Lis Heritage Centre.
*Tourist Information Centre*
☎ (01795) 534542

### Barnsfield M
Listed

Hernhill, Faversham ME13 9JH
☎ Canterbury (01227) 750973 & Deal (01304) 368550
*Listed Grade II country cottages, just off A299, set in 3 acres of orchards, 6 miles from Canterbury.*
Bedrooms: 2 double, 1 twin
Bathrooms: 1 private, 1 public

**Bed & breakfast**

| per night: | £min | £max |
|---|---|---|
| Single | 16.00 | 20.00 |
| Double | 32.00 | 40.00 |

**Half board**

| per person: | £min | £max |
|---|---|---|
| Daily | 24.00 | |

Parking for 10
Cards accepted: Access, Visa

### The Granary M
Listed HIGHLY COMMENDED

Plumford Lane, Ospringe, Faversham
ME13 ODS
☎ (01795) 538416 & Mobile 0860 817713
*Delightfully converted granary in peaceful setting with large garden. Own lounge with colour TV. Close to M2 and Canterbury. Friendly welcome.*
Bedrooms: 2 double, 1 twin
Bathrooms: 1 public

**Bed & breakfast**

| per night: | £min | £max |
|---|---|---|
| Single | 22.00 | 30.00 |
| Double | 32.00 | 38.00 |

Parking for 8

### Leaveland Court M

Leaveland, Faversham ME13 ONP
☎ Challock (01233) 740596
*300-acre arable farm. Enchanting Grade II* listed 15th C timbered farmhouse in quiet rural setting adjacent to Leaveland church. 5 minutes from M2 Faversham, 20 minutes from Canterbury.*
Bedrooms: 1 double, 2 twin
Bathrooms: 3 private, 1 public

**Bed & breakfast**

| per night: | £min | £max |
|---|---|---|
| Single | 20.00 | 20.00 |
| Double | 36.00 | 40.00 |

| Half board per person: | £min | £max |
|---|---|---|
| Daily | 28.00 | 32.00 |
| Weekly | 190.00 | 220.00 |

Evening meal 1830 (last orders 1800)
Parking for 6

### The Oaks
**Listed**

Abbotts Hill, Ospringe, Faversham ME13 0RR
☎ (01795) 532936
*In quiet rural setting with attractive gardens, 1 mile south of Ospringe, via Water Lane. Excellent base for touring Kent.*
Bedrooms: 1 twin
Bathrooms: 1 private

| Bed & breakfast per night: | £min | £max |
|---|---|---|
| Single | 18.00 | 20.00 |
| Double | 32.00 | 34.00 |

Parking for 3

### Owens Court Farm
**COMMENDED**

Selling, Faversham ME13 9QN
☎ Canterbury (01227) 752247
Fax (01227) 752247
*265-acre fruit farm. Lovely Georgian farmhouse on a working hop and fruit farm. Quiet lane, 3 miles from Faversham, 9 from Canterbury.*
Bedrooms: 1 single, 1 twin, 1 triple
Bathrooms: 1 public

| Bed & breakfast per night: | £min | £max |
|---|---|---|
| Single | 15.00 | 16.00 |
| Double | 30.00 | 32.00 |

Parking for 4
Open January-August, October-December

### Preston Lea ⚠
**HIGHLY COMMENDED**

Canterbury Road, Faversham ME13 8XA
☎ (01795) 535266
Fax (01795) 533388

*Beautiful, imposing Victorian house with turrets and other interesting features, set in large secluded grounds. Only 15 minutes from Canterbury and 30 minutes from Channel ports and Eurotunnel.*
Bedrooms: 2 double, 1 twin
Bathrooms: 3 private

| Bed & breakfast per night: | £min | £max |
|---|---|---|
| Single | 25.00 | 30.00 |
| Double | 45.00 | 70.00 |

Parking for 11

### White Horse Inn ⚠
**COMMENDED**

Boughton, Faversham ME13 9AX
☎ Canterbury (01227) 751700 & 751343
Fax (01227) 751090
*15th C coaching inn with oak beams and inglenook fireplace. In centre of village yet only 10 minutes' drive from Canterbury.*
Bedrooms: 7 double, 5 twin
Bathrooms: 12 private

| Bed & breakfast per night: | £min | £max |
|---|---|---|
| Single | 37.50 | |
| Double | 47.50 | |

Lunch available
Evening meal 1900 (last orders 2130)
Parking for 50
Cards accepted: Access, Visa, Diners, Amex, Switch/Delta

West Sussex
Map ref 2D3

Downland village well-known for its annual sheep fair and its racing stables. The ancient landmarks, Cissbury Ring and Chanctonbury Ring, and the South Downs Way, are nearby.

### Findon Tower
**COMMENDED**

Cross Lane, Findon, Worthing BN14 0UG
☎ (01903) 873870
*Elegant Edwardian country house in large secluded garden. Spacious accommodation with en-suite facilities. Warm, friendly welcome, relaxed and peaceful atmosphere. Rural views, snooker room. Excellent selection of food in village restaurants and pubs.*
Bedrooms: 1 double, 1 twin
Bathrooms: 2 private, 1 public

| Bed & breakfast per night: | £min | £max |
|---|---|---|
| Single | 17.50 | 25.00 |
| Double | 35.00 | 45.00 |

Parking for 10

---

Establishments should be open throughout the year unless otherwise stated in the entry.

Kent
Map ref 3C4

Popular resort and important cross-channel port. The town has a fine promenade, the Leas, from where orchestral concerts and other entertainments are presented. Horse-racing at Westenhanger.
*Tourist Information Centre*
*☎ (01303) 258594*

### Beachborough Park ⚠
**APPROVED**

Newington, Folkestone CT18 8BW
☎ (01303) 275432
Fax (01842) 45131
*Beautiful setting, ideal for sightseeing and very convenient for tunnel and ferries. Very comfortable for both active people and those just seeking peace and quiet.*
Bedrooms: 4 double, 2 twin, 1 family room
Bathrooms: 7 private

| Bed & breakfast per night: | £min | £max |
|---|---|---|
| Single | 25.00 | 35.00 |
| Double | 35.00 | 45.00 |

| Half board per person: | £min | £max |
|---|---|---|
| Daily | 27.50 | 32.50 |
| Weekly | 175.00 | 227.50 |

Lunch available
Evening meal 1900 (last orders 2100)

### Harbourside ⚠
**HIGHLY COMMENDED**

14 Wear Bay Road, Folkestone CT19 6AT
☎ (01303) 256528
Fax: (01303) 241299
*En-suite accommodation. Spectacular sea views, and hospitality. Very real value for money. Licensed and fully geared for your comfort.*
Bedrooms: 1 single, 4 double, 2 twin
Bathrooms: 7 private, 2 public

| Bed & breakfast per night: | £min | £max |
|---|---|---|
| Single | 20.00 | 30.00 |
| Double | 40.00 | 50.00 |

Cards accepted: Amex

---

National Crown ratings were correct at the time of going to press but are subject to change. Please check at the time of booking.

## FULKING

West Sussex
Map ref 2D3

Small, pretty village nestling on the
north side of the South Downs
near the route of the South Downs
Way.

### Downers Vineyard ⋀

Listed

Clappers Lane, Fulking, Henfield
BN5 9NH
☎ Brighton (01273) 857484 & Mobile
0850 122991
Fax (01273) 857068
*18-acre vineyard & grazing farm. Quiet
rural position, 1 mile north of the
South Downs and Devil's Dyke, 8 miles
from Brighton.*
Bedrooms: 2 triple
Bathrooms: 2 public

**Bed & breakfast**

| per night: | £min | £max |
|---|---|---|
| Single | 17.00 | 20.00 |
| Double | 30.00 | 33.00 |

Evening meal 1930 (last orders 1930)
Parking for 6

## GATWICK AIRPORT

West Sussex

*See under Crawley, East
Grinstead, Horley, Leigh,
Newdigate, Smallfield*

## GODALMING

Surrey
Map ref 2D2

Several old coaching inns are
reminders that the town was once
a staging point. The old Town Hall
is now the local history museum.
Charterhouse School moved here
in 1872 and is dominated by the
150-ft Founder's Tower.

### Fairfields

The Green, Elstead, Godalming
GU8 6DF
☎ Farnham (01252) 702345
*High quality facilities in quiet modern
detached house with 1 acre of grounds
in centre of village. Guildford 8 miles,
Farnham and Godalming 5 miles.
Excellent pub food adjacent. Non-
smokers only please.*
Bedrooms: 1 double, 2 twin
Bathrooms: 3 private

**Bed & breakfast**

| per night: | £min | £max |
|---|---|---|
| Single | 20.00 | 25.00 |
| Double | 35.00 | 40.00 |

Parking for 4

## GOUDHURST

Kent
Map ref 3B4

Village on a hill surmounted by a
square-towered church with fine
views of orchards and hopfields.
Achieved prosperity through
weaving in the Middle Ages.
Finchcocks houses a museum of
historic keyboard instruments.

### Mill House ⋀

♛♛ COMMENDED

Church Road, Goudhurst, Cranbrook
TN17 1BN
☎ (01580) 211703
*16th C former mill with lots of history
and a smugglers' tunnel. Beautiful
grounds and views. Close to
Sissinghurst, good base for exploring
the Weald.*
Bedrooms: 1 double, 1 family room
Bathrooms: 2 private

**Bed & breakfast**

| per night: | £min | £max |
|---|---|---|
| Double | 35.00 | 40.00 |

Parking for 6

## GUILDFORD

Surrey
Map ref 2D2

Bustling town with many historic
monuments, one of which is the
Guildhall clock jutting out over the
old High Street. The modern
cathedral occupies a commanding
position on Stag Hill.
*Tourist Information Centre*
☎ *(01483) 444007*

### Beevers Farm

Listed

Chinthurst Lane, Bramley, Guildford
GU5 0DR
☎ (01483) 898764
*In peaceful surroundings 2 miles from
Guildford, near villages with pubs and
restaurants. Convenient for Heathrow
and Gatwick. Friendly atmosphere. Non-
smokers only please.*
Bedrooms: 3 twin
Bathrooms: 1 private, 1 public

**Bed & breakfast**

| per night: | £min | £max |
|---|---|---|
| Double | 26.00 | 37.00 |

Parking for 10
Open March-November

### High Edser ⋀

Listed

Shere Road, Ewhurst, Cranleigh
GU6 7PQ
☎ (01483) 278214
*14th-15th C family home set in Area of
Outstanding Natural Beauty. 6 miles
from Guildford and Dorking, within*
*easy reach of airports and many tourist
attractions. Non-smokers only, please.*
Bedrooms: 2 double, 1 twin
Bathrooms: 1 public

**Bed & breakfast**

| per night: | £min | £max |
|---|---|---|
| Single | 22.00 | 22.00 |
| Double | 40.00 | 40.00 |

Parking for 7

### The Old Malt House ⋀

Bagshot Road, Worplesdon, Guildford
GU3 3PT
☎ Worplesdon (01483) 232152
*Old country house in extensive grounds
with swimming pool and ancient trees.
Easy access to Heathrow, Gatwick and
central London.*
Bedrooms: 1 double, 1 family room
Bathrooms: 2 public

**Bed & breakfast**

| per night: | £min | £max |
|---|---|---|
| Single | 18.00 | 20.00 |
| Double | 30.00 | 30.00 |

Parking for 4

## HAILSHAM

East Sussex
Map ref 2D3

An important market town since
Norman times and still one of the
largest markets in Sussex. Two
miles west, at Upper Dicker, is
Michelham Priory, an Augustinian
house founded in 1229.
*Tourist Information Centre*
☎ *(01323) 844426*

### Sandy Bank ⋀

♛♛ COMMENDED

Old Road, Magham Down, Hailsham
BN27 1PW
☎ (01323) 842488
*Well-appointed en-suite rooms in recent
development adjacent to cottage, plus
one en-suite in cottage in attractive
Sussex countryside with easy access to
Downs and sea. Ideal base for touring
Sussex. Friendly atmosphere. Evening
meals by prior arrangement.*
Bedrooms: 3 twin
Bathrooms: 3 private

**Bed & breakfast**

| per night: | £min | £max |
|---|---|---|
| Single | 22.00 | |
| Double · | 38.00 | |

Evening meal 1900 (last orders 2030)
Parking for 3

---

Please mention this guide
when making a booking.

## HARTFIELD

East Sussex
Map ref 2D2

Pleasant village in Ashdown Forest, the setting for A A Milne's "Winnie the Pooh" stories.

### Stairs Farmhouse and Tea Room ⋀

**Listed** **COMMENDED**
High Street, Hartfield TN7 4AB
☎ (01892) 770793
*17th C modernised farmhouse with various period features, in picturesque village. Close to Pooh Bridge and Hever Castle. Views over open countryside. Home produced additive-free meals provided. Tea room and farm shop.*
Bedrooms: 1 double, 1 twin, 1 triple
Bathrooms: 1 private, 2 public

**Bed & breakfast**

| per night: | £min | £max |
|---|---|---|
| Single | 25.00 | 35.00 |
| Double | 38.00 | 42.00 |

**Half board**

| per person: | £min | £max |
|---|---|---|
| Daily | 30.00 | 40.00 |

Lunch available
Evening meal 1800 (last orders 1930)
Parking for 16

## HASLEMERE

Surrey
Map ref 2C2

Town set in hilly, wooded countryside, much of it in the keeping of the National Trust. Its attractions include the educational museum and the annual music festival.

### Town House

**Listed** **COMMENDED**
High Street, Haslemere GU27 2JY
☎ (01428) 643310
Fax (01428) 641080
*Period house in centre of quiet town. Panelled reception rooms, period furniture throughout. Easy walking to restaurants and pubs.*
Bedrooms: 2 single, 1 double, 1 twin
Bathrooms: 2 private, 1 public

**Bed & breakfast**

| per night: | £min | £max |
|---|---|---|
| Single | 20.00 | 21.00 |
| Double | 37.00 | 40.00 |

Parking for 3
Open February-December

We advise you to confirm your booking in writing.

## HAYWARDS HEATH

West Sussex
Map ref 2D3

Busy market town and administrative centre of mid-Sussex, with interesting old buildings and a modern shopping centre.

### The Anchorhold ⋀

**Listed** **APPROVED**
35 Paddock Hall Road, Haywards Heath RH16 1HN
☎ (01444) 452468
*Religious community providing bed and breakfast in a separate cottage within the grounds. Main line station is a quarter of a mile away.*
Bedrooms: 2 single, 2 twin
Bathrooms: 1 public

**Bed & breakfast**

| per night: | £min | £max |
|---|---|---|
| Single | 15.00 | 15.00 |

Parking for 3

## HEADCORN

Kent
Map ref 3B4

Small town with timbered houses used in the 17th C as cloth halls by Flemish weavers. Headcorn Flower Centre and Vineyard is open to visitors.

### Bletchenden Manor Farm

**Listed**
Headcorn TN27 9JB
☎ Maidstone (01622) 890228

*50-acre livestock farm. Listed farmhouse in peaceful position on outskirts of Headcorn village, surrounded by farmland, a mile from mainline station. Gardens, ponds and woodland. Ideal for touring. Close to Sissinghurst and many National Trust properties.*
Bedrooms: 3 twin
Bathrooms: 1 private, 1 public

**Bed & breakfast**

| per night: | £min | £max |
|---|---|---|
| Single | 20.00 | 25.00 |
| Double | 39.00 | 44.00 |

Parking for 2
Open January-November

## HERSTMONCEUX

East Sussex
Map ref 3B4

Pleasant village noted for its woodcrafts and the beautiful 15th C moated Herstmonceux Castle (gardens only open to visitors).

### The Stud Farm

**COMMENDED**
Bodle Street Green, Herstmonceux, Hailsham BN27 4RJ
☎ (01323) 833201
Fax (01323) 833201
*70-acre mixed farm. Upstairs, 2 bedrooms and bathroom let as one unit to party of 2, 3 or 4. Downstairs, twin-bedded en-suite room. Guests' sitting room and sunroom.*
Bedrooms: 1 double, 2 twin
Bathrooms: 1 private, 1 public

**Bed & breakfast**

| per night: | £min | £max |
|---|---|---|
| Single | 22.00 | 25.00 |
| Double | 34.00 | 38.00 |

**Half board**

| per person: | £min | £max |
|---|---|---|
| Daily | 27.50 | 33.50 |
| Weekly | 178.50 | 218.50 |

Evening meal from 1830
Parking for 3

## HOLLINGBOURNE

Kent
Map ref 3B3

Pleasant village near romantic Leeds Castle in the heart of the orchard country at the foot of the North Downs. Some fine half-timbered houses and a flint and ragstone church.

### Woodhouses ⋀

**Listed**
49 Eyhorne Street, Hollingbourne, Maidstone ME17 1TR
☎ Maidstone (01622) 880594
*Interconnected listed cottages dating from 17th C, with inglenook fireplace and exposed wooden beams. Well stocked cottage garden.*
Bedrooms: 2 double, 1 twin
Bathrooms: 3 private

**Bed & breakfast**

| per night: | £min | £max |
|---|---|---|
| Single | 16.50 | 18.00 |
| Double | 32.00 | 32.00 |

**Half board**

| per person: | £min | £max |
|---|---|---|
| Daily | 21.00 | 26.00 |
| Weekly | 132.00 | 164.00 |

Evening meal 1800 (last orders 2000)
Parking for 1

## HORLEY

Surrey
Map ref 2D2

Town on the London to Brighton road, just north of Gatwick Airport, with an ancient parish church and 15th C inn.

### Belmont House M
♛♛
46 Massetts Road, Horley RH6 7DS
☎ (01293) 820500 & 774341
Fax (01293) 783812
*Friendly family guesthouse in pleasant, quiet and green residential area, 2 minutes from shops, restaurants and railway station. 1.5 miles from Gatwick Airport.*
Bedrooms: 1 single, 1 double, 2 twin, 3 triple
Bathrooms: 4 private, 1 public

**Bed & breakfast**

| per night: | £min | £max |
|---|---|---|
| Single | 25.00 | 32.00 |
| Double | 35.00 | 42.00 |

Parking for 22
Cards accepted: Access, Visa, Amex, Switch/Delta
😤👥📞♻❷🛄🏧💳📺🛏️ 🅰✿🛫🚗 T

### Chalet Guest House M
♛♛ COMMENDED
77 Massetts Road, Horley RH6 7EB
☎ (01293) 821666
Fax (01293) 821619
*Comfortable modern guesthouse. Convenient for Gatwick Airport, motorways, railway station, local bus, shops, pubs and restaurants.*
Bedrooms: 3 single, 1 double, 1 twin, 1 triple
Bathrooms: 5 private, 1 public

**Bed & breakfast**

| per night: | £min | £max |
|---|---|---|
| Single | 24.00 | 32.00 |
| Double | 42.00 | 42.00 |

Parking for 14
Cards accepted: Access, Visa
😤👥📞♻❷🛄🏧📺🛄🅰✿🛫 T

### Crutchfield Farm M
♛♛ HIGHLY COMMENDED
Hookwood, Horley RH6 OHT
☎ Norwood Hill (01293) 863110
Fax (01293) 863233
*Listed 15th C farmhouse set in 10 acres, 3 miles from Gatwick. Well-appointed accommodation, tennis court and swimming pool. Parking, transport to airport.*
Bedrooms: 1 double, 2 twin
Bathrooms: 1 private, 1 public

**Bed & breakfast**

| per night: | £min | £max |
|---|---|---|
| Single | 30.00 | 40.00 |
| Double | 40.00 | 50.00 |

Parking for 10
😤👥❷♻🛄📶🅰✻❷📺🛄🅰♺🔍✿🛫🚗🐾 T

### The Gables Guest House M
Listed
50 Bonehurst Road, Horley RH6 8QG
☎ (01293) 774553
*Approximately 2 miles from Gatwick and the railway station. Long term parking. Transport to the airport available.*
Bedrooms: 3 single, 7 double, 9 twin, 3 triple
Bathrooms: 8 private, 3 public

**Bed & breakfast**

| per night: | £min | £max |
|---|---|---|
| Single | 25.00 | 25.00 |
| Double | 32.00 | 38.00 |

Parking for 25
😤👥📞♻❷🛄📺🛄🅰✿🛫 T

### Gainsborough Lodge M
♛♛ COMMENDED ✔
39 Massetts Road, Horley RH6 7DT
☎ (01293) 783982
Fax (01293) 785365
*Extended Edwardian house set in attractive garden. Five minutes' walk from Horley station and town centre. Five minutes' drive from Gatwick Airport.*
Bedrooms: 2 single, 3 double, 4 twin, 2 triple
Bathrooms: 11 private

**Bed & breakfast**

| per night: | £min | £max |
|---|---|---|
| Single | 30.00 | 34.00 |
| Double | 40.00 | 45.00 |

Parking for 16
Cards accepted: Access, Visa, Diners, Amex
😤👥📞♻❷🛄📺🛄🅰✿🛫 SP T

### The Lawn Guest House M
♛♛ HIGHLY COMMENDED
30 Massetts Road, Horley RH6 7DE
☎ (01293) 775751
Fax (01293) 821803

*Ideal for travellers using Gatwick. Pleasantly situated, few minutes' walk to town centre, pubs and restaurants. Good base for London and the south coast. Non-smokers only please.*
Bedrooms: 1 double, 4 twin, 1 triple, 1 family room
Bathrooms: 3 private, 2 public

**Bed & breakfast**

| per night: | £min | £max |
|---|---|---|
| Single | 24.00 | 31.00 |
| Double | 35.00 | 42.00 |

Parking for 10
Cards accepted: Access, Visa, Diners, Amex
😤👥📞♻❷🛄📶❷🛄🅰✿🛫 T

### Prinsted Guest House
Listed
Oldfield Road, Horley RH6 7EP
☎ (01293) 785233
*Detached Edwardian guesthouse in a quiet position, with spacious accommodation, including large family rooms. Close to Gatwick, London 30 minutes by train.*
Bedrooms: 1 double, 2 twin, 2 triple, 1 family room
Bathrooms: 3 public, 1 private shower

**Bed & breakfast**

| per night: | £min | £max |
|---|---|---|
| Single | 27.00 | 37.00 |
| Double | 37.00 | 37.00 |

Parking for 10
Cards accepted: Amex
😤👥📞♻❷🛄📺🛄🅰🛫 T

### Springwood Guest House M
58 Massetts Road, Horley RH6 7DS
☎ (01293) 775998
*Elegant detached Victorian house in pleasant residential road 1 mile from Gatwick Airport. Long-term car parking, courtesy transport. Five minutes from town centre, shops and pubs.*
Bedrooms: 2 single, 1 double, 3 twin, 1 family room
Bathrooms: 1 private, 2 public

**Bed & breakfast**

| per night: | £min | £max |
|---|---|---|
| Single | 21.00 | 25.00 |
| Double | 32.00 | 40.00 |

Parking for 10
Cards accepted: Access, Visa
😤👥📞♻❷🛄🅰🚗

### Victoria Lodge Guest House M
Listed COMMENDED
161 Victoria Road, Horley RH6 7AS
☎ (01293) 785459
*Edwardian detached house, in town centre close to shops, restaurants and pubs. One mile from Gatwick Airport and close to Horley station with direct service to Victoria. Colour TV and tea/coffee in rooms. Full English breakfast.*
Bedrooms: 1 single, 1 twin, 1 triple
Bathrooms: 1 public, 1 private shower

**Bed & breakfast**

| per night: | £min | £max |
|---|---|---|
| Single | 23.00 | 23.00 |
| Double | 35.00 | 35.00 |

Parking for 3
😤3📞♻❷🛄📶✻🐾🛫🚗

## HOVE

East Sussex

*See under Brighton & Hove*

---

**Please mention this guide when making a booking.**

## LEATHERHEAD

Surrey
Map ref 2D2

Old county town in the Green Belt, with the modern Thorndike Theatre.

### Bronwen 🏠

Crabtree Drive, Givons Grove, Leatherhead KT22 8LJ
☎ (01372) 372515
*Large family house in the Green Belt at Leatherhead. Adjoins open farmland and is close to National Trust areas of Headley Heath and Box Hill. 20 minutes from Gatwick, 30 minutes from Heathrow, 40 minutes from central London.*
Bedrooms: 2 single, 1 double, 1 triple
Bathrooms: 1 private, 1 public

**Bed & breakfast**

| per night: | £min | £max |
|---|---|---|
| Single | 18.00 | 24.00 |
| Double | 36.00 | 40.00 |

| Half board per person: | £min | £max |
|---|---|---|
| Daily | 25.00 | 31.00 |
| Weekly | 150.00 | 170.00 |

Lunch available
Evening meal 1900 (last orders 2100)
Parking for 4

## LEIGH

Surrey
Map ref 2D2

### Little Mynthurst

**HIGHLY COMMENDED**

Smalls Hill Road, Leigh, Reigate RH2 8QA
☎ Crawley (01293) 862441

*Spacious, charming country house set in 6 acres with country views. Tastefully renovated. Only 10 minutes from Gatwick Airport yet in a very quiet situation.*
Bedrooms: 2 double, 1 twin
Bathrooms: 1 private, 1 public

**Bed & breakfast**

| per night: | £min | £max |
|---|---|---|
| Single | 20.00 | 30.00 |
| Double | 30.00 | 40.00 |

Parking for 8

## LENHAM

Kent
Map ref 3B4

Shops, inns and houses, many displaying timber-work of the late Middle Ages, surround a square which is the centre of the village. The 14th C parish church has one of the best examples of a Kentish tower.

### Dog and Bear Hotel 🏠

**COMMENDED**

The Square, Lenham, Maidstone ME17 2PG
☎ Maidstone (01622) 858219
Fax (01622) 859415
*15th C coaching inn retaining its old world character and serving good Kent ale, lagers and fine wines with home cooking. En-suite rooms. Large car park and function room.*
Wheelchair access category 3 ♿
Bedrooms: 5 single, 12 double, 5 twin, 3 triple
Bathrooms: 25 private

**Bed & breakfast**

| per night: | £min | £max |
|---|---|---|
| Single | 37.50 | 42.50 |
| Double | 49.50 | 62.50 |

Lunch available
Evening meal 1900 (last orders 2130)
Parking for 26
Cards accepted: Access, Visa, Diners

## LEWES

East Sussex
Map ref 2D3

Historic county town with Norman castle. The steep High Street has mainly Georgian buildings. There is a folk museum at Anne of Cleves House and the archaeological museum is in Barbican House.
*Tourist Information Centre*
☎ *(01273) 483448*

### Felix Gallery

**Listed**

2 Sun Street, (Corner Lancaster Street), Lewes BN7 2QB
☎ (01273) 472668
*Fully-modernised period house in quiet location 3 minutes' walk from town centre, Records Office and castle. Full English breakfast.*
Bedrooms: 1 single, 1 twin
Bathrooms: 1 public

**Bed & breakfast**

| per night: | £min | £max |
|---|---|---|
| Single | 21.00 | 22.00 |
| Double | 34.00 | 36.00 |

Cards accepted: Access, Visa

## LYMINSTER

West Sussex
Map ref 2D3

### Sandfield House 🏠

**Listed** **COMMENDED**

Lyminster, Littlehampton BN17 7PG
☎ Littlehampton (01903) 724129
*Spacious country-style family house in 2 acres. Between Arundel and sea, in area of great natural beauty.*
Bedrooms: 1 double
Bathrooms: 1 public

**Bed & breakfast**

| per night: | £min | £max |
|---|---|---|
| Double | 34.00 | 38.00 |

Parking for 4

## LYNSTED

Kent
Map ref 3B3

Village noted for its charming half-timbered houses and cottages, many of which date from the Tudor period.

### Forge Cottage 🏠

**Listed**

Lynsted, Sittingbourne ME9 0RH
☎ Teynham (01795) 521273
*Historic half-timbered cottage with oak beams, in a picturesque village. Walled garden with terraced lawns. Good touring centre. Strictly non-smoking.*
Bedrooms: 1 double, 1 twin, 1 triple
Bathrooms: 2 public

**Bed & breakfast**

| per night: | £min | £max |
|---|---|---|
| Single | 20.00 | 20.00 |
| Double | 28.00 | 32.00 |

## MAIDSTONE

Kent
Map ref 3B3

Busy county town of Kent on the River Medway has many interesting features and is an excellent centre for excursions. Museum of Carriages, Museum and Art Gallery, Archbishop's Palace, Mote Park.
*Tourist Information Centre*
☎ *(01622) 673581*

### Wealden Hall House

East Street, Hunton, Maidstone ME15 0RB
☎ (01622) 820246
*16th C Grade II Wealden hall house offering comfortable accommodation. Four-poster bed. Set in 1 acre of gardens, 8 miles from Leeds Castle.*

Continued ▶

## MAIDSTONE
### Continued

*Two-night winter breaks available November-February at £55.*
Bedrooms: 2 single, 2 double
Bathrooms: 2 private, 1 public

**Bed & breakfast**

| per night: | £min | £max |
|---|---|---|
| Single | | 18.00 |
| Double | | 36.00 |

Parking for 6

### West Belringham ⋔
**COMMENDED**
Chart Road, Sutton Valence,
Maidstone ME17 3AW
☎ (01622) 843995
Fax (01622) 843995
*Modern bungalow with panoramic views in quaint historic village. Home-made cakes with tea/coffee on arrival. Easy access to London and coast, 10 minutes from Leeds Castle and motorway (M20). Evening meals available at local pubs.*
Bedrooms: 1 twin, 1 triple
Bathrooms: 1 public

**Bed & breakfast**

| per night: | £min | £max |
|---|---|---|
| Double | 34.00 | 38.00 |

Parking for 5
Open March-October

### Willington Court ⋔
**HIGHLY COMMENDED**
Willington Street, Maidstone
ME15 8JW
☎ (01622) 738885

*Tudor-style Grade II listed building. Antiques, four-poster bed. Friendly and relaxed atmosphere. Adjacent to Mote Park and near Leeds Castle.*
Bedrooms: 2 double, 1 twin
Bathrooms: 3 private

**Bed & breakfast**

| per night: | £min | £max |
|---|---|---|
| Single | 25.00 | 33.00 |
| Double | 38.00 | 46.00 |

Parking for 6
Cards accepted: Access, Visa, Diners, Amex

We advise you to confirm your booking in writing.

## MARDEN
Kent
Map ref 3B4

The village is believed to date back to Saxon times, though today more modern homes surround the 13th C church.

### Great Cheveney Farm ⋔
**Listed    HIGHLY COMMENDED**
Goudhurst Road, Marden, Tonbridge
TN12 9LX
☎ Maidstone (01622) 831207
Fax (01622) 831786

*300-acre arable & fruit farm. 16th C farmhouse in Kent Weald, between Marden and Goudhurst villages on B2079. Comfortable, friendly accommodation in peaceful surroundings. Close to Sissinghurst, Scotney and Leeds Castle.*
Bedrooms: 1 single, 1 double
Bathrooms: 2 private showers

**Bed & breakfast**

| per night: | £min | £max |
|---|---|---|
| Single | 21.00 | 25.00 |
| Double | 36.00 | 40.00 |

Parking for 3
Open January-November

## MARGATE
Kent
Map ref 3C3

Oldest and most famous resort in Kent. Many Regency and Victorian buildings survive from the town's early days. There are 9 miles of sandy beach. "Dreamland" is a 20-acre amusement park and the Winter Gardens offers concert hall entertainment.
*Tourist Information Centre*
☎ *(01843) 220241*

### The Malvern Hotel ⋔
**♛♛♛**
29 Eastern Espl, Cliftonville, Margate
CT9 2HL
☎ Thanet (01843) 290192
*Overlooking the sea, promenade and lawns. Close indoor/outdoor bowls complex, Margate Winter Gardens, amenities and Channel ports. Parking (unrestricted) outside and opposite hotel. TV and tea-making facilities - most rooms en-suite with shower and toilet (no baths).*
Bedrooms: 1 single, 5 double, 3 twin,
1 family room
Bathrooms: 8 private, 1 public

**Bed & breakfast**

| per night: | £min | £max |
|---|---|---|
| Single | 20.00 | 30.00 |
| Double | 33.00 | 42.00 |

Evening meal 1800 (last orders 1000)
Cards accepted: Access, Visa, Diners, Amex

## MAYFIELD
East Sussex
Map ref 2D3

On a ridge offering wide views of the Sussex Weald. Fire swept through the village in 1389, thus the oldest houses in the main street date from the 15th C.

### Brook Farm
**♛**
Argos Hill, Salters Green, Mayfield
TN20 6NP
☎ (01435) 873269
*65-acre beef farm. 15th C yeoman's cottage with a wealth of oak beams, on a family-run farm deep in the Sussex countryside.*
Bedrooms: 1 single, 2 triple
Bathrooms: 2 public

**Bed & breakfast**

| per night: | £min | £max |
|---|---|---|
| Single | 14.00 | 14.00 |
| Double | 28.00 | 28.00 |

**Half board**

| per person: | £min | £max |
|---|---|---|
| Daily | 19.00 | 19.00 |
| Weekly | 133.00 | 133.00 |

Evening meal 1900 (last orders 1200)
Parking for 5

## MIDHURST
West Sussex
Map ref 2C3

On the outskirts of the town are the remains of Cowdray Park, a substantial 16th C fortified mansion. There is a museum and the public can watch the famous Cowdray Park polo.

### Crown Inn
**Listed**
Edinburgh Square, Midhurst
GU29 9NL
☎ (01730) 813462
*16th C freehouse behind and below the church. Large selection of real ales and good wine list. Open fires.*
Bedrooms: 1 single, 1 double, 1 twin
Bathrooms: 1 public

**Bed & breakfast**

| per night: | £min | £max |
|---|---|---|
| Single | 15.00 | 20.00 |
| Double | 25.00 | 30.00 |

| **Half board per person:** | £min | £max |
|---|---|---|
| Daily | 21.00 | 33.00 |
| Weekly | 125.00 | 196.75 |

Lunch available
Evening meal 1900 (last orders 2000)
⊠ 🖵 🔒 [S] 🚭 [IIII] 🍴 ✈ 🚜 🏠

## NEWDIGATE

Surrey
Map ref 2D2

Village concerned with the Weald iron industry. The attractive 13th C church was once called "Hunter's Church" because of its connections with deer hunting.

### Sturtwood Farm

♛♛

Partridge Lane, Newdigate, Dorking RH5 5EE
☎ Dorking (01306) 631308
*140-acre mixed farm. Attractive 18th C working farmhouse, 12 minutes from Gatwick. Parking available.*
Bedrooms: 1 single, 1 twin
Bathrooms: 2 private, 1 public

| **Bed & breakfast per night:** | £min | £max |
|---|---|---|
| Single | 18.00 | 22.00 |
| Double | 35.00 | 40.00 |

| **Half board per person:** | £min | £max |
|---|---|---|
| Daily | 26.00 | 30.00 |

Evening meal from 1900
Parking for 6
🐴 🖵 ☕ [UL] [S] 🚭 [IIII] 🚗 ✿ 🚜 🏠

## OLD ROMNEY

Kent
Map ref 3B4

Village on the Romney Marsh with a 13th C church, 2 miles from the Cinque Port of New Romney.

### Rose & Crown Inn ♞

Listed

Old Romney, Romney Marsh TN29 9SQ
☎ New Romney (01679) 67500
Changin to 367500
*17th C traditional country inn with modern chalet accommodation, 100 yards south of A259 at Old Romney crossroad (2.25 miles west of New Romney).*
Bedrooms: 5 twin
Bathrooms: 5 private

| **Bed & breakfast per night:** | £min | £max |
|---|---|---|
| Single | 23.00 | 30.00 |
| Double | 33.00 | 40.00 |

Lunch available
Evening meal 1830 (last orders 2130)
Parking for 20
🐴 1 ♿ 🖵 ☕ [S] 🚭 [IIII] 🍷 30 🍴 ✿ 🚜

## OXTED

Surrey
Map ref 2D2

Pleasant town on the edge of National Trust woodland and at the foot of the North Downs. Chartwell, the former home of Sir Winston Churchill, is close by.

### The New Bungalow Old Hall Farm ♞

Listed

Tandridge Lane, Oxted RH8 9NS
☎ South Godstone (01342) 892508
Fax (01342) 892508
*44-acre mixed farm. Spacious, modern bungalow set in green fields and reached by a private drive. 5 minutes' drive from M25.*
Bedrooms: 1 twin, 1 family room
Bathrooms: 1 public

| **Bed & breakfast per night:** | £min | £max |
|---|---|---|
| Single | 22.00 | 25.00 |
| Double | 32.00 | 35.00 |

Parking for 5
Open January-November
🐴 ♿ ☕ [UL] 🔒 [S] 🚭 [TV] [IIII] 🚗 ✿ 🚜

## PARTRIDGE GREEN

West Sussex
Map ref 2D3

Small village between Henfield and Billingshurst.

### Pound Cottage Bed and Breakfast ♞

♛

Mill lane, Littleworth, Partridge Green, Horsham RH13 8JU
☎ (01403) 710218 & 711285
*Pleasant country house in quiet surroundings. 8 miles from Horsham, 25 minutes from Gatwick. Just off the West Grinstead to Steyning road.*
Bedrooms: 1 single, 1 double, 1 twin
Bathrooms: 1 public

| **Bed & breakfast per night:** | £min | £max |
|---|---|---|
| Single | 16.00 | 16.00 |
| Double | 32.00 | 32.00 |

| **Half board per person:** | £min | £max |
|---|---|---|
| Daily | 22.00 | 22.00 |
| Weekly | 154.00 | 154.00 |

Evening meal from 1830
Parking for 8
🐴 🖵 🖵 [UL] 🔒 🚭 [TV] [IIII] ✿ ✈ 🚜

**Please use the new PhONEday area telephone codes shown in establishment entries.**

## PENSHURST

Kent
Map ref 2D2

Village in a hilly wooded setting with Penshurst Place, the ancestral home of the Sidney family since 1552, standing in delightful grounds with a formal Tudor garden.

### Swale Cottage

Listed HIGHLY COMMENDED

Old Swaylands Lane, Off Poundsbridge Lane, Penshurst, Tonbridge TN11 8AH
☎ (01892) 870738
*Charmingly converted Grade II* listed barn in idyllically tranquil wooded valley. Three attractively furnished en-suite rooms. Close to Penshurst Place, Hever and Chartwell. Gatwick is 30 minutes' drive. Near A26, off the B2176.*
Bedrooms: 2 double, 1 twin
Bathrooms: 3 private

| **Bed & breakfast per night:** | £min | £max |
|---|---|---|
| Single | 30.00 | 36.00 |
| Double | 48.00 | 56.00 |

Parking for 7
🐴 10 🖵 🖵 🖵 ☕ 🧺 [UL] [S] 🚭 🪑 [TV] [IIII] 🚗 ✿ ✈ 🚜 [SP] 🏠

## PETWORTH

West Sussex
Map ref 2D3

Town dominated by Petworth House, the great 17th C mansion, set in 2000 acres of parkland laid out by Capability Brown. The house contains wood-carvings by Grinling Gibbons.

### White Horse Inn ♞

♛♛♛ HIGHLY COMMENDED

The Street, Sutton, Pulborough RH20 1PS
☎ Sutton (01798) 7221
Fax (01798) 7291

*Pretty Georgian village inn close to South Downs Way. Roman villa 1 mile. Garden, log fires. 4 miles Petworth, 5 miles Pulborough.*
Bedrooms: 4 double, 2 twin
Bathrooms: 6 private

| **Bed & breakfast per night:** | £min | £max |
|---|---|---|
| Single | 48.00 | 48.00 |
| Double | 58.00 | 58.00 |

Continued ▶

## PETWORTH

*Continued*

**Half board**

| per person: | £min | £max |
| --- | --- | --- |
| Daily | 41.00 | 60.00 |
| Weekly | 206.00 | 290.00 |

Lunch available
Evening meal 1900 (last orders 2140)
Parking for 10
Cards accepted: Access, Visa

📞 🖵 ♿ 🏵 Ⓢ ▥ 🖴 ➡ ✈ 🚶 🅂🄿 🄼 Ⓣ

## RAMSGATE

Kent
Map ref 3C3

Popular holiday resort with good
sandy beaches. At Pegwell Bay is
the replica of a Viking longship.
Terminal for car-ferry service to
Dunkirk and Ostend.
*Tourist Information Centre*
☎ *(01843) 591086*

### Eastwood Guest House 🏠

| Listed | COMMENDED |
| --- | --- |

28 Augusta Road, Ramsgate CT11 8JS
☎ Thanet (01843) 591505
Fax (01843) 591505

*Pretty Victorian villa, close to ferry port
and amenities. Comfortable rooms,
mostly en-suite. Lock-up garages
available. Breakfast served from 6.45
am, dinner available.*
Bedrooms: 1 single, 5 twin, 2 triple,
5 family rooms
Bathrooms: 8 private, 3 public

**Bed & breakfast**

| per night: | £min | £max |
| --- | --- | --- |
| Single | 18.00 | 25.00 |
| Double | 28.00 | 40.00 |

**Half board**

| per person: | £min | £max |
| --- | --- | --- |
| Daily | 23.00 | 30.00 |
| Weekly | 130.00 | 160.00 |

Evening meal 1830 (last orders 1930)
Parking for 20

🏠 🖵 🗗 ♿ ▥ 🏵 Ⓢ ✂ 🄼 📺 ▥ ➡ ☎
🖐 ❄ 🄿 🚶 🅂🄿 Ⓣ

## ROGATE

West Sussex
Map ref 2C3

### Trotton Farm

| 🏵🏵 | COMMENDED |
| --- | --- |

Trotton, Petersfield, Hampshire
GU31 5EN
☎ Midhurst (01730) 813618
Fax (01730) 816093

---

*Farmhouse just off the A272, access
through yard. Accommodation and
lounge/games room in a converted
cartshed adjoining farmhouse. All rooms
with en-suite shower.*
Bedrooms: 3 twin
Bathrooms: 3 private

**Bed & breakfast**

| per night: | £min | £max |
| --- | --- | --- |
| Single | 25.00 | 25.00 |
| Double | 35.00 | 35.00 |

🏠 🖴 🖵 ♿ 🖐 🏵 Ⓢ ✂ 🄼 📺 ▥ ➡ 🍴 ♦ 🗡
✔ ❄ 🚶

## ROTTINGDEAN

East Sussex
Map ref 2D3

The quiet High Street contains a
number of fine old buildings and
the village pond and green are
close by.

### Braemar Guest House
🏵

Steyning Road, Rottingdean, Brighton
BN2 7GA
☎ Brighton (01273) 304263
*Family-run guesthouse, proud of its
cheerful atmosphere, in an old world
village where Rudyard Kipling once
lived.*
Bedrooms: 5 single, 5 double, 2 twin,
2 triple
Bathrooms: 3 public, 2 private
showers

**Bed & breakfast**

| per night: | £min | £max |
| --- | --- | --- |
| Single | 15.00 | 16.00 |
| Double | 30.00 | 32.00 |

🏠 🖴 ▥ 🄼 📺 ▥ 🄳🄰🄿 🅂🄿

## ROYAL TUNBRIDGE WELLS

Kent
Map ref 2D2

This "Royal" town became famous
as a spa in the 17th C and much
of its charm is retained, as in the
Pantiles, a shaded walk lined with
elegant shops. Heritage attraction
"A Day at the Wells". Rich in parks
and gardens and a good centre for
walks.
*Tourist Information Centre*
☎ *(01892) 515675*

### Chequers

| 🏵🏵 | HIGHLY COMMENDED |
| --- | --- |

Camden Park, Royal Tunbridge Wells
TN2 5AD
☎ Tunbridge Wells (01892) 532299
*Friendly family house, origins 1840.
Part-walled garden. Unique private
location, 10 minutes from Pantiles, high
street, railway station. Peaceful,
comfortable, central base. Non-smokers
only please.*
Bedrooms: 1 single, 1 twin
Bathrooms: 2 private

---

**Bed & breakfast**

| per night: | £min | £max |
| --- | --- | --- |
| Single | 18.00 | 20.00 |
| Double | 30.00 | 35.00 |

Parking for 5

🏠 🖴 🖵 ♿ ▥ Ⓢ ✂ 🄼 📺 ▥ ➡ ❄ 🚶

### Cheviots 🏠

| 🏵🏵 | COMMENDED |
| --- | --- |

Cousley Wood, Wadhurst, East Sussex
TN5 6HD
☎ Wadhurst (01892) 782952

*On B2100 between Lamberhurst and
Wadhurst. Comfortable bed and
breakfast in modern country house with
extensive garden. Home cooking.
Convenient base for walking and
motoring. Close to Bewl Water.*
Bedrooms: 1 single, 1 double, 2 twin
Bathrooms: 3 private, 1 public

**Bed & breakfast**

| per night: | £min | £max |
| --- | --- | --- |
| Single | 20.00 | 25.00 |
| Double | 40.00 | 50.00 |

**Half board**

| per person: | £min | £max |
| --- | --- | --- |
| Daily | 35.00 | 40.00 |

Evening meal from 1800
Parking for 4
Open May-October

🏠 🖴 🖵 ♿ 🖐 ▥ Ⓢ 🏵 ✂ 🄼 ▥ ➡ ❄ ✈ 🚶

### Jordan House 🏠

| 🏵🏵 | COMMENDED |
| --- | --- |

68 London Road, Royal Tunbridge
Wells TN1 1DT
☎ Tunbridge Wells (01892) 523983
*17th C town house with old world
ambience, overlooking Tunbridge Wells
Common and near town centre and
station. Non-smokers preferred.*
Bedrooms: 1 double, 1 twin
Bathrooms: 2 private

**Bed & breakfast**

| per night: | £min | £max |
| --- | --- | --- |
| Single | 18.00 | 20.00 |
| Double | 36.00 | 40.00 |

🏠 🖵 10 🖐 ▥ 🏵 Ⓢ 🄼 📺 ▥ ➡ 🚶 🅂🄿 🄼

### Manor Court Farm 🏠

🏵🏵

Ashurst, Royal Tunbridge Wells
TN3 9TB
☎ Fordcombe (01892) 740279
*350-acre mixed farm. Georgian
farmhouse with friendly atmosphere.
Spacious rooms and near views
overlooking Medway Valley. Good base
for walking and touring. Weekend
cream teas. On the A264, half a mile
east of Ashurst village (Tunbridge Wells
to East Grinstead road).*
Bedrooms: 1 double, 2 twin

Bathrooms: 1 private, 2 public

**Bed & breakfast**

| per night: | £min | £max |
|---|---|---|
| Single | 17.00 | 20.00 |
| Double | 34.00 | 38.00 |

Parking for 15

🐕🕭♨🎏🔌î🅂⅍😾📺▥🗕🚗☎🔾∪♩☼🏍 DAP SP 🏠

## Nellington Mead
♦♦

Nellington Road, Royal Tunbridge
Wells TN4 8SQ
☎ Tunbridge Wells (01892) 545037
*Comfortable modern house with
extensive garden. Easy access to
Kent/Sussex countryside, historic
houses and gardens. London and coast
easily accessible.*
Bedrooms: 1 twin
Bathrooms: 1 private

**Bed & breakfast**

| per night: | £min | £max |
|---|---|---|
| Single | 17.50 | 18.00 |
| Double | 35.00 | 36.00 |

**Half board**

| per person: | £min | £max |
|---|---|---|
| Daily | 25.00 | 28.00 |
| Weekly | 152.50 | 173.50 |

Evening meal from 1900
Parking for 5
Open January-November

🐕🖵♨🔌î🅂⅍📺▥🗕🚗☼♩🏍

## The Old Parsonage ⋔
♦♦♦ DE LUXE

Church Lane, Frant, Royal Tunbridge
Wells TN3 9DX
☎ Frant (01892) 750773
Fax (01892) 750773
*Peacefully situated by the village church
(2 pubs and restaurant nearby), this
classic Georgian country house provides
superior accommodation: en-suite
bedrooms, antique-furnished reception
rooms, spacious conservatory and
ballustrated terrace overlooking the
secluded walled garden.*
Bedrooms: 2 double, 1 twin
Bathrooms: 3 private

**Bed & breakfast**

| per night: | £min | £max |
|---|---|---|
| Single | 32.00 | 42.00 |
| Double | 50.00 | 56.00 |

Parking for 12

🐕🕭🕭🖵🔌♨🅂⅍📺▥🗕🚗☼🏍 🏠

> There are separate
> sections in this guide
> listing groups
> specialising in farm
> holidays and
> accommodation which
> is especially suitable
> for young people and
> organised groups.

---

## RYE

East Sussex
Map ref 3B4

Cobbled, hilly streets and fine old
buildings make Rye, once a
Cinque Port, a most picturesque
town. Noted for its church with
ancient clock, potteries and
antique shops. Town Model Sound
and Light Show gives a good
introduction to the town.
*Tourist Information Centre
☎ (01797) 226696*

## Aviemore Guest House ⋔
♦♦ APPROVED

28/30 Fishmarket Road, Rye
TN31 7LP
☎ (01797) 223052
*Owner-run, friendly guesthouse offering
a warm welcome and hearty breakfast.
Overlooking "Town Salts" and the River
Rother. 2 minutes from town centre. 10
per cent discount for weekly half board
stays.*
Bedrooms: 1 single, 4 double, 3 twin
Bathrooms: 4 private, 2 public

**Bed & breakfast**

| per night: | £min | £max |
|---|---|---|
| Single | 17.00 | 28.00 |
| Double | 30.00 | 38.00 |

**Half board**

| per person: | £min | £max |
|---|---|---|
| Daily | 23.00 | 27.00 |

Evening meal 1800 (last orders 2200)
Cards accepted: Access, Visa, Amex

🐕♨î🅂⅍📺▥🗕🚗◗♩☼ DAP 🔖 SP 🏁

## Furnace Lane Oast ⋔
♦♦

Broad Oak Brede, Rye TN31 6ET
☎ Hastings (01424) 882407
*Beautiful converted double oast house
set in 10 acres of garden and field. One
mile from village shops, wonderful
views, very rural.*
Bedrooms: 1 double, 1 twin, 1 triple
Bathrooms: 3 private

**Bed & breakfast**

| per night: | £min | £max |
|---|---|---|
| Single | 20.00 | 25.00 |
| Double | 40.00 | 50.00 |

**Half board**

| per person: | £min | £max |
|---|---|---|
| Daily | 30.00 | 45.00 |
| Weekly | 190.00 | 290.00 |

Evening meal 1800 (last orders 2000)
Parking for 6

🐕🕭🖵🔌♨🔾🅂⅍📺▥🗕🚗☼🏍 SP 🏠

## Green Hedges ⋔
♦♦♦ HIGHLY COMMENDED

Hillyfields, Rye Hill, Rye TN31 7NH
☎ (01797) 222185
*Country house in a private road. 1.5
acres of landscaped gardens with heated
swimming pool. Short stroll to town
centre. Ample parking. Home- grown
organic produce.*

---

Bedrooms: 2 double, 1 twin
Bathrooms: 3 private, 1 public

**Bed & breakfast**

| per night: | £min | £max |
|---|---|---|
| Double | 23.00 | 28.00 |

Parking for 7

🐕12🕭🖵♨🔾î🅂⅍📺▥🗕🚗🔾 ☼🏍🏠

## Jeake's House ⋔
♦♦♦ HIGHLY COMMENDED

Mermaid Street, Rye TN31 7ET
☎ (01797) 222828
Fax (01797) 222623

*Recapture the past in this historic
building, in a cobblestoned street at the
heart of the old town. Honeymoon suite
available.*
Bedrooms: 1 single, 7 double, 1 twin,
2 triple, 1 family room
Bathrooms: 11 private, 2 public

**Bed & breakfast**

| per night: | £min | £max |
|---|---|---|
| Single | 22.50 | 22.50 |
| Double | 39.00 | 57.00 |

Cards accepted: Access, Visa, Amex

🐕🕭📞🖵♨🔾🅂⅍📺▥🗕🚗🏍 SP 🏠🎬

## Kimblee ⋔
♦♦♦ COMMENDED

Main Street, Peasmarsh, Rye
TN31 6UL
☎ Peasmarsh (01797) 230514 &
Mobile 0831 841004
*Country house with views from all
aspects, 250 metres from pub/restaurant
and 5 minutes' drive on the A268 from
Rye. Warm welcome.*
Bedrooms: 3 double
Bathrooms: 3 private

**Bed & breakfast**

| per night: | £min | £max |
|---|---|---|
| Single | | 17.50 |
| Double | 30.00 | 36.00 |

Parking for 4
Cards accepted: Access, Visa

🐕🕭🖵♨🔾🅂▥🗕🚗☼♩ DAP SP 🎬

## The Old Vicarage
Listed COMMENDED

Rye Harbour, Rye TN31 7TT
☎ (01797) 222088
*Imposing Victorian former vicarage,
quietly situated close to sea and nature
reserve. Antique furniture and open
fires. Good English breakfast.*
Bedrooms: 1 double, 1 twin
Bathrooms: 1 public

Continued ▶

## RYE

*Continued*

### Bed & breakfast

| per night: | £min | £max |
|---|---|---|
| Single | 18.00 | 20.00 |
| Double | 31.00 | 36.00 |

Parking for 4

🛏🍳♿🏃‍♀️🚷ⓊⓁ🔒$✂️🧺⬛🚗🚲 SP

### Saint Margarets ⋔

**Listed**

Dumbwomans Lane, Udimore, Rye
TN31 6AD
☎ (01797) 222586
*Comfortable, friendly chalet bungalow
with sea views. Car parking. En-suite
facilities. B2089, 2 miles west of Rye.*
Bedrooms: 2 double, 1 twin
Bathrooms: 2 private

### Bed & breakfast

| per night: | £min | £max |
|---|---|---|
| Double | 28.00 | 29.00 |

Parking for 3
Open January-October

♿🍳♿🚷ⓊⓁ$🧺⬛🚲 SP

### Strand House ⋔

**☰☰☰ COMMENDED**

Winchelsea TN36 4JT
☎ (01797) 226276

*The old charm of one of Winchelsea's
oldest houses, dating from the 15th C,
with oak beams and inglenooks.
Overlooking National Trust pastureland,
Four-poster bedroom. Residents' licence.*
Bedrooms: 8 double, 1 twin, 1 triple
Bathrooms: 8 private, 1 public

### Bed & breakfast

| per night: | £min | £max |
|---|---|---|
| Single | 28.00 | 32.00 |
| Double | 40.00 | 55.00 |

Evening meal 1830 (last orders 1900)
Parking for 15
Cards accepted: Access, Visa

🛏5🍳🖭🏃‍♀️♿🔒$📺⬛🚗🚲
🚲 SP ♨

### Top o'The Hill at Rye ⋔

**☰☰☰ COMMENDED**

Rye Hill, Rye TN31 7NH
☎ (01797) 223284
Fax (01797) 227030
*Small friendly inn offering fine
traditional food and cottage-style
accommodation. Central for touring
Kent and Sussex, Channel ports nearby.
Large car park, garden.*
Bedrooms: 1 single, 3 double, 2 twin,
1 triple, 1 family room
Bathrooms: 8 private

---

### Bed & breakfast

| per night: | £min | £max |
|---|---|---|
| Single | 22.00 | 25.00 |
| Double | 36.00 | 40.00 |

Lunch available
Evening meal 1900 (last orders 2100)
Parking for 32
Cards accepted: Access, Visa

🛏♿🍳♿🏃‍♀️🚷🕯$📺⬛🚗🖭6-12Ù☀🚲
SP ♨

## ST NICHOLAS AT WADE

Kent
Map ref 3C3

Village in the Isle of Thanet with
ancient church built of knapped
flint.

### Streete Farm House

**Listed**

Court Road, St Nicholas at Wade,
Birchington CT7 0NH
☎ Thanet (01843) 847245
*50-acre arable and mixed farm. 16th C
farmhouse on the outskirts of the
village, with original oak-panelled
dining room.*
Bedrooms: 1 single, 2 double
Bathrooms: 1 public

### Bed & breakfast

| per night: | £min | £max |
|---|---|---|
| Single | 14.00 | 16.00 |
| Double | 28.00 | 32.00 |

Parking for 4

🛏3ⓊⓁ📺📺⬛☀✂️🚲🚲

## SARRE

Kent
Map ref 3C3

### Crown Inn (The Famous
Cherry Brandy House) ⋔

**☰☰☰ COMMENDED**

Ramsgate Road, Sarre, Birchington
CT7 0LF
☎ Birchington (01843) 847808
Fax (01843) 847914
*An ideal centre for exploring
Canterbury, Thanet and east Kent. Our
unique liqueur has been available here
since 1650.*
Wheelchair access category 3 ♿
Bedrooms: 9 double, 2 twin, 1 triple
Bathrooms: 12 private

### Bed & breakfast

| per night: | £min | £max |
|---|---|---|
| Single | 37.50 | |
| Double | 47.50 | |

Lunch available
Evening meal 1900 (last orders 2200)
Parking for 40
Cards accepted: Access, Visa, Switch/
Delta

🛏♿🍳📞🖭🏃‍♀️🕯$🔒📺⬛🚗🖭
☀🚲🚲 SP ♨ Ⓣ

---

## SEVENOAKS

Kent
Map ref 2D2

Set in pleasant wooded country,
with a distinctive character and
charm. Nearby is Knole (National
Trust), home of the Sackville
family and one of the largest
houses in England, set in a vast
deer park.
*Tourist Information Centre
☎ (01732) 450305*

### The Bull Hotel ⋔

**☰☰ ☰ APPROVED**

Wrotham, Sevenoaks TN15 7RF
☎ (01732) 885522 & 883092
Fax (01732) 886288

*Privately-run 14th C coaching inn, in
secluded historic village 15 minutes
from Sevenoaks. Just off M20 and
M25/26, 30 minutes from Gatwick and
London. Oak beams and inglenook
fireplaces. Ideal for local places of
interest.*
Bedrooms: 1 single, 3 double, 6 twin
Bathrooms: 5 private, 1 public

### Bed & breakfast

| per night: | £min | £max |
|---|---|---|
| Single | 35.00 | 40.00 |
| Double | 45.00 | 50.00 |

Lunch available
Evening meal 1900 (last orders 2200)
Parking for 50
Cards accepted: Access, Visa, Diners,
Amex

🛏♿🍳📞🖭🏃‍♀️$🔒📺⬛🚗🖭50☀🚲
🚲 SP ♨ Ⓣ

### Moorings Hotel ⋔

**☰☰☰**

97 Hitchen Hatch Lane, Sevenoaks
TN13 3BE
☎ (01732) 452589
Fax (01732) 456462
*Friendly family hotel offering high
standard accommodation for tourists
and business travellers. 30 minutes from
London. Close to BR station.*
Bedrooms: 5 single, 4 double, 10 twin,
2 triple
Bathrooms: 21 private, 2 public

### Bed & breakfast

| per night: | £min | £max |
|---|---|---|
| Single | 25.00 | 40.00 |
| Double | 35.00 | 58.00 |

### Half board

| per person: | £min | £max |
|---|---|---|
| Daily | 35.00 | 48.00 |
| Weekly | 245.00 | 335.00 |

Evening meal 1900 (last orders 2100)

Parking for 22
Cards accepted: Access, Visa, Amex
🛇🛏📞🖵♿🅪⑤✗🅗📺◐🕮🖕📠
🍴2-45🕨✿🅭�🆂🅿🆃

## SITTINGBOURNE

Kent
Map ref 3B3

The town's position and its ample supply of water make it an ideal site for the paper-making industry. Delightful villages and orchards lie round about.

### The Beaumont
👑👑👑 COMMENDED

74 London Road, Sittingbourne
ME10 1NS
☎ (01795) 472536
Fax (01795) 425921
*17th C farmhouse, conveniently located for historic Canterbury, Rochester and Leeds Castle. Superb prize-winning breakfast menu and picturesque tea garden.*
Bedrooms: 3 single, 3 double, 1 twin, 1 triple, 1 family room
Bathrooms: 5 private, 1 public, 3 private showers

**Bed & breakfast**

| per night: | £min | £max |
| --- | --- | --- |
| Single | 23.50 | 40.00 |
| Double | 42.00 | 48.00 |

Parking for 9
Cards accepted: Access, Visa
🛇🛏📞🖵♿🅪⑤🖙✗🅗📺🕮🖕📠
🍴12✿🅭🆂🅿🆃

## SMALLFIELD

Surrey
Map ref 2D2

Small village between Horley and Lingfield, named after local estate.

### Chithurst Farm
Listed

Chithurst Lane, Horne, Smallfield,
Horley RH6 9JU
☎ (01342) 842487
*92-acre dairy farm. Recently renovated 16th C listed farmhouse, with genuine beamed rooms, inglenook fireplaces and attractive garden. Set in a quiet country lane, yet convenient for Gatwick and motorways.*
Bedrooms: 1 single, 1 double, 1 triple
Bathrooms: 1 public

**Bed & breakfast**

| per night: | £min | £max |
| --- | --- | --- |
| Single | 13.50 | 16.00 |
| Double | 27.00 | 32.00 |

Parking for 3
Open February-November
🛇🏕♿🅪✗📺🖕✿🎿🐎🐕🏠

## SMARDEN

Kent
Map ref 3B4

Pretty village with a number of old, well-presented buildings. The 14th C St Michael's Church is sometimes known as the "Barn of Kent" because of its 36-ft roof span.

### Chequers Inn ♨
🛏

Smarden, Ashford TN27 8QA
☎ Ashford (01233) 770217 & 770623
*15th C inn with oak beams, centrally situated for visiting many stately homes. 5 golf-courses nearby. Food always available - speciality is fresh fish.*
Bedrooms: 1 single, 2 twin, 1 family room
Bathrooms: 2 public

**Bed & breakfast**

| per night: | £min | £max |
| --- | --- | --- |
| Single | 20.00 | 24.00 |
| Double | 36.00 | 45.00 |

Lunch available
Evening meal 1800 (last orders 2200)
Parking for 18
Cards accepted: Access, Visa, Switch/Delta
🛇🖵🖕🐾🛋⑤✗🛲🍴🕮🖐↻🕨✿🐎
🅿🏠

## SOUTHBOROUGH

Kent
Map ref 2D2

### Nightingales ♨
Listed

London Road, Southborough, Royal Tunbridge Wells TN4 0UJ
☎ Tunbridge Wells (01892) 528443
Fax (01892) 511376
*Georgian house situated on A26, convenient for A21, M25 and Tonbridge/Tunbridge Wells.*
Bedrooms: 1 single, 1 double, 1 triple
Bathrooms: 1 public

**Bed & breakfast**

| per night: | £min | £max |
| --- | --- | --- |
| Single | 18.00 | 18.00 |
| Double | 34.00 | 34.00 |

Parking for 3
🛇5🖵♿🅪⑤✗🕮🛲✿✗🐎🏠

## STELLING MINNIS

Kent
Map ref 3B4

Off the Roman Stone Street, this quiet, picturesque village lies deep in the Lyminge Forest, south of Canterbury.

### Great Field Farm
Listed

Misling Lane, Stelling Minnis,
Canterbury CT4 6DE
☎ (01227) 709223

*42-acre mixed farm. Lovely spacious farmhouse with wealth of old pine, fine furnishings, pleasant gardens, paddocks with friendly ponies. Self-contained flat available for B&B or self catering. Quiet location midway Canterbury/Folkestone, adjacent B2068.*
Bedrooms: 2 double, 1 twin
Bathrooms: 2 private, 1 public

**Bed & breakfast**

| per night: | £min | £max |
| --- | --- | --- |
| Single | 15.50 | 20.00 |
| Double | 31.00 | 40.00 |

Parking for 6
🛇🖕♿✗🕮🛲↻✿🐎

## STORRINGTON

West Sussex
Map ref 2D3

Small town within easy reach of walks over the South Downs and the popular Sussex coast.

### Greenacres Country Holidays ♨
👑👑👑 APPROVED

Washington Road, Storrington,
Pulborough RH20 4AF
☎ Worthing (01903) 742538

*Family-run bed and breakfast set in 6 acres at the foot of the downs, 20 minutes from Worthing and the sea. Central for touring the south. Swimming pool.*
Bedrooms: 2 twin, 3 triple
Bathrooms: 5 private, 1 public

**Bed & breakfast**

| per night: | £min | £max |
| --- | --- | --- |
| Single | 20.00 | 35.00 |
| Double | 40.00 | 50.00 |

**Half board**

| per person: | £min | £max |
| --- | --- | --- |
| Daily | 27.00 | 42.00 |
| Weekly | 85.00 | 130.00 |

Evening meal 1830 (last orders 2000)
Parking for 30
Cards accepted: Access, Visa, Amex
🛇🛏📞🖵🖕♿🅪⑤✗🕮🛲🍴14🏕
↻↻✿🐎🅭🆂

National Crown ratings were correct at the time of going to press but are subject to change. Please check at the time of booking.

## SUTTON VALENCE

Kent
Map ref 3B4

Built on a ridge with tiered streets and some interesting 16th C houses. The village commands superb views across the Weald.

### Richmond House ⋒
**Listed**

Rectory Lane, Sutton Valence, Maidstone ME17 3BS
☎ Maidstone (01622) 842217

*Quietly situated with panoramic views of the Weald. Half-mile from Kings Head on A274. Near Leeds Castle.*
Bedrooms: 2 twin
Bathrooms: 1 public

**Bed & breakfast**

| per night: | £min | £max |
| --- | --- | --- |
| Single | 17.00 | 18.00 |
| Double | 34.00 | 36.00 |

Parking for 6

## SWANLEY

Kent
Map ref 2D2

### The Dees ⋒
**Listed** **COMMENDED**

56 Old Chapel Road, Crockenhill, Swanley BR8 8LJ
☎ (01322) 667645
*Crockenhill is 2 miles from M25 and M20. Easy access to Brands Hatch, London, Kent and Sussex coast and country. Nice double room with full private facilities plus single room.*
Bedrooms: 1 single, 1 double
Bathrooms: 1 private, 1 public

**Bed & breakfast**

| per night: | £min | £max |
| --- | --- | --- |
| Single | 12.50 | 17.50 |
| Double | 30.00 | 35.00 |

Parking for 2

---

National Crown ratings were correct at the time of going to press but are subject to change. Please check at the time of booking.

## TENTERDEN

Kent
Map ref 3B4

Most attractive market town with a broad main street full of 16th C houses and shops. The tower of the 15th C parish church is the finest in Kent.

### Finchden Manor
**HIGHLY COMMENDED**

Appledore Road, Tenterden TN30 7DD
☎ (01580) 764719
*Early 15th C manor house, Grade II* listed, with inglenook fireplaces, panelled rooms and beams. Set in 4 acres of gardens and grounds.*
Bedrooms: 1 single, 2 double
Bathrooms: 3 private, 3 public

**Bed & breakfast**

| per night: | £min | £max |
| --- | --- | --- |
| Single | 25.00 | 27.00 |
| Double | 50.00 | 55.00 |

Parking for 3

## TUNBRIDGE WELLS

*See under Royal Tunbridge Wells*

## UCKFIELD

East Sussex
Map ref 2D3

Once a medieval market town and centre of the iron industry, Uckfield is now a busy country town on the edge of the Ashdown Forest.

### Dale Hamme ⋒
**Listed** **APPROVED**

Piltdown, Uckfield TN22 3XY
☎ Nutley (01825) 712422
*15th C hall house with oak beams and inglenook fireplaces in idyllic rural location. On A272 going east, take second left after Piltdown Man pub into Down Street. After 1 mile turn left, house on left hand side.*
Bedrooms: 2 single, 2 twin
Bathrooms: 4 private

**Bed & breakfast**

| per night: | £min | £max |
| --- | --- | --- |
| Single | 15.00 | 15.00 |
| Double | 34.00 | 34.00 |

Parking for 14

### Old Mill Farm ⋒

High Hurstwood, Uckfield TN22 4AD
☎ Buxted (01825) 732279
*50-acre beef farm. Situated in picturesque valley, off A26. Gatwick, Crowborough, Uckfield and Ashdown Forest nearby. All rooms have private facilities.*
Bedrooms: 1 single, 1 twin, 1 family room
Bathrooms: 3 private, 2 public

**Bed & breakfast**

| per night: | £min | £max |
| --- | --- | --- |
| Single | 17.00 | 18.00 |
| Double | 34.00 | 36.00 |

**Half board**

| per person: | £min | £max |
| --- | --- | --- |
| Daily | 25.00 | 26.00 |
| Weekly | 175.00 | 182.00 |

Evening meal 1800 (last orders 2030)
Parking for 6

### South Paddock ⋒
**HIGHLY COMMENDED**

Maresfield Park, Uckfield TN22 2HA
☎ (01825) 762335
*Comfortable quiet country house accommodation set in 3.5 acres of landscaped gardens. Home-made preserves and log fires. Within easy reach of Gatwick, Brighton, Glyndebourne, Hever Castle.*
Bedrooms: 1 double, 2 twin
Bathrooms: 1 private, 1 public

**Bed & breakfast**

| per night: | £min | £max |
| --- | --- | --- |
| Single | 32.00 | 36.00 |
| Double | 50.00 | 53.00 |

Parking for 6

## WARNINGLID

West Sussex
Map ref 2D3

### Gillhurst ⋒

The Street, Warninglid, Haywards Heath RH17 5SZ
☎ Haywards Heath (01444) 461388
*Quiet setting outside beautiful village. Extensive grounds, hard tennis court, lovely decor, large rooms. Walks and lovely gardens in vicinity.*
Bedrooms: 1 double, 2 twin
Bathrooms: 3 private

**Bed & breakfast**

| per night: | £min | £max |
| --- | --- | --- |
| Single | 20.00 | 30.00 |
| Double | 40.00 | 50.00 |

Parking for 10

## WEST CHILTINGTON

West Sussex
Map ref 2D3

Well-kept village caught in the maze of lanes leading to and from the South Downs.

### New House Farm ⋒
**COMMENDED**

Broadford Bridge Road, West Chiltington, Pulborough RH20 2LA
☎ (01798) 812215
*50-acre mixed farm. 15th C farmhouse with oak beams and inglenook for log*

*fires. 40 minutes' drive from Gatwick. Within easy reach of local inns and golf-course.*
Bedrooms: 1 double, 2 twin
Bathrooms: 3 private

**Bed & breakfast**

| per night: | £min | £max |
|---|---|---|
| Single | 25.00 | 35.00 |
| Double | 36.00 | 50.00 |

Parking for 6
Open January-November

🐕 10 ⬚ 🖤 ⬚ ⬚ 🖤 ⬚ 📺 ⬚ 🍴 ⬚ 🌸 ⬚ 🚲 SP 🏫

## WEST CLANDON

Surrey
Map ref 2D2

### Ways Cottage

Listed COMMENDED

Lime Grove, West Clandon, Guildford GU4 7UT
☎ Guildford (01483) 222454
*Rural detached house in quiet location, five miles from Guildford. Easy reach of A3 and M25. Close to station on Waterloo/Guildford line.*
Bedrooms: 1 single, 1 double, 1 twin
Bathrooms: 1 private, 1 public

**Bed & breakfast**

| per night: | £min | £max |
|---|---|---|
| Single | 16.00 | 18.50 |
| Double | 32.50 | 32.50 |

**Half board**

| per person: | £min | £max |
|---|---|---|
| Daily | 26.00 | 28.50 |

Evening meal 1800 (last orders 2100)
Parking for 2

🐕 📫 ⬚ 🖤 ⬚ 🖤 ⬚ 🍴 🌸 ✗ 🚲

## WEST MALLING

Kent
Map ref 3B3

Became prominent in Norman times when an abbey was established here.

### Westfields Farm

Listed

St. Vincents Lane, Addington, West Malling ME19 5BW
☎ (01732) 843209
*A farmhouse of character, approximately 500 years old, in rural setting. Within easy reach of London, Canterbury, Tunbridge Wells and the coast. Reductions for children. Golf nearby.*
Bedrooms: 1 single, 1 double, 1 twin
Bathrooms: 2 public

**Bed & breakfast**

| per night: | £min | £max |
|---|---|---|
| Single | 17.50 | 17.50 |

🐕 ⬚ 🖤 ⬚ 🖤 ⬚ 📺 ⬚ 🍴 🌸 🌸 ✗ 🚲 🏫

## WOKING

Surrey
Map ref 2D2

One of the largest towns in Surrey, which developed with the coming of the railway in the 1830s. Old Woking was a market town in the 17th C and still retains several interesting buildings.

### Elm Lodge 𝍌

Listed

Elm Road, Horsell, Woking GU21 4DY
☎ (01483) 763323
Fax (01483) 845656
*Comfortable Victorian home in a quiet location overlooking woodland, yet just a few minutes from town centre and British Rail main line station.*
Bedrooms: 3 twin
Bathrooms: 1 public

**Bed & breakfast**

| per night: | £min | £max |
|---|---|---|
| Single | 28.00 | 28.00 |
| Double | 40.00 | 40.00 |

**Half board**

| per person: | £min | £max |
|---|---|---|
| Daily | 40.00 | 40.00 |

Evening meal 1800 (last orders 2000)
Parking for 6

🐕 ⬚ S 🖤 📺 ⬚ 🍴 🚲 ✗

## WORTHING

West Sussex
Map ref 2D3

Largest town in West Sussex, a popular seaside resort with extensive sand and shingle beaches. Seafishing is excellent here. The museum contains finds from Cissbury Ring.
*Tourist Information Centre*
☎ *(01903) 210022*

### Park House

Listed

4 St. Georges Road, Worthing BN11 2DS
☎ (01903) 207939
*Small family-run establishment situated just 50 yards from seafront in a quiet road. Five minutes' walk from Worthing town centre.*
Bedrooms: 1 single, 4 double
Bathrooms: 4 private, 1 public

**Bed & breakfast**

| per night: | £min | £max |
|---|---|---|
| Single | 17.00 | 20.00 |
| Double | 34.00 | 40.00 |

Lunch available
Evening meal 1830 (last orders 2030)
Cards accepted: Access, Visa

🐕 ⬚ 🖤 ⬚ S 🖤 🖤 📺 ⬚ 🍴 🌸 🚲 SP

### Tudor Guest House 𝍌

⬚

5 Windsor Road, Worthing BN11 2LU
☎ (01903) 210265

*Comfortable bedrooms, satellite TV, English or continental breakfast. 1 minute from seafront, restaurants. Close to town centre, entertainment, bowling greens, Beach House Park. Parking on premises.*
Bedrooms: 6 single, 2 double, 2 twin
Bathrooms: 3 private, 1 public

**Bed & breakfast**

| per night: | £min | £max |
|---|---|---|
| Single | 12.50 | 14.50 |
| Double | 22.00 | 32.00 |

Parking for 5
Cards accepted: Access, Visa

🐕 1 ⬚ 📫 ⬚ 🖤 S 🖤 🖤 📺 ⬚ 🚲 🌸 🚲 OAP SP

## WYE

Kent
Map ref 3B4

Well known for its agricultural and horticultural college. The Olantigh Tower, with its imposing front portico, is used as a setting for part of the Stour Music Festival held annually in June.

### New Flying Horse Inn 𝍌

⬚⬚⬚ COMMENDED

Upper Bridge Street, Wye, Ashford TN25 5AN
☎ (01233) 812297
Fax (01233) 813487
*17th C former coaching inn with oak beams and gleaming brasses. Ideal for touring and walking the Kent countryside and coast.*
Bedrooms: 1 single, 2 double, 2 twin, 1 triple
Bathrooms: 6 private

**Bed & breakfast**

| per night: | £min | £max |
|---|---|---|
| Single | 37.50 | |
| Double | 47.50 | |

Lunch available
Evening meal 1830 (last orders 2130)
Parking for 30
Cards accepted: Access, Visa

🐕 🌸 📫 📞 📫 ⬚ 🖤 🖤 S ⬚ 🚲 ⬚ 🌸 🚲 SP 🏫

# SURE SIGNS

## OF WHERE TO STAY

**Throughout Britain, the tourist boards now inspect over 30,000 places to stay, every year, to help you find the ones that suit you best.**

Looking for a hotel, guesthouse, inn, B&B or farmhouse? Look for the **CROWN**. The classifications: 'Listed', and then **ONE to FIVE CROWN**, tell you the range of facilities and services you can expect. The more Crowns, the wider the range.

Looking for somewhere convenient to stop overnight on a motorway or major road route? Look for the 'Lodge' **MOON.** The classifications: **ONE to THREE MOON** tell you the range of facilities you can expect. The more Moons, the wider the range.

Looking for a self-catering holiday home? Look for the **KEY**. The classifications: **ONE to FIVE KEY,** tell you the range of facilities and equipment you can expect. The more Keys, the wider the range.
THE GRADES: **APPROVED, COMMENDED, HIGHLY COMMENDED and DE LUXE,** whether alongside the **CROWNS**, **KEYS** or **MOONS** show the quality standard of what is provided. If no grade is shown, you can still expect a high standard of cleanliness.

Looking for a holiday caravan, chalet or camping park? Look for the **Q** symbol. The more ✓s in the Q (from one to five), the higher the quality standard of what is provided.

**We've checked them out before you check in!**

More detailed information on the **CROWNS**, the **KEYS** and the **Q** is given in free *SURE SIGN* leaflets, available at any Tourist Information Centre.

# FARM HOLIDAY GROUPS

This section of the guide lists groups specialising in farm and country based holidays. Most offer bed and breakfast accommodation (some with evening meal) and self-catering accommodation.

To obtain further details of individual properties please contact the group(s) direct, indicating the time of the year when the accommodation is required and the number of people to be accommodated. You may find the Accommodation Coupons towards the back of this guide helpful when making contact.

The cost of sending out brochures is high, and the groups would appreciate written enquiries being accompanied by a stamped and addressed envelope (at least 9" x 4½").

The 'b&b' prices shown are per person per night; the self-catering prices are weekly terms per unit.

The symbol ⛲ before the name of a group indicates that it is a member of the Farm Holiday Bureau, set up by the Royal Agricultural Society of England in conjunction with the English Tourist Board.

---

**Bed & Breakfast (GB)**
PO Box 66, Henley-on-Thames, Oxfordshire RG9 1XS
Tel: Henley-on-Thames (01491) 578803
Fax: (01491) 410806
*Central reservations office for over 500 selected B&B hosts all over Britain, from £14.50 per person. Free mini-guide available.*
500 properties offering bed and breakfast: £14.50–£45 b&b.
Short breaks also available.

⛲ **Cambridgeshire Farmhouse Accommodation**
Mrs Valerie Fuller, Spinney Abbey, Wicken, Ely, Cambridgeshire CB7 5XQ
Tel: Ely (01353) 720971
*Good selection of bed & breakfast and self-catering properties in rural areas. Whether your visit is business or pleasure, we look forward to welcoming you to our farmhouses. Contact Mrs Valerie Fuller at address above for leaflet.*
14 properties offering bed and breakfast: £13–£23 b&b.
2 self-catering units: £175–£300

depending on season.
Short breaks also available.

**"A Cotswold Break"**
Highlands, Stinchcombe Hill, Dursley, Gloucestershire GL11 6AQ
Tel: Stroud (01453) 542539
Fax: (01453) 836737
*A special collection of character B&B accommodation, with excellent facilities, conveniently situated in the Cotswolds. Excellent value, golf packages, gourmet weekends and interesting walks. Half-hour from Cheltenham, Bath, Forest*

of Dean and Cirencester. One hour from Stratford, Stow and Oxford.

Properties offering bed and breakfast: £16–£22 b&b.

Short breaks also available.

###  Cream of Cornwall

Judith Clemo, Rescorla Farm, Rescorla, St Austell, Cornwall PL26 8YT

Tel: St Austell (01726) 850168

Fax: (01726) 850168

*Range of traditional farmhouses, from those nestling under the hills of out-of-the-way villages to the granite lintels of those perched high on the cliffs of the Atlantic coastline.*

31 properties offering bed and breakfast: £12.50–£26 b&b.

65 self-catering units: low season (November–February) £90–£150; high season (March–October) £250–£600.

Short breaks also available.

### East Devon Farm Holidays Group

Mrs Brenda Northam, Bodmiscombe Farm, Blackborough, Cullompton, Devon EX15 2HR

Tel: Kentisbeare (01884) 266315

*A warm welcome and high standards assured in family-run farm and country homes. Explore East Devon's unspoilt rolling countryside with picturesque thatched villages and miles of sandy and pebble beaches. Caravan and tent pitches also available.*

17 properties offering bed and breakfast: £15–£23 b&b.

18 self-catering units: £90–£525 depending on season.

Short breaks also available.

###  Eden Valley & North Pennines

Mrs Ruth Tuer, Meaburn Hill, Maulds Meaburn, Penrith, Cumbria CA10 3HN

Tel: (01931) 715205

Fax: (01931) 715205

*Whether you choose to stay in the caring family atmosphere of a farmhouse bed & breakfast, or a cosy sandstone self-catering cottage, the discerning visitor will appreciate the peace and tranquillity of 'England's last wilderness'. Members are renowned for their hospitality, fresh food and home cooking. Phone or write for brochure.*

11 properties offering bed and breakfast: £13–£20 b&b.

27 self-catering units: low season £92–£150; high season £180–£480.

Short breaks also available.

### Kent Farm Holidays

Mrs D. Day, Great Cheveney Farm, Goudhurst Road, Marden, Tonbridge, Kent TN12 9LX

Tel: (01622) 831207

Fax: (01622) 831786

Mrs R. Bannock, Court Lodge Farm, Teston, Maidstone, Kent ME18 5AQ

Tel: (01622) 812570

Fax: (01622) 814200

*Wide selection, from traditional farm cottages to modern farm-building conversions. Many with interesting architectural features and leisure facilities, many welcome non-smokers. Peaceful touring caravan and camping park.*

20 properties offering bed and breakfast: £16–£30 b&b.

21 self-catering units: low season (October–April) from £95; high season (May–September) £130–£400.

Discounted short breaks available in low season.

### Norfolk & Suffolk Farm Holiday Group

Mrs R Bryce, College Farm, Hintlesham, Ipswich, Suffolk IP8 3NT
Tel: Hintlesham (01473) 652253
Fax: (01473) 652253
*Come to Norfolk & Suffolk and experience farmhouse hospitality on a working farm. We offer quality accommodation in a friendly atmosphere. Enjoy exploring picturesque market towns, heritage coastline and 'Constable country'. Caravan and tent pitches also available.*
34 properties offering bed and breakfast: £13–£21 b&b.
18 self-catering units: low season (October–March) £90–£195; high season (April–September) £160–£350.
Short breaks also available.

### Northumberland and Durham Farm Holiday Groups

Greenwell Farm, Nr. Wolsingham, Tow Law, Co. Durham DL13 4PH
Tel: Weardale (01388) 527248
*Quality bed & breakfast and holiday cottages from Berwick to Barnard Castle. Visit castles on peaceful roads; walk the moors and valleys; see Hadrian's Wall, Durham Cathedral, Beamish Museum and much, much more.*
26 properties offering bed and breakfast: £13–£18.50 b&b.
13 self-catering units: low season (January–December) £100–£200; high season £200–£500.
Short breaks also available.

### South Cotswold Holidays Agency

Mrs Victoria Jennings, Apple Orchard House, Springhill, Nailsworth, Stroud, Gloucestershire GL6 0LX
Tel: Stroud (01453) 832503
Fax: (01453) 836213
*Variety of superior quality bed and breakfast establishments including inns and hotels, ranging from 17th C to modern, in the centre of an area with many visitor attractions, half an hour from Bath and Cirencester and convenient for Cheltenham, Gloucester, Stratford-upon-Avon, Oxford, Wells and Worcester. All have private bathrooms, tea/coffee facilities, friendly, helpful hosts. Colour brochure. Immediate bookings by fax.*
39 properties offering bed and breakfast: £15–£21 b&b. Some rooms for disabled guests. American Express/Visa Mastercard accepted.
6 self-catering units: low season (November–April) £100–£180; high season (May–October) £150–£280.
Short breaks also available.

### Thames Valley Farm & Country Holidays

The Old Farmhouse, Station Hill, Long Hanborough, Oxfordshire OX8 8JZ
Tel: Freeland (010993) 882097
Fax: (010993) 851738
*At the very heart of historical England, and centred on Windsor and Oxford, Thames Valley offers perfect English countryside with the attraction of being easily accessible. Farms and country houses are full of character and each is distinctive in style. Properties vary from elegant village homes to busy farms, and all are committed to ensuring a relaxed and enjoyable stay at an extremely reasonable price.*
25 properties offering bed and breakfast: £16–£28 b&b.
6 self-catering units: £220–£550 depending on season.
Short breaks also available.

### Vale of Lune, Morecambe Bay to Pennine Way

Stirzakers Farm, Barnacre, Garstang, Preston, Lancashire PR3 1GE
Tel: (01995) 603335
*Escape the hustle & bustle and come and stay with us! We offer bed & breakfast or self-catering of high quality on our working farms. Enjoy Northern hospitality, good food and peace & quiet. Explore the coast, Pennines, Forest of Bowland and Lancaster at your leisure. Ideal for overnight break in your journey along the M6. Caravan and tent pitches also available.*
8 properties offering bed and breakfast: £14–£18 b&b.
2 self-catering units: low season (November–March) £85–£120; high season (April–October) £120–£300.
Short breaks also available.

### Warwickshire Farm Holidays

The Secretary, Crandon House, Avon Dassett, Leamington Spa, Warwickshire CV33 0AA
Tel: (01295) 770652
*A warm welcome at farmhouses offering serviced and self-catering accommodation in comfortable and homely surroundings, situated in historic and picturesque 'Shakespeare country'. Caravan and tent pitches also available.*
27 properties offering bed and breakfast: £12–£27 b&b.
25 self-catering units: low season (October–April) £70–£350; high season (May–September) £80–£450.

### Yorkshire Dales & Brontë Country Group

Fold Farm, Kettlewell, Skipton, North Yorkshire BD23 5RJ
Tel: Kettlewell (01756) 760886
Fax: (01756) 760464
*This beautiful region extends from picturesque Kettlewell in the north to Bradford in the south. From mill shops, museums and theatres, to walking in the hills and valleys, we have lovely farmhouses and self-catering cottages where you can enjoy it all in comfort and friendliness.*
11 properties offering bed and breakfast: £16–£30 b&b.
7 self-catering units: low season (November–March) £100–£260; high season (April–October) £120–£480.
Short breaks also available.

# NATIONAL ACCESSIBLE SCHEME FOR WHEELCHAIR USERS

If you are a wheelchair user or someone who has difficulty walking, look for the national 'Accessible' symbol when choosing where to stay.

All the places that display the symbol have been checked by a Tourist Board inspector against criteria that reflect the practical needs of wheelchair users.

**There are three categories of accessibility, indicated by symbols:**

**Category 1:** Accessible to all wheelchair users including those travelling independently

**Category 2:** Accessible to a wheelchair user with assistance

**Category 3:** Accessible to a wheelchair user able to walk short distances and up at least three steps

Establishments in this 'Where to Stay' guide which have a wheelchair access category are listed in the information pages at the back, together with further details of the scheme. Tourist Information Centre staff will also be pleased to help with finding suitable accommodation.

# CHECK THE MAPS

The colour maps at the back of this guide show all cities, towns and villages which have accommodation listings in the guide. They will enable you to check if there is suitable accommodation in the vicinity of the place you plan to visit.

# KEY TO SYMBOLS

Information about many of the services and facilities at accommodation listed in this guide is given in the form of symbols. The key to these symbols is inside the back cover flap. You may find it helpful to keep the flap open when referring to the accommodation listings.

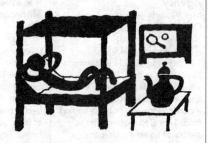

# GROUP AND YOUTH SECTION

*Most of the accommodation establishments listed in this guide are particularly suitable for people looking for relatively low-cost places to stay in England.*

*Some establishments make a special point of providing safe, budget-priced accommodation for young people, for families or for large groups. These places, ranging from Youth Hostels, YMCA and YWCA residences and budget and student hotels to the seasonally available campuses of universities and colleges, are listed individually in the pages which follow.*

*Information on organisations which specialise in accommodation for young people, families and groups is given below – please contact them direct for further details.*

## Youth Hostels

The Youth Hostels Association (England and Wales) provides basic accommodation, usually in single-sex bunk-bedded rooms or dormitories, with self-catering facilities. Most hostels also provide low-cost meals or snacks. At the time of going to press, a night's stay at a Youth Hostel will cost between £3.50 and £15.90 (under 18) and between £5.30 and £18.90 (over 18).

In spite of the word "youth" in the name, there is in fact no upper age limit. Indeed, many Youth Hostels also offer family accommodation, either in self-contained annexes (with kitchen, living room and bathroom) or by letting the smaller, four-to-six bed dormitories as private units.

Groups are very welcome at Youth Hostels, whether for educational or leisure pursuits: some hostels offer field study facilities and many more have classrooms. The YHA also offers a wide range of adventure holidays and special interest breaks.

Youth Hostels – from medieval castles to shepherds' huts – can be found all over the country, both in countryside and coastal locations and in towns and cities.

You need to be a member of the YHA in order to take advantage of the facilities. Membership entitles you to use not only the 240 hostels in England and Wales but also the thousands of Youth Hostels in other parts of the British Isles and around the world. Membership costs £3 (under 18) or £9 (over 18). Family membership is available at £9 (single-parent family) or £18 (two-parent family).

Further information from:
**Youth Hostels Association**
Trevelyan House,
8 St Stephen's Hill,
St Albans,
Hertfordshire AL1 2DY
Tel: (01727) 855215
Fax: (01727) 844126

## YWCA and YMCA

The Young Women's Christian Association, founded in 1855, has grown into the world's largest women's organisation. Among its many activities is the running of over 60 houses in Britain which offer safe, reasonably priced self-catering accommodation, mostly in single rooms, either on a permanent or temporary basis.

Most houses take short-stay visitors only during the summer months. However, some of the

houses do accept short-stay visitors all the year round.

Although the word "women" appears in the name of the organisation, many of the residences now take men and boys as well as women and girls.

The Young Men's Christian Association (YMCA), founded in 1844, operates on much the same basis as the YWCA, taking people of both sexes at its more than 70 residences around the country either on a permanent or short-stay basis.

Special budget accommodation is also available in July and August at some YMCAs as part of the Inter-Point Programme, set up to provide accommodation and advice for Inter-Railers.

Further information from:

**YWCA HQ**
Clarendon House,
52 Cornmarket Street,
Oxford OX1 3EJ
Tel: (01865) 726110

**YMCA**
National Council,
640 Forest Road,
Walthamstow,
London E17 3DZ
Tel: (0181) 520 5599

For details of the Inter-Point Programme, please contact Brian Welters at YMCA on the above telephone number.

## Universities and Colleges

Accommodation in universities and colleges offers excellent value for money at dozens of city centre, seaside and countryside campus locations around England.

This type of accommodation is particularly suitable for groups, whether on a leisure trip or participating in a conference or seminar. Beds available on campus vary from 30 to 3,000. There is a wide selection of meeting room facilities to choose from, with a maximum capacity of 2,000 people, and banqueting facilities for up to 1,500.

Most accommodation is in

single "study bedrooms", with a limited number of twin and family rooms.

Availability is mainly during the academic vacation periods (usually July to September and for four-week periods at Christmas and Easter), with some venues offering short-stay accommodation throughout the year.

For relaxation, there is a wide choice of recreational facilities, with most venues providing TV rooms, bars and restaurants and a variety of sporting activities, ranging from tennis, squash and swimming to team sports.

Activity and special interest holidays are also on offer as are many self-catering flats and houses.

Further information from:

**British Universities Accommodation Consortium (BUAC)**
Box No 1150, University Park,

Nottingham NG7 2RD
Tel: (0115) 950 4571
Fax: (0115) 942 2505

**Connect Venues**
36 Collegiate Crescent,
Sheffield S10 2BP
Tel: (0114) 268 3759
Fax: (0114) 266 1203

## Other Accommodation

In addition to the above main providers on a countrywide basis of budget accommodation for young people and groups, there are, of course, the many individual student and budget hotels around England and also such places as outdoor and field study centres.

Some of these feature in the following pages but for more information on what is available in a particular area, please contact a local Tourist Information Centre.

# WHERE TO STAY

*Accommodation entries in this section are listed in alphabetical order of place name, and then in alphabetical order of establishment.*

*Map references refer to the colour location maps at the back of this guide. The first figure is the map number; the letter and figure which follow indicate the grid reference on the map.*

*Symbols at the end of each accommodation entry give information about services and facilities. A 'key' to these symbols is inside the back cover flap, which can be kept open for easy reference.*

---

## AMBLESIDE

Cumbria
Map ref 5A3

Market town situated at the head of Lake Windermere and surrounded by fells. The historic town centre is now a conservation area and the country around Ambleside is rich in historic and literary associations. Good centre for touring, walking and climbing.
*Tourist Information Centre*
☎ (01539) 432582

### Iveing Cottage Holiday Centre ⋀
YWCA, Old Lake Road, Ambleside LA22 0DJ
☎ (01539) 432340
Contact: The Director
*Centrally located on old coaching road between Ambleside and lake. Ideal for fell-walking, rambling or climbing. Parties or individuals.*
Bedrooms: 1 single, 3 double/twin, 6 dormitories. Total number of beds: 50
Bathrooms: 7 public
**Bed & breakfast**

| per person: | £min | £max |
| --- | --- | --- |
| Daily | 11.75 | 13.25 |

Lunch available
Evening meal 1800 (last orders 1800)
Parking for 9
Open February-November
♿ ♨ Ⓤ 🅸 Ⓢ ✗ 🅜 📺 🛏 ☎ ∪ 🎱 🏕

---

Please mention this guide when making a booking.

---

## BASSENTHWAITE

Cumbria
Map ref 5A2

Standing in an idyllic setting, nestled at the foot of Skiddaw and Ullock Pike, this village is just a mile from Bassenthwaite Lake, the one true "lake" in the Lake District. The area is visited by many varieties of migrating birds.

### Bassenthwaite Parish Rooms
Bassenthwaite, Keswick
Contact: Miss Helen Reb,
Bassenthwaite Parish Rooms, Management Committee, 1 The Avenue, Bassenthwaite, Keswick, Cumbria CA12 4QJ
☎ (01768) 776222
*Village Hall. School Road off A591. Minimum booking 12 people, 3 nights.*
Total number of beds: 50
Bathrooms: 1 public
**Bed only**

| per person: | £min | £max |
| --- | --- | --- |
| Daily | 2.00 | |

Parking for 10
♿ 7 Ⓤ 🏕

### Kiln Hill Barn
Bassenthwaite, Keswick CA12 4RG
☎ (01768) 776454
Contact: Mr. J K Armstrong
*Farmhouse and converted barn in the country. Owned and run by the Armstrongs. Meals served in the barn dining room.*
Bedrooms: 1 single, 2 double/twin, 2 dormitories. Total number of beds: 39
Bathrooms: 4 public

---

**Bed & breakfast**

| per person: | £min | £max |
| --- | --- | --- |
| Daily | 18.00 | 18.00 |

**Full board**

| per person: | £min | £max |
| --- | --- | --- |
| Weekly | 160.00 | 160.00 |

Evening meal 1830 (last orders 1830)
Parking for 15
Open February-October
♿ 🖾 Ⓤ 🅸 Ⓢ 🅜 📺 🛏 ☎ ∪ 🎱 Ⓣ

## BATH

Avon
Map ref 2B2

Georgian spa city beside the River Avon. Important Roman site with impressive reconstructed baths, uncovered in 19th C. Bath Abbey built on site of monastery where first king of England was crowned (AD 973). Fine architecture in mellow local stone. Pump Room and museums.
*Tourist Information Centre*
☎ (01225) 462831

### The City of Bath YMCA ⋀
International House, Broad Street Place, Bath BA1 5LN
☎ (01225) 460471
Contact: Mr A Teasdale
*Open to those of both sexes and all ages. Centrally located and only minutes away from Bath's major attractions. A convenient base for city and West Country tours.*
Bedrooms: 57 single, 21 double/twin, 8 triple, 2 dormitories. Total number of beds: 161
Bathrooms: 29 public

Continued ▶

## BATH

### Continued

**Bed & breakfast**

| per person: | £min | £max |
|---|---|---|
| Daily | 12.50 | |

Lunch available
Evening meal 1700 (last orders 1900)
🏠♿🖥🛆🕇Ⓢ✕🎿📺⛶◨📶🔍✕🏮

## BISHOP AUCKLAND

### Durham
### Map ref 5C2

Busy market town on the bank of
the River Wear. The Palace, a
castellated Norman manor house
altered in the 18th C, stands in
beautiful gardens. Entered from
the market square by a handsome
18th C gatehouse, the park is a
peaceful retreat of trees and
streams.
*Tourist Information Centre*
☎ *(01388) 604922*

### Weardale House ⋀

Ireshopeburn, Bishop Auckland,
County Durham DL13 1HB
Contact: Mr C Jones, Y.M.C.A.
Residential Office, Herrington Burn,
Houghton-le-Spring, Tyne and Wear
DH4 4JW
☎ (0191) 385 2822 & 385 3085
Fax (0191) 385 2267
*Multi-activity outdoor centre. Prices
quoted are for full board Monday-Friday
and include all catering,
accommodation and multi-activity
course.*
Minimum age 7
Bedrooms: 3 single, 8 dormitories.
Total number of beds: 70
Bathrooms: 8 public
**Full board**

| per person: | £min | £max |
|---|---|---|
| Weekly | 116.00 | 128.00 |

Lunch available
Parking for 10
🏠7🖥🛆🕇Ⓢ🎿📺◨◨◨🔍🔍∪✕🛵

## BRADFORD

### West Yorkshire
### Map ref 4B1

City founded on wool, with fine
Victorian and modern buildings.
Attractions include the cathedral,
city hall, Cartwright Hall, Lister
Park, Moorside Mills Industrial
Museum and National Museum of
Photography, Film and Television.
*Tourist Information Centre*
☎ *(01274) 753678*

### University of Bradford ⋀

Bradford BD7 1DP

Contact: Ms A Milton & Ms E
Fazakerley, Conference Officer,
University of Bradford, Bradford, West
Yorkshire BD7 1DP
☎ (01274) 384889 & 733466
Fax (01274) 385505
Telex 51309
*Attractive, compact campus in a
convenient location for touring the
peaks, dales and Bronte country. Sports
facilities including swimming pool,
sauna and solarium.*
Minimum age 13
Bedrooms: 1300 single. Total number
of beds: 1300
Bathrooms: 90 private, 200 public
**Bed only**

| per person: | £min | £max |
|---|---|---|
| Daily | 12.30 | 28.80 |

**Bed & breakfast**

| per person: | £min | £max |
|---|---|---|
| Daily | 15.90 | 33.00 |

Lunch available
Evening meal from 1800
Parking for 150
Open January, March–April, July–
September, December
🏠13🛆🕇Ⓢ🎿📺◨◨◨🔍✕🔍🔍🕇

## BRIGHTON & HOVE

### East Sussex
### Map ref 2D3

Brighton's attractions include the
Royal Pavilion, Volks Railway, Sea
Life Centre and Marina,
Conference Centre and "The
Lanes" and several theatres.
Neighbouring Hove is a resort in
its own right.
*Tourist Information Centre*
☎ *(01273) 323755; for Hove
(01273) 746100 or 778087*

### University of Brighton ⋀

Circus Street, Brighton BN2 2QF
Contact: Mrs Evelyn Mohan, University
of Brighton, Conference Office, Circus
Street, Brighton, East Sussex
BN2 2DF
☎ (01273) 643167 & 643178
Fax (01273) 643149
*The university has a variety of
residential accommodation in Brighton
and Eastbourne available to groups and
conference organisers in April, July,
August and September.*
Bedrooms: 694 single.
Bathrooms: 9 private, 137 public
**Bed & breakfast**

| per person: | £min | £max |
|---|---|---|
| Daily | 15.00 | 19.00 |

Lunch available
Evening meal 1800 (last orders 1900)
Parking for 230
Open April, July–September
🏠14🎿🛆🕇Ⓢ◨◨◨🔍🎿✕🔍🔍✕

## BROMPTON-BY-SAWDON

### North Yorkshire
### Map ref 5D3

William Wordsworth, the renowned
Lakeland poet, was married in the
parish church in 1802 to Mary
Hutchinson of Gallows Hill.

### Wydale Hall ⋀

York Diocesan Centre, Brompton-by-
Sawdon, Scarborough YO13 9DG
☎ Scarborough (01723) 859270 &
859777
Contact: The Warden
*Beside the North York Moors National
Park, 9 miles from the coast. This
conference/holiday centre is ideal for
any holiday group.*
Bedrooms: 10 single, 19 double/twin,
5 triple, 2 dormitories. Total number
of beds: 66
Bathrooms: 16 public
**Bed & breakfast**

| per person: | £min | £max |
|---|---|---|
| Daily | 18.50 | 24.50 |

Lunch available
Evening meal from 1900
Parking for 50
🏠🛆🕇Ⓢ✕🎿📺◨◨◨🔍∪✕🔍SP🏮

## CAMBRIDGE

### Cambridgeshire
### Map ref 2D1

A most important and beautiful city
on the River Cam with 31 colleges
forming one of the oldest
universities in the world. Numerous
museums, good shopping centre,
restaurants, theatres, cinema and
fine bookshops.
*Tourist Information Centre*
☎ *(01223) 322640*

### Cambridge Y.M.C.A.

Queen Anne House, Gonville Place,
Cambridge CB1 1ND
☎ (01223) 356998
Fax (01223) 312749
Contact: Mrs P Bishop
*A young people's residency, in the
centre of Cambridge overlooking
Parkers Piece. Near railway and bus
stations. Very busy - not suitable for
guests expecting peace and quiet.*
Bedrooms: 95 single, 31 double/twin.
Total number of beds: 157
Bathrooms: 24 public
**Bed & breakfast**

| per person: | £min | £max |
|---|---|---|
| Daily | 16.20 | 20.00 |

**Full board**

| per person: | £min | £max |
|---|---|---|
| Weekly | 144.00 | 159.00 |

Lunch available
Evening meal 1715 (last orders 1845)
🏠🎿🛆🕇Ⓢ✕🎿📺◨◨◨🔍✕🕇✕

**Youth Hostel Association ⛰**
97 Tenison Road, Cambridge
CB1 2DN
☎ (01223) 354601
Fax (01223) 312780
Contact: Miss Carol Hancock
*Youth hostel offering a high standard of comfort and facilities, including relaxing lounges, small rooms, an excellent cafeteria and courtyard garden.*
Bedrooms: 23 dormitories. Total number of beds: 128
Bathrooms: 8 public

| **Bed & breakfast per person:** | £min | £max |
|---|---|---|
| Daily | 9.05 | 12.20 |

Evening meal 1800 (last orders 2000)
Cards accepted: Access, Visa, Switch/Delta
🐴 🛏 🔒 [S] 🚭 [TV] ♨ 🧺 🚫 🌿 [SP]

## CIRENCESTER

Gloucestershire
Map ref 2B1

"Capital of the Cotswolds", Cirencester was Britain's second most important Roman town with many finds housed in the Corinium Museum. It has a very fine Perpendicular church and old houses around the market place.
*Tourist Information Centre*
*☎ (01285) 654180*

**Royal Agricultural College ⛰**
Cirencester GL7 6JS
☎ (01285) 652531
Fax (01285) 640644
Contact: Ms T North
*Conference or touring centre in the heart of the Cotswolds offering a very personalised service to all guests.*
Bedrooms: 50 single, 170 double/twin, 20 dormitories. Total number of beds: 430
Bathrooms: 44 private, 53 public

| **Bed & breakfast per person:** | £min | £max |
|---|---|---|
| Daily | 20.00 | |

Lunch available
Evening meal 1800 (last orders 2000)
Parking for 700
Open January, March-April, July-September, December
🐴2 🛏 🫖 🔒 [S] 🪑 [TV] ♨ 🧺 🏋 🏓 ⛳ 🎾 🚫
[OAP] [SP] 🏠 [T]

Individual proprietors have supplied all details of accommodation.
Although we do check for accuracy, we advise you to confirm the information at the time of booking.

## CONSETT

Durham
Map ref 5B2

Former steel town on the edge of rolling moors. Modern development includes the shopping centre and a handsome Roman Catholic church, designed by a local architect. To the west, the Derwent Reservoir provides water sports and pleasant walks.

**Consett Y.M.C.A. ⛰**
Parliament Street, Consett, County Durham DH8 5DH
☎ (01207) 502680 & 501852
Fax (01207) 501578
Contact: Mr A Forsyth

*Leisure holiday facility providing easy access to the Lake District, Weardale, Scotland and Northumbria. Full programme of outdoor activities. Courses for Y.T.S., T.V.E.I., school, college, youth groups, etc, designed. Individuals welcome.*
Minimum age 9
Bedrooms: 2 double/twin, 8 dormitories. Total number of beds: 65
Bathrooms: 5 private, 3 public

| **Bed only per person:** | £min | £max |
|---|---|---|
| Daily | 9.50 | 9.50 |

| **Bed & breakfast per person:** | £min | £max |
|---|---|---|
| Daily | 12.50 | 12.50 |

| **Full board per person:** | £min | £max |
|---|---|---|
| Weekly | 114.00 | 114.00 |

Lunch available
🐴 🔒 [S] 🪑 [TV] ♨ 🧺 🏋 🏓 ⛳ 🐎 🚫 [SP] 🏠

## DARLINGTON

Durham
Map ref 5C3

Industrial town on the River Skerne, home of the earliest passenger railway which first ran to Stockton in 1825. Now the home of a railway museum. Originally a prosperous market town occupying the site of an Anglo-Saxon settlement, it still holds an open market.
*Tourist Information Centre*
*☎ (01325) 382698*

**The Arts Centre**
Vane Terrace, Darlington, County Durham DL3 7AX
☎ (01325) 483271
*Hostel style accommodation housed in one of the country's largest art centres. Offers a wide range of activities.*
Bedrooms: 11 single, 11 double/twin.
Total number of beds: 33
Bathrooms: 6 public

| **Bed only per person:** | £min | £max |
|---|---|---|
| Daily | 6.50 | 9.50 |

| **Bed & breakfast per person:** | £min | £max |
|---|---|---|
| Daily | 9.00 | 13.00 |

Lunch available
Evening meal 1700 (last orders 2000)
Parking for 20
Cards accepted: Access, Visa
🐴 🔒 [S] ♨ 🧺 🚫 🏠

## DURHAM

Durham
Map ref 5C2

Ancient city with its Norman castle and cathedral set on a bluff high over the Wear. A market and university town and regional centre, spreading beyond the market-place on both banks of the river.
*Tourist Information Centre*
*☎ (0191) 384 3720*

**College of St Hild and St Bede ⛰**
University of Durham, Leazes Road, Durham, County Durham DH1 1SZ
☎ (0191) 374 3069
Contact: Mr P A Warburton
*College set in spacious grounds in the medieval City of Durham, providing a splendid base for exploring Northumbria.*
Minimum age 10
Bedrooms: 364 single, 45 double/twin, 1 triple. Total number of beds: 457
Bathrooms: 53 public

| **Bed & breakfast per person:** | £min | £max |
|---|---|---|
| Daily | 12.50 | 15.50 |

| **Full board per person:** | £min | £max |
|---|---|---|
| Weekly | 170.80 | 191.80 |

Lunch available
Evening meal 1800 (last orders 1900)
Parking for 200
Open March-April, July-September
🐴 🛏 🔒 [S] 🪑 [TV] ♨ 🧺 🏓 ⛳ 🎾 🚫 🚌

**Collingwood College ⛰**
South Road, Durham, County Durham DH1 3LT
☎ (0191) 374 4565
Fax (0191) 374 4595
Contact: Mrs Sylvia Hall
*Durham's newest residential college, set in woodland 1 mile south of the city.*
Bedrooms: 485 single, 28 double/twin.
Total number of beds: 301
Bathrooms: 215 private, 56 public

*Continued* ►

## DURHAM

*Continued*

**Bed only**

| per person: | £min | £max |
|---|---|---|
| Daily | 15.00 | 25.00 |

**Bed & breakfast**

| per person: | £min | £max |
|---|---|---|
| Daily | 20.00 | 30.00 |

**Full board**

| per person: | £min | £max |
|---|---|---|
| Weekly | 90.00 | 130.00 |

Lunch available
Evening meal 1800 (last orders 1900)
Parking for 120
Open January, March-April, July-September, December

ﾐﾑ⍓⌂🅢⌖🄽📺🖳⚓☎🔍🔎◡⋔🆂🅿

### Grey College ⋀

University of Durham, South Road,
Durham, County Durham DH1 3LG
☎ (0191) 374 2900
Contact: Mrs V Hamilton
*An attractive venue, just 15 minutes'
walk from the city centre. Reasonable
single and double room rates, lounge,
TV room, bar and sports facilities.*
Bedrooms: 275 single, 12 double/twin,
1 dormitory. Total number of beds:
300
Bathrooms: 28 public

**Bed only**

| per person: | £min | £max |
|---|---|---|
| Daily | 10.00 | |

**Bed & breakfast**

| per person: | £min | £max |
|---|---|---|
| Daily | 16.45 | 16.45 |

Lunch available
Evening meal from 1900
Parking for 60
Open March-April, June-October

ﾐ⍓⌂🅢🄽📺🖳⚓☎🔍⋔🆂

### St. Aidans College ⋀

University of Durham, Windmill Hill,
Durham, County Durham DH1 3LJ
☎ (0191) 374 3269
Contact: Lt. Cdr. J C Bull
*Modern college in beautiful landscaped
gardens overlooking the cathedral.
Comfortable standard and en-suite
single and twin-bedded rooms, bar, TV
lounge, free tennis. Adjacent golf-course.*
Bedrooms: 293 single, 66 double/twin.
Total number of beds: 425
Bathrooms: 94 private, 48 public

**Bed only**

| per person: | £min | £max |
|---|---|---|
| Daily | 10.00 | 15.00 |

**Bed & breakfast**

| per person: | £min | £max |
|---|---|---|
| Daily | 15.00 | 21.50 |

**Full board**

| per person: | £min | £max |
|---|---|---|
| Weekly | 176.00 | 210.00 |

Lunch available
Evening meal 1830 (last orders 1900)
Parking for 80

---

Open March-April, July-September,
December

ﾐﾑ⌂🅢🄽📺🖳⚓☆🔍🔎◡⋔🆂🅿🏨

### Saint Chad's College
### University of Durham ⋀

18 North Bailey, Durham, County
Durham DH1 3RH
☎ (0191) 374 3370 & 374 3364
Fax 374 3360
Contact: Mr I Blacklock
*Historic college welcomes conferences,
groups or individuals at its quiet central
location beside the cathedral,
overlooking gardens and river.*
Bedrooms: 79 single, 54 double/twin,
5 triple. Total number of beds: 202
Bathrooms: 16 private, 38 public

**Bed only**

| per person: | £min | £max |
|---|---|---|
| Daily | 8.50 | 16.50 |

**Bed & breakfast**

| per person: | £min | £max |
|---|---|---|
| Daily | 11.50 | 19.50 |

**Full board**

| per person: | £min | £max |
|---|---|---|
| Weekly | 125.00 | 170.00 |

Lunch available
Evening meal 1800 (last orders 1930)
Parking for 15
Open January, March-April, June-September, December

ﾐﾑ⍓⌂🅢⌖🄽📺🖳⚓🔍🔎🅾🆂🏨

### St. Cuthberts Society

12 South Bailey, Durham, County
Durham DH1 3EE
☎ (0191) 374 3464
Contact: Mrs H Bowler
*Situated in the heart of the old town
and 5 minutes' walk from the cathedral
and city centre. Riverside gardens.*
Bedrooms: 50 single, 23 double/twin,
3 triple. Total number of beds: 114
Bathrooms: 21 public

**Bed & breakfast**

| per person: | £min | £max |
|---|---|---|
| Daily | 15.50 | 15.50 |

**Full board**

| per person: | £min | £max |
|---|---|---|
| Weekly | 171.50 | 171.50 |

Open July-September

ﾐ⍓⌂🆄🅢⌖🄽📺🖳⚓☆⋔🅾

### St John's College ⋀

University of Durham, 3 South Bailey,
Durham, County Durham DH1 3RJ
☎ (0191) 374 3566
Contact: Mr Martin Clemmett
*In the heart of the city, alongside
Durham Cathedral and Castle, offering
good quality student accommodation to
individuals, families and groups.*
Bedrooms: 100 single, 13 double/twin,
1 triple. Total number of beds: 129
Bathrooms: 25 public

**Bed only**

| per person: | £min | £max |
|---|---|---|
| Daily | 13.00 | 13.00 |

---

**Bed & breakfast**

| per person: | £min | £max |
|---|---|---|
| Daily | 15.50 | 15.50 |

**Full board**

| per person: | £min | £max |
|---|---|---|
| Weekly | 199.50 | 199.50 |

Evening meal 1800 (last orders 1930)
Open March-April, July-September,
December

ﾐ⌂🅢🄽📺🖳⚓🔍🅾🏨

### Van Mildert College ⋀

University of Durham, Durham,
County Durham DH1 3LH
☎ (0191) 374 3963
Fax (0191) 384 7764
Contact: Mr Sawyer
*College buildings grouped around a
small lake, in pleasant surroundings, 1
mile from the historic cathedral and
city centre.*
Bedrooms: 390 single, 48 double/twin.
Total number of beds: 438
Bathrooms: 48 private, 68 public

**Bed & breakfast**

| per person: | £min | £max |
|---|---|---|
| Daily | 16.50 | 26.50 |

**Full board**

| per person: | £min | £max |
|---|---|---|
| Weekly | 186.00 | 246.00 |

Lunch available
Evening meal from 1800
Parking for 100

ﾐ⌂🅢🄽📺🖳⚓◡🅣

## GUILDFORD

Surrey
Map ref 2D2

Bustling town with many historic
monuments, one of which is the
Guildhall clock jutting out over the
old High Street. The modern
cathedral occupies a commanding
position on Stag Hill.
*Tourist Information Centre*
☎ *(01483) 444007*

### University of Surrey ⋀

Guildford GU2 5XH
☎ (01483) 259352
Fax (01483) 579266
Contact: Miss J Peberdy
*The university and cathedral occupy
commanding positions on a hill
overlooking this historic town. London
30 miles, coast 40 miles. Self-catering
accommodation also available.*
Minimum age 14
Bedrooms: 6 double/twin. Total
number of beds: 2001
Bathrooms: 360 private, 491 public

**Bed & breakfast**

| per person: | £min | £max |
|---|---|---|
| Daily | 12.86 | 33.95 |

**Full board**

| per person: | £min | £max |
|---|---|---|
| Weekly | 191.23 | 405.08 |

Lunch available
Evening meal 1800 (last orders 1930)
Parking for 1400

Open January, March–April, July–September
Cards accepted: Access, Visa

🛏 14 ♿ ◆ Ⓢ ⎙ ⏏ ▥ ⊟ ✕ ⚘ ☂ ⚓ ✈ ✕ ⑊ ⒹⒶⓅ ⓈⓅ ⌂ ⑂

## HARROGATE

North Yorkshire
Map ref 4B1

A major conference, exhibition and shopping centre, renowned for its spa heritage and award winning floral displays, spacious parks and gardens. Famous for antiques, toffee, fine shopping and excellent tea shops, also its Royal Pump Rooms and Baths.
*Tourist Information Centre*
☎ *(01423) 525666*

### West End Outdoor Centre ⋀

West End, Summerbridge, Harrogate HG3 4BA
Contact: Mrs M Verity, West End Outdoor Centre, Whitmoor Farm, West End, Summerbridge, Harrogate, North Yorkshire HG3 4BA
☎ Blubberhouses (01943) 880207
*Self-catering bunkhouse with panoramic views over Thruscross reservoir. Well-appointed facilities for 30 people. 12 miles from Harrogate and Skipton, 30 miles from York.*
Bedrooms: 4 double/twin, 4 quadruple, 1 dormitory. Total number of beds: 30
Bathrooms: 1 private, 4 public

**Bed only**

| per person: | £min | £max |
|---|---|---|
| Daily | 4.50 | 6.00 |

Lunch available
Parking for 15

🛏 ⚹ ♿ Ⓤ ▤ ♿ ✤ ⏏ ▥ ⚓ ✕

## HATHERSAGE

Derbyshire
Map ref 4B2

Hillside village in the Peak District, dominated by the church with many good brasses and monuments to the Eyre family which provide a link with Charlotte Bronte. Little John, friend of Robin Hood, is said to be buried here.

### Rock Lea Activity Centre ⋀

Station Road, Hathersage, Sheffield S30 1DD
☎ Hope Valley (01433) 650345 & Mobile 0374 112203
Fax (01433) 650342
Contact: Dr Ian Jennings
*Victorian manse in the centre of an unspoilt village, next to a heated swimming pool. Activity holidays and training courses offered all year round.*
Minimum age 16
Bedrooms: 1 double/twin, 1 triple, 2 quadruple, 1 dormitory. Total number of beds: 20
Bathrooms: 3 public

**Bed & breakfast**

| per person: | £min | £max |
|---|---|---|
| Daily | 12.50 | 20.00 |

Lunch available
Evening meal from 1930
Parking for 20
Cards accepted: Access, Visa

⚹ ♿ ⚲ Ⓠ ⚹ ● Ⓢ ✕ ⏏ ▥ ⊟ ⚓ ∪ ⑂ ✕ ⑊ ⚲ ⓈⓅ ⌂ ⑂

## HEBDEN BRIDGE

West Yorkshire
Map ref 4B1

Originally a small town on packhorse route, Hebden Bridge grew into a booming mill town in 18th C with rows of "up-and-down" houses of several storeys built against hillsides. Ancient "pace-egg play" custom held on Good Friday.
*Tourist Information Centre*
☎ *(01422) 843831*

### Hebden Hey Activity Centre ⋀

Hardcastle Crags, Hebden Bridge HX7 7AW
Contact: Mr & Mrs A P Garside, 26 Carlton House Terrace, Haugh Shaw Road, Halifax, West Yorkshire HXL 3LD
☎ Halifax (01422) 347408
*Two purpose-built hostels providing accommodation for up to 28 and 46 persons, in bunk rooms. Price is per person as part of group.*
Bedrooms: 8 dormitories. Total number of beds: 72
Bathrooms: 7 public

**Bed only**

| per person: | £min | £max |
|---|---|---|
| Daily | 1.60 | 2.10 |

Parking for 15

🛏 ⚹ Ⓤ ⏏ ⚲

## HECKFIELD

Hampshire
Map ref 2C2

### Wellington Riding Ltd ⋀

Basingstoke Road, Heckfield, Basingstoke RG27 0LJ
☎ (01734) 326308
Fax (01734) 326661
Contact: Mr John Goodman & Miss Linda Sawyer
*Equestrian centre. Accommodation only for unaccompanied juniors taking riding holiday and for adults on equestrian courses.*
Minimum age 8
Bedrooms: 5 double/twin, 4 dormitories. Total number of beds: 49
Bathrooms: 4 public

**Full board**

| per person: | £min | £max |
|---|---|---|
| Weekly | 246.00 | 425.00 |

Lunch available

Parking for 40
Cards accepted: Access, Visa, Switch/ Delta

🛏 Ⓢ ✕ ⚹ ⏏ ▥ ⊟ ⚓ ∪ ✕ ⚲ ⒹⒶⓅ ⓈⓅ ⑂

## HEPTONSTALL

West Yorkshire
Map ref 4B1

Quaint village above Hebden Bridge with an assortment of narrow streets, weavers' cottages, weather-worn houses and the ruins of a 12th C church. The 17th C grammar school is situated in a churchyard.

### Slack Top Centre ⋀

Mount Zion Baptist Chapel, Heptonstall, Hebden Bridge HX7 7HA
☎ Halifax (01422) 842874
Contact: Mrs E D Hulme
*Chapel converted to form simple sleeping accommodation at gallery level. Ground floor incorporates the chapel, dining area and kitchen.*
Bedrooms: 2 single, 4 dormitories.
Total number of beds: 30
Bathrooms: 4 public

**Bed only**

| per person: | £min | £max |
|---|---|---|
| Daily | 4.25 | 7.25 |

Parking for 12

🛏 ⚹ ♿ Ⓤ ✕ ⚹ ⏏ ▥ ⊟ ⚓ ✕ ⚲ ⒹⒶⓅ ⓈⓅ ⌂

## HORSHAM

West Sussex
Map ref 2D2

Busy town with much modern development but still retaining its old character. The museum in Causeway House is devoted chiefly to local history and the agricultural life of the county.
*Tourist Information Centre*
☎ *(01403) 211661*

### Gaveston Hall Youth & Student Centre ⋀

Nuthurst, Horsham RH13 6RF
☎ (01403) 891 431
Fax (01403) 891439
Contact: Mr C Morris
*In the beautiful Sussex Weald in approximately 100 acres of parks, woodland and streams. School journey and field study centre for youth groups with its own nature trail and many facilities both indoor and outdoor. Coach excursions and special interest courses arranged. 4 miles from Horsham.*
For groups only
Bedrooms: 1 single, 4 double/twin, 7 dormitories. Total number of beds: 90
Bathrooms: 8 public

**Bed & breakfast**

| per person: | £min | £max |
|---|---|---|
| Daily | 11.00 | 12.50 |

*Continued* ▶

## HORSHAM
*Continued*

**Full board**

| per person: | £min | £max |
|---|---|---|
| Weekly | 105.75 | 127.48 |

Lunch available
Parking for 12

🐕🎦ℹ️📺🛏️🚰❄️🔍⚓🚶✈️🏮

## ILKLEY
West Yorkshire
Map ref 4B1

This moorland town is famous for its ballad. The 16th C manor house, now a museum, displays local prehistoric and Roman relics. Popular walk leads up Heber's Ghyll to Ilkley Moor, with the mysterious Swastika Stone and White Wells, 18th C plunge baths.
*Tourist Information Centre*
☎ *(01943) 602319*

### Glenmoor Centre ⚠
Wells Road, Ilkley LS29 9JF
☎ (01943) 816359
Fax (01943) 816359
Contact: Mrs M Cairns
*Attractive accommodation for residential and day conferences in a beautiful setting, just on the edge of Ilkley Moor. Special rates for voluntary organisations and registered charities. Tariffs shown based on minimum 10 delegates.*
For groups only
Bedrooms: 8 single, 12 double/twin.
Total number of beds: 32
Bathrooms: 6 private, 7 public

**Bed only**

| per person: | £min | £max |
|---|---|---|
| Daily | 9.95 | 17.45 |

**Bed & breakfast**

| per person: | £min | £max |
|---|---|---|
| Daily | 12.50 | 20.00 |

Lunch available
Evening meal 1700 (last orders 1900)
Parking for 15

🚰ℹ️§🚪🛏️📺🛏️🚗🅿️🏮

## INGLETON
North Yorkshire
Map ref 5B3

Thriving tourist centre for fell-walkers, climbers and pot-holers. Popular walks up beautiful Twiss Valley to Ingleborough Summit, Whernside, White Scar Caves and waterfalls.

### The Barnstead
Stackstead Farm, Ingleton, Carnforth, Lancashire LA6 3HS
☎ (01524) 241386
Contact: Mr & Mrs J Charlton
*Well-equipped, bunk-style, self-catering accommodation for groups of 2-22 with 4 bedrooms, a communal kitchen and a*

*lounge/dining area. Panoramic views of surrounding limestone countryside. Separate one-bedroomed fully equipped accommodation to sleep 6 also available.*
Bedrooms: 5 dormitories. Total number of beds: 28
Bathrooms: 5 public
**Bed only**

| per person: | £min | £max |
|---|---|---|
| Daily | 7.00 | 7.00 |

Parking for 10

🐕🚰🎦✂️🛏️🛏️🚗🕉️✈️🏮

## LANCASTER
Lancashire
Map ref 4A1

Interesting old county town on the River Lune with history dating back to Roman times. Norman castle, St Mary's Church, Customs House, City and Maritime Museums, Ashton Memorial and Butterfly House are among places of note. Good centre for touring the Lake District.
*Tourist Information Centre*
☎ *(01524) 32878*

### Saint Martins College
Bowerham Road, Lancaster LA1 3JD
☎ (01524) 63446
Fax (01524) 68943
Contact: Mrs Elaine Voyle
*Ideal for individual, group or family holidays, offering a high standard of bed and breakfast accommodation.*
Bedrooms: 399 single, 19 double/twin.
Total number of beds: 437
Bathrooms: 1 private, 101 public

**Bed & breakfast**

| per person: | £min | £max |
|---|---|---|
| Daily | 17.21 | |

**Full board**

| per person: | £min | £max |
|---|---|---|
| Weekly | 120.49 | |

Lunch available
Evening meal 1745 (last orders 1830)
Parking for 200
Open March-April, July-September

🐕🚰🚰ℹ️§🛏️📺🛏️🚗🍴🏹⚓🕉️✈️

> We advise you to confirm your booking in writing.

> Individual proprietors have supplied all details of accommodation. Although we do check for accuracy, we advise you to confirm the information at the time of booking.

## LEICESTER
Leicestershire
Map ref 4C3

Modern industrial city with a wide variety of attractions including Roman remains, ancient churches, Georgian houses and a Victorian clock tower. Excellent shopping precincts, arcades and market, museums, theatres, concert hall and sports and leisure centres.
*Tourist Information Centre*
☎ *(0116)265 0555 or 251 1301*

### Richards Backpackers Hostel
157 Wanlip Lane, Birstall, Leicester LE4 4GL
☎ (0116) 267 3107
Contact: Mr Richard Allen
*A small, cosy, independent hostel catering for backpackers, cyclists and other young tourists. Tent space and camping chalet available. On a bus route. Home-made bread.*
Bedrooms: 1 double/twin, 1 triple, 1 dormitory. Total number of beds: 10
Bathrooms: 1 public

**Bed only**

| per person: | £min | £max |
|---|---|---|
| Daily | | 8.00 |

**Bed & breakfast**

| per person: | £min | £max |
|---|---|---|
| Daily | | 11.00 |

Evening meal 1800 (last orders 2000)

🐕6🐾🚪🛏️ℹ️§✂️🛏️🛏️🚗✈️🏮

## LIVERPOOL
Merseyside
Map ref 4A2

Exciting city, famous for the Beatles, football, the Grand National, theatres and nightlife. Liverpool has a magnificent waterfront, 2 cathedrals, 3 historic houses, museum, galleries and a host of attractions.
*Tourist Information Centre*
☎ *(0151) 709 3631*

### Embassie Youth Hostel ⚠
1 Faulkner Square, Toxteth, Liverpool L8 7NU
☎ (0151) 707 1089
Contact: Mr Kevin Murphy
*Large Georgian hostel 10 minutes' walk from Liverpool's Anglican Cathedral. Cheap, clean and friendly.*
Minimum age 10
Bedrooms: 1 double/twin, 3 dormitories. Total number of beds: 32
Bathrooms: 4 public

**Bed & breakfast**

| per person: | £min | £max |
|---|---|---|
| Daily | | 8.50 |

Parking for 10

🐕❄️🚪✂️📺🛏️🚗⚓✈️🏮🅃

## LONDON

### Greater London

### Anne Elizabeth House Hostel ♠
30 Collingham Place, London
SW5 0QE
☎ (0171) 370 4821
Contact: Mrs. M Lopes
*Convenient for Earl's Court and within easy reach of the West End. Special long-term and student rates.*
Bedrooms: 4 single, 5 double/twin, 8 triple, 4 quadruple, 2 dormitories.
Total number of beds: 64
Bathrooms: 7 public

**Bed & breakfast**

| per person: | £min | £max |
|---|---|---|
| Daily | 7.50 | 21.00 |

🛏 18 ⓤⓛ ♠ ⓣⓥ 📷, 🖪 ✕ 🏌 SP

### Baden Powell House Hostel ♠
Queen's Gate, South Kensington,
London SW7 5JS
☎ (0171) 584 7031
Fax (0171) 581 9953
Contact: Miss A Watson
*International scout hostel with accommodation ranging from single to group. Limited to scout and guide association members, students and other youth organisations.*
Bedrooms: 9 single, 15 double/twin, 4 triple, 4 quadruple, 6 dormitories.
Total number of beds: 112
Bathrooms: 3 private, 23 public

**Bed & breakfast**

| per person: | £min | £max |
|---|---|---|
| Daily | 13.65 | 29.60 |

**Full board**

| per person: | £min | £max |
|---|---|---|
| Weekly | 95.55 | 207.20 |

Lunch available
Evening meal 1800 (last orders 1915)
Parking for 14
Cards accepted: Access, Visa, Switch/Delta

🛏 🛉 S ✕ ♠ ⓣⓥ 📷, 🖪 ✕ 🏠

### Boka Hotel ♠
33-35 Eardley Crescent, Earls Court,
London SW5 9JT
☎ (0171) 370 1388
Contact: Mr. R Gojkovic

*Budget accommodation with a young, friendly atmosphere, for tourists and students. A minute from Earl's Court underground station.*
Bedrooms: 11 single, 30 double/twin, 2 triple, 1 quadruple, 6 dormitories.
Total number of beds: 101
Bathrooms: 10 private, 10 public

**Bed & breakfast**

| per person: | £min | £max |
|---|---|---|
| Daily | 9.00 | 18.00 |

Cards accepted: Access, Visa, Diners, Amex

🛏 🛉 🎮 ⓤⓛ ✕ ♠ ⓣⓥ 📷, 🖪 🍴 SP T

### Brunel University Conference Centre ♠
Conference Office, Brunel University,
Uxbridge, Middlesex UB8 3PH
☎ Uxbridge (01895) 274 000
Fax (01895) 203 142
Telex 261173 G
Contact: Mr Carl Woodall
*En-suite or standard bedrooms, cafeteria or silver service meals, purpose-built theatres and classrooms, audio and visual aids and sports facilities all available.*
Minimum age 12
Bedrooms: 860 single. Total number of beds: 860
Bathrooms: 450 private, 85 public

**Bed only**

| per person: | £min | £max |
|---|---|---|
| Daily | 11.90 | 26.90 |

**Bed & breakfast**

| per person: | £min | £max |
|---|---|---|
| Daily | 16.50 | 31.50 |

**Full board**

| per person: | £min | £max |
|---|---|---|
| Weekly | 210.50 | 290.00 |

Lunch available
Evening meal 1800 (last orders 2000)
Parking for 2000
Open April-September
Cards accepted: Access, Visa

🛏 12 🛉 🎮 S ✕ ♠ ⓣⓥ 📷, 🖪 ✕ 🍴 🏠 ☎ ∪ ↑ ✕ 📷 DAP SP

### Campbell House
Taviton Street, London WC1H 0BX
☎ (0171) 380 7079
Fax (0171) 388 0060
Contact: Mr. R L Sparvell

*Specially reconstructed Georgian housing providing self-catering accommodation in a peaceful, central London location.*
Minimum age 10
Bedrooms: 60 single, 40 double/twin.
Total number of beds: 140
Bathrooms: 25 public

**Bed only**

| per person: | £min | £max |
|---|---|---|
| Daily | 13.50 | 16.00 |

Open June-September

🛏 🛇 🛉 ⓤⓛ ✕ ♠ ⓣⓥ 📷, 🖪 ✕ ✈

### Central University of Iowa Hostel
7 Bedford Place, London WC1B 5JA
☎ (0171) 580 1121
Contact: Mr Roy Oliver
*Old Georgian house near the British Museum. Closest underground stations are Russell Square and Holborn.*
Bedrooms: 1 single, 6 double/twin, 5 dormitories. Total number of beds: 30
Bathrooms: 7 public

**Bed & breakfast**

| per person: | £min | £max |
|---|---|---|
| Daily | 18.00 | 20.00 |

Open May-August

🛏 ♠ ⓣⓥ 📷, 🖪 ✕ 🏠

### Driscoll House Hotel
172 New Kent Road, London SE1 4YT
☎ (0171) 703 4175
Fax (0171) 703 8013
Contact: Mr. T Driscoll

*Long or short term accommodation offered to teachers, students and tourists. Weekly full-board price below excludes weekday lunch.*
Bedrooms: 200 single, 6 double/twin.
Total number of beds: 200
Bathrooms: 14 public

Continued ►

## LONDON

*Continued*

**Bed only**

| per person: | £min | £max |
|---|---|---|
| Daily | 27.00 | 27.00 |

**Bed & breakfast**

| per person: | £min | £max |
|---|---|---|
| Daily | 25.00 | 25.00 |

**Full board**

| per person: | £min | £max |
|---|---|---|
| Weekly | 150.00 | 150.00 |

Lunch available
Evening meal 1730 (last orders 1900)
Parking for 10
⛶ 3 ⌕ 📞 ⓘ 🅂 ⌁ ♿ 📺 🛏 ■ ● ✕ 🐾 🕵 Ⓣ

### Ealing YMCA
25 St Marys Road, Ealing, London
W5 5RE
☎ (0181) 579 6946
Fax (0181) 579 1129
Contact: Judith Birch
*A new residential centre, each room with colour TV. Le Jardin restaurant on premises. Weekly prices shown below are for half board only.*
Bedrooms: 129 single, 13 double/twin, 13 triple. Total number of beds: 157
Bathrooms: 13 private, 28 public

**Bed & breakfast**

| per person: | £min | £max |
|---|---|---|
| Daily | 20.00 | 24.00 |

**Full board**

| per person: | £min | £max |
|---|---|---|
| Weekly | 80.00 | 115.00 |

Lunch available
Evening meal 1745 (last orders 1855)
Parking for 26
Cards accepted: Access, Visa
⛶ 12 ⌕ 📞 ⌨ ⓘ 🅂 ⌁ ♿ 🛏 ■ ● ✕
● ✕

### Ingram Court M
King's College London, Chelsea Campus, 552 Kings Road, London
SW10 0AU
Contact: King's Campus Vacation Bureau, King's College London, 552 Kings Road, London SW10 0UA
☎ (0171) 351 6011
Fax (0171) 352 7376
*Student bedrooms in small residences grouped around a quiet courtyard, on a spacious green campus. Other halls of residence available in Westminster, Wandsworth, Champion Hill and the Sloane Square end of the King's Road.*
Bedrooms: 107 single, 7 double/twin. Total number of beds: 121
Bathrooms: 30 public

**Bed only**

| per person: | £min | £max |
|---|---|---|
| Daily | 11.25 | 13.25 |

**Bed & breakfast**

| per person: | £min | £max |
|---|---|---|
| Daily | 16.50 | 21.50 |

Lunch available
Evening meal 1800 (last orders 1900)
Parking for 20

Open January, March-April, June-September, December
Cards accepted: Access, Visa, Switch/Delta
⛶ ⌕ ⌨ ⓘ 🅂 ⌁ ♿ 📺 🛏 ■ ● ✕ 🐾 Ⓣ

### International House Woolwich M
109 Brookhill Road, London
SE18 6RZ
☎ (0181) 854 1418
Fax (0181) 855 9257
Contact: Mr B Siderman
*Purpose-built student hostel. Self-contained flats for married couples and children. Full en-suite facilities also available. Short-term visitor accommodation available July-September.*
Bedrooms: 85 single, 21 double/twin.
Total number of beds: 127
Bathrooms: 21 private, 18 public

**Bed & breakfast**

| per person: | £min | £max |
|---|---|---|
| Daily | 8.80 | 12.80 |

Parking for 21
Open April, July-September, December
⛶ ⌨ ⓘ 🅂 ⌁ ♿ 📺 🛏 ■ ● ✕ Ⓣ

### International Students House M
229 Great Portland Street, London
W1N 5HD
☎ (0171) 631 3223
Fax (0171) 636 5565
Contact: Ms Martina Downes
*Comfortable accommodation centrally located in West End. Allows easy access to all London's tourist attractions. Close to underground and other public transport.*
Minimum age 17
Bedrooms: 159 single, 107 double/twin, 3 triple, 5 quadruple. Total number of beds: 409
Bathrooms: 4 private, 95 public

**Bed & breakfast**

| per person: | £min | £max |
|---|---|---|
| Daily | 9.99 | 23.40 |

Lunch available
Evening meal 1800 (last orders 1930)
Parking for 10
Cards accepted: Access, Visa, Switch/Delta
⛶ ⓘ 🅂 ♿ 📺 🛏 ■ ● ✕ 🪑 ● ✕ 🐾 🕵 SP 🏍 Ⓣ

### John Adams Hall (Institute of Education) M
15-23 Endsleigh Street, London
WC1H 0DH
☎ (0171) 387 4086
Fax (0171) 383 0164
Telex 94016519 DICE G
Contact: Mr M Lam-Hing
*An assembly of Georgian houses, the hall retaining its old glory. Close to Euston, King's Cross and St Pancras stations.*
Bedrooms: 127 single, 22 double/twin.
Total number of beds: 171
Bathrooms: 1 private, 26 public

**Bed & breakfast**

| per person: | £min | £max |
|---|---|---|
| Daily | 15.00 | 21.40 |

Evening meal 1730 (last orders 1830)
Open January, March-April, July-September, December
Cards accepted: Access, Visa
⛶ ⌕ ⌨ ⓦ ⓘ 🅂 ⌁ ♿ 📺 🛏 ■ ● ✕ 🐾 Ⓣ

### Kent House M
325 Green Lanes, London N4 2ES
☎ (0181) 802 0800 & 802 9009
Fax (0181) 802 9070
*Special off-season and weekly rates for young tourists. Facilities for self-catering. Adjacent to Manor House underground station and 10 minutes from central London.*
Minimum age 16
Bedrooms: 3 single, 13 double/twin, 3 dormitories. Total number of beds: 34
Bathrooms: 6 public

**Bed only**

| per person: | £min | £max |
|---|---|---|
| Daily | 11.00 | 22.00 |

**Bed & breakfast**

| per person: | £min | £max |
|---|---|---|
| Daily | 13.50 | 25.00 |

Parking for 4
⛶ ⌕ ⓦ ♿ 📺 🛏 ■ ● ✕ 🚲 🐾 SP Ⓣ

### Lancaster Hall Hotel (Youth Annexe)
35 Craven Terrace, Lancaster Gate, London W2 3EL
☎ (0171) 723 9276
Fax (0171) 706 2870
Contact: Mr U Maynard
*Within easy walking distance of Hyde Park, Kensington Gardens and Marble Arch. Close to public transport.*
Bedrooms: 3 single, 7 double/twin, 4 triple, 3 quadruple. Total number of beds: 41
Bathrooms: 5 public

**Bed & breakfast**

| per person: | £min | £max |
|---|---|---|
| Daily | 13.50 | 18.00 |

Evening meal 1800 (last orders 2100)
Parking for 13
Cards accepted: Access, Visa, Switch/Delta
⛶ ⌕ ⓘ 🅂 ♿ 📺 🛏 ■ ● ✕ 🏍 Ⓣ

### Lee Abbey International Students Club
57-67 Lexham Gardens, London
W8 6JJ
☎ (0171) 373 7242
Fax (0171) 244 8702
Contact: Miss. J Facey
*A hostel primarily for international students, run by a Christian Community. Short term, non-student visitors welcome in holiday season. Lift serving all floors. Full board weekends; half board weekdays.*
Minimum age 18
Bedrooms: 60 single, 28 double/twin, 10 triple. Total number of beds: 146
Bathrooms: 19 private, 28 public

**Bed & breakfast**

| per person: | £min | £max |
| --- | --- | --- |
| Daily | 14.50 | 22.20 |

Lunch available
Evening meal 1800 (last orders 1900)
Parking for 1

🛏📞🅿🛎Ⓢ🔌🍴📺▦🚭🅰🔍❄SP

## London House Hotel ⚘
81 Kensington Gardens Square,
London W2 4DJ
Contact: Miss Jackie Boughton,
16 Leinster Square, London W2 4DJ
☎ (0171) 727 0696
Fax (0171) 229 3917
Telex 24923 VIEHTL G
*Friendly, comfortable budget hotel,
convenient for shops, theatres and
sightseeing.*
Bedrooms: 4 single, 32 double/twin,
6 triple, 14 quadruple, 11 dormitories.
Total number of beds: 201
Bathrooms: 7 public

**Bed & breakfast**

| per person: | £min | £max |
| --- | --- | --- |
| Daily | 22.00 | |

Cards accepted: Access, Visa, Diners,
Amex

🛏🍴📺▦🚭🅰✗Ⓣ

## Lords Hotel ⚘
20-22 Leinster Square, London
W2 4PR
☎ (0171) 229 8877
Fax (0171) 229 8377
Telex 298716 LORDS G
Contact: Mr. N G Ladas
*Bed and breakfast accommodation in
central London. Residents' bar, direct-
dial telephone, radio. Most rooms with
private facilities.*
Bedrooms: 9 single, 30 double/twin,
12 triple, 14 quadruple. Total number
of beds: 161
Bathrooms: 40 private, 12 public

**Bed & breakfast**

| per person: | £min | £max |
| --- | --- | --- |
| Daily | 16.25 | 40.00 |

Cards accepted: Access, Visa, Diners,
Amex, Switch/Delta

🛏🍴📞🖥🛎📺▦🔍❄SP
♨Ⓣ

## 1 Lynton Road
Kilburn, London NW6 6BD
Contact: Mr K Kuedem, Booking
Office, 1 Lynton Road, Kilburn,
London NW6 6BD
☎ (0171) 328 5249
*Bookings for short/long term
accommodation with very competitive
rates. Suitable for all persons, all the
year round.*
Minimum age 12
Bedrooms: 3 double/twin, 3 triple,
3 quadruple, 3 dormitories. Total
number of beds: 30
Bathrooms: 2 public

**Bed only**

| per person: | £min | £max |
| --- | --- | --- |
| Daily | 7.00 | 14.00 |

Cards accepted: Access, Visa

🛏🚭🔌🍴📺▦🅰❄SPⓉ

## Middlesex University
Wood Green Hall, Station Road,
London N22 6UZ
☎ (0181) 888 4866
Fax (0181) 365 8489
Contact: Ms Celine McCarney
*Modern, self-contained, off campus
building, very close to the underground
(Piccadilly line) and large shopping
centre. Family bookings (children over
10) welcome.*
Minimum age 10
Bedrooms: 150 single. Total number of
beds: 150
Bathrooms: 16 public

**Bed only**

| per person: | £min | £max |
| --- | --- | --- |
| Daily | 9.50 | |

Parking for 8
Open July-September

🛏10👫🚭🔌📺▦🅰✗🐾
🅰 Display advertisement appears on
page 391

## Newham Youth Trust
Newham Youth Lodge, 315 Roman
Rd., East Ham, London E6 3SQ
Contact: Mr G P Owen, c/o Ravenhill
Centre, Ravenhill Road, London
E13 9BU
☎ Administrative secretary (0181) 472
4435
Fax (0181) 470 7302
*Short stay hostel dormitory
accommodation for groups of 12 people
or more only (no individuals please).
Bookings especially welcome from
affiliated members of the Trust,
registered Youth Clubs and
organisations.*
For groups only
Minimum age 10
Bedrooms: 2 double/twin,
4 dormitories. Total number of beds:
26
Bathrooms: 3 public

**Bed only**

| per person: | £min | £max |
| --- | --- | --- |
| Daily | 4.50 | |

Parking for 2

🛏11🔌▦✗🐾

## O'Callaghan's
205 Earls Court Road, London
SW5 9AN
Contact: Mr P J O'Connor,
O'Callaghan's, 205 Earls Court Road,
London SW5 9AN
☎ (0171) 370 3000 & (0181) 540
5958
*Central London low-budget guesthouse
for tourists and students. Open all year
round.*
Bedrooms: 4 double/twin, 3 triple,
3 quadruple. Total number of beds: 26
Bathrooms: 3 public

**Bed & breakfast**

| per person: | £min | £max |
| --- | --- | --- |
| Daily | 8.00 | 12.00 |

🛏5🔌👫🔌🚭📺▦🅰✗🐾SP

## Passfield Hall ⚘
1 Endsleigh Place, London
WC1H 0PW
☎ (0171) 387 7743 & 387 3584
Fax (0171) 387 0419
*University hall of residence with
washbasin in all rooms, suitable for
families. Central for Oxford Street and
the West End.*
Bedrooms: 100 single, 34 double/twin,
10 triple. Total number of beds: 198
Bathrooms: 36 public

**Bed & breakfast**

| per person: | £min | £max |
| --- | --- | --- |
| Daily | 17.50 | 22.00 |

Open March-April, July-September
Cards accepted: Access, Visa, Switch/
Delta

🛏🚭🔌🚭📺▦🅰🔍✗Ⓣ

## "Peace Haven"
London Friendship Centre, 3 Creswick
Road, London W3 9HE
☎ (0181) 992 0221
Contact: Mr. P O'Nath
*Comfortable residential hostel most
suitable for groups of young people and
school parties, open throughout the
year. Individuals also welcome.*
Minimum age 10
Bedrooms: 2 single, 15 double/twin,
1 triple, 2 quadruple, 3 dormitories.
Total number of beds: 53
Bathrooms: 6 private, 8 public

**Bed & breakfast**

| per person: | £min | £max |
| --- | --- | --- |
| Daily | 10.50 | 19.00 |

Lunch available
Evening meal 1700 (last orders 1900)
Cards accepted: Switch/Delta

🛏🍴🔌🖥🔌📺▦🅰✗🐾SP♨

## The Porchester Hotel
33 Princes Square, London W2 4NJ
Contact: Miss Jackie Boughton,
16 Leinster Square, London W2 4DJ
☎ (0171) 286 5294
Fax (0171) 229 3917
Telex 24923 VIEHTL G
*Ideal for youth groups, the Porchester
has its own passenger lift and offers
half the rooms with private facilities.
Value for money, affordable
accommodation.*
Bedrooms: 6 single, 15 double/twin,
21 triple, 13 quadruple, 3 dormitories.
Total number of beds: 170
Bathrooms: 32 private, 10 public

**Bed & breakfast**

| per person: | £min | £max |
| --- | --- | --- |
| Daily | 27.00 | |

Lunch available
Cards accepted: Access, Visa, Amex,
Switch/Delta

🛏🍴📞🖥🛎Ⓢ📺▦🅰Ⓣ

## Queen Alexandra's House ⚘
Bremner Road, Kensington Gore,
London SW7 2QT
☎ (0171) 589 3635
Fax (0171) 589 3177
Contact: Mrs. V E Makey
*A hostel for women students of all ages.
For females only*

*Continued ▶*

## LONDON

### Continued

Minimum age 17
Bedrooms: 75 single, 2 double/twin.
Total number of beds: 81
Bathrooms: 20 public

**Bed & breakfast**

| per person: | £min | £max |
| --- | --- | --- |
| Daily | 23.00 | 23.00 |

Open May-August

### Ramsay Hall ⚔

20 Maple Street, London W1P 5GB
☎ (0171) 387 4537
Contact: Mr Hugh Ewing
*Central London location, good value, comfortable accommodation in pleasant surroundings.*
Minimum age 11
Bedrooms: 364 single, 20 double/twin, 2 triple. Total number of beds: 410
Bathrooms: 70 public

**Bed & breakfast**

| per person: | £min | £max |
| --- | --- | --- |
| Daily | 18.50 | 19.75 |

Evening meal 1800 (last orders 1900)
Open January, March-April, June-September, December

### Rotherhithe Youth Hostel and Conference Centre ⚔

Salter Road, London SE16 1PP
☎ (0171) 232 2114
Fax (0171) 237 2919
Contact: Mr Frank Velander
*Ultra-modern building with every facility for families and individuals. All rooms have en-suite facilities, there is a restaurant and ample street parking. Special prices for family rooms.*
Bedrooms: 22 double/twin, 16 quadruple, 32 dormitories. Total number of beds: 320
Bathrooms: 70 private

**Bed & breakfast**

| per person: | £min | £max |
| --- | --- | --- |
| Daily | 14.00 | 22.00 |

**Full board**

| per person: | £min | £max |
| --- | --- | --- |
| Weekly | 98.00 | 110.00 |

Lunch available
Evening meal 1730 (last orders 2030)
Cards accepted: Access, Visa, Switch/Delta

### Hotel Saint Simeon ⚔

38 Harrington Gardens, London SW7 4LT
☎ (0171) 373 0505 & 370 4708
Telex 269712 GLOBE G
Contact: Mr. J Gojkovic
*Rooms for one, two or three people in central London. Nearest underground station is Gloucester Road.*
Bedrooms: 6 single, 10 double/twin, 5 dormitories. Total number of beds: 41
Bathrooms: 4 private, 6 public

**Bed & breakfast**

| per person: | £min | £max |
| --- | --- | --- |
| Daily | 8.00 | 18.00 |

**Full board**

| per person: | £min | £max |
| --- | --- | --- |
| Weekly | 56.00 | 84.00 |

Cards accepted: Access, Visa, Amex

### Tent City ⚔

Old Oak Common Lane, East Acton, London W3 7DP
☎ (0181) 749 9074 & (0171) 415 7143
Fax (0171) 415 7038
Contact: Ms Maxine Lambert
*"Tented" hostel and campsite close to East Acton tube. On-site snackbar, free baggage and valuables store. Young and fun!*
Bedrooms: 14 dormitories. Total number of beds: 448
Bathrooms: 24 public

**Bed only**

| per person: | £min | £max |
| --- | --- | --- |
| Daily | 4.00 | 5.00 |

Lunch available
Parking for 30
Open June-September

### University of Westminster ⚔

International House, 1-5 Lambeth Road, London SE1 6HU
Contact: Ms Nicole Chanson, University of Westminster, Luxborough Suite, 35 Marylebone Road, London NW1 5LS
☎ (0171) 911 5000
Fax (0171) 911 5141
Telex 25964
*Refurbished Hall of Residence offering good quality accommodation in single and twin rooms on a self-catering basis. Four tube stops away from Piccadilly Circus and within a few minutes' walk of the River Thames, the Houses of Parliament and Westminster Abbey. Ideal for sightseeing and for London's theatreland.*
Bedrooms: 63 single, 9 double/twin. Total number of beds: 81
Bathrooms: 18 public

**Bed only**

| per person: | £min | £max |
| --- | --- | --- |
| Daily | 13.00 | 18.75 |

**Bed & breakfast**

| per person: | £min | £max |
| --- | --- | --- |
| Daily | 15.25 | 21.00 |

**Full board**

| per person: | £min | £max |
| --- | --- | --- |
| Weekly | 175.00 | 200.00 |

Lunch available
Evening meal 1730 (last orders 1930)
Parking for 2
Open April, July-September
Cards accepted: Access, Visa, Switch/Delta

### University of Westminster ⚔

Furnival House, Cholmley Park, Highgate, London N6 5EU
Contact: Ms Nicole Chanson, University of Westminster, Luxborough Suite, 35 Marylebone Road, London NW1 5LS
☎ (0171) 911 5000
Fax (0171) 911 5141
Telex 25964
*Refurbished Edwardian Hall of Residence in Highgate village, situated in its own grounds. Good quality accommodation on self-catering or meals basis. Within easy walking distance of Waterlow Park and Hampstead Heath and half-an-hour from the West End. Some rooms offer panoramic views of London.*
Minimum age 7
Bedrooms: 85 single, 28 double/twin. Total number of beds: 141
Bathrooms: 16 public

**Bed only**

| per person: | £min | £max |
| --- | --- | --- |
| Daily | 13.00 | 18.75 |

**Bed & breakfast**

| per person: | £min | £max |
| --- | --- | --- |
| Daily | 15.25 | 21.00 |

**Full board**

| per person: | £min | £max |
| --- | --- | --- |
| Weekly | 175.00 | 200.00 |

Lunch available
Evening meal 1730 (last orders 1930)
Parking for 6
Open April, July-September
Cards accepted: Access, Visa, Switch/Delta

### Urban Learning Foundation ⚔

56 East India Dock Road, London E14 6JE
☎ (0171) 987 0033
Fax (0171) 538 2620
Contact: Ms Jacqui Duggan
*Purpose-built residential training centre, close to central London. Single study bedrooms arranged in 4-7 bedded apartments.*
Minimum age 12
Bedrooms: 47 single. Total number of beds: 47
Bathrooms: 1 private, 12 public

**Bed only**

| per person: | £min | £max |
| --- | --- | --- |
| Daily | 15.00 | 20.00 |

**Bed & breakfast**

| per person: | £min | £max |
| --- | --- | --- |
| Daily | 18.00 | 24.00 |

Lunch available
Cards accepted: Access, Visa

### Wimbledon YMCA

200 The Broadway, Wimbledon, London SW19 1RY
☎ (0181) 542 9055
Fax (0181) 542 1086
Contact: Mr. A C Rothery
*Modern, purpose-built residence with sports hall, fitness studio, saunas, sunbeds, coffee bar, restaurant and laundry.*
Minimum age 12

Bedrooms: 106 single, 34 double/twin.
Total number of beds: 170
Bathrooms: 1 private, 20 public
**Bed & breakfast**

| per person: | £min | £max |
|---|---|---|
| Daily | 17.00 | 20.00 |

Lunch available
Evening meal 1700 (last orders 1850)
Parking for 30
Cards accepted: Access, Visa

## Y.M.C.A.
Rush Green Road, Romford RM7 0PH
☎ Romford (01708) 766211
Fax (01708) 754211
Contact: Ms Audrey Hylton
*8 minutes' walk from Romford British Rail station, 25 minutes from Liverpool Street station. Easy access to M25 and south coast. Easy travel into London by underground (Elm Park). International hostel with many sports facilities.*
Minimum age 18
Bedrooms: 148 single, 2 double/twin.
Total number of beds: 150
Bathrooms: 4 private, 24 public
**Bed & breakfast**

| per person: | £min | £max |
|---|---|---|
| Daily | 16.50 | 19.50 |

**Full board**

| per person: | £min | £max |
|---|---|---|
| Weekly | 60.00 | 110.00 |

Lunch available
Evening meal 1730 (last orders 1845)
Parking for 120
Cards accepted: Access, Visa

## YWCA Elizabeth House
118 Warwick Way, London SW1V 1SD
☎ (0171) 630 0741
Contact: Ms. F McGinlay
*Clean and secure basic bed and breakfast accommodation in central London for men, women and families. Garden available for guests.*
Bedrooms: 10 single, 13 double/twin, 1 triple, 3 quadruple. Total number of beds: 51
Bathrooms: 9 private, 8 public
**Bed & breakfast**

| per person: | £min | £max |
|---|---|---|
| Daily | 15.00 | 21.00 |

### LONGNOR
Staffordshire
Map ref 4B2

Remote village in farming country between Buxton and Hartington and close to the River Dove.

## High Ash Farm Field Study Centre ⚲
Longnor, Buxton, Derbyshire
SK17 0QY
☎ Buxton (01298) 25727
Contact: Mr & Mrs D Moors
*Rural location for family or group bookings. Ideal venue for children of all ages. Free use of games room and play area.*
For groups only
Bedrooms: 9 dormitories. Total number of beds: 64
Bathrooms: 5 private, 4 public
**Bed only**

| per person: | £min | £max |
|---|---|---|
| Daily | | 12.00 |

**Bed & breakfast**

| per person: | £min | £max |
|---|---|---|
| Daily | | 14.00 |

**Full board**

| per person: | £min | £max |
|---|---|---|
| Weekly | | 140.00 |

Lunch available
Evening meal 1700 (last orders 2100)
Parking for 20

### MANCHESTER
Greater Manchester
Map ref 4B1

The Gateway to the North, offering one of Britain's largest selections of arts venues and theatre productions, a wide range of chain stores and specialist shops, a legendary, lively nightlife, spectacular architecture and a plethora of eating and drinking places.
*Tourist Information Centre*
☎ *(0161) 234 3157/8*

## Holly Royde Conference Centre
56 Palatine Road, West Didsbury, Manchester M20 3JP
Contact: Mrs Lynn Palethorpe, Extra-Mural Department, The University, Manchester M13 9PL
☎ (0161) 275 3274 & 275 3275
Fax (0161) 275 3300
*The residential conference centre of the Extramural department of the University of Manchester, available throughout the year.*
Minimum age 18
Bedrooms: 51 single, 5 double/twin.
Total number of beds: 61
Bathrooms: 2 private, 7 public
**Bed & breakfast**

| per person: | £min | £max |
|---|---|---|
| Daily | 22.35 | 22.35 |

**Full board**

| per person: | £min | £max |
|---|---|---|
| Weekly | 275.00 | 275.00 |

Lunch available
Evening meal from 1845
Parking for 32
Open January-July, September-December

## The Manchester Conference Centre and Hotel ⚲
P.O. Box 88, Sackville Street, Manchester M60 1QD
☎ (0161) 200 4065
Fax (0161) 200 4090
Contact: Mr A F Yates
*Modern year-round conference centre and hotel, in Manchester city centre. Standard and en-suite rooms. Conferences and groups a speciality. Restaurant and bar.*
Bedrooms: 2226 single, 74 double/twin. Total number of beds: 2374
Bathrooms: 1890 private, 300 public
**Bed & breakfast**

| per person: | £min | £max |
|---|---|---|
| Daily | 35.00 | 66.50 |

Lunch available
Evening meal 1830 (last orders 2100)
Parking for 700
Cards accepted: Access, Visa, Diners, Switch/Delta

## University of Manchester ⚲
Dept C736, Oxford Road, Manchester M13 9PL
☎ (0161) 275 2156
Fax (0161) 275 2223
Contact: Miss C S Bolton
*Accommodation for groups and facilities for conferences and exhibitions in university halls of residence. Small or large groups - long or short stay, flexible arrangements, friendly staff.*
Bedrooms: 4272 single, 122 double/twin. Total number of beds: 4516
Bathrooms: 1150 private, 1031 public
**Bed only**

| per person: | £min | £max |
|---|---|---|
| Daily | 11.75 | 28.20 |

**Bed & breakfast**

| per person: | £min | £max |
|---|---|---|
| Daily | 16.00 | 33.30 |

**Full board**

| per person: | £min | £max |
|---|---|---|
| Weekly | 209.00 | 390.80 |

Lunch available
Evening meal from 1800
Parking for 1500
Open January, March-April, June-September, December

### MATFIELD
Kent
Map ref 3B4

Village with Georgian houses, green and pond.

## Old Cryals
Cryals Road, Matfield, Tonbridge TN12 7HN
☎ Brenchley (01892) 722372
Fax (01892) 723311
Contact: Mr C Charrington
*Hostel-type accommodation for 12, in two rooms for 4 and 8. Comfortable*

Continued ▶

## MATFIELD

### Continued

*sitting/dining room with microwave oven, TV, freezer, dishwasher. Self-catering only.*
Bedrooms: 2 dormitories. Total number of beds: 12
Bathrooms: 2 public

**Bed only**

| per person: | £min | £max |
| --- | --- | --- |
| Daily | 6.50 | 7.50 |

Parking for 12
Open March-November
⌂5🏠♿🛏📺▥⚏🚗🔍🍴🚲 SP

## NEWCASTLE UPON TYNE

Tyne and Wear
Map ref 5C2

Commercial and cultural centre of the North East, with a large indoor shopping centre, Quayside market, museums and theatres which offer an annual 6 week season by the Royal Shakespeare Company. Norman castle keep, medieval alleys, old Guildhall.
*Tourist Information Centre*
☎ *(0191) 261 0691 or 230 0030*

### North Eastern YWCA Hostel

Jesmond House, Clayton Road, Newcastle upon Tyne, Tyne & Wear NE2 1UJ
☎ (0191) 281 1233
Contact: Mr M Hutchinson
*New, custom-built accommodation in a good residential area with easy access by Metro and bus to the city centre. All bedrooms have wash basins.*
Minimum age 18
Bedrooms: 80 single. Total number of beds: 80
Bathrooms: 12 public

**Bed & breakfast**

| per person: | £min | £max |
| --- | --- | --- |
| Daily | 16.50 | |

**Full board**

| per person: | £min | £max |
| --- | --- | --- |
| Weekly | 85.00 | |

Parking for 20
♿▥S▥📺▥🚗🍴🚲

### University of Northumbria At Newcastle ⚘

Coach Lane Campus Halls of Residence, Coach Lane, Newcastle upon Tyne NE7 7XA
Contact: Mrs S Cowell, University of Northumbria At Newcastle, Ellison Place, Newcastle upon Tyne, Tyne & Wear NE1 8ST
☎ (0191) 227 4024
Fax (0191) 227 8017
*Accommodation in modern halls of residence, set in pleasant grounds, 3 miles from the city centre. Bed and breakfast with or without evening meal for groups or parties.*
Bedrooms: 186 single, 50 double/twin. Total number of beds: 286

---

Bathrooms: 44 public

**Bed only**

| per person: | £min | £max |
| --- | --- | --- |
| Daily | 10.20 | 13.40 |

**Bed & breakfast**

| per person: | £min | £max |
| --- | --- | --- |
| Daily | 14.80 | 19.15 |

**Full board**

| per person: | £min | £max |
| --- | --- | --- |
| Weekly | 171.75 | 258.80 |

Lunch available
Evening meal 1730 (last orders 1930)
Parking for 200
Open April, July-September
⌂♿♿S▥📺▥🚗🍴🐾🎿

## NEWPORT

Shropshire
Map ref 4A3

Small market town on the Shropshire Union Canal has a wide High Street and a church with some interesting monuments. Newport is close to Aqualate Mere which is the largest lake in Staffordshire.

### Harper Adams ⚘

Newport TF10 8NB
☎ (01952) 815201 & 820280
Fax (01952) 814783
Contact: Mr Ian Barnard
*A country estate of 600 acres. Renaissance architecture with 200 en-suite rooms (300 others). Conference, tutorial and all sports. Groups only (4 plus).*
Minimum age 10
Bedrooms: 443 single, 60 double/twin. Total number of beds: 503
Bathrooms: 180 private, 60 public

**Bed & breakfast**

| per person: | £min | £max |
| --- | --- | --- |
| Daily | 15.00 | 25.00 |

Lunch available
Evening meal 1700 (last orders 2200)
Parking for 4000
Open January, April, July-September, December
⌂♿♿S▥📺▥🚗🍴🐾🎿
🎿🔍🚶🏹 OAP 🚲 SP

## NORWICH

Norfolk
Map ref 3C1

Beautiful cathedral city and county town on the River Wensum with many fine museums and medieval churches. Norman castle, Guildhall and interesting medieval streets. Good shopping centre and market.
*Tourist Information Centre*
☎ *(01603) 666071*

### City College Norwich

Southwell Lodge, Ipswich Road, Norwich NR2 2LL
☎ (01603) 618327 & 660011
Fax (01603) 760326
Contact: Mr John Wheeler

---

*College halls of residence set in a rural tree-screened setting within 10 minutes' walk of Norwich city centre.*
Bedrooms: 270 single, 8 double/twin. Total number of beds: 286
Bathrooms: 13 private, 32 public

**Bed only**

| per person: | £min | £max |
| --- | --- | --- |
| Daily | 12.00 | 18.00 |

**Bed & breakfast**

| per person: | £min | £max |
| --- | --- | --- |
| Daily | 16.00 | 21.00 |

Lunch available
Evening meal 1730 (last orders 1900)
Parking for 500
Cards accepted: Access, Visa, Switch/Delta
⌂♿♿S▥📺▥🚗🔍🍴

### YWCA

Marjorie Hinde House, 61 Bethel Street, Norwich NR2 1NR
☎ (01603) 625982
Contact: Mrs Sylvia Phillips
*Comfortable hostel for long or short stays. Central position near shops, theatres, gardens, library and public transport.*
For females only
Bedrooms: 20 single, 7 double/twin. Total number of beds: 34
Bathrooms: 7 public

**Bed only**

| per person: | £min | £max |
| --- | --- | --- |
| Daily | 7.85 | 9.50 |

♿▥▥📺▥🚗🍴🚲

## OTTERBURN

Northumberland
Map ref 5B1

Small village set at the meeting of the River Rede with Otter Burn, the site of the Battle of Otterburn in 1388. A peaceful tradition continues in the sale of Otterburn tweeds in this beautiful region, which is ideal for exploring the Border country and the Cheviots.

### Otterburn Hall

Otterburn NE19 1HE
☎ Freephone 0800 591527
Fax (0191) 385 2267
Contact: Mrs K Hutchinson
*Family holiday hotel, conference venue and training establishment in 100 acres. Offering special interest holidays. Prices quoted include dinner.*
Minimum age 8
Bedrooms: 3 single, 33 double/twin, 16 triple, 7 quadruple, 1 dormitory. Total number of beds: 136
Bathrooms: 66 private, 8 public

**Bed & breakfast**

| per person: | £min | £max |
| --- | --- | --- |
| Daily | 33.00 | 35.00 |

Lunch available
Evening meal 1900 (last orders 1900)
Parking for 60
Cards accepted: Visa
⌂♿♿S▥📺▥🚗🐾🎿🔍🚶
🚶 OAP 🚲 SP 🏓 T

## RAMSGATE

Kent
Map ref 3C3

Popular holiday resort with good sandy beaches. At Pegwell Bay is the replica of a Viking longship. Terminal for car-ferry service to Dunkirk and Ostend.
*Tourist Information Centre*
☎ *(01843) 591086*

### The Regency Hotel and School of English ⚠
Royal Crescent, Ramsgate CT11 9PE
☎ (01843) 591212
Fax (01843) 850035
Telex 96454 REGRAM G
Contact: Miss J A Beech

*Historic building overlooking flowered lawns and sea. Late-night snack bar, bar and discotheque. Indoor pool, sauna, sandy beaches. Very lively young atmosphere.*
Minimum age 16
Bedrooms: 29 single, 56 double/twin, 4 triple. Total number of beds: 153
Bathrooms: 16 private, 12 public
**Bed only**

| per person: | £min | £max |
| --- | --- | --- |
| Daily | 18.00 | 29.00 |

**Bed & breakfast**

| per person: | £min | £max |
| --- | --- | --- |
| Daily | 18.00 | 29.00 |

**Full board**

| per person: | £min | £max |
| --- | --- | --- |
| Weekly | 126.00 | 203.00 |

Lunch available
Evening meal 1800 (last orders 1915)
Cards accepted: Access, Visa, Diners, Amex

## RIPPONDEN

West Yorkshire
Map ref 4B1

Main Calderdale village on the River Ryburn with walks to Ryburn Reservoir and Blackstone Edge Roman road where part of the Roman pavement is still visible. A pleasant main street of traditional houses leads down to the stocks and there is a spired church and a 16th C packhorse bridge.

### Stones Environmental Training Centre
Rochdale Road, Ripponden, Sowerby Bridge HX6 4LA

Contact: Mr C Haigh, Upper Oakes, Dyson Lane, Ripponden, Sowerby Bridge, West Yorkshire HX6 4JX
☎ Halifax (01422) 824030
*Self-catering activity centre for organised groups such as educational, ecclesiastical and uniformed organisations. Based on a former primary school with opportunities for environmental and outdoor pursuits. Minimum room charge £70 (up to 20 people).*
For groups only
Bedrooms: 2 triple, 2 quadruple, 6 dormitories. Total number of beds: 42
Bathrooms: 4 public
**Bed only**

| per person: | £min | £max |
| --- | --- | --- |
| Daily | 3.50 | |

Parking for 20

## SHEFFIELD

South Yorkshire
Map ref 4B2

Local iron ore and coal gave Sheffield its prosperous steel and cutlery industries. The modern city centre has many interesting buildings - cathedral, Cutlers' Hall, Crucible Theatre, Graves and Mappin Art Galleries - and Meadowhall shopping centre nearby.
*Tourist Information Centre*
☎ *(0114) 273 4671 or 279 5901*

### University of Sheffield ⚠
Conference Office, Octagon Centre, Sheffield S10 2TQ
☎ (0114) 276 8555
Fax (0114) 272 9097
Telex 547216
Contact: Ms C Davies
*Six halls of residence in a quiet suburb near the city centre and adjacent to the Peak District National Park.*
Wheelchair access category 3 ♿
Bedrooms: 2100 single, 100 double/twin. Total number of beds: 2300
Bathrooms: 300 public
**Bed & breakfast**

| per person: | £min | £max |
| --- | --- | --- |
| Daily | 18.95 | |

Lunch available
Parking for 600
Open January, March-April, July-September, December

---

The symbol ⚠ after an establishment name indicates membership of a Regional Tourist Board.

## SHERINGHAM

Norfolk
Map ref 3B1

Holiday resort with Victorian and Edwardian hotels and a sand and shingle beach where the fishing boats are hauled up. The North Norfolk Railway operates from Sheringham station during the summer. Other attractions include museums, theatre and Splash Fun Pool.

### Ye Homesteade Christian Holiday Centre
60 Cliff Road, Sheringham NR26 8BJ
☎ (01263) 822524
Contact: Mr C J Smith
*Small hotel, fully centrally heated. Situated in own garden. Croquet lawn and putting green. 2 minutes from beach and cliffs.*
Bedrooms: 4 single, 4 double/twin, 14 dormitories. Total number of beds: 53
Bathrooms: 3 public
**Bed & breakfast**

| per person: | £min | £max |
| --- | --- | --- |
| Daily | 14.00 | 16.00 |

**Full board**

| per person: | £min | £max |
| --- | --- | --- |
| Weekly | 117.50 | 157.00 |

Lunch available
Open May-September

## STOKE ROCHFORD

Lincolnshire
Map ref 3A1

### Stoke Rochford Hall ⚠
Stoke Rochford, Grantham NG33 5EJ
☎ Great Ponton (01476) 83337
Fax (01476) 83534
Contact: Peter Robinson
*Elegant Victorian mansion house in 28 acres of beautiful parkland and formal gardens, an idyllic setting for that sought-after country holiday retreat. Creche and activity weeks for children in summer, extensive leisure club with indoor heated swimming pool, 18-hole golf-course adjacent.*
Bedrooms: 86 single, 100 double/twin. Total number of beds: 233
Bathrooms: 68 private, 27 public
**Bed & breakfast**

| per person: | £min | £max |
| --- | --- | --- |
| Daily | 27.50 | 45.00 |

Lunch available
Evening meal 1830 (last orders 2030)
Parking for 500
Cards accepted: Access, Visa, Diners, Amex, Switch/Delta

## STREET

Somerset
Map ref 2A2

Busy shoe-making town set beneath the Polden Hills. A museum at the factory, which was developed with the rest of the town in the 19th C, can be visited. Just south, the National Trust has care of woodland on Ivythorn Hill which gives wide views northward.

### Millfield School Village of Education

Millfield School, Street BA16 0YD
☎ (01458) 45823
Fax (01458) 45102
Contact: Mrs C Steer
*Famous independent school with a wealth of facilities and an international reputation as a centre of excellence. Accommodation in association with vast programme of holiday courses.*
Bedrooms: 50 single, 150 double/twin, 150 dormitories. Total number of beds: 800
Bathrooms: 80 public
**Full board**

| per person: | £min | £max |
|---|---|---|
| Weekly | | 143.00 |

Lunch available
Open January, April, July-September, December

## STUDLEY

Warwickshire
Map ref 2B1

This town has been producing needles for several centuries and has some old houses and inns. The Elizabethan Coughton Court (National Trust), the Palladian Ragley Hall with its beautiful plasterwork and Stratford-upon-Avon are easily reached.

### Studley Training Centre Rover Group ♈

Studley Castle, Castle Road, Studley B80 7AJ
☎ (01527) 853111
Fax (01527) 854365
Contact: Miss K Bateman

*Victorian folly, medieval style with towers and turrets. About 1 mile from Studley village, situated on the hilltop long access drive from castle road.*
Bedrooms: 65 single, 12 double/twin.
Total number of beds: 89
Bathrooms: 40 private, 8 public

---

**Bed & breakfast**

| per person: | £min | £max |
|---|---|---|
| Daily | 25.00 | 30.00 |

Lunch available
Evening meal from 1900
Parking for 100
Cards accepted: Visa

## ULLSWATER

Cumbria
Map ref 5A3

This beautiful lake, which is over 7 miles long, runs from Glenridding to Pooley Bridge. Lofty peaks ranging around the lake make an impressive background. A steamer service operates along the lake between Pooley Bridge, Howtown and Glenridding in the summer.

### Patterdale Hall Estate

Glenridding, Penrith CA11 0PJ
☎ Glenridding (01768) 482308
Fax (01768) 482308
Contact: Mr. S Foxall

*Hostel with Victorian features, run as a holiday and outdoor education centre for self-programming groups. Price includes a packed lunch, dinner and breakfast.*
Minimum age 8
Bedrooms: 1 double/twin, 3 quadruple, 10 dormitories. Total number of beds: 62
Bathrooms: 6 public
**Bed & breakfast**

| per person: | £min | £max |
|---|---|---|
| Daily | | 13.07 |

**Full board**

| per person: | £min | £max |
|---|---|---|
| Weekly | 94.63 | 107.55 |

Lunch available
Evening meal from 1800
Parking for 30
Cards accepted: Access, Visa

---

Individual proprietors have supplied all details of accommodation. Although we do check for accuracy, we advise you to confirm the information at the time of booking.

---

## WAREHAM

Dorset
Map ref 2B3

This site has been occupied since pre-Roman times and has a turbulent history. In 1762 fire destroyed much of the town, so the buildings now are mostly Georgian.
*Tourist Information Centre*
☎ (01929) 552740

### Hyde House Leisure & Country Park

Hyde, Wareham BH20 7NX
Contact: Mr C Reynard or Mr C McCarthy, 6 Kew Green, Kew, Richmond, Surrey TW9 3BH
☎ (0181) 940 7782
Fax (0181) 948 4999
*Multi-activity residential centre for holidays and training courses. Maximum 200. Weekend and weeks. Over 30 activities.*
Minimum age 8
Bedrooms: 11 double/twin, 15 dormitories. Total number of beds: 220
Bathrooms: 9 private, 27 public
**Full board**

| per person: | £min | £max |
|---|---|---|
| Weekly | 115.15 | 210.32 |

Lunch available

## WINCHESTER

Hampshire
Map ref 2C3

King Alfred the Great made Winchester the capital of Saxon England. A magnificent Norman cathedral, with one of the longest naves in Europe, dominates the city. Home of Winchester College founded in 1382.
*Tourist Information Centre*
☎ (01962) 840500

### King Alfred's College Conferences ♈

Sparkford Road, Winchester SO22 4NR
☎ (01962) 841515
Fax (01962) 842280
Contact: Mrs S Hogg
*Twelve residential and teaching buildings grouped compactly on a pleasant hillside site, 10 minutes' walk from Winchester city centre.*
Bedrooms: 260 single, 26 double/twin, 14 triple. Total number of beds: 354
Bathrooms: 80 public
**Bed only**

| per person: | £min | £max |
|---|---|---|
| Daily | 12.37 | 14.28 |

**Bed & breakfast**

| per person: | £min | £max |
|---|---|---|
| Daily | 15.23 | 17.13 |

**Full board**

| per person: | £min | £max |
|---|---|---|
| Weekly | 209.65 | 222.95 |

Lunch available
Evening meal 1830 (last orders 1930)
Parking for 200
Open January, March-April, July-September, December

---

## YORK

North Yorkshire
Map ref 4C1

Ancient walled city nearly 2000 years old containing many well-preserved medieval buildings. Its Minster has over 100 stained glass windows. Attractions include Castle Museum, National Railway Museum, Jorvik Viking Centre and York Dungeon.
*Tourist Information Centre*
☎ *(01904) 620557 or 621756 or 643700*

**Fairfax House** Ⓜ
99 Heslington Road, York YO1 5BJ
☎ (01904) 432095
Contact: Mrs. A E Glover
*Student residence in quiet spacious grounds, within walking distance of town centre. Reduced rates for children under 12 and senior citizens.*

Bedrooms: 93 single. Total number of beds: 93
Bathrooms: 14 public

**Bed & breakfast**

| per person: | £min | £max |
|---|---|---|
| Daily | 17.00 | 19.00 |

Open March-April, July-September

---

## University College of Ripon and York Saint John Ⓜ

Lord Mayor's Walk, York YO3 7EX
☎ (01904) 616654/5 & 0800 136171
Fax (01904) 612512
Contact: Mrs A Cheetham
*Well-appointed college accommodation overlooking the city walls. Emphasis on standards of cuisine. Bars, TV, swimming pool, squash and tennis. Full audio-visual service. Suitable for holidays or conferences.*
Bedrooms: 281 single, 12 double/twin.
Total number of beds: 422
Bathrooms: 52 public

**Bed only**

| per person: | £min | £max |
|---|---|---|
| Daily | 14.00 | 19.75 |

**Bed & breakfast**

| per person: | £min | £max |
|---|---|---|
| Daily | 17.50 | 24.25 |

**Full board**

| per person: | £min | £max |
|---|---|---|
| Weekly | 247.80 | 295.00 |

Lunch available
Evening meal 1800 (last orders 2000)
Parking for 180
Open January, March-April, June-September, December

## York Youth Hotel Ⓜ

11-13 Bishophill Senior, York
YO1 1EF
☎ (01904) 625904 & 630613
Fax (01904) 612494
Contact: Ms Maureen Sellers
*Dormitory-style accommodation in the city centre. Private rooms, TV lounge, snack shop, evening meals, packed lunches, games room, residential licence, disco and 24-hour service.*
Minimum age 2
Bedrooms: 7 single, 14 double/twin, 1 triple, 4 quadruple, 5 dormitories.
Total number of beds: 120
Bathrooms: 8 public

**Bed only**

| per person: | £min | £max |
|---|---|---|
| Daily | 8.00 | 12.00 |

**Bed & breakfast**

| per person: | £min | £max |
|---|---|---|
| Daily | 10.30 | 14.30 |

Lunch available
Evening meal 1700 (last orders 1900)
Cards accepted: Access, Visa, Switch/Delta

---

SUNNYSIDE FARM WELCOMES CAREFUL WALKERS.

# COUNTRY CODE

♣ Enjoy the countryside and respect its life and work ♣ Guard against all risk of fire ♣ Fasten all gates ♣ Keep your dogs under close control ♣ Keep to public paths across farmland ♣ Use gates and stiles to cross fences, hedges and walls ♣ Leave livestock, crops and machinery alone ♣ Take your litter home ♣ Help to keep all water clean ♣ Protect wildlife, plants and trees ♣ Take special care on country roads ♣ Make no unnecessary noise

---

RESERVED

# BOOKINGS

When enquiring about accommodation you may find it helpful to use the booking enquiry coupons which can be found towards the end of the guide.
These should be cut out and mailed direct to the establishments in which you are interested.
Do remember to include your name and address.

# Use your *i*'s

There are more than 550 Tourist Information Centres throughout England offering friendly help with accommodation and holiday ideas as well as suggestions of places to visit and things to do.

In your home town there may be a centre which can help you before you set out. You'll find the address of your nearest Tourist Information Centre in your local Phone Book.

## Country Code

♣ Enjoy the countryside and respect its life and work ♣ Guard against all risk of fire ♣ Fasten all gates ♣ Keep your dogs under close control ♣ Keep to public paths across farmland ♣ Use gates and stiles to cross fences, hedges and walls ♣ Leave livestock, crops and machinery alone ♣ Take your litter home ♣ Help to keep all water clean ♣ Protect wildlife, plants and trees ♣ Take special care on country roads ♣ Make no unnecessary noise

## Bookings

When enquiring about accommodation you may find it helpful to use the booking enquiry coupons which can be found towards the end of the guide.
These should be cut out and mailed direct to the establishments in which you are interested. Do remember to include your name and address.

# INFORMATION PAGES

**National Rating Scheme**                                                page 402
All you need to know about the national Crown and Lodge ratings.

**National Accessible Scheme for Wheelchair Users**                       page 404
Information on the scheme which categorises places to stay accessible
to wheelchair users and others who may have difficulty in walking and a list
of establishments in this guide with their wheelchair access category ratings.

**General Advice and Information**                                        page 405
Things to note when making a booking and helpful advice on
cancellations, late arrival, complaints, etc.

**About the Guide Entries**                                               page 408
How to get the best out of the detailed accommodation entries in
this guide, covering locations, prices, symbols, pets, credit cards, etc.

**What's On in England 1995**                                             page 411
A guide to some of the major cultural, sporting and other events
that will be taking place in England during 1995.

**Enquiry Coupons**                    page 417
To help you when making enquiries
about accommodation or seeking
information from advertisers.

**Town Index**                         page 425
Page numbers for all the cities,
towns and villages with
accommodation listings.

**Index to Advertisers**               page 431
A quick-reference index to all
display advertisements.

**Mileage Chart**                      page 432
Distances by road between key cities and towns in Britain.

**Location Maps**                                                         page 433
These colour maps pinpoint all the cities, towns and villages with
accommodation listings in this guide.

**InterCity Rail Map**                                                    page 447
At-a-glance guide to BR InterCity rail services.

# NATIONAL RATING SCHEME

## Sure Signs

The Tourist Boards in Britain operate a national rating scheme for all types of accommodation. The purpose of the scheme is to identify and promote those establishments that the public can use with confidence. The system of facility classification and quality grading also acknowledges those that provide a wider range of facilities and services and higher quality standards.

Over 30,000 places to stay are inspected under the scheme and offer the reassurance of a national rating.

For 'serviced' accommodation (which includes hotels, motels, guesthouses, inns, B&Bs and farmhouses) there are six classification bands, starting with LISTED and then from ONE to FIVE CROWN. For the new generation of 'lodges', offering budget accommodation along major roads and motorways, there are three classification bands, from ONE to THREE MOON.

Quite simply, the more Crowns or Moons, the wider the range of facilities and services offered.

## Quality Grading

To help you find accommodation that offers even higher standards than those required for a Crown or Moon rating, there are four levels of quality grading, using the terms APPROVED, COMMENDED, HIGHLY COMMENDED and DE LUXE.

Wherever you see a national rating sign, you can be sure that a Tourist Board inspector has been there before you, checking the place on your behalf – and will be there again, because every place with a national rating is inspected annually.

Establishments that apply for quality grading – which is optional – are subject to a more detailed inspection that assesses the quality standard of the facilities and services provided. The initial inspection invariably involves the Tourist Board inspector staying overnight, as a normal guest, until the bill is paid the following morning.

This quality assessment includes such aspects as warmth of welcome and efficiency of service, as well as the standard of the furnishings, fittings and decor. The standard of meals and their presentation is also taken into account. Everything that impinges on the experience of a guest is included in the assessment.

Tourist Board inspectors receive careful training to enable them to apply the quality standards consistently and fairly. Only those facilities and services that are provided are assessed, and due consideration is given to the style and nature of the establishment.

B&Bs, farmhouses and guesthouses are not expected to operate in the style of large city centre hotels, and vice versa. This means that all types of establishment, whatever their Crown or Moon classification, can achieve a high quality grade if the facilities and services they provide, however limited in range, are to a high quality standard.

The quality grade that is awarded to an establishment is a reflection of the overall standard, taking everything into account. It is a balanced view of what is provided and, as such, cannot acknowledge individual areas of excellence.

Quality grades are not intended to indicate value for money. A high quality product can be over-priced; a product of modest quality, if offered at a low price, can represent good value. The information provided by the combination of the classification and quality grade will enable you to determine for yourself what represents good value for money.

## All Inspected

All establishments listed in this 'Where to Stay' guide have been inspected or are awaiting inspection under the national rating scheme. The ratings that appear in the accommodation entries were correct at the time of going to press but are subject to change. If no rating appears in an entry it means that the inspection had not been carried out by the time of going to press.

An information leaflet giving full details of the national rating scheme – which also covers self-catering holiday homes and caravan, chalet and camping parks – is available from any Tourist Information Centre.

## Lodge ratings

 In a One Moon 'Lodge', your bedroom will have at least a washbasin and radio or colour TV. Tea/coffee may be from a vending machine in a public area.

 Your bedroom in a Two Moon 'Lodge' will have colour TV, tea/coffee-making facilities and en-suite bath or shower with WC.

 In a Three Moon 'Lodge', you will find colour TV and radio, tea/coffee-making facilities and comfortable seating in your bedroom and there will be a bath, shower and WC en-suite. The reception area will be manned throughout the night.

*Your at-a-glance guide to the minimum facilities and services available at each Listed and Crown rating. Please bear in mind that all Crown classified establishments will provide at least some of the facilities of a higher classification.*

**THE GRADES: APPROVED, COMMENDED, HIGHLY COMMENDED** and **DE LUXE** *indicate the quality standard of what is provided. If no grade is shown you can still expect a high standard of cleanliness.*

| | Listed | One Crown | Two Crown | Three Crown | Four Crown | Five Crown |
|---|:---:|:---:|:---:|:---:|:---:|:---:|
| Clean and comfortable accommodation | ✔ | ✔ | ✔ | ✔ | ✔ | ✔ |
| Adequate heating at no extra charge | ✔ | ✔ | ✔ | ✔ | ✔ | ✔ |
| No extra charge for baths or showers | ✔ | ✔ | ✔ | ✔ | ✔ | ✔ |
| Clean towels, fresh soap | ✔ | ✔ | ✔ | ✔ | ✔ | ✔ |
| Breakfast | ✔ | ✔ | ✔ | ✔ | ✔ | ✔ |
| Fire Certificate (where required) | ✔ | ✔ | ✔ | ✔ | ✔ | ✔ |
| Comfortable lounge or sitting area | | ✔ | ✔ | ✔ | ✔ | ✔ |
| A washbasin in your room or private bathroom | | ✔ | ✔ | ✔ | ✔ | ✔ |
| Beds no smaller than 6' 3" x 3' (single) or 6' 3" x 4' 6" (double) | | ✔ | ✔ | ✔ | ✔ | ✔ |
| No nylon sheets | | ✔ | ✔ | ✔ | ✔ | ✔ |
| Cooked breakfast | | ✔ | ✔ | ✔ | ✔ | ✔ |
| Use of telephone | | ✔ | ✔ | ✔ | ✔ | ✔ |
| Tourist information | | ✔ | ✔ | ✔ | ✔ | ✔ |
| Private bathrooms for at least 20% of the bedrooms | | | ✔ | ✔ | ✔ | ✔ |
| Help with your luggage | | | ✔ | ✔ | ✔ | ✔ |
| Colour TV in the lounge or your bedroom | | | ✔ | ✔ | ✔ | ✔ |
| Double beds with access and table at both sides | | | ✔ | ✔ | ✔ | ✔ |
| Bedside lights | | | ✔ | ✔ | ✔ | ✔ |
| Early morning tea/coffee in your room, hot beverage in the evening | | | ✔ | ✔ | ✔ | ✔ |
| En-suite bathrooms for at least 50% of the bedrooms | | | | ✔ | ✔ | ✔ |
| Easy chair, full length mirror, luggage rack, tea/coffee in your bedroom | | | | ✔ | ✔ | ✔ |
| Hairdryer, shoe cleaning equipment and ironing facilities available | | | | ✔ | ✔ | ✔ |
| A public telephone or one in your room | | | | ✔ | ✔ | ✔ |
| A hot evening meal | | | | ✔ | ✔ | ✔ |
| En-suite bathrooms for at least 90% of the bedrooms, many with bath and shower | | | | | ✔ | ✔ |
| Colour TV, radio and telephone in your bedroom | | | | | ✔ | ✔ |
| Room service – drinks and light snacks between 7am and 11pm | | | | | ✔ | ✔ |
| Lounge service of drinks and snacks to midnight | | | | | ✔ | ✔ |
| Evening meals, with wine, last orders 8.30pm or later | | | | | ✔ | ✔ |
| A quiet sitting area | | | | | ✔ | ✔ |
| Laundry services | | | | | ✔ | ✔ |
| Toiletries, message taking, newspapers on request | | | | | ✔ | ✔ |
| Passenger lift | | | | | ✔ | ✔ |
| All bedrooms with bath, shower and WC en-suite | | | | | | ✔ |
| Direct dial telephone, writing table | | | | | | ✔ |
| Shoe cleaning and daily clothes pressing service | | | | | | ✔ |
| 24-hour lounge service and room service with meals up to midnight | | | | | | ✔ |
| Restaurant open for breakfast, lunch and dinner, with last orders 9pm or later | | | | | | ✔ |
| Full liquor licence | | | | | | ✔ |
| Night porter and porterage | | | | | | ✔ |

# NATIONAL ACCESSIBLE SCHEME
# FOR WHEELCHAIR USERS

Throughout England, the Tourist Boards are inspecting all types of places to stay, on holiday or business, that provide accessible accommodation for wheelchair users and others who may have difficulty walking. Those that meet the criteria can display their wheelchair access category and symbol at their premises and in their advertising – so look for the symbol when choosing where to stay.

The criteria the Tourist Boards have adopted do not, necessarily, conform to British Standards or to Building Regulations. They reflect what the boards understand to be acceptable to meet the practical needs of wheelchair users.

The Tourist Boards recognise three categories of accessibility:

**Category 1**
Accessible to all wheelchair users including those travelling independently

**Category 2**
Accessible to a wheelchair user with assistance

**Category 3**
Accessible to a wheelchair user able to walk short distances and up at least three steps

If you have additional needs or special requirements of any kind, we strongly recommend that you make sure these can be met by your chosen establishment before you confirm your booking.

❏ The National Accessible Scheme forms part of the Tourism for All Campaign that is being promoted by all three National Tourist Boards. Additional help and guidance on finding suitable holiday accommodation for those with special needs can be obtained from:
**Holiday Care Service**
2 Old Bank Chambers, Station Road, Horley, Surrey RH6 9HW.
Tel: (01293) 774535.
Fax: (01293) 784647.
Minicom: (01293) 776943.
The following establishments listed in this 'Where to Stay' guide had been inspected and given an access category at the time of going to press. Use the Town Index at the back of the guide to find page numbers for their full entries.

## Category 1
- CROOKHAM, NORTHUMBERLAND
  - The Coach House
- WIMBORNE MINSTER, DORSET
  - Northill House

## Category 2
- GARBOLDISHAM, NORFOLK
  - Ingleneuk Lodge

## Category 3
- AMBLESIDE, CUMBRIA
  - Borrans Park Hotel
  - Rowanfield Country Guesthouse
- BEVERLEY, HUMBERSIDE
  - Rudstone Walk Farmhouse & Country Cottages
- BOSCASTLE, CORNWALL
  - The Old Coach House
- CHELTENHAM, GLOUCESTERSHIRE
  - Hunting Butts
- CONGLETON, CHESHIRE
  - Sandhole Farm
- ELLERBY, N. YORKSHIRE
  - Ellerby Hotel

- HADLEIGH, SUFFOLK
  - Odds and Ends House
- LENHAM, KENT
  - Dog and Bear Hotel
- LINCOLN, LINCOLNSHIRE
  - Garden House
- NAILSWORTH, GLOUCESTERSHIRE
  - Apple Orchard House
- RICHMOND, N. YORKSHIRE
  - Mount Pleasant Farm
- RINGWOOD, HAMPSHIRE
  - Homeacres
- SARRE, KENT
  - Crown Inn (The Famous Cherry Brandy House)
- SHEFFIELD, S. YORKSHIRE
  - University of Sheffield
- SIDMOUTH, DEVON
  - Wiscombe Linhaye Farm
- STRATFORD-UPON-AVON, WARWICKSHIRE
  - Church Farm
- THIRSK, N. YORKSHIRE
  - Doxford House
- THORALBY, N. YORKSHIRE
  - High Green House

- ULLSWATER, CUMBRIA
  - Waterside House
- WARWICK, WARWICKSHIRE
  - Fulbrook Edge
- WINCHESTER, HAMPSHIRE
  - Shawlands
- WISBECH, CAMBRIDGESHIRE
  - Stratton Farm
- YOXALL, STAFFORDSHIRE
  - The Moat

# GENERAL ADVICE AND INFORMATION

## Making a Booking

When enquiring about accommodation, as well as checking prices and other details you will need to state your requirements clearly and precisely – for example:

1. Arrival and departure dates with acceptable alternatives if appropriate.

2. The accommodation you need. For example: room with twin beds, private bath and WC.

3. The terms you want. For example: room only; bed & breakfast; bed, breakfast and evening meal (half board); bed, breakfast, lunch and evening meal (full board).

4. If you will have children with you, give their ages, state whether you would like them to share your room or have an adjacent room and mention any special requirements such as a cot.

5. Tell the management about any particular requirements such as a ground floor room or special diet.

Misunderstandings can occur very easily over the telephone so we recommend that all bookings should be confirmed in writing if time permits.

When first enquiring in writing about a reservation you may find it helpful to use the Accommodation Coupons (pages 417–422) which can be cut out and mailed to the establishment(s) of your choice.

Remember to include your name and address and please enclose a stamped and addressed envelope – or an international reply coupon if writing from outside Britain.

Please note that the English Tourist Board does not make reservations. You should address

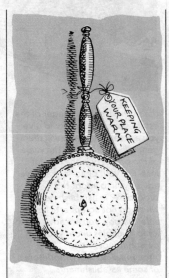

your enquiry direct to the establishment.

## Deposits and Advance Payments

For reservations made weeks or months ahead a deposit is usually payable and the amount will vary according to the length of booking, time of year, number in party and so on. The deposit will be deducted from the total bill at the end of your stay.

Some establishments, particularly larger hotels in big towns, now require payment for the room on arrival if a prior reservation has not been made – especially from guests arriving late and/or with little luggage. Regrettably this practice has become necessary because of the number of guests who have left without paying their bills.

If you are asked to pay on arrival it may be advisable to see your room first to ensure that it meets your requirements.

If you book by telephone and are asked for your credit card number, you should note that the proprietor may charge your credit card account if you subsequently cancel the booking.

## Cancellations

When you accept offered accommodation, on the telephone or in writing, you are entering into a legally binding contract with the proprietor.

This means that if you cancel a reservation, fail to take up the accommodation or leave prematurely the proprietor may be entitled to compensation if the accommodation cannot be re-let for all or a good part of the booked period. If a deposit has been paid it is likely to be forfeited and an additional payment may be demanded.

However, no such claim can be made by the proprietor until after the booked period, during which time every effort should be made to re-let the accommodation. Any circumstances which might lead to repudiation of a contract may also need to be taken into account and, in the case of a dispute, legal advice should be sought by both parties.

It is therefore in your own interests to advise the management immediately if you have to change your travel plans, cancel a booking or leave prematurely.

Travel and holiday insurance protection policies are available quite cheaply and will safeguard you in the event of your having to cancel or curtail your holiday. Your insurance company or travel agent can advise you further on this. Some hotels also offer insurance schemes.

405

## Arriving Late

If you will be arriving late in the evening it is advisable to say so at the time of booking; if you are delayed on your way, a telephone call to inform the management that you will be late might help to avoid problems on arrival.

## Service Charges and Tipping

Many establishments now levy a service charge automatically and if so this fact must be stated clearly in the offer of accommodation at the time of booking. If the offer is then accepted by you the service charge becomes part of the contract.

At establishments where a service charge of this kind is made there is no need for you to give tips to the staff unless some particular or exceptional service has been rendered. In the case of meals the usual amount is 10% of the total bill.

## Telephone Call Charges

There is no restriction on the charges that can be made by hotels for telephone calls made through their switchboard or via direct-dial telephones in bedrooms. Unit charges are frequently considerably higher than telephone companies' standard charges. Hoteliers claim that they need to charge higher rates to defray the cost of providing the service.

Although it is a condition of a national Crown rating that a hotel's unit charges are displayed alongside telephones or with the room information, it is not always easy to see how these compare with the standard charges. Before using a hotel telephone for long-distance calls within Britain or overseas, you may wish to ask how the charges compare.

## Security of Valuables

Property of value may be deposited for safe-keeping with

the proprietor or manager of the establishment who should give you a receipt and who will then generally be liable for the value of the property in the case of loss. For your peace of mind we advise you to adopt this procedure. In establishments which do not accept articles for safe custody, you are advised to keep valuables under your personal supervision.

You may find that proprietors of some establishments disclaim, by notice, liability for property brought on to their premises by a guest; however, if a guest engages overnight accommodation in a hotel the proprietor is only permitted to restrict his liability to the minimum imposed upon him under the Hotel Proprietors Act, 1956. Under this Act, a proprietor of a hotel is liable for the value of the loss or damage to any property (other than a motor car or its contents) of a guest who has engaged overnight accommodation, but if the proprietor has a notice in the form prescribed by that Act, liability is limited to the sum of £50 in respect of one article and a total of £100 in the case of any one guest.

These limits do not apply, however, if you have deposited the property with the proprietor for safe-keeping or if the property is lost through the default, neglect or wilful act of the proprietor or his staff.

To be effective, any notice intended to disclaim or restrict liability must be prominently displayed in the reception area of, or in the main entrance to, the premises.

## Code of Conduct

All establishments appearing in this guide have agreed to observe the following Code of Conduct:
1. To ensure high standards of courtesy and cleanliness; catering and service appropriate to the type of establishment.
2. To describe fairly to all visitors and prospective visitors the amenities, facilities and services provided by the establishment, whether by advertisement, brochure, word of mouth or any other means. To allow visitors to see accommodation, if requested, before booking.
3. To make clear to visitors exactly what is included in all prices quoted for accommodation, meals and refreshments, including service charges, taxes and other surcharges. Details of charges, if any, for heating or for additional services or facilities available should also be made clear.
4. To adhere to, and not to exceed, prices current at time of occupation for accommodation or other services.
5. To advise visitors at the time of booking, and subsequently of any change, if the accommodation offered is in an unconnected

annexe, or similar, or by boarding out, and to indicate the location of such accommodation and any difference in comfort and amenities from accommodation in the main establishment.

6. To give each visitor, on request, details of payments due and a receipt if required.

7. To deal promptly and courteously with all enquiries, requests, reservations, correspondence and complaints from visitors.

8. To allow an English Tourist Board representative reasonable access to the establishment, on request, to confirm that the Code of Conduct is being observed.

## Comments and Complaints

Accommodation establishments have a number of legal and statutory responsibilities to their customers in areas such as the provision of information on prices, the provision of adequate fire precautions and the safeguarding of valuables. Like other businesses, they must

also meet the requirements of the Trade Descriptions Acts 1968 and 1972 when describing and offering accommodation and facilities.

All establishments appearing in this guide have declared that they fulfil all applicable statutory obligations.

The establishment descriptions and other details appearing in this guide have been provided by proprietors themselves and they have paid for their entries to appear.

All establishments in this guide have been inspected or have applied for inspection under the national rating scheme.

The English Tourist Board cannot guarantee the accuracy of the information in this guide and accepts no responsibility for any error or misrepresentation. All liability for loss, disappointment, negligence or other damage caused by reliance on the information contained in this guide, or in the event of bankruptcy or liquidation or cessation of trade of any company, individual or firm mentioned, is hereby

excluded. Prices and other details should always be carefully checked at the time of booking.

We naturally hope that you will not have any cause for complaint but problems do occur from time to time. If you are dissatisfied, make your complaint to the management at the time of the incident. This gives the management an opportunity to take action at once to investigate and to put things right without delay. The longer a complaint is left the more difficult it is to deal with effectively.

In certain circumstances the English Tourist Board may look into complaints. However, the Board has no statutory control over establishments or their methods of operation and cannot become involved in legal or contractual matters.

We find it very helpful to receive comments about establishments in 'Where to Stay' and suggestions on how to improve the guide. We would like to hear from you. Our address is on page 16.

NOBODY'S PERFECT..

BUT WE TRY

# ABOUT THE GUIDE ENTRIES

## Locations

Establishments are listed in this guide under the name of the place where they are situated or, in the case of isolated spots in the countryside, under the nearest village or town. Place names are listed alphabetically within each regional section together with the county name.

Map references are given against each place name. These refer to the colour location maps at the back of the guide. The first figure is the map number; the letter and figure which follow indicate the grid reference on the map. Some entries were included just before the guide went to press and therefore may not appear on the maps.

## Addresses

County names are not normally repeated in the entries for each establishment but you should ensure that you use the full postal address and postcode when writing.

## Telephone Numbers

The telephone number, exchange name (where this differs from the name of the town under which the establishment is listed) and the area code (in brackets) are given immediately below the establishment address in the listings pages of this guide.

All telephone numbers in the editorial and listings pages include the new PhONEday area codes. Please use the new codes when dialling.

## Prices

The prices appearing in this publication will serve as a general guide, but we strongly advise you to check them at the time of booking. This information was supplied to us by proprietors in the summer of 1994 and changes may have occurred since the guide went to press.

Prices are shown in pounds sterling and include Value Added Tax if applicable.

Some, but not all, establishments include a service charge in their standard tariff so this should also be checked at the time of booking. There are many different ways of quoting prices for accommodation and in order to make this as clear as possible and provide a basis for comparison we have adopted a standardised approach.

For example, we show:

1. **Bed and breakfast.** Prices for overnight accommodation with breakfast – single room and double room.

The double room price is for two people. If a double room is occupied by one person there is normally a reduction in the quoted tariff, but some establishments may charge the full rate.

2. **Half board.** Prices for room, breakfast and evening meal, per person per day and per person per week.

Some establishments provide a continental breakfast only in the quoted tariff and may make an extra charge for full English breakfast.

There is a statutory requirement for establishments which have at least four bedrooms, or eight beds, to display overnight accommodation charges in the reception area or at the entrance. This is to ensure that prospective guests can obtain adequate information about prices before taking up accommodation. When you arrive it is in your own interests to check prices and what they include.

A reduced price is often quoted for children, especially when sharing a room with their parents. Some establishments, however, charge the full price when a child occupies a room which might otherwise have been let at the full rate to an adult.

The upper age limit for reductions for children may vary according to the establishment and should therefore be checked at the time of booking.

Prices often vary according to the time of year and may be substantially lower outside the peak holiday weeks. Many hotels and other establishments offer special 'package' rates (for example, fully inclusive weekend rates) particularly in the autumn, winter and spring.

Further details of bargain packages can be obtained from the establishments themselves, from England's Regional Tourist Boards or from local Tourist Information Centres. Your local travel agent may also have information about these packages and can help you make bookings.

## Bathrooms

Each accommodation entry shows the number of private bathrooms available, the number of public bathrooms and the number of private showers.

The term 'private bathroom' means a bath and/or shower plus a WC en-suite with the bedroom or a bathroom with bath and/or shower plus a WC solely for the occupant(s) of one bedroom; 'private shower' means a shower en-suite with the bedroom but no WC.

Public bathrooms are normally equipped with a bath and sometimes also a shower attachment. Some establishments, however, have showers only. If the availability of a bath is an important factor, this should be checked before booking.

## Meals

Where an establishment serves evening meals, the starting time and last orders time are shown in the entry. At some smaller establishments you may be asked at breakfast time or midday whether you will require a meal that evening. So, the last orders time for an evening meal could be, say, 0900 or 1330.

Although the accommodation prices shown in each entry are for bed and breakfast and/or half board, many establishments also offer luncheon facilities and this is indicated by the words 'Lunch available'.

## Opening Periods

Except where an opening period is shown (e.g. Open March–October), the establishment should be open throughout the year.

## Symbols

Information about many of the services and facilities available at establishments is given at the end of each entry in the form of symbols.

The key to these symbols can be found inside the back cover flap. You may find it helpful to fold out the flap when referring to the entries.

## Alcoholic Drinks

Alcoholic drinks are available at all types of accommodation listed in this guide unless the symbol ⓊⓁ appears. However, the licence to serve drinks may be restricted, for example to diners only, so you may wish to check this when enquiring about accommodation.

## Smoking

Many establishments offer facilities for non-smokers, ranging from no- smoking bedrooms and lounges to a no-smoking area of the restaurant/dining room. Some establishments prefer not to accommodate smokers and in such cases the establishment description makes this clear.

## Pets

Many establishments will accept guests with pets but we advise you to confirm this at the time of booking when you should also enquire about any extra charges and any restrictions on movement within the establishment. Some establishments will not accept dogs in any circumstances and these are marked with the symbol 🐾.

Visitors from overseas should not bring pets of any kind into Britain unless they are prepared for the animals to go into lengthy quarantine. Owing to the continuing threat of rabies, penalties for ignoring the regulations are extremely severe.

## Credit/Charge Cards

Indicated immediately above the line of symbols at the end of each accommodation entry are credit/charge cards that are accepted by the establishment. However, you are advised to confirm this at the time you make a booking if you intend to pay by this method. The abbreviations are:

**Access** – Access/ Eurocard/ Mastercard
**Visa** – Visa/Barclaycard
**Diners** – Diners
**Amex** – American Express
**Switch/Delta** – Direct debit card

Where payment for the accommodation is made by credit card, proprietors may charge a higher rate than for payment by cash or cheque. The difference is to cover the percentage paid by the proprietor to the credit card company.

Not all proprietors make this additional charge but if you intend to pay by credit card, it is worth asking whether it would be cheaper to pay by cash or cheque.

When making a booking by telephone you may be asked to give your credit card number as 'confirmation'. **You should note that the proprietor may charge your credit card account if you cancel the booking.** If this is the policy, it must be made clear to you at the time you make the booking.

## Conferences and Groups

Establishments which can cater for conferences and meetings have been marked with the symbol ☎ (numbers following show capacity). Rates are often negotiable and the price may be affected by a number of factors such as the time of year, number of people and any special requirements stipulated by the organiser.

# THE ENGLAND FOR EXCELLENCE AWARDS 1993 WINNERS

The England for Excellence Awards were created by the English Tourist Board to recognise and reward the highest standards of excellence and quality in all major sectors of tourism in England. The coveted Leo statuette, presented each year to winners, has become firmly established as the ultimate accolade in the English tourism industry.

Over the past six years, the Leo has been won by all types and sizes of business with one common attribute – excellence in the facilities and services they offer.

Thames Tower
Black's Road
London W6 9EL

English Tourist Board

Hotel of the Year sponsored by Yellow Pages
SWALLOW HOTEL, BIRMINGHAM

Holiday Destination of the Year sponsored by Marks & Spencer
NOTTINGHAM CITY & NOTTINGHAMSHIRE COUNTY COUNCILS – THE ENGLISH CIVIL WAR 350TH COMMEMORATION

Caravan Holiday Park of the Year sponsored by the National Caravan Council
NEW FOREST COUNTRY HOLIDAYS

Bed and Breakfast of the Year sponsored by Le Shuttle
HALFWAY HOUSE, CRAYKE

Tourism and the Environment Award sponsored by Center Parcs
'ECO-HULL' – BRITISH WATERWAYS & ALVECHURCH BOAT CENTRES

Tourist Information Centre of the Year sponsored by National Express
PICKERING TOURIST INFORMATION CENTRE

Visitor Attraction of the Year sponsored by Embassy Leisure Breaks by Jarvis
EUREKA! THE MUSEUM FOR CHILDREN, HALIFAX

Self-Catering Holiday of the Year sponsored by the Country Holidays Group
LONGLANDS AT CARTMEL

Tourism for All Award sponsored by Blackpool Pleasure Beach
PLYMOUTH DOME

Tourism Training Award sponsored by Poole Pottery
WHITE ROSE LINE, YORK

Travel and Tourism Industry Award sponsored by Sea Containers Ferries
HAVENWARNER

Outstanding Contribution to English Tourism Award sponsored by Hilton UK
SIR BOB SCOTT

# WHAT'S ON IN ENGLAND 1995

*This is a selection of the many cultural, sporting and other events that will be taking place in England during 1995. Dates marked with an asterisk (✳) were provisional at the time of going to press. For details of local events please enquire at the local Tourist Information Centre.*

## JANUARY

**4–29 January**
**Holiday on Ice 1995 – Magic and Illusions**
Brighton Centre, Kings Road, Brighton, East Sussex

**5–15 January**
**London International Boat Show**
Earl's Court Exhibition Centre, Warwick Road, London SW5

**6–8 January**
**Whittlesey Straw Bear Festival**
Various venues, Whittlesey, Cambridgeshire

**25 January ✳**
**Endellion String Quartet Residency 1994–1995**
West Road Concert Hall, 11 West Road, Cambridge, Cambridgeshire

## FEBRUARY

**5–10 February**
**Wordsworth Winter School**
Dove Cottage, Grasmere, Cumbria

**18–19 February**
**Primrose Festival**
By Pass Nurseries, Dobbies Lane, Marks Tey, Essex

**25 February–4 March**
**Bedfordshire Competitive Music Festival**
Corn Exchange, Civic Theatre and Howard Room, St Paul's Square, Bedford, Bedfordshire

## MARCH

**3–5 March**
**Clacton Traditional Ale and Traditional Jazz Weekend**
West Cliff Theatre, Tower Road, Clacton-on-Sea, Essex

**6–10 March**
**Dover Film Festival**
Town Hall, High Street, Dover, Kent

**8–12 March**
**Ilkley Literature Festival**
Various venues, Ilkley, West Yorkshire

**14–16 March**
**Horseracing: Cheltenham Gold Cup Meeting**
Cheltenham Racecourse, Prestbury, Cheltenham, Gloucestershire

**16 March–9 April**
**Daily Mail Ideal Home Exhibition**
Earl's Court Exhibition Centre, Warwick Road, London SW5

## APRIL

**1 April**
**Rowing: Oxford v Cambridge University Boat Race**
Putney to Mortlake, River Thames, London

**1–2 April**
**Thriplow Daffodil Weekend**
Various venues, Thriplow, Cambridgeshire

**6, 7, 8 April ✳**
**Horseracing: Grand National Meeting**
Aintree Racecourse, Liverpool, Merseyside

*4–9 April*
**British International Antiques Fair**
National Exhibition Centre, Birmingham, West Midlands

*12–19 April*
**Harrogate International Youth Music Festival**
Various venues, Harrogate, North Yorkshire

*14–17 April*
**Lancaster Easter Maritime Festival**
Various venues, Lancaster, Lancashire

*16 April* ❋
**Easter Show**
Battersea Park, London SW11

*16–17 April*
**Alford Oyez '95**
Alford Market Place, Alford, Lincolnshire

*23–26 April*
**Harrogate Spring Flower Festival**
Valley Gardens, Harrogate, North Yorkshire

## MAY

*1–8 May* ❋
**Rochester Sweeps Festival**
Various venues, Rochester, Kent

*4–7 May*
**Badminton Horse Trials**
Badminton, Avon

*5–6 May*
**Nottingham County Show**
Newark and Nottinghamshire Showground, Winthorpe, Newark, Nottinghamshire

*5–28 May*
**Brighton International Festival**
Various venues, Brighton, East Sussex

*6 May*
**Helston Furry Dance**
Helston, Cornwall

*6–8 May*
**Spalding Flower Parade and Festival**
Various venues, Spalding, Lincolnshire

*10–14 May* ❋
**Royal Windsor Horse Show**
Home Park, Windsor, Berkshire

*11–14 May*
**Beverley Early Music Festival**
Various venues, Beverley, Humberside

*11–14 May*
**Living Crafts at Hatfield House**
Hatfield House, Hatfield, Hertfordshire

*13–27 May*
**Salisbury Festival**
Various venues, Salisbury, Wiltshire

*13–28 May*
**Bournemouth International Festival**
Various venues, Bournemouth, Dorset

*18–20 May*
**Devon County Show**
Westpoint, Clyst St Mary, Exeter, Devon

*19–21 May*
**Chorley Canal Festival**
Various venues, Chorley, Lancashire

*19–21 May*
**Keswick Jazz Festival**
Keswick, Cumbria

*19 May–4 June*
**Bath International Festival**
Various venues, Bath, Avon

*23–26 May*
**Chelsea Flower Show** (members only on 23–24 May)
Royal Hospital, Royal Hospital Road, Chelsea, London SW3

*26 May–2 June*
**British Open Ballroom and Latin American Dance Championships**
Winter Gardens, Church Street, Blackpool, Lancashire

*26 May–4 June*
**Coniston Water Festival**
Coniston Sailing Club, Coniston Old Hall, Coniston, Cumbria

*27–28 May*
**Air Fete '95**
RAF Mildenhall, Bury St Edmunds, Suffolk

*27–29 May*
**Centenary Spring Craft Fair**
Shugborough, Milford, Staffordshire

*27 May–4 June*
**Saddleworth Festival**
Various venues, Saddleworth, Greater Manchester

*28–29 May*
**North Shields Fishquay Festival**
North Shields, Tyne and Wear

*29 May*
**Northumberland County Show**
Tynedale Park Rugby Ground, Corbridge, Northumberland

# JUNE

*8–14 June*
**Appleby Horse Fair**
Appleby, Cumbria

*11–26 June*
**Whitby Festival**
Various venues, Whitby, North Yorkshire

*8–10 June*
**South of England Agricultural Show**
Ardingly Showground, Haywards Heath, West Sussex

*9–11 June*
**Horseracing: The Derby (9th); Coronation Cup (10th); Oaks Stakes (11th)**
Epsom Racecourse, Epsom, Surrey

*9–11 June*
**Wimborne Folk Festival**
Wimborne Minster, Dorset

*9–25 June*
**Aldeburgh Festival of Music and the Arts**
Various venues, Aldeburgh, Suffolk

*10–11 June*
**Durham Regatta**
River Wear, Durham, Durham

*11 June*
**Centenary Victorian Street Market**
Shugborough, Milford, Staffordshire

*13–16 June* ✶
**Horseracing: Royal Ascot**
Ascot Racecourse, Ascot, Berkshire

*16 June–8 July*
**Bradford Festival**
Various venues, Bradford, West Yorkshire

*17 June*
**Trooping the Colour – The Queen's Official Birthday Parade**
Horse Guards Parade, Whitehall, London SW1

*19–25 June*
**Tennis: Eastbourne International Ladies Tennis Championship**
Devonshire Park, College Road, Eastbourne, East Sussex

*20–25 June*
**International Music Festival**
Various venues, Leicester, Leicestershire

*21–22 June*
**Lincolnshire Show**
Lincolnshire Showground, Grange-de-Lings, Lincoln, Lincolnshire

*24 June–9 July*
**Ludlow Festival**
Various venues, Ludlow, Shropshire

*25 June–1 July*
**Alnwick Fair**
Various venues, Alnwick, Northumberland

*26 June–9 July* ✶
**Lawn Tennis Championships**
All England Lawn Tennis and Croquet Club, Wimbledon, London SW19

*28 June–2 July*
**Henley Royal Regatta**
Henley-on-Thames, Oxfordshire

*30 June–16 July*
**Exeter Festival**
Various venues, Exeter, Devon

# JULY

*July* ✶
**Barbon Sprint Hill Climb**
Barbon Manor, Barbon, Kirkby Lonsdale, Cumbria

*July* ✶
**Keswick Sports**
Fitz Park, Keswick, Cumbria

*1–2 July* ✶
**Kite Festival**
Northern Playing Fields, Washington, Tyne and Wear

*1–16 July*
**Cheltenham International Festival of Music**
Various venues, Cheltenham, Gloucestershire

1–31 July
**Hull Festival**
Various venues, Hull, Humberside

1 July–31 October
**Ellesmere Port Bicentenary Festival**
Various venues, Ellesmere Port and Neston, Cheshire

2–18 July
**Chichester Festivities**
Various venues, Chichester, West Sussex

3–6 July
**Royal International Agricultural Show**
National Agricultural Centre, Stoneleigh Park, Kenilworth, Warwickshire

5–8 July
**Henley Festival of Music and the Arts**
Various venues, Henley-on-Thames, Oxfordshire

7–9 July ✳
**Ely Folk Weekend**
Cresswells Lane Site, Ely, Cambridgeshire

7–9 July ✳
**Grimsby International Jazz Festival**
King George V Stadium, Weelsby Road, Grimsby, Humberside

7–9 July ✳
**Motor Racing: British Grand Prix**
Silverstone Circuit, Towcester, Northamptonshire

7–16 July
**Lichfield Festival**
Various venues, Lichfield, Staffordshire

7–16 July
**York Early Music Festival**
Various venues, York, North Yorkshire

8–16 July
**Wigan International Jazz Festival**
Various venues, Wigan, Lancashire

11–13 July
**Great Yorkshire Show**
Great Yorkshire Showground, Wetherby Road, Harrogate, North Yorkshire

12–15 July
**Claremont Landscape Garden Fete Champetre**
Claremont Landscape Garden, Old Portsmouth Road, Esher, Surrey

15–29 July
**King's Lynn Festival**
Various venues, King's Lynn, Norfolk

16 July
**Tolpuddle Martyrs Rally**
Tolpuddle, Dorset

21–29 July
**Chester Summer Music Festival**
Various venues, Chester, Cheshire

21 July–16 September
**Henry Wood Promenade Concerts – Centenary Series**
Royal Albert Hall, Kensington Gore, London SW7

22 July
**Cleveland County Show**
Stewart Park, Middlesbrough, Cleveland

29 July–5 August
**Sailing: Cowes Week**
Cowes, Isle of Wight

29 July–12 August
**Lake District Summer Music**
Charlotte Mason College, Rydal Road, Ambleside, Cumbria

# AUGUST

2–3 August
**Bakewell Show**
The Showground, Coombs Road, Bakewell, Derbyshire

4–6 August
**Portsmouth and Southsea Show**
Southsea Common, Southsea, Hampshire

4–11 August
**Sidmouth International Festival of Folk Arts**
Various venues, Sidmouth, Devon

5–6 August ✳
**Sunderland International Air Show**
Seaburn and Roker, Coast Road, Sunderland, Tyne and Wear

6–13 August
**Saltburn Victorian Festival**
Various venues, Saltburn-by-the-Sea, Cleveland

11–12 August
**Shrewsbury Flower Show**
Quarry Park, Shrewsbury, Shropshire

12–19 August
**Billingham International Folklore Festival**
Various venues, Billingham, Cleveland

18–25 August
**Broadstairs Folk Week**
Various venues, Broadstairs, Kent

19–26 August
**Castle Park Festival**
Castle Park, Leicester, Leicestershire

*19–26 August*
**Three Choirs Festival**
Gloucester Cathedral,
Gloucester, Gloucestershire

*24–26 August*
**Port of Dartmouth Royal
Regatta**
Dartmouth, Devon

*25–29 August*
**Beatles Festival**
Various venues, Liverpool,
Merseyside

*25 August–3 September* ✳
**Bolton Festival 1995**
Central Library, Le Mans
Crescent, Bolton, Lancashire

*26 August–2 September*
**Bude Jazz Festival**
Various venues, Bude, Cornwall

*27–28 August*
**Notting Hill Carnival**
Ladbroke Grove, London W11

*31 August–3 September*
**Burghley Remy Martin Horse
Trials**
Burghley House, Stamford,
Lincolnshire

## SEPTEMBER

*September* ✳
**375th Anniversary of the
Sailing of the Mayflower**
Various venues, Plymouth, Devon

*1 September–5 November* ✳
**Blackpool Illuminations**
The Promenade, Blackpool,
Lancashire

*2–4 September*
**Wolsingham and Wear Valley
Agricultural Show**
Scotch Isle Farm, Wolsingham,
Durham

*8–10 September* ✳
**Swanage Folk Festival**
Various venues, Swanage,
Dorset

*9–11 September*
**Stanhope Agricultural Show**
Unthank Park, Stanhope, Durham

*12 September*
**Widecombe Fair**
Old Field, Widecombe-in-the-
Moor, Newton Abbot, Devon

*14–17 September*
**Blenheim International Horse Trials**
Blenheim Palace, Woodstock,
Oxfordshire

*16 September*
**Egremont Crab Fair**
Baybarrow, Egremont, Cumbria

*16–17 September*
**Newbury and Royal County of
Berkshire Show**
Newbury Showground,
Chieveley, Newbury, Berkshire

*16–24 September*
**Southampton International
Boat Show**
Mayflower Park, Southampton,
Hampshire

**22–24 September**
*Balloon Fiesta*
Attingham Hall, Attingham Park,
Shrewsbury, Shropshire

**26 September–1 October**
*Showjumping: Horse of the
Year Show*
Wembley Arena, Empire Way,
Wembley, Middlesex

**30 September**
*Eskdale Show*
Brotherilkeld Farm, Boot,
Holmrook, Cumbria

## OCTOBER

**October** ✳
*Leeds International Film
Festival*
Various venues, Leeds, West
Yorkshire

**5–7 October**
*Nottingham Goose Fair*
Forest Recreation Ground,
Nottingham, Nottinghamshire

**5–15 October**
*Norfolk and Norwich Festival*
Various venues, Norwich,
Norfolk

**7–21 October**
*Canterbury Festival*
Various venues, Canterbury,
Kent

**8 October**
*World Conker Championship*
Village Green, Ashton, Oundle,
Northamptonshire

**23–26 October**
*Blackpool Sequence Dance
Festival*
Winter Gardens, Church Street,
Blackpool, Lancashire

## NOVEMBER

**3–19 November**
*Kendal Festival of Jazz and
Blues*
Brewery Arts Centre, Highgate,
Kendal, Cumbria

**11 November**
*Lord Mayor's Procession and
Show*
The City, London

**16 November**
*Biggest Liar in the World*
Bridge Inn, Wasdale, Santon
Bridge, Holmrook, Cumbria

**16–26 November**
*Huddersfield Contemporary
Music Festival*
Various venues, Huddersfield,
West Yorkshire

**27 November–10 December**
*Bonnie Prince Charlie 250th
Anniversary*
City Centre, Derby, Derbyshire

## DECEMBER

**December** ✳
*Lincoln Christmas Market*
Lincoln, Lincolnshire

**2–3 December**
*Dickensian Christmas*
Various venues, Rochester,
Kent

**14–18 December**
*Olympia International
Showjumping Championships*
Olympia, Hammersmith Road,
London W14

**31 December**
*Allendale Baal Festival*
Market Square, Allendale,
Northumberland

# USE YOUR *i*'s

There are more than 550 Tourist Information
Centres throughout England offering friendly help
with accommodation and holiday ideas as well as
suggestions of places to visit and things to do.
In your home town there may be a centre which
can help you before you set out. You'll find the
address of your nearest Tourist Information
Centre in your local Phone Book.

# ACCOMMODATION COUPONS

---

▶ Complete this coupon and mail it direct to the establishment in which you are interested. Do not send it to the English Tourist Board. Remember to enclose a stamped addressed envelope (or international reply coupon).

▶ Tick as appropriate and complete the reverse side if you are interested in making a booking.

❑ Please send me a brochure or further information, and details of prices charged.
❑ Please advise me, as soon as possible, if accommodation is available as detailed overleaf.

Name: _____ (BLOCK CAPITALS)

Address: _____

_____

_____

Postcode: _____

Telephone number: _____ Date: _____

### Where to Stay 1995
**Bed & Breakfast, Farmhouses, Inns & Hostels**

English Tourist Board

---

▶ Complete this coupon and mail it direct to the establishment in which you are interested. Do not send it to the English Tourist Board. Remember to enclose a stamped addressed envelope (or international reply coupon).

▶ Tick as appropriate and complete the reverse side if you are interested in making a booking.

❑ Please send me a brochure or further information, and details of prices charged.
❑ Please advise me, as soon as possible, if accommodation is available as detailed overleaf.

Name: _____ (BLOCK CAPITALS)

Address: _____

_____

_____

Postcode: _____

Telephone number: _____ Date: _____

### Where to Stay 1995
**Bed & Breakfast, Farmhouses, Inns & Hostels**

English Tourist Board

# ACCOMMODATION COUPONS

▶ Complete this side if you are interested in making a booking.

▶ Please read the information on pages 405–409 before confirming any booking.

Please advise me if accommodation is available as detailed below.

From (date of arrival):                  To (date of departure):

or alternatively from:                   To:

Adults          Children          (ages                                    )
Please give the number of people and ages of children

Accommodation required:

Meals required:

Other/special requirements:

▶ Please enclose a stamped addressed envelope (or international reply coupon).

---

▶ Complete this side if you are interested in making a booking.

▶ Please read the information on pages 405–409 before confirming any booking.

Please advise me if accommodation is available as detailed below.

From (date of arrival):                  To (date of departure):

or alternatively from:                   To:

Adults          Children          (ages                                    )
Please give the number of people and ages of children

Accommodation required:

Meals required:

Other/special requirements:

▶ Please enclose a stamped addressed envelope (or international reply coupon).

# ACCOMMODATION COUPONS

▶ Complete this coupon and mail it direct to the establishment in which you are interested. Do not send it to the English Tourist Board. Remember to enclose a stamped addressed envelope (or international reply coupon).

▶ Tick as appropriate and complete the reverse side if you are interested in making a booking.

❏ Please send me a brochure or further information, and details of prices charged.
❏ Please advise me, as soon as possible, if accommodation is available as detailed overleaf.

Name:                                                   (BLOCK CAPITALS)

Address:

                                         Postcode:

Telephone number:                        Date:

## Where to Stay 1995
### Bed & Breakfast, Farmhouses, Inns & Hostels

English Tourist Board

---

▶ Complete this coupon and mail it direct to the establishment in which you are interested. Do not send it to the English Tourist Board. Remember to enclose a stamped addressed envelope (or international reply coupon).

▶ Tick as appropriate and complete the reverse side if you are interested in making a booking.

❏ Please send me a brochure or further information, and details of prices charged.
❏ Please advise me, as soon as possible, if accommodation is available as detailed overleaf.

Name:                                                   (BLOCK CAPITALS)

Address:

                                         Postcode:

Telephone number:                        Date:

## Where to Stay 1995
### Bed & Breakfast, Farmhouses, Inns & Hostels

English Tourist Board

# ACCOMMODATION COUPONS

▶ Complete this side if you are interested in making a booking.

▶ Please read the information on pages 405–409 before confirming any booking.

Please advise me if accommodation is available as detailed below.

From (date of arrival): _____ To (date of departure): _____

or alternatively from: _____ To: _____

Adults _____ Children _____ (ages _____ )

Please give the number of people and ages of children

Accommodation required: _____

_____

Meals required: _____

Other/special requirements: _____

▶ Please enclose a stamped addressed envelope (or international reply coupon).

▶ Complete this side if you are interested in making a booking.

▶ Please read the information on pages 405–409 before confirming any booking.

Please advise me if accommodation is available as detailed below.

From (date of arrival): _____ To (date of departure): _____

or alternatively from: _____ To: _____

Adults _____ Children _____ (ages _____ )

Please give the number of people and ages of children

Accommodation required: _____

_____

Meals required: _____

Other/special requirements: _____

▶ Please enclose a stamped addressed envelope (or international reply coupon).

# Accommodation Coupons

▶ Complete this coupon and mail it direct to the establishment in which you are interested. Do not send it to the English Tourist Board. Remember to enclose a stamped addressed envelope (or international reply coupon).

▶ Tick as appropriate and complete the reverse side if you are interested in making a booking.

❏ Please send me a brochure or further information, and details of prices charged.
❏ Please advise me, as soon as possible, if accommodation is available as detailed overleaf.

Name: _____ (BLOCK CAPITALS)

Address: _____

_____

_____ Postcode: _____

Telephone number: _____ Date: _____

## *Where to Stay 1995*
**Bed & Breakfast, Farmhouses, Inns & Hostels**

English Tourist Board

---

▶ Complete this coupon and mail it direct to the establishment in which you are interested. Do not send it to the English Tourist Board. Remember to enclose a stamped addressed envelope (or international reply coupon).

▶ Tick as appropriate and complete the reverse side if you are interested in making a booking.

❏ Please send me a brochure or further information, and details of prices charged.
❏ Please advise me, as soon as possible, if accommodation is available as detailed overleaf.

Name: _____ (BLOCK CAPITALS)

Address: _____

_____

_____ Postcode: _____

Telephone number: _____ Date: _____

## *Where to Stay 1995*
**Bed & Breakfast, Farmhouses, Inns & Hostels**

English Tourist Board

# ACCOMMODATION COUPONS

▶ Complete this side if you are interested in making a booking.

▶ Please read the information on pages 405–409 before confirming any booking.

Please advise me if accommodation is available as detailed below.

From (date of arrival): _____ To (date of departure): _____

or alternatively from: _____ To: _____

Adults _____ Children _____ (ages _____ )

Please give the number of people and ages of children

Accommodation required: _____

_____

Meals required: _____

Other/special requirements: _____

▶ Please enclose a stamped addressed envelope (or international reply coupon).

▶ Complete this side if you are interested in making a booking.

▶ Please read the information on pages 405–409 before confirming any booking.

Please advise me if accommodation is available as detailed below.

From (date of arrival): _____ To (date of departure): _____

or alternatively from: _____ To: _____

Adults _____ Children _____ (ages _____ )

Please give the number of people and ages of children

Accommodation required: _____

_____

Meals required: _____

Other/special requirements: _____

▶ Please enclose a stamped addressed envelope (or international reply coupon).

# Advertisement Coupons

▶ *Complete this coupon and mail it direct to the advertiser from whom you would like to receive further information. Do not send it to the English Tourist Board.*

To (advertiser's name): _____

*Please send me a brochure or further information on the following, as advertised by you in the English Tourist Board's* Where to Stay 1995 *Guide:*

_____

_____

*My name and address are on the reverse.*

---

▶ *Complete this coupon and mail it direct to the advertiser from whom you would like to receive further information. Do not send it to the English Tourist Board.*

To (advertiser's name): _____

*Please send me a brochure or further information on the following, as advertised by you in the English Tourist Board's* Where to Stay 1995 *Guide:*

_____

_____

*My name and address are on the reverse.*

---

▶ *Complete this coupon and mail it direct to the advertiser from whom you would like to receive further information. Do not send it to the English Tourist Board.*

To (advertiser's name): _____

*Please send me a brochure or further information on the following, as advertised by you in the English Tourist Board's* Where to Stay 1995 *Guide:*

_____

_____

*My name and address are on the reverse.*

# ADVERTISEMENT COUPONS

Name: _____ (BLOCK CAPITALS)

Address: _____

_____

Postcode: _____

Telephone number: _____ Date: _____

*Where to Stay 1995*
**Bed & Breakfast, Farmhouses, Inns & Hostels**

English Tourist Board

---

Name: _____ (BLOCK CAPITALS)

Address: _____

_____

Postcode: _____

Telephone number: _____ Date: _____

*Where to Stay 1995*
**Bed & Breakfast, Farmhouses, Inns & Hostels**

English Tourist Board

---

Name: _____ (BLOCK CAPITALS)

Address: _____

_____

Postcode: _____

Telephone number: _____ Date: _____

*Where to Stay 1995*
**Bed & Breakfast, Farmhouses, Inns & Hostels**

English Tourist Board

# TOWN INDEX

The following cities, towns and villages all have accommodation listed in this guide. If the place where you wish to stay is not shown, the location maps (starting on page 433) will help you to find somewhere suitable in the same area.

## A      page no

| | |
|---|---|
| Abbotsbury *Dorset* | 257 |
| Abingdon *Oxfordshire* | 318 |
| Abthorpe *Northamptonshire* | 196 |
| Alcester *Warwickshire* | 136 |
| Aldeburgh *Suffolk* | 220 |
| Alderley Edge *Cheshire* | 88 |
| Aldham *Essex* | 220 |
| Aldington *Kent* | 354 |
| Aldwark *Derbyshire* | 196 |
| Alford *Lincolnshire* | 196 |
| Alkham *Kent* | 354 |
| Alkmonton *Derbyshire* | 196 |
| Allendale *Northumberland* | 66 |
| Allerford *Somerset* | 257 |
| Alnmouth *Northumberland* | 66 |
| Alnwick *Northumberland* | 66 |
| Alston *Cumbria* | 40 |
| Alton *Hampshire* | 318 |
| Alton *Staffordshire* | 136 |
| Altrincham *Greater Manchester* | 88 |
| Ambergate *Derbyshire* | 196 |
| Amble-by-the-Sea *Northumberland* | 67 |
| Ambleside *Cumbria* | 40 |
| Amersham *Buckinghamshire* | 318 |
| Amesbury *Wiltshire* | 257 |
| Ampleforth *North Yorkshire* | 104 |
| Ampney Crucis *Gloucestershire* | 137 |
| Amport *Hampshire* | 318 |
| Ampthill *Bedfordshire* | 220 |
| Ancaster *Lincolnshire* | 197 |
| Andover *Hampshire* | 319 |
| Appleby-in-Westmorland *Cumbria* | 42 |
| Appledore *Kent* | 354 |
| Ardingly *West Sussex* | 354 |
| Arnside *Cumbria* | 43 |
| Arundel *West Sussex* | 355 |
| Ascot *Berkshire* | 319 |
| Ashbourne *Derbyshire* | 197 |
| Ashbrittle *Somerset* | 258 |
| Ashburton *Devon* | 258 |
| Ashford *Kent* | 355 |
| Ashford in the Water *Derbyshire* | 198 |
| Ashover *Derbyshire* | 198 |
| Ashton Keynes *Wiltshire* | 258 |
| Askrigg *North Yorkshire* | 104 |
| Avebury *Wiltshire* | 258 |
| Avon Dassett *Warwickshire* | 137 |
| Aylesbury *Buckinghamshire* | 319 |
| Aylesford *Kent* | 356 |
| Aylsham *Norfolk* | 221 |
| Aysgarth *North Yorkshire* | 105 |

## B      page no

| | |
|---|---|
| Babraham *Cambridgeshire* | 221 |
| Bacton *Suffolk* | 221 |
| Bainbridge *North Yorkshire* | 105 |
| Bakewell *Derbyshire* | 198 |
| Balsall Common *West Midlands* | 138 |
| Bamburgh *Northumberland* | 67 |

| | |
|---|---|
| Bamford *Derbyshire* | 198 |
| Bampton *Oxfordshire* | 320 |
| Banbury *Oxfordshire* | 320 |
| Bantham *Devon* | 259 |
| Bardon Mill *Northumberland* | 67 |
| Barlaston *Staffordshire* | 138 |
| Barnard Castle *Durham* | 67 |
| Barnham *Suffolk* | 221 |
| Barnstaple *Devon* | 259 |
| Barton on Sea *Hampshire* | 320 |
| Bath *Avon* | 259 |
| Battle *East Sussex* | 356 |
| Beadnell *Northumberland* | 68 |
| Beaminster *Dorset* | 263 |
| Beaulieu *Hampshire* | 320 |
| Beccles *Suffolk* | 222 |
| Beckington *Somerset* | 263 |
| Bedford *Bedfordshire* | 222 |
| Beetley *Norfolk* | 222 |
| Bellingham *Northumberland* | 68 |
| Belper *Derbyshire* | 199 |
| Berkeley *Gloucestershire* | 138 |
| Berrynarbor *Devon* | 263 |
| Berwick-upon-Tweed *Northumberland* | 69 |
| Beverley *Humberside* | 105 |
| Bewdley *Hereford and Worcester* | 138 |
| Beyton *Suffolk* | 222 |
| Bibury *Gloucestershire* | 138 |
| Bicester *Oxfordshire* | 321 |
| Biddenden *Kent* | 356 |
| Bideford *Devon* | 263 |
| Bidford-on-Avon *Warwickshire* | 139 |
| Bingley *West Yorkshire* | 106 |
| Birchington *Kent* | 357 |
| Birdlip *Gloucestershire* | 139 |
| Birkenhead *Merseyside* | 88 |
| Birmingham *West Midlands* | 139 |
| Birmingham Airport *West Midlands* (See under Balsall Common, Coleshill, Coventry, Hampton in Arden, Meriden, Solihull) | |
| Bishop Auckland *Durham* | 70 |
| Bishop Thornton *North Yorkshire* | 106 |
| Bishop's Castle *Shropshire* | 139 |
| Bishop's Lydeard *Somerset* | 263 |
| Bishop's Stortford *Hertfordshire* | 222 |
| Blackburn *Lancashire* | 89 |
| Blackpool *Lancashire* | 89 |
| Blagdon *Avon* | 263 |
| Blakeney *Gloucestershire* | 140 |
| Blakeney *Norfolk* | 222 |
| Blandford Forum *Dorset* | 321 |
| Bledington *Gloucestershire* | 140 |
| Bletchingdon *Oxfordshire* | 321 |
| Blockley *Gloucestershire* | 140 |
| Blythburgh *Suffolk* | 223 |
| Bodenham *Hereford and Worcester* | 140 |
| Bodmin *Cornwall* | 264 |
| Bolton *Greater Manchester* | 89 |
| Bolton-le-Sands *Lancashire* | 89 |

| | |
|---|---|
| Boroughbridge *North Yorkshire* | 106 |
| Borrowdale *Cumbria* | 43 |
| Boscastle *Cornwall* | 264 |
| Boston *Lincolnshire* | 199 |
| Bournemouth *Dorset* | 321 |
| Bourton-on-the-Water *Gloucestershire* | 140 |
| Bovey Tracey *Devon* | 264 |
| Bowes *Durham* | 70 |
| Bowness-on-Solway *Cumbria* | 43 |
| Box *Wiltshire* | 264 |
| Brackley *Northamptonshire* | 199 |
| Bracknell *Berkshire* | 323 |
| Bradford *West Yorkshire* | 106 |
| Bradford-on-Avon *Wiltshire* | 265 |
| Bradwell *Derbyshire* | 199 |
| Brailes *Warwickshire* | 142 |
| Braintree *Essex* | 223 |
| Braithwaite *Cumbria* | 43 |
| Bramdean *Hampshire* | 323 |
| Bramerton *Norfolk* | 223 |
| Brampton *Cumbria* | 43 |
| Bransgore *Hampshire* | 323 |
| Brede *East Sussex* | 357 |
| Bredenbury *Hereford and Worcester* | 142 |
| Bredon's Norton *Hereford and Worcester* | 142 |
| Brendon *Devon* | 265 |
| Bretforton *Hereford and Worcester* | 142 |
| Brewood *Staffordshire* | 142 |
| Bridestowe *Devon* | 265 |
| Bridgnorth *Shropshire* | 142 |
| Bridgwater *Somerset* | 265 |
| Bridport *Dorset* | 266 |
| Brigg *Humberside* | 106 |
| Brighton & Hove *East Sussex* | 357 |
| Brimpton *Berkshire* | 323 |
| Bristol *Avon* | 267 |
| Brixham *Devon* | 267 |
| Brize Norton *Oxfordshire* | 323 |
| Broad Chalke *Wiltshire* | 267 |
| Broad Hinton *Wiltshire* | 268 |
| Broadway *Hereford and Worcester* | 143 |
| Brockdish *Norfolk* | 223 |
| Bromsgrove *Hereford and Worcester* | 145 |
| Bromyard *Hereford and Worcester* | 145 |
| Brooke *Norfolk* | 223 |
| Broseley *Shropshire* | 145 |
| Broughton Astley *Leicestershire* | 200 |
| Broughton-in-Furness *Cumbria* | 44 |
| Broxted *Essex* | 223 |
| Bruisyard *Suffolk* | 223 |
| Brundall *Norfolk* | 224 |
| Buckfastleigh *Devon* | 268 |
| Buckingham *Buckinghamshire* | 323 |
| Buckland Monachorum *Devon* | 268 |
| Bucknell *Shropshire* | 145 |
| Bude *Cornwall* | 268 |
| Bulphan *Essex* | 224 |
| Bungay *Suffolk* | 224 |

425

Buntingford *Hertfordshire* 224
Burbage *Wiltshire* 269
Burford *Oxfordshire* 323
Burley *Hampshire* 324
Burnham-on-Sea *Somerset* 269
Burnham Overy Staithe *Norfolk* 224
Burnley *Lancashire* 89
Bursledon *Hampshire* 324
Burton Bradstock *Dorset* 269
Burton upon Trent *Staffordshire* 146
Burwardsley *Cheshire* 90
Burwash *East Sussex* 357
Burwell *Cambridgeshire* 224
Bury St Edmunds *Suffolk* 225
Buxton *Derbyshire* 200

**C**       page no

Cadnam *Hampshire* 324
Caldbeck *Cumbria* 44
Callington *Cornwall* 269
Cambridge *Cambridgeshire* 225
Canterbury *Kent* 358
Cardington *Shropshire* 146
Carlisle *Cumbria* 45
Carterway Heads *Northumberland* 70
Cartmel *Cumbria* 46
Cartmel Fell *Cumbria* 46
Castle Bytham *Lincolnshire* 201
Castle Cary *Somerset* 269
Castle Donington *Leicestershire* 201
Castle Hedingham *Essex* 227
Castleside *Durham* 70
Castleton *Derbyshire* 201
Cawston *Norfolk* 227
Chagford *Devon* 270
Chalfont St Giles
*Buckinghamshire* 325
Chandlers Ford *Hampshire* 325
Chard *Somerset* 270
Charlbury *Oxfordshire* 325
Chatteris *Cambridgeshire* 227
Cheddar *Somerset* 270
Chediston *Suffolk* 227
Chelmsford *Essex* 227
Cheltenham *Gloucestershire* 146
Chelwood Gate *East Sussex* 360
Chester *Cheshire* 90
Chester-Le-Street *Durham* 70
Chesterfield *Derbyshire* 202
Chew Magna *Avon* 270
Chichester *West Sussex* 360
Chickerell *Dorset* 270
Chiddingstone *Kent* 360
Chideock *Dorset* 271
Chilham *Kent* 360

Chippenham *Wiltshire* 271
Chipping Campden *Gloucestershire* 147
Chittoe Heath *Wiltshire* 271
Chorley *Lancashire* 91
Choseley *Norfolk* 228
Chulmleigh *Devon* 271
Church Stretton *Shropshire* 148
Cirencester *Gloucestershire* 149
Cleeve Hill *Gloucestershire* 150
Cleobury Mortimer *Shropshire* 151
Cliftonville *Kent*
(See under Margate)
Clitheroe *Lancashire* 91
Cloughton *North Yorkshire* 107
Clovelly *Devon* 272
Clun *Shropshire* 151
Clungunford *Shropshire* 151
Cockermouth *Cumbria* 46
Coddenham *Suffolk* 228
Codsall *Staffordshire* 152
Colchester *Essex* 228
Coleford *Gloucestershire* 152
Coleshill *Warwickshire* 152
Colne *Lancashire* 91
Coltishall *Norfolk* 228
Colwall *Hereford and Worcester* 152
Colyton *Devon* 272
Compton *Berkshire* 325
Compton *Hampshire* 325
Congleton *Cheshire* 91
Coningsby *Lincolnshire* 202
Coniston *Cumbria* 46
Consett *Durham* 71
Corbridge *Northumberland* 71
Corfe Castle *Dorset* 325
Corse *Gloucestershire* 152
Corsham *Wiltshire* 272
Cossington *Somerset* 272
Cotgrave *Nottinghamshire* 202
Cotherstone *Durham* 71
Cotswolds
(See under Ampney Crucis,
Berkeley, Bibury, Birdlip,
Bledington, Blockley, Bourton-on-
the-Water, Bretforton, Broadway,
Cheltenham, Chipping Campden,
Cirencester, Cleeve Hill,
Donnington, Fairford, Gloucester,
Great Rissington, Guiting Power,
Lechlade, Long Compton,
Minchinhampton, Moreton-in-
Marsh, Nailsworth, Naunton,
Northleach, Nympsfield, Painswick,
Rendcomb, Slimbridge,
Stonehouse, Stow-on-the-Wold,
Stroud, Teddington, Tetbury,
Tewkesbury, Winchcombe)

Coventry *West Midlands* 153
Coxwold *North Yorkshire* 107
Crackington Haven *Cornwall* 272
Cranborne *Dorset* 326
Cranbrook *Kent* 361
Craster *Northumberland* 72
Craven Arms *Shropshire* 153
Crawley *West Sussex* 361
Crayke *North Yorkshire* 107
Crediton *Devon* 273
Crewkerne *Somerset* 273
Cricklade *Wiltshire* 273
Cromer *Norfolk* 229
Crookham *Northumberland* 72
Cropton *North Yorkshire* 107
Croyde *Devon* 273
Croydon *Greater London* 32
Cucklington *Somerset* 274
Cuddesdon *Oxfordshire* 326
Cullompton *Devon* 274
Curdridge *Hampshire* 326

**D**       page no

Dalston *Cumbria* 47
Danbury *Essex* 229
Danby *North Yorkshire* 108
Darley *North Yorkshire* 108
Darsham *Suffolk* 229
Dartmoor
(See under Ashburton, Bovey
Tracey, Bridestowe, Buckfastleigh,
Buckland Monachorum, Chagford,
Drewsteignton, Dunsford, Holne,
Ilsington, Lustleigh, Lydford,
Peter Tavy, Tavistock, Widecombe-
in-the-Moor, Yelverton)
Dartmouth *Devon* 274
Dawlish *Devon* 274
Deal *Kent* 361
Debden Green *Essex* 229
Deddington *Oxfordshire* 326
Dedham *Essex* 229
Deerhurst *Gloucestershire* 154
Denmead *Hampshire* 326
Derby *Derbyshire* 202
Dereham *Norfolk* 229
Dersingham *Norfolk* 230
Desborough *Northamptonshire* 202
Devizes *Wiltshire* 275
Dibden *Hampshire* 327
Didmarton *Gloucestershire* 154
Dilwyn *Hereford and Worcester* 154
Diss *Norfolk* 230
Doddiscombsleigh *Devon* 275
Donnington *Gloucestershire* 154

# PHONEDAY

All telephone numbers in the editorial and listings sections of this guide include the new PhONEday area codes. Please use the new codes when dialling.

*THINK OF A NUMBER ... ADD ONE.*

Dorchester *Dorset* 275
Dorking *Surrey* 362
Dover *Kent* 362
Doveridge *Derbyshire* 202
Downham Market *Norfolk* 230
Drewsteignton *Devon* 276
Droitwich *Hereford and Worcester* 154
Dulverton *Somerset* 276
Dunsford *Devon* 277
Dunster *Somerset* 277
Duntisbourne Abbots
*Gloucestershire* 155
Durham *Durham* 72
Dymock *Gloucestershire* 155

**E**      page no

Easingwold *North Yorkshire* 108
East Allington *Devon* 277
East Bergholt *Suffolk* 230
East Budleigh *Devon* 277
East Dean *East Sussex* 363
East Grinstead *West Sussex* 363
East Hendred *Oxfordshire* 327
Eastbourne *East Sussex* 363
Ebberston *North Yorkshire* 108
Eccleshall *Staffordshire* 155
Edale *Derbyshire* 202
Edwinstowe *Nottinghamshire* 203
Elham *Kent* 364
Ellerby *North Yorkshire* 108
Elmesthorpe *Leicestershire* 203
Elmley Castle
*Hereford and Worcester* 155
Elmswell *Suffolk* 230
Elsing *Norfolk* 230
Ely *Cambridgeshire* 231
Embleton *Northumberland* 73
Enford *Wiltshire* 277
Englefield Green *Surrey* 364
Epping *Essex* 231
Escrick *North Yorkshire* 108
Evesham *Hereford and Worcester* 156
Ewen *Gloucestershire* 156
Exeter *Devon* 278
Exmoor
(See under Allerford, Brendon,
Dulverton, Dunster, Lynton,
Parracombe, Timberscombe, West
Anstey, Wheddon Cross, Winsford)
Exmouth *Devon* 278
Eyam *Derbyshire* 203
Eyke *Suffolk* 231

**F**      page no

Fairford *Gloucestershire* 156
Fairlight *East Sussex* 364
Fakenham *Norfolk* 231
Falstone *Northumberland* 73
Fareham *Hampshire* 327
Faringdon *Oxfordshire* 327
Farnham *Surrey* 364
Farnsfield *Nottinghamshire* 203
Faversham *Kent* 364
Felixstowe *Suffolk* 232
Felsted *Essex* 232
Fenny Bridges *Devon* 279
Figheldean *Wiltshire* 279
Findon *West Sussex* 365
Flamborough *Humberside* 109
Flaxton *North Yorkshire* 109
Fleet *Hampshire* 327
Folkestone *Kent* 365
Fonthill Gifford *Wiltshire* 279
Fordingbridge *Hampshire* 328
Forest-in-Teesdale *Durham* 73
Forest of Dean
(See under Blakeney, Coleford,
Corse, Newent, Newland)
Fowey *Cornwall* 279
Fownhope *Hereford and Worcester* 157
Foxton *Leicestershire* 204
Framlingham *Suffolk* 232
Fressingfield *Suffolk* 233
Frinton-on-Sea *Essex* 233
Frome *Somerset* 279
Fulking *West Sussex* 366

**G**      page no

Garboldisham *Norfolk* 233
Garforth *West Yorkshire* 109
Garstang *Lancashire* 92
Gatwick Airport *West Sussex*
(See under Crawley, East
Grinstead, Horley, Leigh,
Newdigate, Smallfield)
George Nympton *Devon* 279
Gerrards Cross *Buckinghamshire* 328
Gillamoor *North Yorkshire* 109
Gissing *Norfolk* 233
Glastonbury *Somerset* 280
Glooston *Leicestershire* 204
Gloucester *Gloucestershire* 157
Godalming *Surrey* 366
Golcar *West Yorkshire* 109
Goosnargh *Lancashire* 92
Goring *Oxfordshire* 328
Goudhurst *Kent* 366
Grampound *Cornwall* 280

Grange-over-Sands *Cumbria* 47
Grasmere *Cumbria* 47
Grassington *North Yorkshire* 109
Grayrigg *Cumbria* 48
Grays *Essex* 233
Great Bardfield *Essex* 233
Great Bircham *Norfolk* 233
Great Dunmow *Essex* 234
Great Eccleston *Lancashire* 92
Great Horwood *Buckinghamshire* 328
Great Rissington *Gloucestershire* 157
Great Yarmouth *Norfolk* 234
Green Hammerton
*North Yorkshire* 110
Greenodd *Cumbria* 48
Greinton *Somerset* 280
Guildford *Surrey* 366
Guilsborough *Northamptonshire* 204
Guiting Power *Gloucestershire* 158
Gunnerside *North Yorkshire* 110

**H**      page no

Hacheston *Suffolk* 234
Hadleigh *Suffolk* 234
Hailsham *East Sussex* 366
Hale *Cheshire* 92
Halifax *West Yorkshire* 110
Hallington *Northumberland* 74
Haltwhistle *Northumberland* 74
Hambledon *Hampshire* 328
Hampton in Arden *West Midlands* 158
Hamsterley *Durham* 74
Hamsterley Forest *Durham*
(See under Barnard Castle, Bishop
Auckland, Tow Law)
Harrogate *North Yorkshire* 110
Harrow *Greater London* 32
Hartest *Suffolk* 235
Hartfield *East Sussex* 367
Hartland *Devon* 280
Haseley *Warwickshire* 158
Haslemere *Surrey* 367
Hathersage *Derbyshire* 204
Havant *Hampshire* 329
Haverthwaite *Cumbria* 48
Hawes *North Yorkshire* 111
Hawkshead *Cumbria* 48
Hawnby *North Yorkshire* 111
Haworth *West Yorkshire* 111
Haydon Bridge *Northumberland* 74
Hayfield *Derbyshire* 204
Hayling Island *Hampshire* 329
Haywards Heath *West Sussex* 367
Headcorn *Kent* 367
Heathrow Airport *Greater London*
(See under West Drayton)

| | | |
|---|---|---|
| Hebden Bridge *West Yorkshire* | 112 | |
| Heighington *Durham* | 74 | |
| Hellifield *North Yorkshire* | 112 | |
| Helmsley *North Yorkshire* | 112 | |
| Helston *Cornwall* | 281 | |
| Hemingford Grey *Cambridgeshire* | 235 | |
| Henley-in-Arden *Warwickshire* | 158 | |
| Henley-on-Thames *Oxfordshire* | 329 | |
| Henstridge *Somerset* | 281 | |
| Hereford *Hereford and Worcester* | 158 | |
| Herstmonceux *East Sussex* | 367 | |
| Hesleden *Durham* | 75 | |
| Hethersett *Norfolk* | 235 | |
| Hevingham *Norfolk* | 235 | |
| Hexham *Northumberland* | 75 | |
| Higham *Suffolk* | 236 | |
| Highworth *Wiltshire* | 281 | |
| Hintlesham *Suffolk* | 236 | |
| Hinxton *Cambridgeshire* | 236 | |
| Hitcham *Suffolk* | 236 | |
| Holbeach *Lincolnshire* | 205 | |
| Hollingbourne *Kent* | 367 | |
| Holmes Chapel *Cheshire* | 92 | |
| Holmfirth *West Yorkshire* | 113 | |
| Holne *Devon* | 281 | |
| Holnest *Dorset* | 281 | |
| Holy Island *Northumberland* | 76 | |
| Hook Norton *Oxfordshire* | 330 | |
| Hope *Derbyshire* | 205 | |
| Horley *Surrey* | 368 | |
| Horton *Dorset* | 330 | |
| Hove *East Sussex* | | |
| (See under Brighton & Hove) | | |
| Huntingdon *Cambridgeshire* | 236 | |
| Hunton *North Yorkshire* | 113 | |
| Husbands Bosworth *Leicestershire* | 205 | |
| Husthwaite *North Yorkshire* | 113 | |
| Hyde *Greater Manchester* | 93 | |
| Hythe *Hampshire* | 330 | |

### I page no

| | | |
|---|---|---|
| Ilkley *West Yorkshire* | 113 | |
| Ilsington *Devon* | 282 | |
| Ingatestone *Essex* | 236 | |
| Ingleby Greenhow | | |
| *North Yorkshire* | 114 | |
| Ingleton *North Yorkshire* | 114 | |
| Inglewhite *Lancashire* | 93 | |
| Ingoe *Tyne and Wear* | 76 | |
| Ironbridge *Shropshire* | 159 | |
| Isle of Wight | | |
| (See under Ryde, Ryde-Wootton, | | |
| Shalfleet) | | |
| Ivybridge *Devon* | 282 | |

### K page no

| | | |
|---|---|---|
| Kendal *Cumbria* | 49 | |
| Kenilworth *Warwickshire* | 159 | |
| Kentisbeare *Devon* | 282 | |
| Kersall *Nottinghamshire* | 205 | |
| Kersey *Suffolk* | 237 | |
| Kessingland *Suffolk* | 237 | |
| Keswick *Cumbria* | 50 | |
| Kettering *Northamptonshire* | 205 | |
| Kettlewell *North Yorkshire* | 114 | |
| Kidderminster | | |
| *Hereford and Worcester* | 159 | |
| Kielder *Northumberland* | 76 | |
| Kielder Forest *Northumberland* | | |
| (See under Bellingham, Falstone) | | |
| Kimmeridge *Dorset* | 330 | |
| Kineton *Warwickshire* | 160 | |
| King's Lynn *Norfolk* | 237 | |
| Kings Caple | | |
| *Hereford and Worcester* | 160 | |
| Kings Langley *Hertfordshire* | 237 | |
| Kingsbridge *Devon* | 282 | |
| Kingston Lisle *Oxfordshire* | 330 | |
| Kingstone *Hereford and Worcester* | 160 | |
| Kinnersley *Hereford and Worcester* | 160 | |
| Kirby Muxloe *Leicestershire* | 205 | |
| Kirkby *North Yorkshire* | 114 | |
| Kirkby Stephen *Cumbria* | 51 | |
| Kirkbymoorside *North Yorkshire* | 114 | |
| Knutsford *Cheshire* | 93 | |

### L page no

| | | |
|---|---|---|
| Lambourn *Berkshire* | 330 | |
| Lamplugh *Cumbria* | 52 | |
| Lancaster *Lancashire* | 93 | |
| Langdale *Cumbria* | 52 | |
| Langham *Leicestershire* | 206 | |
| Langton Herring *Dorset* | 283 | |
| Lanivet *Cornwall* | 283 | |
| Launceston *Cornwall* | 283 | |
| Lavenham *Suffolk* | 237 | |
| Lawshall *Suffolk* | 238 | |
| Lazonby *Cumbria* | 52 | |
| Leamington Spa *Warwickshire* | 160 | |
| Leatherhead *Surrey* | 369 | |
| Lechlade *Gloucestershire* | 161 | |
| Ledbury *Hereford and Worcester* | 161 | |
| Leeds *West Yorkshire* | 115 | |
| Leeds/Bradford Airport | | |
| (See under Bingley, Bradford, | | |
| Leeds, Otley) | | |
| Leek *Staffordshire* | 161 | |
| Leeming Bar *North Yorkshire* | 115 | |
| Leicester *Leicestershire* | 206 | |
| Leigh *Surrey* | 369 | |

| | | |
|---|---|---|
| Leintwardine | | |
| *Hereford and Worcester* | 162 | |
| Lenham *Kent* | 369 | |
| Leominster | | |
| *Hereford and Worcester* | 162 | |
| Lesbury *Northumberland* | 76 | |
| Levisham *North Yorkshire* | 115 | |
| Lewdown *Devon* | 284 | |
| Lewes *East Sussex* | 369 | |
| Lichfield *Staffordshire* | 162 | |
| Lincoln *Lincolnshire* | 206 | |
| Liskeard *Cornwall* | 284 | |
| Little Bedwyn *Wiltshire* | 284 | |
| Little London *Hampshire* | 331 | |
| Little Tey *Essex* | 238 | |
| Little Walsingham *Norfolk* | 238 | |
| Little Wittenham *Oxfordshire* | 331 | |
| Liverpool *Merseyside* | 94 | |
| Loddiswell *Devon* | 284 | |
| London | 24 | |
| Long Buckby *Northamptonshire* | 206 | |
| Long Compton *Warwickshire* | 163 | |
| Long Marston *North Yorkshire* | 115 | |
| Long Melford *Suffolk* | 238 | |
| Long Sutton *Somerset* | 285 | |
| Looe *Cornwall* | 285 | |
| Lorton *Cumbria* | 52 | |
| Loughborough *Leicestershire* | 206 | |
| Louth *Lincolnshire* | 207 | |
| Lowestoft *Suffolk* | 238 | |
| Loweswater *Cumbria* | 53 | |
| Ludford *Lincolnshire* | 207 | |
| Ludham *Norfolk* | 239 | |
| Ludlow *Shropshire* | 163 | |
| Lund *Humberside* | 115 | |
| Lustleigh *Devon* | 285 | |
| Lydford *Devon* | 286 | |
| Lyme Regis *Dorset* | 286 | |
| Lymington *Hampshire* | 331 | |
| Lyminster *West Sussex* | 369 | |
| Lyndhurst *Hampshire* | 331 | |
| Lynsted *Kent* | 369 | |
| Lynton *Devon* | 286 | |

### M page no

| | | |
|---|---|---|
| Maidenhead *Berkshire* | 332 | |
| Maidstone *Kent* | 369 | |
| Malham *North Yorkshire* | 116 | |
| Malmesbury *Wiltshire* | 287 | |
| Malpas *Cheshire* | 94 | |
| Malvern *Hereford and Worcester* | 164 | |
| Manchester *Greater Manchester* | 94 | |
| Manchester Airport | | |
| (See under Alderley Edge, | | |
| Altrincham, Hyde, Knutsford, | | |
| Manchester, Salford, Stockport) | | |

# COUNTRY CODE

♣ Enjoy the countryside and respect its life and work
♣ Guard against all risk of fire ♣ Fasten all gates
♣ Keep your dogs under close control ♣ Keep to
public paths across farmland ♣ Use gates and stiles
to cross fences, hedges and walls ♣ Leave livestock,
crops and machinery alone ♣ Take your litter home
♣ Help to keep all water clean ♣ Protect wildlife,
plants and trees ♣ Take special care on country
roads ♣ Make no unnecessary noise

SUNNYSIDE FARM WELCOMES CAREFUL WALKERS.

| | | |
|---|---|---|
| Marden *Kent* | 370 | |
| Margaret Roding *Essex* | 239 | |
| Margate *Kent* | 370 | |
| Market Deeping *Lincolnshire* | 207 | |
| Market Drayton *Shropshire* | 165 | |
| Market Harborough *Leicestershire* | 207 | |
| Market Weighton *Humberside* | 116 | |
| Marlborough *Wiltshire* | 287 | |
| Marlow *Buckinghamshire* | 332 | |
| Martinstown *Dorset* | 288 | |
| Martock *Somerset* | 288 | |
| Marton *North Yorkshire* | 116 | |
| Masham *North Yorkshire* | 116 | |
| Matlock *Derbyshire* | 207 | |
| Mayfield *East Sussex* | 370 | |
| Melton Constable *Norfolk* | 239 | |
| Melton Mowbray *Leicestershire* | 208 | |
| Meriden *West Midlands* | 165 | |
| Mevagissey *Cornwall* | 288 | |
| Middlesbrough *Cleveland* | 76 | |
| Middleton *Northamptonshire* | 208 | |
| Middleton *Suffolk* | 239 | |
| Middleton-in-Teesdale *Durham* | 77 | |
| Midhurst *West Sussex* | 370 | |
| Milton Abbas *Dorset* | 333 | |
| Milton Keynes *Buckinghamshire* | 333 | |
| Minchinhampton *Gloucestershire* | 165 | |
| Minehead *Somerset* | 289 | |
| Minstead *Hampshire* | 334 | |
| Minster Lovell *Oxfordshire* | 334 | |
| Minsterley *Shropshire* | 165 | |
| Mockbeggar *Hampshire* | 334 | |
| Monyash *Derbyshire* | 208 | |
| Moreton-in-Marsh *Gloucestershire* | 166 | |
| Moreton Pinkney *Northamptonshire* | 208 | |
| Moretonhampstead *Devon* | 289 | |
| Morwenstow *Cornwall* | 290 | |
| Mountsorrel *Leicestershire* | 208 | |
| Much Hadham *Hertfordshire* | 239 | |
| Much Wenlock *Shropshire* | 167 | |
| Mullion *Cornwall* | 290 | |
| Mundesley *Norfolk* | 239 | |
| Mylor Bridge *Cornwall* | 290 | |
| Myton-on-Swale *North Yorkshire* | 117 | |

**N**      page no

| | |
|---|---|
| Nailsworth *Gloucestershire* | 167 |
| Nantwich *Cheshire* | 95 |
| Naunton *Gloucestershire* | 168 |
| Nayland *Suffolk* | 239 |
| Nether Wallop *Hampshire* | 335 |
| New Forest (See under Barton on Sea, Beaulieu, Bransgore, Burley, Cadnam, Dibden, Fordingbridge, Hythe, Lymington, Lyndhurst, Minstead, Mockbeggar, Ringwood, Sway, Tiptoe, Totton) | |
| Newark *Nottinghamshire* | 208 |
| Newbury *Berkshire* | 335 |
| Newcastle upon Tyne *Tyne and Wear* | 77 |
| Newdigate *Surrey* | 371 |
| Newent *Gloucestershire* | 168 |
| Newland *Gloucestershire* | 168 |
| Newmarket *Suffolk* | 240 |
| Newport *Shropshire* | 168 |
| Newquay *Cornwall* | 290 |
| Newton Ferrers *Devon* | 291 |
| Newton Longville *Buckinghamshire* | 335 |

**O**      page no

| | |
|---|---|
| Oakamoor *Staffordshire* | 169 |
| Oakham *Leicestershire* | 209 |
| Okehampton *Devon* | 291 |
| Old Romney *Kent* | 371 |
| Oldham *Greater Manchester* | 96 |
| Ombersley *Hereford and Worcester* | 170 |
| Onneley *Staffordshire* | 170 |
| Orton *Cumbria* | 53 |
| Osmington *Dorset* | 292 |
| Osmotherley *North Yorkshire* | 117 |
| Oswaldkirk *North Yorkshire* | 117 |
| Oswestry *Shropshire* | 170 |
| Otley *West Yorkshire* | 117 |
| Otterton *Devon* | 292 |
| Ottery St Mary *Devon* | 292 |
| Oundle *Northamptonshire* | 209 |
| Ovington *Northumberland* | 78 |
| Owslebury *Hampshire* | 335 |
| Oxen Park *Cumbria* | 53 |
| Oxford *Oxfordshire* | 335 |
| Oxted *Surrey* | 371 |

**Norfolk Broads** (See under Aylsham, Beccles, Brundall, Bungay, Cawston, Coltishall, Great Yarmouth, Hevingham, Lowestoft, Ludham, North Walsham, Norwich, Rackheath, Rollesby, Salhouse, South Walsham, Stalham, Wroxham)

| | |
|---|---|
| Norham *Northumberland* | 77 |
| North Walsham *Norfolk* | 240 |
| Northallerton *North Yorkshire* | 117 |
| Northampton *Northamptonshire* | 209 |
| Northleach *Gloucestershire* | 169 |
| Northwich *Cheshire* | 95 |
| Norwich *Norfolk* | 240 |
| Noss Mayo *Devon* | 291 |
| Nottingham *Nottinghamshire* | 209 |
| Nuneaton *Warwickshire* | 169 |
| Nunnington *North Yorkshire* | 117 |
| Nympsfield *Gloucestershire* | 169 |

**P**      page no

| | |
|---|---|
| Padstow *Cornwall* | 292 |
| Painswick *Gloucestershire* | 171 |
| Parracombe *Devon* | 293 |
| Partridge Green *West Sussex* | 371 |
| Patrley Bridge *North Yorkshire* | 118 |
| Patterdale *Cumbria* | 53 |
| Peak District (See under Aldwark, Ashbourne, Ashford in the Water, Bakewell, Bamford, Buxton, Castleton, Edale, Eyam, Hathersage, Hayfield, Hope, Monyash, Rowarth, Rowsley, Tideswell, Winster) | |
| Peak Forest *Derbyshire* | 209 |
| Pelynt *Cornwall* | 293 |
| Pendeen *Cornwall* | 293 |
| Penrith *Cumbria* | 53 |
| Penruddock *Cumbria* | 54 |
| Pensford *Avon* | 293 |
| Penshurst *Kent* | 371 |
| Pentewan *Cornwall* | 293 |
| Penzance *Cornwall* | 293 |
| Perranuthnoe *Cornwall* | 294 |
| Peter Tavy *Devon* | 294 |
| Peterborough *Cambridgeshire* | 241 |
| Petersfield *Hampshire* | 337 |
| Petworth *West Sussex* | 371 |
| Pickering *North Yorkshire* | 118 |
| Piddletrenthide *Dorset* | 294 |

| | |
|---|---|
| Pillaton *Cornwall* | 294 |
| Plawsworth *Durham* | 78 |
| Plymouth *Devon* | 295 |
| Poole *Dorset* | 337 |
| Porthleven *Cornwall* | 295 |
| Portland *Dorset* | 296 |
| Portreath *Cornwall* | 296 |
| Portsmouth & Southsea *Hampshire* | 337 |
| Powerstock *Dorset* | 296 |
| Preston *Lancashire* | 96 |
| Priddy *Somerset* | 296 |

**Q**      page no

| | |
|---|---|
| Quidenham *Norfolk* | 241 |

**R**      page no

| | |
|---|---|
| Rackheath *Norfolk* | 241 |
| Radwinter *Essex* | 241 |
| Ragnall *Nottinghamshire* | 210 |
| Ramsey *Cambridgeshire* | 242 |
| Ramsgate *Kent* | 372 |
| Ravenscar *North Yorkshire* | 119 |
| Reading *Berkshire* | 338 |
| Redcar *Cleveland* | 78 |
| Redlynch *Wiltshire* | 296 |
| Reeth *North Yorkshire* | 119 |
| Rendcomb *Gloucestershire* | 171 |
| Ribble Valley (See under Clitheroe) | |
| Richmond *North Yorkshire* | 119 |
| Rickmansworth *Hertfordshire* | 242 |
| Rillington *North Yorkshire* | 120 |
| Ringwood *Hampshire* | 339 |
| Ripon *North Yorkshire* | 120 |
| Robin Hood's Bay *North Yorkshire* | 120 |
| Rocester *Staffordshire* | 171 |
| Rochdale *Greater Manchester* | 96 |
| Rock *Hereford and Worcester* | 171 |
| Rogate *West Sussex* | 372 |
| Rollesby *Norfolk* | 242 |
| Romsey *Hampshire* | 339 |
| Rosley *Cumbria* | 54 |
| Ross-on-Wye *Hereford and Worcester* | 172 |
| Rothbury *Northumberland* | 78 |
| Rottingdean *East Sussex* | 372 |
| Rowarth *Derbyshire* | 210 |
| Rowlands Gill *Tyne and Wear* | 78 |
| Rowsley *Derbyshire* | 210 |
| Royal Tunbridge Wells *Kent* | 372 |
| Rufforth *North Yorkshire* | 121 |
| Rugby *Warwickshire* | 173 |
| Rushton Spencer *Staffordshire* | 173 |
| Ruyton-XI-Towns *Shropshire* | 173 |
| Ryde *Isle of Wight* | 339 |
| Ryde-Wootton *Isle of Wight* | 339 |
| Rye *East Sussex* | 373 |
| Ryton *Tyne and Wear* | 79 |

**S**      page no

| | |
|---|---|
| Saffron Walden *Essex* | 242 |
| St Agnes *Cornwall* | 297 |
| St Albans *Hertfordshire* | 243 |
| St Bees *Cumbria* | 55 |
| St Ives *Cornwall* | 297 |
| St Kew *Cornwall* | 297 |
| St Michael's on Wyre *Lancashire* | 96 |
| St Neot *Cornwall* | 297 |
| St Nicholas at Wade *Kent* | 374 |
| Salcombe *Devon* | 298 |
| Salford *Greater Manchester* | 97 |
| Salhouse *Norfolk* | 243 |
| Salisbury *Wiltshire* | 298 |

**Salisbury Plain**
(See under Amesbury, Figheldean,
Salisbury, Shrewton, Warminster,
Winterbourne Stoke)
**Saltburn-by-the-Sea** *Cleveland* 79
**Sandbach** *Cheshire* 97
**Sandy** *Bedfordshire* 244
**Sarre** *Kent* 374
**Saunderton** *Buckinghamshire* 339
**Saxilby** *Lincolnshire* 210
**Saxlingham Thorpe** *Norfolk* 244
**Saxmundham** *Suffolk* 244
**Scarborough** *North Yorkshire* 121
**Seahouses** *Northumberland* 79
**Sedbergh** *Cumbria* 55
**Selborne** *Hampshire* 340
**Selby** *North Yorkshire* 121
**Settle** *North Yorkshire* 122
**Sevenoaks** *Kent* 374
**Severn Stoke**
*Hereford and Worcester* 174
**Shaldon** *Devon* 299
**Shalfleet** *Isle of Wight* 340
**Shap** *Cumbria* 55
**Shearsby** *Leicestershire* 210
**Sheffield** *South Yorkshire* 122
**Shelley** *Suffolk* 244
**Shepton Mallet** *Somerset* 299
**Sherborne** *Dorset* 300
**Sheringham** *Norfolk* 244
**Sherwood Forest**
(See under Edwinstowe, Kersall,
Newark, Ragnall, Southwell,
Upton)
**Shifnal** *Shropshire* 174
**Shipton Bellinger** *Hampshire* 340
**Shipton-under-Wychwood**
*Oxfordshire* 340
**Shrewsbury** *Shropshire* 174
**Shrewton** *Wiltshire* 300
**Sidcup** *Greater London* 32
**Siddington** *Cheshire* 97
**Sidmouth** *Devon* 300
**Silloth** *Cumbria* 55
**Singleton** *Lancashire* 97
**Sittingbourne** *Kent* 375
**Sixpenny Handley** *Dorset* 340
**Skegness** *Lincolnshire* 210
**Skillington** *Lincolnshire* 211
**Slaley** *Northumberland* 79
**Slapton** *Devon* 300
**Slimbridge** *Gloucestershire* 176
**Sloley** *Norfolk* 244
**Smallfield** *Surrey* 375
**Smarden** *Kent* 375
**Solihull** *West Midlands* 176
**Souldern** *Oxfordshire* 340

**South Creake** *Norfolk* 245
**South Lopham** *Norfolk* 245
**South Mimms** *Hertfordshire* 245
**South Molton** *Devon* 301
**South Walsham** *Norfolk* 245
**Southampton** *Hampshire* 340
**Southborough** *Kent* 375
**Southend-on-Sea** *Essex* 245
**Southport** *Merseyside* 97
**Southsea** *Hampshire*
(See under Portsmouth &
Southsea)
**Southwell** *Nottinghamshire* 211
**Southwold** *Suffolk* 245
**Spennymoor** *Durham* 79
**Staindrop** *Durham* 80
**Stalham** *Norfolk* 246
**Stamford** *Lincolnshire* 211
**Standlake** *Oxfordshire* 341
**Stanley** *Durham* 80
**Stanton Drew** *Avon* 301
**Starbotton** *North Yorkshire* 122
**Starcross** *Devon* 301
**Steel** *Northumberland* 80
**Stelling Minnis** *Kent* 375
**Stiperstones** *Shropshire* 176
**Stockbridge** *Hampshire* 341
**Stockport** *Greater Manchester* 98
**Stockton-on-Tees** *Cleveland* 80
**Stoke-by-Nayland** *Suffolk* 246
**Stoke Holy Cross** *Norfolk* 246
**Stoke-in-Teignhead** *Devon* 301
**Stoke-on-Trent** *Staffordshire* 176
**Stoke St Gregory** *Somerset* 301
**Stone** *Staffordshire* 177
**Stonehouse** *Gloucestershire* 177
**Storrington** *West Sussex* 375
**Stourbridge** *West Midlands* 177
**Stow-on-the-Wold** *Gloucestershire* 177
**Stratford St Mary** *Suffolk* 246
**Stratford-upon-Avon** *Warwickshire* 178
**Stroud** *Gloucestershire* 181
**Studland** *Dorset* 341
**Styal** *Cheshire* 98
**Sudbury** *Suffolk* 246
**Sunderland** *Tyne and Wear* 80
**Sutton-on-Trent** *Nottinghamshire* 212
**Sutton Scotney** *Hampshire* 341
**Sutton Valence** *Kent* 376
**Swanley** *Kent* 376
**Sway** *Hampshire* 341
**Swindon** *Wiltshire* 302
**Sydling St Nicholas** *Dorset* 302

**T** page no
**Tarporley** *Cheshire* 98
**Taunton** *Somerset* 302
**Tavistock** *Devon* 302
**Teddington** *Gloucestershire* 182
**Telford** *Shropshire* 182
**Tenterden** *Kent* 376
**Tetbury** *Gloucestershire* 183
**Tewkesbury** *Gloucestershire* 183
**Thaxted** *Essex* 247
**Thetford** *Norfolk* 247
**Thirsk** *North Yorkshire* 122
**Thompson** *Norfolk* 247
**Thoralby** *North Yorkshire* 123
**Thornham** *Norfolk* 247
**Thornton Watlass** *North Yorkshire* 123
**Thorpe Morieux** *Suffolk* 247
**Thurlstone** *South Yorkshire* 124
**Tideswell** *Derbyshire* 212
**Timberscombe** *Somerset* 303
**Tintagel** *Cornwall* 303
**Tiptoe** *Hampshire* 342
**Tiptree** *Essex* 247
**Tiverton** *Devon* 303
**Tivetshall St Mary** *Norfolk* 248
**Toft** *Cambridgeshire* 248
**Tolpuddle** *Dorset* 304
**Torquay** *Devon* 304
**Torrington** *Devon* 305
**Totnes** *Devon* 305
**Totton** *Hampshire* 342
**Tow Law** *Durham* 80
**Troutbeck** *Cumbria* 55
**Trowbridge** *Wiltshire* 306
**Truro** *Cornwall* 306
**Tunbridge Wells**
(See under Royal Tunbridge
Wells)
**Tynemouth** *Tyne and Wear* 81

**U** page no
**Uckfield** *East Sussex* 376
**Uffington** *Oxfordshire* 342
**Ugborough** *Devon* 306
**Ullswater** *Cumbria* 55
**Uppingham** *Leicestershire* 212
**Upton** *Nottinghamshire* 212
**Upton-upon-Severn**
*Hereford and Worcester* 184
**Uttoxeter** *Staffordshire* 184

**V** page no
**Vowchurch**
*Hereford and Worcester* 184

# KEY TO SYMBOLS

Information about many of the services and
facilities at accommodation listed in this guide
is given in the form of symbols. The key to
these symbols is inside the back cover flap.
You may find it helpful to keep the flap open
when referring to the accommodation listings.

| W | page no |
|---|---|
| Waddington *Lancashire* | 98 |
| Wallingford *Oxfordshire* | 342 |
| Warborough *Oxfordshire* | 342 |
| Ware *Hertfordshire* | 248 |
| Warkworth *Northumberland* | 81 |
| Warminster *Wiltshire* | 306 |
| Warnford *Hampshire* | 342 |
| Warninglid *West Sussex* | 376 |
| Warter *Humberside* | 124 |
| Warwick *Warwickshire* | 185 |
| Watchet *Somerset* | 307 |
| Waterhouses *Staffordshire* | 186 |
| Watford *Hertfordshire* | 248 |
| Weedon *Northamptonshire* | 212 |
| Wells *Somerset* | 307 |
| Wells-next-the-Sea *Norfolk* | 248 |
| Wem *Shropshire* | 186 |
| Wendover *Buckinghamshire* | 343 |
| Wenlock Edge *Shropshire* | 187 |
| Weobley *Hereford and Worcester* | 187 |
| Wessington *Derbyshire* | 212 |
| West Anstey *Devon* | 308 |
| West Bagborough *Somerset* | 308 |
| West Bay *Dorset* | 308 |
| West Bergholt *Essex* | 248 |
| West Chiltington *West Sussex* | 376 |
| West Clandon *Surrey* | 377 |
| West Drayton *Greater London* | 32 |
| West Haddon *Northamptonshire* | 213 |
| West Lulworth *Dorset* | 343 |
| West Malling *Kent* | 377 |

| | page no |
|---|---|
| West Stour *Dorset* | 343 |
| West Witton *North Yorkshire* | 124 |
| Westbury *Buckinghamshire* | 343 |
| Westgate-in-Weardale *Durham* | 81 |
| Weston-super-Mare *Avon* | 308 |
| Wetherby *West Yorkshire* | 124 |
| Weybread *Suffolk* | 248 |
| Weymouth *Dorset* | 308 |
| Wheddon Cross *Somerset* | 309 |
| Whitby *North Yorkshire* | 124 |
| Whiteparish *Wiltshire* | 309 |
| Whitley Bay *Tyne and Wear* | 81 |
| Wickham *Hampshire* | 343 |
| Widecombe-in-the-Moor *Devon* | 309 |
| Willoughby Waterleys *Leicestershire* | 213 |
| Wilmcote *Warwickshire* | 187 |
| Wimborne Minster *Dorset* | 344 |
| Wincanton *Somerset* | 309 |
| Winchcombe *Gloucestershire* | 187 |
| Winchester *Hampshire* | 345 |
| Windermere *Cumbria* | 56 |
| Windsor *Berkshire* | 346 |
| Winsford *Somerset* | 309 |
| Winslow *Buckinghamshire* | 346 |
| Winster *Derbyshire* | 213 |
| Winterborne Stickland *Dorset* | 347 |
| Winterbourne Stoke *Wiltshire* | 310 |
| Winwick *Northamptonshire* | 213 |
| Wirral *Merseyside* (See under Birkenhead) | |
| Wisbech *Cambridgeshire* | 249 |
| Witney *Oxfordshire* | 347 |
| Wix *Essex* | 249 |

| | page no |
|---|---|
| Woking *Surrey* | 377 |
| Wokingham *Berkshire* | 347 |
| Woodbridge *Suffolk* | 249 |
| Woodbury *Devon* | 310 |
| Woodham Ferrers *Essex* | 249 |
| Woodstock *Oxfordshire* | 347 |
| Wooler *Northumberland* | 82 |
| Wootton Bassett *Wiltshire* | 310 |
| Wootton Wawen *Warwickshire* | 188 |
| Worcester *Hereford and Worcester* | 188 |
| Workington *Cumbria* | 59 |
| Wormsley *Hereford and Worcester* | 189 |
| Worthing *West Sussex* | 377 |
| Wroxham *Norfolk* | 250 |
| Wye *Kent* | 377 |
| Wye Valley (See under Fownhope, Hereford, Ross-on-Wye) | |
| Wylam *Northumberland* | 82 |
| Wymondham *Norfolk* | 250 |

| Y | page no |
|---|---|
| Yarkhill *Hereford and Worcester* | 189 |
| Yarnton *Oxfordshire* | 348 |
| Yelverton *Devon* | 310 |
| Yeovil *Somerset* | 310 |
| Yeovilton *Somerset* | 311 |
| York *North Yorkshire* | 124 |
| Yoxall *Staffordshire* | 189 |

| Z | page no |
|---|---|
| Zeals *Wiltshire* | 311 |

# INDEX TO ADVERTISERS

*You can obtain further information from any display advertiser in this guide by completing an advertisement enquiry coupon. You will find these coupons on pages 423–424.*

| | | | |
|---|---|---|---|
| **Abbey Court Hotel**, London W2 | 33, IBC | **Middlesex University**, London N22 | 391 |
| **The Abbotts Hotel**, London NW2 | 28 | **Oxstalls Farm Stud**, Stratford-upon-Avon | 179 |
| **Apple Orchard House**, Nailsworth | 167 | **The Penny Farthing Hotel**, Lyndhurst | 331 |
| **The Beeches**, Doveridge | 203 | **Rudstone Walk Farm**, Beverley | 105 |
| **Browson Bank Farmhouse**, Richmond | 129 | **Sass House Hotel**, London W2 | 33, IBC |
| **Corona Hotel**, London SW1 | 26 | **The Turret**, Lynton | 311 |
| **Elizabeth Hotel**, London SW1 | 26 | **Westpoint Hotel**, London W2 | 33, IBC |
| **Granada Lodges** | IFC | **Windsor House Hotel**, London SW5 | 28 |

# MILEAGE CHART

The distances between towns on the mileage chart are given to the nearest mile, and are measured along routes based on the quickest travelling time, making maximum use of motorways or dual-carriageway roads.
The chart is based upon information supplied by the Automobile Association.

*(Map of Great Britain showing town locations: Inverness, Fort William, Aberdeen, Perth, Glasgow, Edinburgh, Stranraer, Carlisle, Newcastle upon Tyne, Middlesbrough, Kendal, York, Leeds, Hull, Holyhead, Liverpool, Manchester, Sheffield, Lincoln, Nottingham, Norwich, Aberystwyth, Birmingham, Cambridge, Carmarthen, Gloucester, Colchester, Cardiff, Bristol, Oxford, London, Barnstaple, Guildford, Maidstone, Dover, Taunton, Southampton, Dorchester, Exeter, Plymouth, Brighton, Penzance.)*

| | Aberdeen | Aberystwyth | Barnstaple | Birmingham | Brighton | Bristol | Cambridge | Cardiff | Carlisle | Carmarthen | Colchester | Dorchester | Dover | Edinburgh | Exeter | Fort William | Glasgow | Gloucester | Guildford | Holyhead | Hull | Inverness | Kendal | Leeds | Lincoln | Liverpool | Maidstone | Manchester | Middlesbrough | Newcastle upon Tyne | Norwich | Nottingham | Oxford | Penzance | Perth | Plymouth | Sheffield | Southampton | Stranraer | Taunton | York |
|---|---|---|---|---|---|---|---|---|---|---|---|---|---|---|---|---|---|---|---|---|---|---|---|---|---|---|---|---|---|---|---|---|---|---|---|---|---|---|---|---|---|
| Aberystwyth | 471 |
| Barnstaple | 607 | 222 |
| Birmingham | 434 | 123 | 178 |
| Brighton | 609 | 290 | 203 | 171 |
| Bristol | 518 | 132 | 100 | 88 | 170 |
| Cambridge | 465 | 230 | 267 | 113 | 121 | 171 |
| Cardiff | 538 | 118 | 137 | 108 | 205 | 47 | 206 |
| Carlisle | 235 | 237 | 372 | 282 | 259 | 302 |
| Carmarthen | 521 | 50 | 199 | 157 | 267 | 110 | 269 | 68 | 286 |
| Colchester | 518 | 289 | 292 | 171 | 112 | 196 | 48 | 231 | 312 | 293 |
| Dorchester | 599 | 214 | 94 | 170 | 117 | 62 | 181 | 129 | 364 | 191 | 208 |
| Dover | 587 | 322 | 275 | 205 | 81 | 209 | 121 | 244 | 398 | 306 | 113 | 204 |
| Edinburgh | 126 | 336 | 472 | 298 | 474 | 382 | 336 | 402 | 99 | 386 | 389 | 464 | 458 |
| Exeter | 591 | 206 | 55 | 161 | 172 | 83 | 251 | 121 | 356 | 183 | 275 | 364 | 247 | 455 |
| Fort William | 157 | 447 | 582 | 409 | 585 | 492 | 469 | 513 | 210 | 496 | 522 | 574 | 608 | 133 | 567 |
| Glasgow | 149 | 336 | 472 | 298 | 475 | 382 | 359 | 402 | 99 | 386 | 412 | 464 | 498 | 46 | 456 | 102 |
| Gloucester | 483 | 110 | 126 | 54 | 156 | 36 | 123 | 65 | 248 | 127 | 171 | 118 | 195 | 347 | 110 | 458 | 348 |
| Guildford | 567 | 226 | 174 | 128 | 44 | 106 | 91 | 142 | 332 | 204 | 104 | 97 | 100 | 431 | 146 | 542 | 431 | 101 |
| Holyhead | 463 | 105 | 341 | 168 | 344 | 251 | 226 | 205 | 228 | 155 | 334 | 333 | 367 | 327 | 326 | 439 | 328 | 217 | 301 |
| Hull | 361 | 229 | 322 | 141 | 283 | 232 | 140 | 252 | 172 | 300 | 193 | 314 | 262 | 232 | 306 | 382 | 271 | 241 | 220 | 301 |
| Inverness | 106 | 497 | 632 | 458 | 635 | 542 | 519 | 562 | 259 | 546 | 572 | 624 | 658 | 157 | 616 | 65 | 174 | 508 | 592 | 488 | 431 |
| Kendal | 287 | 191 | 326 | 153 | 329 | 236 | 253 | 256 | 52 | 240 | 319 | 318 | 352 | 152 | 311 | 263 | 152 | 202 | 286 | 182 | 165 | 312 |
| Leeds | 328 | 174 | 310 | 120 | 263 | 220 | 148 | 240 | 122 | 201 | 302 | 269 | 199 | 294 | 333 | 222 | 185 | 220 | 166 | 60 | 382 | 71 | 312 |
| Lincoln | 390 | 199 | 274 | 88 | 215 | 184 | 94 | 204 | 184 | 253 | 148 | 262 | 216 | 260 | 259 | 394 | 283 | 150 | 173 | 205 | 48 | 444 | 177 | 73 |
| Liverpool | 361 | 111 | 274 | 101 | 277 | 184 | 217 | 205 | 126 | 168 | 267 | 266 | 300 | 225 | 259 | 336 | 225 | 150 | 234 | 102 | 129 | 386 | 79 | 74 | 141 |
| Maidstone | 550 | 285 | 232 | 168 | 49 | 166 | 84 | 202 | 361 | 264 | 76 | 161 | 44 | 421 | 205 | 572 | 461 | 52 | 57 | 329 | 225 | 621 | 315 | 233 | 179 | 263 |
| Manchester | 356 | 131 | 262 | 88 | 265 | 172 | 161 | 192 | 121 | 181 | 214 | 254 | 288 | 220 | 246 | 331 | 220 | 138 | 222 | 122 | 99 | 380 | 74 | 44 | 85 | 35 | 251 |
| Middlesbrough | 276 | 245 | 359 | 178 | 321 | 269 | 200 | 289 | 95 | 294 | 353 | 351 | 322 | 147 | 343 | 279 | 194 | 235 | 278 | 236 | 89 | 306 | 83 | 64 | 125 | 145 | 285 | 115 |
| Newcastle upon Tyne | 237 | 277 | 391 | 211 | 353 | 302 | 233 | 322 | 59 | 327 | 406 | 354 | 108 | 376 | 242 | 102 | 96 | 157 | 177 | 317 | 147 | 40 |
| Norwich | 489 | 293 | 329 | 176 | 170 | 233 | 63 | 268 | 283 | 330 | 59 | 242 | 170 | 360 | 314 | 494 | 383 | 186 | 161 | 305 | 152 | 543 | 277 | 173 | 103 | 241 | 134 | 185 | 225 | 257 |
| Nottingham | 395 | 160 | 234 | 54 | 196 | 145 | 87 | 165 | 189 | 213 | 140 | 226 | 216 | 266 | 219 | 400 | 289 | 110 | 153 | 174 | 93 | 449 | 149 | 74 | 36 | 108 | 170 | 70 | 131 | 163 | 119 |
| Oxford | 506 | 159 | 170 | 68 | 110 | 74 | 100 | 109 | 271 | 115 | 115 | 149 | 370 | 154 | 481 | 371 | 48 | 371 | 128 | 173 | 106 | 161 | 162 | 103 |
| Penzance | 701 | 316 | 109 | 272 | 283 | 193 | 361 | 231 | 466 | 293 | 386 | 165 | 359 | 565 | 109 | 676 | 566 | 219 | 258 | 434 | 415 | 726 | 420 | 404 | 368 | 368 | 316 | 356 | 452 | 485 | 423 | 328 | 264 |
| Perth | 87 | 385 | 520 | 346 | 523 | 430 | 381 | 450 | 147 | 434 | 434 | 512 | 546 | 42 | 504 | 103 | 62 | 396 | 480 | 376 | 277 | 114 | 200 | 244 | 306 | 273 | 509 | 268 | 192 | 153 | 405 | 311 | 420 | 614 |
| Plymouth | 632 | 247 | 81 | 215 | 125 | 125 | 293 | 163 | 398 | 225 | 317 | 97 | 290 | 496 | 45 | 608 | 497 | 151 | 97 | 398 | 408 | 202 | 351 | 335 | 300 | 248 | 287 | 384 | 417 | 354 | 299 | 195 | 77 | 546 |
| Sheffield | 369 | 166 | 272 | 92 | 234 | 183 | 123 | 203 | 163 | 251 | 177 | 264 | 254 | 207 | 373 | 263 | 148 | 192 | 157 | 67 | 423 | 120 | 36 | 48 | 78 | 217 | 37 | 104 | 137 | 148 | 44 | 142 | 366 | 285 | 298 |
| Southampton | 572 | 226 | 140 | 134 | 63 | 76 | 131 | 141 | 337 | 203 | 158 | 54 | 155 | 436 | 112 | 548 | 437 | 100 | 48 | 305 | 257 | 597 | 291 | 238 | 213 | 239 | 112 | 227 | 294 | 327 | 193 | 170 | 66 | 223 | 485 | 155 | 208 |
| Stranraer | 241 | 344 | 480 | 306 | 483 | 387 | 410 | 410 | 107 | 394 | 407 | 506 | 540 | 64 | 502 | 164 | 106 | 440 | 336 | 279 | 266 | 160 | 382 | 469 | 228 | 202 | 164 | 391 | 297 | 379 | 573 | 154 | 505 | 171 | 432 |
| Taunton | 559 | 174 | 50 | 130 | 154 | 51 | 219 | 89 | 324 | 151 | 244 | 45 | 227 | 423 | 35 | 534 | 424 | 77 | 126 | 292 | 273 | 584 | 278 | 261 | 226 | 184 | 214 | 310 | 343 | 281 | 186 | 122 | 144 | 472 | 75 | 224 | 91 | 432 |
| York | 322 | 201 | 315 | 134 | 277 | 225 | 157 | 245 | 116 | 251 | 210 | 307 | 278 | 193 | 300 | 327 | 216 | 191 | 234 | 192 | 38 | 376 | 90 | 24 | 81 | 101 | 241 | 71 | 50 | 90 | 181 | 87 | 184 | 409 | 238 | 340 | 60 | 250 | 224 | 267 |
| London | 549 | 238 | 216 | 120 | 60 | 120 | 60 | 155 | 314 | 217 | 62 | 129 | 78 | 413 | 200 | 524 | 413 | 103 | 30 | 282 | 188 | 574 | 268 | 199 | 142 | 216 | 38 | 203 | 256 | 288 | 115 | 131 | 56 | 309 | 462 | 241 | 169 | 80 | 441 | 167 | 212 |

# Location Maps

Every place name featured in the accommodation listings pages of this 'Where to Stay' guide has a map reference to help you locate it on the maps which follow. For example, to find Colchester, Essex, which has 'Map ref 3B2', turn to Map 3 and refer to grid square B2.

All place names in the listings pages are shown in black type on the maps. This enables you to find other places in your chosen area which may have suitable accommodation – the Town Index (preceding pages) gives page numbers.

MAP 5

Newcastle upon Tyne

Carlisle

MAP 4  York

Manchester

Lincoln

Birmingham

Ipswich

MAP 2

MAPS 6&7

Oxford
Bristol

London

MAP 1

Southampton

Dover

MAP 3

Exeter

# MAP 1

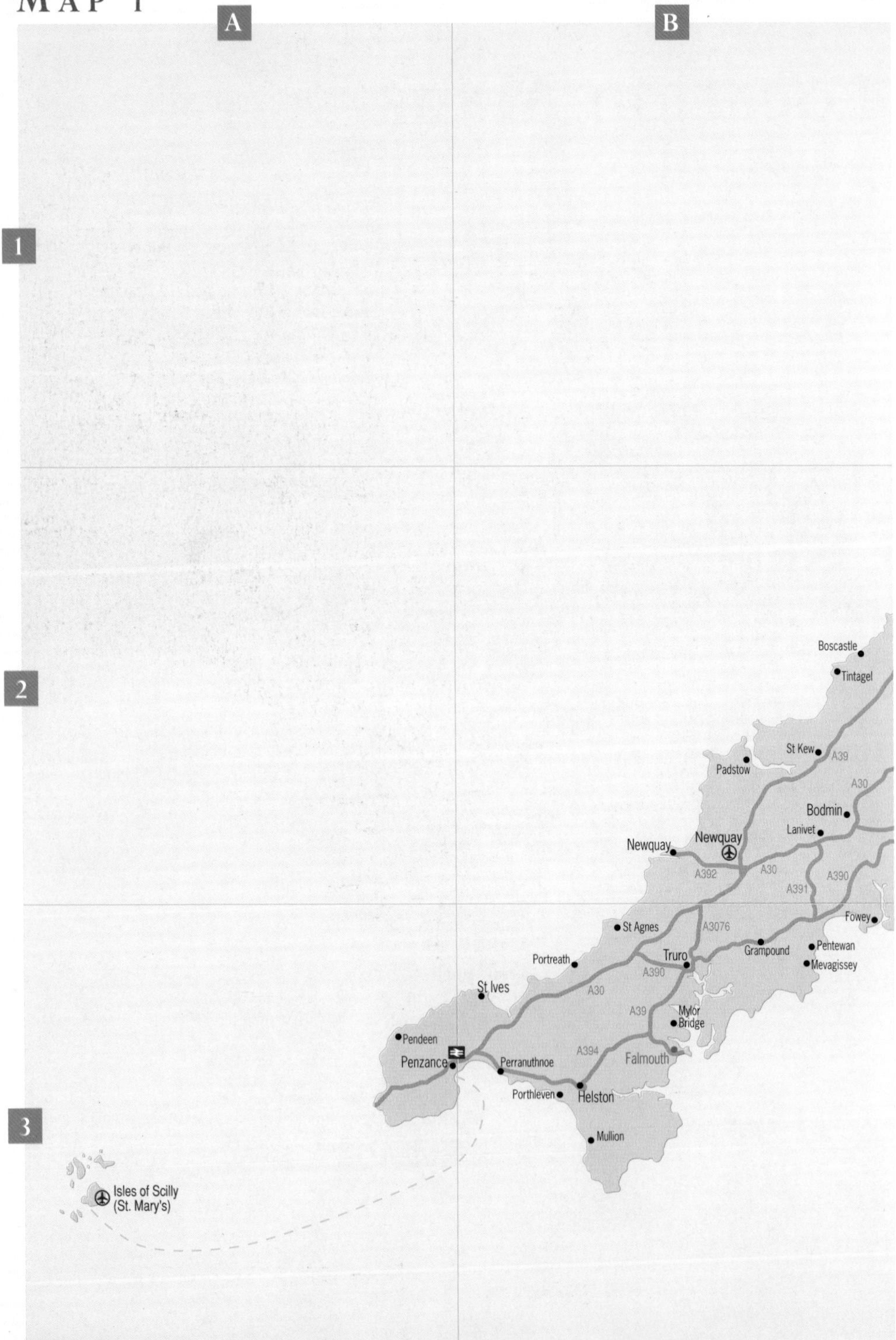

A    B

1

2

Boscastle
Tintagel
St Kew
A39
A30
Padstow
Bodmin
Lanivet
Newquay
Newquay
A392    A30    A390
A391
St Agnes    A3076    Fowey
Portreath    Truro    Grampound    Pentewan
A390    Mevagissey
St Ives    A30
A39    Mylor
Bridge
Pendeen    A394    Falmouth
Penzance    Perranuthnoe
Porthleven    Helston

3

Mullion

Isles of Scilly
(St. Mary's)

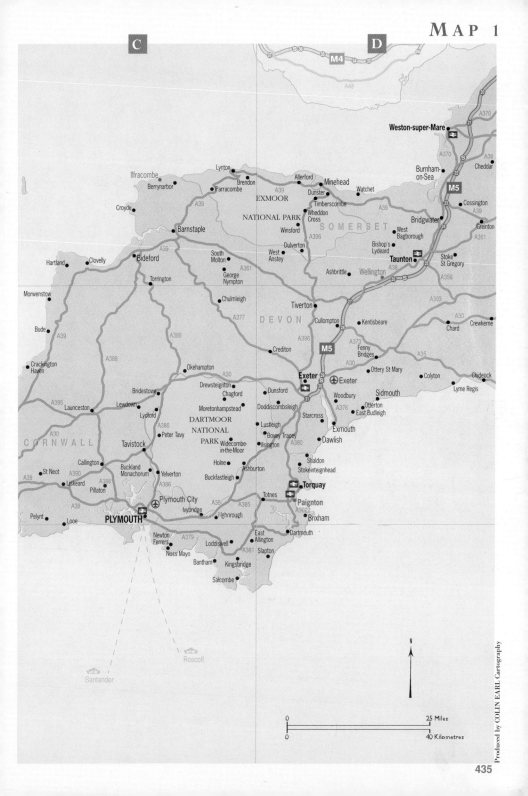

MAP 1

C D

Weston-super-Mare

Burnham-on-Sea

Cheddar

M4

A48

A370

A370

A38

M5

Ilfracombe

Lynton

Allerford

Minehead

Watchet

Cossington

Berrynarbor

Brendon

Dunster

Parracombe

EXMOOR

Timberscombe

A39

Bridgwater

Croyde

A39

NATIONAL PARK

Wheddon Cross

SOMERSET

West Bagborough

Winsford

Greinton

Barnstaple

Dulverton

Bishop's Lydeard

A361

Hartland

Clovelly

South Molton

West Anstey

Taunton

Stoke St Gregory

Bideford

A39

A361

George Nympton

Ashbrittle

Wellington

A358

Morwenstow

Torrington

Chulmleigh

A38

A377

Tiverton

DEVON

Kentisbeare

A303

Bude

A39

Cullompton

Chard

Crewkerne

A388

Crackington Haven

A386

Crediton

A396

Fenny Bridges

A35

A395

Okehampton

M5

A373

A30

Launceston

Bridestowe

Drewsteignton

A30

Dunsford

Ottery St Mary

Colyton

Chideock

Lewdown

Chagford

Doddiscombsleigh

Woodbury

A376

Sidmouth

Lyme Regis

Lydford

A386

Moretonhampstead

Starcross

Otterton

East Budleigh

CORNWALL

A30

DARTMOOR

Lustleigh

Exeter

Exmouth

Peter Tavy

NATIONAL

Bovey Tracey

Tavistock

PARK

Widecombe-in-the-Moor

Ilsington

A380

Dawlish

St Neot

Callington

Holne

Ashburton

Shaldon

A38

A390

Buckland Monachorum

Yelverton

Stokeinteignhead

Liskeard

A388

Buckfastleigh

Torquay

Pillaton

A386

A38

Plymouth City

Totnes

Paignton

Pelynt

Looe

Ivybridge

A38

A385

A3022

Brixham

PLYMOUTH

Ughrough

Newton Ferrers

A379

Dartmouth

Noss Mayo

Loddiswell

East Allington

Bantham

A381

Slapton

Kingsbridge

Salcombe

Roscoff

N

Santander

0 25 Miles

0 40 Kilometres

Exeter

Produced by COLIN EARL Cartography

435

# MAP 2

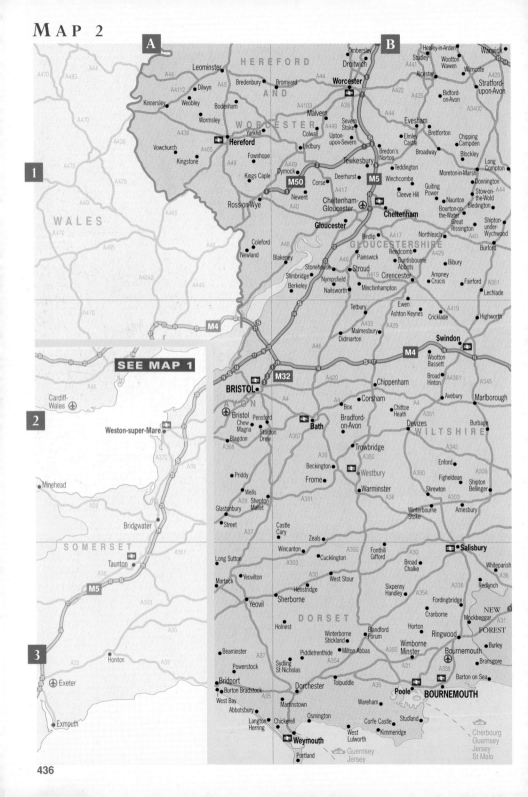

**A**

**B**

HEREFORD
AND
WORCESTER

WALES

GLOUCESTERSHIRE

AVON

SOMERSET

WILTSHIRE

DORSET

NEW
FOREST

SEE MAP 1

Ombersley
Droitwich
Worcester
Henley-in-Arden
Studley
Wootton Wawen
Wilmcote
Warwick
Alcester
Stratford-upon-Avon
Bidford-on-Avon
Leominster
Bredenbury
Bromyard
Malvern
Severn Stoke
Evesham
Elmley Castle
Bretforton
Chipping Campden
Blockley
Long Compton
Droitwich
Dilwyn
Weobley
Bodenham
Kinnersley
Wormsley
Yarkhill
Hereford
Colwal
Ledbury
Upton-upon-Severn
Bredon's Norton
Broadway
Donnington
Stow-on-the-Wold
Bledington
Shipton-under-Wychwood
Vowchurch
Fownhope
Kingstone
Kings Caple
Dymock
Corse
Newent
Tewkesbury
Teddington
Winchcombe
Cleeve Hill
Guiting Power
Naunton
Bourton-on-the-Water
Great Rissington
Burford
Ross-on-Wye
Deerhurst
Cheltenham-Gloucester
Cheltenham
Birdlip
Northleach
Gloucester
Rendcomb
Bibury
Coleford
Newland
Blakeney
Stonehouse
Painswick
Duntisbourne Abbots
Ampney Crucis
Fairford
Lechlade
Slimbridge
Nympsfield
Stroud
Cirencester
Berkeley
Nailsworth
Minchinhampton
Ewen
Highworth
Tetbury
Ashton Keynes
Cricklade
Malmesbury
Didmarton
Swindon
Wootton Bassett
Broad Hinton
Avebury
Marlborough
Chippenham
Corsham
Chittoe Heath
Devizes
Burbage
Bristol
Pensford
Box
BRISTOL
Chew Magna
Stanton Drew
Bath
Bradford-on-Avon
Cardiff-Wales
Blagdon
Trowbridge
Enford
Figheldean
Shipton Bellinger
Weston-super-Mare
Priddy
Beckington
Westbury
Shrewton
Amesbury
Wells
Frome
Warminster
Minehead
Shepton Mallet
Glastonbury
Winterbourne Stoke
Bridgwater
Street
Castle Cary
Zeals
Salisbury
Taunton
Long Sutton
Wincanton
Cucklington
Fonthill Gifford
Broad Chalke
Whiteparish
Martock
Yeovilton
West Stour
Sixpenny Handley
Redlynch
Sherborne
Henstridge
Fordingbridge
Cranborne
Mockbeggar
Yeovil
Horton
Ringwood
Burley
Holnest
Bransgore
Beaminster
Winterborne Stickland
Blandford Forum
Wimborne Minster
Bournemouth
Powerstock
Sydling St Nicholas
Piddletrenthide
Milton Abbas
Barton on Sea
Honiton
Bridport
Dorchester
Tolpuddle
Poole
BOURNEMOUTH
Burton Bradstock
West Bay
Abbotsbury
Martinstown
Osmington
Wareham
Corfe Castle
Studland
Exeter
Langton Herring
Chickerell
West Lulworth
Kimmeridge
Cherbourg
Guernsey
Jersey
St Malo
Exmouth
Weymouth
Portland
Guernsey
Jersey

436

# MAP 2

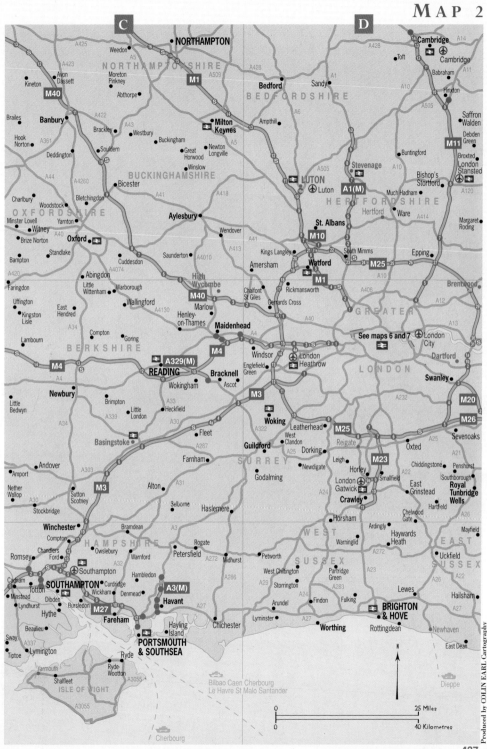

# MAP 3

1   2

C

Great Yarmouth   Lowestoft   Kessingland   Southwold   Blythburgh   Darsham   Middleton   Aldeburgh

Mundesley   North Walsham   Stalham   Ludham   Rollesby   South Walsham   Wroxham   Salhouse   Rackheath   Brundall   Blofield   THE BROADS   Beccles   Bungay   Chediston   Weybread   Brockdish   Fressingfield   Bruisyard   Framlingham   Hacheston   Saxmundham   Eyke   Woodbridge   Felixstowe   Frinton-on-Sea

Cromer   Sheringham   Aylsham   Cawston   Hevingham   Sidley   Coltishall   NORWICH   Norwich   Stoke Holy Cross   Brooke   Saxlingham Thorpe   Twetshall St Mary   Diss   Gissing   South Lopham   Coddenham   Ipswich   Wix   Hintlesham   Shelley   Higham   East Bergholt   Dedham   Colchester

Blakeney   Melton Constable   Elsing   Hethersett   Wymondham   Qudenham   Garboldisham   Bacton   Manningtree

Wells-next-the-Sea   Little Walsingham   South Creake   Beetley   Dereham   Swaffham   Thompson   Thetford   Barnham   Elmswell   Beyton   Thorpe Morieux   Hitcham   Kersey   Hadleigh   Lavenham   Stoke-by-Nayland   West Bergholt   Stratford St Mary   Nayland

Burnham Overy Staithe   Great Bircham   Dersingham   NORFOLK   Fakenham   Bury St Edmunds   SUFFOLK   Lawshall   Hartest   Long Melford   Sudbury   Castle Hedingham   Aldham   Little Tey

Thornham   Choseley   King's Lynn   Downham Market   Ely   Burwell   Newmarket   Radwinter   Thaxted   Great Dunmow   Felsted   Great Bardfield   Braintree

Boston   Holbeach   Spalding   Wisbech   CAMBRIDGESHIRE   Chatteris   Ramsey   Hemingford Grey   Huntingdon

Sleaford   Ancaster   Grantham   Stoke Rochford   Skillington   Castle Byham   Market Deeping   Stamford   Oundle   Peterborough   Kettering   LINCOLNSHIRE

SEE MAP 2   Cambridge   London Stansted   Stevenage   Luton   Bedford   BEDFORDSHIRE   M11

Esbjerg   Gothenburg   Hamburg   Hook of Holland   Zeebrugge

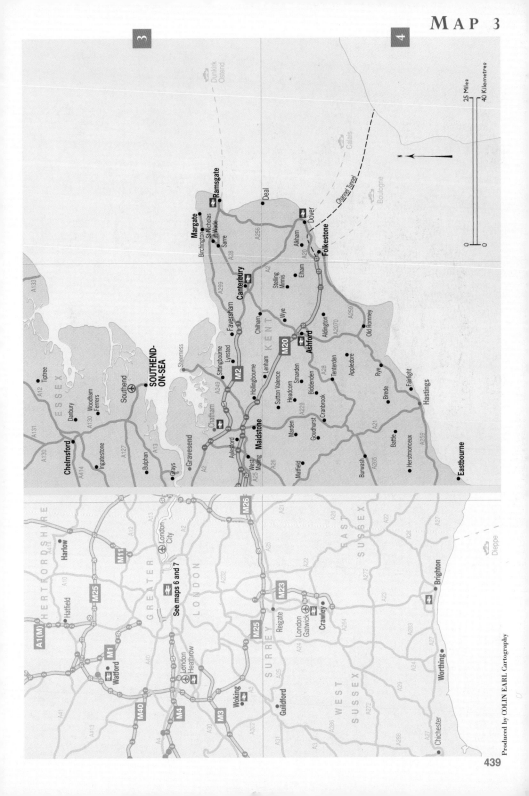

MAP 3

Produced by COLIN EARL Cartography

439

# MAP 4

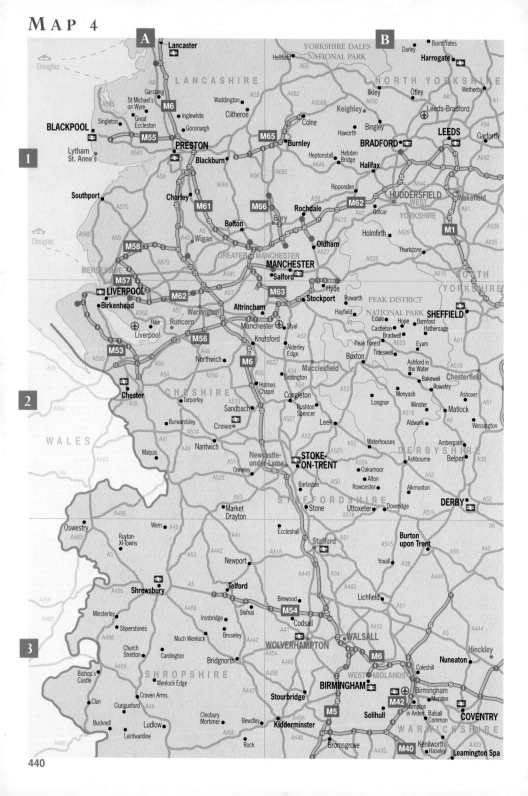

A

B

Douglas

Lancaster

Morecambe

**YORKSHIRE DALES NATIONAL PARK**

Hellifield

Darley

Burnt Yates

A65

Harrogate

LANCASHIRE

Garstang

A6

St Michael's on Wyre

Waddington

A59

A682

Ilkley

Otley

A61

Wetherby

A6068

Keighley

A650

Leeds-Bradford

M6

Inglewhite

Clitheroe

Colne

Haworth

Bingley

NORTH YORKSHIRE

Singleton

Great Eccleston

Goosnargh

M65

Burnley

BRADFORD

LEEDS

A64

Garforth

BLACKPOOL

M55

PRESTON

Blackburn

Heptonstall

Hebden Bridge

Halifax

A642

Lytham St. Anne's

A583

A59

A56

A682

A646

Ripponden

A644

HUDDERSFIELD

WEST

Wakefield

Southport

A570

A59

A666

Chorley

A58

Golcar

YORKSHIRE

M1

A565

A6

M61

M66

Rochdale

M62

Holmfirth

A629

A628

A635

Douglas

M58

Wigan

A49

Bolton

Bury

Oldham

A627

Thurlstone

A616

MERSEYSIDE

A570

A580

**GREATER MANCHESTER**

A628

SOUTH YORKSHIRE

M57

M62

Salford

MANCHESTER

M63

Hyde

Rowarth

PEAK DISTRICT

LIVERPOOL

Birkenhead

A57

Warrington

Altrincham

Stockport

Hayfield

NATIONAL PARK

SHEFFIELD

A562

Hale

Runcorn

Manchester

Styal

A6

Edale

Hope

Bamford

A53

M56

Knutsford

A52

Castleton

Bradwell

Hathersage

M53

A49

Alderley Edge

Peak Forest

A623

Eyam

A61

A550

A56

Northwich

A537

Siddington

A34

Tideswell

Ashford in the Water

A619

A54

A556

Holmes Chapel

Buxton

Bakewell

Chesterfield

A55

M6

A50

Congleton

A53

Rowsley

Ashover

Chester

CHESHIRE

Tarporley

Sandbach

Rushton Spencer

Monyash

Winster

Matlock

A61

A494

A55

Burwardsley

A534

Crewe

A527

Leek

A515

Aldwark

A6

Wessington

Malpas

A41

A49

Nantwich

A53

Waterhouses

A52

Ambergate

WALES

A483

Onneley

A51

Newcastle-under-Lyme

A520

Ashbourne

DERBYSHIRE

Belper

A38

A5

A525

Barlaston

STOKE-ON-TRENT

A50

Oakamoor

A52

Alkmonton

Alton

Rowcester

Oswestry

A495

Market Drayton

Stone

Uttoxeter

Doveridge

A516

DERBY

A52

Ruyton-XI-Towns

Wem

A49

A41

Eccleshall

A518

A51

Burton upon Trent

A50

A6

A483

A5

A442

Newport

A449

A34

A515

A444

Minsterley

Shrewsbury

A458

A5

Telford

Brewood

Lichfield

A51

Stiperstones

A458

Ironbridge

Shifnal

M54

Codsall

Church Stretton

Cardington

Broseley

A442

A460

A452

Hinckley

A489

Much Wenlock

Bridgnorth

WOLVERHAMPTON

WALSALL

Nuneaton

Bishop's Castle

SHROPSHIRE

Wenlock Edge

A454

A449

WEST MIDLANDS

Coleshill

M6

Clun

Craven Arms

A442

BIRMINGHAM

Birmingham

Meriden

Clungunford

A49

Cleobury Mortimer

Bewdley

Stourbridge

M42

Hampton in Arden

Balsall Common

COVENTRY

Bucknell

Ludlow

A456

Kidderminster

M5

Solihull

WARWICKSHIRE

Leintwardine

A456

Rock

A448

Bromsgrove

A435

M40

Kenilworth

Haseley

Leamington Spa

A423

440

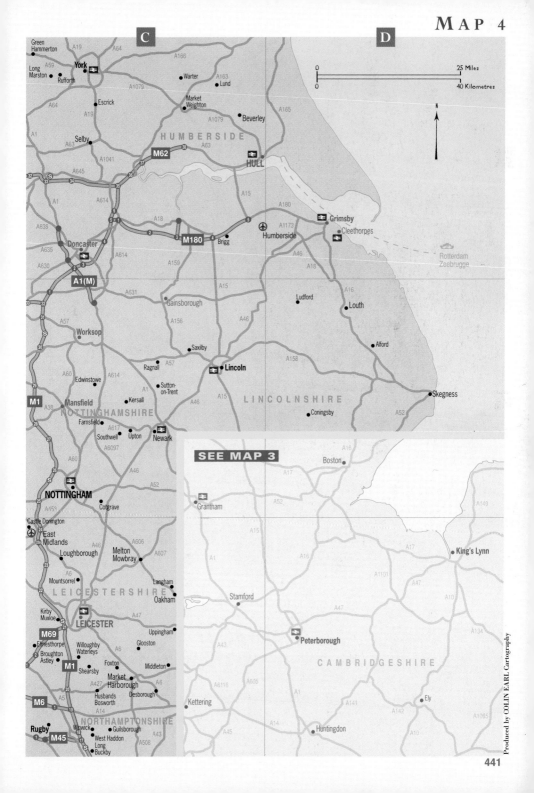

C

D

Green Hammerton
Long Marston
Rufforth
York
A19
A64
A59
A1079
Escrick
A64
A19
Selby
A63
A1
A1041
A645
32
S
33
A1
A614
A638
Doncaster
A635
A630
A1(M)
33
A57
37
A1
S
Worksop
30
A60
Edwinstowe
M1
A38
Mansfield
NOTTINGHAMSHIRE
Farnsfield
A617
Southwell
Upton
Newark
29
A60
A6097
A46
A52
NOTTINGHAM
A453
Cotgrave
Castle Donington
East Midlands
24
A6
Loughborough
A46
Melton Mowbray
A606
A607
Mountsorrel
Langham
LEICESTERSHIRE
Oakham
Kirby Muxloe
LEICESTER
A47
M69
Uppingham
Elmesthorpe
Willoughby Waterleys
A6
Glooston
Broughton Astley
M1
Foxton
Middleton
Shearsby
Market Harborough
A6
M6
A5
A427
Husbands Bosworth
Desborough
Rugby
M45
NORTHAMPTONSHIRE
Warwick
Guilsborough
West Haddon
Long Buckby
A43
A508
A14

A64
A166
Warter
A163
Lund
Market Weighton
A1079
Beverley
A165
HUMBERSIDE
A63
M62
32
HULL
A15
A180
Brigg
M180
2
3
4
Humberside
A1173
A159
A18
A631
A15
Gainsborough
A156
A15
A46
Saxilby
A57
Ragnall
Lincoln
Sutton-on-Trent
A1
Kersall
A46
A15
Coningsby

A46
Grimsby
Cleethorpes
Rotterdam Zeebrugge
A46
A18
A16
Ludford
Louth
A158
Alford
LINCOLNSHIRE
Skegness
A52

SEE MAP 3

A16
Boston
A17
Grantham
A52
A149
A15
A16
A17
King's Lynn
A1
A1101
A47
Stamford
A47
A10
A43
Peterborough
A134
Kettering
CAMBRIDGESHIRE
A6116
A605
A1
A141
Ely
A1065
A14
Huntingdon
A142
A45
A10

0
40 Kilometres
0
N

Produced by COLIN EARL Cartography

441

# MAP 5

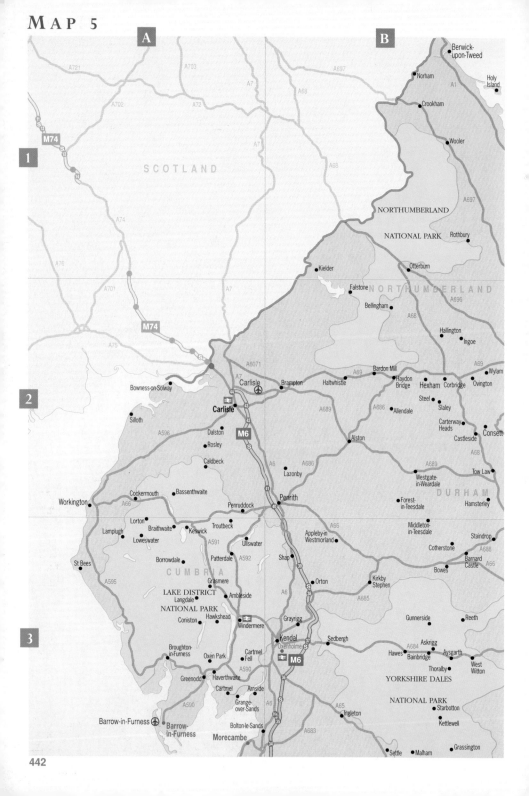

A    B

1

2

3

SCOTLAND

M74

M74

NORTHUMBERLAND

NATIONAL PARK

NORTHUMBERLAND

DURHAM

CUMBRIA

LAKE DISTRICT
NATIONAL PARK

YORKSHIRE DALES

NATIONAL PARK

Berwick-upon-Tweed
Norham
Holy Island
Crookham
Wooler
Rothbury
Kielder
Otterburn
Falstone
Bellingham
Hallington
Ingoe
Bardon Mill
Wylam
Haltwhistle
Haydon Bridge
Hexham
Corbridge
Ovington
Brampton
Steel
Slaley
Carlisle
Allendale
Carterway Heads
Consett
Bowness-on-Solway
Castleside
Alston
Tow Law
Silloth
Dalston
Westgate-in-Weardale
Rosley
Lazonby
Forest-in-Teesdale
Hamsterley
Caldbeck
Penrith
Cockermouth
Bassenthwaite
Middleton-in-Teesdale
Workington
Penruddock
Staindrop
Lorton
Troutbeck
Appleby-in-Westmorland
Cotherstone
Braithwaite
Keswick
Barnard Castle
Lamplugh
Loweswater
Ullswater
Bowes
Borrowdale
Patterdale
Shap
St Bees
Grasmere
Orton
Kirkby Stephen
Langdale
Ambleside
Gunnerside
Reeth
Coniston
Hawkshead
Windermere
Grayrigg
Broughton-in-Furness
Askrigg
Oxen Park
Cartmel Fell
Kendal
Sedbergh
Hawes
Aysgarth
West Witton
Oxenholme
Bainbridge
Greenodd
Haverthwaite
Thoralby
Cartmel
Arnside
Grange-over-Sands
Starbotton
Barrow-in-Furness
Kettlewell
Bolton-le-Sands
Ingleton
Morecambe
Grassington
Settle
Malham

# MAP 5

C

D

0 ———————————————————— 25 Miles
0 ———————————————————— 40 Kilometres

N

Bamburgh
Seahouses
Beadnell
A1
Embleton
Craster
Alnwick
Lesbury
Alnmouth
Warkworth
Amble-by-
A1068    the-Sea

A697

A1    A189

A696    A19
**Whitley Bay**
Newcastle    **NEWCASTLE** ● Tynemouth
**UPON TYNE**
Ryton
Rowlands  Gateshead    **TYNE AND WEAR**
Gill
A692    A19    **SUNDERLAND**
**Stanley**  Chester-  Washington
le-Street
Plawsworth    A690
A691
**Durham**
A19
A167    Hesleden
Spennymoor    **Hartlepool**
A68  A688
Bishop    **A1(M)**    A689
Auckland

Heighington
**CLEVELAND**    **Redcar**
Saltburn-
Stockton-    by-the-Sea
on-Tees    **MIDDLESBROUGH**
**Darlington**    A66    A171    Ellerby
Tees-side    A174    Whitby
A66    A19    A172  Ingleby  Danby    Robin Hood's Bay
Kirkby  Greenhow    Ravenscar
Richmond    A1
Osmotherley    **NORTH YORK MOORS**
Hunton    A684    **NORTH**  **NATIONAL PARK**    A169  A171  Cloughton
Northallerton    A170
Leeming Bar    Hawnby  Gillamoor    Levisham    **Scarborough**
**YORKSHIRE**    Kirkbymoorside  Cropton
Thornton    Helmsley    Ebberston  A170
Watlass    Thirsk    A170  Marton    Pickering
Masham    Ampleforth    Nunnington    Bromptn-
Coxwold  Oswaldkirk    by-Sawdon
A168  A19  Husthwaite    A64    A165
Ripon    Crayke    Rillington
A61  A1  Easingwold    Flamborough
Pateley  Boroughbridge  Myton-    A166
Bridge    on-Swale
Bishop    Flaxton
Thornton

Produced by COLIN EARL Cartography

# MAP 6

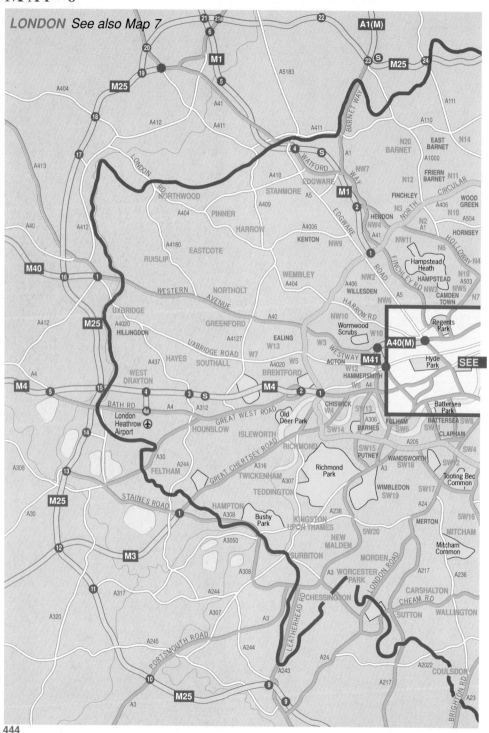

# MAP 6

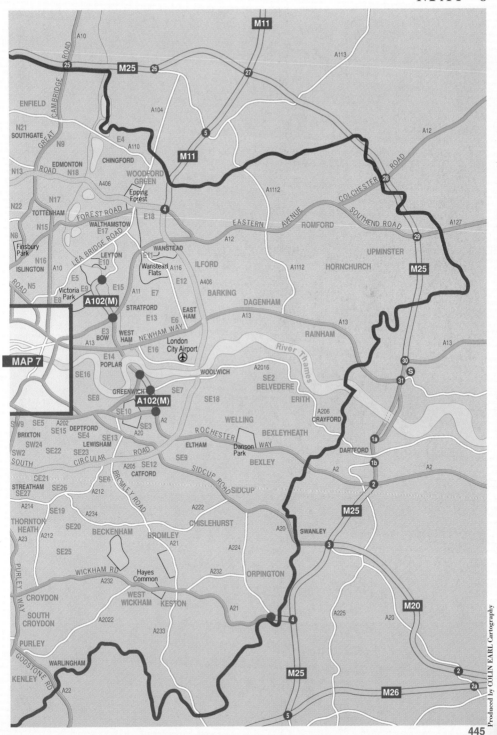

Produced by COLIN EARL Cartography

# MAP 7

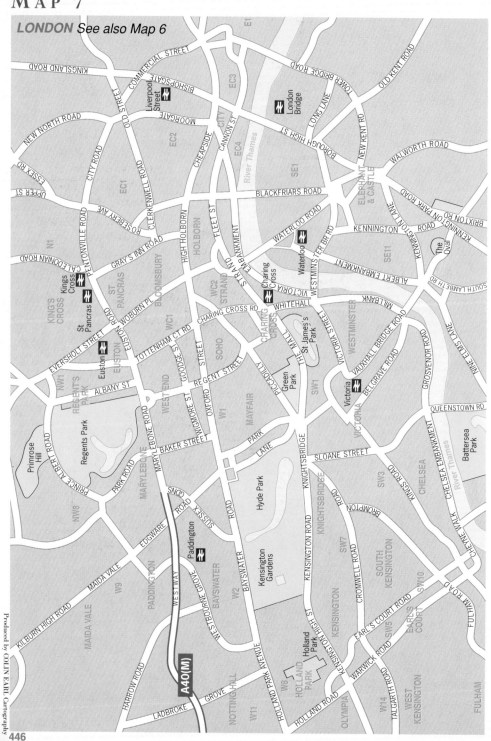

KINGSLAND ROAD

NEW NORTH ROAD

COMMERCIAL STREET

BISHOPSGATE

OLD STREET

CITY ROAD

ESSEX RD

UPPER ST

Liverpool Street

MOORGATE

EC3

EC2

EC1

CLERKENWELL ROAD

CHEAPSIDE

CANNON ST

CITY

EC4

River Thames

London Bridge

LONG LANE

BOROUGH HIGH ST

TOWER BRIDGE ROAD

OLD KENT ROAD

WALWORTH ROAD

SE1

ELEPHANT & CASTLE

NEW KENT RD

BLACKFRIARS ROAD

BRIXTON RD

KENNINGTON PARK ROAD

KENNINGTON PARK LANE

KENNINGTON ROAD

SE11

The Oval

CALEDONIAN ROAD

PENTONVILLE ROAD

ROSEBERY AVE

N1

FLEET ST

HIGH HOLBORN

HOLBORN

WATERLOO ROAD

Waterloo

WESTMINSTER BR RD

SOUTH LAMBETH RD

ALBERT EMBANKMENT

MILLBANK

KING'S CROSS

Kings Cross

St Pancras

GRAY'S INN ROAD

ST PANCRAS

WOBURN PL

BLOOMSBURY

WC1

CHARING CROSS RD

STRAND

WC2

VICTORIA EMBANKMENT

STRAND

Charing Cross

WHITEHALL

CHARING CROSS

St James's Park

VICTORIA STREET

WESTMINSTER

SW1

VAUXHALL BRIDGE ROAD

GROSVENOR ROAD

NINE ELMS LANE

EVERSHOLT STREET

EUSTON ROAD

Euston

NW1

EUSTON ROAD

TOTTENHAM CT RD

GOODGE ST

WEST END

OXFORD STREET

GOODGE STREET

REGENT STREET

SOHO

W1

PICCADILLY

MAYFAIR

THE MALL

Green Park

St James's Park

Victoria

VICTORIA

BELGRAVE ROAD

QUEENSTOWN RD

ALBANY ST

REGENT'S PARK

Regents Park

MARYLEBONE

WIGMORE ST

BAKER STREET

MARYLEBONE ROAD

PARK LANE

KNIGHTSBRIDGE

SLOANE STREET

Battersea Park

CHELSEA

SW3

CHELSEA EMBANKMENT

River Thames

Primrose Hill

PRINCE ALBERT ROAD

PARK ROAD

NW8

PARK ROAD

EDGWARE

SUSSEX GDNS

Paddington

BAYSWATER

W2

ROAD

Hyde Park

Kensington Gardens

KNIGHTSBRIDGE

KENSINGTON ROAD

BROMPTON ROAD

SW7

SOUTH KENSINGTON

KINGS ROAD

SW10

CHEYNE WALK

KILBURN HIGH ROAD

MAIDA VALE

W9

PADDINGTON

WEST WAY

WESTBOURNE GROVE

PADDINGTON

BAYSWATER

HARROW ROAD

LADBROKE GROVE

NOTTING HILL

W11

A40(M)

HOLLAND PARK AVENUE

W8

HOLLAND PARK

Holland Park

HOLLAND PARK HIGH ST

HOLLAND ROAD

OLYMPIA

W14

WEST KENSINGTON

TALGARTH ROAD

WARWICK ROAD

EARL'S COURT ROAD

SW5

EARLS COURT

CROMWELL ROAD

KENSINGTON

SW7

FULHAM RD

FULHAM

Produced by COLIN EARL Cartography

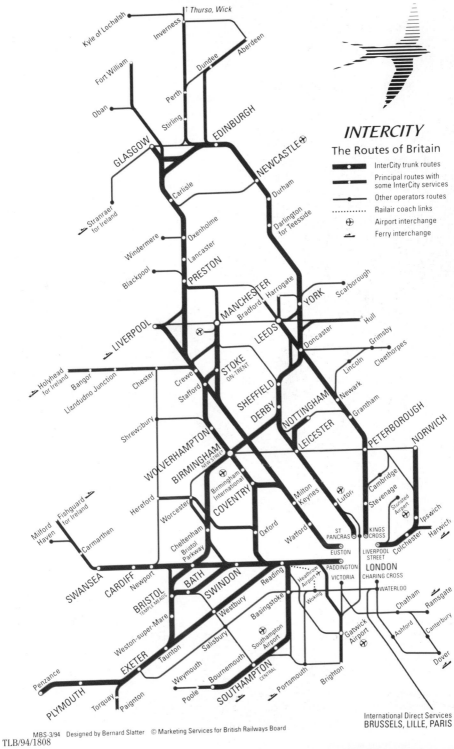

*INTERCITY*
## The Routes of Britain

| | |
|---|---|
| ▬▬●▬▬ | InterCity trunk routes |
| ▬▬▬▬ | Principal routes with some InterCity services |
| ●——● | Other operators routes |
| ········· | Railair coach links |
| ⊕ | Airport interchange |
| ⛴ | Ferry interchange |

International Direct Services
**BRUSSELS, LILLE, PARIS**

MBS-3/94  Designed by Bernard Slatter   © Marketing Services for British Railways Board
TLB/94/1808

# Your Quick Guide to Finding a Place to Stay

*This **'Where to Stay'** guide makes it quick and easy to find somewhere suitable to stay.*

The TOWN INDEX (starting on page 425) and the LOCATION MAPS (starting on page 433) show all cities, towns and villages with accommodation listings in this guide.

### 1 TOWN INDEX
If the place you plan to visit is included in the town index, turn to the page number given to find accommodation available there. Also check that location on the colour maps to find other places nearby which also have accommodation listings in this guide.

| | |
|---|---|
| Avon | 259 |
| | 356 |
| Battle *East Sussex* | 68 |
| Beadnell *Northumberland* | 263 |
| Beaminster *Dorset* | 320 |
| Beaulieu *Hampshire* | 222 |
| Beccles *Suffolk* | 263 |
| Beckington *Somerset* | 222 |
| Bedford *Bedfordshire* | 222 |
| Beetley *Norfolk* | 68 |
| Bellingham *Northumberland* | 199 |
| Belper *Derbyshire* | 138 |
| Berkeley *Gloucestershire* | 263 |
| Berrynarbor *Devon* | |
| Berwick-upon-Tweed *Northumberland* | 69 |
| Beverley *Humberside* | 105 |
| Bewdley *Hereford and Worcester* | 138 |
| Beyton *Suffolk* | 222 |

also confirm any other information in the published entry which may be important to you (price, whether bath and/or shower available, children/dogs/credit cards welcome, months open, etc).

If you are happy with everything, make your booking and, if time permits, confirm it in writing.

### 2 LOCATION MAPS
If the place you want is not in the town index – or you only have a general idea of the area in which you wish to stay – use the colour location maps to find places in the area which have accommodation listings in this guide.

When you have found suitable accommodation, check its availability with the establishment and

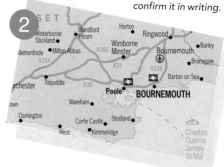